EUROPE

Director of Publishing
Will Holub-Moorman

Editorial Director
Priyanka Sen

Production Manager
Michael Goncalves

Researcher-Writers
Meg Bernhard
Ana Chaves
Tim Doner
Dan Fulop
Ryan Furey
Zeb Goodman
Miles Hewitt
Claire McLaughlin
Petey Menz
Wesley Rivera
Haley Rue
Priyanka Sen
Matt Shuham

EUROPE OVERVIEW

NORWAY

DENMARK

North Sea

IRELAND

GREAT BRITAIN

THE NETHERLANDS

GERMANY

BELGIUM

LUX.

Rhine

Atlantic

Ocean

Seine

Mosel

Danube

LICHTENSTEIN

Loire

SWITZER-LAND

Dordogne

Po

Bay of Biscay

FRANCE

Rhône

MONACO

PORTUGAL

Duero

ANDORRA

Corsica

SPAIN

Menorca

Sardinia

Guadalquivir

Ibiza

Mallorca

GIBRALTAR (U.K.)

CEUTA (SPAIN)

MELILLA (SPAIN)

MOROCCO

ALGERIA

TUNISIA

CONTENTS

RESEARCHER-WRITERS

MEG BERNHARD: A sophomore from Temecula, a small city in Southern California whose name means "sun shines through the mist," Meg bus-hopped coast to coast on the Iberian Peninsula this summer. Living like the Madrileños (even when she was in Portugal), Meg climbed Moorish fortresses, ate a lot of ham, and even walked 20km across Ibiza.

ANA CHAVES: Ana took her sass and humor from Prague to Warsaw this summer. Sipping coffee with the locals, trying to fall in love with Gothic architecture, and researching multi-story clubs were all in a day's work. When Ana wasn't getting caffeinated, she committed herself to writing up hilarious copy.

TIM DONER: Hopping from Oslo to Stockholm to Copenhagen, Tim traversed Scandinavia this summer. He reveled in all things Viking while munching on reindeer meat and enjoying a ridiculously high standard of living. Being a budget traveller in some of the most expensive destinations was never easy, but Tim always managed to turn in kick-ass copy.

DAN FULOP: Dan is a daring traveler from New York who made his first trip overseas right out of the womb. Although Dan was raised in Westchester suburbia, he took every opportunity he could to venture into the outdoors. While making his way from the Dolomites to the Matterhorn this summer, outdoor enthusiast met urban explorer during a thrilling journey characterized by a "healthy" combination of hiking the Bernese Oberland, imbibing with locals, and sampling regional delicacies in a gourmand's heaven.

RYAN FUREY: The globetrotting Ryan took a break to call Germany his home for two months this summer. He sampled every beer he could get his hands on waited long hours to get into Berlin's prestigious clubs, and still had time to go surfing on the side. When he wasn't taking killer shots for his Instagram, Ryan always made time for his one true love: currywurst.

ZEB GOODMAN: Zeb spent the better part of two months wandering around the southern coast of France, offending locals everywhere with his American accent and claiming he was Canadian in an poor attempt to avoid propagating American stereotypes. In the name of "research" and "journalism," Zeb train-hopped and hitchhiked his way to every beach and vineyard from Nice to Biarritz, narrowly escaping homelessness and all the while reassuring his editors and parents that he was visiting museums and living a healthy lifestyle.

MILES HEWITT: Miles took his poetry and flair to London and Amsterdam where he battled his verses against the Bard himself and spent more time than he'd like to admit rummaging around record shops. As Let's Go's official cool-cat-in-residence, Miles brought hipster charm and literary wit to everything he did across the pond.

CLAIRE MCLAUGHLIN: After devoting her college years to Let's Go in the office, our beloved former Director of Publishing decided to give up corporate meetings for a life roughing it on the road in Italy. From experiencing majestic sunsets over the Tiber to eating delicious paninis in Florence, Claire did it all while sending in hilarious copy and great Instagram photos all summer long.

PETEY MENZ: This year, Petey gave up Scottish lochs for pristine beaches and scalding temperatures as he traveled through Slovenia and Croatia. Petey always went above and beyond for his job whether he was dressing up as a gladiator, discovering the alleged hometown of Marco Polo, or turning in killer copy every week.

WESLEY RIVERA: Wesley traversed northern Spain, from Salvador Dalí's home in the eastern tip of the Iberian peninsula to Galicia, the westernmost Spanish region once considered to be the end of the earth. Along the way he savored all the tapas and sangria that Spain has to offer and was awestruck by beautiful Spanish castles and cathedrals. His favorite memories include hiking through mountains along the border of France, living with a DJ in Barcelona, witnessing the running of the bulls, and watching the locals of Blanes catch an octopus with their bare hands.

HALEY RUE: A native of Washington state, Haley took her love of mountains and indie-rock to the Alps of Austria and the hipsters of Hungary. As she made her way across Central Europe, Haley crowd-surfed in Budapest, charmed Mozart men in Vienna, wandered and pondered in Graz and Innsbruck, and drank plenty of coffee all the while. With her goofy spirit, unbridled openness, and adorable dimples, she made friends everywhere she went and ensured that her travels were anything but boring (her least favorite word).

PRIYANKA SEN: For her second summer with Let's Go, Priyanka hopped a few islands in Greece before returning to Europe's boot and her one true love, Italy. From the ruins of the Acropolis to the bumpin' beats of Rimini, Priyanka's journey around the Mediterranean featured the perfect combination of all things ancient and modern. Once again testing the limits of propriety with her sometimes risque and always hilarious reviews, Priyanka kept the office staff laughing while turning in kickass content all summer long.

MATT SHUHAM: Hopping from Paris to Blois to Bayeaux, Matt explored all things French this summer as he made his way from the nation's capital to the chateaus of the Loire Valley to the shores of Brittany. To cap off his route, he crossed the border into Belgium, making stops in Brussels, Bruges, Antwerp, and Ghent.

DISCOVER

EUROPE

Everyone you know—parents, friends, and especially random old men in parks—probably has a few stories that start, "When I was in Europe..." For all the shenanigans that ensue, these tales might as well begin with, "Once upon a time..." Still, for the most part, they're true stories. A kindly matriarch will cook you dinner and insist on setting you up with one of her children; a shop owner will convince you to buy mooncakes before you figure out what's really in them; you'll spend all night trying to dodge a neighborhood's worth of stray cats who seem to think you're their king; you'll meet a princess disguised as a pixie-haired commoner and fall in love over Vespa rides and one hilarious prank at the Bocca della Verità. Wait, that last one was *Roman Holiday*—but you get the point.

The unifying theme of this guide is adventure. Not geography, not sights, not history. Europe has been the stomping ground of students for generations, precisely because of the opportunities for escapes and escapades it provides. It has the whole gamut of architectural periods and incredible renovations, brogues and rolling r's, and residents who drink alcohol like water. And you're always in the good company of fellow travelers, both young and old, out on adventures like you. Give Europe a chance, think outside of the box, and you can make your trip something worth bragging about. Who knows? Maybe *Roman Holiday* was based on a true story.

1

when to go

Summer is the busiest time to travel in Europe. The season's many festivals can jack up prices, but it might be worth it to catch Madrid's bullfighting festival or London's Proms. Late spring and early autumn bring fewer tourists and cheaper airfares—meaning they're good times to go, if you can get the days off. Winter travel is great for those looking to hit the ski ranges around the mountains, but not the best time to take a walking tour through Prague. Plus, you'll find that some hotels, restaurants, and sights have limited hours or are on vacation—from you.

what to do

FOOD FOR THOUGHT

From French *patisseries* to Italian *pizzerie*, the sheer wealth of cuisine options across Europe could keep your palate entertained for several lifetimes. It's a miracle that all travelers don't return home 50lb. heavier and desperately in need of a larger pant size.

- **CIP CIAP (VENICE, ITALY).** The crispy crust. Gooey, melted cheese. The smell of tomatoes and basil...we think it's the best pizza and Venice, and we're hungry just thinking about it.
- **EL SOBRINO DE BOTÍN (MADRID, SPAIN):** If reading *The Sun Also Rises* made you think, "Gee, I'd like to eat that suckling pig Hemingway mentioned," you're weird. You should also go to this upscale restaurant.
- **STEINHEIL 16 (MUNICH, GERMANY):** Schnitzel and beer. What did you think you would eat in Munich?
- **RESTAURANT 3FC (PARIS, FRANCE):** Once you've eaten your weight in bread, cheese, and pastries, leave France for North Africa for an irrestistible kebab from Restaurant 3FC.
- **MATHALLEN (OSLO, NORWAY):** A collection of pop-up restaurants right below a culinary school. Prepare your tastebuds.
- **PIEMINISTER (LONDON, GREAT BRITAIN):** You've likely heard not-too-great things about British food. These pies will certainly change your mind.

THE GREAT INDOORS

Let's get real: you didn't come to Europe for the trees—except the ones in the background of the *Mona Lisa*. These museums could keep you distracted for a lifetime or four.

- **THE LOUVRE (PARIS, FRANCE):** We promise it was famous before *The Da Vinci Code*.
- **THE BRITISH MUSEUM, THE NATIONAL GALLERY, THE TATE MODERN, AND THE VICTORIA AND ALBERT MUSEUM (LONDON, UK):** We couldn't pick just one—nor should you, because they're all free!
- **UFFIZI GALLERY (FLORENCE, ITALY):** Venus's flowing locks, a swan-like depiction of Mary with Jesus, and 43 other rooms full of art are waiting for you (and thousands of other sightseers) to appreciate their magnificence.
- **MOSTEIRO DOS JERÓNIMOS (LISBON, PORTUGAL):** Okay, so it's more of a church than a museum. But it's remained in near-perfect condition for over 500 years, so if you want to party (maybe pray is more appropriate) like it's 1502, this is the place.
- **MUZEJ MIMARA (ZAGREB, CROATIA):** You've probably never heard of this museum. But have you heard of Botticelli, Caravaggio, or Manet? Yes? Then add this place to your must-see list.

discover

- **MOST BLING:** The Pope's crib (a.k.a. Vatican City), where you'll find the sickest frescoes and some Swiss guards in tricked out uniforms.

- **WORST MUSEUM TO VISIT WITH YOUR FAMILY (ESPECIALLY CREEPY UNCLE NICK):** The Amsterdam Sex Museum.

- **BEST WAY TO RELIVE YOUR CHILDHOOD:** Visit the fantastic home of Hans Christian Andersen in Odense, Denmark. Become a swan and never need to fly Ryanair again. Dreams do come true.

- **BEST WAY TO CONTRACT EARLY-ONSET DIABETES:** Cologne's Schokoladenmuseum, where gold fountains spurt out samples of sweet, sweet, chocolate goodness.

- **BEST PLACE TO TURN LEAD INTO GOLD:** Alchemia, a triple threat restaurant-pub-music venue in Kraków, Poland.

- **DOX (PRAGUE, CZECH REPUBLIC):** If you're in Europe for more than 10min., you're bound to see something from (a) Anticuity or (b) the Renaissance. DOX and its constantly rotating contemporary art exhibits are a welcome and insightful reprieve.

- **VAN GOGH MUSEUM (AMSTERDAM, THE NETHERLANDS):** Come see a museum dedicated to everyone's favorite bad boy painter. Let's van Gogh.

- **FUNDACIÓ MIRÓ (BARCELONA, SPAIN):** Do you like bright colors, abstract shapes, and staring slightly puzzled to fully understand a piece of art? You'll love Joan Miró and this collection of his works and others inspired by him.

DON'T BE A SQUARE

Just hang around in one. While strolling along winding avenues and exploring tiny alleyways is certainly necessary, European life shines in its open spaces: Italy's *piazze*, Spain's *plazas*, and even Hungary's *tere* are not only beautiful to look at, but they are home to festivals, outdoor (free!) art, and even bustling nightlife. You might cut through on your way to a world-famous museum, but be sure to stop and appreciate what these outdoor spaces have to offer.

- **NIEUWMARKT (AMSTERDAM, THE NETHERLANDS):** This one's a two-for-one: see the largest medieval building in Amsterdam while gorging on fresh cheeses, breads, and other snacks.

- **MONASTIRAKI (ATHENS, GREECE):** Descend from the Acropolis to discover an expanse of cheap souvlaki, street dancers, and the famous Athens flea market.

- **PIAZZA DELLA SIGNORIA (FLORENCE, ITALY):** Disclaimer: there are a lot of *piazze* in Florence—and across Italy, for that matter. But this one, just outside the famed Uffizi Gallery, houses a portico of statues that rivals the museum itself.

- **WENCESLAS SQUARE (PRAGUE, CZECH REPUBLIC):** The square features a sprawling green, cobblestone streets lined with department stores, and the National Museum. But if you happen to be visiting in December, you're in for a treat: the annual Christmas Market, which lights up the city and features holiday food, drink, and (of course) merriment.

- **HEROES' SQUARE (BUDAPEST, HUNGARY):** This enormous stone slab is a bit bizarre at first glance, but it's home to the iconic Millennium Monument as well as two museums.

- **PLAZA MAYOR (MADRID, SPAIN):** As with Italy's *piazze*, Spain (and, specifically, Madrid) is full of *plazas*. But Plaza Mayor—the "main square"—is the king of them all.

what to do

suggested itineraries

THE GRAND TOUR

Brace yourself. This is one serious trip, but it's absolutely worth it. We recommend you tackle it with the help of budget airlines or a railpass.

- **LONDON (4 DAYS):** Load up on history, tweed, and tea. Make every attempt to serendipitously run into William, Kate, and baby George.

- **AMSTERDAM (3 DAYS):** Amsterdam has it all: imperial history, artistic pedigree, great music. Plus, coffeeshops and legalized prostitution! You might not want to write home to mom about this leg of the trip.

- **BRUSSELS (2 DAYS):** Go beyond the waffles, the chocolate, and the beer to find...a peeing statue. Well, that's something.

- **PARIS (4 DAYS):** The quintessential European city will have you singing of *la vie en rose* in no time.

- **NICE (2 DAYS):** The best of the Riviera is hiding somewhere between tourist flocks.

- **BARCELONA (3 DAYS):** Stroll through the medieval streets of Barri Gòtic in search of damsels to rescue and **dragons** to slay.

- **LISBON (2 DAYS):** Sip *vinho do porto* while gazing at the sunset over the Rio Tejo.

- **MADRID (2 DAYS):** Eat dinner at midnight, go out until dawn, and explore the city between siestas.

- **ROME (4 DAYS):** Get the best of the old—the Colosseum owes a lot to facelifts—and the new—bars in the Centro Storico and clubs in Testaccio—in the Eternal City.

- **FLORENCE (3 DAYS):** Throw yourself into the Renaissance, which seems to live on in every Florentine building.

- **VENICE (2 DAYS):** You don't have to ride gondolas to enjoy the nooks and crannies of this lagoon island. They're overpriced anyway.

- **PRAGUE (3 DAYS):** During the day, the Charles Bridge is overrun with tourists and vendors, but there's nothing quite so magical at night.

- **MUNICH (2 DAYS):** Oktoberfest will leave you wishing for some January- through December-fests.

discover

- **BERLIN (3 DAYS):** Look out for horn-rimmed glasses and cardigans among Friedrichshain's nightclubs, which are housed in former DDR buildings.
- **ATHENS (2 DAYS):** By now you've seen much of Western Europe—now see the city where modern civilization all began.
- **SPLIT (2 DAYS):** Explore the palm tree-lined waterfront and the remains of Diocletian's palace before raging the night away at one of Split's many night clubs.

ISLAND HOPPING

No, you haven't accidentally picked up a copy of *Let's Go Caribbean*. While much of Europe is landlocked, there are still plenty of opportunities to be surrounded by water. And we're not just talking the UK and Greece—the British and Greek Isles aren't the only way to get off the mainland. You'll be exchanging a boat ride to a palm-tree lined oasis for quick ferries and walks over bridges, but it's still a slice of "island life."

- **PARIS, FRANCE:** The city's neighborhoods spiral outward from the Seine, in the middle of which are two islands: Île de la Cité and Île St-Louis. Here you'll find one of Paris's most famous landmarks, the Notre Dame Cathedral.
- **BERLIN, GERMANY:** There's almost no way to avoid a trip to Museumsinsel (Museum Island), home of the Neue Gallery, the Berlin Dom, and—most notably—the Pergamon Museum.
- **VIENNA, AUSTRIA:** Go dancing on the Danube at Summer Station, an outdoor dance party every night of the week during the summer months.
- **PALERMO, ITALY:** Discover a whole other Italy once you ferry over to Sicily. See the influence of Byzantine, Norman, and Spanish conquests of the island as you wander through ancient churches and taste unique Sicilian flavors.
- **MYKONOS, GREECE:** Athens by day, island by night. Only a short ferry ride from the capital city, this island is your destination for a little Dionysian revelry.
- **IBIZA, SPAIN:** It almost doesn't need mention: it's the destination for constant partying, and a trip to Spain wouldn't be complete without this island getaway.

STOP AND SMELL THE ROSES

In case you didn't know: you're going to spend a lot of time in Europe inside (with good reason—see "The Great Indoors" a few pages back). But that doesn't mean you shouldn't get a little fresh air, since Europe is packed with as many parks and gardens as it is with museums and cathedrals.

- **SEVILLA, SPAIN:** You didn't think you'd be getting a safari in Europe, did you? You can—though you'll see forests, swamps, and dunes instead of giraffes on the savannah—at the Parque Nacional de Doñana.
- **VIENNA, AUSTRIA:** Roam the gardens of the Hapsburgs at the Belvedere and pretend for an afternoon that you'll ever live in such lavish opulence.
- **EDINBURGH, UK:** Sometimes flowers and trees aren't just for aesthetic beauty. Visit the Royal Botanic Gardens a scientific plant experience.
- **PARIS, FRANCE:** If you're looking to see green, you've come to the right place. There's certainly no shortage of grassy knolls in this city.
- **PRAGUE, CZECH REPUBLIC:** The walk up to Petřin Hill won't exactly be relaxing, but the views and sights throughout the tree-topped area is worth the hike.
- **LJUBLJANA, SLOVENIA:** The ultimate outdoors experience awaits travelers at Park Tivoli. A stroll in the garden? A walk around the pond? A few games of tennis? The choice is yours. (And if you're sick of being outside by now—or it's, you know, raining—Tivoli Castle offers an indoor respite from the elements.)

THE ULTIMATE PUB CRAWL

Partying is as legitimate a reason to go to Europe as any other. Drinking customs say a lot about a city's culture, and... who are we kidding? It's fun. Don't be ashamed!

- **DUBLIN, IRELAND:** Perhaps, more aptly, Publin?
- **OXFORD, UK:** Party with the best and brightest in this university town.
- **AMSTERDAM, THE NETHERLANDS:** We recommend the GLBT nightlife. Other activities are yours to choose.
- **COLOGNE, GERMANY:** This city has some of the best of Germany's party scene.
- **BUDAPEST, HUNGARY.** Down pálinka in the city's many ruin pubs.
- **PRAGUE, CZECH REPUBLIC:** The beer is cheaper than water!
- **MUNICH, GERMANY:** This is the birthplace of Oktoberfest and the beer garden.
- **BORDEAUX, FRANCE:** We get it, too much beer. Welcome to wine country!
- **ROME, ITALY.** Casually sip wine on the Spanish Steps. Classic.
- **BARCELONA, SPAIN:** Every good night ends with a beautiful sunrise. Well done.

discover

how to use this book

CHAPTERS

Conquering the great continent of Europe is no easy task. Many have tried—from Julius Caesar to Napoleon—and all have failed. That's why you've come to us. We've been criss-crossing the continent for 55 years, smelling out the sightliest sights and the homiest hostels, and now, dear reader, we will pass on all of our knowledge to you. Let's get this show on the road with the travel coverage chapters—the meat of any *Let's Go* book.

We'll start off with Austria, where you can embark on your own Alpine adventure, à la *The Sound of Music*. From there, we trek on over to feast on *frites* in Belgium, enjoy Adriatic views in Croatia, and take in the old-world magic of the Czech Republic. Get a little closer to *The Little Mermaid* and its author, Hans Christian Anderson, in Denmark. Trek to France to explore fine art and finer dining, and meet Beethoven and Berliners in Germany. We cross the Channel to get our fill of Beefeaters and double-decker buses in Britain, make a pit stop at the Parthenon in Greece, and head north to Hungary's thermal baths before returning to the Emerald Isle to drink Guinness over Joyce. Get the lowdown on Italy's artistic treasures. Learn how to navigate canals in the Netherlands. Become a viking (well, at least try to) in Norway. Give props to *pierogies* in Poland. We'll show you where to find Portugal's finest port and take a cruise or Slovenia's Lake Bled. Then, complete your grand tour on the sun-drenched beaches of Spain and the Baltic coast of Sweden.

But that's not all, folks. We also have a few extra chapters for you to peruse:

CHAPTER	DESCRIPTION
Discover Europe	Discover tells you what to do, when to do it, and where to go for it. The absolute coolest things about any destination get highlighted in this chapter at the front of all *Let's Go* books.
Essentials	Essentials contains the practical info you need before, during, and after your trip—visas, regional transportation, health and safety, phrasebooks, and more.

ACCOMMODATIONS

In this book, we've listed our favorite hostels, hotels, B&Bs, and guest houses, along with helpful information about navigating the accommodations market, in the "Accommodations" sections and "Get a Room!" boxes. Our full list of reviews—along with our hotel and hostel booking engine powered by ⬛**Hostelworld**—can be found at **www.letsgo.com**.

LISTINGS

Listings—a.k.a. reviews of individual establishments—constitute a majority of *Let's Go* coverage. Our Researcher-Writers list establishments in order from **best to worst value**—not necessarily quality. (Obviously a five-star hotel is nicer than a hostel, but it would probably be ranked lower because it's not as good a value.) Listings pack in a lot of information, but it's easy to digest if you know how they're constructed:

ESTABLISHMENT NAME   TYPE OF ESTABLISHMENT $-$$$$
Address   ☎phone number website
Editorial review goes here.

i Directions to the establishment. Other practical information about the establishment, like age restrictions at a club or whether breakfast is included at a hostel. Prices for goods or services. ☒ *Hours or schedules.*

ICONS

First things first: places and things that we absolutely love, sappily cherish, generally obsess over, and wholeheartedly endorse are denoted by the all-empowering **Let's Go thumbs-up**. In addition, the icons scattered at the end of a listing (as you saw in the sample above) can serve as visual cues to help you navigate each listing:

✎	Let's Go recommends	☎	Phone numbers
✈	General information	🕐	Hours

PRICE DIVERSITY

A final set of icons corresponds to what we call our "price diversity" scale, which approximates how much money you can expect to spend at a given establishment. For **accommodations,** we base our range on the cheapest price for which a single traveler can stay for one night. For **food,** we estimate the average amount one traveler will spend in one sitting. The table below tells you what you'll *typically* find in Europe at the corresponding price range, but keep in mind that no scale can allow for the quirks of all individual establishments.

ACCOMMODATIONS	WHAT YOU'RE LIKELY TO FIND
$	Campgrounds and dorm rooms, both in hostels and actual universities, as well as some convents in Italy. Expect bunk beds and a communal bath. You may have to provide or rent towels and sheets.
$$	Upper-end hostels and lower-end hotels. You may have a private bathroom, or a sink in your room with a communal shower in the hall.
$$$	A small room with a private bath. Should have some amenities, such as phone and TV. Breakfast may be included.
$$$$	Large hotels, chains, and fancy boutiques. If it doesn't have the perks you want (and more), you've paid too much.
FOOD	**WHAT YOU'RE LIKELY TO FIND**
$	Street food, fast-food joints, university cafeterias, and bakeries (yum). Usually takeout, but you may have the option of sitting down.
$$	Sandwiches, pizza, low-priced entrees, ethnic eateries, and bar grub. Either takeout or sit-down service with slightly classier decor.
$$$	A somewhat fancy restaurant. Entrees tend to be heartier or more elaborate, but you're really paying for decor and ambience. Few restaurants in this range have a dress code, but some may look down on T-shirts and sandals.
$$$$	Your meal might cost more than your room, but there's a reason—it's something fabulous, famous, or both. Slacks and dress shirts may be expected.

discover

AUSTRIA

The Seine has its lovers' trysts. The Thames has its bridges. The Tiber has Romulus and Remus. The Danube has—well, put on the Blue Danube and lace up your waltzing shoes, traveler, because this river will have you dancing. For joy, that is. This area has been inspiring troubled writers, wacky musicians, and singing families for centuries, but it's still hard to pinpoint exactly what is special about Austria and its iconic waterway. Maybe it's that Austria has maintained much of the charming 17th- and 18th-century architecture built along the river, resulting in a picturesque scene whether you stay in Vienna or venture into von Trapp territory in Salzburg. Or you can experience Austria's second-largest but often overlooked city, Graz, whose local university makes it a haven for students. Or maybe it's that the Viennese really do dance the waltz en masse on New Year's Eve. We haven't found one, all-encompassing answer yet (though not for lack of trying). We challenge you to find it, one cup of Viennese coffee and Danube backdrop at a time.

greatest hits

- **CAPTAIN KIRCHE.** While Vienna boasts a number of churches—what European capital doesn't?—the most impressive of all is **St. Stephen's Cathedral** in the first district. (p. 11)

- **DRINK LIKE A LOCAL.** Tone your drinking muscles at **Flex**, a popular Vienna club with an offbeat vibe. (p. 22)

- **THE HILLS ARE ALIVE.** Let your inner Von Trapp child sing as you stroll through **Salzburg**, where you can see nearly endless renditions of the musical. (p. 26)

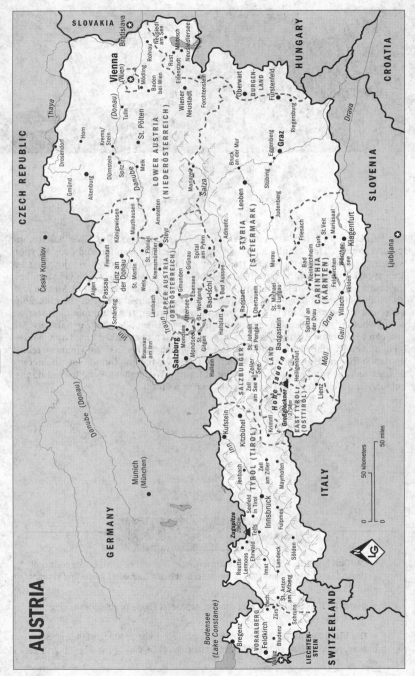

vienna

Austria's capital city is an ancient maze of breathtaking old buildings rooted in a rich history of rising and falling empires and wars. Wandering down the stone city streets, you may find yourself at the steps of a palace or a magnificent church. The spirits of Mozart, Beethoven, and many famous composers that even the biggest of Beliebers would recognize still linger in Vienna, from the city's famous opera to the countless citizens who work to preserve Vienna's rich musical heritage. While much of the city is rooted in classics and tradition, newer generations of the Viennese are bringing a modern edge to the historical city. Contemporary art is on the ups, and its cool presence stands out even more clearly when juxtaposed with the old world. The pace of Vienna is relaxed. Here, loitering for hours in coffee shops and parks is a right. Yet amongst the loiterers and on nearly every street corner, you'll find some of the most talented philosophers, artists, and musicians in the world, making Vienna the magical place it is today.

SIGHTS

▨ ST. STEPHEN'S CATHEDRAL   CHURCH
Stephansplatz 3   ☎001 515 52 30 54 www.stephanskirche.at

Perhaps the most monstrous thing ever to possess a pet name, St. Stephen's Cathedral (which the native Viennese call "Steffl") stands looming in Vienna's ever-busy first district. The cathedral's history is as deep as the dirt and grime that give the once white building its black tint. St. Stephen's Cathedral was built atop the ruins of two churches in 1106, but its expansion lasted into the 16th century. While you can get a glimpse into the beautifully ordained baroque interior of the cathedral without handing over any euro, this is only the tip of iceberg. If you decide to stop being cheap and are willing to cough up €4.50, you'll find yourself immersed in the cathedral's history (and potentially dust), as the giant limestone church holds many treasures, including the sepulcher of Emperor Frederik III, the Altarpiece of Wiener Neustadt, and a lot of old tombs. Guided tours of the cathedral catacombs and historical artifacts are given regularly, making sure you won't miss out on a single famous dead guy. Take a hike up the 300+ stairs, and you can see a spectacular view of Vienna from St. Stephen's south tower. Equally as beautiful as what you see from the inside is roof above your head. The cathedral's giant roof is adorned with colored tiles that are definitely Insta-worthy. Vivaldi's "Four Seasons" is played each year during the annual summer cathedral concert—haunting, considering the church was the site of the famous composer's funeral. And if you're not into real historic facts, the church is also rich in myths and legends about anything from forbidden romances to bread loafs (ask a guide to learn more!).

i €4.50. ☑ Open M-Sa 6am-10pm, Su 7am-10pm. Guided tours M-Sa 10:30am and 3pm, Su 3pm.

SPANISH RIDING SCHOOL   HORSEBACK RIDING
Michaelerplatz 1   ☎01 5339031 www.srs.at/en

While Vienna has world-renowned ballets and operas, what really puts the city a step (or gallop) above the rest is its dancing horses. Okay, so the world-class equestrians of the Spanish Riding School in Vienna's Hofburg Palace might resent someone referring to their haute ecole (classical equestrian training) as "dancing," but their practice is as marvelous as any ballet. Vienna's Spanish Riding School is the oldest of its kind and has preserved its traditional art throughout the years. And despite its name, the horses of the riding school are as Austrian as Mozartkugeln, bred at Piber Federal Stud in Western Austria. The school gets its name not from the home of the horses but rather from their breed, which is the Lipizzan Spanish breed. Once "enrolled" in the Spanish Riding School, the

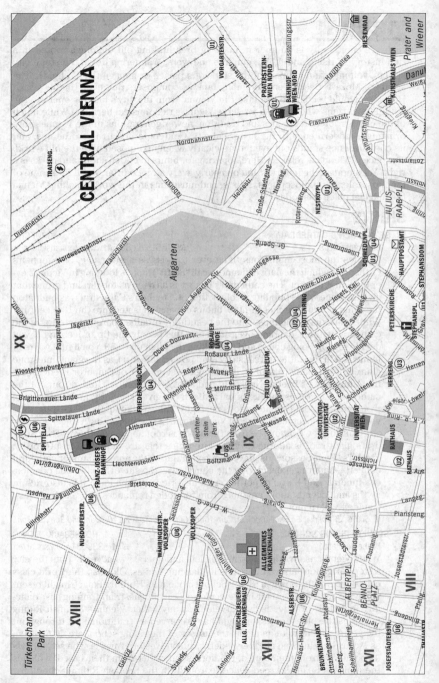

CENTRAL VIENNA

Türkenschanz-Park

XVIII

XX

Augarten

Prater and
Wiener

RESENRAD

KUNSTHAUS WIEN

Danu

Weiße

Dampfschiffstr.

Krieger

PRATERSTERN-
WIEN NORD

BAHNHOF
WIEN-NORD

VORGARTENSTR.

Nordbahnstr.

Heinestr.

Große Stadtgut

Nordbahnstr

Rotensteng.

NESTROYPL.

Praterstr.

Ausstellungsstr.

Hauptallee

Franzensbrstr.

Zollamtssr.

mtssr.

TRAISENG.

Dresdnerstr.

Rauscherstr.

Jägerstr.

Nordwestbahnstr.

Taborstr.

Obere-Augarten-Str.

Leopoldsgasse

Gr. Sperlg.

Obere-Donau-Str.

Lilienbrunng.

JULIUS-
RAAB-PL.

SCHWEDENPL.

HAUPTPOSTAMT

STEPHANSDOM

Stromstr.

Pappenheimg.

Wallensteinstr.

Wexstr.

Reinprechtsdsl.

Klosterneuburgerstr.

Brigittenauer Lände

Spittelauer Lände

SPITTELAU

FRIEDENSBRÜCKE

Rembrandtstr.

Obere Donaustr.

Unt. Augarten

ROSSAUER
LÄNDE

Rossauer Lände

SCHOTTENRING

Franz Josefs Kai.

Rotenturmstr.

PETERSKIRCHE

STEPHANSPL.

Maria-Theresien-Str.

Werdertorg.

Neutor.

Börsg.

Wipplingerstr.

Tiefer Graben

HERRENG.

Herren

Althanstr.

Rögerg.

Hahng.

Pramerg.

FREUD MUSEUM

Börse

Schottenring

Schottentor

HERRENG.

R.-T.-R.-Ring

Döblingergürtel

FRANZ-JOSEFS-
BAHNHOF

Rotenlöweng.

Glaserg.

Seeg.

Müllnerg.

Porzellang.

Liechtensteinstr.

Thurn-Wasser-Str.

Türken-

SCHOTTENTOR
UNIVERSITÄT

Unt.-Str.

UNIVERSITÄT
WIEN

Döblinger Hauptstr.

Liechtensteinstr.

Liechten-
stein
Park

Fürsteng.

Boltzmanng.

US

Strudelhofg.

IX

RATHAUS

RATHAUS

Landesge-
richtsstr.

NUSSDORFERSTR.

Sobieskig.

Sechsschimmelg.

Nußdorferstr.

Alserbachstr.

Währingerstr.

Spitalg.

Aue

Billrothstr.

NUSSDORFERSTR.

W.-Exner-G.

Sechsschg.

Lazarettg.

Langeg.

Piaristeng.

VOLKSOPER

WÄHRINGERSTR.-
VOLKSOPER

Günmp.

ALLGEMEINES
KRANKENHAUS

Währinger Gürtel

Alserstr.

Skodag.

Laudong.

Florianig.

Josefstädterstr.

VIII

Gymnasiumstr.

Schopenhauerstr.

MICHELBEUERN
ALLG. KRANKENHAUS

ALSERSTR.

Martinstr.

Buschbeg.

Kinderspitalg.

ALBERTPL.

BENNO-
PLATZ

Blindeng.

Pfeilg.

Lenaug.

XVII

Geitzg.

Antonig.

Kreuzg.

Staudig.

Heindler-Haupt-Str.

BRUNNENMARKT

Ottakringerstr.

Payerg.

Scheithammerg.

Hernaiser Gürtel

XVI

JOSEFSTÄDTERSTR.

THALIASTR.

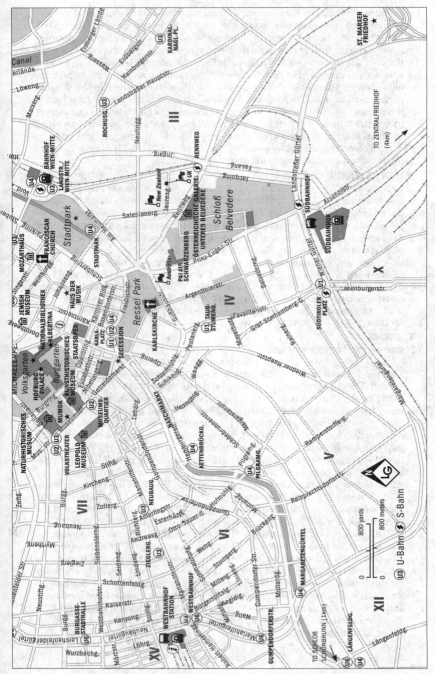

vienna

stallions are trained for six years to do things as simple as changing legs to more complicated moves like pirouetting—so maybe making the comparison to a ballet isn't so ridiculous. While many horses go through this intensive training, only a few make the final cut and have a chance to perform. Of course, horses are not the only animals trained at the Spanish Riding School, as teenagers and young adults are also trained to ride and control the animals, and the horse and rider ultimately perform as one unit. You can see the incredible acts in the school's gorgeous riding hall. The exquisite baroque architecture itself is worth a visit to the school. Tours of the school are given throughout each day. If you're dying to see the horses in action but can't make it to a gala performance, morning trainings with music are also offered to give visitors a glimpse of the show.

i Tour of school and other Hofburg museums €22. Show tickets €20-160. ⏰ Open daily 9am-4pm. (Times may vary based on performance. Check website for details.)

WIENER RIESENRAD   AMUSEMENT PARK
Riesenradplatz 1   ☎01 7295430 www.wienerriesenrad.com/de

Construction in 1897, Wiener Riesenrad is no longer the world's tallest big wheel, but it is still a famous symbol of Vienna and perhaps an even more famous date place, with its two luxurious gondolas, the Jubilaum and Kaiserwaggon. Today, the Ferris wheel stands at the entrance of Vienna's Prater amusement park, so after you take your touristy photos, you can spend your whole day (and budget) on a host of rides, from ones that whirl you backwards to ones that whirl you upsidedown and spin you all around. Just be sure to give yourself enough time to get your bearings before checking out the delicious Eisvogel in the square surrounding the park, which fittingly serves award-winning Viennese cuisine.

i Entrance to park free. Ride tickets €9, children €4. ⏰ Open daily Jan-Feb 10am-7:45pm, March-Apr 10am-9:45pm, May-Sept 9am-11:45pm, Oct 10am-9:45pm, Nov-Dec 10am-7:45pm.

STADTPARK   PARK
Main entrance from Johannesgasse   ☎01 40 00 80 42
                        www.wien.gv.at/umwelt/parks/anlagen/stadtpark.html

Vienna's first public park, Stadtpark is a must for photos, walks, or just lying around. The huge green covers 28 acres and stretches from the city's first district to the third. Stadtpark is more than just a great place to loiter; it is also home to many famous statues of dudes we should all know but probably don't, such as Franz Schubert, Anton Bruckner, and the mayor who created the park, Andreas Zelinka. Zelinka doesn't ring a bell? Don't worry, you're in good company. One guy you should definitely know is Johann Strauss. Not only did he compose the Blue Danube Waltz, but his memorial in Stadtpark is one of the most photographed monuments in the world—yes, shocking that it isn't Mozart! The gilded bronze monument of the composer playing the violin has been housed in Stadtpark since 1921 and has been selfie central since the birth of the iPhone. Also of note is the picturesque stone bridge that connects the two halves of the park, which are divided by the Wienfluss river. While the bridge, constructed in 1857, may not be as popular as Strauss's memorial, it is equally photogenic and a beautiful place to take a stroll and some snapshots. For kids or anyone who just really likes to swing, Kinderpark was added to the park only one year after its opening and continues to operate as a playground and site for many pickup football games. For the "I'm-an-artist-not-an-athlete" types, Stadtpark's Kursalon is a beautiful Italian Renaissance-style building that is used for dances and concerts. And uniting the sporty and artistic is the Kursalon's delicious Cafe Restaurant Johann—apple strudel is the only way to end a day at Stadtpark.

i Free. ⏰ Open daily 24hr.

austria

KARLSKIRCHE

Kreuzherrengasse 1

CHURCH

☎1 505 62 94 www.karlskirche.at

The green dome of Karlskirche peaks its head between the rows of buildings of Karlsplatz, sparking the curiosity of all who catch a glimpse. Upon closer investigation, you'll find a beautiful opening in the streets and stores of Karlsplatz that houses this fantastic baroque church. Karlskirche or St. Charles's Church, was built in 1739, fulfilling a vow taken by Emporer Charles VI during a plague epidemic—history's ultimate pinky promise. The famous church, often cited as one of the most beautiful churches in Vienna, was consecrated for St. Charles Borromeo, and the exhibits inside display some of his possessions. But perhaps more exquisite than the exhibits (and free) is the view you'll get by just standing in the breathtaking cathedral and looking up. The entire building is a true baroque masterpiece: its high alter has been restored to look as spectacular as ever, with an abundance of golds and marble; at the top of the alter is a triangular window letting in an almost heavenly light; and its ceiling is painted fantastically. Karlskirche also allows you to climb up to the second floor and get an up-close look at the intricate colors and detailing of the famous building.

i €6. ☼ Open M-Sa 9am-6pm with 30min. lunch break at 12:30pm, Su noon-5:45pm.

TIERGARTEN SCHONBRUNN

Maxingstraße 13b

ZOO

☎1 87 79 29 40 www.zoovienna.at

The Tiegarten Schonbrunn, located at Vienna's biggest castle, the Schonbrunn, is the oldest (and one of the largest) zoo in the world. It was constructed in 1752 by Emperor Franz I as the royal menagerie. The circular structure that now operates as one of many restaurants in the zoo was originally constructed as the breakfast pavilion for the emperor and his wife, Maria Theresia. Talk about upper crust. One of the most popular exhibits in the zoo is its giant pandas, Yang Yang, Long Hui, Fu Hu, and Fu Long, whose natural birth in 2007 was the first of its kind in all of Europe. Don't think that because Tiegarten Schonbrunn is old it's also out of date. In fact, the zoo has aged like wine and gotten better with time. While it preserves its old charm and character, Tiegarten has become quite modern. Its over 500 species are housed in a simulated rainforest house, flooded Amazon, and an arctic region for the zoo's new polar bears. Tiegarten Schonbrunn was also awarded the title of Europe's best zoo three times. Make sure to head to the zoo well before its 6:30pm closing time, as many of the animals start falling asleep and hiding around 5:30pm.

i €16.50. ☼ Open daily Apr-Sept 9am-6:30pm, Oct 9am-5:30pm, Nov-Jan 9am-4:30pm, Feb 9am-5pm, Mar 9am-5:30pm.

SIGMUND FREUD MUSEUM

Berggasse 19

MUSEUM

☎1 319 15 96 www.freud-museum.at

Suffering from disruptive creams? In need of a way to train your pet mouse? Check out Vienna's Sigmund Freud museum in the ninth district. The museum, located in Vienna's former Jewish district, is the former residence of the famous psychologist before he emigrated from Austria to Britain during World War II. While you may not work out your Oedipus complex here, you will find a great deal of original Freud paraphernalia displayed in the small museum. It is furnished with couches and chairs that once cushioned the legend and the crazy patients he studied. Also on display are a number of Freud's papers and studies as well as a documentary on Freud's life. The museum was started with help from Freud's daughter, Anna, in 1971 and continues to grow. If you, like most college students, took any type of psychology class during your studies, then getting a look into the digs of the man who caused you all that grief during exam week is a fascinating experience.

i €8. ☼ Open daily 9am-5pm.

vienna

austria

HOSTELING INTERNATIONAL MYRTHENGASSE
HOSTEL $

Myrthengasse 7 ☎01 52 36 31 60 www.hihostels.com

As part of an international hostel chain, Hostelling International has the formula for mediocre living down: bed, sheets, and a roof over the head... and maybe some butter and toast to really entice the guests. While a stay at Hosteling International Myrthengasse is definitely preferable to bumming it under a tree, it's more basic than a 12-year-old Instagramming a pumpkin spice latte. Hosteling International Myrthengasse is all about functionality. The hostel's location makes it easy to escape into Old Town Vienna, and it's only a short walk to the bustling downtown. If you are a Hosteling International member, Hosteling International Myrthengasse is perhaps your most economically intelligent move.

i *Dorms starting at €22.* ☉ *Reception 24hr.*

MY MOJO VIE HOSTEL
HOSTEL $

Kaiserstrasse 77, Apt. 8 ☎676 55 111 55 www.mymojovie.at

The danger with staying at Mojo Hostel is that you'll probably never want to leave. In fact, some guests have been known to book the minimum two nights and ended up staying six weeks. Lucky ducks. In order to book a room at this beautiful converted apartment, you must plan far in advance—don't rely on doing the classic student traveler move of booking the night before. While the hostel may be a decent walk from the city center, it is very close to a metro station that'll get you to Vienna's first district in a flash. But honestly, with all the free hostel food and great amenities, you might find yourself staying in more often than you'd think. For your comfort, the hostel offers a full bath (that's right, even a tub!), towels, comfortable beds, a TV and cozy living room, and a laptop for use in each room. Mojo's prices may seem a little steep for a hostel, but in the end, the high quality amenities are worth a few extra euro, and the friends you'll make are priceless.

i *Rooms starting at €34.* ☉ *Reception 24hr.*

BELIEVE IT OR NOT HOSTEL
HOSTEL $

Myrthengasse 10/14 ☎0676 55 00 055 www.believe-it-or-not-vienna.at

Ripley's Believe It or Not Museum boasts freaking bizarre things. Vienna's Believe It or Not Hostel boasts the freaking best. A self-proclaimed "all inclusive apartment," Believe It or Not has the feel of a home more than that of a hostel. It's interior is stylish, with wood floors, animal skin rugs, white furniture, pillows, steel, guitars, a hammock—the list of chicness is so long that to name everything making Believe it or Not Hostel more put together than you would take up this whole listing. Its location is convenient, as it is in a quiet neighborhood in the old town but is still less than a mile from Hofburg Castle and the busy city. And when hostel host Lilly is around to make breakfast and chat up guests, she acts as though she is inviting you into her home rather than just taking your cash. She is incredibly warm, kind, and personable. The price for perfection is not cheap as Believe It or Not is a bit expensive for a hostel, but look at it this way: skip one meal and instead fill up on the hostel's free Nutella.

i *8-bed dorms €35. 4-bed dorms €40. Breakfast free.* ☉ *Reception open daily 8am-noon, if arriving before or after, buzz in with the intercom.*

BURGGARTEN

Josefsplatz 1

PARK

☎1 533 90 83 www.bmlfuw.gv.at

Of Vienna's many parks, Burggarten definitely wins "Most Likely to be Full On Any Given Day of the Week." The park, which is as large as its accolade, is often filled with many picnic blankets and bodies sprawled across its grass. Primarily young Viennese and tourists can be found throughout the historic park, with everyone eating, playing music, juggling, and, more often than not, getting a bit tipsy. The park has two main sections divided by a strip of large trees. Its main entrance on the side of the Ringstrasse opens up to the Mozart Memorial and flowers in the shape of a treble clef. This side is more likely to have tourists taking goofy pictures, so if you can ignore the constant cheesing, you'll find that this side is less crowded in terms of loiterers and often full of street musicians and jugglers hoping to benefit from the international disturbers of the peace. Behind the barrier of trees is the more popular side for Viennese youth. It is a huge open field adjacent to the Schmetterling Haus (Butterfly House) and the Burggarten Cafe. It's the perfect place to enjoy Frisbee, footsie, and wine straight from the bottle.

i Free. ☺ Open daily 24hr.

RATHAUS

Friedrich-Schmidt-Platz 1

CULTURAL SITE

☎01 525 50 www.wien.gv.at

Rathaus means "town hall," which to you probably means boring meetings or local crazies arguing about noise complaints. But the Rathaus of Vienna is far from mundane. Not only is this gorgeous gothic building, which serves as the city's town hall, the home of the mayor, but it is also the backdrop of the beautiful Rathauspark. The park is huge and has many green fields and fountains, perfect for wasting away a lazy afternoon. But even the opportunity to loiter in luxury is not the best feature of Rathaus. Throughout the summer, the mayor hosts a number of cultural events in his ultimate front yard throughout the summer. The Rathaus brings the locals of Vienna and tourists together through film, art, and cultural festivals, such as the huge, annual Vienna Pride and Rainbow Parade. If you visit Vienna's town hall in the summer, you are likely to find yourself in the middle of one of these many fests. But if you miss out and catch the park at one of its quieter moments, embrace the peace of the park and the breathtaking architecture of Vienna's town hall.

i Free. ☺ Open daily 24hr.

CAFE CENTRAL

Herrengasse 14

CAFE

☎01 5333763 www.palaisevents.at/cafecentral.html

Once a grand bank and stock market house, Palais Ferstel opened Cafe Central as its focus in 1876. The interior of this coffee house looks like it could be located in the Hofburg rather than on a city center street corner. It is composed of huge arches, plush red seating, and perhaps its greatest crown: the best applestrudel in Vienna (making it the best in the world). Famous intellectuals such as Freud and infamous dictators like Hitler have all graced Central's booths to ponder humanity for hours over the cafe's near-perfect melanges. But today, one thing you're almost guaranteed to not see at Cafe Central is any locals. The cafe is a hub for tourists with big cameras and iPhones, taking photos of nearly every bite. Not that anyone can blame them after seeing the decadent, flaky, layer upon layer of warm cinnamon perfection that is the applestrudel or the mountain of whipped cream it comes with. If the strudel isn't enough sugar for you, you probably have a problem. Still, do yourself a favor and at least look at the other cakes on display in the front of the cafe. Indulge all your senses, fulfill your daily calorie count, and embrace your touristy side—Cafe Central is worth it.

i Coffee €3-7. Cakes €3-6. ☺ Open M-Sa 7:30am-10pm.

vienna

FOOD

MOMEN
HEALTH FOOD $$

Neuer Markt 8a

www.momen.at

Face it, if you've been in Vienna for any time at all, you've probably had at least one of these three things: schnitzel, apple strudel, or McDonald's. Which means that eating healthily isn't easy with the plethora of sweets and fried food waiting for you around every corner in Vienna. Fortunately, Momen, located in Vienna's first district, changes the game and offers a selection of healthy, organic, and delicious food. Momen's menu primarily consists of three things: hummus, steak, and salad. You can get hummus and guacamole, hummus and chicken, and even hummus and either New York Strip or Flank Steak. If you aren't into hummus, 1) What is wrong with you? 2) Momen's other main entrees have just as many unique, fresh, and delicious choices. On top of being a health foods restaurant, Momen is also an outdoor hookah bar—interesting combo, but we won't question it because it gives the restaurant a cool vibe and makes it a true hummus hangout.

i *Hummus €9-16. Steak €13-20.* 🕑 *Open daily 11am-11pm.*

CAFE ESPRESSO
CAFE $

Burggasse 57

☎0676 596 16 45 www.myashoka.de

The bamboo wall blocking the outdoor seating from the street and the Hawaiian flowered umbrellas blocking customers from UV rays make Cafe Espresso stand out from the millions of other coffee shops in Vienna. The beach feel, juxtaposed with the beautiful old world feel that is inescapable in Vienna, gives the cafe a stylish but chill vibe. It's the perfect place to relax with a cappuccino and your computer (or, who knows, a real book). Not only is Cafe Espresso good for espresso (duh) and loitering, it also serves delicious food. Start the day off right by devouring a "Fluffy Omelette" that lives up to its name or, if still recovering from the night before, try Espresso's hangover cure of eggs with cheese and ham on a delicious roll. And when that doesn't quite rid you of the jackhammer in your head, don't be afraid to flop out on Espresso's retro booths or lay your head on the table. That's not rude. It's just that chill here.

i *Coffee €2-5.* 🕑 *Open M-F 7:30am-1am, Sa-Su 10am-1am.*

EIS-GREISSLER
ICE CREAM $

Rotenturmstraße 14

☎664 311 91 95

Despite being a tiny shop surrounded by the big department stores of Vienna's Rotenturmstraße street, Eis-Greissler is impossible to miss (largely due to the women's-restroom-length line stretching from its counter out onto the sidewalk). When you realize that Eis-Greissler is just another ice cream shop, the long line might have you scratching your head. But just wait. Flavors like goat cheese, sour cream blueberry, and elder flower are just a few of the options you'll find on Eis-Greissler's menu. Goat cheese ice cream might sound freaking bizarre, but one lick and you'll wonder why you ever settled for basic bitches like vanilla and chocolate (although those classics are available as well). Apart from its unique flavors, Eis-Greissler's ingredients also make it special—everything that goes into your heavenly scoop(s) are from local farms and 100% organic. (Organic means healthy right?) Whether you're in Vienna for a month, a day, or a mere 30min. stop by Eis-Greissler ASAP. You'll never look at ice cream the same way.

i *1 scoop €2. 2 scoop €3.40.* 🕑 *Open daily 11am-11pm.*

FREIRAUM
RESTAURANT, BAR $$$

Mariahilfer Straße 117

☎01 59 69 600 www.freiraum117.at

If Freiraum's chic appearance doesn't intimidate you, step into this huge restaurant, bar, lounge, and cafe that is just as trendy as it appears. Freiraum's menu

has as many types of cuisine as a hipster has favorite foreign films. You can choose anything Thai to Italian to American to good old schnitzel. Its cocktails, as expensive as they are trendy, are refreshing and delicious; its delicious, thin crust pizza is so good it'll be gone in seconds; and its curry has the perfect amount of kick. Freiraum even makes schnitzel elegant. On a sunny day, Freiraum's open windows make this a place you could waste your whole day.

i Entrees €12-25. Drinks €5-12. ⏰ Open M-Th 8am-2am, F-Sa 8am-4am, Su 8am-2am.

LE BOL
CAFE $$

Neuer Markt 14 ☎06 99 10 30 18 99 www.lebol.at

True coffee lovers know that a cup is simply not enough. A bowl, on the other hand, is every coffee lover's fantasy. If the name isn't a dead giveaway, Le Bol is where these dreams come true. This French-inspired cafe in Vienna's first district is popular for its bowls of delicious joe as well as its fine pastries, sandwiches, and snack plates. Even more unique about than the dishware is where Le Bol serves its espresso: while it has a large outdoor dining area and a few intimate tables inside, Le Bol calls itself "la table commune de Vienna." For those of you who don't speak French and can't figure out the rather obvious translation, this means "the common table of Vienna." Step inside the warm cafe, and you'll understand why. In the center of the cafe's main dining room is a large rectangular table that seats nearly 20 people. Here people come together to share interesting conversation and loads of dinner stories—like your family's Christmas dinner, except with less dysfunction. In true Viennese style, people sit for hours reading, conversing, and relaxing at the cafe's tables, big or small.

i Coffee €2.50-5. Entrees €6-13. ⏰ Open daily 8am-10pm.

BITZINGER WURSTELSTAND ALBERTINA
VIENNESE $

Augustinerstraße 1 ☎1 533 10 26 www.bitzinger.at

Bitzinger Wurstelstand Albertina may look like just another food stand selling hotdogs and pretzels, but there's a reason its line is so impressive: it's that damn good. The wursts of Bitzinger Wurstelstand Albertina are known throughout Vienna for being among the top street foods. Juicy, tender, and savory, these wursts are heavenly on a sober day and downright orgasmic on a drunken nights. And just because Bitzinger Wurstelstand Albertina is a food stand doesn't mean it's simple. You can choose from a variety of hotdogs and wursts here—some served spicy with curry, others traditional with mustard. The most popular wurst is a classic filled with pockets of melted cheese. The dogs can be served in a bun for easy transport or sliced on a plate. Either way, the location of Bitzinger Wurstelstand Albertina right next to Burggarten park makes it the perfect place to get cheap eats on the go.

i Wursts €3-6. ⏰ Open daily 11am-midnight.

CASTELLETTO
CAFE $$

Rotenturmstraße 24 ☎01 535 44 83 www.castelletto.at

If the dangling gold lights of Castelletto don't catch your eye, the even more fantastical gelato creations here surely will. Located in the busy Schwedenplatz, Castelletto is a popular summer hangout for both locals and tourists. The cafe, restaurant, and gelato stand has very limited indoor seating, but it has a huge dining space outside. If ice cream, cookies, and fudge aren't at the bottom of your food pyramid, you should first try reevaluating your priorities, but if that doesn't work for you, go ahead and check out the rest of Castelletto's menus. The cafe has a number of options, from salads to soups to steak and salmon. With its perfect location and sell-your-soul-for-them sweets, Castelletto is a worthwhile stop on any day in Vienna.

i Entrees €8-15. Gelato €1.50-6. ⏰ Open daily 7am-midnight.

austria

STEINDL

VIENNESE $$

Stumpergasse 59   ☎1 596 52 76 www.restaurant-steindl.at

While only a turn away from the busy city center, Steindl is a quiet, chill spot to get a good meal. With its relaxed bar, simple decor, and all too cool owners, Steindl will wrap you in relaxation with or without the help of wine. Its menu includes traditional Viennese delicacies but with Steindl's own gourmet touches. Schnitzel is served with tomato and mozzarella, and pastas include exotic mushrooms and rich cream sauces. Like your mom's home cooking, this cuisine somehow hits the spot. But unlike your mom's home cooking, the flavors here are a bit more creative and complex. The food of Steindl looks as fancy as it sounds, and while dishes are chic and stylish, the restaurant itself is casual. You might feel so comfortable in Steindl's wooden booths that you get the urge to sling off your shoes and put up your feet. Although frequented by many tourists, especially due its proximity to a popular hostel, Steindl's crowd includes many locals.

i Entrees €7-20. Drinks €2-10. ✪ Open M-F 10am-10pm, Sa 3-8pm. Bar open M-Sa until midnight.

INDISCHES NAMASTE

INDIAN $$

Seidengasse 41   ☎01 523 80 60

Indisches Namaste is the underdog you love to root for. It's a small, family owned Indian restaurant just a few blocks from Vienna's Westbanhof train station. Run by an Indian husband and wife duo, Namaste is quite the mom and pop operation, with the wife cooking and the husband serving. This makes sitting down at Namaste feel almost like stepping into someone's home for dinner instead of going to a restaurant. When you eat at Namaste, you're never quite sure what you're going to get—sometimes its doors may not open until 20min. after their 6pm dinner service begins, and you aren't guaranteed to find chicken tandoori being served here, but as they say, when one door closes, another one opens. And any one of Namaste's open doors is delicious and authentic and full of flavor. But beware, when you are warned of the dark green sauces' spiciness, it isn't because your waiter thinks you're a lightweight—it will truly make your mouth burn.

i €8-15. ✪ Open for lunch daily 11am-3pm. Dinner daily 6-11pm.

CAFE PRUCKEL

CAFE $

Stubenring 24   ☎01 5126115 www.prueckel.at

Cafe Pruckel is perhaps the least touristy of the traditional cafes in Vienna's city center. Stepping into Pruckel is like stepping into the '60s. The decor is retro, with old cafe booths and beautiful chandeliers. Perhaps the nicest modern addition to Pruckel is the distinct smoking section, which is separated from the rest of the restaurant by a large glass door, keeping the main dining area smelling like cappuccino rather than cigarettes. Overall, Cafe Pruckel lives up to its title as a classic Viennese cafe. If you aren't diehard enough to trade occasionally slow service for authenticity, its convenient location across from Stadtpark and delicious cakes might sway you to give this famous cafe a go.

i Coffee €2-6. Cakes €2-4. ✪ Open daily 8:30am-10pm.

FIGMULLER

VIENNESE $$

Wollzeile 5   ☎01 59 69 600 www.figlmueller.at/en

It's no secret that Figmuller is the place to get Wiener Schnitzel. It's also no secret that Wiener Schnitzel is the food to get in Vienna. Put these two facts together, and it means you will definitely be making a trip to this small, traditional Viennese restaurant. Although all the food served at Figmuller is Viennese, its clientel is anything but. This historical restaurant opened over 100 years ago and has since become a hot spot for tourists in search of the world's best schnitzel. While words like "best" are hard to quantify, "bigggest" is easily measurable, and

Figmuller's larger-than-your-face-sized schnitzel are pretty incomparable. Along with the giant fried meat, you'll need to pack in some fruits and vegetables, too; Figmuller suggests pairing its famous schnitzel with traditional potato salad cranberry sauce. While all the add-ons might make for a pricey meal, live it up and indulge.

i Entrees €12-20. 🕰 Open daily 11am-10:30pm.

PHIL
CAFE $

Gumpendorfer Straße 10-12   ☎01 5810489   phil.info

With its shelves full of books ranging from the mainstream Hunger Games series to artsy picture books, Phil feels more like an intellectual hipster's living room than a cafe. While all Viennese cafes expect loitering, Phil is designed for it. In the back, it has good work tables surrounded by comfortable couches and plush chairs, and its library-sized book collection is free for hours of consumption. Along with all the delectable artsiness waiting to be devoured is a delicious selection of coffee, tea, breakfasts, and sandwiches. Here, you can get anything from just a cup of tea to a food baby-worthy meal and then sit around for hours. If its interior and customers weren't hip enough, Phil also boasts a wide range of organic, vegetarian, and vegan food. So ditch your touristy ways for a few hours and lose yourself in a world of literature, comfy couches, and caffeine.

i Meals €8-10. Drinks €2-6. 🕰 Open M 5pm-1am, Tu-Su 9am-1am.

NIGHTLIFE

TEL AVIV BEACH
BAR

Donaukanal Straße 26   de-de.facebook.com/telavivbeach

The resort town of Vienna is known for its sandy white beaches and crashing ocean waves. That last sentence was a lie. Have you seen a map recently? Austria is landlocked. But this geographical problem doesn't keep the bars of Vienna from adopting a beach theme. Tel Aviv Beach Bar is one of many resort-themed bars along the Danube—or as the Viennese call it, Donau—River. Its (imported) white sand, beach chairs, and umbrellas transport you to the beautiful coast of Israel...even if you can't so much as dip your toes in the Donau. While Tel Aviv Beach Bar closes fairly early and is no real place to party, it has a chill, come-as-you-are vibe that is perfect for relaxing or pregaming before hitting some of the clubs along the river. If there is a big sports game going on, Tel Aviv is the place to go to avoid the feel of a standard sports bar while still keeping an eye on the score. If you aren't into watching the big screen, you can dangle your feet over the edge of the Danube's wall and chat or relax. Although Tel Aviv Beach is a big date spot or place to hang out with a group of friends, it's easy to bond with fellow sports fans or mojito lovers. Tel Aviv Beach does a wonderful job supplying all the sand and drinks necessary to make you think you're at a real beach resort, but don't take the theme too far: while shorts and bare feet are both acceptable, leave the bikini back in the backpack.

i Beer and wine €2-6. Mixed drinks €5-12. 🕰 Open daily noon-midnight.

FLEX
CLUB

Augartenbrücke 1   ☎01 5337525   flex.at/flex_frontend

Are you into guys with gauges, chicks with shaved heads, or jumping around like no one is watching? If you answered yes to any of the above, Flex just might be the club for you. If you answered yes to all of the above, this small club along the side of the Danube was literally made for you. Although a popular club in Vienna, Flex maintains an offbeat vibe. Its crowd is young and casual and generally grungy. You probably won't be hearing any of your favorite top 40 jams at Flex, but rather a mix of electronic, house, and reggae. The unassuming, unpretentious vibe of Flex allows for great dancing, which really means horrible dancing that is a tremendous amount of fun. Feeding off the high energy, you'll find yourself jumping from corner to corner, not afraid of who is watching. Flex is an ideal club for those looking to burn off the calories of booze. With its cool crowd and ultra-trippy clips from Alice and Wonderland that are projected on the wall, Flex is the perfect, balls-to-the-wall party zone in Vienna.

i *Cover €12. Drinks €5-12.* ⏰ *Open daily 8pm-6am.*

SUMMER STATION

Floridsdorf

DANCING

☎650 50 06 954 www.summerstation.at

Looking to escapes your fellow overly-eager tourists and the overly-commercial areas of the city? Summer Station is the place for you. Located on the Danube Island (or the Donau, as Austrians call it), Summer Station is an island retreat in an ocean of loud, high-heeled nightlife. It hosts outdoor parties on the little strip of land in the Danube every night of the week, and its large dance floor sees everything from Salsa Thursdays to "Freaky" Fridays. Regardless of the music style, locals make the trek to the island club for one reason: to dance. While big sporting events may be played on screens in the background and delicious Indian food is served at the bar, the dance floor is constantly packed. Couples and friends of all ages storm the floor to show off their moves—and we're not talking about dropping, dipping, or dougying anything. Instead, Summer Station is full of people who love to swing dance or salsa or who are willing to try their hand at real dancing. Don't be intimidated by the twirling pros before you—the crowd at Summer Station is excited to help newcomers pick up a few cha-cha steps and spins. And whether you find that you have two left feet or were born to dance, all levels are encouraged to groove to the DJ's superb music selection.

i *Free.* ⏰ *Open daily 11am-11pm.*

L..K BAR

Salzgries 17

☎067 67 06 81 24 paddysco.at

You know that big comfy couch that seems to eat everything? Once something disappears into the cracks of its huge, plushy cushion, there is no hope in getting it back. At the L..k Bar near Vienna's Schwedenplatz, the unreachable sofa items are people, usually intoxicated, usually having the times of their lives. The L..k Bar takes Vienna's traditional loitering to a whole new level, as the walls of the second floor of this two-story bar are lined with giant sofas and TVs. In between is a hip bar serving decently priced beer and a plethora of shots. The service is fast and efficient for the young international and local crowd. This stylish, reasonably priced joint may seem like a perfect pregaming option, but this only stands true if your company remains downstairs in the more hyped, pool table environment. Upstairs, the drunker the crowd gets, the more appealing the couches become, and the more likely it is that you'll skip the club for a good snooze. L..k Bar is a great place to go with a group of friends who you neither mind drooling in front of nor chatting with for hours.

i *Beer €2.20. Shots €1.20.* ⏰ *Open M-Sa 8pm-4am.*

WIEN&CO

Universitätsring 12

WINE BAR

☎050 706 3142 www.weinco.at

Want to step away from the craziness of the club for a sophisticated night out? Head to Vienna's popular Wien&Co wine bar. The concept of Wien&Co is unique. On one side is a little wine store with a large selection of Austria's finest wines, along with international brands. The prices range greatly, from inexpensive favorites to bottles for high rollers only. Just don't expect to be finding your favorite Three Buck Chuck here—you said you wanted a sophisticated night, remember? Once you make your selection, head to the opposite side of the building, where you'll find a restaurant and bar. You can sit outside or indoors and satisfy your incoming drunchies by munching on delicious gourmet breads and cheeses or a full meal as a waiter pours you your wine selection at the perfect temperature. If you're not looking to buy a whole bottle of wine, the bar serves individual glasses as well as a variety of liquors. Despite its location in the tourist-infested Stephenplatz, the bar is mainly full of elegant locals, yet the cool environment is still welcoming to the stray traveler, and after a few glasses of wine, conversation rolls easily despite possible language barriers. Like many Viennese bars, Wien&Co allows smoking indoors, which is still considered fashionable in here. If you're sensitive to smoke, definitely grab a place outside the bar.

i *Prices vary greatly based on wine quality.* 🕐 *Open daily 10am-1am.*

SAULENHALLE
CLUB

Heldenplatz ☏1 532 42 41 www.facebook.com/Saeulenhalle

Standing only a door away from the famous, very posh Volksgarten, Saulenhalle is like a beauty queen's up-and-coming little sister. While it may not be on as high of a pedestal as its neighboring club, Saulenhalle is constantly boasting a line of high-heeled girls and blazered boys. The club is composed of a huge, long room with a bar at the entrance and a dance floor toward the rear. Along its walls are huge TVs and couches, and DJs often make appearances here, playing R&B and hip hop and proving that Pit Bull's status as Mr. Worldwide truly extends beyond the Americas. If the cool interior gets a bit too stuffy, the club has an outdoor area for warm summer nights, with yet another dance floor surrounded by candlelit tables and a bar. Unfortunately, classy clubs mean fucking expensive booze, so do yourself a favor and pregame on that bottle of wine before coming face to face with Saulenhalle's beastly glasses. But in the end, whether you're wine wasted or sober as can be, Saulenhalle's good music and beautiful crowd promises a good night under the Viennese stars.

i *Prices vary based on event. See online for details.* 🕐 *Open W 10pm-6am, Th-Sa 11pm-6am.*

IF DOGS RUN FREE
BAR

Gumpendorfer Straße 10 ☏01 913 21 32 www.ifdogsrunfree.com

While it's named after an old Bob Dylan song, this bar, located on Vienna's all too hip Gumpendorfer Strasse, also lends its name out to some pretty entertaining drinking games and profound rounds of the "what if" game. One thing Vienna is not lacking in is hipster bars, perhaps making chic, minimalistic joints such as If Dogs Run Free the new mainstream. Either way, the bar stands apart from its crunchy peers simply due to its high level of execution. Everything, from the bar's sleek, futuristic interior—red geometric sculptures hang over a cool gray bar—to its unique cocktails, is spot on. If you are looking to get the basic cocktails, If Dogs Run Free is not your place. But then again, if you are looking to get the basic cocktails, maybe you aren't off-beat enough for the bar in the first place. While If Dogs Run Free can whip up some classic cocktails, it is best known as serving interesting, less mainstream mixes like concoctions famous during the American Prohibition Era. Note: If Dogs Run Free isn't the place to get your dance on. (Twerking will most surely be frowned on.) However, it is a chill bar to pregame at or to get lost in sharing ideas and discussing art well into the wee hours of the morning.

i *Wine €3.20-5, cocktails €8-9.* 🕐 *Open Tu-W 5pm-2am, Th-Sa 5pm-4am, Su 5pm-2am.*

PRATERSAUNA
CLUB

Waldsteingartenstraße 135 ☏1 729 19 27 www.pratersauna.tv

Nightclub Pratersauna is a pool party unlike any you've ever experienced. While this is in part due to the fact that the pool isn't actually open for swimming on most nights (for obvious safety reasons), it is also due to the fantastic quality of parties promised at the popular club. Pratersauna is the place to be after dark in Vienna. It has multiple dance floors, which play primarily electronic, techno, and house music. Despite the club's size, it is almost guaranteed to be packed and have a line out the door. As suggested by its name, Pratersauna is a renovated sauna turned club in Prater park. Hints of the old, retro design can be found throughout the club, but they are masked by modern lighting and contemporary furniture, bars, and surprisingly beautiful bathrooms. If dancing is not your thing, you can lounge poolside on one of the love seats or in Pratersauna's large garden.

i *Price ranges from €8-12 based on event. ⌚ Club open daily 9pm-6am. Pool open 1pm-9pm.*

BABENBERGER PASSAGE   CLUB
Burgring 3 / Babenbergerstrasse 1   ☎01 961 88 00 www.club-passage.at

If you ask any young Viennese party animal where the "poshest" place to get down is, he or she will probably point you to Babenberger Passage Nightclub. Passage is pronounced so it rhymes with "massage," making it sound even cooler and more into itself. The entrance to this popular underground nightclub is a bit hard to find, as the club is literally under the sidewalks outside Burggarten Park. Its door can easily be mistaken for a metro entrance during the day, but at night, there is no mistaking the pounding base and red lights radiating from the tunnel entrance for your average U-bahn. Once underground, you'll find a huge open room with a dance floor surrounded by four bars, a DJ, and luxurious white couches—some of which are roped off for the club's VIPs. Although the blue and purple dance floor is pretty empty before midnight, many students and frugal party animals filter in before the witching hour to save a good deal of euro, as the club offers discounts before the clock strikes midnight. You'll need the extra cash if you plan on indulging in one of the bars well crafted, extremely overpriced drinks. Around 1am, the VIPs flood in and order buckets of vodka; this is when the club really starts picking up and the dance floor is crowded with Vienna's best dressed. The music and attire depend on what day of the week you're there. Wednesday is Club Cosmopolitan's R&B, Thursday is KutKlub's nostalgic retro hip hop, Friday is Flash Friday rap and R&B, and Saturday is Posh Club's hip hop. Real talk: basically all of these themed nights are the same, but the different names give you an excuse to try out the club night after night. If you were sensible enough not to pack your high heels and nicest clothes in your travel bag, don't worry: some of Passage's younger crowd are more concerned with showing off their moves than their Gucci, and your go-to jeans and nightout shirt won't be turned down.

i *Price ranges from €10-15 based on event. ⌚Open Tu 8pm-4am, W-Th 10pm-4am, F-Sa 11pm-6am.*

ESSENTIALS
Practicalities

- **TOURIST OFFICE:** Friedrich-Schmidt-Platz 1 (☎1 525 50 ⌚ Open daily M-F 8am-6pm.) The City Information Centre at Vienna's City Hall has brochures and pamphlets about Vienna's many attractions as well as onsite staff to answer any of your questions regarding the city.

- **POST OFFICE:** Most of Vienna's post offices are open daily 8am-6pm. Two post offices with extended hours are Post Office 1010 Wien (Fleischmarkt 19), which is open M-F 7am-10pm and weekends 9am-10pm, Post Office at the West Train Station (Fleischmarkt 19), which is open M-F 7am-7pm, Sa 9am-6pm, Su 9am-2pm.

- **GLBT:** Austria is considered a conservative country. While same-sex partnerships have been recently legalized, the country's strong Catholicism has stood in the way of complete equality. **HOSI (Homosexual Initiative)** provides a list of GLBT-friendly establishments in Salzburg. (Gabelsbergerstr. 26 ☎662 43 59 27 www.hosi.or.at/english ⌚ Open M-W 10am-5pm, F 10am-5pm.)

Emergency

- **AMBULANCE:** ☎112
- **FIRE DEPARTMENT:** ☎122
- **POLICE:** ☎133
- **24-HOUR MEDICAL ASSISTANCE:** ☎1 513 95 95
- **PHARMACY:** Pharmacies in Vienna are called Apotheke. Medicine can only be bought at pharmacies and not drugstores. Apothekes take turns operating at nights and on weekends, so you must check online at www.apotheker.or.at to see which pharmacy is open if you need to purchase something past 6pm or on a weekend.
- **MEDICAL SERVICES:** Vienna's hospitals are internationally renowned. The biggest is General Hospital AKH (Währinger Gürtel 18-20). It can be reached at }01 40 4000. This hospital has English speakers, although you may also contact Vienna Medical Society Service Bureau for Foreign Patients at }01 501 51253 with inquiries for English-speaking doctors and hospitals.

Getting There

By Plane

Vienna International Airport is about 16km east of the city in Schwechat. There are many public transportation options to quickly and easily get into the city:
The City Airport Train (CAT) operates daily between 5:30am-11:30pm every 30min. and takes about 16min. to get from the airport to Vienna. It costs €11 for a one-way ticket, which can be bought from ticket machines and tourists offices at the airport as well as at www.cityairporttrain.com.

Airport buses stop at City Centre, Westbanhof Station, and Kaisermühlen Vienna International Centre VIC. Buses run every 30min. from around 5am-11:30pm, depending on the bus. Tickets are €8 and may be purchased from ticket machines and tourists offices at the airport. Check www.postbus.at/en/Airportbus/Vienna_AirportLines for specific route and time details.

Getting Around

By Public Transportation

Getting around Vienna on public transportation is easy with the city's buses, trams, trains, and new metro lines. The U-Bahn is Vienna's subway. Tickets for public transportation are a uniform €1.70 , but you can purchase the Vienna card for €19, which allows unlimited use of public transportation in 72hr. increments. These are sold at information, tourist, and public transportation offices, as well as over the phone at ☎01 798 44 00148. For more information about transportation in Vienna, call Vienna Public Transport Information Center at ☎01 790 9100.

By Taxi

Taxis in Vienna have a basic, regulated fare of €2.50, plus €1.20 per kilometer.

salzburg

Salzburg has gone soft. What used to be the site of pillaging and burning, churches falling into piles of divine rubble, and Mozart clawing around the edges of truth sonata after sonata is now perfectly content to orient most of the typical tourist experience around an admittedly well-shot but absurdly plotted movie starring Julie Andrews and Christopher Plummer. Alas, all cities cannot retain their crusading kick-assery, and it's probably a good thing for Salzburg's architecture, considering everything in the city has been destroyed and rebuilt multiple times. But then again, you would be remiss to define Salzburg solely by mountain-twirling and wistful singing about Edelweiss. For one thing, the definitive symbol of Salzburg is a fortress **(Festung Hohensalzburg)** that has never once been conquered. If you fancy yourself an ascetic or devotee more than a war-buff, Salzburg boasts a dozen more-famous-than-the-next cathedrals (the **Dom**), abbeys **(Nonnberg Abbey)**, churches **(Franziskaner Kirche),** and monasteries (the **Augustinian Monastery**) and then there's the shopping. **Getreidsgasse** is the Diagon Alley of Europe; its hundreds of stores are packed along the street, each with a classy metal banner hanging outside the front

ORIENTATION

Salzburg is divided into East and West Salzburg by the blue-green river Salzach. On the west side lies most of the **Old Town,** a maze of plazas and alleyways and, yes, Catholic cathedrals. The dominant feature of this side of town is the looming **Festung Hohensalzburg,** the large white fortress that spits out a small train car every 10min. to bring weary sightseers back to ground level after carrying them up to enjoy the view. The fun extends to the north of the area with Mönchsberg, the long, narrow mountain upon which the fortress sits. Four bridges connect the older part of the city to East Salzburg, which has a more open, boulevard city layout. More than likely, you'll be entering this part of the city through the Hauptbahnhof.

East Salzburg

East Salzburg is a series of shady lanes, wide streets, and some of the city's newer sights. The main place to visit is the **Mirabell Palace and Gardens,** which lies just east of the river Salzach and has a fabulous view of the **Festung Hohensalzburg** opposite the fast-flowing stream. Most of the main attractions lie within the ring of **Franz-Josef-Straße** that encircles the part of the Old Town that bleeds into East Salzburg and runs between the Salzach and the Kapuzinerberg Hill. Unless you're looking for something specific, there really is no reason to go north of the Hauptbahnhof, as this area is mostly industrial and corporate, offering little in the way of sightseeing joys.

West Salzburg

West Salzburg is where all of the tourists dwell. The streets are charming and nestled between sights more famous than the next, and every business has a small metal plaque outside to satisfy foreign curiosity. Once you enter the city proper, the main thoroughfare is **Getreidegasse,** along which every international store and chain restaurant (as well as some choice local places and Mozart's birthplace) lies. Between Getreidegasse and the blockade of Mönchsberg are huge open plazas that crop up one after the other, as is the case with Mozartpl., Residenzpl., and Dompl. The pedestrian area extends throughout this whole area, reaching an eastern boundary at Nonntaler Hauptstr. Past this point, the area again becomes commercialized, and there isn't much to see. Working in from the river, the nightlife area is concentrated around **Rudolfskai,** which lies along the river banks south of the Staatsbrücke.

SIGHTS

East Salzburg

🏰 EAGLE'S NEST (KEHLSTEIN)

VIEW

Kehlstein, Germany ☎490 86 52 29 69 www.kehlsteinhaus.de

When der Führer reached his 50th birthday, you can imagine there was a bit of a scramble to pick a present for his special day. The answer? A super-high lookout point in the Bavarian mountains. The lookout point now hosts a restaurant that tries not to dwell upon what happened here 70 years ago. However, tourists still shoot up in a 40-story elevator to view the Octagonal Room (where Hitler entertained dignitaries) and the Pine Room (Eva Braun's favorite) as well as for the tremendous views of the mountains themselves. Be advised that visiting the Eagle's Nest involves crossing the border into Germany; there are rarely border controls, but bring your passport just in case.

i Salzburg Hauptbahnhof to Berchtesgaden Hauptbahnhof. Take bus #838 and get off at the Dokumentation stop. You'll have to pay to take the special shuttles up to the top; otherwise you can take the 2-3hr. hike on the clearly marked path for free. Bus and lift return trip €15.50, children under 14 €9. Fun Fact: At the end of The Sound of the Music, when the von Trapp family climbs over the mountains, they are actually crossing over into Germany and would have been in the line of sight of Kehlstein. ☼ Open May 17-Oct 8:20am-5pm.

⬛ MIRABELL PALACE
PALACE, GARDENS

Mirabellpl. 4 ☎66 28 07 20

Are those drag queens? Yes. A man playing "Kalinka" on the accordion? Yes. Is that a string quartet playing Mozart? Of course. Is there any reason why you should not visit the Mirabell Gardens? No. The Pegasus statue and rainbow explosion of flower formations define Austrian aesthetics in one fell swoop: a love of mythology and outrageous beauty. The drag queens are a bit outside of this purview, but you might still find them dressed up in traditional Austrian garb and willing to take pictures with confused tourists.

i Bus #1, 2, 3, 5, 6, 25, or 32 to Mirabellpl. (Schloss). Gardens free. ☼ Palace open M 8am-4pm, Tu 1-4pm, W-Th 8am-4pm, F 1-4pm. Gardens open daily 6am-dusk.

SALT MINES
MINES

Bergwerkstr. 83, Germany ☎49 (0)86 52 60 02 20 www.salzzeitreise.de

If we were to time travel, the number one commodity we would take with us to fifth-century Salzburg would be salt itself (a pound of which in die gute alte Zeit costs as much as a pound of gold). The Reichenbach mines are now in Germany after the principality of Salzburg was cut down to size in the 19th century, and they're still churning out good ol' NaCl to this day. The tour is a bit like a mining amusement park tour, with a train that brings you to the center, a series of slides from one part of the cave to the other, and a boat ride across a lake complete with technicolor lighting effects. Be advised that visiting the Salt Mines involves crossing the border into Germany; there are rarely border controls, but it is advised that you bring your passport.

i Take the ÖBB rail to Berchtesgaden Hauptbahnhof. Take bus #840 from the Bahnhof Berchtesgaden. Get off at the Salzbergwerk. €15, with Salzburg card €12. ☼ Open daily May-Oct 9am-5pm; Nov-Apr 11am-3pm.

CAPUCHIN MONASTERY
HIKING, VIEW

Kapuzinerberg 6 ☎662 87 35 63 0

If you want The Passion of the Christ without all of the crazy Mel Gibson Aramaic, then the Capuchin monks have something for you. The monastery is a place of pilgrimage due to its stunning, 17th-century Baroque Stations of the Cross running up the side of the hill that overlooks all of East Salzburg. An expansive parking garage now lies under the mountain, but ignore that and use your own two feet for a mini-climb up the city's most accessible mountain.

i Bus #4 to Hofwirt. Walk along Linzergasse and turn left onto Kapuzinberg. Climb the mountain. Free. ☼ Open M-Sa 6am-6pm, Su 8am-6pm.

West Salzburg

⬛ FESTUNG HOHENSALZBURG
FORTRESS

Mönchsberg 34 ☎662 84 24 30 11 www.salzburg-burgen.at

The only thing that has ever invaded this millennium-old fortress are tourists streaming from either the funicular that runs up the mountain or the perilous footpath (by which you literally have to pass through die Höllenpforte—"The

get a room!

YOHO INTERNATIONAL YOUTH HOSTEL
HOSTEL $$

Paracelsusstr. 9 ☎662 87 96 49 www.yoho.at

No pirates to be found here, but you will discover pretty much every other treasure a traveler could want—including Wi-Fi, a bar, breakfast, a Nintendo Wii, and the requisite The Sound of Music nightly screening—at this large hostel. All rooms have decor that shies away from institutional metal bunks in favor of light wood and buttercup-yellow sheets. The hostel bar serves €3.50 mojitos and usually ends up packed with a cheery, somewhat-raucous crowd watching the soccer game.

i Bus #22 to Wirtschaftskammer. Walk east along Lasserstr. and turn right onto Paracelsusstr. 4- and 6-bed dorms (male, female, and mixed) €20-23; singles €40. Linens and keycard €5 deposit. ✪ Reception 24hr.

HAUS CHRISTINE
B&B $$

Panoramaweg 3 ☎662 45 67 73 www.haus-christine.org

If you and a friend or two came to Austria to experience the bright, scenic side of the alpine country, then this B&B nestled in the hills will be perfect to feast your eyes upon. The rooms are done up in light pastels, with a breakfast room that looks out into the surrounding forest. It's a blessing and curse that the location is so beautiful, as it is a bit more of a hassle to get into the city than at other hostels, but the view comes at a price that's worth paying.

i Bus #21 to Werner-von-Siemens-Platz. Go east on Söllheimer Straße and turn left onto Bergstr. Haus Christine is clearly marked on the left. Breakfast included. Doubles €40; triples €57; quads €72. ✪ Reception flexible depending on guests' schedule.

GASTHAUS HINTERBRÜHL
GUESTHOUSE $$$

Schanzlgasse 12 ☎662 84 67 98 www.fam-wagner.at

With its pine-carved headboards, you'd think that this hotel was pulled straight from the Laura Ingalls Wilder prairie. Bizarrely enough, it's only a 2min. walk from the Old Town and is a good bet for those who want old-fashioned Austrian charm (the building is 800 years old) as opposed to the über-modern spaceship style that most chain hotels favor. The best part is the garden and the views of the Dom against a mountain backdrop.

i Bus #5 or 25 to Justizgebäude. Walk away from the river and turn right onto Schanzlgasse. Breakfast included. Singles €42; doubles €66; triples €79. ✪ Call ahead if arriving on Sunday.

Gates of Hell"). Overlooking the rest of the city, the castle provides the requisite beautiful view along with a series of eccentric attractions, such as a torture chamber and a marionette museum. (We know that, somewhere, Chuckie is proud). The best way to attack the castle is by avoiding the pricey souvenir gambits; instead, work your way down the castle from the top parapet that the on-site maps recommend as the second stop.

i Bus #3, 5, 6, 8, 20, 25, or 28 to Rathaus. Enter the Old Town by walking south along the river and head toward the Dom (with the green domes). Go toward the mountain until you get to Festungsgasse. The sign for the funicular is large. If you want to walk up the footpath, turn right and continue along the road uphill until you reach the entrance. Fortress via Festungbahn €11, via footpath €7.80. Ticket includes admission to all museums in the fortress as well as an audio guide. ✪ Open daily Jan-Apr 9:30am-5pm; May-Sept 9am-7pm; Oct-Dec 9:30am-5pm.

🏛 DOM
CATHEDRAL

Dompl. ☎662 80 47 79 50 www.salzburger-dom.at

If the Salzburg Dom represents anything, it's the utter absurdity of war and religious feuds. In 1167, the whole shebang was burned down because pyromaniac Frederick Barbarossa refused to acknowledge the "anti-Pope" Paschal. Like seemingly everything in Western Europe, the church was also destroyed in 1944 when an American bomb collapsed the cathedral completely. Despite all the trials and tribulations, the organ is still in good condition, and frequent concerts emphasize the visual delight with auditory stimuli.

i Bus #3, 5, 6, 8, 20, 25, or 28 to Rathaus. From the stop, go into the Old Town and turn left onto Getreidegasse until you come out onto the huge Residenpl. The cathedral is on the opposite side of the plaza. Donations encouraged. ☼ Open Jan-Feb M-Sa 8am-5pm, Su 1-5pm; Mar-Apr M-Sa 9am-6pm, Su 1-6pm; May-Sept M-Sa 8am-7pm, Su 1-7pm; Oct M-Sa 8am-6pm, Su 1-6pm, Nov M-Sa 8am-5pm, Su 1-5pm; Dec M-Sa 8am-6pm, Su 1-6pm.

MOZART'S BIRTHPLACE
MUSEUM

Getreidegasse 9 ☎662 84 43 13 www.mozarteum.at

While Vienna tries to emphasize that it's the city Mozart actually wanted to live in, Salzburg is indeed where the prodigious story began. This museum provides a startlingly cumulative portrait of what it was like to dwell among the 16,000 Salzburg residents of Mozart's time and also houses the master's own tiny violin and dozens upon dozens of original works. The museum is a study in romanticizing Mozart's life, and as a particularly apt plaque for the boy-turned-man-wonder states: "In the Romantic era, Mozart's allegedly tragic life circumstances corresponded to the romantic image of the unappreciated genius who had do die at such an early age."

i Bus #3, 5, 6, 8, 20, 25, or 28 to Rathaus. Walk away from the river into the Old Town and turn right onto Getreidegasse. The museum is on the left in a bright yellow building. €7. ☼ Open daily 9am-5:30pm.

ST. PETER'S ABBEY
MONASTERY, CHURCH, CEMETERY

St. Peter Bezirk 1/2 ☎662 84 45 76 www.erzabtei.at

If you happen to be the sibling of a famous German-speaking musician, you're probably buried in St. Peter's Friedhof along with Mozart's sister, Haydn's brother, and a litany of other notables-by-connection. The monastery and church date back to the eighth century, making the complex the oldest monastery in the German-speaking world. The cool and somewhat creepy icing on the abbey's cake are the catacombs, which you can experience in a Hunchback of Notre Dame fashion for a small fee.

i Bus #3, 5, 6, 8, 20, 25, or 28 to Rathaus. From the stop, walk away from the river into the Old Town and turn left onto Getreidegasse until you come out onto the huge Residenpl. Go past the cathedral; the abbey is located up against the mountain. Catacombs €1.50, students €1. ☼ Church open daily 8am-noon and 2:30-6:30pm. Cemetery open daily 6:30am-dusk. Catacombs open May-Sept Tu-Su 10:30am-5pm; Oct-Apr W-Th 10:30am-3:30pm, F-Sa 10:30am-4pm.

ROYAL PALACE RESIDENCES
STATE ROOMS

Residenzpl. 1 ☎662 80 42 26 90 www.salzburg-burgen.at

In a world where IKEA holds a monopoly on our lives and our collective goal is a sofa unit with green stripes, these state rooms serve as a comforting reminder that the consumers of years past were 100 times worse than us. The Royal Palace Residences not only boast the requisite giant crystal chandeliers but are also home to the room that hosted a six-year-old Mozart sawing away on his tiny violin.

i Bus #3, 5, 6, 8, 20, 25, or 28 to Rathaus. Walk away from the river into the Old Town and walk toward the Dom. You'll come out onto Residenzpl.; the residence is on the right. €9. ☼ Open daily 10am-5pm; check website as dates vary.

NONNBERG ABBEY

Nonnberggasse 2

☎662 84 16 07

This would be the point where we start bursting into "Climb Every Mountain," but alas, there's only one mountain you need to climb (and sadly no streams to ford). Nestled under Festung Hohensalzburg, this abbey has hosted nuns for almost a millennium. In the olden days, the abbey was actually the site of some gender parity when an archbishop decreed the abbess of Nonnberg equal to the abbot of St. Peter's in 1241. It has retained its quiet, royal beatitude with a darkened, romantic chapel and well-groomed graves outside.

i Bus #3, 5, 6, 8, 20, 25, or 28 to Rathaus. Enter the Old Town and walk toward the Dom (with the green domes). Go toward the mountain behind it until you get to Festungsgasse. Walk left along the mountain on this street and turn right when you get to the building with the onion dome. Free. ☒ Open daily 7am-dusk.

MUSEUM OF NATURAL HISTORY AND TECHNOLOGY

Museumspl. 5

MUSEUM

☎662 84 26 530 www.hausdernatur.at

With everything in Salzburg clocking in at hundreds upon hundreds of years old, this museum is perfect for those more excited about the Higgs boson than hellacious stories of power-driven priests. The aquarium is the highlight of the complex, with thousands of fish streaming in between carefully placed barnacles; the interactive part of the museum is worth checking out as well. The museum can't completely escape its Salzburg location, though, and one of the coolest exhibits is the "walk-in violin."

i Bus #20, 24, or 28 to Ferdinand Hanusch Platz (Franz-Josef-Kai). Walk with traffic along Franz Josef Kai and turn left onto Museumspl. €7.50, students €5. ☒ Open daily 9am-5pm.

HELLBRUNN PALACE

Fürstenweg 37

PALACE, FOUNTAINS

☎662 82 03 72 0 www.hellbrunn.at

It's no wonder this place starts with "Hell," as the devil surely lives in the trick fountains that dot this massive palatial complex. The Austrians are crazy about commissioning palaces for themselves, and Hellbrunn was the brainchild of Prince Archbishop in 1615 (talk about separation of church and state). The trick fountains are definitely the best part, as jets of water suddenly shoot out at random passersby to great giggles and some grimaces. The folklore museum will satisfy the less spontaneous with beautiful examples of traditional costume as well as a number of relics.

i Bus #25 to Fürstenweg. There are clear signs to the entrance. Guided tour of fountains, palace, and folklore museum €9.50; students €6.50. Park free. ☒ Open daily Apr 9am-4:30pm; May-Jun 9am-5:30pm; Jul-Aug 9am-6pm; Sept 9am-5:30pm; Oct 9am-4:30pm.

AUGUSTINIAN BREWERY

Lindhofstraße 7

BREWERY

☎662 43 12 46 www.augustinerbier.at

Tourists come from hundreds of miles around to taste the purest beer on earth. While we really don't ask what's in the beers of today, the brewery here still follows the Purity Law of 1516, which, despite what it sounds like, has nothing to do with virgins. It's all about ingredients, and the beers here are guaranteed to contain only hops, water, malt, and yeast.

i Bus #7, 8, 20, 21, 27, or 28 to Bärenwirt. Walk north on Müllner Hauptstr and turn left onto Augustinergasse. Tokens for beer €3. ☒ Open M-F 3-11pm, Sa-Su 2:30-11pm.

FOOD

East Salzburg

CAFE SHAKESPEARE
CAFE $$

Hubert-Sattler-Gasse 3 ☎650 77 35 357

Cafe Shakespeare is a cafe and bar named after the Bard, with a healthy dose of anti-American alternative art for good measure. The outdoor terrace has a clear view of the Mirabell Palace, while the interior has comforting wood paneling that's overlooked by a distressed bald eagle and a choice four-letter word to describe patriotism. The bar is where the youth gather to smoke and drink white beer after white beer, but the menu has some special items—the Hausgemachtes toast is a small but simple step in your pursuit of happiness.

i Bus #1, 2, 3, 5, 6, 25, or 32 to Mirabellpl. (Schloß). It's on the left side of the church. Entrees €8.50-12.40. Dessert €3.20-4.20. ⏱ Open M-F 10am-1am, Sa 4pm-2am, Su 4pm-midnight.

RISTORANTE DA ALBERTO
ITALIAN $$

Franz-Josef-Straße 37 ☎662 88 10 81

Occasionally, it's nice when the menu is in eight different languages or tries to attempt three different cuisines, but most of the time, it ends up feeling like a bad trip to Disney World. Fortunately, Alberto is full-and-out Italian—none of those shenanigans of overly deferential cuisine to suit the capricious whims of English speakers. The restaurant is secluded in a quieter part of the New Town, and the pizza is crispy, delicious, and cheaper than what it'll cost you to enter most museums in the city. And who's to say that a good pizza isn't a comparable form of art?

i Bus #2 or 4 to Wolf-Diestrich-Straße. Walk in the direction the bus came in and turn right onto Franz-Josef-Straße. Pizza €8-11. Pasta €9-12. ⏱ Open daily 11:30am-2:30pm and 5:30-10pm.

CAFE BAZAR
CAFE $$

Schwarzstr. 3 ☎662 87 42 78

It's a bit bizarre that you might be sitting in the same seat that Marlene Dietrich once lounged in. However, the only angels you'll be seeing presently are the fantastically down-to-earth waiters and waitresses at this classiest of cafes in the New Town. The menu is the typical toast, soup, and occasional entree that so defines the Salzburg scene, but the hanging newspapers, free-standing coat hangers, and wood-and-gold decor give the guests an easier time of imagining what the cafe was like in its heyday as the center of artistic thought.

i Bus #27 to Landestheater. Walk down Schwarzstr.; the cafe is on the left. Small eats €4-12. Coffee €2.70-6. ⏱ Open M-Sa 7:30am-11pm, Su 9am-6pm.

West Salzburg

EISGROTTE
GELATO $

Getreidegasse 40 ☎662 84 31 57 www.eisgrotte.at

The name means "Ice Cave," but the theme of this gelato joint is more '50s diner, with neon signs and the svelte red leather seats we've come to associate with soda fountains. During the day, the servers dole out scoops like mad to clamoring tourists, but if you go during slower hours, after the nearby shops have closed around 6pm, you'll have a chance to breathe and enjoy your ice cream in your own personal cave of happiness.

i Bus #3, 5, 6, 8, 20, 25, or 28 to Rathaus. Walk away from the river into the Old Town and turn right onto Getreidegasse. The store is on the right. 1-scoop cone €1. ⏱ Open daily 9am-midnight.

austria

CAFE PAMINA

CAFE $$

Judengasse 17 ☎662 84 23 38 www.cafepamina.at

Cafes and bakeries are like rabbits in Salzburg—they multiply like crazy and their food is super-light. Pamina is what you could call an antithetical hearty cafe, with some of the best ice cream variations around (try the eponymous, big-as-your-face Pamina with frozen yogurt, strawberry ice cream, strawberries, and whipped cream). The location on the quiet Judengasse is ideal for enjoying Salzburg without feeling rushed by tourists waiting outside.

i Bus #3, 5, 6, 8, 20, 25, or 28 to Rathaus. Walk away from the river and into the Old Town. Turn left onto Getreidegasse, which becomes Judengasse. Ice cream €3-7. ☑ Open M-Sa 9am-6pm.

CARPE DIEM

RESTAURANT $$$$

Getreidegasse 50 ☎662 84 88 00 www.carpediemfinestfingerfood.com

Carpe Diem takes its name seriously, making delicious gourmet food available for the seizing at every price range. If you live by a YOLO philosophy (carpe diem for stupid people), find a friend and order the €98 menu for two. If you're not insane, you can order something nice like strawberries with white chocolate and basil (€13.50) or one of the many finger food options for under €10. The best part about a restaurant that goes from €10-100 is that the decor has to suit the people paying €100, so relish the classy, super-modern black leather furnishings.

i Bus #3, 5, 6, 8, 20, 25, or 28 to Rathaus. Walk away from the river into the Old Town and turn right onto Getreidegasse. The restaurant is on the right. 3-course lunch menu €19.50. Desserts €11.50-13.50. A la carte €5.40-10.90. ☑ Open daily from 8:30am-midnight.

REPUBLIC

CAFE $$

Anton-Neumayr-Platz 2 ☎662 84 34 48 www.republic.at

Republic, conveniently, is more like its own little republic than a cafe. The sprawling, orange-themed cafe takes up most of Anton-Neumayr-Platz and publishes its own magazine, has a radio channel, bar, restaurant, and club. Packed at all hours, it's great if you want to have large chunks of time to people-watch, as the waiters aren't rushing to get you out of your seat despite the teeming crowds.

i Bus #3, 5, 6, 8, 20, 25, or 28 to Rathaus. Walk away from the river into the Old Town and turn right onto Getreidegasse. Walk all the way down and turn right once you hit the mountain. Republic is in the plaza. Sandwiches €4-13. Meat entrees €14-19 60 ☑ Open M-Th 8am-1am, F-Sa 8am-4am, Su 8am-1am.

NIGHTLIFE

East Salzburg

▨ PEPE COCKTAIL BAR

BAR

Steingasse 3 ☎662 87 36 62 www.pepe-cocktailbar.at

It's nice when you find a place that doesn't serve only 10 variations of beer to a rowdy crowd. Pepe definitely caters well to its ZARA-clad crowd as they throw back cocktail after cocktail in this remarkably chic bar. While most of the drinks are tropical-themed, with daiquiris given ample advertisement, we recommend the Schwermatrose (rum, kahlua, lime, and lemon) for a fresh beginning to a pub crawl along Steingasse.

i Bus #3, 5, 6, 8, 20, 25, or 28 to Rathaus. Cross the bridge into East Salzburg and take a quick right onto Steingasse. The bar is on the left. ☑ Open Tu-Sa 7pm-3am.

▨ MONKEYS CAFE.BAR

BAR

Imbergstr. 2A ☎662 87 66 52 www.monkeys-salzburg.at

In between two streets along the Salzach, this bar seemingly contains all of the city's young students and tourists in its laser-lighted interior. The inside is modern without being too yuppie and caters to its international clientele by hosting

Latin disco nights as well as City of the Week events on Friday evenings. During the winter, the bar also becomes a thriving cafe.

i Bus #3, 5, 6, 8, 20, 25, or 28 to Rathaus. Cross the bridge over into East Salzburg and take a quick right onto Giselakai, which turns into Imbergstr. ☾ Open M-Th 11:30am-2am, F-Sa 11:30am-4am, Su 11:30am-2am.

SAITENSPRUNG
PUB, BAR

Steingasse 11 ☎662 87 34 55 www.shamrocksalzburg.com

This youth-oriented club's back wall is dug straight out of the side of Kapuzinerberg Hill. The music is the latest Top 40 hits, and the martinis are a particularly popular option for the under-25 crowd. The best part of this place, however, is just sitting in the bar feeling serene in the understated, natural decor.

i Bus #3, 5, 6, 8, 20, 25, or 28 to Rathaus. Cross into East Salzburg and turn right onto Steingasse. The bar is on the left. ☾ Open daily 9pm-4am.

CHEZ ROLAND
MUSIC, BAR

Giselakai 15 ☎662 87 43 35 www.chez-roland.com

Since Salzburg doesn't have in much in the way of dive bars, it is best to remain in the realm of the classy with Chez Roland. Around since the '70s, the archway-dominated bar has been a rotating door for luminaries of the Salzburg Festival scene. Don't go crazy on the liquor here—instead, blend in and order anice Austrian wine for only €3 a glass.

i Bus #3, 5, 6, 8, 20, 25, or 28 to Rathaus. Cross over to east Salzburg and turn right onto Giselakai. ☾ Open daily 7:30pm-late.

West Salzburg

⚅ MURPHY'S LAW IRISH PUB
IRISH, PUB

Gstättengasse 33 ☎662 84 28 82

Murphy's Law reminds us that "if anything can go wrong, it will." We suppose that this Irish pub adds the corollary, "When it does indeed go wrong, drink up!" The spirit of this place is infectious, with riotous laughter and sometimes unintelligible jabber between friends filling the air. The bonhomie extends to betting pools and trips to see games that are organized to keep the patrons coming back.

i Bus #1, 4, 5, 7, 8, 20, 21, 22, 24, 27, or 28 to Mönchsbergaufzug. Take a quick left onto Griesgasse until you reach the end; cross the street onto Gstättengasse. The bar is on the left. ☾ Open M-F 2pm-2am, Sa-Su 11am-2am.

⚅ SODA CLUB
ELECTRONIC MUSIC, BAR

Gstättengasse 17 ☎650 31 17 761 www.sodaclub.cc

What better place to lose yourself in electronic beats and dubstep drops than a bar built into the side of a mountain (even if it once was filled with monks)? Exposed cave walls put exposed brick to shame as a decor option, and the drinks are surprisingly cheap given the upscale vibe.

i Bus #1, 4, 5, 7, 8, 20, 21, 22, 24, 27, or 28 to Mönchsbergaufzug. Take a quick left onto Griesgasse and continue until you reach the end; cross the street onto Gstättengasse. The bar is on the left. ☾ Open Tu 9pm-4am, W-Sa 9pm-5am.

SHAMROCK IRISH PUB
PUB, BAR

Rudolfskai 12 ☎662 84 16 10 www.shamrocksalzburg.com

Shamrock gets a little bit too into the Irish campiness (the first indicator is the sign that says "Irish Food! Irish Staff! Irish Music!"). Regardless, the place is packed with Austrian and international students watching soccer and kicking back cider after beer after Guinness. The decor reminds us inextricably of the Prancing Pony of The Lord of the Rings fame, with thick, dark wooden benches and a general sense of camaraderie, until the Ringwraith called morning comes.

i Bus #3, 5, 6, 8, 20, 25, or 28 to Rathaus. Walk with traffic along Rudolfskai. .5L Guinness €4.50. ☾ Open M-W noon-3am, Th-Sa noon-4am, Su noon-2am.

VIS A VIS   MUSIC, PUB

Rudolfskai 24   ☎662 84 12 90 www.visavis-bar.at

VisÁ Vis caters to an under-30 crowd that doesn't feel as sporty as the football-salivating group at the nearby Irish pubs. The emphasis here is a bit on excess, as the bar pushes groups to buy bottles of Absolut with four Red Bulls to wash it down. Nothing gets too out of hand under the exposed brick archway, which has enough lights to provoke an awed comment of "double rainbow" every now and then. Each night has a different theme, but it's worth it to go on Wednesdays when the cocktails (the bar's specialty) are under €4 before midnight.

i Bus #3, 5, 6, 8, 20, 25, or 28 to Rathaus. Walk with traffic on Rudolfskai; the bar is on the left.
🕐 *Open daily 8pm-4am.*

ARTS AND CULTURE

▨ LANDESTHEATER   THEATER

Schwarzstr. 22   ☎662 87 15 120 www.salzburger-landestheater.at

The Landestheater is the premier Salzburg option for those looking for a warm glass of Deutsche Kultur. The opera performances tend to stick to Wagner and cartoon villain soundtracks, while the non-musical theater side sports an ambitious line-up of Chekhov, Frisch, Schiller, Mann, and everyone's favorite—Kafka. While the theater's regular season isn't open until the fall, the theater also hosts some Salzburg Festival events.

i Bus #27 to Landestheater. Ticket price varies according to performance. Check website during the season for details. 🕐 *Late Aug-Jun M-F 10am-1pm and 2-4pm.*

MARIONETTEN THEATER   THEATER

Schwarzstr. 24   ☎662 87 24 06 www.marionetten.at

We're not a fan of beating the dead horse that is *The Sound of Music*, but a scene along the lines of "The Lonely Goatherd," with preciously floating marionettes, is what you can expect from this summer theater. The performances tend to go straight for the German classics, with The Magic Flute, Hansel and Gretel, and Die Fledermaus among the repertoire. This place also stands out from other Austrian theaters with its English subtitles. Even if you think puppets are a bit juvenile, you might revise your opinion after seeing a blow-out rendition of Don Giovanni.

i Bus #27 to Landestheater. The Marionnetten Theater is just past the Landestheater on the side of the street opposite the river. €18-35, students €18. 🕐 *Open May-Sept 9am-1pm and 2hr. before each performance.*

MOZARTEUM   MUSIC

Theatergasse 2   ☎662 87 31 54 www.mozarteum.at

The students of Salzburg's Mozarteum frequently branch out to play Mendelssohn quartets in the nearby Mirabell Gardens, but the graded performances can be viewed by the public as well. The university has a full orchestra and smaller chamber music groups that give performances throughout the year. A special schedule run during the festival month is also played by students of the summer academy. Tickets can be purchased through the Mozart Foundation.

i Bus #1, 3, 4, 5, 6, 21, 22, 25, or 27. Prices vary by event. Check website before ordering tickets.
🕐 *Open Sept-Jun M-F 9am-5pm, Sa 9am-noon.*

SALZBURG FESTIVAL   FESTIVAL

Hotstallgasse 1   ☎662 80 450 www.salzburgerfestspiele.at

For a brief moment, the tourist trap of Julie Andrews is forgotten in favor of an aspect of Salzburg culture that was, interestingly enough, featured in The Sound of Music: the Salzburg Festival. Operas, concerts, and other performances play continuously for days upon days upon days as a blow-out approach to the arts that will make you never want to hear Mozart again. As a bonus, the Salzburg Festival actually has some English events that will leave you feeling künstlerisch instead of künstlich (artistic, not artificial).

i The festival takes place at many different venues throughout the city. Tickets vary greatly depending on performance. Check website for details. ☿ Late Jul-early Sept.

SHOPPING

▧ RED BULL WORLD   CLOTHING
Getreidegasse 34   ☎662 84 36 05 www.redbullworld.at
The flagship Red Bull store will give you wings—for a price. If you want to be the Icarus of credit cards, by all means, max out your limit on Red Bull-emblazoned paraphernalia. For those less in love with labels, the store also sells a variety of merely kick-ass effects, such as AWOLNATION CDs.

i Bus #3, 5, 6, 8, 20, 25, or 28 to Rathaus. Walk away from the river into the Old Town and turn right onto Getreidegasse. The store is on the left. Shirt €35. CDs around €15. ☿ Open M-F 9:30am-6pm, Sa 9:30am-5pm.

▧ HÖLLRIGL   BOOKS
Sigmund-Haffnergasse 10   ☎662 84 11 460
Unlike Salzburg's oldest cathedral and fortress, there are reasons other than fire and acid rain that there aren't any millennia-old bookstores in town. Mainly, no one back then was literate. Höllrigl, however, is the oldest bookstore you'll find in Austria (founded in 1519) and operates on an indie-style set-up, with recommendations by staff members, dim lighting, and not much room between the shelves. Needless to say, you can lose hours in here.

i Bus #3, 5, 6, 8, 20, 25, or 28 to Rathaus. Walk away from the river into the Old Town, turn left when you hit Getreidegasse and Judengasse, then take a quick right onto Sigmund-Haffnergasse. Paperbacks from €9. ☿ Open M-F 9am-6:30pm, Sa 9am-6pm.

ESSENTIALS
Practicalities

- **SALZBURG TOURIST OFFICE:** Mozartpl. 5 (☎662 88 98 73 30 www.salzburg.info ☿ Open daily June-Aug 9am-7pm; Sept-May 9am-6pm.) Other tourist offices located at the airport (Innsbrucker Buddesstr. 95) and the train station (Südtiroler Platz. 1).

- **INTERNET:** Salzburg has recently begun a free Wi-Fi program in the city, with coverage around the Salzach river from 5am-midnight. Coverage includes Mozartpl., Volksgarten, Mirabell Palace, and Max-Reinhardt-Platz.

- **GLBT:** Austria is considered a conservative country. While same-sex partnerships have been recently legalized, the country's strong Catholicism has stood in the way of complete equality. **HOSI (Homosexual Initiative)** provides a list of GLBT-friendly establishments in Salzburg. (Gabelsbergerstr. 26 ☎662 43 59 27 www.hosi.or.at/english ☿ Open M-W 10am-5pm, F 10am-5pm.)

Emergency

- **AMBULANCE:** ☎112

- **FIRE DEPARTMENT:** ☎144

- **POLICE:** ☎133

- **DENTIST ON CALL:** ☎662 87 34 66

- **DOCTOR ON CALL:** ☎662 87 13 27

austria

Getting There

By Plane

To fly into Salzburg, travelers will pass through the **W.A. Mozart International Airport** (Innsbrucker Bundesstr. 95 ☎662 85 80 79 11). Many places fly directly from other European cities to Salzburg, but those who are traveling overseas might find it easier to fly into Flughafen München in southern Germany and take the airport shuttle to Ostbahnhof, then a DB or ÖBB train to Salzburg Hauptbahnhof (€24). To get to the city center from the Salzburg airport, take bus #2 (Ⓩ Every 10-20min., M-F 5:30am-10:30pm, Sa 6am-11pm, Su 6:30am-11pm) to the Hauptbahnhof train station, from which you can take a number of buses to various locations in the city.

By Train

The **Salzburg Hauptbahnhof** receives a large number of international trains, including trains to and from Zürich (€51 Ⓩ 6hr.), Munich (€25 Ⓩ 2hr.), Budapest (€44 Ⓩ 5½hr.), and Frankfurt (€107 Ⓩ 5hr.) as well as trains to and from Vienna (€50 Ⓩ 3hr.) and Innsbruck (€41 Ⓩ 2hr.). There is reduced coverage on Sundays, so check the ÖBB website at www.oebb.at, where you can reserve your tickets ahead of time. If traveling within Austria, simply buy a ticket at the offices in each major train station.

Getting Around

By Foot

The best way to see most of the Old Town is by walking, as even bicycles have a hard time navigating these pedestrian-crowded streets.

By Bike

If you're planning to spend an extended period of time in Salzburg, renting or buying a bike will probably be your best bet. Because the public transportation system relies on buses, traffic can build up around the Old Town. For shorter stays, **TopBike** provides bike rentals. (Staatsbrücke, Franz-Josef-Kai www.topbike.at *i* €7 per hour, €20 per day. Ⓩ Open daily Apr-June 10am-5pm, July-Aug 9am-7pm, Sept-Oct 10am-5pm.)

By Car

If you consider yourself the outdoorsy sort, then a car might come in handy to explore the surrounding Bavarian Alps and other mountaineering options. The downside is that many rental companies have a 3-day minimum rental period; nevertheless try **AutoEurope** if you're interested. (12 Gniglerstrasse ☎1 866 16 51 From €150 for 3 days.)

By Bus

Bus fares cost €2.10 per trip, €5 for a 24hr. pass, and €13.10 for a week-long pass. If you purchase the **Salzburg Card,** you have access to all public transportation (including the funicular to the top of Festungs Hohensalzburg and the Mönchsberg Elevator) for free. (Mozartpl. 5 ☎3662 88 93 70 www.salzburg.info *i* Includes admission to all sights in Vienna and use of public transportation network. 24hr. card €25, under 15 €12.50; 48hr. €34/17; 72hr. card €40/20.)

austria essentials

MONEY

Tipping and Bargaining

Service staff is paid by the hour, but a service charge is not usually included in an item's unit price. Cheap customers typically just round up to the nearest whole euro, but it's customary and polite to tip 10-15% if you are satisfied with the service. If the service was poor, you don't have to tip at all. To tip, tell the waiter the total of the bill with the tip included. Do not leave the tip on the table; hand it directly to the server. It is standard to tip a taxi driver at least €1, housekeepers €1-2 per day, and public toilet attendants around €0.50.

Taxes

Most goods in Austria are subject to a value added tax (VAT) of 20% (a reduced tax of 10% is applied to accommodations, certain foods, and some passenger transportation). Non-EU visitors who are taking these goods home unused may be refunded this tax for purchases totaling over €75 per store. When making purchases, request a VAT form and present it at a Tax Free Shopping Office, found at most airports, road borders, and ferry stations, or by mail. Refunds must be claimed within six months.

SAFETY AND HEALTH

Local Laws and Police

Certain regulations might seem harsh and unusual (e.g. jaywalking is a €5 fine), but abide by all local laws while in Austria; your embassy will not necessarily get you off the hook. Always be sure to carry a valid passport, as police have the right to ask for identification.

Drugs and Alcohol

The drinking age in Austria is 16 for beer and wine and 18 for spirits. The maximum blood alcohol content level for drivers is 0.05%. Avoid public drunkenness; it can jeopardize your safety and earn the disdain of locals. While possession of marijuana or hashish is illegal, possession of small quantities for personal consumption is decriminalized in Austria. Each region has interpreted "small quantities" differently (anywhere from 5 to 30g). Carrying drugs across an international border—considered to be drug trafficking—is a serious offense that could land you in prison.

BELGIUM

Belgium may not rank near the top of most people's lists of must-see European vacation spots. Next to the Netherlands or Greece, Belgium doesn't scream party central, and it doesn't have famous sights like you can find in Italy and France. But many people spend a whole Eurotrip searching for, and failing to find, the kind of small-town charm that is this entire country's specialty. Shift your vacation into a different gear and indulge in Belgium's own version of whimsy. Plus, Belgian cuisine revolves around fries, waffles, chocolate, and beer. It's basically the best Sunday brunch you've ever had, and it never ends.

If you have a penchant for public urination, you'll probably enjoy yourself in Brussels. Peeing statues aplenty await you; it's hard to turn the corner without seeing something taking a leak. It's cute when you're made out of bronze, but Let's Go doesn't recommend trying it yourself—indecent exposure charges don't make good souvenirs. While you're avoiding criminal charges, you might want to swing by the European Quarter, where you'll find more ambassadors and Eurocrats than you can shake a roll of red tape at. Brussels is also home to dozens of museums, art galleries, and theaters for the cultural traveler in you. And don't forget Bruges, one of Europe's most charmingly preserved medieval cities. It's not just small-town charm you'll find in Belgium; this is the place for small-country charm.

greatest hits

- **MELT IN YOUR MOUTH.** Belgian chocolate is famous for a reason. Head to the **Musée du Cacao et du Chocolat** in the Grand Palace to stare at more than you could ever possibly eat. (p. 43)

- **2001: A BEER ODYSSEY.** With over 2000 beers available (and counting), **Delirium** will quickly become your favorite nighttime hangout in Brussels. (p. 49)

- **IN BRUGES.** Climb the **Belfort** (p. 54) or sample tradition Belgian fare at **Pas Partout** (p. 55). Maybe you'll even run into Colin Farrell. (You probably won't.)

brussels

ORIENTATION

The center of Brussels is roughly split between **Upper Town,** on the hill, and **Lower Town,** at the foot of that hill. These neighborhoods bleed into each other a bit, but the clear heart of the city is the **Grand Place** in Lower Town. These two areas are encircled by a guitar-pick shaped loop of main roads and part of the metro. The biggest metro stops that serve this area are **Gare du Nord** in the north, Arts-Loi in the east, Place Louise in the south, **Gare du Midi** in the southwest, and Comte de Flandre in the west, with **Gare Centrale** smack-dab in the middle. Going east of Arts-Loi will take you to **Place Schuman,** the neighborhood that houses the EU and its parliamentary big-wigs along with the grand Parc du Cinquantenaire/Jubelpark and some of the city's coolest museums. South of the city center is **Louise,** best known for its shopping, and Place Flagey, where a picturesque pond is dotted with funky bars. These four areas—Upper and Lower Town in the center, Place Schuman in the east, and Louise in the south—make up the meat of Brussels. A bit farther northwest, at the end of the metro, is **Heysel,** where you will find some of Brussels's more concentrated tourist traps, including the Atomium (which, however tourist trappy, you should still see).

Lower Town

Brussels is not a huge tourist destination, but those who do visit tend to stay near the **Grand Place,** or "Grand Plaza," where the **Musée de la Ville** (city museum) and the **Hôtel de Ville** (town hall) are located. The busy Grand Place is the heart of Brussels, where you will find the best of the city's waffles, chocolate, and tourists, but venturing away from this center and through the smaller, winding streets will allow you to really experience the city. **Manneken Pis** is a straight shot from the Grand Place down **rue de L'Etuve;** going farther east and south will lead you into the Upper Town. Northwest of the Grand Place, **boulevard Anspach,** accessible by metro stop Bourse, is a diagonal that bisects the city where you will find basic needs like ATMs, pharmacies, and *alimentations.* Farther west of the Bourse and bd Anspach is **Place Saint-Géry,** home to most of Brussels's night owls. To the north is **rue Neuve,** a central shopping district filled with clothing outlets and fast food. Rue Neuve is flanked to the west by the beautiful neighborhood of **Sainte Catherine,** which is a bit pricey but still a welcome respite from the noise of the Grand Place.

Upper Town

Upper Town is divided into a number of smaller neighborhoods that wrap around the eastern and southern ends of Lower Town, each of which maintains a distinct personality despite rather blurred borders. These areas are home to Brussels's best museums and some fancy shopping—great places to spend the day before heading to the city center for an evening beer.

Broad, traffic-laden streets and long city blocks make Upper Town difficult to navigate by foot, so take advantage of the metro and tram lines. Use the **Mont des Arts** and the **Place Royale** as your central anchors when navigating Upper Town. From there, the **rue Royale** will take you past the **Parc de Bruxelles** and many of the Upper Town's museums, galleries, and grand palaces, not to mention the Belgian Parliament. Be careful going much farther north than La Botanique, especially at night; this area is unofficially known as Brussels's red light district. South of Place Royale are **boulevard de Waterloo** and **avenue de la Toison d'Or,** which hug the eastern edge of Upper Town and extend down to shopaholic heaven, **avenue Louise.**

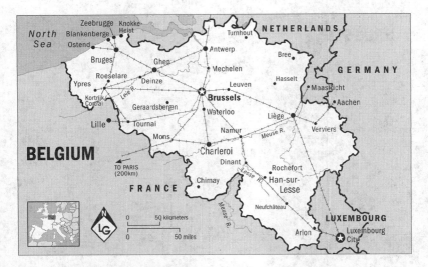

Place Schuman and Heysel

Venturing outside the loose bounds of Upper and Lower Towns will take a few metro stops, but it's worth leaving the busy city center for a day. Place Schuman (which typically refers to the metro stop and its surrounding buildings) is just east of the city center and home to the **European Commission** and **European Parliament.** The area is much nicer than central Brussels but consequently is populated almost entirely by Eurocrats and doesn't really cater to the student crowd or the student budget. Parc du Cinquantenaire Jubelpark is a few steps farther east of Place Schuman and houses the **Musée Royal de l'Armée et d'Histoire Militaire** and **Autoworld,** which are definitely worth visiting after a picnic in the big park. To the south of Place Schuman is the European Parliament and Place du Luxembourg (or P'Lux), which feeds and waters all the tired politicians.

On the opposite side of town, northeast of the city center, is **Heysel,** the last major stop on the Brussels metro. It seems far but only takes 20min. to reach and is worth the ride if only to see the **Atomium,** the signature structure from the 1958 World Expo. **Mini-Europe** is a fun little excursion if you're feeling the need to get in touch with your inner child.

SIGHTS

Brussels is definitely underrated in the things-to-see category. Aside from its notorious and unusual statues and the **Grand Place,** Brussels has a diverse array of museums and several lovely city parks that are worth your time. Parc Leopold and the Square Marie Louise Plein are beautiful respites from the city noise. So while you definitely shouldn't miss everyone's favorite urinating boy, don't let anyone fool you into thinking that's all there is to see in Brussels.

Lower Town

The Lower Town has most of Brussels' famous sights.

▨ MANNEKEN PIS   STATUE

Intersection of rue de l'Étuve and rue du Chêne

Prepare to be both amused and underwhelmed by the icon of Brussels—a 2ft. tall statue of a little boy peeing into a pond. Don't ask us what it means (his actual origins are unknown); all we know is that he is continually swamped

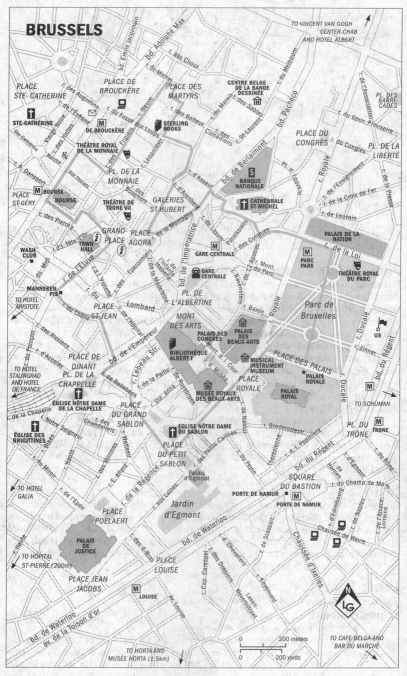

BRUSSELS

PLACE STE-CATHERINE

STE-CATHÉRINE

PLACE DE BROUCKÈRE

DE BROUCKÈRE

PLACE DES MARTYRS

STERLING BOOKS

CENTRE BELGE DE LA BANDE DESSINÉE

PLACE DES BARRICADES

PL. DES BARRICADES

PLACE DU CONGRÈS

PL. DE LA LIBERTÉ

bd. Adolphe Max

r. aux Choux

r. St-Michel

bd. Émile Jacqmain

r. des Augustins

de l'Évêque

r. du Fossé aux Loups

r. Neuve

r. du Persil

r. des Bouchers

r. des Comédiens

r. du Marais

r. des Sables

r. St-Laurent

bd. Pachéco

r. du Meiboom

TO VINCENT VAN GOGH CENTER-CHAB AND HOTEL ALBERT

r. de l'Association

r. du Gouv. Provisoire

THÉÂTRE ROYAL DE LA MONNAIE

PL. DE LA MONNAIE

BOURSE

BOURSE

THÉÂTRE DE TOONE VII

GALERIES ST-HUBERT

PLACE ST-GÉRY

WASH CLUB

GRAND PLACE

TOWN HALL

PLACE AGORA

MANNEKEN PIS

TO HOTEL ARISTOTE

PLACE ST-JEAN

r. du Lombard

PL. DE L'ALBERTINE

BANQUE NATIONALE

CATHÉDRALE ST-MICHEL

bd. de Berlaimont

r. d'Assaut

r. d'Arenberg

r. de la Montagne

r. de l'Impératrice

bd. de l'Impératrice

r. de Loxum

Parvis

r. des Colonnes

GARE CENTRALE

GARE CENTRALE

PALAIS DE LA NATION

PARC PARK

THÉÂTRE ROYAL DU PARC

Parc de Bruxelles

r. Royale

r. de l'Enseignement

r. de la Croix de Fer

r. de la Presse

r. de Louvain

r. de la Loi

US

r. Ducale

r. Zinner

r. de la Loi

PLACE DE DINANT

PL. DE LA CHAPELLE

PLACE DE LA CHAPELLE

ÉGLISE NOTRE DAME DE LA CHAPELLE

ÉGLISE DES BRIGITTINES

MONT DES ARTS

PALAIS DES CONGRÈS

BIBLIOTHÈQUE ALBERT I

PALAIS DES BEAUX-ARTS

MUSICAL INSTRUMENT MUSEUM

PLACE DES PALAIS

PALAIS ROYALE

PALAIS ROYAL

PLACE ROYALE

MUSÉE ROYAUX DES BEAUX-ARTS

bd. de l'Empereur

TO HOTEL STALINGRAD AND HOTEL DE FRANCE

de la Rollebeek

r. Ste-Anne

r. de Ruysbroek

r. de la Paille

r. du Musée

Mont d. l. Cour

r. Baron

r. Royale

r. Brederodestr.

r. de Namur

TO SCHUMAN

PL. DU TRÔNE

TRÔNE

PLACE DU GRAND SABLON

ÉGLISE NOTRE DAME DU SABLON

PLACE DU PETIT SABLON

Palais d'Egmont

r. des Petits Carmes

Thérésienne

r. d. l. Pépinière

r. du Régent

TO HOTEL GALIA

PLACE JEAN JACOBS

PLACE POELAERT

PALAIS DE JUSTICE

TO HÔPITAL ST-PIERRE (200m)

Jardin d'Egmont

PORTE DE NAMUR

PORTE DE NAMUR

SQUARE DU BASTION

r. du Champ de Mars

r. d'Edimbourg

r. de Naples

Chaussée de Wavre

bd. de Waterloo

av. de la Toison d'or

LOUISE

PLACE LOUISE

des 4-Bras

r. de la Régence

aux Laines

r. aux Laines

r. de Stassart

Chaussée d'Ixelles

av. Louise

Kemmeld

Lakenstraat

Weverstraat

bd. de Waterloo

TO HORTA AND MUSÉE HORTA (1.5km)

N

LG

TO CAFÉ BELGA AND BAR DU MARCHÉ

0   200 meters

0   200 yards

belgium

with giggling tourists and that he likes to celebrate certain national holidays and events.

i Head southwest from the Grand Place along rue de l'Étuve. The Manneken is 3 blocks down. Check the vendor's calendar to see what the Manneken Pis will be wearing and when.

GRAND PLACE
SQUARE

Grand Place

The historic center of Brussels is a grand place known, naturally, as the Grand Place. Many of the tourists are too focused on what's in front of them to look up—that's a mistake, as the really worthwhile, intricate architecture is actually above you. Make sure to return once the sun goes down, when the famous Guildhall buildings, including the Hôtel de Ville and the Maison de Roi, are dramatically illuminated.

i ⓂBourse. Head straight down rue de la Bourse, which leads to the northeast corner of the square.

MUSÉE DU CACAO ET DU CHOCOLAT
MUSEUM

9-11 rue de la Tête d'Or   ☎02 514 20 48 www.mucc.be

What's more Belgian than peeing statues? Chocolate, that's what. Opened in 1998 by Jo Draps, the daughter of one of the founders of Godiva, the Musée du Cacao et du Chocolat is a chocoholic's dream (or worst nightmare, if it's Lent). Fresh milk chocolate is churned in the entrance, and the backroom allows you to watch a chocolate chef work his magic.

i ⓂBourse. Head straight down rue de la Bourse, which leads to the northeast corner of the Grand Place. The museum is just south of the Grand Place. €5.50; students, seniors, and ages 12-16 €4.50; under 12 free with parent. ☒ Open Tu-Su 10am-4:30pm.

MUSÉE DE LA VILLE DE BRUXELLES (LA MAISON DU ROI)
MUSEUM

Grand Place   ☎02 279 43 50 www.bruxelles.be

The dignified building that houses the Musée de la Ville de Bruxelles is arguably a bigger deal than the museum itself. La Maison du Roi (King's House) was built in the 13th century to both demonstrate the power of the Belgian prince and serve as an economic center for the city. Make sure to check out the stone remains from the original building on the first floor and the room with model replicas of 13th-century Brussels.

i In the northeast corner of Grand Place €4; students, seniors, and groups €3; children €2. Under 18 free on weekends. ☒ Open Tu-W 10am-5pm, Th 10am-8pm, F-Su 10am-5pm.

JEANNEKE PIS
STATUE

Off rue des Bouchers

The poor lonely sister of Manneken Pis is locked away behind bars (albeit pretty ones) down a tiny alleyway and isn't even listed by the Tourist Office in its official guides—where women's rights activists when you need them? Jeanneke Pis shows no shame as she squats down to do her business in a small pond. Conceived by Denis Adrien Debourvrie in 1985, the statue doesn't actually urinate anymore, but local lore has it that if you toss a coin in Jeanneke's puddle, the little girl will bring you luck. So throw a penny in the pond for good fortune and feminism.

i ⓂBourse. Just off rue des Bouchers. Take a right after Chez Léon.

Upper Town

▨ MAGRITTE MUSEUM
MUSEUM

3 rue de la Régence   ☎02 508 32 11 www.musee-magritte-museum.be

René Magritte may not be the most famous painter in the Musées Royaux des Beaux-Arts collection, but he's certainly one of the most interesting. The paintings of this master of Surrealism question the relationship between words, images, and reality. Start your tour at the glass elevator, where Magritte paintings

get a room!

Accommodations in Brussels fill up quickly. The EU Parliament attracts Europe's elite and the pricey, bougie hotels that come with them. Most student-friendly accommodations are located slightly north of the **Grand Place** and are within walking distance of Lower Town. Hotels will get more expensive in Upper Town, and the neighborhoods will generally get more unsafe for solo travelers the further south you get. There is no clearly defined high or low season in Brussels, although prices drop significantly in July and August.

☒ 2GO4 HOSTEL   HOSTEL $$
99 bd Emile Jacqmain   ☎02 219 30 19 www.2go4.be

2go4 is a haven for young solo travelers thanks to its strict no-large-groups policy. Shared spaces like the funky common room and the well-trafficked communal kitchen make for good opportunities to meet your fellow travelers. Amenities like individual reading lights and power outlets, plus the convenient location, make up for the sub-standard showers.

i Ⓜ*Rogier. Follow bd d'Anvers and turn left onto bd Emile Jacqmain. Linens included. Towels available for rent. Max. 6 people per group. Free Wi-Fi. Computers available. Dorms €21-29; singles €50-55.* ☒ *Reception 7am-1pm and 4-10pm.*

☒ SLEEP WELL   HOSTEL, HOTEL $$
23 rue du Damier   ☎02 218 50 50 www.sleepwell.be

Sleep Well has hostel and hotel components. Both are bright, cheerful, and cheap, and they share huge common areas and a popular bar. The hostel, though, has an inconvenient lockout between 11am and 3pm.

i Ⓜ*Rogier. Follow rue Neuve and turn left onto rue de la Blanchisserie. Rue du Damier is on your right. Breakfast and linens included. Towels available for rent. Wi-Fi €1 per 30min. Dorms €20-24; singles €36; doubles €54.* ☒ *Reception 24hr. Lockout 11am-3pm.*

☒ JACQUES BREL   HOSTEL $$
30 rue de la Sablonnière   ☎02 218 01 87 www.laj.be

Surprisingly lively, Jacques Brel provides a modern bar and lounge in its reception area. Rooms are comfortable, priced for budget travelers, and not nearly as boring as the exterior suggests. The hostel is conveniently located right at a 20min. walk from the Grand Place.

i Ⓜ*Botanique. Head south down rue Royale (away from Botanique) and take the 1st left. Breakfast and linens included. Reserve 4 weeks in advance. Free Wi-Fi and computer access. 6- to 8-bed dorms €21; 3- to 5-bed dorms €23; singles €36. Over age 25 add €2.* ☒ *Reception daily 7am-midnight. Lockout 10am-3pm.*

on the opposite wall blur together eerily as the elevator rushes by. Make sure to check out the collection of hand-drawn images—compiled by Magritte, Scutenaire, Hamoir, and Nougé—in which each of the friends took turns drawing a different limb or cross-section of the human form without looking at what their colleagues had previously drawn.

i Ⓜ*Parc. Walk south down rue Royale. €8, seniors €5, students €2, under 19 and 1st W of each month after 1pm free. Audio tour €4. Combined ticket with Musées Royeaux des Beaux-Arts €13, students €3.* ☒ *Open Tu 10am-5pm, W 10am-8pm, Th-Su 10am-5pm.*

☒ CATHÉDRALE DES SAINTS MICHEL ET GUDULE   CATHEDRAL
15 rue du Bois Sauvage   ☎02 217 85 45 www.cathedralestmichel.be

Perhaps the grandest cathedral in Brussels, Saint Michel et Gudule expects respectful silence from all its visitors. Blabbermouths have no fear: when you hear the grand organ mysteriously playing from the lofty stretches above, you'll have no problem shutting up. 11th-century architecture snobs didn't like its original design, so the church was rebuilt in the Gothic style over the next three centuries. As you wander through the splendor of the Catholic cathedral, gaze up to the saintly statues guarding the walls.

i ⓂGare Centrale. Free. Crypt €1. Free choir concerts throughout the year. ☒ Open M-F 7:30am-6pm, Sa-Su 8:30am-6pm. Mass in French Su 10, 11:30am, and 12:30pm.

MUSICAL INSTRUMENTS MUSEUM (MIM)   MUSEUM
2 montagne de la Cour   ☎02 545 01 30 www.musicalinstrumentsmuseum.be

If you have the slightest interest in music, the history of instruments, or just cool art deco buildings, you should get yourself on down to MIM. This museum just celebrated its 10th anniversary, and the 10 floors of its collection feature impressive interactive exhibits, though not every floor has something to look at. A large glass elevator leads to the top floors and the rooftop restaurant, which boasts a panoramic view of the city. The most ingenious part of the museum is the audio tour, which, instead of being vocal, is just music.

i ⓂParc. Permanent collection free 1st W of each month after 1pm. €5, under 26 and over 64 €4, under 13 free. Audio guide free with admission. ☒ Open Tu-F 9:30am-5pm, Sa-Su 10am-5pm. Last tickets sold 4:15pm.

CENTRE BELGE DE LA BANDE DESINÉE   MUSEUM
20 rue des Sables   ☎02 219 19 80 www.cbbd.be

Don't expect to find Marvel or DC on the shelves of this comic book museum, dedicated to the likes of Tintin and Boulle and Bill. Real comic book nerds head downstairs to the library, where you can read as many comics as you want, or pop next door to the bookshop where you can purchase your own to take home with you.

i ⓂRogier. ☒ Open Tu-Su 10am-6pm. Reception closes at 5:30pm.

MUSÉES ROYAUX DES BEAUX-ARTS   MUSEUM
3 rue de la Régence   ☎02 508 32 11 www.fine-arts-museum.be

The Musées Royaux des Beaux-Arts, attached to the Magritte Museum, holds a vast collection split between modern and ancient works. The modern arts section displays mind-boggling works from the 19th through 21st centuries, including provocative paintings and sculptures that will either fascinate you or make you wonder why you bought a ticket.

i ⓂParc. Walk south down rue Royale. €8, students €5, under 18 and 1st W of each month after 1pm free. Combined ticket with Magritte Museum €13, students €3. ☒ Open Tu-Su 10am-5pm. Last entry 4pm.

Place Schuman and Heysel

🏛 MUSÉE ROYAL DE L'ARMÉE ET D'HISTOIRE MILITAIRE   MUSEUM
3 Parc du Cinquantenaire   ☎02 737 78 33 www.klm-mra.be

This grand museum is absolutely massive, and you can easily get lost among the weapons and swords on display here. The aviation hall is the largest part of the museum; you'll spend most of your time here, where light aircraft from WWI and WWII abound. History buffs and war nerds could easily spend a couple of hours here, but those of you who aren't impressed by generations of war technology may want to just do a quick in-and-out while at the nearby park.

i ⓂSchuman. Head through the Arcade du Cinquantenaire; the museum is on the left, through the parking lot and across from Autoworld. Free. Audio guides €2-3. ☒ Open Tu-Su 9am-noon and 1-4:45pm. Aviation hall open Tu-Su 9am-4:45pm. Sky Cafe open 11am-4pm.

🏛 PARC DU CINQUANTENAIRE   PARK
This park's Arcade Cinquantenaire looks like a cross between the Arc de Triomphe and the Brandenburg Gate, so take some pictures of it and try to convince

your gullible/clueless friends that you went to Paris or Berlin (for bonus points, use two different photos of it and convince them you went to both).

i ⓂSchuman. At the end of rue de la Loi.

ATOMIUM   MONUMENT
Sq. de l'Atomium   ☎02 475 47 77 www.atomium.be

For some, the Atomium is a horrific eyesore in the Brussels skyline; for others, it's a stroke of architectural genius. Built for the 1958 World Expo, André Waterkeyn designed this monument to resemble the atom of an iron crystal—just 165 billion times bigger. The top of the Atomium offers a panoramic view of the city, as well as a restaurant and cafe, and a permanent exhibition on the '58 Expo and the Atomium's construction.

i ⓂHeysel €11, students and ages 12-18 €8, ages 6-11 €4, under 6 free. Audio tour €2. Ⓩ Open daily 10am-6pm. Last entry 30min. before close.

FOOD

Even though it's the capital of the EU, Brussels does not have capital prices. With *friteries* and waffle joints on every other corner, in addition to the traditionally meat-and-potato heavy Flemish diet, don't expect to tighten the notches on your belt any time soon. ost restaurants have outdoor terraces, and the weather is almost always pleasant enough to enjoy the fresh air.

Lower Town

The Lower Town offers some of the best places to get all your artery-clogging cravings met. There are also plenty of touristy rip-offs, most of which are centered on the **rue des Bouchers.** For late-night munchies or a meal on the run, try the **rue du Marché aux Fromages,** just off the Grand Place—it's sometimes called the "rue des pittas" or "kebab street."

🔲 FRITLAND   FRITERIE $
49 rue Henri Maus   ☎02 514 06 27

Forget about arteries: we'll gladly wash down as many fistfuls of creamy, mayonnaise-dipped French fries with as many cans of blonde Belgian beer as we like, merci beaucoup. Especially when the whole thing only costs €5 per round (seriously, €3 for a mountain of fries and sauce, €2 for the beer).

i ⓂDe Brouckere. Head northwest on rue de l'Evêque and turn left onto bd Anspach. Turn left onto rue des Pierres; Fritland is on the left. Beer €2. Fries €3. Chicken kebab €3. Ⓩ Open M-Th 11am-1am, F-Sa 11am until dawn, Su 11am-1am.

🔲 MOKAFE   CAFE $
9 Galerie du Roi   ☎02 511 78 70

Tucked inside the fancy (and expensive) Galerie du Roi is the charming Mokafe, a cafe specializing in waffles—not the €1 sugar balls sold around Manneken Pis, but the proper Belgian kind, served on a real plate with powdered sugar on top. You'll be dining with locals, a few tourists, and the biggest waffle snobs of them all: little old Belgian ladies.

i From the Grand Place, take the rue de la Colline on the eastern side to reach the Galerie du Roi. It looks like a shopping center inside a palace. Sandwiches €2-4. Waffles €3-5. Ⓩ Open daily 7am-8pm, but hours are flexible.

🔲 IN'T SPINNEKOPKE   TRADITIONAL, BELGIAN $$$
1 pl. Jardin aux Fleurs   ☎02 511 86 95 www.spinnekopke.be

Spinnekopke (that's "spider's head" in Flemish) might not sound like an appetizing name for a restaurant. But once you take in this rustic tavern's candlelit tables and crowds of locals, you'll know that you've stumbled across something very exciting. Green-aproned waiters will attend to your table with the utmost attention. For a really tasty meal, try one of the many sauces available for their steak (steak €17.50, with sauce €3), including a brilliant cheese, lambik beer, and cream sauce.

i ⓂBourse. Head down rue Orts and turn left onto rue des Charteux, which leads to pl. du Jardin aux Fleurs. English menus available. ⓒ Open M-F noon-3pm and 6-11pm, Sa-Su 24hr.

FIN DE SIÈCLE
BELGIAN $$

9 rue des Charteux ☎2 513 51 23

Don't let the borderline pornographic prints of greased up hands caressing female lady parts turn you off (or on). Aside from the uncomfortable choice of wall art, Fin de Siècle is a perfect gem. With a small patio, a deep interior, and high ceilings, Fin de Siècle caters to a relaxed, intimate crowd of regulars looking to enjoy a respite from the rowdy bar scene of nearby pl. St Géry.

i ⓂBourse. Head down rue Auguste Orts and take a left onto rue des Charteux. Plats €12-19. ⓓ Open daily in the evening until late.

Upper Town

If you're near the **Place de la Liberté,** a number of convenience stores carry snacks and sandwich fixings for a picnic in the **Parc de Bruxelles.** In the southern part of Upper Town, the area around **Place Flagey**—though far from the city center—boasts a number of interesting and moderately priced eateries.

🏮 EAT PARADE
SANDWICHES $$

87 rue de Namur ☎02 511 11 95

The only procession here is the line of Brussels's businessmen stretching out the door, and if you can make it past the packed crowd to the counter of this cozy lunchtime joint, you'll see why they're eager to be part of the spectacle. Do as the locals do and take your chef d'œuvre to the nearby Parc de Bruxelles for the perfect summer picnic in front of the Royal Palace.

i ⓂPort de Namur. Walk northwest on rue du Namur; Eat Parade is on the next corner after the big intersection. Sandwiches €4. ⓓ Open M-F 7am-3:45pm, Sa 9:30am-4pm.

🏮 LE PERROQUET
SALADS AND PITA $$

31 rue Watteeu ☎02 512 99 22

If you're starting to feel weighed down by all those fries and waffles drowned in chocolate, head to Le Perroquet for a vegetable cleanse. The menu was created in collaboration with a dietician, and the servings are healthy enough to keep your cardiologist at bay. Butterfly chairs make the quiet terrace a great place to enjoy a drink with your health-conscious significant other.

i ⓂLouise. Head northwest on av. de la Toison d'Or; at the roundabout, take the 3rd exit onto rue des Quatre Bras; continue onto pl. Poelaert. At the next roundabout, take the 2nd exit onto rue de la Régence and turn left or to rue Van Moer. Continue onto rue Watteeu; Le Perroquet is on the left. €12 min. credit cards. ⓓ Open M noon-11:30pm, Tu-W noon-midnight, Th-Sa noon-1am, Su noon-11:30pm.

THE MERCEDES HOUSE
BRASSERIE $$$

22-24 rue Bodenbroek ☎02 400 42 63

Looking for a way to combine your love of cars with some fine Belgian dining? This brasserie is part of the Mercedes House, which showcases Mercedes-Benz cars, and is an ideal location for a coffee or light lunch. Hot drinks are available and can be enjoyed on the terrace outside, where you can also admire the shop's crop of shiny cars. At lunchtime, you can sample traditional dishes that won't drive away with your money, but if you want to take a different kind of spin, order a bottle of champagne at €50 a pop.

i ⓂParc. Entrees €11.50-15.50. Plats €15.50-24. ⓓ Open M-F 11:30am-3pm.

brussels

Place Schuman and Heysel

◪ ANTOINE'S
FRITERIE $

1 pl. Jourdan

Around lunchtime, crowds of businessmen, children, students, and tourists descend on Brussels's oldest friterie for large, piping-hot portions of some of the city's best frites. Many people head to grassy Parc Léopold to enjoy their fries alfresco.

i Ⓜ*Schuman. Pl. Jourdan is just off rue Froissart. Frites €2-2.20. Sauce €0.50. ⓧ Open M-Th 11:30am-1am, F-Sa 11:30am-2am, Su 11:30am-1am.*

◪ CHEZ MOI
PIZZERIA, BAR $

66 rue du Luxembourg
☎02 280 26 66

Avoid the expensive eateries in and around the EU area and join the young workers devouring their delicious (and dirt-cheap) pizza slices on the grass of pl. du Luxembourg. Chez Moi offers a daily menu of classic flavors (mushroom, pepperoni, etc.).

i Ⓜ*Maelbeek. Turn left onto rue de la Loi after exiting the station. Take the 1st left onto rue de Trèves, walk 4 blocks, then turn right onto pl. du Luxembourg. Head right across the square to get to rue du Luxembourg. Takeout and delivery available. Slices €2-3.50. ⓧ Open M-W 11am-11pm, Th-F 11am-midnight.*

CAFÉ PARC AVENUE
CAFE $$$$

50 av. d'Auderghem
☎02 742 28 10 www.parc-avenue.be

Eating out in the EU area can be expensive. Fortunately, this upscale cafe has €16 lunch special that includes the entree and plat of the day. It may not sound like much, but after mounds of greasy fries and sweet waffles, this meal will leave you feeling as satisfied and as slick as the suits lunching next to you.

i Ⓜ*Schuman. Walk toward the park and to the right; the cafe is on the corner of rue Belliard and av. d'Auderghem. Entrees €8-12. Salads €12-14. Plats €16-34. ⓧ Open M-F 11am-2:30pm and 6:30-11pm.*

NIGHTLIFE

We encourage you to sample as many **good Belgian brews** as humanly possible, but remember: the metro stops at midnight. The cheapest and most popular bars are in Lower Town, which features a decent mix of tourist traps and well-kept local secrets. Upper Town nightlife is less vibrant and more expensive, with bars and lounges full of 30-somethings in abundance but fewer options for students.

Lower Town

The Lower Town has the liveliest nightlife in Brussels.

◪ DELIRIUM
BAR

4A Impasse de la Fidélité
☎02 514 44 34 www.deliriumcafe.be

If you want to party hard in Brussels, Delirium is the place to do it. While its immense popularity means that all of the drunkest tourists (and Belgians) will be here, Delirium is a large enough place that you won't mind. Shenanigans and revelry abound, and with a selection of more than 2000 beers, this bar provides the opportunity to get drunk on new brews every night. Beware: these beers are strong (10% alcohol), so exercise some caution when you go out—it's not called Delirium for nothing.

i Ⓜ*De Brouchere. Walk south on bd Anspach 1 block, turn left onto rue Grétry, and continue about 2 blocks; the bar is on the left. Beer €2-6. ⓧ Open daily 10am-4am.*

◪ L'ESTAMINET TOONE
PUB

Impasse Schuddeveld 6
☎02 511 71 37 www.toone.be

You are likely to run into a chill, older crowd at l'Estaminet Toone, but occasional live music, marionettes dangling from the ceiling, and laughter keep this

brussels

place light-hearted and young. This tavern neighbors le Royal Théâtre Toone, where you can enjoy an evening marionette show before heading down to the bar for some brews. The bar is accessed through a long tunnel, so although it may get a bit noisy inside, the hubbub from rue des Bouchers is (thankfully) drowned out.

i Ⓜ️De Brouckère. Walk 1 block south on bd Anspach to rue Grétry and turn left. Continue down rue des Brouchers; a big sign over the road points to Toone, on the right. Cash only. Beers €2.50-6.50. ✆ Open Tu-Su noon-midnight.

🏛 BONNEFOOI
BAR
8 rue des Pierres   ☎048 762 22 31   www.bonnefooi.be

Bonnefooi is one of Brussels's most pleasant bars, and it attracts a steady stream of young tourists to its unobtrusive side street near Bourse. It's not as wild as its 8am closing time might suggest, but it is a great place to relax at the end of a night of partying.

i Ⓜ️Bourse. Just off of bd Anspach. Beer €2-4. Mixed drinks €7. ✆ Open daily 6pm-8am.

GOUPIL LE FOL
BAR
22 rue de la Violette   ☎02 511 13 96

This eclectic estaminet is one of the Lower Town's best finds. A sign outside explains that the bar will not serve Coca-Cola to its patrons (except as a vehicle for alcohol). Step inside and you'll be enveloped in a world of revolution, literature, and art. Goupil le Fol is packed with an intellectual crowd of alternative students and older art-lovers, and the owner, Abel, counts the Princes of Spain and Belgium among his patrons.

i Ⓜ️Bourse. From the Grand Place, head down rue des Chapeliers and turn left onto rue de la Violette. Beer €3-6. ✆ Open daily 6pm-6am.

Upper Town

Apart from one of the city's best clubs, Upper Town nightlife tends to be less vibrant and more expensive than in the Lower Town.

🏛 FUSE
CLUB
208 rue Blaes   ☎02 511 97 89   www.fuse.be

Fuse proudly proclaims itself "Best Belgian Club Ever." That might be overdoing it, but it is one of Brussels's biggest and liveliest clubs, with pounding music and drinks that will make even the worst dancing excusable.

i Ⓜ️Port de Hal. Head north on bd du Midi, then turn right onto rue Blaes. Cover Sa before midnight €6, after midnight €11. Drinks €4-10. ✆ Open on club nights Th-Sa 11pm-late.

🏛 LA FLEUR EN PAPIER DORÉ
PUB
55 rue des Alexiens   ☎02 511 16 59   www.lafleurenpapierdore.be

A mix of older locals and young artsy types crowd this historic pub just off of the Sablon area. Now protected by the Belgian government, it counts the artist Magritte and Tintin author Hergé among its former clientele. Temporary art exhibits fill the kooky space, making for a nice break from the monotonous profusion of Irish pubs and dark taverns.

i Ⓜ️Gare du Midi. Beer €2-7. ✆ Open Tu-Sa 11am-midnight, Su 11am-7pm.

Place Schuman and Heysel

🏛 JAMES JOYCE
IRISH PUB
34 rue Archimède   ☎04 7162 05 80

If you show up to James Joyce solo, never fear—you will surely depart among (new) friends. This pub caters a bit more to the middle-aged crowd than the student scene, but as some travelers might say, every hour is happy hour here. The only Brussels bar with a full dartboard, a smoke room, and a reading corner with books that include (you guessed it) Ulysses, James Joyce ensures that there will be no shortage of conversation topics.

i Ⓜ*Schuman. Walk north on rue Archimède 1½ blocks. James Joyce is on the left just past the Hairy Canary. Bartenders will make mixed drinks on request but no fancy mixed drinks. Live music 1st Th of each month.* ⏰ *Open M-Th 5pm-late, F 5pm-7am, Sa noon-7am, Su noon-late.*

SOHO
CLUB

47 bd du Triomphe ☎02 649 35 00 www.soho-club.be

Soho is one of Brussels's liveliest clubs, despite being situated near the EU district. The 20-something crowd on the gigantic dance floor is a welcome break from the older Eurocrats found in the area. Expect a wide variety of music and theme nights.

i Ⓜ*Hankar. Head west on Chaussée de Wavre and turn left onto rue de la Chasse Royale, then right onto bd du Triomphe. The Hankar stop is serviced by the night bus. Cover €10. Drinks €5-10.* ⏰ *Open Th-Sa 11pm-late.*

ARTS AND CULTURE

⬛ BEURSSCHOUWBURG
THEATER

20-28 rue Auguste Orts ☎02 550 03 50 www.beursschouwburg.be

A haven for up-and-coming artists, the Beursschouwburg hosts modern theater productions along with film and documentary screenings, dance performances, and temporary art installations. On Wednesdays, they host a free, student-oriented show with the superb title SHOW, which stands for "Shit Happens on Wednesday."

i Ⓜ*Bourse €12, students €10.* ⏰ *Box office open M-F 10am-6pm.*

LE BOTANIQUE
CONCERTS

bd du Jardin. 29-31 Botanique ☎02 218 37 32 www.botanique.be

The Botanical Gardens make for a beautiful stroll during the day, but things get a little raunchier at night, when the grand building that towers above the gardens hosts some of the best concerts in the city. Three different stages provide an intimate performance space for artists from the UK, continental Europe, and on occasion the US; past heavyweight performers include Ellie Goulding, Marina and the Diamonds, and Kate Nash. Brussels's student crowd can't get enough of Le Botanique, and in recent years it has become the city's most popular venue for live music.

i Ⓜ*Botanique. Buy tickets online. Some tickets available at the door. Prices vary by show.* ⏰ *Box office open daily 10am-6pm.*

THÉÂTRE ROYAL DU PARC
THEATER

3 rue de la Loi ☎02 505 30 30 www.theatreduparc.be

If you're game for a laugh, then get yourself down to the Parc and pick up a ticket to see a variety of performances. The early 2013 season included Sherlock Holmes, Around the World in 80 Days, Oedipus, and Les Misérables.

i Ⓜ*Troon. Walk toward the park and to the left; the theater is in the corner of the park. Ticket €5-30. Student tickets €9.50.* ⏰ *Box office open Sept-May M-Sa 11am-6pm, Su 11am-5pm; Jun and Aug Tu-F 11am-6pm. Closed all of Jul.*

ESSENTIALS

Practicalities

- **TOURIST OFFICES:** ⬛**Use-it** makes maps especially for student travelers that are available for free at many hostels as well as at their office and on their website. The office staff can give advice on nightlife, food, shopping, GLBT life, and more. They also provide a list of festivals and events, have free internet (computers available), and free coffee. (8 Steenkoolkaai www.use-it. be Ⓜ*Ste-Catherine.* ⏰ *Open M-Sa 10am-1pm and 2-6pm.)* The **central tourist office,** in the east corner of the Grand Place (Ⓜ Bourse), sells the **Brussels Card,** which includes free public transport, a city map, free museum access, and discounts at a few shops and restaurants for one, two, or three days (€24/34/40). There is also a second, less central office (2-4 rue Royale) and another at the central concourse of Gare du Midi (open daily 9am-6pm). (☎02 513 89 40 www.brusselsinternational.be ☒ Open daily 10am-6pm.)

- **CURRENCY EXCHANGE: CBC Automatic Change ATMs.** (7 Grand Place ☎02 546 12 11 ☒ Open 24hr. Also at Ⓜ De Brouckere and Ⓜ Gare du Midi.)

- **INTERNET: CyberCafés.** (86 bd Émile Jacqmain *i* €1.50 per 30min. ☒ Open daily 9am-10pm.) Free Wi-Fi is available at **McDonald's, Exki,** and **Quick** on rue Neuve.

- **POST OFFICES: Central Office.** (1 bd Anspach ☎02 201 23 45 *i* Ⓜ De Brouckère. Belgium €0.75, EU €1.09, other countries €1.29. ☒ Open M-F 8:30am-6pm, Sa 10am-4pm.)

- **POSTAL CODE:** 1000.

Emergency

- **EMERGENCY:** For police, ambulance, or fire, call ☎100 or ☎101.

- **POLICE: Police headquarters** are located at 30 rue du Marché au Charbon. (☎02 279 77 11 *i* Ⓜ Bourse. From the Grand Place, follow rue du Marché au Charbon from the northwest corner of the square. ☒ Open 24hr.)

- **LATE-NIGHT PHARMACIES:** Pharmacies in Brussels rotate hours, so there will always be one reasonably close to you that's open late. Pharmacies will usually display hours on a sign. **Pharmacie Fripiers** is closest to the Grand Place. (24B rue des Fripiers ☎02 218 04 91 ☒ Open M-F 9am-7pm, Sa 9:30am-7pm.) To find one open near you, visit www.servicedegarde. be or call ☎0800 20 600.

- **HOSPITALS/MEDICAL SERVICES:** The Saint-Pierre University Hospital has two locations. **Saint-Pierre University Hospital–Site César de Paepe** is a 10min. walk from the Grand Place. (11 rue des Alexiens ☎02 506 71 11 www.stpierre-bru.be *i* Ⓜ Bourges. From the Grand Place, exit through the southernmost corner of the square and turn left onto rue des Alexiens.) **Saint-Pierre University Hospital (International Patients Service)** is to the south. (322 rue Haute ☎02 535 33 17 www.stpierre-bru.be *i* Tram #3, 4, 33, or 51 to Ⓜ Porte de Hal. Head south on rue Haute. ☒ Open 24hr.)

Getting There

BY PLANE

The **Brussels airport** (BRU ☎090 07 00 00 www.brusselsairport.be) is 14km from the city center. Trains run between the airport and Gare du Midi every 20min. (€6-7 max; 5am-midnight). STIB bus #12 runs until 8pm, later on weekends and public holidays; bus #21 runs every 30min. (☒ 5am-11pm, until midnight during the summer). **Brussels South Charleroi Airport** (CRL ☎090 20 24 90 www.charleroi-airport.com) is a budget airline hub 45km south of Brussels. A shuttle runs from the airport to Gare du Midi. (€13, round-trip €22. ☒ Every 30min.)

BY TRAIN

Brussels has three main train stations: **Gare du Midi, Gare Centrale,** and **Gare du Nord.** All international trains stop at Gare du Midi, and most stop at Gare Centrale and Gare du Nord as well. Gare Centrale is the closest to the center and the Grand Place. Gare du Nord is in the north just past Botanique. Gare du Midi is in the southwest on bd du Midi. Brussels can be reached from Bruges (€12 ☒ 30min.), Amsterdam (€43 ☒ 3hr.), and Paris (€55-86 ☒ 1hr. from Ⓜ Midi); trains also run from London (www.eurostar.com €60-240 ☒ 2hr.). There are also normal commuter trains that run between Amsterdam and Brussels that you can board without advance booking, but you can (and probably should) book in advance.

Getting Around

Getting around Brussels is cheap and simple on foot, especially in Lower Town. With skinny, winding streets that change names often (and often have two names to begin with), it's easy to get lost. Luckily, it's also easy to get found: look for tall signposts around Lower Town and the major museum districts of Upper Town. These will point you in the direction of major attractions and metro stations and will even suggest whether to walk or take the metro based on how far your destination may be. Cars rule the roads in Brussels, so bikes are only advisable for the truly brave. If you want to bike around Brussels, there are **villo** (bike rental) points located at key locations throughout the city; the first 30min. is free, but you pay incrementally for each 30min. thereafter (www.villo.be).

BY PUBLIC TRANSPORTATION

The metro system rings the city, with a main **tram** running vertically through the middle and two other lines running east to west. There are 18 trams in total. The **bus** and tram system connects the various quarters of the city, and night buses service major stops on Friday and Saturday nights every 30min. until 3am. All public transport in Brussels is run by the **Société des Transports Intercommunaux Bruxellois (STIB)**. (☎07 023 20 00 www.stib.be ☑ System operates daily 5am-midnight.) The **metro**, tram, and bus all use the same tickets. (€2, purchased inside vehicle €2.50; round-trip €3.50; day pass €6; 10-trip ticket €13.) It's a good idea to pick up a copy of the metro map, which also contains information about transfers and night buses. The map is free and available at ticket counters and at the Gare du Midi.

BY TAXI

After the metro stops running, you can call Taxi Bleus (☎02 268 00 00), Taxi Verts (☎02 349 49 49), **Taxis Oranges** (☎02 349 43 43), **Autolux** (☎02 411 41 42), or **CNTU** (☎02 374 20 20). Official taxi signs are yellow and black. Taxi prices are calculated by distance (€1.66-2.70 per km), plus a fixed base charge (€2.40, at night €4.40). **Collecto** is a shared taxi system that has 200 pickup points in Brussels (☎02 800 36 36 www. collecto.org *i* €6. ☑11pm-6am. Call 20min. or more in advance).

bruges

There's a reason you'll meet cute old couples on second honeymoons in Bruges: with its picturesque canals and narrow old houses, it looks a little like a fairy-tale land. The cobbled streets are often clogged with tourists wearing fanny packs and toting cameras; most congregate around the museums, which range from the history of the *frite* to Flemish art. Put in a little extra effort, and locals will happily share with you all of Bruges's ghost stories, weird secrets, and small-town charm.

ORIENTATION

Thanks to its small size, Bruges is very easy to navigate. Getting lost in the city is more fun than worrying, since it takes only 10min. to get back on track. Bruges is surrounded by a canal which cuts through the center of the city, so if you do get lost, just follow the water. **The Markt** is the center of town, and is recognizable by the large **belfry tower**, which can be seen from almost any part of town. Four of Bruges's main roads emanate from the Markt: **St-Jakobstraat** to the northwest, **Vlamingstraat** to the northeast, **Wollestraat** to the southeast, and **Steenstraat** to the southwest. East of the Markt along Breidelstraat is **the Burg**, Bruges's other main square, which boasts the Town Hall and Holy Blood Chapel. **Hoogstraat** runs east from the Burg, while **Blezelstraat** runs south. You can easily find all destinations in Bruges from the Markt and the Burg.

get a room!

Bruges draws a fair amount of young backpackers, so hostels are plentiful in the city center and just outside the city walls. Visit **www.letsgo.com** for more hostel and hotel recommendations.

CHARLIE ROCKETS
HOSTEL $

19 Hoogstraat ☎050 33 06 60 www.charlierockets.com

It's all American at Charlie Rockets, so you'll feel right at home in this hostel off of Bruges's main square. The large dorm rooms are spacious and the bathrooms are clean and modern, but Charlie is really out of this world compared to its competition due to its rocking bar, which is actually one of the highlights of a night out in Bruges. Save yourself the trouble and literally live at the bar.

i Hoogstraat runs southeast from the Burg. Free Wi-Fi. Breakfast and sheets included. 6- to 8-bed dorm €19-21. Doubles €43-55 ☒ Reception open 6am-4am.

SIGHTS

Bruges loves young people, leading to huge discounts for those under 26.

BELFORT
TOWER

7 Markt ☎050 44 87 78 www.museabrugge.be

If you've bribed the weather gods into giving Beligum a cloudless day, the gorgeous view from the Belfort can extend all the way to the North Sea. Keep in mind that the 83m structure was built centuries before the age of elevators so you'll have to climb a lot of stairs to get that photo-op. But the panoramic view over the entire city is well worth the huffing and puffing.

i Grand Markt. €8, under 26 €6, seniors €6. ☒ Open daily 9:30am-5pm.

HOLY BLOOD CHAPEL
CHURCH

10 Burg ☎050 33 67 92

This small church has one main draw which brings religious visitors and tourists by the thousands every year: a vial containing what the church claims to be the blood of Christ. The prized possession is displayed every day from 2-4pm; head up the flight of stairs and pay your respects (or even kiss!) the glass container containing one of Christianity's most prized possessions. In mid-May, the city of Bruges holds the annual Holy Blood Procession, a tradition dating back to the 14th century.

i In the southwest corner of the Burg. Free. Tickets must be purchased in advance at www.tick-etsbrugge.be. ☒ Open daily Apr-Sept 9:30am-noon and 2-5pm; Oct-Mar 10am-noon and 2-5pm.

GROENINGE MUSEUM
MUSEUM

12 Dijver ☎050 44 87 43 www.museabrugge.be

The Groeninge Museum houses Bruges's best collection of Flemish and Belgian artists from the 15th-20th centuries. As you move through the rooms, you'll begin to appreciate the talent that went into some of these obscure religious paintings, particularly Provost's various intriguing depictions of the life of Saint Nicolas. However we also particularly enjoyed the more modern interpretation of the Last Supper by Gustave van de Woestyne. The ticket also gets you access to the temporary exhibition in the Arentshuis as well as The Forum, which is Bruges center for contemporary art.

i From the Markt, head south along Wollestraat and cross the bridge. Take a right onto Dijver and through the archway on your left €8. ☒ Open Tu-Su 9:30am-5pm.

belgium

FOOD

Bruges is brimming with restaurants—unfortunately, the local specialty is pawning small portions of overpriced food off on unsuspecting tourists. These places cluster around the Markt, but you know better than to fall into these traps. Instead, head a little farther out from the Markt to find a quality place, which will leave neither your wallet nor your stomach empty.

◪ PAS PARTOUT   TRADITIONAL $
1 Jeruzalemstraat   ☎050 33 51 16 srpaspartout@busmail.net

This restaurant used to be a three-star Michelin restaurant where it cost a fortune just to look at the menu, but a few years ago it was taken over and turned into a social service project, in an attempt to serve high quality food to those who wouldn't normally be able to afford it. Now the older locals of Bruges come to Pas Partout to have cheap meals (under €10) of the highest quality in the area. Besides the food not much matches the restaurants origins for in many ways the place kinda feels like a cafeteria, but not in a bad way it is just plain and with a nondescript atmosphere. Do not let this stop you from coming here though for you will not regret taking your lunch at this hidden treasure.

i From the Burg, head along Hoogstraat to the east, cross the bridge and continue onto Molenmeers. Turn left onto Jeruzalemstraat just past the laundrette and continue to the end of the road. Meal €7.30-10.75. ☑ Open M-Sa 11:45am-2:15pm.

MÉDARD   TRADITIONAL $
18 Sint Ammandstraat   ☎050 34 86 84

Médrad has a history which goes back all the way to the 1930s, when the current owner's grandparents first opened their first little restaurant in Bruges. Food has been in the family for generations, and in 2003 the current owner moved back into what was once her parents' house to reopen the doors of Médrad. Locals started flocking back almost immediately, and after a look at the menu we can see why. The specialty spaghetti (€6.50) comes with cheese, vegetables, and plenty of ground beef—and this is just one of the small dishes. If you're really hungry try the large dishes, if you dare.

i Just off of the Markt. Reservations recommended. Meals €6.50. Sandwiches €3-5. ☑ Open Tu-Sa noon-3pm and 6:30-7:30pm. Closed in the evenings on W and Su.

GRAND KAFFEE DE PASSAGE   TRADITIONAL $$
26-28 Dweerstraat   ☎050 34 01 40 www.passagebruges.com

The Grand Kaffee is deeply traditional, and proud of it. Portraits of family members spanning the generations hang on the walls, but this doesn't make the place feel like some sort of creepy memorial, for even these pics have character to them as they are all different sizes and housed in different style frames. The large interior matches by carrying a dim and classic feel to it that is exactly what you will want when enjoying the traditional Flemish cuisine offered here. Even the menu looks like a storybook, and the intricate writing is translated into English to make choosing even easier.

i From the Markt, head down Steenstraat which leads into Zuidzandstraat. Dweerstraat is on the right. Meal €9-16. ☑ Open daily 6-10pm.

NIGHTLIFE

Nightlife in Bruges is pretty easy-going; the only things that stay open until 7am are the *frites* stands. Locals enjoy a quiet drink in some hidden spots, while the tourists congregate near the Markt to down pricey pints. For a more authentically Belgian experience, head to one of the bars below. This is a place to drink slowly and strike up conversations with the locals.

LUCIFERNUM
8 Twijnstraat

BAR

Ring the bell here on a Saturday night, and the doors of Lucifernum swing open, unleashing a series of the weird and wonderful. The scaffolding is a piece of permanent artwork that Willy Restin, the owner of the bar and a local Mephistopheles (in a good way), refuses to take down. During the summer months, the crowds head outside to lounge in Willy's garden, which feels more like the backyard of someone's house. Locals consider this to be one of the hidden gems of Bruges, so don't turn up expecting to down shots and stumble out wasted. Pay Willy and his friends some respect and treat this treasure for what it is: an absolutely fantastic venue for you to channel your inner Oscar Wilde. Keep in mind that Willy doesn't let his place fill up passed capacity, so don't arrive too late if you want to get in.

i From The Burg, head along Hoogstraat. Take a left up Kelkstraat and turn right onto Twijnstraat. Ring the doorbell (indicated with à sign). Entry to either bar includes a free drink. No official dress code, but leave your sneakers at the hostel. Rum Bar cove €5; includes 1 free drink. Absinthe Bar cover €6; includes 1 drink. Drinks €5-6. ☼ Open Su 6:30pm-2am.

'T POATERSGAT
82 Vlamingstraat

BAR

The owner of this bar bought the underground passage which connects the church above with the outside world. The owner claims that the monks that used to live in the church used the passage to sneak out, change into civilian clothes, and head down to the brothel at the end of the road. Nowadays the brothel no longer exists, but the underground passage is home to 't Poatersgat and still keeps the locals of Bruges pretty happy. Those who aren't in the know often miss the rabbit hole of an entrance; the door is embedded in the wall of the church, very low down, and many say the only way to find it is to "stumble down the steps by chance." (Be careful not to hit your head if you've had a few drinks already.) Once inside you will discover an elegant and rather cozy bar, fit with plenty of seating and plenty of young locals filling up those seats. Definitely a highlight of the Bruges nightlife.

i Vlamingstraat is just off the Markt. Free Wi-Fi. Beer €2.50-5. ☼ Open daily 5pm-late.

DE GARRE
1 De Garre

PUB
☎050 34 10 29

They say no one just stumbles across De Garre—if you manage to find it, you were destined to visit. That's because De Garre is one of Bruges's best hidden pubs. Located down a small alleyway between the Markt and the Burg, De Garre is the only place to sample the smooth and tasty De Garre beer (€4). This 11.5% beer is a strong brew, so strong that the pub only allows you to have three in one sitting. Inside, the two-story house-like seating area is very typical of Belgian watering holes, and the cheese which comes with every beer helps the drinks along nicely.

i De Garre is just off of Breydelstraat, in between the Markt and the Burg. Bee €2-3.50. ☼ Open M-F noon-midnight, Sa 11am-1am, Su noon-midnight.

ESSENTIALS
Practicalities

- **TOURIST OFFICES: In and Uit Brugge.** (Concertgebouw 34 't Zand ☎050 44 46 46 www. bruges.be/tourism ☼ Open daily 10am-6pm.) A smaller branch is in the train station, **Stationsplein.** (☼ Open M-F 10am-5pm, Sa-Su 10am-2pm.)
- **ATMS:** In the **Markt,** on **Vlamingstraat,** and in **Simosteviplein.**

belgium

- **INTERNET:** There's free Wi-Fi at the train station, at the bars of central hostels, and at a few bars like **'t Poatersgat** (see **Nightlife**).

- **POST OFFICES:** The central post office is at **5 Markt.** (☎050 33 14 11 www.depost.be ☒ Open M-F 9am-6pm, Sa 9am-3pm.)

- **POSTAL CODE:** 8000.

Emergency

- **POLICE:** The police headquarters are at **7 Hauwerstraat.** (☎050 44 88 44 From the Markt, exit on the northwest side and turn left onto Geldmuntstraat, which becomes Noordzandstraat. Turn left onto Vrijdagmarkt, then right onto Hauwerstraat.)

- **LATE-NIGHT PHARMACIES:** Call the 24hr. pharmacy hotline. (☎0900 10 500 ☒ Operates 10pm-9am.)

- **HOSPITALS/MEDICAL SERVICES: Hospital AZ St-Jan.** (Riddershove 10 ☎050 45 21 11 www.azbrugge.be Bus #13 to AZ Sint-Jan AV.)

Getting There

Bruges is really only reachable by train, but its train station has services that run to several Belgian and international cities and the three stations in Brussels. (€13. ☒ 50min.) To reach Bruges from other major European cities, you will have to change at Brussels Midi/Zuid or Brussels Nord. (☒ Ticket office open June-Aug M-Sa 10am-7pm, Su 10am-7pm; Sept-May M-Sa 10am-6pm, Su 10am-7pm.)

Getting Around

Bruges is a rather simple city for tourists to navigate, thanks to the abundance of pedestrian walkways and bike lanes; in fact, you'll find more bikes on the road than you will cars, especially in the center. Most visitors tackle the city by foot, heading from the station into the center and exploring the cobbled streets and densely clustered sights. If you're hoping to explore further afield, or if you have more time to spend in Bruges, then renting a bike may be a good idea. Try Ropellier Bikes at 26 Mariastraat. (☎050 34 32 62 *i* €4 per hr., €8 per 4hr., €12 per day. ☒ Open daily 9am-7pm.) Bruges Bike Rental offers a student discount on single-day rentals. (17 Desparsstraat ☎050 61 61 08 *i* €4 per hr.; €6 per 2hr; €8 per 4hr.; €12 per day, students €8. ☒ Open daily 10am-10pm.)

The bus system in Bruges is run by De Lijn, whose office is at the train station (Stationsplein. ☎070 220 200; €0.30 per min. wwww.delijn.be). Buses #1, 6, and 11 go from the station into the town center. Buses #58 and 62 stop at Memling Campsite (see p. 178). Bus #2 stops at Europa HI Youth Hostel. Tickets are valid for 1hr. (€1.20 if bought at the station booth, €3 if bought on board.)

belgium essentials

MONEY

Tipping

In Belgium, service charges are included in the bill at restaurants. Waiters do not depend on tips for their livelihood, so there is no need to feel guilty about not leaving a tip. Still, leaving 5-10% extra will certainly be appreciated. Higher than that is just showing off. Tips in bars are very unusual; cab drivers are normally tipped about 10%.

Taxes

The quoted price of goods in Belgium includes value added tax (VAT). This tax on goods is generally levied at 21% in Belgium, although some goods are subject to lower rates. Non-EU visitors who are taking these goods home unused may be refunded this tax for purchases totaling over €125 per store. When making purchases, request a VAT form and present it at a Tax Free Shopping Office, found at most airports, road borders, and ferry stations, or by mail. Refunds must be claimed within six months.

SAFETY AND HEALTH

Drugs and Alcohol

Belgium has fairly liberal attitudes regarding alcohol, with no legal drinking age. You have to be 16 to buy your own alcohol (18 for spirits), but it's perfectly legal for someone else to buy alcohol and pass it to someone under 16. Public drunkenness, however, is frowned upon.

Belgium's attitude toward even soft drugs is traditional and conservative. Marijuana is illegal and not tolerated. Coffeeshops in Belgium are just that.

belgium

CROATIA

With attractions ranging from sun-drenched beaches and cliffs around Dubrovnik to dense forests around Plitvice, Croatia's wonders and natural beauty never cease to amaze. With a history full of political divides and conflict, Croatia has a few skeletons in its closet. After the devastating 1991-1995 ethnic war, however, Croatia finally achieved full independence for the first time in 800 years. Nowadays, the major threat comes from the hordes of tourists who make their way to the Adriatic coast to check out Roman ruins or dance all night at summer music festivals like Ultra Europe. Despite the crowds and the rising prices, this friendly and upbeat country demands to be seen at any cost.

greatest hits

- **THE WALL:** Stunning views of the Adriatic, the city, people's backyards; you'll get it all on your walk along Dubrovnik's **City Walls** (p. 68).
- **DO AS THE ROMANS DO:** Visit the **Pula Arena** (p. 83), one of the best-preserved ancient amphitheaters in the world. Caveat emptor: they no longer hold gladiator fights.
- **MY PRECIOUS:** One does simply walk into **Tolkien's House** (p. 64) in Zagreb, a world-class beer bar with a *Lord of the Rings* obsession. Prepare for walls decked out with swords and chainmail.

zagreb

About a million of Croatia's 4.3 million residents live in the Zagreb metropolitan area, so it's no surprise that this very, very old city (Romans founded a town nearby in the first century; more recognizable settlements followed around 1094) boasts a fair bit of activity. Though no sea coasts are to be found—even the river Sava lies outside the main urban area—Zagreb's museums, eclectic architecture, and gorgeous urban parks mean there's no shortage of things to do. At night, enjoy a glass of Croatian wine in a quiet bar, or take a bus out to Lake Jarun to rage at one of the city's infamous clubs. Or, given that most of these clubs are open until 6am, you could do both.

ACCOMMODATIONS

MY WAY HOSTEL
HOSTEL $

Trpimirova 4 ☎95 462 22 60 www.mywayhostel.com

No, it's not affiliated with Burger King, nor does it allow you to redesign your rooms to your liking (wouldn't that really make it your way?). But My Way Hostel does provide comfortable accommodation, clean bathrooms, and extensive common space, all within a short walk from the train and bus stations. There's also a community kitchen and an outdoor seating area. The bright orange walls downstairs may be a tad garish, but the neutral tones in the dorms ensure you won't be kept awake by poor palette choices. Though none of the doors to the dorms have locks, each resident is provided with a large storage locker. This may be all too secure—in the event you lose your key, the staff may have to break the lock open to retrieve your things. But so long as you don't lose your key, your stay at My Way Hostel is sure to be a comfortable one.

i *Doubles 330 kn. Dorms 70-90 kn. ☒ Reception 24hr.*

HOSTEL SWANKY MINT
HOSTEL $$

Ilica Ulica 50 ☎01 400 42 48 www.swanky-hostel.com

There can't be many contenders in the "post-industrial loft-style hostel" category, but Swanky Mint would be top of the heap no matter what. This hostel, organized around a courtyard just off Ilica Ulica, is housed in a former textile factory, but there's nothing gritty about its sleek, modern bedrooms and bathrooms. Certain dorms open directly onto the courtyard, making it feel like you have your very own studio apartment (that you share with three to seven roommates, of course). If you don't feel like leaving the confines of the hostel, you still won't lack for nightlife; Swanky Mint has a large bar located within the hostel itself. The outdoor terrace is particularly popular during the summer months. With tables reserved for hostel guests, you'll be sure to find a spot.

i *Singles 350 kn. Dorms 140-160 kn. ☒ Reception 24hr.*

HOSTEL CHIC
HOSTEL $

Pavla Hatza 10 ☎01 779 37 60 www.hostel-chic.com

Despite the name, Hostel Chic is not located in a particularly chic area (although it is only a few blocks from the train station), nor are its purple and green rooms particularly, shall we say, fashionable. But if you're not looking for a trend-setting place to rest your head at night, Hostel Chic will certainly do the job. Free Wi-Fi? Check. Community kitchen? Check. Reading lights, laundry facilities, safety deposit box? Check, check, check. With a friendly staff and cheap prices, this is a solid choice for your stay in Zagreb.

i *Dorms 98 kn. ☒ Reception 24hr.*

croatia

CHILL OUT HOSTEL $

Tomićeva Ulica 5a ☎01 484 96 05 www.chillout-hostel-zagreb.com

You'd be hard-pressed to find a better location for a hostel than Chill Out's; not only are you right off Ilica Ulica, Zagreb's main commercial drag, you're right at the base of the Zagreb funicular, meaning access to the Upper Town is just 4 kn and 66 meters away. But this large hostel is comfortable enough for you to not want to leave. Wi-Fi, free printing, lockers, and towels are all available for free. Though breakfast is not included, the hostel does include a restaurant focusing on Croatian cuisine—and yes, it serves a distinctly Croatian breakfast.

i Dorms 75 kn. ☑ Reception 24hr.

HOSTEL SARA HOSTEL $$

Vlaška Ulica 17 ☎09 827 93 06

This recently opened hostel still maintains a fair bit of cozy charm. Located on the upper floors of an old building on Vlaška Ulica, the clean design and white wooden beds make the dorms seem more like IKEA than an unfortunately cramped cabin at camp. Large windows let in tons of light, and the small but friendly staff can easily answer your questions or direct you to a nearby restaurant or bar. And since it's within walking distance of Tkalčićeva Ulica, there are a lot of potential recommendations.

i Singles 192 kn. Dorms 100-125 kn. ☑ Reception 24hr.

SIGHTS

MUZEJ MIMARA MUSEUM

Rooseveltov Trg 5 www.mimara.hr

The Strossmayer Gallery of Old Masters may have the words "old masters" in its name, but make no mistake: the Muzej Mimara is Zagreb's strongest collection of classic art. Botticelli? Check. Caravaggio? Check. Rubens, Degas, Manet? Check, check, and check. All the more impressive is that the museum's treasures were once the private collection of one man, Ante Topić Mimara, for whom the museum is named. Think of it as Zagreb's version of the Frick Collection, complete with a portrait of Sir Thomas More by Hans Holbein—now that's a weird coincidence. Painting is the museum's strong suit, although there are more than a few fascinating pieces in the sculpture and design collections. After working your way through the museum's three large floors, treat yourself to a drink in the improbably well-stocked in-house bar, Café Gymnasium.

i 40 kn, students 30 kn. 20 kn for special exhibitions. ☑ Open July-Sept Tu-F 10am-7pm, Sa 10am-5pm, Su 10am-2pm; Oct-June Tu-W 10am-5pm, Th 10am-7pm, F-Sa 10am-5pm, Su 10am-2pm. Closed Mondays.

MUSEUM OF BROKEN RELATIONSHIPS MUSEUM

Ćirilometodska 2 ☎01 485 10 21 www.brokenships.com

If you're traveling without your significant other, this museum will make you give him or her a call immediately, roaming services be damned. If you've just gotten out of a relationship, this museum will make you cry. If you're not sure about whether or not to start a relationship, this museum may cause you to join the church. This is the Museum of Broken Relationships, one of Zagreb's smallest and strangest institutions. People from all over the world have sent in mementos of their failed relationships, along with brief explanations or summaries: they range from poetically cryptic to way-too-much-information. The museum can only show a small segment of its total collection, but there's always tons of variety: anything from Magic 8 Balls to heroin tests can pop up. Bring a date—you never know what can happen.

i 25 kn, students 20 kn. ☑ Open daily June-Sept 9am-10:30pm; Oct-May 9am-9pm.

zagreb

MODERNA GALERIJA
Andrije Hebranga 1   ☎01 241 68 00 www.moderna-galerija.hr
MUSEUM

Don't know the first thing about Croatian art? Well, Moderna Galerija might not be the best place to start; there's very little wall text, so you can't learn that much about the various movements that shaped Croatian art in the 19th and 20th centuries. On the other hand, that lets the art speak for itself—you might know nothing about Croatian art going into the Moderna Galerija, but you also might love it when you come out. The German artist Joseph Beuys, who collaborated with a Croatian artist on one work, is likely the only recognizable name here—still, that work hardly compares to the massive canvases on display by the Croats, which range from the romantic to the aggressively primitive.

i 40 kn, students 20 kn. ☒ Open Tu-F 11am-7pm, Sa-Su 11am-2pm. Closed Mondays.

MUSEUM OF CONTEMPORARY ART
Avenija Dubrovnik 17   ☎01 605 27 00 www.msu.hr
MUSEUM

The Museum of Contemporary Art is not near anything else you will visit in Zagreb. It is also not like anything else you will visit in Zagreb. Sure, there are other modern art museums, but none of them have a giant metal slide that spans three stories. And yes, you're allowed to slide down it—just not headfirst. Though Croatian artists are well represented, the Museum of Contemporary Art has a truly international scope; there's everyone from California conceptualist John Baldessari to Belgian provocateur Jan Fabre. Similarly, there's a wide tonal range—you're just as likely to see a political work about spousal abuse as you are to see a sly conceptual joke. Highlights include the mind-bending collection of op art (you may leave with your eyes crossed), early graphic works made with a computer, and the transplanted studio of sculptor Ivan Kozarić.

i 30 kn, students 15 kn. Free for toddlers and the unemployed. Free every first Wednesday of the month. ☒ Open Tu-F 11am-6pm, Sa 11am-8pm, Su 11am-6pm.

CROATIAN MUSEUM OF NAÏVE ART
Cirilometodska 3   ☎01 485 21 25
MUSEUM

Thought the Museum of Contemporary Art was weird? All that avant-garde posturing is nothing compared to what's on display in the Croatian Museum of Naïve Art, which features work made by untrained Croatians. Marvel at surreal depictions of peasant landscapes, gory crucifixions, and women with huge goiters. Consider the numerous portraits of cross-eyed people. Peruse the obsessive renderings of cathedrals in Vienna and Milan. And stop short in front of Guiana '78, a large work depicting a crowd of passed-out junkies sticking hypodermic needles into each other. There are also some very nice and placid landscapes, just to balance everything out.

i 20 kn, students 10 kn. ☒ Open Tu-F 10am-6pm, Sa-Su 10am-1pm. Closed Mondays.

FOOD

◪ BISTROTEKA
Ulice Nikola Tesle 14   ☎01 483 77 11
BISTRO $

Sleek black furniture, exposed white brick walls, a well-stocked bar alongside an appealing breakfast menu—yep, Bistroteka is the place to go if you want to look cool while you're scarfing down a meal. If you sit outside, you don't even need to take your sunglasses off. Surprisingly enough, that sense of chic is coupled with refreshingly low prices; full-sized sandwiches only cost about 30 kn. With all your savings, maybe you can even buy another pair of sunglasses. We're not sure how Bistroteka can keep its food prices so low—maybe it's subsidized by Veuve Clicquot, which has seemingly provided aprons for the waitstaff to wear, or maybe it's the fact that you get to serve your own water. Who knows how much money that saves?

i Sandwiches 30 kn. Meals 40-50 kn. ⏰ Open M-Th 8:30am-midnight, F-Sa 8:30am-1am.

STARI FIJAKER
CROATIAN $

Mesnička Ulica 6

Stari Fijaker is located just off Ilica Ulica, one of Zagreb's busiest and most modern streets. But the vibe inside this massive restaurant is pure old world. Start out with some hearty tomato soup, then move onto deer medallions. Have a glass of Croatian wine. Marvel at the photos of Old Zagreb and the distinctive light fixtures—the bulbs are housed in models of old cars. Despite the strong sense of tradition, Stari Fijaker is highly accessible to those who don't speak fluent Croatian (the extensive menu is available in English) as well as to vegetarians (there are quite a few alternatives to those deer medallions). Be warned, though, that if you order the fish, it'll probably arrive with its head. We told you—this place is old school.

i Starters 20 kn. Entrees 50-70 kn. ⏰ Open M-Sa 11am-11pm, Su 11am-10pm.

ROUGEMARIN
INTERNATIONAL $$

Ulica Frana Folnegovića 10 ☎01 618 77 76 www.rougemarin.hr

It's out of the way, even if you're headed to the Museum of Contemporary Art, but the oft-crowded tables at RougeMarin are a clear sign it's worth the trip. With a menu that rotates monthly, RougeMarin is committed to exciting ingredients and novel combinations: one recent item combined lamb, chickpeas, and blueberries. Despite this variety, RougeMarin has its staples: namely, the hamburgers that are always on the menu. Simple as they may be, these burgers are made with the same devotion as the more eclectic menu items—and the homemade fries are to die for. Wash it all down with some pomegranate juice, or choose from one of their carefully selected wines or beers. Then start on the long walk home—you'll need it after ingesting all these calories.

i Starters 30 kn. Burgers 48 kn. Entrees 60-70 kn. ⏰ Open M-Th 11am-11pm, F 11am-3pm.

... NISHTA
INTERNATIONAL $

Masarykova Ulica 11 ☎01 889 74 44 www.nishtarestaurant.com

Croatian cuisine is known for meat and seafood, but vegans and vegetarians need not worry; Zagreb has a number of excellent meatless restaurants, chief among them being the interestingly punctuated ...Nishta. We suggest saying it with a pause. The menu's almost as eclectic as the decor (check out the Barbie and Ken dolls on the doors of the bathrooms), with Mexican and Indian touches. Highlights include the burritos and the banana curry, both of which will satisfy your stomach without a hint of animal byproducts. And every dish is worthy of being posted to your Instagram—did we mention they've got free Wi-Fi? The homey interior—check out the yellow and purple walls—might also be worth a quick snapshot.

i Starters 30 kn. Entrees 50-60 kn. ⏰ Open Tu-Su noon-11pm.

MUNDOAKA STREETFOOD
SEAFOOD $$

Petrinjska 2 ☎01 788 87 77

Mundoaka Streetfood doesn't make a lot of sense. Why do they serve their food on imposing slabs of wood instead of plates? Why do they serve beer from a Catalan brewery that's impossible to find elsewhere? Why do they put their vinegar and olive oil in little test tubes? And, most importantly, why is this one of Zagreb's best restaurants? Yes, you heard us right. This tiny joint (they've got a mirror on one wall to make it look bigger), complete with a name that screams "straight outta Greenpoint!", is one of the best places to grab a bite in Croatia's capital. And Croatia's yuppies know it; you'll likely have to wait for a table, even if you arrive before 6pm. But once you get a seat, the food will convince you it was worth the wait. The menu is heavy on seafood and meats with Asian touches; order the massive pizza for two if you really want to chow down.

i *Entrees 70-90 kn.* ☒ *Open M-Th 9am-midnight, F-Sa 9am-1am.*

FINI ZALOGAJ
SANDWICHES $
Radićeva Ulica 8
www.fini-zalogaj.hr

Want a fast bite that's more authentic than McDonald's? Look no further than Fini Zalogaj, a self-described "fine food bar" on Radićeva Ulica. Its stock in trade? Hearty sandwiches filled with huge hunks of meat (as an added plus, you can have them wrapped in bacon or sprinkled with sesame seeds!). Though the sandwiches are not always structurally sound (we recommend not unwrapping the paper container you'll be given), they are always delicious.

i *Sandwiches 25 kn.* ☒ *Open daily 8am-4pm.*

ROCKET BURGER
BURGERS $
Tkalčićeva Ulica 44
☎01 557 91 75

Here's the deal: burger restaurants are a legitimate trend in Zagreb now. You can weep about globalization and how American culture devours all, or you can shut up and enjoy a great meal at Rocket Burger, one of the best products of this trend. Located near the many bars of Tkalčićeva Ulica, Rocket Burger is the perfect thing to chow down on after a few pints of Ožujsko—or you could enjoy a pint of craft beer from local brewers Nova Runda, available on tap at Rocket Burger.

i *Burgers 40 kn.* ☒ *Open M-Th 11am-11pm, F 11am-midnight, Sa 10am-midnight, Su 10am-10pm.*

PIZZERIA ZERO ZERO
PIZZA $
Vlaška Ulica 35
☎01 889 70 00

Pizza doesn't have the same cachet in Zagreb that it has along other regions of Croatia, like the Istrian Coast. But that doesn't mean the capital city totally lacks for good 'za; for proof of that, just swing by Pizzeria Zero Zero, which is not code for how many calories are in its pizzas. Choose from a variety of toppings, including a strong selection of white pies (read: no tomato sauce); if you're not too hungry, best to opt for a salad, as it only serves one size of pizza.

i *Pizzas 50-60 kn.* ☒ *Open M-Th 10:30am-11pm, F-Sa 10:30am-midnight, Su noon-11pm.*

NIGHTLIFE

☒ TOLKIEN'S HOUSE
BAR
Opatovina 49
☎01 485 20 50

Some of the bars on Tkalčićeva Ulica can feel a little juvenile—did you really come all the way to Croatia to watch American tourists chug cheap beer (even if it's cheap Croatian beer)? If the shots and EDM get to be too much for you, fear not; Tkalčićeva's cool older sibling, Opatovina, is just a few steps away. And there's nothing that sums Opatovina up quite like Tolkien's House. Featuring walls decked out with swords, chain mail, and giant clubs, Tolkien's House is a world-class beer bar with an inexplicable Lord of the Rings obsession. But even if you can't tell an elf from an orc, this cozy space will still hold some appeal—just have a pint of pale ale from Zmajska Pivovara, some of the first craft brewers in Croatia.

i *Beers from 20-30 kn.* ☒ *Open M-F 7am-midnight, Sa 8am-midnight, Su 9am-11pm.*

☒ RAKHIA BAR
BAR
Tkalčićeva 45

Rakija, for all intents and purposes, is Balkan schnapps—fruit-flavored liqueur, flavored with everything from plums to wild berries. They say the best rakija is made at home. But in case you don't feel like following a stranger home to try their homemade spirits, just find yourself a seat at Rakhia Bar. With over 30 types of rakija in its vaults, Rakhia lets you sample to your heart's content; with most of them priced between 10 and 16 kn, your wallet won't be complaining either. The vibe inside is low-key, with lots of exposed brick—though it's located on Tkalčićeva Ulica, its upstairs location means it's a bit removed from that street's excesses.

i Shots of every liquor you can imagine from 10-16 kn. ☺ Open M-Th 8am-midnight, F-Sa 8am-2am, Su 8am-midnight.

PINTA ZAGREB   BAR
Radićeva Ulica 3a   ☎01 483 08 89 www.pinta.hr

There are no frills to Pinta Zagreb—the inside's smoky, the draft selection is small (Tomislav and two Ožujsko taps), and there's minimal decor. It's a dive bar in the heart of Zagreb (right next to a backpackers' inn, no less), but that doesn't stop the locals from streaming to it. The perfect antidote to some of the flashier bars that have opened up recently, as the city adds hostels and gains tourists. Chill out with the eclectic soundtrack (Sex Pistols, Bob Marley, etc) and enjoy a nice creamy pint of Tomislav.

i Beers 15 kn. Wine and cocktails 20 kn. ☺ Open daily 8am-11pm.

PIVNICA MALI MEDO   BAR
Tkalčićeva 34-36-38-42   ☎01 492 96 13 www.pivnica-medvedgrad.hr

The cheapest beer in Zagreb is, by some miracle, not synonymous with the worst beer in Zagreb. That's because the cheapest pints to be had are at this brewpub, and it makes beer that's a lot better than Ožujsko and Staropramen. If you can't decide which of the five regular and one rotating taps to choose from, order a taster of all six—only 20 kn! Evidently it's a business model that works—this is less of a bar and more of an empire, with its address stretching across nearly an entire block of Tkalčićeva Ulica. Even with all that real estate, the bar still manages to be packed on a regular basis—those prices, after all, are pretty darn low.

i Beers 10-15 kn. Taster of every beer available for 20 kn. ☺ Open M-W 10am-midnight, Th-Sa 10am-1am, Su noon-midnight.

SAVSKA 14   BAR
Savska Cesta 14

This large bar lacks a name, but it does have an address—and after all, which one is more important? Be sure you know that address, as there's no signage to indicate exactly where the bar is; look for a big hedge and listen for a fair bit of noise. In short, this is where you should go if you want to feel like a local—a cool local, even! At most hours of the night, you'll find big crowds excitedly talking and downing bottles of Staropramen and Karlovačko. The large tables, inside and out, will soon be filled with empties. One element of the sparse decor is a large painting of a girl puking into a toilet. Make sure you bring a friend to walk you home.

i Beers 10-15 kn. ☺ Open daily 8pm-2am.

VINTAGE INDUSTRIAL BAR   BAR
Savska Cesta 160   ☎01 619 17 15 www.vintageindustrial-bar.com

No, this is not a place where they play Skinny Puppy and Nine Inch Nails on loop. Located in what looks like a former auto body shop, Vintage Industrial Bar is not for the faint of heart. With a gritty rock-and-roll soundtrack and restored cars out front, VIB is a spot where alternative types throw down. Given its massive space and slightly removed location, it's no surprise that it has hosted bands and after-parties for concerts. If there are no events going on, however, the vibe is likely more reservedly cool than loud and raucous—though, of course, all that can change by the time the bar closes at 5am.

i Beers 15-20 kn. Cocktails 20 kn. Shots of rakija 10 kn. ☺ Open Tu-Th 10pm-2am, F-Sa 10pm-5am, Su 10am-1am.

AQUARIUS

Aleja Matije Ljubeka ☎01 3640 231 www.aquarius.hr

Looking to party in Zagreb? No, not drinking a few glasses of wine with friends, not having a few pints and singing along to the jukebox, not discussing the finer points of a certain blend of rakija—partying. The kind with dry ice, strobe lights, glow sticks, and a cover charge. If this is the sort of party you are looking for, then you absolutely must go to Aquarius. Located on Lake Jarun, Aquarius boasts two floors, cutting-edge electronic music, and a lot of alcohol. Unfortunately, it also has a lot of cigarettes—sometimes it's hard to tell if the smoke on the dance floor is coming from dry ice or Pall Malls. Still, when it comes to clubbing in Zagreb, Aquarius is the best game in town.

i Cover 20 kn. Shows often require tickets. Beers and cocktails 20-30 kn. ⚅ Café open daily 9am-9pm, club open 11pm-6am.

ESSENTIALS

Practicalities

- **MONEY:** ATMs are located throughout the city. An exchange office is located at the bus station. Most ATMs will disperse money in 200 and 100 kn bills, which may earn some annoyance from locals.

- **POST OFFICE:** There is a large post office located just to the left of the train station, on Ulica Kneza Branimira. It is open daily 7am-midnight.

- **TOURIST INFO CENTER:** Tourist Information Centre, Trg Bana J. Jelačića 11 ☎01 481 40 51. ⚅ Open M-F 8:30am-9pm, Sa-Su 9am-6pm.

Emergency

- **GENERAL EMERGENCY NUMBER:** ☎112. The American Embassy in Croatia also maintains an emergency number for American citizens: ☎01 661 2400.

- **POLICE:** ☎192

- **PHARMACIES:** Gradska Ljekarna Zagreb, Trg Petra Svačića 17 ☎01 485 65 45. ⚅ Open M-F 7am-8pm, Sa-Su 7:30am-3pm.

Getting Around

Zagreb is well served by a tram system; major hubs are located in Ban Jelačić Square and by the train station, at Kralja Tomislava Square. Tickets are 10 kn during the day and can be purchased on the tram; they are valid for 90 minutes. At the city outskirts, buses take over.

If you don't want to walk to the Upper Town (the site of St. Mark's Church, the Croatian Museum of Naïve Art, and the Museum of Broken Relationships, among other attractions), take the funicular, which costs 4 kn. With a length of only 66 meters, it's the shortest inclined railway in the world.

dubrovnik

Dubrovnik is commonly known as the Pearl of the Adriatic, but we prefer to call it the tourist trap of Dalmatia. That doesn't mean it's not fun to visit, though. Come for the striking city walls, the rocky beaches, and the unparalleled wine bars; stay because you ran out of money for a bus ticket and need your mom to wire some cash. Kidding—kind of.

ACCOMMODATIONS

HOSTEL VILLA ANGELINA OLD TOWN
HOSTEL $$$

Plovani Skalini 17a
☎091 893 9089

One of three hostels actually located within Dubrovnik's Old Town, Hostel Villa Angelina is a low-key delight. If Dubrovnik's nightlife doesn't impress you, you can always curl up in the large beds, each of which is equipped with a reading light, or you can watch TV in the common room. But if getting into the city is all you want to do, Villa Angelina's awesome location makes it as easy as stepping out the door. Bathrooms are well kept, and free towels are provided.

i *Dorms 290 kn. ✪ Reception 24hr.*

HOSTEL MARKER
HOSTEL $$

Svetog Djurdja 6
☎091 739 75 45

A fantastic location near the Old Town and Pile Bay (where you can rent a kayak and explore Dubrovnik from the sea) distinguishes Hostel Marker. Though it lacks a large common area, the dorms and other rooms are decently furnished, and the hostel is clean and well maintained on the whole. Let's be honest—you're paying for the location. Free towels, blankets, and Wi-Fi provided.

i *Dorms 230 kn. ✪ Latest check-in at 12:30am. No curfew.*

HOSTEL CITY CENTRAL
HOSTEL $

Ulica U Pilama 7
☎092 150 70 46

Located a few minutes from the Old Town, Hostel City Central is a solid choice for housing during your stay in Dubrovnik; you'll be able to get to the Old Town in minutes, and its close proximity to the Pile Gate bus stop means you can catch a bus going anywhere (not that there are tons of places worth visiting besides the Old Town). It's also noticeably cheaper than many other hostels in the Old Town; with prices like these, you'll think you're staying out in Dubrovnik's suburbs.

i *Dorms from 200 kn. ✪ Latest check-in 10pm. No curfew.*

KINGS LANDING HOSTEL
HOSTEL $$$

Boškovićeva 5

Some people only go to Dubrovnik because they film *Game of Thrones* there. If you are one of these people (you know who you are), you will need to stay at the Kings Landing Hostel. Located in a centuries-old building, the staff has preserved tons of period touches and added some *Game of Thrones* touches. If you want the vibe to keep going once you step outside, have them arrange a GOT-themed tour. Most of the dorms are on the smaller side (about four beds), but the beds are comfortable and the bathrooms are well kept.

i *Dorms 300 kn. ✪ Reception open 11am-6pm.*

OLD TOWN HOSTEL
HOSTEL

Od Sigurate 7
☎020 322 007

Like Kings Landing Hostel, but without the themed door knockers and nerdy patrons. Housed in a 400-year-old building, Old Town Hostel offers amenities ranging from 24-hour breakfast to a communal hookah pipe (follow-up doctor appointments not covered). Rooms go quickly, so be sure to book far in advance. Convenient and comfortable.

i *Singles 200 kn. Doubles 350 kn. ✪ Reception open 8am-11pm.*

VILLA BANANA
HOSTEL $

Gornji Kono 58a
☎095 569 5407

It's far from the Old Town, but it's cheap. If you've got time to spend walking up stairs and taking buses, then Villa Banana is a fine choice for your trip to Dubrovnik. Be sure to call ahead and arrange to be picked up from the bus station (free) or the airport (not free). You'll be served free juice and cookies when you check in and can buy beer, wine, or soda from their fridge. Rooms are large,

dubrovnik

comfortable, and far homier than the average anonymous hostel. Some rooms are equipped with balconies, which provide fantastic views of Dubrovnik; that's the advantage of being so far away.

i Dorms 180 kn. ◷ Reception 24hr.

SIGHTS

▨ DUBROVNIK CITY WALLS
LANDMARK

Let's be honest. The walls are why you came to Dubrovnik. Without these bad boys, it's just another random Croatian port town. So are they worth the journey? And once you get there, is walking around on them worth the 100 kn entrance fee? Yes and yes. Stunning views of the Adriatic, the city, people's backyards—you'll get it all on your walk along the city walls. And despite Dubrovnik's reputation as a city-turned-tourist-trap, the walls are so big and so well organized (traffic can only proceed one way) that it's possible to enjoy a smooth, largely crowd-free experience. Be sure to keep your ticket on you, as there are several checkpoints along the way. Street vendors provide water and other amenities inside, though you may want to bring your own supplies to save money. Make sure your camera is all charged up, as you'll be snapping pictures every step of the way.

i There are three entrance points, but the most prominent is directly next to Pile Gate. 100 kn. ◷ Open daily 9am-7:30pm.

FRANCISCAN MONASTERY AND PHARMACY MUSEUM
MUSEUM

Placa 2 ☎020 321 410

You know that old pharmacy in your neighborhood that seems like it's been around forever, and you always wonder how they stay in business? Well, think of how the people in Dubrovnik must feel; within the walls of the Franciscan Monastery is a pharmacy that's been operating since 1317. Though the one that's used today (don't worry, you don't need to pay the 30 kn admission fee to enter) doesn't use the same shelves and ceramic jars that are lovingly preserved in the museum, the monastery is still worth a visit. The art collection is decent (it includes what may be the world's worst Rubens), but the old pharmacy collections are fascinating to look at, and the church still bears some historically intriguing scars from the Siege of Dubrovnik. Visited by Jackie Kennedy, Dick Cheney, and possibly you!

i 30 kn. ◷ Open daily 9am-6pm.

DUBROVNIK AQUARIUM AND MARITIME MUSEUM
AQUARIUM, MUSEUM

Ulica Kneza Damjana Jude 2 ☎021 427 937

In general, you're best off exploring Adriatic ocean life in Croatia's restaurants rather than in its (generally lackluster) aquariums. The Dubrovnik Aquarium and Maritime Museum is a happy exception. Here, you'll see everything from sea turtles to locust lobsters in large tanks or giant pools of water. Housed in St. John's Fortress, a medieval structure with cavernous stone chambers, the aquarium has a quiet, serene feel. The English wall text is fairly comprehensive and includes information on how every fish is caught. We can't guarantee you won't work up an appetite here.

i 60 kn. ◷ Open daily 9am-10pm.

RECTOR'S PALACE
PALACE

Pred Dvorom 1 ☎020 321 422

The Rector's Palace is sort of a one-stop shop for museum-going in Dubrovnik. Want to see some art? Some historical interiors and centuries-old jail cells? Vintage weaponry and silverware? Contemporary war photography? The Rector's Palace has it all, and with the large space set aside for rotating exhibitions, it's a safe bet you'll find something of interest. Highlights include the two large bronze

Dubrovnik may be familiar to you even if you've never been to Croatia. That's because this coastal city stood in for the fictional city of "King's Landing" on popular fantasy show/masturbation fodder *Game of Thrones*. That means that if you visit Dubrovnik today, you'll find street performers dressed up like characters and run into tours where people say stuff like "in season 5, Cersei walks down this flight of stairs." Thrilling stuff. If you're a fan, be sure to check out Fort Lovrijenac, Pile Gate, Lokrum Island, and of course those famous city walls, all of which have made appearances on the show.

figures that struck Dubrovnik's town bells for centuries, a painting showing the seals of every noble family in Dubrovnik, and the well-preserved dragon cells, tiny prison chambers that housed especially tough criminals. In the gift shop, you'll find scarves inspired by the collections, posters of past exhibits, replicas of small sculptures, and much more.

i *100 kn, students 25 kn for the Dubrovnik Museums ticket (includes admission to Maritime Museum, Ethnographic Museum Rupe, Revelin Fortress Archaeological Collections, House of Marin Držić, Dubrovnik Art Gallery, Natural History Museum, Museum of Modern Art, and Rector's Palace).* 🕐 *Open daily 9am-6pm.*

FORT LOVRIJENAC   FORTRESS
Općina Dubrovnik

The one problem with Dubrovnik's city walls is that it's hard to get a really good look at them. Sure, you can marvel at them from up close, whether you're walking along them or just staring from Pile Gate, but does that really give a sense of just how impressive these babies are? Short of renting a helicopter, your best bet is to make the quick hike up to Fort Lovrijenac, an old military fortress-cum-tourist attraction and concert venue. You may not learn too much about Dubrovnik's history as a fortified city state, but the views of the city and the Adriatic are the best you'll find. As a plus, the shady walk to the top won't leave you drenched in sweat.

i *30 kn.* 🕐 *Open daily 8am-5pm.*

MUSEUM OF MODERN ART   MUSEUM
Frana Supila 23   ☎020 426 590

There's a lot of cool stuff outside Dubrovnik's city walls, like bottles of water that don't cost 15 kn. On a more cultural note, there's Dubrovnik's Museum of Modern Art, a charming collection distinguished by its outdoor sculpture garden. Here, you'll find bronze figures that range from the geometrically stylized to the grotesquely bizarre; even if you don't like them, you'll have to appreciate the view from the giant balcony they stand on. Elsewhere in the museum, you'll find a brief overview of modern art in Croatia (yes, there are sculptures by Ivan Meštrović), along with a vast space for special exhibitions.

i *Individual ticket free for students. 100 kn, students 25 kn for the Dubrovnik Museums ticket (includes admission to Maritime Museum, Ethnographic Museum Rupe, Revelin Fortress Archaeological Collections, House of Marin Držić, Dubrovnik Art Gallery, Natural History Museum, Museum of Modern Art, and Rector's Palace).* 🕐 *Open Tu-Su 9am-8pm.*

LOKRUM ISLAND   ISLAND
                                                                             ☎020 323 554

If you ended up booking a hostel or hotel outside of the whole town, you'll be doing a lot of hiking on your trip to Dubrovnik. Odds are, however, that hiking alongside strip malls and suburban homes isn't exactly what you had in mind.

dubrovnik

For a more "scenic height," take a short ferry to Lokrum Island, a.k.a. that large land mass just off the coast of Dubrovnik. Here, you'll find miles of trails, a botanical garden that was nearly destroyed in the 1990s war, and a restaurant and a cafe-bar to stave off your hiking-induced hunger. We particularly recommend going to the top of Fort Royal, which provides great views of Dubrovnik.

i *Ferries leave every half hour from the Old Harbor. 80 kn for a round-trip ticket. ☒ The island closes at 8pm when the last ferry leaves.*

KUPARI
RUINS

Some 8km southeast of Dubrovnik's Old Town lies one of the clearest signs that 20-some years ago, Croatia was indeed in the midst of a bloody war for independence. This is Kupari Beach, once a military resort filled with thriving hotels. They're still there, but they've been bombed out and deserted; balconies and staircases have collapsed, while windowpanes lie shattered on the ground. There are still tons of people on the largely untouched beaches, but only squatters live in the hotel now.

i *Free.*

FOOD

🏷 TAJ MAHAL
BOSNIAN $$

Ulica Nikole Gučetića 2   ☎020 323 221

"Hungry?" asks the first page of Taj Mahal's menu. You better be. This Bosnian restaurant is not for the faint of heart or the vegetarian of diet. If you want big hunks of meat on a skewer, potatoes stuffed with Bosnian cream cheese, and a rich cup of Turkish coffee—sorry, Bosnian coffee—to wash it all down with, this place is for you. Unlike most of Dubrovnik's restaurants, there are no seafood options, but if you need some protein to propel you around the city walls, there's no better place. Enjoy a nice chunk of baklava afterward.

i *Entrees 70-150 kn. ☒ Open daily 10am-2pm.*

… NISHTA
VEGETARIAN $

Corner of Palmotićeva Ulica and Prijeko Ulica   ☎020 322 088

Are you a vegetarian in Croatia who's sick of asking the waitress if you can have the octopus salad without the octopus? Are you sick of having the same tomato sauce and pasta entree that every restaurant seems to offer? Did you skip dinner last night and just eat the six bananas you bought at Konzum? Then steer yourself to …Nishta, a small vegetarian restaurant in the heart of Dubrovnik's Old Town. Seitan burgers, tempeh burritos, and, yes, pasta with tomato sauce are all available for your consumption. Homemade juices, health food shots, and a selection of organic beers and wines round out the menu. Just try not to get a headache from the hot pink bathrooms.

i *Entrees 60-80 kn. ☒ Open M-Sa 11:30am-11pm.*

PIZZERIA OLIVA
PIZZA $

Lučarica Ulica 5   ☎020 324 594 www.olivadubrovnik.com

Yes, Pizzeria Oliva's pizzas cost a good 10 kn more than pizzas anywhere else in Croatia. But Dubrovnik is expensive enough to make this one of the cheaper meals in the city. Besides, the varied toppings—arugula with pesto, prosciutto, and the mushroom-ham-peppers combination are all worth exploring—make it some of the best food you're likely to find in the city. Inside, whirring fans keep it cool; outside, you'll find comfortable if not spacious seating.

i *Pizzas 60-80 kn. ☒ Open daily noon-midnight.*

BARBA
SEAFOOD $

Boškovićeva 5   ☎091 205 34 88

Barba is perhaps the only fast food joint in the world where you can get oysters. Surprisingly enough, they're really good too, whether you get them fresh or fried. This small restaurant (you can eat the food there or get it to go) is maybe the only place in Croatia to serve truly affordable seafood. Surprisingly enough, it's located in Dubrovnik, possibly the most expensive city on Croatia's Adriatic coast. Try the octopus burger or salad if you're looking for something especially hearty; otherwise, just grab some fried fish or a fish sandwich. And, of course, a few oysters.

i *Sandwiches 30-40 kn. Burgers 40-50 kn. Fish entrees 39-54 kn. Oysters 12 kn each.* ✪ *Open daily 10am-2am.*

POKLISAR
CROATIAN $$

Ribarnica Ulica 1 ☎020 322 176 www.poklisar.com

Dubrovnik's Above 5 restaurant may have a flashier vantage point, but it's hard to beat the views of the Old Harbor that Poklisar provides. Whether you're chowing down on a full meal or just enjoying cocktails and ice cream, Poklisar is a great option for food in Dubrovnik. The menu focuses on Dalmatian cuisine, though it's a little more offbeat than your standard *konoba*; dig the shrimp skewers with blue cheese, or the beef tournedos with black truffle sauce.

i *Entrees 90-180 kn.* ✪ *Open daily 9am-midnight.*

SEGRETO PASTA AND GRILL
ITALIAN S$

Cvijete Zuzorić 5 ☎020 323 392 www.segretodubrovnik.com

Sometimes Croatia feels a lot closer to Italy than other former Yugoslav countries, and this delicious Italian joint is a perfect example of that. The entrees can get a little pricey, so if you're trying to save, either go for lunch (meals are a good 10-20 kn cheaper) or order something off the pasta menu, which is also generally cheaper. Vegetarians will be enthused by the hearty eggplant parm, while meat eaters can pig out on the steak and seafood entrees. Be sure to wash it all down with a glass of Birra del Borgo beer, made by a cult-favorite Italian brewery.

i *Pasta dishes 70-90 kn. Entrees 90-160 kn.* ✪ *Open daily 11:30am-midnight.*

AZUR
FUSION $

Pobijana 10 ☎020 324 806 www.azurvision.com

If you tire of Dubrovnik's many Dalmatian restaurants (pork medallions, prawns, octopus salads; we get it!), head to Azur, an Asian-Mediterranean fusion restaurant located in an Old Town back street. The curries and sauces are certainly less spicy than you'll find in India or China (or, to be honest, in any American Chinatown or Indian restaurant), but the varied menu is still packed with flavor. The wine list is on the pricier side, but most of the entrees are affordably priced. Bring a group and order one of the sharing plates—salmon tacos, anyone?

i *Entrees 70-150 kn. Sharing plates 50-90 kn.* ✪ *Open daily 12:30pm-11pm.*

DOLCE VITA
ICE CREAM

Ulica Naljeśkovićeva 1a ☎098 944 9951

Avoid the ice cream shops on Stradun; they're generic, overpriced, and overflowing with customers. Instead, turn onto Ulica Naljeśtovićeva and grab a cone at Dolce Vita, Dubrovnik's finest purveyor of frozen treats. Flavors range from the super sweet Dolce Vita to the Earl Grey-like bitter orange, but you're likely to pick a winner no matter what you choose. Crepes and cakes are also available if you're trying to avoid a brain freeze, though that might not be a bad thing in the middle of a Dubrovnik summer.

i *8 kn for one scoop, 17 kn for two scoops.* ✪ *Open daily 9am-midnight.*

NIGHTLIFE

D'VINO
WINE BAR

Palmotićeva Ulica 4a ☎02 032 11 30 www.dvino.net

Dubrovnik's best wine bar is also one of its most accessible. If you know nothing about wine, order one of its helpful tasting flights: everything from an overview of the wines of Croatia to a comparison of several wines made with Plavac Mali grapes. If you know everything about wine and have tons of money to burn, ask about its vintage collection. No matter your wine knowledge, you'll enjoy this funky wine bar's comfortable leather seats, comprehensive snacks menu, and hipper-than-thou soundtrack.

i *Glass of wine 40-60 kn. ⏰ Open daily noon-2am.*

BUZA   BAR

Crijevićeva Ulica 9   ☎098 361 934

Outside Buza, which is located on some rocks jutting out from the city walls, you'll see a sign that reads "Cold Drinks and the Most Beautiful View." Notice they didn't say anything about good drinks. By most standards, Buza is not a great bar—the menu is limited, they make you drink out of plastic cups, and there are way too many alternatives available—but the view is indeed tremendous. Sit down, enjoy a beer or a mini-bottle of wine, and gaze out at the Adriatic. Then buy a commemorative postcard, hat, or T-shirt. Yes, these are actually available for purchase.

i *Beer 40 kn. ⏰ Open 9am-2am.*

ONOFRIO ICE BAR   BAR

Poljana Paska Miličeva 3   ☎091 152 0257

You've walked along the walls of Dubrovnik, you've hiked on Lokrum Island, and you carried your bags from the bus station all the way to the Old Town. One thing's certain: you're a sweaty mess. But there's a bar in Dubrovnik that can correct all that. A bar made of ice that, for reasons unknown, shares space with a Korean restaurant. This is Onofrio Ice Bar, perhaps the only place in Dubrovnik where you'll feel you're not wearing enough layers. The 75 kn cover charge includes a free drink, perhaps the only one you will have in Dubrovnik without feeling that it got a little too warm while you were drinking it. No windows and, in general, very little that would suggest you are not just partying in a meat locker, but the temperature is low enough to assuage any and all complaints.

i *75 kn cover, includes free drink. ⏰ Open daily 7pm-2am.*

CAFFE BAR NONENINA   BAR

Pred Dvorom 4   ☎098 825 844 www.nonenina.com

If you're looking for a place to sip sophisticated cocktails and relax, you can't do too much better than Caffe Bar Nonenina. Located just across from the Rector's Palace and next to the cathedral, Nonenina will provide you with some serious eye candy while you sink into one of their large wicker chairs. The cocktail list is no slouch, whether you're looking for a classy aperitif or want to get seriously messed up; in the latter event, order an XXL cocktail, for three to six patrons.

i *Cocktails 60-90 kn. XXL cocktails 185-205 kn. ⏰ Open daily 9am-2am.*

BUZZ BAR   BAR

Prijeko Ulica 21   ☎020 321 025. www.thebuzzbar.wix.com

As cafe-bars go, Buzz Bar is clean, has a slightly more expansive beer and liquor list, and has a helpful staff. There are quotes from Ernest Hemingway and Frank Sinatra on the menu (we get it, they drank alcohol), but the menu also has prices that are far better than most nightlife joints in Dubrovnik. Order a San Servolo or a medica (a sweet, honey-based liquor) and enjoy the free Wi-Fi.

i *Beers 20-40 kn. Liquors 12-20 kn. ⏰ Open daily 8am-2am.*

RAZONADA   WINE BAR

Od Puča 1   ☎020 326 222 www.thepucicpalace.com

A hotel wine bar sounds like a recipe for a very large bill, but Razonada, a clean, well-lit joint in Dubrovnik's Old Town, manages to keep prices fairly reasonable—unless you go for champagne or one of the cigars in its walk-in humidor.

More to the point, the wine list is large and varied, making room for such oddities as orange wine, made by leaving the grape skins with the fermenting juice. The rest of the menu is similarly offbeat: check out the cold-brew coffee that comes in a wine glass or the flavorful olive-leaf tea. Atmosphere is friendly and low-key.

i Wines 30-60 kn by the glass. ☒ Open daily 11am-midnight.

ESSENTIALS
Practicalities

- **MONEY:** There are numerous ATMs and exchange offices up and down Stradun, the main street in the Old Town.
- **POST OFFICE:** Central Post Office, Vukovarska 16 ☎020 362 068. ☒ Open M-F 7am-8pm, Sa 8am-3pm. Closed Sunday. In addition, there are numerous post office boxes on Stradun.
- **TOURIST INFORMATION CENTER:** Brsalje 5 ☎020 312 011. ☒ Open daily 8am-8pm.

Emergency

- **EMERGENCY NUMBER:** ☎112
- **HOSPITALS:** Dr. Roka Mišetića 2, Dubrovnik ☎020 431 777.
- **PHARMACY:** Ljekarna Kod Zvonika, Placa 2 ☎020 321 133. ☒ Open M-F 7am-8pm, Sa 7:30am-3pm. Closed Sunday.

Getting Around

Dubrovnik's Old Town is small and easily navigable by foot. You will most likely not be staying in the Old Town, but 99% of what's interesting in Dubrovnik is located in it. Buses regularly connect the various parts of Dubrovnik to the Old Town; if you exit from the Pile Gate, you'll find a major hub for buses. Pro tip: if you're staying outside the city, walk to the Old Town and take a bus home (otherwise, you'll likely be walking uphill).

hvar

Like many of Croatia's islands, Hvar is blessed with gorgeous beaches, delightful restaurants, and fine wines. The thing about Hvar, of course, is that it's also a party island; the fact that you can buy Grey Goose in souvenir shops should tip you off. The empty Coronas on the streets and the massive yachts docked in the harbor signal that this is a destination for everyone from drunken chavs to the 0.001%. Though you may enjoy those beaches, those restaurants, those wines, you are here to party in this strange, strange place: one part incredibly well-preserved natural beauty, one part playground for the rich, one part frat star paradise. Plan to stay up until 5am at least one night; plan to be so hungover that you curse the fact that Hvar is the sunniest island in the Adriatic. In short, go Hvard.

ACCOMMODATIONS

WHITE RABBIT HOSTEL
HOSTEL $

Stjepana Papafave 6 ☎095 849 37 46

If you want convenience, head to the White Rabbit Hostel. Located just off Trg Sv. Stjepana (a.k.a. the dead center of Hvar's old town), White Rabbit Hostel is a comfortable and secure place to crash while you explore Hvar's beaches, restaurants, and nightlife. The rooftop allows for a cool view of the maze-like old town, while the air-conditioned rooms and soft beds will provide you all the comfort you need after a long night on the town. Lockers provided.

i Dorms 250 kn. Cash only. ⏰ Reception 24hr.

HOSTEL VILLA ZORANA
HOSTEL $$
Domovinskog Rata 20 ☎091 723 17 37 www.villazorana.hostel.com

Large dorm rooms, couch-filled terraces, and a massive outdoor kitchen; Villa Zorana is a comfortable hostel, and that's even before you get to the incredible water pressure in the shower. The large terrace and big kitchen make it easy to hang out with big groups, although quiet time is imposed after 10:45pm; at that point, head to the Riva with your new friends. Bathrooms, like the rest of the facilities, are well kept, and you can rent a scooter through the hostel. Best of all, they serve you orange juice and ice cream when you check in.

i Dorms 270 kn. Privates 450 kn. ⏰ Reception 24hr.

YOUTH HOSTEL VILLA SKANSI
HOSTEL $$
Domovinskog Rata 18 ☎091 906 52 52

Liked Hostel Villa Zorana? You'll love Hostel Villa Skansi. Located just next door, Skansi is housed in a similar setup (big dorm rooms that open onto terraces with sliding doors) but has the added amenity of an in-hostel bar. That makes pregaming for a night on the town extremely easy. Beds are comfortable, bathrooms are well kept, and if they don't give you orange juice and ice cream, that's no big deal. Towels are 10 kn to rent, and the private rooms boast views of the ocean. By the way, you have to be under 40 to stay here.

i Dorms from 280 kn. ⏰ Reception 24hr.

HVAR OUT HOSTEL
HOSTEL $
Burak 23 ☎021 717 375

If the name of the hostel didn't tip you off, know that it's run by the same people who own Hostel Booze & Snooze in Split. Yep—this is a party hostel, and its close proximity to the Riva, Jazz Barrr, and the Carpe Diem Beach boats will be highly appreciated when you're walking back after a crazy night. Fortunately, as close as this hostel is, it's not in the absolute middle of the action; tucked away in a small street halfway up a small hill, Hvar Out is plenty isolated from the noise and hubbub (though that doesn't guarantee a bit of noise when your dorm-mates head to bed). Common areas include a kitchen and a terrace.

i Dorms 240 kn. ⏰ No curfew.

DINK'S PLACE
HOSTEL $
Ive Roića 5 ☎091 786 69 23

Though it's a bit of an uphill walk from the ferry depot in Hvar Town, Dink's Place's combination of comfortable rooms, shady terraces, and dedicated staff (sometimes they'll even organize barbecues for you!) makes for a winning combination. Dorms are equipped with multiple bathrooms and large lockers, the beds are large and comfortable, and the terraces provide you with plenty of room to stretch out (although they are closed after 10:30pm).

i Dorms 240 kn. Cash only. ⏰ Reception 24hr.

SIGHTS

FORTRESS (ŠPANJOLA)
LANDMARK

To be perfectly frank, Hvar is not known for its historical sights. It has beaches, it has clubs, and occasionally some of those clubs throw parties on some of those beaches. But no visit to this Dalmatian island would be complete without a trek up to the fortress. Built at the start of the 16th century, when Hvar was under Venetian rule, the fortress has served as a military outpost as well as a prison (you can still see some of the tiny cells!), and today it houses everything from a cafe-bar (you'll need a drink after the long trek uphill) to a small exhibit of amphorae found in a shipwreck. Of course, the best reason to visit is the panoramic views of Hvar you get; make sure your camera is ready.

i *Admission 30 kn, discounted 15 kn.* 🕐 *Open daily 8am-10pm.*

STARI GRAD PLAIN
ARCHAEOLOGICAL SITE

As a human settlement, Hvar is old; there were people here about 5,500 years ago. Before you ask, "Gee, what did they do before Carpe Diem opened?", remember that Hvar is unusually fertile for an island in the middle of the sea. Nowhere is that clearer than at Stari Grad Plain, the largest fertile plain in the Adriatic. It's been farmed since Neolithic times, but things didn't take off for another couple thousand years; the Greeks started farming it in the mid-300s BCE, setting out land divisions that endure to this day. Taking a few hours to hike around the fields is highly recommended; maps near Stari Grad highlight the archaeological sites on the plain, which range from medieval churches to Greek fortresses.

i *Between Stari Grad and Vrboska, Hvar. Free.* 🕐 *Hours vary; go during daylight.*

FRANCISCAN MONASTERY MUSEUM
MUSEUM

Put Križa 15 ☎021 741 193

Relics, modern art, and a 500-year-old cypress tree—there's something for everyone at the small but eclectic Franciscan Monastery Museum, located just off Hvar's coastline. Breeze through the heavily restored Church of St. Mary of Grace before exploring the museum's traditional collection of religious art, then its more eclectic selection of modern art, which puts abstract works alongside religious sculptures by Ivan Meštrović. The wall text is nonexistent, and most of the older works don't even give an artist—just a century, or the vague "Venetian School." Downstairs, you'll find some barnacle-encrusted amphorae and a selection of old Croatian banknotes. Venture outside to the small but well-kept garden, which houses one of the oldest trees in Croatia.

i *25 kn.* 🕐 *Open M-Sa 9am-3pm and 5-7pm.*

CATHEDRAL OF ST. STEPHEN
CHURCH

Trg Sv. Stjepana

You can't miss Hvar's Cathedral of Saint Stephen. Sooner or later, you'll come by Trg Sv. Stjepana, and you're not exactly going to be distracted by the town pharmacy. This church, built in the 1400s and 1500s after an earlier Gothic Church was destroyed (the bell tower was added later), is not only the best example of architecture you're going to find in Hvar (the Church of St. Mary of Grace, located by the Franciscan Monastery, has been much more heavily restored), but it's also a great way to quickly escape the heat, as the stone walls keep it relatively cool all day.

i *10 kn.* 🕐 *Open daily 9am-noon and 5-7pm.*

FOOD

🔖 GIAXA
CROATIAN $$$

Trg Tv. Petra Hektorovića 3 ☎021 741 073 www.giaxa.com

So you come to Hvar and you decide to splurge. Who can blame you? If you want to blow your hard-earned kuna, this splashy island is a perfect place to do it. And when it comes to splurging on food, we recommend you head straight to Giaxa. Not only is the Adriatic cuisine sprightly and delicious, you get to eat inside (or just outside, should you choose to sit outside) a real palace—the Jakša Palace, a noble residence built near the end of the 15th century. Inside, you'll eat alongside centuries-old stone arches; outside, you'll be shaded by an overhead passageway, which keeps the space cool all day.

i *Entrees 90-220 kn. 3-course lunch menu 120 kn.* 🕐 *Open daily noon-midnight.*

W BURGER & STEAKHOUSE

STEAKHOUSE **$$**

Trg Sv. Stjepana 28 ☎099 359 3391 www.wsteakburger.com

Vegans and vegetarians, steer clear. Everyone else, settle in for one of the heartiest meals you'll have in Hvar. For about 70 kn (on average), you'll enjoy a real burger—big, packed with toppings, and sandwiched in a bun that can stand up to the juicy meat. Wash it down with a selection from the small but well-curated wine list or a hefty glass of draft beer. The steaks may be a bit pricier, but they're just as juicy and even more likely to fill you up. Though seafood may be Hvar's stock in trade, W Burger & Steakhouse shows that this island knows how to handle the beef too.

i Burgers 65-80 kn. Steaks 140-190 kn. ☒ Open daily 10am-2am.

C'EST LA VIE

CROATIAN **$**

Križna Luka ☎021 717 012

Given its status as a hoity-toity tourist destination, Hvar has more than its share of pretentious restaurants. For a breezy antidote (and we mean breezy; this place is right on the water), check out C'est La Vie, an unassuming bistro whose main claim to fame is offering the cheapest beer in town (14 kn for 300mL of Ožujsko). True as that may be, it's a deal easily matched by any grocery store. No matter: you're not coming here for the cheap beer, but for the small but spot-on menu. Calamari, *cevapčići*, fries, three types of burgers, three types of salads. That's all you can get, and that's all you'll want. Given its prime location near the small beaches close to Hvar Town, you may find yourself unable to resist a quick bite after taking a swim.

i Entrees 40-60 kn. ☒ Open daily 9am-late.

FRESH PASTA HOUSE

ITALIAN **$**

Riva 27 ☎021 750 750

Croatia has a few restaurants like Fresh Pasta House, where you choose a base pasta and then an accompanying sauce. In practice, the choose-your-own-"pasta"dventure gimmick can prove a little stressful—what if you come up with a bad combination and the waiter starts laughing at you? Tagliatelle with a white wine sauce—have you gone mad? Luckily, Fresh Pasta House has a non-judgmental staff and an absolutely stacked list of pastas and sauces to choose from. Order blind and you'll be sure to pick a winner, though you may also be picking a sauce that costs 200 kn—fresh lobster doesn't come cheap. Caveat emptor, y'know? Be sure to grab the house-made focaccia, which comes adorned with spicy sea salt and delicious Croatian olive oil.

i Pastas 25-35 kn. Sauces 40-200 kn. ☒ Open daily 11am-11pm.

MAMA LEONA SPAGHETTERIA AND PIZZERIA + VITA HEALTH FOOD BAR

ITALIAN **$**

Riva 13 ☎091 120 0303 www.vitahvar.com

Pasta joint? Pizzeria? Weird, New Age-y place where you can order green shakes? Don't bother trying to wrap your head around how this business fits together (and yes, it is one business; don't freak out when you sit down for Vita and find menus for Mama Leona). Just know that here, you'll find one of the cheapest and best breakfasts in town. And even if you're not typically into health food, you'll no doubt be impressed by Vita's selection of smoothies, teas, and coffee: there's no better way to wake up.

i Breakfast 20-60 kn. Entrees 60-100 kn. ☒ Open M-F 10am-10pm, Sa-Su 9am-11pm.

GRABIĆ

BAKERY **$**

Trg Sv. Stjepana

The local bakery chain Grabić, operating since 1956, boasts several locations in Hvar, including ones in Hvar Town and Jelsa. Whether you're headed to the bus station and need a quick bite, or if you're in the process of discovering that tapas do not a meal make, Grabić is the right choice for a gluten-based snack.

The pastries range from chocolate croissants to something resembling Croatian jelly donuts (except with chocolate instead of jelly). For more savory fare, there are sandwiches and a selection of mini pizzas. None of this is particularly mind-blowing, but it's easy, cheap, and central—what's to critique about that?

i *Sandwiches 35 kn. Pizza 14 kn. Pastries under 10 kn. ☒ Open daily 8am-8pm.*

ARTICHOKE
CROATIAN $$

Obala Ćire Gamulina ☎098 908 86 67

Should you find yourself in Jelsa for the day—and we highly recommend a trip out here, and to Stari Grad—you'll have to grab lunch at this restaurant. Not only is the hearty Dalmatian fare tasty and filling, it offers a 20% discount until 6pm. That is not nothing. Enjoy beef braised in red wine, fresh fish, or fresh gnocchi; if you want something lighter, order something from its extensive tapas menu.

i *Entrees 90-150 kn. 20% discount for lunch. ☒ Open daily 10am-2am.*

CAFFE BAR FIG
CAFE $

Off Trg Sv. Stjepana ☎099 267 9890 www.figcafebar.com

Typically, when you see the word "*konoba*" on the side of a Croatian restaurant, it signifies a sort of traditional grill. Not so with Fig, a small establishment that serves fresh ingredients in novel combinations. Though it's just steps away from Trg Sv. Stjepana, it feels miles away from that square's bustling atmosphere. And its tasty, light cuisine feels miles away from the heavier fare you'll find elsewhere. Like 99% of the restaurants in Croatia, you'll find prosciutto on the menu here; unlike 99% of the restaurants in Croatia, it's served here as part of a salad that also includes watermelon, red onion, and feta cheese. You can also get it on a flatbread alongside cranberries and toasted brie. The rest of the menu is similarly eclectic. Want watermelon gazpacho? Vegetarian curry? A full English breakfast? It's all available here. The inside is air-conditioned, so be sure to duck inside on a hot day; if the weather permits, however, nab a seat on one of the outdoor benches, adorned with plush cushions.

i *Walk down the alleyway between two restaurants (Mizzarola and Ex Rocco). Entrees 50-100 kn. ☒ Open daily 10am-10pm.*

NIGHTLIFE

CARPE DIEM BEACH
CLUB

Stipanska Island www.carpe-diem-beach.com

What to say about Carpe Diem Beach? Should we mention the Moët & Chandon signs plastered everywhere? The bottle service that leads 18-year-old Spanish heirs to wave around 3L bottles of Belvedere? The pool that goes unoccupied until 3 or 4am, when it's suddenly full of so many fully clothed patrons that the water spills onto the pavement? Or maybe the fact that you absolutely need cash—no cards accepted at the door for the 150 kn cover, and 1000 kn minimum charge at any of the bars. This, for better or for worse, is Hvar—the party central that represents either your ideal vacation or a nightmarish vision of Europe's tourism-driven future. You'll know if it's for you.

i *Taxi boats leave from Riva starting at 12:30am. Cover 150 kn, drinks upward of 60 kn. ☒ Open daily 12:30-5 am.*

ROOFTOP BARS (TOP BAR & TERASA BAR)
BAR

Top Bar: Fabrika 28; Terasa Bar: Trg. Sv. Stjepana

No question about it—the streets of Hvar get wild after dark. Just try pushing your way through the crowds of people clustered around Kiva Bar and Nautical Bar. If you appreciate the action but would appreciate it more from a slightly removed perspective, we suggest you check out two of Hvar's best-kept secrets: Top Bar and Terasa Bar. These are both located in the center of town, but most people miss them—probably because they're both at least two stories off the ground. Top Bar is located, somewhat confusingly, on the second-highest floor of the Adriana Hotel. Despite its luxe interior, stunning views of the harbor, and location within a luxury hotel, there's no cover charge or other fee to enter, and the prices are generally reasonable (30 kn for beers, about 75 for cocktails). Moreover, the space is large, there are lots of tables and couches, and sometimes people even start dancing. Perhaps Hvar's best-kept secret. If you want a more low-key vibe at a slightly lower altitude, head to Terasa Bar, which overlooks Trg Sv. Stjepana.

i *Beers 30 kn. Cocktails 70-80 kn.* ☺ *Top Bar open daily 10pm-2am. Teasa Bar open daily 7pm-2am.*

JAZZ BARRR
BAR

Svetega Križića 1   ☎091 956 16 96

Most of the crowd heads straight to Kiva Bar and Nautica Bar, but if you're look-ing to pregame before Carpe Diem, this small joint is the place. Cocktails are cheaper (25 kn for a very strong vodka Sprite, and only 160 kn for a liter cock-tail), the crowd is more local, and the atmosphere seems even more raucous than the Riva scene. Though it closes down at 2am, the crowd will definitely be ready for more; follow them to Pink Champagne, Veneranda, or Carpe Diem Beach.

i *Cocktails 25-60 kn. Cash only.* ☺ *Open daily 9pm-2am.*

PRSUTA 3
BAR

Trg Tv. Petra Hektorovića 5   ☎098 969 61 93

Despite the impressions you may have gotten from Hvar's party scene, this tiny Dalmatian island does not produce vodka by the 3L bottle-load. When it comes to alcoholic beverages, Hvar is all about wine—white wine grapes are grown on the Stari Grad Plain, while grapes for the red wine Plavac are grown elsewhere. If you read that last sentence with an unhealthy amount of interest, Prsuta 3 is for you. But if you just want a great bar where you can drink fine wine and have loud conversations, Prsuta 3 is also for you. Located on a small street just steps from Hvar's main square, Prsuta 3 claims to be the island's first wine bar, and it may as well be the most definitive. The bottle list covers all of the Dalmatian islands, and the wines available by the glass are no slouch either—look for the hyper-rare Grk, a Korčula wine made from grapes that only have female flowers. If you're feeling celebratory, go wild and order a magnum, or indulge in some Croatian sparkling wine. The vibe is excited, raucous, unpretentious—if you're looking for a more mature party scene, go here.

i *Glasses 30-60 kn.* ☺ *Open daily 6pm-2am.*

KA'LAVANDA MUSIC BAR HVAR
BAR

Dr. Mate Milićića 7   ☎021 718 721 www.kalavanda.com

Ka'Lavanda should be intolerable; it is, after all, a place where you can order a magnum of Dom Pérignon, and the prices are a good 10 kn more expensive than you'll find elsewhere in Hvar. But if you want decent cocktails—rather than a half-assed Cuba Libre or Long Island iced tea—you'll have to suck it up, because Ka'Lavanda is the best cocktail bar in Hvar, if not all of Croatia. Most bars here get no more inventive than the Negroni; Ka'Lavanda has a whole page of sours, including a Zegroni made with 20-year-old Zacapa rum. It may cost 128 kuna, but hey. If you're a cocktail geek, the presence of French 75s, Kir Royals, watermelon mojitos, and rosemary truffle martinis will send you into waves of ecstasy. Of course, they also have trashy shooters like the Mexican Asshole (tequila, sambuca, tabasco—charming).

And despite the house music and bottle service (4480 kn for a 3L bottle of Belvedere, anyone?), Ka'Lavanda attracts a surprisingly relaxed and mature

croatia

crowd. Besides, the gray couches outside are pretty darned comfortable—and unlike at Carpe Diem, you don't need to order a bottle to sit at one.

i *Cocktails 50-130 kn. ☑ Open daily 2pm-late.*

ESSENTIALS

Practicalities

- **MONEY:** The most ATMs are located in and around Trg Sv. Stjepana. This area is also home to several exchange offices.
- **POST OFFICE:** Obala Riva 19. ☑ Open June 15-Sept 15 M-Sa 7am-9pm; Sept 16-June 14 open M-F 7am-7pm, Sa 8am-noon.
- **TOURIST INFORMATION CENTER** Trg Sv. Stjepana 42 ☎021 741 059.

Emergency

- **EMERGENCY NUMBER:** ☎112
- **AMBULANCE:** ☎021 717 099
- **POLICE:** ☎021 741 100
- **FIRE:** ☎021 741 200
- **PHARMACY:** Trg Sv. Stjepana 15. ☑ Open M-F 8am-9pm, Sa 8am-1pm and 6-9pm, Su 10am-noon.

Getting Around

The individual towns on Hvar Island—Hvar, Jelsa, and Stari Grad, to name a few— are all quite small and have no public transportation. To get from town to town, you can rent a scooter, a car, or a bike; these prices range from 70-100 kn a day for a bike to upward of 300 kn a day for a car. You can also take a bus—check the local station for the most up-to-date times. Tickets can be purchased on the bus and are generally between 20 and 40 kn. Your ferry will either land at Stari Grad or in Hvar town; be sure to check this in advance, as they are separated by 20 kilometers. Getting between the two is easy (take those buses!) but not fun to deal with at the last minute.

korčula

Idyllic views of the Adriatic, magnificently preserved city walls, and streets that somehow aren't packed with tourists. No, this isn't what you wish Dubrovnik was— this is Korčula, a small town on a small island also named Korčula. Here, you'll find those stunning city walls, great wine bars, and more information (and misinformation) about Marco Polo than you ever wanted to know. Elsewhere on the island, you'll find pristine beaches and acres of vineyards. Korčula is known for its white wines, so be sure to wash your seafood dinner down with a glass of Grk, Pošip, or Rukata. If Hvar's party atmosphere and heavy red wines left you cold, spend a few days in Korčula.

ACCOMMODATIONS

HOSTEL CAENAZZO
Trg Svetog Marka

HOSTEL $

As a general rule, hostels that are affiliated with pizzerias are to be avoided, but Hostel Caenazzo is a notable exception. And Pizzeria Caenazzo is pretty decent too. The dorms are not exceptionally large, but the beds are quite comfortable and the bathrooms are exceptionally well kept. Plus, you get those little shampoo and soap capsules, so you can pretend you're in a fancy hotel. The sometimes-effective A/C may be brutal, but Hostel Caenazzo's extreme proximity to the Adriatic means you can pop in for a quick dip whenever things get too heated.

i Dorms 150 kn. Check-in 2-9pm. No curfew.

SIGHTS

MARCO POLO MUSEUM
Trg. Plokata 33

MUSEUM
☎098 970 53 34

Marco Polo was probably not born in Korčula, Croatia. But why spoil the fun? Why not live the lie by attending this museum, which presents a (largely) factual look at the extraordinary life of Mr. Polo? As you examine six elaborate dioramas, complete with creepily lifelike human figures, you'll hear some very dramatic narration (Memorable Excerpt #1: "memories burst like a volcano") detailing Marco Polo's journey from Italy to China. Whoops! Did we say Italy? We meant Croatia. Did you know that when Marco Polo was crossing the desert to get to China, he was thinking about Korčula? Memorable Excerpt #2: "Korčula. How he loved that town." Be sure to buy some Marco Polo olive oil in the gift shop.

i 60 kn, students 50 kn. Open daily 9am-midnight.

CATHEDRAL OF ST. MARK, BELL TOWER, AND TREASURY MUSEUM
Trg Svetog Marka

CHURCH

You pay the 10 kn admission, you walk into Korčula's Cathedral of St. Mark, and you think you're getting a pretty good deal. Then you realize that the admission is separate for the bell tower and for the treasury museum, and the main attraction of the actual cathedral is that it's shaped kind of strangely. Though the three separate admissions may be a trick to increase revenue, it also allows you to optimize your tourism experience. Go to the treasury during the day to look at religious art. Walk to the top of the bell tower at night (it's open until 11pm) for the best views. Skip the cathedral entirely. Capisce?

i Cathedral 10 kn. Bell tower 20 kn. Treasury 20 kn. Hours vary, usually open 9am-9pm. Bell-tower open 9am-11pm.

KORCULA TOWN MUSEUM
Trg Svetog Marka

MUSEUM
☎020 711 420

The lack of air conditioning means this museum can't be your respite from the summer heat, but just chalk it up to historical accuracy and go anyway. Interested in archaeology? Traditional Korčulan dress? The partisan movement during World War II? Maybe you just haven't seen enough barnacle-encrusted amphorae? If you answered yes to any of these questions (and if you answered yes to the last one, you're lying), then you'll enjoy the Korčula Town Museum, housed in Gabriellis Palace. Of particular interest is the authentically preserved kitchen on the top floor, which may whet your appetite for some Dalmatian specialties.

i 20 kn. Open daily Apr-June 10am-2pm; July-Sept 9am-9pm; Oct-Mar 10am-1pm.

FOOD

ATERINA
Trg Korčulanskih Klesara i Kipara 2

CROATIAN $
☎091 986 18 56

Unless you have never had Italian food, you will not be extremely surprised by Dalmatian cuisine, which boils down to Italian food with fresher fish. Point being, nothing at Aterina (except for the octopus and polenta special) is that out of the ordinary. But don't let yourself skip over Aterina for that reason; its homemade ingredients and extensive wine list make it a great place to grab a meal in

Korčula. The entrees, most of which are pasta dishes, range in price from 70 to 120 kn, but a perfectly filling meal can also be created by combining a few of the appetizers. If you really can't make up your mind, you have the option to get a plate with a sample of every appetizer. If it's hot out (and believe us, it will be), we recommend the gazpacho-like cold tomato soup, which pairs perfectly with one of the many types of bruschetta offered. If you get seafood (or even if you don't), be sure to order a glass of white wine. Aterina has three varieties of the hyper-rare Grk (the grape vine only produces female flowers, making cultivation difficult), two of which are available by the glass.

i *Appetizers 25-60 kn. Entrees 70-120 kn. ☼ Open daily noon-midnight.*

BISTRO GAJETA
PIZZA, CAFE $
Šetalište Petra Kanavelića
☎020 716 359

Korčula's city walls may not be as dramatic as Dubrovnik's, but eating alongside them still provides a pretty decent view. Though many of the restaurants along Šetalište Petra Kanavelića are on the expensive side, Bistro Gajeta provides a tasty, filling, and affordable alternative. The best offer? The varied pizzas, although some of the meat dishes come close. Be sure to grab some ice cream from their stand afterward—or don't, as you may be too full from the pizza.

i *Pizzas 50-70 kn. Entrees 70-100 kn. ☼ Open daily 9am-midnight.*

FUNDAMENTUM
TAPAS $
Kanona a Rozanovica 3
☎099 681 04 99

For lighter fare in Korčula (maybe you had a whole pizza for lunch and that wasn't such a great call, you know?), you can't do much better than Fundamentum, a wine bar and tapas joint just off Trg Svetog Marka. If you're with a big group, order one of the cheese or meat plates to share; smaller parties can make do with the varied bruschetta offerings. Pasta dishes round out the menu. And of course there's plenty of wine to wash it all down. Indoor seating is limited.

i *Dishes 10-30 kn. ☼ Open daily noon-midnight.*

NIGHTLIFE

CAPERS
BAR
Šetalište Petra Kanavelića 1
☎099 411 73 79

Korčula's best cocktail bar doesn't have the views that Massimo (below) has, but it does have a far more comprehensive menu and live entertainment at night. And the view isn't half bad here either. Choose from a lengthy list of (somewhat pricey) cocktails while you enjoy acoustic sets after midnight. The attentive, knowledgeable waitstaff can whip up whatever concoction you request quickly and efficiently.

i *Cocktails 60-80 kn. ☼ Open daily noon-4am.*

MASSIMO
BAR
Kula Zakerjan, Šetalište Petra Kanavelića
☎020 715 073

Yes, Massimo is a tourist destination. But, crucially, it is not a tourist trap. The prices are decent and the experience is well worth the crowd. So put on your fanny-pack and embrace your black-socks-and-sandals-wearing self, because this cocktail bar in a 15th-century tower is a mandatory stop in Korčula. Yes, you read that right. Massimo is located in Zakerjan Tower, built from 1481 to 1483 under the order of the doge of Venice. He probably didn't think, "Gee, this would be a great place to sip a daiquiri while watching the sunset," but we're happy it worked out that way. Careful not to drink too much, however—to get to the top, you need to climb a narrow ladder. Space is so limited, in fact, that drinks are ferried to the top via dumbwaiter.

i *Cocktails 50-70 kn. ☼ Open daily 6pm-2am.*

korčula

VINUM BONUM

Punta Jurana

BAR

☎020 715 014

Croatia is not known for its cutting-edge nightlife, but Vinum Bonum is something truly new: an unholy, unhealthy, and altogether delightful combination of dive bar and upscale bottle shop. Interested in getting sloshed for next to nothing? Then get a glass of house wine for 5 kn. Then get another, and another, and another. Throw in a shot of homemade liquor for 10 or 12 kn. Then go back to the wine. Interested in getting sloshed while also emptying your wallet? You might consider buying a bottle from their archives. Snacks run the gamut from hot dogs to prosciutto. Be sure to try the house cognac, Mr. Konjak, before you leave.

i House wine 5-8 kn. Bottled wines 30-40 kn by the glass. ☼ *Open daily 6pm-midnight.*

ESSENTIALS

Practicalities

- **MONEY:** There are numerous ATMs and exchange offices by the ferry port and near the bus station. Inside Korčula's town walls, there are fewer ATMs, but exchange offices can still be found.

- **POST OFFICE:** Kalac 1 ☎0800 303 304. ☼ Open daily 8am-8pm.

- **TOURIST INFORMATION CENTER:** Open daily 8am-10pm during the summer. ☎020 715 701.

Emergency

- **EMERGENCY NUMBER:** ☎112

- **HOSPITAL:** Dom Zdravlja Korčula, Ulica 575 ☎020 711 137.

- **PHARMACY:** Ulica Kralja Tomislava ☎020 711 057.

Getting Around

Korčula is, simply put, tiny. Buses and cars can't operate in the pedestrian town center anyway.

pula

Want to experience Istria but don't think you can last a day in a small town like Rovinj? Head directly to Pula, the largest urban area in Istria. While the 60,000-person city isn't exactly a metropolis, it boasts more than its share of clubs, bars, and Roman ruins to complement the stunning rock beaches. Check out the well-preserved Roman amphitheater (it dates back to the time of Augustus!), stuff your face with *ćevapčići* at one of the town's many grills, then make your way down to the beach and dip your feet in the wavy Adriatic. Just watch out for sea urchins.

ACCOMMODATIONS

DREAMBOX HOSTEL

Ruže Petrović 14

HOSTEL $

☎915 65 14 76

You better be sure of Dreambox's address—there's no way you'll recognize it from the street. This family-run hostel is located in a very large house on an entirely residential lane—before you find the reception desk, you'll be certain you're trespassing in someone's backyard. That hominess, however, is key to the appeal of Dreambox. Where else will you sleep in rooms with 14-foot ceilings? Where else will the owner brew you Turkish coffee in a traditional copper džezva? At Dreambox, you'll feel like you have your own home on the Croatian seaside. Though it's not at all close to the bus station, an 11 kn ticket on the 1 bus will take you just a few blocks away—this is crucial to know before you arrive in Pula. There are several restaurants and a market close by; you can also walk to the coastline. Should you want to visit Premantura and Kap Kamenjak, the owner can arrange for a taxi to pick you up, or he can drive you himself: his prices are the best in town.

i Dorms start at 85 kn. Private rooms 350 kn. ☼ Reception 8am-10pm.

RIVA HOSTEL
HOSTEL $

Riva 2A ☎95 827 0243 www.rivahostel.com

Waterfront real estate tends to be luxurious. Such is the case with Riva Hostel, even if Pula's largely industrial harbor isn't exactly the most scenic seascape. In addition to the usual amenities (Wi-Fi, 24-hour security, no curfew, and bike rental), you'll find a rooftop bar, as well as multiple kitchens and common spaces. The spacious rooms (with A/C!) aren't too shabby either. In keeping with all this luxury, Riva Hostel will actually take your credit or debit card—not always a given in Croatia. However, there's also an ATM right around the corner. Also just around the corner—OK, well, maybe a few minutes walk—are the Pula Arena and the rest of the old town.

i Dorms 120 kn. Private rooms 400 kn. ☼ Reception 9am-midnight.

HOSTEL PIPISTRELO
HOSTEL $$

Flaciusova 6 ☎052 393 568

Hostel Pipistrelo bills itself as an "art" hostel. It's heavy on character—rooms have names like "Chandelier" or "Prose," and old LPs and movie posters line the walls. Sometimes that forced quirkiness can get a little bizarre—the logo depicts a man in bed screaming "argh!" Despite that unfortunate instance of branding, you'll get a good night's sleep here. The rooms are spacious and comfortable, and the attentive staff is happy to answer questions or arrange trips for you; if you're a couple on your honeymoon, you can get discounts on packages that include a rental car, but there are multiple arrangements with tourist agencies regardless of your marital status.

i Dorms 145 kn in the summer, 130 kn in the off season. ☼ Reception 8am-9pm.

SIGHTS

PULA ARENA
ANCIENT ROME

Flavijevska Ulica

You can't miss Pula's ancient amphitheater, which was originally constructed in Augustan times and enlarged by Vespasian; this massive structure dominates Pula's town center. And with a variety of concert events during the summer, it also dominates Pula's entertainment scene—for better or for worse, they no longer hold gladiator fights. Caveat emptor. Fair warning: the frequent concerts mean that your appreciation of this archeological treasure may be impeded by temporary stages, speakers, and the like. If you're just looking for a quick photo, you might as well walk around outside; there are plenty of opportunities for striking shots, especially during the evening. If you're looking to learn a bit about Istria's Roman history, plunk down the admission fare and enjoy the large exhibit, housed in a subterranean gallery where wounded and dead gladiators were brought. Here, you'll see plenty of amphorae (the practice of consuming liters of wine is apparently an ancient one) along with old water pumps, olive oil works, and other such artifacts.

i 40 kn, students 20 kn. ☼ Open daily May-June 8am-9pm; July-Aug 8am-midnight; Sept-Apr 8am-7pm.

TEMPLE OF AUGUSTUS

Forum

There's no way around it: in the great Pula-Roman-ruins race, the Temple of Augustus runs a distant second to the arena (it was originally one of three temples, which explains its small size). But once you've had your share of gladiators and amphorae, mosey on over to this small but appealing museum. If you're obsessed with antiquity and the Archaeological Museum is still closed (one of those things is far more likely than the other), then the fragmentary artifacts inside are well worth the 10 kn. Otherwise, the friezes outside and the scenic steps, with great views of the surrounding square will easily satisfy you.

i *10 kn, students 5 kn.* ☼ *Open M-F 9am-10pm, Sa-Su 9am-3pm.*

CAPE KAMENJAK (DAY TRIP)

Premantura

Pula's beaches are nice, but the nicest in Istria are just a few hours down, at Cape Kamenjak. Located just outside the tiny town of Premantura (population less than 1000), a day trip to Cape Kamenjak is absolutely essential if you're spending any time in Pula. Situated on a peninsula that forms the very southern tip of Istria, Kamenjak is a nationally protected area, which means the miles and miles of beaches are totally unspoiled. Swim out to an island if you're up for it. Its vast size means you might want to bring a bike to get around, though walking is also an option; its vast size also means that you can find a private spot despite the hundreds and hundreds of Croats that flow in daily. If you're looking for something a little more stimulating than sun and sand (well, sun and pebbles), keep a look out for petrified dinosaur footprints, which have been observed on the island of Veli Brijuni.

i *Free.*

FOOD

PIZZERIA JUPITER

Castropola 42   ☎052 214-333 www.pizzeriajupiter.com

Jupiter, in Roman parlance, was the king of the gods. Pizzeria Jupiter is by no means the king of the pizza places, but its prices and large upstairs terrace make it worth a visit anyway. Expect to pay about 30-40 kn for an individual pie; the toppings are varied, but not exactly novel. Still, who ever went wrong with pizza margherita? If you're with a big group and everyone agrees on what to order (and you're in Pula, not fantasyland), then go for one of the jumbo pizzas, which'll run you between 60 and 80 kn. Though you'll find pizza as an option at many of Pula's bistros, this is where you should go for the real deal (and, given their prices, a good deal at that).

i *Pizzas 30-40 kn for individuals, 60-80 kn for "jumbo."* ☼ *Open M-F 10am-midnight, Sa noon-midnight, Su 1pm-midnight.*

BISTRO ODISEJ

Arsenalska Ulica   ☎052 223 288

Pula doesn't have the same classy establishments as nearby Rovinj. What it has in spades are meat-heavy bistros. And the Bistro Odisej, nestled between a sheer cliff and a gigantic gray wall, may not have the most appealing location (Arsenalska Ulica is not exactly the Champs-Elysées), but its protein-packed menu makes a visit mandatory. *Cevapčići* sausages, veal, burgers—if it's meaty, they've got it, and you can probably have it wrapped in a big puffy bun with fresh white onions. Not for the pretentious eater, but who needs those anyway? And with most of the menu available for under 50 kn, the price is certainly right.

i *Entrees 30-50 kn.* ☼ *Open M-F 6:30am-11:30pm, Sa-Su 9am-11:30pm.*

GOSTIONICA GALEB

CROATIAN $

Osječka Ulica 37

☎052 386 361

If you've spent the day lounging along the Lungomare, don't worry about enduring a long walk in town before you can eat. Just grab a bite at Gostionica Galeb, a small bistro near the water. Surrounded by residential streets, Galeb boasts sunny outdoor seating filled with charmingly misshapen tables; they look like they've come from a tree that's just been knocked down. Maybe it used to stand next to the tree that's randomly standing in the middle of the terrace. Arbor-related mysteries aside, the meat-focused menu (look for the mix grill!) will surely quell the appetite you've built up at the beach. Maybe you'll feel the urge to pound a few half-liters of *Ozujško*; they've got it on draft. Grab a bit of ice cream for dessert—the sugar high is the rush you need to hustle back to the beach for sunset.

i Mains from 35-55 kn. ⚇ Open Tu-Su 10am-6:30pm.

BISTRO COLOSEUM

MEDITERRANEAN $

Istarska 36

☎98 285 903

Walking around Pula, you'll see legions of people sitting outside, sipping a cappuccino or nursing a beer (*Ozujško*, naturally). They are not in restaurants. They are in cafes. Pula has cafes in spades. Take heed: very few of these cafes serve food. You could starve a man in Pula by throwing him in the town center and not telling him where a restaurant is. Maybe that's an exaggeration, but it's still good to know where Bistro Coloseum is. Here, you'll find such stomach-fillers such as stuffed burgers—no bun but there's ham and cheese inside! Wash it down with a soda-wine cocktail—Fanta and wine, anyone? This is what white-wine spritzers hath wrought. It may not be "classy," but the Roman decor at least gives it a certain air of decadence

i Entrees 50-80 kn. ⚇ Open daily 8am-11pm.

NIGHTLIFE

BEER CLUB PULA

BAR

Tomasinijeva Ulica 34

www.beerclubpula.com

No, this isn't a place where people sit around and discuss the minute differences between Karlovačko, Ožujsko, and Laško. Beer Club Pula is one of the few honest-to-goodness beer bars in Croatia: you'll often find the latest in Croatian craft beer on tap, while the extensive bottle lists includes everything from Belgian monk's brews to weird stuff by cutting-edge Danes. Of course, you can also get cheap half-liters of Staripronan or Ožujsko; a good choice if you want to have more than a few drinks but don't want to empty your wallet.

i Prices highly variable; most beers 20-40 kn, but some beers can cost as much as 90 kn. ⚇ Open M-Sa 7am-midnight, Su 9am-midnight.

KLUB ULJANIK

CLUB

Dobrilina 2

☎95 901 8811

Looking to rage in Pula? You've come to the place. Is it the right place? Well, it's the place: draw your own conclusions. There's no cover, shots will run you between 16 and 20 kn, and the music is loud enough for people to miss the fact that you don't speak Croatian. That's the good news. The not-so-good news is that the crowd skews male and not a lot of people like to dance. The upshot of the not-so-good news is that it's easy to get up on stage and start dancing. You may not want to rage in Pula. But if you are looking to rage in Pula, you've come to the place.

i No cover. Shots 10-20 kn. ⚇ Open Th-Sa 8pm-6am.

Lehartova Ulica 1

Looking for a relaxing evening in Pula? Don't laugh when we say that the best place is in the shadow of the Ministry of Defense. But yes, the Terasa Mozart, an open-air bar located in the courtyard of the House of Croatian Defenders, is indeed a great place to grab a drink, enjoy the summer air, and listen to relaxing live music: acoustic covers of Prince and Tom Petty, anyone?

i *Mixed drinks 40-50 kn. Beers and wines 20-30 kn.* ◪ *Open 8am-10pm.*

ESSENTIALS

Practicalities

- **MONEY:** ATMs are everywhere; look for the Bankomat sign. An exchange office can be found a few minutes walk from the bus station, at Giardini Ulica 12.

- **POST OFFICE:** Danteov Trg 4.

- **TOURIST INFO CENTER:** Forum 3 ☎385 52 219 197.

Emergency

- **EMERGENCY NUMBER:** ☎112

- **HOSPITAL:** Opca Bolnica Pula, Zagrebacka ☎385 52 376 000.

- **PHARMACY:** Giardini 14 ☎385 52 222 551. ◪ Open daily 7am-8pm.

Getting Around

By Bus

Though it's the largest city in Istria, Pula's town center is compact; most of the town lives in sprawling residential areas. Buses come frequently; the 1 bus, which leaves from the bus terminal and terminates at Stoja, and the 2 bus, which leaves from the bus terminal and terminates at Verudela, will likely be able to deliver you to an out-of-the-way hostel. Tickets can be purchased on the bus for a fee of 11 kn, or you can get a card (75 kn for a first time purchase, includes 40 kn for fare) and pay 7 kn per ride.

By Taxi

Taxi Duka is open 24hr. (☎385 97 600 88 90)

rovinj

Am I in Italy or Croatia? That's what you'll be asking yourself if you visit Rovinj (a.k.a. Rovigno), a small town on Croatia's Istrian coast. This is a truly bilingual town, where you can wash down pizza with pelinkovac. But while the dizzying mix of Italian and Croatian traditions is nice, Rovinj's true appeal lies in its curvy coasts and tiny islands. That's why visitors from all over Europe flock here—in addition to Italian and Croatian, expect to hear German, French, and the Queen's English—and, consequently, why the place is so expensive. Just lie down on a smooth slab of rock (the beaches may be free, but they sure ain't sandy), close your eyes, and let the warmth of the sun help you forget about your bank account.

ACCOMMODATIONS

ROOMS MONTALBANO
HOTEL $$

Ulica Montalbano 14 ☎052 814 074

Walking through the narrow streets of Rovinj, you might be seized by an irresistible impulse to live there, in these romantic cobblestoned alleys. You also might be seized by a desire to get back to streets where you don't trip. Assuming you're seized by the first impulse, make sure you're staying at Rooms Montalbano, a charming family-run hotel in the heart of Rovinj's old town. Here, you'll find wooden floors, quaint rooms, and windows with adorable views of the surrounding streets. Bathrooms are compact but contain all the necessities. Pay in cash.

i Doubles 350 kn.

APARTMENTS ROMANO
HOTEL $$

Vukovarska Ulica 2 ☎052 817 275

Though it's a bit removed from Rovinj's main town, Apartments Romano is the perfect place to go if you're looking for a beach vacation. Located on a residential street, the hotel is just five minutes away from the pebbly shore. Forgot suntan lotion in your room? Just run back and get it. Cooking up dinner and want to catch the sunset? Run on down—just don't leave the gas on. And yes, Apartments Romano, in both its apartments and studio rooms, includes a kitchen complete with fridge and oven (there's a market located just a few minutes away). Should you tire of cooking, you'll have to endure a walk into town—but the owners will drive you to the bus station when you check out. If you want to be picked up, just email in advance.

i Doubles 300 kn.

SIGHTS

SAINT EUPHEMIA'S BASILICA
CHURCH

Trg Sv. Eufemije

Rovinj's most famous structure is probably this baroque church, built in 1736. Euphemia was a Christian who was martyred under the Emperor Diocletian; her remains legendarily disappeared from Constantinople and ended up in Rovinj. Large, dramatic paintings show her getting fed to the lions and her sarcophagus ending up on the rocky beaches outside the city. It all seems more miraculous when you take a look at the sarcophagus itself—to be perfectly clear, this is a gigantic chunk of rock.

Admission to the church is free, but it costs 20 kn to walk up to the top of the bell tower. Is it worth it? Long answer: you can see the tower from just about anywhere in Rovinj, which gives you an idea of just how good its view is. Short answer: yes.

i Basilica free; tower 20 kn. ☑ Open daily May 10am-4pm; June-Sept 10am-6pm; Oct-Apr 10am-2pm.

MINI CROATIA
GALLERY

Milana Macana 5 ☎052 830 877

A visit to Rovinj can easily make you want to visit the rest of Croatia. But if you lack the funds or time to mount a full trip down the Adriatic coast, rejoice: just two kilometers out of Rovinj's old town, there exists Mini Croatia. This miniature model of the entire country, complete with streams, highways, and a pond standing in for the sea, can be walked easily. Marvel at the tiny models of famous buildings and landmarks while reading up on the history of each town in the detailed guidebook. Zagreb is represented by its cathedral and the Ban Jelačić statue, while towns with lesser-known buildings sometimes get another item to represent them; the model of Krk, for instance, boasts the Baška tablet, a 12th-century artifact. By the end of the line, you'll have learned more than your share of Croatian geography and history—in cocktail party conversation, you could probably fool everyone into thinking you actually made the trip. As an added bonus, Mini Croatia is approved by none other than former Croatian president Stjepan Mesić; a picture of him at the site proudly hangs near the entrance. Sadly, there's no miniature version of him.

i *Walk or drive west along Ulica Giordana Palliate until it turns into the 303 highway; continue along for approximately 2km. Mini Croatia will be on your right. Admission 25 kn. ☼ Open daily May 10am-6pm; June-Aug 9am-8pm; Sept-Oct 10am-6pm.*

ULICA GRISIA
NEIGHBORHOOD

Ulica/Via Grisia

Rovinj's old town is full of narrow, winding, and slippery streets—some call them romantic, others call them poor urban planning. The Rovinj-iest street, of course, is the steep Ulica Grisia, which runs from St. Euphemia's Basilica down to Veli Trg. Here, you'll find wine shops, craft shops, shops selling paintings of rock stars, galleries of naïve art (look out for those oil paintings on glass!), jewelry shops, handmade leather shops, handmade soap shops (everything from bubblegum to rosemary), shops selling olive oil, shops selling truffles, shops selling pelinkovac, shops selling antiques, and, of course, the inimitable Pizzeria Da Sergio. If you want to shop in Rovinj, this is the place to do it; if you want to get a sense of this romantic/poorly planned Istrian town, this is the thoroughfare to walk down. Just don't wear high heels; these cobblestones aren't forgiving.

i *Free, unless you buy something.*

FOOD

Maybe it's all the tourists, maybe it's all the seafood, maybe it's all the restaurants being right on the water. Whatever the reason, there's no question that Rovinj is expensive. Since you're already staying in an apartment, the cheapest option is to hit up the supermarket and put your kitchen and/or refrigerator to use. But if you can't cook or don't want to do so on vacation, look for the following restaurants.

PIZZERIA DA SERGIO
PIZZA $$

Ulica Grisia 11
☎052 81 69 49

Beloved by locals and tourists alike, Pizzeria da Sergio is a sort of miracle; not only does it serve some of the best food you'll find in Rovinj, it's easily one of the cheapest restaurants around. Granted, some of the seafood pizzas can get a little pricey—such is the case with *frutti di mare*—if you want to stuff your face for less than 70 or 80 kn, this place is your best bet. Whether you're looking for artichokes, prosciutto, olives, or calamari, there's a pizza here to satisfy you: if you can't make up your mind, turn to the "Da Casa" page to find local favorites like the Pizza Rovignese. Though you may need to wait for a table, the service is startlingly quick—but once you sit down, who wants to leave?

i *Pizzas 50-60 kn. ☼ Open daily 11am-3pm and 6-11:30pm.*

B052
ICE CREAM $

Carera 65
☎052 818 006

Located on Via Carera, b052 doesn't have the same great views as the ice cream shops along the harbor. What it does have, however, is truly incredible ice cream—especially if you're into chocolate. Like regular chocolate? They've got it. Plus white chocolate. And chocolate with hazelnut. Chocolate mixed with oranges or strawberries. If your breath smells bad, they've got chocolate with mint. If you need a drink, they've got chocolate with rum. If you like it bitter, they've got dark chocolate. If you like it sweet, they've got milk chocolate. If you like it spicy, they've got chocolate with chili. Did we forget anything? Oh yeah, there's chocolate with cinnamon too. Other sweets on the menu include crois-

croatia

sants, muffins, and macaroons. Or you can just enjoy an espresso or Istrian craft beer, either in the sleek white interior or their gorgeous backyard courtyard.

i Scoops of ice cream 10 kn.

SEGUTRA
TAPAS $

Vrata Pod Zidom 4   ☎05 281 20 04

"Tapas bar" and "reasonable prices" are not words that usually pop up in the same sentence. But Segutra, located on a small side street near Rovinj's harbor, makes that combination seem as natural as prosciutto on melon: most of the tapas can be had for between 12 and 17 kn, whether you're interested in fish, cheese, veggies, or meat (if you like prosciutto, you're in luck). The sandwiches and main courses aren't badly priced either. Perfect for a full meal or if you just need a quick bite to tide you over. The service is fast and the staff is friendly. And despite being located on a very narrow street, Segutra has a fair bit of outdoor seating—and free Wi-Fi. Doubles as an excellent place to grab a drink (beers and wines are both 20-30 kn) while nibbling on a bit of truffle cheese.

i Tapas 12-17 kn. Sandwiches 25-40 kn. Entrees 45-80 kn.

BALBI
ITALIAN $$

Trg G. Matteottija   ☎05 281 72 00

Tapas bar, pizzeria, ice cream joint—great, but where do I go in Rovinj if I want a real sit-down meal and don't want to break the bank? The answer is simple: Balbi. Located in a small square in the heart of Stari Grad, Balbi offers Italian cuisine and seafood at exceptionally reasonable prices. Maybe that's because the actual restaurant takes up so little real estate; almost all of the seating is outside, so be sure to bring a sweater if the temperature's dropping. For the cheapest options, turn to the pasta dishes, which have portions that far outstrip the 60 or 70 kn costs.

i Appetizers 50-70 kn. Pastas 60-70 kn. Entrees 80-100 kn.

NIGHTLIFE

PIASSA GRANDA
WINE BAR

Veli Trg 1   ☎098 824 322

The knowledgeable waitstaff is quick to call Piassa Granda the best wine bar in Istria, and its selection of wines from the region is unparalleled. But if you're the type who can't tell Riesling from Reese's Pieces, don't worry: the vibe is "relaxed drinking," not "Wine Snobs R Us." Relax at the small tables outside, covered with blue gingham tablecloths and bolted to the ground (otherwise, the uneven Rovinj streets would make spilling drinks inevitable). Chuckle at the slogans painted all around the walls "a meal without wine is breakfast," "wine is cheaper than therapy and you don't have to make an appointment." Then ask the waiters what they recommend. or just start out with malvazija, the local favorite: it's a dry white wine from Istria, and they've got more than a few varieties available. If a glass or two turns into a full bottle (definitely a possibility here), you can order some prosciutto, seafood, polenta, or a cheese plate: and again, you can ask them for help with pairings.

i Glasses of wine from 25-45 kn. Bottles 150-350 kn. ⏱ Open daily 10am-1am.

MEDITERRANEO
BAR

Sv. Križa 24   ☎091 160 7451

Rovinj does not have insane nightlife; no clubs or discotheques of note are to be found here. Instead, you'll find seaside cocktail bars, deplorable in theory but irresistible in practice. The best of these is Mediterraneo. Cheaper and more enjoyable than its next-door neighbor, Valentino (fewer canoodling couples), Mediterraneo boasts stunning views of Katarina Island to complement its extensive cocktail menu. The aesthetic is surreal, though not in a disturbing, David

rovinj

Lynch-ian kind of way—more like Lilly Pulitzer on Mars. Atop a rocky, uneven bit of coastline sit pastel-colored cushions, chairs, and wooden tables. Sit too close to the water and you'll risk getting doused with ocean spray every now and then. If it's sunny out, that might be just what you need to cool yourself off. If you're not feeling the cocktails (everything from sweet piña coladas to bitter Negronis), enjoy some San Servolo beer, a local wine, or some of the local liquors (pelinkovac, grappa, etc). If it's before 5pm or you just don't want to indulge, coffee and mocktails are well represented as well. Grab a cushion, lean up against the stone walls, and soak up the view. It may not be a rager, but it's pretty darned nice.

i *Cocktails 50-65 kn. Beers 20-40 kn. Wine 20-40 kn. ☼ Open daily 9am-2am.*

ESSENTIALS
Practicalities

- **MONEY:** ATMs are everywhere; look for the Bankomat sign. An exchange office can be found a few minutes walk from the bus station, at Trg na lovki.

- **POST OFFICE:** Via Matteo Benussi 4 ☎05 237 26 18. ☼ Open M-Sa 7am-8pm.

- **TOURIST INFO CENTER:** Obala Pina Budicina 12 ☎385 52 811 566.

Emergency

- **EMERGENCY NUMBER:** ☎112

- **HOSPITALS:** Rovinj Emergency Clinic, includes the Tourist Medical Center ☎52 813 004 ☼ Open 24hr.

- **PHARMACIES:** Pharmacy Blitva, Ulica Carrera 22a ☎52 830 832

Getting There

The closest airport to Rovinj is in Pula, about 25 miles south of Rovinj. Regular bus routes go from Pula to Rovinj. The route takes approximately 40 minutes and can cost 30-40 kn, though prices vary.

Getting Around

Rovinj is a small town and is easily walkable (especially if you stick to the Old Town on the peninsula). Be sure to wear shoes with traction, as the smooth-cobblestone streets are always slippery. Taxis can be hailed by the bus station, though check in advance if your hotel will send a car to pick you up; some family-run hotels will arrange this. Bikes and electric scooters can be rented from vendors in town. Boats can be hailed from around the harbor, either to take you to Saint Katarina Island or to take a tour. Most tours leave around 11:30am, and can last anywhere from an hour to all day.

split

Zagreb may be Croatia's official capital, but let's be frank: the action is here in Split. Located on a peninsula jutting into the Adriatic, Split is the gateway to Hvar, Brač, Korčula, and other famed Croatian islands. Here, you'll find world-class restaurants, beautiful beaches (some with actual sand!), and an old town built into a former Roman palace. Walk along the palm-tree-lined waterfront or explore the remains of Diocletian's Palace before jetting off to one of the many beaches for a swim. At night, take it easy at a wine bar or rage at one of the many clubs, which cater to tastes from techno to karaoke.

ACCOMMODATIONS

HOSTEL SPLIT BACKPACKERS (1 AND 2)
HOSTEL $

Kralja Zvonimira 17; Poljišanska 18   ☎02 178 24 83 www.splitbackpackers.com

A hostel so nice they made it twice, Hostel Split Backpackers has two locations in Split. Both are great places to crash. The beds are roomy and large, with personal outlets, lights, and curtains for added privacy. Each also comes with a locker for extra security. Showers and common spaces are well maintained in both locations. The atmosphere is a little more low-key than some of Split's party hostels, but you'll still be able to find a crew of tourists ready to rage. Even better is the late checkout: sleeping until 11am never felt so good.

i *Dorms 170 kn. ☑ Reception 24hr.*

KISS HOSTEL
HOSTEL $

Stari Pazar 2   ☎095 838 4437

This is the rare hostel where top bunks are preferable to those on the bottom, the reason being the exceptionally small space between the two. That unfortunate fact aside, Kiss Hostel is a solid choice for accommodation in Split. Located in the heart of the city (it's just steps from the Peristyle and the cathedral), Kiss Hostel offers comfortable beds, air conditioning, and well-kept showers. Common areas are small, but that encourages bonding.

i *Dorms 140 kn in the summer, 100 kn during the off season. ☑ Reception 24hr.*

HOSTEL MANUELA
HOSTEL $

Radmilovića Ulica 14   ☎098 954 14 51

Hostel Manuela may not be the most polished hostel in Split, but its comfy beds and secure location make it a solid place to crash. The hostel, frankly, looks like your run-of-the-mill household; there is little to suggest that this is a professional hostel, beyond the locks on every door and the presence of four or five bunk beds in every dorm room. Still, the staff is friendly, the beds are comfortable, and it is a professional hostel: Wi-Fi, computer access, and laundry (for 50 kn) all provided.

i *Dorms 180 kn. ☑ Hours vary; call to be let in.*

HOSTEL SPLIT WINE GARDEN
HOSTEL $

Poljana Tina Ujevica 3/3   ☎09 848 08 55

Don't let the name put you off (or entice you beyond reason). Hostel Split Wine Garden is not a boozer's paradise, but rather a perfectly nice hostel with a terrace partially covered by a grapevine. Located just behind the national theater (dangerously close to the best ice cream shop in town, Luka Ice Cream and Cakes), Hostel Split Wine Garden offers comfortable rooms and a tranquil terrace to relax on—you'll need it after hiking up and down Marjan, which is also nearby. Lockers and air conditioning provided.

i *Dorms from 160 kn. ☑ Reception 24hr.*

SIGHTS

GALERIJA MEŠTROVIĆ
GALLERY

Šetalište Ivana Meštrovića 46   ☎02 134 08 00

One visit to Galerija Meštrović, and you'll know that sculptor Ivan Meštrović was no starving artist. Though he fled to the US in the 1940s (he was no fan of Marshal Josip Broz Tito), he intended this palatial villa to be his place of retirement. Today, it stands as a museum devoted to his idiosyncratic work. Meštrović was deeply concerned with religious themes, a fact that's very much evident in his striking sculptures of Jesus Christ, St. John, Moses, and a host of other biblical figures. Further proof can be found in a renovated chapel down the road (your admission ticket can be used here), which houses a series of Meštrović's wooden reliefs depicting the life of Christ. If the art isn't your cup of tea, just revel in the splendor of the estate. In terms of retirement homes, it's no palace of Diocletian, but it's still pretty darn nice.

i *Admission 40 kn; also buys admission to the Crikvine-Kaštele.* ⏰ *Open May-Sept Tu-Su 9am-7pm; Oct-Apr Tu-Sa 9am-4pm, Su 10am-3pm.*

CATHEDRAL OF SAINT DOMNIUS
CHURCH

Near Peristil

The oddest thing about Split's cathedral is just how hard it is to take in. This is a monumental building, but the narrow streets of Split (it's located within the framework of Diocletian's Palace) make it difficult to really see; dig all the camera-happy tourists desperately trying to fit it into their frames. Of course, there's an easy solution: just go inside. From the relics in the treasury to the stunning heights of the bell tower, Split Cathedral is a dazzling monument that reminds you that, yes, things happened here post-Diocletian (even though it was originally built as the emperor's mausoleum, which explains its decidedly non-orthodox architecture). You'll see the bones of saints, a very mildewy crypt, and some wood purportedly from the cross Christ was crucified on. Climb up to the bell tower for the best view of Split; not even the top of Marjan can beat this.

i *15 kn for admission to the cathedral, crypt, and nearby Jupiter's Temple. 45 kn for all that jazz plus the bell tower and the treasury.* ⏰ *Open M-Sa 8am-7pm, Su 12:30-6pm.*

FROGGYLAND
GALLERY

Ulica Kralja Tomislava 5   ☎098 264 373 www.froggyland.net

Do cathedrals make you yawn? Do Roman ruins leave you unmoved? Are art galleries your cure for insomnia? Then proceed with haste to Split's weirdest attraction, a museum unlike any other in Croatia (and possibly the world). This is Froggyland, a century-old collection of stuffed frogs created by taxidermist Ferenc Mere. Yet this is no ordinary collection of stuffed frogs (if such a thing exists): these frogs, 507 of them in total, are posed in a variety of comic scenes that mimic human life. We see frogs getting shaved at the barber, going to school, cheating at cards. This is not a museum of students of biology, but for students of humanity. Our foibles, our fears, our frailties are captured in these frogs.

i *Admission 35 kn.* ⏰ *Open daily 10am-10pm.*

GALLERY OF FINE ARTS
MUSEUM

Ulica Kralja Tomislava 15   ☎02 135 01 12 www.galum.hr

Due to its stunning location on the coast, the Galerija Meštrović is undoubtedly the flashiest art museum in Split. But visitors to the city's Gallery of Fine Arts won't be disappointed; this is one of the best institutions in Split. The collection focuses on Croatian artists, though there are a few foreign heavyweights—including Albrecht Dürer, represented by a print of Melencolia I. The museum is organized chronologically, though the 1400 to 1900 section is tiny. Aside from a few highlights, like the Dürer and a striking stone relief of Saint Jerome, you can speed through this section quickly and head over to the selection of modern, high modern, and postmodern works. These range from naïve oil and glass paintings to satirical sketches of Croatian cultural bigwigs (including Ivan Meštrović himself) to vibrantly colored abstract works from the 1960s. The collection is large, varied, and impressive.

i *20 kn.* ⏰ *Open Tu-Sa 10am-9pm.*

SPLIT CITY MUSEUM (MUZEJ GRADA SPLITA)
MUSEUM

Papalićeva Ulica 1   ☎02 136 01 71 www.mgst.net

With daily opening hours from 9am to 9pm, Muzej Grada Splita is the city museum that never sleeps. That gives you all the time you'll need to explore these varied, intriguing collections, which cover just about every aspect of Split's history. We recommend going after a few days in the city, which'll give you a new perspective on now-familiar sights. Here's an example: that black sphinx by the cathedral? Farmers used to cover their eyes as they walked past, for fear that they would be cursed by the pagan evil eye.

The museum is not organized chronologically, but you'll get a sense of Split's rollicking history (it was ruled by Venetians at one point, and some wanted it to join with Italy rather than a unified Croatian state) while marveling over swords, vintage photographs, and original sculptural decorations from the cathedral's bell tower.

i *20 kn, students 10 kn. ☑ Open daily 9am-9pm.*

FOOD

BUFFET ŠPERUN
Sperun 3
CROATIAN $$
☎02 134 69 9

Hearty Dalmatian cuisine is the order of the day at Buffet Šperun, a small, appealingly rustic restaurant just steps from Split's waterfront. The cozy interiors and painted wooden walls give it a sort of country inn feel, even though you can easily walk here from Split's urban center. Seafood and meat dominate the menu, though pasta dishes pop up here and there. Check out the specials menu, which is usually very affordable. If you're not impressed by Split's flashier restaurants, set up shop here. You'll leave full, and so will your wallet.

i *Appetizers 50-70 kn. Entrees 50-130 kn. ☑ Open daily 9am-11pm.*

KOBAJE
Vukovarska 35a
CROATIAN $
☎02 153 70 09

Beer and sausages. That's what Kobaje offers—their slogan is "craft beer and street food"—and how can you argue with that? Not only is their selection of beer among the best in Split (certain bars specialize in Croatian craft beer, but nowhere else has the international selection), their meat-heavy menu is one of the cheapest. Most sausages can be had for under 20 kn, while the sandwiches and burgers fall between 30 and 60 kn. More money for you to spend on beer! The crisp house lager is only 15 kn for half a liter—again, a better deal than you'll find anywhere else in town. Aside from a few poorly named menu items ("Afternoon Quickie," "Ménage à Trois," and "One Night in BangCock" all make appearances), Kobaje is a home run. It's a bit of a walk from Split's center, but definitely worth it.

i *Sausages 20 kn. Entrees 30-60 kn. ☑ Open M-F 10am-midnight, Sa-Su 5pm-midnight.*

MAKROVEGA
Leština Ulica 2
VEGETARIAN $
☎02 139 44 40 www.makrovega.hr

If you're a vegetarian, you're probably used to having your meals at restaurants dictated for you. The one salad on the menu? Yeah, that's what you're having. Makrovega, despite being a vegetarian/vegan restaurant, won't buck that trend: they have a daily menu available for 60 kn, and that's what you're going to get. Lack of choice aside, the folks at Makrovega know how to put on a fantastic meal: Dalmatian classics like gnocchi happily rub shoulders with seitan and tofu. Just make sure you have Makrovega's address written down before going out—you'll never find it otherwise.

i *Daily menu 60 kn. ☑ Open M-F 9am-9pm, Sa 9am-5pm. Closed Sunday.*

ADRIATIC SUSHI AND OYSTER BAR SPLIT
Carrarina Poljana 4
SUSHI, SEAFOOD $$
☎02 161 06 44

Do you love fish but hate Croatian cuisine? Just head over to Adriatic Sushi and Oyster Bar, where you can savor fresh fish in a wholly different manner. The prices may be a little steep—expect to pay between 40 and 60 kn for four sushi rolls—but it's still one of the best places to indulge in seafood. At 14 kn, however, the oysters are reasonably priced—and given the fact that *Condé Nast*

Traveler named "eating oysters in Croatia" as one of the essential things to do in Europe before you die, there's no reason not to indulge. To accompany all this, we recommend a glass of Pošip.

i Sushi rolls 40 and 60 kn. Oysters 14 kn. ☉ Open daily 1-11pm.

KITCHEN 5
CROATIAN $$

Ulica Kraj Sv. Marije 1 ☎02 155 33 77

Spend a little time in Split and you'll realize one thing: these restaurants are big on tradition. For a fresher take on Dalmatian cuisine, check out Kitchen 5, a hip new spot just steps from Narodni Trg. Menu highlights include the very filling salads (if the tuna salad is on the specials list, be sure to order that) and the charmingly small hamburger. Sit at a high table inside or in the small outdoor terrace.

i Salads 40 kn, entrees 80-100 kn. ☉ Open M-F 8am-midnight, Sa-Su 8am-1am.

VEGE
VEGAN $

Off Poljana kneza Trpimira ☎095 896 51 86

Split can get expensive, and one of the easiest ways to cut costs is by avoiding sit-down restaurants. If you want to stay healthy while sticking to fast food stands, then head directly to Vege, a vegan fast food joint located near Split's port. Enjoy a soy burger, fried seitan, or just a healthy helping of basmati rice with rich tomato sauce. Once your meal is served, you get free rein with a variety of spices and sauces, letting you add all the savory delight you need to a vegetarian meal.

i Meals 40-50 kn. ☉ Open daily 9am-11pm.

NOSTRESS BISTRO
CROATIAN $$$

Ulica Iza Lože 9 ☎099 498 18 88 www.bistro-nostress.com

We'll be frank. NoStress Bistro's name makes it sound like a budget hostel. Besides, unless you're eating at one of those sushi places where they serve the fish that kills you if it's not prepared right, how stressful is eating at a restaurant? Issues of branding aside, NoStress Bistro is an excellent choice for lunch or dinner in Split. Located in Narodni Trg, NoStress Bistro offers a menu full of Dalmatian classics, from fish stew to gnocchi with octopus. Regional specialties like olive oil and truffles are often highlighted in these dishes. For dinnertime entertainment, try to nab one of the tables that looks out onto the square; all the better for people watching.

i Meals 90-300 kn. ☉ Open M-Th 7am-1am, F-Sa 7am-2am, Su 7am-1am.

BRASSERIE ON 7
RESTAURANT $

Obala Hrvatskog Narodnog Preporoda 7 ☎02 127 82 33

You may not be able to wake up for breakfast after a night out in Split, but should you find yourself awake before 11:30am, proceed directly to Brasserie on 7, a resort-like restaurant on the waterfront. The lunch and dinner menus verge on the wallet-busting, but breakfast entrees are kept between 60 and 80 kn; highlights include the fresh fruit platter, cinnamon toast, and omelettes made with prawns. If you need a little hair of the dog to get you through a nasty hangover, know that Brasserie on 7 has the best beer list on the Riva. Smoothies, however, are upwards of 40 kn and not exceptionally large: they're tasty, but not necessarily worth it.

i Breakfast 60-80 kn. ☉ Open daily 8am-11pm.

DIOCLETIAN'S WINE HOUSE
WINE HOUSE $$

Julija Nepota 4 ☎099 564 71 11 diocletianswinehouse.com

If you can't enjoy any meal without the accompaniment of fermented grape juice, we have just the restaurant for you. Diocletian's Wine House, located on a narrow street in the former palace area, offers tasty chicken, beef, and fish dishes, all of which taste much better with a glass of Pošip, Malvazija, Crljenak

Kaštelanski, or whatever unpronounceable wine you choose from the extensive menu. Sit outside on the quiet street, or relax in the air-conditioned interior. Despite the restaurants name, the decor is more Restoration Hardware than Roman Empire.

i *Entrees 70-140 kn. ☺ Open daily 8am-1am.*

NIGHTLIFE

PARADOX WINE & CHEESE BAR
Utica Poljana Tina Ujevica 2

WINE BAR

☎02 139 58 54

Despite the name, there's nothing difficult to understand about Paradox Wine & Cheese Bar: it's simply the best place to get a glass of wine in Split. The selection of Croatian grapes is unparalleled, and since you likely haven't heard of any of them, you'll be delighted to learn that the menu is organized by taste and strength. Of course, some of these are far more familiar than you think—if you get a glass made from Crljenak grapes, know that you're ordering Croatian Zinfandel. Be sure to supplement your boozing with a cheese plate, most of which come with Croatian jam as well; these cheeses are slightly more international, though Croatia is obviously well represented.

i *Wines by the glass 20-35 kn. ☺ Cheese plates served M-Sa 11am-11pm, Su 3-11pm. Open M-Sa 9am-midnight, Su 3pm-midnight.*

LEOPOLD'S DELICATESSEN BAR
Ujevićeva Poljana 3

BAR

☎095 538 5129

You've probably guessed that a "delicatessen bar" isn't exactly the liveliest place in Split, but it's hard to argue with a place where you can down a great beer, then make your own sandwich. Leopold's is devoted to Croatian craft beer—their lengthy menu includes tasting notes for each brew—and the low-key atmosphere makes it a perfect place to really savor your glass of Nova Runda pale ale. The seating is almost exclusively outdoors, which is perfect for the warm Croatian summers. For the adventurous, the bar offers donkey sausage.

i *Beers 13-40 kn. ☺ Open M-Th 8am-1am, F-Sa 8am-2am, Su 8am-1am.*

TO JE TO
Ulica Tome Nigerova

BAR

www.facebook.com/ToJeToCaffe

You don't like techno or flashing lights, so the bigger clubs are out of the question, but you also want a right that's a little less sedate than chilling at a wine bar. It's a dilemma, but the solution is simple: go to To Je To. This small bar, located near Marmontova Ulica, is well worth a visit for its cheap prices, selection of Croatian craft beers, and appealingly rowdy atmosphere. Trivia nights, live music, and karaoke are all part of the weekly schedule. The last of these occurs every Friday, and its low-rent energy makes it absolutely essential for any vacationer in Split. Even if you don't get to scream into a microphone, TJT is a load of fun. Best deal beyond beer: a Croatian rakija taster for 50 kn.

i *Beers 16-20 kn. ☺ Open M-Th 8am-1am, F-Sa 8am-2am, Su 9am-midnight.*

FIGA
Ulica Andrije Buvine 1

BAR

☎02 127 44 91

Figa bills itself as a cocktail party in the street and that's impossible to dispute. Located on a stepped street just off of Maruliceva Ulica, a thoroughfare connecting Narodni Trg and Figa, this bar puts out cushions and small tables for its customers to chill out on. Walk by and you'll feel like you've crashed a party—so why not sit down and join it? The cocktail list stretches ever so slightly more than the usual fare, while beers from Istrian craft brewery San Servolo liven up the menu. If you need something to slow down your alcohol consumption, grab a tasty fruit smoothie.

i *Beers 20-25 kn. Cocktails 40-50 kn. ☺ Open M-Th 8am-1am, F-Sa 8am-2am.*

split

CAFFÉ GALERIJA
BAR

Ulica Kralja Tomislava 15   ☎02 135 01 12 www.galum.hr

Why is Split's best cafe-bar located in the city's Gallery of Fine Arts? We have no clue, but the combination of solid drinks, live music, and a garden courtyard turns out to be damn near irresistible and far more unique than the other cafe-bars in the city. Enjoy piano music as you sip a local liquor (try borovnica, based on blueberries, for an exceptionally sweet drinking experience), or take advantage of the long list of teas.

i Liquors 10-18 kn. Beers and wines 20-30 kn. ☺ Open Tu-Su 10am-9pm.

RIVA BARS
BARS

Riva

It's difficult to recommend any particular bar on the Riva, but it's also impossible to ignore them. This is one of the nicest streets in Split; even after dark, the view of the port is magnificent. Crowds gather nightly; the energy is palpable. It's a great place to spend a few hours talking or to get riled up before heading to a club. The bad news, of course, is that most of these bars are fairly generic. They all serve more or less the same cocktails (mojitos, check; Long Island iced teas, check) and shooters (you can gauge how "classy" a particular establishment is by whether they offer BSOs or Bloody Screamin' Orgasms). They all have approximately the same prices (that is, slightly too high). Here are a few distinguishing characteristics: Caffé Gentile offers a martini endorsed by Dolce & Gabbana. Twins and St. Riva both offer two slightly different varieties of Long Island iced tea; one with Coca Cola, and one with cranberry juice. Adriana has comfy seats. Cakula has a better than average beer selection: Brooklyn Lager, anyone?

ESSENTIALS

Practicalities

- **MONEY:** ATMs are located throughout the town; there are several Splitska Banka ATMs located on the Riva, for instance.

- **POST OFFICE:** Papandopulova Ulica 1 ☎02 134 80 74. ☺ Open M-F 7am-8pm, Sa 7am-1pm. Closed Sunday.

- **TOURIST INFORMATION CENTER:** Peristil ☎02 134 56 06. ☺ Open M-Sa 8am-9pm, Su 8am-8pm.

Emergency

- **EMERGENCY NUMBER:** ☎112

- **HOSPITALS:** Klinički Bolnički Centar Split, Spinčićeva 1 ☎02 155 61 11.

- **PHARMACIES:** Gundulićeva 52 ☎02 134 07 10. ☺ Open M-F 7am-8pm, Sa 7:30am-3pm. Closed Sunday.

Getting Around

The attractions in Split's old town are easily walkable; in fact, the narrow nature of many of these streets makes car or rail transport impossible. Public buses connect the Split city center with the suburbs, as well as neighboring cities like Omis (bus number 60) and Trogir (bus number 37). Tickets can be purchased at Tisak kiosks or on the bus.

croatia

trogir

You ever see that mo̶In Bruges? With the two Irish gangsters hiding out in a small, well-preserved med̶ ̶town in Belgium? Where all the streets are narrow, all the art is religious, and̶ ̶y other staircase is too small for fat American tourists to fit through? Well, im̶ ̶that with the temperature doubled, and you've got a pretty good picture of ̶a time machine of a city located near Split. But despite its proximity to on̶ ̶batia's party havens, Trogir is a quiet, placid town; one of the coolest sights̶ ̶eum run by nuns, for heaven's sake. Come for the food, the architecture, ̶a sponges they sell at every street corner. Stay for the relaxed cafe bars on̶ ̶ront, or hop on the bus to Split when night falls; you'll be there soon enoug̶

ACCO̶ ̶IONS

HOST̶

HOSTEL $
☎091 579 21 90

̶stel isn't in the main town, don't let that dissuade you. Trogir is ̶ting to this hostel from the bus station takes minutes, despite ̶u cross two bodies of water while doing it. This one-floor hostel ̶arge dorm rooms. Lockers and towels are provided.

i ⏱ *Reception open until 11pm.*

̶IR
̶27

HOSTEL $
☎092 305 20 05

̶s are not UNESCO-listed. Technically, neither is City Hostel Trogir. ̶ostel, housed in a 14th-century building, is located within Trogir's ̶which is UNESCO-listed as a whole. So that's probably as close as ̶get. But hey—that's pretty darn close! Fortunately, the rooms have ̶vated significantly since the 14th century, and the plumbing goes way ̶chamber pots. Rooms boast big beds and lockers; if you need a bite, ̶a restaurant downstairs. If you're flying into Split Airport, transportation ̶e arranged.

̶orms 149 kn. ⏱ *Reception 24hr.*

̶HTS

̶OWN OF TROGIR MUSEUM

MUSEUM

Ulica Gradska Vrata 4   ☎02 188 14 06 muzejgradatrogira.blogspot.com

This museum is actually composed of three separate parts: one focuses on life in Trogir generally, one pays particular attention to stone working in Trogir, and one houses the works of Cata Dujšin, a Croatian painter born in Trogir in 1897. Naturally, the one focusing on life in general is the biggest; there's information about the city's many rulers, from the French to the Venetians. Marvel at remnants of figureheads from Turkish ships, old native dress, and photographs of Trogir in the early 19th century. Though smaller, the stoneworking rooms and the Dujšin Gallery have their own charms: Dujšin's self-portraits are particularly captivating.

i *20 kn, students 15 kn.* ⏱ *Open daily June 9am-noon and 5-8pm; July-Aug 9am-noon and 6-9pm; Sept 9am-noon and 5-8pm; Oct-May 9am-2pm.*

CATHEDRAL OF ST. LAWRENCE

CHURCH

Gradska Ulica

If you do one thing in Trogir, make it going to this cathedral. Even the entrance is historic—the portal is the one surviving work of Radovan, a mysterious sculptor who lived in Trogir (maybe) and attained legendary status due to... well, this portal. It all sounds a little circular, but the art itself hold *up. Inside, you've got* shockingly high ceilings, as well as a treasury chock full o*elics: bones, fingers,* you name it. The treasury also includes a gift shop, but *ar as we could tell* they weren't selling off any relics. It'd be too difficult to *a finger through* customs anyway. If you're not feeling dizzy, then take a wa *to the top of the* bell tower. Though it's a bit cramped at the top, the view is *it.*

i 25 kn. Children under 14 not allowed in bell tower. ⏰ Open M-Sa 8an

KAIROS COLLECTION
Trg Ivana Pavla II

11am-6pm.

MUSEUM

What's the Kairos collection like? Well, we'll give you one h is run by a nun, which should give you an idea of what you'l *ket desk* paintings? Check. (Who is Saint Spiridion, anyway?). Churc *ligious* Check—hymns in Croatian, old vestments, etc. And then there *lalia?* fragment that gives the museum its name: a third-or-fourth-c *tone* carving depicting Kairos, Zeus's youngest son and god of the f Isn't this a little too pagan for the Benedictine monastery the K° *a* is housed in? We don't care; the art is good, and well worth the 3c

i 30 kn. ⏰ Open daily 8am-1pm and 3-6:30pm.

FOOD

KONOBA TOMA
Šubićeva Ulica 44

CRC

☎091 781 71 42 ʋww.konoba

For hearty grill fare, there's no better choice in Trogir than Konoba meat-centric tavern just steps from the water. Beef marinaed in wine, ti sages with raw onions, and, of course, a whole lot of fish: nese are just so the highlights. Though the prices are on the higher side, hey're far lower the nearby Restoran Don Dino.

i Most entrees 80-100 kn. Cevapčići 58 kn. ⏰ Open daily 11am-midnight.

POP-UP SHOPS ON THE MAINLAND

STREET FOOD

Here's a fun game to play: walk through the old town of Trogir and try to find restaurant that does not boast "Dalmatian Specialties" and is not affiliated wit a hotel. These are all fine dining options, but as you might imagine, they're a little on the pricier side. For the best fast food in Trogir, walk across Trogirski Most and take a left, where you'll find a small array of pop-up shops and fast food stands. Though the many souvenir stands may make this look like a tourist trap, you're likely to find more locals hanging out around here; if you want to eat cheaply in Trogir, this is where you go. Check out sandwich joint Big Mama or the eclectic TUO Bikoni (open daily 9am-11pm), which serves shrimp for 20 kn and pizza for 10 kn; the shrimp is fried right in front of you.

⏰ Hours vary.

NIGHTLIFE

CAFFE TROGIR
Trg Ivana Pavla II

BAR

You might think the Trogir waterfront is the most scenic place to drink, but you'd be wrong. Here in Trg Ivana Pavla II, you've got the Cathedral of St Lawrence on one side, the Duke's Palace on the other—the very essence of this medieval town can be found here. Naturally, that makes cocktail bar Caffé Trogir a pretty decent place to grab a drink. What distinguishes it from Trogir's many other cafe-bars? Well, primarily the location. And the slightly higher prices. But when you're kicking back with a Campari-orange and gazing up at the cathedral—well, you'll probably find that it's all worth it.

i Liquors 20 kn. Beers 20-25 kn. Cocktails 45-50 kn. ⏰ Open late.

croatia

BIG DADDY

Obana Bana Berislavića

We get it, Trogir; you're classy. You've been around for 2300 years. You have swanky hotels and classy restaurants galore. To be honest, it can be sickening. That's why it's good to have a bar like Big Daddy to add a little good-natured sleaze to Trogir. Why is it mafia-themed? Who knows, but it's certainly a nice contrast to the upscale hotel bars along the waterfront. Get a fifth of Smirnoff and four Red Bulls for 400 kn if you're feeling aggressive, or just stick to the beers and domestic liquors: kruškovac, anyone? Of course, sometimes it gets a little too trashy and depressing, such as when they have a promotion with Captain Morgan and the waitresses dress up like pirates. Oh well.

i Liquors 10-20 kn. Beers 20 kn. Cocktails 40-50 kn. ☼ Open late.

MARTININO

BAR

Hrvatskih Mučenika 2　　　　　　　　　　　　　　　☎021 882 515

Most of Trogir's cafe-bars are cafes first, bars second. Sure, you'll find people drinking at them, but it always seems so casual. Of course these people are drinking beer in the middle of the day, you think. This is Europe, after all! Martinino is not like that. It is a proper bar, and its plush black seating and snazzy, dimly lit interior reflects that. Don't worry—you can still get a coffee. The menu? Standard fare: Karlovačko, the regular assortment of cocktails and shooters. But despite its upscale look, Martinino has the best prices in town. Visit after 9pm on Wednesday or Saturday and all cocktails are only 25 kn. That's good at any exchange rate. Located just steps from the Trogirski Most, a bridge connecting the historic island to the mainland, Martinino is conveniently located—although you'll have to contend with heavy foot traffic as well as heavy noise from actual traffic. If it all gets to be too much, just duck inside—unlike most cafe-bars in Trogir, Martinino has a large interior.

i Beers 20-30 kn. Cocktails 40-60 kn. ☼ Open late.

ESSENTIALS

Practicalities

- **MONEY:** ATMs can be found easily in town; exchange offices are also prevalent.
- **POST OFFICE:** Gradska Ulica 53. ☼ Open daily 7am-9pm.
- **TOURIST INFO CENTER:** Trg Ivana Pavla II., Br. 1 ☎02 188 14 12.

Emergency

- **EMERGENCY NUMBER:** ☎112
- **HOSPITALS:** Hitna Pomoć Trogir. Kardinala Alojzija Stepinca 17 ☎02 188 14 61.
- **PHARMACIES:** Obala Bana Berislavića 15 ☎02 188 15 35. ☼ Open M-F 7am-7pm, Sa 7:30am-3pm.

GETTING AROUND

As a whole, Trogir is tiny. The part you want to see (the medieval town) is even smaller. Walking is the best bet.

zadar

Churches, liquor, and a pipe organ played by the ocean. What's not to like about Zadar? This Dalmatian city, the fifth-largest in Croatia, is widely renowned for its many churches and its natural beauty (just try to find space on the waterfront at sunset). But it's got far more than old buildings and clear water: with a thriving restaurant scene and decadent clubs in public parks, Zadar is a great place to indulge your inner hedonist. Not sure if you're ready for Split or Hvar? Warm up here. Just don't drink too much maraschino.

ACCOMMODATIONS

HOUSE HOSTEL ZADAR

HOSTEL $

Ulica Ljudevita Posavskog 14 ☎098 139 23 87 www.zadarhostel.weebly.com

Sure, it's not located within Zadar's old city walls, but House Hostel Zadar's spacious rooms and numerous amenities easily make up for the few extra minutes of walking—no bus or taxi necessary. Besides, you'll appreciate the proximity to the bus station if you oversleep and need to get there in two minutes (it's possible!). The large bedrooms are the main draw. The kitchen is neat and provides a variety of plates, cups, and utensils, but it's on the smaller side. The roomy bathrooms, however, provide some of the best water pressure in Croatia—you'll have a hard time dragging yourself out of the shower. Towels can be rented for 10 kn, and you can have laundry done for 40. Dorms only, although they're thinking of expanding soon.

i Dorms 150 kn in the summer, 100 kn during off season. ☷ Reception open daily 9am-2pm and 5-9pm, although late arrivals can be arranged.

OLD TOWN HOSTEL

HOSTEL $

Mihe Klaića 5 ☎099 809 32 80

For better or for worse, most of the action in Zadar is contained within its old city walls. So if you're spending more than a few nights in this Dalmatian city, you might as well book a room at the Old Town Hostel. Cheaper than renting one of the many private rooms in the city (dorms start at 120 kn during the summer), Old Town Hostel is conveniently located for just about anything you might want to do in Zadar. Housed in a centuries-old building, the rooms are surprisingly comfortable and spacious, though you should take advantage of the location by spending as little time inside as possible.

i Dorms 120 kn in the summer, 88 kn during off-season. ☷ Reception 24hr.

RETRO ROOMS ZADAR

GUESTHOUSE $$

Široca Ulica 12 ☎091 763 21 19 www.retroroomszadar.com

Truth be told, we have no idea what makes these rooms "retro"—the building they're housed in is surely one of the most modern in Zadar's old town. But let's not quibble about a name. The important thing is that Retro Rooms Zadar has rooms that are spacious, air-conditioned, and come with a kitchen (if Zadar's excellent-but-a-little-pricey restaurant scene isn't your jam).

i Rooms 380 kn. ☷ Owner available by phone or email anytime.

SIGHTS

SEA ORGAN

LANDMARK

They say there's nothing more relaxing than listening to the waves. Zadar's sea organ takes that thought to a whole new level. After the waterfront was destroyed during WWII, the city rebuilt it as one of the world's largest musical instruments. As waves crash against the stone waterfront, they produce alien harmonics—somewhere between whale song and Steve Reich's *Pendulum Music*. You'll hear low rumblings as you get closer, but the organ is best appreciated up close—dip your feet in the water and watch as different waves produce different sounds. If a boat comes by, get excited—the ripples are going to make things interesting. If that's not enough sensory stimuli for you, come during sunset.

i *On the northwest corner of the Old City peninsula. Admission free. ☾ Open 24hr.*

CHURCH OF ST. DONATUS
Trg Rimskog Foruma

CHURCH

☎02 331 61 66

Most of the churches in Zadar are pretty normal. St. Donatus? Not so much. Dating back to the ninth century, St. Donatus looks like nothing you've ever seen, unless you're a student of pre-Romanesque architecture. From outside, it looks like a stone cylinder with no windows; inside, it's a vast, cavernous space. Most striking is its sparseness; don't come here looking for shiny reliquaries or religious painting. You're here for the architecture, which is just as stunning if you're on the ground or upstairs in the gallery. We recommend saving it until last—it's the perfect antidote to all those boring normal churches.

i *20 kn, students 12 kn. ☾ Open daily Apr-May 9am-5pm; June 9am-9pm; Julu-Aug 9am-10pm; Sept-Oct 9am-5pm; closed Nov-March.*

MUSEUM OF ANCIENT GLASS
Poljana Zemaljskog odbora 1

MUSEUM

☎023 363 831 www.mas-zadar.hr

Is the Museum of Ancient Glass right for you? Well, try reading the following: Small bottles with bell-shaped body. Juggles with square body. Balsamarium with bell-shaped body. Bottles with flattened body. Bottles with biconical body. Bottles with spherical body. Bottles with belly-shaped body. Bottles with spindle-shaped body. Juglet with polygonal body. Still awake? You just might be able to handle the well-executed, well-laid-out, but stunningly narrow Museum of Ancient Glass. Housed in a 19th-century palace, the Palača Cosmacendi, this museum focuses on one thing and one thing only. You'll see glass urns from the first and second centuries, ancient materials for raw glass found in a shipwreck, and bizarre oddities like a fish-shaped bottle. You'll learn about the history of glass making and its history in Croatia. You probably already know whether or not you want to visit this museum.

i *30 kn, students 10 kn. ☾ Open daily 9am-9pm.*

FOOD

GROPPO
Široka Ulica 22

CROATIAN $

☎02 377 89 81 www.restaurant-groppo.com

Široco Ulica is filled with ice cream stands and cheap pizza joints, all housed in modern buildings that feel more like strip malls than Roman ruins. And then you get to Groppo. Shut off from the streets by an old stone wall, Groppo offers delicious Dalmatian fare (don't worry, there are no dogs on the menu), along with a carefully chosen wine and cocktail list. If you're going to splurge in Zadar, this is the place. You know it's a classy joint when they wrap the napkins with little pieces of twine.

i *Starters 60-80 kn. Entrees 70-140 kn. ☾ Open daily 8am-11:30pm.*

ATRIJ
Jurja Barakovića 6

CROATIAN $

☎02 331 64 24

What's the appeal of Atrij? Is it the distinctive outdoor seating, which consists of booths lined up along the outside wall? Is it the unparalleled people-watching that comes from such an arrangement? Is it the menu, which boasts tuna steak and pork medallions? No need to narrow it down to one: these are all good reasons to pay a visit to Atrij, located just a few minutes from Zadar's Museum of Ancient Glass. Perfect for a drink as well as a full meal, Atrij's location on a busy

zadar

pedestrian walkway means there's no shortage of entertainment to accompany a delicious meal or a tasty cocktail.

i *Entrees 70-90 kn. ⏲ Open daily 8am-1am.*

PASTA & SVAŠTA
ITALIAN $

Poljana Šime Budinića 1 ☎02 331 74 01 www.pastasvasta.com

Zadar has no shortage of places where you can really stuff yourself. Hunks of meat? Sure. Fish plates for two? No problem. But if the broiling sun doesn't exactly whet your appetite (or if you just want something that doesn't come with eyes), Pasta & Svašta is an excellent choice for some lighter fare. As you might be able to guess from its very rhyming name, it's all about pasta here. Choose from fusilli, pappardelle, gnocchi, or a variety of other types of pasta, then find a sauce that'll fit it best. Vegetables, prosciutto, bits of seafood—it's all up for grabs. If you're not sure that fusilli will stuff you, opt for stuffed ravioli for 10 kn extra, or explore their small but delectable meat and fish options. Best of all—they serve breakfast 9-10:30am and have a 45 kn brunch special (bruschetta and daily soup) 10:30am-noon.

i *Pasta with sauce 70-90 kn. Meat and fish entrees 100 kn. ⏲ Open daily 9am-11pm.*

IL PICCOLO
INTERNATIONAL $

Stomorica 6 ☎097 636 80 38 www.facebook.com/doportuna

Tucked away in a small street near the river, Il Piccolo is your best bet for cheap, fast food in Zadar; that is, cheap, fast food that doesn't come from a takeout joint unappealingly titled "FAST FOOD." The menu is small but covers a lot of ground: fish, pasta, salads, and wraps are all on the table, though there are only a few choices for each. You can take the meal away and eat down by the river, or just sit outside and people watch. See that dude at the other restaurant? He's paying more than you!

i *Entrees 40-60 kn. ⏲ Open daily until 10pm.*

NIGHTLIFE

LA BODEGA
BAR

Kalelarga, Široka Ulica ☎095 456 45 56 www.facebook.com/LaBodegaZadar

Want good Croatian wine? Go to La Bodega. End of story. Do not pass go, do not try the house malvazija at the random cafe/bar you just found. With over 300 varieties of fermented grape juice, La Bodega is undoubtedly the best wine bar in Zadar. For those who can't tell the difference between white and red, don't worry: they've got all the beer, spirits, and cocktails you need. And if you need a few munchies to sate you, they've got Dalmatian cheeses and meats to accompany all that fine wine. In general, these lean toward the pricier side; the wines, thankfully, are generally reasonably priced. They also offer brunch, although there is no such thing as a bottomless pitcher of Pošip. Get boozy anyway.

i *Glasses of wine 20-50 kn. Bottles 165-300 kn. Prosciutto and cheese 70-100 kn. ⏲ Open daily 7am-2am.*

LEDANA
CLUB

Perivoj Kraljice Jelene Madijevke ☎09 863 07 60 www.ledana.hr

When traveling in foreign countries, it's usually best to avoid parks after nightfall. If you do that in Zadar, however, you'll be missing out on one of the city's best clubs. Ledana, located in a mouthful of a park (ask directions at your peril, as it will mean pronouncing "Perivoj Kraljice Jelene Madijevke"), is not the pit of Bacchanalian decadence that an open-air club could be, but it's still great fun. Regular events like DJ battles and themed parties keep the atmosphere fresh, while illuminated fountains and cushions on the ground remind you that, yes, you're partying in a park. And not like in high school when you drank 40s at the local playground and got chased away by cops. Drinks are fairly standard, though not at all overpriced.

i No cover. Cocktails 40-50 kn. Shots 16-20 kn. ✪ Open daily 8pm-4am. Club open 11pm-4am.

THE GARDEN
BAR

Liburnska Obala 6   ☎02 325 06 31 www.watchthegardengrow.eu

Yes, Zadar has more than one club that's housed outside in a parklike area. But the Garden is not a poor man's Ledana. It's more like a bar that just happens to be outside (except for the bathrooms, thankfully), which gives it a casual, relaxed vibe. Located in a grassy area atop the city walls, this bar offers fantastic views of the inlet between the old town and the mainland. And since there's no shortage of couches to lie down on, you can also get some serious stargazing in. Or maybe you'll just feel the need to lie down after having a bit too much to drink. You see, the Garden is a real bar—not a cafe-bar with generic cocktails and the same three Euro light lagers. They've got Belgian, Scottish, and Croatian craft beer, cocktails that were invented after 1950 (dig the Barbarella, made with gin, ginger, lemon and apple juice, and mint), and food like algae and spring rolls. OK, so it's a hipster joint—but with that view, who can complain?

i Beers 18-30 kn. Cocktails 40-50 kn. ✪ Open daily 10am-1:30am.

ESSENTIALS
Practicalities

- **MONEY:** ATMs are plentiful. There is an exchange office at the bus station.

- **POST OFFICE:** Kralja S. Držislava 1. ☎02 322 23 55 ✪ Open M-F 7am-8pm, Sa 7am-7pm. Closed Sunday.

- **TOURIST INFO CENTER:** Mihovila Klaića 1 ☎02 331 61 66.

Emergency

- **EMERGENCY NUMBER:** ☎112

- **HOSPITALS:** Opća Bolnica Zadar, Bože Peričića 5 ☎02 331 56 77.

- **PHARMACIES:** Ulica Jurja Barakovića 2. ☎02 330 29 20 ✪ Open M-F 7am-8pm, Sa 7:30am-1:30pm, Su closed.

Getting Around

Zadar's town center is easily walkable. The bus station is about a 15min. walk from the old town.

croatia essentials

VISAS

Croatia is a member of the EU. Citizens of Australia, Canada, New Zealand, the US, and many other non-EU countries do not need a visa for stays of up to 90 days. Citizens of other EU countries may enter Croatia with only their national identity cards. Passports are required for everyone else. Despite being part of the EU, Croatia is not in the Schengen area, however holders of a Schengen visa are allowed to visit Croatia for up to 90 days without the need of an additional visa.

MONEY

Despite being a member of the EU, Croatia is not in the Eurozone and uses the Croatian kuna (HRK or kn) as its currency.

Tipping is not always expected, but often appreciated in Croatia. For bars and cafes, tips are not expected, but it is common to round up the bill. So if the bill comes to 18 kn, leave 20 kn. Tipping in restaurants is much more common, and you should tip your server about 10%, or 15% for really exceptional service. Taxi drivers also do not expect tips, but customers generally round up the bill.

ATMs in Croatia are common and convenient. They are often located in airports and major thoroughfares. Just look for a sign that says "Bankomat." The two major international money networks are MasterCard/Maestro/Cirrus and Visa/PLUS. To find out what out-of-network or international fees you may be subject to by using ATMs, call your bank.

DRUGS AND ALCOHOL

The minimum age to purchase alcohol in Croatia is 18, though technically there is no minimum age to drink alcohol (cheers!). Remember to drink responsibly and to never drink and drive. The legal blood alcohol content (BAC) for driving in Croatia is under 0.05%, significantly lower than the US limit of 0.08%.

CZECH REPUBLIC

Throughout the Czech Republic, the vestiges of Bohemian glory and communist rule can be found on the same block. More recently, the'90s sparked the transformation of this country into an alternative, electrifying country. Döner kebabs, bockwurst, and Czech cheeses are peddled side by side. Freewheeling youth and a relentless drive toward the modern mean endless streets of hip hangouts and vehemently chill attitudes, making Czech cities, especially Prague, some of the best student destinations in Europe. And even though the locals might be too cool for school they do appreciate a tenacity to learn, evident from all the Czechs who cheer your blatantly wrong attempts at their language. Whether they're dishing heapings of local cuisine onto your plate, sharing beers with you at a low-key Prague pub, or inviting you to a local party, the citizens will open their arms to you.

greatest hits

- **ART NOUVEAU'S POSTER BOY.** Get the full picture of the artist at the **Alfons Mucha Museum** (p. 113), which features original posters as well as other designs.

- **VITUS IS VITAL.** A trip to the Czech capital would not be complete without a visit to Prague Castle, in particular **St. Vitus Cathedral** (p. 123).

- **DRINK DRINK.** In case you had doubts, they named it twice: **Bar Bar** (p. 133) is one of the best spots in the city for nighttime drinks and international cuisine. Yum yum.

prague

Prague is the idyllic European city that European inflation hasn't yet found. Paris, budget version. In Prague, century-old tradition collides with Jewish history and modernization to bring you a city with a royal castle, the oldest operating synagogue in Europe, and quaint minimalist cafes. A true definition of Prague, however, would be: Gothic churches on Gothic churches. In Prague, you'll find all the Gothic churches you never knew you needed. If your visit is limited to the areas by the river—Old Town and the castle district—you'll hit the major sights, but will miss out on much of the city's charm. Tourists own the areas by the Vltava (you'll get really good at Segway-dodging), but the locals prefer neighborhoods like Vinohrady and Žižkov. Farther neighborhoods hold a reputation of a lively and interesting cafe and pub culture; Vinohrady is particularly well-known for catering to the LGBTQ+ community. Orienting yourself in Prague is made easy by the presence of the Vltava River, splitting the city in two. The most famous pedestrian bridge is the Charles Bridge, named after Prague's beloved Charles IV. Prague had more kings than just him, but you wouldn't know it by looking at its history. Not saying that the other kings were slackers, but Charlie was the real MVP. Besides the Charles Bridge, the castle in Hradčany, the astronomer's clock in Staré Město, and Letná Park in Holesovice are must-sees. As you cover the city on foot, consider seeing it from above at Letná Park (home to a giant metronome that replaced a Stalin statue), at the top of the clock tower, or at Vyšehrad (an old fortress). Prague's characteristic red rooftops and cobbled streets, somehow, look even more beautiful from on high.

ORIENTATION

The Vltava River runs through Prague, separating the city in two and making navigation infinitely easier. The more touristy areas hug the edges of the river—Josefov, Staré Město (Old Town), and Nové Město (New Town) can be found along the Vltava on the right bank from top to bottom, and Hradčany and Malá Strana on the left bank. On the left bank, farther from the center, you'll find Holesovice above Hradčany, and Smíchov below Malá Strana. On the right bank, farther out, you'll find Žižkov to the right of Staré Město, and Vinohrady to the right of Nové Město. Each neighborhood has its own reputation, though in general, the closer to Staré Město, the more touristy the establishments. On the other hand, the more there is to see. Neighborhoods like Staré Město, Nové Město, and Hradčany are replete with sights, while farther areas like Vinohrady and Žižkov feature fewer sights but a more authentically Czech experience.

ACCOMMODATIONS

Nové Město

MOSAIC HOUSE
HOSTEL $$

Odborů 278/4   ☎221 595 350 www.mosaichouse.com

True to its name, art installations greet you before you even step through the doors of Mosaic House. Giant mushroom sculptures stand close to the entrance; sculptures of men with umbrellas hang above. Inside, sculptures of headless human figures display information. The hostel is pricier than other Nové Město and Prague places, but the quality of the hostel reflects the extra cost. The common spaces look like the apartment you always thought you'd have in your 20s before you realized you were broke. Mosaic House also features their own Music Bar and Lounge, La Loca, revolutionizing the concept of "staying in." A fun night starts right downstairs. Moreover, Mosaic House sets itself apart by its commitment to their green initiative, realized through their energy, insulation, and water systems. Not to mention how green with envy your friends at other hostels will be.

i B: Národní třída. Turn left onto Spálená and then right onto Odborů. The hostel is on the right. Dorms 400-550Kč. Laundry 280 Kč. ☒ Check-in 3pm. Check-out 11am. Reception 24hr.

HOSTEL ANANAS
HOSTEL $

Václavské nám. 846/1   ☎775 112 405 www.hostelananas.com

Located off of Wenceslas Square, Hostel Ananas is new to the hostel scene, having opened in 2015 as the latest in the fruit-themed hostel collection. Close to both New Town and Old Town sights, Ananas, and the 24-hour McDonald's on the same street, could not be more convenient. While some of McDonald's portion sizes may seem huge, nothing about Ananas' rooms could be described similarly. The 8-bed rooms seem better equipped to be four-bed-rooms—as of now, only one thin person can fit between some of the bunk beds. Moreover, while some of McDonald's snacks are disappointingly low on meat, at Ananas, the see-through shower doors bring meat in great abundance. If communal nudity is bonding, visitors to Ananas are the best of buddies. Regardless, Ananas offers 24-hour reception, remarkably reliable Wi-Fi, and laundry facilities, making it one of the best options in the area.

i A: Můstek – A. From the station, walk down towards 28. října. The hostel is on your right. Dorms 330-400Kč. ☒ Check-in 1:30pm Check-out 10:30am. Reception 24hr.

HOSTEL ORANGE
HOSTEL $

Václavské nám. 781/20   ☎775 112 625 www.hostelorange.cz

Another in the fruit hostel series, Hostel Orange can be found on Wenceslas Square, close to the New Town sights and reasonably close to the Old Town ones as well. Each floor of the hostel is painted in a different color, which is probably best for getting lost college-aged kids back to their proper rooms. Among its facilities, Hostel Orange counts a common room, Wi-Fi, free towels, 24-hour reception and laundry services. Orange you happy you chose to stay here? Orange puns not included.

i A: Můstek – A. From the station, turn left to stay on Václavské náměstí. The hostel is on the right. Dorms 320-500Kč. ☒ Check-in at 1pm. Check-out at 11am. Reception 24hr.

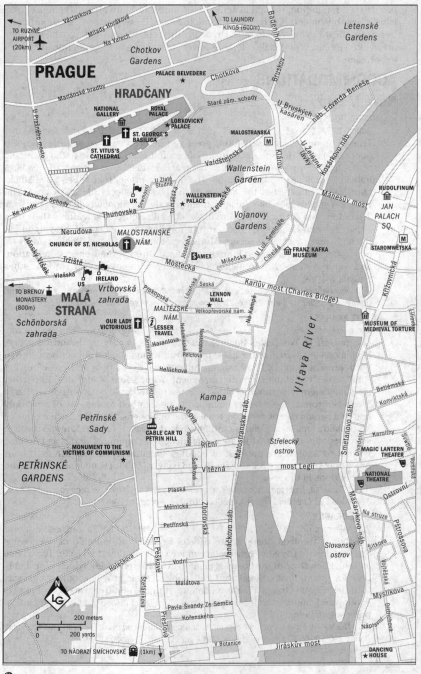

PRAGUE

HRADČANY

Letenské Gardens

Chotkov Gardens

TO LAUNDRY KINGS (600m)

TO RUZYNĚ AIRPORT (20km)

Václavkova

Milady Horákové

Na Valech

Badeniho

Bruskov

PALACE BELVEDERE ★

Chotkova

Mariánské hradby

Staré zám. schody

U Bruských kasáren

náb. Edvarda Beneše

NATIONAL GALLERY

ROYAL PALACE

LOBKOVICKÝ PALACE

ST. GEORGE'S BASILICA

MALOSTRANSKÁ Ⓜ

ST. VITUS'S CATHEDRAL

U Prašného mostu

Valdštejnská

Klárov

U železné lávky

Kosárkova náb.

Zámecké Schody

U Zlaté Studně

Wallenstein Garden

Mánesův most

RUDOLFINUM

JAN PALACH SQ.

Ke Hradu

Jánský Vršek

Thunovska

Sněmovní

UK

Tomášská

Letenská

WALLENSTEIN PALACE ★

Vojanovy Gardens

U Luž. Semináře

STAROMWĚTSKÁ Ⓜ

Nerudova

MALOSTRANSKÉ NÁM.

CHURCH OF ST. NICHOLAS ✝

Josefská

Cihelná

Křižovnická

Tržiště

Vlašska

US

IRELAND

AMEX

Mišeňská

FRANZ KAFKA MUSEUM

TO BRENOV MONASTERY (800m)

MALÁ STRANA

Vrtbovská zahrada

Mostecká

Lázeňská

Saská

Karlův most (Charles Bridge)

Schönborská zahrada

OUR LADY VICTORIOUS ✝

Prokopská

MALTÉZSKÉ NÁM.

LENNON WALL

Velkopřevorské nám.

Na Kampě

ⓘ LESSER TRAVEL

Harantova

Nebovidská

Nostecova

Pelcova

MUSEUM OF MEDIEVAL TORTURE

Hellichova

Karmelitská

Újezd

Kampa

Betlémská

Vltava River

Konviktská

Petřínské Sady

Všehrdova

CABLE CAR TO PETRIN HILL

Besední

Říční

Šeříková

Střelecký ostrov

Smetanovo náb.

Karoliny

Světlé

Vořišilská

Divadelní

MAGIC LANTERN THEATER

MONUMENT TO THE VICTIMS OF COMMUNISM ★

PETŘINSKÉ GARDENS

Vítězná

most Legií

NATIONAL THEATRE

Ostrovní

Masarykovo náb.

Plaská

Zborovská

Janáčkovo náb.

Na struze

Pštrossova

Mělnická

Petřínská

Slovanský ostrov

Sítkova

Voitěšská

Holečkova

Štefánikova

Preslova

El. Peškové

Vodní

Malátova

Myšlikova

Dittrichova

Náprstní

Pavla Švandy Ze Semčíc

Kořenského

V Botanice

Jiráskův most

DANCING HOUSE ★

TO NÁDRAŽÍ SMÍCHOVSKÉ 🚆 (1km)

N LG

0 — 200 meters

0 — 200 yards

czech republic

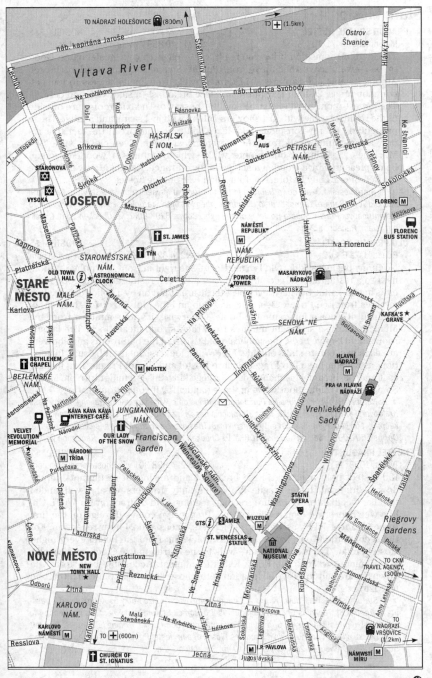

Staré Město

PRAGUE SQUARE HOSTEL

HOSTEL $$$

Melantrichova 471/10   ☎224 240 859 www.praguesquarehostel.com

The kind of rooms that bring you really, really close to your hostelmates. Good or bad—we'll leave that up to you. Prague Square is your standard hostel. Among its amenities are free Wi-Fi, free towels, free linens, access to lockers, common areas, 24-hour reception, and free breakfast (a sandwich and cereal). The largest rooms host eight; the smallest host two. The bathrooms are outside of the rooms—some with just showers, others with just a sink and a toilet. Those particularly energy-conscious (aka lazy) will take comfort in the fact that it's only a two-minute walk from the Astronomical Clock. Even closer is the Sex Machines Museum—a one-minute walk—which features a wooden woman being pleasured by a wooden machine in the entrance. Repent afterwards at the Church of our Lady Before Týn, four minutes from the hostel.

i A: Staroměstská. Walk down Kaprova in the direction of Maiselova toward St. Vitus Cathedral and Old Town Square. Turn right onto U Radnice, then left onto Staroměstská nám. Turn right onto Melantrichova. Prague Square Hostel is on the right. Dorms 620-780Kč. Check-in 2pm. Check-out 10am. Reception 24hr.

OLD PRAGUE HOSTEL

HOSTEL $$

Benediktská 685/2   ☎224 829 058 www.oldpraguehostel.com

No funny business, kids. Old Prague Hostel sits right in front of a police station, next to a restaurant-club combo, and near a Korean restaurant. Any good night ends in handcuffs, but maybe it's best those aren't put on by a police officer. Two minutes from the Prague Beer Museum Pub and the club Roxy, for the alcohol inclined, it's not a long stumble home. Otherwise, it's four minutes from the Municipal House and eight minutes from the Astronomical Clock. The largest rooms hold twelve beds, the smallest hold two, and the bathrooms and showers are each in separate stalls outside. Free Wi-Fi, lockers, linens, the usual. In addition, as a sister hostel to Prague Square Hostel and Hostel Prague Týn, meager as it may be, breakfast is included. As college kids, this is a major turn on. Mmm. Something to think about while in those handcuffs, if you get our drift.

i B: Náměstí Republiky. Cross Na Poříčí, and continue onto Palladium. Keep walking as you pass Králdovorská/Truhlářská street. Pass Revoluční, pass Pizza Nuova and turn immediately after, keeping it on your right. Turn left onto Benediktská. The hostel is on the left. Wheelchair accessible. Dorms 560-700Kč. Security deposit 100Kč. Check-in 2pm. Check-out 10am. Reception 24hr.

HOSTEL PRAGUE TÝN

HOSTEL $$

Týnská 1053/19   ☎224 808 301 www.hostelpraguetyn.com

Kid tested, nom approved. Free breakfast and an Indian restaurant literally downstairs from Hostel Prague Týn keep cranky travelers fed and well-tended to. Like wee babes, we require frequent feedings and distraction via Wi-Fi. Unlike wee babes, we require alcohol too. Prague Týn comes through on the first front with free Wi-Fi, as well as free lockers, linens and 24-hour reception. For the second, the Clock Tower Pub Crawl picks up from the hostel every night. Hostel Prague Týn is a four-minute walk to the Astronomical Clock, and equally, a four-minute walk to the Franz Kafka Monument. Accessible both from Old Town Square and Josefov, the location of this hostel is a major point of attraction for visitors.

i A: Staroměstská. Walk down Kaprova. Continue onto Nám Franze Kafky as Kaprova ends, passing in front of St. Nicholas Church. Continue as it becomes Staroměstské nám. As you reach the Ministerstvo pro místní rozvoj, turn right. Walk until you reach Týnská, turning left onto it. Turn left onto Týnská ulička, continuing as it becomes Týnská again. Hostel Prague Týn is on the left. Dorms 560-700Kč. Check-in 2pm. Check-out 10am. Reception 24hr.

HOSTEL HOMER

HOSTEL $

Melantrichova 465/11   ☎722 661 922 www.hostelhomer.com

They're like really into their own Simpsons theme, but it also feels like they've never actually watched the show. A sign in the bathroom informs you that Lisa would never flush a tampon, Maggie would never throw up all over the bathroom, and Bart would never leave a toilet unflushed. In our opinion, Bart would find that shit hilarious. Anyway. There's only one bathroom per floor—though the bathroom is really well cleaned and spacious. Rooms range from doubles to 16-beds with TJ-Maxx-y dividers stuffed between adjacent bunks. These beds are probably good for your back. In the same vein, the towels exfoliate nicely. If your hostelmates keep you up at night, turn to the pretty decent Wi-Fi for comfort. In addition to access to the internets, HomeR boasts 24-hour reception, free linens, free towels, a kitchen/common area, and free lockers. Also free smells. Next to an Italian restaurant, the entrance often smells like good eats. Among the hostel's redeeming factors, the location. This hostel is only two minutes away from the Astronomical Clock, and a short walk from quirky cafes and popular nightlife spots. For the stubbornly lazy, this place will be a home(R) for you.

i A: Staroměstská. Walk down Kaprova in the direction of Maiselova. Turn right on U Radnice, then left on Staroměstská nám. Turn right onto Melantrichova. Hostel HomeR is on the right, in the same entrance as Pizzeria Pulcinella. Dorms 450-590Kč. Security deposit 200Kč. Laundry available for 270Kč. ☼ Check-in 2pm. Check-out 10:30am. Reception 24hr.

FRANZ KAFKA HOSTEL

HOSTEL $

Kaprova 14/13   ☎222 333 116 www.hostelfranzkafka.com

A one-minute walk from St. Vitus Cathedral and, more importantly, adjacent to a pizza place, Franz Kafka Hostel's location does not disappoint. Throw in the free linens, free towels, free Wi-Fi, free lockers, and you could certainly do worse than this place. The rooms are spacious and well-kept and come equipped with a TV. They don't have 24-hour reception, but if you let them know when you plan to arrive, they will inconvenience someone on your behalf and make them let you in. On the other hand, the lights in the bathrooms and kitchen/common space turn off every few seconds or so, leaving you in the dark until you get the will to throw your hands in the air and wave them like you just don't care. But you do. You do care. It's especially fun when you're showering. Surprise bonus round: you picked one of the showers with low water pressure. Hop while rinsing your eye with a stream not unlike that of your grandpa with an enlarged prostate. Sorry, gramps. Wi-Fi doesn't quite reach the fifth floor, though fourth-floor folk seem to fare better. May the odds be ever in your favor. Showers and toilets are all found in one room, each in separate stalls. Though the person-to-shower ratio is high, as is the norm in hostels, you probably won't find yourself waiting for too long, particularly if you shower at odd hours. If you're morning-breathy, eye-squinty at like noon, you might have to ask the receptionist to turn on the electricity again. It's unclear if this a regular thing, but it seems this is the hostel's way of saying, "Who the hell wakes up past noon?" Really though, who the hell wakes up before noon?

i A: Staroměstská. Walk down Kaprova in the direction of Maiselova. The hostel is on the left. Dorms 400Kč. Security deposit 200Kč. Breakfast 110Kč. ☼ Check-in 2pm. Check-out 11am. Reception 9am-8pm.

Malá Strana

HOSTEL SANTINI PRAGUE

HOSTEL $$

Nerudova 211/14   ☎257 316 191 www.hostelsantiniprague.com

Hostel Santini can be found on Nerudova, a street that couldn't get more touristy if it wore an I <3 Prague shirt. Actually, it sells those. But here, touristy translates to safe, and slightly inflated prices come with the benefit of shops and restaurants that crowd this street and cater to visitors. In a time of desperate hunger or desperate souvenir needs, Nerudova does not disappoint. Santini faces the Romanian embassy, recognizable by its sculptures of two muscular men holding the weight of the structure. It's refreshing to see men carry their own weight for once. Hostel Santini occupies a historical building, reflected by the elegant interior that could be a hotel were it not for the snoring German next to you. Breakfast in the morning—a pre-packed sandwich and cereal—are not always satisfying, but free. While in Malá Strana, Santini is remarkably close to Hradčany as well, making it an ideal choice for the tourist trying to cover both.

i A: Malostranská. From the Metro, take tram 12, 20, or 22 in the direction of Smíchovské nádraží, and get off at Malostranské náměstí. From here walk onto Malostranské náměstí and continue onto Nerudova. The hostel is on the left. Dorms 560-600Kč. Laundry 200Kč. ☒ Check-in 2pm. Check-out 10am. Reception 24hr.

HOSTEL MANGO HOSTEL $
Míšeňská 68/8 ☎775 112 625 www.hostelmango.cz

Part of the fruit hostel group, Hostel Mango is the Malá Strana one of the bunch. Close to Karlův Most and the Lennon Wall, the sweetest thing about this mango is its proximity to both Malá Strana and Staré Město sights. The bathrooms, admittedly, leave much to be desired – when the showers become unintentional baths, you learn the importance of carrying shower shoes. This isn't where Kim Kardashian would stay, but you aren't Kim Kardashian. Unless you are. Hey, Kim K! While more luxurious options exist, Mango is cheap and accessible. 24-hour reception, free Wi-Fi, free towels, and laundry services certainly sweeten the deal some.

i A: Malostranská. From the station, turn right onto Klárov. Continue onto U lužického semináře. Turn right onto Míšeňská. The hostel is on the right. Dorms 369-539Kč. ☒ Check-in 1:30pm. Check-out 10:30am. Reception 24hr.

Hradčany

ARPACAY BACKPACKERS HOSTEL HOSTEL $$
Nerudova 223/40 ☎251 552 297 www.arpacayhostel.com

Straddling Malá Strana and Hradčany, Arpacay is your girl Miley, in multiple-bed dorm form. The best of both worlds, Arpacay offers easy access to the Prague Castle, as well as the Charles Bridge. What we mean to say is that Arpacay is hella convenient. Planted on picturesque (and equally, touristy) Nerudova Street, Arpacay is in the part of Prague that ends up on postcards. Though the building that Arpacay occupies hails from the 16th century, its facilities have caught up to the needs of present-day. Arpacay serves all-you-can-eat breakfast for 130Kč, and boasts 24-hour reception, free towel rental, free padlock rental, and free Wi-Fi in its included services. Unlike much of its competition, Arpacay's rooms—even those with the most beds—embrace the idea of "personal space." Sardines no more, visitors have plenty of room to be.

i A: Malostranská. From the subway stop, turn right onto Klárov. Walk down this street for one block, then turn right onto Letenská. Continue onto Malostranské náměstí, and then onto Nerudova. The hostel is on the right. 10-bed dorm 440-490Kč; 4-bed dorm 540-590Kč. Laundry 149Kč. Breakfast 130Kč. ☒ Check-in 2pm. Check-out 11am. Reception 24hr.

Vinohrady

CZECH INN HOSTEL $
Francouzská 240/76 ☎420 267 267 612 www.czech-inn.com

Planted in trendy Vinohrady, the Czech Inn offers everything ranging from private singles to 36-bed dorms, and a comfortable first-floor lounge with alcohol and coffee to tie it all together. The shared facilities are sleek and modern, and the hostel is outfitted with a basement bar, laundry services, and the ever-essential Wi-Fi. If you're toward the 36-bed end of the range, the experience in the actual dorm room is about as pleasant as an experience with 35 other people can be. It's something like Russ an Roulette, but chances are pretty good you won't get shot. Breakfast is served in the morning until noon for 150Kč, though there are also plenty of nearby cafes and restaurants for those willing to put on pants before eating.

i A: Náměstí Míru. Walk down Francouzská, which is on the southwest of the Metro station, near Retro Music Hall. The hostel is on your right. Dorms 400-500Kč, doubles 800-900Kč, singles 1800Kč. ☑ Check-in 3pm. Check-out 12pm. Reception 24hr.

Holešovice

▨ SIR TOBY'S HOSTEL
HOSTEL $
Dělnická 1155/24 ☎246 032 610 www.sirtobys.com

Equipped with a pub, breakfast for 150Kč, and reliable Wi-Fi, Sir Toby's is the whole package. Holešovice is at a distance from the center—accepting that, however, Sir Toby's is a solid deal. A well-kept kitchen and a nearby supermarket give thrifty travelers the option to cook rather than eat out. In addition, Sir Toby's offers 24-hour reception and free use of computers, hair dryers, converters, irons, and alarm clocks. Towels come at a 100Kč deposit and a 25Kč rental fee, but that's probably not a cost you'll want to skip out on. While "Sir Toby" may sound like a sex act, or something you'd name your miniature schnauzer, the hostel actually has pretty good vibes. All the shared rooms are reserved for those 18-39 years old, so there's a wealth of friends/drinking partners wandering about.

i C: Vltavská. Upon exiting the station, find Nábřeží Kapitána Jaroše on the south end of the station. Continue down this street onto Za Viaduktem and then onto Argentinská. Turn right onto Dělnická. The hostel is on the right. 12-bed dorms 400-500Kč; 4 or 5-bed dorms 500-800Kč. Self-service laundry 190Kč. ☑ Check-in 3pm. Check-out 11am. Reception 24hr.

PLUS PRAGUE
HOSTEL $
Privozni 1 ☎220 510 046 plushostels.com/plusprague

Sauna and pool access wir this hostel major points. And then a large lounge area, vending machines, and a nearby restaurant give this hostel the air of a nice hotel, but at broke backpacker prices. How else are you going to afford beer? It's at a bit of a distance from the center—approximately a 20-minute metro ride to the Astronomical Clock—but the facilities are nicer than what you'd find closer to Prague 1. 24-hour reception gives you the luxury of coming and leaving as you please and always finding staff available when you need them. Their restaurant and bar simplifies getting into bed after a crazy night; their 135Kč breakfast simplifies getting back out in the morning. For a little extra, you can get a padlock and a towel, and do your laundry here. Protect the bank; ward off the stank.

i C: Nádraží Holešovice. Upon exiting the station, turn left onto Plynární. Continue walking onto Ortenovo nám and then onto Přívozní. The hostel is on the left. Dorms 300-500Kč. Laundry 100Kč wash, 100Kč dry. ☑ Check-in 3pm. Check-out 10am. Reception 24hr.

SIGHTS

Nové Město

▨ ALFONS MUCHA MUSEUM
MUSEUM
Kaunický Palác, Panská 7 ☎420 224 216 415 www.mucha.cz

Much(a) to no one's surprise, the Alfons Mucha Museum exhibits a body of works by Alfons Mucha, as well as information on the artist and his life. Czech-born, Mucha's claim to fame came as he accepted a last-minute offer to create a poster for the Parisian actress Sarah Bernhardt. Bernhardt loved the poster, prompting Mucha's career. Mucha is best known for his representation of beautiful blonde

women (in case you were wondering where Cosmo gets their ideals), within the Art Nouveau style. Okay, sometimes they're brunette. Mucha himself rejected this label, however, claiming that his style was not tied to the artistic style of the time, rendering Mucha the original hipster. After World War I, Mucha designed Czechoslovakian banknotes and stamps, featuring images of the Prague Castle found in Hradčany. The bills were widely circulated, granting Mucha a significant position in both the artistic and political history of the region. As fascism entered the scene, Mucha was arrested, interrogated, and then he died. The museum honors the artist's legacy, and like any decent establishment, has a gift shop with Mucha to offer.

i B: Můstek - B. From the station, walk down Jungmannovo nám. toward Na Můstku, and continue onto Na Příkopě. Take the pedestrian tunnel, from which you'll exit onto Panská. The museum is on your left. 240Kč, reduced admission 160 Kč. ☑ Open daily 10am-6pm.

WENCESLAS SQUARE (VÁCLAVSKÉ NÁMĚSTÍ) SQUARE

Wenceslas Square, named after Bohemia's patron saint, Saint Wenceslas, functioned as a horse market in the Middle Ages. Quite a lot has changed since then—showering as a daily habit, for one, and the relevance of horse markets. Today's Wenceslas Square is a bustling block full of chain stores and vendors alike. The square serves as a central site in Prague, and fills regularly with tourists and locals passing through or visiting the National Museum, restaurants, or stores that stand on the Square. Throughout history, Wenceslas Square has held an important presence—in 1969, for example, Wenceslas Square was the site of Jan Palach's self-immolation protesting Soviet invasion. Today, Wenceslas is less about stirring up trouble, and more about stripping down. The Square is known for its strip clubs, and other similar services. During the day, it's much tamer however. Most tourists who visit New Town end up around the Square at some point. Stop by to see the statue of St. Wenceslas, and then check out David Černý's parody in the Lucerna Complex.

i A: Můstek - A. From the station, walk down Jindřišská.

DANCING HOUSE LANDMARK
Jiráskovo nám. 1981/6 ☎420 605 083 611

Nicknamed "Fred and Ginger," after the beloved dance duo in the early 1900s, the Dancing House presents a unique architectural feat. The building appears almost to be crooked or warped, and is said to resemble a pair converging together in dance, from where it gets its name and nickname. At the time of its construction, the building attracted significant criticism by critics who felt it clashed with its Art Nouveau surroundings. But buildings can have curves too, and public opinion has now grown to love and appreciate the Dancing House. At the top, the building features an international restaurant with a focus on French cuisine, appropriately named "Ginger & Fred" Restaurant. Precisely because the Dancing House was controversial at its inception, it has become a great tourist attraction and made an appearance on a series of architecture-themed 2000 koruna coins. Next in line: The Twerking House.

i B: Karlovo náměstí. From the Metro station, turn left onto Palackého nám. Turn right onto Rašínovo nábř. The building is on your right.

ST. HENRY'S TOWER TOWER
Jindřišská ☎420 224 232 429

The tallest freestanding belfry in Prague, St. Henry's Tower offers a view literally like that of no other bell tower. Despite its size, St. Henry's is often overlooked for other more out-there, in-your-face towers. St. Henry's has been reconstructed multiple times, following attacks and weather damage. The current tower stands at about 65 meters, composed of ten floors. Like any tourist site in Prague, St. Henry's has a restaurant, Zvonice, as well as a whiskey bar, a gallery, a museum,

prague

and an observation desk. St. Henry's Tower also features a carillon, and a bell preserved from 1518 on display in the restaurant.

i C: Hlavní nádraží. From the station, walk down Jeruzalémská. Turn left onto Senovážné nám. The tower is on the left. 100Kč, students 70Kč. ☼ Open daily Apr-Oct 10am-7pm; Nov-Mar 10am-6pm.

THE CHURCH OF OUR LADY OF THE SNOWS (KOSTEL PANNY MARIE SNĚŽNÉ)   CHURCH
Jungmannovo náměstí 753/18

The Church of Our Lady of the Snows was designed ambitiously, in the hopes of building a church comparable to the magnificent St. Vitus Cathedral. It never did realize the goals of its creators, however, and that is a sentiment we relate deeply to. Sorry, mom. As legend has it, the Virgin Mary came to a merchant in a dream and told him that she would make it snow, despite the heat, and that he should construct a church on that site. Hence, The Church of Our Lady of the Snows. War wreaked havoc on the structure, and it has undergone several renovations throughout history. While not built according to the original plans, the church is still considered significant in Prague, and features a notably high altar and impressive vaulted ceilings.

i B: Můstek – B. The church is right outside the station. ☼ Open daily 9am-6pm.

FRANCISCAN GARDENS (FRANTIŠKÁNSKÁ ZAHRADA)   GARDENS
A little patch of hidden greenery, this park is lined with rows of roses, hedges, and benches. The Gardens offer respite from the chatter of Nové Město. While centrally located, the Gardens are easily overlooked, making it one of our favorite spots in the area. Previously a monastery, and a police station at one point, the site has now found its chill. Bringing a date here is highly recommended. Winking and whispering "I wanna see your secret garden next," not so much.

i B: Můstek – B. Turn left onto Jungmannovo nám. The gardens are on your left. ☼ Open daily Apr 15-Sept 14 7am-10pm; Sept 15-Oct 14 7am-8pm; Oct 15-Apr 14 8am-7pm.

EMMAUS MONASTERY (EMAUZSKÝ KLÁŠTER)   MONASTERY
Vyšehradská 49/320   ☎224 917 662 www.emauzy.cz

The Emmaus Monastery was founded by Charles IV in 1348, and is associated with figures such as Jan Hus and Johannes Kepler. As legend has it, the monks of this monastery were so good that Hell sent the Emmaus Devil to distract them from their duties. Disguised as a cook, the Devil used food to interrupt the monks' piety, but was turned into a black cock when his intents were revealed. Never trust the cocks. Spared from destruction during the Hussite Wars, this building was briefly a Hussite monastery, though it has since been returned to the Benedictines. Despite the monastery's luck with the Hussites, Emmaus carries a history of trauma, like most significant Prague sites. Many of its monks were sent to concentration camps during World War II, and the structure was damaged by American bombings. The Emmaus Monastery has since been restored, however, and is notable for its preserved, elaborate frescoes and Gothic style.

i B: Karlovo náměstí. From the station, turn right onto Palackého nám and continue onto Zítkovy sady. Turn left onto nám. Pod Emauzy. Turn right on the next corner onto Pod Slovany. The monastery is on the left. 50Kč, reduced admission 30Kč. ☼ Open May-Sept M-Sa 11am-5pm; Oct M-F 11am-5pm; Nov-Mar M-F 11am-2pm; Apr M-F 11am-5pm.

Staré Město

CHARLES BRIDGE (KARLŮV MOST)   BRIDGE
Bridge the gap between you and a date with a visit to Karlův Most, one of the oldest and most popular Prague attractions. Overlooking the Vltava River, the Charles Bridge offers a stunning view of lively Staré Město and Malá Strana, complemented by the calm of the river. There is something undeniably romantic about bodies of water, or so our YA novels have promised. It is said that Charles

IV laid down the first stone for this bridge, back in the times where there was royalty who were "the Fourth" and people ran around marrying their uncles and shit. Old Charlie Boy married IV times—because monogamy was only in if you were a woman—and fathered 13 children. One too many to star in Cheaper by the Dozen. You overshot it, dude. The bridge today is lined with statues of saints, and its footpath is a hub for street vendors selling jewelry, portraits, and the like. This gothic bridge boasts a tower at each end of the bridge, and the kind of grim history that can only come with living alongside humanity. Floods and severed heads mark the past of the Charles Bridge, but the greatest threat you'll face today is a dress-lifting gust of wind or an errant selfie stick. Fear not, however, for the selfie you'll get out of it will definitely be worth it. Nothing says "I had a great time" like "I have a million pictures to prove it; believe me I had a great time."

i A: Staroměstská. Walk down Žatecká. Turn left onto Platnéřská and then another left onto Křižovnická. Follow Křižovnická, then turn right onto Křižovnické nám. Continue onto Karlův most. The bridge is within sight from here. Free.

ASTRONOMICAL CLOCK TOWER AND OLD TOWN HALL LANDMARK

Staroměstská náměstí   ☎236 002 629 www.staromestskaradnicepraha.cz

Clocks and cocks hold a lot in common. For starters, size—over-exaggerated. The Astronomical Clock, while a Prague favorite, may disappoint. Initial reactions often include, "...Oh," "That's it?" and "Even my dick's bigger than that!" (it's not). Hang around for a little longer though—the clock's got a little more than meets the eye. While the creator was first believed to be some poor fellow who was blinded so he could never make another clock like it, that is, in fact, nothing more than the product of some poor research. Oedipal themes aside, the real story is far tamer. The true creator was Miklaus of Kadan; it was made in 1410; no eyeballs were harmed in the construction of this clock. The clock features apostles that emerge every hour to figuratively wag their fingers at four figures representing Death, Greed, Pleasure, and Vanity. The clock is embedded in the Astronomical Clock Tower, part of the buildings that compose Old Town City Hall, notable for its historical function as a prison and damage at the hands of the Nazis. If you're looking to get high, this is worth the climb. Standard admission to the Astronomical Clock Tower is 120Kč, for students under 26 only 70Kč. As a quick way to see the whole city at once, the view from the top of the Astronomical Clock Tower offers a magnificent glimpse into the happenings of the city, far above the red-shingled roofs. For 100Kč (70 Kč for students under 26), tack on the historical halls tour.

i A: Staroměstská. Head down Kaprova toward Maiselova. Upon reaching Maiselova, turn left onto Nám. Franze Kafky, and continue down this street and make a slight right turn onto Staroměstské nám. Turn right around the corner and the Astronomical Clock Tower will be on the right. Tower is wheelchair accessible. Astronomical Clock Tower 120Kč, students under 26 70Kč. Historical halls tour 100Kč, students under 26 70Kč. ⏰ Tower open M 11am-10pm, Tu-Su 9am-10pm. Historical halls open M 11am-6pm, Tu-Su 9am-6pm.

CHURCH OF OUR LADY BEFORE TÝN (KOSTEL MATKY BOŽÍ PŘED TÝNEM) CHURCH

Staroměstská náměstí

Prague's more goth than that choker you wore everyday in sixth grade. You tried to add black lipstick to the mix, but your mom wouldn't let you out of the house like that, and looking back that was really best for everyone. A softer side of the Gothic aesthetic, perhaps, the Church of Our Lady Before Týn is yet another Gothic church in Prague. You might have seen one around. Prague's kinda into them. This particular church resides in Old Town Square and replaced a similar predecessor, a replacement itself of a Romanesque church. The two spires of the church frame the skyline, though they are not of equal heights. One represents masculinity, the other femininity, and with a basic understanding of the patriarchy, you could probably guess which is which. Your mom always said that it's what's on the inside that counts, but this church is like Miley Cyrus—it's got the best of both worlds. The inside does not disappoint in the slightest. Sweeping high ceilings and gold-gilded errything, the building stands as a reminder that mankind produces beautiful things. It's rumored that the church inspired the architecture of the castle in Disney's Sleeping Beauty. Standing under its arches, it's quite easy to understand why. No prince in sight yet, but we'll definitely keep you updated.

i A: Staroměstská. Head down Kaprova toward Maiselova. Upon reaching Maiselova, turn left onto Nám. Franze Kafky. Make a slight right turn onto Staroměstské nám. Church of Our Lady Before Týn is on the left. Wheelchair accessible. Free. ☼ Tu-Sa 10am-1pm and 3pm-5pm, Su 10:30am-noon.

MUNICIPAL HOUSE (OBÉCNI DUM) CONCERT HALL
Nameští Republiky ☎222 002 129 www.obecni-dum.cz

The Municipal House, the creation of artists in the early 1900s, today hosts a number of functions, among them Smetana Hall, a remarkable concert hall that plays a chief role in the music festival Prague Spring. Obécni Dum was built on the old site of the Royal Court, and in 1918, served as the location at which the new republic was declared. The Municipal House is known for its architectural style of Art Nouveau, a French term that translates directly to "New Art", proving once again that artistic talent does not extend to creative naming abilities. Like any attraction worth visiting, there's a restaurant inside, outfitted with the kind of chandeliers that imply you should probably find somewhere cheaper to eat. Enjoy a performance by the Prague Symphony Orchestra, and partake in the Prague Spring Festival if you're there in mid-May or early June. The official website encourages parents to bring their children, claiming that they will never forget "where the Royal Court was once located, which witnessed the proclamation of independent Czechoslovakia in 1918." They will most definitely forget this, but hey, you tried. That's almost enough.

i B: Náměstí Republiky. Tours 290Kč, students under 26 250Kč. ☼ Open daily 10am-8pm.

CHURCH OF ST. JAMES (SVATÝ JAKUB VĚTŠÍ) CHURCH
Malá Štupartská 6

The Church of St. James was originally constructed in a Gothic style, but then it got Baroque-n. A fire in 1689 consumed the church, and it was rebuilt as a Baroque building. This gem of Prague serves as the resting place of Count Vratislav of Mitrovice, though he hardly rests in peace. They accidentally buried him alive—no one bothered to check, eh?—and for days after the count's burial, people heard noises coming from the tomb. As is logical, no one stopped to think, "Yo, maybe he's alive," and they just sprinkled holy water on him and went on with their days. Shit friends ya got, Count. If that's not creepy enough, a mummified arm hangs in The Church of St. James, supposedly the arm of a thief who tried to steal from the high altar of the church. Mary's got a side gig in law enforcement it seems, because legend has it she snatched the thief's arm and wouldn't release it until it had to be amputated. An interesting interpretation of "it'll cost you an arm and a leg," surely. A mural graces the top of the Church of St. James, and baby angels abound. Beautiful, yes, but the Church has got some skeletons in its closet. Literally.

i B: Náměstí Republiky. Free. ☼ Open Tu-Su 9:30am-noon and 2pm-4pm.

ESTATES THEATER (STAVOVSKÉ DIVADLO) THEATER
Železná 11 ☎224 901 448 www.narodni-divadlo.cz

A cultural center of Prague, the Estates Theater represents the caliber of the fine arts in Prague, presenting Opera, Ballet and Drama performances. Constructed in the 18th century, its architecture emulates a neoclassical style, and bears the motto "Patriae et Musis," proposed by its founder, Count Frantisek Antonin Nostitz-Rieneckwhich. This is a splendid name, the third part of which we can only imagine is pronounced "Nose Tits." Mozart's Don Giovanni premiered here in 1878, one of many fine works to be performed at the Estates Theater. Indecisive as ever, the theater has undergone many name changes, only to settle back down at where it started. Located near a major university, professors seem to have feared students would find performances at the theater more interesting than their lessons. What they seem to have overlooked is that essentially anything is more interesting than university lectures. The truth hurts, Professor.

i B: Můstek – B. Head down Na můstku and continue onto Na příkopě. Turn left onto Havířská and continue until you reach Ovocný trh. The Estates Theater is right around the corner, to your left. Open during performances. Ticket prices vary. Visit website for the most up-to-date information.

POWDER TOWER   TOWER
Na příkopě

The Powder Tower, the result of a renovation on one of Prague's 13 original city gates, hearkens back to a time in which gates actually kept people out. Only true 11th century kids will understand. Once known as the New Tower, and for some time, Horská Tower, its name was changed to the Powder Tower when it started being used to store gunpowder. The Powder Tower, originally built in the Gothic style, was used for coronation ceremonies. The road from Kutná Hora also passed through here, connecting the city with Eastern Bohemia. Inside, a spiral staircase leads up 186 steps; a gallery near the top is accessible to the public and features an exhibition as well as a superb view of Prague.

i B: Náměstí Republiky. Head down Nám. Republiky onto Na příkopě. Make a slight right onto U Prašné brány. The Powder Tower is on the right. 95Kč, students 65Kč. ⚭ Open daily Nov-Feb 10am-6pm, March 10am-8pm, April-Sept 10am-10pm, Oct 10am-8pm, .

ST. NICHOLAS CATHEDRAL (CHRÁM SV. MIKULÁŠE)   CHURCH
Staroměstské náměstí

If you Google, "St. Nicholas Church Prague," you'll pull up the one in Malá Strana instead, and that's probably what it feels like to have an older, much more successful sibling. St. Nicholas Cathedral—the one in Staré Mešto—stands as an architectural testament to the Baroque style. The green-spired cathedral, like almost any church in Prague, is a breath-taking sight; this one in particular serves a concert hall to the Czechoslovak Hussite Church, putting on performances everyday from April to November at 5pm and 8pm. On the inside, a large, flower-shaped crystal chandelier hangs, donated by Tsar Nicholas II.

i A: Staroměstská. Head down Kaprova toward Maiselova. Turn left onto Nám. Franze Kafky. Continue onto Staroměstské nám. St. Nicholas Cathedral is on the left. Free. ⚭ Open M-Sa 10am-4pm, Su 11:30am-4pm. Mass at 10am on Sundays.

Josefov

A joint ticket (300Kč for adults, 200Kč reduced price) covers admission to the Pinkas Synagogue, the Maisel Synagogue, the Old Jewish cemetery, the Klausen Synagogue, the Ceremonial Hall, the Spanish Synagogue, and temporary exhibitions in the Robert Guttmann Gallery. Men are asked to cover their heads before entering the Jewish sites. All sights are within comfortable walking distance from the Information and Reservation Center of the Jewish Museum in Prague, where you can find tickets for tours and sites, as well as information maps and audio guides.

i A: Staroměstská. From the station, walk down Kaprova toward Valentinská, and turn left onto Valentinská. Turn right onto Široká. Walk down two blocks, and turn left onto Maiselova. The Information and Reservation Center will be on your left. Sites open Apr-Oct M-Th 9am-6pm, F 9am-Sabbath, Su 9am-6pm, closed Saturdays; Nov-Mar M-Th 9am-5pm, F 9am-Sabbath, Su 9am-5pm, closed Saturdays.

PINKAS SYNAGOGUE
SYNAGOGUE

The names of nearly 80,000 victims of the Holocaust cover the inner walls of Pinkas Synagogue, a memorial to the suffering borne by the Jews of Bohemia. Black and red prints span the synagogue, a visual reminder of the extent of tragedy the Holocaust brought. Additionally, the synagogue contains a permanent exhibit of children's drawings, kept from the concentration camp Theresienstadt. Originally a private prayer house, the Pinkas Synagogue is the second-oldest synagogue in Prague. Though closed during the Communist Era, the building was later reopened and now commemorates the loss of the Jewish community at the hands of the Nazis.

i From the information center, walk down Maiselova, and turn right onto Široká. The synagogue is on your right.

OLD JEWISH CEMETERY
CEMETERY

About 12,000 tombstones fill the Old Jewish Cemetery, marking the remains of figures like Aaron Meshulam Horowitz, Mordecai Maisel, and Rabbi Judah Loew Ben Bezalel. The second oldest Jewish cemetery in Europe, demand for burials exceeded supply of plots, and much of the space now contains multiple bodies stacked on top of each other. The oldest tombstone at the site is marked with the year 1439, meaning the poor dude died during a time in which humanity still had not accepted that Earth revolves around the sun. Gray slabs stick out of the cemetery haphazardly like our teeth before braces and also after braces because we never wore our retainers. Pebbles lay at the base of the tombstones, commemorating the people who lay there in a Jewish tradition that swaps the perceived paganism of flowers for small stones. By the exit visitors will find the Ceremonial Hall, a two-floor museum on the history of Jewish burials.

i The entrance to the Old Jewish Cemetery is through the courtyard in the Pinkas Synagogue and behind the Information and Reservation Center.

SPANISH SYNAGOGUE

Complex geometric patterns outlined in red, green, and gold fill the interior of the Spanish Synagogue, known for its Moorish style produced by Josef Niklas and Jan Bělský. The youngest of the synagogues in Jewish Old Town, it is also perhaps the most beautiful, like the new kid at school that displaces the previously most popular. Better watch your back, Spanish Synagogue. The walls of the interior meet the ceilings at a curve, contrasting the straight lines of the floors and pews outlined with circular designs. The synagogue serves as both a concert hall and a museum, featuring exhibits on Czech Jewish history and silver artifacts.

i From the Information and Reservation Center, walk down Maiselova and turn left onto Široká. Walk down three blocks and at the roundabout, the Spanish Synagogue is to your left, right by the Statue of Franz Kafka.

OLD-NEW JEWISH SYNAGOGUE
SYNAGOGUE

Despite the name, the Old-New Jewish Synagogue is—as historians put it—hella old. The oldest operating synagogue in Europe, while actually new in the 13th century, the synagogue is now older than yo momma jokes. Like essentially all of Prague's churches, the synagogue was built in an early Gothic style. Legend claims that the remains of a golem, a protective monster in Jewish tradition lay in the attic of the Old-New Jewish Synagogue, after having been created by Rabbi Loew to defend the Prague Jews. Another tale posits that angels protect the synagogue from fire. So don't try dropping your mixtape here.

i From the Information and Reservation Center, walk down Maiselova. The Old-New Jewish Synagogue is on the right, by the corner between U starého hřbitova and Maiselova.

STATUE OF FRANZ KAFKA

STATUE

This statue commemorating beloved Prague native, Franz Kafka, is the work of sculptor Jaroslav Rona, and features a large headless man with a small one riding on his shoulders (see also: Hagrid and his father, headless). The sculpture draws its subject matter from Kafka's own writing, a short story titled "Description of a Struggle." This memorial to Kafka, one of Prague's greatest, was given a Grand Prix award, and now stands near the site of Kafka's former home on Dušní Street. Though not directly related to the Jewish synagogues and cemetery, it happens to be remarkably close to the rest of the sites.

i *From the Information and Reservation Center, walk down Maiselova, Turn left onto Široká. The statue is right by the Spanish Synagogue.*

Malá Strana

▨ PETŘÍN HILL

PARK, OBSERVATORY

Prague has its highs and lows, and this is quite literally one of the highs. Petřín Hill, home to Petřín Tower, holds everything from a mirror maze to a memorial to the victims of communism. To the Czechs, it's just a nice park. The mirror maze, originating from the 1891 Jubilee Exposition, can be found near the tower, a favorite for children, narcissists, and people who just like mirrors, okay? For when Tinder pulls through the Rose Gardens are the best place to break out into Shakespearean iambic pentameter. Success rate: mixed. On a similar topic, different direction, there's nowhere better than the observatory to break out the line "Are you from outer space? Because your butt is out of this world." Success rate: no data yet. With three telescopes and space exploration exhibits though, we'd say your chances look pretty good. At the base of the hill, you'll find a memorial to the victims of communism. If you're looking to spend a calm afternoon on the hill, bring along Milan Kundera's *The Unbearable Lightness of Being*. The hill is referenced multiple times in the novel, and that's some nice meta shit.

i *A: Malostranská. Walk southwest toward the hill. Or, take the funicular. The funicular is considered part of the public transport system, and you can buy the same kind of ticket to use it (24Kč). The funicular starts at the Újezd tram stop.*

▨ PETŘÍN TOWER

TOWER

If being cheap has taught us anything, it's how to appreciate a good knockoff. The Eiffel Tower gets plenty of love, sure, but there's no reason to trek all the way to Paris when you can get (almost) the same thing right here in Prague. The structure of the tower is very deliberately modeled after that of the Eiffel Tower, resulting from a visit to Paris in 1889. 299 steps bring you to the top of the approximately 60-meter tower, shorter and fatter than the building that inspired it (see also: Angelina Jolie, us). The top floor offers a panoramic view of the city; the journey there offers quivering calves of steel. If the latter doesn't appeal, an extra 60Kč grants elevator access.

i *Walk up Petřín Hill or take the funicular from Újezd. From the funicular stop, turn right and walk along the wall until you see the tower. Admission 120Kč, reduced admission 65Kč. Elevator 60Kč. Admission combined with Mirror Maze 190Kč.* ☒ *Open daily Apr-Sept 10am-10pm; Nov-Feb 10am-6pm; Mar-Oct 10am-8pm.*

CHURCH OF ST. NICHOLAS (KOSTEL SVATÉHO MIKULÁŠE)

CHURCH

Malostranské nám.

The Church of St. Nicholas is considered one of the most beautiful examples of the High Baroque style. For the High Broke, admission isn't too bad either. One hundred years of construction went into the masterful structure that is now the Church of St. Nicholas. From the outside, the church is easily recognizable by its large green dome that stands tall against the Malá Strana skyline. On the inside, the ceilings are covered in elaborate frescoes—you've got your angels, your saints, your divine basics. Everything that could be gilded, is. For avid classical music fans, St. Nicholas Church holds frequent concerts.

i A: Malostranská. Turn right onto Klarov and follow Letenská to Malostranské náměstí. 70Kč, students 50Kč. Concerts 490Kč, students 300Kč. ☒ Open daily 9am-5pm. Concerts everyday except Tu 6pm-7pm.

LENNON WALL   MONUMENT
Velkopřevorské náměstí

Everyone's favorite new cover photo, the John Lennon Wall came to be during the Czech Republic's communist era. Under the regime, western music was banned. The painting of Lennon's face onto a wall was an explicit act of defiance. Attempts to cover the face were all in vain; no matter how many times it was painted over, the Czech people replaced the image, expressing their hopes for peace through graffiti. This wall was, at its start, a countercultural symbol, art against the Man. Since then, the wall has gone the way of essentially everything notable ever: tourist magnet, beloved selfie background, cherished place to spray paint your name and that of your significant other. Put a big heart around it. The owners of the property have let the tourists and graffiti-ers have their way with the wall, filling it with, well, usually their names. Humans, we're a narcissistic people.

i From the Charles River, make a left turn onto Lázeňská after the bridge ends. Stay on it, then turn left onto Velkopřevorské náměstí. The wall is on the left. Free. ☒ 24hr.

WALLENSTEIN PALACE AND GARDENS   PALACE, GARDENS
Valdštejnské nám. 162/3   ☎257 010 401

The Wallenstein Palace and Gardens bear the name of the nobleman who commissioned them, General Albrecht Vaclav Eusebius of Wallenstein, intending them to be his private residence. At the time of construction, the site occupied the space of over 20 houses. If that sounds excessive and unnecessary, that's because it totally was. Currently the site of the Czech Senate, the Wallenstein Palace and Gardens are still quite opulent and attract many visitors. The palace is built in an early Baroque style, and features stellar frescoes by Baccio del Bianco. In the gardens, you'll find plenty of peacocks (not a Katy Perry metaphor), and plenty of peacocks (definitely a Katy Perry metaphor). Statues of muscular men wrestling stand alongside the rows of trimmed hedges in the gardens, no censorship in sight. One wall of the gardens is filled with artificial stalactites that contrast sharply with the rest of the carefully-kept area. At the end of the wall, an aviary stands.

i A: Malostranská. From the station, walk onto Valdštejnská. Turn left onto Valdštejnské nám. The palace is on the left. Admission free. ☒ Gardens open Apr-May M-F 7:30am-6pm, Sa-Su 10am-6pm; June-Sept M-F 7:30am-7pm, Sa-Su 10am-7pm; Oct M-F 7:30am-6pm, Sa-Su 10am-6pm. Palace open Apr-May Sa-Su 10am-6pm; June-Sept Sa-Su 10am-6pm; Oct Sa-Su 10am-6pm; Nov-Mar first weekend of the month 10am-4pm.

KAFKA MUSEUM   MUSEUM
Cihelná 635/2b   ☎257 535 373 www.kafkamuseum.cz

"The little mother with claws," said Kafka about Prague. It is now this mother that bears claim to Kafka, commemorating the writer's prolific legacy. In addition to the Kafka Statue in Old Town, Prague honors its city native with the Kafka Museum in Malá Strana. Outside the entrance of the museum stands one of David Černý's works, depicting two men pissing on the Czech Republic, moveable dicks in their hands. The top five reactions in this museum, in order: delight, shock, embarrassment, arousement, and apathy. Inside the museum, the designers create a Kafkaesque environment, as disorienting as the man's works. The museum exhibits a range of documents related to Kafka's life, including sketches, letters, and diary entries, with an emphasis on the interaction between Prague and Kafka's writing.

i A: *Malostranská. From the station, turn right onto Klárov and continue onto U lužického semináře and then Cihelná. The museum is on the left. 100Kč, reduced admission 60Kč.* ⏰ *Open daily 10am-6pm.*

CHURCH OF OUR LADY VICTORIOUS (KOSTEL PANNY MARIE VÍTĚZNÉ)   CHURCH
Karmelitská 9   ☎257 533 646 www.pragjesu.cz

The first Baroque church in Prague—you read that right, Baroque—the Church of Our Lady Victorious dates back to the early 1600s. The church is not best known for its architectural style however, but for its figurine of the baby Jesus, donated by Polyxena of Lobkovic in 1628. The statue is believed to have healing powers, and to have served as a protectorate of the city during the Thirty Years' War. For this, the effigy has gained international recognition, receiving gifts from figures as famous as Pope Benedict XVI. All in all, the baby Jesus has amassed over 100 robes, a number that fills us with serious wardrobe envy. In the spirit of capitalism, take home your own replica from the souvenir shop.

i A: *Malostranská. From the Metro, take tram 12, 20, or 22 in the direction of Radošovická , to Hellichova, which is 2 stops away. The church is right at the stop.* ⏰ *Open M-Sa 8:30am-7pm, Su 8:30am-8pm.*

Hradčany

Around Prague Castle

The following sights are only a small sampling of what the castle complex has to offer. Both free and paid tours are available of this area. For the paid tour, two different possible routes. Route A (350Kč) covers: The Old Royal Palace, a permanent exhibition "The Story of Prague Castle," St. George's Basilica, the Golden Lane, the Powder Tower, St. Vitus, Wenceslas and Adalbert Cathedral, and the Rosenberg Palace. Route B (125Kč) covers: The Old Royal Palace, St. George's Basilica, the Golden Lane, St. Vitus, and Wenceslas and Adalbert Cathedral.

▨ PRAGUE CASTLE   CASTLE
24 373 368; www.hrad.cz

Since the 10th century, Czech royalty and leaders have occupied the Prague Castle, the largest ancient castle in the world. In the castle complex remains the office of the President of the Czech Republic, and as such, is guarded by the Castle Guard. With all the contemporary enemies of the Czech Republic (like none), this position is primarily one of standing still in a fancy get-up without any of the fanbase of the beefeaters. Charles IV, of course, took his place in the Prague Castle for some time, and in 1918, the first President of the Czechoslovak Republic took up office here. During Nazi occupation, Reinhard Heydrich lived in the castle. Legend has it that anyone who unlawfully wears the crown jewels will die within a year. True or not, Heydrich fulfilled the legend, dying soon after wearing the jewels.

i A: *Malostranská. From the station, walk down Klárov and continue onto Pod Bruskou. Turn left onto Staré zámecké schody, and follow the road to take the stairs towards Prague Castle.* ⏰ *Open daily Apr-Oct 5am-midnight; Nov-Mar 6am-11pm.*

▨ ST. VITUS CATHEDRAL   CHURCH

Known colloquially as St. Vitus Cathedral, the building's full name is actually "The Metropolitan Cathedral of Saints Vitus, Wenceslaus, and Adalbert." We'd ask why Vitus gets all the credit, but with a name like Adalbert, the answer is pretty clear. Much to no one's surprise, St. Vitus Cathedral is an example of Gothic architecture and follows in the long history of multiple churches dedicated to St. Vitus, the first dating back to the year 930. St. Vitus Cathedral holds an important position in Czech history, and serves as the resting place of multiple queens, kings, and saints like Charles IV and his four wives. The Wenceslas Chapel is quite literally the gem of the site, adorned with 1300 gems, gold, original 14th century depictions of the Passion of Christ, and paintings of St. Wenceslas. The Czech Crown Jewels are also held in the chapel, though they are very infrequently accessible to the public and are protected by seven locks, the keys to which are in the possession of seven different Czech leaders. For a striking view of the city, head up the Great South Tower's 237 steps.

i *A: Malostranská. The cathedral is slightly further behind the Prague Castle. To get there from the station, head down Klárov and continue onto Pod Bruskou. Turn left onto Staré zámecké schody and take the stairs. Continue onto U Svatého Jiří, then onto Hrad III. Nádvoří from which the cathedral is visible. Bell tower admission 150 Kč.* ☑ *Open Apr-Oct M-Sa 9am-5pm; Su noon-5pm; Nov-Mar 9am-4pm, Su noon-4pm. Last entry to cathedral is 20min. before close.*

OLD ROYAL PALACE
PALACE

"If it ain't broke don't fix it," is a saying best left to peasants. Royalty much prefer living by: "If it vaguely bores you, go ahead and get a new one"—a philosophy applied to servants, castles, and wives. While the Old Royal Palace was good enough for the likes of Charles IV and Vladislav Jagiello, later rulers just weren't feelin' it. The Old Royal Palace has remained relevant, nonetheless, resurfacing with different important functions. Vladislas Hall of the Old Royal Palace has served in the past as the site of tournaments and royal ceremonies and remains politically relevant. Vladislas Hall is perhaps best known by AP Euro and Latin students alike, however, for the Defenestration of Prague aka that time two Catholic governors were thrown out of a window. They survived the fall because of a pile of shit. Bullshit, if you ask us.

i *A: Malostranská. The palace is right next to St. Vitus Cathedral. To get there from the station, head down Klárov and continue onto Pod Bruskou. Turn left onto Staré zámecké schody and take the stairs. Continue onto U Svatého Jiří, then onto Hrad III. Nádvoří from which the palace is visible.* ☑ *Open daily Apr-Oct 9am-5pm; Nov-Mar 9am-4pm.*

Other Sights

STRAHOV MONASTERY (STRAHOVSKÝ KLÁŠTER)
MONASTERY

Strahovské nádvoří 1/132 ☎233 107 704 www.strahovskyklaster.cz

Founded in 1143, the Strahov Monastery has survived wars, fires, and communism, and today you can go in to check out the library and gallery it houses. The works in the Strahov Book Collection number about 260,000, covering a diverse range of themes. In addition to books, the library houses a "cabinet of curiosities," which is quite different from your cabinet of curiosities next to your bed. Among the oddities are elephant trunks, a narwhal tooth previously believed to be a unicorn horn, and the remains of a dodo bird, a species that is now extinct. The Strahov Gallery, instead, features paintings from the 14th to 19th century. Expect a lot of paintings of landscapes, fruit, and constipated looking people. And if all this hasn't convinced you that monk lyfe can be fun, wrap up your time here with a beer at the monastic brewery.

i *A: Malostranská. From the subway station, walk to the tram stop and get on the 22 tram going towards Bílá Hora. Ride for 4 stops and get off at Pohořelec. Walk down Pohořelec, and then continue onto Dlabačov. Turn right onto Strahovské nádvoří. The monastery is on the right. Gallery 100Kč. Library 100Kč.* ☑ *Gallery open daily 9:30am-11:30am and noon-5pm. Library open daily 9am-noon and 1pm-5pm. Brewery open daily 10am-10pm.*

LORETO
CHAPEL

Loretánské nám. 102/8 ☎233 310 510 www.loreta.cz

The Loreto in Prague holds great significance for Christians and, as such, is the starting site of many pilgrimages. A replica of the Santa Casa, or the "Holy House," stands as the focal point of the complex, believed by Christians to be the house in which the angel Gabriel visited Mary and announced her Immaculate

prague

trdelník

This street food is a sweet, doughy cylinder rolled in sugar, and you don't earn your Prague tourist badge until you've tried one. Staré Město, in particular, has plenty of trdelník stands lining Old Town Square and its outskirts. At about 60Kč, it's a little over $2, and well worth the price, at least once. A traditional Slovak treat, trdelník is hardly unique to Prague—in Hungary, it goes by kürtőskalács, prügelkrapfen in Austria, etc. If you're trying to figure out where to try the treat, the answer is definitely Prague. Who are you kidding? You can't pronounce prügelkrapfen.

Conception. The walls of the house were transported from Bethlehem to their current location at the Italian Loreto in the late 1200s, and a copy stands at the site in Prague. The site also incorporates the Church of the Nativity of Our Lord, notable for its 27-bell complex and beautiful carillon, as well as a treasury, which holds the "Prague Sun." This treasure holds 6,222 diamonds, making it quite a valuable artifact. Worldly goods are beautiful too.

i A: Malostranská. From the subway station, walk to the tram stop and get on the 22 tram going towards Bílá Hora. Ride for 4 stops and get off at Pohořelec. Walk down Pohořelec then continue onto Loretánské. Loreto is within sight after a block. 150Kč, students 110Kč. Audio guide 150Kč. Photo permission 100Kč. ☒ Open daily Apr-Oct 9am-5pm; Nov-Mar 9:30am-12:15pm and 1pm-4pm.

Vinohrady

VYŠEHRAD
MONUMENT

V pevnosti 159/5b ☎420 241 410 348 www.praha-vysehrad.cz

Vyšehrad, the site of a fortress overlooking the Vltava, dates back to about the 10th century, servicing Vratislav II and Charles IV at the height of its glory. Once a royal residence and military stronghold, Vyšehrad now lives out its days as a beautiful park with striking views over Prague. Beloved by families and tourists alike, it's the Bob Ross of places. From war to tug-of-war, kings to engagement rings, Vyšehrad has now turned over to the peasants—a lovely, peaceful place to take a walk with kids or romantic prospects. Left over from its past are the St. Peter and Paul Church, the Devil's Column and the Vyšehrad Cemetery, where the Czech Republic's finest rest in peace. The graves of Antonín Dvořák and Alphonse Mucha, among others, can be found on the grounds. The Slavín tomb, the focal point of the cemetery, holds the remains of only the most important interred in the cemetery. You can't decompose with us. The Devil's column, a pile of three small columns, is said to have resulted from a bet between the priest and the Devil. Why the Devil himself hasn't more important things to do (does hell run itself?) is beyond us. Another legend claims that Libuse's Bath, part of a watchtower in Vyšehrad, was where the Princess Libuse threw her lovers to their deaths as she bored of them. A woman after our hearts.

i C: Vyšehrad. From the station, head north on Na Bučance. Turn right onto Lumírova. You will see Vyšehrad on your left.

Holešovice

LETNÁ PARK
PARK

The only kind of exercise you'll ever get us to do. A killer walk for a killer view, Letná Park sits atop a hill and offers the best view you'll ever get of the Vltava and of the city without getting on a plane. A bird-eye's view, no TSA-groping involved. The park is a popular destination for cyclists, skaters and runners—the winding paths and respite from the bustling streets offer a bubble of nature and calm in the heart of Prague. At the top, a large metronome marks the site where a Stalin statue used to stand. Up here, you can see the Vltava snake under bridges, red roofs in the background. It's Prague's best angle, and absolutely worth it.

i A: Malostranská. Upon exiting the station, walk down Nábřeží Edvarda Beneše. Letná Park is on your left.

PRAGUE ZOO

ZOO

U trojského zámku   ☎296 112 230 www.zoopraha.cz

Petition to make elephants the dominant species. Do elephants bully others? Do elephants make others cry? Do elephants wear socks and sardals? They seem to be much more evolved than we are. The Prague Zoo is ranked as one of the best zoos in the world, making it a lovely place to visit in the afternoon. The baby chimp swings from rope to rope, egged on by audience amusement, while its parents lazily sunbathe. The giraffes stand perfectly still, seeing no reason to exert unnecessary energy. The polar bears swim laps all day because fitness is important. These animals have figured life out, and we have so much to learn. Spend a day among fur, claws, and scales and forget your obligations. They're social constructs anyway.

i C: Nádraží Holešovice. From the Metro, take bus 112. Take the bus sever stops and get off at Zoologická zahrada, or Prague Zoo. 200Kč, students 150Kč. ✪ Open daily June-Aug 9am-7pm; Sept-Oct 9am-6pm; Nov-Feb 9am-4pm; Mar 9am-5pm; Apr-May 9am-6pm.

DOX CENTRE FOR CONTEMPORARY ART

MUSEUM

Poupětova 1   ☎295 568 123 www.dox.cz

Long gone are the days of vain Renaissance portraits and classical sculptures. Now is the age of—well, we're not sure. Photographs, yes, and twig and yarn sculptures. There's one of a twisted tire, another of a paper covered in ballpoint ink. There are murals, electrical schematics, and pornography covered in doodles. Contemporary art calls into question the substance of art itself. Is a twisted tire art? Is a piece of paper scribbled out art? Oh god, are we art? (We think you're a masterpiece btw). Find the answers to all these questions and more at the Dox Centre for Contemporary Art, a museum that houses the art the creative world is churning out nowadays, as well as a stellar cafe and design shop.

i C: Nádraží Holešovice. From the station, walk down Plynární. Turn right onto Osadní, and then after a block, turn left onto Poupětova. The Dox Centre is on your left. 180Kč, students 90Kč. ✪ Open M 10am-6pm, W 11am-7pm, Th 11am-9pm, F 11am-7pm, Sa-Su 10am-6pm. Closed Tuesdays.

NATIONAL GALLERY

MUSEUM

Dukelských hrdinů 47   ☎224 301 122 www.ngprague.cz

Parts of the National Gallery can be found all over Prague, with the largest here in Holesovice. Like all great things, the National Gallery arose from a hint of elitism—an art collection formed by the doing of the "Society of Patriotic Friends of the Arts," with the aim of remedying the city's "debased artistic taste." The original hipsters, perhaps? The Veletržní palác is a functionalist building, with a wide space conducive to the exhibits it holds. Among the works displayed, you'll find names like Alphonse Mucha—the permanent exhibit emphasizes Czech artists while still including foreign talent, and centers on art in the 19th, 20th, and 21st century. With so many different National Gallery buildings out there, we're expecting to see a Buzzfeed quiz soon: "Which National Gallery is your spirit animal? And related Mean Girls gifs." This one may not be most relevant to your interests, but if the content does appeal, the site is sure to please.

i C: Vltavská. Walk down Heřmanova street. Turn right onto Dukelských hrdinů. The museum is on the left. Admission 200Kč. ✪ Open daily 10am-6pm.

prague

FOOD

Nové Město

LEMON LEAF
THAI $

Myslíkova 260/14 ☎224 919 056 www.lemon.cz

Lemon Leaf is cheaper than it looks—in this case, that's a compliment. Large portions here will keep your energy up as you tour the city on foot. The dishes are altered to fit the European palate, but make for a lovely break from the traditional pork-heavy Czech cuisine. The restaurant's décor, unsurprisingly, yellow-themed, is inviting, without being over-the-top. Less Kris Jenner, more Chris Pratt. For the picky eater, yes, there is Pad Thai.

i B: Národní třída. From the station, turn left onto Spálená. Two blocks down, turn right onto Myslíkova. The cafe is on the left. Noodle dishes 149-219Kč. Salads 189-199Kč. Alcoholic beer 39-59Kč. ☼ Open M-Th 11am-11pm, F 11am-midnight, Sa noon-midnight, Su noon-11pm.

GLOBE CAFÉ
AMERICAN $$

Pštrossova 6 ☎224 934 203 globebookstore.cz

For when your attempts at Czech pronunciation have been laughed at just one too many times. Globe Café, an American expat favorite, is a taste of Prague with a nod toward the western. American foods dominate the restaurant's menu, English fills the air, and the bookstore works in Czech and English alike. Globe Café distinguishes itself further with cultural events at night, including film screenings, author readings, and live music. Escape the (dia)critics for a slice of America in the heart of Prague: wings, burgers, and grilled cheese sandwiches are all you need to feel at home. Star spangled banners not included. Healthcare, of course, also not included.

i B: Národní třída. From the station, turn left onto Opatovická. On the next corner, turn left onto Pštrossova where the cafe is on the left. Hot coffee drinks 45-80Kč. Pasta dishes 150-170Kč. Sandwiches 150-185Kč. Burgers 170-295Kč. ☼ Open M-F 10am-midnight, Sa-Su 9:30am-10pm. Kitchen open until 11pm. Happy hour M-F 5pm-7pm.

CAFÉ NEUSTADT
CAFE $

Karlovo nám. 23/1 ☎775 062 795 www.cafeneustadt.cz

Wire sculptures dangle overhead; a piano stands next to them. Café Neustadt, a hip haven in the New Town Hall courtyard, boasts ample outside seating options and an equally charming inside. The chairs all seem semi-thrifted, but given Café Neustadt's clientele, this was likely on purpose. Neustadt has made a name for itself among the young and happening community, and keeps its cultured reputation up with frequent concerts. Across the street from Mamacoffee, this is reason enough to drink more coffee. Stop by both, and bask in the glory that is a crippling caffeine dependence.

i B: Národní třída. From the station, turn left onto Spálená. Turn left onto Karlovo nám, where the cafe is on the left. Beer 25-38Kč. Wine 45Kč. Espresso drinks 38-57Kč. ☼ Open M-Th 8am-midnight, F 8am-4am, Sa 10am-4am, Su 10am-midnight.

Q CAFÉ
CAFE $

Opatovická 166/12 ☎776 856 361 www.q-cafe.cz

We'll give it to you straight—Q Café is anything but. A rainbow flag flutters outside the establishment, and a line of rainbow light bulbs hang over the bar by the entrance. One of the walls displays artsy photos of naked men modeling together. The really naughty bits are all covered up, but if that's what you're looking for, you've probably heard of "the Internet." More than just an LGBT+-specific establishment, Q Café takes its commitment to the community seriously, and offers literature and products related to this topic, and more importantly, a safe space. While particularly loved by the gay male community, Q cafe is welcoming to all, within and outside of the community. Beers and queers, get your fill of both here.

i B: *Národní třída. From the station, walk onto Ostrovní toward Spálená. Turn left onto Opatovická. The cafe is on the left. Nonalcoholic coffee 37-65Kč. Teas 37-80Kč. Salads 75-135Kč.* ☼ *Open daily 1pm-2am.*

CAFÉ NONA
Národní 1393/4

CAFE $

☎775 755 147 www.cafenona.cz

Short for Nova Scena, or New Scene, the building containing Café Nona hosts modern theater performances, and looks like a physical manifestation of Jaden Smith's tweets. An ice-cube-alien-submarine something. The cafe occupies a floor of this space, and carries a confused public library aesthetic. Tables and comfortable couches are scattered throughout, illuminated by the light that streams through the waffle ceiling structure. The tables against the windows are particularly ideal for lunch dates, while the inner tables and couches are suited for reading or getting work done. At night, the patrons turn from caffeine to alcohol, the lights dim, and the place gets clubby.

i B: *Národní třída. From the station, walk down Ostrovní toward Spálená. On the next corner turn right onto Mikulandská. Walk a block and then turn left onto Národní. The cafe is on the left. Coffee drinks 34-110Kč. Cocktails 70-120Kč. Beer 22-55Kč.* ☼ *Open M-F 9am-midnight, Sa-Su 11am-midnight.*

Staré Město

ORIGINAL COFFEE
Betlémská 12

CAFÉ $

☎777 263 403 www.originalcoffee.cz

Did we just step into Anthropologie? Wonderland-esque sketches and Polaroids line the minimalist white walls—sunsets, hands, signs in foreign languages, coffee cups. One of them is of a banana. We tried to find meaning in this, but it really might just be a banana. Or a phallic euphemism. As you mull over the Freudian implications, take a cappuccino and a slice of cake—for the more hipster among you, a vegan rhubarb and poppy strudel. Bring a laptop; this cafe is an ideal place to delude yourself into thinking you'll do any work. Instead, update your Tumblr among potted succulents, an out-of-place coat rack, and casually white we're-trying-to-look-like-we're-not-trying-but-that's-hovadina shutters. Unlike Anthropologie, you won't have to sell an arm, a leg, and your most photogenic kid to afford it. Maybe just like a finger or something.

i B: *Národní třída. Turn right onto Lazarská, and then right again onto Spálená. Follow onto Na Perštyné and then take a left onto Betlémské nám. Follow this street, sticking to the right. On the following fork, stay to the left to turn onto Betlémské. Original Coffee is on the left. Wheelchair accessible. Cash only. Coffee 50-60Kč.* ☼ *Open M-F 8am-7pm, Sa-Su 10am-7pm.*

EBEL CAFÉ
Řetězová 9

CAFÉ $

☎603 823 665 www.ebelcoffee.cz

The teacup pig of cafes. It's got two, maybe two-and-a-half coffee tables squeezed into a room that we imagine is comparable to Harry Potter's cupboard. And you'll love it. A visit to Café Ebel is probably the only time you'll get elbowed by another patron trying to pull out a chair and find it effing adorable. Small but mighty, Café Ebel serves quality espresso, desserts, and chocolate. A flyer on their coffee tables boasts Colombian coffee; their menu presents a United Nations spread of coffee beans for sale, hailing from Brazil to Zimbabwe. Phenomenal desserts proffer the sweet to coffee's natural bitter—try their apple pie (80Kč) with a cappuccino (55Kč). The small space isn't ideal for long stays, but free Wi-Fi keeps visitors to this cupboard of a cafe well-connected.

i A: *Staroměstská. Walk down Kaprova in the direction of Maiselova. The cafe is on the left. Coffee 45-90Kč. Alcoholic drinks 40-295Kč. Pastries 80Kč.* ☼ *Open M-F 8am-8pm, Sa-Su 8:30am-8pm.*

STANDARD CAFÉ

CAFÉ $

Karoliny Světlé 321/23 ☎606 606 806 www.standard-cafe.cz

A dented yellow canoe hangs from the ceiling of the middle room, and it's probably a symbol for something. Something deep. Nietzschean, surely. This slightly grungy cafe encompasses three rooms—the front naturally lit, the back two furnished with dim lamps, and all three filled with cigarette smoke. The artsy-fartsy vibes are strong with this one. The place boasts exposed pipes, mismatched chairs, an indie music selection, and aesthetic young people bent over journals and pints of beer. They all have cooler piercings than you and know like 34 bands you've never heard of. The menu offers a solid range of alcoholic, caffeinated, and none of the above drinks, in addition to dessert-y items, salads and paninis. The chocolate cake and espresso drinks shine as solid options for those who realize that life is too short to be putting vegetables in your desserts.

i B: Národní třída. Turn right onto Lazarská, and then right again onto Spálená. Follow Spálená until you reach Národni. Turn left onto Národni, and then turn right onto Karoliny Světlé. Standard Café is on the left. Coffee 29-75Kč. Cake 26Kč. Beer 20-70Kč. Salads 84-94Kč. Paninis 45-74Kč. ☼ Open M-F 10am-1am, Sa-Su 12pm-1am.

CHOCO CAFÉ U ČERVENÉ ŽIDLE

CAFÉ $

Liliová 3/250 ☎222 222 519 www.choco-cafe.cz

Hot chocolate thicker than a porn star. There's no faking your moans here though; a cup of Choco Café's hot chocolate running down your throat will bring you actual eye-rolling pleasure. Essentially a melted bar of chocolate, a mug of Choco Café's finest is no light dessert. Probably best to take on not-an-empty stomach but also not a too full one either to minimize ralphing potential. This, sadly, comes from the personal experience of one of our researchers. Strike the perfect balance and you'll achieve visceral satisfaction with Choco Café's hot chocolate with chili, orange, ginger or your favorite alcoholic indulgence. Complement your drink nicely with a croissant on the side (20Kč), and take it all in alongside vintage-y postcards. cats, gardens, crosses, and the like. The kind of shit that reminds you that you haven't called your grandma in ages. Even though she sent you a card and a check on your birthday. Shit.

i A: Staroměstská. Turn right onto Platnéřská. Then turn left on Mariánské nám. Turn right on the first side street, and then turn left. Follow this street until you reach Karlova. Turn right and then immediately turn left onto Liliová. Choco Café is on the left. Hot chocolate 59-99Kč. Chocolate 89-195Kč. Coffee 39-95Kč. Hot alcoholic drinks 55-69 Kč. ☼ Open M-Sa 10am-9pm, Su 10am-8pm.

HAVELSKÁ KORUNA

SELF-SERVE $

Havelská 501/23 ☎224 439 331 www.havelska-koruna.com

Not exactly Instagram material. The plastic trays and lunch-line serving style give off a middle school vibe, minus the trauma of puberty and bad haircuts. As a self-serve joint, enjoy authentic Czech eats here alongside real-life Czechs, not just aging Americans trying to make the most out of retirement. You'll be handed a slip as you enter; as you order, the employees will write what you got on the slip. Unless you're finding your finances about 500Kč too solid, hold on to it. The menu is in both Czech and English, but most of the employees only speak Czech so go ahead and butcher their language a little. Whatever it gets you will probably be good anyway. And most importantly, cheap. Sorry Jessie J—it really is all about the money, money, money. Despite what the name may imply, eating at Havelská Koruna won't eat up all your korunas. There is definitely a good slogan somewhere in there. They should pay us for this.

i A or B: Můstek. Follow Václavské nám as it becomes Na můstku. Turn right onto Rytířska, and then left onto Havelská ulička. Turn left onto Havelská. Havelská Koruna is across the street. Wheelchair accessible. Entrees 33-89Kč. Desserts 12-27Kč. ☼ Open daily 10am-8pm.

bitcoin coffee (paralelní polis)

The future is upon us, and the future is bitcoins. People thought we'd be wearing space suits by now and eating our meals in pill form. Instead, we've invented cronuts and buy $60 Urban Cutfitter flannels. But the future is still relentless. Bitcoin Coffee, or Paralelní Polis, is a café located on Dělnická 43 that accepts only bitcoins. Yes, that's right. Bitcoins. The first of its kind, this Prague café leads the way in the acceptance of the famed cryptocurrency. The concept is highly radical. The structure of the institution seeks to eliminate hierarchies, removing ranks within their own staff, even. Staff members don't wear aprons, making accidental interaction with other people much more probable—"Could I have another cappuccino?" "Oh, I don't work here. But I'm John, what's your name?"—ah damnit, a conversation has begun. The café is run by a bunch of radicals trying to make a statement on, well, something. The government. The man. Rules. Decaffeination. Your pick. (Espresso drinks 45-60Kč. ☏ Open M-F 8am-8pm, Sa-Su 10am-8pm.)

LA CASA BLŮ LATIN AMERICAN $
Kozí 857/15 ☏224 818 270 www.lacasablu.cz

Latin American eats? Let's taco 'bout it. Colorful knickknacks originating from various Latin American countries outfit the walls of Casa Blů, a restaurant that counts Argentinian chimichurri, Uruguayan beef, and tacos with pico de gallo among its offerings. Munching on Latin American cuisine in the Czech Republic minutes from the Jewish Quarter sounds like the start of some shitty joke—what do you get when you cross a Czech, a Jew and a churrasco? We didn't get around to making up a punchline to that, but anyway, globalization. A cultural hub, La Casa Blů played host to a 2000 Czech film, Samotáři, and regularly invites Latin American artists to perform or display their art. Swing by during happy hour to score a meal on the cheap (everyday until 5:30pm). The tacos chile con carne (175Kč, 120Kč during happy hour) are a huge hit and go nicely with a beer or Chilean wine. To be fair though, anything goes nicely with a beer or Chilean wine.

i A: Staroměstská. Turn right on Široká, and then left onto Kozí. The restaurant is on the left. Burritos 158-195Kč (Happy Hour 130-150Kč). Quesadillas 150-190Kč (Happy Hour 98-140Kč). Beer 21-44Kč. ☏ Open M-F from 11am, Sa from noon, Su from 2pm. Closing times vary. Happy Hour until 5:30pm.

KABUL RESTAURANT MIDDLE EASTERN $$
Krocínova 316/5 ☏602 212 042 www.kabulrestaurant.cz

Culture in the form of a hunkering skewer of life-giving meat. Mm, not that kind of skewer of meat. Better. The only Afghan restaurant in Prague, this place reps damn well. Arabic music videos play on the TV overlooking Afghan decorations. The famous National Geographic magazine photograph of a young Afghan girl hangs, framed. The seating is a mix of tables and chairs, and rugs with cushions circling a table. The food is, plainly put, delicious. Spring for one of the lamb dishes (220-290Kč) or a vegetarian dish (80-170Kč). The free Wi-Fi and (not-free) alcoholic drinks seal the deal. Is this true love or just lust? Who knows, but damn are we ready for that meat.

i B: Národní třída. Turn right onto Lazarská, and then right onto Spálená. Continue on this street and then turn left onto Národní and right onto Karoliny Světlé. Follow this street until reach a fork. Take the left fork onto Krocínova and arrive at Kabul Restaurant. Beef entrees 90-240Kč. Lamb entrees 220-290Kč. Vegetarian entrees 80-170Kč. Dessert 50-90Kč. ☏ Open daily 11:30am-11pm.

prague

LOKÁL
CZECH $

Dlouhá 33 ☎222 316 265 lokal-dlouha.ambi.cz

Size matters—and this place knows it. The restaurant spans the length of a block, but they don't seem to have trouble filling up. Cheap meals and quality tank beer draw in crowds looking for an authentic taste of Prague. If you didn't come to Prague for the absinth, maybe you came for the beer, and if PBR's all you've known till now, it's probably best you don't mention that. Czech out the beer (32-45Kč) and have a meal while you're at it. For vegetarians, the daily menus feature two salads and one non-salad vegetarian dish.

i B: Náměsti Republiky. Cross Na Poříčí, and continue on Palladium. Pass Pizza Nuovo and turn right immediately after. Follow this path as it merges with Benediktská. Turn left onto Dlouhá. Lokál is on your right. Wi-Fi available. Beer 32-45Kč. Sides 35-45Kč. Entrees 105-195Kč. ⚇ Open M-Sa 11am-1am, Su 11am-midnight. Express meal available M-F 11am-3pm.

CAFÉ KAMPUS (KRÁSNÝ ZTRÁTY)
CAFÉ $

Náprstkova 10 ☎775 755 143 www.cafekampus.cz

Heavy smoke with a side of—well, snobbery? F. Scott Fitzgerald vibes. Black-and-white photographs line the walls; the cafe-restaurant's alternate name, Krásný Ztráty, translates to "beautiful losses." Yup. They've got a room that looks like a private library converted into a restaurant and scattered tables and couches. The tortured artist clientele keeps this place running, but its offerings aren't too shabby either. Quesadillas, pork dishes, coffee and the like. Enough alcohol to get through a conversation with someone here. Ponder what the hell "beautiful losses" means over a Caesar Salad (130Kč) and a beer (20-49Kč). If you figure it out, please tell us—we want to be cultured, too.

i A: Staroměstská. Turn right onto Platnéřská, and then left onto Mariánské nám. Turn right on the first side street you pass, and then left. Follow this street until you reach Karlova. Turn right and then immediately left onto Liliová. Walk down Liliová and turn left onto Náprstkova. Café Kampus is on your left. Wi-Fi available. Coffee 29-69Kč. Salads 110-130Kč. Quesadillas 95-99Kč. ⚇ Open M-F 10am-1am, Sa noon-1am, Su noon-11pm.

Josefov

⊠ KAFKA SNOB FOOD
CAFÉ $$

Široká 64/12 ☎420 725 915 505

In a swarm of overpriced tourist traps, Kafka Snob Food escapes the worst of it. The restaurant has an edgy industrial aesthetic, mixed with bright lights and KAFKA spelled out in big letters, should you forget for a moment where you are. Snobs or not—we'll leave that up to you to determine—the food does not disappoint. Should Josefov leave you tired out, this place has all the trappings of a cafe, and can make cappuccinos just as good as those of that minimalist Tumblr-looking cafe you probably prefer. A short walk from the sights, Kafka Snob Food is an ideal place to sit, recharge, and nom the ache in your feet away.

i A: Staroměstská. From the station, walk down Kaprova and turn left onto Valentinská. On the next corner, turn right onto Široká. The restaurant is on the right. Espresso drinks 55-80Kč. Entrees 195-350Kč. ⚇ Open M-Sa 8am-10pm, Su 10am-10pm.

KOLONIAL
CZECH $$

Široká 25/6 ☎224 818 322 www.kolonialpub.cz

Inexplicably, wheely attached to a bicycle theme. On Kolonial's windows are printed outlines of people on bicycles. The motif carries on to the interior as well with cycle pieces displayed throughout the space. Kolonial serves Czech cuisine and the kind of portion sizes you like to see when you've done more walking than your feet ever asked for. If you judge your food by literal height, go for one of the skewers. Served vertically, it gives the illusion of consuming a small edible tower; admittedly, somewhat amusing. Like Kafka Snob Food, Kolonial is quite close to the sights.

i A: Staroměstská. *From the station, walk down Kaprova and turn left onto Valentinská. On the next corner, turn right onto Široká. The restaurant is on the right. Skewers 178-278Kč. Grill entrees 158-285Kč. Bottled beer 42-49 Kč.* ✪ *Open M-F 9am-midnight, Sa-Su 9am-midnight.*

Malá Strana

⚅ CUKRKÁVALIMONÁDA CZECH $$
Lázeňská 7 ☎257 225 396

The name is the second best thing to have been on your tongue. First is their food. Come on, don't be dirty. A cafe-restaurant, Cukrkávalimonáda has all the trappings of a trendy Prague spot—magnificent chalkboard art, wooden stools and tables—with the menu of a restaurant to round it all out. Minutes from the Lennon Wall, Cukrkávalimonáda is the perfect place to unwind and process Lennon's revolutionary messages. If you're aching for Western ways, try the Camembert sandwich, a Czech twist on the classic American grilled cheese. Say yes to the dess(ert), and finish your meal with something sweet from their display.

i A: Malostranská. *From the station, turn right onto Klárov. Continue onto U lužického semináře. Turn right onto Saská, and then a left onto Lázeňská. The restaurant is on the right. Breakfast 69-249Kč. Sandwiches 159-249Kč. Coffee drinks 65-149Kč.* ✪ *Open daily 9am-7pm.*

BAR BAR CZECH $$
Všehrdova 436/17 ☎257 312 246

Somewhat hidden, Bar Bar can be found on a street off of the main street in Malá Strana, and is truly a gem. Inside, wine bottles decorate the shelves built into one of the walls, imbuing the place with a sense of elegance. Sure, our collection of wine bottles is "concerning" and "a way of avoiding our problems," but Bar Bar's is "fancy" and "a nice touch." Anyway, the restaurant looks far more upscale than its prices reflect—the wine bottles and polished interior make a cheap meal feel like a splurge. The daily menu also often includes vegetarian options, which can be a difficult find in pork-loving Prague. If you're looking for drinks instead, Bar Bar is unsurprisingly, also a bar.

i A: Malostranská. *From the Metro, take tram 12, 20, or 22 in the direction of Radošovická , to Hellichova, which is 2 stops away. From the stop continue walking down Újezd. Turn left onto Všehrdova. The restaurant is on the left. Coffee and tea 37-54Kč. Entrees 155-235Kč. Burgers 180-190Kč.* ✪ *Open daily 11:30am-11:30pm.*

GREEN SPIRIT VEGETARIAN BISTRO & CAFÉ VEGETARIAN $
Hellichova 397/14 ☎257 317 459 www.greenspiritbistro.cz

Vegetarian food as delicious as this? Your friends will be green with envy. Meatless munchies can be difficult to track down in Prague, a city known for its meat-heavy cuisine. You'll pass restaurant after restaurant advertising pork knuckles, but very few vegetarian options, much less healthy ones. How many times can you eat fried cheese without having a heart attack? Actually, not the worst way to go. If you're looking for a vegetarian meal in Malá Strana, head to Green Spirit Vegetarian Bistro & Café, located a few blocks from Petřín Hill and the Church of Our Lady Victorious. You too will be left victorious here—the menu is all vegetarian and no, we don't just mean "has salads." Fettucine, tofu burgers, and paella are just some of the main dishes the restaurant offers, in addition to fruit cocktails to wash it all down.

i A: Malostranská. *From the Metro, take tram 12, 20, or 22 in the direction of Radošovická, to Hellichova, which is two stops away. From the stop, continue walking down Újezd. Turn right onto Hellichova. The restaurant is on the right. Coffee drinks 35-60Kč. Appetizers 60-65Kč. Entrees 129-159Kč.* ✪ *Open daily 10am-8pm.*

BELLA VIDA CAFÉ
CAFE $

Malostranské nábř. 563/3   ☎221 710 494 www.bvcafe.cz

In Spanish, the name Bella Vida translates to "Beautiful Life," strikingly appropriate for a cafe that overlooks the Vltava. The outdoor seating of this establishment hangs over the quiet river, a view worth more than what you'll pay. On the inside, the décor is refined and elegant, filled with dark polished wood and a small collection of books. The establishment has a romantic ambiance—bring the cutest person you see along and let the place work its magic. We, for example, brought ourselves. #selflove. More than just a cafe, Bella Vida has plenty of food options. A meal here in their outside seating makes for the perfect lazy summer afternoon, a reminder that life is indeed beautiful.

i A: Malostranská. From the Metro, turn right and onto Klárov. Continue onto U lužického semináře. Turn left onto Na Kampě. Continue onto U Sovových mlýnů, and then take the stairs and turn left onto Malostranské nábř. The cafe is on the right. Coffee drinks 50-145Kč. Salads 155-265Kč. Pasta 155-185Kč. ☼ Open daily 8:30am-10pm.

Hradčany

KÁVARNA NOVÝ SVĚT
CAFÉ $

Nový Svět 2   ☎242 430 700 kavarna.novysvet.net

Meaning "New World," Nový Svět is a short distance from the tourist-overrun sites in Hradčany, tucked just far away enough to escape the crowds of tourists. A New World, indeed. Nový Svět is your classic minimalist, delicate Prague cafe with drinks and desserts that put Starbucks to shame. To be fair, it doesn't take much to put Starbucks to shame. Located on a small winding cobble-stoned street, the cafe has a romantic small European town feel. Outdoor seating and indoor seating are both available, to suit your current outlook on nature, humanity, and how close you want to be to each. They don't have much on the menu besides caffeine and simple carbs; if your diet consists of more than that (why?), it's best to stop for a bite to eat beforehand.

i A: Malostranská. From the subway station find the tram stop, and get on the 22 tram heading towards Bílá Hora. Ride this for 3 stops, and get off at Brusnice. From this stop, turn right onto Jelení. Turn left onto Černínská, then left onto Nový Svět. The cafe is on the left. Espresso drinks 35-45Kč. Beverages 35-38Kč. Savory food 38-68Kč. ☼ Open daily 11am-7pm.

U ZAVĚŠENÝHO KAFE
CZECH $

Úvoz 6   ☎605 294 595 www.uzavesenyhokafe.cz

Kindness is a universal concept, and one that reigns at U Zavěšenýho Kafe. This pub, a local favorite, sets itself apart from the flock of traditional Czech restaurants with its "pay-it-forward" coffee initiative. At U Zavěšenýho Kafe, patrons can pay for an extra cup of coffee or redeem an already-paid-for cup, as tracked by an abacus that hangs inside. Apart from their "hanged coffee" scheme, from which they derive their name, the pub displays comical, eclectic murals and equally odd sculptures. Not to mention their cult-like following. There are religions in this world with less devoted followers than this place. Salvation, U Zavěšenýho Kafe, does not promise—but good food and a relaxed quirky dinner atmosphere, yes.

i A: Malostranská. From the subway stop, turn right onto Klárov. Walk down one block then turn right onto Letenská. Follow onto Malostranské náměstí, then Nerudova, and then onto Úvoz. The cafe is on the right.Vegetarian dishes 85-145Kč. Entrees 65-175Kč. Salads 40-70Kč. ☼ Open daily 11am-midnight, kitchen closes at 10pm.

CRÊPERIE U KAJETÁNA
CREPES $

Nerudova 278/17   ☎773 011 031

Crêperie U Kajetána knows its target group well: humans. Is there anything we love more than ourselves? Of course not, and Crêperie U Kajetána celebrates that charming narcissism. Black walls and chalk mean that every visitor and their favorite grandma can have their name written on the interior of the restaurant. The black walls are covered in the notes of everyone who stopped by recently, some reaching heights that make you question who stood on who and how, in order to write their name there. The other walls display pretty outlines by artists better than those employing the chalk. Sorry, grandma. As for the food, U Kajetána successfully does not screw up one of the easiest foods to screw up. The crêpes—or palačinky, as the Czechs call them—come in sweet or savory variations, including toppings like chocolate and raspberries, goat cheese and pear, and grilled chicken and mushroom.

i A: Malostranská. Turn right onto Klárov. Walk down for one block then turn right onto Letenská. Continue onto Malostranské náměstí, and then onto Nerudova. The Crêperie is on the left. Sweet crêpes 99-149Kč. Savory galettes 129-169Kč. Trdelník 60 Kč. ☼ Open daily 9:30am-8pm.

Vinohrady

MONOLOK CAFÉ
CAFÉ $
Moravská 1540/18   ☎739 018 195 www.monolok.cz

Metal abstract sculptures resembling twisted paper clips or tin foil after you unwrap your sandwich decorate the walls of this bright, naturally lit cafe. Art? Scrap metal? ¿Por qué no los dos? In addition to all that vitamin D, Monolok's menu provides plenty of healthy dining choices, among them a stellar open-faced salmon, spinach, lemon, thyme, and yogurt sandwich. When's the last time you put thyme in anything? We're not sure we could answer this question ourselves. Clean neutral tones dominate this cafe, and make it a lovely place to do work.

i A: Náměstí Míru. Walk down Korunní toward Blanická. Turn right onto Budečská. Walk down another block, and turn left onto Moravská. The cafe is on your right. Espresso 39-110Kč. Burgers 139-179Kč, Breakfast options 69-99Kč. ☼ Open M-F 8am-10pm, Sa-Su 10am-7pm.

MOZAIKA BURGER
BURGERS $
Nitranská 13   ☎420 224 253 011 www.mozaikaburger.cz

A classic for a reason. When all else goes wrong, beef and cheese do not. When trying new things leaves you battered and bruised, turn to an old comfort for the kind of love drunk guys in clubs will never give you. Mozaika Burger wins the burger award (does not exist, we think), and consequently, wins our hearts. They've got the tried and true burger varieties, but branch out with pesto, different kinds of cheese, cilantro, and the like. Cheesecake, cookies or ice cream, as these things tend to do, end your meal on a perfect, sweet note.

i A: Jiřího z Poděbrad. From the station, walk down Vinohradská toward Nitranská. Turn right onto Nitranská. The restaurant is on your right. Burgers 154-195Kč. Desserts 39-95Kč. ☼ Open M-Sa 11:30am-11pm.

CAFÉ JEN
CAFÉ $
Kodaňská 553/37   ☎420 604 329 904 www.cafejen.cz

Hipster Vinohrady cafes are a cliché but there are worse things in the world than really good coffee. A sweet brunch place, Café Jen has caffeine and meals on the cheap, all sold within the confines of white walls, arches, and slightly nautical pillows. Brunch-y offerings until 6pm, coffee, and dessert mean that you could easily spend all day here—which considering the effort it takes to go places, is not a bad idea. We don't know who this Jen is, with her overly American name and business casual abbreviation, but we like where she's going with this.

i A: Jiřího z Poděbrad. Walk down Vinohradská toward Nitranská. Turn right onto Řipská. After two blocks, turn left onto Korunní, and then right onto Chorvatská. Turn left onto Kodaňská. The cafe is on your left. ☼ Open M 8am-7pm, Tu-F 8am-9:30pm, Sa 9:30am-7pm, Su 9:30am-7pm.

prague

CAFÉ MEZI ZRNKY

CAFÉ $

Sázavská 19 ☎420 732 238 833

Your typical cute cafe with really, really good cappuccinos, Café Mezi Zrnky makes for a lovely stop in your day. Benches line the sides of the cozy room, and the baristas seem to have impeccable taste in American indie music. A chalkboard hangs above the kitchen part of the cafe listing the espresso options, the ceiling is covered by a draped white sheet, the wooden boards of the kitchen area are casually white-washed, and the entire thing looks vaguely like something we've seen on Pinterest. Yeah, we'd pin dat.

i A: Náměstí Míru. Walk down Korunní toward Blanická. Turn left onto Sázavská. The cafe is on your left. 🕐 Open M-F 7:30am-6:30pm, Sa 9:30am-3:30pm.

DISH FINE BISTRO

BURGERS $

Římská 1196/29 ☎420 222 511 032

The name sounds like a bad translation or a poetic statement—and yeah, we'd spit a few verses for these burgers. Dish Fine keeps it short and sweet—burgers, salads and desserts, strong emphasis on the first one. For the stubborn (we prefer well-accustomed), you've got your basic beef-cheddar burger; for everyone else, combos like cured ham and eggplant, pickled shiitake mushrooms and spicy kimchi sauce, and rucola and sundried tomatoes. The restaurant itself is slightly upscale with nice wooden tables, which we'd describe as "good for pretending you're not just eating a burger." Denial is the best state of them all, friends.

i A: Náměstí Míru. Turn right onto Ibsenova. After a block, turn left at Římská. The restaurant is on your right. Burgers 165-195Kč. 🕐 Open M-Sa 11am-10pm, Su noon-10pm.

U DĚDKA

INTERNATIONAL $$

Na Kozačce 12 ☎420 222 522 784 www.udedka.cz

Czech pubs abound, but some are better than others, and this is one of the best. U Dědka is more than meets the eye—chicken wings, duck confit, and quesadillas all find themselves on the same menu here. The pub is a little more upscale than one might expect for their prices, outfitted with paintings and complemented by Wi-Fi. One of the paintings is of a naked woman, which offends us deeply. Sure, when she's naked in the restaurant it's all "art" and "classy," but when we start taking off our clothes it's all "stop," and "please don't." Ugh.

i A: Náměstí Míru. Turn right onto Máchova, and then take the next left onto Rybalkova. Turn right onto Na Kozačce. The restaurant is on the left. Salads 140-145Kč. Main Dishes 140-235Kč. Desserts 80-85 Kč. 🕐 Open M-F 11am-1am, Sa-Su 4pm-1am.

MAMACOFFEE

CAFÉ $

Londýnská 122/49 ☎420 773 263 333 www.mamacoffee.cz

Mothers and coffee do indeed both give life, but so does Wi-Fi and on that front, Mamacoffee just doesn't come through. In the spirit of compensation, this cafe offers quality espresso drinks in delicate blue and white mugs with mild Martha Stewart vibes. You wouldn't think it if you saw it, but Mamacoffee is indeed a chain with multiple stores throughout Prague. The cafes maintain a small-cafe feel still, masking well their mitosis. In addition to prepared drinks, Mamacoffee sells a fine selection of beans and grounds so you too can engage in the process of quality caffeination.

i A: Náměstí Míru. From the station, turn right. Make a left onto Londýnská. Mamacoffee is on the right. Coffee 39-62Kč. Breakfast 45-75Kč. Entrees 105-135Kč. 🕐 Open M-F 8:30am-8pm, Sa-Su 9am-6pm.

KAFÉ KAKAO

CAFÉ $

Americká 2 ☎777 903 902 www.kafekakao.cz

A relaxed coffee spot, Kafé Kakao drops all pretenses and does good food, good coffee, and good prices all within a pretty enough place. Kakao buys into none of the hipster thing, leaving abstract art and IKEA vibes to the young mustachioed crowd. A room of the cafe is dedicated to babies and kids, inviting families to stop by and let their snot-nosed miracles crawl around for a bit. Head to the adult section to enjoy a small meal and a coffee. Among the options are bruschetta, baked goat cheese, and couscous salad.

i A: Náměstí Míru. Walk down Americká for about for about five minutes. Kafé Kakao is on the left. Breakfast 45-92Kč, Salads 69-129Kč. ☑ Open daily 10am-7pm.

Holešovice

BIBLIOTECA DEL VINO
WINE BAR $

Komunardů 894/32 ☎775 506 606 www.bibliotecadelvino.cz

Despite the name, there aren't really books, but there's plenty of alcohol. The semblance of class without any of the effort-consuming parts. The ceiling is detailed in graffiti, there's a wall entirely filled with wine bottles, and they serve damn good rosé. Pick your poison—in addition to wine, Biblioteca sells espresso drinks, delectable chocolate cake, and a respectable array of cheese. There's also salad, but we figured we'd start with the good things. On the downside, they're closed past 11pm and on weekends. On the upside, this is the perfect excuse for day drinking.

i C: Vltavská. Walk onto Nábřeží Kapitána Jaroše at the south end of the station. Continue onto Za Viaduktem and then onto Argentinská. Turn right onto Dělnická and then left onto Komunardů. Biblioteca is on the right. Wine by glass 70-90Kč. Espresso drinks 35-145 Kč. Chocolate cake 75 Kč. ☑ Open M-F 3:30pm-11pm.

OUKY DOUKY COFFEE
CAFÉ $

Janovského 14 ☎266 711 531 www.oukydouky.cz

Ouky Douky doesn't look like much from the outside, but the inside is something like an espresso/book paradise. Shelves of worn books for sale line the walls, making this feel like a cafe plopped down in the heart of your favorite used bookstore. In addition, the expansive menu, which ranges from soup to sandwiches, mean that you could stay there all day, and finally make it through your summer reading. Refresh yourself and your soul with a visit to this literary hotspot. Read a book while enjoying your cappuccino and pretend you're Fitzgerald. Or substitute coffee for alcohol and pretend you're Hemingway.

i C: Vltavská. Upon exiting the station, turn left onto Heřmanova. Walk down this street and then turn left onto Janovského. The coffee shop is on your left. Espresso drinks 34-58Kč. Sandwiches 86-126Kč. ☑ Open daily 8am-midnight.

BISTRO ŠPAJZ
CAFÉ $

Na Maninách 796/9 ☎731 217 376 www.spajzka.cz

Bistro Špajz plays into none of the new-age hipster vibes of Prague cafes and skips right down to the basics: good food at good prices. What you lose in fuss and frills, you regain entirely in solid deals. Hearty meals served on plain wooden tables make this a solid lunch spot for any traveler on a budget. You can't go wrong with roast beef (89Kč) or for the beef-averse, the chicken gyros (89Kč). The portion sizes are generous and will keep you full when you find yourself koruna-counting. Margaritas ain't cheap, we get it.

i C: Vltavská. Upon exiting the station, walk onto Nábřeží Kapitána Jaroše. Continue onto Za Viaduktem and then onto Argentinská. Turn right onto Tusarova. Turn left onto Na Maninách. The bistro is on your left. Soups 25Kč. Entrees 86-94Kč. ☑ Open M-Th 7:30am-5pm, F 7:30am-4pm.

RESTAURANT BATERKA
INTERNATIONAL $$

Dělnická 71 ☎266 711 185 www.baterka.com

For those staying at Sir Toby's Hostel, Restaurant Baterka is but a short walk for large portions at reasonable prices. The restaurant's bright orange walls and tables look clean and nice, but the greatest appeal comes in Baterka's low prices. Perhaps not the best logic for picking a prostitute, but for a restaurant, it'll get

prague

you satisfied. This place serves respectable carb and crêpe options, two of our favorite c-words, right under "cocktails," and some other words we can't say. But if you're looking for a cheap and delicious dinner, stop by here.

i C: Vltavská. Upon exiting the station, walk onto Nábřeží Kapitána Jaroše. Continue onto Za Viaduktem. Continue walking onto Argentinská. Turn right onto Dělnická. The restaurant is on the left, about five blocks down the street. Pasta dishes 115-195Kč. Entrees 133-255Kč. ☼ Open M-Sa 11am-11pm, Su 11am-10pm.

SASAZU
ASIAN $$$

Bubenské nábřeží   ☎284 097 455 www.sasazu.com

Definitely not for those just rich at heart; you better find yourself some deep pockets if you're hoping to eat here. Before you eat, someone comes around and places a mint leaf in your hand. "Rub it around; it'll make your hands smell good." The mint is then replaced by a hot towel. No one's rubbing any part of you for free, we are sorry to tell you. This upscale Asian place featuring stunning lantern decorations, serves some damn fine food. The portions are small, and it'll probably take quite a few orders to get you anywhere near full, but the food is delicious. Treat. Yo. Self.

i C: Vltavská. Upon exiting the station, walk onto Nábřeží Kapitána Jaroše. Turn right onto Argentinská and continue onto Bubenské nábř. The restaurant is at the corner of the street on your left. Entrees 290-495Kč. Soups 175 Kč. Desserts 210 Kč. ☼ Open M-Th 12pm-midnight, F-Sa 12pm-1am, Su 12pm-midnight.

NIGHTLIFE
Nové Město

VINARNA U SUDU
BAR

Vodičkova 677/10   ☎222 232 207 www.usudu.cz

There's more to Vinarna U Sudu than meets the eye. Seemingly your typical Czech pub, a walk inside exposes room after room in this underground semi-maze. Several bars and tables fill the entirety of the space, as well as a small level filled with just foosball tables. More complex than you'd think (less, though, than your teen angst), Vinarna U Sudu has both the elements of a lively Czech pub and that of a hidden stone wine cellar. From outside, it's easy to overlook this gem of a pub, but this place is always full nonetheless. A wine bar, Vinarna U Sudu serves quality wine for anyone looking for something to add to their Snapchat story.

i B: Národní třída. From the station, turn right onto Purkyňova toward Vladislavova, and then turn right onto Vladislavova. Walk about a block and then turn left onto Lazarská. On the next block, turn the corner to the right and the pub is on your left. Beer 30-45Kč. Wine (by glass) 33Kč. Cocktails 80-84Kč. ☼ Open M-Th 9am-4am, F 9am-5am, Sa 10am-5am, Su 10am-3am.

JAMPA DAMPA
CLUB

V Tůních 1770/10   ☎704 718 530

Lesbian? Lez Go. Jampa Dampa, an LGBT club and bar in the area shows love to the ladies who like showing love to the ladies. While open and inviting to all, the place keeps a solid Sapphic vibe, ideal for the female traveler who's even less straight than these Prague streets. A small dance floor takes up half of the lower level; tables occupy the rest. At night, women fill up the place, dancing together to pop-y songs and taking breaks at the tables. The atmosphere is lively, and more importantly, safe and welcoming to anyone inside or outside of the LGBT+ community. If you're looking to eat out—and we don't mean restaurants—Jampa Dampa is worth a visit.

i C: I. P. Pavlova. From the station, walk out and turn right Onto Sokolská. On the next corner turn left onto Ječná and then turn right onto V Tůních. The bar is on your right. Wine 42-240Kč. Beer 25-85Kč. Whiskey drinks 65-120Kč. ☼ Open Tu-W 6pm-4am, Th 6pm-2am, F-Sa 6pm-6am.

REDUTA JAZZ CLUB JAZZ CLUB

Národní třída 20 ☎224 933 487 www.redutajazzclub.cz

Got the blues? Hop out of bed, and jazz things up with a trip to Reduta. Live musicians perform every night at this venue, in a luxurious red-clad, dimly lit lounge. The oldest jazz club in the city, Reduta has existed since 1957, but the aesthetic is that of the 1920s. Reduta is particularly famous for President Bill Clinton's 1994 sax performance at the venue (sex performance reserved for the American public). Reduta has brought to light many influential performers in the genre, and a night at the bar is a display of both history and talent.

i B: Národní třída. From the station, turn right onto Spálená. Walk a block and then turn left onto Národní. The bar is on the left. Entrance 225-350Kč. ☺ Open 9pm-midnight, performances start at 9:30pm.

Staré Město

ROXY CLUB

Dlouhá 33 ☎602 691 015

Men are always lying when they say, "It's bigger than you'd think." We're not. The outside of Roxy doesn't do the inside justice. Roxy rox pretty hard; it's easily one of the hottest clubs in the Josefov/Staré Mesto area, perhaps both literally and figuratively. The huge dance floor fills up quickly, and things heat up fast. Free Monday entrance gives us all a reason to look forward to the start of the week, because 9am lecture just ain't doing it. DJs got you dancing the night away, and it's almost like Tuesday will never come. It will, but that's a problem for future you. Roxy leans toward electronic and dance vibes, and easily attracts the young and hip of Prague.

i B: Náměstí Republiky. Walk down Havlíčkova. Turn left onto V Celnici, following it as it becomes nám. Republiky.Turn left onto Pa ladium. Turn right onto Benediktská, and then left onto Dlouhá. Roxy is on your right. Cover varies, usually either free or between 100-200Kč. ☺ Open daily 11pm-late.

KARLOVY LÁZNĚ CLUB

Smetanovo nábřeží 198/1 ☎222 220 502 www.karlovylazne.cz

A huge, five-story middle finger to the idea of quality, not quantity. Boasting the title of "the largest club in Central Europe," Karlovy lázně is a one-stop shop for any tourist hoping to spend a night rubbing against sweaty college-aged kids. Each story of the club plays a different style of music—among them are radio hits, dance, oldies, hip hop, and chill out. Some floors have novelty elements like a dancing hologram skeleton and an oxygen bar; all floors offer horny masses. If you're willing to shell out extra, you can visit the Ice Pub inside of Karlovy lázně. It's cool as hell for maybe five minutes, cold as balls for the rest. Most pub-crawls end at this club, and understandably so. Every young tourist and their friend they just met from Canada end up here, and you probably will too. So leave the regret and bad taste in your mouth for the morning, and dance.

i A: Staroměstská. Head down Žatecká then turn right on Platnéřská. Follow Platnéřská onto Křižovnická and then onto Smetanovo nábř. Karlovy lázně is on the right. Cover Su-W 180Kč, Th-Sa 200Kč. ☺ Open daily 9pm-5am.

DRUNKEN MONKEY PUB CRAWL

U milosrdných 848/4 ☎773 683 003 www.drunkenmonkey.cz

This pub, founded by Americans, offers one of the main pub crawls in Prague: the Drunken Monkey Pub Crawl. Not to be taken literally—the hope is that you will still be able to stand by the end of a visit to pubs and clubs around town. Start off the night at the Drunken Monkey, and make your way through some of Staré Město's most popular watering holes. In a true American spirit, everyone plays fratty drinking games and gets smashed. Land of the free and all, but this

prague

crawl will set you back 500Kč. If you're feeling lonely or in need of guidance, cough up the dough and hand the reins over to a pro.

i A: Staroměstská. Head north on Žatecká toward Široká, turning right when you reach it. Turn left onto Dušní and walk down until you reach U milosrdných. The destination is on the right. Pub crawl 500Kč. ☼ Open daily noon-late night.

DÉJÀ VU
BAR, CLUB

Jakubská 648/6 ☎222 311 743 www.dejavuclub.cz

You haven't déjà vu-ed a pub-club duo like this one. A two-story bar and club, Déjà Vu offers bright colored lights and a large image of Jim Morrison watching you get smashed. It's a great place to meet people, slurring their words as they hit on each other over Cuba Libres. From 6-9pm, indulge hedonistically in 50% off quality cocktails. The upper level, a bar, caters to those looking to talk and unwind; the lower level, a club, is for those looking to grind. Good vibes, literally and figuratively, this pub/club is known for its quality beats and ambiance.

i B: Náměstí Republiky. Walk down Nám. Republiky. Turn right onto U Obecního domu and right again onto Rybná. Then turn left turn onto Jakubská. Déjà Vu is on the left. No cover. Cocktails 105-185Kč. ☼ Bar open Su-Tu 6pm-2am, W-Th 6pm-3am, F-Sa 6pm-4am. Happy hour daily 6-9pm. Club open W-Th 8pm-3am, F-Sa 8pm-4am.

CHAPEAU ROUGE
BAR, CLUB

Jakubská 2 ☎222 316 328 www.chapeaurouge.cz

French appears to be a go-to for bar names. While this may imply some extra sense of class, this place is just as much ass as any other quality Prague club. Chapeau is part-dance club, part-pub, and part-concert venue for bands too alternative for you to know. The lowest level boasts exposed stone walls, live music, and a wall covered in what appears to be math and chem scribbles. If you don't know what they mean sober, you won't know what they mean drunk. Established on the old site of a pub known as the "Devil's Pub," Chapeau knows how to show visitors a hell of a good time. Stop by—we promise, you won't Hades it.

i B: Náměstí Republiky. Walk down Nám. Republiky. Turn right onto U Obecního domu and right again onto Rybná. Then turn left turn onto Jakubská. Déjà Vu is on the left. Cover varies. ☼ Bar open M–Th midnight-3am, F midnight-4am, Sa 4pm-4am. Underground concerts begin at 8pm.

Malá Strana

◈ U MALÉHO GLENA JAZZ AND BLUES CLUB
JAZZ CLUB

Karmelitská 374/23 ☎257 531 717

This pub serves up some serious talent—U Malého Glena has made a name for itself among the musical crowds. Take your beer with a side of beats; this is one of the classiest ways to spend a night drinking. If you're missing the Western world, the pub is owned by an American, and the menu knows it. Tex Mex in Prague? You bet. Live shows are put on every night in the lower part of the place, and the beer keeps flowing throughout. The venue is small, but it's all about the motion of the ocean, baby—and the talent is strong in this one. Sundays are jam sessions for any visitor who takes their music game past, "Anyway, here's Wonderwall."

i A: Malostranská. From the Metro, take tram 12, 20, or 22 to Malostranské náměstí. From the stop, turn left onto Karmelitská. The club is on the right. Cover M-Tu 200Kč, W-Th 170Kč, F-Sa 200Kč, Su 100Kč. Blues shows 130Kč. Grill items 159-199Kč. Salads 125-165Kč. Breakfast 95-159Kč. ☼ Open M-F 10am-2am, Sa-Su 10am-3am. Kitchen closes at midnight. Jazz/Blues Club doors open 7:30pm, shows start 9pm.

KLUB ÚJEZD
BAR

Újezd 422/18 ☎251 510 873 www.klubujezd.cz

Sea monsters greet you upon entrance (not a mirror, actually), setting the tone nicely for this bar. Klub Újezd is a multi-story bar with an eclectic character and equally unique client base. The basement is particularly interesting, with a quite literal underground vibe. Upstairs, the ambiance is more lounge-y and smoky. The décor is at best, odd, but the place is well-known and well-loved, giving hope to weirdos everywhere. Maybe high school just didn't get you, but this place does. The space is filled with peculiar original art, and the overall effect is very alt.

i A: Malostranská. From the Metro, take tram 12, 20, or 22 to Újezd. The club is right by the tram stop. Rum 46-220Kč. Whisky 60-140Kč. Beer 24-60Kč. Ⓧ Club open daily 6pm-4am. Bar open daily 2pm-4am.

POPOCAFEPETL
BAR
Újezd 19   ☎739 110 021 www.popocafepetl.cz

The Popos—so loved, they made more of them. As of now, there's the Újezd one, the Michalská one, the Na Struze one, and the Italska one. Each has a different personality, but all are student hotspots. This particular PopoCafePetl is more barlike, and has a relaxed ambiance. The décor is very underground cellar, as is the trend in Prague. Popo stays open quite late, if you find yourself with desperate needs at 3:30am. If you get a chance, swing by the other Popos to compare and contrast, and pick your favorite. If you happen upon a slow night, the place is quite close to Klub Újezd as well.

i A: Malostranská. From the Metro, take tram 12, 20, or 22 to Újezd. The club is right by the tram stop. Beer 22-45Kč. Rum 29-95Kč. Short cocktails 35-85Kč. Ⓧ Open daily 3pm-4am.

Vinohrady

RADOST FX
BAR
Bělehradská 234/120   ☎224 254 776 www.radostfx.cz

We can't promise you an orgasm, but at the very least, an Orgasm. Bols Amaretto, Finlandia Vodka, and Bailey's Cream—that's probably what sexual satisfaction feels like anyway. If your exes are anything like ours, maybe even be better. In addition to "Orgasms," Radost FX's list of cocktails features names like FX Spaceship, Ice Gimlet, and Make Love. Radost FX is everything weird still within the realms of not-creepy. Eclectic sofas, chandeliers, and mirrors compose the bulk of the place's décor, and make for a cool, chaotic ambiance. The second floor of Radost FX serves as a lounge, best for when you want to consume your alcohol in a sitting position. Standing takes so much effort.

i C: I. P. Pavlova. Turn left onto Legerova. Walk down about a block and turn right onto Jugoslávská. Turn left onto Bělehradská. The club is on the right. Club is free for women, 100Kč for men. Vodka cocktails 105-145Kč. Rum cocktails 90-145 Kč. Ⓧ Club open Th-Sa 10pm-5am. Lounge open daily 11am-2am. Café open daily 11am-midnight.

CLUB TERMIX
CLUB
Třebízského 1514/4a   ☎222 710 462 www.club-termix.cz

A favorite for Prague's gay community, Club Termix is the universe's apology for Grindr. A small club with no cover charge, Termix fills up consistently with men looking for men. For the rest of the spectrum of people, the pickings are scarce—the club attracts many more men than women—but for those who fall into the target group, the ratio couldn't be better. The club's space hangs odd things from the ceiling, but here, it's really what's on the inside that counts. Catering to the gay community, Termix fills a rare niche so that you can fill your rare niche (too far?), and for that, the club is beloved.

i A: Jiřího z Poděbrad. From the station, walk down Vinohradská toward U vodárny. Turn right onto Třebízského. The club is on the right. No cover charge. Beer 25-85Kč. Cocktails 30-130Kč. Ⓧ Open W-Sa 10pm-5am.

SOKOOL
BAR
Polská 1   ☎222 210 528 www.sokool.cz

The kind of building only a mother could love, the space occupied by SoKool, previously a restaurant in Prague's communist past, isn't doing anyone any visual favors. The inside—a classic pub preferred by locals—serves as a reminder of the dangers of judging a book by its cover (thanks, mom). Wooden chairs, wooden tables, and a seemingly random assortment of framed items fill the place and give it an informal relaxed feel. SoKool stands by the park Riegrovy sady, a favorite look-out over Prague. Indeed, in Riegrovy sady, with your back to SoKool, your view of Prague improves immediately.

i A: Jiřího z Poděbrad. Walk down Vinohradská toward U vodárny. Turn right onto Budečská. Turn left onto Polská. The bar is on the right. Cocktails 64-89Kč. Wine (by glass) 19Kč. Beer 19-30Kč. ☑ Open M-F 11am-midnight, Sa noon-midnight, Su noon-11pm.

BAR & BOOKS   BAR
Mánesova 64   ☎222 724 581 www.barandbooks.cz
If drunk texting proves anything, it's that alcohol and words go together like Netflix, flunking your biochem final, and bitching about how unfair that curve was anyway. Chugging wine alone is frowned-upon, but add books into the mix and it becomes "having refined tastes." The inside of Bar & Books—the one in Mánesova, one of two Bar & Books in Prague with counterparts in Warsaw and New York City—is lined with shelves of books that whisper "culture" in soothing British accents. The dimly-lit bar has a romantic atmosphere, best for the couple with exquisite tastes looking for a relaxed, sophisticated night. The elegant décor transports visitors back to 1940s New York, and the bar hosts events including karaoke, live music, neo-burlesque, and complimentary cigars for ladies's nights.

i A: Jiřího z Poděbrad. From the station, head north and turn left onto Mánesova. Walk down about two blocks, and the cafe will be on your left. Cocktails 145-295Kč. Wine (by glass) 135-155Kč. ☑ Open daily 5pm-3am.

ZANZIBAR   BAR
Americká 152/15   ☎222 520 315 www.kavarnazanzibar.cz
A slightly upscale cafe + restaurant + bar, Zanzibar is your standard Czech pub plus better lighting, polished wood, and a touch of elegance. Patrons can find full meals, espresso drinks, and alcohol enjoyed alongside locals out with their friends or coworkers. Casually sophisticated, Zanzibar attracts clientele looking for a calm drink with friends, leaving behind the hordes of horny teens hoping to get plastered in Prague. Whether you're looking for a meal, a drink, or somewhere to go when your hostelmates are too annoying—Zanzibar has a little something for everyone.

i A: Náměstí Míru. From the station, walk down Americká for about 5 minutes. The cafe is on the right. Cocktails 129-139Kč. Wine (by glass) 32-45Kč. Beer 39-45Kč. Sandwiches 95-129Kč. ☑ Open M-Th 8am-11pm, F 8am-midnight, Sa 10am-midnight, Su 10am-11pm.

Holešovice

CROSS CLUB   CLUB
Plynární 1096/23   ☎736 535 053 www.crossclub.cz
Decked out in more metal than a Hot Topic employee, Cross Club is Henry Ford's assembly line meets the Transformers meets drunk Europeans. Industrial vibes, complemented by electronic and alt music, dominate the bar/club/restaurant, meaning there are pipes everywhere and the entire thing feels like the coolest robot's body you've ever been in. More than just your average robot, however, Cross Club's ambiance, food, and drinks keep this place popular and one of Prague's best nightlife offerings.

i C: Nádraží Holešovice. Turn left onto Plynární. Cross Club is on the left. Cover varies. ☑ Bar open daily 2pm-2am. Club open F-Sa 6pm-7am, Su-Th 6pm-5am.

czech republic

MECCA CLUB

CLUB

U průhonu 799/3   ☎734 155 300 www.mecca cz

A mecca of what remains unclear, but this club certainly is the center of a lot of attention. The décor of the club implies luxury and class, though it draws the same crowd as any other big Prague club. Open for only two days a week, Mecca Club has got the exclusivity thing down on lock. Supply and demand, bitches. Equipped with five bars, Mecca keeps the alcohol flowing, like any respectable club should. International DJs fill the space with the kind of music ideal for rubbing against other people. If your money is just weighing you down too much, spring for a VIP table. One step closer to living out your dream of being a Kardashian.

i C: Nádraží Holešovice. Turn left onto Plynární and then right onto Osadní. Walk down this street until you turn left onto U průhonu. Mecca Club is on the left. Often no cover, but check website for specific events. ۩ Open Fr-Sa 8pm-6am.

FRAKTAL

BAR

Šmeralova 1 Praha 7   ☎222 946 845 www.fraktalbar.cz

Vera Bradley + the southwestern United States + the fashion sense of your aunt who did a lot of drugs in the 70s but is now a nice eclectic lady give this restaurant and bar happy vibes. Fraktal serves Mexican and pub food, and most importantly, plenty, plenty of beer. It's not a place for a rowdy night, but a nice spot to eat and drink among friendly people. There's outdoor seating for warm nights and a more casual ambiance. A nice respite from the throbbing music of clubs, a trip to Fraktal is worth it for everyone that understands it's so much nicer to consume alcohol sitting down.

i C: Vltavská. Walk down Heřmanova, then turn right onto Kamenická. Walk down half a block and turn left onto Městský Okruh/Pražský okruh/Veletržní. Continue until you reach Šmeralova. Fraktal is on your left. Nachos 110-155Kč. Burritos 155-145Kč. Beer 22-65Kč. ۩ Open daily 11am-midnight.

ESSENTIALS

Practicalities

- **TOURIST INFORMATION CENTRE** (Staroměstské náměstí 1, Staré Město. www.prague.eu. Open daily 9am-7pm.) Other branches in Wenceslas Square (Václavské náměstí. ۩ Open daily 10am-6pm) and Lesser Town Bridge Tower (Mostecká. ۩ Open daily 10am-6pm).

- **BANKS/ATMS:** ATMs can be found in the city center by Czech and international banks, of which many are located around Wenceslas Square. Cash machines in general can be found in large shopping centers as well as metro stations. Most accept regular international cards with Visa, Plus, Mastercard, Cirrus or Maestro symbols.

- **INTERNET:** Free Wi-Fi can be found in most McDonalds and KFC restaurants as well as Starbucks around Czech Republic. Look around for the 'Wi-Fi Zdarma,' or Free Wi-Fi signs on windows of cafes and restaurants to find Wi-Fi zones. There are also Internet cafes around the city for those unable to find Wi-Fi elsewhere. Click Internet Café (Malé nám. 13 ۩ Open daily 10am-11pm). Interlogic Internet Café (Budějovická 1123/13. Open M-F 9am-10pm, Sa-Su 11am-10pm.)

- **POST OFFICE:** Main Post Office (Jindřišská 909/14 ☎221 131 111; www.ceskaposta.cz. ۩ Open daily 2am-midnight.) Most other post offices are open M-F 8am-6pm.

Emergency Numbers

- **EMERGENCY NUMBER:** 112

- **POLICE:** 156 (city police), 158 (Police of the Czech Republic)

- **AMBULANCE:** 155

- **FIRE:** 150

- **RAPE CRISIS CENTER:** The White Circle of Safety (U Trojice 2. Hotline: ☎257 317 100. 🛈 Open M-Th 5pm-8pm; F by appointment 9am-1pm)

- **HOSPITALS:** Public hospitals that treat foreigners without European insurance and have English-speaking staff and emergency care: University Hospital in Motol (V Úvalu 84 ☎224 431 111). Nemocnice Na Homolce (Roentgenova 37/2 ☎257 271 111).

- **PRIVATE CLINIC:** Poliklinika Na Národní (Národní 1010/9 ☎222 075 119). Unicare Medical Cente (Na Dlouhém Lánu 563/11 ☎420 608 103 050).

- **24/7 PHARMACIES:** Lékárna Palackého (Palackého 5 ☎224 946 982 / 222 928 220). Lékárna U Svaté Ludmily (Belgická 37 ☎222 513 396 / 222 519 731). Ústavní lékárna FTNsP (Thomayerova nemocnice, Vídeňská 800 ☎261 081 111 / 261 084 019).

Getting There

There are no direct trains or buses that will get you from the airport to the city center, but there are bus lines that will connect you to metro lines in the city. Tickets for buses or trams should be purchased at the Public Transport counters at the arrivals halls of Terminal 1 or Terminal 2, open from 7am-10pm. If they are closed, you can use the vending machines at the bus stop or purchase one from the driver. Note that the drivers will only accept small notes and change, and may require exact amounts.

Tickets are valid based on the amount of time passed since validating. A 32Kč ticket will be valid for 90 minutes for any type of public transport including transfers. You may need to purchase an extra half-price ticket for large pieces of luggage. Upon boarding the train, bus, or tram, make sure to validate your ticket by sliding your ticket into the yellow validating machines on the poles next to vehicle doors.

Bus 119 - leaves from Terminal 1 (Exit D, E, F) and Terminal 2 (Exit C, D, E). Get off at the last stop, Nádraži Veleslavín (Metro line A). The bus runs every 5 to 20min from 4:15am to 11:30pm, and the journey takes about 20min. From Nádraži Veleslavín, the Metro connects to Malostranská in Mala Strana, Staroměstské náměstí in Old Town or Můstek near Wenceslas Square.

Getting Around

Public Transportation

The same ticket is used for all forms of public transportation, and different tickets are valid for different amounts of time. A standard adult single ticket costs 32Kč and is valid for 90 minutes. Shorter tickets for 30 minutes can be bought 24Kč and longer tickets can be bought for 24 hours (110Kč), 3 days (310Kč), or 5 days (550Kč). Once the ticket is bought and you have boarded, be sure to validate your ticket by sliding it into the yellow validating machines that are next to poles on trams and buses and by the entrance of the metro station for metros.

Metro

The Prague Metro runs on 3 lines: A (green), B (yellow), and C (Red). It operates daily from 5am-midnight, and each train runs every 2-10 minutes. Maps of the metro system can be found in metro stations and in the trains.

Trams

Day trams operate between 4:30am-12:15am, and run every 8 minutes in the morning, and 10 minutes during the day. During the weekend, these intervals may increase to 15 minutes during the day. Night trams operate between 12:15am-4:30am and run every 30 minutes. The central point of night-time transfers is Lazarska.

Buses

Day buses operate between 4:30am-12:15pm, and run every 5-15 minutes in the morning, and 10-20 minutes during the day. During the weekend these intervals may increase to 10-60 minutes during the day. Night buses operate between 12:15am-4:30am and run every 30-60 minutes.

Taxis

Ubers are usually readily available, but taxis are also available in Prague. The maximum fare for taxis is 28 Kč/km, with a boarding fee of 40Kč. You can board taxis by waiting at taxi stands that can be found on roads including Jelení, Loretánské nám. 2, Malostranské nám., nám. Republiky, and more, but it is recommended that you order a taxi through a dispatching office where you can get information on fares in advance. Dispatching companies that speak English and also allow you to order a taxi online include AAA radiotaxi (☎222 333 222, www.aaataxi.cz/en), Citytaxi Praha (☎257 257 257 www.citytaxi.cz/en/praha), and Modrý anděl (☎240 727 222 333,www.modryandel.cz/en).

czech republic essentials

MONEY

Tipping and Bargaining

Like most European cities, Prague's policy on tipping is pretty relaxed: most locals will just round up. Aim for around 5-10% if you're satisfied with your service. Touristy restaurants in the center of town will expect a 15-20% tip, but it's best to avoid those places anyway. Bargaining is only done in open-air markets or antique shops.

SAFETY AND HEALTH

Local Laws and Police

You should not hesitate to contact the police in the Czech Republic. Be sure to carry a valid passport, as police have the right to ask for identification. Police can sometimes be unhelpful if you are the victim of a currency exchange scam; in that case, you might be better off seeking advice from your embassy or consulate.

Drugs and Alcohol

If you carry insulin, syringes, or any prescription drugs on your person, you must also carry a copy of the prescriptions and a doctor's note. The drinking age in the Czech Republic is 18. Avoid public drunkenness, as it will jeopardize your safety. The possession of small quantities of marijuana (less than 15g) was decriminalized in 2009. Carrying drugs across an international border—drug trafficking—is a serious offense that could land you in prison.

Smoking is incredibly popular in the Czech Republic. If you are sensitive to cigarette smoke, ask for a non-smoking room in a hotel or hostel or to be seated in the non-smoking area of restaurants.

SPECIFIC CONCERNS

Petty Crime and Scams

Scams and petty theft are unfortunately common in the Czech Republic. An especially common scam in bars and nightclubs involves a local woman inviting a traveler to buy her drinks, which end up costing exorbitant prices; the proprietors of the establishment (in cahoots with the scam artist) may then use force to ensure that the bill is paid. Travelers should always check the prices of drinks before ordering. Another common scam involves a team of con artists posing as metro clerks and demanding that you pay large fines because your ticket is invalid. Credit card fraud is also common in Eastern Europe. Travelers who have lost credit cards or fear that the security of their accounts has been compromised should contact their credit card companies immediately.

Con artists often work in groups and may involve children. Beware of certain classics: sob stories that require money, rolls of bills "found" on the street, mustard spilled (or saliva spit) onto your shoulder to distract you while they snatch your bag. **Never let your passport or your bags out of your sight.** Hostel workers will sometimes stand at bus and train arrival points to recruit tired and disoriented travelers to their hostel; never believe strangers who tell you that theirs is the only hostel open. Beware of **pickpockets** in large crowds, especially on public transportation.

Visitors to Prague should never enter a taxi containing anyone in addition to the driver and should never split rides with strangers. While traveling by train, it may be preferable to travel in cheaper "cattle-car" type seating arrangements; the large number of witnesses makes such carriages safer than seating in individual compartments. Travelers should avoid riding on night buses or trains, where the risk of robbery or assault is particularly high. *Let's Go* does not recommend hitchhiking and picking up hitchhikers.

DENMARK

Straddling the border between Scandinavia and continental Europe, Denmark packs majestic castles, pristine beaches, and thriving nightlife onto the compact Jutland peninsula and its network of islands. Vibrant Copenhagen boasts busy pedestrian thoroughfares and one of the world's tallest carousels in Tivoli Gardens, while beyond the city, fairytale lovers can tour Han Christian Andersen's home in rural Odense. In spite of the nation's historically homogenous population, its Viking past has given way to a dynamic multicultural society that draws in visitors as it turns out Legos and Skagen watches.

greatest hits

- **#NOFILTER:** For one of the most iconic views of Copenhagen, take a walk down **Nyhavn** (p. 150), a famous waterfront area with colorful buildings.

- **UGLY DUCKLINGS UNITE:** Pay your respects to the man who invented your childhood at the **Hans Christian Andersen Museum** (p. 162) in Odense.

- **OH DEER: BAMBI FANS TAKE NOTE:** Aarhus's **Deer Park** (p. 158) is a relaxing place to contemplate life while also petting deer.

copenhagen

Most pollsters rank Denmark as the happiest country on earth. It's easy to brush that away. Happiness is so subjective, ya know? But then you'll get to Copenhagen, and it will slowly dawn on you: damn, these people are happy. As the capital city, Copenhagen is colorful, relaxed, and close to nature. Their greatest cultural creation is not the Vikings, but a concept called hygge that's best described as "being cozy with friends and family."

Copenhagen is the kind of place where you can spend the day cafe-hopping in search of the perfect chai, or strolling through palaces and gardens before sampling the newest sushi-tapas fusion. It's a city where the old and the new have reached a harmony, and it may just be the liveliest place you visit. Given the city's size, there are plenty of cheap hotels and hostels around. Unlike other Scandinavian cities, it really is possible to have fun here without emptying your wallet. The nightlife runs the gamut from hedonistic nightclubs and punk rock bars to microbreweries and jazz clubs—and all at an affordable price. For foodies, the city has everything you can imagine, especially at massive "food halls" where dozens of stands hawk the latest trends in Nordic cuisine, dessert-making, and Middle Eastern street food. You can spend a month here and still not see everything, so whether it's art museums or coffee shops, bookstores or bars, we trust you'll get up to plenty of exciting adventures while you're here.

ACCOMMODATIONS

GENERATOR HOSTEL   HOSTEL $

Adelgade 5   ☎78 77 54 00 generatorhostels.com/en/destinations/copenhagen

Generator has everything you could want in a hostel: comfy rooms, a restaurant and bar, a huge outdoor space, and, best of all, hammocks. Everywhere. The main floor is littered with blackboards giving advice on the best things to do in Copenhagen, and the staff seem particularly well-equipped to help you build an itinerary. Generator feels part hotel, part tourist agency, and it might just be the best decision you make while in town.

i Singles 480 DKK. Doubles 960 DKK. Dorms 150 DKK. Breakfast 70 DKK. 🕐 Reception 24hr.

DOWNTOWN   HOSTEL $$

Vandkunsten 5   ☎70 23 21 10 www.copenhagendowntown.com

Walk by this place and the first thing you'll notice is its guests: they're strewn out on beanbags or crashed on couches. Many are sipping Carlsbergs or pouring over maps in what looks like a commercial for budget cartography school, but this is just another day at one of Copenhagen's most popular hostels. With its sidewalk lounge area, free pasta, 2-for-1 happy hour, and a slew of other goodies specially tailored to backpackers, Downtown runs an operation that's hard to beat. Yoga? They got it. Free tours? Yep. Double shots for under 40 DKK? That's the price of half a beer in Norway—sign us up!

i Singles 686-931 DKK. 6-person dorm 225-284 DKK. 10-person dorm 200-236 DKK. Reception 24hr.

SLEEP IN HEAVEN   HOSTEL $

Struenseegade 7   ☎35 35 46 48 www.sleepinheaven.com

This hostel with a cutesy name is located in Nørrebro, a leafy neighborhood of Copenhagen filled with kebab shops, cafes, and microbreweries—and it hosts a decent bar and cafe onsite. Sleep in Heaven has a much more intimate feel than other hostels because it's a much smaller operation, but the rooms are spacious and well-ventilated (while the lockers are a definite plus). Consider this place

hygge

Look up *hygge* (pronounced something like hoo-guh) in a dictionary and you're likely to find something like "coziness," "warmth," or "intimacy," but those don't quite do it justice. As one of our Danish friends explained: "*Hygge* is when you sit around with family and drink wine and eat grilled pork and everyone is happy." What's so complicated about that? Well, that's technically hygge, but it encompasses a lot of other things, too. *Hygge* is creamy porridge and rye bread that makes you reminisce about childhood (think "comfort food"). *Hygge* is ugly Christmas sweaters and beer as you sit by the Yule log and watch the snowy weather. Hygge can even be simply sitting in a café soaking up your friends' beaming Danish smiles. Yet, bizarrely, we've also heard that bicycling can be a form of *hygge*, as is any intimate setting lit by candles. For all the different definitions, though, it seems to be the epitome of the Danish social experience and something no Dane can live without—so consider yourself honored if you can *hygge* your way into a family dinner and spend the night basking in each other's *hygge*-ty.

the Ed Sheeran of hostels: it's charming, hip, and bearded, but with enough business acumen to be attractive to a wider demographic.

i 6-person dorm 185 DKK. 9- or 12-person dorm 170 DKK. Reception 24hr.

URBAN HOUSE
HOSTEL $$
Colbjørnsensgade 5
☎33 23 29 29 www.urbanhouse.me

Urban House is a solid place to stay in Copenhagen. The rooms have en suite bathrooms, the lobby has a sizable bar, and Central Station is only five minutes away. However, be ready for a more depersonalized experience than what you'll get at Generator or Downtown: the place is entirely self-check in, and while assistants and bartenders are around, there is no official reception. If independence rings your liberty bell, though, then this hostel was made for you.

i Singles 950-1100 DKK. 6-person dorms 179-264 DKK. 8-person 174-259 DKK. Entirely self-check in: pay online and receive a code to get into your room. No official reception, but staff usually available 24hr.

WAKEUP COPENHAGEN
HOTEL $
Borgergade 9

If the idea of spending the night with strangers doesn't float your boat, WakeUp will probably be the best (and most affordable) option for you in Copenhagen. With basic economy rooms going for around 500 DKK, it's certainly not ideal for those on a budget, but as FDR once said, "When you gotta splurge, you gotta splurge." The rooms at WakeUp are chic and well-designed, with comfortable mattresses, en suite bathrooms, and a TV, while the hotel itself is in a superb location right off of Gothersgade (around the block from Generator Hostel, Kongens Have, and many of the bars and restaurants listed here).

i Singles 500 DKK. Often 100 DKK cheaper if booked directly on their website. Reception 24hr.

SIGHTS

CHRISTIANSBORG
CASTLE
Prins Jørgens Gård 1
☎33 92 64 92 www.christiansborg.dk

Danes are absolutely in love with their royal family and now, for only 100 DKK you can take part in that experience. Walking through Christianslott is like being in a fairy tale: there's a Rapunzel-worthy tower overlooking the whole city, stables to house the royal ponies, and banquet halls that look like something out of fairy tale (though, presumably, with better mother figures and fewer talking animals). The best part of the palace tour is the tapestry room, showcasing eleven massive tapestries which depict Danish history from the beginning till now. Apparently each one has a small "mistake" for intrepid museum goers to find — so if you happen to catch a glimpse of Donald Duck above Hitler's head, congratulations! You may just be knighted…

i *Combination ticket 120 DKK, students 100 DKK. Open 10am-5pm.*

NYHAVN
Nyhavn 1-71

NEIGHBORHOOD
www.nyhavn.com

You've probably seen this place on postcards, but that's nothing compared to what it looks like in real life. Nyhavn (meaning "new harbor") is one of the main waterways in Copenhagen and it's surrounded by some very Nordic-looking buildings: almost every house overlooking the port is yellow, red, green, or blue. Like everything else Scandinavian, they look happy, old-fashioned and immaculately put together. From the port, you have the added bonus of being able to take guided tours of the harbor…because if anything screams "Eurotrip" it's canal boat ride selfie.

i *Free. Open 24hr. Companies like Stromma offer sightseeing boat tours leaving from Nyhavn. Adults 80 DKK. Tours last an hour and depart one to four times every hour until 6pm. Check www.stromma.dk for more information.*

KONGENS HAVE
Gothersgade 11

GARDEN

Kongens Have is the epitome of everything Danish: it's got nature, it's got public drinking, and it's got roughly a metric ton of *hygge*. The park, one of Copenhagen's biggest and most centrally located, is an absolute must if you're looking

christiana

Walking into Christiania is like taking a step into a different planet. From the moment you pass the giant wooden gates, there are three rules every traveller must abide by: 1) have fun, 2) don't run, and 3) for the love of God do not take photos. Often referred to as Freetown Christiania, this community is in a curious legal limbo that makes it an autonomous state with very… different practices from the rest of Copenhagen. From the moment you enter, you'll notice everyone is smoking a spliff in the open. Walk down the community's charmingly named Pusher Street, and you'll get a contact high stronger than a whiff of Bob Marley's dreams.

And while Let's Go in no way endorses the use of illegal drugs, there's a very important reason we're mentioning this place at all. Denmark is already one of the most progressive countries in the world. But when Christiania declared itself an independent commune in the 70s, it pushed the limits of what Danish society found acceptable. After dramatic clashes with police and organized crime in the 90s, the commune enacted a zero tolerance policy for selling or using hard drugs and has since then achieved a fragile de facto independence from Copenhagen and its police force. If you spend two seconds at any hostel in Copenhagen, someone is guaranteed to mention Christiania and how cool it is that they sell pot there. But we assume you're smarter than the average plebeian, so you should know that this place is much, much more than a drug haven. It's a self-sufficient community with fully-functional cafés, restaurants, markets, and a population that has equal say in its policies. Christiania is a real life experiment in anarchist living and, as long as you follow the rules, a perfectly safe and cool place to visit.

to kick back and relax for any afternoon. The gardens are immaculately kept, there are often concerts there in summer, and it overlooks a number of beautiful Baroque buildings. Spend a day here and tell us the Danes aren't going to save the world.

i Free. Open daily 11am-7pm.

STATE ART MUSEUM (STATENS MUSEUM FOR KUNST) MUSEUM

Sølvgade 48-50 ☎33 74 84 94 www.smk.dk

Whether you want Renaissance landscapes or Greek statues, three-nippled goats or trippy expressionism, this has got to be the best art museum in Scandinavia. Even if you're not an art-lover, the roaming exhibits are bizarre and alarmingly fun to visit. The modern section houses Danish work from the last 50 years, and it's incredibly interesting to see how much they've changed. If you don't believe us, try explaining how else the country went from Virgin Mary to midgets riding toothless prostitutes in under a century.

i Permanent exhibitions free. Special exhibitions 110 DKK, students 90 DKK. Open M-Tu 10am-5pm, W 10am-8pm, Th-Su 10am-5pm.

FOOD

▓ COPENHAGEN STREET FOOD STREET FOOD $

Trangravsvej on Papirøen (Paper Island)

There are over 30 restaurants and food trucks on these premises, with everything from Moroccan barbecue to local ice cream to a place called "OK Thai" that serves pretty bitchin' Thai food. Our recommendations: go by Anatolia for some gozleme (flatbread with feta and eggs), Latinda for plantains with guacamole, Pølse Kompagniet for organic sausages, and end with a bucket of booze at the Bucket Bar. Wandering through the stalls here is like being a child on Christmas morning. So get on over to Papirøen and prepare yourself for the culinary experience of a lifetime.

i Price varies based on restaurant. Most dishes under 80 DKK. Open M-Sa 11-10pm, Su 11am-8pm. Coffee available at 11am, food trucks open at noon.

▓ ZAFRAN PERSIAN $$

Blågårdsgade 9 ☎35 34 90 95

Zafran is one of Copenhagen's best Persian restaurants. Our personal favorite dish is the joojeh kebab—tender strips of marinated beef resting on a bed of buttery rice—though pretty much everything here is fresh and delicious. For starters, you can't go wrong with the mast-o-khiar (cucumber in mint yogurt) or the sabzi khordan (feta, dill, parsley, and onion scooped up with flatbread). Better yet, this place has a bring-your-own-wine policy because why not.

i Appetizers 40 DKK. Entrees 85-140 DKK. Open daily 5pm-10pm.

BEYTI KEBAB MIDDLE EASTERN $

Blågårdsgade 1 ☎32 17 00 03

These guys are the MLB to the pee-wee league kebab shops you'll find in most Copenhagen neighborhoods. They have a huge menu (50+ items) and offer everything from your standard shish kebabs and hamburgers to vegetarian mixes and more esoteric Turkish specialties. The bigger dishes (~75 DKK) include juicy skewers of meat, rice, yogurt and pita bread soaked in various sauces. For the more broke among you, Beyti also whips up the classics like durum shish kebab and shawarma for under 40 DKK. If the price and quality weren't enough, they have free Wi-Fi, so you can continue watching Top Chef as you scarf down your meat sticks and wonder when the crème freeeeche is coming.

i Entrees 75 DKK. Wraps and burgers 40 DKK. Salads 30 DKK. Open M-Th 11am-midnight, F-Sa 11am-6am, Su noon-midnight.

copenhagen

TORVEHALLERNE

Frederiksborggade 21 ☎70 10 60 70 www.torvehallernekbh.dk

There are a staggering 60 shops in Torvehallerne, so if you don't find something you like, there's a chance you are actually a lump of coal. While the center boasts too many places to list by name, we particularly enjoyed Banh Mi Daily (Vietnamese buns and spiced meat/herb baguettes; 58 DKK), Grøn (porridge is astounding) and Granny's House (Danish pastries—go for the peanut butter brownies and traditional rye bread; most under 30 DKK). Whether you're looking for coffee, sushi, wine or hand cream, you can be sure that a) they'll have it and b) it's more artisanal than a curated vegan cube of sustainably harvested oxygen.

i Price varies based on restaurant. Most dishes under 80 DKK. Open M-Th 10am-7pm, F 10am-8pm, Sa 10am-6pm, Su 11am-5pm.

SLIDERS

BURGERS $

Peblinge Dossering 2 ☎31 32 26 20

Sliders is like McDonald's older cousin who quit the fast food game and decided to make something of itself. That gamble has clearly paid off, as all nine burgers on the menu—from the BBQ pork to truffle cheese and hoisin duck—are leagues beyond what most places serve, and you can order them in batches of three. Though the restaurant can get packed, the communal table seems to turn over customers fast. If you're heading out for drinks in Nørrebro, Sliders is the perfect place to stock up on carbs and feel satisfied with your choices.

i Single slider 45 DKK. Three sliders and a side 119 DKK. Open Tu-Sa 11am-10pm, Su 11am-9pm; closed Mondays.

NIGHTLIFE

ALPEHYTTEN

BAR

Gothersgade 33A (in the basement) ☎51 29 51 20 www.alpe-hytten.dk

This place is unapologetically simple, and that's the source of all of its charm. It's a small, local joint where everyone seems to know each other—the staff, in fact, seemed perfectly at home chatting up the regulars and playing beer pong as they were working behind the counter. On weekends, you can get endless refills on beer for 50 DKK, and, if you're clumsy enough to spill your drink, there's a high chance you'll have to take the Punishment: a skull-shaped glass jar packed with tequila, salt, and God knows what else. If you want a good taste of Danish hygge and place that'll go easy on your wallet, Alpehytten should be your go-to spot.

i Drinks 40-90 DKK. Open Tu-W 8pm-3am, Th 8pm-4am, F 4pm-5am, Sa 9pm-5am.

BUTCHER'S

CLUB

Vestergade 10 ☎31 37 86 18 www.butcherscph.dk

Butcher's is great if you want a nightclub but hate the anonymity of 8,000 drunk teens humping in the dark. The lighting here is dim, but it's intimate enough to have a conversation, or at least make eye contact with the person you're grinding on. With admission at 30 DKK and most drinks below 80 DKK, it's not terrible on the wallet (though if you want to pop bottles, it's going to cost significantly more). For best results, drink somewhere cheap, come here on the later side, and spend the night bumping, twisting and twerking the night away.

i Cover 30 DKK. Beers 50 DKK. Mixed drinks 70-100 DKK. Th are 18+; F-Sa are 21+. Open Th 10pm-5am, F-Sa 9pm-5am.

TYROLIA BIER KLUB

CLUB

Vestergade 12 ☎61 67 29 62 www.tyrolia.dk

If you arrive at Tyrolia before 11pm on the weekend, there's no entrance fee and there's cheap (and sometimes free) beer. That's actually all you need to know. Granted, you can only choose between Carlsberg and Tuborg. But beggars can't be choosers, right? Go to Australian Bar around the corner at the same times and

top danish foods you need to devour

1. STEGT FLÆSK: It's fried bacon, parsley sauce, and potatoes, and it's washed down with beer. Ain't nothing better (or more likely to give you a heart attack) than this classic Danish dish.

2. SMØRREBRØD: This Scandinavian classic is as simple as they come: it's an open sandwich with endless possibilities. Fish? Fo' sho. Meats and cheeses? Obviously. Chocolate? No, that's gross, but you can probably pay someone to throw some chocolate on there. No questions asked.

3. RUGBRØD: Don't ask us how to say this. Just know that it's absolutely delicious. Apparently all Danish children (and adults) eat this bread, and it's easy to see why: it's jampacked with seeds like it just survived a sunflower explosion, and the dough itself has a slightly acidic taste somewhere between sourdough and rye. It's tasty, healthy, and apparently available only in Denmark—so make sure you get a bite in before it's confiscated at border control!

4. FRIKADELLER: Meatballs. As in balls of meat. Rolled in breadcrumbs. Fried with onion and eggs. Served in mouthwatering garlic gravy. You can cry now.

---

there's also free entrance and often free beer at 11pm. You probably don't want to spend the whole night at either of these places, but your inner economist is beaming.

i *Cover 50 DKK. No cover 10pm-11pm. Beer 30 DKK. Shots 20-30 DKK. Open F-Sa 10pm-5am.*

NØRREBRO BRYGHUS
BAR

Baldersbuen 25 ☎46 55 04 70 www.noerrebrobryghus.dk

Microbreweries, like hula hoops and the Facebook, seem to be "all the rage" these days, so a trip here is definitely worth it if you want to see how the times they are a changin'. Bryghus seems to be a massive hit with the locals (making it difficult to get a table or even a spot on the floor during music performances) but it's profoundly worth it. The Bombay Pale Ale and Nørrebro Pilsner are both delicious, while you can also try a number of experimental flavors (From Latvia With Love, a porter clocking in at 7.7% alcohol content, almost gave us enough courage to stand up to Vladimir Putin). If you're out on the town in Nørrebro, this may be one of the smartest decisions you'll make all night.

i *Beers: 25cl (small) 48 DKK; 40cl (medium) 69 DKK; 60 cl (large) 85 DKK. Brewery open M-Th 5:30pm-10pm, F-Sa 5:30pm-11pm.*

KARUSELLEN
BAR

Ægirsgade 10 ☎35 83 29 16

Remember how we said there's nothing fancy about Alpehytten? Well, there's really nothing fancy about this place—yet many of the locals we met called it their favorite bar in Copenhagen. The atmosphere inside feels like a Viking mead hall: loud, smokey and pretty frickin' raucous. Its location deep in Nørrebro means that most of the crowd are locals (and young ones at that), but both the clientele and staff are friendly and eager to chat. If you're looking for a slightly rough, no-nonsense spot, this is your place: the prices are great and the inevitable walk home sends you past a hundred kebab spots to satisfy your drunk needs.

i *Drinks 20-30 DKK. Open M-W 10am-2am, Th 10am-3am, F-Sa 10am-4am, Su 10am-8pm.*

SUNDAY
CLUB

Lille Kongensgade 16 ☎53 66 82 28 www.sundayclub.dk

If you're an Ibiza-type clubber and need a minimum of 2,000 people in the same room to feel comfortable, this is the place for you. Between the dance floor,

bars, and terrace, it's impossible not to find one cutie that you'd like to dance with. In any event, all of that debauchery comes at a cost: most drinks are in the 100 DKK range and above, and the entrance can be steep (and come with an hour-long wait.) However, every city has that one club whose name is whispered with the same fear and admiration as "Voldemort" and, after a night here, you'll see why for Copenhagen, it's Sunday.

i Cover varies, usually over 100 DKK. Drinks 100 DKK. Open F-Sa 11:30pm-5am.

ESSENTIALS
Practicalities

denmark

- **TOURIST OFFICES:** Copenhagen Visitor Center (Vesterbrogade 5 ☎70 22 24 42; www.visitco-penhagen.dk. ⏰ Open M-Sa 9am-7pm.)

- **TOURS:** Hostels such as Generator, Downtown, and Sleep in Heaven often arrange free walking tours in the mornings—simply ask reception for times and details. As Copenhagen is one of the most bike-friendly cities in the world, bike tours are very popular, but consult the Tourist Information Center website for full listings. **Grand Tour** (www.stromma.dk. Tickets for one hour boat tour 80 DKK): sightseeing by boat around Copenhagen's harbor and coastline. Leaves one to four times per hour from Nyhavn harbor until 6pm; tickets can be bought on-site. **Pub Crawl** Copenhagen (www.pubcrawlcopenhagen.dk. 140 DKK): A five-hour long pub crawl that comes with free entrance at night clubs, discounts on beers and mixers, and free shots. Meets at Black Memorial Anchor in Nyhavn every Tu and Th-Sa at 8pm.

- **CURRENCY EXCHANGE:** Possible at Copenhagen Airport, Forex stores, and most banks.

- **ATMS:** You're never more than five minutes away from an ATM in Copenhagen. They are often in front of banks and especially visible around major pedestrian spots like Stortorget, Central Station, and Gothersgade.

- **LUGGAGE STORAGE:** Available at Copenhagen Airport (small box 50 DKK, larger box 75 DKK) and at Copenhagen Central Station (small box 50 DKK, large box 60 DKK. ☒ Open M-Sa 5:30am-1am, Su 6am-1am.)

- **GLBT SERVICES:** LGBT Denmark (Nygace 7 ☎33 13 19 48. ☒ Best to call on Thursdays 2pm-5pm. www.lgbt.dk.)

- **LAUNDROMATS:** Easily done at hostels such as Generator or Downtown, but there are laundromats (Danish: vaskeri) all over Copenhagen. One centrally located one is Renseriet (Borgergade 18 ☎33 14 04 53. ☒ Open M-F 8am-5pm.)

- **INTERNET:** Wi-Fi is available widely throughout Copenhagen, with hotspots in the Copenhagen Visitor Center, Kastrup Airport, many train stations, and most hostels and hotels. Additionally, many chain stores such as 7-11 and Baresso Coffee also have free connectivity.

- **POST OFFICE:** Posthus Købmagergade (Købmagergade 33 ☎70 70 70 30. ☒ M-F 10am-6pm, Sa 10am-2pm, closed Sundays.)

Emergency

- **EMERGENCY NUMBER:** ☎112

- **POLICE (NON-EMERGENCY):** ☎114

- **MEDICAL EMERGENCY:** ☎1813

- **SEXUAL ASSAULT:** Thora Center for Sexual Assault ☎33 32 86 50

- **24 HOUR PHARMACIES:** Lyngby Svane Apotek (Lyngby Hovedgade 27 ☎45 87 00 96. ☒ Open 24/7.) Steno Apotek (Vesterbrogade 6C ☎33 14 82 66. ☒ Open 24/7.) Glostrup Apotek (Hovedvejen 101 ☎43 96 00 20. ☒ Open 24/7.)

- **PRIVATE DOCTORS:** Doctors at Laegelinien (☎25 96 93 75. www.laegelinien.dk.) Phone consultations and prescriptions from 130 DKK. House calls from 1200 DKK.

- **HOSPITALS:** Bispebjerg Hospital (Bispebjerg Bakke 23. 35 31 35 31.) Herlev Hospital (Herlev Ringvej 75 ☎38 68 38 68.) Hvidovre Hospital (Kettegårds Alle 30 ☎36 32 36 32.) Note: Foreign visitors are entitled to free medical treatment in case of an emergency.

Getting There

By Plane

Copenhagen Airport, also known as Kastrup, is the main airport servicing Denmark's capital city as well as much of southern Sweden. To get from the airport to Copenhagen Central Station takes less than 15 minutes by train. A one-way ride costs 48 DKK (if you're travelling to spots outside of the city limits, it's 75 DKK), and the train makes stops in Copenhagen at Central Station, Nørreport, and Østerport.

By Taxi

Taxis are much more expensive than public transportation and may take slightly longer. Most cab companies have fixed fares to and from the airport and can be booked in advance, but the 20min. ride will cost at least 250 DKK, often 300 DKK or higher.

By Train

All trains coming in from other parts of Denmark or Europe will arrive at Copenhagen Central Station (Københavns H). The train from Malmö takes under 30 minutes and leaves at least twice per hour, at a cost of under 130 DKK. Central Station is also the drop off point for trains from other major Danish cities such as Odense (roughly 2hr. away, one-way tickets around 270 DKK) and Aarhus (roughly 4 hours away, one-

copenhagen

way tickets around 600 DKK). Tickets can either be purchased at the station, online, or, for those with a European sim card, via the DSB app.

Getting Around

By Public Transportation

Copenhagen's transportation is run by the DSB, the Danish national railway company. To ride the metro, you can purchase tickets at most 7-11's and train stations, or with the app "Mobilbilletter Hovedstaden." Note: Transportation is on the honor system here, but know that if you are asked for a ticket and cannot produce one you can be fined up to 750 DKK. A single ride ticket for 2 zones (covers most of the city) costs 24 DKK; 24-hour ticket 80 DKK; 72-hour ticket 200 DKK.

The Copenhagen Card provides free admission to 74 museums, free public transportation, and discounts on restaurants and parking. 24 hours 360 DKK; 48 hours 500 DKK; 72 hours 590 DKK.

By Taxi

Taxis are more expensive than using public transportation, but given the size of Copenhagen, they are often your best choice on late nights out. You'll often find them lingering outside of popular tourist destinations or nightlife hotspots, but you can also book in advance. Taxa (☎35 35 35 35. www.taxa.dk.) Hailing off the street can have a base fee of 24-40 DKK and booking in advance will be 37-50 DKK. From there, it's 7 DKK per minute and 19.5 DKK per km.

Uber is widely available throughout Copenhagen, with a base fare of 40 DKK and a price of 4 DKK per minute and 20 DKK per km (minimum fare of 100 DKK).

aarhus

Aarhus is the second largest city in Denmark, and it's about as wet as your dreams. The main pedestrian walkways all follow the winding route of the Aarhus River, and most attractions are never more than ten minutes away from the ocean. With Parisian cafes and Viking cathedrals, Turkish kebab and massive Irish pubs, it's a city that straddles the old and the new. It has all the food options of an international city, alongside a vibrant Nordic cuisine culture, and you'll find cafes and coffee shops on nearly every block. In terms of nightlife, Aarhus can be as raucous as a frat house or as cool, calm and collected, as a scene from Mad Men—whatever your preference, you'll find it here. Perhaps most importantly, penny-pinching travellers will be happy to know that the city is not as expensive as Copenhagen, though the limited hostelling opportunities make budget hotels your best option. Whatever your reason for coming here, you may find Aarhus to be the most charming "little" big city you've ever visited.

ACCOMMODATIONS

CABINN AARHUS   HOTEL $$

Kannikegade 14   ☎86 75 70 00 cabinn.com/CABINN-Aarhus-Hotel

Much like its Odense cousin, this Aarhus branch of the Danish hotel chain is pleasant, affordable, and located just steps from the Cathedral and Åboulevard. The hotel is in the process of doubling its capacity to 400 rooms, and we'd say it's best described as cheap and cozy without being cramped. Though the amenities may be simple—showers, Wi-Fi, TV, free coffee, and a bed—it's got a bang for your buck.

i Standard economy rooms 495 DKK. Larger rooms from 545 DKK. Book online to save 100 DKK.
🕐 Reception 24hr.

HOSTEL CITY SLEEP-IN
HOSTEL $

Havnegade 20 ☎86 19 20 55 www.citysleep-in.dk

City Sleep-In is a pretty simple place—clean, compact, and perhaps a bit drab in the lobby—but the price tag of 190 DKK makes it too attractive a bargain to pass up. It may not be the best place to socialize (it's about as quiet as watching an unexpected sex scene while at the movies with your parents), but there are plenty of good bars and restaurants nearby to make up for it.

i 6-bed dorm 190 DKK. ☼ Reception open M-F 8am-11am and 4pm-9pm, Sa-Su 8am-11am and 4pm-11pm.

SIMPLE BED HOSTEL
HOSTEL $

Åboulevarden 86 ☎24 25 97 02 www.simplebedhostel.com

We have to admire these people's upfront, no-bullshit naming policies. Simple Bed provides an entirely self-check in service with simple beds, a common room (the TV has Netflix!), and a shared kitchen. Everything is clean and comfortable enough to make it a livable and affordable spot for those passing through town, and the location just five minutes away from sites like the Cathedral only adds to the bargain.

i Singles 425 DKK. Doubles 525 DKK. 6-bed dorm 225 DKK. ☼ No reception, but owners live upstairs.

SIGHTS

AARHUS CATHEDRAL
CHURCH

Store Torv ☎86 20 54 00 www.aarhusdomkirke.dk

It may be hard to wax poetic on cathedrals when you see them so often in Europe, but the Aarhus Cathedral is pretty remarkable. The building itself dates back to the 900s, a time when Aarhus was a B-list Viking city, and it's still one of the tallest buildings there today. The inside is open to the public on weekdays and it's beautifully decorated. The frescoes of Jesus are fabulous and the small boats hanging from the ceiling are de-lish. This is one of the most iconic spots in Aarhus, and as a good tourist, you absolutely must visit it.

i Free. ☼ Open M 9am-1pm, Tu 10:30am-1pm, W-Th 9am-1pm and 4pm-6pm, F 9am-1pm.

ÅBOULEVARD
BOARDWALK

Meaning "River Boulevard" (because Danish would call a river "Å"), this narrow walkway travels along the water and brings you past the main shopping attractions and cafes that define urban life in Aarhus. Whether it's parks full of smooching couples, teens breakdancing in a public square, or sidewalk coffee shops staffed by neckbearded baristas, a walk along the boulevard shows a slice of Aarhus that brings a whole new meaning to the concept of people-watching.

i Free. ☼ Open 24/7.

KUNSTMUSEUM (ART MUSEUM)
MUSEUM

Aros Allé 2 ☎87 30 66 00 www.aros.dk

We imagine many visitors may be a bit shocked by a billboard of a naked woman pissing into a wine glass, but this newest ad for an art exhibition is just an everyday experience at the Aarhus Kunstmuseum. The white, angular awnings of the building's interior feel part Twilight Zone, part 2001: A Space Odyssey, and the exhibits mimic that diversity. Here you'll find French impressionists next to warzone photos, Chinese political posters next to pictures of pubic hair, and it all feels weirdly zen. The biggest reason to stop by, though, is the rainbow panorama: a 360 degree walkway on the museum's roof that overlooks the entire city and is covered by glass from every color on the spectrum. If you've ever wanted to see Aarhus in red, blue, pink or indigo, now's your chance.

i 90 DKK if under 28 years old above 28 110 DKK. Free for under 18. ☼ Open Tu 10am-5pm, W 10am-10pm, Th-Su 10am-5pm; closed Mondays.

aarhus

DEER PARK

Ørneredevej 6

If you're the kind of person who reads Walden Pond more than the Bible, you're in luck: Aarhus has the perfect place for you to kick back and contemplate civil disobedience—and better yet, there are deer! This park is roughly an hour south of downtown by foot, and it's positively swarming with deer (while it's unclear if they tease the ones with the funny noses, we suggest you find the one that looks most like Rudolf and give it extra love). As long as you don't feed the critters something stupid like Fruit Loops or pot brownies, you're more than welcome to interact with and pet them. And that really does make up for all the childhood trauma you suffered after watching Bambi.

i Free. ☼ Open daily 8am-sunset.

VIKING MUSEUM
MUSEUM

Sankt Clemens Torv 6 ☎87 16 10 16 www.moesgaardmuseum.dk/vikingemuseet

In case you needed a reminder that this country made its career pillaging and looting Europe, the Viking Museum has got you covered. The exhibits, located several feet underground in a basement darker than a Scandinavian winter, you can see the exploits of Denmark's first Christian king, the dentally-challenged Harald Bluetooth (and yes, he's the namesake for Bluetooth devices!). The museum gives interesting insight into Norse mythology and the founding of Aarhus, and its location directly across from the cathedral makes it a must-go on the list of sights to explore in the city.

i Free. ☼ Open M-F 10am-5pm.

DEN GAMLE BY
OPEN-AIR MUSEUM

Viborgvej 2 ☎86 12 31 88 www.dengamleby.dk

Want to see what life was like in Ye Olde Denmark? Want to eat homemade bread baked by women in bonnets or walk past charming wooden houses? Den Gamle By—Danish for "the old town"—is Aarhus's biggest attraction, and it's easy to see why. It's a massive, open air museum with recreations of life in the 1800s, 1920s, and 1970s. At each part, you can interact with park employees who discuss the relative merits of, we assume, burning coal, the Aryan race, and maybe LSD. If conversation is too much for you, simply seeing the development of architecture is interesting enough. Den Gamle By hosts buildings dating as far back as 1550, and truly immerses visitors in what Denmark looked like "back in the day." While the 135 DKK adult price tag may seem a bit high, we trust there is nowhere else in Europe where you can feel what it was like to be Hans Christian Andersen, a World War I vet, and a commune hippie all in one day.

i Entrance during the summer 135 DKK, students 70 DKK. Hours and prices vary each month, so check the website. Summer schedule listed here. ☼ Open Mar 28-June 26 10am-5pm; June 27-Aug 9 10am-6pm; Aug 10-Nov 13 10am-5pm.

FOOD

MACKIE'S PIZZA
PIZZA $$

Sankt Clemens Torv 9 ☎86 12 36 61 www.mackiespizza.dk

The restaurant's motto is "all people smile in the same language," and the food is definitely enough to leave you smiling and satisfied. It has all the deep fried, cheesy dishes we love and know mixed with just enough salads and wraps to make us feel almost good about ourselves. Add to that a full drink menu with dozens of spirits and beers, and you'll be singing the pledge of allegiance too. (Our personal favorite order: pulled pork BBQ pizza with a brown ale; 130 DKK.)

i Pizzas 100 DKK. ☼ Open M-Sa noon-11pm, Su noon-10pm.

JAKOB'S PITA BAR
Vestergade 3

MIDDLE EASTERN $

☎87 32 24 20 www.jacobsbarbq.dk

Jakob's is more than a Pita Bar—it's a brand, it's an idea, it's a lifestyle. For 50 DKK, you can stuff toasty bread with tasty meats like lamb, falafel, or chicken all topped with a kaleidoscope of sauces. More importantly, you can enjoy your treat while sitting in Jakob's Café next door or having a drink at the bar.

i *Pitas 50 DKK.* ☒ *Open M-Th 5pm-11pm, F-Sa 5pm-midnight, Su 5am-10pm.*

MEXICAN GRILL BURRITOPLUS
Guldsmedgade 15

MEXICAN $

☎22 30 92 48

Though critics and naysayers may opine that there's something rotten in the kingdom of Denmark, it's certainly not the burritos. This place serves up a tasty tortilla with chicken, sour cream, and all them fixings for only 49 DKK (add 20 DKK for guac) and, unlike whatever you told your prom date at 4am, it really is big enough. The place is located near one of Aarhus's biggest shopping streets and, for all of you who are aching under Europe's anti-Chipotle tyranny, it's a little taste of home.

i *Burrito 49 DKK. Guac 20 DKK.* ☒ *Open daily 11am-9pm.*

RESTAURANT RIVAS
Fredensgade 22

PERSIAN $$

☎86 13 15 17 www.restaurantrivas.dk

Rivas is a taste of Iran in Denmark. The interior feels almost like an homage to golden-age Hollywood, though instead of Elizabeth Taylor they have photos of famous Persian stars from the same era. The wine selection is great, the prices aren't bad, and dishes like the jujeh kebab are juicier than any gossip you'll hear all month. If you're looking for Middle Eastern food with a touch of elegance and meat that's been perfectly spiced and cooked, Rivas makes for a wonderful evening visit.

i *Entrees 89-150 DKK.* ☒ *Open daily 4pm-9:30pm.*

CAFÉ FAUST
Åboulevarden 38

CAFE $

☎86 19 07 06 www.cafefaust.dk

Located right on the Aarhus River, Faust feels like the kind of place where you wile away the hours smoking cigarettes and plotting the overthrow of the Czar. That may just be the European romantic in us, but the cafe definitely seems to be a magnet for all kinds of Danes: students, pensioners, families—there's got to be a revolutionary or two in the mix! The 10am-2pm brunch may feel a bit pricey, but the scent of cheeses, smoothies, eggs, bacon, nutella, nuts, and more made us open our wallets faster than China, 1979.

i *Brunch 115 DKK. Sandwiches 120 DKK.* ☒ *Open M-W 10am-midnight, Th 10am-1am, F-Sa 10am-2am, Su 10am-midnight.*

NIGHTLIFE

WAXIES
Frederiksgade 16

IRISH PUB

☎86 13 83 33 www.waxies.dk

Waxies advertises itself as "the biggest and best Irish pub in Aarhus," and this place does have a certain charm when you spend enough time inside. Like a decadently alcoholic wedding cake, Waxies has three floors with three different bars and hosts activities like quizzes and music shows in case all that booze still can't get you to socialize. With pints of beer going for as little as 30 DKK and weekend nights that last till 5am, this may be one of the best watering holes you find while in Aarhus.

i *Pints of beer 30-40 DKK. Drinks 50 DKK.* ☒ *Open M-T noon-2am, W-Th noon-3am, F-Sa noon-5am, Su noon-2am.*

aarhus

Skolegade 23   ☎86 93 77 27 www.meatpackers.dk

Meat Packers may not be the fanciest club, but, it's a cheap-beer, good-music kind of place, and it doesn't need to serve Cristal to deserve our write-up. In fact, it's better that this place doesn't serve Cristal, because then you and we probably couldn't afford it. With free entrance, 4-beers-for-50 DKK deals and latenight 2-for-1 cocktails, Meat Packers is affordable and packed as the party drags on. For those looking to get crunk in central Aarhus, the bumping beats and thankfully meat-free stench of Meat Packers makes it an ideal stopover as the sun is coming up.

i No cover. Beers 10-20 DKK. Shots 10 DKK. Ask about the happy hour deals. ✪ *Open W 8pm-3am, Th-F 8pm-5am, Sa 10pm-5am.*

ESSENTIALS
Practicalities

- **TOURIST OFFICES:** Visit Aarhus (Fredensgade 45 inside the bus station. www.visitaarhus.com. ✪ Open daily 7am-10pm.)

- **CURRENCY EXCHANGE:** A branch Forex Bank is located directly outside of Aarhus Central Station

- **ATMS:** ATMs can be found outside of Central Station, as well as along busy pedestrian walkways such as Park Alle, Rådhusplænen, or Østergade. Additionally, there is a Nordea Bank with an ATM directly across the street from the Aarhus Cathedral

- **LUGGAGE STORAGE:** Available at Aarhus Central Station from 30 DKK a day and up. Lockers take coins and cards.

- **GLBT SERVICES:** LGBT Danmark (located in Café Sappho, Mejlgade 71 ☎86 13 19 48 ✪ Open every Th 2pm-5pm.)

- **LAUNDROMATS:** Møntvaskeriet (Østbanetorvet 8 ☎86 27 73 84 ✪ Open daily 7:30am-10pm.)

- **INTERNET:** Internet is widely available in hotels, hostels, the train station, and coffee shops. Additionally, many places advertise free Wi-Fi on their shop windows—you'll see these especially along Sønder Alle, Åboulevard, and Jaegårdsgade.

Emergency

- **EMERGENCY NUMBER:** ☎112

- **NON-EMERGENCY POLICE NUMBER:** ☎114

- **MEDICAL EMERGENCY:** ☎1813

- **PHARMACY:** Løve Apoteket (Store Torv 5 ☎86 12 00 22. ✪ Open 24/7.)

- **HOSPITALS:** Aarhus University Hospital (Nørrebrogade 44 ☎70 11 31 31)

Getting There
By Plane

Aarhus is serviced by a small airport called Aarhus Lufthavn about 20 miles north of the city. There are less than a dozen flights a day and most go to Copenhagen or London. If you're coming from the airport, the airport shuttle bus leaves from directly in front of Aarhus Central Station (Aarhus H) on a schedule tailored to the flights coming in that day. The price of the bus is 100 DKK.

denmark

hans christian anderson

You're probably coming to this town to pay your respects to Denmark's literary giant. Maybe The Princess and the Pea made you set the bar in your love life way too high. Maybe The Emperor's New Clothes left you with a fear of intimacy. Maybe you just saw the Mermaid Statue in Copenhagen and didn't understand what all the big fuss was. However you know him, it's important to understand that Danes, and especially Odense-ites, worship this man the way Americans worship the second amendment. So here's the sparknotes version of all you need to know:

- Born in Odense in 1805 and died in 1875, an era characterized by war, industrialization, and collective nouns like "the poor"

- Grew up the son of a cobbler and washerwoman and escaped to Copenhagen to be a writer (cue Don't Stop Believing by Journey)

- Achieved major fame with his Fairy Tales (Eventyr) in 1835, which included most of his famous stories like The Little Mermaid

- Published a new set of fairytales in 1838 which included classics like The Steadfast Tin Soldier (though this was an era when sequels weren't automatically shitty, we still don't know if fangirls camped outside the town printing press waiting for the book's release).

- Met Charles Dickens in 1847 and, if sources are to be trusted, actually fangirled

- Much like fans of Twilight, spent the majority of his life confused and sexually frustrated when it came to love

- Much like Genghis Khan, said "eff it" to finding true love and died from a combination fall/liver disorder at the age of 70 (which in 1800s years was around 160).

By Train
Trains from Copenhagen Central Station leave for Aarhus Central Station regularly. The ride is roughly 4 hours long, and a one way tickets costs around 600 DKK. Tickets can either be purchased at the station, online, or, for those with a European sim card, via the DSB app.

Getting Around
Public Transportation
Public transportation in Aarhus is run by a company called Midttrafik and the cost of a single ride is 20 DKK for 2 zones (which covers most of the city). You can buy tickets at the machines at bus stops or from the driver when you enter the bus.

The Aarhus Card offers free admission at 16 museums and 30% discount at the Old Town and Aros Art Museum. Cards can be bought at the Bus Station, City Sleep-in Hostel, most hotels and the Bruuns Galleri shopping center, among other locations. 24-hour card 129 DKK. 28-hour card 179 DKK.

Taxis
Aarhus Taxa (☎89 48 48 48. www.aarhustaxa.dk.) Weekday rates start at 33 DKK and go up 7.81 DKK per km. At night, rates start at 44 DKK and go up 9.21 DKK per km.

aarhus

odense

If New York City is the city that never sleeps, Odense is the city that took NyQuil and slept through all of its alarms. Though it's the third largest city in Denmark, it feels much more like a sleepy village than anything else: you can hit all of the main sights in a single day and your nightlife options are limited. Even so, the town has a special charm once you walk around: it's the childhood home of Hans Christian Andersen (the author of every fairy tale ever) and has a surprisingly large selection of cafés, restaurants, and stores. If you're looking for a quaint trip away from the hustle and bustle of Copenhagen, you're only two hours away from a town whose name means "Odin's Sanctuary." So let's go relax.

ACCOMMODATIONS

CABINN ODENSE
Østre Stationsvej 9 ☎63 14 57 00 www.cabinn.com/en/hotel/cabinn-odense-hotel

HOTEL $$

This budget hotel is about as basic as a sorority girl with a pumpkin spice latte, but for the penny-pinching traveller it's a godsend. The rooms are compact—they take the term "Cabinn" quite literally here—but they're on the cheaper end of Odense accommodations and in a perfect location next to the train station. Every room has a TV, shower, and wifi, and most come with bunkbeds (in case, you know, you need a physical reminder of how lonely you are). The lobby has snacks, drinks, and computers and is a good launching point for a day of adventuring, as you're only ever five minutes away from the city's main attractions.

i Economy rooms 495 DKK. Larger rooms 545 DKK. Book online to save 100 DKK. ✆ Reception 24hr.

DANNHOSTEL ODENSE CITY
Østre Stationsvej 31 ☎63 11 04 25 www.odensedanhostel.dk

HOSTEL $

This is the only hostel in central Odense, and what you see is what you get. Its location right next to the train station makes it ideal for backpackers, and the quality, services, and discounts they offer are identical to what you'll find in other Hostelling International locations throughout Europe. If you're only staying a night or two Odense, it may make sense to shell out the extra money for a single. You might not be able to fit you and your ego into the smaller 4-bed dorms.

i Singles 435 DKK. Doubles 570 DKK. Dorms 250 DKK. ✆ Reception daily 8am-noon and 4-8pm.

SIGHTS

🏛 HANS CHRISTIAN ANDERSEN MUSEUM
Bangs Boder 29 ☎65 51 46 01 www.museum.odense.dk/hcandersenmuseum

MUSEUM

Hans Christian Andersen practically invented childhood: whether you like The Little Mermaid, The Princess and the Pea or The Ugly Duckling, there's a fat chance you read this guy as a tot. He even inspired the movie Frozen…and while that might actually make you despise the man, please take your prejudice, let it go, and visit the quaint yellow house where he grew up. The displays tell his rags-to-moderate-income story as the son of a humble cobbler whose imagination and wordplay brought him international renown. He was pretty much the Kanye of the 19th century. While the entire museum will take you 30min. max, Danes get really, really excited about this guy—the least you can do is pay your respects (and 95 DKK for entrance).

i 95 DKK, children under 17 free. ✆ Open daily 10am-5pm.

ST. CANUTE'S CHURCH

Klosterbakken 2

☎66 12 03 92

You know how they say that death and taxes are the only unavoidable things in life? For Europe, they add one more category: churches. So if you truly want to experience Odense, you'll need to visit St. Canute's Church. It's medieval. It's huge. It's got more Gothic architecture than the entire Yale campus. Even better, the backstory to its construction reads like a Game of Thrones episode: murder, intrigue, kings blaming women for bad weather, and characters with unpronounceable names. What more could you ask for from a church? (besides, you know, spiritual salvation).

i Free. ☼ Open M-Sa 10am-5pm, Su noon-4pm.

KONGENS HAVE

Directly across from Odense Central Station

PARK

Kermit the Frog once famously opined that it's not easy being green. While we sympathize with his plight, we believe Kongens Have is a counterargument to this statement. Indeed, in clear juxtaposition to the industrial-looking train station, this park hosts a sea of green grass, the majestic white pillars of the Odense Palace, and a clear view of nearby architectural wonders like the Odense Theater. This is an excellent spot for reading a book or taking an early-morning still-hungover nap.

i Free. ☼ Open 24hr.

MUNKE MOSE

PARK

Was Kongens Have too small for you? Did the imposing architecture of the Soviet-style train station turn you off? Then consider that park your mistress and this one your wife: Munke Mose is located on a gorgeous tree-lined river that looks something out of the Shire, and the animal statues littered throughout the grounds resemble Aslan's camp from The Lion, the Witch and the Wardrobe. This city is basically a living monument to nostalgia and this park continues that theme—just ten minutes south of Central Station, you can relive your favorite childhood adventures in this majestic setting.

i Free. ☼ Open 24hr.

FOOD

CAFÉ BIOGRAFEN

Brandts Passage 39-41

CAFE $

☎66 13 16 16 www.cafebio.dk

Biografen is a solid place to sip coffee, poke at your smoked salmon, and contemplate the inherent folly of Man. With both indoor and outdoor seating, and an interior theme that evokes Hollywood's Golden Age, this place is a local haunt for students and adults alike. Better yet, it's connected to an actual movie theater that shows films every day—because while Vince Vega may have bragged that you can buy beer at European movie theaters in Pulp Fiction, it's an entirely different experience when you do it firsthand. All you need now is a Royale with Cheese to make your European adventure complete.

i Coffee 25 DKK. Dishes 70 DKK. ☼ Open M-Th 10am-11pm, F-Sa 10am-midnight, Su 10am-11pm.

CAFE CUCKOO'S NEST

Vestergade 73

CAFE $$

☎65 91 57 87 www.cuckoos.dk

Cafe Cuckoo's Nest offers a fresh, delicious and professionally curated buffet. The bacon is crisp, the cheese selection is on point, and the salmon is more tender than your feelings. And they're right on the money with the tasty rugbrød, pastries, and fruit. It may all be a bit pricey (the brunch buffet will set you back 135 DKK) but why not treat yo self?

i All-you-can-eat brunch buffet 135 DKK. Coffee 25 DKK. ☼ Open M-Th 9am-11pm, F-Sa 9am-2am, Su 10am-10pm.

odense

MAMMAS PIZZERIA

ITALIAN $

Klaregade 4   ☎66 14 55 40 www.mammas.dk

A simple Italian restaurant serving up all the classic dishes from Europe's favorite boot. Our personal recommendation if you're craving a taste of the Old Country: try the pizza siciliana with a side of gnocchi and a Peroni beer. It feels so authentically Italian that it almost catcalls you, "Ciao bella!" The atmosphere here is great, so if you're looking to please a special someone while in Odense, Mammas got you covered.

i *Full pizzas 100 DKK. Beer 30-40 DKK.* ☒ *Open M-W 11:30am-9:30pm, Th-Sa 11:30am-11pm, Su noon-9pm.*

FROGGY'S CAFÉ

INTERNATIONAL $$

Vestergade 68   ☎65 90 74 47 www.froggyscafe.dk

Just off of Odense's main pedestrian walkway, this café is a hipster's wet dream: its English, Mexican, Indian, and Nordic menu is a taste of everything that is multicultural, and the late-night jazz and cocktails will have your fedora-wearing self quoting Allen Ginsberg until the wee hours of the morning. Whether you need a 4am nightcap or a late Sunday brunch, think of this place as an excellent spot to park your cash and escape from the real world for a bit.

i *Entrées 90-140 DKK.* ☒ *Open M-W 9am-midnight, Th 9am-2am, F 9am-4am, Sa 9:30am-5am, Su 9:30am-midnight.*

RED CHILLI

INDIAN $

Vesterbro 8   www.redchilli-odense.dk

In a town that's more Scandinavian than a socialized meatball dinner, this place is a surprisingly tasty injection of foreign culture. Most appetizers are in the 30 DKK range (we recommend the samosas) and the larger dishes are between 79 and 104 DKK. If you're looking for Indian food without the monsoons this summer, Red Chilli is the place for you.

i *Appetizers 30 DKK. Entrées 79-104 DKK.* ☒ *Open M-Th 3pm-9pm, F-Sa 3pm-9:30pm, Su 3pm-9pm.*

NIGHTLIFE

BLOMSTEN AND BIEN

CLUB

Overgade 45   ☎26 11 76 58 www.blomstenogbien.nu

If you've ever seen Inglourious Basterds, you'll know Aldo Rayne's number one rule is that you never fight in a basement. While we wholeheartedly agree with him, we must admit that dancing in a basement can be pretty fun. This particular basement is a nightclub offering music and libation until the wee hours of the morning—giving you time to kick back with an Old Fashioned or a Heineken as you compete with man-bunned Danes on the dance floor. Odense is a small town and it seems like half of the city comes here on Saturday nights, so plan on popping your collar, taking that cologne bath, and coming over before midnight if you want to beat the crowds.

i *Cocktails 75 DKK. Beers 40 DKK.* ☒ *Open Th-Sa 10pm-5am.*

BOOGIE DANCE CAFÉ

CLUB

Nørregade 21   ☎22 30 43 39 www. boogiedance.dk

This is the place to be after 1am. The rooftop terrace is buzzing with young people until well after the sun has come up, and the dance floor and drink prices will have you screaming "Let's Go!" as you deftly slip our new European guidebook into your purse. Spend the night making friends and banging out 15 DKK shots in Hans Christian Andersen's hometown, and you'll never be able to describe your night with depressing adjectives like lonely.

i *Cover 40 DKK. Beers 30 DKK. Shots 15 DKK.* ☒ *Open Tu-W 11pm-4:30am, Th-Sa midnight-5am.*

ESSENTIALS
Practicalities

- **TOURIST OFFICES:** VisitOdense (Vestergade 2 ☎63 75 75 20; www.visitodense.com. Open M-F 9:30am-6pm, Sa 10am-3pm, Su 11am-2pm.)
- **CURRENCY EXCHANGE:** There s a Forex exchange center in Odense Central Station
- **ATMS:** ATMs can be found in Central Station, at the BankNordik one block east, and along major pedestrian paths such as Vesterbro and Kongensgade
- **LUGGAGE STORAGE:** You can use the lockers at Central Station at a rate of 40 DKK for 24 hours.
- **LAUNDROMAT:** Byens Møntvask (Nyborgvej 35 ☎40 11 15 51. Open daily 7am-9pm.) Washing a small load costs 35 DKK. Bigger loads cost 50 DK.
- **INTERNET:** You can get online at Central Station, certain buses, and many hotels. Additionally, you can go to the public library (Odense Centralbibliotek, Stationsvej 15 ☎66 13 13 72. Generally open daily 10am-4pm.)
- **POST OFFICE:** Posthus Odense City (Vesterbro 39. Open M-F 10am-6pm, Sa 10am-3pm.)

Emergency

- **EMERGENCY NUMBER:** ☎112
- **NON-EMERGENCY POLICE NUMBER:** ☎114
- **MEDICAL EMERGENCY:** ☎1813
- **PHARMACY:** Apoteket Ørnen (Filosofhaven 38B ☎66 12 29 70. Open 24hr.)
- **HOSPITALS:** Odense University Hospital (Søndre Blvd. 29 ☎65 41 21 00. Open 24hr.)

Getting There

Odense technically has an airport, but only offers a few flights a day—and, weirdly enough, none of those flights are domestic. If you come to the city, you will most likely do so by train.

All trains coming in to Odense arrive at Odense Central Station. The journey from Copenhagen takes around 2 hours and costs 240 DKK (270 DKK if you want to reserve a seat). Trains leave every 30min. or so from Copenhagen Central Station. Tickets can be purchased at the station, online or, for those with a European sim card, via the DSB app.

Getting Around
By Public Transportation

This town is the size of a hamburger and you can walk pretty much anywhere. However, there is a local bus system, for which single tickets cost 23 DKK, a 24-hour ticket costs 40 DKK, and a 10-trip ticket costs 150 DKK.

The Odense City Pass gets you free entrance in over a dozen museums, a 50% discount at the zoo, and free public transportation. A 24-hour pass costs 169 DKK.

By Taxis

Odense Taxa (☎66 15 66 31; www.odensetaxa.dk.) Fares on weekends and nights start at 36 DKK and go up 5.83 DKK per minute.

odense

denmark essentials

VISAS

Denmark is a member of the EU. Citizens of Australia, Canada, New Zealand, the US, and many other non-EU countries do not need a visa for stays of up to 90 days. Denmark is a member of the Schengen area, so if you plan to spend time in other Schengen countries, note that the 90-day period of time you are allowed to visit without a visa applies cumulatively to all Schengen countries.

MONEY

Despite being a member of the EU, Denmark is not in the Eurozone and uses the Danish krone, (DKK or kr.) as its currency.

All service bills in Denmark tend to include a gratuity, so tipping is not expected. In restaurants, if no gratuity is added for some reason, you should tip your server 10%. If a gratuity is added, it is not uncommon to still leave a small tip in the form of rounding up the bill. Taxis in Denmark also often include a gratuity in the final charge, but if you would like to leave an extra tip, round up the bill.

ATMs in Denmark are common and convenient. They are often located in airports, train stations, and major pedestrian areas. The two major international money networks are MasterCard/Maestro/Cirrus and Visa/PLUS. To find out what out-of-network or international fees you may be subject to by using ATMs, call your bank.

ALCOHOL

The minimum age to purchase alcohol in Denmark is 16 for drinks below 16.5% ABV and 18 for drinks above 16.5% ABV. There is no minimum age to drink alcohol. To be allowed into bars, clubs, or discos that serve any kind of alcohol, you must be 18 or older. Remember to drink responsibly and to never drink and drive. The legal blood alcohol content (BAC) for driving in Denmark is under 0.05%, significantly lower than the US limit of 0.08%.

denmark

FRANCE

Think of a famous idea. Any famous idea. Or for that matter any brushstroke, article of clothing, architectural style, camera technique, great thinker that should have been medicated, or hip reason to brew a Molotov cocktail. If that idea is Western, then it is probably French (or at least hotly contested and contributed to a French intellectual movement). Your first walk around Paris will be defined by a paralyzing level of excitement. Your first party in Monaco might result in a Hangover-esque situation. It's no secret that young Americans "backpack" through France to lose their virginity and construct their identity at a safe distance from their parents. The successes of James Baldwin, Gertrude Stein, and Ernest Hemingway suggest that we couldn't have chosen a better spot; there is a pervading sense in France that everything is here.

Students might go to France to be fashionably disaffected artists in boho-chic corner cafes, but this isn't the land of berets and baguettes anymore: it's the land of sustainable energy and the 35hr. work week. As France wrestles with the economic and cultural ramifications of a globalized world, this is also, increasingly, the country of parkour and veil bans, sprawling Chinatowns and the Marie Leonie case of 2004. Nowhere is the cognitive dissonance of these cultural collisions more evident than in Marseille, whose burgeoning Little Algeria encroaches upon the city's Old World streets. In the midst of these transitions, the most sacred of French traditions remain gloriously preserved—you might eat a lot of kebabs while you're here, but you can still riot against The Man in the morning and commit adultery by noon.

greatest hits

- **WE'LL ALWAYS HAVE PARIS.** From the "metal asparagus" of the **Eiffel Tower** (p. 184) to the bars of **St-Germain**, you'll have plenty to do in France's capital.

- **THAT'LL DO NICELY. Nice** (p. 228) might be the best city on the Côte d'Azur for backpackers, and it's definitely the cheapest.

- **RAISE THE ROOF.** Dance the night away with a view overlooking two rivers and the entire city of Lyon at **Le Sucre** (p. 263), a bar sitting atop a defuncy sugar factory.

FRANCE

North Sea

BRITAIN

Manchester

Amsterdam

NETHERLANDS

Rotterdam

Münster

Bristol

London

Düsseldorf

Dover

Folkestone

Dunkerque

Antwerp

BELGIUM

Brussels

GERMANY

Portsmouth

Calais

Lille

Mainz

Plymouth

Boulogne-sur-Mer

Arras

LUX.

English Channel
(La Manche)

Somme R.

Amiens

Metz

Channel
Islands

Cherbourg

Le Havre

Rouen

Reims

Nancy

Strasbourg

Roscoff

Bayeux

Caen

Sélestat

Brest

St-Malo

Mont-St-Michel

Paris

Seine R.

Marne R.

Épernay

Colmar

Quimper

Dinan

Chartres

Troyes

Mulhouse

Rennes

Le Mans

Fontainebleau

Besançon

SWITZ.

Angers

Orléans

Blois

Loire R.

Dijon

Pontarlier

Bern

Nantes

Tours

Amboise

Beaune

Haut-Jura
Mts.

Lake
Geneva

Belle Ile

Saumur

Bourges

Nevers

Geneva

Île d'Yeu

Poitiers

Vienne R.

Cluny

Lyon

Annecy

Chamonix

ATLANTIC
OCEAN

La Rochelle

Vichy

Mont Blanc
4810m

ITALY

Cognac

Angoulême

Limoges

Clermont-
Ferrand

Grenoble

Gironde R.

Montignac

Le-Mont-Dore

Cévennes
Mts.

Bay of Biscay

Les Eyzies-
de-Tayac

Le Puy de Sancy

Rhône R.

Bordeaux

Sarlat

Dordogne R.

Castelnaud-la-Chapelle

MONACO

Menton

— TGV Line

Garonne R.

Avignon

Nice

Biarritz

Adour R.

Nîmes

Aix-en-
Provence

Antibes

Cannes

Bayonne

Toulouse

Arles

St-Raphaël

CÔTE
D'AZUR

St-Jean-
Pied-de-Port

Montpellier

Marseille

St-Tropez

Lourdes

Carcassonne

Toulon

Bilbao

Cauterets

Golfe du Lion

TO CORSICA

Burgos

Perpignan

P Y R E N E E S

Aude R.

ANDORRA

SPAIN

Cap Corse

Bastia

Calvi

CORSICA

Corte

Zaragoza

Barcelona

Ajaccio

Mediterranean Sea

Porto-
Vecchio

Bonifacio

SARDINIA
(ITALY)

N

LG

0   150 kilometers

0   150 miles

Valencia

france

paris

Paris leaves an impression on everyone, from students perfecting their *langue française* to tourists who wonder why the French don't pronounce half the consonants in each word. This city has been home to countless films, daydreams, and kings named Louis, and it easily destroys all diets with its arsenal of buttery croissants and delicate pastries. Nearly everyone in the world idealizes Paris, whether it's for the Eiffel Tower, the intellectual literary cafes, or the impossibly chic and be-scarfed denizens of the city. But don't let yourself be disillusioned by ideals—yes, everyone is in love with Paris, but this place can be rough, and that waiter over there? Yeah, he's judging you. When you get Englished for the first time (when your mangled French inquiry is interrupted with an English response), you'll start to realize that your Converse won't cut it after all and that maybe you should have paid more attention in French class. Parifs will charm and bitchslap you with equal gusto, but don't get too le tired—think of it as a gentle form of Parisian hazing. Once you learn your way around the narrow, cobblestoned streets and nail down your *merci, beaucoup*, Paris will be more spectacular than ever. Some tiny corner of it will be yours in memory and experience, whether it's admiring a painting in an empty room at the Louvre (they exist), listening to the bells of Notre Dame chime as you sit by the Seine, sunbathing in the gorgeous Jardin du Luxembourg, or biting into your first Nutella banana crêpe. Slow down and don't worry about how well you're fitting in—this city is big and captivating enough for everyone to claim their little slice.

ORIENTATION

Despite all the invasions, revolutions, and riots throughout French history, Paris was still meticulously planned. The Seine River flows from east to west through the middle of the city, splitting it into two sections. The *Rive Gauche* (Left Bank) to the south is known as the intellectual heart of Paris, while the *Rive Droite* (Right Bank) to the north is famous for fashion, art, and commerce. The two islands in the middle of the Seine, the Île de la Cité and Île St-Louis, are the geographical and historical center of the city. The rest of Paris is divided into 20 *arrondissements* (districts) that spiral outward from the islands. These *arrondissements* are numbered; for example, the Eiffel Tower is located in *le septième* (the seventh), abbreviated 7ème.

If the simplicity of this layout sounds too good to be true, it is. Neighborhoods frequently spread over multiple *arrondissements* and are often referred to by name rather than number. The Marais, for example, is in both the 3ème and the 4ème. Neighborhood names are based on major connecting hubs of the Métro or train (Montparnasse, Bastille) or major landmarks and roads (Champs-Élysées, Invalides). Streets are marked on every corner, and numerous signs point toward train stations, landmarks, and certain *triomphant* roundabouts. You can try to walk through it all, but the size of the city is deceiving. So when your feet start to fall off, remember that buses and the subway go almost everywhere in the city, and your hostel is just a short ride away.

Île de la Cité and Île St-Louis

Some 2000 years ago, the French monarchy claimed Les Îles as the geographic center of its kingdom and the royal and governmental seat of power. The islands were perfectly located and easily defendable in the middle of the Seine—think castles, drawbridges, fire-breathing **dragons**, and then don't because you're probably thinking of a bad *Shrek* sequel. Today, you can see how Paris grew outward, both physically expanding beyond the islands and politically distancing itself from the monarchy.

Île de la Cité, the larger of the two islands, is still considered the city's center and is home to Paris's *kilomètre zéro*, from which distances are measured and where

paris

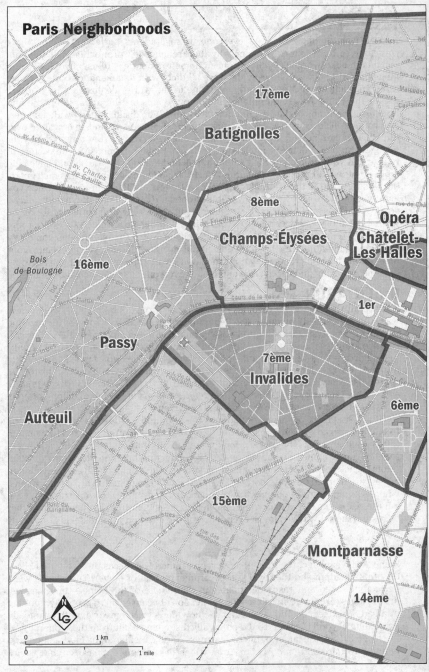

Paris Neighborhoods

17ème

Batignolles

8ème

Champs-Élysées

Opéra

Châtelet-
Les Halles

Bois
de Boulogne

16ème

1er

Passy

7ème

Invalides

6ème

Auteuil

15ème

Montparnasse

14ème

N

0   1 km

0   1 mile

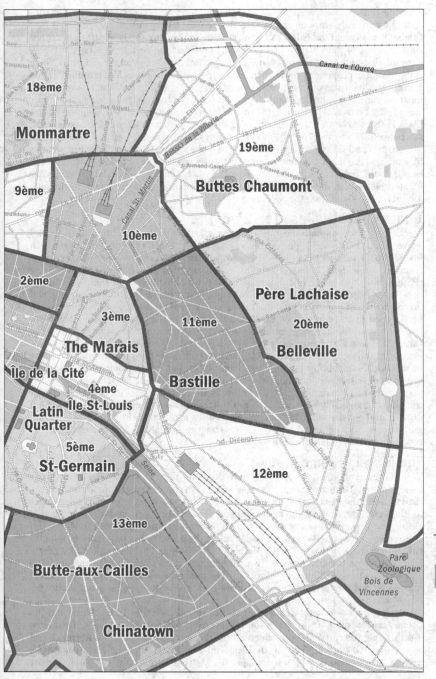

France's major roads originate. Trigger-happy tourists congregate on two streets that cut vertically through the island: the Boulevard du Palais, where you'll find **Sainte-Chappelle** and the **Palais du Justice**, and rue de la Cité, the next street over that runs in front of **Notre Dame.** Unsurprisingly, most of the restaurants here are less than interested in fair prices and authenticity, particularly as you get closer to Notre Dame, but it is possible to find worthy spots tucked in the nooks and crannies of this island. Although the physical center of the city sounds like an ideal place to stay, most accommodations are overpriced, and once the tourist traffic clears out after sunset, the islands tend to become uncomfortably quiet, with the exception of the plaza in front of Notre Dame. Île St-Louis, the quiet younger sister of the two islands, sits peacefully beside its impressive big brother and provides a welcome escape from the crowds and bustle across the way. The restaurants and shops here are smaller in scale and are mostly located on **rue Saint-Louis en l'Île.** The only Métro stop on the islands is Ⓜ**Cité,** between bd du Palais and rue de la Cité, but several other stops are located just across the bridges that connect the islands to the mainland of the city, including Paris's largest stop, Ⓜ Châtelet.

Châtelet-Les Halles (1er, 2ème)

Les Îles are the geographic center of the city, but, with the exception of the Eiffel Tower, Paris's 1er and 2ème arrondissements are the fountainhead from which everything flows. Most famously, the **Louvre** and **Les Halles** marketplace draw crowds from far and wide to Paris's bellybutton. Naturally, this area is tourist-heavy during the daytime, especially in the summer. Unfortunately, Les Halles and the Jardin des Halles have been under serious renovation and reconstruction since 2011 and are currently an unsightly block of cranes and concrete; the project is expected to be finished in bits and pieces through 2016. Ⓜ**Châtelet-Les Halles** is the city's main transportation hub and is located in the southeast corner of these neighborhoods; three RER and five Métro lines can be accessed between here and the two connecting stations, Ⓜ**Châtelet** and Ⓜ**Les Halles.** The Ⓜ**Opéra** stop is a prominent point in the northwest corner of the neighborhood, topped off by **boulevard Haussmann/Montmartre/Poissonnière** and hugged in the east by **boulevard de Sébastopol.** The closer you are to the Louvre, the more likely prices are to be unnecessarily high, so make the effort to go a few blocks farther north, east, or west to get away from the loud crowds and equally annoying prices. **Rue St-Denis** runs parallel to bd de Sébastopol and is generally a dependable strip for good but pricey nightlife and more reasonable food and accommodation options.

The Marais (3ème, 4ème)

The Marais embodies the ultimate ugly duckling tale. Originally a bog (*marais* means"marsh"), the area became livable in the 13th century when monks drained the land to build the **Right Bank.** When Henri IV constructed the glorious **place des Vosges** in the early 17th century, the area suddenly became the city's center of fashionable living, and luxury and scandal soon took hold. Royal haunts gave way to slums and tenements during the Revolution, and many of the grand *hôtels particuliers* fell into ruin or disrepair. In the 1950s, the Marais was revived and declared a historic neighborhood; since then, decades of gentrification and renovation have restored the Marais to its pre-Revolutionary glory. Once palatial mansions have become exquisite museums, and the tiny, twisting streets are crowded with hip bars, avant-garde galleries, and one-of-a-kind boutiques.

    Boulevard de Sébastopol divides the Marais from Les Halles in the west, and the **Centre Pompidou** anchors down the southwest portion of the neighborhood. The Métro 1 runs along the rue de Rivoli, which marks the southern border. The northern and eastern borders are defined by the **Boulevard Saint-Martin** and the **Plaza République,** and bd Beaumarchais, which runs along the Métro 8, forms a quarter-circle border around the Marais. The quickest way to go north-south is to take the Métro 11 beginning from the **Hôtel de Ville** along the rue de Beaubourg. Today, the Marais is known as a center of Parisian diversity. **Rue des Rosiers,** in the heart of the 4ème, is the center of Paris's Jewish population, though the steady influx of hyper-hip clothing and rising rents have led to a significant loss of Jewish establishments. But the Marais remains lively on Sunday and quieter on Saturday, the Jewish day of rest. The neighborhood is also unquestionably the GLBT center of Paris, with the community's hub at the intersection of **rue Sainte-Croix de la Brettonerie** and **rue Vieille du Temple.** Though the steady stream of tourists has begun to wear on the Marais's eclectic personality, the district continues to be a distinctive mix of old and new, queer and straight, cheap and chic.

Latin Quarter and St-Germain (5ème, 6ème)

The Latin Quarter and St-Germain are two of Paris's primary tourist neighborhoods, second only to the areas around the Louvre, Notre Dame, and the Hôtel de Ville. The Latin Quarter, however, got its name from the many institutions of higher learning in the area, including the famous **Sorbonne,** where Latin scriptures and studies were more prevalent than kissing couples along the Seine. To this day, these neighborhoods—the Latin Quarter in particular—are the student hubs of Paris, mixing overpriced tourist traps with budget-friendly student hangouts. **Boulevard St-Michel** divides the two areas, with St-Germain to the west and the Latin Quarter to the east. Meanwhile, **Boulevard du Montparnasse** and **Boulevard de Port Royal** separate both areas from southern Paris, with the **Jardin du Luxembourg** and the **Panthéon** being the central icons of each *arrondissement*. As tempted as you may be to shell out your money in St-Germain-des-Prés, your wallet will thank you if you head to the 5ème and roam **rue Monge** and **rue Mouffetard** for affordable food, nightlife, and accommodations.

Invalides (7ème)

If Paris was Jay-Z, then the **Eiffel Tower** would be his Beyoncé—both are icons in their own right, and together, they are absolute magic. Everyone that comes to Paris will want to see the world's greatest power couple, so prep yourself for the higher prices and overeager tourists who are crazy in love with snapping pics left and right. The Eiffel Tower(s) over the 7ème, but the rest of Destiny's Child is nearby and have more than made it on their own. Starting from the west, the **Champs de Mars** stretches southeast in front of the Eiffel Tower, with Ⓜ**École Militaire** at its feet. In the middle of the neighborhood is the **Esplanade of Les Invalides,** topped off in the north with Ⓜ**Invalides** and to the south with the **Musée de l'Armée.** Continue east to find the **Musée d'Orsay** (and its long lines) on the banks of the Seine. The **Quai d'Orsay, rue de l'Université,** and **rue St-Dominique** run West to East through the neighborhood and make for great strolls past the brasseries and cafes. And if you don't want to walk, the RER C chugs along the Seine and will conveniently drop you off right in front of the biggest attractions, but for a scenic route, take the 69 bus, which travels from the Eiffel Tower all the way to the Musée d'Orsay.

Champs-Élysées (8ème)

The Champs-Élysées is a whole other kind of Paris, where even the Métro stops seem to sparkle with glamor. This is the Paris where the daughters of American millionaires throw their bachelorette parties and where fashion moguls wipe their you-know-whats with only the finest of handwoven silks. It's a fun place to window shop and daydream about the finer things in life, but the buck stops there.

   Avenue des Champs-Elysées is the heart of this area, pumping life from the **Arc de Triomphe** through the rows of designer shops and out-of-this-world expensive restaurants and nightclubs. If you want to continue to immerse yourself in all the beautiful things you will probably never have, head for **Avenue Montaigne, rue du Faubourg St-Hon-**

oré, or the side streets around **La Madeleine.** The #2 Métro line separates the 8ème from the 16ème in the north, but the closer you get to this area, the fewer tourists you will find.

Opéra (9ème) and Canal St-Martin (10ème)

Although they follow the spiral pattern from the center of the city along with the other *arrondissements,* the 9ème and 10ème feel a bit ambiguously plopped in the middle of the *Rive Droite.* The 9ème can be particularly difficult to navigate, especially since its namesake Métro stop and tourist site, the Paris Opéra, is positioned at its southern tip rather than at the center. The 9ème is roughly surrounded by the #2 Métro line in the north along bd de Clichy, Gare St-Lazare in the west, and Ⓜ Opéra in the south. Navigating the Opéra neighborhood by rail will generally mean traveling in the east-west directions: The #8 and #9 Métro runs along bd Haussmann in the south and conveniently begins at **Opéra Garnier** and will drop you off at Ⓜ République, near the Canal St-Martin. To the north, the #2 runs along bd Clichy and intersects with the #12, which actually cuts vertically through the neighborhood to reach **Notre Dame de Lorette** and eventually Gare St. Lazare. Finally, the #7 runs diagonally from the southwest corner of the *arrondissement* from Ⓜ Opéra to the northeast corner of the Canal St-Martin neighborhood.

Right next to the 9ème, the 10ème is known (and named for) the **Canal Saint-Martin,** which runs along the eastern border of the *arrondissement.* Stray too far from this "mini-Seine" (i.e., anywhere west of bd Magenta), and you'll find yourself smack in the middle of the sketchy area that surrounds the **Gare du Nord** and **Gare de l'Est.** If the gun armories and cash-for-gold stores didn't give you a hint, we'll tell you now: stay clear of this area at night.

Bastille (11ème, 12ème)

The Bastille is home to the famous prison where the French Revolution kicked things off with a bang on July 14, 1789. A few centuries later, Parisians still storm this neighborhood nightly in search of the latest cocktails, culinary innovations, and up-and-coming musicians in the city. Five Métro lines converge at Ⓜ République and Ⓜ Nation, and three lines at Ⓜ Bastille, making this district a busy transport hub. Although the area is still a bit worn around the edges, Bastille is a neighborhood that is well known for its cheap food, red-hot nightlife, and uncrowded stores for those in search of stress-free shopping. The highest concentration of all three is in the area between **rue de Charenton,** in the south of the 11ème, and **rue de la Roquette,** running northeast away from the Bastille. Late-night cheap eats, youth hostels, and bars where memories are made and forgotten line the streets east of République and particularly along **rue Oberkampf.** The Algerian community offers countless dining options at the **Marché d'Aligre,** where the weekly outdoor market sets up. The **Viaduc des Arts** and the gorgeous **Promenade Plantée** (see **Sights,** p. 188) will lead you toward the more expensive shops and galleries in the 12ème.

Montparnasse and Southern Paris (13ème, 14ème, 15ème)

These three *arrondissements,* which make up nearly one-sixth of Paris, lack the photo-ops and famous sights that attract tourists elsewhere in the city. They do, however, tend to comprise Paris's so-called better half, where locals dominate the tourists and the pace of life is more relaxed. The neighborhoods spread east to west in ascending order, with Montparnasse somewhere in between the 14ème and 15ème in the area immediately surrounding the **Montparnasse Tower** and the **Cimetière du Montparnasse** in the 14ème. Your best mode of transportation between here will be the #6 Métro line, which runs aboveground along bd du Grenelle and bd Garibaldi on the northern edge of the 15ème, then cuts a bit farther down into the 14ème and 13ème along bd St-Jacques and bd Vincent. The 15ème and 14ème are divided by the train tracks that stem from the SNCF station behind the Montparnasse Tower, and **rue de la Santé** roughly divides the 14ème and the 13ème. The 13ème has a strange combination of characters thanks to **Chinatown**, nestled south of rue de Tolbiac, and the small hippie enclave surrounding **rue de la Butte aux Cailles**, which avoids the capitalist drive to overcharge for meals or entertainment. The bank of the River Seine along the 13ème is home to a series of floating bars and restaurants, especially opposite the Parc de Bercy, though many travelers don't make it this far south or east.

Auteuil, Passy & Batignolles (16ème, 17ème)

The 16ème and 17ème are almost devoid of tourists. More residential, these neighborhoods are home to ladies who lunch, their beautiful children, and their overworked husbands. The 16ème is frequented by Parisian elites who have money and are willing to spend it in the expensive boutiques and cafe lounges lining the main roads around ⓜ**Trocadéro**. The 17ème, meanwhile, is far more relaxed in terms of its residents and prices. Its sheer size and lack of notable sights make this area a retreat for working class citizens and overly earnest teenagers who take leisurely strolls or sit in the many cafes.

The 16ème covers the area west of the 8ème, where the Seine dives sharply south. Auteuil and Passy are loosely defined, if at all, but Auteuil generally covers the southern half of the *arrondissement*, while Passy makes up the northern half (although you probably won't hear many Parisians refer specifically to either one). Most tourist traffic converges at ⓜ**Trocadéro** at the **Palais de Chaillot;** many major sights are scattered about the banks of the river, especially near ⓜ**Passy** (between the **Musée du Vin** and **Maison de Radio France**), where you can find some of the best views of the Eiffel Tower. The northern border of this area is generally marked by the **Arc de Triomphe.**

The 17ème consists of the area directly north of the Arc de Triomphe and the 8ème. Batignolles tends to refer just to the eastern corner of this *arrondissement*, around the **Square des Batignolles** It is in and around the square that most of the best bars and restaurants in the neighborhood can be found, especially along and just off **rue des Dames.** Pl. du Maréchal Juin anchors the other side of town and is connected to bd des Batignolles and bd de Courcelles by av. de Villiers.

Montmartre (18ème)

Montmartre is easily the most eccentric of Paris's *arrondissements*, with religious landmarks like the **Basilique du Sacré-Cœur** looming over the infamous **Moulin Rouge** and the land of the scantily-clad **Red Light District.** Half the fun around here is bumbling about the cobblestone streets and posing next to the street art and graffiti as you huff and puff your way up and down the stairs. There's a super-touristy area on **rue de Steinkerque** if you want to pick up some postcards, but please, stay away from the corny berets and the overpriced food around these parts. The 18ème has recently exploded with youth hostels that keep bars full at night but also attract pickpockets. The neighborhood sits on top of a huge hill that is a bit of a hike, so plan your sightseeing accordingly. The bottom of the hill is lined by **boulevard de Clichy** and **boulevard de Rochechouart,** under which the #2 Métro line runs and where you can find a lot of great bars. **Boulevard Barbès** roughly borders the eastern end of this area, and the Cimetière de Montmartre borders it to the west.

Buttes-Chaumont & Belleville (19ème, 20ème)

The Buttes-Chaumont and Belleville neighborhoods cover a huge area, but several well-placed Métro lines make them easy to navigate. Even though this corner of Paris may be a bit far, in a city where green space comes at a premium, these neighborhoods have more than their fair share of beautiful parks—**Parc de Belleville** comes with sweeping views of the Parisian skyline. At night, the bars in this area come alive with artsy locals who love to kick back cheap booze or dance the night away at **Rosa Bonheur** or **La Bellevilloise**. Running along the northern edge of the 19ème is av. Jean Jaurès and the #5 Métro, which lead straight to Parc de la Villette. To the west, the #2 Métro runs straight down bd de la Villette and stops near the Parc de Belleville, Père-Lachaise Cemetery, and nearly every main street from the 19ème to the 20ème. The #9, #3, and #11 Métros run horizontally through the area, and the #11 runs through rue de Belleville, which is home to Paris's second largest Chinatown and host to a number of cheap eateries. While this area is full of goodies, it can also be a little rough around the edges when the sun sets, so we advise caution after dark.

SIGHTS

Seeing everything in Paris is exhausting if not impossible (even we struggled a bit). For a short trip, visiting the main attractions can mean waiting in lines, feeling the urge to add the annoying couple in front of you to the body count at the Catacombs, and becoming completely desensitized to some of mankind's greatest feats of engineering and art. Give yourself a break. Before heading off to see something because you saw it on a postcard, check this section for what's really worth it. Some of Paris's most interesting sights are devoid of tourists.

Île de la Cité and Île St-Louis

NOTRE DAME   CATHEDRAL
Île de la Cité   ☎01 42 34 56 10 www.notredameparis.fr

If you've read this far, stay with us for a little longer. Here is what you need to see and do when visiting Notre Dame. First, as you enter, notice the headless figures above the doors. Revolutionaries thought that the King of Judah was somehow related to the French monarch (he's not) and decapitated him. From the entrance, you'll see massive crowds. Keep to the right and follow the arrows past Joan of Arc to the Treasury, where you can see Napoleon's sweet emperor cloak as well as relics like St. Louis's tunic. Jesus's thorny crown rests here too, but it's only revealed on the first Friday of the month at 3pm. The *crème de la crème* is the 13-ton bell in the South Tower that requires eight men—or one hunchback—to ring.

i Ⓜ*Cité. Walk down the street away from the quai onto rue de la Cité. Free. Audio tour €5, includes treasury visit. Towers €8.50, reduced €5.50, under 18 and EU citizens under 26 free.* ⚄ *Cathedral open daily 8am-6:45pm. Towers open daily Apr-Sept 10am-6:30pm; Oct-Mar 10am-5:30pm. Last entry 4:45pm. Free tours in French M-F 2 and 3pm, Sa-Su 2:30pm; English W-Th 2pm, Sa 2:30pm. Treasury open M-F 9:30am-6pm, Sa 9:30am-6:30pm, Su 1:30-6:30pm; last entry 15min. before close. Su Mass 8:30am (French), 10am (Gregorian Chants), 11:30am (easy French with some English thrown in), 12:45pm, and 6:30pm.*

SAINTE-CHAPELLE   CHURCH
6 bd du Palais   ☎01 53 40 60 80 www.monuments-nationaux.fr

Everybody needs the occasional diversion to get through a service. Take the 13th-century equivalent of TVs in church: the stunning floor-to-ceiling stained glass windows in the **Upper Chapel** of Sainte-Chapelle, illuminating dreamscapes of no fewer than 1113 individual Biblical stories. They really tried, but you just can't squeeze that many depictions onto stained glass and make it understandable without a priest (or tour guide) explaining each one. The easiest to make out is the Passion of the Christ, located at the apex of the chapel. The **Lower Chapel** has a blue, vaulted ceiling dotted with the golden symbol of the French monarchy, the *fleurs-de-lis*, and contains a few "treasures" (i.e., platter-sized portraits of saints). This was where mortals served God, while royalty got to get a little closer in the Upper Chapel.

i ⓂCité. Walk away from the quai, turn right onto the sidewalk, and turn left onto bd du Palais. Within Palais de la Cité. €8.50, ages 18-25 €5.50, under 18 and EU citizens under 25 free. Audio guide €4.50. Twin ticket with Conciergerie €12.50, ages 18-25 €8.50, under 18 free. ☒ Open daily Mar-Oct 9:30am-6pm; Nov-Feb 9am-5pm. Last entry 30min. before close. Open W evenings May 15-Sept 15, last entry 9pm.

CONCIERGERIE
PALACE, PRISON

2 bd du Palais   ☎01 53 40 60 80   www.monuments-nationaux.fr

It can't compete with Versailles in grandeur, but the Conciergerie has hosted over four centuries worth of French royalty and functioned as the administrative headquarters for the city for much longer. Perhaps most famously, the Conciergerie is best known for its other function: a prison where revolutionary celebrities like Robespierre and the unforgettable Queen Marie Antoinette were put behind bars. During the Reign of Terror, over 2000 executions took place over the course of a single year—if you have a common French last name, check the list of executed prisoners to see if you have any long-lost guillotined relatives.

i ⓂCité. Walk toward the quai, then turn left onto bd du Palais. The entrance is on the right. €8.50, students €5.50, EU citizens ages 18-25 and under 18 free. Combined ticket with Sainte-Chapelle €12.50, students €8.50, under 13 and EU citizens ages 18-25 free. ☒ Open daily 9:30am-6pm, last entry 5:30pm.

PONT NEUF
BRIDGE

Though its name might suggest otherwise, the bridge cutting through the western tip of Île de la Cité is the oldest in Paris. Completed in 1607, it was the center of Paris until the end of the 18th century—street performers, pickpockets, traders, and curious members of the bourgeoisie would congregate around this bustling bridge. The occasional gargoyle and a statue of Henri IV are all that Pont Neuf has to offer nowadays.

i ⓂPont Neuf.

CRYPTE ARCHEOLOGIQUE
MUSEUM

7 Parvis Notre-Dame, pl. Jean-Paul II   ☎01 55 42 50 10   www.crypte.paris.fr

Hidden beneath feet of countless tourists traipsing about the plaza in front of the Notre Dame lies the Crypte Archeologique. This museum displays the excavations of 2000-year-old archaeological layers, from the fortified walls from the 4th century to the foundations of medieval homes to ancient bath houses. The museum is rather small and dimly lit, and while the museum does its best to explain the various ruins, the remains of the ancient city are quite underwhelming—it's difficult to make out any structures when everything looks like various piles of eroded gray stones.

i ⓂCité. Walk down the street away from the quai onto rue de la Cité. There is a set of stairs at the end of the plaza in front of Notre Dame that looks like an entrance to the Métro. €5, seniors €3.50, ages 14-26 €2.50, under 14 free. Audio guide €3. ☒ Open Tu-Su 10am-6pm, last entry 5:30pm.

Châtelet-Les Halles

Châtelet-Les Halles is perhaps Paris's densest tourist area, and that's saying something.

▨ MUSÉE DU LOUVRE
MUSEUM

rue de Rivoli   ☎01 40 20 53 17   www.louvre.fr

On the **second floor,** only Sully and Richelieu are accessible. In Sully, all of the rooms are filled with French paintings that typically require some background study in art history to fully appreciate. Richelieu is filled with student groups and more obscure tours checking out the remaining Belgian, Dutch, German, Russian, and Scandinavian works. These are pretty to look at, but you may be

get a room!

Budget accommodations (or budget anything, for that matter) can be difficult to find in Paris. But there are still deals for savvy travelers who know where to look. Expect to pay about €40-60 for the best budget hotels, which can be very quirky or forgettable but are always clean and more peaceful than the alternatives. If you're doing Paris on the cheap, be warned that you can't always count on having your own bathroom or shower, even if you shell out for a single. For more recommendations, visit **www.letsgo.com**.

⬛ CENTRE INTERNATIONALE DE PARIS (BVJ): PARIS LOUVRE
HOSTEL $$

20 rue Jean-Jacques Rousseau   ☎01 53 00 90 90 www.bvjhotel.com

With 240 beds, this hostel knows how to run a clean and efficient enterprise, with bare bones but spacious dormitories of four to 10 beds. In the summer, it's packed with international youths and backpackers looking to capitalize on the cheap prices and prime location.

i Ⓜ*Louvre-Rivoli. Walk north on rue du Louvre and turn left onto rue St-Honoré. Turn right onto rue Jean-Jacques Rousseau. 3-night max. stay; extensions can be arranged upon arrival. Breakfast included. Dorms €30; doubles €70. Cash only.* ☒ *Reception 24hr.*

⬛ HÔTEL JEANNE D'ARC
HOTEL $$$

3 rue de Jarente   ☎01 48 87 62 11 www.lesvoixdejeanne.com

Hotel Jeanne d'Arc will brighten up any traveler's day with fun and artistic decor in the lobby and common area. And best of all, it's a cheaper option than most of the hotels in the area and only a few steps away from the Métro. A deal this good fills up quickly during the summer, so be sure to book ahead.

i Ⓜ*St-Paul. Walk against traffic onto rue de Rivoli; turn left onto rue de Sévigné, then right onto rue de Jarente. Breakfast €8. Reserve 2-3 months in advance (earlier for stays in Sept-Oct). Singles €65; 1-bed doubles €81-96; 2-bed doubles €119.*

⬛ YOUNG AND HAPPY HOSTEL
HOSTEL $$

80 rue Mouffetard   ☎01 47 07 47 07 www.youngandhappy.fr

A funky, lively hostel with 21 clean rooms, some with showers and toilets, Young and Happy Hostel is where you want to stay in the 5ème, if not in all of Paris. It's a great option if you're young, fun, and on a budget. Light sleepers, however, should consider staying elsewhere—rue Mouffetard gets quite noisy at night. While impromptu, their reception doubles as a bar and serves drinks if you ask for them.

i Ⓜ*Place Monge. From rue Monge, walk behind the pl. Monge on rue Ortolan and turn left onto rue Mouffetard. The hostel is on the righ. Breakfast included. Twins €30-45; 3- and 5-person dorms €22-38; 10-person €19-33.* ☒ *Reception 24hr. Lockout 11am-4pm.*

⬛ OOPS!
HOSTEL $$

50 av. des Gobelins   ☎01 47 07 47 00 www.oops-paris.com

It's easy to see why young backpackers flock to this hostel in droves: from the fun patterns in the rooms to the lists of clubs and parties in the lobby to the fast Wi-Fi, Oops! is designed for the young, wild, and free. Top it all off with cheap prices and ensuite bathrooms (so clutch), it's understandable that you have to book in advance.

i Ⓜ*Les Gobelins. Walk south on av. des Gobelins toward pl. d'Italie. The hostel is 3 blocks from the Métro, on the right. Cash only. Breakfast included. Lobby computers available. Reserve online. Mar-Oct dorms €30-42, private rooms €70-115; Nov-Feb dorms €23-28, private rooms €60-80.* ☒ *Reception 24hr. Lockout 11am-4pm.*

france

better off spending a little more time getting friendly with your favorites from earlier. Unless you're planning on bunking up next to the *Venus de Milo*, seeing everything at the Louvre is impossible. Just getting a glimpse of what's in front of you, though, is a pretty good start.

i ⓜPalais Royal-Musée du Louvre. Follow the crowds. Walk past the rue de Rivoli with the flow of traffic on rue de Rohan. All-day access, access to Musée Delacroix included. The Carte Louvre Jeunes entitles the owner to 1-year unlimited access without waiting in line and free access for the owner and a guest on W and F after 6pm. €11, under 18 and EU citizens ages 18-25 free. Special exhibits €12. Combined ticket €15. Carte Louvre Jeunes ages 26-29 €35, 18-25 €15. 1st Su of every month (does not include special exhibits) free. F after 6pm free for under 26 of all nationalities. Audio tour €5, under 18 €3. ☑ Open M 9am-6pm, W 9am-9:45pm, Th 9am-6pm, F 9am-10pm, Sa-Su 9am-6pm. Last entry 45min. before close; rooms begin to close 30min. before museum.

JARDIN DES TUILERIES   GARDEN
pl. de la Concorde, rue de Rivoli   ☎01 40 20 90 43

Covering the distance from the Louvre to the pl. de la Concorde, the Tuileries and their colorful green chairs are a favorite of tourists during the summer and with Parisians who like to drag them off and sit with them alone (chairs, not tourists). As with the gardens of Versailles and the Palais du Luxembourg, something as fabulous as the Louvre requires a massive complex of hedges, trees, and a very large fountain. The gardens grew as each successive king added something to call his own. Today, the Tuileries are filled with food stands, merry-go-rounds, and a huge Ferris wheel near the rue de Rivoli entrance, rendering it all quite different from the Tuscan sanctuary Henry originally intended.

i ⓜTuileries. Between pl. de la Concorde and Musée Louvre. Free. ☑ Open daily Jun-Aug 7am-11pm; Sept 7am-9pm; Oct-Mar 7:30am-7:30pm; Apr-May 7am-9pm. Amusement park open Jun-mid-Aug.

MUSÉE DE L'ORANGERIE   MUSEUM
Jardin des Tuileries   ☎01 44 50 43 00 www.musee-orangerie.fr

Although this was once the greenhouse of the Jardin des Tuileries, the only flowers that the Musée de l'Orangerie holds now are Monet's *Water Lilies*, which remains a surprisingly serene exhibit despite the crowds. The museum displays primarily works by Impressionist and post-Impressionist painters such as Monet, Picasso, and Renoir and received the collection of renowned dart collector Paul Guillaume in the 1960s. Show up at 9am or on free Sundays (the first Sunday of every month) if you don't want to roast in the sun for most of the day.

i ⓜConcorde. Walk down pl. de la Concorde along the Tuileries Gardens to its main entrance and turn right immediately; the museum is in front. €7.50, students and after 5pm €5. Combined ticket with Musée d'Orsay €16. Free 1st Su every month. ☑ Open M 9am-6pm, W-Su 9am-6pm. Last entry 5:30pm, rooms cleared at 5:45pm.

MUSÉE DES ARTS DÉCORATIFS   MUSEUM
107 rue de Rivoli   ☎01 44 55 57 50 www.lesartsdecoratifs.fr

Fashion-conscious Francophiles and lovers of pretty things could easily spend a full day perusing the Musée des Arts Decoratifs. Spanning 10 floors, this enormous museum complex is comprised of three different collections, in addition to many smaller exhibits. **Arts Décoratifs** (Interior Design), **Mode et Textile** (Fashion and Fabric), and **Publicité** (Advertisement) are all dedicated to *haute couture* designs that the average tourist has probably never experienced. The Arts Décoratifs have exhibits on interior design, from period rooms of the Middle Ages to part of Jeanne Lanvin's house to some groovy, Proust-inspired furniture from the '70s. The Mode et Textile has exhibits on the evolution of fashion from the '70s to the '90s and features small exhibits on prominent fashion designers, including

paris

Yves Saint Laurent. The jewelry collection, **Galerie des Bijoux,** will make anyone's engagement ring look embarrassing.

i Ⓜ*Palais Royal-Musée du Louvre. Walk with the traffic on rue de Rivoli; the museum is on the left. Free audio tour. All 3 museums €9.50, ages 18-25 €7.50, under 18 and EU citizens 18-25 free.* ⏰ *Open Tu-Su 11am-6pm, temporary exhibitions have extended hours Th until 9pm. Last entry 30min. before close.*

ÉGLISE SAINT-EUSTACHE
CHURCH

2 rue du Jour   ☎01 42 36 31 05 www.saint-eustache.org

With so many cathedrals in Paris, it can quickly seem like a competition of "Whose is bigger?" And while size doesn't matter to God, Église St-Eustache probably never worried about pleasing Jesus. The Romanesque church boasts incredibly tall, 34m vaulted ceilings, the largest pipe organ in France, its fair share of stained glass, paintings by Rubens, and a silver sculpture dedicated to the victims of the AIDS epidemic.

i Ⓜ*Les Halles. Walk up Allée André Breton and turn left onto rue Rambuteau; the church is on the right. Audio tours available in English, ID required. Free. Audio tour suggested donation €3.* ⏰ *Open M-F 9:30am-7pm, Sa 10am-7pm, Su 9am-7pm. Mass Sa 6pm; Su 9:30am, 11am, 6pm.*

PALAIS-ROYAL
PALACE

8 rue de Montpensier   ☎01 47 03 92 16

This palace has a history plagued with abandonment, debauchery, and low funding. Louis XIV lived here as a child before moving on to bigger and better digs at Versailles. Henrietta Maria, the wife of the deposed English king Charles I, called the palace home after being kicked out of her own country for being Catholic. (The French reaction to her showing up was apparently, "You're Catholic? Move into this palace!") In the 18th century, Louise Henrietta de Bourbon moved in, and the palace was the site of her numerous debaucheries and extramarital affairs—at least a palace is far classier than a motel room. Finally, in 1781, the broke Duke of Orléans had to rent out the space to raise money. Today, the palace is a government building and closed to the public, but you can still see the impressive façade facing the Louvre and visit the Cour d'Honneur and the inner courtyard, which contains artist Daniel Buren's *Les Colonnes de Buren.* The gardens are nowhere near as nice as the nearby Tuileries, and the famous arcades are priced exclusively for window shopping.

i Ⓜ*Palais Royal-Musée du Louvre. Cour d'Honneur accessible from entrance on rue St-Honoré at the front of the palace. Free.* ⏰ *Fountain, galleries, and garden open Jun-Aug daily 7am-11pm; Sept 7am-9:30pm; Oct-Mar 7:30am-8:30pm; Apr-May 7am-10:15pm.*

The Marais

🏛 CENTRE POMPIDOU
MUSEUM, LIBRARY

pl. Georges Pompidou, rue Beaubourg   ☎01 44 78 12 33 www.centrepompidou.fr

The exterior of the Pompidou is a crazed network of yellow electrical tubes, green water pipes, and blue ventilation ducts, leaving plenty of space inside for all the good stuff. The center's functions are as varied as its colors; it serves as a cultural theme park of ultra-modern exhibition, performance, and research space. It is home to Europe's largest modern art museum, **Musée National d'Art Moderne,** which occupies the fourth, fifth, and sixth floors with a collection of over 60,000 works dating from 1905. Be sure to check out Duchamp's infamous *Fountain,* which is just a urinal that he signed "R. Mutt," because, hey, it's modern art. Temporary exhibits on international modern art fill the sixth floor. Other parts of the complex to explore include **Salle Garance,** which runs an adventurous film series; **Bibliothèque Publique d'Information,** a free library; **Institut de la Recherche de la Coordination Acoustique/Musique (IRCAM),** an institute and laboratory for the development of new technology; and the rooftop restaurant, **Georges.**

i Ⓜ*Rambuteau or Hôtel de Ville. From* Ⓜ*Rambuteau, walk down rue Beaubourg with the flow of traffic, turn right onto rue Rambuteau, then left at the plaza; the entrance is on the left. From* Ⓜ*Hôtel de Ville, walk up rue de Renard against the flow of traffic, turn left onto rue St-Merri, then right into the plaza; the entrance is on the right. Free Wi-Fi. Museum €13, under 26 €11, under 18 and EU citizens ages 18-25 free. 1st Su of the month free. Library and forum free. Ⓒ Center open M 11am-10pm, W-Su 11am-10pm Museum open M 11am-9pm, W-Su 11am-9pm. Last tickets sold at 8pm. Library open M noon-10pm, W-F noon-10pm, Sa-Su 11am-10pm.*

MUSÉE CARNAVALET
MUSEUM
23 rue de Sévigné   ☎01 44 59 58 58 www.carnavalet.paris.fr

Located in Mme. de Sévigné's beautiful, 16th-century *hôtel particulier* and the neighboring Hôtel Le Peletier de St-Fargeau, this meticulously arranged and engaging museum traces Paris's history from its origins to Napoleon III. The history of Paris is long, and this museum is pretty large, so we recommend grabbing a map and taking your time as you stroll through ornate 18th-century apartments. The city's urban development is conveyed through small-scale models, paintings (expect to see a lot of portraits), antique furniture, and sculptural fragments. Highlights include the famous *The Tennis Court Oath*, Marcel Proust's fully reconstructed bedroom, and a piece of the Bastille prison wall. (We tried, but shouting *"Vive la Revolution!"* doesn't entitle you to touch it.)

i Ⓜ*Chemin Vert. Take rue St-Gilles, which becomes rue du Parc Royal, and turn left onto rue de Sévigné. Free. Audio tour €5. Ⓒ Open Tu-Su 10am-6pm. Last entry 5:15pm.*

MUSÉE DE LA CHASSE ET DE LA NATURE
MUSEUM
62 rue des Archives   ☎01 53 01 92 40 www.chassenature.org

Yes, yes, we all love animals, but please save your horror for PETA meetings. This eclectic museum isn't just about bloodshed—it displays hunting-themed arts, weaponry, and stuffed animals that explore man's relationship with nature through the history and practices of hunting. The museum's interior is reminiscent of the sumptuous living rooms in a hunting lodge and contains a variety of cabinets for animals like the owls, boars, and stags, with drawers you can pull out to see their droppings. By far the most impressive room is the Trophy Room, with a stuffed polar bear on its hind legs, cheetahs in a glass case, heads of a rhinoceros, lion, tiger, moose, deer, boars, etc.

i Ⓜ*Rambuteau. Walk against traffic on rue Beaubourg, turn right onto rue Michel le Comte, then left onto rue des Archives €6, ages 18-25 and seniors €4.50, under 18 free. 1st Su of each month free. Ⓒ Open Tu-Su 11am-6pm.*

PLACE DES VOSGES
PARK

Paris's oldest and perhaps snootiest public square has served many generations of residents, from the knights who clashed swords in medieval tournaments to the hipsters who tan and swap bottles during picnics today. All 36 buildings that line the square were constructed by Baptiste du Cerceau in the same architectural style; look for pink brick, slate roofs, and street-level arcades. The quaint atmosphere attracted **Cardinal Richelieu** (who lived at no. 21 when he wasn't busy mad-dogging musketeers), writer **Alphonse Daudet** (who lived at no. 8), and **Victor Hugo** (no. 6). It was also the venue for one of seven-year-old prodigy **Mozart's** concerts, inspiring every "My Child is an Honor Student" bumper sticker that has been printed since. Come here to people watch, sunbathe, nap in the grass, and wish you were friends with Molière or Voltaire.

i Ⓜ*St-Paul or Bastille. Follow rue St-Antoine and turn onto rue de Birague. Free Wi-Fi.*

MAISON DE VICTOR HUGO

MUSEUM

6 pl. des Vosges   ☎01 42 72 10 16 www.maisonvictorhugo.paris.fr

Dedicated to the father of French Romanticism and housed in the building where he lived from 1832 to 1848, this museum displays memorabilia from his pre-exile, exile, and post-exile days, including his family's little-known paintings and the desk where he wrote standing up. On the first floor, the collection reveals paintings of scenes from *Les Misérables* and other works. On your way up, don't miss the caricatures of good ol' Hugo by André Gill. Upstairs, you'll find Hugo's apartments, a recreation of the bedroom where he died, and the *chambre chinoise*, which reveals his flamboyant interior decorating skills and just how romantic he really was.

i Ⓜ St-Paul or Bastille. Follow rue St-Antoine and turn onto rue de Birague. Free. Special exhibit €5, students and under 26 €2.50. Audio tour €5. ☒ Open Tu-Su 10am-6pm. Last entry 5:40pm.

GALERIE THUILLIER

GALLERY

13 rue de Thorigny   ☎01 42 77 33 23 www.galeriethuillier.com

One of Paris's most active galleries, Galerie Thullier has exhibits that rotate every two weeks, which means that there's always something new to see when you visit. The art displayed here ranges across all styles, and the gallery exhibits a number of different artists at any given time. Although there is no real permanent exhibit, some artists have close relationships with the gallery and show their work here as often as possible.

i Ⓜ St-Sébastien-Froissart. Walk down rue du Pont aux Choux and turn left onto rue de Turenne, then right onto rue de Thorigny. ☒ Open Tu-Sa 1-7pm.

Latin Quarter and St-Germain

🏛 PANTHÉON

HISTORICAL MONUMENT, CRYPT

pl. du Panthéon   ☎01 44 32 18 04 http://pantheon.monuments-nationaux.fr

If there's one building that doesn't know the meaning of antidisestablishmentarianism, it's the Panthéon. Because the Neoclassical building went back and forth between a church and a "secular mausoleum" over the years, it contains some surprising eternal residents. Within the crypt, tombs alternate between Christian heroes, such as St. Louis, and Enlightenment thinkers like Voltaire, Rousseau, and Descartes (who would probably object to being placed so close to icons of church dogma). What's worse, both Foucault's pendulum and revolutionary statues lie above the remains of Joan of Arc and Ste. Geneviève. Other famous graves include those of Victor Hugo, Émile Zola, and Marie Curie, the only female resident. The trip up the dome has three stops, with 360-degree views of the Marais and the Latin Quarter, and you can meander the colonnade at the top for the allotted 10min. before being herded back down.

i Ⓜ Cardinal Lemoine. Head away from the river on rue du Cardinal Lemoine and turn right onto rue Clovis. Walk until you reach pl. du Panthéon. Dome visits Apr-Oct in Dutch, English, French, German, Russian, and Spanish. €7.50, ages 18-25 €4.50, under 18 and EU citizens under 26 free. ☒ Open daily Apr-Sept 10am-6:30pm, Oct-Mar 10am-6pm. Last entry 45min. before close.

🏛 LE JARDIN DU LUXEMBOURG

GARDEN

Main entrance on bd St-Michel   ☎01 42 34 23 62 www.senat.fr/visite/jardin

As with most ornate things in Paris, these gardens and the Palais du Luxembourg used to be exclusively for royalty until the revolutions began in 1789. Today, the park is a favorite among Parisians, who love to hole up with a book on a bench by the apple orchards or snag a colorful aluminum chair and bask in the sun during their lunch break. Children run around this park like they own it, and with a carousel, numerous playgrounds, and 1920s wooden sailboats by the Grand Bassin Pond, the kiddos are definitely getting the most out of it. Don't get too excited about picnicking, though—perfectly manicured lawns like these are off-limits, and the one patch of grass that is open is unsurprisingly crowded. The Palais, which now houses the Sénat, is still off-limits, but the best and most sought-after spot in the garden is the **Fontaine des Médicis**, a vine-covered grotto east of the Palais that features a murky fish pond and Baroque fountain sculptures.

i Ⓜ*Odéon or RER B: Luxembourg. Guided tours in French Apr-Oct 1st W of each month 9:30am. Tours start at pl. André Honorat behind the observatory. Free.* Ⓐ *Open daily in summer 7:30am-1hr. before sunset; in winter 8am-1hr. before sunset.*

▩ SHAKESPEARE AND CO. BOOKSTORE   BOOKSTORE

37 rue de la Bûcherie   ☎01 43 25 40 93 www.shakespeareandcompany.com

Sylvia Beach's original Shakespeare and Co. at 8 rue Dupuytren (later at 12 rue de l'Odéon) is legendary among Parisian Anglophones and American literature nerds alike. An alcoholic crew of expat writers gathered here in the '20s, and Hemingway described the bookstore in *A Moveable Feast.* After closing during World War II, George Whitman—no relation to Walt—opened the current ragtag bookstore on the shores of the Seine in 1951, dubbing it "a socialist utopia masquerading as a bookstore." This certainly isn't your run-of-the-mill, money-making Barnes&Noble; they're in it for the love of the game at Shakespeare and Co. Grab a book off the shelves and head to the quiet library overlooking the Seine on the second floor.

i Ⓜ*St-Michel. Take quai de Montebello toward Notre Dame and turn right onto rue St-Jacques. Rue de la Bûcherie is on the left.* Ⓐ *Open M-F 10am-11pm, Sa-Su 11am-11pm.*

MUSÉE ZADKINE   MUSEUM

100B rue d'Assas   ☎01 55 42 77 20 www.zadkine.paris.fr

Installed in the former house and studio of Russian sculptor Ossip Zadkine (1890-1967), this pleasantly tourist-free museum houses a terrific collection of his extensive work in a minimalist, modern setting of clean-cut white walls. While most artists tend to stick to one area, Zadkine worked in 12 different styles, from Primitivism to Neoclassicism to Cubism, and the museum's collection includes all of his creative periods. Visitors can pore over his classical masterpiece, *L'hommage à Apollinaire,* then immerse themselves in his more modern and strikingly disembodied *Le Torse de la Ville Détruite.* The tiny forested garden, realized by landscape painter Gilles Clément, is a welcome retreat from the busier northern part of the 6ème. Don't forget to indulge in a free cup of hot tea, served in a bamboo cup on your way out.

i Ⓜ*Vavin. At the intersection, turn left onto rue de la Grande Chaumière, then right onto rue Notre-Dame des Champs. Turn left onto rue Joseph Bara, then left onto rue d'Assas. Guided tours available by reservation. Permanent exhibit free; temporary exhibits vary.* Ⓐ *Open daily 10am-6pm.*

ARÈNES DE LUTÈCE   PARK, HISTORIC MONUMENT

49 rue Monge   ☎01 45 35 02 56

Back in the days of the Romans in the first and second centuries, this amphitheater was used for spectacles like **gladiator battles** and animal fights attended by as many as 15,000 people. Tamer audiences came for the plays and comedies, but we bet the place only really filled up for the bloodbaths. In the 13th century, the amphitheater, long out of use, was completely filled in and remained undiscovered until 1869. Today, the seating around the amphitheater has been restored and opened to the public. Occasionally, there are summertime performances that feature music, comedy, theater, and dance, but this circular sandpit is generally used for pick-up soccer games and various other forms of public folly (some things never change). Around the amphitheater are some small walking paths and dense foliage that provides some much-needed shade during the hot summer.

i Ⓜ*Place Monge. At the intersection of rue de Navarre and rue des Arènes; the Métro stop is beneath it. Occasionally hosts outdoor performances.* Ⓐ *Closing times vary during the year, open M-F 8am, Sa-Su 9am. Open May-Aug M-F 8am-9:30pm, Sa-Su 9am-9:30pm.*

paris

Invalides

◪ EIFFEL TOWER
TOWER

Champs de Mars   ☎08 92 70 12 39   www.tour-eiffel.fr

At 324m—just a tad shorter than New York City's Chrysler Building—the tower is a tremendous feat of design and engineering, though wind does cause it to occasionally sway 6 to 7cm (nobody's perfect). The lines are unsurprisingly long, but the unparalleled view from the top floor deserves a visit. The cheapest way to ascend the tower is by burning off those *pain au chocolat* calories on the world's most iconic Stairmaster, although the third floor is only accessible by elevator. Waiting until nightfall to make your ascent cuts down the line and ups the glamour; buying your ticket online can also save you hours—we mean that literally. At the top, captioned aerial photographs help you locate other famous landmarks; on a clear day it is possible to see Chartres, 88km away. From dusk until 2am (Sept-May 1am) the tower sparkles with light for 10min. on the hour.

i Ⓜ*Bir-Hakeim,* Ⓜ*Trocadéro, or* Ⓜ*École Militaire. From* Ⓜ*Bir-Hakeim, walk toward the Seine, turn right onto quai de Grenelle, and the Eiffel Tower is on the right. From* Ⓜ*École Militaire, walk up av. de la Bourdonnais against traffic. Elevator to 2nd fl. €8.50, ages 12-24 €7, ages 4-11 and handicapped €4; under 4 free; elevator to top €14.50/13/10/free; stair entrance to 2nd fl. €5/3.50/3/ free. Buy your ticket online and pick your time to climb in order to cut down the wait.* ☒ *Elevator open daily Jun 15-Sept 1 9am-12:45am; rest of year 9:30am-11:45pm. Last entry 45min. before close. Stairs open daily Jun 15-Sept 1 9am-12:45am, last entry midnight; rest of year 9:30am-6:30pm, last entry 6pm.*

◪ MUSÉE D'ORSAY
MUSEUM

1 Rue de la Légion d'Honneur   ☎01 40 49 48 14   www.musee-orsay.fr

Aesthetic taste is fickle. When a handful of artists were rejected from the Louvre salon in the 19th century, they opened an exhibition across the way, prompting both the scorn of stick-up-their-arses *académiciens* and the rise of Impressionism. Today, people line up at the Musée d'Orsay to see this collection of groundbreaking rejects. Originally a train station, the museum is fairly large and is best seen over several visits so you don't become art-ed out. The first and second floors contain pre-Impressionist works and lesser-known artists, with all the big names and famous works of Impressionist and Post-Impressionist art on the more crowded top floor. Everything at the museum is practically a must see, but if you're really crunched for time, limit yourself to Van Gogh's portraits and *Starry Night*, Degas's ballerinas, Cézanne's *Apples and Oranges* and other still lifes, and Seurat and Signac's Pointillism. Avoid the long lines by buying a ticket beforehand and hopping over to Entrance C.

i Ⓜ*Solférino. Access at entrance A off the square at 1 rue de la Légion d'Honneur. €9, ages 18-25 €6.50, under 18 and EU citizens 18-26 free, joint ticket with Musée Rodin €15.* ☒ *Open Tu-W 9:30am-6pm, Th 9:30am-9:45pm, F-Su 9:30am-6pm. Visitors asked to leave 30min. before close.*

◪ MUSÉE DE L'ARMÉE
MUSEUM

129 rue de Grenelle   ☎08 10 11 33 99   www.musee-armee.fr

Americans in favor of the Second Amendment, European empire enthusiasts, and war buffs will all find a visit to the Musée de l'Armée a surefire good time. Housed inside the grand Hôtel des Invalides and built by Louis XIV for his war veterans, the museum is comprised of six main parts. The impressive **Église du Dôme** is the most recognizable part of the museum and holds the **tomb of Napoleon** surrounded by sculptures and inscriptions celebrating our favorite *petit* emperor. The dome and the Saint-Louis des Invalides chapel are flanked by the Charles de Gaulle historical exhibit and collections covering Louis XIV to Napoleon III in the East Wing and the fantastic World War I and World War II exhibit and ancient armor and arms collections in the West Wing. Even for those who aren't crazy about ordnance will find something fascinating here. Whether it's the shiny street taxi used to shuttle soldiers in WWI, animated maps of major battles and conquests, or the collection of armor for children (both terrifying and strangely cute), the museum covers quite a bit of ground.

i ⓂInvalides or ⓂLa Tour-Maubourg. The museum is located in the center of the park. Admission to all museum €9.50, students under 26 €7.50, EU citizens and under 18 free; €7.50 after 5pm in the summer, after 4pm in the winter, and late on Tu. Temporary exhibits €8.50; entrance to both permanent and temporary €12. Audio tour €6, under 26 €4. ⏰ Open daily Apr-Oct 10am-6pm; Nov-Mar 10am-5pm. Dome Church and Modern Department are open Apr-Sept until 9pm; Jul-Aug until 7pm. Except Jul-Sept, 1st M of every month only Dome Church and artillery trail are open. Charles de Gaulle Monument closed every M.

🖼 MUSÉE RODIN   MUSEUM
79 rue de Varenne   ☎01 44 18 61 10 www.musee-rodin.fr

After Auguste Rodin (1840-1917) was rejected by the most prestigious art school in Paris, he rejected the idealized styles and themes in sculpture to create works of vivid realism. Living well is the best revenge—today the art world considers him the father of modern sculpture. This museum houses three of Rodin's most famous sculptures, *Le Penseur* (The Thinker), *La Porte de L'Enfer*, and *Le Baiser*. For one of the best photo ops of all time, strike a pose like *Le Penseur* contemplating *Le Penseur*—so meta. Meanwhile, *The Gates of Hell* is a bronze mess of lustful pairs swirling in the violent turbulence of the second ring of Hell from Dante's *Divine Comedy*. Rodin's lesser-known sculptures are inside the Hôtel Biron, the 18th-century building where he lived and worked.

i ⓂVarenne. Temporary exhibits housed in the chapel, to the right as you enter. Museum €9, ages 18-25 €5, under 18 and EU citizens under 26 free; garden €1/1/free; joint ticket with Musee d'Orsay €15. 1st Su of the month free. Audio tours in 6 languages €4 each for permanent and temporary exhibits, combined ticket €6. ⏰ Open Tu-Su 10am-5:45pm, last entry 5:15pm.

🖼 CHAMPS DE MARS   PARK
Lined with more lovers than trees, the expansive lawn that stretches from the École Militaire to the Eiffel Tower is called the Champs de Mars (Field of Mars). Close to the neighborhood's military monuments and museums, it has historically lived up to the Roman god of war for whom it was named. The open field has been used for military boot camp and as a convenient place for violent demonstrations, including but not limited to a slew of civilian massacres during the Revolution. At the end of the Champs de Mars, toward the Military School, is the "Wall of Peace," a glass structure that has 32 languages' worth of the word "peace" inscribed on its walls in an attempt to make up for the field's bloody past. For a picnic with a view, head over to rue Cler to buy some baguettes and charcuterie from the open-air markets as you watch the sun set behind the Eiffel Tower.

i ⓂLa Motte Picquet-Grenelle or ⓂÉcole Militaire.

MUSÉE DE LÉGION D'HONNEUR   MUSEUM
2 rue de la Légion-d'Honneur   ☎01 40 62 84 25 www.musee-legiondhonneur.fr

This museum is worth a brief (and free) visit when you're all art-ed out by the Musée d'Orsay across the street. It showcases France's highest honors, decorations, and orders—in other words, there are some very ornate pendants, medallions, and insignias on display here. The most famous and prestigious items here are the royal collars of the Legion of Honor, a national order established in 1802 by Napoleon, who understood the importance of shiny objects when he famously declared, "It is with such baubles that men are led." Other must-sees here are the foreign orders from countries such as Madagascar to Japan and the enormous black velvet royal capes.

i RER Musée d'Orsay or ⓂSolférino. Across the street from Musée d'Orsay. Handicapped entrance at 1 rue de Solférino. Free entrance and audio tour. ⏰ Open W-Su 1-6pm.

paris

MUSÉE MAILLOL

MUSEUM

61 rue de Grenelle   ☎01 42 22 59 58   www.museemaillol.com

The museum was founded by Aristide Maillol's muse, Dina Vierny, who was 15 when she met the French sculptor. Unlike Georgia O'Keefe's ambiguous "lady" flower images, the work of Maillol is pretty straightforward. Nude sculptures and paintings form the backbone of this museum's permanent collection on the upper levels, although the first and second floors are dominated by detailed and well-curated temporary exhibits that range from art from Pompeii to work by Murano glass makers.

i Ⓜ*Rue du Bac. Walk down rue de Bac along the flow of traffic and turn left onto rue de Grenelle. The museum is on the right €11; ages 11-25, unemployed, and handicapped €9; under 11 free. Audio tour €5.* ☐ *Open daily 10:30am-7pm, last entry 45min. before close.*

MUSÉE DU QUAI BRANLY

MUSEUM

37 quai Branly   ☎01 56 61 70 00   www.quaibranly.fr

Museums can get old real quick, but before you can even think about how tired your feet are, this time machine/museum of natural history will shower you with its theatricality—every which way you turn will be a new video about Indian shadow puppets, a collection of wooden Polynesian ancestral poles, or a group of noisy school children (no, they're not on display, but they're essentially permanent fixtures here). The museum doesn't have any rooms, which creates some rather abrupt transitions from the four organized regions (Africa, Asia, the Americas, and Oceania). In case you can't tell the difference between a Nepalese tunic and an African one, look at the floor: the color under your feet corresponds to what section of the world you are in. Be sure to sit in one of the many hidden sound caves to take in some tribal noises in solitude, but beware of local high school students using the dark spaces as personal make-out rooms.

i Ⓜ*Alma-Marceau. Cross Pont de l'Alma and follow quai Branly toward the Eiffel Tower. €8.50, under 18 and EU citizens 18-25 free. Temporary exhibit €7. Joint ticket €10. Audio tour €5.* ☐ *Open Tu-W 11am-7pm, Th-Sa 11am-9pm, Su 11am-7pm.*

Champs-Élysées

🏛 ARC DE TRIOMPHE

HISTORIC MONUMENT

pl. Charles de Gaulle-Étoile   www.arc-de-triomphe.monuments-nationaux.fr

Probably the second most iconic structure in the whole city, the Arc de Triomphe dominates the Champs-Élysées and remains strikingly powerful even when viewed from a distance. The original architect imagined an unparalleled tribute to France's military prowess in the form of a giant, bejeweled elephant. Fortunately, Napoleon had the more restrained idea of building an arch. You could probably pull together an exhibition of French history since the arch's 1836 completion based purely on photos of the Arc's use in ceremonial celebrations. It stands both as a tribute to French military triumphs and as a memorial to those who have fallen in battle. The Tomb of the Unknown Soldier, added in 1920, lies under the arch. Every day at 6:30pm, the tomb's eternal flame is re-lit in a ceremony. The Arc is spectacular to look at, and it returns the favor by being spectacular to look from. The observation deck offers a brilliant view of the Historic Axis, which stretches from the Louvre to the Grande Arche de la Défense.

i Ⓜ*Charles de Gaulle-l'Étoile. You will die (and face a hefty fine) if you try to dodge the 10-lane merry-go-round of cars around the arch, so use the pedestrian underpass on the right side of the Champs-Élysées, facing the arch. Expect long waits, although you can escape the crowds if you go before noon. Buy tickets in the pedestrian underpass. €9.50, ages 18-25 €6, under 18 and EU citizens 18-25 free.* ☐ *Open daily Apr-Sept 10am-11pm; Oct-Mar 10am-10:30pm. Last entry 45min. before close.*

▓ PINACOTHÈQUE · MUSEUM

28 pl. de la Madeleine · ☎01 42 68 02 01 www.pinacotheque.com

A young contender in Paris's competitive museum scene, Pinacothèque has held its own since it opened in 2007. When director Marc Restellini, a little-known art scholar not backed by any large foundation, decided to open up his own museum, the museum world refused to take him seriously. To their great surprise (and chagrin), temporary exhibits on Edvard Munch, Jackson Pollock, and the terracotta warriors from China drew round-the-block visitors. Unbeholden to any higher powers, this museum runs entirely on gift shop and ticket sales, so it can afford to be a little more experimental in its exhibitions—the permanent collection contains startling juxtapositions, with works by Picasso next to pieces by 17th-century Dutch painter Frans Hals next to one of Warhol's stereographs of Marilyn Monroe. The permanent collection is worth a visit, although the stars here are the more extensive temporary exhibits.

i Ⓜ*Madeleine. Facing the front of the church, turn around to the right, and the ticket office is located on the corner of rue Vignon and rue de Sèze. Audio tours available for download online. Permanent collection €8, ages 12-25 and students €6, under 12 free; temporary collections €12/10; combined tickets €18-22. ☒ Open M-Tu 10:30am-6:30pm, W 10:30am-9pm, Th 10:30am-6:30pm, F 10:30am-9pm, Sa-Su 10:30am-6:30pm. Last entry 45min. before close.*

AVENUE DES CHAMPS-ÉLYSÉES · SHOPPING DISTRICT

From pl. Charles de Gaulle-Étoile to pl. de la Concorde

There's a reason we included it here and not in **Shopping**—you can't afford it. The Champs-Élysées seems to be a magnificent celebration of the elite's pomp and fortuitous circumstance, but it's mostly filled with flashy cars, expensive cafes packed with rich foreigners, and kitschy shops. On the plus side, it does offer some of the best people watching in Europe. The avenue also hosts most major French events: on **Bastille Day,** the largest parade in Europe takes place here, as does the final stretch of the **Tour de France.** Huge national celebrations, like FIFA World Cup championships and political demonstrations, also love to clog up this commercial artery. While the Champs itself may be deteriorating in class (with the invasion of chain stores), many of its side streets, like **Avenue Montaigne,** have picked up the slack and ooze sophistication.

i Ⓜ*Charles de Gaulle-l'Étoile.* Ⓜ*George V,* Ⓜ*Franklin D. Roosevelt, or* Ⓜ*Champs-Élysées-Clemenceau stops all along the avenue.*

PLACE DE LA CONCORDE · PLAZA

pl. de la Concorde

Constructed by Louis XV in honor of himself, the Place de la Concorde quickly became ground zero for all public grievances against the monarchy. During the Reign of Terror, the complex of buildings was renamed Place de la Révolution, and 1343 aristocrats were guillotined here in less than the span of one year. Louis XVI met his end near the statue that symbolizes the French town of Brest, and the obelisk marks the spot where Marie Antoinette, Charlotte Corday (Marat's assassin), Lavoisier, Danton, and Robespierre lost their heads. Flanking either side of Concorde's intersection with the wide **Champs-Élysées** are reproductions of Guillaume Coustou's **Chevaux de Marly;** also known as *Africans Mastering the Numidian Horses,* the original sculptures are now in the Louvre to protect them from pollution. At night, the Concorde's dynamic ambiance begins to soften, and the obelisk, fountains, and lamps are dramatically illuminated. On **Bastille Day,** a military parade led by the President of the Republic marches through the Concorde (usually around 10am) and down the Champs-Élysées to the Arc de Triomphe, and an impressive fireworks display lights up the sky over the plaza at night. At the end of July, the **Tour de France** finalists pull through the Concorde and into the home stretch on the Champs-Élysées. Tourists be warned: between the

paris

Concorde's monumental scale, lack of crosswalks, and heavy traffic, crossing the street here is impossible at best and fatal at worst. Unless you want to see the obelisk up close, it's best to admire it from afar and circle around the plaza to get to Madeleine or the Champs-Élysées, rather than cross the plaza directly.

i ⓂConcorde.

OBÉLISQUE DE LUXOR
HISTORIC MONUMENT

pl. de la Concorde

In the center of Paris's largest and most infamous public square, the 3300-year-old Obélisque de Luxor stands at a monumental 72ft. The spot was originally occupied by a statue of Louis XV (after whom the square was originally named) that was destroyed in 1748 by an angry mob. King Louis-Philippe, anxious to avoid revolutionary rancor, opted for a less contentious symbol: the 220-ton, red granite, hieroglyphic-covered obelisk presented to Charles X from the Viceroy of Egypt in 1829. The obelisk, which dates back to the 13th century BCE, recalls the royal accomplishments of Ramses II and wasn't erected until 1836. Today, it forms the axis of what many refer to as the "royal perspective"—a spectacular view of Paris from the Louvre, in which the Place de la Concorde, the Arc de Triomphe, and the Grande Arche de la Défense appear to form a straight line through the center of the city. The view serves as a timeline of Paris's history, from the reign of Louis XIV all the way to the celebration of modern commerce.

i ⓂConcorde.

GRAND PALAIS
PALACE

3 av. du Général Eisenhower ☎01 44 13 17 17 www.grandpalais.fr

Designed for the 1900 World's Fair, the Grand Palais and the accompanying Petit Palais across the street were lauded as exemplary works of Art Nouveau architecture. Today, the Grand Palais is used as a concert venue and an exhibition space for wildly popular temporary installations on artists such as Klimt and Monet. It is also well known as the annual host of Chanel's elaborate fashion shows. For the temporary exhibits, it's best to buy a ticket in advance and skip the lines. Otherwise, most of the building's beauty can be admired outside for free, especially at night, when the 6000 metric ton glass ceiling glows, lighting up the French flag that flies above it.

i ⓂChamps-Élysées-Clemenceau. Prices vary depending on exhibitions. €8-16, ages 18-26 €6-10. ☒ Hours vary widely based on the exhibition. Closed Tu.

Bastille

▨ VIADUC DES ARTS AND PROMENADE PLANTÉE
PARK, SHOPPING STRIP

10 cour du Marché Saint-Antoine ☎01 44 75 80 66 http://www.leviaducdesarts.com

An oft-overlooked sight, the elevated Promenade Plantée runs along the old Vincennes railway line and was the inspiration for New York City's High Line. The 4.5km pathway and its fragrant flowers make for a terrific afternoon stroll, or at least a greener alternative to the busy streets below. If you're short on time, the Jardin de Reuilly is a much larger, beautiful place for a picnic before you have to scramble back down to the concrete streets when the sun sets. Below the Promenade on av. Daumesnil, Paris's contemporary artists occupy the shops under the heavy archways of the **Viaduc des Arts.** You can find everything from flashy *haute couture* to workshops that use leather, wood, copper, and glass to create trendy art collections that scream, "Look at me! I'm artistic!" from the windows.

i ⓂBastille. Promenade runs from the Bois de Vincennes to the rue de Lyon. The Viaduc des Arts runs along av. Daumesnil from rue de Lyon to rue de Charenton. Entrances to the Promenade are at Ledru Rollin, Hector Malot, and bd Diderot. ☒ Park opens M-F 8am, Sa-Su 9am. Closing hours vary, around 5:45pm in winter, 9:30pm in summer. Stores open M-Sa; hours vary, with many taking a 2hr. lunch break at noon.

BASTILLE PRISON
HISTORIC SITE

Visitors to the prison subsist on symbolic value alone—it's one of the most popular sights in Paris that doesn't actually exist. On July 14, 1789, an angry Parisian mob stormed this bastion of royal tyranny, sparking the French Revolution. They only liberated seven prisoners, but who's counting? Two days later, the Assemblée Nationale ordered the prison to be demolished. Today, all that remains is the fortress's ground plan, still visible as a line of paving stones in the pl. de la Bastille. But it was hardly the hell hole that the Revolutionaries who tore it down imagined it to be. Bastille's elite inmates were allowed to furnish their suites, use fresh linens, bring their own servants, and receive guests; the Cardinal de Rohan famously held a dinner party for 20 in his cell. Notable prisoners included the **Man in the Iron Mask** (made famous by writer Alexandre Dumas), the Comte de Mirabeau, Voltaire (twice), and the Marquis de Sade. The anniversary of the storming is celebrated every year on July 14 and (much like a certain celebration 10 days earlier across the Atlantic) is a time of glorious fireworks and copious amounts of alcohol, with festivities concentrated around pl. de la Bastille (but note that the fireworks are over the Eiffel Tower).

i Ⓜ*Bastille.*

MALHIA KENT
FASHION

19 av. Daumesnil   ☎01 41 92 88 88 www.malhia.fr

Fulfilling every *Project Runway* fantasy, this workshop gives an up-close, behind-the-scenes look at fashion. High-end fabrics made out of colorful threads of glitter, lace, and feathers will delight any aspiring seamstress, but for those who don't know how to make it work with a sewing machine, there's not much to see other than a ton of really expensive, shiny pieces of cloth. Maybe they would make fancy, albeit rough, hand towels? Or place mats?

i Ⓜ*Bastille. In the Viaduc des Arts. Items usually run from €75-300.* ☑ *Open Tu-F 10am-7pm, Sa 11am-7pm.*

Montparnasse and Southern Paris

🔲 CATACOMBS
HISTORIC LANDMARK

1 av. du Colonel Henri Roi-Tanguy   ☎01 43 22 47 63 www.catacombes.paris.fr

The Catacombs were the original site of Paris's quarries, but they were converted into an ossuary in 1785 to help alleviate the stench rising from overcrowded cemeteries—somehow, burying six million people at once seemed like a better idea. Not for the claustrophobic or faint of heart, this 45min. excursion leads visitors down a winding spiral staircase to a welcoming sign: "Stop! Here is the Empire of Death." Stacks of skulls and femurs line the walls, with the highlight being the barrel-shaped arrangement of skulls and shinbones. Try to arrive before the opening at 10am; hordes of tourists form extremely long lines hoping to escape the pressing sun. The visitors' passage is well marked, so don't worry about getting lost. Try trailing behind the group a little for the ultimate creepy experience—you won't be disappointed.

i Ⓜ*Denfert Rochereau. Cross av. du Colonel Henri Roi-Tanguy with the lion on the left. Audio tour €3. €8, over 60 €6, ages 14-26 €4, under 14 free.* ☑ *Open Tu-Su 10am-5pm. Last entry 4pm.*

TOUR MONTPARNASSE
TOWER

33 av. du Maine   ☎01 45 38 52 56 www.tourmontparnasse56.com

Everyone loves a great panorama of Paris, but the perennial problem is that no matter how many stairs you climb or elevators you take, you can't see the landmark you're standing on. Tour Montparnasse solves this problem with a 196m vantage point over the city and a terrific view of nearly all of Paris's famous landmarks, all without forcing you to see the stark and monolithic tower itself. The elevator is allegedly the fastest in Europe (moving at 19ft. per second—not a lot of time to clear the pressure in your ears) and spits you out at a mandatory photo line on the 56th floor. After being shoved in front of a fake city skyline and forced to smile for a picture that you probably don't want, you're finally allowed up to the 59th floor to take in the beauty and meticulous planning of Paris's historic streets. Thankfully, the city ruled that similar eyesores could not be constructed in Paris's downtown shortly after this one was built.

i Ⓜ*Montparnasse-Bienvenue. Entrance on rue de l'Arrivée. €13.50, students and under 20 €7, under 15 €8, under 7 free.* ⏰ *Open Apr-Sept daily 9:30am-11:30pm, Oct-Mar M-Th 9:30am-10:30pm, F-Sa 9:30am-11pm, Su 9:30am-10:30pm. Last entry 30min. before close.*

MÉMORIAL DE LA LIBÉRATION DE PARIS   MEMORIAL, MUSEUM
23 allée de la 2ème DB, Jardin Atlantique   ☎01 40 64 39 44 www.ml-leclerc-moulin.paris.fr
Opened in 1994 for the 50th anniversary of the liberation of Paris from Nazi control, this memorial is composed of the **Mémorial du Maréchal LeClerc** and the **Musée Jean Moulin,** named for two celebrated World War II heroes. French hero Jean Moulin organized and unified the French resistance before his arrest, interrogation, and death under the Gestapo. The whole memorial is located above the SNCF station, where LeClerc set up his command post in 1944, and in the neighborhood where Moulin lived under the artist guise *Romanin* prior to his military success. The two galleries are symbolically connected by the Liberation Gallery, which is meant to represent the remarkable unification of resistance forces to fight the Nazi regime and liberate France. The galleries contain an impressive array of 13 screens that play a harrowing series of video footage chronicling the tragedies and victories Paris experienced over the course of Nazi occupation and liberation.

i Ⓜ*Montparnasse-Bienvenue. Follow signs for the Memorial Leclerc from the Métro stop to the Memorial; the museum is on top of the SNCF terminal. Permanent collection free. Audio tour €5. Rotating exhibits vary, usually €5, ages 14-26 €2.* ⏰ *Open Tu-Su 10am-6pm.*

Auteuil, Passy & Batignolles

▣ PALAIS DE TOKYO   MUSEUM
13 av. du President Wilson   ☎01 81 97 35 88 www.palaisdetokyo.com
The Palais de Tokyo rejects the label "museum," and prefers to call itself a site "devoted to contemporary creativity." The artistic creations of future Duchamps, Basquiats, and Harings are featured here in all forms imaginable, from paintings and sculpture to projections, videos, dance, and fashion. If the world of art, with all of its hallowed names and iconic images, seems a bit stuffy and staid to you, you'll be glad to know that very little at this site is permanent—exhibitions are only up for a few months. Although the stuff here may seem ridiculous and esoteric (someone explain to us how trapezoids count as modern art), the museum's unpretentious attitude toward art and its anti-museum stance make it a liberating and surprisingly personal visit.

i Ⓜ*lena €10, under 26 and seniors €8, under 18 free. When there are no exhibits, the Palais is open for free.* ⏰ *Open M noon-midnight, W-Su noon-midnight.*

▣ PALAIS DE CHAILLOT   MUSEUMS, HISTORIC BUILDING
1 pl. du Trocadéro   ☎01 58 51 52 00
To prep for the 1937 World's Fair, the French government tore down the old Palais du Trocadéro and built the current Palais de Chaillot. With its stellar view of the Eiffel Tower from across the Pont d'Iéna, the Palais has attracted its share of visitors, from Adolf Hitler to the UN General Assembly (to make up for the former). In 1948 they adopted the Universal Declaration of Human Rights at the Palais, and today the wide esplanade between the two wings is known as the "Esplanade of Human Rights." On either side of the esplanade are the arching wings of the Palais. The southern wing houses the Musée National de la Marine

(The National Navy Museum) and the Musée de l'Homme (Museum of Man). The eastern wing contains the Cité de l'Architecture and Théâtre National de Chaillot. For those who don't want to pay to enter the museums, the esplanade and the view are free, although the food stands nearby are not.

i Open M 11am-6pm, W-F 11am-6pm, Sa-Su 11am-7pm.

◩ MUSÉE D'ART MODERNE DE LA VILLE DE PARIS   MUSEUM
11 av. du President Wilson   ☎01 53 67 40 00 www.mam.paris.fr

If the Centre Pompidou is too high a price to pay for modern art, the free permanent collection at this museum features works by major figures like Picasso, Duchamp, and Matisse and is every bit as wonky. The highlight of this museum is usually the well-attended and excellent temporary exhibitions. Most recently, the museum did a retrospective on Keith Haring with a focus on his political artwork, which is essentially all of his work. During the summer, the museum cafe opens up to a gorgeous terrace with a river view.

i ⓜIéna. Cross the street to av du President Wilson and walk with the Seine to your right. Permanent collection free. Temporary exhibits €10, students €5. ⓩ Permanent collection open Tu-Su 10am-6pm. Last entry 5:45pm. Special exhibits open Tu-W 10am-6pm, Th 10am-10pm, F-Su 10am-6pm.

◩ LA GRANDE ARCHE DE LA DEFENSE   MONUMENT
1 parvis de la Défense   ☎01 49 07 27 55 www.grandearche.com

When French President François Mitterand created an international design competition for Paris's newest monument, those who entered the artistic fray faced some intimidating predecessors—who wanted to compete with Gustave Eiffel? Danish architect Johan Otto Von Spreckelsen took the plunge in 1983 and submitted his design for an arch that matches the glassy skyscrapers of this ultramodern business district and has become one of Paris's defining monuments. Made of 300,000 tons of white marble and standing taller than the Notre Dame, the arch was inaugurated on July 14, 1989, on the bicentennial of the French Revolution. It lies on the same boulevard as the Arc de Triomphe, and on a clear day, you can take the stairs to the top and see the Louvre. Since 2010, however, the elevator to the roof has been shut down, along with the museums that were located on the roof. The stairs remain open, and the plaza still offers a great view of the boulevard and the Arc de Triomphe in the distance.

i ⓜLa Défense.

MUSÉE MARMOTTAN MONET
2 rue Louis-Boilly   ☎01 44 96 50 33 www.marmottan.fr

For those who want some breathing room while appreciating Impressionist art—kisses to the Musée d'Orsay, but the Musée Marmottan Monet is free from crowds and filled with over 100 Impressionist and Post-Impressionist paintings, from Claude Monet's *Water Lilies* and other pieces from his personal collection. If you tire of Manet, Degas, or Gauguin, you can admire the grandiose collection of Napoleonic furniture (including Napoleon's bed, which is unsurprisingly *petit*). Be sure to pay a visit to the exhibit on illuminated manuscripts and medieval artwork, which is surprisingly captivating—this is probably the closest you'll ever get to stained glass from a 13th-century cathedral.

i ⓜLa Muette. Walk with traffic on av. Mozart, turn left onto Chaussée de la Muette, walk through the Jardin de Ranelagh on av. Jardin de Ranelagh, turn right onto av. Raphael, then left onto rue Louis-Boilly; the museum is on the right. €10, under 18 and students under 26 €5. Audio guides €3. ⓩ Open Tu-W 10am-6pm, Th 10am-8pm, F-Su 10am-6pm. Last entry 30min. before close.

MUSÉE GALLIERA   MUSEUM
10 av. Pierre 1er de Serbie   ☎01 56 52 86 00 www.palaisgalliera.paris.fr

There's no denying it—the French dress to impress. This museum elegantly displays the history of fashion from the 18th to the 20th century. With 30,000 outfits, 70,000 accessories, and not much space in which to display them, the museum organizes its exhibits by century and rotates them more swiftly than a Lady Gaga costume change.

i Ⓜléna. Walk down av. Pierre 1er de Serbice. Entrance is on the right side of the street. Entrance on pl. Rochambeau. €7, students and seniors €5.50. Ⓩ Open Tu-Su 10am-6pm. Last entry 5:30pm.

MUSÉE DU VIN
MUSEUM

5 sq Charles Dickens ☎01 45 25 63 26 www.museeduvinparis.com

A wine museum in Paris has so much potential, but you would need to pregame the Musée du Vin to make it interesting. The museum is located in the underground tunnels of limestone quarries and contains various displays of many highly technical tools such as "bunghole openers" and "tasting pliers," with confusing and terse explanations of their functions. The creepily lifelike figures in the museum don't help much with the explanation of the winemaking process, and the bulletins are almost completely in French. At the end of your tour of the museum, there is a tasting of a glass of rosé, white, or red wine—but for €12, you may be better off just buying a bottle elsewhere.

i ⓂPassy. Go down the stairs, turn right onto pl. Albioni, then right onto rue des Eaux; the museum is tucked away at the end of the street. Self-guided tour and 1 glass of wine €12; students, seniors, and visitors with disabilities €10. Ⓩ Open Tu-Su 10am-6pm.

STATUE OF LIBERTY
STATUE

Pont de Grenelle

Most things in Paris are done with flourish and a sense of grandeur—this, however, is more of an afterthought. Not even 40ft. tall, this replica of France's famous gift to the US is not worth your precious time. But you know what is? The man-made island it sits on. The Île aux Cygnes floats in the middle of the Seine and offers great views of Paris and the Eiffel Tower, while the leafy trees provide welcome shade for a pleasant picnic.

i ⓂJavel or ⓂPassy. From ⓂJavel walk toward the Seine, turn right onto quai André Citroen, turn left onto Pont Grenelle, and take stairs down to the Île aux Cygnes. From ⓂPassy walk down rue d'Albioni toward the Seine and cross av. du President Kennedy to the Pont Bir-Hakeim; turn right onto Île aux Cygnes and walk all the way down.

Montmartre

🏛 BASILIQUE DU SACRÉ-CŒUR
CHURCH

35 rue du Chevalier-de-la-Barre ☎01 53 41 89 00 www.sacre-coeur-montmartre.com

Situated 129m above sea level, this splendid basilica was first planned in 1870 to serve as a spiritual bulwark for France and the Catholic Church, which were facing an imminent military defeat and German occupation. The basilica was commissioned by the National Assembly and was initially meant to be an assertion of conservative Catholic power, but the only people that assert themselves on the steps today are the scammers offering "free" bracelets, so keep your wits about you after you reach the top of the exhausting climb. Inside, the basilica's dome is dominated by an image of Jesus Christ with his arms outspread, and if you're up for more stairs, climb up to the dome for an even better (and still free) view of the Parisian rooftops. Return to the steps of the basilica at night to watch the Eiffel Tower light up and sparkle.

i ⓂLamarck-Caulaincourt. Take rue Caulaincourt and turn right onto rue Lamrack. Follow rue Lamrack until you reach the basilica. Free. Ⓩ Basilica open daily 6am-10:30pm. Dome open daily Mar-Nov 9am-7pm; Dec-Feb 9am-6pm. Mass M-F 11:15am, 6:30pm, 10pm; Sa 10pm; Su 11am, 6pm, 10pm.

Buttes-Chaumont & Belleville

PARC DE BELLEVILLE
PARK

27 rue Piat

Parc de Belleville is the place to get lost. Get lost in a book. Get lost in a meal of baguettes, cheese, apples, and wine. Get lost in a game of badminton. Or get lost just wandering about the terraces and smelling the endless colorful flowers. The park is located on a slope, resulting in gorgeous views from the top of Parisian landmarks like the Eiffel Tower and the Panthéon. Come at sundown, when you can see the reds and yellows of the sky above the Parisian skyline. Gently bubbling fountains decorate different parts of the park and add a pleasant ambient soundtrack to the landscape. The park is divided into terraces and different grassy areas that are used for pick-up soccer games or picnics. Be sure to check out the summer schedule of the public amphitheater for concerts and festivals. Although Parc de Belleville closes after dark and many patrons clear out by late evening, fences are low and often breached by bored teenagers looking for a place to rendezvous after hours. (*Let's Go* does not recommend hopping fences like a hoodlum).

i Ⓜ*Pyrénées. Walk west on rue de Belleville, then turn left onto rue Piat. Entrances on rue Piat, rue des Couronnes, rue Bisson, and rue Jouye-Rouve. Free. ☼ Open daily dawn to dusk.*

CITÉ DE LA MUSIQUE
MUSEUM

221 av. Jean Jaurès ☎01 44 84 44 84 www.citedelamusique.fr

The Cité de la Musique is an institution that offers concerts, practice rooms, a media library, and workshops, although the highlight is the Musée de la Musique. The museum takes visitors on a tour of music from prehistoric times, with flutes and mammoth tusk horns, to ornate 16th-century Venetian pianos (a must-see) to early 20th-century radios. With over a thousand instruments and a fantastic free audio tour with music clips (we wouldn't expect anything less), the museum shows you how wonderful the world sounded pre-Autotune. Highlights include instruments formerly owned by greats like Frédéric Chopin, Stradivarius violins, gilded baroque-style harpsichords, and a small collection of world instruments. Temporary exhibits hit the museum's lower levels twice a year and cover a range of musical styles and time periods; a recent exhibit was dedicated entirely to Bob Dylan.

i Ⓜ*Porte de Pantin. Extra charges may apply for temporary exhibits. Concert €8-41, 50% discount under 16, under 26 €9 if tickets are available. Museum €7, under 26 free; joint with temporary exhibits €9/5. ☼ Info center open Tu-Sa noon-6pm, Su 10am-6pm. Musée de la Musique open Tu-Sa noon-6pm, Su 10am-6pm. Last entry 5:15pm.*

PARC DES BUTTES-CHAUMONT
PARK

1 rue Botzaris

Not your average Parisian park, the Buttes-Chaumont was modeled after Hyde Park in London, but it seems more like Pandora from *Avatar*. In the 13th century, this area was the site of a gibbet (an iron cage filled with the rotting corpses of criminals), a dumping ground for dead horses, a haven for worms, and a gypsum quarry (the origin of the term "plaster of Paris"). Thankfully, it's come a long way since then. Around the park and walkways, a barrier of trees provides shade, but there is more than enough sun for a picnic or laying out on the steep grassy slopes that overlook the high cliff. Bridges lead over the surrounding lake to the top, where designer Adolphe Alphand decided (why? we don't know) to build a small Roman temple. For some solitary ambling and a rare moment of peace and greenery, mosey along one of the many narrow footpaths.

i Ⓜ*Buttes-Chaumont. Free. ☼ Open daily Apr 7am-9pm; May-Aug 7am-10pm; Sept 7am-9pm; Oct-Mar 7am-8pm.*

paris

FOOD

Say goodbye to foot-long subs and that sticky pre-sliced cheese they sell at Costco; you're not in Kansas anymore. Food is an integral part of French life—while world-famous chefs and their three-star prices are valued Parisian institutions, you don't have to break the bank for excellent cuisine, especially if you come at lunchtime (when prices are nearly half what they are at dinner). Brasseries are even more casual and foster a lively and irreverent atmosphere. The least expensive option is usually a creperie, which specialize in thin Breton pancakes filled with meat, vegetables, cheeses, chocolate, or fruits. Creperies might conjure images of yuppie brunches and awkward first dates for Americans, but here in Paris, you can often eat a crepe for less than you'd pay for a patty at the great Golden Arches. Specialty food shops, including *boulangeries* (bakeries), *patisseries* (pastry shops), and *chocolatiers* (chocolate shops), provide delicious and inexpensive picnic supplies. A number of cheap kebab and falafel stands around town also serve quick, cheap fare. *Bon appétit!*

Île de la Cité and Île St-Louis

▨ CAFÉ MED   RESTAURANT, CREPERIE $$
77 rue St-Louis-en-l'Île   ☎01 43 29 73 17

On an island dominated by tourists, Café Med is a welcoming and surprisingly affordable spot for lunch and dinner. This usually packed cafe has prix-fixe meals for under 10 euro and enormous, crispy crepes. Colorful Moulin Rouge posters decorate the walls, but this small cafe has a much more laid-back and casual vibe thanks to the French locals and experienced travelers who chatter away over hot apple tarts.

i Ⓜ️Pont Marie. Cross Pont Marie, turn right onto quai de Bourbon, left onto rue le Regrattier, then right onto rue St-Louis-en-l'Île. Café Med is on the left. Prix-fixe menus from €9.90-19.90. ⏰ Open daily 11:45am-3:15pm and 6:45pm-10:30pm.

▨ MA SALLE À MANGER   RESTAURANT, COCKTAIL BAR $$
26 pl. Dauphine   ☎01 43 29 52 34 www.masalleamanger.com

If a cafe is located in the quiet pl. Dauphine, why not make the plaza your dining room? Seat yourself outside at Ma Salle à Manger, a tiny restaurant featuring food from the southwest region of France. Feast on their Basque specialties like the celebrated Basque pâté surrounded by vintage posters from the Bayonne festivals and red-and-white checkered aprons hanging on the walls.

i Ⓜ️Cité or Ⓜ️Pont Neuf. From Pont Neuf, cross the bridge and turn left into the square. Plats €15-18. Prix-fixe menu (entree and plat or plat and dessert) for lunch €19.50, dinner €22.50. ⏰ Open daily from 9:30am-10:30pm.

LE PETIT PLATEAU   CAFE $$
1 quai aux Fleurs   ☎01 44 07 61 86

With beautiful views of the Seine and a nice breeze to boot, this affordable cafe fills up quickly at lunchtime. Le Petit Plateau is located around the corner from the main street but is close enough to the foot traffic for some excellent people watching in relative peace and quiet. The stars of the show here are the quiches, which are made fresh every day, although the establishment also has its share of quality salads (the one with goat cheese is a popular choice).

i Ⓜ️Cité. Walk toward the Seine, turn right onto quai de la Corse, then walk until Pont Saint-Louis; the cafe is on the right, next to Esmeralda. Quiches from €8.50. Salads €10.5-11.50. Sandwiches €5-15. Lunch €12.50-16.50. ⏰ Open daily 10am-6pm.

LA RÉSERVE DE QUASIMODO   CAFE $$
4 rue de la Colombe   ☎01 46 34 67 67

Conversations flow freely here, just as they have for the last seven centuries. The food here is as good as that of the next French cafe, but this establishment operates a small wine cellar to pair perfect selections with each dish (or with an assortment of cheese or charcuterie if you're not feeling too hungry). This restaurant also offers sandwiches and the cheapest takeaway crepes on the island—don't be fooled into paying more than 3 euro for a Nutella crepe!

i Ⓜ*Cité. Walk toward the Seine, turn right onto quai de la Corse, then left onto rue de la Colombe; Quasimodo is on the left. Plats €11-13. Salads €6.5-11. Sandwiches €4-7. Entrees €5. Lunch special €16.* Ⓩ *Open M-Sa noon-11pm. Kitchen open until 10 pm.*

The Marais

▨ L'AS DU FALLAFEL
FALAFEL $

34 rue des Rosiers ☎01 48 87 63 60

L'As du Fallafel has become a landmark, and with good reason. Get a view into the kitchen, and you'll see giant tubs of freshly cut veggies and the chef frying falafel as fast as it's ordered. Patrons line up outside for the famous "falafel special"—we think of it as more of a magic trick, because we still don't know how they managed to fit everything into that pita. With greasy fried eggplant, hummus, pickled cabbage, cucumber, and, of course, plenty of crunchy falafel balls, it's huge, and it's especially fun to watch everyone try to eat it as neatly as possible. Avoid this place during dinner hours, as the wait can reach 30min.

i Ⓜ*St-Paul. Take rue Pavée and turn left onto rue des Rosiers. Falafel special €5.50. Shawarma €8. Eat-in falafel €8.* Ⓩ *Open M-Th 11am-midnight, F 11am-5pm, Su 11am-midnight.*

▨ BREIZH CAFÉ
CAFE $$

109 rue Vieille du Temple ☎01 42 72 13 77 breizhcafe.com

The crepes here are easy, Breizh-y, beautiful. The galettes are made with organic eggs and flour from Brittany, and Breizh Café also serves fancy shmancy hand-made Bordier butter to smear on your crepe. Quality is king here, and nearly everything is made from some sort of premium product that melts foodies right then and there. Those on a budget will doubly appreciate the prices, with numerous options that easily ring in to under €10. Complete your meal with one of nearly 20 different ciders to wash it all down.

i Ⓜ*St-Sébastien-Froissart. Walk down rue du Pont aux Choux with the traffic and turn left onto rue Vieille du Temple; Breizh Cafe is on the right. Savory crepes €4.50-11.80. Sweet crepes €3.30-7.50. Ciders €3.50.* Ⓩ *Open W-Sa 11:30am-11pm, Su 11:30am-10pm.*

▨ PAIN VIN FROMAGE
TRADITIONAL $$$

3 rue Geoffrey L'Angevin ☎01 42 74 07 52 www.painvinfromage.com

Gee, wonder what they serve here? Perhaps, bread, wine, and cheese? Nobody does the Holy Trinity of French cuisine quite as well as this rustic Parisian gem. If you can handle the rich, ripe smell of cheese and hot fondue for an evening, it will be worth it. With a selection of fine cheeses from seven different regions in France and the perfect wine selection to pair them with, the gentlemen might as well twist their handle-bar mustaches with a *hoh hoh hoh* while the ladies puff on their long cigarette handles with an *ooh là là!* For a more romantic experience—you're in Paris, make the most of it—head downstairs to the quieter, dimmed, and intimate stone basement.

i Ⓜ*Rambuteau or* Ⓜ*Hôtel de Ville. Reservations recommended. Entrees €4-9.50. Charcuterie platters €8.50-10. Fondue €14-16.50. Regional cheese platters €18.* Ⓩ *Open daily 7-11:30pm. Closed Jul 15-Aug 15.*

Latin Quarter and St-Germain

▨ AU P'TIT GREC
CREPERIE $

62 rue Mouffetard ☎01 43 36 45 06

Forget about all the other crepes you've eaten—the *crepes salées* (savory crepes) at Au P'tit Grec laugh at the other crepes you've eaten. You think you've had crepes? Think again. Filled with anything from chorizo to chèvre to mushrooms to bacon, these enormous crepes are stuffed to their physical limit with everything you've ever wanted and combinations you didn't even know you desired. Be sure to add in salad, tomatoes, and onions at no extra charge. This takeout joint has a few bar stools if you can snag a seat, but on a busy day, expect quite a crowd outside of its blue doorway, with everyone clamoring for the cheap crepes before hitting up the nearby bars.

i Ⓜ*Place Monge. Walk down rue Monge, turn right onto rue Ortolan, then left onto rue Mouffetard. Au P'tit Grec is on the right. Crepes salées €3-5.80, crepes sucrées €1.50-4.50.* ⏰ *Open daily 11am-midnight.*

▨ HUÎTRERIE RÉGIS
OYSTERS $$$

3 rue de Montfaucon ☎01 44 41 10 07 http://huitrerieregis.com

Oysters are the only child at Huîtrerie Régis and are showered with the utmost care and affection of the restaurant, which is dedicated entirely to the dish. The oysters are undeniably the stars of the restaurant, and Huîtrerie Régis is arguably the gem of Paris's oyster bars. The tiny, whitewashed dining room with sky blue plates feels like a Mediterranean cottage and is usually packed for dinner. If the restaurant is too crowded, Huîtrerie Régis also sells shucked oysters to go, and with oysters this good, not too much preparation is needed for a delicious meal at home.

i Ⓜ*Saint-Germain-des-Prés or Mabillon. From Saint-Germain, walk down bd Saint-Germain in the direction of the traffic, turn right onto rue du Four, then left onto rue de Montfacon; Huîterie is on the left. From Mabillon, walk up rue du Four in the direction of traffic, turn right onto rue de Montfacon; Huîtrerie is on the left. Dozen oysters €18.50-59, to-go €15-37.* ⏰ *Open Tu-Su noon-2:30pm and 6:30-10:30pm.*

▨ PATISSERIE VIENNOISE
CAFE $

8 rue de l'École de Médecine ☎01 43 26 60 48

Competition is justly fierce when it comes to patisseries in Paris, but Patisserie Viennoise takes the cake, pun fully intended. This tiny shop and small, two-room *salon de thé* is famous among Paris locals for their sumptuous hot chocolate and *café viennois*, a piping hot espresso with a very generous serving of whipped cream (Cholesterol? What's that?). Their pastries are also pretty good, but puts you in grave danger of a sugar coma when coupled with one of their hot drinks.

i Ⓜ*Odeon or Cluny-La Sorbonne. From Odeon, walk down bd Saint-Germain in the direction of traffic for 1 block, turn right onto rue Hautefeuille, then left onto rue de l'École de Médecine; Patisserie is on the left. From Cluny-La Sorbonne, walk up bd Saint-Germain against traffic, turn left onto bd Saint-Michel and right onto rue de l'École de Médecine; Patisserie is on the right. Cafe €2. Hot chocolate €3-3.50. Café viennois €3.50-4.* ⏰ *Open M-F 9am-7pm.*

▨ LA BOTTEGA DI PASTAVINO
ITALIAN, EPICERIE $

18 rue de Buci ☎01 44 07 09 56

Every boulangerie in Paris sells panini, but at Pastavino, the sandwiches seem to come straight from the Italian motherland. Served on hot, thick focaccia, with mozzarella so good you'll wonder which country really knows its cheeses, the panini are the main draw of this tiny establishment and are a great deal in this expensive area. Pastavino also doubles as an Italian *épicerie*—sorry, we mean *bottega*—filled with specialty pastas, cannoli, antipasti, gnocchi, and a slew of sauces.

i Ⓜ*Mabillon. Walk up rue du Four, past bd Saint-Germain, onto rue de Buci. Pastavino is on the left. Panini €4.50-6.* ⏰ *Open M-Sa 9:30am-8:15pm.*

DE CLERQ
BELGIAN FRIES $

184 rue Saint-Jacques ☎01 43 54 24 20

Everybody, from students from the nearby Sorbonne to professionals in sharp suits to policemen, gets in line at De Clerq for the excellent and cheap Belgian

france

fries. The potatoes are hand-peeled, imported fresh daily, and dipped twice in beef grease before being drizzled in house sauces. The fries are the main draw here, although the burgers and the *liège* waffles are quite popular as well. This is a takeaway joint, so grab your meal and head to the Jardin du Luxembourg to munch away.

i RER Luxembourg. Walk up the bd Saint-Michel toward the Jardin du Luxembourg, turn right onto rue le Goff, right onto rue Gay-Lussac, left onto rue Royer-Collard, left onto rue Saint-Jacques, and walk 1 block; De Clerq is on the left. Fries €2.50-4.50. Burgers €3.50-5.80. Waffles €2.50. ☒ Open M-Th 11am-10pm, F-Sa 11am-midnight, Su 6:30-10pm.

LES PAPILLES
TRADITIONAL, WINE BAR $$$$

30 rue Gay Lussac   ☎01 43 25 20 79 www.lespapillesparis.fr

Part wine shop, part épicerie, part restaurant, and all delicious, Les Papilles ranks as a top choice of food critics and is always packed during dinner. The small restaurant has an old-world charm, with tiny tables, a zinc bar, a colorful mosaic floor, and an entire wall of neatly arranged bottles of wine. Although there is a fair share of tourists in this restaurant, the food remains faithful to French cuisine, and the prix-fixe, four-course menu (the only option in the house) is always expertly prepared. If you're looking to splurge for a meal, this is the place to do it.

i RER Luxembourg. Walk up the bd Saint-Michel toward the Jardin du Luxembourg, turn right onto rue le Goff, and right onto rue Gay-Lussac; Les Papiles is up the block on the right. Reservations recommended €7 corkage fee. Prix-fixe meals €35. ☒ Open Tu-Sa noon-2pm and 7-10pm.

LE CAFÉ DE LA NOUVELLE MAIRIE
CAFE, WINE BAR $$$

19 rue des Fossés Saint-Jacques   ☎01 44 07 04 41

After hipsters go through their rough, transitional 20s, the successful survivors morph into incredibly self-assured, unpretentious, and impeccably styled 30-somethings, and those 30-somethings come to this cafe. Here, they sip espressos as they read the latest novel and swap literary criticism over glasses of fine wine excellently paired with the small plates of French dishes. Those that aren't huddled over a two-person table are at the bar or are holding hands with their partners on the peaceful terrace outside.

i RER Luxembourg. Walk toward the Jardin du Luxembourg, turn right onto rue le Goff, right onto rue Gay-Lussac, left onto rue Royer-Collard, left onto rue Saint-Jacques, and right onto rue des Fossés Saint-Jacques; the cafe is on the left. Wine €5-7 per glass. Entrees €5-12. plats €9-15. Dessert €6-8. Cash only ☒ Open M-F 8am-midnight.

Invalides

The chic 7ème is low on budget options, but there are a number of quality restaurants here that are worth the extra euro.

◾ BARTHÉLÉMY
FROMAGERIE $

51 rue de Grenelle   ☎01 42 22 82 24

The French go hard on cheese, and every square inch of this famous fromagerie is packed with every type of (expensive) cheese imaginable. This store is frequently filled with older French customers who know their brie and hang tight with Madame Barthélémy. Barthélémy is quite small and crowded, so the staff may not be able to give those without a cheese palate the low-down on the goods—it's best to know your preferences before you go. The limiting factors here are your wallet and how long you can endure the sharp, pungent scent of ripening cheese.

i ⓂRue de Bac. Walk south down bd Raspail and turn right onto rue de Grenelle; the shop is on the right, just before the next corner. Cheese from €3-12. ☒ Open M-F 8:30am-1:30pm and 4-7pm, Sa 8:30am-1:30pm and 3-7pm.

paris

CHEZ LUCIE
CREOLE $$

15 rue Augereau   ☎01 45 55 08 74 www.restuarant-chez-lucie.fr

You've been working that French scowl to perfection, but at this creole hole-in-the-wall, it's actually okay to grin and chat up the owner, who regularly shoots the breeze with his customers and will gladly show you pictures of his wife. Specializing in dishes from Martinique, Chez Lucie has options you won't normally see in Paris, from fish in coconut milk to spicy catfish to the more adventurous shark toufée. The portions are enormous for such a low price, and the *ti'ponch* (rum punch) will knock you on your ass.

i Ⓜ*École Militaire. Walk toward the Eiffel Tower on av. de la Bourdonnais, turn right onto rue de Grenelle, and take an immediate left onto rue Augereau. The restaurant is on the right (with a bright yellow awning). Entrees €7. plats €13-20. 3-course lunch special €16. Dinner menu with entree, plat, and dessert €26.* 🕐 *Open daily noon-2pm and 7-11pm.*

LE SAC À DOS
TRADITIONAL $$$

47 rue de Bourgogne   ☎01 45 55 15 35 www.le-sac-a-dos.fr

This restaurant is near some of Paris's biggest attractions, but its location on a quiet street saves it from mobs of tourists. Le Sac à Dos is a small, unassuming French restaurant that buys ingredients fresh every morning from local markets. For budget travelers, this place is on the pricier end, but you're paying for some peace to go with your *foie gras* and *mousse au chocolat* (served in a cookie bowl).

i Ⓜ*Varenne. Walk away from Pont d'Alexandre III on bd des Invalides and turn left onto rue de Varenne. Walk 1 block, past the Musée-Rodin, to rue de Bourgogne and turn left. The restaurant is on the right. Prix-fixe dinner €20. Plats €12-18. Desserts €6.* 🕐 *Open M-Sa 11am-2:30pm and 6:30-11pm.*

DEBAUVE&GALLAIS
CHOCOLATIER $

30 rue des Saints-Pères   ☎01 45 48 54 67 www.debauve-et-gallais.com

Around here, DG isn't short for a fashion house—cue Debauve&Gallais, former royal chocolate suppliers for the rulers of France. Sulpice Debauve, chemist-turned-chocolatier, landed his cushy gig when Marie Antoinette complained that her medicine tasted bad, and Debauve, unlike parents worldwide who would ignore these complaints, created *pistoles* (chocolate coins) for her. Debauve later took in his nephew, Gallais, and today the family-owned chocolate shop continues to sell its renowned and pricey currency alongside a variety of nougats, ganaches, and other assorted bonbons.

i Ⓜ*St-Germain-des-Prés. Walk west on bd St-Germain and turn right onto rue des Saints-Pères. Boite de Pistoles de Marie-Antoinette €34.* 🕐 *Open M-Sa 9am-7pm.*

Champs-Élysées

TY YANN
CREPERIE $

10 rue de Constantinople   ☎01 40 08 00 17

The ever-smiling Breton chef and owner, M. Yann, cheerfully prepares outstanding and relatively inexpensive *galettes* (€7.50-11) and crepes in this tiny, unassuming restaurant, where the walls are decorated with his mother's pastoral paintings. Many of the crepes here are expertly flambéed for meals that are too hot to handle, and some creative concoctions include La Vannetaise (sausage sauteed in cognac, Emmental cheese, and onions; €10). The *galettes* will more than fill you for a meal, so come with a friend and split a sweet crepe for dessert—we recommend the honey almond lemon. Wash it all down with a bowl of cider in an adorable ceramic mug.

i Ⓜ*Europe. Walk up rue de Rome with the train tracks on the right and turn left onto rue de Constantinople; Ty Yann is on the right. Crepe €7.50-11. Credit card min. €12.* 🕐 *Open M noon-2:30pm, Tu-F noon-2:30pm and 7:30-10:30pm, Sa 7:30-10:30pm.*

france

LADURÉE
TEA HOUSE $

18 rue Royale ☎01 49 60 21 79 www.laduree.com

Opened in 1862, Ladurée started off as a modest bakery. It has since become so famous that a *Gossip Girl* employee was flown here to buy macaroons so Chuck could properly offer his heart to Blair. On a more typical day the rococo decor of this tea salon—the original location of a franchise that now extends to 13 countries—attracts a jarring mix of well-groomed shoppers and tourists in sneakers. Along with the infamous mini macaroons arranged in pyramids in the window (beware: the rose flavor tastes like bathroom freshener), most items here are liable to induce a diabetic coma. Ladurée also sells other pastries, but save your money for their expensive macaroons. Dine in the salon or queue up for a culinary orgasm to go.

i Ⓜ*Concorde. Walk up rue Royale toward the Church Madeleine, away from the pl. de Concorde. Ladurée is on right. Other locations at 75 av. des Champs-Elysées, 21 rue Bonaparte, and 64 bd Haussmann. Box of 6 mini macaroons €15.80.* ⚄ *Open M-Th 8am-7:30pm, F-Sa 8am-8pm, Su 10am-7pm.*

AMOUR DE BURGER
BURGERS $$

7 rue Godot de Mauroy ☎01 53 30 09 72 www.amourdeburger.com

Amour de Burger will have you falling in love with burgers all over again. Set up like an American greasy spoon, this affordable French burger joint still maintains a European air, with most patrons sipping on white wine or watching a soccer match on the TV above the bar. Like all French bread, the brioche buns rank better than their American counterparts, and the patties are a bit thicker and stockier than those from American diners. The portions, however, are not quite as French and will leave you both stuffed and head-over-heels in love with this Parisian anomaly. Pescetarians and vegetarians should spring for the salmon or veggie burgers, and those who want a French twist can order a burger foie gras.

i Ⓜ*Madeleine. Facing the church, turn around to the left, toward Pinacotheque; pass Pinacotheque and take the 1st left. Amour de Burger is on the left. Burger €12-18.50. Dinner menu €10 and 13.* ⚄ *Open M noon-3pm, Tu-F noon-3pm and 7-11:30pm.*

Opéra and Canal St-Martin

CHARTIER
TRADITIONAL $$

7 rue du Faubourg Montmartre ☎01 47 70 86 29 www.restaurant-chartier.com

Even with the swift-footed waiters and the two huge floors packed with Parisians and tourists, there just isn't enough Chartier to go around. On a busy night, you'll just have to wait your turn to eat in the famous restaurant's glam, art deco interior. Chartier has been in business for over 100 years, and with its fame, it could easily charge out the you-know-what for its menu, but thankfully for budget travelers, it has held true to its original purpose of hearty French meals at decent prices. Its popularity, however, means that efficiency is prized here, so don't expect an intimate, drawn-out meal. Seat, order, food, check, and don't even try to pull any funny business with special requests.

i Ⓜ*Grands Boulevards. Walk with traffic down bd Poissonnière and turn right onto rue du Faubourg Montmartre. Reservations recommended for larger groups. Menu €18. Entrees €2-7. plats €8.50-13.50. Cheese plates €2-2.60. Desserts €2.20-4.* ⚄ *Open daily 11:30am-10pm.*

SUPERNATURE
BRUNCH, ORGANIC $

12 rue de Trévise ☎01 47 70 21 03 www.super-nature.fr

After all that cheese and wine, it's time to feel good about your life choices, and Supernature is here to help. The restaurant serves up quite a few delicious healthy options, with a few non-vegetarian choices tossed in—this is France after all. Expect to see and hear buzzwords like "local" and "organic" around here and a packed crowd at the incredible Sunday brunch. For those looking for a cheaper meal, get in line with the Parisians at the takeout joint down the block, with its generous *formules* for €7.60.

i Ⓜ*Grands Boulevards. Walk against the traffic on bd Poissonière, turn left onto rue Rougemont, then right onto rue Bergère, then left onto rue de Trèvise. Supernature on right. Reservations recommended for Su brunch. Brunch €20. Lunch menu €16-20. Takeout formules €7.60-8.60. ✆ Open M-F noon-4pm, Su 11:30am-4pm.*

🦪 BOB'S JUICE BAR   SMOOTHIES, BAGELS $
15 rue Lucien Sampaix   ☎09 50 06 36 18 www.bobsjuicebar.com

This juice bar wouldn't raise an eyebrow in Brooklyn, but its vegetarian fare (read: not just salads) and health-food focus make it stand out in Paris. The communal table at this small, hippie, eco-conscious smoothie and lunchtime spot is usually filled with backpackers and locals alike. Those looking to detox with veggies and superfoods will find more than enough acai and quinoa salad in the house, although Bob's also serves homemade pastries for those with a sweet tooth.

i Ⓜ*Jacques Bonsergent. Walk up bd Magenta toward Gare du Nord and turn right onto rue Lucien Sampaix. Juice Bar is ½ a block up on the left. Smoothies €6. Bagel sandwiches €6. ✆ Open M-F 7:30am-3pm.*

🦪 CHEZ MAURICE   BISTRO $$
26 rue des Vinaigriers   ☎01 46 07 07 91

Finally, a real, dirt cheap French meal. While the inside may seem standard for a bistro—think red-checkered tablecloths and curtains, dark wood interiors, and framed, vintage-y posters—the *escargot* and steak tartare here make it a favorite of young locals with scruffy beards. Hold out for the desserts, where you'll be hard-pressed to choose between crème brûlée or chocolate fondue.

i Ⓜ*Jacques Bonsergent. Walk up bd Magenta toward Gare du Nord and turn right onto rue Lucien Sampaix. Walk 1 block to rue des Vinaigriers and turn right. The restaurant is on the right. Menu formule €11-18. ✆ Open M-F noon-3pm and 6:30-11pm, Sa 6:30-11pm.*

Bastille

🦪 RESTAURANT 3FC   KEBABS, ALGERIAN $
16 rue d'Aligre   ☎01 43 46 07 73

If you're starving, only have a meager supply of coins jangling in your pocket, and don't want to eat out of the garbage, hit 3FC. Not only is the food cheaper than dirt (€0.70 per kebab—we estimate that the current market price for dirt is at least €0.90 per handful), but it's bangin' delicious. Choose from a selection of raw kebabs in the front freezer, take them to the kitchen, and wait for the fresh-grilled meat to be brought back to your seat. This place is packed on a nightly basis (note: kebabs are particularly popular among the drunk-munchies crowd), but the beauty of food on a stick is that it's just as mobile as you are.

i Ⓜ*Ledru-Rollin. Walk east on rue du Faubourg St-Antoine away from Bastille, take the 3rd right onto rue du Cotte, and turn left onto rue d'Aligre. Kebab €0.70-2. Sandwiches with fries €4. Couscous €7. Entrees €3.50. plats €6. ✆ Open Sept-Jun daily 11am-midnight.*

🦪 WEST COUNTRY GIRL   CREPERIE $$
6 passage St-Ambroise   ☎01 47 00 72 54 www.westcountrygirl.com

West Country Girl is where Parisians take their lucky visiting friends for an excellent taste of the city's quintessential dish. This small creperie is tucked into a quiet side street in Bastille, and its simple wooden furniture, large open windows, and white walls with flecks of pink paint make the place feel like someone's extended dining room. The galettes here are simple, and the menu is short and filled with classics, like goat cheese and spinach and ham, cheese, and eggs. To top it all off, the lunch menu is unbeatable, ringing in at €10.50

for a savory and dessert crepe with a glass of Breton cider. Be sure to order the melt-in-your-mouth house specialty, a homemade salted caramel butter crepe.

i *Parmentier. Walk down av. Parmentier toward rue Oberkampf, turn left onto rue Lechevin, then left onto Passage St-Ambroise: West Country Girl is on the left. Lunch menu €10.50. Savory crepes €4-8, sweet €2.60-7.50. ☼ Open Tu-Sa noon-2pm and 7:30-10pm.*

🍽 AUGUSTE   SANDWICHES $

10 rue St-Sabin   ☎01 47 00 48 20   www.augusteparis.com

Shame on all the other *sandwicheries* when AUGUSTE sells 'em at €2-3 apiece (with organic ingredients!) without breaking a sweat. Nothing too fancy here, just the good old staples that you can wash down with their freshly made smoothie of the day. Pinch some pennies with trendy adults and students in this sparsely designed, stone-walled spot and marvel at the deal you're getting.

i *ⓂBréguet-Sabin. Walk against the traffic on bd Richard-Lenoir and continue down rue St-Sabin against the traffic; AUGUSTE is on the left. Sandwiches €2-4. Soups €3-5. Smoothies €3-5. Cash only. ☼ Open Sept-Jun M-Sa noon-2:30pm and 5pm-1am; Jul-Aug noon-2:30pm.*

🍽 LE GOYAVIER   CREOLE $$$

4 rue St-Bernard   ☎01 43 79 61 41

Hailing from the Réunion Island in the Indian Ocean, the chef here knows how to cook up a real South Asian meal and cooks it damn well. The place doesn't hide behind any fancy, ornamental decor—the sign out front is plain and the tables are unremarkable. The only complaint around here is about the prices, with each dish coming in at €20 and over. If you're willing to splurge, though, the generous servings and superb *rougail* sausages straight from the pot are worth your while.

i *ⓂLedru Rollin. Walk east on rue du Fauberge St-Antoine and turn left onto rue St-Bernard. The restaurant is on the right behind the scaffolding. Reservations recommended. Entrees €6-10. plats €20-22. House punch €6. Cash or check only. ☼ Open M-Tu and Th-Su 8pm-midnight.*

CANNIBALE CAFÉ   TRADITIONAL $$

93 rue Jean-Pierre Timbaud   ☎01 49 29 95 59   cannibalecafe.com

Don't be turned off by the name—believe it or not, this restaurant has a decent list of vegetarian options, and its Rococo bar and creative and stylish clientele are leagues beyond any cannibalistic barbarianism. Intellectuals and artistes frequent this bar during the day to loiter over coffee and the free Wi-Fi. Come dinnertime, classier friends turned off by the hedonism of Oberkampf pop over for a late night drink or a dish of rich tuna rilletes or duck confit.

i *ⓂCouronnes. Walk down rue Jean-Pierre Timbaud; Cannibale is on the right. Weekday lunch menu €9.90-13.90. Entrees €6.50-9.50. plats €13-23. Platters €14. Desserts €7-9. ☼ Open daily 8am-2am.*

PAUSE CAFE   CAFE $$

41 rue de Charonne   ☎01 48 06 80 33

Hipster glasses are an unofficial prerequisite for working here. People climb over themselves to get a seat on the large outdoor terrace to peruse the straight-forward menu of salads, beer, tartare, and honey-glazed duck breast. French people adore this place and chatter away all day on the terrace devoid of any Anglophones. This place is so hip that it was featured in the '90s hit film, *Chacun Cherche Son Chat*, which we suspect is the main reason people come here.

i *ⓂLedru-Rollin. Take av. Ledru-Rollin north and turn left onto rue de Charonne. Entree €6-11. plats €12-15.80. Desserts €5.50-6. Brunch €19.50. ☼ Open M-Sa 7am-2am, Su 7am-8pm.*

Montparnasse and Southern Paris

CHEZ GLADINES — BASQUE $$

30 rue des 5 Diamants — ☎01 45 80 70 10

Chez Gladines has the exposed brick walls and red-checkered tablecloth of any other French bistro, but the jam-packed restaurant and prominent Basque flag tells a different story. This joint and its enormous salads are hugely popular with customers, who will gladly wait for an hour for a table during dinner rush. Dishes are relatively cheap for the amount of food you get, making it a great place to share dishes.

i ⓂPlace d'Italie. Take bd Auguste Blanqui away from pl. d'Italie and turn left onto rue des 5 Diamants. Salads €7-11. plats €10-15. Wine €2.40-3 per glass. Cash only. ☒ Open M-F noon-3pm and 5pm-midnight, Sa-Su noon-4pm and 5pm-1am.

PHO 14 — VIETNAMESE $

129 av. de Choisy — ☎01 45 83 61 15

If you're hankering for good *pho*, there's no need to fly to Vietnam—make it Pho 14. A local favorite that draws starving students and penny-pinching barmen, Pho 14 (not to be confused with Pho 13 next door) serves huge bowls of *pho* beef (flank steak in spicy soup with rice) for reasonable prices. The hot meals and crowded tables make for a steamy restaurant during the summer, but you can cool down with red bean, coconut milk, and cane sugar drink. This restaurant usually has a line out the door at night and during the lunch rush, so try to arrive on the early or late side of dinner.

i ⓂTolbiac. Walk east on rue de Tolbiac and turn left onto av. de Choisy. Pho €7-8.50. Drinks €3.60. ☒ Open daily 9am-11pm.

LE DRAPEAU DE LA FIDELITÉ — TRADITIONAL, VIETNAMESE $

21 rue Copreaux — ☎01 45 66 73 82 http://phamconquan.free.fr

The owner is a former philosophy professor from Saigon University who decided to switch things up and opened this hole-in-the-wall dive that serves up delicious bowls of *pho*, *beef bourguignon*, and other goodies at €6 a plate. The university air still lingers in the reams of books on the wall, the crowds of students, and the prices: for his students, whom he affectionately calls his *"chouchous du quartier,"* or "favorites of the neighborhood," the price drops to €5. Don't forget to drink some beer for €2—the cheerful red font outside reminds you to "Drink a little bit. It's pleasant." We couldn't agree more.

i ⓂVolontaires. Walk against the traffic on rue de Vaugirard, turn right onto rue Copreaux; Le Drapeau is on the right. plat €6, students €5. Coffee €1. Beer €2-2.50. Wine €2-2.60. Cash only. ☒ Open daily 11:30am-10pm. Kitchen open 11:30am-8:30pm.

KHAI TRI — BANH MI $

93 av. d'Ivry — ☎01 45 82 12 40

You think you know cheap? Your local banh mi joint at home is probably pricier, and less delicious, than Khai Tri. At €3.20 for a half-baguette bursting with all the usual goodies of sliced pork, pâté, and pickled carrots, the banh mi here is simply unbeatable. With only three different types of sandwiches and not much else on the menu, this tiny sandwich shop is wildly popular with customers, who frequently line up outside for a cheap lunchtime sandwich.

i ⓂTolbiac. Walk down rue de Tolbiac toward av. de Choisy Banh, away from the McDonald's. Walk 1 block, turn right onto av. d'Ivry; Khai Tri is on the right. Banh mi €2.90-3.20. ☒ Open Tu-Sa 9:40am-5:40pm, Su 10am-5:30pm.

CREPERIE JOSSELIN — CREPERIE $$

67 rue du Montparnasse — ☎01 43 20 93 50

In a city where you can't walk two blocks without passing a crepe stand and on a block teeming with creperies, Josselin still manages to stand out thanks to

france

its delicious dedication to the culinary craft of crepe-making. Miniature violins, lace window curtains, and little porcelain teacups decorate the wooden interior of this cozy, grandmotherly restaurant. The edges of the Breton crepes here are thin, crisp, and dainty, and the pocket inside is full of terrific combinations, like warm goat cheese drizzled with honey or banana and chocolate flambéed with rum. The wait can be long for dinner, so come for the lunch special (€12 for a savory crepe, a dessert crepe, and a drink).

i Ⓜ*Edgar Quinet. Walk up rue du Montparnasse with traffic; Crêperie Josselin is on the right. Savory crepes €5-9.80. Sweet crepes €5-7.80. Cash only.* ☒ *Open Tu-F 11:30am-3pm and 6-11:30pm, Sa noon-midnight, Su noon-11pm.*

LE TEMPS DES CERISES   TRADITIONAL $$
18 rue de la Butte aux Cailles   ☎01 45 89 69 48

Not only is this place an excellent French bistro, but in line with the hipster-activist background of the neighborhood, Le Temps is an anti-cellphone (turn it off!) worker's cooperative since 1976. Their history may give them major street cred, but this place is popular with locals and students for the quality of its food and lively atmosphere during the dinner hours. It's location at the heart of Quarter Butte-aux-Cailles also makes it a perfect jumping off point for drinks later in the night.

i Ⓜ*Corvisart. Walk toward rue Corvisart away from Pizza Hut on the same side of bd Auguste-Blanqui as Pizza Hut. Turn left onto a passageway and take the stairs through Jardin Brassai, pass rue des 5 Diamants, turn right onto rue Gérard, turn left onto rue de la Butte aux Cailles; Le Temps is on the left. plat du jour €11. Lunch menu M-F, Su €12-15. Dinner menu €19.50-24.50. Entrees €4.5-15. plats €11-20. Wine €3-5.* ☒ *Open daily 11:45am-2:30pm and 7:15-11:45pm.*

ATELIER AUBRAC   TRADITIONAL $$$$
51 bd Garibaldi   ☎01 45 66 96 78 http://www.atelieraubrac.com/

This cool, traditional French restaurant is a carnivorous cavern. With hefty plates full of the kind of meat you'd expect a lumberjack or quarterback to enjoy, Atelier Aubrac is a place you want to come to with an empty stomach. If you're not sure what to order, have a chat with the gregarious chef, although it'd be hard to go wrong with a 10oz. rib eye steak or a 7oz. rump steak. Lunchtime tends to bring in a professional crowd, but the clientele gets more diverse at dinner.

i Ⓜ*Sèvres-Lecourbe. Walk northwest on bd Garibaldi; the restaurant is on the right. Lunch menu €16-19. Dinner menu €23.50-27.50. Entrees €7-13. plats €14-29.* ☒ *Open M-F 12:30-2:15pm and 7:30-10:15pm, Sa 7-10:15pm.*

Auteuil, Passy & Batignolles

BATIGNOLLES ORGANIC PRODUCE MARKET   MARKET $
bd de Batignolles

There are only two organic markets of note in Paris, and in comparison to the larger, more crowded market at bd Raspail, the one at Batignolles is smaller, less chaotic, and, as a result, much more fun. Stretching across bd de Batignolles every Saturday morning, the Batignolles Organic Produce Market is a delectable jumble of singing shoppers, hats, flowers, bottles of apple cider, honey, textiles, loaves of bread, and obscenely large hunks of cheese, not to mention gorgeous, organic fruits and vegetables. You can buy a crêpe here, nibble on samples as you stroll through, or construct a gourmet picnic with ease and schlep it to the nearby Square des Batignolles.

i Ⓜ*Rome. On the traffic divider along bd des Batignolles, at the border of the 8ème and 17ème.* ☒ *Open Sa 9am-2pm.*

3 PIÈCES CUISINE

BRUNCH, TRADITIONAL $$

25 rue de Chéroy   ☎01 44 90 85 10

3 Pièces Cuisine keeps things casual with (surprise!) just three spacious rooms and a bar that comes alive at night. The one-page menu is equally simple, with a variety of burgers, tartines, sandwiches, and salads. The restaurant's bright red, green, purple, and yellow colors match the lively clientele, who pack 3PC on Sundays for the ultra-cheap brunch (€11) and at night for the mojitos before heading out into the night.

i ⓂVilliers. Head east down bd de Batignolles (which is bd de Courcelles in the other direction) and take a left onto rue de Chéroy. The restaurant is on the next corner on the left. Brunch €11. Prix fixe menus €10-15. Plats €7.50. Cocktails €5-7. ☒ Open daily 8:30am-1:30am.

LE CLUB DES 5

TRADITIONAL $$

57 rue des Batignolles   ☎01 53 04 94 73 www.leclubdes5.fr

The five friends who founded this fun restaurant wanted to bring the vibe of their childhood in the '80s to the place. Le Club des 5 is a combination of nostalgia and hipster, with street signs and cartoon characters decorating the walls of this casual restaurant and one entire section plastered with colorful magazine cutouts. The menu contains grown-up dishes, such as rotisserie chicken and hanger steak, alongside the ones for the kid in you, like the Megacheeseburger and Oreo cheesecake.

i ⓂPl. de Clichy. With your back to Montmartre, walk 3 blocks down bd des Batignolles and turn right onto rue des Batignolles. The cafe is 2 blocks down on the left. Lunch plat €11; entree and plat €14; entree, plat, and dessert €17. Dinner plats €16-20. Brunch €26. ☒ Open M 7:30-11pm, Tu-Su noon-2:30pm and 7:30-11pm. Brunch served Sa-Su noon-4pm.

LE PATIO PROVENÇAL

TRADITIONAL $$$

116 rue des Dames   ☎01 42 93 73 73 www.patioprovencal.fr

Those in the market for an intimate meal--couples and double daters alike--should head to Le Patio Provençal for expertly done French dining. A wonderful skylight brightens the seating in the middle of the restaurant, while several wooden booths allow for more private dining. In the background, Norah Jones serenades your indoor garden dinner to round out the relaxed vibe. The menu may not be exotic for Paris, but you won't hear any complaints about their duck confit and lamb chops, and vegetarians rejoice at their options at this restaurant. Be sure to leave enough room for all three courses—you won't want to miss out.

i ⓂVilliers. Follow rue de Levis away from the intersection and turn right onto rue des Dames. Lunch men €17. Dinner menu from €24, weekends €28. Entrees €9. plats €17-20. Desserts €8. ☒ Open M-Sa noon-2:30pm and 7-10:30pm.

Montmartre

Montmartre has tons of great food options at relatively reasonable prices, especially considering how popular the area is with tourists.

🔖 LE CAFÉ LOMI

CAFE $

3 Rue Marcadet   ☎09 80 39 56 24 www.cafelomi.com

This isn't a cafe that you just "happen" upon—this coffee shop is a bit far flung, which saves it from the hordes of tourists who would drink up all the carefully crafted *noisettes* and the hipsters who would take up all the comfortable leather chairs and couches. Le Café Lomi used to just be in the business of hand-selecting coffees from all over the world and expertly roasting it on site, but thankfully for us, it now also serves espressos made from the roasted beans to neighborhood patrons.

i ⓂMarcadet Poissonniers. Walk down rue Ordener, past bd Ornano, 4 blocks. The cafe is on the right. Espresso €2-2.40. Cappuccino €3.90-4.30. ☒ Open W-Su 10am-7pm.

☒ LE POTAGER DU PÈRE THIERRY
TRADITIONAL $$

16 rue Trois Frères   ☎01 53 28 26 20

Almost as soon as this tiny bistro opens its doors, couples and friends swoop in, grab a coveted table, and settle in for a somewhat cramped but masterfully prepared dinner. The red-checkered napkins and smooth stone walls set the scene for a traditional French bistro experience, but the light fixtures made from colanders and the shiny wooden tables add a more modern twist to this restaurant. The specialty of the house is undoubtedly the *l'œuf cocottes au foie gras* (eggs baked in foie gras; €7), although the catch of the day and the filet mignon are also standouts on the menu.

i ⓂAbbesses. Walk down rue Yvonne le Tac, turn left onto rue des Trois Frères; Le Potager is on the right. Reservations recommended. Entrees €6-7. plats €12-16. Dessert €6-8. ② Open daily 8pm-midnight.

☒ LE BAL CAFÉ
BRUNCH $$$

6 Impasse de la Défense   ☎01 44 70 75 51 www.le-bal.fr

Nobody does brunch quite like the British, and with the stellar combination of truly exceptional coffee (none of that overpriced instant stuff found in Parisian cafes) and former chefs from Rose Bakery running the kitchen, Le Bal Café has become quite the darling of food critics. Throw in an art exhibition space in a former ballroom next to the minimalist dining space, and you've got yourself a bona fide hipster hangout.

i ⓂPlace de Clichy. Walk up av. de Clichy away from the roundabout for 2 blocks, turn right onto Impasse de la Défense; the cafe is on the right. Reservations recommended for brunch. Entrees €6-8. plats €13-16. Dessert €6. ② Open W-F noon-2:30pm and 8-10:30pm, Sa 11am-3pm and 8-10:30pm, Su 11am-4pm.

Buttes-Chaumont & Belleville

☒ LA BOULANGERIE PAR VÉRONIQUE MAUCLERC
BOULANGERIE, PATISSERIE

83 rue de Crimée   ☎01 42 40 64 55

Baking its divine bread in one of only four remaining wood-fired ovens in France, this *boulangerie* uses only organic ingredients in its creations. Run by Véronique herself, the bakers here begin mixing their mythical, organic dough at 2am. She doesn't even use yeast—instead, *levain*, a natural riser, is added to the bread, which is then left for up to 15hr. to rise. While on the outside this *boulangerie* may seem similar to all the other ones you'll come across in Paris, don't make the mistake of walking blithely by. People make the pilgrimage here for the bread, so for once, skip the croissant (gasp). Trust us—the pistachio, almond, hazelnut bread is worth your precious cash. If you don't want to buy a whole loaf, ask for a *tranche* (slice) instead. Be sure to stop by the *salon de thé* tucked in the back for a spoil-me-rotten Sunday brunch.

i ⓂLaumière. Walk northeast on av. Jean Jaurès, then turn right onto rue de Crimée; the boulangerie is near the end of the block on the right. Chocolate chip cookies €2.10. Chocolate tarts €3.80. Lemon meringue tarts €4.10. ② Boulangerie open Tu-F 9am-2pm and 3:30-8pm, Sa-Su 8am-8pm. Salon de thé open Tu-Sa 9am-5:30pm.

☒ L'ATLANTIDE
NORTH AFRICAN $$$

7 av. Laumière   ☎01 42 45 09 81 www.latlantide.fr

Moroccan food is all the rage in Paris, but for L'Atlantide, it's more than a trend. Cough up a pretty penny because this Berber restaurant knows what it's doing and isn't afraid to charge top dollar for its tajines and couscous dishes. Traditional North African rugs hang from the ceiling, and wood carvings and driftwood room dividers create a decidedly Moroccan air. Even though "As Time Goes By" may not be playing in the background, with all the

paris

dim lighting and imported North African wine, we bet that a meal here could be the start of many beautiful friendships.

i Ⓜ*Laumière. Walk south down av. de Laumière toward the park. L'Atlantide is near the end of the road on the right. Entrees €6-10. Couscous €13-19.50. Tajines €14-19.50.* Ⓧ *Open M-F 7-10:30pm, Sa-Su noon-2:30pm and 7-10:30pm.*

NIGHTLIFE

You may have told your parents, professors, and prospective employers that you've traveled to Paris to compare the works of Monet and Manet (hint: it's not just one letter), but after more than 50 years in the business, we at *Let's Go* know it isn't just art that draws the young and the restless to Europe. If you're traveling to drink and mingle, Paris will not disappoint. Nightlife here is debaucherous, and there's something for everyone. Bars are either chic cafes bursting with people watching potential, party joints all about rock and teen angst, or laid-back local spots that double as havens for English-speakers. Clubbing in Paris is less about hip DJs and cutting-edge beats than it is about dressing up and being seen. Drinks are expensive, so Parisians usually stick to the ones included with the cover. Many clubs accept reservations, which means there's no available seating on busy nights. It's best to be confident (but not aggressive) about getting in. Bars in the 5ème and 6ème draw international students, while Châtelet-Les Halles attracts a slightly older set. The Marais is the center of Parisian GLBT nightlife.

Île de la Cité and Île St-Louis

Far from a party spot, the islands are a bit of a nightlife wasteland. If you're looking for a quiet terrace on which to share a beer and conversation, this is your spot. Tourists tend to clear out of les Îles after dark, so the pace is comfortably slower here.

LE SOLEIL D'OR   BRASSERIE
15 bd du Palais   ☎01 43 54 22 22

This place is a tourist magnet during the day thanks to its location at a busy intersection, faux-modern seating, and Berthillon ice cream. You may not want to stay here all night, but come get schwasty during happy hour, with pints of beer and cocktails for €6 until 9pm.

i Ⓜ*Cité. Turn left down bd du Palais from the Métro; the brasserie is on the corner. Happy hour 3-9pm. Beer €6-8. Cocktails €6-9. Happy hour drinks €6.* Ⓧ *Open daily 6:15am-10pm.*

Châtelet-Les Halles

The bars in Châtelet are close together and easy to find. This neighborhood has its fair share of GLBT bars (though it's no Marais) and smaller establishments that are packed until dawn.

🏳 BANANA CAFÉ   BAR, CLUB, GLBT
13 rue de la Ferronnerie   ☎01 42 33 35 31 www.bananacafeparis.com

Situated in the heart of Châtelet, Banana Café is the GLBT capital outside of the Marais. The club suits a wide clientele that ranges from the young crowds taking advantage of the cheap happy hour on the terrace to the erotic dancers stationed outside. Head downstairs after midnight for a lively piano bar and more dance space before hopping out at dawn to catch the Métro back home. There are weekly themed nights that take place Th-Sa from midnight to dawn.

i Ⓜ*Châtelet. Walk 3 blocks down rue St-Denis and turn right onto rue de la Ferronerie. Cover F-Sa €10; includes 1 drink. Beer €5.50. Cocktails €11. Happy hour pints €3; cocktails €4-5.* Ⓧ *Open daily 6pm-6am. Happy hour 6-11pm.*

LES CARIATIDES

BAR, CONCERT VENUE

3 rue de Palestro   ☎01 42 36 19 72 www.lescariatides.com

Clearly this bar's signs about moderate drinking are less than effective, and the only thing that's louder than the music here is the sound of drunk partiers trying to sing along. Downstairs in the basement, Les Cariatides has gigs playing anything from rock to pop to indie nearly every night, and it quickly becomes full on the weekends. For some fresh air, wrangle your way to the bar and order some decently priced tapas before heading back down to dance the night away.

i ⓂEtienne Marcel. Walk up rue de Turbigo against the flow of traffic, turn left onto rue de Palstre; Les Cariatides is on the left. Shot €4. Pint of beer €6-8. Tapas €10 for 5. Happy hour pint €4-5; cocktails €6. Extra €1 on all drinks after 1am. Ⓩ Open M-Sa 6pm-4am, Su 2-4pm. Happy hour M-Sa 6-9pm.

The Marais

There are about as many bars and clubs in the Marais as there are people, and the establishments you'll find here are just as diverse as the crowds.

CANDELARIA

BAR, TACOS

52 rue de Saintonge   ☎01 42 74 41 28 www.candelariaparis.com

This bar takes hole-in-the-wall to a completely new level. Fronted by a greasy tacos joint, Candelaria is easy to miss and just looks like an oddly popular bougie dive where you can get some good guac. But wiggle past the crowds (and there are always crowds), and you will happen upon a small, unmarked door—make your way inside and fall through the proverbial rabbit hole into one of Paris's most popular bars. This hidden, stone-walled bar is much larger than the tapas joint outside and is even more crowded. The dim bar is usually standing room only and is quite popular with the locals, hipsters, and intellectuals, with a healthy presence of Anglophone students thrown in. The house punch, made with cognac and spiced wine, is pricey but a must, and their cocktails are absolutely delicious.

i Filles du Calvaires. Walk down rue des Filles du Calvaire with traffic, turn right onto rue de Bretagne, then right onto rue de Saintonge; Candelaria is on the right. House punch €54 for 4-6 people. Cocktails €12. Guac and chips €5.50. ⓏKitchen in front open W 12:30-11pm, Th-Sa 12:30pm-midnight, Su 12:30-11pm. Bar open daily 6pm-2am.

RAIDD BAR

BAR, CLUB, GLBT

23 rue du Temple   ☎01 53 01 00 00

If you want a penis, or just want to see one, come here. Sparkling disco balls light up Raidd Bar, as do the muscular, tank-topped torsos of the sexy male bartenders. After 11pm, performers strip down in the glass shower built into the wall and begin to rub themselves clean while your mind gets dirty. There's a notoriously strict door policy: women aren't allowed unless they are outnumbered by (gorgeous) men, and since this place has no cover, prepare for a long wait on the weekends.

i ⓂHôtel de Ville. Walk up rue du Renard, turn right onto rue de la Verrerie, then left onto rue du Temple; Raidd Bar is on the left. Beer €6.50. Mixed drinks €8.70, €6 before 9pm. Cocktails €8.70-11, €6-8 before 9pm. Happy hour beer €4.20. ⓏOpen M-Th 5pm-4am, F-Su 5pm-5am. Happy hour 5-11pm.

LE BARAV

WINE BAR

6 rue Charles François Dupuis   ☎01 48 04 57 59 www.lebarav.fr

Even the staunchest, frown-iest Parisians manage to have a good time at this *très* popular wine bar. Old hipsters, young hipsters, students, and professionals—everyone makes the trek to the northern reaches of the Marais to dine at this dimly lit, wooden bar for the delicious tapenades, large antipasti, charcuterie platters, and perfectly paired cheap glasses of wine from the cave next door. Reservations are recommended in the evening unless you want to be unceremoniously bounced from your table when your time is up.

i ⓜTemple. *Head down Passage Sainte-Elisabeth with the traffic, turn right onto rue du Temple, left onto rue Dupetit-Thouars, then left onto rue Charles-François Dupuis; Le Barav is on the right. Reservations recommended. Lunch menu €10. Entrees €5.50. plats €11.50-12.50. Salads €10.50. Platters €5.50-16. Glass of wine €5. Pint €6. ☾ Open M noon-3pm, Tu-F noon-3pm and 6pm-12:30am, Sa 6pm-12:30am.*

LE KOMPTOIR   BAR

27 rue Quincampoix   ☎01 42 77 75 35 www.lekomptoir.fr

Head to this tapas bar for some of the cheapest happy hour pints and cocktails in the Marais. Le Komptoir's distinctive backwards "K" in its name hints at its backwards (but awesome) behavior of offering cheap drinks, free entry to concerts, and a long food menu, complete with paella (€13). There are plenty of tables on the ground floor and in the basement, making this a great bar for groups.

i ⓜHôtel de Ville. *In the pl. Michelet. Walk up rue du Renard, turn right onto rue St-Merri, then left onto rue Quincampoix. Jazz concerts Th 9pm. No cover, but must buy a drink. Beer €6.20-6.80. Cocktails €7.50-8.50. Tapas €7.50-13. Happy hour pints €4.40-4.80; cocktails 2 for 1. ☾ Open Tu-Su 10am-2am. Happy hour 5:30-8:30pm.*

STOLLY'S   BAR

16 rue Cloche Percé   ☎01 42 76 06 76 www.cheapblonde.com

This small Anglophone hangout takes the sketchy out of the dive bar but leaves the attitude. Older, non-trendy locals in tattoos and strict black attire kick back pitchers of cheap blonde beer (€12) to ensure that the bar lives up to its motto: "Hangovers installed and serviced here." Come inside, have a pint, and shout at the TV with the regulars that stake out a seat before the place fills up at night.

i ⓜSt-Paul. *From the Métro, turn right onto rue Pavée, then left onto rue du Roi de Sicile. Turn left onto rue Cloche Percé. Shooters €3-6. Beer pints €5-6; pitcher of blond beer €12. Cocktails €7-8. Happy hour pints and cocktails €6. ☾ Open daily 4:30pm-2am. Happy hour 4-8pm. Terrace open until midnight.*

LE YONO   BAR, CLUB

37 rue Vieille du Temple   ☎01 42 74 31 65 www.leyono.fr

It's easy to walk past Le Yono, as it's set back from the street through a stone corridor that makes for a grand entrance (and later a perfect smoker's getaway) to this cave-like club. The bar area is big and open and makes a great space for chatting on weekdays under the translucent ceilings, but on weekends, the real party is downstairs. The mosaics on the walls light up a dance floor packed with students dancing along with DJs that rock the house with electronic beats.

i ⓜHôtel de Ville. *Walk against traffic on rue de Rivoli and turn left. Or from* ⓜSt-Paul, *walk with traffic on rue de Rivoli and turn right. Live music 2-3 times per week. Downstairs open F-Sa. Cocktails €10-12. Happy hour cocktails €5.50, pint of Heineken €5.50. Mojitos 10-12. Pint of beer €7-8. Tapas Th-Sa €5-9. ☾ Open Tu-Sa 6pm-2am.*

O'SULLIVAN'S REBEL BAR   BAR

10 rue des Lombards   ☎01 42 71 42 72 chatelet.osullivans-pubs.com

O'Sullivan's Rebel Bar makes Paris's chain bars look like classy English tea rooms. The walls are covered with graffiti, the menus are unapologetically sticky, and the place can get pretty crowded on a game night. The patrons, complete with piercings and shaved heads, couldn't care less about noise levels or their livers and make this place a riot almost as soon as it opens.

i ⓜHôtel de Ville. *Walk up rue du Renard and turn left onto rue de la Verrerie, which becomes rue des Lombards. M all-night happy hour. Pints €6-7. Shots €5-9. Cocktails €7-16. Happy hour pints €4; cocktails €5.50. ☾ Open M-Th 5pm-2am, F 5pm-5am, Sa 2pm-5am, Su 2pm-2am. Happy hour 5-9pm.*

france

L'ART BRUT
BAR

78 rue Quincampoix   ☎01 42 72 17 36 www.artbrutbistro.fr

In case the crowds didn't tip you off, this bar is a favorite in the neighborhood. Young locals come here in groups and easily fill up this small, narrow bar and spill out onto the street during the warmer months. Changing art installations hang on the walls of wood and stone, giving this place a hipster-artsy vibe, just in case the low prices didn't attract enough attention and adoration. Sip some organic wine a €3.50 a pop as you nod along to the rock and Balkan folk music and fill yourself with cheap dishes of charcuterie and cheese platters.

i Ⓜ Rambuteau or Ⓜ Etienne-Marcel. From Rambuteau, walk down rue Beaubourg with traffic, turn right onto rue Rambuteau, then right onto rue Qincampoix; L'Art Brut is on the right. From Etienne-Marcel, walk down rue-aux-Ours and turn right onto rue Quincampoix; L'Art Brut is on the left. Organic wine €3.50 per glass. Pints of beer €4.50-6.50. Cocktails €6-9. Platters €9.50. Ⓓ Open daily 4pm-2am.

L'ATTIRAIL
BAR

9 rue au Maire   ☎01 42 72 44 42 www.lattirai.fr

On a street filled with subpar Asian *traiteurs* and seemingly nothing else, L'Attirail shines through like a cabin in the woods, a light through the expensive darkness, an oasis in the midst of €10 cocktails. Here, 20-somethings and students clink glasses and swap stories on the warm terrace or inside the bar, where the walls are covered with passport photos of past patrons. Drinks here are cheap, and happy hour starts early, making this a great place to get schwasty before hitting up more active venues later on in the night.

i Ⓜ Arts et Métiers. Walk down rue Réamur with traffic, turn right onto rue Volta, then left onto rue au Maire; L'Attirail is on the left. Salads €9.50. plats €9.50-12. Drinks €4.50-5.50. Ⓓ Open M-Sa 10:30am-2am, Su 5pm-2am. Happy hour 3.30-8pm.

Latin Quarter and St-Germain

The neighborhoods are where you'll find the majority of Paris's students spending their intellectual (or not so intellectual) nights out.

✒ L'ANTIDOTE
BAR

45 rue Descartes   ☎01 43 54 69 78 www.lantidote-paris.com

If you've got problems, alcohol is not the answer, but hey, if you're just having a poisonously boring weekend and want a morerambunctious night out, L'Antidote may be your answer. During the week, the two enormous television screens make this place more of a sports bar, but come weekend, crowds of young Parisians and backpackers from nearby hostels flock to this bar to shake it like a Polaroid picture on the sweaty, stone-vaulted dance floor. Drinks flow freely thanks to the superb happy hour, and the prime location on rue Mouffetard makes it easy to bar hop, though we doubt you'll want to leave.

i Ⓜ Place Monge. Walk down rue Lacépède, turn right onto rue Mouffetard, and walk 1 block; L'Antidote is on the right. Happy hour pint of beer €3-5.50; cocktails €5.50-7.50. Shots €25 for 10, €3 for 1. Pint of beer €4.80-6.80. Cocktails €7-8.50. Ⓓ Open daily 5pm-2am. Happy hour 5pm-9pm.

✒ LE PANTALON
BAR

7 rue Royer-Collard   ☎01 40 51 85 85

If there was ever such a thing as a takeaway beer and cocktail bar, this is it. Packed to the gills with laid-back Sorbonne students and recent college grads in suits, this narrow bar is a student epicenter, drawing crowds on the weekends with its cheap drinks and specialty shots. It can sometimes be a bit claustrophobic inside, and the tap by the window and the extra cents it costs to drink indoors directs a lot of traffic onto the streets. On the cobblestoned sidewalk, patrons mill about in their T-shirts and take long draws from ciga-

paris

rettes after a long day. Grab a group of friends, or just work on your tolerance and order the 10 shots for €5 deal to start (or end) your night with a schwasty bang.

i RER Luxembourg. Walk toward the Jardin du Luxembourg, turn right onto rue le Goff, right onto rue Gay-Lussac, and left onto rue Royer-Collard; Le Pantalon is on the right. Bee €2.50-7. Cocktails €7. Shots €2.50, €10 for 5. Cash only. ⊠ Open daily 3pm-2am. Happy hour 5:30pm-7:30pm.

LE PIANO VACHE
DIVE BAR

8 rue Làplace   ☎01 46 33 75 03 http://lepianovache.fr

Le Piano Vache is all about vintage rock and has remained largely unchanged since opening in 1969. Plastered with old posters and filled with equally ancient couches, this bar looks like it was decorated by a tipsy, nostalgic rockstar. This dive oozes 1970s underground cool, and the live music, themed nights, and terrific happy hour specials attract a mélange of regulars and students who spread out at the large wooden tables.

i ⓂMaubert-Mutualité. Walk down rue des Carmes against the flow of traffic 4 blocks, turn left onto rue Làplace; Le Piano Vache is on the left. M live jazz 9:30pm-1:30am, Tu '80s night 9:30pm-2am, W Goth music DJ 9pm-2am, Th discounted prices all night, F rock DJ 9pm-2am, Sa DJ 9pm-2am. Coffee €1. Beer €4-7. Cocktails €7-8. M night pints €7; cocktails €10. Th night pints €5; cocktails €5; tapas €5. ⊠ Open M-Sa noon-2am; during school holidays 6pm-2am.

⚑ L'ACADÉMIE DE LA BIÈRE
BAR

88 bd de Port-Royal   ☎01 43 54 66 65 www.academie-biere.com

With 12 beers on tap and 150 bottled varieties, L'Académie de la Bière is as serious about its brews as Parisians are about their wine. Popular with students looking to unwind on the weekend, the bar itself is minuscule, but the extensive patio (which is covered and sometimes heated, depending on the weather) is filled end-to-end with those spirit-seeking students. Most drinkers come to L'Académie to study the brews, but any smart student knows not to drink on an empty stomach—the steaming hot plates of mussels and German sausages alone are worth a visit to this restaurant.

i ⓂVavin. Walk southeast on bd du Montparnasse as it turns into bd du Port-Royal. The bar is on the left. Beer €6-8. Mussels €8-9. Sausages €8-14. ⊠ Open M-Th 10am-2am, F-Sa 10am-3am, Su 10am-2am. Happy hour daily 3:30-7:30pm.

LE BAR DIX
BAR

10 rue de l'Odéon   ☎01 43 26 66 83 lebar10.com

Founded in 1955, Le 10 Bar has become quite the silver fox as it ages gracefully while retaining its 1950s charm—even Clooney could take some pointers. The itsy bar is a bit musty smelling, and the posters from 1950s plays are fading fast, but the antique woodwork and jukebox that croons Édith Piaf and Aretha Franklin will take you on your own *Midnight in Paris* field trip. This bar is for the nostalgic and those who fancy themselves intellectuals or artists with a penchant for sangria. At 9pm, head downstairs to the basement where Ernest Hemingway used to write inspired tales after amorous encounters with his mistress who lived above the bar. Although we don't recommend trespassing above the bar in search of a lover, you may still feel literary love in the air at Le Bar 10; memorize a few lines of French poetry and flirt the night away.

i ⓂOdéon. Walk south to where the road splits into 3 forks and take the middle fork; Le 10 Bar is on the right. Sangria €3.50 per glass. Beer €4-5.50. Cash only. ⊠ Open daily 6pm-2am. Basement opens at 9pm.

LE VIOLON DINGUE
BAR, CLUB

46 rue de la Montagne Ste-Geneviève   ☎01 43 25 79 93

Known as "le VD" to locals, this bar has some of the cheapest happy hour drinks around, and it's open the latest. The upstairs feels like a pub with a strong American influence, complete with football from the US. After 1am, though, the place floods with young French students and American tourists who swarm to get into the downstairs club, where the latest top 40 hits blast against the vaulted stone ceilings until 5am.

i Ⓜ*Cardinal Lemoine. Walk uphill on rue du Cardinal Lemoine and turn right onto rue Clovis. Walk 1 block and turn right onto rue Descartes. When you hit the plaza, the bar is on the left. Beer €6. Cocktails €7-10. Happy hour beer €3-4; cocktails €5-6; jagerbombs €5. Prices increase €1 after 1:30am. ☎ Open Tu-Sa 8pm-5am. Club open Tu-Sa midnight-5am. Happy hour Tu-Sa 7-10pm.*

Invalides

LE CONCORDE ATLANTIQUE
CLUB

23 quai Anatole France   ☎01 40 56 02 82 www.bateauconcordeatlantique.com

Take a three-story club with half thought-out themed *soirées*, add copious amounts of booze deals, and transform it into a boat right on the Seine. You have just imagined Le Concorde Atlantique. On Friday and Saturday nights there's usually a line to enter this club, where the party can start as early as 10pm and keeps going until 5am. Expect to find a healthy number of tourists here in the packed crowd, although there are no swim trunks or flippy-floppies in sight—only well-dressed 20-somethings who are less interested in keeping it classy and more interested in making it nasty. Keep an eye out during the summer for the Terrassa parties, with a series of locally famous DJs. *Soirées* are shamelessly promoted, often with cover charges that include free drinks and the occasional ladies' night. The deals don't end there: the website **www.parisbouge. com** is an invaluable resource here, giving out cheap tickets and drink passes that can save travelers as much as 50%.

i Ⓜ*Assemblée Nationale, right on the Seine in between Pont de la Concorde and walking bridge Solferino. Cover from €10-20, includes (sometimes up to 5) free drinks. Some nights men pay extra €5-10. ☎ Open Tu-Sa 8pm-5am.*

Champs-Élysées

🏳️‍🌈 LE QUEEN
CLUB

102 av. des Champs-Élysées   ☎01 53 89 08 90 www.queen.fr

Le Queen is a renowned Parisian institution where drag queens, superstars, tourists, and go-go boys get down and dirty to the mainstream rhythms of a 10,000-gigawatt sound system. Open all night, every night, Le Queen has *soirées* for just about every party demographic you can think of, although the hot-mess and perennially-drunk crowd is well attended here. Be prepared to show ID to gain entrance to this flashy disco with a light-up dance floor, which features theme nights that include the occasional gay *soirée*.

i Ⓜ*Georges V. Disco on M. Ladies night on W; no cover for women 11:30pm-1am. Live DJ on F. Cove €20, includes 1 drink. Drinks €15. ☎ Open daily 11:30pm-6am.*

LE SHOWCASE
CLUB

Under Pont Alexandre III, Port des Champs Elysées   ☎01 45 61 25 43 www.showcase.fr

One of the most popular clubs with the bohemian bourgeoisie in Paris (kids with money), Le Showcase's limited operation days and even more limited entrance make it nearly impossible to get in without some good-looking friends. Every Friday and Saturday night, live international DJs spin techno and electro beats for the well-heeled crowds in this super-dim club. To be sure you'll make it in, get on the "guest list" by registering your name for free online, then dance 'til dawn in this dungeon-esque club.

i Ⓜ*Champs-Élysées-Clemenceau. Entry typically free before midnight. Register for free on their website or Facebook page to be added to the guest list. Cover €10-15. Beer €9. Cocktails €15. ☎ Open F-Sa 11pm-dawn.*

THE FREEDOM
BAR

8 rue de Berri ☎01 53 75 25 50

To hear some English and catch a game or two, visit The Freedom and hang out with the regulars here. This pub is more low-key than the usual English joint and is more of a watering hole for local Anglophones than a buzzing joint at which to start the night—although the cheap drinks on student nights make it worth a quick stop.

i Ⓜ*George V. Walk away from the Arc de Triomphe and turn left down rue de Berri. Student Night on Th; pint €4, vodka shots €2.50. DJs F-Sa. Ladies night F-Sa; cocktail and vodka shots €6. Beer €6-7. 🕐 Open M-W 11:30am-2am, Th 11:30am-4am, F-Sa 11:30am-5am, Su 11:30am-2am.*

LE SENS UNIQUE
WINE BAR

47 rue de Ponthieu ☎01 43 59 76 77

In an area writhing with girls who don't know how to walk in their 5in. stilettos and guys who spend as much time on their hair as their outfits, Le Sens Unique manages to keep it classy—and we mean really classy. Silver couches, a wine bar with dried vines wrapped over the bar, a brick interior, and street signs decorating the walls, this mellow local hideout is almost entirely devoid of tourists. The gentle owner welcomes everyone with open arms to sample hand-selected fine wines from Périgord, in the Bourdeaux region of southern France. Although the wines here aren't super cheap and only a few are sold by the glass, the quality of the drinks and the relaxing atmosphere are well worth the price. Those with a little more than $20 in their pockets should splurge on the foodie-approved dishes here, too.

i Ⓜ*Franklin D. Roosevelt. Walk up the Champs-Élysées toward the Arc de Triomphe, turn right onto rue La Boétie, then left onto rue de Ponthieu. Or Ⓜ George V. Walk down the Champs-Élysées away from the Arc de Triomphe, turn left onto rue de Berri and right onto rue de Ponthieu. Beaujoulais Nouveau 3-day wine tasting event starts 3rd Th in Nov. Wine €4.50-6. 🕐 Open M-Sa noon-11pm.*

Opéra and Canal St-Martin

⬛ LE VERRE VOLÉ
RESTAURANT, BAR

67 rue Lancry ☎01 48 03 17 34 www.leverrevole.fr

This restaurant is tiny, but that's not the only reason why you'll need a reservation here for lunch and dinner. This unassuming wine bar and restaurant has developed quite the cult following by food critics and bobos who pine after the generous dishes paired with the organic and natural wines. While you won't hang out here all night, this great location on the canal is the perfect spot to mingle with young Parisian hipsters over a glass of one of the restaurant's many wines.

i Ⓜ*Jacques Bonsergent. Walk down bd de Magenta and turn left onto rue de Lancry; it's just before the canal. Wine from €5.50 per glass. Corkage fee €7. Entrees €6.50-9. plats €11-13. 🕐 Open Tu-Su noon-3:30pm and 6:30-11:30pm.*

⬛ CHEZ PRUNE
CAFE, BAR

36 rue Beaurepaire ☎01 42 41 30 47

In case the colorful graffiti didn't tip you off, this neighborhood is artsy. And in case the fedora-ed, scruffed-up clientele didn't tip you off, Chez Prune is the water cooler for all the young bohemians in this neighborhood. The cafe has a spacious terrace that is nearly always full of groups of friends sharing the terrific charcuterie and cheese platters or couples chowing down on zucchini pancakes. Located along the canal and various bike and footpaths, Chez Prune is the place to see the trendy folk of Paris pass by on their bikes or with a cigarette in hand. At night, you can cozy up next to the canal with a *vin chaud*, as this bar fills up with 20-somethings looking to get tipsy off a few cheap drinks.

i Ⓜ*Jacques Bonsergent. Walk up rue de Lancry with the flow of traffic and turn right onto quai de Valmy. Cocktails €8.50. plats €14. 🕐 Open M-F 8am-2am, Su 10am-2am.*

france

CORCORAN'S

IRISH PUB, CLUB

23 bd Poissonnière   ☎01 40 39 00 16 www.corcoransirishpub.fr

During the day, this Irish pub serves up all the greasy Anglo-Saxon goods, like fish and chips and Irish stew for the few customers that come through. At night, Corcoran's comes alive as a hoppin' nightclub Th-Sa nights. A flurry of French and English speakers alternately populate the dance floor, so if you're looking to play it smooth in your native tongue, throw back a Guinness and party like a rockstar at Corcoran's, where you'll find the best of both worlds. Don't show up too sloshed if you want the bouncers to let you in.

i Ⓜ*Grands Boulevards. Upon exiting the Métro, look for the green awning. Other locations in the Bastille, St-Michel, and Clichy areas. Happy hour M-F 5-9pm. Karaoke Th 9pm. Live music 4 times a week. Su 3pm traditional irish music and step dancing. Shots €4. Beer €6.50-7. Mixed drinks €8. Happy hour mixed drinks €6, pints €5. ☼ Open daily 10am-dawn.*

LE BRÉBANT

CAFE, BAR

32 bd Poissonnière   ☎01 47 70 01 02 www.cafelebrebantparis.com

Of all the bars in this concentrated nook around Ⓜ Grands Boulevards, Le Brebant has the privilege of occupying the largest corner of the intersection, thereby outdoing all its neighbors in size and noise. Open late into the night, this cafe has an impressive selection of seafood, though the non-happy hour drinks are quite pricey. The art deco interior makes for a pretty sight, although we recommend people watching the plastered partiers exiting from Corcoran's across the street.

i Ⓜ*Grands Boulevards. Across from Corcoran's. Free Wi-Fi. Happy hour mixed drinks and beer €6. ☼ Open daily 7pm-6am.*

Bastille

Nightlife in the 11ème has long consisted of Anglophones who drink too much and rockers and hipsters who intend to stay out until the Métro starts up again.

🎖 LE BARON ROUGE

WINE BAR

1 rue Théophile Roussel   ☎01 43 43 14 32

This wine bar is doing it right with a 45 bottle selection of reds and whites that start from as low as €1.50 a glass, leaving you with plenty of money left over for a rich *assiette* of charcuterie, cheese, or oysters. The pros and regulars bring their own bottles and fill them up straight from the barrels before taking their drinks outside to the pavement. If you're lucky, you can nab an impromptu barrel table surface for you drink. With booze this good and this cheap, the crowd really doesn't need much to keep the conversation and laughter going.

i Ⓜ*Ledru-Rollin. Walk south with traffic on av. Ladru-Rollin, then turn left onto rue de Prague. Turn left with traffic onto rue Traversière. Wine €1.50-3.60. Platters €7-16. ☼ Open Tu-F 10am-2pm and 5-11pm, Sa 10am-10pm, Su 10am-4pm.*

🎖 UFO

BAR

49 rue Jean-Pierre Timbaud   ☎06 09 81 93 59

UFO's pricing is out of this world, with happy hour pints for €3.50 and pastis for €1.50. The super-scuffed and worn furniture also looks like it's been through a wormhole and back. Cheap drinks and a short happy hour means that the student and young rockers here down their drinks at inhuman speeds before dancing to garage rock, punk, and funk. Weekend DJs make this dive bar a prime destination for an invasion.

i Parmentier. Walk up av. Parmentier toward the brasserie Le Plein Soleil, turn right onto rue Jean-Pierre Timbaud; UFO is on the left. Cocktails €5-10. Beers €4-7. Happy hour pints €3.50, glass of wine €1.50, pastis €1.50. ☼ Open daily 6pm-2am. Happy hour daily 6-8pm.*

paris

Montparnasse and Southern Paris

BATOFAR
BOAT, BAR, NIGHTCLUB

Across from 11 quai Francois Mauriac   ☎01 53 60 17 00 www.batofar.org

You might feel like T-Pain at this nightclub, which occupies the lowest level of a boat and leads a quadruple life as a nightclub, concert venue, restaurant, and bar. Ideally located on the quiet eastern end of the Seine, the Batofar brings the area alive at night with its live concerts and bangin' DJs. If you're not interested in sweaty dancing, singing, and bumpin' and grinding, hit the bar on the breezy top level of the boat. You can also head for the shore and relax on the patio, also known as *La Plage*, where you can enjoy fresh rum punch made with pineapples, oranges, mangoes, or cranberries. Locals love this increasingly popular locale as much as the savvy backpackers who know it exists.

i ⓂQuai de la Gare. Go to the Seine and head down the stairs to the riverbank, then turn right so the river is on your left. Walk about 5min. DJ every night and after concerts. Tickets can be bought at the door, usually €3-25. White sangria €5. Punch €6. Cocktails €10. Tapas €5. ⌚ Open daily noon-late. Patio on the bank (La Plage) open May-Sept noon-1am; brunch on Su. Terrace on the boat open daily 6pm-midnight. Happy hour Oct-Apr 6-8pm; May-Sept 5-7pm. Restaurant open Tu-Sa noon-2:30pm and 7:30-11:30pm. Concerts usually start 7pm or later.

LA FOLIE EN TÊTE
BAR

33 rue de la Butte-aux-Cailles   ☎01 45 80 65 99 http://lafolieentete.wix.com/lesite

Decorated with musical instruments, street signs, and newspaper clippings announcing Bob Marley concerts, this bar loves its reggae, rock, and world music. This bar has one of the cheapest happy hours in the neighborhood and is well known for its strong ti' punch and excellent mojitos. Hipsters, poets, musicians, broke students, and the occasional suit and tie keep it packed and steamy until closing.

i ⓂPlace d'Italie. From pl. d'Italie, follow rue Bobillot. Turn right onto rue de la Butte-aux-Cailles and follow it as it turns right. Beer €5-6. Cocktails €7.50. Happy hour cocktails €5, pints €3-3.50. ⌚ Open M-Sa 5pm-2am, Su 6pm-midnight. Happy hour daily 5-8pm.

LE MERLE MOQUEUR
BAR

11 rue de la Butte aux Cailles   ☎01 45 65 12 43

Capturing the spirit of the neighborhood with its eclectic mix of color block walls, uneven stools, spray-painted doors, '80s music, and a rather random selection of art, this bar is a little funky and not at all fussy. The naked lady and her pig friend painted near the door are here to offer you a plastic patio chair and a selection of over 20 different types of rum.

i ⓂCorvisart. Follow the signs to Butteaux Cailles, south of the Métro stop. Drinks €4-6. Happy hour pints €3, rum punch €5. ⌚ Open daily 5pm-1:30am. Happy hour 5-8pm.

CAFE OZ: DENFERT ROCHEREAU
BAR

3 pl. Denfert-Rochereau   ☎01 45 38 76 77 www.cafe-oz.com

Opened in May 2011, the newest and largest iteration of this Australian chain is rumored to have the largest terraces in Paris. The view from the terrace in front of the bar is more likely to be of hurried travelers lugging suitcases than of a chic Parisian sidewalk, so we recommend heading to the other terrace in the back. After midnight, the older crowd vacates, and the massive interior becomes packed with young bodies dancing on tables, stairs, and wherever there's room. Things are kept cool thanks to the drafty, 30ft. ceilings. Despite Oz's size, the giant kangaroo out front and walls covered in boomerangs still make you feel like you're in a packed hut on a beach in Queensland.

i ⓂDenfert-Rochereau, behind the RER station. Cover charg €15 with drink, depending on the night. Shooters €5. Beer €7-8. Cocktails €10. Happy hour cocktails €7. Bar snacks €6-9. ⌚ Kitchen open M-Sa noon-4pm. Bar open M noon-2am, Tu-W noon-3am, Th-Sa noon-5am. Snacks served W-Sa 5pm-9pm. Happy hour M 5pm-midnight, Tu-Sa 5-8pm, Su 5pm-midnight.

Auteuil, Passy & Batignolles

Just like the food, the nightlife in these *arrondissements* tends to be cheaper, younger, and chiller in the 17ème than in the 16ème, where you'll find a bevy of overpriced bars and nightclubs.

LES CAVES POPULAIRES   BAR
22 rue des Dames   ☎01 53 04 08 32

For some cheap drinks, bohemian company, and some good cheese and charcuterie platters, Les Caves Populaires is the bar of choice. The bar stands out from the relatively quiet rue des Dames with its noise—this place is full even in the afternoon—and with its red mosaic exterior and whitewashed stone walls. In a place where the coffee is organic, served with a stick of cinnamon, and only €1, it only makes sense that the groups of friends here have rosy cheeks from laughter (although the cheap glasses of wine can't hurt).

i Ⓜ*Place de Clichy. Walk down bd des Batignolles with the flow of traffic (away from the traffic circle). Turn right onto rue Lecluse, turn left onto rue des Dames; Les Caves is on the right. Wine from €2 per glass. Shot €3-4. Cocktails €3-12.* ☒ *Open M-Sa 8am-1am, Su 11am-1am.*

FROG XVI   BAR
110 bis av. Kleber   ☎01 47 27 88 88 www.frogpubs.com

One of several English Frog pubs across Paris, Frog XVI is the trendier cousin of the more traditional Frog and Rosbif. With two levels, rock music, large comfortable leather seats, and the microbreweries downstairs in full view, this is the place to loosen up and hang out with old friends or make new ones over a quality beer. The crowd here is a healthy mix of young locals and tourists, which means this place can fill up quickly, so plan your arrival accordingly, especially on a game day.

i Ⓜ*Trocadéro. Free Wi-Fi. DJ Th Sa. Brunch Sa-Su noon-4pm. Happy hour M-F 5:30-8pm. Lunch menu M-F €12.50. Pints €5. Beer €7.* ☒ *Open daily noon-2am.*

LE BLOC   CAFE, BAR
21 rue Brochant   ☎01 53 11 02 37

Formerly a warehouse, this cafe was updated with a super modern, minimalist exterior, with clean cut lines and an enormous window for the first floor. The walls of this multi-level cafe are decorated with photographs, and there's a nook under the stairs with a cramped but comfortable array of lounge chairs, including a creatively redesigned shopping cart (yes, it is somehow comfortable). Parisians who want to associate themselves with chicness—or who are actually chic—park it here for a decent meal, and in the evenings lo-fi electro music plays in the background as the Parisians get ready for the rest of the night.

i Ⓜ*Brochant. From the Métro, walk straight onto rue Brochant. Free Wi-Fi. Half beer €2.70. Cocktails €7. Salads €8-11.50. Daily specials for €10.* ☒ *Open daily 8:30am-2am.*

DUPLEX   CLUB
2 bis av. Foch   ☎01 45 00 45 00 www.leduplex.com

Stories of this late-night disco make their way around Paris, and we mean that in an infamous way. The three-story subterranean club has several rooms with different music playing, but you can expect to hear the usual techno, house, top 40, and some throwback hip hop. Women in heels and snappy looking men pack this club and don't stop until 6am—just in time to go home on the Métro.

i Ⓜ*Charles de Gaulle-Étoile. Half block from the Circe. Cover (includes 1 drink) M-Th €15, F-Sa €20, Su €15. Drinks M €8, Tu-Th €9, F-Sa €11, Su €9.* ☒ *Open daily midnight to 6am.*

L'ENDROIT   BAR, CAFE
67 place du Dr Félix Lobligeois   ☎01 42 29 50 00

L'Endroit is French for "the place," and this is definitely the place to be. The Parisians who gather here suck down pint-sized mojitos and laugh carelessly over a shared pack of cigarettes. When the sun's out, chowing down on massive burgers accompanied by even more massive salads seems to be a popular activity. Once darkness strikes, so do those midnight munchies, and with L'Endroit closing shop on the weekends at 5am, there's nothing like a pre-dawn meal.

i Open M-Th 11am-2am, F-Sa 11am-5am, Su 11am-2am.

Montmartre

With sex shops and strippers galore, Montmartre can be sketchy at night, with some loud drunkards making quite a scene and pickpockets eyeing the tipsy tourists.

MARLUSSE ET LAPIN   BAR
14 rue Germain Pilon   ☎01 42 59 17 97

Even in a neighborhood teeming with sex shops and cabarets, a place like Marlusse et Lapin stands out for its weirdness. In the back of this tiny bar is "Grandma's Chamber," with flowery wallpaper, a sewing machine, a bed that now functions as seating, and black and white photos of grandparents. In case this scene isn't bizarre enough for you, order a glass of authentic absinthe for a truly down-the-rabbit-hole experience. In case wormwood isn't your thing, this place also serves up popular flavored shots for €3 if you can elbow your way to the bar.

i ⓂPigalle or Abbsesses. From Pigalle, facing the rounded plaza, turn right and walk down bd de Clichy, then turn right onto rue Germain Pilon; Marlusse is on the right. From Abbsesses, facing the church, head right on rue des Absesses, then left onto rue Germain Pilon; Marlusse is on the left. Shot €3. Half pint beers €2.80. Cocktails €5-7. Absinthe €6-9. Happy hour beer €3-4; mixed drinks €4.50. ⓀOpen daily 4pm-2am. Happy hour 4-8pm.

Buttes-Chaumont & Belleville

Instead of clubs and dirty dancing, the loud, artsy bars in 19ème and 20ème are the centers of nightlife around here and attract mostly the hipster locals.

ROSA BONHEUR   BAR, GLBT
2 av. des Cascades   ☎01 42 00 00 45 www.rosabonheur.fr

Nestled in the Parc des Buttes Chaumont, Rosa Bonheur has arguably the best setting in all of Paris. As it gets dark, the mystery of the forest and the fading colors of the sunset infect all the young people here with a romanticism reminiscent of *A Midsummer Night's Dream*—left and right, everyone is dancing, fumbling, laughing, and locking lips. Groups of friends settle down at tables outside or stand around barrels to polish off bottles of wine, while couples dance and grind about indoors on the crowded dance floor. In addition to all this laid-back hedonism, Rosa has a conscientious heart: this restaurant also hosts a lot of community service and charity events for GLBT rights and environmental awareness, along with Paris's *Silence de Danse*, an event where you put on headphones, dance, and look really funny.

i ⓂBotzaris. Entrance at the gates facing 74 Botzaris. Tapa €5-8. Sangria €4. Pints €5. Mojitos €8. ⓀOpen W-Su noon-midnight. Last entry 11pm.

LES PÈRES POPULAIRES   BAR
46 rue Buzenval   ☎01 43 48 49 22

"Père" means "father" in French, and we wish our dads were this cool. This bar is filled with 20-somethings unchained to any commitments, much less fatherhood, who gather here to drink cheap beer or sip €1 espressos at the mismatched tables, cozy couches, or the bright green bar. And when shots are €3 and beer is €2.60, it's no wonder that the booze flows freely and the Parisians (you won't find a single tourist here) become uncharacteristically loud. Les Pères has no sign on the outside, and it doesn't need one—it's the loudest, happiest place on the block.

i ⓂBuzenval. Walk down rue Buzenval against the flow of traffic; the bar is on the left. Coffee €1. Shots €3. Beer €2.60-6.50. Wine €2.70-9. Sandwiches €3.90. ⓀOpen M-F 8am-2am, Sa-Su 10am-2am.

LA BELLEVILLOISE

BAR, CONCERT

19-21 rue Boyer

☎01 46 36 07 07 www.labellevilloise.com

La Bellevilloise is the multi-tasking, effortlessly cool older sister you always wish you were. A hugely popular institution in Paris, this establishment is a restaurant, bar, and club in one. Whether or not you want a delicious brunch with live jazz, a night of electro-swing music by an up-and-coming band, or a chance to admire some contemporary art as you take a break from swinging to Creole beats, La Bellevilloise has you covered. Even though it may be far from the center of the city, Parisians from *arrondissements* all over venture here for the music and the food, so be sure to make a reservation for meals and be prepared to share some personal space as you shake about.

i ⓂMénilmontant. Walk along rue de Ménilmontant with traffic until rue Boyer. Turn right onto rue Boyer; La Bellevilloise is on the right. Concerts and club 19+, some events 21+. Live music in the restaurant 4-5 times per week. Su brunch with live jazz. Reservations recommended for dinner and brunch. Concerts €10-15. Wine €4. Beer €4-9. Shots €5. Cocktails €9. ☼ Open W-F 7pm-2am, Sa 11am-2am, Su brunch 11am-4:30pm.

O' PARIS

CAFE, BAR

1 rue des Envierges

☎01 43 66 38 54 www.le-o-paris.com

For one of the best terraces in all Paris, come to O' Paris. Located at the top of steep slope, this cafe/bar overlooks the gorgeous Parc de Belleville, with the Eiffel Tower and the Parisian rooftops all at your feet. With a view this great, it's no wonder that this cafe is the spot of choice for the fashionable denizens of the 20ème and bobos from all over Paris. And as if the view wasn't enough, the €2 coffee and €10 lunch menu make it hard to find a seat on the packed street corner when the sun's out. The dinner menu here is a little pricey, and it's the view that's most important, so save your evening dining money for elsewhere or, better yet, pack a picnic and tan in the park right in front of you. During the evening, O' Paris is buzzing with patrons who refuse to budge from their seats and stay for drinks and a relaxed and beautiful midnight in Paris.

i ⓂPyrénées. Facing McDonald's, head left and walk up rue de Belleville, then turn left onto rue Piat; O' Paris is on the left. Lunch menu €10. Brunch €17-22. ☼ Open M-W 10:30am-2am, Th-Su 10am-2am.

AUX FOLIES

BAR

8 rue de Belleville

☎06 14 17 91 33

If you ever need to feel cool or, damn, if you just are cool, you should be at this bar. Frequented by everyone from suave and collected older men to young, frenetic locals to graffiti artists who have tagged the nearby alleyways, Aux Folies is nearly always packed with an artsier crowd that doesn't mind a little dirt, drinks their coffee black, and likes their booze cheap (beers start at €2). This bar was once a mini-theater where Edith Piaf used to sing, and the unchanged decor and neon lights help maintain an old-school vibe. The terrace gets a rare bit of sunlight on this crowded, narrow street, but just be prepared to elbow your way into a seat.

i ⓂBelleville. Walk up rue de Belleville; Aux Folies is on the left. Beer €2-4. Wine €3 per glass. Cocktails €4.50. ☼ Open M-Sa 6am-2am, Su 7am-1am.

ARTS AND CULTURE

A trip to the Opéra Garnier, comic relief at the Odéon Théâtre, or late-night wining and dining at the Moulin Rouge are all possibilities for total cultural immersion and will leave you with more memories than that one night on the Mouffetard. If this sounds boring to you (hopefully it doesn't, but we cater to all tastes), you'll be pleased to know that Paris's concerts get just as rowdy as its clubs. Whether you

paris

have a solid grasp of French or are a novice who's just laughing because everyone else is, you'll definitely leave feeling a bit more *je ne sais quoi*.

Theater

⛭ ODÉON THÉÂTRE DE L'EUROPE
LATIN QUARTER AND ST-GERMAIN

2 rue Corneille ☎01 44 85 40 40 www.theatre-odeon.eu

The Odéon is a classically beautiful theater: gold lines the mezzanine and muted red upholstery covers the chairs. Many plays at this national theater are performed in foreign languages, with French translations shown above on a screen, which can make if frustrating if you don't *parler* the language. If you do, though, or if you just don't mind, the prices here are stunningly reasonable, and standing tickets are dirt cheap. The under-26 crowd can score the luxury of a seat for the same price, so save your young legs—watching foreign performances of *As You Like It* or *Platonov* takes enough energy already.

i ⓜOdéon. Limited number of rush tickets available 2hr. before the start of the show. Shows €10-36, under 26 €6-18. Rush tickets €6. ⓩ Performances generally M-Sa 8pm, Su 3pm.

⛭ THÉÂTRE DE LA VILLE
CHÂTELET-LES HALLES

2 pl. du Châtelet ☎01 42 74 22 77 www.theatredelaville-paris.com

Since the'80s, the Théâtre de la Ville has become a major outlet for avant-garde theater, dance, and music for those who aren't afraid to go far out in performances titled "Disabled Theater" and "The Pornography of Souls." The theater is a bit more traditional and puts on classics by the likes of Shakespeare and Balzac, along with more contemporary German, Japanese, and American playwrights.

i ⓜChâtelet. Walk down rue de Rivoli toward Hôtel de Ville. Tickets €19-25, under 30 €9-20. ⓩ Box office open M 11am-7pm, Tu-Sa11am-8pm.

Cabaret

⛭ AU LAPIN AGILE
MONTMARTRE

22 rue des Saules ☎01 46 06 85 87 www.au-lapin-agile.com

Halfway up a steep, cobblestoned hill that American tourists describe as "just like San Francisco," Au Lapin Agile has been providing savvy Parisians and tourists with traditional music, dance, and theater since the late 19th century. The performers present old French songs, ballads, lively sing-alongs, and guitar performances that last well into the night. The tiny theater was a popular spot for the 20th-century bohemian art scene—Picasso, Utrillo, and Max Jacob are on the list of people who cabareted here.

i ⓜLamarck-Coulaincourt. Follow rue St-Vincen to rue des Saules. Tickets €24, students under 26 €17. Tu-F and Su cover includes 1 drink. Drinks €6-7. ⓩ Shows Tu-Su 9pm-1am.

BAL DU MOULIN ROUGE
MONTMARTRE

82 bd de Clichy ☎01 53 09 82 82 www.moulin-rouge.com

The Moulin Rouge promises to be as trippy and over-the-top as Baz Luhrmann's film, but at €99 a show, the famed glam and glitz just isn't worth it. The world-famous home of the can-can opened in 1889 and has hosted international superstars like Ella Fitzgerald and Johnny Rey, and it now welcomes a fair crowd of tourists for an evening of sequins, tassels, and skin. The shows remain risqué, and the late show is cheaper, but be prepared to stand if it's a busy night.

i ⓜBlanche Sarl. Elegant attire required; no shorts, sneakers, or sportswear. 9 and 11pm show €99, with ½-bottle of champagne €109. 7pm dinner and 9pm show €180-210. Occasional lunch shows €100-130; call for more info. ⓩ Dinner daily 7pm. Shows daily 9 and 11pm.

Cinema

▥ L'ARLEQUIN
LATIN QUARTER AND ST-GERMAIN
76 rue de Rennes
☎01 45 44 28 80

A proud revival theater, L'Arlequin mixes modern French films with artsy selections from a pool of international award-winners. Four films are featured each week, undoubtedly decreasing the prevalence of adolescent movie-hopping. Some films are in English, but the vast majority are in French.

i Ⓜ*St-Sulpice. Walk down rue ce Rennes toward the Café de Métro; L'Arlequinon is on the right. €9.60; students, under 18, and over 60 €7.10.*

CINÉMATHÈQUE FRANÇAISE
BASTILLE
51 rue de Bercy
☎01 71 19 33 33   www.cinematheque.fr

Though it's had some problems settling down (it's moved over five times, most recently in 2005), the Cinémathèque Française is dedicated to all things film. On the upper levels, the excellent Musée du Cinéma showcases old projectors and photographic plates alongside grand costumes and set pieces from movies like *Psycho* and *Métropolis*. The well-curated temporary exhibits on periods of film history and cinematic icons like Bette Davis, Tim Burton, and Jacques Demy draw a crowd of devoted cinephiles and casual moviegoers. And of course, the center screens multiple classics, near-classics, or soon-to-be classics per day; foreign selections are usually subtitled in French. Films by directors like Hitchcock, Fellini, Clément, and Matarazzo might be hard to understand in French, but hey, the picture's worth a thousand words.

i Ⓜ*Bercy. Musée du Cinéma €5; ages 13-26 and seniors €4, under 18 €2.50, Su 10am-1pm free; temporary exhibition €10/8/5; films €6.50/5.50/3. Joint ticket Musée with temporary exhibition €12, Musée and film €7. ☒ Musée open M-Sa noon-7pm, Su 10am-8pm. Temporary exhibition M 10am-8pm, W 10am-8pm, Th 10am-10pm, F-Su 10am-8pm. Ticket window open M noon-last showing, W-Sa noon-last showing, Su 10am-last showing.*

ACTION CHRISTINE
LATIN QUARTER AND ST-GERMAIN
4 rue Christine
☎01 43 33 85 78   www.actioncinemas.com

This small theater plays restored American flicks from the 1930s through the '70s, like *African Queen*, *Bedlam*, and (of course) *King Kong*. This is a nice way to escape the heat, and the films are voiced over with French subtitles for Anglophone enjoyment.

i Ⓜ*Odéon. Follow rue de L'Éperon and turn right onto rue St-André des Arts. Turn right onto rue Grands Augustins, then left onto rue Christine. Films in English with French subtitles. €8, under 20 and students €6. ☒ Shows 2-10pm.*

Music

▥ POINT EPHÉMÈRE
OPÉRA AND CANAL ST-MARTIN
200 quai de Valmy
☎01 40 34 02 48   www.pointephemere.org

Located in the bobo Canal St-Martin area, Point Ephémère is a mecca for hipsters who smoke to be ironic and artistes who probably know cooler bands than you do. Bringing in lesser-known rock bands from France, Belgium, the UK, the US, and elsewhere, this concert hall is crowded with young people four or five days a week. And as if hosting urban gospel rock and psychedelic bands didn't give it enough street cred, outside the concert hall is a bar, restaurant, and art expo space with artists' residences upstairs.

i Ⓜ*Louis Blanc. Walk down rue Louis Blanc toward the canal. Entrance is on the canal side, not the street. Buy tickets at the box office inside Point Ephémère in advance, online, or at the door, cheaper in advance. Be careful after dark. Concerts €15-20. Lunch menus €11.50-14.50. Brunch €16. Dinner à la carte. ☒ Bar open M-Sa noon-2am, Su noon-9pm. Restaurant open M-F 12:30-2:30pm and 8-11:15pm, Sa 12:30-2:30pm, Su noon-4:30pm. Brunch Su, in the summer Sa-Su. Snacks daily noon-1am.*

paris

LE BATACLAN
BASTILLE

50 bd Voltaire ☎01 43 14 00 30 www.le-bataclan.com

In French, *bataclan* is slang for "stuff" or "junk." In French music culture, Bataclan means a packed, 1500-person Chinese pagoda that hosts alternative and indie rock, synthetic pop, hip hop, reggae, and folk acts like Local Natives, Bastille, and Fabolous. The craziest venue in Bastille, Le Bataclan attracts a more local crowd, since the French love their more obscure bands (who are usually cheaper than those playing at La Cigale). Be sure to pregame with Capri Sun for their themed '80s or '90s parties that easily go until 6am.

i ⓂOberkampf. Tickets €15-50. ⚄ Shows start at 7:30pm.

Opera and Dance

PALAIS GARNIER (OPÉRA GARNIER)
OPÉRA AND CANAL ST-MARTIN

pl. de l'Opéra ☎01 71 25 24 33 www.operadeparis.fr

You can tour it during the day, but going at night is a whole different ball game. The chandeliers dim, the stage lights up, and you are thrown back to the *fin de siècle* with ballet performances ranging from *Orpheus and Eurydice* to the *Bolshoi Ballet*. Although the Opéra Garnier confusingly no longer performs operas, its ballets, chamber music concerts, and choral performances still draw crowds of older adults and the lucky holders of youth rush tickets who are interested in more than the ornate architecture of the building.

i ⓂOpéra. Tickets usually available 2 weeks before the show. Tickets generally €10-110. Under 28 rush tickets sold 1hr. before show starts based on availability, operas €25, ballets €15, concerts €10. ⚄ Box office open M-Sa 11:30am-6:30pm.

OPÉRA BASTILLE
BASTILLE

pl. de la Bastille ☎01 40 01 19 70 www.operadeparis.fr

Although considered Opéra Garnier's "ugly" other half, the Opéra Bastille has been the primary home of the Paris Opera since 1989. Matching its tiered glass exterior and geometric interior, the Opéra Bastille puts on classical pieces with a modern spin. There may not be gilded columns, but the breathtaking performances more than compensate.

i ⓂBastille. Tickets can be purchased online, by mail, by phone, or in person. Tickets €5-140. Under 28 rush tickets sold 1hr. before show starts based on availability, operas €25, ballets €15, concerts €10. 32 spots are reserved for €5 each and are sold 1½hr. before performance. ⚄ Box office open M-Sa 2:30-6:30pm.

SHOPPING

"Shopping" and "Paris" are almost synonymous. But the excessive wealth of the Champs-Élysées and Île St-Louis are not for the faint of heart—they're for the rich. Indeed, the many antiques, rare books, and tempting tourist trappings you'll find across the city could easily empty pockets. No one likes credit card debt, so we recommend the vintage shops and quirky boutiques in the youthful Marais and Bastille neighborhoods.

Books

▨ SHAKESPEARE AND CO.
LATIN QUARTER AND ST-GERMAIN

37 rue de la Bûcherie ☎01 43 25 40 93 www.shakespeareandcompany.com

This is more than just a bookstore. See **Sights**.

i ⓂSt-Michel. Take quai de Montebello toward Notre Dame and turn right onto rue St-Jacques. Rue de la Bûcherie is on the left. ⚄ Open daily 10am-11pm.

GIBERT JEUNE

15 bd Saint-Denis   ☎01 55 34 75 75 www.gibertjeune.fr

If you're studying abroad in Paris, this is probably where you'll want to buy your textbooks—Gibert Jeune carries over 300,000 titles, and with this many books, the store has multiple locations within walking distance for different genres. Buy a book and get the Gibert Jeune bag to blend in with the rest of Paris's literary crowd. Bonus: it's air-conditioned, which makes for a cool, intellectual getaway on a hot summer day.

i Ⓜ St-Michel. *Multiple locations along quai St-Michel, pl. Saint-Michel, and rue de la Huchette.* ② *Open M-Sa 9:30am-7:30pm.*

SAN FRANCISCO BOOK CO.

17 rue Monsieur le Prince   ☎01 43 29 15 70 www.sanfranciscobooksparis.com

San Francisco Book Co. is a quaint little English-language bookshop filled floor to ceiling with used books. If you're running low on cash, you can rummage through the €1-3 books outside or sell or trade your own books here. Find some summer fiction or mysteries on your own, or ask the gentle owner from Lincoln, Nebraska, about his more rare finds. You may not guess that among the Jodi Picoult novels and Michelin travel guides lie first edition copies of James Joyce's *Ulysses* or prints of Latin classics from the 17th century.

i Ⓜ Odéon. *From the intersection, walk down rue Dupuytren. Turn left at the end of the street onto rue Monsieur le Prince.* ② *Open M-Sa 11am-9pm, Su 2-7:30pm.*

POP CULTURE SHOP

23 rue Keller   ☎01 43 55 34 68 www.popcultureshop.fr

Pop Culture Shop is focused on a specific kind of pop culture: comic books and superhero memorabilia. Shelves upon shelves of comic books make this a geek's gold mine in Bastille's shopping district. The shop is only a few years old, but the owner's collection has been in the works for many more. Find all your Batman and Green Lantern classics as well as some less mainstream names. In the back you can browse a decent collection of vinyls and figurines.

i Ⓜ Bastille. *Walk down rue de la Roquette and turn right onto rue Keller. Comic book €5-10. Vinyls €12-24.* ② *Open Sept-Jun M 2-7:30pm, Tu-Sa 11am-7:30pm; Jul-Aug M-W 2-7:30pm, Th-Sa 11:30-7:30pm.*

LES MOTSÀ LA BOUCHE

6 rue Ste-Croix de la Bretonnerie   ☎01 42 78 88 30 www.motsbouche.com

Logically located in the Marais, this two-story bookstore offers mostly GLBT literature, photography, magazines, and art, with everything from Proust to guides on lesbian lovemaking. Straight guys could probably learn a few pointers from that last one, too. And right next to the gay pornzines are some works by Foucault and Arendt because, you know, it's all interchangeable. Most books are in French, but there is an English section with books by David Sedaris and, of course, *Brokeback Mountain*. Head downstairs for the international DVD collection (€7-25); titles range from the artistic to the pornographic.

i Ⓜ Hôtel de Ville. *Take a left onto rue Vieille du Temple and a left onto rue Ste-Croix de la Bretonnerie. Books €8-21.* ② *Open M-Sa 11am-11pm, Su1-9pm.*

Clothing

Parisians know how to dress well. It's in their blood. If you want to dress like them, you don't have to drain your bank account—or as they say in French, *"fais chauffer ta carte bleu"* ("heat up your credit card"). **Galeries Lafayette** is the French equivalent of Macy's and will save you time and money, not to mention the embarrassing experience of being asked to leave Louis V. For everything vintage, from pre-World War II garb to totally radical Jeff Spicoli get-ups, head to the Marais and Bastille. **Les Halles**

paris

are also a mega complex of stores that sell everything from clothing to music and provide all that your average supermall has to offer.

FREE'P' STAR
MARAIS

8 rue Ste-Croix de la Bretonnerie   ☎01 42 76 03 72 www.freepstar.com

Enter as Plain Jane and leave as Madonna—from the '80s or '90s, that is. Choose from a wide selection of vintage dresses (€20), velvet blazers (€40), boots (€30), and military-style jackets (€5) that all seem like a good idea when surrounded by other antiquated pieces but require some gumption to be worn out in the open—maybe shoulder pads are making a comeback? Dig around the €10 denim pile and €3 bin for ripped jeans that died out with Kurt Cobain.

i Ⓜ*Hôtel de Ville. Follow rue de Renard and turn right onto rue St-Merri, which becomes rue Ste-Croix de la Bretonnerie. There are 2 other locations at 61 rue de la Verrerie (01 42 78 076) and 20 rue de Rivoli. Credit card min €20.* ✿ *Open M-F 11am-9pm, Sa-Su noon-9pm.*

SOBRAL
LES ÎLES

79 rue St-Louis-en-l'Île   ☎01 43 25 80 10 www.sobraldesign.fr

Brazilian artist Sobral is inspired by nature and makes all of his products with natural elements. Tiny Eiffel Towers, bangle bracelets, and elaborate necklaces are all made from natural resin infused with colors and objects in patterns reminiscent of tie-dye. The prices here may be fairly expensive, but it's a fun place to window shop. After all, Sobral only has three locations outside of Brazil, and this is one of them.

i Ⓜ*Pont Marie. Walk across the bridge and continue straight, then turn right onto rue St-Louis-en-l'Île. Rings €35. Bracelets €28-56. Earrings €18-40. Necklaces €78-120. Mirrors from €110.* ✿ *Open daily 11am-7:30pm.*

Vintage

COME ON EILEEN
BASTILLE

16-18 rue des Taillandiers   ☎01 43 38 12 11

Forget tacky vintage blazers and enormous shoulder pads—this vintage paradise is full of timeless designer goods, thank you. From Vanessa Bruno dresses to Marc Jacobs heels, your finds will leave you dying to brag to your friends about what a savvy thrift shopper you are. Look Faye Dunaway-chic in your Lanvin flats and not Bill Cosby-itchy in those, ahem, memorable sweaters.

i Ⓜ*Voltaire or*Ⓜ*Bastille. Walk up rue de la Roquette; rue des Taillandiers is about halfway between the 2 stops. Items from €30-80.* ✿ *Open M 11am-8:30pm, Tu 3-8:30pm, W-F 11am-8:30pm, Su 2-8pm. Store opens at 2pm in Aug; closes at 5pm in winter.*

MAMIE SHOP
OPÉRA

69 rue de Rochechouart   ☎01 42 81 10 42

Right next door to Mamie Blue, Mamie Shop offers a bigger selection and a little more flair than its sister store. The shop feels a bit like Willy Wonka's version of a clothing store, with spaces narrow enough for just one person to fit at a time, but with so many rooms and clothing, you could easily get lost. Sadly, there are no glass elevators for sale, just some interesting articles of clothing. Mamie Blue specializes in clothing from the 1920s to the 1970s, with flowery dresses and Mad Men-esque blouses, although we're thinking the prices might be a little over-adjusted for inflation.

i Ⓜ*Anvers or Barbès. From bd de Rochechouart, turn onto rue de Rochechouart, which is located between the 2 Métro stops. Tailoring available. Men's jackets from €30. Dresses €40-175.* ✿ *Open M 3-6pm, Tu-Sa 11am-12:30pm and 3-6pm.*

Specialty

PALAIS DES THÉS
MARAIS

64 rue Vieille du Temple   ☎01 43 56 90 90 www.palaisdesthes.com

Le Palais des Thés lives up to its name with a grand, handpicked selection of teas. Tea experts travel to 20 countries in Asia, Africa, and South America to find the highest quality supplies. By personally traveling to each tea estate, the owners are able to ensure fair trade and labor practices and keep an eye on local environmental issues, so you can steep your organic jasmine tea with a clean conscience. Teas can be as inexpensive as €3-4 or as pricey as €100 for 100g. Describe your preferences and tastes to the welcoming staff, and they will point you in the direction of the tea that best fits your needs (and your pocketbook).

i Ⓜ️St-Paul. *Walk up rue Malher as it turns into rue Payenne. Turn left onto rue des Francs Bourgeois, then turn right onto rue Vieille du Temple. 4 other locations around the city. Most tea €3.50-17 per 100g.* ⏲ *Open M-Sa 10am-8pm.*

CAILLES DE LUXE
BASTILLE

15 rue Keller   ☎09 53 02 65 22 www.caillesdeluxe.com

When the owners of this glam little shop decided they were fed up with quality jewelry costing a fortune, they decided to go into the business themselves. Bright colors and simple geometric shapes mark the staples of this shop and make for fantastic statement pieces. Go a notch or two above with some of the more unusual items, like necklaces with Scrabble ornaments or fun Ghostbusters earrings. This is definitely a place for the ladies, so guys might want to find a nice place to sit for a while.

i Ⓜ️Voltaire. *Walk southwest on rue de la Roquette and turn left onto rue Keller; the store is about halfway down on the left. Earrings from €9. Rings from €5.* ⏲ *Open Tu-Sa 11am-8pm.*

LE MARCHÉ AUX FLEURS
ÎLE DE LA CITÉ AND ÎLE ST-LOUIS

pl. Louis-Lépine

The flower market at the center of Île de la Cité brings a welcome scene of green and freshness to the city streets. Go traditional and buy your sweetheart a dozen roses or a wild orchid. Or go rogue and opt for a birdhouse, seeds for an herb garden, or a rare tree from Madagascar.

i Ⓜ️Cité. *Flowers from €5.* ⏲ *Open M 10am-6:30pm, W-Su 10am-6:30pm.*

ESSENTIALS

Practicalities

- **TOURIST OFFICES: Bureau Central d'Accueil** provides maps and tour information and books accommodations. (25 rue des Pyramides ☎01 49 52 42 63 www.parisinfo.com *i* Pyramides.⏲ Open daily May-Oct 9am-7pm; Nov-Apr 10am-7pm.) Also located at Gare de Lyon (☎01 43 33 24 ⏲ Open M-Sa 8am-6pm); Gare du Nord (☎01 45 26 94 82 ⏲ Open daily 8am-6pm); Gare de L'est (⏲ Open M-Sa 8am-7pm); Anvers facing 72 bd Rochechouart (⏲ Open daily 10am-6pm). **Tourist kiosks** at Ⓜ️ChampsÉlysées-Clemenceau, Ⓜ️Cité in front of Notre Dame, Ⓜ️Hôtel de Ville inside the Hôtel de Ville, Ⓜ️Anvers, and Ⓜ️Bastille. All offices and kiosks have tourist maps; Métro, bus, and RER maps; and walking guides to Paris produced by the Paris Convention and Visitors Bureau. Most hotels and hostels also offer these resources for free.

- **TOURS: Bateaux-Mouches** offers boat tours along the Seine. (Port de la Conférence, Pont de l'Alma ☎01 42 25 96 10 www.bateaux-mouches.fr *i* Ⓜ️Alma-Marceau or Ⓜ️Franklin Roosevelt. Tours in English €12.50, under 12 €5.50, under 4 free. ⏲ Cruise about 70min. Apr-Sept M-F every 20-30min. 10:15am-10:30pm; Oct-Mar M-F every 11am-9pm, Sa-Su 10:15am-9pm every 45-60min.)

paris

- **GLBT RESOURCES: Paris Gay Village.** (61-63 rue Beaubourg ☎01 77 15 89 42 www. parisgayvillage.com *i* ⓂRambuteau. English spoken. ☑ Open M 6-8pm, Tu-Th 3:30-8pm, F 1-8pm, Sa 1-7pm.) Recommends GLBT accommodations, listings, and networking. SKOPIK map can be found at most tourist offices. Map of GLBT friendly establishments throughout Paris. **Centre Gay et Lesbien** (63 rue Beaubourg ☎01 43 57 21 47 www.centrelgbtparis.org *i* ⓂRambuteau. English spoken. Provides legal assistance, networking. ☑ Open M 6-8pm, Tu 3-8pm, W 12:30-8pm, Th 3-8pm, F-Sa 12:30-8pm, Su 4-7pm.

- **STUDENT RESOURCES: Centre d'Information et de Documentation pour la Jeunesse** provides information on temporary work, job placement, tourism info, and housing for students studying in Paris. (101 quai Branly ☎01 44 49 12 00 www.cidj.com *i* ⓂBir-Hakeim. ☑ Open Tu-F 1-6pm, Sa 1-5pm.)

- **TICKET AGENCIES: FNAC.** (74 av. des Champs-Élysées ☎08 25 02 00 20 www.fnacspec-tacles.com *i* ⓂFranklin D. Roosevelt.ⓂChâtelet/Les Halles. Various other FNAC stores throughout Paris; check the website for more locations. ☑ Open M-Sa 10am-11:45pm, Su noon-11:45pm.)

- **INTERNET: American Library in Paris** has computers and internet access for members or guests with day passes. (10 rue du Général Camou ☎01 53 59 12 60 www.americanlibrary-inparis.org *i* ⓂÉcole Militaire. ☑ Open Tu-Sa10am-7pm, Su 1-7pm; Jul-Aug Tu-F 1-7pm, Sa 10am-4pm.) There is also free Wi-Fi at **Centre Pompidou** and in its **Bibliothèque Publique d'Information.** (pl. Georges Pompidou, rue Beaubourg 8 ⓂRambuteau or ⓂHôtel de Ville. ☑ Center open M 11am-9pm, W-Su 11am-9pm. Library open M noon-10pm, W-F noon-10pm, Sa-Su 11am-10pm.) There is also always free Wi-Fi at McDonald's, Starbucks, and shaky Wi-Fi in public parks.

- **POST OFFICES: La Poste** runs the French postal system (www.laposte.fr). There are many post offices in Paris that are generally open M-F 8am-7pm and Sa 8am-noon. The most centrally located post offices are in **Saint-Germain** (118 bd St-Germain *i* ⓂOdéon. ☑ Open M-F 8am-8pm, Sa 9am-5pm) and **Châtelet-Les Halles.** (1 rue Pierre Lescot *i* ⓂLes-Halles. ☑ Open M-F 8am-6:30pm, Sa 9am-1pm.) The **Paris Louvre** post office is also easily accessible. (52 rue du Louvre *i* ⓂLouvre-Rivoli. ☑ Open 7:30am-6pm.)

Emergency

- **POLICE: 17. Préfecture de la Police.** (9 bd Palais ☎01 53 71 53 71 *i* ⓂCité. Across the street from the Palais de Justice. ☑ Open 24hr.)

- **CRISIS LINE: SOS Help!** is an emergency hotline for English speakers. (☎01 46 21 46 46)

- **DOCTORS:** ☎36 24, Dentist: ☎01 43 37 51 00. (☑ Available daily 3-11pm.) Ambulance (SAMU): ☎15. Fire: ☎18.

- **LATE-NIGHT PHARMACIES: Pharmacie Les Champs.** (84 av. des Champs-Élysées ☎01 45 62 02 41 *i* ⓂFranklin Roosevelt. ☑ Open daily 24hr.) **Grande Pharmacie Daumesnil.** (6 pl. Félix Eboué ☎01 43 43 19 03 *i* ⓂDaumesnil. ☑ Open daily 8:30am-10pm.) **Pharmacie européenne.** (6 pl. de Clichy ☎01 48 74 65 18 *i* ⓂPl. de Clichy. ☑ Open daily 24hr.) **Pharmacie Première.** (24 bd de Sébastopol ☎01 48 87 62 30 *i* ⓂChatelet. ☑ Open daily 8am-midnight.)

- **HOSPITALS/MEDICAL SERVICES: American Hospital of Paris.** (Pedestrian entrance at 63 bd Victor Hugo, vehicle entrance at 84 bd de la Saussaye. ☎01 46 41 25 25 www.ameri-can-hospital.org *i* ⓂPort Maillot, then bus 82 to last stop Hôpital Américain. Or ⓂPonte de Neuilly, then bus #93 to Hôpital Américain. Or ⓂPont de Levallois-Bécon, walk down rue Anatole France, turn right onto rue Baudin, walk 4 blocks, continue down rue Greffulhe and rue de Villiers, turn right onto bd du Château, walk 1 block, and turn right onto bd Victor Hugo; Hospital is on the left.) **Hôpital Bichat.** (46 rue Henri Huchard ☎01 40 25 80 80 *i* ⓂPorte de St-Ouen.)

france

Getting There

How you arrive in Paris will be dictated by where you are traveling from. Those flying across the Atlantic will most likely end up at **Paris-Charles de Gaulle,** one of Europe's main international hubs. If flying from within Europe on a budget airline, you'll probably fly into **Orly.** Though it hardly counts as arriving in Paris, flying into **Beauvais** from other European cities will often save you a lot of money even with the €16, 75min. shuttle ride into the Porte Maillot station in Paris. RER lines, buses, and shuttles run regularly from all three airports to Paris; however, time and price vary with each airport. With its confusingly endless number of train stations, Paris offers options for both those coming from within France and those who are traveling by train from elsewhere in Europe.

BY PLANE

PARIS-CHARLES DE GAULLE (CDG)

Roissy-en-France, 23km northeast of Paris   from landline in Paris☎3950
from abroad ☎01 70 36 39 50 www.adp.fr.

Most transatlantic flights land at Aéroport Paris-CDG. The two cheapest and fastest ways to get into the city from Paris-CDG are by RER and by bus. The RER train services Terminals 1, 2, and 3. The RER B (€9.50, includes Métro transport when you get off the RER) will take you to central Paris. To transfer to the Métro, get off at Gare du Nord, Châtelet-Les Halles, or St-Michel. The **Roissybus** (☎01 49 25 61 87 *i* €10 ☒45-60min., every 15-20min. during day; 20-30min. at night. Departures from Opéra 5:45am-11pm, from CDG 6am-11pm.) departs from Terminals 1,2 and 3 and arrives at Opéra. **Les Cars Air France** (☎08 92 35 08 20) departs from Terminals 1, 2, and 3 and connects to Étoile and Porte Maillot (Line 2) or Gare de Lyon and Gare Montparnasse (Line 4).

ORLY (ORY)

Orly, 18km south of Paris   ☎01 49 75 15 15 www.adp.fr.

Aéroport d'Orly is used by charters and many continental flights. From Orly Sud Gate G or Gate I, platform 1, or Orly Ouest level G, Gate F, take the **Orly-Rail** shuttle bus to the Pont de Rungis/Aéroport d'Orly train station, where you can board the RER C for a number of destinations in Paris, including Châtelet, St-Michel, Invalides, and Gare d'Austerlitz (RER C). Another option is the RATP ☒**Orlybus** (☎08 36 68 77 14 *i* €7.20 ☒ 30min., every 15-20min.), which runs between Métro and RER stop Denfert-Rochereau and Orly's south and west terminal. RATP also runs **Orlyval** (☎01 69 93 53 00 *i* VAL ticket €8.40, VAL-RER ticket €11.30), a combination Métro, RER, and VAL rail shuttle. The VAL shuttle goes from Antony (RER B) to Orly Ouest and Sud. Buy tickets at any RATP booth in the city or from the Orlyval agencies at Orly Ouest, Orly Sud, and Antony. See www.aeroportsdeparis.fr for maps of transportation between Orly and different locations in Paris. **Les Cars Air France** (☎08 92 35 08 20) connects from Orly Sud and Ouest terminals to Gare Montparnasse, Invalides, and Étoile (Line 1).

BY TRAIN

SNCF (www.sncf.com) sells train tickets for travel within France and abroad and offers *la Carte 12-27,* which guarantees reduced prices of up to 60% after you pay a one-time €50 fee. **Rail Europe** (www.raileurope.com) also sells tickets for travel within France and abroad, but prices for US residents tend to be higher than those offered by SNCF. There are several major train stations in Paris: **Gare d'Austerlitz** services southwest France, Spain, Portugal; **Gare de l'Est** for eastern France, Germany, Switzerland, eastern Europe; **Gare de Lyon** for southeast France, Italy; **Gare de Nord** for northern France, Germany, Belgium, Netherlands, UK. From Gare de Lyon, there are trains to Lyon (2hr., €25-92), Marseilles (3-4hr., €25-120), and Nice (5hr. 30min., €25-125). For London and the UK, book up to 120 days in advance with **www.eurostar.com**

(€42-183, 2hr. 30min. to London from Gare du Nord). For Brussels (1hr. 30min., €29-99) and Amsterdam (3hr. 15min., €35-130) from Gare du Nord, use **www.thalys.com.** For Switzerland from Gare de Lyon to Geneva, book through www.sncf.com (3-4hr., €25-130). For Italy, trains depart from Gare de Lyon; for overnight sleepers, book with **www.thello.com** (Milan, 10hr. €35-220; Rome, 15hr., €100-275). For Spain, book through www.sncf.com; overnights from Gare d'Austerlitz (Barcelona, 11hr. 30min., €96-211); daytime trains from Gare de Lyon (Barcelona, 6hr. 30min., €106-175). For Germany, book through www.sncf.com (Cologne, 3-4hr. direct, €99-120; Frankfurt, 4hr. direct, €89-119) for overnights and daytime trains.

Thalys.com offers reduced prices for those under 26. **Gare du Nord** (112 rue de Maubeuge) is the arrival point for trains from northern France and Germany as well as Amsterdam (From €65, 3½hr.), Brussels (From €50, 1hr.), and London €50-120, 2½hr.). **Gare de l'Est** (78 bd de Strasbourg) receives trains from eastern France and southern Germany, Austria, Hungary, Munich, (€125-163, 9-10½hr.), and Prague (€118-172, 12-15hr.). **Gare de Lyon** (20 bd Diderot) has trains from Florence (€135-170, 9-12hr.), Lyon (€60-70, 2hr.), Marseille (€45-70, 3-4hr.), Nice (€100, 5½hr.), and Rome (€177-200, 12-15hr.). **Gare d'Austerlitz** (85 quai d'Austerlitz) services the Loire Valley and the Iberian peninsula, including Barcelona (€135-170, 7-12hr.) and Madrid (€220-300, 12-13hr.). **Gare St-Lazare** (13 rue d'Amsterdam) will welcome you from northern France, while **Gare Montparnasse** (17 bd Vaugirard) is the destination of trains from northeastern and southwestern France.

Getting Around

BY Métro

In general, the Métro is easy to navigate, and trains run swiftly and frequently. Most of Paris lies within zones 1-2, so don't worry about the suburbs in zones 3-5. Pick up a colorful map at any station. Métro stations themselves are a distinctive part of the city's landscape and are marked with an "M" or with *"Métropolitain,"* but along the Champs-Élysées, they are unmarked stairs leading underground. The earliest trains start running around 5:30am, and the last ones leave the end-of-the-line stations (the *portes de Paris*) at about 12:15am during the week and at 2:15am on Friday and Saturday. In general, be at the Métro by 1am if you want to take it home at night. Connections to other lines are indicated by *correspondance* signs, and exits are marked by blue *sortie* signs. Transfers are free if made within a station, but it's not always possible to reverse direction on the same line without exiting. Hold onto your ticket until you exit the Métro and pass the point marked **Limite de Validité des Billets;** a uniformed RATP *contrôleur* (inspector) may request to see it on any train. If you're caught without a ticket, you will have to pay a €30 fine on the spot. It's a good idea to carry one more ticket than you need, although most, but not all, stations have ticket machines that now accept both bills and coins. Tickets cost €1.70 per journey, although it's much more useful to buy a *carnet* of 10 tickets for €13.30. You can also buy unlimited Métro passes for 1 day (€6.60), and on the weekend, young'uns under 26 can buy a day pass for €3.65. For longer visits, you can buy a week- or month-long (€19.80/65.10) **Navigo Découverte Pass**, which costs an additional €5 and requires a passport photo to attach to the card. Month-long passes begin the 1st day of the month, and week-long passes begin on Monday. You can also buy a *Paris Visite* pass (meant for tourists) for unlimited travel for 1-5 days with rather meager discounts (1-day pass €10.55; 2-day €17.15; 3-day €23.40; 5-day €33.70.)

When it's getting really late, your best chance of getting the train you want is heading to the biggest stations, like Gare du Nord, Gare de l'Est, and Châtelet-Les Halles. However, these stations are often full of tourists and pickpockets, so stay alert when traveling at night or avoid it altogether. If you must travel by public transport late at night, get to know the Noctilien bus (see below). When in doubt, take a taxi.

BY RER

The **RER** *(Réseau Express Régional)* is the RATP's suburban train system, which passes through central Paris and travels much faster than the Métro. There are five RER lines, marked A-E, with different branches designated by a number. The newest line, E, is called the Eole *(Est-Ouest Liaison Express)* and links Gare Magenta to Gare St-Lazare. Within central Paris, the RER works just like the Métro and requires the same ticket for the same price (if you have to transfer from the RER to the Métro or vice versa, however, you will need another ticket). The principal stops within the city that link the RER to the Métro are Gare du Nord, Nation, Charles de Gaulle-Étoile, Gare de Lyon, Châtelet-Les Halles, St-Michel, and Denfert-Rochereau. The electric signs next to each track list all the possible stops for trains running on that track. Be sure that the little square next to your destination is lit up. Trips to the suburbs require more expensive tickets that can also be bought at the automatic booths where you purchase Métro tickets. You must know what zone you're going to in order to buy the proper ticket. In order to exit the RER station, insert your ticket just as you did to enter and pass through. Like the Métro, the RER runs 5:30am-12:30am on weekdays and until 2:30am on weekends, but never wait until 2:30am to get to the Métro or RER. Again, if you must travel by public transportation late at night, get to know the Noctilien bus.

BY BUS

Although slower than the Métro, a bus ride can be a cheap sightseeing tour and a helpful introduction to the city's layout. Bus tickets are the same as those used for the Métro and can be purchased in Métro stations or from bus drivers (€1.70). Enter the bus through the front door and punch your ticket by pushing it into the machine next to the driver's seat. Inspectors may ask to see your ticket, so hold on to it until you get off. When you want to get off, press the red button so the *arrêt demandé* (stop requested) sign lights up. Most buses run daily 7am-8:30pm, although those marked **Autobus du nuit** continue until 1:30am. The **Noctilien** runs all night (daily 12:30am-5:30am) and services more than 45 routes throughout the city. If you plan to use this frequently, get a map of the routes from a Métro station and study it. Hard. Look for bus stops marked with a moon sign. Check out www.noctilien.fr or inquire at a major Métro station or Gare de l'Est for more information on Noctilien buses. Complete bus route maps are posted at the bus stops, while individual lines only give out maps of their own routes. Noctilien #2 runs to all the major train stations along the periphery of the city, while #12 and #13 run between Châtelet and Gare de Montparnasse.

BY TAXI

Traveling by taxi in Paris can be intimidating. Parisian taxis usually have three fares that change based on the time of day and day of the week. Rush hours and early morning hours on the weekends are the priciest, while morning to midday fares on weekdays are the cheapest. Fares are measured out by the kilometer and only switch to waiting time if a trip is over an hour. The pick-up base charge is €2.40, and minimum fare is €6.40. Each additional person after three passengers costs €3, and each additional piece of luggage after the first costs €1. A typical 20min. taxi ride costs €12-20, and a 40min. ride can be as much as €50. Taxis are easily hailed from any major boulevard or avenue, but stands are often outside major Métro intersections. If the taxi's green light is on, it is available. From the airport, prices skyrocket and begin at €50. It's never a bad idea to ask for a receipt at the end of your trip in case of dispute or lost property.

BY BIKE

If just don't feel like walking or gambling with timetables, bike rentals may be for you. There are many **Vélib'** stations around the city where you can rent a public bike for prices ranging from €1.70 for the day, €8 for the week, and €29 for the year. Each time you take it out, the first 30min. are free, the next 30min. are €1, 2nd additional 30min. are €2, and each additional 30min. thereafter €4. You can return the bike at any Vélib' station. If you arrive at a station and there are no open spots, go to the machine, punch in your number, and receive an additional 15min. to find another open station. Stations at the top of hills are generally open, and those at the bottom are typically not; spots near major tourist destinations and the quais are often a safe bet. If you want to rent on the spot, you must have a credit card with a chip on it to use the automatic booths where you can rent a bike; otherwise, you can rent from www.velib.fr to receive a subscription code. **Paris Bike Tour** also offers bike rentals for €20 for a 24hr. period; each extra day costs €10 (13 rue Brantôme ☎01 42 74 22 14 ☒ Open daily 9:30am-6:30pm). The bad news is they also require €250 deposit and a copy of your photo ID.

nice

Nice is undoubtedly a tourist's city, with a large population of the city's inhabitants visiting for holiday and the rest of the population living off of the money those vacationers shell out. Asking a local for a "non-touristy restaurant" will cause a legitimate laughing fit and you won't find a street without a hotel or hostel's blinking sign out front. Nonetheless, as far as vacation spots go, Nice is a tough one to beat. The weather is perfect, the water is refreshing, the food is delicious, and the views are amazing (not to mention the women, but I guess that's included in the view). The typical American dreams of traveling to Paris, while the Parisians, who know what's up, travel instead to Nice.

Nice has a little something for everyone, whether you're visiting from the jersey shore and just want to drink on the beach, or even if you're a total nerd and just want to visit some museums, you'll be able to find what you're looking for in Nice. (Full disclosure: we went to the museums too. And what's more, we liked them). In the heart of Nice you'll find a unique mix of hardcore backpackers, wealthy vacationing families, and a whole lot of French-speaking Nicoise (...duh?). A 20 min bus ride east, however, will help you escape the crowds and venture into Nice's surrounding seaside towns for a authentic grasp on native Riviera life.

The most important thing about Nic is that within the confines of the city and the towns surrounding it, it's borderline impossible to be bored. Bask in the sun on the shores of the Plage Mala, stroll down the Promenade des Anglais, snack on a crepe at Le Circuit, or drink 'til you fall off the table at Wayne's. Or even better, do them all in one day -there's more to do tomorrow and even if you had to repeat it all again, would that really be so bad?

SIGHTS

FRENCH RIVIERA
COASTLINE

☎1-800-PARADISE (but really) http://www.frenchriviera-tourism.com/

If you're vacationing in Nice you certainly don't need to be told to visit the French Riviera as you're essentially already there. The Riviera or the Côte d'Azur extends along the southern shores of France from the country's easternmost boundary towards the western edge of Cassis. Obvious stops include Nice and Cannes but some of the best beaches, views, and restaurants are tucked into the cliffs between Monaco and Nice. The locals will boast that Plage Mala (Mala

Beach) of Cap D'ail, the little seaside village northeast of Nice, is the most beautiful beach in the world. Let's Go challenges you to prove us wrong and clue us in, but it's doubtful that that will happen. Ten mins by bus west of Plage Mala is Villefranche, a quiet village embedded in the seaside cliffs. The icing on the cake for both Villefranche and Cap D'ail is their sense of authenticity. You won't find nearly as many tourists in either of these two towns, offering a peaceful and genuine glimpse into the lifestyles of the southern French.

For a more lively (or touristy) piece of the Riviera, Monaco, Nice, and Cannes are just as gorgeous, albeit a bit more crowded. Monaco's coastline harbors some of the world's most expensive yachts, which are available for charter assuming you just hit the jackpot on every slot machine in the country's famous Monte Carlo casino. For students a bit less lucky, a stroll down by Monaco's harbor to glimpse the wealthiest 1% of the world live their lives is entertaining in and of itself.

The opportunities waiting within the French Riviera are limitless – from jumping off five story cliffs into the ocean, to enjoying a quiet view with a glass of wine. It's difficult to go wrong along the coast. If you need more convincing, you probably shouldn't travel because you don't understand what awesome is. But just in case, think about this: Americans travel to Europe for vacation, but Europeans (and smart Americans) travel to the French Riviera.

i Priceless. ☼ Open Year Round.

PLAGE MALA
BEACH
Cap d'Ail
http://riviera-beaches.com/CapdAil/Mala.html

Plage Mala (Mala Beach) is the number one place to soak up the sun in Nice as recommended by the native Niçoise. Unlike some of the other beaches along the Côte d'Azur, Plage Mala has both components that make a beach great – water AND sand. Thankfully, this beach has more than just the bare minimum. It's quietly tucked in between a set of intimidating cliffs making for a pleasantly relaxing afternoon of sun bathing, and the lack of tourists gives the sensation of a private beach without the price tag. Lining the cliff faces along the water are a few small caves that seasoned swimmers can venture into, and stand-up paddleboards can make the journey easier for just a few euros.

The route from Nice to Plage Mala by bus is perhaps just as beautiful as the beach itself. The number 100 bus picks up beach-goers at Garibaldi Square and drops them off twenty minutes later at Cap D'ail, the tiny beachside town just uphill from Plage Mala. Along the way, the bus cruises through the hills and tunnels of Villefranche and Eze – quiet, tourist-free towns with streets carved into the mountains and tiny cafés by the sea. The bus route is perched a few hundred feet above sea level, offering panoramic views of the towns, and frequent stops leave room to hop out and take a closer look if the urge strikes.

Finally, by hopping back on the number 100 bus after Cap D'ail, you'll find yourself in Monaco after only five mins. Wander into the famous Monte Carlo casino and blow the rest of your vacation budget or play it safe by strolling along the shore for a peek at the multimillion-dollar yachts in the harbor.

In conclusion: Plage Mala is perfect. It's the perfect beach, in the perfect town. It's the number one must-see while in Nice and its location will get you out of the tourist-ridden areas of Old Town and Massena square and into the oasis that showcases the best that the French Riviera has to offer.

i Free!

CASTLE HILL
CHATEAU
Quai des Etats-Unis
http://en.nicetourisme.com/things-to-do/50

Castle Hill, known locally as "the chateau" is a must-see in Nice for one specific reason: never in your life will you come closer to seeing your desktop wallpaper in person. Even with the world's worst camera-phone, a picture of the Promenade des Anglais from atop Castle Hill is enough to give a blind man wanderlust. From the first lookout point, the view is breathtaking and the higher you climb, the better it gets. The chateau is less touristy than other sites in Nice because you have to have some serious quads to make it to the top.

The route up the hill is visible from the Promenade des Anglais and is as steep as it is long (it's steep and long). If you're too out of shape or you're traveling with your infant child (this is a student travel guide… check yourself), there is a little train that runs up to the top and back down, offering historical information about Nice as you sit back for the ride, wondering when you let yourself go and couldn't handle a ten minute hike.

A few levels from the top, a man-made waterfall crashes towards the lower levels, emitting a blanket of steam that cools you off and makes for the most instagrammed photo ever. The crashing gallons of water are visible from the beaches below, calling to the tourists of Nice as if to say, "come to me! There are more photos to be taken!" The sad truth, however, is that if you don't make the hike and take a selfie from the peak of Castle Hill, no one will believe that you've been there, including yourself in five years.

🕐 *Open every day, 8am - 8pm*

CHAGALL MUSEUM   MUSEUM

Avenue du Docteur Ménard   ☎493 53 87 20 http://www.musees-nationaux-alpesmaritimes.fr
The Marc Chagall Museum is one of the better-known and more appreciated museums in Nice. It's perched atop the Avenue du Docteur Menard and is just a ten-minute walk North from L'avenue D'Anglaterre. The museum primarily features Chagall's religious works documenting his life as a Russian Jew within the context of famous biblical stories. His intensely colorful paintings line the walls of the museum for you to browse, and if the art isn't really your thing, the museum is well air conditioned which you'll soon come to value during your time in the French Riviera.

The layout of the museum is quietly pleasant with a small cafe out front and a well-manicured lawn and garden leading towards the entrance. The museum is fairly close to both the Matisse Museum and the Archeology Museum. Visiting the three will make for a relaxing and easy half-day excursion that will cause you to break neither the bank nor a sweat (seriously, the AC is nice).

Tickets will run you €9 but you'll be able to knock it down to €7 with a student ID. Groups of ten or more can squeeze in for €7.50 but that likely won't help you unless you're chaperoning a field trip. Included in the admission fee is an audio guide (in French or English), which provides some background information on each painting. If you're not in the mood to trek up the hill to get there, the #15 and #22 buses both stop just out front and a round trip bus pass from the square is only €3.

Ultimately, the Chagall Museum is worth a quick visit if you're at all interested in art. The pleasant atmosphere is a peaceful escape from the bustle of Old Town and Massena Square and the opportunity to examine the prolific artist's lesser known works is a great opportunity.

i €9. Students €7. Groups of 10+ €7.50. 🕐 *Open 10am - 6pm everyday, Closed all day on Tuesday.*

OLD TOWN   NEIGHBORHOOD

Old Town is Nice's crown jewel, which is immediately apparent given the number of tourists wandering about. On the bright side, this might give you a rare opportunity to hear more English than French as the rest of Nice stays impressively faithful to the country's native language. Old Town has a touch of everything, from kitschy tourist trinkets, to soap vendors from Marseille, to the city's best restaurants. Regardless of what you're looking for, wandering through

A few minutes north of Place Massena by foot will lead you into what can only be called the backpacker's sector of Nice. Every other building is either a kebab shop or a hostel (if you find a building that's both, please let us know). But much like feeling of grocery store anxiety when choosing a box of cereal, it can be difficult to choose a place to stay. Despite all the options however, three hostels outshine the rest by leaps and bounds Baccarat, Antares, and Villa St. Exupery are what backpackers' dreams are made of. They're irresistible, and they rank amongst the top tier on Hostelworld for good reason.

HOTEL BACCARAT

39 rue d'Angleterre   ☎04 93 88 35 73

The Hotel Baccarat is kind of like the stray dog that was underfed when it was younger but has since been adopted and now, though it's still a bit mangy, has a vibrant and energetic spirit that makes it impossible not to love. (That was a serious analogy). If you're looking for a hotel-type living situation with quiet bedrooms, down comforters and ample space, the Baccarat is not your hostel. However, if you're looking for the best hostel staff and a big population of fellow backpackers, Baccarat is as good as they come. And if you're a seasoned backpacker, it doesn't take long to discover that the staff and the hostelmates overshadow the physical amenities every time. Once you stop lying to yourself and admit that you're in Nice to drink and sunbathe, you'll realize that the Baccarat is your best option by a long shot. The hostel is ten minutes by foot from Place Massena, Old Town and the beaches, and the minor walk is outweighed by the staff and hostelmates you'll find at the Baccarat.

i *Dorms €20-40; Private rooms €50-80.* ⏰ *Lockout from 3am-6am (though if the staff know you, they'll let you in).*

HOTEL ANTARES

5 avenue Thiers   ☎04 3 88 22 87

If the hotel Baccarat is the slightly mangy dog with the happy, vibrant personality, the Antares is that dog's slightly less mangy, slightly less vibrant brother. (Yay! More dog references). As a sister hotel of the Baccarat, the Antares operates similarly. The prices are comparable, as are the amenities. The two hostels are linked by a courtyard and share a kitchen for guest-use. The Antares faces the train station, which is convenient for arrival but slightly less appealing because of the view and the sounds. It is under ten mins by foot from the beach, Old Town, and Place Massena, making its location incredibly convenient. The Antares has a spacious lobby and resembles that of a real hotel more than the Baccarat. However, the lack of a "chill-out room" gives the hotel slightly less of a sense of community (though many clever Antarians mooch off of Baccarat's common space, blending in with the Baccaratians and making friends in the process).

i *Dorms: €20 -30; Private rooms: €70-90.* ⏰ *Curfew 3-6am.*

nice

the narrow alleyways and soaking in the colorful architecture of Southern France is a great experience.

The must-sees in Old Town are many – the Opera House that watches over the beach with the same name, the Palais Lascaris that houses the world's weirdest musical instruments, and Fennochio's famous glacier (or gelateria for the

Italians). If you have the time, the best way to experience Old Town is to walk into the center and get lost. Each narrow alleyway includes a variety of small mom and pop shops, from art dealers, to incense vendors, to yes, even a sex shop. More importantly, Old Town is the hub of Nice's nightlife. Bars, discotechs, clubs, it's all in Old Town.

Old Town's charm is matched by convenience as it lies smack in the middle of Massena Square and Garibaldi Square. The further towards the latter you find yourself, the quieter and less touristy the streets become. The restaurants in this area will cost a bit less and the service will be a bit better, but you'll miss out on the people-watching that the more touristy areas of Old Town are great for.

MUSEUM OF MODERN AND CONTEMPORARY ART   MUSEUM
Place Yves Klein   ☎497 13 42 01 http://www.mamac-nice.org/

The Museum of Modern and Contemporary Art is a behemoth of modern art and architecture sitting just to the east of Old Town. The museum's layout itself is a work of art and it's worth a visit just to wander about in the garden outside. Built in the shape of a square, the museum sits three stories tall with galleries on every floor. Each corner of the square features large, spacious exhibits filled with works of art ranging from paintings, to cleverly arranged trash, to an old desk with various objects on top (or maybe that was just the reception desk… modern art is weird). In the middle of the museum is a courtyard filled with interesting sculptures such as giant mobiles and a loch ness monster created out of shattered mirrors. Behind the museum is a sprawling garden with statues, the most notable of which is a giant human head also in the shape of a square.

The art inside is interesting to say the least, but as anyone who's been to a modern art museum will tell you, it's not for everyone. There is, however, a feature of the Museum of Modern and Contemporary Art that is for everyone (except maybe those with a fear of heights) and that's the 360 degree panoramic view of all of Nice from the top of the museum. Just like the layout below, the roof of the museum features walkways across the perimeter of the building's roof with lookout points on all four corners, one of which is adorned with a rainforest-like garden named after the garden of Eden.

Logistically, the museum is a student's paradise. It's entirely free. It's air-conditioned. It's in the center of Nice and within walking distance from almost everything. And last but not least, the cafeteria serves alcohol (as does essentially every place in Nice). Stop by on a cloudy day when the beach seems less appealing and browse some of France's best works of modern art – you have nothing to lose. Literally. It's free. What do you have to lose?

i Admission is free, Guided tours for €5. ☒ Open 10am-6pm. Everyday except Monday.

PLACE MASSENA   SQUARE
Place Massena, or Massena Square, is the epicenter of downtown Nice that connects the beaches of the Promenade des Anglais to Old Town and the hostels to the North. The square is as spacious and well thought-out as it is beautiful, making for a fantastic place to wander. During the daytime, the square buzzes with tourists and locals alike, snapping photos, commuting, and lazing about on the benches.

In the center of the square, a giant statue of Poseidon stands in the middle of a beautiful stone fountain and watches over the Avenue D'Anglaterre to the north. To his right lies a plaza erupting with streams of water inhabited by both children and sweaty tourists. To the left, a similar plaza emits cool vents of steam for those who, for some reason or another, can't commit to slightly more moisture. Straight ahead, along the Avenue D'Anglaterre, naked man-statues crouch in different poses atop metal pillars that glow in different colors throughout the night. The combination of these statues with the one of Poseidon in the center

creates a borderline overwhelming amount of naked men in the square, which I guess can be entertaining if that's what you're into.

The tram runs through the middle of the square and is a quick way to get around but the best way to experience Place Massena is by foot. The square is within walking distance of most everything you'd want to see and the real experience comes from immersing yourself in the crowds of the square.

The square is free (obviously), but the shops and restaurants surrounding it will likely lure you in at least for a moment. The entrance to Old Town borders the Southeast side of the square and the beach lies a few hundred meters to the South of Poseidon. Grab your swimming trunks, some walking shoes, and a few spare euros and hit the square for a taste of all things Nice.

PALAIS LASCARIS   MUSEUM
15 rue Droite ☎493 62 72 40 http://nice.fr/Culture/Musees-et-expositions/Le-palais-Lascaris

The Palais Lascaris is a fun little museum tucked into the winding side streets of Old Town. But be warned: it's difficult to find, as despite the beautiful and ornate paintings of of its anterior, its outer appearance is unremarkable and easy to miss (insert joke about ex-girlfriend here). If you manage to find the palace, the scattered rooms inside are exquisitely decorated and entertaining to browse through. Some rooms appear to be turned upside down—expertly woven carpets with detailed murals sewn in adorn the walls, and intense, beautiful frescos are strewn across the ceilings. In other rooms, you'll find the typical paintings of an old rich person with interspersed musical instruments that you've almost undoubtedly never seen before. In fact, the original inhabitant of the Palais Lascaris was a collector of rare and interesting musical instruments, which is one of the primary reasons for the preservation of the museum today. If you're interested in browsing through the world's largest collection of the world's smallest violins, this is the place to go.

If rare and exotic instruments isn't your cup of tea, the Palais Lascaris is still quite a visual treat. The artwork lining the walls, ceilings, and essentially every surface of the building is expertly painted and impossibly ornate. Depictions of Greek mythology tower above you as you sneak past sculptures of ancient biblical women. And even many of the instruments themselves are painted with colorful murals.

For residents of the U.S. or students under 26 years of age, the entrance to the museum is free. Guided tours are available, but are entirely in French and are geared towards the field trips of 8 year-old schoolchildren that they're overrun with and are consequently not recommended. Access to the palace is limited to bipedal organisms (namely humans with legs) as the entrance is not accessible by car or bus and the primary focus of the palace is up a few flights of stairs. Nonetheless, for those tackling the palace on foot, the museums convenient location right in the heart of Old Town makes it easy to visit.

i *Free admission. Guided tours for €5. ☼ Open 10am-6pm every day but Tuesday. Closed on holidays.*

PROMENADE DES ANGLAIS   STREET
Promenade des Anglais   http://en.nicetourisme.com/promenade-des-anglais

The Promenade des Anglais lines the southern coast of France and looks out onto the Mediterranean Sea. The Niçois Travel Bureau calls it the "most famous promenade in the world," and between the sculptures, palm trees, and beaches you'll quickly see why. The building of the promenade was originally proposed by the wealthy English vacationers who spent their winters in Nice to avoid the cold weather back home. This in turn led to its name, translated from French as: "the promenade of the English."

france

The coastline along the promenade is packed with beach-goers of all walks of earth, soaking up the sun on a variety of public and private beaches. The common motif amongst them all, however, is rocks. Along the promenade's coast you won't find any sand, as the beaches consist of medium-sized pebbles. In the hotter months, these will heat up quite a bit and you'll be given the luxury of choosing whether you'd rather burn your feet by walking slowly along the coals or bruise them by stumbling across them quickly. On the bright side, the water is objectively perfect; cool enough to be refreshing while warm enough fend off any shivers.

Depending on your location, the side of the promenade opposite the beach will change from parks, to restaurants, to the famous Nice Opera House. If your ADHD kicks in and walking along the promenade is too slow, clearly labeled bike lanes allow you to triple the speed of your promenade-viewing pleasure. For the best view of the promenade in all its glory, take a hike up Castle Hill towards the chateau. The entire walk is lined with jaw dropping views of the coast and the steep incline will help you burn off enough calories to improve your beach body for your afternoon dip.

i Free, Prices vary for private beach admission. ☼ Open all day, every day. Skinny dipping at night is borderline legal and worth the rush.

FOOD

Nice has a bit of everything in terms of food, and since there's so much competition for tourists' hard-earned cash, most restaurants bring their A game. Old Town is saturated with restaurant after restaurant and while you could subsist off of Fennochio's 100+ flavors of glace during your stay, we suggest you try a few other options (and then subsist off of Fennochio's 100+ flavors of glace).

FENOCCHIO	ICE CREAM $
2 Place Rosetti	☎493 80 72 52 http://fenocchio.fr/
6 Rue de la Poissonerie	☎493 62 88 80

Fenocchio is Nice's famous Glacier (the French word for gelateria) which serves more than 100 different flavors of glace. Choices range from the basic (think chocolate and vanilla) to the more eccentric (think avocado, beer, or Irish whiskey). However, even the most basic flavors have variations that make deciding what to order a nightmare, albeit a great nightmare to have. In addition to chocolate, the gelateria offers dark chocolate, cacao, chocolate chili, mocha, chocolate-ginger, chocolate-orange, and other chocolate based flavors (the best of which is obviously cacao). Given that there are literally 100+ flavors, you would be remiss not to try one of the more eccentric ones. Speculoos is flavored after the gingerbread cookie butter spread and is objectively the greatest tasting substance known to man. A popular flavor amongst the staff is pecan and maple syrup, which is also delectable. As a rule of thumb, you can't go wrong here unless you order the olive flavor in which case you still may not have gone wrong, we just haven't tried it ourselves.

Fenocchio exists in two separate locations which are located just far enough apart for you to finish your first helping of glace before arriving at the next location for seconds (we see what you did there, Fenocchio...) The prices are reasonable (€2.50 for one scoop and €1.50 for each additional scoop) and especially when you give up on eating real food and decide to subsist on Fenocchio's glace alone. It's possible and it's recommended, and we'll even allow you a few cheat days when you can add alcohol into your diet to supplement the ice cream.

i 1 scoop €2.50. Each additional scoop is €1.50. ☼ Open daily 9am-12am. (Poissonerie location closed Tuesdays).

STUZZICO

4 Rue St. Gaetan

PIZZA $$

☎493 92 70 42

Drunchies joints in Nice are few and far between. A typical night out lasts 'til around 2 am and once you stumble out of the bar looking for something greasy that you'll likely regret in the morning, it can be a bit heartbreaking to realize the lights of your favorite kebab stop are out. Fortunately for you, there's Stuzzico. This hole-in-the-wall Italian pizzeria is just a few hundred yards away from Wayne's and Pompeii, making the time frame between your last beer and your first slice conveniently short. Although the actual quality of the pizza is mostly irrelevant to you at that point in the night, you can sleep soundly knowing that, unlike everyone else, the determined field researchers of Let's Go tasted Stuzzico while sober, and it has our stamp of approval.

Stuzzico itself is actually a fully functioning restaurant during the daytime. The seating is mostly indoors with ample space and a pleasant, if not the most fancy, atmosphere. As the sun sets, the staff close up shop, and serve delicious foodstuff out of the exterior counter. You can browse the available toppings (flavors?) and order from the sidewalk. For obvious reasons (aka everyone is drunk when they order), there is no outdoor seating at night. The building across the street however, has a wide ledge conveniently placed at butt-height. This is where the majority of nightclub escapees choose to eat, as is apparent by the greasy paper plates littering the ground in the immediate area. While cheap pizza at midnight in a narrow alleyway with standing room only may sound depressing while sober, all you'll really understand of that sentence while drunk is the word "pizza," which is just as well, as you won't regret a Stuzzico slice.

i Slices: €3.50 Euro; Small Pizza: €7-10; Large: €11.50-15. ◵ Open daily 10am-12am (though tends to close later depending on the circumstances).

LA MAMA

17 Rue Pairolière

NIÇOISE $$$

☎493 85 70 85

La Mama is your go-to for French food specific to Nice. Plates from this seaside city (say that 10 times fast) range from deep fried zucchini fritters with a hint of lemon juice to decadent beef stew poured over polenta. If you have a few spare euros, the menu prix fixe runs about €24 but will provide an entree (appetizer), a plat (real entree), and a dessert (dessert). If that type of cash makes your wallet sad, opt for the mussels instead. They're so fresh they're almost alive, will run you half the price of the menu prix fixe, and can be prepared a variety of different ways. What's more–they come in a really cool cauldron so you can feel like an underwater witch when you eat them (if you want to do that… you might not).

La Mama's atmosphere adds to its quiet French charm in the same way its food does. It's tucked away behind Place Garibaldi (the significantly less touristy of the two plazas) and is hidden along a tiny winding alleyway. The seating is primarily outside and the only other inhabitants of the street are other folks eating dinner in the same fashion. Overall, the restaurant is a cute and secluded way to experience Niçoise food and culture while distancing yourself a bit from the mob of Old Town. You can also justify a trip here as French lesson, as the menus are written entirely in French, and only one of the waiters knows English (though this is not atypical for a Niçoise restaurant. If you're going to splurge on dinner, you may as well do so in an authentically French fashion.

i €10-30. ◵ Open daily 11:30am-10pm.

LE CIRCUIT

29 Palace Saetone

BREAKFAST $

☎493 88 94 93

Le Circuit is your best value-per-cost breakfast in Nice assuming you eat more than a single egg when you wake up. This simple little cafe overlooks a side street roundabout and has a sunny, pleasant atmosphere. It is entirely family-run and the staff is enthusiastic about their customers and will often sit and chat with the regulars with a cup of espresso or a warm croissant.

The food is superb and for the money it costs, can't be beat within the limits of the city. Crepes will run anywhere from €2 - €7.50 but the greatest feature of Le Circuit is the "breakfast." Not only is it the only title on the menu in English, but its also a complete breakfast unlike the average French cafe's misleading title for a piece of bread and a cup of coffee. For €7.50 you can get a cup of orange juice, an espresso or cafe americain, half a baguette with butter and jam, and an omelet (or sunny side up eggs). For breakfast in France, that's about as much physical food-mass you can get for €7.50, and if you're still hungry, you can either start your diet right then and there or head over to the McDonalds a few blocks away and binge eat your problems away (we've all been there, its just more sad on vacation). The bottom line is this: If you, like most people, wake up hungry, and if you, like most students, wake up poor, Le Circuit is a gem of a breakfast joint. When you find yourself frequenting it, you'll know who to thank.

i Coffee €2. Crepes from €2. Full breakfasts from €6.

CREPERIE BRETONNE
CREPES $
85 Avenue du 3 Septembre
☎493 78 20 02

The Creperie Bretonne is one of the more perplexing cafes in the area as the entire operation from seating, to taking orders, to cooking and even cleaning seems to be undertaken by one single man. This feat is more impressive considering the quality of the food, the actual size of the cafe, and the reviews that the creperie gets. While not exactly in Nice proper, the creperie is located just down the street from the bus stop in Cap d'Ail. What this means for the creperie is that it gets a lot of visits from passersby. What this means for you is that you can enjoy one of the best crepes of your life on you way to Plage Mala.

The first thing you'll need to understand about the Creperie Bretonne (and all French creperies for that matter), is the two distinct categories of crepes: sweet or savory. The savory crepes here are much like breakfast sandwiches and often include delicious breakfast ingredients such as eggs, ham, cheese, mushrooms, etc. They're somewhat like the French interpretation of the omelet (which the Creperie Bretonne also serves). These crepes are not so much a means to an end when you're hungry, but rather a work of art in and of themselves. Perfectly sculpted crepes dripping with meat and cheese are the best way to wake up. If you're still hungry (which you won't be, but remember that the meal isn't over until you hate yourself), try one of the dessert crepes. These feature assorted fruit jams, chocolate spread, or even just plain sugar for those who like to get straight to the point.

i Crepes €4-8. Coffee €1.50.

NAN KEBAB
KEBABS $
Rue de Belgique

Nan Kebab is somewhat of a hybrid kebab place with a creative take on kebabs. Here the kebabs are wrapped up in nan, a type of thick pita bread with melted cheese baked into the inside. The result is interesting, filling and separates Nan Kebab from the three other kebab vendors on that street alone. Nan Kebab is also fairly cheap, as a kebab, fries and drink will run just under €8 (okay that's not that cheap but you're in Nice and beggars can't be choosers).

Besides the price, the other tangible benefit to Nan Kebab is its location. Most hostels are situated roughly ten min north from Place Massena, and the majority of the best food venues in Nice are around Old Town. If you need a quick bite and are teetering on the edge of a hypoglycemic coma, Nan Kebab is just around the corner from most hostels in the area and will happily fill you're stomach for just a few euros. It's worth noting, however, that the staff here

nice

doesn't speak English, which poses a slight difficulty in terms of ordering. Don't be surprised if what you think you ordered isn't what you really ordered and consequently isn't what you get. Regardless, the mystery adds to the fun and most meals on the menu are delicious anyway.

i Kebabs €5 (+€1 for fries, +€1 for drink). ⏰ Open daily 10am-8pm.

PLANET SUSHI   SUSHI $$

42 blvd Jean Jaures   ☎497 08 08 08 http://www.planetsushi.fr/restaurant/planet-sushi-nice/
Planet Sushi is not exactly what you'd expect when dining out in Nice but the set up of the restaurant is too interesting to pass up with out trying. The venue is something straight out of Lost in Translation (aka Tokyo), with its clean white walls, neon pink lights, and purple chairs. Seating is available outside and in, but the real experience comes from sitting at the sushi bar. The sushi bar is in the middle and left side of the restaurant and has chairs on each side facing one another. In the middle, a conveyor belt continuously runs in front of your place setting, transporting little plates of sushi by your nose and begging you to snatch one. The plates are color coded according to three apparent criteria: 1. How fancy the sushi looks, 2. How good the sushi is, and 3. Price.

Planet Sushi's interesting set up does, however, come with a few drawbacks. First of all, you have no idea what you're eating as none of the plates are labeled. This is not a huge issue, but it can be disconcerting to bite into a piece of sushi hoping for fish and getting a mouthful of cream cheese. The second issue is that you can't really tell how long each sushi roll has been on the conveyor belt. There's a frightening chance that, against all odds, one little California roll missed everyone's chopsticks for the past four hours and now you're the shmuck who's going to eat it. You pay for Planet Sushi for the atmosphere, and the sushi, though not the greatest you'll ever eat, is an added bonus. Not the best decision for the budget-travel backpacker, but a fun decision nonetheless.

i Meals €10-25. ⏰ Open daily 11am-11pm.

GRANNY'S CRÊPERIE ET SALON DE THÉ   CAFE $

5, place de l'Ancien Sénat
If your grandmother was a little bit eccentric, had a house in rural France that you visited every summer, and collected colorful knickknacks, this cafe would probably remind you of her. Granny's is located right in the middle of Old Town, just past the flower market and around the corner. It's in a slightly less trafficked area and is tucked into shady alcove that will help you escape the heat and the noise. Vintage toy robots line the walls and the menu is written on a giant toy xylophone, causing flashbacks to a time when your parents paid for all your meals and you didn't know what having a job meant.

Seating is entirely outside, and the patio is fenced in by an array of plants on one side and a boutique toy store on the other. The tables are a soft yellow and the chairs are covered in sun-bleached pink and yellow cushions, ultimately encasing the cafe in a warm, comfortable aura (unless like, you hated your grandma or something). The crepes are tasty but won't make your head explode with amazement. Though in such a popular area of Nice, and for a measly €3-€7, Granny's crepes are worth a bite.

i Crepes from €3-7. Coffee €2. Open daily 10am-5pm.

NIGHTLIFE

Nightlife in Nice can be a bit picky and a bit sporadic. As many of locals will be quick point out, backpackers in Nice don't know where to go, so the best bar or club on a given night generally tends to be the one that the most backpackers accidentally wander into...Nonetheless, Wayne's, Pompeii, and Checkpoint are the most consistent and generally the best options. Weekends tend to usher in uncomfortably

france

crowded dance floors making week nights more comfortable options at the popular hangouts. Unlike the nocturnal discotheques of Madrid, nightlife in Nice slows down after 2am, with only a handful of options open later than that. Your best bet is to pre-game with your hostel friends (you've made friends, haven't you?) and then venture down to Old Town to scope out the best venue for the night.

WAYNE'S BAR & RESTAURANT
RESTAURANT, BAR

15 Rue de la Prefecture ☎493 13 46 99 www.Waynes.fr

Wayne's is more or less the heart and soul of Nice's young adult nightlife. Catering to backpackers and locals alike, you'll be hard pressed to spend a night out in Nice without ending up at Wayne's at least for a drink or two. Among the hostel community, it has the famous reputation of being "the bar where everyone dances on the tables and chairs." This reputation is entirely well deserved, as the average night at Wayne's is distinctly similar to the old playground game where you can't touch the ground because it's lava.

Most nights feature live music based mostly around alternative rock cover bands, which is typical of Niçoise nightlife and a welcome break from the thumping bass of a discotech. The staff aren't so much friendly as they are forgiving – the sound of broken glass accompanies the bad on most every song – but we hope that you're not heading to the bar with the intention of hanging out with the bartender anyways.

Wayne's is right in the middle of Old Town, as with much of Nice's nightlife, making it easy to access and easy to leave if it's having an off night (be wary of weekends, as it often gets uncomfortably crowded). Drinks are fairly expensive and a cheap beer or a shot will run you upwards of €5 with a mixed drink cashing in at around €7. As such, most folks will solve this cost conundrum with a serious pregame, leaving the necessity for only a drink or two once at Wayne's. Finally, its peak hours are from about 12am til 2am when the bar closes. Nice's nightlife is a testament to the adage, early to bed, early to rise, makes a man healthy, wealthy, and… not hungover.

i No cover charge. Beers € 5+; shots and mixed drink €7+. ⏰ Open daily 10am-2am.

BULLDOG PUB POMPEII
PUB

16 Rue de l'Abbaye ☎699 29 89 10 https://www.facebook.com/16abbayepompei

Bulldog Pub Pompeii has a bit more of a club feel than Wayne's, if only in name (note: the common vernacular name is just Pompeii). There is more open space and the live music is similar, if not a bit better, (think Kings of Leon cover band with a lady singer who sings only in French). The pub is separated into three distinct areas, all with a very specific function. In the front is the bar. This is self-explanatory – order your drink, and move on. To the right is the stage and the dance floor, where the majority of the crowd congregates for obvious reasons. Finally, upstairs are the restrooms and the balcony which doubles as a smoking room (read: cigarette tornado). The balcony looks out onto the dance floor and stage, which is actually quite cool, and even more so if your lungs inhale more tobacco and nicotine than they do oxygen.

Pompeii is located in a quiet little alleyway in Old Town and is only about five min from Wayne's by foot. It opens at 11pm and closes at 5am, making it one of the latest available options for nightlife in Nice. Like most of the better bars in the area, drinks aren't cheap. A beer will run you around €7 and a cocktail is a steep €9. The crowd here leans a bit more towards locals than at Wayne's, but backpackers are welcome and often present. To prevent the suffocating crowds that can be found elsewhere, the bouncers here are a bit stricter with regards to maximum capacity. They aren't choosy per se, but they'll make you wait until someone leaves before letting you in if the dance floor is a bit tight. Overall,

Pompeii is a lively and entertaining pub and is a welcome break from Wayne's, which, while also fun, can get a bit monotonous after too many nights in a row.

i *Beer €7; Cocktails €9.* ☼ *Open daily 11pm-5am.*

CHECKPOINT PUB
PUB

2 rue Desboutin   ☎666 39 64 94 http://www.checkpointpub.com/

Checkpoint is the third of the three most popular bars in Nice and resembles your typical Irish Pub (its logo is a green, white, and orange shamrock). Depending on the night, Checkpoint may be the cheapest option for nightlife in Nice. Monday nights provide €.50 glasses of champagne (unfortunately, only for girls). Tuesday night includes a happy hour before midnight that provides €4 pints and €5 cocktails. Wednesday is karaoke night with €2 shots and Thursday night is open mic night with the same happy hour options as Tuesday. Friday and Saturday the drinks will be full price (€5 a beer and €8 per cocktail) and Sunday is back to karaoke, this time offering cocktails instead of shots at €5 a pop.

While Checkpoint can be a bit of a mixed bag with slightly cheaper drink options, the atmosphere is generally a bit lacking when compared to Wayne's or Pompeii. The crowds will be thinner, which is preferable if that's what you're looking for, and if you arrive with some good friends, Checkpoint is a good option for just chilling and chatting. Ruling Checkpoint out would be a disservice as on the occasional odd night, the population of backpackers will congregate here rather than at Wayne's, making Checkpoint the better option by a landslide.

Like all of Nice's nightlife, Checkpoint is in the middle of Old Town, and is therefore easy to get to and easy to bail on if something better calls your name. The pub is friendly to backpackers and locals alike and the ratio between the two varies significantly on a nightly basis. If you're sick of Wayne's or if, for some reason, you'd rather be in Ireland than in the French Riviera, head down to Checkpoint for a pint of Guinness and a chance to make a fool of yourself singing karaoke, even if its not karaoke night.

i *No Cover Charge. Prices vary by night, full prices: €5 beer; €8 cocktails.* ☼ *Open daily 4pm-2:30am.*

OPERA PLAGE
BEACH

Promenade des Anglais

When the financial burden of hitting the bars or clubs becomes too much to bear, the frugal backpacker will join his or her fellow travellers on Opera Beach for cheap wine and chill vibes. Drinking on the beach is inexpensive, fun, and much more intimate than the bar scene in Old Town. What's more, if you drink enough, you'll no longer notice that the beach is entirely pebbles and not sand (on the bright side, you won't get sand in your sneakers while you're there).

While the bars in Nice lack nothing in energy, they do lack somewhat in variety. Hitting Wayne's, Pompeii, or Checkpoint every night can get exhausting (oh poor you) and on a night off when you still want to hang with some friends, the beach is the budget traveller's dream come true. A bottle of rosé or red wine will run you just north of €5 at the local Monoprix and 12 pack of beer can be had for under €8 (those are some appetizing prices).

The beach is conveniently located next to a large body of water. Once your inebriated self becomes uninhibited, strip down to your birthday suit and jump in the water. There is no better icebreaker than an ice bath and once you leave nothing to the imagination, there is nowhere to go but up.

i *Free (well, buy some wine first).*

THE BAY FESTIVAL
FESTIVAL

Promenade des Anglais (Subject to change)   http://thebayfestival.fr

The Bay Festival is an indie electronic music festival featuring lots of international artists such as Bondax, Ryan Hemsworth, Flume, and Cashmere Cat. The festival is targeted heavily towards college-aged delinquents and its location right along the Promenade des Anglais makes for a perfect sun-drenched summer festival. Hit the festival with your friends and vibe out to some chillwave, dreamwave, and all other kinds of waves that make you feel like your floating.

The festival exists in four parts, spanning all of June and then a finale in August. The lineups improve as time passes with the August date boasting the better known artists. As can be expected, the price increases with each event as well, with the first night running you only €16 but the finale costing a pricey €28. The opening acts begin around 6pm and the headliner makes an appearance after 11pm. Liking the festival's Facebook page will conveniently provide you with updates about the whereabouts of the after party, which lasts till the brutal hours of the morning.

While the locations are subject to change, all are within a few minutes of the Promenade des Anglais. Popular venues include Florida Beach and Theatre of Green, both outdoors and both ideal for a festival of this size. Expect just under 1,000 people ready to dance for hours in an intoxicated daze of electro indie-pop.

i Admission €16- 28, depending on date. ☼ Open 6pm-1am.

LE GRAND CAFE DE LYON
BAR

33 Avenue Jean Medecin   ☎493 88 13 17 http://www.cafedelyon.fr/

The Grand Café de Lyon is the most misleading venue you'll find in the nightlife section of Nice. It is not a cafe in the general sense. It is not necessarily nightlife per se. It is not in Lyon. What it is, however, is essentially is a daytime bar with extensive outdoor seating which makes for some of the best people-watching that exists in Nice. Structurally, the cafe is something straight out of a Wes Anderson film. Golden chairs, red neon trim, soft lighting, mirrored walls, and a glassware collection that seems never ending. Furthermore, the infinite selection of beers, cocktails and all forms of alcohol leaves room for experimentation and a trial by error way of getting wasted.

The cafe is located just north of Place Massena along the avenue Jean Médecin, a bustling street populated by both tourists and locals. For the typical backpacker living a few blocks north of the beach, the cafe splits the distance and provides an opportunity to rehydrate on your way to the water.

Anticipating a visit here to be that of a typical cafe will leave you disappointed and hungry as the food is expensive and by no means the cafe's forte. Instead opt for a bottle of Delirium Tremens, a beer named after the hallucinations that occur during alcohol withdrawal. The tastelessness of the name is masked by the tastiness of the beer, which has been frequently hailed as the best beer in the world. While the drinks are more expensive than those in the corner store, the selection is vast and the atmosphere is uniquely enjoyable, making day drinking feel slightly less shameful.

i Beer from €5. Cocktails from €7. Snacks from €3. ☼ Open daily 7am-11pm.

YOUR NEIGHBORHOOD HOSTEL
HOSTELS

Believe it or not, one of your best bets for nightlife (depending on where you're staying of course) is your own hostel. Nice is inherently a tourist's city, and the backpackers that stay there are, for the most part, dirt poor. Somewhere down the line they realized that the best hostels are the ones that allow them to buy alcohol from the liquor store (or any store, because, well, France) and bring it to the hostel to rage. Enter the party hostel – the temporary housing situation for young folks trying to get their drink on without getting their debt on. Thanks to the creation of the party hostel, 8pm til midnight in Nice is all about the hostel pregame. This pregame will vary widely depending on where you're staying, but most good hostels will have some get together or another. Villa St. Exupery

nice

hosts a happy hour while Hotel Baccarat boasts a full-blown champagne party every other night.

The other primary reason why the hostel pregame is an essential part of Nice nightlife is as follows. Backpackers make up a huge portion of the bar and club population on a given night. The average backpacker knows between 0 and 4 fellow backpackers in his or her given city. The average backpacker wants to meet more than just those 0-4 people and this is intrinsically difficult in a crowded nightclub. Thus, the hostel pregame allows people to meet each other and hangout, all with the glorious social lubricant of alcohol. Rolling up to a club solo and sober is an interesting game plan (read: it's a bad game plan). Rolling up to a club with several other inebriated backpackers whom you just met is awesome. Ipso facto, the hostel pregame is as much a necessity as it is a luxury.

i Varies by location. Liquor store beers: €1+; Wine: €5+. ☼ Generally speaking, 8pm-12am.

ESSENTIALS
Practicalities

- **TOURIST OFFICE:** Avenue Thiers - Gare SNCF. (☎892 70 74 07; www.nicetourisme.com. This tourist office is incredibly convenient as it's located directly outside of the train station in Nice. The office provides maps, brochures, and other touristy information and a receptionist is available for interrogation from 8am-8pm.)

- **POST OFFICE:** 21 Avenue Thiers. (Open M-F 8am-7pm and 8am-12pm on Saturday.). Additional post offices are scattered all throughout the city.

- **POSTAL CODE:** 06000

- **EMBASSY:** 7 Avenue Gustave V. (☎04 93 88 89 55; http://www.marseille.usconsolate.gov/nice/.html. Open M-F 9-11:30am and 1:30-4:30pm.)

Emergency

- **POLICE:** 1 Avenue Marechal Foch. (☎492 17 22 22)

- **HOSPITAL:** Hospital Saint Roch. (5 Rue Pierre Devoluy ☎493 62 06 91)

- **PHARMACY:** Pharmacies are located on essentially every street in Nice and are easily spotted due to the flashing neon green crosses out front (no these are not medical marijuana dispensaries).

Getting There

By Plane

Nice-Cote d'Azur (☎08 20 42 33). Shuttles from the airport to the train station run every thirty minutes.

By Train

Gare SNCF Nice-Ville. (Avenue Thiers ☎04 93 14 82 12 www.sncf.com) Trains run to Cannes, Marseille, Monaco, and Paris.

By Bus

Gare Routiere. (5 blvd. Jean Juares ☎04 92 00 42 93) Number 100 bus runs from Nice to Monaco/Menton. Tickets are €1.50 one way.

By Ferry

Corsica Ferries. (☎04 92 00 42 93 corsicaferries.com)

Getting Around

velo Blue (velobleu.org) is much like citybike or other comparable companies. rent a bike for roughly 1 euro per hour and return the bike to any veloblue stand in Nice.

cannes

Cannes is one of three cities along the French Riviera whose net worth wouldn't increase if every notable movie star the world over congregated in the city for a festival. It's also the only city along the French Riviera where this actually happens. Home to the famous Cannes Film Festival, Cannes is a city of glamour, riches, and excess. As a student traveler on a budget, your dollar won't stretch too far here but that doesn't mean you can't have a great time. For those with a lot of money there are three things to do: Shop, lie on the beach, and party. For those without: eliminate the first option and just lie on the beach and party. Or better yet— party on the beach.

Unfortunately, with the glamour and glitz of Cannes comes a bit of superficiality. Poor students in dirty clothes aren't always treated the same as the billionaires and their trophy wives in €6000 designer dresses. As the natives will eloquently inform you: you won't get into any nightclub worth going to unless you're wearing heels or smell like money.

At the end of the day, though Cannes is a little slice of paradise. The beaches are blanketed in soft, imported sand. The restaurants are delicious. The women are beautiful, (and the men are rich if that's what you're into). And if you can sneak your way in, the nightlife is exhilarating. What more could you really want?

SIGHTS

There's quite a lot to do in Cannes, but at the end of the day, no matter how much you read about the culture, and art, and history of the city, you'll spend most of your time at the beach or at the bar. Nonetheless, if you hate the sand and the sun (which not-coincidentally also means that you probably hate world-peace and love communism), there are still some great things to do in Cannes. Below you'll find some tips on the best beaches, the best sights, and the best beaches (see what we did there?).

LE SUQUET
NEIGHBORHOOD

Le Suquet is the old quarter of Cannes located just East of La Croisette. The area is populated primarily with restaurants and tiny boutique shops which, oddly enough for Cannes, aren't selling €5000 designer dresses. Le Suquet starts near the Bay of Cannes which is crowded with multimillion dollar yachts during the summer months. Climbing up the winding streets will eventually lead you to Place de la Castre, the site of the Musee and Eglise de la Castre. This modest hill will also afford you the best view of Cannes without a helicopter or private jet (which is kind of a joke, but not really considering the wealth in this city).

Le Suquet is an attraction in Cannes for a variety of reasons in addition to those mentioned above. First and foremost, while not technically a part of Le Suquet, Midi Plage and the beaches next to it are a few minutes away by foot and are some of the best public beaches in the city. Le Marché Forville takes place within the confines of Le Suquet each morning. The market is a large indoor venue that resembles a train station (without any trains) and hosts a variety of vendors in the morning and early afternoon of most weekdays. The primary focus of the vendors is often fresh fruits and vegetables and the occasional baguette.

All things considered, Le Suquet's primary draw is food. Some of the best restaurants in Cannes are nestled into the neighborhood's narrow winding streets. Bring your camera and your appetite and grab some oysters at Astoux et Brun after your hike back down from Place de la Castre.

cannes

get a room!

There is no shortage of hotels in Cannes, but there are very few which cater to the student traveller. In fact, none of them really cater to students, but some of them are at least kind of affordable. If you're looking to stay along La Croisette be prepared to shell out €1000 per night. A few minutes north however, rooms can be had for under €50 if you play your cards right. Hotel PLM is your best bet on a budget while La Villa Tosca is an upgrade of the same style for a higher price. Whatever you do, just stay away from the Hotel Claremont.

HOTEL PLM

3 rue Hoche   ☎493 38 31 19 http://www.hotel-cannes-plm.com/en/

The Hotel PLM is your best bet in Cannes assuming you can get the right room. It's a small boutique hotel just north of La Croisette and within five minutes by foot from anywhere you'd want to go. Unfortunately, however, it's generally a bit expensive. Rooms start a €50 and up unless you plan ahead and book the "petit single." This room (and I say "room" because there seems to be only one of them), is €35 a night and is more than comfortable enough for a stay in Cannes.

Nonetheless, the PLM is your cheapest option in Cannes. Call ahead, book that petit single, and enjoy your stay. Though on second thought, you probably don't need to call ahead. The petit single will probably be vacant because everyone else visiting the city is rich enough to afford their own bathroom.

i Petit Singles €35; Singles €50.

HOTEL LA VILLA TOSCA

11 rue Hoche   ☎493 38 34 40 http://www.villa-tosca.com/en/

Hotel La Villa Tosca is more or less the older brother of Hotel PLM. They're operated by the same staff, owned by the same person, and are less than 100 meters apart from each other. The primary difference between the two is quality. This doesn't mean that Hotel PLM is bad by any means, it simply means that La Villa Tosca is better. As you can imagine, that also means it's more expensive. La Villa Tosca is probably where your parents would stay in Cannes if they didn't want to empty your college fund, while the PLM is where you'd stay.

Villa Tosca features bigger and better rooms as well as a large, open first floor with a living room, dining room, bar, and the whole works. The location is difficult to beat — the hotel is right on Rue Hoche where many of the better restaurants are. It's 5 mins from La Croisette and the Palais des Festivals, and ten mins from Le Suquet.

The gist of what you need to know is this: La Villa Tosca and the PLM are like genetically similar brothers, with one being the strong, handsome son who makes his parents proud, while the other is more like the runt of the family, but who's still loved by his parents just the same. If you have some extra money, you can't go wrong with La Villa Tosca. It really is just an upgraded version of the PLM. If you're strapped for cash, however, the PLM is everything you need without the bells and whistles of La Villa Tosca.

i Singles: €61-91 (depending on the season); Doubles: €82-125 (depending on season).

CENTRE D'ART LA MALMAISON AT CANNES

47 Blvd. de la Croisette ☎497 06 44 90 http://www.cannes.com/fr/mairie/annuaire-pratique/
lieux/serv_munic/centre-d-art-la-malmaison.html

The Centre d'art La Malmaison is the closest thing there is to a museum for
young adults insomuch as there are no oil paintings of old rich people on the
walls and no statues of greek gods/goddesses. In fact, the museum is dedicated
to contemporary art from the 20th and 21st century and houses an ever-changing
array of interesting exhibits. The most recent exhibition housed more than 100
African tribal sculptures with a variety of works from other artists who sought
inspiration from such sculptures. Featured artists include Picasso and Warhol,
each of whom you should probably have heard of before and if not, you probably
won't enjoy this museum.

The museum itself is rather small but it's centrally located, making a visit
both quick and convenient. Its entrance is along the boulevard de la Croisette
and is hard to miss thanks to the giant and colorful humanoid sculptures
towering over the doorway. The museum exhibits are well arranged, making
an exploration of the artwork on display pleasantly uncomplicated. Finally the
museum is well air-conditioned, which, if nothing else, is always worth a few
minutes of your time.

As is the case with most museums in France, the Centre d'Art la Malmaison
is free for students, which is a welcome relief from the expenses of staying in
Cannes. The museum is great for a quick one-hour break from the beach during
which you can soak up some culture rather than more UV rays—stop by any day
during July or August before 8pm.

i *Full Price: €6; under 25 years old: €3; Students: Free with ID.* ☼ *Closed May & June; July-August
open daily 11am-8pm.*

PLAGE DU MARTINEZ

Hotel Martinez, Rue de la Croisette ☎493 90 12 34
http://cannesmartinez.grand.hyatt.com/en/hotel/home.html

Plage Martinez in and of itself is not necessarily your best bet in terms of beaches
along La Croisette. Yes, it's linked with the famous Hotel Martinez which makes
you feel fancy and all that, but remember that the hotel is famous, not the beach.
Honestly, the beach has good reviews on Trip Advisor probably because those
reviewing it do not understand that all the beaches along La Croisette are not
encapsulated by the title "Plage du Martinez."

Okay, so you shouldn't go to the beach specifically associated with Hotel
Martinez, where should you go instead? Well, the beach slightly east of Plage
Martinez (or left, if you're facing the beach) is one of the best public beaches
along La Croisette. It's technically called Plage Zamenhoff, but that's somewhat
irrelevant. The important aspects of the beach are that it's a) better than the other public beach (Plage Mace), b) less crowded than Plage Mace, and c) totally,
100% free.

If you are looking for a private beach, all of your options along La Croisette
are more or less interchangeable. Baoli Beach is known as the best, but it's also
the most expensive (read: 100 euros for a beach bed). Plage 45 next door to Baoli
is almost identical but really, if you're trying to escape the peasants on the public
beaches, you can't really go wrong with any of the spots along La Croisette.

☼ *Open daily July-August 9:30am-7pm; September-June daily 9:30am-6pm.*

MUSEE DE LA CASTRE

Le Suquet, Rue de la Castre ☎04 93 38 55 26
http://www.cannes.com/fr/culture/musee-de-la-castre.html

The Musee de la Castre exhibits a collection of various works of art and artifacts
from around the world, many of which will provide inspiration for your night-

mares if you were running out of terrifying horror-thoughts. This is only partially a joke as the first exhibit upon entering is a collection of ancient masks from Oceania, the Americas, and the Himalayas, some of which include fragments of (human?) teeth and (human?) bones and all of which vaguely resemble the pig-mask man from Saw II. If you venture past the mask section without turning and running from the museum, the proceeding collections are much less intimidating and range from classical paintings of the French Riviera, to a collection of eclectic musical instruments from every corner of the world.

One of the primary draws of the museum, however, is its location. The museum sits atop Le Suquet, offering the best view of Cannes by a long shot. Outside the entrance to the museum is a quiet courtyard that houses a giant square tower overlooking the city and the ocean. Further out towards the front of the museum lies L'Eglise de la Castre, a beautifully ornate church that is said to have once almost bankrupted the city because of the expenses of the church's interior. Crystal chandeliers, stained glass windows, hanging model sailboats, and iconic religious statues fill the nave to point that borders on excess, which is strangely appropriate for Cannes general theme of indulgence. The church itself is free of charge (while the museum will cost you without a student ID), and it's well worth a peek if you have a few extra minutes.

Overall, a trip atop Le Suquet will run you no more than €6(and will likely be free assuming you're a student). The price, or lack thereof, is well worth the view, museum, and church all in one. Climb up to the top of the hill, take some pictures of the view, take a look at the masks, and then say a prayer in the church on your way out to ask for eternal safety from the masks you just escaped from.

i Full Price €6; Under 25 Years €3; Under 18 or students free. ☾ Open June Tu-Su 10am-1pm and 2pm-6pm; July-August daily 10am-7pm.

LA CROISETTE   STREET
Blvd. de la Croisette

La Croisette is, more or less, the main attraction of Cannes. Its unavoidable centrality to the city makes it a must-see even if you're trying not to as you'll inevitably have to walk along the street to get somewhere else. La Croisette is bookended by the Palais de Festival and the Palm Beach Casino, allowing it to effectively span the coastline just south of anything worth seeing in Cannes.

On one side of the street are the majority of Cannes' private beaches, where a sun bed ranges in price from €6 for the day to north of €100. The beaches on each end of La Croisette are public, and only slightly rockier than the private ones (interesting that works out...). On the other side of the street is the shopping mecca for billionaires the world over. Every high-fashion brand in existence has a storefront along the street in addition to one mediocre gelateria who's ability to afford such expensive real estate is a question for the ages (*cough cough drug front cough*).

In addition to the private beaches and high-end stores, you can also spend even more money along La Croisette at one of the luxury hotels along the street. Buying a sandwich from the Carleton's lobby restaurant will run you almost €50 which is probably comparable if not more expensive than your actual hotel room somewhere else.

As a student traveler, La Croisette is not where you'll want to spend your money. However, a stroll down the promenade will give you a glimpse of the world's richest 1% as they park their Bentley in front of the Hotel Martinez after their multimillion dollar shopping spree. There's no better place to laugh at the ridiculous excess of Cannes while silently wishing you were a trust-fund baby.

i Free (unless, of course, you're a trust fund baby and can afford a sandwich here.

PALAIS DES FESTIVALS

VENUE

Boulevard de la Croisette   ☎492 99 84 00   http://en.palaisdesfestivals.com/

The Palais des Festivals is the building responsible for roughly 90% of the general population's perception of Cannes. This is the venue for the Cannes Film Festival—also known as the only time Hollywood's biggest stars visit a city all at once and actually decrease the city's average annual income per capita. The famous red carpet in front of the venue is the subject of millions of photos populating the hard drives of tourists and paparazzi alike, and the feet that have walked up the steps out front belong to the same superstars whose handprints are embedded in the bricks surrounding the building.

Unfortunately for the average tourist, however, after posing for a photo on the front steps, there's not much else you can do at the Palais des Festivals. The venue is closed to the public and is only open and functioning during one of the many private events held there. There are no guided tours, no public access, no real substance to a visit to the Palais. On the bright side, however, that means there are no entry fees, right?

For the most part, there isn't much entertainment to be had here. Nonetheless, you can spend a few minutes walking around the building without having to go out of your way, as the Palais is central to Cannes most heavily trafficked areas. The building sits essentially between La Croisette and Le Suquet, and is just West of one of Cannes primary public beaches. Cannes' tourist office is located on the ground floor of the Palais, adding to the building's centrality and convenience. Take a look around when you're in the area, but don't spend too much time here.

i Closed to the general public.

CIMITIERE GRAND JAS

CEMETERY

205 Avenue de Grasse   ☎493 99 48 18

The Cimitiere Grand Jas is far from everything that Cannes represents by pretty much every definition of the word "far." Not only will it take you about an hour to walk here from the center of Cannes, but the mentality of this cemetery is so distant from the ethos of everything that Cannes represents. Without sounding too cheesy, Cannes is the embodiment of the accumulation of wealth, while the cemetery towering above the city is a testament to the fact that sooner or later, you will die, and all that money you earned will be for nothing, and everyone will forget you, and then the world will end, and all of your offspring will perish, and there is no God, etc.

Okay maybe that went a little bit too far, but you get the point—the cemetery exists as an interesting yet oddly appropriate juxtaposition to Cannes. A quick trip to the cemetery is a good way of putting some perspective on the mentality of Cannes. Standing in silence and pacing through the peaceful, flower-laden graves prevents you from getting caught up in all of that materialistic superfluity that you'll find on every street corner in Cannes.

Stop by the cemetery, pay your respects to the dead, and if nothing else, enjoy the view of the ocean from atop the hill. Or don't. You're young, you're on vacation, maybe the last thing you want to do is walk between a bunch of spooky tombs and think about all the dead people you know.

i Free.

PLAGE MIDI

BEACH

Boulevard du Midi Jean Hibert

Plage Midi is, by popular opinion, the best public beach in Cannes. Its 5 min separation from La Croisette is enough to make all the difference in terms of crowds and real estate. The beach itself is much larger than either of the two

cannes

public beaches that bookend La Croisette, and the human per square-foot-of-beach ratio is far more favorable than elsewhere.

What really separates Plage Midi from the rest of the public beaches in Cannes, however, are the rafts. Roughly 200 meters offshore giant square rafts are tethered to the ground. The rafts exist for your diving pleasure or, for the more boring folks who are opposed to getting sand in their unmentionables, they exist for sunbathing without sandbathing.

The other benefit to Plage Midi is the view from the shore. Rather than staring at the yachts and private beaches that surround the public beaches of La Croisette and serve as reminders of how much money you don't have, the shoreline of Plage Midi looks out towards the mountains to the west of Cannes. In the evening, the sun begins to sink behind the mountains, reducing them to silhouettes reflecting the blue color of the water, which is actually really cool despite how corny it sounds in a sentence. Finally, the lack of a port between Plage Midi and those same mountains eliminates any reason for yachts to anchor between the two, giving you an unobstructed view and allowing you to forget the likelihood that you'll never own a yacht yourself. Ultimately, if you're heading to the beach and not planning to spend some cash for a seat at any of the private ones, Plage Midi is your best bet.

i Free, with various public beaches along the same street.

FOOD

Restaurants in Cannes vie over tourists' money and, as such, maintain quite high standards as far as food goes. This being the case, however, you're not gonna leave any of the best restaurants without shelling out quite a few euros. Unless you know where to go. Some of the choices are obvious ones and though they may be touristy (where in Cannes isn't), they're at least worth a bite. Our list has got everything, from the 3am dive, to the best seafood in the city.

LE PAIN QUOTIDIEN
BREAKFAST $$

5 square Merimée ☎497 06 53 78 http://www.lepainquotidien.fr/en/store/cannes

Okay okay, this place is about as authentically France as Au Bon Pain but it's still some of the best breakfast you're going to find in the area (unless you're planning to spend more on breakfast than you did for your hotel room...) The petit dejeuner comes with an espresso, a glass of fresh orange juice, a basket of freshly baked bread, and either a croissant or some pan au chocolat (a croissant with chocolate inside – it's awesome). The bread is served with a variety of homemade jams and marmalades with an occasional jar of dutch chocolate spread (aka fancy Nutella). The best thing about the breakfast here, however, might be the price tag – the whole shebang will run you just south of €10 which is on the lower end of the spectrum for a hearty meal in Cannes.

The location of Le Pain Quotidien is about as convenient as it gets. The cafe sits across the street from Le Palais de Festival and is within crawling distance (read: really close by) to the beach, le Suquet, and La Croisette. Convenient location aside, the interior of the cafe is similar if not identical to every picture in your Pinterest folder titled: "Dream Kitchen." The walls are bare and the brickwork underneath peaks through in patches, giving the cafe a homely, comfortable feel. The kitchen is open and pots and pans hang down from racks on the ceiling, and a soft light filters in from the windows. The whole atmosphere is like comfort food for your eyes. Seating is available both inside and out, with an additional communal table for parties bigger than six or for strangers looking for friends. Finally, apart from their bread, Le Pain Quotidien's signature is their assortment of tartines, or Belgian open faced sandwiches. And if you've never

france

eaten a sandwich before, there is an informational graphics conveniently placed along the side wall explaining the proper way to do so, (just in case).

i Breakfast from €8; lunch and dinner from €10. ⏰ Open daily 8am-11pm.

LE CIRQUE
FRENCH $$

30 Rue Hoche ☎493 30 02 38 lecirquecannes.fr

The French equivalent for the English term "hipster" is "bobo," and Le Cirque is where the "bobos" eat. It's a cool, under the radar restaurant with great food and relaxed vibes. The only thing slightly non-hipster about the restaurant is its lack of a vegetarian/vegan/gluten-free/trending-diet-fad option. The menu's entree section is titled "Terre & Mer" and is essentially a list of different dead animals prepared in fancy ways, whether they once lived on land ("terre") or in the sea ("mer"). Despite the unappetizing tone of the previous sentence, the dead animals served here are actually incredibly delicious, and the menu is less macabre than the review here (due to a possible error in translating the menu to english, one of the listed plates is titled "smiling lamb").

The restaurant itself is affordable in comparison to the rest of Cannes. Entrees range between €10 and €20 but never rise above the latter. Le Cirque boasts an extensive wine list as well, so if you are a vegetarian and the menu turns you off, you could just drink until you either leave the restaurant or become a carnivore again. Finally, the atmosphere of the restaurant adds substantially to its charm. Unique newspaper sketches of circus acts line the walls to create a lighthearted, colorful decor. Seating is available outside along the street with plenty of space inside as well. Escape from the touristy eats alongside La Croisette or near Le Palais de Festival and grab a bite of something that used to bite things itself at Le Cirque.

i Entrees €10; Plats €15. Drinks from €6. ⏰ Open M-F 9am-midnight, Sa 1-10pm, Su noon-2am.

AU PETIT CREUX D'AZUR
RESTAURANT $

17 Rue du Maréchal Foch ☎664 82 55 69 https://www.facebook.com/auptitcreuxdazur

Hallelujah! The concept of 24-hour food joint does exist in the French Riviera after all! Well, it almost exists. Au Petit Creux d'Azur, the Cannes equivalent to a food truck, is open every day from 2am till 8pm. Not quite 24-hours, but as close as it gets in Cannes. This tiny sandwich shop and bakery exists just across the street from the train station and serves an interesting customer base consisting of police officers, homeless people, and heavily intoxicated college students (who on certain night could also be mistaken for homeless people).

The "restaurant" could hardly be called glamorous, but it satisfies the specific needs of the late night binge eating population who, for the most part, are looking for anything but glamorous restaurants. The food is an interesting creation in itself. The "menu" revolves around a series of sandwiches which are either flatbread paninis or footlong baguette subs depending on the night as well as your comprehension of French. The lack of seating turns every meal into a "to-go" meal, consequently meaning that an order of fries ensures that they are jammed right into the heart of the sandwich, which is sometimes surprising but mostly delicious.

In addition to the sandwiches, Au Petit Creux d'Azur also sells baked goods out of the front display. While the majority of the pastries here will be far from the freshest you'll find in France, the thick slices of chocolate cheesecake are nothing to shake a stick at. For the budget traveler living far away from La Croisette, this tiny cafe will likely be closer to your headquarters as it's located towards the more reasonably-priced end of Cannes. Sandwiches run about €5, providing a serious meal for a not-so-serious price tag.

i Sandwiches €5. Pastries €3. ⏰ Open daily 2am-8pm.

RAINBOW KEBAB KEBAB $

22 Rue Jean Juares

Rainbow Kebab has one of the best value-per-cost ratios for food vendors in Cannes, and we're talking both quantity and quality here. €5.50 will get you a big Kebab Galette and€ 8 will get you an XL Kebab Galette. Both options are filling and satisfying, and combo meals exist with fries and drinks included for marginally more cash.

Rainbow Kebab is conveniently located just across the street from the train station, making it easy to access and easy to find—just don't mix it up for the other kebab stop a few storefronts down, as you'll leave there disappointed and with a lighter wallet. The staff here are friendly and speak English, which may not be essential but if you're not a kebab veteran, the ordering process goes a lot more smoothly when you can ask questions in a language you understand. For example: No, hot sauce, garlic sauce, and ketchup don't mix well—but it's easy to understand why one would think that. (Just kidding... What were you thinking?)

As a general rule of thumb, the farther you get from La Croisette, the less expensive the restaurants become. As a rule for your other thumb, kebabs are generally cheaper than pretty much anything else in the South of France. And finally, as a rule for your tastebuds, Rainbow Kebab is one of the better options for cheap food in Cannes. Part with your precious €6 and grab a kebab before catching the train.

i Kebabs €5.50; with fries: €6.50; with fries and drink €7.50. ⏱ Open M-Sa 11am-12am.

GELATERIA DI TORINO L'ILE DE GLACE GELATO $

2 avenue de Grasse https://www.facebook.com/pages/

L%C3%AEle-de-la-glace/459831490714690

There are a lot of options for glace in Cannes, but an overwhelmingly large amount of them will leave you disappointed. Taking a walk past the train station and into the less touristy sector of Cannes will solve this problem quickly and effectively. L'Ile de Glace is owned by Giovanni Torino who makes all his glace in-house and only from the ingredients he deems fresh enough to flavor his incredible boules (scoops) of frozen sugar-milk. As a result, you won't find an overwhelming array of flavors, but those that are offered are guaranteed to satisfy your craving. The sorbet has bits of fresh fruit mixed inside and the sweeter, chocolatey flavors have bits of magical tasty goodness mixed inside.

Since the glacier is located a few minutes north of La Croisette, the prices won't bleed you as much as the more touristy glaciers will. This comes in handy since you can then pay the same amount for twice the glace and then forego eating a real, more nourishing meal but who cares because #vacation. One scoop will run you €2.50 with an additional €1 for each extra scoop. You can attempt the L'Ile de Glace challenge in which you pay full price for each flavor and if you can finish all of it in under one hour you win a really bad stomachache and an awesome sense of accomplishment. (Note: This isn't a real challenge but the temptation to try it will probably be there anyway now that we've given you the idea).

i 1 Scoop €2.50; additional Scoops €1. ⏱ Open daily 11am-9pm.

AT'HOME CAFE CAFE $

11 Rue Felix Faure ☎650 09 42 44

At'Home Cafe is tucked into a quiet alleyway just outside Le Suquet and invites passersby in for a quick bite. Maybe you got sick of Le Pain Quotidien and wanted something more authentic to start your day, or maybe you got a bit lost in your search for Place de la Castre and wandered in for directions and a cup of coffee. Either way, you can't go too wrong with At'Home Cafe, but you haven't really gotten it right.

At'Home Cafe is quiet, tiny, and a bit cramped, which could be cute if it panned out the right way but after bumping into the door with your arm every time you try to stab a piece of your crepe with you fork it becomes a bit less cute and a bit more confusing as to why they put a table so close to the entrance. Furthermore, hopefully your date enjoys a lengthy game of footsie, as there's only room for one pair of legs under the table, and those belong to the table.

On the bright side, At'Home seems to reject the French idea of eating only a piece of bread and an espresso for breakfast. €8.50 will buy you a breakfast complete with an omelette, a basket of bread, and a coffee, which, for Cannes in not a bad deal. The value of the food, however, is unfortunately not matched by taste. The food isn't bad by any means, it just isn't great, and if you're in Cannes, a city where the food is generally above average, you'd be unwise to settle for anything less.

i Breakfast from €5. Espresso €1.50.

RESTAURANT ASTOUX & BRUN

RESTAURANT $$$$

27 rue Félix Faure et Louis Blanc ☎493 39 21 87 http://www.astouxbrun.com

Restaurant Astoux & Brun is one of the most popular seafood restaurants in Cannes, and for good reason. The restaurant specializes in shellfish and doubles as a take-out vendor from the side street for those with enough hubris to think they can out-cook the chefs who work here. The restaurant is located between Le Suquet and La Croisette and the outdoor seating, which includes a view of the port, is also great for people-watching.

Despite being a bit touristy, the food here is delicious. Mussels are a specialty of Cannes (as well as the Riviera as a whole) and you'd be remiss not to try them. Keep in mind that the locals use one mussel as a pincher to grab the rest rather than a fork— follow suit or risk looking like the clueless tourist that you truly are. In addition to the food, the atmosphere is uniquely charming. All of the tables have original paintings of different fish, and the elevated platters of various crustaceans will get your saliva flowing before you can even read the menu.

The only downside to Astoux & Brun is the price tag. You can get away with a giant plate of mussels for less than €15 but ordering anything else like oysters will quickly exceed your budget. Nonetheless, grab a seat on the terrace, order up a plate of mussels and practice using a pair of Riviera chopsticks (using the mussels to pinch other mussels like we talked about).

i Entrees range from €15 to €50 . Order the mussels, seriously. ☒ Open daily 12pm-2:30pm and 7pm-11pm.

NIGHTLIFE

As you now know, Cannes is alluring for three reasons: the beaches, the shopping, and the nightlife. It's also well-known for being an incredibly wealthy city. And anyone with the math skills of a first grader and the common sense of a fourth grader knows that wealth + parties = good parties. Unfortunately, anyone with the common sense of a fourth grader also knows that wealth + parties = expensive parties. The nightlife in Cannes is some of the best in the French Riviera, but indulging in the fun will take a serious toll on not only your liver, but also your bank account. The clubs in Cannes are great but they're alarmingly expensive. Affordable options exist but if you want to do Cannes right, save your money before you arrive and when you do, hit the following venues.

ZOA

2 Place Charles de Gaulle ☎493 30 00 30 http://www.zoasushibar.com

Zoa is the most relaxed of the popular nightlife venues in Cannes and can occasionally be the most touristy due to its location just across from the Palais des Festivals. It operates as a restaurant during the evening and is rumored to have the best sushi in Cannes. The bar however, is also one of the better options in the city–their gin and tonic is a game changer (think cucumber instead of lime), and is conveniently more gin than tonic, making the price tag easier to swallow but perhaps not the drink. Like most bars and clubs in Cannes, Zoa features a live DJ most nights who, like most DJs in Cannes, spins a mix primarily featuring deep house vibes.

Zoa gets fairly calm during weeknights but picks up during July and August (as does the whole city). The club is clean and minimalist, giving it a chic, almost sterile feel, which sounds a bit off but in this case works. The bar is well-stocked and pop-culture bearbricks are hidden among some of the bottles, which is an interesting and subtle nod to the art and culture for which Cannes is well-known. They were also almost certainly expensive, which is the other thing Cannes is well-known for. If it's within your budget, stop by Zoa early in the night for some sushi, and stay for drinks and good music.

i *No Cover Charge. Cocktails from €10.* ☒ *Open daily 5:30pm-2:30am.*

BAOLI

Porto Canto, Blvd. de la Croisette ☎493 43 03 43 http://www.lebaoli.com/baoli

you haven't heard people raving about Baoli yet, you should leave your hotel room for more than five minutes or invest in a hearing aid. Baoli is arguably the best club in Cannes (but only in argument, as Gotha probably takes that title). Nonetheless, the runner up for such an award in a city teeming with nightlife venues is nothing to shake a stick at. If it's the weekend, and you're at Baoli, you'd have to try reallllly hard to have a bad time.

Baoli is located nearby the Palm Beach Casino, which is somewhat unfortunate as that places it about 20 mins away from the center of Cannes by foot. If you are heading there on foot, make sure you have good directions, as it's somewhat easy to miss if you don't know what you're looking for. The building is one story tall and is surrounded by overgrown vines and tropical-looking plants, which is cool once you realize its a nightclub, but is easy to write off as just another one-story building with overgrown vegetation if you're not paying attention.

Bear in mind that Baoli, being one of the better options in Cannes, is fairly exclusive. flats and flip-flops are a big no-no and if you look like you came from the beach, that's where you'll be heading back to. Drinks are expensive (surprise!) but the prices are worth it to experience the club at least once. Bust out your highest heels and double-check your bank's overdraft fees, you'll need the former to get in and you won't leave without the latter.

i *Cocktails from €15. Open April-October daily 8pm-5am; November-March weekends 8pm-5am.*

B. PUB

22 rue Mace ☎493 38 17 30 https://www.facebook.com/BPubCannes

B. Pub is somewhat of a hybrid between the energy-packed nightclubs of Cannes and the slightly more relaxed bar life. It has the energy of a bar with the atmosphere of a club, which, on paper makes it sound like a really bad club though in actuality it's more like a really cool bar.

Tables line the walls of the club with high seating and dim, purple lights. In the center, the bar is crowned with a clean array of illuminated Grey Goose bottles with seating available around the bar. B. Pub hosts fairly good DJs who spin sets chilled out deep house music to match the discotech-y atmosphere.

Any Cannes local will tell you to show up to B. Pub for a pre-game session before hitting Bâoli or Gotha. That Cannes local will also ask you which yacht is yours and will order a bottle of Grey Goose assuming you're good to split the cost because the Cannes local has more money than you know how to count. As a student traveler, your best bet is to pre-game B. Pub as drinks range between €10 and €15 a pop (just wait 'til you see the prices at Bâoli or Gotha…). Limiting yourself to one drink and then nursing it as long as possible is a good way to survive the night financially. Finally, the bouncers are heelists and will turn away any female wearing flats or flipflops. They'll also turn away any male not accompanied by a female in heels, so figure that out before showing up at the door.

All in all, despite its cost and exclusivity, B. Pub is one of the more popular nightlife venues for the front end of the night in Cannes. Sure, you can choke out some karaoke in the Station Tavern by the Gare S.N.C.F. but you're in Cannes to live it up, and if your idea of living it up is train station karaoke, you're doing it wrong.

i Beers from €7. Cocktails from €10. ~ Open daily 9pm-2:30am.

BACKSTAGE
CLUB

Rue Gerard Monod

Backstage is your most affordable late-night club option but is also ranked third in terms of popularity. Gotha and Baoli are generally more populated, but are both farther away from the center of Cannes, and can be a bit too much effort during the weeknights. Backstage is more down to earth and more manageable of a venue, not to mention slightly cheaper than the rest of the exclusive clubs.

Fortunately, you might even get past the bouncer in flats at Backstage, especially on an uncrowded night, which may seem unimportant but can be a nice change of pace from the occasionally suffocating exclusivity of Baoli and Gotha. The venue is set up similarly to B. Pub, with neon purple and blue lights and a well-stocked bar in the center. Don't ask the bartender to mix you "his favorite drink" however, as you might end up drinking what is, for all intents and purposes, Listerine.

Backstage is situated towards the easternmost edge of central Cannes, conveniently close to the Pint House, making the gap between your last pre-game drink and your first game time drink under 5 mins. If you're too lazy to make a big ordeal out of going out or you need a break from the popular kids at the other clubs, Backstage will suit you just fine.

i Beer from €6. Mixed drinks from €10. ✆ Open daily 8pm-5am.

LES MARCHES
CLUB

Palais des Festivals, Blvd. de la Croisette   ☎493 39 77 21 http://www.lesmarches-club.com

Les Marches operates under the philosophy that the more bouncers a club has, the more exclusive it is. In a way, they aren't wrong, as getting past all three checkpoints on your way into the club will either make you feel attractive, important, lucky, or all three. Although while you have to give the club credit here for their business strategy, they lose credit in other areas.

Les Marches isn't a bad club by any stretch of the imagination, it's just not where you should go as a student in Cannes. The majority of the people here are in their thirties or beyond, which is a little weird given the club's young attitude. Though in a way it makes sense because of the club's convenience and centrality to Cannes (it's located on top of the Palais des Festivals). Furthermore, while the Victoria's Secret fashion show playing on all the TVs behind the bar is a nice touch while waiting for a drink, it starts to feel a little bit creepy when you think about all the forty year-old men with their eyes glued to the screen.

cannes

If you had no other option, Les Marches would still be a fun club to hit. However, the abundance of nightlife venues in Cannes makes it easy and somewhat smart to avoid. Yes, they sometimes have high profile DJs and artists perform, but at the same time, if you're excited for a Fat Joe concert, you're living in the wrong decade and you should go "make it rain on dem hoes" somewhere else.

i €10 cover charge. Mixed drinks from €10. ⏰ Open daily 8pm-5am.

LA CROISETTE / THE BEACH
BEACH
Blvd. de La Croisette

Yep, you're too poor to afford any of the popular clubs in Cannes. It's sad but true. Nonetheless, you can still get drunk with all the other kids at the beach and unless you're sense of FOMO is so strong that you're having a panic attack from not being at Baoli, you can still have a pretty fun time. The peasant's oldest trick in the book is to grab a bottle of rose and a six pack and head down to the beach. Unlike everywhere else, you won't need heels and a dress to get in, and its recommended that you don't wear heels because a) you'll look like a stripper drinking cheap alcohol at the beach in stilettos, and b) the legality of drinking at the public beaches at night is blurry, and your escape plan will fall to pieces as quick as you will when you try to run from the cops a few drinks in.

Fortunately, almost every corner store in Cannes hosts a collection of wine, liquor and beer, and even more fortunately, they won't cost you your first born son. You can get enough rotten grape juice to blur your vision for under € 15 euros which is comparable to the price of a single drink anywhere else. You can actually enjoy your drinks while thinking of how much money you're not spending, whereas the opposite is true when you go to any of the real clubs in Cannes.

i Free! (Except the drinks part. Find a place to buy 'em.)

GOTHA
CLUB
Palm Beach, Place Franklin Roosevelt, Pointe Croisette ☎493 45 11 11 www.gotha-club.com/

Gotha club is like that club you see in movies all the time then say to yourself "man, I wish clubs like this were actually real!" Well, it turns out they are. Enter: Gotha Club. Exit: Your entire life savings. Gotha club is an absurdly over the top establishment in terms of both awesomeness and exclusivity. It all makes sense if you think about it – the best club in a city that somewhat revolves around nightlife? Yeah, it's gonna be a good time.

Taking a look at the summer lineup is like scrolling through the hip-hop and house music genres on your iTunes—Wiz Khalifa, Rick Ross, Snoop Dogg, Nervo, David Guetta... You get the point—and that's just July's schedule. The only problem with Gotha? You probably won't get in. Okay, that's not necessarily true, but you're gonna have to pull out all the stops if you want a chance to see the other side of the door. Guys: Call that Victoria's Secret model who gave you her number the other night. (Oh, that didn't happen?). Girls: Be that Victoria's Secret model. Maybe that's an exaggeration but you get the point—You have to look nice. Rumor has it the club literally hires a small team of fashion experts to judge who to let in and who to turn away.

Do you need admission to Gotha to have a good time in Cannes? Absolutely not. If you do get turned away you have plenty of other, almost just as good options. And you can at least feel like your soul remains pure and unadulterated by the superficial glitz and glamour that is Cannes nightlife.

i Cover charge depending on the event. Cocktails €15. ⏰ Open April-September 8pm-5am.

THE PINT HOUSE
BAR
17 Rue Frères Pradignac ☎493 38 90 10 http://www.pinthouse.fr

Woah—A nightlife venue in Cannes that you can actually afford and that isn't the street or the beach! The Pint House is not only one of the few affordable bars in Cannes, it's one of the only fun ones. Unlike the sketchy, dirty bars where the not-so-friendly natives and clueless backpackers congregate (though that's usually a recipe for an interesting night), The Pint House is actually a popular venue among the youth of Cannes. In the summer months, you'll find a mix of students home for the summer, yachties (people who work on yachts rather than own them), and the culturally literate backpacker (that's you!).

The Pint House is conveniently located along Rue Hoche, the easternmost blocks of which is home to some of the less exclusive bars of Cannes. If you get bored, you can walk next door for a different beer list or across the street to talk to that French girl who you've been making eye-whoopie with for the last twenty minutes. The seating along the street is primarily outside, as are all the other bars, making the street seem like one big, drunken party.

A beer will run you around € 5 which, while not necessarily cheap, is about as low as it gets in Cannes without sneaking in your own alcohol. Speaking of which, we know from experience that actually sneaking in your own alcohol is weird and usually pretty obvious, and the staff will be quick to point out that either the six-pack of Heineken leaves or you do. If you're not into the exclusive club scene but want to be more social than the sad beach-drinkers, grab a pint here. Or if you want to be more economical in your pursuit of drunkenness, put the following adage into practice: "one tequila, two tequila, three tequila, floor."

i No cover charge. Pints €4. Shots €5-10. 🕗 Open daiy 6pm-6am.

ESSENTIALS
Practicalities

- **TOURIST OFFICE:** Underneath the Palais des Festivals. (1 Blvd. de la Croisette ☎492 99 84 22; www.cannes.fr. Open July-Aug 9am-8pm, Sep-Jun 9am-7pm.) Additional branch next to the train station.

- **POST OFFICE:** 22 rue de Bivouac Napoleon. (☎493 06 26 50. Open M-F 9am-7pm; Sa 9am-12pm.) Additional post office at 34 rue Mimont.

- **POSTAL CODE:** 06400

Emergency

- **POLICE:** 1 av. de Grasse. (☎4 93 06 22 22) Additional location at 2 quai St-Pierre (08 00 11 71 18).

- **HOSPITAL:** Hospital des Broussailles. (13 av. des Broussailles ☎493 69 70 00)

- **PHARMACY:** Pharmacies are located on essentially every street in Cannes and are easily spotted due to the flashing neon green crosses out front.

Getting There
By Train
Gare de Cannes. (1 ave. Jean Juares. Open daily 5:55am - 8:55pm) Trains run to Antibes, Grasse, Marseille, Monaco, Nice, Saint-Raphael, and Paris

By Plane
The closest airport is Nice-Cote d'Azur. Fly into Nice, take the bus to the train station, and the train to Cannes takes only 30 minutes.

By Bus
Rapide Cote d'Azur. (pl Hotel de Ville ☎493 48 70 30)

Getting Around

The easiest way to get around in Cannes is by foot. Everything worth seeing is within walking distance of La Croisette.

cassis

Cassis is one of the smaller towns along the southern French coasts but is nonetheless worth visiting. Locals and visitors alike brag that Cassis is one of the most beautiful, if not the most beautiful, place in Southern France. It's up to you whether or not you agree, but even if you don't you'll still want to stop by at some point during your trip to Provence. From the harbor to the calanques, the shoreline around Cassis is breathtaking. In some areas, the crystal clear, aquamarine seawater allows you to see the ocean floor with complete clarity from depths of almost 50 feet. Furthermore, Calanque d'En Vau is one of the only places in Southern France where the beach is naturally sandy, which is convenient if you don't like getting an unwanted deep-tissue foot massage every time you hit the beach. Further west, the beaches give way to flat, solid rock ledges perfect for lounging on or launching off. Cool off at the beach during the day and then stroll around the town center at night where you'll find locally sourced seafood, homemade ice cream, and quiet plazas to enjoy it all in.

SIGHTS

CALANQUE D'EN VAU   CALANQUE

Have you ever seen those breathtaking pictures of the fjords in Norway and then told yourself you'd visit them one day knowing full well that you'll never go to Norway? Well now you don't have to! The calanques in Cassis look almost the same as the Norwegian fjords except they're in southern France, they're warm enough to swim in, and they're easy to access. Okay, France, you win.

Calanque d'En Vau is the crown jewel of Cassis and debatably one of the most beautiful sights in all of Southern France. Picture a small sandy beach with rocky white cliffs stretching up over one hundred feet and wrapping around the beach on all sides. Then picture the cliffs leading out into a narrow canyon which opens up into the ocean a few hundred yards away. And then fill the entire canyon from the beach to the ocean with crystal clear water that shines with an aquamarine color that looks so perfect that you're convinced someone photo shopped real life. That's Calanque d'En Vau, except the real thing is even better because there's no effective way to capture its beauty with words.

So now that you're committed to checking it out, here's the catch – Calanque d'En Vau is crowded. Very very crowded. It's a small beach with a lot of hype, so every tourist and their mother are going to check it out. There is, however, a way around the crowds if you hit the beach early. The crowds roll in (or paddle in, as the beach is easiest to access by kayak), around 12pm on most weekdays. Getting there around 10am will give you a much calmer and more secluded beach experience, and arriving any time before 10am will likely give you the beach all to yourself.

PLAGE BLEUE   "BEACH"

Route des Calanques Port Miou

Plage Bleue, or Blue Beach, is not actually a beach. It's known locally as "flat rocks" which is decidedly appropriate considering the "beach" is actually just a group of smooth, flat rocks extending out above the water. The rocks are littered with sunbathers and cliff jumpers alike giving the beach a very Mediterranean

france

get a room!

As is the case with many of the smaller towns in Southern France, affordable housing options in Cassis are few and far between. The best option is to book somewhere through Airbnb as t will give you the best shot and staying somewhere central to Cassis without break ng the bank. The only hostel in Cassis is the Auberge de Jeunesse, the government funded hostel which is so far outside the center of Cassis that it might as well be in Marseille. If airbnb doesn't pan out, you're better off searching on couchsurfing.com for a place to crash in an attempt to avoid the lengthy trek to and from the Auberge de Jeunesse.

AUBERGE DE JEUNESSE

La Fontasse   ☎044 201 0272   www.hifrance.org/auberge-de-jeunesse/cassis.html

The Auberge de Jeunesse is the government funded hostel in Cassis and is comparable to the DMV of accommodations. The staff at most of these locations are often not the most friendly of folks, and while the rates are cheaper than any of the hotels in Cassis' center, you'll understand why when you make the hour-long trek from the harbor to the hostel.

The location of the Auberge in Cassis seems alluring given its proximity to the calanques but make no mistake – the calanques are good for spending the day at, but are otherwise in the middle of nowhere. Furthermore, the Auberge is still far enough away from the calanques that you'll still have to take a day trip there from the hostel anyways. You could comfortably camp closer to the center of Cassis than if you stayed at the Auberge (and this might not actually be a bad idea).

Ultimately, if you're looking to stay in Cassis, your best bet is to either book through airbnb or couchsurfing.com or else fork over the extra cash for a hotel in the town center. Unless you're looking to spend your time in Cassis power walking to burn off all the croissants you've eaten, the Auberge de Jeunesse is not an ideal place to stay.

i Dorms €22. 🕐 Reception 8-10:30am, 5-9pm.

feel with the groups of Europeans occupying different ledges of flat stone on which to soak up the sun.

Plage Bleue offers a place to tan without getting sucked in with the crowds in the more local beaches next to the town center. Swimming at Plage Bleue, however, is a bit of a struggle. Ignore for a moment that the water feels like it's below freezing, the only way to access it from Plage Bleue is to jump. This option is fairly safe given the depth of the water and the varying heights from which to leap – the real struggle, however, comes with trying to get out of the water. The rocks leading out are covered in seaweed and as the surf comes in and out, you'll find yourself quite literally sliding up and down slabs of slimy rock (which is actually kind of fun if you can forget about how foolish you look).

If cliff jumping or polar plunges aren't your thing, Plage Bleue still comes with it's own entertainment. The rocks are frequented by groups of local kids who put on a show for the less adventurous beach-goers by flipping, twisting, and twirling off of the highest points and into the water. Each kid tries to one-up the last in terms of difficulty which is endlessly entertaining for the not-so-faint of heart.

cassis

FOOD

LE ROMARIN
RESTAURANT $$
5 Rue Docteur Séverin Icard
☎442 01 09 93

As the locals of Cassis will eloquently explain to you, "the restaurants along the harbor are shit." Rather than testing the validity of that statement with firsthand experience, we recommend you walk two minutes north of the harbor and eat at Le Romarin. Le Romarin is a small, unremarkable-looking restaurant stretching out into one of the side streets of Cassis. Though while the décor of the restaurant leaves room for improvement, the food itself does not.

The restaurant's specialty is beef tartar, which is served in one of five different ways. The tartar is great, but it might not change your life. The fried calamari with pasta, however, will. It's that good. Order the calamari, and then once you finish it, just sit there for a few hours until your hungry again and order another plate. We can't say we did this ourselves, but we can say that we wish we had.

The restaurant is convenient to get to from just about anywhere in Cassis given the size of the city. It's a short walk from the harbor and is fairly easy to find. As mentioned earlier, the ambience isn't the best in the city, and the service won't impress you with speediness, (although the wait staff are all very friendly). At the end of the day, however, you're going to a restaurant for the food, right? Well, good food is in abundance at Le Romarin.

i Entrees start at €10. ☐ M-Su 11am - 10pm

AMORINO
ICE CREAM $
4 Avenue Victor Hugo
☎04 42 04 65 94 http://www.amorino.com

Okay, you caught us – Amorino is somewhat of a chain and now we're recommending it on Let's Go. Maybe you think we're sellouts but the cold hard truth is that Amorino serves damn good ice cream – and we would know because we eat a lot of ice cream.

Amorino prides itself on making its ice cream with no artificial colors or flavoring, which is actually somewhat impressive considering the array of chemicals masquerading as ice cream at this point in time. This being the case, however, you won't find one hundred different flavors like you might at a different glacier. Amorino offers just over ten ice cream flavors and ten sorbets. Oddly enough, within those ten ice creams are three types of chocolate and two types of vanilla. Even more odd is the fact that there are distinctly perceptible differences between all of them, so you could order three scoops of chocolate and not get bored.

Unlike everywhere else in France, Amorino doesn't charge in terms of "boules" (the French word for scoops). Amorino fills the cone with "florets" of ice cream, sculpting each bit of heavenly sweetness around the mouth of the cone and creating what looks like a frozen flower of godlike tastiness. If one floret isn't enough, however, you can order a tub of ice cream to go. And while you don't necessarily have to leave the store in order to eat the entire contents of that tub, you might get some weird looks if you don't.

i Small €2.50; Medium €3.80; Large €4.90. ☐ M-Su 10am-10pm.

NIGHTLIFE

LE BIG BEN
CLUB
Place Georges Clemenceau

Cassis is a small town and Le Big Ben is the only worthwhile nightlife joint within it borders. This is a sad truth to hear, but on the bright side, Le Big Ben is actually a pretty good club. It's easy to miss from the outside, as the exterior isn't much more than a windowless doorway squeezed in between a few other shops and restaurants. If the doorway doesn't catch your attention, however, the bouncers

france

will. Being the only fun club in the area without making the trip to Marseille, Le Big Ben has the privilege of being picky about who they let in. Keeping this in mind, however, the bouncers are fairly lenient and seem relatively good-natured.

If you make it through the door, you'll find yourself walking down a lengthy flight of stairs into the basement/dungeon that makes up the entire club. The bar sits immediately to the left of the stairs with tables and booths lining the walls and a dance floor in the middle. Strategically placed mirrors make it look like there are other rooms in the club where people are mimicking the people in the room you're in. Maybe that's how all mirrors work, maybe you're witnessing a parallel universe in which everything is exactly the same except for the fact that everyone's hands are sewn on backwards and no one can pronounce consonants, or maybe you drank way too much. We're not here to judge, but the mirror thing is a nice touch. If you're a vampire and the mirrors don't do much for you, the TVs inside the club play full-length feature films (Forrest Gump, for example), which is weird, but kind of fun at the same time.

The best thing about Le Big Ben, however, just might be the prices. Cassis is sandwiched between some of the most expensive cities on a backpacker's itinerary, so the €7 drinks at Le Big Ben feel like Christmas morning after the assault and battery that your wallet has likely seen over the past few days. If you read that past sentence and are thinking to yourself that €7 drinks are expensive, then our helpful travel tip to you would be to avoid southern France altogether or else smuggle your own alcohol in with a Poland Springs bottle like you did at your seventh grade dance.

i Drinks €7. ☑ Open Tu-Su 11pm - 5am. Closed Monday.

ESSENTIALS
Getting There
BY TRAIN
Getting into Cassis by train is the easiest way to access this seaside village. The train station is only 20 minutes from Gare St. Charles in Marseille, making Cassis an easy spot to get to. Trains run between Marseille and Cassis every 30 minutes or so, and given the duration of the journey, tickets are refreshingly cheap.

BY BUS
Buses run from the Gare SNCF into the town center roughly every 20 minutes. The easiest stop to get off and hit the town center is at La Poste (rue L'Arene). One trip is €0.80 and the bus runs from 7am until 7pm every day.

Getting Around
By Bus
Buses run from the Gare SNCF to the center of town every twenty minutes. Beyond that, taking a bus anywhere else in Cassis would be foolish if not impossible, considering how small the city is.

By Taxi
Taxis can be had by calling (04 42 01 78 96) but you're better off hoofing it, as everywhere within the town limits is easily within walking distance.

By Foot
Cassis is small and as such, everywhere within the town is accessible by foot. The longest walk you'll have to take is that from the center of town to the first calanque, and that will only run you thirty minutes maximum.

Practicalities

- **TOURIST OFFICE:** quai des Moulins. (☎08 92 25 98 92 www.ot-cassis.com. Summer hours daily 9am-7pm.)
- **TOURIST INFORMATION:** 08 92 25 98 92

Emergency

- **EMERGENCY TELEPHONE:** 17
- **FIRE:** 18
- **POLICE:** 17 or 04 42 01 17 17
- **HOSPITALS:** Blvd. Lamaritine, 13600, Cassis (04 42 08 76 00)
- **PHARMACIES:** 34 rue l'Arene (04 42 01 71 71)

lyon

Lyon is a serious contestant for the best city in France. Yes, you read that correctly, we said Lyon, not Paris – hear us out. Lyon is a thriving French city that is only slightly smaller than Paris. It has a perfect mix of historical significance and thriving youth culture. It is the gourmet capital of France and boasts several Michelin-rated restaurants, world-famous chefs, and culinary schools. It has the best rooftop club in all of France as well as a bar with a bartender who's ranked #5 in the world (yeah, apparently bartenders can be ranked). Lyon has a thriving arts community with up-and-coming musicians, artists, actors, designers etc. And, the icing on the cake is that Lyon is not the crowded, over-commercialized, snobbish and somewhat stereo-typically French Paris. Almost everything you're looking for in Paris can be found in Lyon (there's even a radio tower that looks kind of like the Eiffel Tower). There's a reason why the people of Lyon are unanimously and outrageously proud of their city and they will go out of their way to show you why they love it so much. To write Lyon off as just another French city subpar to Paris is more of a disservice to you than to Lyon. Lyon will survive without you, but you won't have an authentic impression of France without checking out this grounded, genuine, and impressively cool city.

SIGHTS

BASILIQUE NOTRE DAME DE FOURVIÈRE   BASILICA
8 Place de Fourvière   ☎04 78 25 13 01 www.fourviere.org

The Basilique Notre Dame is that big church you've been looking at on the hill above Lyon but have been too lazy thus far to visit it. While it would be convenient for you if we told you it's not worth the trek, it is worth the trek, so you should stop eating croissants and guzzling red wine for long enough to pay a visit.

Fourvière is a giant behemoth of a building with enough gold leaf and intricately carved figures on the ceiling to make Versailles nervous. The best thing about the basilica, however, is its location. Fourvière sits on top of a giant hill to the west of Lyon and the view from the basilica's rear is one of the best (if not the best) of the entire city. The basilica is within climbing distance from the city proper, and we say "climbing" because to get there you'll be doing exactly that. The streets running up towards Fourvière are anything but level and if you're quads aren't on fire by the time you summit then you should stop blood doping because its cheating.

france

The basilica, despite being somewhat out of the way, sits along a route that loops you around the western edge of the city and is worth visiting. Fourvière overlooks Old Town, and that's where you should logically start. Leaving Old Town and hiking up to the basilica will only take about 10-15 mins. The basilica itself is free and you can visit for as long as you'd like. Leaving Fourvière, head south and pay a visit to le Jardin des Curiosites for the only view in Lyon that gives Fourvière's a run for its money.

i Free. ⏰ Everydya: 9am-12:30pm, 2-6pm.

MUSEE DES BEAUX ARTS

MUSEUM

20 place des Terreaux ☎04 72 10 17 40 www.mba-lyon.fr

Lyon's fine arts museum is somewhat underwhelming given the otherwise rich culture present throughout the city. Structurally, the museum itself is beautiful. The inner courtyard inside the museum mutes the crowds from the plaza and gives the museum a quieter more intimate feeling. The exhibitions within, however, could be improved.

There's no doubt that France houses some of the most impressive museums in the world but these historical and artistic powerhouses are certainly not found in Lyon, and even more certainly, not in Lyon's Musee des Beaux Arts. The exhibitions within the museum are unmemorable and unremarkable to say the least. This is a fine arts museum where even the art-history majors struggle to recognize a single noteworthy piece or artist.

Lyon's fine arts museum is not one that will attract visitors the world over, and you likely won't find a work here that will change your life, or even your mind about the museum. You obviously won't be worse off for visiting the fine arts museum here, but you could probably spend your time in a much more entertaining or enlightening way while in Lyon (like getting hammered and eating delicious gourmet food). If art is hugely important to you, the Musee des Beaux Arts is worth a quick visit but for the average tourist who isn't inexplicably aroused by oil on canvas, perhaps sit this one out.

i Free for persons under 25 years; €7 for all others. ⏰ Open M and W-Su 10am-6pm, except opens 10:30am on Fridays. Closed Tuesday.

FOOD

YAAFA

FALAFEL $

17 Rue D'Algerie ☎06 61 35 03 73 www.facebook.com/Yaafa

Yaafa stands for "you are a falafel addict" which is hilarious but also totally accurate once you've eaten here. This falafel joint is, in many ways, the food venue from heaven. It's cheap (€5 euros for a falafel). It's open late (and serves perfect drunk food). And it's really fucking good (apologies for the language, but if you ask the chef for his best falafel, he'll make you one that is, in his words, not ours, "really fucking good."

The trifecta of cheap, drunk-friendly, and good, justifies the title of the restaurant and makes its customers very likely to return time and time again. Furthermore, the restaurant itself hires some of the best staff in Lyon – don't be surprised if you bring your sandwich outside to eat and five mins. later the guy who made it sits down at your table and tells you some of his favorite places in Lyon. (Full disclosure: eating a meal with your falafel guy can sometimes be creepy, but in the case of Yaafa, the staff is all 30-somethings with great tips and good conversation.

Finally, Yaafa is entirely vegetarian. This is good for vegetarians (obviously) but it's also not bad for carnivores, who generally shy away from these types of venues. The falafel here is great, and doesn't taste anything like a veggie-burger or any of that vegan cardboard stuff. If you've never had a falafel before, or if

lyon

you've never had a good falafel before (which you haven't if you haven't tried Yaafa), then search your pockets for €5 and become a falafel addict.

i *Falafel €5.* ⏲ *Mon-Wed: 11:30am-10pm; Thurs-Sat: 11:30am-12am*

BUTCHER BROTHER
AMERICAN $$

4 Rue Longue ☎04 78 30 41 92 www.facebook.com/ButcherBrother1

You are in an authentically French city and now you're being told to go to a very American restaurant... We understand that this might not be what you were expecting but sometimes you need a break from snails and frog's legs. Butcher Brother is a New York inspired burger joint with a hamburger that will make New Yorkers question their nationality. Everything about this burger is made entirely in-house – even the bun. Ask for the most popular burger and then pretend you can understand the waitress when she explains what's on it in French. We guarantee once you try it you really won't care too much about the ingredients.

get a room!

For once you actually have a choice as to where to stay in a city as there are multiple affordable options. There is, however, one obvious winner and that is Slo Living Hostel. Beyond the first choice, you have Cool & Bed (www.coolandbed.com, ☎426 18 05 28) with airbnb or couchsurfing coming in a close third. Finally, you also have your local Auberge de Jeunesse, but with so many more attractive options, book a room at the Auberge only as a last resort.

SLO LIVING HOSTEL

5 rue Bonnefoi ☎478 59 06 90 http://slo-hostel.com

If your Pinterest board and your Tumblr feed had sweet sweet intercourse and that lovechild emerged onto this good green earth in the form of a youth hostel (why that would happen is beyond us), it would undoubtedly emerge in the form of Slo Living Hostel. If you're confused by that previous sentence and by what it could possibly mean, all you need to gather from it is that Slo Living is f***ing cool.

The hostel was created by a group of three friends who traveled the world for a year, gathering data on what the liked and didn't like about each hostel they stayed at, and then combined all the good things to make their own, which they opened to the public in June of 2014. Even the actual building was designed by one of the three who conveniently studied architecture for a short time. The lobby is high-ceilinged with copious amounts of natural light flooding in through the towering windows. Beyond the lobby is an inner courtyard with deck chairs on grassy lawn and a natural wood porch lining the outskirts. Hallways lead out into the courtyard with dorms and bathrooms on the inside.

The hostel embraces Lyon's gourmet culture and serves a traditional French, three-course meal every evening for a small additional charge, as well as a small French breakfast in the morning with cereal, croissants, coffee, and juice. One of the greatest aspects of Slo Living, however, is the staff. Everyone at Slo Living is unreservedly proud of Lyon and will be eager to point out the dos and don'ts of the city. The staff's recommendations for bars, clubs, restaurants, and sights within the city are absolute gems and if, for some reason, Let's Go's guide to Lyon disappeared off the face of this earth (which it won't, don't worry), Slo Living's staff would probably do the next best job of giving you the ins and outs of Lyon.

i *Dorms €25; Doubles €75; Deluxe Doubles €85.*

The restaurant is open for lunch and dinner every day but Monday, but lunch is your best bet. Diners who show up before sunset have the option to get a burger, a side of potatoes, a side of salad and a glass of (really good) wine for just €12. Not necessarily cheap, but if there's one French city where you don't want to skimp on the food budget it's Lyon.

Butcher Brother is tucked away into one of the side streets of the 2eme Arrondissement (the neighborhoods of Lyon are numbered 1-9), which is convenient as its fairly central to Lyon as a whole. It's just around the corner from The Ou where you can grab a homemade pastry for dessert inside a modern Victorian tearoom (try the carrot cake and the iced tea). Get rid of your homesick food-feelings and grab the best burger of your life at Butcher Brothers.

i *Burgers range from €10; Lunch Special: €15 for burger, sides, glass of wine. ☒ Open Tu-Sat 12-2:30pm; 7:30-10:30pm.*

CAFE THOMAS
RESTAURANT $$

1 Rue Laurencin   ☎04 72 16 28 64 www.restaurant-thoomas.com

It's probably a good sign to walk into a restaurant in the gourmet capital of France and find it teeming with locals (good sign #1). It's probably also a good sign when every single person in the restaurant is ordering the meal of the day because it's so damn good (good sign #2). Finally, it's probably a good sign when the waiter knows enough about each of the wine options to fuel a two-hour conversation (good sign #3). In conclusion, all you really have to do is find Café Thomas (which isn't hard) and everything else will be taken care of–meal of the day with the best wine pairing–that's pretty painless. If you really want to make your own decisions, you can order a few of the French tapas written on the chalkboard in the back of the restaurant. You'll save a bit of money and stomach-space this way, but honestly just get the meal of the day, there's no need to be difficult.

If this cafe doesn't help you understand why people rave about the food in Lyon, then you have the palate of an earthworm and should just save your money and go to Subway. The food and wine are both locally sourced, and the chefs probably are too but that's slightly less relevant as long as they continue to churn out the plates they've been creating. The cafe is open for lunch and dinner Tuesday through Sunday but sometimes opens up on Mondays just for fun. It's nestled into a side street running perpendicular to the Saone in the second arrondissment. It's easy to get to, fairly easy to find, and difficult to leave. The wait-staff are very friendly and all speak English, which is somewhat interesting considering there is an alarming lack of tourists here. (Good news for you, bad news for the other tourists). Grab a bite at Café Thomas on Tuesday and then book a hotel for the rest of the week so you can keep coming back to try tomorrow's plate of the day.

i *€9-16. ☒ Open Tu 6pm-12am; W-F 11am-2pm, 6pm-12am; Sa 11am-2pm.*

NIGHTLIFE

LE SUCRE
CLUB

50 quai Rambaud   ☎04 27 82 69 40 www.le-sucre.eu

Le Sucre is celebrated as the "best rooftop in all of France," and we're inclined to agree. The nightclub is perched on the rooftop of a now-defunct sugar factory on the southern tip of Lyon where the two rivers converge. As such, you end up with a nightclub, on top of a defunct factory, with a view of two rivers and the whole of Lyon. Yeah, that's not a bad venue.

Le Sucre is known for being somewhat of an electronic mecca. Live DJs perform several nights per week and the club is frequented by electro-snobs and EDM-fiends alike. You won't be an outcast here if you're not a diehard Radiohead fan, just don't start going off about how the music sounds like a malfunctioning elevator with a broken radio inside, because you might get thrown out (or off).

Any local with more than two friends will tell you Le Sucre is the best bet for clubbing in Lyon. The good news is that it's popular and will rarely, if ever, have a slow night. The bad news is that the club owner knows this and therefore charges admission and occasionally requires tickets for the more popular DJs. The tickets usually run about €10 which isn't too bad, but you won't get a free drink with the cover charge like you might elsewhere. Check online before heading out to see if you can buy a ticket, as this will get you through the door much quicker and will save you some money by not having to buy a ticket at the venue. If you like music, alcohol, or fellow humans, check out Le Sucre for a sweet time (get it?!).

i *Cover Charge up to €10. Drinks €6-15. Open 10pm-12 am Thurs; Fri-Sat 11pm-5am; Sun 3pm-10pm.*

REDWOOD   BAR

1 Rue Chavanne   ☎04 72 26 62 27

Redwood is a Rum Bar situated in the second district of Lyon. Yes, Rum Bars apparently exist outside of Pirates of the Caribbean and yes, they're just as awesome as they sound. This small bar has a clean and minimalist vibe with both terrace seating as well as tables on the inside. You won't find the pounding music or the squad of bouncers outside the door like you will at some other venues, which is a refreshing change and somewhat of a surprise given the chic vibes of the bar.

If you've ever been to one of those slightly tacky restaurants where they cook your meal on the stovetop in the center of your table, ordering a drink at Redwood is a somewhat similar experience without the tackiness. The bartender is an expert in his craft and mixes a drink with such showmanship and finesse that you'll be unconvinced he doesn't have more than two arms. More importantly, he churns out some of the better rum-based drinks in France.

Finally, Redwood's location in the center of Lyon leaves you some options for your next post-rum stop. Heading south will bring you to Le Sucre, while a quick trek north will bring you to Le Terminal. Stop in for a Moscow Mule or ask for the bartender's choice. You'll end up with a damn good cocktail for an even €10 and the show is free.

i *All cocktails €10.* 🕐 *Open Tu-Su 6:30pm-1am; opens 8pm Su. Closed Mon.*

ESSENTIALS
Getting There
By Train
Trains to Lyon run through either Gare de la Part-Dieu or Gare de Perrache. Part-Dieu is the larger of the two and is where all national or international trains depart from. It's located on 5 pl. Beraudier and the ticket desk is open 8am-8pm M-Th and Sunday, and from 7am-10pm on Friday.

By Plane
Lyon's main airport is Aeroport Lyon-Saint-Exupery. The airport itself is small as most international flights fly out of Paris. From the airport, Rhonexpress trains shuttle passengers from the airport into the main part of the city.

Getting Around
By Metro
Public transport in Lyon is run by TCL (08 20 42 70 00 / www.tcl.fr) and includes access to buses, trams and the metro. Tickets to any of the above run €1.70 and public transit runs from 5am - 12:20am. Metro trains via line T1 run directly to Gare Part-Dieu.

By Bus

Public transport in Lyon is run by TCL (08 20 42 70 00 / www.tcl.fr) and includes access to buses, trams and the metro. Tickets to any of the above run €1.70 and public transit runs from 5am - 12:20am. Bus routes and maps are available at the touris office.

By Taxi

Taxi Lyon: 04 72 10 86 86

By Foot

Lyon is large enough that getting around on foot can be inconvenient if you plan to cover lots of ground in one day. Nonetheless, the city is certainly manageable to experience by foot.

By Bike

Lyon has Velo'v bike stands all throughout the city where you can pick up or drop off rental bikes. Tickets can be purchased at the stand, online, or at the tourist office.

Practicalities

- **TOURIST OFFICE:** Place Bellecour (☎04 72 77 69 69 www.lyon-france.com. Open daily 9am-6pm. The tourist office offers accommodation bookings, maps, and a Lyon City Card: €20 for access to museums, public transport, a city tour and a boat tour.)

- **TOURIST INFORMATION:** ☎04 72 77 69 69

- **ATMS:** 24hr. ATMs in Bellecour Square.

Emergency

- **EMERGENCY TELEPHONE:** 17

- **FIRE:** 18

- **POLICE:** 17

- **HOSPITALS:** Hopital Hotel-Dieu (1 pl. de l'Hopital, 2eme / 08 20 08 20 69)

- **PHARMACIES:** Marked by glowing green crosses.

bordeaux

Bordeaux is the wine capital of the world and that's about all the convincing you should need to book a ticket there. That isn't even a joke. That really is all the convincing you should need. So since you've already made up your mind to visit Bordeaux, we'll at least give you an idea of what else you'll find there besides wine. For starters, you'll find more wine. Beyond that, you'll find a city with incredibly rich history, buildings that could be classified as works of art in and of themselves and life size reflections of those buildings in the Miroir d'Eau. Furthermore, you'll find the world's largest continuous pedestrian street, and the world's largest pedestrian crowd walking down it at all times (that second fact probably isn't even remotely true, but the street is pretty crowded). You'll find a lively student body, gourmet French restaurants to feed them in, and several bars and clubs to "hydrate" them in. At the end of the day though, if Bordeaux had none of those things but the wine, it would still be worth visiting. Go drink the wine.

SIGHTS

BORDEAUX CATHEDRAL
CATHEDRAL

Place Pey Berland   ☎05 56 52 68 10   www.cathedrale-bordeaux.fr

The Bordeaux Cathedral (also known as the Saint Andrew Cathedral) is the biggest, most centrally located cathedral in Bordeaux and in terms of sight-seeing, is really the only cathedral worth visiting. It's likely not the most impressive cathedral you'll see during your time in France, but given its centrality to downtown Bordeaux and its free admission, you'd be foolish not to stop in and take a look around.

The building itself is formatted in the shape of a cross with several different chapels hidden behind the center of the cathedral. These chapels shockingly cost a bit extra however, so bring some change with you if you're looking to thoroughly investigate the sights within the cathedral.

The cathedral is located in the heart of Bordeaux, and is just around the corner from La Musee de Beaux Arts, allowing you to knock out both sights in an afternoon if you're ambitious. Be wary of the somewhat odd hours within the cathedral however, as a lack of planning will end with you showing up to locked doors. During the summer the cathedral is open from 10am - 1pm and 3pm - 7pm everyday except Monday during which it's open only during the afternoon.

i Free. 🕑 Open Monday 3-7:30pm; Tuesday-Saturday 10am-1pm, 3-7:30pm; Sunday 9:30am-1pm, 3-7:30pm.

MUSEE DES BEAUX-ARTS DE BORDEAUX
MUSEUM

20 cours d'Albret   ☎05 56 10 20 56   www.musba-bordeaux.fr

The Musee des Beaux-Arts de Bordeaux is one of the better fine arts museums in non-Parisian France. The layout of both the museum's interior and exterior is expertly done, and the entire venue is well cared for and well curated. The entrance to the museum features an inner courtyard with a charming garden and expansive lawn which offers a peaceful escape from the steady hum of Bordeaux. On either side of the courtyard you'll find the North or South gallery which host the artwork.

Since it is a fine arts museum, you can expect to see an overwhelming amount of oil paintings of old men with the occasional slightly plump naked woman. However, the Musee des Beaux-Arts features more than just that— there you'll find sculptures of wolves attacking deer, paintings of pastoral landscapes, yard sculptures of cubism-inspired women, and a significant portion of art inspired by Greek mythology.

The interior of the museum has a slightly modern feel which pairs well with the classic, formal feel of the artwork. Paintings are arranged in several open rooms with walls in the middle, making the entire gallery feel somewhat like a large, extended hallway with random slabs of wall jutting into the center. Finally, if the courtyard, artwork, and location aren't enough to lure you in, keep in mind that the museum is well air-conditioned during the summer months.

i Free for anyone under the age of 25 years. 🕑 Open M, W-Su 11am-6pm; closed Tuesday.

FOOD

LE PETIT COMMERCE
CAFE $$$

22 rue Parlement Saint-Pierre   ☎05 56 79 76 58   https://www.facebook.com/pages/
LE-PETIT-COMMERCE/151929008218963

This little cafe is nestled into the wall on Rue Parliament – one of the better streets for dining out in all of Biarritz. Here you'll find traditional French food as well as an assortment of seafood, but don't even bother glancing at the menu – you want to order the magret de canard. Southwestern France is famous for its duck and while you could settle for the confit de canard, the quality (and

get a room!

Cheap accommodations in Bordeaux are slightly hard to come by, but those that exist are good enough to comfortably stay in the city for reasonable prices. With careful planning, airbnb may offer the best options, but the Auberge de Jeunesse which was renovated in 2011 is more than good enough for the average student traveler.

AUBERGE DE JEUNESSE
22 cours Barbey   ☎556 33 00 70 www.auberge-jeunesse-bordeaux.com

The Auberge de Jeunesse is the only youth hostel in Bordeaux and while it could use a bit of friendly competition, it's still more than comfortable enough to stay in. The biggest downfall of the Auberge is the location. It's located in what seems to be the red light district of Bordeaux. This is good news if you're a big fan of strip clubs, (and good news if you're a stripper looking for work), but bad news if you're a God fearing Christian or something like that. Furthermore, while the Auberge's location in the red light district isn't ideal, it's not as unfortunate as the twenty-minute walk into the city center. Nonetheless, a tiny bit of exercise is worth the €30+ you'll pay to stay closer to the center of Bordeaux.

Apart from the location, the Auberge in Bordeaux is pretty standard. The rooms are, for the most part, clean, and spacious enough to accommodate the four people per room. Don't be turned off by the reviews online claiming the hostel has extensive water damage, as the hostel is newly renovated and is actually fairly well maintained. The staff could be a bit more friendly, however, as some of the receptionists are comparable to Roz, the secretary from Monster's Inc.

All in all, the Auberge de Jeunesse is more than good enough for a stay in Bordeaux assuming you're not vehemently opposed to a bit of walking. You'll have a clean room, a shower, and a place to sleep for €22 a night. Who knows, you might even change your mind about the strip clubs!

i €23 per night. ☼ Reception 7:30am-1pm; 3-10pm.

---

quantity) of the magret at the Le Petit Commerce can't be beat. One glance at the slab of duck on your plate will have you wondering how many ducks they seem to have glued together to produce it, and one bite will have you questioning why they didn't glue on more. Imagine cutting through a crispy, salty outer crust to find delicious, tender, moist duck meat underneath. Pair that with a side of mashed potatoes, green salad, and a bottomless glass of red wine and you're good to go.

Aside from the food, (as if anything else matters at this point), the Le Petit Commerce has a very charming ambiance and is a joy to eat at. The restaurant has indoor seating, but the tables set out on the terrace are much more pleasant, as they provide a view of the old cobble stone streets of Bordeaux as well as a great vantage point for people-watching. The waitstaff are friendly, English-speaking, and are quick to offer advice or a good wine pairing.

If you still need convincing, Le Petit Commerce is located in the heart of Bordeaux, making it easily accessible and in a prime location to head down to the Miroir d'Eau afterwards to catch the sunset. If you like food, or if you like edible happiness, head down to Le Petit Commerce for some of the better food and drink in Bordeaux.

bordeaux

i Entrees €15-30. ☑ Open daily 10am-1am.

LA PETIT MAISON DE PIERRE
RESTAURANT $$

10, Place Saint Pierre ☎05 57 34 48 76

La Petit Maison (de Pierre) is a tiny restaurant tucked into the corner of the square at the end of Rue Parliament. The restaurant is hidden enough that it stays out of the average tourist's line of sight, but is still right in the heart of the city, offering an optimal location.

The size of the restaurant itself provides a few minor problems, as the lack of space on the terrace causes uncomfortably close seating arrangements. You may have gotten used to eating alone by now but when you're sandwiched in between two couples on dates, you have to have some serious self-confidence to not feel slightly awkward.

If you don't mind eating your meal while bumping elbows with couples who will almost certainly be bumping uglies later that night, La Petit Maison de Pierre serves some seriously delicious French cuisine that will leave you reconsidering whether Lyon deserves its title as the gourmet capital of France. We suggest that you order the confit de canard, as duck is somewhat of a specialty in southwestern France. Grab a glass of red to go with it (because Bordeaux) and you should be set for a great meal.

i Entrees: €10-20. ☑ Open Th-M 11am-10pm. Closed Tu-W.

LA MAISON DU VIN
WINE BAR $

1 Cours du 30 Juillet ☎05 56 00 22 88

This venue isn't so much about food as it is about wine, but it's the perfect place to justify day-drinking, so you should pay it a visit nonetheless. The wine bar is located directly underneath L'ecole de Vin, one of the most prestigious wine schools in the world. We recommend taking one of their wine-tasting courses in English before attempting to discern the subtleties of wine at the bar below, but then again the teachers at the school advise you to spit your wine out after tasting it, while the waiters at the bar below prefer you to do just the opposite.

La Maison du Vin serves some of the cheapest good wine in Bordeaux, and each glass ranges from €2 – €5. They offer dry white, sweet white, rose, and red wine, and our professional opinion is that you should try one of each. The venue also offers small assiettes to accompany each glass ranging from charcuterie, to cheese, to chocolate. These assiettes are more expensive, however, at €7, and will slowly rob you blind as you knock back glass after glass.

If you're in Bordeaux, you should be heading to at least one wine bar, and La Maison du Vin is one of, if not the, cheapest option in the city. Furthermore, La Maison du Vin is a perfect example of getting more than what you paid for, seeing as the wine is cheap in price but rich in taste. Lastly, while you might not expect a cheap wine bar to be all fancy and whatnot, but La Maison du Vin is a glorious temple to alcoholic grape juice that is anything but dingy. Lounge chairs are arranged around low tables and light filters in through stained-glass windows depicting portraits of Dionysus, the Greek god of wine. Do Bordeaux justice by heading to La Maison du Vin and sampling some of Bordeaux's best (affordable) wine.

i Glasses of wine: €2-5 ; Snacks: €7. ☑ Open M-Sa 11am-10pm.

NIGHTLIFE

THE DOG & DUCK
PUB

3 Quai Louis XVIII ☎09 67 05 07 7 0 www.facebook.com/thedoganddduckbordeaux

For the size of the city, Bordeaux boasts an impressive amount of English Pubs, and The Dog & Duck is easily in the top three. A solid beer list, relaxed atmosphere, good location, and English-speaking staff make the Dog & Duck a great place to grab a pint, but what you really want to head there for is trivia night. The Dog & Duck hosts a trivia night every Sunday where crowds congregate to answer questions based on a certain theme. Examples include war, rugby, St. Patrick's Day, and pretty much everything in between. The entire contest takes place in three parts: picture identification, thematic trivia, and general knowledge. The best thing about trivia night, however, is the prize for winning. The first place team earns a bottle of their choosing behind the bar, be it vodka, whiskey, gin, etc. The runner up team gets a meter of shots – 10 shots lined up on a block of wood filled with assorted types of alcohol. Finally, third place gets a bottle of wine from behind the bar. Prizes one through three are all solid rewards for the collection of useless facts that's been taking up real estate in your head since your family started playing Trivial Pursuit. Unleash the contents of your memory bank, claim your prize, drink it, and then prepare to add nothing new to your memory bank for the remainder of the night.

If Sunday night trivia isn't exactly your thing, you should make it your thing. Until then, the Dog & Duck is still a great place to grab a beer with friends during the rest of the week. The beers on tap are fairly priced and the staff is entertaining and easy to talk to. Grab a table inside with your friends or, if you went to the bar alone for some reason, head outside to the terrace and make some new ones. If you're looking for a fun night out without the excess and overload of a nightclub, the Dog & Duck is your go-to.

i *Pints €6. ☑ Open M-F 3pm-2am; Sa-S 12pm-2am.*

HOUSES OF PARLIAMENT PUB
11 rue de Parliment ☎05 56 79 38 03 http://www.hop-pub.com

Okay, recommending three English pubs in a very French city is an interesting choice, but the students and young adults of Bordeaux tend to hang out at such venues, and so should you. Houses of Parliament is probably the smallest of the three English Pubs listed here, but what it lacks in size, it makes up for in upkeep. The pub is clean and well built, with a pool table in the back and plenty of tables in the middle and front rooms of the pub. The pub hosts a collection of beers on tap and houses enough booze to keep you drunk for the better (or worse) part of a year.

While Houses of Parliament lacks the terrace seating that you'll find at the Dog & Duck or HMS Victory, it claims the best location of the three in the heart of Bordeaux. Houses of Parliament is just down the street from all of the best restaurants in the city. Furthermore, Houses of Parliament is almost directly next door to Club 07, which is one of the better places to spend the later half of the night.

If you churn out an English pub-crawl, save Houses of Parliament for last and you'll be ideally situated to jump from the rowdy British bar scene into the chic French club scene. It might be an interesting transition, but then again, if you've completed your English pub-crawl in Bordeaux, you probably won't even notice you've swapped nightlife environments, let alone the fact that the people surrounding you are now speaking French.

i *Pints €6; Cocktails €8. ☑ Everyday: 3pm - 2am*

HMS VICTORY BAR
3 Place Général Sarrail ☎05 56 92 78 47

The HMS Victory is an English Bar where a significant portion of Bordeaux's student body congregates. The drinks are affordable to begin with, and every Thursday night is student night, discounting each pint to an even more palatable price. The atmosphere at the HMS is friendly and upbeat and the English waitstaff are a breath of fresh (English) air after attempting to order drinks in

bordeaux

French, (Gin and Tonics in France are called "Gin Tonics..." It's tough to wrap your head around, we know, but you'll get used to it eventually).

The HMS offers indoor and outdoor seating, but you'd probably never realize that even after a few trips there. The outdoor seating is extensive and much more appealing, as the HMS' terrace spills out into the plaza and provides a laidback yet still somewhat lively atmosphere. And the waitstaff walk around and serve drinks, which eliminates the need to ever step foot inside the actual building. Just be aware that the Bollywood bar next door is almost certainly a drug front and the bouncers there will protect it physically if need be. (Just kidding, but the Bollywood does send out some slightly uneasy vibes).

The HMS Victory is your best bet if you're looking to grab a beer outside with some friends or mingle with the student population of Bordeaux in the early hours of the night. You might not get the most extensive beer list here and you won't win a meter of shots on trivia night, but you can't go wrong with a few terrace beers before hitting the club later in the night.

i *Beer pints €6. Cocktails €8. ☼ Open M- Sa 12pm-2am; closed Sunday.*

ESSENTIALS
Practicalities

- **TOURIST OFFICE:** 12 Cours de 30 Juillet. (☎05 56 00 66 00 www.bordeaux-tourisme.com. M-Sa 9:30am-1pm, 2-7pm. It also provides city guides to Bordeaux, maps, brochures, reservations, information on vineyard visits and wine tastings.)
- **TOURIST INFORMATION:** ☎05 56 00 66 00

Emergency

- **EMERGENCY TELEPHONE:** 17
- **FIRE:** 18
- **POLICE:** 17
- **HOSPITALS:** Hopital St-Andre (1 rue Jean Burguet) (05 56 79 56 79)
- **PHARMACIES:** Marked by neon green crosses

Getting There
By Train

Trains to Bordeaux run through Gare St-Jean (rue Charles Domercq) and run from the city to Lyon, Marseille, Nantes, Nice, Paris, Poitiers, and Toulouse)

BY BUS: Buses depart from Reseau TransGironde and run to many smaller vineyard towns neighboring Bordeaux which is the quickest way to get from the city to wine country. Bus stops and schedules are somewhat tricky within Bordeaux, so your best bet is to double check with the Tourist Office.

By Taxi

Taxi Tele (05 56 96 00 34).

Getting Around
By Tram

The Tramway snakes throughout the city and is accessible from any stop along the tracks. This is the cheapest and most convenient way to get around Bordeaux via public transportation, as the trams run to each stop every five mins or so.

By Bus

Buses depart from Reseau TransGironde and run to many smaller vineyard towns neighboring Bordeaux which is the quickest way to get from the city to wine country. Bus stops and schedules are somewhat tricky within Bordeaux, so your best bet is to double check with the Tourist Office.

By Taxi

Taxi Tele (05 56 96 00 34).

By Foot

Bordeaux isn't a huge city, but it can take a toll on your energy if you try to tackle the whole thing on foot. Make use of the tram system to expedite longer walks, but if need be, nothing is out of walking distance.

biarritz

During the summer months tourists swarm to the south of France to escape the monotony of city life and bathe in the Mediterranean. While the French Riviera was once a pleasant escape from the crowds of bigger cities, it has become more and more crowded with international tourists with each passing year. Biarritz, however, is slightly different than the Riviera in this sense. Biarritz, the ritzy resort town on the southwestern coast of France, is more of a vacation getaway for French natives looking to relax amidst a crowd that's primarily made up of their fellow countrymen. The international tourists in this area generally end up in San Sebastian, the Spanish beach town a few miles to the south. Therefore, much to the delight of the Biarritz regulars, this beach town remains relatively unspoiled by outsiders.

If you don't let the somewhat unwelcoming natives ruin your mood, Biarritz is just about as close as you can get to paradise. The town is the surfing capital of France, and the epic wave breaks make the sandy beaches wildly entertaining. If you ever leave the beach, Biarritz boasts several excellent restaurants as well as a waterfront casino in case you haven't wasted all your money on alcohol yet. Ultimately, head to Biarritz if you're looking for a French beach town without the stereotypically American Americans that you'll find along the Riviera.

SIGHTS

VIRGIN ON THE ROCK   SCULPTURE
Rocher de la Vierge

The Virgin on the Rock is a small sculpture of the Virgin Mary. On a rock. Surprise! The sculpture was allegedly commissioned by Napoleon, who also ordered that the rock on which the sculpture is perched to hollowed out to allow people to pass through to witness the sculpture from both sides. The rock sits in the middle of the water and is only accessible by what was once a swinging wooden bridge but has since been replaced by a metal footbridge built by the same architect who designed the Eiffel Tower.

In the grand scheme of things, the Virgin on the Rock isn't exactly the most overwhelming thing to witness. In fact, the statue of the Virgin is perhaps the least impressive aspect of the venue. But the platform where visitors stand to observe the statue is most useful for catching one of the best views of the Basque regions. The Grand Plage is visible in its entirety from the outcrop, as is a portion of the Spanish coast jutting out into the distance. The Virgin herself seems to be watching over Biarritz, which is nice in theory but not nice if you're trying to catch a glimpse of the statue's front (the statue is conveniently positioned in such a way that makes it impossible to see Mary's face). The bridge and outcrop

get a room!

Hotels along Southwestern France put the "Ritz" in "Biarritz," and if you're vaguely fluent in English, you'll know that this doesn't bode well for the budget-conscious traveler. Biarritz in and of itself caters to the more financially stable (read: rich), so if you're one of the sad souls looking to skimp on your housing arrangements, you should expect to a) Bring a tent and book a campsite, or b) Make reservations at one of the two surf-hostels far in advance. However, if you're a trust fund baby you can choose option c) None of the above, and book a room at Hotel Le Cafe de Paris (it's not actually a cafe) where you'll enjoy a quiet room overlooking the Pacific ocean complete with a private balcony and nauseating price tag.

SURF HOSTEL BIARRITZ
HOSTEL $$

Batiment E, Domaine de Migron ☎760 55 81 33 www.surfhostelbiarritz.com

Surf Hostel Biarritz is your best budget-friendly housing option in the area. No, it's not the cheapest possible option, but for €36 per night you get a bed, breakfast, a bike and a surfboard, which effectively covers your housing, transportation, and a third of your meals in one fell swoop. Also, unlike some of the other hostel-options in the area, Surf Hostel Biarritz is within walking distance from both the beaches and the city center, unlike other hostels that forget to inform you that they're practically not even in the same time-zone as the beaches.

However, what Surf Hostel Biarritz offers in good vibes, well-packaged deals, and friendly staff, it lacks in room availability. There are only five rooms which range from singles to quads, but in the peak of tourism season (a.k.a. all summer long, a.k.a. the only time worth going to Biarritz), these rooms fill up fast. But if you're not about to shell out a few hundred euros to stay in the city center, and you're not planning to train for a marathon by commuting from hostels elsewhere, Surf Hostel Biarritz is your best bet.

i €36; includes bed, breakfast, bike, and surfboard. Free Wi-Fi. Washer, drier, and kitchen access available. ☑ Reception M-Sa 8am-noon, 2-5pm.

AUBERGE DE JEUNESSE BIARRITZ
HOSTEL

8 rue Chiquito Cambo ☎559 41 76 00 www.hifrance.org

The name of the Auberge de Jeunesse de Biarritz is misleading, as it is hardly even in Biarritz. In fact, it would take you almost an hour to walk to Biarritz's city center from the Auberge, which really takes away from the experience of vacationing in a coastal town. In the Auberge's defense, its price tag is quite a bit more palatable than the other venues at just €22 per night—just know that the trade-off between price and location for the Auberge is a risky one.

On the bright side, a night at the Auberge includes complimentary breakfast, free Wi-Fi, and (non-complementary) dinner, cocktails from the bar, access to washers and dryers, and bike rentals. Furthermore, if you're not looking to bike the 4km into town every day, there are various public transportation options to expedite the process.

If you've planned far enough in advance, try for Surf Hostel Biarritz, but if it's all filled up, the Auberge is the next best option on a budget.

i Rooms start at €22. ☑ Reception Jan. 20-Apr. 30 8:30-11:30am, 6-9pm; May 1-August 31 8:30am-12:30pm, 6-10pm; Sept. 1-30 8:30am-12:30pm, 6-9:30pm; Oct. 1-Dec. 15 8:30-11:30am, 6-9pm.

france

offer profile and rear views so if you're hoping to snap a picture from the front end, you'd better be an accomplished rock climber.

The statue is centrally located and is situated between the Grande Plage and Le Plage de la Cote des Basques. It's in the perfect spot for those hoping to take a walk down the coastline of Biarritz and is just across the street from La Musee de la Mer, making the two sights easy to knock out at once.

i Free.

MUSEE DE LA MER DE BIARRITZ   MUSEUM
Plateau de l'Atalaye   ☎05 59 22 75 40 www.museedelamer.com/en

La Musee de la Mer de Biarritz is half nautical museum and half aquarium, which is to say, half of the museum is cool. This is somewhat of an overgeneralization, but unless you traveled to Biarritz to look at a variety of differently tied knots behind museum glass, the other half of this museum is knot that cool (GET IT!?). Aside from the knots and the model ships, the aquarium aspect of La Musee de la Mer is quite cool.

The aquarium tanks are filled with a variety of fish (and non-fish sea creatures), which make up a quite prolific collection that's worth checking out. The highlights include sea turtles, seals, and sharks, although the sharks look like they could star in the movie "Honey, I Shrunk the Kids." The seals have the potential to be the most entertaining exhibit given the tank's size and outdoor component. However, the seals' tendency to play dead occasionally makes for a slightly less captivating exhibit.

The museum's location across the street from the Virgin on the Rock makes it convenient to visit via a 10min. walk from downtown Biarritz. The admission fee is a bit steep at €10 per person, but if you're interested in fish tanks or want a closer look at the sardines you've been eating all week, La Musee de la Mer de Biarritz is worth an hour or two of your time.

i Adult €14, students €9.80. ☼ Open Apr-July daily 9:30am-10pm; Aug daily 9:30am-midnight; Sept-Oct daily 9:30am-10pm.

COTE DES BASQUES   SHORELINE
The Cote des Basques is a fancy way of saying "shoreline," but nonetheless, the shoreline in Biarritz is incredible. Fancy name or not, it's very difficult to go wrong with the beaches lining southwestern France. Biarritz may not be the French Riviera, but as far as shoreline and beaches go, Biarritz may actually take the cake. If you're not too keen on the pebbly coast of Nice or the lifelessly flat water of Cannes, Biarritz has just about anything you could want from a coastal town. Think long sandy beaches, powerful rolling waves, warm Atlantic water, and topless sunbathers. Okay, the topless sunbathing thing turns out to be more of a curse than a blessing, but either way, the beaches are better in Biarritz.

However, the Cote des Basques technically encompasses more than just the beaches. The pathways along the shoreline snake along winding, rocky outcrops jutting into the water, not unlike the coastline of California's Big Sur. If you need a break for sunbathing or surfing, a walk south from the Grande Plage will lead you along some of Biarritz's most impressive viewpoints and provide hours of picturesque beauty.

Ultimately, if you're heading to Biarritz for vacation, you certainly don't need to be told why you should visit the Cote des Basques. Biarritz is famous almost solely for its coastal beauty, and the entire town was built around the ocean and the beaches that touch it.

PHARE DE BIARRITZ   LIGHTHOUSE
Esplanade Elisabeth II   ☎05 59 22 37 10

The Phare de Biarritz is a giant lighthouse overlooking the Cote des Basques and offers one of the best views in Biarritz. The lighthouse itself is fairly, old and

biarritz

there's not much to the actual structure other than a long ,windy staircase and a panoramic perch up top. If you're looking to get a good view of the Grande Plage, or all of Biarritz for that matter, the Phare de Biarritz is your best bet.

The lighthouse is located in the middle of Pointe St. Martin, a small outcrop to the North of the Grande Plage. The point itself is a quiet, secluded area devoid of the crowds found at the beach or the tourists found in the town center. An expansive green lawn surrounds the lighthouse with public benches, small gardens, and quiet pathways. And while the point itself provides an incredible view of the ocean and the beaches, a hike up to the peak of the lighthouse provides a breathtaking panorama that could breath life into even the most underwhelming Instagram feed.

Unless shelling out €1.50 is a legitimate problem for you, there's no reason to not visit the Phare de Biarritz. If nothing else, justify your trip up the spiral staircase as your cardio for the day.

i €1.50 to climb to the top. ☼ Open daily 9am-6pm.

FOOD

CAFE JEAN
FRENCH, SPANISH $$
13 rue des Halles ☎05 59 24 13 61 http://cafejean-biarritz.com

Cafe Jean is your go-to tapas joint in Biarritz, serving a mixture of French and Spanish cuisine. The restaurant is a few blocks from rue de Centre, the gourmet hotspot in Biarritz, making Cafe Jean close to the action without being overwhelmed by crowds. The little cafe boasts a friendly and helpful (and English-speaking) staff who will recommend certain dishes with ease and help the tapas-selection process move smoothly.

Start your meal with an aperitif of the house sangria. You've got a red and white option, but given your proximity to Bordeaux, it'd be a shame to pass on the red. Once you're comfortably sipping your sangria, the problem of choosing from the tapas menu awaits. To be fair, struggling to decide what to eat because each option looks so damn good is a true first-world problem and one you should consider yourself lucky to have. Nonetheless, don't pass on the magret de canard or the fois gras—you're only in southwestern France every so often, so take advantage of the duck delicacies while you can.

Ultimately, Cafe Jean is a great venue to grab a light dinner without breaking the bank or your diet plan. You won't end up gorging yourself here unless you dig into each and every possible tapas choice (which wouldn't be the worst idea). The ambiance within the cafe gives off a chic, slightly modern vibe with a few subtle nods to the cafe's Spanish roots. If you're looking for a casual dinner in one of the more popular neighborhoods in Biarritz, you can't go wrong with Cafe Jean.

i Tapas €5-10. ☼ Open daily 9am-3pm, 6:30pm-1am. Closed Su evenings and M Sept-June.

LA TIREUSE
WAFFLES $
29 rue Mazagran ☎05 59 24 26 18 www.facebook.com/latireuse.biarritz

La Tireuse is a beer-drinking waffle-eater's paradise, which would be somewhat of a niche market if it didn't cater to the rest of the world as well. This bar/food stand is reminiscent of a Belgian ski cabin nestled in the mountains, with enough beer decor to furnish several bars twice the size of La Tireuse. The bar area boasts over 20 beers on tap as well as over 50 varieties of bottled beers from around the world. The selections on tap rotate weekly, with a few relatively constant world-renowned brews such as Delirium Tremens. Furthermore, the bar houses a collection of custom glassware for each different beer on tap, ranging from the boringly standard pint glass to the unnecessarily peculiar, bong-shaped glass which is so unstable that it requires its own wooden stand.

The bar serves a selection of "homemade artisan chips," which seem like somewhat of a gimmick but in reality taste phenomenal. (This is even more the case after you've pushed your way through 1/4 of the beers on tap). As far as food goes, however, your best bet is to leave the bar area and head outside toward the waffle stand attached to the side of La Tireuse. This small waffle stand generally serves a standing line about 10 folks long from 8pm onward as every sweet tooth in Biarritz waits their turn to choose from over 10 different waffle choices. Oh, you've never had a Belgian waffle with melted Nutella drizzled over it and a scoop of vanilla ice cream on top? That's a shame because no matter how delicious you're imaging it to be, it's incomprehensibly better than you could imagine. What's more, the waffles are delicious when you're sober, better when you're drunk, and then even better once you're sober again. And that's not even possible!

In short, head to La Tireuse for a beer, or for a waffle, or for both. Bide your time at the pool table in the bar or grab a waffle to go. It doesn't really matter what your plans are for the evening because if they don't involve a pint and a waffle, they probably suck.

i *Waffles starting at €5. Beer starting at €4. ☼ Open W-Su 3pm-2am.*

BALEAK   RESTAURANT $$$$
8 rue du Centre   ☎05 59 24 58 57 http://www.baleak.fr

If you go to only one restaurant during your stay in Biarritz, it should, without a doubt, be Baleak. Baleak translates to "whale" in english, which is more or less how you'll feel if you leave the restaurant having eaten everything on the menu that looks appealing. The food is perfect, the atmosphere both within the restaurant and outside on rue du Centre is lively and energetic, and the food is perfect (in case we forgot to mention that).

Assuming you take our advice and check out Baleak for dinner, know this as well: if there is one restaurant to splurge at in Biarritz, it's Baleak. This is the place to treat yourself to a three-course meal with a glass or two (or five) of wine. You'll start your meal with some tuna and mango tartar if you know what's good for you. And if you're looking to crush the seafood selection, opt next for the seafood platter—a giant bowl of mussels, clams, prawns, calamari, etc. If you're not into the shellfish scene, try the duck or perhaps anything else on the menu, because you literally cannot go wrong.

The ambiance inside the restaurant is energetic yet calm all at once, but if you want the true rue du Centre experience, grab a table in the middle of the street. Rue du Centre is one of the more popular, up and coming gourmet destinations in Biarritz, and, given the lack of terrace space for the many different restaurants lining the street, the eateries have since banded together to close off the entire street at night, moving tables and chairs onto the road for a makeshift dining terrace. The end result is more or less a giant restaurant party in the middle of the street catered by some of the best restaurants in southwestern France. Are you really not going to check that out?

i *Meals starting at €20. ☼ Open for dinner daily July - Aug. Open for lunch and dinner Jan-June Tu-Sa; Sept-Dec Tu-Sa.*

NIGHTLIFE

DUPLEX   CLUB
24 av. Édouard VII   ☎05 59 24 65 39 http://nightclub-biarritz.com/en/

The best word to describe Duplex is "meh" based on the fact that, while there's nothing inherently wrong with it, there's nothing memorably right with it. If you had to describe the most general nightclub ever with three words, you'd probably be describing Duplex, and you probably wouldn't really need more words than three anyway. Dancing, people, alcohol. That's your three word summary. On the bright side, however, it's certainly better than "dancing, empty, alcohol."

Duplex's major appeal is its proximity to the beach and its location in central Biarritz. If you're in downtown Biarritz, you'll never really be more than 10min. away by foot, and you'll more than likely be under 5min. away if you aren't in Old Town. Apart from the convenience factor, there aren't many other reasons to spend the night at Duplex. On the one hand, it's better than Play Boy Club, the other central nightclub in Biarritz. On the other hand, it's so much less fun than Blue Cargo that if you have 15min. and 80 cents to spare, hop on the bus and head there. In all honesty, there is really no reason to head to Duplex before 3am (and if you have other options, there is no reason to head there afterwards).

The cover charge at Duplex earns you one free drink (assuming you couldn't piece together the fact that paying for entry to earn a free drink is just paying for a drink). The most appealing aspect of drinking at Duplex is the fact that if you can round up a couple friends and piece together the funds for a bottle, you can then get a table to sit at. Furthermore, you can drink half the bottle, then essentially check the remaining alcohol behind the bar to drink it the following night, which conveniently allows you to wave the cover charge when you return.

i Cover €10, includes 1 free drink. Mixed drinks €10. 🕐 Open daily midnight-6am.

BLUE CARGO CLUB
Plage d'Ilbaritz ☎05 59 23 54 87 www.bluecargo.fr
If you're in Biarritz and you've spoken with anyone under the age of 30 regarding nightlife venues, you've either heard about Blue Cargo or you're deaf. Blue Cargo is leaps and bounds ahead of any other nightlife venue within a 20mi. radius of Biarritz (full disclosure: we haven't tested every club within that actual radius, but we're still pretty confident Blue Cargo is the best).
🕐 Open daily noon-2am.

ESSENTIALS
Practicalities

- **TOURIST OFFICE:** Sq. d'Ixelles. (☎05 59 22 37 10 www.biarritz.fr. Open July-Aug 9am-7pm. Also offers same-day hotel reservations, campsite reservations, Guide Loisirs, Biarritzscope, and Hebergement city guides.)
- **TOURIST INFORMATION:** 05 59 22 37 10

Emergency

- **EMERGENCY TELEPHONE:** 17
- **FIRE:** 18
- **POLICE:** 17
- **HOSPITALS:** Centre Hospitalier Cote Basque. (13 av. Interne Jacques Loeb, Bayonne ☎05 59 44 35 35) Medecin en Garde. (☎05 59 24 01 01)
- **PHARMACIES:** Marked by green crosses.

Getting There
By Plane

Planes fly into Aeroport de Parme (7 esplanade de l'Europe, 05 59 43 83 83). Bus #6 runs directly to and from the airport. Flights within France and internationally to Dublin, London, Birmingham, Amsterdam, and Helsinki.

france

By Bus
Buses stop at Sq. d'Ixelles and run to St-Jean de-Luz, Hendaye, and San Sebastian.
By Taxi
Taxi de Biarritz (05 59 03 18 18, www.taxis-biarritz.fr)

Getting Around
By Bus
VTAB buses run around the city and stop in front of the tourist office.

By Taxi
Taxi de Biarritz (05 59 03 18 18, www.taxis-biarritz.fr)

By Foot
Biarritz is small enough to make conquering the town on foot fairly simple. Be warned, however, that the town is very hilly, and if you're not one to enjoy walking up hills all day, you'd be wise to consult the bus schedule.

france essentials

MONEY
Tipping
By law in France, a service charge, called "service compris," is added to bills in bars and restaurants. Most people do, however, leave some change (up to €2) for sit-down services, and in nicer restaurants it is not uncommon to leave 5% of the bill. For other services, like taxis and hairdressers, a 10-15% tip is acceptable.

Taxes
The quoted price of goods in France includes value added tax (VAT). This tax on goods is generally levied at 19.6% in France, although some goods are subject to lower rates. Non-EU visitors who are taking these goods home unused may be refunded this tax for purchases totaling over €175 per store. When making purchases, request a VAT form and present it at a Tax Free Shopping Office, found at most airports, road borders, and ferry stations, or by mail. Refunds must be claimed within six months.

SAFETY AND HEALTH
Drugs and Alcohol
Although any mention of France often conjures images of black-clad smokers in berets, France no longer allows smoking in public as of 2008. The government has no official policy on berets. Possession of illegal drugs (including marijuana) in France can result in a substantial jail sentence or fine. Police may arbitrarily stop and search anyone on the street.

There is no drinking age in France, but restaurants will not serve anyone under the age of 16, and to purchase alcohol you must be at least 18 years old. Though there is no law prohibiting open containers, drinking on the street is considered uncouth. The legal blood-alcohol level for driving in France is 0.05%, which is less than it is in the US, UK, New Zealand, and Ireland, so exercise appropriate caution if operating a vehicle in France.

KEEPING IN TOUCH

Cellular Phones

In France, mobile pay-as-you-go phones are the way to go. The two largest carriers are SFR and Orange, and they are so readily available that even supermarkets sell them. Cell-phone calls and texts can be paid for without signing a contract by using a Mobicarte prepaid card, available at Orange and SFR stores, as well as tabacs. You can often buy phones for €20-40, which includes various amounts of minutes and 100 texts. Calling the US from one of these phones is around €0.80 a minute, with texts coming in at around €0.50.

GERMANY

Anything that ever made it big is bound to attract some stereotypes, and Germany is no exception. Beer, crazy deaf composers, robotic efficiency, sausage, Inglourious Basterds—just to name a few. Germany has some of the best collections of art in the world, incredible architecture, and a history that makes it clear no one bosses Germany around. Whether giving the ancient Romans a run for their money or giving birth to Protestantism, Germany has always been a rebel. Even behind its success as a developed country, it hasn't given that up.

The damage from World War II still lingers in city skyscapes, and the country is keenly embarrassed of its Nazi and communist pasts. Even though its concrete wall has been demolished, Berlin, the country's capital, still retains a marked difference between east and west after decades of strife, tempering the picturesque castles and churches of earlier golden ages.

Plenty of discounts, cheap eats, and a large student population make Germany an exciting place to visit and study. It's also incredibly accessible for Anglophone visitors, as many Germans have no qualms about slipping from their native tongue into English. The nightlife and culture of Berlin or Munich will grab you and never let you go, while thriving smaller university towns will charm you into wanting to stay another semester.

greatest hits

- **COLD WAR KIDS.** Admire the Berlin Wall murals painted by artists from around the world at the **East Side Gallery** (p. 299).
- **BEAMER, BENZ, OR BENTLEY.** Sport the classiest threads you own, and head to the **BMW Welt and Museum** (p. 349) to test drive a new whip.
- **DOWN IN ONE.** Pace yourself and avoid using the vomitorium at Munich's most famous beer hall, **Hofbräuhaus** (p. 353).

berlin

So you've decided to visit Berlin. Congratulations. Your pretentious friends went to Paris. Your haughty friends went to London. And your lost friends went to Belarus. But you decided on Berlin. You've probably heard that Berlin is the coolest city in the world, or that it has one of the best clubs in Europe, or that it sleeps when the sun comes up. Well, don't believe the hype. It's not the coolest city in the world; it's several of the coolest cities in the world. It doesn't have one of the best clubs in Europe; it has 10. And to top it off, Berlin never sleeps.

Berlin's rise began with some normal history, taken to epic heights. King Friedrich II and his identically named progeny ruled from canal-lined boulevards, built palaces like middle-fingers to all the haters, and developed Prussia into an Enlightened European powerhouse, with Berlin at the helm. But after centuries of captaining Europe, Berlin went crazy in the 20th. As the seat of Hitler's terror and with World War II drama in its streets, Berlin rebooted in the '50s, only to become a physical manifestation of Cold War divisions. The Berlin Wall rose in 1961, slicing the city and fueling the enmity of a radical student and punk population. Ten years after the Wall crumbled in 1989, the German government decided to relocate from Bonn to Berlin. And from there, Berlin became today's European champion of cool.

Sorry about your friends.

ORIENTATION

Charlottenburg

Should you tire of the immense bustle or forget that Berlin was an old European capital, venture into Charlottenburg. Originally a separate town founded around the grounds of Friedrich I's palace, it became an affluent cultural center during the Weimar years and the Berlin Wall era thanks to Anglo-American support. The neighborhood retains its original old-world opulence, from the upscale Beaux-Arts apartments to the shamelessly extravagant **Kurfürstendamm**, Berlin's premiere shopping strip. **Ku'damm,** as the locals call it, runs from east to west through southern Charlottenburg. Popular sights include the Spree River in the northwest and the absurdly splendiferous **Schloß Charlottenburg** to the north, both of which bolster Charlottenburg's old-Berlin appeal. Aside from the sights, the neighborhood's high rents keep out most young people and students, so the Charlottenburg crowd tends to be old and quiet and prefers the sidewalk seating of expensive Ku'Damm restaurants to crazy ragers in the area's few clubs.

Schöneberg and Wilmersdorf

South of Ku'damm, Schöneberg and Wilmersdorf are primarily quiet residential neighborhoods, remarkable for their world-class cafe culture, bistro tables, relaxed diners, and coffee shops spilling out onto virtually every cobblestone street. Also, nowhere else in Berlin, and perhaps in all of Germany, is the GLBT community quite as spectacularly ready to party as in the area immediately surrounding **Nollendorfplatz.** To the west lies one of Berlin's most convenient outdoor getaways: **Grunewald** rustles with city dwellers trading their daily commute for peaceful strolls with the family dog among the pines. But if you don't have the time for the 20min. bus or tram ride—or if a palm reader once predicted that you would be mauled by dogs in a German forest—then Schöneberg and Wilmersdorf offer a gracious handful of shady parks scattered among their apartment façades, where you can sit in the grass and kick back the cups of joe.

Mitte

Mitte lives up to its name. Literally, Mitte means "center" in English, and every second you spend in Mitte will remind you that it is, in fact, the center of everything in Berlin. You're going to find thousands of tourists in Mitte, and you'll also find anything and everything political, historical, and cultural. Southwest Mitte boasts the **Brandenburg Gate**, the **Reichstag**, and the exceedingly famous **Jewish Memorial.** At the very center of it all, you'll find **Museuminsel**, literally an island of museums that piles some of the world's most awe-inspiring sights practically on top of each other. In the north, Mitte borders **Prenzlauer Berg** starting at **Rosenthaler Platz.** This area has Mitte's cheapest eats and tons of techno clubs you're sure to encounter. Some of the world's most famous performance halls, including the **Berlin Philharmonic** and the **Deutscher Staatsoper,** grace this cultural capital. Then, of course, there's the forest-like **Tiergarten** at the center of Mitte, which shelters sunbathers, barbecuers, pensive wanderers, and probably

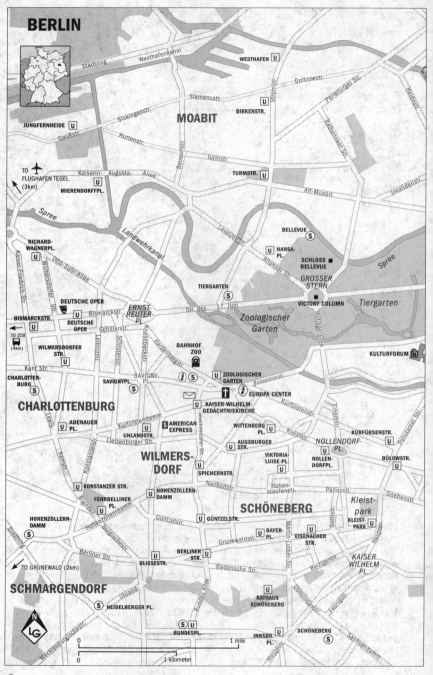

BERLIN

WESTHAFEN

Stadtring · Westhafenkanal

Quitzowstr.

Siemensstr.

JUNGFERNHEIDE

Gaußstr.

Sickingenstr.

MOABIT

BIRKENSTR.

TO FLUGHAFEN TEGEL (3km)

Kaiserin- Augusta- Allee

MIERENDORFFPL.

Huttenstr.

Turmstr.

TURMSTR.

Alt-Moabit

Invalidenstr.

Spree

Landwehrkanal

Leverpostr.

BELLEVUE

RICHARD-WAGNERPL.

Otto-Suhr-Allee

Kaiser-Friedrich-Str.

Wilmersdorfer Str.

HANSA-PL.

SCHLOSS BELLEVUE

Spree

DEUTSCHE OPER

Bismarckstr.

TIERGARTEN

GROSSER STERN

BISMARCKSTR.

DEUTSCHE OPER

ERNST-REUTER-PL.

Schillerstr.

Str. des 17. Juni

VICTORY COLUMN

Tiergarten

TO ZOB (4km)

WILMERSDORFER STR.

Kant Str.

Hardenbergstr.

BAHNHOF ZOO

Zoologischer Garten

Budapesterstr.

KULTURFORUM

CHARLOTTEN-BURG

SAVIGNYPL.

SAVIGNY-PL.

ZOOLOGISCHER GARTEN

CHARLOTTENBURG

Leibnizstr.

Schlüterstr.

EUROPA CENTER

Kurfürstenstr.

ADENAUER PL.

Kurfürstendamm

UHLANDSTR.

Lietzenburger Str.

AMERICAN EXPRESS

KAISER-WILHELM-GEDÄCHTNISKIRCHE

WITTENBERG PL.

Kleiststr.

KÜRFÜRSTENSTR.

Tauentzienstr.

NOLLENDORF-PL.

BÜLOWSTR.

WILMERS-DORF

Konstanzer Str.

AUGSBURGER STR.

VIKTORIA-LUISE-PL.

NOLLEN-DORFPL.

SPICHERNSTR.

Nachodstr.

Hohenstaufenstr.

Pallasstr.

Goebenstr.

KONSTANZER STR.

FEHRBELLINER PL.

HOHENZOLLERN-DAMM

SCHÖNEBERG

Kleist-park

HOHENZOLLERN-DAMM

Hohenzollerndamm

Güntzelstr.

GÜNTZELSTR.

Grunewaldstr.

Martin-Luther-Str.

KLEIST-PARK

Stadtring

Berliner Str.

BERLINER STR.

BAYER-PL.

EISENACHER STR.

KAISER WILHELM PL.

TO GRUNEWALD (2km)

BLISSESTR.

Badensche Str.

Bundes Allee

Dominicusstr.

SCHMARGENDORF

Uhland-

HEIDELBERGER PL.

RATHAUS SCHÖNEBERG

N

LG

BUNDESPL.

INNSBR. PL.

SCHÖNEBERG

0 — 1 mile

0 — 1 kilometer

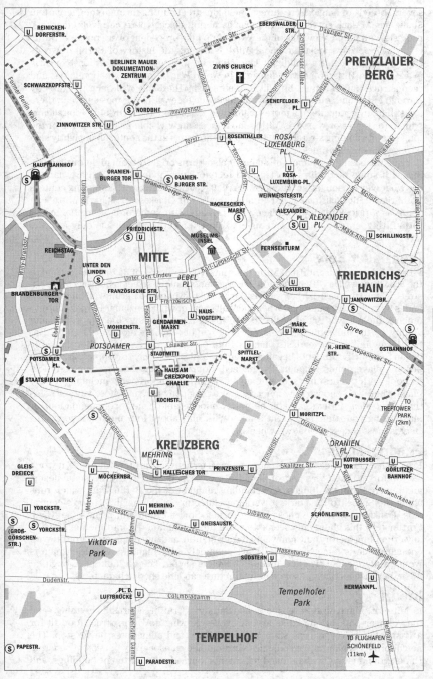

berlin

several breeds of magical creatures. The main street cutting through the Tiergarten, **Straße des 17 Juni,** serves as a popular gathering place where carnivals, markets, protests, and public viewings of the World Cup take precedent over constant traffic.

What's perhaps most fun about Mitte is tracing the history of Berlin down its streets and through its buildings. One common phrase used in relation to nearly every sight in Mitte is "heavily damaged in World War II," and original buildings and reconstructions are often difficult to distinguish. The **Berlin Wall** once ran directly through Mitte, and, though the signs of the divide fade with every passing year, there are still many remnants of a more fragmented Berlin, like the DDR-built **Fernsehturm,** which, for better or worse, is Mitte's most incessantly visible landmark. One of the longest still-standing stretches of the Wall deteriorates in the south, an unsightly sign of unsettling recent times.

But Mitte isn't just about the sights; it also burns brightly from night until morning with some of Berlin's most prized techno clubs, many of which are named, for whatever reason, after baked goods (e.g., **Cookies**). Plus, with shopping centers both ritzy (**Friedrichstraße**) and intimidatingly hip (**Hackescher Markt**), Mitte can serve as a pricey place to replace your threads with something more flannel or form-fitting; entry into the sometimes exclusive nightlife options is only a flashy strut away.

Prenzlauer Berg

P'Berg is the area just north of Mitte that runs from the edge of **Rosenthaler Platz** up to the **Schönhauser Allee** U-Bahn station. P'Berg's most famous street is **Bernauer Strasse,** a street which runs east(ish) to west(ish), parallel to where the Berlin Wall once stood, and is dotted with memorials. When the Wall came down, Prenzlauer Berg was pretty much a ghost town. But after decades of lower rents drawing students, youth, and vitality, by the millennium, Prenzlauer Berg had become the hippest of the hip. But hip, by definition, never lasts, and as time progressed, Prenzlauer Berg steadily began to gentrify: students became parents, hippies gave way to yuppies, and parks became playgrounds. Though it's changed, Prenzlauer Berg hasn't completely lost its cool: with the best bar scene of any of Berlin's neighborhoods, including a wine place where you choose how much to pay, a ping-pong bar, and more vintage sofas than *Mad Men*, P'Berg can still be pretty unbelievable. One recommendation for maximizing your time here: rent a bike. With only about four metro stations, this Berg is most accessible on two wheels.

Friedrichshain

Friedrichshain is one of Berlin's cheaper districts. It's rough around the edges, it won't let you forget that it was part of the DDR, and it's plastered in graffiti, metal-heads, and punks. From the longest still-standing remnant of the Berlin Wall, which runs along the Spree, to the stark, towering architecture of the neighborhood's central axis, **Frankfurter Allee**, the ghost of the former Soviet Union still haunts the 'Hain. Fortunately, this ghost only seems to scare the population out into the night, when any crumbling factory, any cobwebbed train station, and any complex of graffiti with enough grime is fair game for F'Hain's sublimely edgy nightlife. Friedrichshain is wonderfully inexpensive and unique. Travelers should keep a lookout, though, at night, because its often desolate infrastructure can hide shady characters.

Kreuzberg

If Mitte is Manhattan, Kreuzberg is Brooklyn. Graffiti adorns everything, and the younger population skulks around while chowing down on street food fit for a Last Supper. The parties start later, end later, and sometimes never stop. The neighborhood's alternative soul sticks around like an especially persistent squatter. Underground clubs in abandoned basements, burned-out apartment buildings, and oppressive warehouse complexes shake off their dust when the sun disappears and rage until well after it reappears. The area is also home to most of Berlin's enormous Turkish population (hence the nickname "Little Istanbul"). *Döner* kebabs, the salty scraps cut from those gigantic meaty beehives in every other storefront, go for €2-3 all across this district, and the **Turkish Market** along the southern bank of the **Landwehrkanal** is one of the most exciting, raucous, cheap, and authentic markets in Western Europe. If you want to learn about Berlin, head to Mitte. If you want to not remember what you learned, come to Kreuzberg.

ACCOMMODATIONS

Charlottenburg

HAPPY GO LUCKY HOTEL
HOSTEL $
Stuttgarter Platz 17
☎30 327 09 072

The Germans tend to be straightforward, and this quiet hostel is no exception. With friendly staff and friendlier prices, Happy Go Lucky is just that. We appreciated the festive graffiti (did you know you were in Berlin?), over-ate from the €6 breakfast buffet, and filled the peaceful courtyard with cigarette smoke. Although it's far from the rush of the city's center, its proximity to cute cafes, cheap eats, and the U-bahn and S-bahn will certainly make you happy (though you might not get lucky). Until recently, this stop was called the Berolina Backpacker, and much of the integrity of the original backpacker's oasis remains the same. Large groups (like high-school field trips) commonly book here, so it might be worth it to book ahead of time.

i *Dorms from €9. Singles €38. Doubles from €65.* ☒ *Reception 24hr.*

ALETTO KUDAMM
HOSTEL $
Hardenbergstr. 21
☎30 233 214 100

Though the logo frightens us (we think it was inspired by a bad trip in a sex shop), the Aletto Hotel and Hostel makes up for this colorful cactus-dildo with immaculately clean rooms (personal air-conditioning and a TV?!), inviting staff, and more ballsy activities in the common spaces than we have time for (quite literally: foosball, futballs, ping-pong balls, billiard balls, and metal balls in a sand pit are just the start). A 2min. walk from the Zoologischer Garten, the Aletto Kudamm is an ideal location for less-than-ideal Charlottenburg. Aletto also has this wonderful hotel/hostel combination in Schoeneberg and Kreuzberg, so it maintains high standards that give this contemporary stop an almost sanitized feel.

i *Dorms €12. Singles €39. Doubles €49.* ☒ *Reception 24hr.*

Schöneberg and Wilmersdorf

GRAND HOSTEL BERLIN
HOSTEL $
Tempelhofer Ufer 14
☎30 200 95 450

Though technically this hostel is located in neighboring Kreuzberg, it's only a 10min. walk from the heart of Schöneberg (and 10 seconds from Mockenbrucke station) and well worth the commute. Upon arrival at the grand 19th-century building, you'll be greeted with a complimentary beer or coffee while you're waiting to get checked into your room. On top of this unexpected hospitality, the reception is warmly welcoming and adjacent to a cozy bar/library where you'll find many of the hostel's residents working while they drink or drinking while they work. Are you starting to understand why it's won all those awards? A royal staircase bridges the old to the new where rooms and amenities are consistently spotless and spacious. The only downside? Its reputation attracts a ton of fellow travelers, so make sure to book in advance. Regardless, this is one of our favorite spots to come back to in Berlin.

i Dorms €14. Singles €39. Doubles €44. Breakfast €6. ☉ Reception 24hr.

JUGENDHOTEL BERLINCITY
HOTEL $$

Crellestr. 22

Nestled in a cozy nook of peaceful Schöneberg, Jugendhotel Berlincity is a great option for travelers looking to cafe-hop by day and avoid the clubs by night. Our only hesitation is the lack of dormitory option; the only choice is to book a private room regardless of whether you are a one-woman wolfpack or a six-person group. Given the location and private-room-only option, this hotel is better suited for older couples or younger groups who are traveling for the first time.

i Singles from €35. Doubles from €50.

Mitte

CIRCUS HOSTEL
HOSTEL $$

Weinbergsweg 1A   ☏30 2000 3939

Don't be fooled by the colorful interior; this circus isn't joking around. With exceptionally clean rooms overlooking the bustling Rosenthaler Platz, outstandingly helpful and friendly staff, a famous breakfast buffet, and even a microbrewery bar in the basement, we couldn't ask for much more. You might not even leave the hostel the entire time you're in Berlin. But given the Circus Hostel's proximity to Mitte's greatest bars and restaurants, you might just have to. Don't fear—you can bring the hostel with you; they run weekly pub crawls, and sightseeing tours, and offers bike rentals, along with so many more extras that you'll extend your stay. Oh, don't forget to pay respect to the shrine for David Hasselhoff in the basement—the mural even has real chest hair.

i Dorms €23-27. Singles €50. Doubles €66. ☉ Reception 24hr.

WOMBAT'S CITY HOSTEL
HOSTEL $

Alte Schönhauser Str. 2   ☏30 8471 0820

Wombat's is a hostel disguised as a hotel, or a hotel disguised as a hostel. We can't exactly figure it out, but whatever they're doing we don't want them to stop. In addition to their spacious rooms, spotless interior, and spirited employees, they have a rooftop bar and terrace with a great view of the Fersehturm. Don't sweat the slightly more expensive rates—the first beer at their bar is on them.

i Dorms €17. ☉ Reception 24hr.

HEART OF GOLD HOSTEL
HOSTEL $

Johannisstr. 11   ☏30 2900 3300

Heart of Gold has the answer to the ultimate question, and it's 42. If you're confused, don't panic! You'll soon discover that Heart of Gold is *Hitchhiker's Guide to the Galaxy*-themed, and Google will help you with any references you don't get. The rooms are so large they feel like deep space, but they're much cleaner than the atmosphere. The wall-sized windows and quaint courtyard provide the perfect vantage points for stargazing or day drinking, whichever you prefer. You won't leave saying, "So long, and thanks for all the fish," but you will be thanking the Heart of Gold for much more.

i Dorms from €17. ☉ Reception 24hr.

EASTENER HOSTEL MITTE
HOSTEL $

Novalisstr. 14   ☏175 1123 515

The Eastener is the coziest hostel we've found in Mitte. Matt (the owner) and the rest of the staff are outgoing and accommodating and are perpetually willing to help. The rooms, as advertised, are tiny, but the location is prime and on a surprisingly quiet street given its proximity to main attractions of Mitte. The

berlin

Eastener is a perfect hostel for a quick one- to three-night stay, but any longer and you should look for somewhere a bit more spacious.

i *Dorms from €17. ☺ Reception until 8pm.*

ST. CHRISTOPHER'S HOSTEL
Rosa-Luxemburg-Straße 41

HOSTEL $$
www.st-christophers.co.uk

St. Christopher's embodies the backpacker's spirit. The culture is youthful and energetic, and the vibrant common areas attract a lively crowd. The best part of St. Christopher's might be Belushi's, which is its famous UK-style sports pub that runs great happy hours and is the perfect start to any night out in Berlin. The rooms uphold the same standard of spaciousness and cleanliness as just about every other hostel chain, so you won't have any surprises except how much fun you're going to have. Enjoy.

i *Dorms €20-27. ☺ Reception 24hr.*

BAXPAX DOWNTOWN
Ziegelstr. 28

HOSTEL $
☎30 2787 4880 www.baxpax.de

Baxpax Downtown has got it goin' on. They've figured out everything a youthful traveler could want or need and set a new standard for the all-inclusive hostel. It has a bar and lounge downstairs with enough cheap snacks to satiate your whole group for under €10, and there's even a club in the basement. On top of that, they have two pop-up pools for the summertime heat waves. Brightly colored walls and wooden floors give Baxpax Downtown plenty of character, and comfortable rooms promise a much-deserved night's rest.

i *Dorms €15-23. ☺ Reception 24hr.*

GENERATOR HOSTEL
Oranienburger Str. 65

HOSTEL $$
☎30 9210 37680

Like a new flavor of Pringle, Generator is trendy and crisp. With locations in some of the more fashion-forward cities around the globe, Generator hostels are meant to reflect the design-oriented spaces they accommodate. The result is a perfect spot for those who wish they could stay at the 25hour hotel but can't afford it. The staff can tell you the best 400 places in Berlin to get single-sourced cold-pressed coffee and will gladly do so. Overall, Generator is a comfortable option with an artsy, urban twist.

i *Dorms €20. ☺ Reception 24hr.*

MEININGER HOTEL AND HOSTEL HUMBOLDTHAUS
Oranienburger Str. 67-68

HOSTEL $
☎30 3187 9816 www.meininger-hotels.com

Meininger is another chain that combines the hostel concept with a hotel feel. It has a high standard of cleanliness almost to a sanitized degree and space-filling decorations that remind you that you're staying here for function, not fashion. The rooms err on the smaller side, but given the prices and proximity to Mitte's most popular attractions, restaurants, and bars, you might run into us staying here again.

i *Dorms €12-20. ☺ Reception 24hr.*

Prenzlauer Berg

EASTSEVEN HOSTEL BERLIN
Schwedter Str. 7

HOSTEL $$
www.eastseven.de

East Seven is cozy and opinionated, and we absolutely love it. Nestled on a quiet street in Prenzlauerberg (which is everywhere, but you get the idea), East Seven caters to the backpacker who has taste. With an indoor lounge and beautiful patio area equipped with a grill, this place understands how to make travelers feel at home. Rooms are spacious with hardwood floors, elegant windows, and subtle-hued stripes that your grandmother would approve of. The young, knowledgeable staff makes checking-in welcoming and easy; just make sure you take advantage of their expertise of all things Berlin.

i *Dorms from €23. ⏰ Reception 7am-midnight.*

ALCATRAZ HOSTEL
HOSTEL $

Schönhauser Allee 133A — www.alcatraz-backpacker.de

If the real Alcatraz took some lessons from this hostel, they'd never again have problems with people trying to escape because no one would want to leave. The staff is friendly and accommodating, the common spaces (a.k.a. the chillout room and common kitchen) are tidy and outfitted with foosball along with some well-worn couches, and the location is uber-close to the U-bahn. The only commonality we can find between this Alcatraz and the prison is that the hostel rooms err on the cozier side and the decorations are pretty minimal. Instead of sitting in your room contemplating these similarities, take a stroll into the central courtyard or enjoy the bright murals lining the walls.

i *Dorms from €12. ⏰ Reception 7am-1am.*

Friedrichshain

U INN BERLIN HOSTEL
HOSTEL $

Finowstr. 36 — ☎30 330 24410 www.uinnberlinhostel.com

In one of the busiest nightlife districts in Berlin, U Inn Berlin Hostel is a restful refuge, quiet sanctuary, and peaceful perch amid the never-ending nocturnal abyss that is Friedrichshain. Though still proximal to the busiest parts of the nightlife districts, U Inn Berlin is nestled on one of the quieter streets in northern Friedrichshain and is only a stone's throw from the best restaurants and cafes anywhere in Berlin. Exceptionally friendly staff will invite you to cook dinner with them, similarly congenial travelers will invite you to party with them, and this cozy hostel will definitely look forward to having you back.

i *Dorms €18. Singles €34. Doubles €54. ⏰ Reception 7am-11pm.*

INDUSTRIEPALAST
HOSTEL $$

Warschauer Str. 43 — ☎30 7407 8290 www.ip-hostel.com

We can't really think of a better way to describe the vibe of Friedrichshain than an industrial palace. We also can't really think of a better place to stay than Industriepalast. Rising along with the tide of the hotel/hostel combo, Industriepalast is the perfect amount of professional while still staying on a budget. Especially given its proximity to every club in the Kreuzberg/Friedrichshain area, Industriepalast is the perfect place from which to stage your 48hr. techno marathon.

i *Dorms €22. Doubles €80. ⏰ Reception 24hr.*

SCHLAFMEILE
HOSTEL $

Weichselstr. 26a — ☎30 2068 7314 www.schlafmeile.de

Boxhagener Platz is the place to start any night out in Berlin, and Schlafmeile is the place to crash after any night (or morning) out in Berlin. Luckily for you the two are synonymous, so begin your day in one of the hundreds of idyllic cafes surrounding Schlafmeile, grab a quick burger before the long night out, and look forward to coming back to the cozy nook that is Schlafmeile Hostel. With the reception doubling as a bar, we give Schlafmeile a 10/10 for having their priorities straight.

i *Dorms €15. ⏰ Reception 8am-midnight.*

SUNFLOWER HOSTEL
HOSTEL $$

Helsingforser Str. 17 — ☎30 4404 4250 www.sunflower-hostel.de

Sunflower isn't quite is pretty as the name suggests, but you really couldn't get much closer to Berghain. Depending on who you are, this could either be perfect or horrible. Regardless, the young, hip staff bump indie-rock and techno music

24/7, so even if you don't get into Berghain you can come back and drink the night away to drum-and-bass anyway. Sarcastically encouraging quotes decorate the walls, a strange collection of dolls hang from the ceiling in the lounge, and a whole range of characters who might not even be staying there gather for drunken evenings (and mornings) every night of the week.

i *Dorms €20-28.* 🕐 *Reception 24hr.*

EASTERN COMFORT HOSTELBOAT
HOSTEL $

Mühlenstr. 73-77 ☎30 6676 3806 www.eastern-comfort.com

That's right. This hostel is on a boat. We don't even really care about anything else—we're happy enough that we're floating and get to spend the night. Especially given the potential for this to be the most kitschy, gimmicky tourist trap known to traveler-kind, we were delighted that the accommodations were surprisingly acceptable. You can even camp on deck and have a view of the East Side Gallery. We wouldn't not do it again.

i *Camping €15. Dorms from €16.* 🕐 *Reception 24hr.*

Kreuzberg

THE CAT'S PAJAMAS
HOSTEL $

Urbanstr. 84 www.thecatspajamashostel.de

The Cat's Pajamas is the cat's meow; seriously, this fabulous feline hostel is far from a flophouse. Modern, minimalist, and magnificently clean, the Cat's Pajamas is the attenuated accommodation in an ideal location. Right on the border of New Age Neukolln and creative Kreuzberg, the Cat's Pajamas is equipped with every amenity a backpacker could need or want. This hostel puts the icing on the cake with artful decor that continues to convince you you're in one of the most creative and progressive places in the world, with one of the hippest hostels to boot.

i *Dorms from €15. Singles €49. Doubles €60.* 🕐 *Reception 24hr.*

THREE LITTLE PIGS HOSTEL BERLIN
HOSTEL $

Stresemannstr. 66 www.three-little-pigs.de

The big bad wolf of Berlin is a daunting beast. The Three Little Pigs Hostel has outsmarted its perpetrator, though, with a location that locals are envious of. The hostel is equidistant from both the cultural epicenter of Mitte and the nocturnal haven of Kreuzberg and Friedrichshain. If you have to see everything Berlin has to offer in little to no time, the Three Little Pigs Hostel will be a perfect perch from which to explore the city. The hostel is much more than just a location, though, with amenities that are far from a pig sty. This place isn't just for youthful swine; appreciate their taste in decor, knack for cleanliness, and overall hospitality that will make you proud to be a little pig.

i *Dorms from €13.* 🕐 *Reception 24hr.*

COMEBACKPACKERS HOSTEL
HOSTEL $

Adalbertstr. 97 www.comebackpackers.com

Kottbusser Tor has two rush hours. The first is 5-7pm on weekdays, and the second is any time after midnight on Friday until Sunday morning. Seriously. This nocturnal haven is buzzing all weekend. And Comebackpackers Hostel is the perfect refuge to take a break from the hustle and bustle of Kreuzberg, or to bring the bustle with you into Comebackpackers's super-social common space. "By travellers, for travellers," Comebackpackers is a hostel purist's heaven, with no indication of a sanitized hotel atmosphere now or to come. This place has soul, and for that we love it.

i *Dorms from €14.* 🕐 *Reception 24hr.*

BAXPAX KREUZBERG   HOSTEL $

Skalitzer Str. 104   www.baxpax.de/kreuzberg

Baxpax Hostels are scattered about Berlin, and all offer the same grungy grit-
tiness that reflects the spirit of Berlin perfectly. Although the amenities might
not be the same caliber as many of the Newer-Age hotel/hostels that seem to be
trending all throughout Europe, Baxpax Kreuzberg embodies the traveler spirit
that hasn't changed since the '60s. All youthful spirits welcome.

i Dorms €10-15. ☎ Reception 24hr.

SIGHTS

Charlottenburg

OLYMPIASTADION   STADIUM

Olympischer Platz 3   ☎30 306 88 100

Originally erected for the 1936 Olympics, the Olympiastadion operates today
as, well, a stadium. Occasionally hosting major sporting events (such as the
2006 FIFA World Cup final) and concerts, the stadium generally functions as
a tourist attraction for those interested in seeing one of the three Nazi-built
monumental structures, but really the stadium acts as an unofficial monument
to Jesse Owens. If you've never heard of him, he was an African American track
and field athlete in the 1936 Games who won four gold medals, but some dude
with a mustache refused to recognize his wins due to his race. Because of the
significance of the fact that Germany hosted the Olympics in 1936, it is definitely
worth the trip out west to check this place out and reflect on the turbulence
Berlin has experienced throughout the last century.

i €7, students €5.50. Audio guide €4. Guided tour €11, students €9.50. ☎ Open daily Apr-July
9am-7pm; Aug 9am-8pm; Sept-Oct 9am-7pm; Nov-Mar 10am-4pm.

SCHLOSS CHARLOTTENBURG   PALACE

Spandauer Damm 20-24   ☎30 320 911

Sprawling extravagance shouldn't repel you from this garish Baroque palace, but
man does strolling through the inside make your wallet feel thin. Not only does
entrance cost €12 (€8 for students), but there is so much rich people stuff on the
inside, you'd think they would be more careful about who they let in. From the
outside this place is no joke either. Commissioned as a gift for his wife in the
1600s, Friedrich I must have screwed up bad if he built a palace to get out of
the doghouse. Be sure to stroll along the beautiful and immaculately maintained
garden, which spans for acres behind the palace (all for free!). The weaving
network of paths wrap around gardens, fountains, and even a summer residence
called Belvedere (tours from €4). All of this makes it the perfect destination for
a summer picnic or romantic stroll.

i €12, students €8. Photo pass €3. Audio tour free. Garden free from sunrise to sunset. ☎ Open
Tu-Su 10am-6pm.

MUSEUM BERGGRUEN   MUSEUM

Schloßstr. 1

Need a break from the beautiful faces all around Berlin? Soak up Picasso in all of
his asymmetrical glory and gain some appreciation for those good-lookin' folks
at your hostel. There are two whole floors dedicated to Picasso's work, so even
if you're not a Picasso enthusiast you might be by the time you leave. Along with
the expansive Picasso collection, Museum Berggruen has a room dedicated to
Matisse, some Paul Klee scattered about, and a few creepy humanoid statues
made by Alberto Giacometti (one extra-tall one standing guard as you walk
in—look out).

i €10, students €5. Audio guide free. ☎ Open Tu-F 10am-6pm, Sa-Su 11am-6pm.

berlin

BROHANMUSEUM
MUSEUM

Schloßstr. 1a

You'll never again forget what Art Deco means, but you might want to after sponging up so much functional Cubism. The Brohanmuseum houses an expansive collection of furniture, paintings, sculptures, and posters highlighting the origins and progressions of the Art Nouveau and Art Deco era (roughly 1889-1940). For those of us rusty with art history, this essentially means that every item at the cat lady's eclectic garage sale can be found here. Seriously. This place is like the collection of leftovers from the set of *That 70's Show*.

i €6, students €4. ☒ Open Tu-Su 10am-6pm.

KATHE-KOLLWITZ MUSEUM
MUSEUM

Fasanenstr. 24

Though not as large as many of the museums in Berlin, the Kathe-Kollwitz Museum is one of the most moving. Through WWI and WWII, Kathe Kollwitz was a member of the Berlin Sezession, and through her haunting depictions of wartime suffering, she became one of the most prominent German artists of the 20th century. Her illustrations and sculptures are tonally dark and elicit equally dark feelings from emotionally trying times. You can feel the presence of death and suffering in each of her pieces, which is both an incredible feat and emotionally draining. The experience is not one to miss.

i €6, students €3. ☒ Open daily 11am-6pm.

C/O BERLIN
MUSEUM

Hardenbergstr. 22-24 ☎30 284 441 662

C/O Berlin is one of Berlin's newest museum additions. It operates as both a performance space and photography museum. The installations rotate every few months but attract a diverse range of artists and photographic styles. Whether you're a fine-art photographer or daily selfie-stick user, C/O Berlin is worth a visit. In addition to its neatly curated photo spaces, it also has a quaint cafe bustling with aspiring artists. We recommend C/O Berlin for a lunch-break museum tour and coffee or for one of its many events (which are often free!).

i €10, students €5. ☒ Open daily 11am-8pm.

Schöneberg and Wilmersdorf

Schöneberg sights are a mix of pastoral parks and whatever cultural bits and pieces ended up in this largely residential neighborhood. Travelers with limited time in Berlin should note that attractions here are few and far between and aren't easily and efficiently visited. If you want to see them all, attack these sights in groups.

🖼 GRUNEWALD AND THE JAGDSCHLOSS
PARK

Am Grunewaldsee 29 (Access fromPücklerstr.) ☎030 813 35 97 www.spsg.de

This 3 sq. km park, with winding paths through wild underbrush, gridded pines, and a peaceful lake, is popular dog-walking turf and a great change from the rest of bustling Berlin. About a 1km walk into the woods is the **Jadgschloß,** a restored royal hunting lodge that houses a gallery of portaits and paintings by German artists like Anton Graff and Lucas Cranach the Elder. The one-room hunting lodge is worth skipping, unless you find pottery shards particularly enthralling. Instead, walk around the grounds or take a hike north in the forest to **Teufelsberg** ("Devil's Mountain"), the highest point in Berlin that was made from WWII rubble piled over a Nazi military school.

i U3 or U7: Fehrbelliner Pl., or S45 or S46: Hohenzollerndamm, then bus #115 (dir. Neuruppiner Str. or Spanische Alle/Potsdamer): Pücklerstr. Turn left onto Pücklerstr., follow the signs, and continue straight into the forest to reach the lodge. Check the Jadgschloß visitor center for a map. Hunting lodge €4, students €3. Tours in German €1) offered on weekends. ☒ Open spring-fall Tu-Su 10am-6pm, last entry 5:30pm; winter Sa-Su 10am-4pm, last entry 3:30pm.

BRÜCKE MUSEUM
MUSEUM

Bussardsteig 9 ☎030 831 20 29 www.brueckemusuem.de

The Brücke (The Bridge) houses a number of brightly-colored oil paintings which you'd think were put together by Monet. Think again. For us non-artistic folk, no-names line every wall of this museum. Their works are part of *Die Brücke* movement, which showcases thick brushstrokes, super-bright yellows, and other energetic colors. This museum is tiny and extremely far from almost everything else, but for anyone who's heard of *Die Brücke* before, it'll be worth the trek. It's not often you get to experience your passion in a modern building nestled at the edge of a German wood.

i *U3 or U7: Fehberlliner Pl., ther bus#115 (dir. Neuruppiner Str. to Spanische Allee/Potsdammer): Finkenstraße, then walk back up Clayallee about 50ft. and turn left onto the footpath leading into the woods. Look for signs. €5, students €3. Cash only. ◲ Open M 11am-5pm and W-Su 11am-5pm.*

ALTER SANKT-MATTHÄUS-KIRCHHOF
CEMETERY

On Großgörschen Str. ☎030 78 11 850

We're fairly sure Hansel and Gretel and the mean-nasty witch they killed are all buried in this cemetery. Well, maybe not, but both of the Grimm brothers are. This *Kirchhof* is an expansive and sloping retreat from the city around, and it's isolated from the bustle by tall trees and hushed gardens. Besides the infamous Brothers Grimm, this cemetery is the eternal resting place of Romantic composer Max Bruch. A grand, mid-19th-century chapel juts out from the shrubbery, as do a number of gigantic and increasingly impressive structures that old Berlin families built for their deceased. After you've spent an hour grave hunting, stop by the cafe and flower shop to ease yourself back into the hassles of the living.

i *U7, S2, S25: Yorckstr. ◲ Open in summer M-F 8am-8pm, Sa-Su 9am-8pm; winter M-F 8am-4pm, Sa-Su 9am-8pm. Hours vary by month. Cafe open M-Sa 9am-6pm.*

VIKTORIA-LUISE-PLATZ
PARK

Intersection of Motzstr. and Winterfeldstr.

Come young, come homeless! Like the best German *Plätze*, Viktoria-Luise-Platz just seems to bring everyone together during those blissfully sunny afternoons. There's probably a kid trying out his new skateboard tricks on one side and a young mother watching her child take its first steps on the other. This oasis of a park is named after Wilhelm II's daughter and, in keeping with its name, channels the extravagance of an older, pre-war, bourgeois Berlin, with a central geyser of a fountain and a Greco-Roman-looking row of columns standing guard at one side. Take advantage of the lack of an open container law and bring your booze collection and a blanket to sip lazily amid the perfectly green grass and flowers.

i *U4: Viktoria-Luise-Pl.*

RATHAUS SCHÖNEBERG
COURTHOUSE

John-F.-Kennedy-Pl. 1

The *Rathaus* (literally, "courthouse") here is pretty unremarkable, being the stark, early 19th-century building that it is (so many straight lines!). Still, JFK came here to establish that he was a jelly-filled doughnut during his Translation 101 case study-worthy speech in which he declared, "Ich bin ein Berliner." But this place isn't just a dull and historical courthouse. It also houses a flea market every Saturday and Sunday on the *Platz* out front bearing Jack's name. Even if you come here midweek, the huge park is an ideal spot to romp around, catch some sun, and nibble on whatever foodstuffs you happen to bring with you.

i *U4: Rathaus Schöneberg. ◲ Flea market open Sa-Su 10am-6pm.*

GAY MEMORIAL
MEMORIAL

Just outside the Nollendorf U-Bahn station

Don't blink! You might miss it. This slightly hidden memorial is shaped like a Crayola crayon, with six ultra-neon colors running down its sides. The small monument commemorates homosexuals killed during World War II. There's not a whole lot to see here—the memorial is tiny, and the markings are virtually nonexistent. Still, it's worth turning your head if you happen to pass by on the way to the Nollendorfplatz U-Bahn stop.

i *U1, U3, U4, or U9: Nollendorfpl.*

Mitte

MEMORIAL TO THE MURDERED JEWS OF EUROPE
MEMORIAL

Cora-Berliner-Straße 1

Simple, haunting, and beautiful, the Memorial to the Murdered Jews of Europe is well worth a visit. Stark concrete blocks arranged in a grid pattern over an entire city block, the location is not one you'd expect for a place of reflection. As you walk deeper into the grid, though, you'll become surrounded by towering blocks in a maze of gray and the noise of the city will recede into silence. After losing yourself among the concrete labyrinth, head below ground for a moving, informative exhibit on the history of Judaism during World War II. Especially devastating is the "family" room, which presents pre-war Jewish family portraits and then investigates the individual fates of the family members. The last room continuously plays one of the thousands of compiled mini-biographies of individuals killed in the Holocaust.

i *Free.* ☒ *Open Tu-Su 10am-7pm; closed Mondays.*

BRANDENBERG GATE
GATE

Pariser Pl. ☎030 250 02 333

You've already seen its image obnoxiously covering the windows of every passing U-Bahn train, but upon approaching the real Brandenburg Gate for the first time, trumpets may still blare in your head. During the day, tourists swarm this famous 18th-century gate; however, the wise traveler will return at night to see it ablaze in gold. Friedrich Wilhelm II built the gate as a symbol of military victory, but Germans these days prefer to shy away from that designation. A system of gates (and, independently, a certain famous wall) once surrounded it, but today only this most famous gate remains.

i *S1, S2, or S25: Brandenburger Tor.*

PERGAMON MUSEUM
MUSEUM

Bodestr. 1-3

We aren't kidding when we say that people come all the way to Berlin just to check this place out. Here's why: Pergamon was the capital of a Hellenistic kingdom, and the museum reconstructs its temple to nearly its full size, so you can walk up its steep steps. The awe-inspiring battle relief on the wall displays jagged toothed snakes ripping off heroes' arms while titans tear lions' mouths apart. The Mesopotamian Ishtar Gate, reconstructed tile-by-tile from the original, rises 30m into the air, then stretches 100m down a hallway. You'll hardly believe it, so come see it. But wait! The Pergamon Museum is under renovation until 2019, so if you want to get the full effect you should wait to book your tickets until then. The closures affect the Pergamon Altar, the North Wing, and the Hall of Hellenistic Architecture. The Market Gate of Miletus, the Ishtar Gate and Processional Way from Babylon, and the Museum of Islamic Art will remain open during this time.

i *€12, students €6. Museum Island Pass (Museuminsel ticket; €18, students €9) is a one-day pass to all of the museums on Museum Island (hint: it's worth it). For an even better deal, get the Museum Pass, which is a 3-day (consecutive) ticket to all of the National Museums of Berlin (Staatliche Museen zu Berlin) and a few others (hint: it's even more worth it). €24, students €12.* ☒ *Open daily 10am-6pm.*

BERLINER DOM
LANDMARK
Am Lustgarten

As one of Berlin's most magnificent buildings, this landmark is impossible to miss and would be a mistake not to visit. Unfortunately, you have to pay a small fee to enter the church, but the grandeur of the inside will quickly wipe your memory bank of any fiscal resentment. After thoroughly exceeding your aesthetic expectations, take a walk up the stairway to heaven (it never ends), stop to gaze at the museum of the church's construction along the way, and then enjoy a stroll around the dome itself and find some spectacular views of the city. Just don't fall down the stairway on your way down—you wouldn't want to end up in the spooky crypt beneath the church.

i €7, students €5. ☑ Open M-Sa 9am-8pm, Su noon-8pm.

NEUES MUSEUM
MUSEUM
Bodestr. 1-3

Ironically, the Neues Museum (literally translated to New Museum) houses one of the best collections of ancient artifacts in the world. In addition to the incredible collection of sarcophagi, jewelry, and sculptures throughout the space, the museum itself is a remarkable work of modern architecture and worth a visit by itself. Don't miss Nefertiti—she's kinda famous. Then learn about your origins from the "time machine" and massive collection of prehistoric artifacts. Wander into the central chamber on the second floor, and you might just feel like the slab of granite you're standing on is floating through some esoteric Egyptian incantation. Given that the Neues Museum is one of the best museums in Berlin, it manages to attract quite a crowd, so get here early or reserve tickets online to avoid lines.

i €12, students €6. ☑ Open M-W 10am-6pm, Th 10am-8pm, F-Su 10am-6pm.

ALTE NATIONALGALERIE
MUSEUM
Bodestr. 1-3

This expansive collection of late-19th- and early-20th-century, mostly German artwork pays its dues to *fin de siècle* greats such as Adolph von Menzel, Paul Cezanne, Auguste Rodin, Caspar David Friedrich, and many more. The first floor is an ode to Realism with canvases depicting everything from France to feet, while the second floor reminds us of artwork that could be on the cover of some elven fantasy novel (apparently they call that Romanticism). Additionally, there's a small collection of works by the French Impressionist masters like Monet, Manet, Munet, Bidet (OK, maybe not the last two), and Renoir.

i €12, students €6. ☑ Open Tu-W 10am-6pm, Th 10am-8pm, F-Su 10am-6pm; closed Mondays.

ALTES MUSEUM
MUSEUM
Am Lustgarten

Standing as a pillared fortress across the courtyard from the Berliner Dom, the Alte (meaning "old") Museum has an expansive collection of things that are, well, pretty darn old. With mostly Roman and Etruscan antiquities like vases, sculptures, jewelry, and tons of other artifacts from the daily lives of the long-dead, the Altes Museum can be a bit overwhelming after visiting the much more grandiose Pergamon and Neues Museums. Don't brush this one under the rug, though, because it has a world-famous collection of Greek sculptures, terracotta, and ancient coins that is worth checking out.

i €10, students €5. ☑ Open Tu-W 10am-6pm, Th 10am-8pm, F-Su 10am-6pm; closed Mondays.

BODE MUSEUM
MUSEUM
Am Kupfergruben

The Bode Museum houses a gigantic collection of sculptures dating back to the Middle Ages. Basically this means there are a ton of crazy fold-out nativity scenes made out of wood, more sculptures of Jesus than you'd expect to find in the Pope's house, and a whole range of Byzantine art. The museum itself is gorgeous, but after walking through the whole place you'll definitely appreciate a beer and a seat in Monbijou Park. You'll realize that the Bode Museum is pretty darn good-lookin' from the outside, too.

i €10, students €5. ⏰ Open Tu-W 10am-6pm, Th 10am-8pm, F-Su 10am-6pm; closed Mondays.

NEUE WACHE
MEMORIAL

Unter den Linden 4   ☎030 250 023 33

Neue Wache (literally "New Watch") originally housed the royal palace guards. In 1969, after both devastating World Wars, an unnamed soldier and an unnamed concentration camp victim were laid to rest here. The memorial is nothing short of eerie, with a small amount of light propagating from the roof toward a mesmerizing sculpture by Käthe Kollwitz. The sculpture is aptly titled "Mother with her Dead Son." Aside from this grand adornment, the room is empty. There's little so affecting as the echo of a footstep within this room.

i U2: Hausvogteipl. From the metro, walk north along Oberwallstr. Free. ⏰ Open daily 10am-6pm. The interior of the monument is still visible when the gate is closed.

FERNSEHENTURM
TOWER

Panoramastr. 1A   ☎030 247 575 875 www.tv-turm.de

At 368m the Fernshehturm (literally "TV Tower") trumps all other sky pokers in the EU. It's shaped like a lame 1950s space probe on purpose: the East Berliners wanted their neighbors to the west to remember Sputnik every time they looked out their windows in the morning. For better or for worse, capitalism has since co-opted the DDR's (East Germany's) biggest erection, giving you the chance to rocket up into the tower's crowning Christmas ornament for a steep fee. Fortunately, in spite of the hordes of tourists that will inevitably get in your way, the view is incredible and especially worth checking out at the end of your stay, once you have a working vocabulary of Mitte's sights. Otherwise, it's just a big, beautiful mess of towers and roofs.

i U2, U5, or U8: Alexanderpl. €13, ages 3-16 €8, under 3 free. Entrance requires you to pass through security, so be sure to leave any pocket knives at your hostel. ⏰ Open daily 10am-midnight.

KULTURFORUM

Matthäikirchplatz

Located right next to Potsdamer Platz, Kulturforum is a collection of significant architectural buildings that house some of Berlin's most prominent museums and event halls. The most notable among this group is the Neue Nationalgalerie, which has been temporarily closed for renovations with expectations to re-open around 2018. That said, the Kulturforum is absolutely worth visiting, with both the Gemaldegalerie holding one of the world's most expansive and important collections of European paintings. There are 2700 paintings covering the time and styles between the 13th and 18th centuries, so bring your walking shoes and thinking cap—you'll be sure to need them. In the same vicinity are both the Art Library and Museum of Decorative Arts, which both warrant their own visit. Often, though, the Art Library will have temporary exhibits like work from photographer Mario Testino. Oh, and on your way out, make sure to take a stroll by the Berlin Philharmonie, which is a landmark for unique architecture in Berlin and will entice you to snap a few photos.

i Prices and hours vary at each of the museums, but the Museum Pass is accepted at all of them except at special exhibits.

HAMBURGER-BAHNHOF MUSEUM
MUSEUM

Invalidenstr. 50-51

Although this used to be a major train station connecting Berlin to Hamburg, the space has nothing to do with transportation. Instead, the building has been transformed into the museum for contemporary art, exhibiting a mixture of paintings, sculptures, photography, and mixed-media installations from a variety of noteworthy artists (there's some Warhol in there, just to namedrop). You'll find yourself confused, exhausted, inspired, and reborn through your trek around this gigantic exhibition space; just make sure you don't get too frustrated with the conceptual nature that is modern art.

i €14, students €7. ⏰ *Open Tu-W 10am-6pm, Th 10am-8pm, F-Su 10am-6pm; closed Mondays.*

THE KENNEDYS
MUSEUM

August Str. 11-13   ☎030 206 53 570 www.thekennedys.de

The Kennedys is half museum, half art gallery. It houses an exhibit of photographs and rare memorabilia— JFK's suitcases, matches, and pens—and shows museum-goers the Kennedys' progression from Irish immigrants to America's political elite. Berlin seems to be extremely fond of the Kennedys, and not just for JFK's über-famous *"Ich bin ein Berliner"* comment—the city's relationship with the Kennedys started what the museum repeatedly refers to as the great German-American friendship. You may end up learning more about the Kennedys than you ever wanted to know, and the exhibition can often seem far too starry-eyed for its handsome protagonist, but the photographs are engaging, especially the ones you don't recognize. Anticipate seeing hundreds of pics of the Kennedys playing with their children, but don't expect to see any snaps of JFK wearing his reading glasses. After learning about the Germans' American hero, treat yourself to an American delicacy at Mogg & Melzer on your way out—you won't regret it.

i S1, S25, or U55: Brandenburger Tor. From the metro, walk west toward Brandenburg Gate, then turn right into the square immediately before the Gate. €5, students €2.50. ⏰ *Open Tu-Su 11am-7pm.*

Prenzlauer Berg

Prenzlauer Berg isn't the place for sightseeing. There are a couple of treasures, namely **Mauerpark** and random bits of the remaining Berlin Wall, but this part of the city is mostly about hip bars, boutiques, and cafes.

▨ MAUERPARK
PARK

Extends north of the intersection between Eberswalder Str. and Schwedter Str.

Mauerpark is the heart and soul of Prenzlauer Berg. It's a grungy, sprawling, all-in-one park: you'll find a flea market, a stadium, some unique graffiti (if your name is Alex, there's even a marriage proposal!), day-drinking, a huge playground, men walking their dogs, and Sunday afternoon karaoke. In summary, Mauerpark is a park designed to exemplify the very essence of Berlin—perhaps as a thesis, spoken through a loudspeaker. We don't recommend taking a nap here, but we do recommend spending some time appreciating everything it has to offer.

i U2: Eberswalder Str. From the metro, walk west on Eberswalder Str. Mauerpark extends far to the north after you pass the stadium. Free.

▨ BERLINER MAUER DOKUMENTATIONSZENTRUM
MUSEUM, MONUMENT

Bernauer Str. 111   ☎030 467 986 666 www.berliner-mauer-gedenkstaette.de

A remembrance complex, museum, chapel, and entire city block of a preserved portion of Berlin Wall (complete with watch tower) come together in this memorial to "victims of the Communist tyranny." The church is made of an inner oval of poured cement walls, lit from above by a skylight and surrounded by a transparent skeleton of two-by-fours. The museum has assembled a comprehensive collection of all things Berlin Wall, including original recordings, telegrams, blueprints, film footage, and photos. Climb up a staircase to see it from above.

i U8: Bernauer Str. From the metro, walk north on Brunnen Str., then turn left onto Bernauer Str. The church and memorial are on the left before Ackerstr., and the Dokumentationszentrum and exhibition are on the right immediately after Ackestr. Free. ⏰ *Open Apr-Oct Tu-Su 9:30am-7pm; Nov-Mar 9:30am-6pm.*

JÜDISCHER FRIEDHOF

CEMETERY

Schönhauser Allee

Prenzlauer Berg was one of the major centers of Jewish Berlin during the 19th and early 20th centuries. This ivy-covered Jewish cemetery contains the graves of composer Giacomo Meyerbeer and artist Max Liebermann and is studded by impressively high, dark tombs under towering trees. It's currently in a disappointing state of disrepair, with countless overturned tombstones and fallen trees, but it's still a beautiful grove worth wandering through. Nearby, **Synagogue Rykstrasse** (Rykestr. 53, right next to the Wasserturm) is one of Berlin's loveliest synagogues and one of the few spared on *Kristallnacht*. Since the synagogue still operates as a school, visitors aren't allowed to enter, but the red-brick, turn-of-the-century façade is impressive enough to warrant a visit.

i U2: Senefelderpl. From the metro, walk north on Schönhauser Allee. The gate to the cemetery is on the right, near the Lapidarium. Free. ☉ Open M-Th 8am-4pm, F 8am-1pm.

ZEISS-GROSS PLANETARIUM

PLANETARIUM

Prenzlauer Allee 80   ☎030 421 84 50 www.astw.de

In 1987, this spherical planetarium opened as the most modern facility of its kind in the DDR. Would you believe that they had technology as advanced as the radio? The technology paled in comparison to what was going on in the West at the time, but today it can still show you the stars, sometimes with accompanying Bach or commentary for children. There are no exhibits, only shows, so check the website or call ahead for times.

i S8, S41, S42, or tram M2: Prenzlauer Allee. From the metro, the planetarium is across the bridge, on the left €5, students €4. ☉ Shows Tu-Th 9am-noon and 1-5pm, F 9am-noon and 1-9:30pm, Sa 2:30-9pm, Su 1:30-5pm.

Friedrichshain

▨ EAST SIDE GALLERY

MONUMENT

Along Mühlenstr.   www.eastsidegallery.com

The longest remaining portion of the Berlin Wall, this 1.3km stretch of cement slabs has been converted into the world's largest open-air art gallery. The Cold War graffiti is unfortunately long departed; instead, the current murals hail from an international group of artists who gathered in 1989 to celebrate the Wall's fall. One of the most famous contributions is by artist Dmitri Wrubel, who depicted a wet, wrinkly political kiss between Leonid Brezhnev and East German leader Erich Honecker. The stretch of street remains unsupervised and, on the Warschauer Str. side, open at all hours, but vandalism is surprisingly rare.

i U1, U15, S3, S5, S6, S7, S9, or S75: Warschauer Str. or S5, S7, S9, or S75: Ostbahnhof. From the metro, walk back toward the river. Free.

▨ VOLKSPARK FRIEDRICHSHAIN

PARK

Volkspark Friedrichshain isn't the largest park in Berlin; it loses out to the **Tiergarten** in Mitte in terms of both size and class. But this brings us to the age old question: does size really **matter**? Volkspark compensates by attracting tons of people, from dog-walkers to kite-fliers to sunbathers. Monuments have popped up around the park as well, the most popular being the **Märchenbrunnen,** or the "Fairy Tale Fountain," a fountain that depicts 10 Grimm characters around a tremendous cascade of water. **Mount Klemont** gained its mass from the enormous pile of rubble swept beneath it in 1950 from two bomb-destroyed World War II bunkers; today, it occasionally serves as a platform for open-air concerts and movie screenings.

i S8 or S10: Landsberger Allee or U5: Strausbgr. Pl. From Strausbgr. Pl., walk north on Lichtenberger Str. Bounded by Am Friedrichshain to the north, Danziger Str. to the east, Landsberger Allee to the south, and Friedenstr. Str. to the south.

berlin

STASI MUSEUM

Ruschestr. 103, Haus 1   ☎030 553 68 54 www.stasimuseum.de

It's odd to imagine that this was once the most feared building in all of Germany: the Stasi Museum is housed in the gigantic headquarters of the East German secret police, the **Staatssicherheit**, or **Stasi**. During the Cold War, the Stasi kept dossiers on some six million of East Germany's own citizens, an amazing feat and a testament to the huge number of civilian informers in a country of only 16 million people. Since a 1991 law made the records public, the "Horror Files" have rocked Germany, exposing millions of informants and destroying careers, marriages, and friendships at every level of German society. The museum exhibition presents a wide array of original Stasi artifacts, among which is a mind-blowing collection of concealed microphones and cameras. All we want to know is how nobody noticed the bulky microphone concealed under a tie.

i *U5: Magdalenenstr €6, students €4.50. Exhibits in German; English info booklet €3. ⌚ Open M-F 10am-6pm, Sa-Su 11am-6pm.*

Kreuzberg

None of Kreuzberg's sights are essential, especially compared to their glamorous cousins in Mitte, but if you're interested in something other than grunge, there are several museums, parks, and buildings you should consider stopping at. In addition to the sights we've listed, Kreuzberg also has several beautiful 19th-century churches that are worth a peek, including **Saint-Michael-Kirche** (Michaelkirchpl.), the **Heilig-Kreuz-Kirche** (Zossener Str. 65), and **Saint Thomas-Kirche** (Bethaniendamm 23-27).

▨ DEUTSCHES TECHNIKMUSEUM BERLIN

Trebbiner Str. 9   ☎030 902 54 0 www.sdtb.de

With 30 full-size airplanes, 20 boats—including a full-size Viking relic—and a train from every decade since 1880, this museum could be a city in itself. Its permanent exhibitions cover everything from aerospace to road traffic to photo technology, but the special exhibitions also manage to be enticing. Most recently, Technikmuseum showed off 30 years in 30 photographs, a small but incredibly charming tour of the museum's technological prowess. But if photographs don't appeal, we find it hard to believe that World War II planes used for the Berlin Airlift, a U-boat, and a WWII rocket won't please.

i *U1 or U2: Gleisdreieck. From the metro, head east on Luckenwalder Str. and turn right onto Tempelhofer Ufer. Walk under the train tracks and turn right onto Trebbiner Str. The entrance is about¾ of the way down Trebbiner Str. Many exhibits in English. €8, students €4; after 3pm, admission is free for children and students under 18. ⌚ Open Tu-F 9am-5:30pm, Sa-Su 10am-6pm.*

▨ TOPOGRAPHY OF TERROR

Niederkirchner Str. 8   ☎030 254 50 90 www.topographie.de

The Topography of Terror takes you way back to 1930, and from then it takes you to explore the development of Nazi-/Gestapo-/Secret Service-induced terror. Seriously, prepare to be terrorized. The main exhibit consists of an extended series of maps, graphs, photographs, and an enormous amount of context—you could spend an entire afternoon reading through all the captions and explanations, which are fortunately provided in both German and English. That said, the images are so consistently powerful—and the exhibition so unbelievably exhaustive—that it is a must for any nuanced understanding of the development of Nazi terror. Outside, a newer exhibition of the development of Nazi influence in Berlin runs along the block-long remaining segment of the Berlin Wall.

i *U6: Kochstr., or U2: Potsdamer Pl. From the metro, head east on Leipziegerstr. and take a right onto Wilhelmstr. Free. ⌚ Open daily 10am-8pm.*

BERLINISCHE GALLERY
MUSEUM

Alte Jakobstr. 124-128

Berlin is a modern city, and a modern city needs a good museum for modern art. Despite the fact that the majority of Berlin has acted as a canvas for contemporary artists over the last 50 years, the Berlinische Gallery does a pretty good job keeping us entertained. With rotating exhibits, there's always something waiting to surprise us. There's also a concise collection outlining the history of architectural progression after the war along with some paintings highlighting the rebelliousness of an era.

i €8, students €5, under 18 free. ⏰ Open M 10am-6pm, W-Su 10am-6pm.

SOVIET WAR MEMORIAL
MEMORIAL

Treptower Park

This memorial, a commemoration of Soviet soldiers who gave the ultimate sacrifice during the Battle of Berlin, is humongous. At 20,000 sq. m, it puts Mitte's **Soviet Memorial** to shame. Two jagged triangular slabs, each bearing the hammer and sickle, guard a tremendous rectangular square lined by exquisitely cut shrubs and surrounded by marble reliefs of Soviet soldiers helping the poor and the huddled. Quotes from Stalin in the original Russian and in German surround you at every step. But the most impressive piece stands at the end of the square: a tremendous, grassy mound bears a giant bronze statue of a Soviet soldier crushing a broken swastika and lugging a sword.

i U1 or U15: Schlesisches Tor. From the metro, walk southeast on Schlesische Str. Cross both canals and continue until you reach a fork in the road, between Puschkinallee and Am Treptower Park. Take Puschkinallee and walk along the park until you reach a large, semicircular courtyard with an entrance gate. Turn into this courtyard; the memorial is on the left. Free. ⏰ Open 24hr.

JEWISH MUSEUM
MUSEUM

Lindenstr. 9-14   ☎030 259 93 300 www.jmberlin.de

You'd know the Jewish Museum was important just from a single glance from outside the building: traffic blockades and security personnel swarm around the place, and you have to go through a security checkpoint to enter the museum. The building itself plays a significant role in the portrayal of its exhibitions: Daniel Libeskind designed the building to reflect the discomfort, pain, and the inherent voids in Jewish history, manifesting these characteristics as tremendous, triangular shafts, inaccessible rooms, and uneven floors. It's an amazing museum that actually succeeds at being experiential: it's disorienting, frightening, and historical.

i U1 or U6: Hallesches Tor. From the station, head east on Gitschinerstr. and take a left at Lindenstr. €7, students €3.50, under 5 free. Audio tour €3. ⏰ Open M 10am-10pm, Tu-Su 10am-8pm. Last entry 1hr. before close.

CHECKPOINT CHARLIE
HISTORIC SITE

Zimmerstr. and Friedrichstr.

Though we really don't like this place, we can't leave it out: Checkpoint Charlie is incredibly popular, absurd, and has hundreds of tourists and multiple Starbucks cafes (which practically don't exist in Berlin) on one street. Never, ever have we seen more of a tourist trap. Though Checkpoint Charlie was once important to Berlin as the entrance to the American sector of West Berlin, today it's nothing but a mock entrance point, with German men dressed as American soldiers. You guessed it—you can take your picture with them for two badly-spent euro. A set of placards along Kochstr. provides a somewhat interesting history on the checkpoint and the various escapes it witnessed. Skip the museum: with admission at €12.50, you're better off buying a few beers.

i U6: Kochstraße. From the metro, walk north on Friedrichstr. Free. Museum €12.50, students €9.50. ⏰ Open 24hr.

PRINZESSINNEN GARTEN GARDEN

Prinzenstr. 35-38 www.prinzessinnengarten.net

This difficult-to-pronounce public garden is a rags-to-riches story. Left as abandoned wasteland by the city for years, a group of volunteer friends and neighbors transformed the unused space into a blooming and booming public garden and social space. In addition to the ecologically diverse landscape, the space also is host to diverse exhibitions and vendors that not only set the example for urban gardening projects around Europe, but also finance the rent of the space from the city. Impressive. Delicious. Trendy. Green. Pay a visit and appreciate the progressiveness of Berlin's public spaces.

i Free. ⚇ Open daily 11am-6pm.

FOOD

Charlottenburg is not known for its budget-friendly fare, so head north to Moabit for cheap, authentic Turkish or Vietnamese food. Check out Schöneberg's relaxed cafe culture around the intersection of Maaßenstr. and Winterfeldstr. In Mitte, it's best to avoid overpriced restaurants and cafes near major sights. Prenzlauer Berg is another cafe capital: check out Kastanienallee or the streets around Helmholtzpl. for the highest concentration of caffeine. Some of Friedrichshain's narrow cobblestone streets are lined with cheap cafes, ice cream joints, and reasonably priced restaurants. The intersection of Simon-Dach-Str. and Grünbergerstr. is a good place to start. For the best international cuisine in a city known for cheap ethnic fare, head to Kreuzberg, where incredible restaurants line Oranienstraße, Bergmannstraße, and Schlesische Straße.

Charlottenburg

KASTANIE GERMAN $

Schloßstr. 22

If you've been dreaming about the idyllic German meal of meat, Wießbier, and more meat, make this your first stop. Best enjoyed on a sunny afternoon, settle into the classic wooden table and chairs beneath the shade of kastanie trees, dig your feet into the gravel courtyard, and indulge in Bavarian specialties like six Nürnberger sausages, served with a side of pretzel, mustard, and an enthusiastic "Guten tag." You can self-diagnose an extreme case of gout upon departure, but it will be worth it.

i Food €2-10. Beer €3. Breakfast €3-8. ⚇ Open daily 10am-2am.

LONMENS NOODLE HOUSE TAIWANESE $

Kantstr. 33 ☎30 3151 9678

We know you didn't come to Berlin for Taiwanese food, but maybe you should have. Authentic and dirt-cheap, LonMens is a hidden gem that fills its hole-in-the-wall status with the freshest dumplings west of the East. We guarantee that everything you order will be delicious, and it won't break your already-suffering bank account. Though not on the menu, the chili wontons are divine and will leave you salivating until you return the next night. The best part? You can strut your steamed duck buns (not kidding—order them) right by the tourists disappointed in their less authentic, more expensive Chinese food right next door (we're talking about you, Good Friends).

i Food €4-8. ⚇ Open daily noon-11pm.

WUSTEREI GERMAN $

Hardenbergstr. 29d

It's tough to recommend currywurst stands in Berlin because they're all so damn delicious, cheaper than using the toilette, and more common than Starbucks in Manhattan. Wusturei caught our attention just because it seemed to have the

germany

top currywurst in west berlin

1. CURRY 36: This place is so popular they started selling their own t-shirts. Though they're speckled all over the city, the one right outside of the Zoologischer Garten almost always has a line for a reason. Order it any time of the day, but try it ohne darm (without casing—it's the Berliner style)

2. WITTY'S: Bio-markets are around every corner, but Bio-wurst? You'll have to go to Witty's. Promising all organic meat and oils, Witty's is your best bet when you are environmentally and health conscious.

3. WURSTEREI: Some claim that the best currywurst is all about the sauce. Those people go to Wursterei. Not too spicy, not to sweet, just enough pizazz, and still dirt-cheap.

4. KU'DAMM 195: If you want your currywurst served up with a bit of class, head to Ku'damm 195. Need some champagne to wash it down? They've got you covered.

5. BRUTZELSTUBCHEN: Delivered fresh from the butcher every morning, the sausage here is incredible. Plus, the name is so fun to say it doesn't even matter how good the food tastes.

perfect sauce: not too ketchupy, with just enough kick, and we didn't feel too much like a giant sausage after eating it. *Das ist gut!* If for whatever inhuman reason you don't enjoy indulging in this version of Germany's fast-food staple, walk across the street and try it again at Curry 36, which we also found to be amongst the best of the 'wurst. Regardless of what you choose, grab a Berliner Kindl, ask for extra mayo on the *pommes frites*, appreciate the posture-correcting standing barrel-tables, and enjoy the view of the Kaiser-Wilhelm Memorial Church while you gorge yourself like the pig you're eating.

i Food €4-10, but you should realistically get out of there too full to walk on about €7, including the beer (€3). ⏰ Open M-Th 10am-midnight, F-Sa 10am-3am, Su 10am-midnight.

WINDBURGER BURGERS $
Windscheidstr. 26 ☎30 437 27 177

As we're sure you will discover, Berlin has a bit of an obsession with New Age burger joints. There seems to be one around every corner, and we aren't complaining. If you find yourself missing good old-fashioned American food, head to WindBurger. You can snag a burger and fries on the go here for just a euro or two more than you'd spend at a doner kebab or currywurst stand. Meat not your thing? You should probably leave Germany, or at least order the veggie burger. The homemade fries will bring you right back to all that time you've never spent sitting at those classic American sports bars.

i Food €6-12. ⏰ Open M-Sa noon-10pm.

CAFÉ AM NEUEN SEE BIERGARTEN $
Lichtensteinallee 2 ☎30 254 4930

If you came to Berlin yearning for Oktoberfest-like biergartens only to discover that the authentic ones are in Bavaria, this place will grant you reprieve. Perched on the Neuen See Pond in the southwest of the Tiergarten, this cafe and biergarten could have been Disney's inspiration for Epcot Germany. Best enjoyed on a sunny afternoon when you're craving a romantic setting and an unromantic amount of beer, Café am Neuen See is a peaceful refuge hidden from the rush of the Ku'damm just 5min. away. The best thing about this biergarten is that no matter how much beer you've had, they'll still let you rent a rowboat (€5 per 30min.). Dissatisfied with the selection? Compare beer, garden, and biergarten at the Schleusenkrug on the northern side of Tiergarten, only a 15min. walk away.

i Pizza, pretzels from €5. Beer €3-6. ⏰ Open M-F 11am-late, Sa-Su 10am-late.

SCHWARZES CAFÉ
CAFE $

Kantstr. 148   ☎30 3138 038

Craving absinthe at 4am? This is your place. Schwarzes serves up an extravagant menu 24hr. a day, but don't be fooled: Schwarzes is not your average late-night drunken pitstop. Its range is expansive and eclectic, from homemade hummus to indulgent dessert crepes, but it doesn't sacrifice quality for quantity. Enjoy the antique decor, contemporary artwork, indie music, and diverse crowd while you decide whether absinthe is more like an alcohol or a drug. Be careful—your bill will rise faster than the sun.

i *Food €6-13. Drinks €3-7.* ☼ *Open daily 24hr., except closed Tu 3-10am.*

WINTERGARTEN CAFÉ IN LITERATURHAUS BERLIN
CAFE $$

Fasanenstr. 23   ☎30 882 5414

If you have one hungover breakfast splurge in Charlottenburg, you should make it at this place. Before you arrive, though, brush up on your manners, brush your hair, put on your cleanest (or should we say least dirty) clothes, and warm up your pinky fingers. With an idyllic courtyard, glass-roofed terrace, and regal dining room, you'll feel like you're eating a breakfast fit for royalty. You'll be reminded that you are far from royalty once you get the check, but it's OK since you saved a bunch of money visiting the Kathe-Kollwitz Museum instead of the much more expensive museums near Ku'damm.

i *Food €8-17.* ☼ *Open daily 9am-midnight.*

Schöneberg and Wilmersdorf

CAFÉ BILDERBUCH
CAFE $

Akazienstr. 28

Whoever opened Café Bilderbuch seemed to have a conflict between starting an antique shop or a cafe. Well, the cafe won out, and we're glad it did. Though the cafe was seemingly designed by an eclectic Francophile and collector of regal antiques, you'll overlook the fringed lamps and well-worn leather couches for the delicious brunch menu, which is printed on the restaurant's own press. Anything you order will undoubtedly be great, but you can't go wrong with a plate of fruit and cheese accompanied by a coffee and a bread basket.

i *Breakfast and brunch options €5-8.* ☼ *Open daily 9am-11pm.*

SOFRAM
TURKISH $

Potsdamer Strasse 137

Berlin has a huge Turkish population, and the natural consequence of this is unbelievable Turkish food. Don't be fooled, this isn't another introduction to a doner kebab stand; Sofram is a tried-and-true Turkish restaurant where you can eat an authentic, home-cooked meal for €6. The staff will do their best with your broken German or English sign-language, and when they offer their Turkish black tea (complimentary), you'd be mistaken to turn it down.

i *Food €5-9.* ☼ *Open M-Sa 10am-11pm.*

IMREN GRILL
TURKISH $

Hauptstr. 156

This is the best doner kebab place you'll find in Schöneberg, hands down. The durum (they make their own bread) is €4, the Turkish pizza is €3, and the end-less, guilt-free joy you and your tastebuds will experience is priceless. Perfect for a late-night snack or a lunch on the go, Imren Grill has got you covered.

i *Food €3-6.* ☼ *Open daily 10am-11pm.*

EULE'S CAFÉ
CAFE $

Über die Parkeingänge

Nestled among gardens on the west side of Gleisdreieck Park, Eule's Café is a safe haven for parents, children, cyclists, skateboarders, and park-goers alike looking for a Milchkaffee and pastry. The tiny shack might not be all that impressive, but the ambience makes up for the appearance. With a sign out front stating: "No Wi-Fi, talk to each other, pretend it's 1993, live!" and a crowd who couldn't be happier to be enjoying their coffee off the grid, Café Eule is a perfect oasis away from the hustle and bustle of the city next door. So sit back, relax, and enjoy your cappuccino while you watch fashionable moms push very impressive strollers all around Gleisdreieck.

i Food €2-6. 🕐 Open daily 10am-6pm.

DOUBLE EYE COFFEE
COFFEE HOUSE $
Akazienstr. 22

Double Eye is a coffee purist's dream. It's as serious about its coffee as it is about the amount of time the staff lets you relax (exactly none) in their shop, so come to Double Eye only if you're ready to take care of business. Don't let this dissuade you from coming, though—we had the most delicious coffee we've ever had here. And the espresso went down smoother than water. We've never experienced anything quite like it. If you come before or after work hours, though, get ready to wait in line.

i Coffee €2-6. 🕐 Open M-F 8:45am-6:15pm, Sa 9:15am-5:45pm; closed Sundays.

CARAMIA FOCACCERIA
BAKERY $
Goltzstr. 32

Simple and unassuming, Caramia Focacceria served us the best personal-sized pizzas for €2.50 we've ever had. We ordered one, and then we ordered one more (OK, OK, we ordered one after that, too). Nobody in there speaks English, but everyone speaks the language of Italian delicacies, so point and smile, then eat and enjoy. If you have any room left over in your stomach, you will definitely give in to temptation with gelato staring at you while you ravenously scarf down Berlin's best impression of NYC's dollar pizza.

i Pizza €2.50-5. 🕐 Open daily 11am-midnight.

Mitte

DJIMALAYA
TURKISH $
Invalidenstr. 159

The combination of affordability, location, atmosphere, and unbelievable hummus makes Djimalaya one of our top stops for a relaxed lunch or low-key dinner in Mitte. The wraps are killer and on a different planet from even the best doner kebab stands. We opted for the fried cheese hummus wrap and wish we could have eaten ten. On a hot summer day, order a pitcher of the homemade lemonade and sit curbside; you won't want to leave.

i Food €4-10. 🕐 Open daily noon-11pm.

CHAY VIET
VIETNAMESE $
Brunnenstr. 164

The amount of authentic, delicious Vietnamese food in Mitte will astound you. Chay Viet is no exception, but stands out from the most trafficked Vietnamese spots because it's a bit farther away from bustling Rosenthaler Platz. As a result of being a bit off the beaten path, Chay Viet serves up delicious, affordable vegetarian soups and curries with a more peaceful atmosphere that is well worth the five-minute walk.

i Food €6-14. 🕐 Open M-F 11:30am-10pm, Su 1-10pm.

DUDU
ASIAN $$
Torstr. 134

We are going to skip all of the immature Dudu jokes that you know we want to make and cut straight to the chase. Sure, this place might seem like just another chic, Asian-fusion trend-follower that attracts gullible yuppies into its makeshift jungle, but stave off your judgments until you take your first bite. Its yellow coconut curry over rice was da bomb, and its sushi was some of the best we've ever had. If you're pinching pennies, you can walk away only spending €10, but you won't want to. The cocktails are pretty damn tasty, too.

i Food €10-20. ⏰ Open M-Sa noon-midnight, Su 1pm-midnight.

NOLA'S AM WEINBERG
SWISS $$

Veteranenstr. 9

Talk about picturesque. Then pay for it. We're only kind of kidding. Nola's is a Swiss restaurant that does Sunday brunch particularly well. Apparently it does fondue too, but we'd really only recommend coming here for a lazy Sunday brunch when you don't mind forking over €12 for a beautiful (all-you-can-stuff-your-face) buffet of meats, cheeses, eggs, and pastries. Perched on the top of the hill overlooking Weinsburgsweg Park, Nola's is a pretty idyllic spot to enjoy a sunny Sunday afternoon.

i Food €8-18. All-you-can-eat brunch €12. ⏰ Open daily noon-1am.

MOGG & MELZER
SANDWICHES $$

Auguststr. 11-13

Sometimes you just need a good ol'-fashioned sandwich. Well, this place doesn't have anything like that. Instead, they have mountains of thick-sliced pastrami towering between slices of homemade bread. We're not really sure these behemoths are really sandwiches, but they're effing delicious. They also come with coleslaw so tasty you won't even know it's coleslaw. The only downside to Mogg & Melzer is that the sandwich options come in two styles: "there-goes tomorrow's budget" expensive and it has "Well, damnit, now I'm homeless" expensive. We chose the latter, and it was well worth it. Could you spare any change?

i Food €8-15. ⏰ Open M-Sa 10am-10pm, Su 7am-8pm.

FATHER CARPENTER COFFEE BREWERS
CAFE $

Münzstr. 21

There are roughly two million minimalist, succulent-loving, hipster-esque coffee shops hidden in nooks and crannies all over Berlin, but especially in Mitte. That said, some of them are well worth a visit. Father Carpenter is definitely one of these worthwhile coffee adventures. We can't say we've ever tasted espresso as smooth as this. Even if you self-identify as a Starbucks-loving basic bitch, you'll appreciate Father Carpenter's selection of coffee and surprisingly delicious breakfast sandwiches. What's even greater than its coffee is the beautiful courtyard it's nestled in; even if you're not a coffee-lover, its outdoor seating is a must-visit for a relaxing afternoon pit stop.

i Food €2-8. ⏰ Open M-Sa 9am-7pm.

CURRY MITTE
GERMAN $

Torstr. 122

There are simply too many currywurst stands in Berlin to choose a favorite. For us, Curry Mitte has the perfect balance of sweet and spicy sauce, fresh meats, and proximity to the late-night scene that deems Curry Mitte the best of the 'wurst. It really doesn't get any better when your midnight raving gives you a midnight craving. So go indulge in Berlin's favorite fast food and forget about feeling guilty.

i Food €3-7. ⏰ Open M-Th 11am-midnight, F-Sa 11am-6am.

JORIS BERLIN
GERMAN $

Brunnenstr. 158

You've been clubbing nonstop and taking inconsistent, inadequate breaks to refuel at currywurst stands. You're hurting, bad, and we understand. What we understand even more is that the road to recovery begins at Joris. Nothing fancy, nothing frilly, just a good, old-fashioned, healthy bowl of vegetables big enough to feed a small family or a very hungover tourist. We suspect you're the latter, so head to Joris and get yourself a salad, baked potato, or soup that will turn your nausea into energy before you can say "Supa Lecka!" Although the menu is a bit difficult to comprehend for a (post-inebriated) foreigner, the staff is friendly enough to walk you through the options without getting frustrated with you for being so slow.

i Food €6-12. ☑ Open M-F 9am-5pm.

EISMANUFAKTUR
Auguststr. 63

ICE CREAM $

To our pleasant surprise, Berlin's ice-cream culture is nearly as strong as its coffee culture (and that's really saying something). The ice cream at every place we tried was incredible and often had delicious flavors we'd never heard of and will never forget. However, Eismanufaktur stood above the rest with ice cream, gelato, and sorbet only fit for gods and goddesses. We tried the guava and mango flavors, and then went back for the rhubarb. Rhubarb? That's right: rhubarb. Get it; you won't regret it.

i Ice cream €2-5. ☑ Open M-Th 1-8pm, F-Sa 1-9pm, Su 1-8pm.

Prenzlauer Berg

Prenzlauer Berg is smitten with its cafes: nearly every street hides a cafe (or six), so a cheap, tasty cup of joe or a small, inexpensive meal are never hard to come by. Check out **Kastanienallee**, **Kollwitzstrasse**, or the streets around **Helmholtzplatz** for the highest concentration of caffeine. If your place is kitchen equipped, stock up at any of the several **REWE** stores around P'Berg.

PIZZA NOSTRA
Lychener Str. 2

PIZZA $$

Seriously delicious pizza at a reasonable price? Yes please. Sometimes you just gotta stuff your face with pizza, so why not make it the best pizza in Prenzlauer Berg? What makes Pizza Nostra so damn delicious is its history; run by two Italian dudes with roots going back to a Napoli bakery over a century ago, this place has Italian style in its DNA. Using their family dough recipe, they serve up unique slices with pick-your-own toppings from the simple to the extravagant—all for a decent price.

i Pizza €7-12. ☑ Open M-Sa noon-midnight, Su 1pm-midnight.

W-DER IMBISS
Kastanienallee 49

FUSION $$

This place should be on your radar from the second you step foot in Berlin. Signifying their mission in a simple act of rebelliousness, W-Der Imbiss is easily identified by the upside down McDonald's logo. You'll understand more about this stance against shitty food more once you taste the Mexi-Indi-talian fusion goodness. Basically, they've taken naan and used it as a burrito wrap, pizza dough, bread dip, and, well, just naan. It's all great, so make sure to bring a friend in order to taste more of the menu.

i Food €6-12. ☑ Open M-Th noon-10pm, F-Sa noon-11pm, Su noon-10pm.

THE BIRD
Am Falkplatz 5

BURGER $$

Berlin has a sweet spot for trendy American-style burger places with German twists. The Bird is one of the better places for an over-the-top, US-style sloppy burger with a bowl full of fries on the side, and it has attracted quite a bit of notoriety because of it. This means a packed *haus* every day of the week, so you might have to end up waiting a while to get a seat. Despite the wait, The Bird manages to pull off an American-style burger pretty damn well, and you might see us waiting in line to get one. The biggest downside to this trendy establishment, though, is a price tag that might make you want to flip them the bird as you walk out.

i *Food €10-20.* ☼ *Open M-Th 6pm-midnight, F 4pm-midnight, Sa-Su noon-midnight.*

CAFÉ KRONE
CAFE $

Oderberger Str. 38

Café Krone embodies Prenzlauer Berg's cafe culture in one meal. Elegant yet relaxed, this cafe is the perfect place to enjoy a lazy morning's breakfast and coffee while watching the hoards of Berliners walking to Mauerpark flea market. Just know that you're getting the better deal with delicious charcuterie plates, pancakes, or muesli. You'll have as hard of a time deciding as we did. The chef apparently has a sweet spot for egg dishes as well, and the egg salad redefined the dish for us. Give it a try, fellow egg-lovers.

i *Food €4-14.* ☼ *Open M-F 9:30am-6:30pm, Sa-Su 10am-7pm.*

Friedrichshain

SILO COFFEE
CAFE $

Gabriel-Max-Straße 4   www.silo-coffee.com

We know this place is overcrowded with coffee snobs and yuppies. We understand that there are often long waits for food and seating. We, too, spent all of our money between 2 and 6am last night. We get it. Really. But great food is great food is great food. And Silo serves up one of the best breakfasts we've had in a long while. Especially given that they're coffee specialists, we couldn't believe how delicious the food was. The classic baked eggs (€8) are out-of-this-world good. To make things even better, the staff is super nice and entirely makes up for the often-snobby crowd this place attracts.

i *Coffee €2-5. Food €4-10.* ☼ *Open M-Th 8:30am-5pm, F 8:30am-7pm, Sa 9:30am-7pm, Su 10am-7pm.*

SCHILLER BURGER
BURGERS $$

Herrfurthstr. 7   www.schillerburger.com

There are more American-style burgers in Berlin than in a McDonald's. Seriously, it's weird, but we can't really complain when they rival the burgers Americans are so proud of. Schiller burger serves up a no-frills, no-wait, and delicious burger for about the same amount you'd spend on a doner kebab. The sweet potato fries alone make the visit worth it.

i *Burgers €5-10.* ☼ *Open M-Th noon-midnight, F-Sa noon-3am, Su noon-midnight.*

LOUISE CHERIE CAFÉ
CAFE $

Gruenbergerstr. 91   ☎30 6807 0609 www.louisecheriecafe.de

If you weren't already linguistically challenged enough with German, Louise Cherie speaks French. And we mean that in more ways than one. This cozy cafe is a slice out of Paris's pie, complete with zesty coffee, homemade tarts and pies, and cheese and bread trays that make Francophiles flock from miles around. Oui would come for brunch here every day if we could.

i *Coffee €2-4. Breakfast €6. Dessert €3-6.* ☼ *Open M-W 10am-7pm, F-Su 10am-7pm; closed Thursdays.*

GOODIES
CAFE $$

Warschauer Str. 69   ☎30 8965 4973 www.goodies-berlin.de

Anything that was directly on Warschauer Str. we turned a blind eye to, assuming that it would either be overpriced or catering to tourists. After one particularly long night (read: it was 10am) we sacrificed our food-tegrity and ate at this funky-looking grocery store/cafe right on the busiest part of the street (you can see both Berghain and the Warschauer train station from here). Goodies was exactly what we needed to replenish after a long night of Club Mate and beer.

Organic smoothies, vegan breakfast wraps, and tempting cookies just scratch the surface of their extensive, though expensive, menu. Think Whole Foods, but more German.

i Food €4-10. ☒ Open M-F 7am-8pm, Sa-Su 9am-8pm.

REMBRANDT BURGER
BURGERS S$$

Richard-Sorge-Straße 21 ☎30 8999 7296 www.rembrandt-burger.de

We know, we know. Another burger place?! You came all the way to Berlin to eat shitty American-style food? Well, friends, rid yourself of your dubiousness or you shalt be duped. Not only was Rembrandt one of the craziest-ass mofos with a cool hairdo to run the art world, Rembrandt Burger is his modern-day equal in burger form. Their burgers are damn good, and their fries are even better. We had the Old Amsterdam Burger in the spirit of Rembrandt's hometown, and we weren't disappointed. Why don't Americans think of burger combinations like this?

i Food €8-12. ☒ Open daily noon-10pm.

Kreuzberg

MUSTAFAS GEMUSE KEBAP
TURKISH $

Mehringdamm 32

If we could, we'd smuggle the mountain of meat responsible for filling Mustafa's kebabs home with us and eat durum every day for the rest of our lives. It's seriously good and the most filling, delicious lunch you'll have for €4. As far as doner kebab stands go, we think Mustafa's may very well be the best in Berlin, if not the whole world. Go. Eat. Enjoy.

i Food €3-8. ☒ Open daily 10am-2am.

GASTHAUS FIGL
PIZZA $$

Urbanstr. 47 www.gasthaus-figl.de

There are places to grab a quick pizza pie all over Berlin. Gasthaus Figl is not one of these places. For Figl, Pizza is their craft, created with only the utmost care and freshest ingredients. They make each of their pies with a hefty dose of love, and we love eating it. Rumor has it that Figl makes the best pizza in Berlin, and we'd be lying if we said we didn't believe it. If you don't think they make the best pizza, you can't deny that they have the best website. Get hungry at gasthaus-figl.de.

i Food €8-15. ☒ Open Tu-Su 6pm-midnight.

DOYUM GRILL HOUSE
TURKISH $

Admiralstraße 36

One of the largest immigrant populations in Berlin is from Turkey. Along with this massive influx of Turkish immigrants comes a culture of Turkish food that can only be beaten in Turkey itself. We think that the best Turkish restaurant in Berlin is an unassuming place on an unimpressive street right outside the overwhelmingly busy Kotbusser Tor. But, holy shit, is its food incredible. Far from the average doner kebab stand, Doyum Grill House is a proper Turkish restaurant offering authentic Turkish eats. We had the Adana Kebab mit Aubergines (eggplant). We had never really had anything like it, but we would definitely get it again.

i Food €5-11. ☒ Open M-Th 11am-10pm, F 11am-11pm, Sa 11am-10pm, Su 3-10pm.

HALLESCHES HAUS
CAFE $

Tempelhofer Ufer 1

Hallesches Haus is like an all-in-one store for hipsters. Not only is it a third-generation coffee shop serving up pristine brews and super sandwiches, it's also a general store selling all sorts of handmade appliances for the young urban professionals who appreciate thoughtfully designed silverware. What's not to love?

Even if you're not into hand-crafted knives or self-bound books, Hallesches Haus is the perfect place to start your day with a cappuccino and croissant.

i Coffee €2. Pastries and sandwiches €2-6. ☼ Open M-F 9am-7pm, Sa 11am-4pm; closed Sundays.

MARKETHALLE NEUN
Eisenbahnstr. 42-43

MARKETPLACE $
www.markethalleneun.de

Street food Thursdays are a sensory experience to behold. The weekly gathering of eclectic food vendors attracts flocks of foodies from around the globe, all gathering to get a taste of Berlin's diverse food culture. From ice cream to empanadas to barbecue, you can probably find anything you have a hankering for and more. The only catch is that the best vendors tend to have a line akin to Berghain, and if you're particularly famished, you may have to opt for the less popular options (vegan schnitzel? uhh, no thanks). Already had dinner? Every third Sunday there's a breakfast market with brunch until 6pm. Sound like heaven? It is.

i Food €3-10. ☼ Open Th 5-10pm, Su 10am-6pm.

NIGHTLIFE

If you're reading this section and thinking, "I'm not sure I want to go clubbing in Berlin," then stop it. Stop it right now. Take a hint from Lady Gaga, patron saint of Berlin, and just dance... you won't regret it. The true *Diskotheken* await in the barren cityscape of Friedrichshain and the notoriously nocturnal Kreuzberg. Mitte does not disappoint, either—its tremendous multi-room clubs filled with exquisitely dressed 20-somethings are generally worth their hefty covers. The major parties in Schöneberg are at the GLBT clubs in the northern part of the neighborhood. For tamer nightlife, try the jazz clubs in Charlottenburg or the bar scene in Prenzlauer Berg.

Charlottenburg

Don't go to Charlottenburg expecting a wild time. We're pretty sure you won't be able to get *that* crazy here, since Charlottenburg is known for its residential feel, quiet cafes, and the 30-somethings who are busier starting families than throwing crazy ragers. The neighborhood is great for a mellow evening or some live jazz, but the real parties are eastward. The **Ku'damm** is best avoided after sunset, unless you enjoy chatting up drunk businessmen.

MONKEY BAR
Budapesterstr. 40

BAR
☎30 120 221 210

If yuppies were modern-day Puritans, this would be their city on a hill. On the 10th floor of the exceptionally trendy hotel in Bikini Haus Berlin, the Monkey Bar offers panoramic views of West Berlin so you can drink cocktails looking at the Kaiser-Wilhelm Memorial Church or at the monkeys just below in Zoologischer Garten. We think some lucky hipster from a graduate school of design was given too much money to decorate the interior, so the result is quirky decor with plenty of succulents, rough (yet intentional) unfinished wood, and handmade pillows on all of the seating. Brush up on your history of architecture and man-buns and prepare to empty your bank account before going. The cocktails are *superlecker* but range from €10-14. They also have a Caesar salad that should rewrite history, but at €13, you can decide between a night spent under a tree in the Tiergarten or dinner and a drink. Your choice!

i Cocktails €8-15. Beer €3-6. Food €8-16. ☼ Open M-Th noon-1am, F-Sa noon-2am, Su noon-1am.

GALANDER CHARLOTTENBURG
Stuttgarter Pl. 15

BAR
☎30 364 65 363

Galander is designed with the intention of eliciting a 1920s feel, but instead it feels like everyone there was born in the 1920s. The bar just continues Charlottenburg's trend of old trying to be young and cool. The drinks won't wreck

germany

your paycheck but aren't going to surprise your tastebuds, which are already suffering from the haze of cigarette smoke drifting through the air. We suggest Galander if you're looking for a classier pregame or smoky postgame, but this shouldn't be your only destination.

i Drinks €8-12. ☼ Open daily 6pm-2am.

DAS KLO BAR

Leibnizstr. 57 ☎30 437 27 219

Translating to "The Loo," Das Klo takes its shit seriously. Well, kind of. Food is served in mini porcelain toilets, and beer is served in urine collectors (never used—don't worry). Every kitschy antique neglected by upscale antique shops has been claimed and vomited onto Das Klo's walls, only adding to the confusion you'll feel after being squirted by water when walking through the door and insulted in German by its DJ/comedian/porcelain-priest. If you don't take yourself too seriously and have always wanted to eat out of the toilet, it might be worth the experience.

i Beer €4-8. ☼ Open M-W 7pm 2am, Th-F 7pm-4am, Sa 7pm-2am.

QUASIMODO MUSIC VENUE

Kantstr. 12a ☎30 318 04 560

Great music every night of the week with genres from blues to jazz to funk, or some eclectic combination of each. The only problem is that the crowd tends to be representative of Charlottenburg, which means older and boring. If you want deep house until the sun comes up, you should go somewhere else, but if you don't mind getting funky next to a 40-something who has to put the kids to bed after the next song, Quasimodo is the place for you!

i Tickets €8-15. ☼ Doors open at 9pm. Restaurant open M-F 4:30pm-midnight, Sa-Su noon-1am.

A-TRANE JAZZ CLUB

Pestalozzistr. 105 ☎30 313 2550

Unless you're a passionate jazz fan, you shouldn't board the A-Trane. For those of you who enjoy hearing the brass wail and the strings dance, then A-Trane is definitely worth stopping by. Though small in size, the internationally acclaimed jazz club attracts some big names (Herbie Hancock, Wynton Marsalis, just to name a couple) and has been the recording site for many live albums. Expect to groove well into Sunday morning with a crowd that has been doing the same thing since '92.

i Cover €10-20. ☼ Doors open at 9pm.

Schöneberg and Wilmersdorf

Schöneberg is Berlin's unofficial gay district, so most of the nightlife here caters to the GLBT community. A couple of distinctive cocktail bars may be worth visiting in the interest of broadening your buzz, but the neighborhood's real parties happen at the GLBT clubs and bars in northern Schöneberg.

KUMPELNEST 3000 BAR

Lützowstr. 23

Imagine every person you've ever seen who you've looked at and thought, "Wow, that person looks crazy." Now imagine them all in the same place. Well, Kumplenest 3000 is that place. In what used to function as a brothel, Kumpelnest 3000 now acts as a disco-themed dive bar and attracts everyone from shirtless transvestites to the average college partygoer—even on Wednesday nights. German for "nest of friends," the Kumpelnest is surprisingly friendly—and we mean really friendly. When you're ten Pilsners deep and it's 3am (and only then), you should venture to the Kumpelnest for an experience you probably won't forget or won't remember one second of.

i Drinks €4-12. ☼ Open M-Th 7pm-6am, F-Sa 7pm-8am, Su 7pm-6am.

THE GREEN DOOR
BAR

Winterfeldtstr. 50

Step behind the green door and enjoy some of the most creative cocktails in Schöneberg. You'll have to ring the bell to be let in, but unless you look like you're going to attempt something crazy, you shouldn't have any problems. The inside of the bar exudes cool, with simple, funky decor straight from a '70s porno. Speaking of porno, the bar is a reference to the movie, Behind the Green Door, which is a kitschy porno from way back when lava lamps were trending. You'll never guess that from the much classier inside, but it's always worth getting references. The classed-up inside comes at a cost, though, with cocktails tending toward the expensive side.

i Drinks €8-15. ☼ Open M-Th 6pm-3am, F-Sa 6pm-4am, Su 6pm-3am.

MISTER HU'S COCKTAIL BAR
BAR

Goltzstr. 39
☎30 217 2111

Our favorite part about Mister Hu's was that, at 2am on a Thursday, there were tons of people chilling in the outdoor seating. The cocktails are good but not terribly original or impressive. The bar and music were pretty standard, but the crowd enjoying the laid-back atmosphere is what makes this place great. If you're looking to sit down and drink for an extended period of time without a worry in the world, we recommend checking out Mister Hu's.

i Drinks €7-13. ☼ Open daily 6pm-3am.

Mitte

Mitte's techno clubs often offer the height of Berlin's dance scene. Nowhere else will you find clubs so well attended by exquisitely dressed locals in their early 20s, and, despite high covers, these tremendous multi-room clubs rarely disappoint. Most of these places are pretty close to **Rosenthaler Platz**, but some club is always just around the corner in Mitte. Don't expect to get a full night's sleep; the parties generally don't heat up until 2am.

MUSCHI OBERMAIER
CLUB

Torstr. 151

Named after the iconic sex symbol from left-wing Berlin in the late '60's, Uschi Obermaier, this place reeks of grit, grunge, and rock-and-roll. The place is dark, sweaty, and saturated with cigarette smoke, and we suspect it hasn't changed much since its prime. The music makes up for the tiny dance floor, and the crowd ranges from young and naïve to old and weathered. Everyone seems to have the same idea, though, which is to have a damn good time. The drinks aren't particularly special, but the atmosphere is unique enough to pay it a visit.

i Cover varies but usually under €5. ☼ Open M-Sa 8pm-2am.

MEIN HAUS AM SEE
BAR

Torstr. 125

Vintage decor, well-worn couches, a miniature cafe next to the bar, and a constant horde of youngsters teeming with angst make Mein Haus am See a popular destination for backpackers passing through Mitte. In addition to a range of funky seating upstairs, there is also a downstairs with a club-like atmosphere and club-like lighting (a.k.a. no lighting). Not your scene? Grab a book and latte at 4am because this joint plays 24/7 and used to be a library. Don't misinterpret us though—most don't come here to catch up on literature.

i Usually no cover unless there's a live music event. Beer €2.50. Cocktails €6-8. ☼ Open 24hr.

NEU ODESSA
BAR

Torstr. 89

The bright entrance light will guide you straight into some of the better cocktails in Mitte. The vintage parlor look and smoke stained couches give Neu Odessa its upscale atmosphere and attract a group of night-owls who aren't just there to get hammered. The well-dressed hipsters who frequent this bar know to order the whiskey and stay away from the overpriced beer, but either way you aren't going to get out of here on a budget.

i Beer €4. Cocktail €8-15. ☒ Open daily 7pm-late.

KITTY CHENG
BAR

Torstr. 99

Kitty Cheng might be disguised as an antique, posh bar, but it has much more soul than it alludes to. One of the only bars that regularly bumps to old-school and new-school hip-hop, it has created one of the more interesting spots for higher-end cocktails in Mitte but they know it and make you pay for it. It's pretty stringent about the guy-to-girl ratio, so if you're a group of excited dudes, you might want to think about bringing a date or you won't be let in. And maybe spiff up a bit—they don't take too kindly to sloppily dressed partygoers.

i Beer €4. Cocktails €8-15. ☒ Open M-Th 9pm-2am, F-Sa 9pm-5am.

Prenzlauer Berg

Prenzlauer Berg has one of the highest birth rates in all of Germany, meaning that you aren't going to find many crazy clubs that rage until the sun comes up. There's less techno, more lourging, and far earlier quiet hours (starting around midnight) than other parts of Berlin. Prenzlauer Berg's nightlife is calm but still worth checking out. The bars are some of the most unforgettable in town, and, since they fill and empty a bit earlier, they're perfect before you head out to later, clubbier climes.

▧ THE WEINEREI: FORUM
BAR

Fehrbelliner Str. 57 ☎030 440 69 83 www.weinerei.com

With its dim lighting and kitschy, mismatched, super comfy furniture, Weinerei Forum dillies up some of the best and cheapest coffee and food in the neighborhood. Wait, it gets better. From 8pm to midnight, this place holds Berlin's most lively wine tasting: you pay €2 for a glass, you try any of their several wine varieties, and at the end of it all, you put as much money as you "think you owe" in a jar. Now, if you just read this as "€2 for unlimited wine!!!" you're not the kind of cool cat the forum is trying to attract. As you leave without putting any money or just a few euro cents in that jar, you'll get scowled at and possibly called out. Weinerei Forum wants you to be the judge of the value of your wine and food; while that's totally awesome and a great way to spend an evening, it doesn't mean it's a freebie.

i U2: Senefelderpl. From the metro, exit by the northern stairs, then head west on Schwedter Str. Turn left onto Kastanienalle, then veer right onto Veteranenstr., a block down the hill. The bar is on the corner of Veteranenstr. and Fehrbelliner Str. Cash only. ☒ Open daily 10am-late. Wine flows 8pm-midnight every night, so let that guide you.

SCOTCH AND SOFA
BAR

Kollwitzstr. 18 ☎030 440 42 371

Retro. Stylish. Classic. Scotch and Sofa defines what a bar should be, with comfortable spaces to lounge about. Come to Scotch and Sofa to sip your scotch or whiskey, talk about something intellectual, and osmose the coolness of the atmosphere. Take some advice, though: if you aren't already experienced in the whole classy-scotch-drinking game, pick the cheapest option on the mile-long menu. It all tastes good, and your wallet will thank you.

i U2: Senefelderpl. From the metro, exit by the northern stairs, then head southeast on Metzer Str. After passing the grocery store, turn left onto Kollwitzstr. The bar is on the right, half a block up Kollwitzstr. Scotch from €5. ☒ Open daily 6pm-very late. Happy hour daily 6-7pm; cocktail of the day €3.80.

WOHNZIMMER
BAR

Lettestr. 6 ☎030 445 54 58 www.wohnzimmer-bar.de

This bar is laid back, and when we say that, we mean grab a beer (€2.60) and lie on a chaise lounge or one of the many super comfy couches in the "living room." Wohnzimmer is a smoking bar, so the patrons tend to be in their late 20s and exude philosophical vibes. Nostalgia abounds.

i U2: Eberswalder Str. From the metro, head east on Danziger Str., turn left onto Lychener Str., then right onto Lettestr., just past the park. The bar is on the left, at the corner of Lettestr. and Schliemannstr. Beer €2.50-3. Cocktails €4-5. Cash only. ☼ Open daily 10am-late.

DUNCKER
CLUB

Dunckerstr. 64 ☎030 445 95 09 www.dunckerclub.de

Duncker used to be a stable, and it still kinda looks like one. In all of Prenzlauer Berg, this is the craziest club, and it might even rival Stasi-bunker clubs. The interior is decorated with chain mail and armor and pretty much anything else you associate with horses. Dunker is frequented by 20-somethings and serves as a venue for a host of live music events. Ring the bell for entry.

i U2: Eberswalder Str. From the metro, head east on Danziger Str., then turn left on Dunckerstr. Walk north on Dunckerstr. until you reach the bridge over the train tracks. The club is on the left, in the darkened building immediately past the bridge. Goth music M. Eclectic DJs Tu-W. Live bands Th. "Independent dance music" F-Sa. Throwback DJs Su. "Dark Market" goth flea market Su 1pm. Cover varies, usually less than €5; no cover on Th. Beer €2.50. Long drinks €4.50. F-Sa all drinks max. €2. Cash only. ☼ Open M-W 9pm-late, Th 10pm-late, F-Sa 11pm-late, Su 10pm-late.

BADFISH BAR
BAR

Stargarder Str. 14 www.badfishbarberlin.com

Badfish has an unbeatable atmosphere that's only trumped by the friendliness of the bartenders. It's not often you find a bar that has a great drink selection coupled with friendly staff and reasonable prices to boot. It has every alcoholic beverage variety your thirsty self could want to consume, from frozen margaritas to ciders to craft beers to high-end whiskeys—just don't try them all at once. Oh, and it has picklebacks. Don't know what those are? Order one anyway.

i Beer €3-5. Cocktails €6-10. ☼ "Angry" hour daily 5-7pm. Open daily 5pm-5am.

Friedrichshain

Barren factory-scapes, heavily graffitied walls, and blinding floodlights may not be the most inviting obstacles to navigate in the dead of night, but such is the environment that hides some of Friedrichshain's—and Berlin's—biggest and most bangin' techno clubs. The old warehouses along **Revaler Strasse** hold the lion's share of sprawling dance floors, but you might want to branch out a little to avoid a double-digit cover.

BERGHAIN AND PANORAMA BAR
CLUB

Am Wriezener Bahnhof www.berghain.de

Even if we told you not to, we know you're going to end up going to Berghain. It's the unofficial electronic epicenter of the world—a techno temple that offers a church service for house worshippers from Friday until Monday. If this is your culture and you came to Berlin to go to Berghain, you must go. For those of you who didn't know what Berghain was until now, you should think about going somewhere else. The line to get in (even at 3am on Saturday or 10am on Sunday) is usually over two hours long (should be named Berg-line, amirite?), and there's a good chance Sven will shake his head in disapproval and you'll be sent packing. Although it definitely has one of the most unique venues in the world, an incredible sound system, and a cult following, we believe Berghain contradicts the spirit of Berlin by using good advertising to generate global hype, making the countercultural mecca surprisingly commercial. Oh, if you decide to go, make sure you wear all black.

i *Cover €14. Drinks €4-10. ☼ Open F-Sa noon-late.*

CASSIOPEIA
CLUB

Revaler Str. 99 ☎30 4738 5949 www.cassiopeia-berlin.de

Cassiopeia is in the RAW Temple, which still stands as an act of defiance to the gentrification of Berlin. The party zone bordering the train tracks is filled with broken bottles, graffiti, and industrial buildings giving off the vibe of third-world country meets clubbing sanctuary. You might see the lights shining out of Cassiopeia like the queen in her starry chair, beckoning you to come and take a shot, but we reckon you'll hear Cassiopeia before you get anywhere close enough to see it. This place is just as raucous as the rest of 'em and will give you a hell of a night if you show up with the right attitude.

i *Cover €5-15. Beer €2-4. Shots €2-5. Cocktails €5-10. ☼ Hours vary, usually open 11pm-late. Check website for the most up-to-date times.*

CLUB ZUR WILDEN RENATE
CLUB

Alt-Stralau 70 ☎30 2504 1426 www.renate.cc

Club Zur wilden Renate is everything you'd expect from the lovechild of a circus and a typical Berlin industrial club. Kitschy, psychedelic, and just plain crazy is the result, and we love every second of it. It might not have the same revered status as many of the other techno temples around Berlin, but nobody there seems to give a damn about what anyone thinks anyway. Respect.

i *Cover €6-10. ☼ Hours vary, check website for most up-to-date show times.*

SISYPHOS
CLUB

Hauptstr. 15 ☎30 9836 6839 www.sisyphos-berlin.net

We don't know why they named this club after the famous punishment of Sisyphus. Sure, they could be insinuating that you should party for eternity. But really this place would be more accurately named if Sisyphus grew dreadlocks, chiseled his boulder into a snowboard, and slid down that damn hill like the wild hippie that he is, all while smoking the fattest of joints. Then we'd understand the name. There's even an old truck-school-bus thing in the middle of the open-air venue. One word of caution (though mothers would probably give at least 2000 words of caution) is that Sisyphos is pretty far out. Literally—it's a hike to get there. And they usually don't get going until 4am. Worth the experience? We think so.

i *Cover €10. Beer €2-4. Shots €2-4. Cocktails €5-10. ☼ Open nonstop from Friday at midnight until Monday. Hold onto your horses.*

Kreuzberg

If you came to Berlin for nightlife and you've visited some places in other neighborhoods, you've probably been left wondering why on earth Berlin has the reputation it boasts. And the answer, dear friend, is Kreuzberg. Kreuzberg is world-renowned for its unbelievable techno scene. Converted warehouses, wild light displays, destructive speaker systems, and packed dance floors cluster around **Schlesisches Tor,** but some of the best spots are scattered more widely. Kreuzberg is one of Berlin's most notoriously nocturnal neighborhoods, so expect the parties to rage from about 2am to well past dawn.

TRESOR
CLUB

Köpenicker Str. 70 www.tresorberlin.com

Housed inside an old, derelict heating plant, Tresor is a modern techno tabernacle and legendary labyrinth of some of the best electronic music to come out of Berlin. With an industrial dance floor in the basement and more laid-back house lounge upstairs, the sheer size of the space will impress you. Globus on the third floor produces some of the smoothest house vibes we've found, +4 is the laboratory where the techno-technicians experiment, and the vault is where Tresor's signature sound staves off the morning and then charges straight through to the next day. Anywhere within this once-machine-filled maze makes for the perfect place to dance the night away, and a crowd with similar interests puts Tresor at the top of our list of clubs to visit in Kreuzberg.

i *Cover varies, usually €7-15.* 🕐 *Open W and F-Sa midnight-late.*

WATERGATE
CLUB

Falckensteinstr. 49   www.water-gate.de

Compared to many of the other factory-style clubs around Kreuzberg, Watergate is surprisingly small. That said, what it lacks in floor space it makes up for with quality of music, wall-to-wall LED lighting, and the perfect lounge outside right on the River Spree. Given its central location and popular reputation, Watergate can amass quite a line at the door, but the door policy is relaxed. As long as you don't look like you're there to hurt someone, you should have no problem getting in and having a great time. This house of house thumps well into the AM, so bring your stamina.

i *Cover €5-10.* 🕐 *Open W and F-Sa 10pm-5am.*

LIDO BERLIN
MUSIC VENUE

Cuvrystr. 7   www.lido-berlin.de

Lido is one of the most renowned institutions for live music in Berlin. What? Not another techno-house factory? Yup, that's right. Lido has been hosting some of the greatest indie rock bands to come out of and visit Berlin for the last decade. Housed in a 1950s style movie theater, the venue is a welcome change of pace from the industrial drum-and-bass warehouses, with a stage and dance floor big enough for you and a couple hundred of your newfound best friends and an outdoor lounge that is the perfect place to rest your ears and your feet. If live music is your thing and techno doesn't float your boat, Lido will be your flagship.

i *Cover varies, usually €4-10.* 🕐 *Hours vary depending on the concert; check website for the most up-to-date schedule.*

LUZIA
BAR, CAFE

Oranienstr. 34   ☎030 817 99 958 www.luzia.tc

Kreuzberg is covered with clubs, but where are all the bars? Well, they're superfluous because Luzia is such a great bar that they'd all fall short in comparison. Luzia is huge and tremendously popular with the Kreuzberg locals, most of whom are UK transplants who think of themselves as German artists. Whatever, this is still a great bar. Gold-painted walls glow softly in the light of flickering candles. The huge, L-shaped design allows for long lines of vintage, threadbare lounge chairs, cafe tables, and a bar so long that it can easily serve the crowd that swarms here at peak hours.

i *U1 or U8: Kotbusser Tor. From the metro, head northeast up Aldabertstr. and turn left onto Oranienstr. The bar is on the right. The only sign is a large, black rectangle with a gold coat of arms in the middle. Beer €2.50-3.50. Long drinks €5-6. Absinthe €3-7. Cash only.* 🕐 *Open daily noon-late.*

MAGNET CLUB
CLUB, MUSIC VENUE

Falckensteinstr. 48   ☎030 440 08 140 www.magnet-club.de

Magnet wishes it were in New Orleans: it's the sort of place that hosts ladies' cage wrestling competitions. Patrons include locals who come for the DJ and furious tourists who got rejected from Watergate next door. Indie bands play on a short, shallow stage that makes it seem as though they're part of the crowd, and DJs spin a much lighter mix than their Kreuzberg counterparts—think indie electropop. Magnet tries hard to one-up its peaceful indie followers, offering free Jager shots (while the stock lasts) a couple of nights a week.

i U1: Schlesisches Tor. From the metro, head toward the bridge. An "M" hangs above the door. Cover €3-7. Shots €2-2.50. Beer €2.50-3. Long drinks €6-6.50. Ⓧ Usually open Tu-Su from 10pm. Check online for exact schedule.

SO36
BAR, CLUB
Oranienstr. 190 ☎030 614 01 306 www.so36.ce

SO36 was probably amazing in 1970. For one thing, seeing David Bowie on a dance floor might make your heart stop. But today, SO36 is less of a club and more of a relic, a tribute to better music and better times. The various parties, live shows, and cultural presentations that fill this huge hall attract a mixed gay/straight clientele whose common denominator is that they like to party hardy. Gayhane, a gay cabaret that performs the last Saturday of every month, has become a staple of the Berlin GLBT scene and can get pretty epic.

i U1 or U8: Kottbusser Tor. From the metro, walk north on Adalbertstr. and turn right onto Oranienstr. The club is on the right. Cover varies. Shots €2.20. Beer €2.80-3.50. Wine €3. Long drinks €5.50, with Red Bull €6. Cash only. Ⓧ Hours vary, but usually open F-Sa 10pm-late.

ROSES
GLBT, BAR
Oranienstr. 187 ☎030 615 65 70

At first glance, it might look like a kink shop, but, rest assured, the fuzzy pink walls and the omnipresent cheetah print make this gay bar a sight for sore eyes. Gay men, some lesbian women, and a couple of straight groups (there to camp out in campy glory) join together for small talk over some clean electronic. The bar's small size makes mingling easy, and the endless assortment of wall trinkets (glowing mounted antlers, twinkling hearts, a psychedelic Virgin Mary) keep everyone giggling.

i U1 or U8: Kottbusser Tor. From the metro, head northwest on Oranienstr. past Mariannenstr. The bar is on the left. Beer €2.50. Cocktails €5, with Red Bull €6. Cash only. Ⓧ Open daily 9pm-late.

ARTS AND CULTURE

As the old saying goes, "Where there be hipsters, there be Arts and Culture." Though the saying's origins are unclear, it certainly applies to Berlin. Whether it's opera, film, or Brecht in the original German that you're after, Berlin has got you covered. For a magical evening at the symphony, grab a standing-room-only ticket to see the Berliner Philharmoniker or grab a rush seat to see the Deutsche Oper perform Wagner's four-opera cycle, *The Ring of the Nibelung*. If rock, pop, indie, or hip hop are more your style, head to Kreuzberg to check out Festsaal Kreuzberg and Columbiahalle. Nearby, English Theater Berlin will satisfy any Anglophone's theater cravings, while the Deutsches Theater in Mitte hosts performances of the German classics as well as the English canon in translation. The truly hip should head straight to Lichtblick Kino or Kino Babylon to find radical documentaries, avant-garde films, and a sea of retro frames and flannel.

Music and Opera

BERLINER PHILHARMONIE
MITTE
Herbert-von-Karajan-Str. 1 ☎030 254 88 999 www.berlin-philharmoniker.de

If you fancy yourself to be a fan of classical music, you'd better have heard of the **Berlin Philharmoniker.** Led by Sir Simon Rattle, the Philharmoniker is considered one of the world's finest, if not the finest, orchestras. Concerts take place in the Philharmonie, a decidedly huge and weird-looking concert hall near Potsdamer Platz. The bright yellow building was designed to be pitch perfect: every member of the audience gets an adequately full view and incredibly full sound. With most concerts selling out about a month in advance, it can be pretty tough to get a seat, so check the website for availability. For sold-out concerts, some tickets and standing room may be available 90min. before the concert begins, but only at the box office. Stand in line, get some cheap tickets if you're lucky, and enjoy some of the sweetest sounds known to mankind.

i *S1, S2, S25, or U2: Potsdamer Pl. From the metro, head west on Potsdamer Str. Tickets for standing room from €7, for seats from €15. ☼ Open from Jul-early Sept. Box office open M-F 3-6pm, Sa-Su 11am-2pm.*

DEUTSCHE STAATSOPER   MITTE

Unter den Linden 7   ☎030 203 54 555 www.staatsoper-berlin.de

The Deutsche Staatsoper is notorious for its splendor. Though its presence and patronage suffered during the years of separation, this opera house is rebuilding its reputation and its repertoire of Baroque opera and contemporary pieces. Unfortunately, its exterior is under extensive renovation, and the usual opera house is closed until mid-2014. Until its main building reopens, the Staatsoper presents performances in the sticks—Schiller Theater in Charlottenberg.

i *U6: Französische Str. Or bus #100, 157, or 348: Deutsche Staatsoper. Tickets €14-260. For certain seats, students can get a ½-price discount, but only within 4 weeks of the performance and only at the box office. Unsold tickets €13, 30min. before the show. ☼ Open Aug through mid-Jul. Box office open daily noon-7pm and 1hr. before performances.*

DEUTSCHE OPER BERLIN   CHARLOTTENBURG

Bismarckstr. 35   ☎030 343 84 343 www.deutscheoperberlin.de

The Deutsche Oper Berlin's original home, the Deutsches Opernhaus, was built in 1911 but (surprise!) was decimated by Allied bombs. Today, performances take place in Berlin's newest opera house, which looks like a gigantic concrete box. If you have the chance, don't pass up a cheap ticket to see one of Berlin's most spectacular performances.

i *U2: Deutsche Oper. Tickets €16-122. 25% student discount when you buy at the box office. Unsold tickets €13, 30min. before the show. ☼ Open Sept-Jun. Box office open M-Sa 11am until beginning of the performance or 11am-7pm on days without performances, Su 10am-2pm. Evening tickets available 1hr. before performances.*

FESTSAAL KREUZBERG   KREUZBERG

Skalitzerstr. 130   ☎030 611 01 313 www.festsaal-kreuzberg.de

Free jazz, indie rock, swing, electropop—you never know what to expect at this absurdly hip venue. A tremendous chasm of a main hall accommodates acts of all shapes and sizes, plus an overflowing crowd of fans packed together on the main floor and the mezzanine. A dusty courtyard out front features a bar and novelty acts like fire throwers. Poetry readings, film screenings, and art performances fill out the program with appropriately eclectic material, making this one of Berlin's most exciting venues.

i *U1 or U8: Kottbusser Tor. From the U-Bahn, head east on Skalitzerstr. The venue is on the left. Tickets €5-20. Shots €2. Long drinks €6. ☼ Hours vary. Usually open F-Sa 9pm-late.*

COLUMBIAHALLE   KREUZBERG

Columbiadamm 13-21   ☎030 698 09 80 www.c-halle.com

Any venue that features Snoop Dogg, The Specials, and Bon Iver in a matter of a couple months has a special place in our hearts. With a wildly eclectic collection of superstars and indie notables from all over the world, Columbiahalle's calendar is bound to make you gasp and say, "I definitely wanna see that," at least twice. Once a gym for American service members in south Kreuzberg, Columbiahalle may look dated and innocuous, but its standing-room-only floor and mezzanine sure can rage.

i *U6: Platz der Luftbrücke. From the metro, head east on Columbiadamm. The venue is in the 1st block on the right. Tickets €20-60, depending on the act. ☼ Hours and dates vary, but concerts tend to start at 8pm. Check the website for more details.*

Film

Finding English films in Berlin is almost as easy as finding the Fernsehturm. On any night, choose from over 150 different films, marked **O.F.** or **O.V.** for the original version (meaning not dubbed in German), **O.m.U** for original version with German subtitles, or **O.m.u.E.** for original film with English subtitles.

LICHTBLICK KINO

PRENZLAUER BERG

Kastanienallee 77   ☎030 440 58 179 www.lichtblick-kino.org

Lichtblick is a charming cinema. The 32-seat theater presents avant-garde films and radical documentaries, as well as a wildly eclectic range of movies. English films are intermixed with all sorts of other international fare and all films are shown with the original sound and accompanied by German subtitles, so you won't need to perform any amazing feats of lip-reading for any of the many English films. With a bar in the main entrance and a couple guys reading philosophical novels by candlelight, this is the quintessential art house experience.

i U8: Eberswalder Str. From the metro, walk southwest on Kastanienallee, past Oderberger Str. The theater is near the end of the next block on the left. Tickets €5, students €4.50. ⏲ 2-5 films shown every night, check the website for a calendar. Usually 5-10pm.

KINO BABYLON

MITTE

Rosa-Luxemburg-Str. 30   ☎030 242 59 69 www.babylonberlin.de

Americans, Brits, and Berliners alike flock to this spunky, independent film house with a commitment to classic international cinema. Silent films, fiction readings, and constant themed retrospectives guarantee that you'll have a chance to see something new and interesting alongside the classics. Casanova, anyone? Occasional summer screenings happen outdoors on the beautiful Rosa-Luxemburg-Pl.—and epic screenings of *Rocky Horror Picture Show* go down regularly. Unfortunately, outside of the frequent American classics, English is a bit hard to come by, as most subtitles are in German.

i U2: Rosa-Luxemburg-Pl. From the metro, walk south on Rosa-Luxemburg-Str. Tickets €4-8. ⏲ The schedule changes daily; check website for details. Box office open M-F from 5pm until the 1st film of the evening.

ARSENAL

MITTE

In the Filmhaus at Potsdamer Pl.   ☎030 269 55 100 www.arsenal-berlin.de

Run by the founders of Berlinale and located just below the **Museum for Film and Television,** Arsenal showcases independent films and some classics. Discussions, talks, and frequent appearances by guest directors make the theater a popular meeting place for Berlin's filmmakers. With the majority of films in the original with English subtitles, non-Germans can watch easy.

i U2, S1, S2, or S25: Potsdamer Pl. From the metro, head west on Potsdamer Str. and go into the building labeled "Deutsche Kinemathek." Take the elevator down to the 2nd basement level. Tickets €6.50, students €5. ⏲ 3-5 films shown each night. Films usually start 4-8pm. Check the website for a full calendar.

CENTRAL KINO

MITTE

Rosenthaler Str. 39   ☎030 285 99 973 www.kino-central.de

A small theater right in the middle of Mitte, this place shows indie German fare, award-winning American films, and other international cinema, mostly in the original language with German subtitles. While the screens aren't huge, the location is prime. It's located near Hackesher Markt in a heavily graffitied courtyard; one theater is even outside.

i S3, S5, or S7: Hackescher Markt. From the metro, walk north on Rosenthaler Str., past the Hackesche Höfe, and the theater is in a courtyard next door. €6.50, students €6. ⏲ Open daily before the 1st movie noon-3pm.

Theater

ENGLISH THEATER BERLIN
KREUZBERG

Fidicinstr. 40   ☎030 693 56 92 www.etberlin.de

Though all the shows here are presented in English, it's hard to find a theater that is more "Berlin." From 10min. skits to full-out festivals, the English Theater tries out every edge of the spectrum, and, boy, is this place ever edgy. We hear that most shows feature naked people and cabbages.

i U6: Pl. der Luftbrücke. From the metro, head north on Mehringdamm for 2 blocks and turn right onto Fidicinstr. The theater is on the left, within the 1st block. €13, students €8. ☒ Box office opens 1hr. before show. Shows are at 8pm unless otherwise noted. Check the website for a calendar of performances.

DEUTSCHES THEATER
MITTE

Schumann Str. 13a   ☎030 284 41 225 www.deutschestheater.de

Built in 1850, this world-famous theater was once controlled by legendary director Max Reinhardt and is still a cultural heavy hitter in Berlin. With even English dramas in translation (Shakespeare and Beckett are rockstars here), Anglophones shouldn't expect to understand any of the words. Fortunately, the productions are gorgeous enough that they're worth seeing in spite of the language barrier.

i U6: Oranienburger Tor. From the U-Bahn, head south on Friederichstr., take a right onto Reinhartstr., then another right onto Albrecthstr €5-30. ☒ Box office open M-Sa 11am-6:30pm, Su 3-6:30pm. Shows are at 8pm unless otherwise noted.

VOLKSBÜHNE
MITTE

Linienstr. 227   .   ☎030 24 06 55 www.volksbuehne-berlin.de

Originally established to house productions of Socialist Realism at prices accessible to the working class, this imposing "people's theater" looks like it came straight out of a utopian sci-fi thriller. While the enormous stage goes dark during the summer, alive with concerts, German and English theater, and touring performances and festivals from Sept-May. Productions range from Büchner to Brecht to an interactive contemporary work called "Revolution Now!"—you'll probably leave more convinced of capitalist injustice than ever before. Before and after the shows, crowds gather in the beautiful plaza to smoke and talk.

i U2: Rosa-Luxemburg-Pl. From the metro, walk south down Rosa-Luxemburg-Str. Tickets €6-30. Students get a 50% discount on certain performances; check the website. ☒ Box office open daily noon-6pm and 1hr. before performances. Shows are at 8pm unless otherwise noted.

SHOPPING

Books

Finding English books in Berlin is about as easy as finding someone who speaks English: they're everywhere, but they're not always very good. Secondhand is the best way to offset the extra cost of English books.

▨ ST. GEORGE'S BOOKSTORE
PRENZLAUER BERG

Wörtherstr. 27   ☎030 817 98 333 www.saintgeorgesbookshop.com

You'd be hard-pressed to find a better English-language bookstore on the continent. St. George's owner makes frequent trips to the UK and US to buy the loads of titles that fill the towering shelves. The books are stacked from the floor to the ceiling, and picturesque ladders stretch upward. Over half of the books are used and extremely well-priced (paperbacks €4-8), with a number of books for just €1. Pay in euro, British pounds, or American dollars (oh my!).

i U2: Senefelderpl. From the metro, head southeast on Metzerstr. and turn left onto Prenzlauer Allee. Follow Prenzlauer Allee 3 blocks, then turn left onto Wörtherstr. The bookstore is halfway down the block, on the right. Used hardcovers €10. ☒ Open M-F 11am-8pm, Sa 11am-7pm.

Riemannstr. 7   ☎030 694 01 160 www.anothercountry.ce

Browsing this cluttered secondhand English bookstore feels a little like walking around some guy's house, but a wide and unpredictable collection rewards your searching, especially since all books are €2-5. Another Country doesn't just want to be that forgettable place where you can buy a cheap copy of *Twilight* (which is in stock; €5); it wants to be a local library and cultural center. A small percentage of the books are labeled "lending only," meaning they're priced a little higher (around €10), and you get back the entire price, minus €1.50, when you return them. Plus, live acoustic performances, readings, and trivia add further incentive to return again and again. Check out the wide selection of "Evil Books," which includes a copy of L. Ron Hubbard's *Dianetics*, a book entitled *The Quotable Richard Nixon*, and *Bradymania*.

i U7: Gneisenaustr. From the metro, walk south on Zossener Str. Turn right onto Riemannstr., and Another Country is on the left. ⏰ Open Tu-F 11am-8pm, Sa-Su noon-4pm.

Music

SPACE HALL   KREUZBERG
Zossenerstr. 33, 35   ☎030 694 76 64 www.spacehall.de

They don't make them like this anymore in the States—maybe they never did. With two addresses (one of just CDs, the other strictly vinyl), Space Hall makes it nearly impossible *not* to find what you're looking for. The vinyl store never misses a beat, with the longest interior of any Berlin record store (painted to resemble a forest, of course) and easily one of the widest selections to boot. They also have an inspiring collection of rubber duckies.

i U7: Gneisenaustr. From the metro, head south on Zossenerstr. The record store is on the left. CDs regular €10-20, discounted €3-10. LPs €10-30. ⏰ Open M-W 11am-8pm, Th-F 11am-10pm, Sa 11am-8pm.

HARD WAX   KREUZBERG
Paul-Lincke-Ufer 44a   ☎030 611 30 111 www.hardwax.com

Walk down a silent alleyway, through an eerily quiet courtyard, up three flights of dim, graffitied stairs, and suddenly, you're in one of Berlin's best record stores for electronic music. Bare brick and concrete walls make it feel aggressively nonchalant, while an entire back room dedicated to private listening stations for patrons proves that Hard Wax is dedicated to helping you get out of the House. Here, you'll find dubstep, IDM, ambient, and subgenres upon subgenres. Fortunately, nearly every CD and LP bears a short description in English courtesy of Hard Wax's experts, so you'll never feel like you're randomly flipping through a lot of crap. Though the selection is small compared to some of Berlin's other electro-record stores, the offerings seem hand-picked.

i U1 or U8: Kottbusser Tor. From the U-Bahn, head south on Kottbusserstr. Take a left just before the canal, then enter the courtyard on the left just after crossing Mariannenstr. Records €5-30; most €8-12. CDs €10-20. ⏰ Open M-Sa noon-8pm.

ESSENTIALS
Practicalities

- **TOURIST OFFICES:** Now privately owned, tourist offices merely give you some commercial flyer or refer you to a website instead of guaranteeing human contact. Visit **www.berlin.de** for reliable info on all aspects of city life. **Tourist Info Centers.** (Berlin Tourismus Marketing GmbH, Am Karlsbad 11 ☎030 25 00 25 www.visitberlin.de. *i* On the ground floor of the Hauptbahnhof, next to the northern entrance. English spoken. *Siegessäule, Blu,* and *Gay-Yellowpages* have GLBT event and club listings. Transit maps free; city maps €1-2. The monthly

berlin

Berlin Programm lists museums, sights, restaurants, and hotels as well as opera, theater, and classical music performances, €1.75. *Tip* provides full listings of film, theater, concerts, and clubs in German, €2.70. *Ex-Berliner* has English-language movie and theater reviews, €2. ☺ Open daily 8am-10pm.) **Alternate location.** (Brandenburger Tor S1, S2, S25, or bus #100: Unter den Linden. *i* On your left as you face the pillars from the Unter den Linden side. ☺ Open daily 10am-6pm.)

- **STUDENT TRAVEL OFFICES: STA** books flights and hotels and sells ISICs. (Dorotheenstr. 30 ☎030 201 65 063 *i* S3, S5, S7, S9, S75, or U6: Friedrichstr. From the metro, walk 1 block south on Friedrichstr., turn left onto Dorotheenstr., and follow as it veers left. STA is on the left. ☺ Open M-F 10am-7pm, Sa 11am-3pm.) **Second location.** (Gleimstr. 28 ☎030 285 98 264 *i* S4, S8, S85, or U2: Schönhauser Allee. From the metro, walk south on Schönhauser Allee and turn right onto Gleimstr. ☺ Open M-F 10am-7pm, Sa 11am-4pm.) **Third location.** (Hardenbergstr. 9 ☎030 310 00 40 *i* U2: Ernst-Reuter-Pl. From the metro, walk southeast on Hardenbergstr.Open M-F 10am-7pm, Sa 11am-3pm.) **Fourth location.** (Takustr. 47. ☎030 831 10 25 *i* U3: Dahlem-Dorf. From the metro, walk north on Brümmerstr., turn left onto Königin-Luise Str., then turn right onto Takustr. ☺ Open M-F 10am-7pm, Sa 10am-2pm.)

- **TOURS: Terry Brewer's Best of Berlin** is legendary for its vast knowledge and engaging personalities, making the 6hr.+ walk well worth it. Tours leave daily from in front of the Bandy Brooks shop on Friedrichstr. (☎017 738 81 537 www.brewersberlintours.com *i* S1, S7, S9, S75, or U6: Friedrichstr €12. ☺ Tours start at 10:30am.) **Insider Tour** offers a variety of fun, informative walking and bike tours that hit all the major sights. More importantly, the guides' enthusiasm for Berlin is contagious, and their accents span the English-speaking world. (☎030 692 3149 www.insidertour.com. ☺ Tours last 4hr.)

- **CURRENCY EXCHANGE AND MONEY WIRES:** The best rates are usually found at exchange offices with **Wechselstube** signs outside, at most major train stations, and in large squares. For money wires through Western Union, use **ReiseBank.** (M: Hauptbahnhof ☎030 204 53 761 ☺ Open M-Sa 8am-10pm.) **Second location.** (M: Bahnhof Zoo ☎030 881 71 17.) **Third location.** (M: Ostbahnhof 030 296 43 93.)

- **LUGGAGE STORAGE:** In the M: Hauptbahnhof, in "DB Gepack Center," 1st fl., east side €4 per day). Lockers also at M: Bahnhof Zoo, M: Ostbahnhof, and M: Alexanderpl.

- **INTERNET ACCESS:** Free internet with admission to the **Staatsbibliothek.** During its renovation, Staatsbibliothek requires €10 month-long pass to the library. (Potsdamer Str. 33 ☎030 26 60 ☺ Open M-F 9am-9pm, Sa 9am-7pm.) **Netlounge.** (Auguststr. 89 ☎030 24 34 25 97 www.netlounge-berlin.de *i* M: Oranienburger Str. €2.50 per hr. ☺ Open daily noon-midnight.) **Easy Internet** has several locations throughout Berlin. (Unter den Linden 24, Rosenstr. 16, Frankfurter Allee 32, Rykestr. 29, and Kurfürstendamm 18.) Many cafes throughout Berlin offer free Wi-Fi, including **Starbucks,** where the networks never require a password.

- **POST OFFICES: Bahnhof Zoo.** (Joachimstaler Str. 7 ☎030 887 08 611 *i* Down Joachimstaler Str. from Bahnhof Zoo on the corner of Joachimstaler Str. and Kantstr. ☺ Open M-Sa 9am-8pm.) **Alexanderplatz.** (Rathausstr. 5, by the Dunkin Donuts. ☺ Open M-F 9am-7pm, 9am-4pm.) **Tegel Airport.** (☺ Open M-F 8am-6pm, Sa 8am-noon.) **Ostbahnhof.** (☺ Open M-F 8am-8pm, Sa-Su 10am-6pm.) To find a post office near you, visit the search tool on their website, www.standorte.deutschepost.de/filialen_verkaufspunkte, which is confusing and in German but could help.

- **POSTAL CODE** 10706.

Emergency

- **POLICE:** Pl. der Luftbrücke 6. U6: Pl. der Luftbrücke.
- **EMERGENCY NUMBERS:** ☎110.

- **AMBULANCE AND FIRE:** ☎112.

- **NON-EMERGENCY ADVICE HOTLINE:** ☎030 466 44 664.

- **MEDICAL SERVICES:** The American and British embassies list English-speaking doctors. The **emergency doctor** (☎030 31 00 31 or ☎018 042 255 23 62) service helps travelers find English-speaking doctors. **Emergency dentist.** (☎030 890 04 333)

- **CRISIS LINES:** English spoken on most crisis lines. **American Hotline** (017 781 41 510) has crisis and referral services. **Poison Control.** (030 192 40) **Berliner Behindertenverband** has resources for the disabled. (Jägerstr. 63d ☎030 204 38 47 www.bbv-ev.de ☼ Open W noon-5pm and by appointment.) **Deutsche AIDS-Hilfe.** (Wilhelmstr. 138 ☎030 690 08 70 www.aidshilfe.de) **Drug Crisis Hotline.** (☎030 192 37 24hr.) **Frauenkrisentelefon.** Women's crisis line. (☎030 615 4243 www.frauenkrisentelefon.de ☼ Open M 10am-noon, Tu-W 7-9pm, Th 10am-noon, F 7-9pm, Sa-Su 5-7pm.) **Lesbenberatung** offers counseling for lesbians. (Kulmer Str. 20a ☎030 215 20 00 www.lesbenberatung-berlin.de) **Schwulenberatung** offers counseling for gay men. (Mommsenstr. 45 ☎030 194 46 www.schwulenberatungberlin.de.) **Maneo** offers legal help for gay victims of violence. (☎030 216 33 36 www.maneo.de ☼ Open daily 5-7pm.) **LARA** offers counseling for victims of sexual assault. (Fuggerstr. 19 ☎030 216 88 88 www.lara-berlin.de ☼ Open M-F 9am-6pm.)

Getting There

By Plane
Capital Airport Berlin Brandenburg International (BBI) is currently under construction and will be opened at an unknown future date. Until then, **Tegel Airport** will continue to serve travelers. (☎018 050 00 186 www.berlin-airport.de *i* Take express bus #X9 or #109 from U7: Jakob-Kaiser Pl., bus #128 from U6: Kurt-Schumacher-Pl., or bus TXL from S42, S41: Beusselstr. Follow signs in the airport for ground transportation.)

By Train
International trains (☎972 226 150) pass through Berlin's **Hauptbahnhof** and run to: Amsterdam, NTH (€130. ☼ 7hr., 16 per day); Brussels, BEL (€140. ☼ 7hr., 16 per day); Budapest, HUN (€140. ☼ 13hr., 4 per day); Copenhagen, DNK (€135. ☼ 7hr., 7 per day.); Paris, FRA (€200. ☼ 9hr., 9 per day.); Prague, CZR (€80. ☼ 5hr., 12 per day); Vienna, AUT (€155. ☼ 10hr., 12 per day.)

By Bus
ZOB is the central bus station. (Masurenallee 4. ☎030 301 03 80 *i* U2: Theodor-Heuss-Pl. From the metro, head southwest on Masurenallee; the station is on the left. Alternatively, S4, S45, or S46: Messe Nord/ICC. From the metro, walk west on Neue Kantstr. The station is on the right. ☼ Open M-F 6am-9pm, Sa-Su and holidays 6am-8pm.)

Getting Around

By Public Transportation: The Bvg
The two pillars of Berlin's metro are the **U-Bahn** and **S-Bahn** trains, which cover the city in spidery and circular patterns, (somewhat) respectively. **Trams** and **buses** (both part of the U-Bahn system) scuttle around the remaining city corners. (BVG's 24hr. hotline ☎030 194 49 www.bvg.de.) Berlin is divided into three transit zones. **Zone A** consists of central Berlin, including Tempelhof Airport. The rest of Berlin lies in **Zone B**. **Zone C** covers the larger state of Brandenburg, including Potsdam. An **AB** ticket is the best deal, since you can later buy extension tickets for the outlying areas. A **one-way** ticket is good for 2hr. after validation. (Zones AB €2.30, BC €2.70, ABC €3, under 6 free.) Within the validation period, the ticket may be used on any S-Bahn, U-Bahn, bus, or tram.

Most train lines don't run Monday through Friday 1-4am. S-Bahn and U-Bahn lines do run Friday and Saturday nights, but less frequently. When trains stop running, 70 night buses take over, running every 20-30min. generally along major transit routes; pick up the free *Nachtliniennetz* **map** of bus routes at a **Fahrscheine und Mehr** office. The letter "N" precedes night bus numbers. Trams continue to run at night.

Buy tickets, including monthly passes, from machines or ticket windows in metro stations or from bus drivers. **Be warned:** machines don't give more than €10 change, and many machines don't take bills, though some accept credit cards. **Validate** your ticket by inserting it into the stamp machines before boarding. Failure to validate becomes a big deal when plainclothes policemen bust you and charge you €40 for freeloading. If you bring a bike on the U-Bahn or S-Bahn, you must buy it a child's ticket. Bikes are prohibited on buses and trams.

Single-ride tickets are a waste of money. A **day ticket** (AB €6.30, BC €6.60, ABC €6.80) is good from the time it's stamped until 3am the next day. The BVG also sells **7-day tickets** (AB €27.20, BC €28, ABC €33.50) and **month-long passes** (AB €74, BC €75, ABC €91). The popular tourist cards are another option. The **WelcomeCard** (sold at tourist offices) buys unlimited travel (AB 48hr. €17, ABC €19; 72hr. €23/26) and includes discounts at 130 sights. The **City TourCard** is good within zones AB (48hr. €16, 72hr. €22) and offers discounts at over 50 attractions.

By Taxi

Call 15min. in advance for a taxi. Women can request female drivers. Trips within the city cost up to €30. (☎030 261 026, toll-free ☎0800 263 00 00)

By Bike

Biking is one of the best ways to explore the city that never brakes. Unless your hostel is out in the boonies, few trips will be out of cycling distance, and given that U-Bahn tickets verge on €3 and that the average long-term bike rental costs €8 per day, pedaling your way can be a better deal and a simpler way to navigate. **Fat Tire Bike Rental** (Panorama Str. 1a ☎016 389 26 427)and **Prenzlberger Orange Bikes** (Kollwitzstr. 35 ☎030 240 47 991 www.berlinfahrradverleih.com) are both great options.

dresden

Dresden should win an award for being the best overlooked city in Germany. If we're being honest, there's a good chance you haven't even heard of this Bavaradise unless you remember passing it on your bus from Prague to Berlin (or unless you're a WWII history buff, in which case, we're sorry). With museums that would delight your history professor, enough biergartens to give us an immediate beer belly, and a laid-back youth culture that synthesizes rebellious punk-rockers and dreadlocked hippies, Dresden is not a city to neglect. All you need to fully absorb this Saxon capital is one weekend. Be surprised by the elegant skyline of Alstadt and educated by expansive collections in the museums, then recuperate while relaxing at one of the Elbe's many riverside biergartens. We guarantee you'll love Dresden's disposition so much you might not take that bus to Berlin.

ORIENTATION

Much of Dresden was leveled in air raids during February 1945. Although the city's architectural prowess never fully recovered to its previous status of "the Florence of the north," the Saxon capital's culture persevered and remains today in an idyllic Bavarian village with a grungy twist. Many of the iconic landmarks were rebuilt in all of their sparkling grandeur and stand now as cultural relics that draw flocks of camera wielding tourists from around the world.

Separated by the River Elbe, Dresden is divided into two major neighborhoods: Neustadt (meaning "new town") to the north and Altstadt ("old town") to the south. You'll find armies of map-reading camera clickers bewildered by the Baroque beasts clustered in Altstadt, while the majority of Dresden's young people seek refuge in Neustadt's many pubs, biergartens, or spontaneous curbside gatherings. If you are looking to immerse yourself in the treasures in Dresden's museums but don't want to spend all of your money on a hotel, or if you consider yourself a traveler who prioritizes experience with local people as opposed to local attractions, we definitely recommend that you find a place to stay somewhere in Neustadt. Not only will you be surrounded by tons of options for cheap food and cheap beer, but you'll also be surrounded by tons of young folk taking full advantage of both of these things every night of the week. We were pleasantly surprised to find impromptu curbside gatherings of young locals that were as vibrant on Wednesday as they were on Saturday.

ACCOMMODATIONS

HOSTEL LOLLIS HOMESTAY DRESDEN   HOSTEL $
Görlitzer Str. 34

The Bavarian accent requires some adjustment, especially for those of you coming down from Berlin. Fear not, Hostel Lollis Homestay offers free German lessons that double as a pre-pre-game and a way to meet some pretty cool polyglots. It also offers a free home-cooked meal one night a week, and the stuff can tell you exactly where to get one if you happen to miss theirs. The staff will quickly become your friends, and it's possible someone staying at the hostel might one day become your family. Making Lollis all the more enticing, it's situated only a 30-second walk from the most buzzing corners of Neustadt. Could it really get any better? Actually, yes. It has free bike rentals.

i Dorms €15-20. Linens €2, free with €5 deposit if staying longer than 4 nights. Breakfast €4. ⊡ Reception 24hr.

HOSTEL MONDPALAST DRESDEN   HOSTEL $
Louisenstr. 77

Although theiitsr bar bids you *bon voyage*, the only things you'll be saying farewell to at Hostel Mondpalast are your worries. On the bustling Louisenstr., everything you need is right at your doorstep. There's not much of a reason to leave, anyway, with the hostel bar, Bon Voyage, right next to the reception. In the chance that you can pry yourself off the barstool, Mondpalast is the ideal place to start any adventure you could hope to find in Dresden.

i Dorms €15-19. Breakfast €7. Linens €2. ⊡ Reception 24hr.

KANGAROO STOP HOSTEL   HOSTEL $
Erna-Berger-Str. 8

If you weren't aware, Germans are passionate about nature. The Germans who founded Kangaroo Stop just so happened to be passionate about Australia's nature. Only a quick hop from the Banhof-Neustadt, Kangaroo Stop's Down-Under theme was just the right thing to bring us back up above. Cozy, comfortable, and convenient, the gecko-adorned walls of the Kangaroo Stop were the only barriers keeping us from booking a flight to the land of the greatest barrier. Especially given that Kangaroo Stop doesn't have any vegemite, we have all the more reason to stay.

i Dorms €13-19. Breakfast €6. Linens €2.

SIGHTS

When you cross over the Augustusbrucke from Neustadt, you'll immediately be immersed in a mythical land with an overwhelming amount of beautiful buildings. There's not as much to see as you might think on first glance, but Dresden's museum list and information centers really make you think there is. Don't be confused: we'll break it down for you. Oh, and get used to hearing the name August the Strong. You'll see his gilded greatness all throughout Dresden. We can only speculate what he was compensating for, but it must have been bad.

RESIDENZSCHLOSS (ROYAL PALACE)
PALACE

Taschenberg 2

After crossing the Augustusbrucke into Schlossplatz and through the arched pathway, you'll arrive in a narrow cobblestone path that is as idyllic as it is historic. To your right, you'll see Dresden's Royal Palace, which now houses a significant portion of Dresden's attractions. You'll be thoroughly confused by the options for tickets that are outlined in detail at the information kiosks, but your best bet is to grab a pass to the Historic Green Vault and hold off on the pass for the Residenzschloss until after your walk through treasured halls. If you're left wanting more of royal collections, you can grab a Residenzschloss pass (€12, students €9) that gets you access to the New Green Vault, the Reisenaal (meaning "giant's hall," it's a sweet collection of armor and swords and other King Arthur shit), the Turkish Chamber (rugs!), the Munzkabinett (coin cabinet, it's like your dad's coin collection but larger), and the Cabinet of Prints and Drawings. All of these are worthwhile, but it can be a lot of museum at once. Oh, this palace is a reconstruction—most of the palace was destroyed in the air raids of 1945.

i €12, students €9, Historic Green Vault €10. ⏰ Open M 10am-6pm, W-Su 10am-6pm; closed Tuesdays.

ZWINGER PALACE
PALACE

Right behind the Semperoper building (which is a beautiful attraction in and of itself) rests the magnificent Zwinger Palace. As one of the most grandiose Baroque palaces in Germany, just visiting the palace and Nymphenbad (Nymph's Bath—it's a huge fountain) is worth it even if you don't care about the exhibits. The galleries and collections the palace holds are equally as impressive as the palace itself, with the Gemaldegalerie Alte Meister taking the cake for most awe-inspiring. There's also the largest collection of specialist ceramics in the world (woohoo pottery class!), along with a museum of scientific instruments, which is unexpectedly awesome. We think you'll be satisfied after the Alte Meister Gallery, but how much museum power-walking you want to do is up to you.

i Each exhibit requires a separate ticket. Alte Meister €10, students €7.50. Mathematics/Physics Gallery and Porcelain Collection €6, students €4.50. ⏰ Open Tu-Su 10am-6pm; closed Mondays.

FRAUENKIRCHE
CHURCH

Neumarkt

Arguably the most prominent landmark in Dresden, the Frauenkirche (Church of Our Lady) stands as a beacon of reconstruction over the city. Completely demolished in the air attacks of WWII, the building was globally crowdsource-funded and rebuilt in 2005. From the outside, the building is magnificent and impressive, and from the inside the building looks like a shrine to Easter (we think Vineyard Vines may have funded the pastel paint). You can even take an elevator (almost) all the way to the top, and then hike the remaining stairs to get a panorama view of Dresden from Frauenkirche dome. At €8 (students €5) we like the view from the ground.

i Dome €8, students €5. ⏰ Open M-Sa 10am-6pm, Su 12:30-6pm.

FURSTENZUG AND BRUHLSCHE TERRASSE
LANDMARKS

Schlossplatz; Georg-Treu-Platz 1

Though technically they're not next to each other, we're grouping these two sights together because we think they're the best free sights in Dresden. The Furstenzug is claimed to be the largest porcelain mural in the world, with the mosaic stretching for 100m and depicting a procession of nearly a millennium of Saxony's important people. It survived the air raids of WWII, so the original is still there for all of your viewing glory. The Bruhlsche Terrasse, known as the Balcony of Europe, overlooks the Elbe River valley and Neustadt to the north and the royal promenade of Dresden to the south. It's the perfect place to catch some shade during the day or view the illuminated buildings of Dresden at night. If you go during the day, just watch out for the crowds of camera clickers.

i Free. ☑ Open 24hr.

KUNSTHOFPASSAGE
Görlitzer Str. 23

ART CENTER

Enter the through the archway under the sign with the flying yellow cow and find yourself in a hidden courtyard passageway filled with art installations and architectural anomalies. It even has a building that plays music through a series of pipes and tubes whenever it rains, or every half hour when water is filtered from the roof. The shops and cafe/restaurants in here are pricey, but it's definitely worth it to walk through the passage and experience the art culture of Neustadt.

i Free. ☑ Open 24hr.

FOOD

BAUTZNER TOR
Hoyerswerdaer Str. 37

GERMAN $$

Not only will Bautzner Tor fulfill every Bohemian food fantasy you've ever had, it'll top you off with some of the best home-brewed beer in Dresden. Don't be fooled by it punk-rock attitude; this rustic tavern is a classic German dining establishment with a Neustadt attitude (or Neustadttitude, if you will). If you plan to start your night at Bautzner Tor, we suspect you'll end up staying until they kick you out. With hearty meals, heartier beers, and a healthy mix of locals and tourists, why leave?

i Beer €3-5. Food €6-11. ☑ Open daily 5-11pm.

CURRY & CO
Louisenstr. 62

GERMAN $

Curry & Co is a modern take on a classic German delicacy: currywurst. *Imbisses* (snack stands) line the streets all throughout German cities delving out spiced sausages to starving sightseers 24/7. Quite frankly (heh), Curry & Co does it best. With vegan options and special sauces, there are enough options to keep your culinary inquisitiveness entertained every day you're in Dresden.

i Classic currywurst with fries €4.30. ☑ Open M-W 11am-10pm, Th 11am-midnight, F-Sa 11am-2am, Su 11am-10pm.

MARMARIS KEBAB HAUS
Louisenstr. 57

TURKISH $

Doner kebab rules Germany's fast food market. Spectacular spinning spits of meat mesmerize us on every busy street corner and tempt our drunken selves every night we're out. We'll be honest; we gave into temptation once and for all (OK maybe thrice and for all) at Marmaris. In addition to the uber-friendly staff, Marmaris kebabs got better each time we indulged. With pita toasted to perfection and beef that gave us an erection, Marmaris is more than worth an inspection.

i Kebabs €3-7. ☑ Open daily 11am-2am.

LILA SOSSE
Alaunstr. 70

GERMAN $$

Hidden in the eclectic Kunsthofpassage, Lila Sosse serves up German-style tapas in glass jars. It might sound a bit strange, but it's not nearly as odd as the building that makes music when it rains just next door. The food is almost as great as the atmosphere, with almost everyone at the restaurant choosing to sit outside on

dresden

the cobblestone passage (at least when the weather's nice). What are German tapas anyway? Well, at Lila Sosse, they're a creative twist on classic German cuisine. From potatoes with mustard to Waldorf salads, Lila Sosse does it all. And on a warm evening, its lemonade will be the best thing you've ever had.

i *Food €7-12. Beer €3-6. ☏ Open M-F 4-11pm, Sa-Su noon-11pm.*

CAFÉ ECKSTEIN
CAFE $

Alaunstr. 47

From the outside, Café Eckstein looks like every other laptop-party-hosting coffeeshop we've ever checked in at on Facebook. We stumbled into Eckstein assuming we'd check our email, have a coffee, and leave. But we stayed because the food (especially the breakfast) was delicious, the staff have unbelievably friendly, and it played the most refined playlist of roots reggae we've heard since Jamaica. To make things even better, we couldn't believe how packed it was with locals at 11pm on a weeknight, all of whom were there to have any number of Café Eckstein's great cocktails.

i *Breakfast €5-9. Cocktails €4-8. Beer €2-4. ☏ Open M-Th 9am-midnight, F-Sa 9am-1am, Su 9am-midnight.*

RASKOLNIKOFF
RUSSIAN $$

Böhmische Str. 34

Unless you have keen observation skills, you'll pass right by Raskolnikoff's unimpressive exterior without realizing you just missed one of the best restaurants in Dresden. The lesson, friends, is that what's on the inside counts. And Raskolnikoff serves delicious Russian-style meals inside one of Neustadt's oldest buildings. The only downside is that Raskolnikoff is a bit pricey for the budget traveler, so pretend you're in a biergarten and just order a few of in own Raskolnikoff beers instead of missing this hidden gem entirely.

i *Food €8-14. Beer €3-5. ☏ Open M-F 10am-2am, Sa-Su 9am-2am.*

CAFÉ AHA
CAFE $

Kreuzstr. 7

Altstadt is filled with restaurants, biergartens, and cafes that all cater to tourists. Although we're sure you'll end up spending way too much money for a *bratwurst mit brot* at one of these all-too-common establishments, do your best to make it to Café Aha instead. With an extensive coffee list, plenty of vegetarian options, and a few local specialties sprinkled in, Café Aha is sure to have exactly what you need during a day of museum-hopping.

i *Coffee €2-5. Food €4-10. ☏ Open daily 9am-midnight.*

EVA'S PIZZA
PIZZA $

Görlitzer Straße 29

There will come a point when you need to maximize your ratio of calories consumed to euros spent. At first, you're likely to run rampant in doner kebab and currywurst stands. After a while, though, the novelty of these fast-food staples wears off, and you'll be left craving something you haven't realized you've been craving. And that's when you go to Eva's and eat €5 pizzas until you can't feel your feet. Stand up and waddle away with pride.

i *Pizza €5. ☏ Open daily noon-late.*

NIGHTLIFE

SCHEUNE
BIERGARTEN

Alaunstr. 36 — www.scheune.org

Scheune is a block party. Scheune is a concert venue. Scheune is a biergarten. And Scheune is one hell of a good time. In fact, we're not sure we found anything that Scheune's not. Every night of the week, we were amazed to find a huge crowd of local beer-sippers kicking back outside Scheune's walls with no intention of going anywhere. Even if you don't want to take part in Scheune's festivities, we still think it's worth taking part in in the unofficial block party that slows down more than just traffic.

i Hours and prices vary depending on the event. ☎ Check the website for the most up-to-date information. Or just show up at 10pm on a Friday—you're bound to find something going on.

HEBEDAS   CLUB
Rothenburger Str. 30

If you want to experience the spirit of Neustadt, head to Hebedas. Especially for Friday and Saturday's "Zebra Disco," this place gets absolutely mad. The free spirits flock, the punk-rockers rock, and the university students lock (lips, that is). Tired of the hustle? Follow the hordes of sweaty peace-seekers out onto the curbside lounge and kick back with the locals.

i Beers €2-5. Cocktails €4-8. ☎ Open daily 7:30pm-late.

GROOVESTATION   CLUB
Katharinenstr. 11-13

Whether you want to vibe out to some roots reggae, hipster-hustle to indie-tronic, rock out to some good ol' fashioned hard rock, or get lost in the house music, Groovestation has it all. Dresdeners seem to like doing all of these things, so join a healthy host of locals and tourists alike at one of Dresden's most popular nightlife destinations. Still not convinced? Every Monday you can challenge seasoned veterans to a round of unexpectedly intense foosball. Loser buys.

i Cover varies, usually free-€10. Beer €3-5. Cocktails €4-10. ☎ Open M-Th 7pm-3am, F-Sa 7pm-5am, Su 7pm-3am.

OSTPOL   BAR
Königsbrücker Str. 47

Ostpol has some serious Neustadttitude. In addition to being a GDR-themed bar fully equipped with communist propaganda and '60s furniture, it also has some of the cheapest beer we've seen since Prague. With bands you've never heard of most nights of the week, you're bound to have a good time and drink way too much of that cheap beer. Did we mention they have really cheap beer?

i Beer €1-5. ☎ Open M-Sa 8pm-late. Events start at 9pm.

BLUE NOTE   MUSIC VENUE
Görlitzer Str. 2B

For the musically inclined among us, Blue Note has music flowing through its veins. Luckily for the less musically inclined among us, it also has beer flowing through its veins, so you shouldn't have any problem dragging your tone-deaf friends along. With performances from some heavy hitters (and their pictures lining the wall), Blue Note has arguably the greatest blues and jazz music performances in Dresden.

i Cover €5. Beer €3-6. Cocktails €4-9. ☎ Open daily 8pm-5am.

ESSENTIALS
Practicalities

- **TOURIST OFFICES:** The tourist office books rooms and tours for free (M-Sa only) and sells the Dresden City Card and the Dresden Regio Card. (Pragerstr. 2b ☎0351 50 16 01 60 www.dresden-tourist.de.)

- **LUGGAGE STORAGE:** Lockers are located in all train stations. Look for the suitcase symbol. (€3-4 per 24hr.)

- **POST OFFICE:** Königsbrücker Str. 21-29. (☎0180 304 05 00 Western Union available.) 2nd branch in the Altstadt (Wilsdruffer Str. 22).

- **POSTAL CODE:** 01099.

Emergency

- **EMERGENCY NUMBERS:** ☎112.
- **POLICE:** ☎110.
- **LATE-NIGHT PHARMACY: Saxonia Apotheke Internationale.** (Prager Str. 8a ☎0351 490 49 49 www.saxoniaapotheke.de *i* Carries international medicines. The Notdienst sign outside lists rotating 24hr. pharmacies.)

Getting There

By Plane

The **Dresden Airport** information desk (☎0351 881 33 60 www.dresden-airport.de) is reachable by public transit on the S-Bahn, line S2. (🖾 Every 30min. from Hauptbahnhof 4:48am-11:48pm, from Neustadt 4:55-11:55.) The **shuttle** (€1.90) will pick up or drop off at Dresden-Neustadt and most Dresden hotels (15min.), or the Dresden Hauptbahnhof. ((20min.)

By Train

Dresden has two main stations: the **Hauptbahnhof** (south of Altstadt) and **Bahnhof-Dresden-Neustadt** (on the other side of the Elbe on the western edge of the Neustadt). Nearly all intercity trains arrive at the Hauptbahnhof. S2 trains run every 30min. from Hauptbahnhof to Bahnhof-Dresden-Neustadt, so it's easy to get from one to the other. A third station, **Dresden Mitte,** lies between the two but is rarely used. Trains run from the Hauptbahnhof to: Berlin (€37. 🖾 3hr., 1 per hr.); Frankfurt am Main (€87. 🖾 5hr., every hr.); Munich (€101. 🖾 6hr., 2-4 per hr.); Budapest, HUN (€103. 🖾 11hr., 6 per day.); Prague, CZR. (€31. 🖾 2hr., every hr.)

Getting Around

By Tram

Dresden is largely a walking city, and there aren't many places you'll need to go that you can't easily reach by foot. The only time you may find it necessary to move a little more quickly is to move between the Altstadt and the Neustadt, for which you should use the tram system (single ticket €2; 4-trip card €5; 1-day ticket €5; 1-week travel pass €15). Tickets are available on trams and from **Fahrkarten** dispensers at major stops. Validate your tickets in the red boxes on board. For information and maps, visit **www.vvo-online.de,** or try the **Service Punkt** stands in front of the Hauptbahnhof or at Postpl., Albertpl., and Pirnaischer Pl. Most major lines run every 10min. or so during the day, and every 30min. after midnight—look for the moon sign marked "Gute-Nacht-Linie."

By Metro

The **S-Bahn,** or suburban train, travels along the Elbe from **Meißen** to the **Czech border.** Buy tickets from the Automaten and validate them in the red machines at the bottom of the stairwells to each track.

By Taxi

Reach **Taxi Dresden** at ☎0351 21 12 11. There's a flat fee of €2.50, plus €1.50 per km.

By Bike

Biking in Dresden is not a very pleasant experience, because most of the roads are bumpy cobblestone, and the ones that are paved are cobbled on the sides, so you'll often have to ride on the sidewalk to avoid a slow, bumpy ride. A bike still is recommended, though, as there's no quicker or more reliable way to travel between the north and south sides of the river. Bike rental is available at all train stations.

Deutsche Bahn at Neustadt station and Hauptbahnhof offers bikes for €8 per day. Ask at the **Gepäck Zentrum** (Luggage Center), indicated by the signs with suitcase symbols. (☎1805 15 14 15.)

cologne

Cologne is the fourth largest city in Germany (after Berlin, Hamburg, and Munich), but it feels decidedly provincial. Perhaps it's the way that its famous cathedral owns all the other buildings in town, or maybe it's because the locals speak their own funky dialect, called Kölsch. Cologne became a major pilgrimage destination in the 12th century, after relics of the Three Wise Men were transferred to its cathedral. Many know "cologne," thanks to Eau de Cologne, an 18th-century perfume that was all the rage back in the day and now makes for the perfect passive-aggressive gift. The city center was almost completely razed by bombings during World War II and has since been meticulously reconstructed.

The city never regained the power it once had in the Middle Ages, but that doesn't mean that it lives in the past. Trade fairs and conventions regularly bring in throngs of businesspeople. The city is also home to many art museums, and the nightlife scene stays vibrant thanks to the presence of the University of Cologne (Universität zu Köln), one of Germany's largest universities. Known as the "Gay Capital of Germany," Cologne is also the site of an enormous Pride parade every summer. Don't be fooled: Kölsch beer may be served in the smallest glasses you'll find in Germany, but people here like to enjoy life in big gulps.

ORIENTATION

The Rhein runs north to south through the middle of the city. The historic center is located on the west bank, where a semi-circle of streets, made up of the Hansaring, Hohenzollernring, Hohenstaufenring, Sachsenring, and Ubierring, separates the city's Altstadt (Old Town, inside the ring) from the Neustadt (New Town, outside the ring). On the other side of the river is Deutz, home to Cologne's trade fairs.

Altstadt-Nord

The northern part of the Old Town is home to the majestic **Dom,** which sits next door to the **Hauptbahnhof,** Cologne's transportation hub. Many of the city's museums and churches can be found here, rubbing elbows with Western shops and overpriced German brewhouses. **Hohe Straße** and **Schildergasse** are the main shopping streets, stretching from the cathedral all the way to Ⓜ️Neumarkt. This district is also where you'll find Eau de Cologne stores, including the famous **4711-Haus.**

Altstadt-Sud

The southern part of the Old Town begins at roughly the Deutzer bridge. **The Chocolate Museum** and the **Rautenstrauch-Joest Museum** remain this neighborhood's greatest assets, but recent construction along the banks of the Rhein has transformed the once-defunct **Rheinauhaufen** (Rhein harbor) into a posh residential area. The three inverted, L-shaped apartment buildings, called the **Kranhaus** (Crane House), have brought the city some modern architectural street cred. Cologne's gay hubs (the Heumarkt area and Rudolfpl.) can be found on the border between the northern and southern sections of the Old Town.

Neustadt

Thanks to the presence of the University of Cologne (located in the southwest part of Neustadt), this district has some of Cologne's most student-friendly restaurants and bars. The area around **Zülpicher Platz** has great restaurants and stores on every corner, while the **Belgisches Viertel** to the northwest has a reputation for trendy stores and bars. **Hohenzollernring** and the surrounding side streets make up another lively area that boasts many cafes, movie theaters, and nightclubs.

SIGHTS

Altstadt-Nord

🔲 KÖLNER DOM (COLOGNE CATHEDRAL)   CATHEDRAL

Domkloster 3   ☎0221 17 94 05 55 www.koelner-dom.de

To ascend the Südturm (southern tower), exit the church through the main gate and turn left to head down the stairs. The climb up the tower's 533 steps will take at least 15min. and will leave you wobbly-legged, but it offers a panoramic view of the city. Though Cologne's skyline sans cathedral is pretty underwhelming, the climb is definitely worth it. Catch your breath about three-quarters of the way up at the Glockenstube, a chamber for the tower's nine bells. Four of the bells date from the Middle Ages, but the loudest one is the 20th-century upstart called Der Große Peter, which is the world's heaviest swinging bell at 24 tons.

i *By the Hauptbahnhof. The Dom Forum (☎0221 92 58 47 20www.domforum.de), across the street, organizes guided tours in English. A 20min. film in English shown inside the Dom Forum provides an introduction to the cathedral. Cathedral free. Schatzkammer €5, students €2.50; tower €2.50/1; combined €6/3; Dom Forum tours €6 €4; film €2 €1,free with a tour. ☒ Church open daily May-Oct 6am-9pm; Nov-Apr 6am-7:30pm. Schatzkammer open daily 10am-6pm. Tower open daily May-Sept 9am-6pm; Oct 9am-5pm; Nov-Feb 9am-4pm; Mar-Apr 9am-5pm. Dom Forum open M-F 10am-6:30pm, Sa 10am-5pm, Su 1-5pm. Tours M-Sa 10:30am and 2:30pm, Su 2:30pm. Dom Forum film M-Sa 11:30am and 3:30pm, Su 3:30pm.*

🔲 MUSEUM LUDWIG   MUSEUM

Heinrich-Böll-Pl.   ☎0221 22 12 61 65 www.museum-ludwig.de

If you thought Cologne was too focused on its past to collect modern art, you were wrong. The interesting exterior of this building is a work of art in itself that contrasts beautifully with the historical cathedral next door. Still, the metal curves are nothing compared to the astronomic collection of 20th-century art inside. With almost 800 works by Pablo Picasso, the museum has the third largest Picasso collection in the world, documenting all stages of the artist's career. The entire bottom floor is dedicated to the biggest names in Pop Art, such as Andy Warhol, Roy Lichtenstein, and Robert Rauschenberg. Expressionism and the Russian avant-garde art also dominate the permanent collection.

i *Behind the Dom, close to the Römisch-Germanisches Museum. Audio tour €3. €10, students €7; 1st Th of the month ½-price after 5pm. ☒ Open Tu-Su 10am-6pm. Open until 10am 1st Th of the month.*

KOLUMBA   MUSEUM

Kolumbastr. 4   ☎0221 933 19 30 www.kolumba.de

This contemporary art museum run by the Church—yes, you read that right—displays religious artwork from the Middle Ages to the present. The museum is an amazing combination of past and present. Not only is the contemporary museum built upon the ruins of a church, but it is probably one of the few places where you can see centuries-old crucifixes side-by-side with contemporary installations, photographs, and paintings, often dramatically emphasized by spotlights in dark rooms. The museum was constructed over the ruins of the Gothic cathedral of St. Kolumba, which you can see on the ground floor.

i *U3, U4, U5, U16, U18: Appellhofpl. Walk through the Opern Passage and turn left onto Glockengasse; Kolumba is 1 block past 4711-Haus. Free guidebooks available in English €5, students €3, under 18 free. ☒ Open M noon-5pm, W-Su noon-5pm.*

get a room!

Below are a couple of Let's Go's top recommendations for catching some Z's in Cologne; for more, visit **www.letsgo.com**.

▨ STATION HOSTEL FOR BACKPACKERS
HOSTEL $$

Marzellenstr. 44-56 ☎0221 912 53 01 www.hostel-cologne.de

This five-floor backpacker haven has the best location of any hostel in town and a lively atmosphere to match. The "What's On" part of their website and the knowledgeable staff will direct you to all the cool places in Cologne. The bar and lobby are on the smaller side, but the upstairs seating area with a great kitchen makes up for this. The building is far from new, but the young guests' spirits make the stay here worth it.

i Exit the Hauptbahnhof with the Dom to the left and walk past the Rolex building. At the roundabout, turn right onto Marzellenstr. Free Wi-Fi in common areas and free computer use. Linens included. Lockers outside of the room. 6-bed dorm €17-23; singles from €32; doubles from €48. ⛺ Recept on 24hr.

MEININGER HOTEL COLOGNE CITY CENTER
HOSTEL $$

Engelbertstr. 33-35 ☎0221 99 76 09 65 www.meininger-hotels.com

Meininger is as young and interesting as its guests: the intriguing velvet wallpapers are almost as cool as the hostel's location near the great nightlife around Zülpicher Pl. The hostel does everything right: the guest kitchen, game room, lounge, and bar are great for relaxing and socializing, while the colorful rooms with private bathrooms are quiet and clean. The free maps of the city, cheap snacks, and affordable bike rentals are extra perks.

i U1, U7, U12, or U15: Rudolfpl. From the station, walk south on Habsburgstr., turn right onto Lindenstr., then left onto Engelbertstr. Free Wi-Fi. Breakfas €5.90. Linens and towels included. Computers €1 per 20min. or €2 per hr. Bike rental €12. Women-only dorms available. Dorms €24, but the price can go up to €35 on Sa-Su; singles from €39; doubles from €79. ⛺ Reception 24hr.

NAZI DOCUMENTATION CENTER (EL-DE HAUS)
MUSEUM

Appellhofpl. 23-25 ☎0221 22 12 63 32 www.nsdok.de

Cologne had its own share of Nazi history, and this museum documents that very powerfully. The former Gestapo headquarters and jail here were converted into a museum that educates visitors on the city's history under the Nazis. Make sure not to miss the basement, where you can see original prison cells, where pleas, poems, and even self-portraits were all scratched into the plaster walls by the (mostly political) prisoners. The exhibit documents a number of individual stories, ranging from successful escape attempts to torture and executions. Although the top floors only have German explanations, the large black-and-white photographs transcend language barriers.

i U3, U4, U5, U16, or U18: Appelhofpl., then follow the signs. English explanations in the basement jail but not in the exhibits upstairs €4.50, students €2. Audio tour available in English and 5 other languages €2. Cash only. ⛺ Open Tu-F 10am-6pm, Sa-Su 11am-6pm.

TWELVE ROMANESQUE CHURCHES OF KÖLN
CHURCHES

Twelve churches containing the bones of saints were built in a semicircle around the Altstadt during the Middle Ages to protect Cologne. Though each is dwarfed by the Dom, the churches attest to the glory and immense wealth of what used to be the most important city north of the Alps. The most memorable of these is probably **Saint Ursula Church** (Ursulapl. 24), dedicated to the

British princess St. Ursula, who was so fond of her celibacy that she delayed her marriage to take a religious trip around Europe, during which she and her virgin companions were killed by the Huns. The church's treasury contains hundreds of human skulls wrapped in fabric, and the walls are decorated with bones. Another interesting church is the **Groß Saint Martin** (An Groß St. Martin 9-11), which was re-opened in 1985 after near destruction in WWII. The excavated cellar dates to the first century CE and once served as a training ground for wrestlers. St. Gereon has a history that dates back to the fourth century as well as a beautiful dome with interesting stained glass windows. Entry to the churches is free, so if you don't feel like paying for museums, you can get your dose of sightseeing simply by touring these. As not many people choose to do this, you won't be surrounded by tourist crowds.

i St. Ursula is northwest of the Hauptbahnhof. Groß St. Martin is close to the river, between the Deutzer and Hohenzollern bridges. Churches free. St. Ursula treasury €2. Groß St. Martin excavations €0.50. ☼ St. Ursula treasury open M 10am-1pm, W 10am-1pm, and F-Sa 10am-1pm and 2-5pm. Groß St. Martin open Tu-F 9am-7:30pm, Sa 9:30am-7:30pm, Su 10am-7pm.

Altstadt-Sud

🔲 SCHOKOLADENMUSEUM (CHOCOLATE MUSEUM) MUSEUM

Am Schokoladenmuseum 1a ☎0221 931 88 80 www.schokoladenmuseum.de

Give in to the temptation: it's worth it. Cologne's Chocolate Museum is every child's dream and is equally interesting for adults. What we appreciate most about this amazing place is that even though it has all the fun of free samples (check out the chocolate fountain—for best results, show up several times wearing different wigs), there's still a lot to be learned here, too. Besides exploring the complex history that turned our favorite dessert from a spicy drink into sweet candy, you can also see cocoa plants in the mini greenhouse, pyramids of Kinder Egg toys, and even a purple Milka cow. You'll also learn how hollow chocolate bunnies are made, and you can watch the stony-faced, lab-coated Oompa-Loompas—er, museum employees—make and package chocolates behind glass walls.

i U1, U7, or U9: Heumarkt. Walk east to the river, turn right, and continue along the bank. When you reach the island, turn left onto the small footbridge. All explanations in English €8.50, students €6, family €24. Cash only. ☼ Open Tu-F 10am-6pm, Sa-Su 11am-7pm. Last entry 1hr. before close.

MUSEUM SCHNÜTGEN AND RAUTENSTRAUCH-JOEST MUSEUM MUSEUM

Cäcilienstr. 29-33 ☎Rautenstrauch-Joest:0221 221 31 356 www.museenkoeln.de

These two establishments follow Cologne's trend of museums with incredible architecture. Although located in the same building, the two museums seem to be polar opposites. The Schnütgen showcases one of world's largest collections of European medieval art; one of the most interesting parts, though, is the contrast between the plain, modern walls of the museum and the gorgeous stained glass taken out of its ordinary setting. The Rautenstrauch-Joest welcomes visitors with a video of people greeting each other in different languages. This ethnological museum examines artifacts from Africa, Asia, Australia, and America through themes such as prejudice, funerals, clothing, and religion. Again, the presentation of these exhibits alone, with large curtains and state-of-the-art interactive screens, makes for a worthwhile visit.

i U1, U3, U4, U7, U9, U16, or U18: Neumarkt. Head east a tiny bit on Cäcilienstr. Schnütgen €6, students €3.50. Rautenstrauch-Joest €7/4. Combined €10/7. Cash only. ☼ Both open Tu-W 10am-6pm, Th 10am-8pm, F-Su 10am-6pm.

FOOD

Altstadt-Nord

◙ WEINHAUS VOGEL

GERMAN $$

Eigelstein Str. 74   ☎0221 139 91 34

Don't be fooled by the wine glasses in the window: Weinhaus Vogel is an authentic local restaurant where great beer is more important than fancy wine. If you're still not convinced, just take a look around at the enormous collection of beer posters. Daily local specialties go for €5-6, but we also recommend entrees from the main menu, like the delicious *wienerschnitzel*.

i From the Hauptbahnhof, head past the Rolex building, then turn right at the roundabout. Continue straight through the tunnel; the restaurant is on the right about 300m down the street. Meal €6-18. Daily specials €5-6. Kölsch €1.30. Cash only. ☒ Open M-Th 10am-midnight, F-Sa 10am-2am, Su 10am-midnight.

FRÜH AM DOM

GERMAN $$$

Am Hof 18   ☎0221 261 32 11 www.frueh.de

The enormous, red Gothic letters that spell out the name of this restaurant are only an introduction to the establishment's grandeur. Früh am Dom has colossal rooms, tile stoves, large wooden cabinets, an outside seating area, and even its own stained glass panel of the Cathedral. Due to its proximity to the famous Dom and the large plates of traditional food, Früh am Dom is the kind of landmark where locals send their out-of-town guests to get the typical Cologne experience. However, as great as this may sound (and it is pretty great), the prices aren't exactly geared toward the starving student.

i Walk south from the plaza of the Dom, then turn left onto Am Hof. The restaurant is on the right. Soup €4-4.60. Entrees €7.50-22.50. Kölsch €1.80. ☒ Open daily 8am-midnight. Warm food served until 11:30pm.

Altstadt-Sud

TOSCANINI

ITALIAN $$

Jakobstr. 22   ☎0221 310 99 90

Swinging green leaves near the entrance mixed with red brick arches and large windows make Toscanini a sweet and casually romantic restaurant. It is a bit of a trek from the main tourist path, but it's worth the trip if you're looking for authentic Italian food. The restaurant is best known for its pizza, served fresh from the stone oven: try the Rustica, a delicious combination of cheese, prosciutto, and arugula. It's also one of the few places where the wait staff doesn't bring you a little *Kölsch* glass right away—wine is the beverage of choice here.

i U3 or U4: Severinstr. Head south down Severinstr. and turn right onto Jakobstr. Toscanini is on the right. Pizza €5.30-9.50. Pasta €6.10-12.90. Beer €2.10. Wine €2.10 per 0.1L. ☒ Open M-Sa noon-3pm and 6-11pm, Su 6-11pm.

Neustadt

◙ HABIBI FALAFEL

MIDDLE EASTERN $

Zülpicherstr. 28   ☎0221 271 71 41 www.habibi-koeln.de

The marvelous aura of this tiny restaurant makes even the delicious smells and handsome, well-dressed men on their lunch breaks seem unimportant. The small, mosaic-covered tables and hanging newspaper articles come together to create a place very popular with local students, especially on late nights after a few rounds of drinks. The cheap falafel (€1.90) and shawarma (€2.50) are in demand at all times of the day, and the takeout is extremely cheap. If you have time to stay for a while, we recommend the generous plates, which come with a cup of cinnamon tea.

i *U9, U12, or U15: Zülpicher Pl. Head down Zülpicherstr.; the restaurant is on the right. Plates €6.70-7.70, takeout €1.90-4. Espresso €0.70. Cash only. ☒ Open M-Th 11am-1am, F-Sa 11am-3am, Su 11am-1am.*

▨ BEI OMA KLEINMANN
SCHNITZEL $$$

Zülpicherstr. 9   ☎0221 23 23 46 www.beiomakleinmann.de

Perhaps the best-known *schnitzel* restaurant in Cologne, Bei Oma Kleinmann offers more than a dozen varieties, from "Weiner Art" to "Chili Lili" and "Olaf Maria," all of which are equally enormous. This place, full of old radios and taxidermied mountain goats, knows that dinner is the most important meal of the day (for your soul, not your health). Thus, the restaurant is open only in the evenings, and it gets crowded fast. Though the founder, Oma Kleinmann, recently passed away at the age of 95, she is remembered with framed photographs on the walls.

i *U9, U12, or U15: Zülpicher Pl. Head down Zülpicherstr.; the restaurant is on the left. Schnitzel €12.90-20.90. Kölsch €1.50-2.50. Cash only. ☒ Open Tu-Th 5pm-midnight, F-Sa 5pm-1am, Su 5pm-midnight. Kitchen open 5-11pm.*

NIGHTLIFE

Altstadt-Nord

▨ GLORIA
VENUE, GLBT

Apostelnstr. 11   ☎0221 66 06 30 www.gloria-theater.com

Gloria is a must-see landmark of Cologne's GLBT scene. Not just a cafe and not just a club, this former movie theater offers the best of all worlds and hosts all sorts of awesome events, from parties to films to stand-up comedy. Although the cafe is nice, the real deal is the multi-purpose theater in the back, with red velvet walls and clusters of disco balls. Call or visit the website for the schedule of events; in the past, big names such as Sufjan Stevens and Coldplay have performed here.

i *U1, U3, U4, U7, U9, U16, or U18: Neumarkt. Walk west toward St. Aposteln church and follow Apostelnstr. as it curves right. Cover €8-15. Theater tickets €15-25. Beer €1.90. Long drinks €6.50. Cash only. ☒ Cafe open M-Sa noon-8pm. Club hours vary based on event schedule.*

Neustadt

▨ DIE WOHNGEMEINSCHAFT
BAR

Richard-Wagner-Str. 39   ☎0221 39 76 09 04 www.die-wohngemeinschaft.net

Whoever had the idea for this bar was a genius: the interior design combines cute, hipster, and awesome in the best possible way. The bar consists of four rooms, each decorated in the style of a fictitious university roommate—Annabel's cutesy vintage bed is good for chit-chatting, and JoJo's minibus is really cool to sit in (though we've never seen a dorm that would fit a minibus). Play ping-pong in Mai Li's smoky room, or listen to eclectic DJ mixes in Easy's abode. The adorable details don't stop at the rooms: the large bar has vintage fridges and awesome chairs. Aside from the bar, DW also runs a hostel with rooms just as creative as the bar.

i *U1, U7, U12, or U15: Rudolfpl., then walk south 1 block to Richard-Wagner-Str. and head west. The bar is on the left. Live DJs W-Sa. Beer €1.60- 2.60. Long drinks €5-6. Cash only. ☒ Open M-Th 3pm-2am, F-Sa 3pm-3am, Su 3pm-2am.*

DAS DING CLUB

Hohenstaufenring 30-32 ☎2233 71 42 06 www.dingzone.de

"The Thing" is a smokey student disco with a bunch of neon lights everywhere, and it's the best place to show off your dance moves to your new hostel friends. Das Ding is incredibly student (and budget traveler) friendly, with dirt-cheap specials every night of the week. Tuesdays, for example, offer €1 vodka energy shots in addition to free-beer-o'clock from 9-11pm. And it doesn't stop there: the club even has a birthday special that includes 10 free shots, a bottle of champagne, and party goods. Student IDs are not required, but the bouncer outside keeps the crowd young.

i U9, U12, or U15: Zülpicnerpl. Just past the Rewe supermarket. Cover €3-5. Beer €1.20. Shots €1.50-3. Cash only. ☼ Open Tu-W 9pm-3am, Th 10pm-4am, F-Sa 10pm-5am.

ESSENTIALS
Practicalities

- **TOURIST OFFICES:** KölnTourismus. (Kardinal-Höffner-Pl. 1, across from the Dom. ☎221 34 64 30 www.koelntourismus.de *i* Books accommodations for a €3 fee. Inquire about local bus tours, which cost about €15. English-language walking tour €9, students €8. DIY iGuide €8 per 4hr. ☼ Open M-F 9am-8pm, Sa-Su 10am-5pm. English-language walking tour Sa 11:30am.)

- **CURRENCY EXCHANGE:** Reisebank. (Inside the Hauptbahnhof. ☎0221 13 44 03 www.reisebank.de *i* Exchanges traveler's checks for a €6.50 commission. ☼ Open daily 7am-10pm.) Exchange. (Kardinal-Höffner-Pl. 1, inside the tourist office ☎0221 92 52 596 ☼ Open M-F 9am-6pm, Sa 9am-4pm.)

- **WOMEN'S RESOURCES:** Frauenberatungszentrum. (Friesenpl. 9 ☎0221 420 16 20 ☼ Open M 2-5pm, Tu 9am-noon, W 2-5pm, Th-F 9am-noon.)

- **GLBT RESOURCES:** SchwIPS Checkpoint. (Pipinstr. 7, just around the corner from Hotel Timp. ☎0221 92 57 68 11 www.checkpoint-koeln.de ☼ Open M-Th 5-9pm, F-Sa 2-7pm, Su 2-6pm.) LSVD Emergency Hotline. (☎0221 19 228)

- **INTERNET:** Many cafes offer free Wi-Fi, including Starbucks in the Hauptbahnhof. Gigabyte. (Across the street from the Hauptbahnhof. *i* €2 per hr. ☼ Open 24hr.) A cheaper option is the Film Cafe. (Eigelstein Str., 40 *i* €1 per hr.)

- **POST OFFICES:** Breite Str. 6-26, near Appellhofpl. (☼ Open M-F 9am-7pm, Sa 9am-2pm.)

- **POSTAL CODES:** Cologne postal codes start with 50 or 51. The code for the post office listed above is 50667.

Emergency

- **112. POLICE:** ☎110.

- **DOM APOTHEKE:** (Courtyard between the Dom and the Hauptbahnhof. ☎0221 20 05 05 00 www.dom-apotheke-koeln.de ☼ Open M-F 8am-8pm, Sa 9am-8pm.)

Getting There
By Plane

Flights from **Köln-Bonn Flughafen** (☎02203 40 40 01 02 www.koeln-bonn-airport.de), located halfway between Cologne and Bonn, serve most major European cities, in addition to Turkey and North Africa. The airport is also a budget airline hub. The **S13** runs between the Cologne Hauptbahnhof and the airport. *i* €2.50. ☼ 15min., every 20-30min.) A taxi from Cologne to the airport costs no more than €30.

By Train

The Cologne Hauptbahnhof is located right by the Dom in the Altstadt-Nord. Trains go to: **Berlin** (€109. ⏱ 5hr., 1-2 per hr.); **Bonn** (€6.80. ⏱ 30min., 2 per hr.); **Frankfurt** (€64. ⏱ 1½hr., every hr.); **Munich** (€129. ⏱ 5hr., every hr.); **Amsterdam** (€58. ⏱ 3hr., every 2hr.); **Basel** (€111. ⏱ 4hr., every hr.); **Brussels** (€46. ⏱ 2hr., 4 per day); **London** (€400. ⏱ 5hr., 2 per day); **Vienna** (€154. ⏱ 10hr., 5 per day.) Prices may be lower if booked at least three days in advance.

Getting Around

By Public Transportation

Cologne's buses, trams, and subways are served by the **KVB**, or Kölner Verkehrs-Betriebe (☎0221 26 313 www.kvb-koeln.de). A **Kurzstrecke** ticket (€1.70, ages 6-14 €1) is good for a ride of four stops or less. A ride to anywhere in the city is €2.50 (ages 6-14 €1.30), but you can save money by buying a carnet of four (€9/4.90). A day pass is €7.30 for individuals, and €10.70 for groups of up to five. Validate tickets at the validating machines before boarding or face a €40 fine.

By Ferry

Köln-Düsseldorfer leaves from the dock in the Altstadt, between the Deutzer and Hohenzollern bridges, and offers trips up and down Rhein. (☎0221 208 83 18 www.k-d.de *i* To the Mainz €55, round-trip €60; to Bonn €14/16. Up to 50% discounts for students with valid ID. 1hr. panoramic cruises up and down Rhein in the Cologne area €7.80. 2hr. afternoon cruises €12. ⏱ Panoramic cruises Apr-Oct daily 10:30am, noon, 2pm, and 6pm. Afternoon cruises 3:30pm.)

By Gondola

Kölner Seilbahn sells scenic gondola trips across the Rhine, from the Zoo to the Rheinpark. (Riehlerstr. 180 ☎0221 547 41 83 www.koelner-seilbahn.de *i* U18: Zoo/Flora. 1-way €4; round-trip €6. ⏱ Open Apr-Oct daily 10am-6pm).

By Bike

Cologne is a big city, and renting a bike can help you conquer the distances more easily. Pay attention to the direction of bike traffic, as bike lanes are often one-way. In general, keep to the right side of the street. **Radstation** offers bike rental near the Hauptbahnhof. (Breslauer Pl. ☎0221 139 71 90 *i* Exit the Hauptbahnhof through the rear exit, then turn right. €50 deposit. €5 per 3hr., €10 per day, €40 per week. ⏱ Open M-F 5:30am-10:30pm, Sa 6:30am-8pm, Su 8am-8pm.)

hamburg

As the waterway to the North Sea, some claim that Hamburg has 2579 bridges, but the official count is "more than 2300." Whichever way you count, Hamburg has more bridges than Venice, London, and Amsterdam combined. And that's really something; the city's water is breathtaking. But if water, water, and more water isn't your thing, Hamburg's also the perfect place to try donning high heels on cobblestone streets. Or just take a break and explore Hamburg's copper roofs, fantastic parks, awesome boating opportunities, chic shops, and old factories. Like any good quintessential German city, Hamburg has been burned, bombed, and bisected with nightlife trashier than garbage (again outdoing Venice, London, and Amsterdam combined). Still, the city has somehow managed to draw in corporations, lawyers, and a whole bunch of immigrants. Maybe it's the nightlife. Hamburg is a port, after all.

ORIENTATION

Hamburg's geography is notoriously complex, so consider pulling out a map to look over as you read through this. Hamburg lies on the northern bank of the **Elbe River.** The city's **Altstadt,** full of old façades and labyrinthine canals, lies north of the Elbe and south of the **Alster lakes. Binnenalster,** the smaller of the two Alster lakes, is located in the heart of the Altstadt, with the bustling **Jungfernstieg** on the south corner. The much larger **Außenalster,** popular for sailing in the summer and skating in the winter, is slightly farther north, separated from the Binnenalster by the **Kennedy- and Lombardbrücken.**

Five unique spires outline Hamburg's Altstadt. Anchoring the center of the Altstadt is the palatial **Rathaus,** the ornate town hall, and its exquisite doorstep and regular home to both political protests and farmers' markets, the **Rathausmarkt. Alsterfleet Canal** bisects the downtown, separating Altstadt on the eastern bank from the **Neustadt** on the west. The city's best museums, galleries, and theaters are within these two districts.

The **Hauptbahnhof** lies at the eastern edge of the city center, along **Steintorwall.** Starting from the **Kirchenallee** exit of the Hauptbahnhof, Hamburg's gay district, **St. Georg,** follows the **Lange Reihe** eastward. Outside the Hauptbahnhof's main exit on Steintorwall is the **Kunstmeile** (Art Mile), a row of museums extending southward from the Alster lakes to the banks of the Elbe. Perpendicular to Steintorwall, **Mönckebergstraße,** Hamburg's most famous shopping street, runs westward to the **Rathaus.** Just south of the Rathaus, **Saint Pauli** bears long waterside walkways and a beautiful copper-roofed port along the towering cranes of the Elbe's industrial district. Horizontally bisecting St. Pauli is the infamously icky **Reeperbahn** (disingenuously pronounced "RAPER-bawn"), which is packed with strip joints, erotic shops, and a tourist mecca of clubs on the pedestrian off-shoot **Große Freiheit.**

To the north of St. Pauli, the **Schanzenviertel** is a radically liberal community on the cusp of gentrification. Here, rows of graffiti-covered restaurants and a busy, late-night cafe and bar scene show little edge but attract fleets of bargain-hunting students. In late summer, the **Schanzenfest** illegal street market consistently breaks out into a full-fledged war of Molotov cocktails and tear gas between cops and civil discontents. On the westernmost side of Hamburg, **Altona** celebrates with a mini-Schanzenviertel nightlife and restaurant scene; the area was an independent city ruled by Denmark in the 17th century before Hamburg absorbed it. Altona's shop-lined pedestrian zone, the **Ottenser Hauptstrasse,** runs west from the Altona train station.

SIGHTS

▓ PLANTEN UN BLOMEN   BOTANICAL GARDEN

Next to the Hamburg Messe   ☎040 428 232 125 www.plantenunblomen.hamburg.ce

This park is fantastic. It's huge, it's laden with lily pads and manicured gardens, and it has something for everyone. There's a real botanical garden, a greenhouse growing things which we thought could only grow south of the Equator, coffee and bananas among them. There's a Japanese garden. There's a charming little rose garden. There are a whole handful of cafes and ice cream stands. There are wading pools. There are fountains. For the Harry Potter enthusiast, a giant (though inanimate) chess set is the arena of competition for many a muggle. Daily performances by groups ranging from Irish step dancers to Hamburg's police choir fill the outdoor Musikpavillion Sundays at 3pm May-Sept. The nightly Wasserlichtkonzerte draws crowds to the lake with fountains and choreographed underwater lights.

i S11, S21, or S31: Dammtor. ⊶ U1: Stephanspl. ⌗ Open daily 7am-11pm. Hours of the other attractions (Japanese garden, botanical garden, golf course, etc.) vary.

▨ HAMBURGER KUNSTHALLE (HALL OF ART)   MUSEUM

Glockengießerwall   ☎040 428 131 200 www.hamburger-kunsthalle.de

The Kunsthalle is the Louvre of Germany. The museum is stately, massive, and located on prime Hamburg turf. Staring at every piece of artwork for 10 seconds each would take a few days, and just running quickly through the place sucks up a good two hours. Either way, it's time well spent. With an incredible collection of canvases from every period in art history—from early medieval religious paintings through Modernism—arranged chronologically across its spacious, skylit halls, this museum is freakishly gorgeous. After you've gotten your fill of everything pas, enter the cafe and take the underground passage behind you to the *Galerie der Gegenwart* (Gallery of the Present) for an expertly curated series of contemporary art exhibits, which may include anything from photographs to the skins of stuffed animals.

i Turn right from the "Sitalerstr./City" exit of the Hauptbahnhof and cross the street. The Kunsthalle has the domed ceiling. €12, students €6, under 18 free. Audio tour €2. ⌚ Open Tu-W 10am-6pm, Th 10am-9pm, F-Su 10am-6pm.

▨ RATHAUS   TOWN HALL

Rathausmarkt   ☎040 428 312 064

With more rooms than Buckingham Palace, the 1897 Hamburger Rathaus is an ornately carved stone monument to Hamburg's long history as a wealthy port city. Today, we have the privilege of seeing the post-fire original: during the extensive Allied bombing of the Innenstadt, a bomb fell on the Rathausmarkt just out front, but, due to the quick thinking of some invisible, architecture-loving time traveler, it never exploded. Accessible only with a thorough 40min. tour, the lavish chambers of the Rathaus overflow with expansive murals, disorienting ornate molding, and wedding-cake chandeliers.

i U3: Rathaus. Tours don't run on days that the state government convenes. Even on open days, certain rooms may be closed due to meetings, so call ahead. Tours €3, under 14 €0.50. ⌚ English tours M-Th every hr. 10:15am-3:15pm, F 10:15am-1:15pm, Sa 11:15am-5:15pm, Su 11:15am-4:15pm.

MUSEUM FÜR KUNST UND GEWERBE   MUSEUM

Steintorpl.   ☎040 428 134 880 www.mkg-hamburg.de

This museum aims to confuse: the complex is a concoction of 19th-century and hyper-modern construction, and the exhibited art and design is similarly varied. Works hail from everywhere and anywhere: a hall of 17th- and 18th-century pianos borders a room of Middle Eastern carved tile; Art Deco pottery squares off against a gigantic collection of 18th-century porcelain arranged by region of origin; and a hallway of late 20th-century chairs challenges your backside to figure out how to sit in them. And this is just the permanent collection. Special exhibits range from 1980s and '90s Japanese fashion to Art Nouveau advertisements. Yes, it's a disorienting jumble, but it's a pleasing one.

i S1, S2, S3, S11, S21, S31, U1, U2, or U3: Hauptbahnhof. Leave through the Hauptbahnhof's south exit; the museum is across the street. €10, students €7, under 18 free. Admission €5 on Th after 5pm. ⌚ Open Tu-W 10am-6pm, Th 10am-9pm, F-Su 10am-6pm.

Outside Central Hamburg

KZ-GEDENKSTÄTTE NEUENGAMME   CONCENTRATION CAMP

Jean-Dolidier-Weg 75   ☎040 428 131 500 www.kz-gedenkstaette-neuengamme.de

It's quite a trek from Hamburg, but it's one you should make: seeing the complex that once housed a concentration camp is nothing short of a chilling experience. Since the camp lies out in the rolling Hamburg countryside, a visit will take at least three hours, but this lesser known center of Nazi terror is a humbling experience worthy of the trip. Between 1938 and 1945, this camp held more

get a room!

Accommodations in Hamburg can get freakishly expensive, especially in the summer months. But like the good, cheap food, the good, cheap hostels are located in the Schanzenviertel and out west in Altona.

▨ INSTANT SLEEP   HOSTEL $$

Max-Brauer-Allee 277   ☎040 431 82 310 www.instantsleep.com

Instant Sleep combines the feel of a summer camp and the set-up of an institution: the beds aren't bunked, but they feel like cots and are all quite close together. Instant Sleep keeps a fully stocked kitchen and an awesomely social common room. Expect to find foosball, hammocks, and a comfy loft with bean bags and a television. A young backpacking crowd gathers here to hang out or fans out onto the balcony for a smoke.

i U3, S11, S21, or S31: Sternschanze. Free Wi-Fi. Linens included. Laundry available. 12-bed dorm €15; 6- to 8-bed dorms €17; 4- to 5-bed €21; singles €39; doubles €54; triples €72. Cash only. ☒ Reception open M-W 8am-11pm, Th-Sa 8am-2am, Su 8am-11pm. Balcony open until 10pm.

SCHANZENSTERN ALTONA   HOSTEL $$

Kleiner Rainstr. 24-26   ☎040 399 19 191 www.schanzenstern.de/hotel/altona

Altona has a hotel atmosphere, with a silent courtyard, a residential street, and a lack of common space. Still, the rooms here are tremendous, the beds are comfy and rarely bunked, every room comes with its very own bathroom, and the wide view of Altona will make you swoon. With the Altstadt and the Schanzenviertel each about a 5-10min. train ride away, the location can feel a little remote. Good thing there's a bustling shopping and nightlife center nearby.

i S1, S2, S3, S11 or S31: Altona. From the metro, exit at Ottenser Hauptstr. and head west along the pedestrian walkway. Turn right at Spritzenpl. and take the right fork in the road. Turn left onto Kleiner Rainstr.; the hostel is on the left, just before the bend in the road. Free Wi-Fi and internet terminals available. Breakfas €6.50. Linens included. Dorms €19; singles €44; doubles €59-69; triples €74; quads €84; apartments €79-100. Cash only. ☒ Reception 24hr. Common room open 7am-2am.

than 100,000 forced laborers. Close to half the occupants died from overwork, disease, or execution. Walk around the camp buildings, from the cafeteria and dorms—now reduced to stark piles of rubble—to the work camps, and browse the thorough and moving collection of photographs and artifacts, which includes artwork by some of the prisoners.

i S21: Bergedorf. Then take bus #227 or #327: KZ-Gedenkstätte, Ausstellung (about 35-45min.). Buses leave the train station and the camp M-Sa every 30min., Su every 2hr. Free. ☒ Museum and memorial open Apr-Sept M-F 9:30am-4pm, Sa-Su noon-7pm; Oct-Mar M-F 9:30am-4pm, Sa-Su noon-5pm. Paths open 24hr. Tours in German Su noon and 2:30pm.

FOOD

▨ RISTORANTE ROCCO   ITALIAN $$$

Hofweg 104   ☎040 22 31 88

From the outside, with its spot next to a small canal and outdoor tables tiered to approach the water, Ristorante Rocco looks way too cla$$y for budget travelers. Even on weekdays, Rocco always hosts business peeps out on date night. Despite the pretentious atmosphere, though, the food is unpretentious and the prices unassuming. For the local all-time favorite, opt for the *lasagne* (€9), which is baked in its own little dish and covered in deliciously-crispified cheese. Or, if you rather, satisfy your taste for Hamburg's seafood with any of the dishes containing scampi or *Meeresfrüchten*.

i U3: From the metro, walk north on Winterhuder Weg for 3 large blocks. Then keep left as Winterhuder Weg splits off of Herderstr. Turn right onto Hofweg, and the restaurant is on the right, right next to the canal. Pasta €8-10.50. Entrees €10.50-18. ☺ Open M-F noon-3pm and 6-11:30pm, Sa-Su 6-11:30pm.

▨ AZEITONA
MIDDLE EASTERN $

Beckstr. 17-19   ☎040 18 00 73 71

They say that Hamburg is famous for its €2.50 falafel, and we think Azeitona scored the reputation for the whole city. This cafe is tiny and all vegetarian, and the falafel is pretty darn good. For the perfect sandwich, add some of Azeitona's antipasti for €0.50. The restaurant is decorated like a little slice of the Middle East, and even the benches are carpeted.

i U3: Feldstr. From the metro, walk north on Sternstr. After a short block, turn left onto Beckstr. Azeitona is on the right. Entrees €2.50-6. Caipirina €4. ☺ Open M-Th noon-11pm, F-Sa noon-late, Su noon-11pm.

▨ EISCAFE AM POELCHAUKAMP
ICE CREAM $

Poelchaukamp 3   ☎040 27 25 17

It's just an ice cream parlor, but it's an exceptionally good one. The owners are Italian, and the *eis* is authentic, too. Get a couple scoops—the rum flavors, rum truffle and *malaga* or rum raisin, are the best. Take it to explore the nearby residential neighborhood.

i U3: Sierichstr. From the metro, walk south on Sierichstr. for about 10min. Then turn right onto Poelchaukamp, and the Eiscafe is on the left near the canal. Each scoop €1. ☺ Open daily 11am-10pm.

LA SEPIA
SEAFOOD $$

Neuer Pferdemarkt 16   ☎040 432 24 84

When in Hamburg, eat seafood. It's simply a must, and this Spanish and Portuguese restaurant serves some seriously generous portions at seriously affordable prices (at least in comparison to similar cafes). The low prices justify the interior, which is impersonal and loaded up with tanks of crustaceans. Avoid the expensive dinner entrees and catch the lunch special (noon-5pm) for around €5-7, or try the fish sampler (€6) to get the full cornucopia of Hamburg's *Meeresfrüchte* (fruit of the sea).

i U3, S11, S21, or S31: Sternschanze. Entrees €7.50-22. Soups €4.50. ☺ Open daily noon-3am.

HATARI PFÄLZER CANTINA
GERMAN $$

Schanzenstr. 2   ☎040 43 20 88 66

You'll be glad to hear that the word "eclectic" sums this cafe up quite nicely: it's decorated with Chinese **dragons** and hunting trophies. Students flock here for hamburgers (€7.80-8.20) and Hamburger-watching on the busy street corner. Hatari also serves German specialties, including *schnitzel* (€11-12) and *Flammkuchen* (€7.30-8.30), or "French pizza," a Bavarian thin crust spread with thick cream and piled with toppings.

i U3, S11, S21, or S31: Sternschanze. Entrees from €7. Cash only. ☺ Open daily noon-late.

HIN&VEG
VEGETARIAN $

Schulterblatt 16   ☎040 594 53 402

This veggie diner is fittingly dog-friendly. As you enter, you might hear one of the servers adoring a dog: *"Wasser für den Hund."* If you're intimidated by meaty German classics, this is your chance to fill up on veggie versions of Deutschland staples. Hin&Veg serves dishes like vegetarian currywurst (€3) and *döner* (€4), all with vegan sauces. Also, a delicious collection of veggie burgers makes for a light, refreshing way to gain the requisite Hamburg/hamburger bragging rights.

i U3, S11, S21, or S31: Sternschanze. From the metro, head south on Schanzenstr. and take the 3rd left onto Schulterblatt. The restaurant is on the right. Burger €2-4. Pizza €5.90-7.50. Cash only.
🕐 Open M-Th 11:30am-10:30pm, F-Sa 11:30am-midnight, Su 12:30-10pm.

NIGHTLIFE

⬛ AUREL
BAR

Bahrenfelderstr. 157 ☎040 390 27 27

Aurel identifies itself as a*Kneipe*, which is basically a pub. Despite the prevalence of beer drinking, one of the main attractions at Aurel is their delicious mojito special (€6.50 before 9pm). An early crowd sticks around Aurel until bedtime. A small, beleaguered bar keeps tabs on the incessantly large crowd, which packs the small tables and inevitably spills out onto the sidewalk. Check out the stained glass on the back wall (don't worry—we don't get it either).

i S1, S3, or S31: Altona. From the metro, exit onto Ottenser Hauptstr., walk east, then turn right onto Bahrenfelderstr. The bar is on the left at the corner of Bahrenfelderstr. and Nöltingstr. Beer €2.60-3.50. Mojitos €8 after 9pm. Mixed drinks €6-8. Cash only. 🕐 Open daily 10am-late.

⬛ SHAMROCK IRISH BAR
BAR

Feldstr. 40 ☎040 432 77 275 www.shamrockirishbar.com

Our researchers were mystified by the outdoor flower garden at this punk bar: how, oh how, could leather-clad, whiskey-drinking old boys frequent this dark, smoky Irish bar without treading on them? True to its Irish heritage, Shamrock often fills to capacity with Guinness-drinking English-speakers. Irish football banners hang from the ceiling, and some of the funniest bartenders this side of the Channel fill huge steins with Guinness, Kilkenny, and Irish Car Bombs. Come Thursday nights at 9pm for a hilarious pub quiz and watch Germans mutter to each other in broken English about topics ranging from Bolshevism to Batman to beer.

i U3: Feldstr. From the metro, head east on Feldstr. The bar is on the left. Guinness and Kilkenny 0.3 €2.90, 0.4L €3.80. 🕐 Open Tu-Th 6pm-1am, F 5pm-late, Sa 1pm-late, Su 6pm-midnight.

ROSI'S BAR
BAR

Hamburger Berg 7 ☎040 31 55 82

In an area famous for debauchery, Rosi's sets the standard. Though this bar is located on a strip of seemingly identical bars, nowhere else comes close to Rosi's age-old(going on 60 years) notoriety, fame, or motley collection of DJs. Come for soul one night and return for goth-rock the next; no two evenings are alike. Rosi, the one-time wife of Tony Sheridan, became the bar's manager at the tender age of 18 and still runs it now with her son. Dark wood walls are dressed up with a single disco ball and layers of music posters, all of which contribute to Rosi's wild nights.

i S1, S2, or S3: Reeperbahn. Go east on Reeperbahn, take a left onto Hamburger Berg, and walk about 75m. DJs most nights from 11pm. Beer €2.50-3. Cocktails €5. Cash only. 🕐 Open M-Th 9pm-4am, F-Sa 9pm-6am, Su 9pm-4am.

CAFÉ GNOSA
CAFE, BAR, GLBT

Lange Reihe 93 ☎040 24 30 34 www.gnosa.de

Café Gnosa is a Hamburg institution. It's a great cafe and perfect for a visit during the day, but it's most famous for its fabulous GLBT nightlife. Full of bright lights and decorated with dark wood, Café Gnosa has been serving warm and cold drinks and famous cakes since World War II. Hamburg's first gay bar attracts an older crowd—gay and straight—who remember its early days, plus some younger faces eager to enjoy the exquisite cakes and talk with the refreshingly friendly staff. You can also pick up free GLBT publications like *hinnerk* and Hamburg's Gay Map here.

i *From the north entrance of the Hauptbahnhof, follow Ernst-Mecke-Str. as it becomes Lange Reihe. Beer €2.70-3.60. Cocktails €5.50-8. Champagne €8.70. Coffee €1.90. Cakes €2-5. Cash only. ☼ Open daily 10am-1am.*

KYTI VOO
BAR, GLBT

Lange Reihe 82 ☎040 280 55 565 www.kytivoo.de

Red neon lights and loud electro suggest a small club, but Kyti Voo is really a large, chic gay bar with an insatiable hunger for heavy beats. The bar inside is massive and many-sided, so it's too bad no one uses it in the summer, when 20- to 40-somethings snatch up the extensive outdoor seating. By about 10:30pm, Kyti Voo's sidewalk is one of the most popular places in St. Georg. Sip coffee or cocktails or chow down on a steaming hot *Flammkuchen* (€6.90-8.90).

i *From the north entrance of the Hauptbahnhof, follow Ernst-Mecke-Str. as it becomes Lange Reihe. The bar is on the right, about halfway down the block. Espresso €1.60. Beer on tap 0.3L €2.80, 0.5L €3.60. Cocktails €5.50-8. Wine €3.40-6.50. Cash only. ☼ Open M-F 9am-late, Sa-Su 10am-late.*

YOKO MONO
BAR

Marktstr. 41 ☎040 431 82 991 www.yokomono.de

Yoko Mono is situated on the edge of a trash-covered, motor-biker-frequented park. The crowd that gathers here is student heavy and generally under 25. Yoko Mono is pretty much the ideal place to chat to someone about how much you love Bon Iver. A pool table heats up the side room, while the small main bar is dark, cozy, and packed. With all the cool, attractive friends it encourages you to meet, this bar could've easily broken up the Beatles.

i *U3: Feldstr. From the metro, head north on Laeiszstr., then west on Marktstr. Wine €2.50-2.80. Beer €2.80-3.50. Cash only. ☼ Open daily noon-2am or later.*

FABRIK
CLUB

Barnerstr. 36 ☎040 391 070 www.fabrik.de

Fabrik used to be a factory for machine parts. Complete with a rusted crane on the roof, Fabrik is perhaps the only appropriate place to do the robot. Actually, no one does the robot, even here, though you can engage in some Fabrik boogie woogie. For years, crowds have packed this two-level club to hear live DJs, big-name rock acts, and an eclectic mix of other bands, with styles ranging from Latin to punk.

i *S1, S3, or S31: Altona. From the metro, exit at Ottenser Hauptstr., walk along the pedestrian walkway to the east, turn right onto Bahrenfelderstr., and walk north until you reach Barnerstr. The club is on the right. Check the website for a schedule of events. Live DJ most Sa nights at 10pm. The club hosts a "Gay Factory" night each month. Cover €7. Tickets €17-36. ☼ Hours vary, and most acts start at 9pm.*

ESSENTIALS
Practicalities

- **TOURIST OFFICES:** Hamburg's main tourist offices supply free English-language maps and pamphlets. All sell the Hamburg Card (€8.90), which provides discounts for museums, tours, and particular stores and restaurants, plus unlimited access to public transportation. The Hauptbahnhof office books rooms for a €4 fee and offers free maps. (☎040 300 51 300. *i* In the Wandelhalle, the station's main shopping plaza, near the Kirchenallee exit. ☼ Open M-Sa 9am-7pm, Su 10am-6pm.) The Sankt Pauli Landungsbrücken office is often less crowded than the Hauptbahnhof office. (Between piers 4 and 5. ☎040 300 51 203. ☼ Open M-W 9am-6pm, Th-Sa 9am-pm.)

germany

- **CURRENCY EXCHANGE:** ReiseBank arranges money transfers for Western Union and cashes traveler's checks. (☎040 32 34 83 *i* 2nd fl. of the Hauptbahnhof near the Kirchenallee exit. Also sells telephone cards. Other branches in the Altona and Dammtor train stations as well as in the Flughafen. 1.5% commission. €6.50 to cash 1-9 checks, €10 for 10 checks, and €25 for 25 checks. Exchanges currency for a fixed charge of €3-5. ☒ Open daily 7:30am-10pm.) Citibank cashes traveler's checks, including AmEx. (Rathausstr. 2 ☎040 302 96 202 *i* U3: Rathaus. ☒ Open M-F 9am-1pm and 2-6pm.)

- **GLBT RESOURCES:** St. Georg is the center of the gay community. Hein und Fiete, a self-described "switchboard," gives advice on doctors, disease prevention, and tips on the gay scene in Hamburg. (Pulverteich 21 ☎040 240 333. *i* Walk down Steindamm away from the Hauptbahnhof, turn right onto Pulverteich, and look for a rainbow-striped flag on the left. ☒ Open M-F 4-9pm, Sa 4-7pm.) Magnus-Hirschfeld-Centrum offers film screenings, counseling sessions, and a gay-friendly cafe. (Borgweg 8 ☎040 278 77 800. *i* U3: Borgweg. ☒ Cafe open M-Th 5:30-11pm, F 5pm-late, Su 3-8pm.) Magnus-Hirschfeld-Centrum also offers gay and lesbian hotlines. (Gay hotline ☎040 279 00 69. Lesbian hotline ☎040 279 0049. ☒ Gay hotline open M-W 2-6pm and 7-9pm, Th 2-6pm; Lesbian hotline open W 5-7pm, Th 6-8pm.)

- **INTERNET ACCES:** Free Wi-Fi is available in Wildwechsel (Beim Grünen Jäger 25 ☒ Open daily 4pm-late), at the Altan Hotel (Beim Grünen Jäger 23 *i* You don't have to be a guest to use internet in the lobby/bar. ☒ Open 24hr.), and at Starbucks. (Neuer Jungfernstieg 5 ☒ Open M-F 7:30am-9pm, Sa-Su 8am-6pm.) Staats- und Universitätsbibliothek has computers on the 2nd floor, but internet access is limited to library cardholders. (Von Melle-Park 3 ☎040 428 38 22 33. *i* Library car €5 per month, €13 per 6 months. ☒ Open M-F 9am-9pm, Sa-Su 10am-9pm.)

- **POST OFFICE:** Hauptbahnhof. (At the Kirchenallee exit. ☒ Open M-F 8am-6pm, Sa 8:30am-12:30pm.)

- **POSTAL CODE:** 20095.

Emergency

- **EMERGENCY NUMBERS:** ☎112.

- **POLICE:** 110. (*i* From the Kirchenallee exit of the Hauptbahnhof, turn left and follow signs for "BGS/Bahnpolizei/Bundespolizei." Another branch is located on the Reeperbahn, at the corner of Davidstr. and Spielbudenpl., and in the courtyard of the Rathaus.)

- **PHARMACY:** Adler Apotheke.(Schulterblatt 106 ☎040 439 45 90 *i* Schedule of emergency hours for Hamburg pharmacies out front. ☒ Open M-F 8:30am-7pm, Sa-Su 9am-4pm.) Hauptbahnhof-Apotheke Wande halle. (☎040 325 27 383. *i* In the station's upper shopping gallery. ☒ Open M-W 7am-9pm Th-F 7am-9:30pm, and Sa-Su 8am-9pm.)

Getting There

By Plane

Air France (☎018 058 30 830) and **Lufthansa** (☎018 058 05 805), among other airlines, serve Hamburg's **Fuhlsbüttel Airport** (HAM; ☎040 507 50). **Jasper Airport Express** buses run from the Kirchenallee exit of the Hauptbahnhof directly to the airport. (☎040 227 10 610. *i* €5, under 12 €2. 25min. ☒ Every 10-15min. 4:45am-7pm, every 20min. 7-9:20pm.) Alternatively, you can take U1, S1, or S11 to Ohlsdorf, then take an express bus to the airport. (*i* €2.60, ages 6-14 €0.90. ☒ Every 10min. 4:30am-11pm, every 30min. 11pm-1am.)

By Train

The **Hauptbahnhof**, Hamburg's central station, offers connections to: Berlin (€56; 2hr., about 1 per hr.); Frankfurt (€109; 4hr., 1 per hr.); Hannover (€40; 1½hr., 2 per hr.); Munich (€185; 6hr., about 1 per hr.); and Copenhagen (€80; 5hr., 6 per day). The efficient staff at the **DB Reisezentrum** sells tickets (⌚ Open M-F 5:30am-10pm, Sa-Su 7am-10pm), which are also available at the ticket machines located throughout the Hauptbahnhof and online at. **Dammtor** station is near the university, to the west of Außenalster; **Harburgdorf** is to the southeast. Most trains to and from Schleswig-Holstein stop only at **Altona,** while most trains toward Lübeck stop only in the Hauptbahnhof. Stations are connected by frequent local trains and the S-Bahn.

By Bus

The **ZOB** terminal is across Steintorpl. from the Hauptbahnhof. (☎040 24 75 76 ⌚ Open M-Tu 5am-10pm, W 5am-midnight, Th 5am-10pm, F 5am-midnight, Sa-Su 5am-10pm.)

Getting Around

By Public Transportation

HVV operates the efficient U-Bahn, S-Bahn, and bus network. Tickets are validated upon purchase according to the station or time you buy them. Short rides within downtown cost €1.30, and one-way rides farther out in the network cost €0.80; when in doubt, use the starting point/destination input tool on any ticket machine to figure out which of the one-way tickets will suffice. Two different day cards may cause confusion: the **9-Uhr Tageskarte** (9hr. day card €5.50) works for unlimited rides midnight-6am and 9am-6pm on the day of purchase. A **Ganztageskarte** (full-day pass; €6.80) works for unlimited rides at any point throughout the day of purchase until 6am the next morning. A **3-Tage-Karte** (3-day ticket; €16.50) is also available. Passes are available for longer time periods, though anything over a week requires a photo. Frequent riders can bring a photo or take one in the nearby ID booths for €5.

By Ferry

HADAG Seetouristik und Fährdienst AG runs ferries. (☎040 311 70 70 *i* Departs the docks at St. Pauli Landungsbrücken. 21 stops along the river. Price included in HVV train and bus passes; €2.60 for a new ticket. ⌚ All 21 stops 75min., every 15min.) Take the HVV-affiliated ferries in lieu of the expensive tour boats for an equally impressive view of the river Elbe.

By Taxi

All Hamburg taxies charge the same rates. Normally, it's about €2.70 to start, then about €1.80 per km for the first 10km and €1.28 per km thereafter. Try **Autoruf** (☎040 441 011), **Das Taxi** (☎040 221 122), or **Taxi Hamburg**. (☎040 666 666)

By Bike

Hamburg is wonderfully bike-friendly, with wide bike lanes on most roads. Rent a bike at **Fahrradstation Dammtor/Rotherbaum** (Schlüterstr. 11 ☎040 414 68 27 *i* €4-8 per day ⌚ Open M-F 9am-6:30pm) or **Hamburg City Cycles**. (Bernhard-Nocht-Str. ☎040 742 14 420 *i* Offers guided bike tours €12 per day, €23 per 2 days, €7 per day thereafter. ⌚ Open Tu-F on request, Sa-Su 10am-6pm.)

munich

If you ask the average traveler about this Bavarian capital, you'll hear beer, beer, and more beer. The birthplace of Oktoberfest, Munich is the third largest city in Germany (pop. 1,380,00) and one of the country's most expensive. It's difficult to believe that this affluent, beer-soaked city is where the Nazi NSDAP Party had its first headquarters. Hitler's first attempt to seize power took place in Munich, and the Führerhimself spoke at some of the beer halls that you can still visit today. The first Nazi concentration camp, Dachau, is just 30min. away from the city. Today, Munich is trying to put much of this history behind it and has become a thriving center of European commerce, with world-class museums, parks, and architecture. Salzburg (only 1½hr. away by train) is a popular daytrip for many Munchkins—er, Müncheners—and the fairytale castle of Neuschwanstein is a major tourist attraction.

ACCOMMODATIONS

EURO YOUTH HOTEL
Senefelderstr. 5

HOSTEL $$

Hostels are really scaling up these days, and the Euro Youth Hotel is one of them. The grand staircase and wood-paneled reception are batting way out of their league, and the surprisingly cheap rooms aren't far behind. Don't let all the luxuries fool you, though, your stay includes a mean breakfast buffet and access to the hopping hostel bar, which features quiz nights, karaoke, and daily specials. Grab one of the hostel's city maps—it will help you a ton. And book in advance, as rooms fill up fast.

i Dorms from €20. ☪ Reception 24hr.

WOMBAT'S CITY HOSTEL MUNICH
Senefelderstr. 1

HOSTEL $$

Wombat's is a constant party with a hostel on the side. The party-hostel vibe is kicked into gear with a free drink voucher that will surely be followed by many more drinks in their always-hopping "Wombar". The free drink voucher is just one of their many bonuses for guests, which include an excellent breakfast buffet (€4) and parking in their basement. Those looking for more restful activities can find reprieve in one of the hammocks hanging in the courtyard garden. Dorms include high-tech key card lockers and private bathrooms, and the hostel's custom city map is a big plus.

i Dorms from €22. ☪ Reception 24hr.

HI MUNICH PARK YOUTH HOSTEL
Miesingstr. 4

HOSTEL $$

Located a bit outside the city's bustling center, HI Munich Park is worth the trip. Especially for travelers seeking peace and quiet while maintaining accessibility to Munich's sights and sounds, this modern abode is the perfect place to call home. Although you'll be nestled in a green oasis of forest and natural space, proximity to the metro means central Munich is less than 10 minutes away. Maybe it's all the trees, but the exceptionally welcoming staff was a breath of fresh air. The breakfast was the perfect start to our day, too.

i Dorms from €20. HI membership required, can be purchased on-site for €3.50, or €7 per year. ☪ Reception 24hr.

SIGHTS

City Center

MARIENPLATZ
Marienpl. 1

SQUARE

The pedestrian area around Marienpl. is the heart of Munich. Its name comes from the Mariensäule, a 17th-century monument to the Virgin Mary that sits at the center of the large square as a tribute to the city's miraculous survival of the Swedish invasion and the plague. The square is dominated by the impressively ornate Neo-Gothic Neues Rathaus, or new city hall, which was built in the early 20th century. Camera-toting tourists gawk at its central tower during the thrice-daily Glockenspiel mechanical chimes displays, which may be one of the most underwhelming tourist attractions you'll ever see and hear. At the eastern end of the square, the Altes Rathaus (Old Town Hall) houses a small and boring toy museum.

To the north of Marienplatz are Frauenkirche, Max-Joseph Platz, and Odeons-platz, all of which are worth a stroll through for their beautiful architecture and to take an SD card's worth of pictures. Don't forget the Hofbrauhaus, which is just as easily recognized as a landmark sight as it is a restaurant, tavern, and biergarten.

i S1, S2, S3, S4, S5, S6, S7, S8, U3 or U6: Marienpl. ⏲ *Glockenspiel displays in summer 11am, noon, and 5pm; in winter 11am and noon.*

ALTER PETER (SAINT PETER'S CHURCH) CHURCH
Rindermarkt 1 ☎089 210 237 760

As the poster inside explains, Alter Peter was severely damaged during World War II. The Gothic-inspired church was then meticulously rebuilt, but most of the interior walls remain plain and white. However, you can still see an original cannonball lodged in the church wall (behind the church, take the steps leading up to Cafe Rischart and look around the top right corner of the window frame). Check out the freakish, gem-studded skeleton of St. Mundi-tia, exhibited in a glass case that looks more like a diamond ad gone wrong than holy remains. The church's tower offers a bird's-eye view of Munich and is definitely worth climbing. However, the ascent to the (almost) heavens is challenging, as the staircase of 306 steps is too narrow for two-way traffic. Watch out for others and observe the decades of cool signatures and stickers on the walls.

i S1, S2, S3, S4, S5, S6, S7, S8, U3 or U6: Marienpl. *Church free. Tower €1.50, students and children €1. Cash only.* ⏲ *Tower open in summer M-F 9am-6:30pm, Sa-Su 10am-6:30pm.; in winter M-F 9am-5:30pm, Sa-Su 10am-5:30pm.*

RESIDENZ MUSEUM AND HOFGARTEN MUSEUM
Residenzstr. 1 ☎089 26 06 71 www.residenz-muenchen.de

The 130-room Residenz palace, once home to Bavarian dukes and electors, is now a museum that takes the word "excess" to new dimensions, with mirrors, porcelain, and blinding gold leaves galore. Highlights include the ancestral gallery, hung with over 100 family portraits tracing the royal lineage, and the spectacular Renaissance antiquarium, replete with stunning frescoes. A separate ticket is needed for the Treasury, full of shiny expensive stuff.

i U3, U4, U5, or U6: Odeonspl. *Residenz and treasury each €7, students €6, under 18 free; combined Residenz and treasury ticket €11/9/free; Cuvilliés Theater €3.50/2.50/free; combination Residenz, treasury, and theater €13/10.50/free. Audio tours included.* ⏲ *Residenz and Treasury open Apr-Oct daily 9am-6pm; Oct-March 10am-5pm. Last entry 1hr. before close. Theater open Apr-Jul M-Sa 2-6pm, Su 9am-6pm; Aug-Sept daily 9am-6pm; Sept-Oct M-Sa 2-6pm, Su 9am-6pm; Oct-Mar M-Sa 2-5pm, Su 10am-5pm.*

University Area

▨ PINAKOTHEKEN MUSEUMS
Barrerstr. ☎089 23 80 52 16 www.pinakothek.de

Don't let the whole "five museums" thing scare you away from Pinakothek-en: think of all these museums as just one giant and super impressive art gallery. The five buildings are part of the Kunstareal, a museum district in Maxvorstadt that comprises the majority of Munich's art museums. Start with **Alte Pinakothek,** the one with the collection that some would affectionately call "boring, old art" (14th- to 17th-century art, including works of European masters such as da Vinci and Dürer). What's surprisingly cool is that the whole collection is arranged in one giant hallway of multiple rooms, so you can really experience how much art changed over the course of 300 years. Also in the Kunstareal are the New Pinakothek (which is architecturally beautiful and has a great cafe) and the Pinakothek der Moderne (which is our favorite). The Pinakotheken can be a lot of art all at once, so consider visiting over several days or run (not literally) through the museums on Sundays, when admission is only €1.

i U2: Theresienstr. Walk east on Theresienstr. until you see the big museum complex. Museum Brandhorst and Neue Pinakothek each €7, students €5; Pinakothek Alte €4, students €2. Pinakothek der Moderne €10/7; Sammlung Schack €4/3; 1-day pass to all 5 €12/9; 5-entry pass €29. All museums €1 on Su. ⓐ Alte Finakothek open Tu 10am-8pm, W-Su 10am-6m. Neue Pinakothek open M 10am-6pm, W 10am-8pm, Th-Su 10am-6pm. Pinakothek der Moderne open Tu-W 10am-6pm, Th 10am-8pm, F 10am-6pm, Sa 10am-10pm, Su 10am-6pm; closed M. Museum Brandhorst open Tu-W 10am-6pm, Th 10am-8pm, F-Su 10am-6pm. Sammlung Schack open daily 10am-6pm.

▥ ENGLISCHER GARTEN   PARK

Strolling through the open emerald fields and leafy paths of the enormous Englischer Garten may be one of the most relaxing things you can do on a summer day in the city. The park is one of the largest metropolitan public parks in the world, dwarfing both Central Park in New York and Hyde Park in London. The amazingly healthy residents of Munich do everything from walk their dogs, ride their bikes, and bathe in the sun here. Some choose to do this last activity in the nude, in areas designated FKK or *Frei Körper Kultur* ("Free Body Culture"). There are also several beer gardens here, but the most famous one surrounds a wooden Chinese pagoda. In the southern part of the garden, a former Nazi art exhibition space, Haus der Kunst (Prinzregentenst.1 089 21 12 71 13 www.hausderkunst.de), is now Munich's premier venue for contemporary art, with changing international and domestic exhibitions. Right next to the Haus der Kunst, surfers have found their way into the Eisbach, and surf the standing wave created by a pinch point in the river 365 days a year.

i U3: Universität, Giselastr., or Münchner Freiheit. Park free. Haus der Kunst €5-12. Student discounts available. ⓐ Haus der Kunst open M-W 10am-8pm, Th 10am-10pm, F-Su 10am-8pm.

KÖNIGSPLATZ   SQUARE

The Königsplatz was comissioned by King Ludwig I to be Munich's tribute to Greek and Roman antiquity. During the Third Reich, the Nazis, who also admired ancient Rome, made the square their headquarters and used the large roads for rallies. The infamous book burning of 1933 took place here, and the famous Munich Accord was signed in Hitler's "Führerbau," just east of the square (strangely, the building is now home to a music and theater university). The square is not just for squares though; or sunny days, dozens of people spend their time just chilling on the stairs or sunbathing in the large grassy fields.

i U2: Königspl. Glyptothek and Antikensammlungen each €3.50, students €2.50; combined ticket €5.50/3.50. Every Su €1. ⓐ Antikensammlungen open Tu 10am-5pm, W 10am-8pm, Th-Su 10am-5pm. Glyptothek open Tu-W 10am-5pm, Th 10am-8pm, F-Sa 10am-5pm.

Olympic Area

▥ BMW WELT AND MUSEUM   MUSEUM

Am Olympiapark 1   ☎018 02 11 88 22 www.bmw-welt.com

Do you know what BMW stands for? Regardless of your answer, you must stop by the BMW Welt and Museum. (BMW stands for "Bayerische Motoren Werke," by the way.) The amazing, futuristic architecture of the entire BMW complex alone would make your visit worthwhile. However, you can also jump into all sorts of cars, play racing computer games, and watch shows of handsome Germans driving motorcycles up and down stairs while you're here. And this is only in the BMW Welt, which is the car company's showcase. The museum is almost as cool (although perhaps not as interactive), with state-of-the-art exhibits detailing the history, development, and design of Bavaria's second-favorite export. Frosted glass walls and touch-sensitive projections lead visitors past engines, chassis, and concept vehicles with exhibits in both English and German. Visitors can also make reservations to tour the adjacent production factory, with a tunnel that runs through the entire assembly line.

i U3: Olympiazentrum. BMW Welt is the large steel structure visible upon exiting the metro; the museum is located across the street. Factory and BMW Welt tours available only with a reservation. BMW Welt free. Museum €10, students €7, family €12. Special discounts with Olympiapark ticket or the City Tour Card. ☎ BMW Welt open daily 7:30am-midnight. Museum open Tu-Su 10am-6pm; last entry 5:30pm. 2 factory tours in English daily 11:30am and either noon or 4pm.

OLYMPIAPARK
SPORTS COMPLEX

Olympiapark ☎089 30 67 24 14 www.olympiapark.de

Built for the 1972 Olympic Games, the lush Olympiapark contrasts with the curved steel of the Olympic Stadium and the 290m Olympiaturm, Munich's tallest tower. The Olympic area can be accessed for free, but you can buy a self-guided audio tour for in-depth information about the various structures. Otherwise, three English-language tours are available. The Adventure Tour gets you into many of the buildings and introduces you to Olympiapark's history; the Stadium Tour focuses just on the stadium; and the Roof Climb lets you unleash your inner Spider-Man and climb the stadium's roof with a rope and a hook. The building where Palestinian terrorists captured Israeli athletes during the Munich Massacre is in the northern half of the park (Connellystr. 31).

i U3: Olympiazentrum. Audio tours and tickets for tours can be purchased at the information desk in the southeast corner of the park (close to the ice rink). Audio tour €7, deposit €50. Adventure Tour €8, students €5.50. Unguided entrance to stadium €3. Stadium Tour €7.50, students €5. Roof climb €41, students €31. Tower and Rock Museum €5.50, under 16 €3.50. Admission includes discounts at Sea Life and the BMW Museum. ☎ Tours offered daily Apr-Nov. Adventure Tour 2pm. Stadium Tour 11am. Roof Climb 2:30pm (weather permitting). Tower and Rock Museum open daily 9am-midnight. Audio tour available 9am-5pm, but can be returned any time before 11:30pm.

Au-Haidhausen

DEUTSCHES MUSEUM
MUSEUM

Museumsinsel 1 ☎089 217 91 www.deutsches-museum.de

An hour or so in the Deutsches Museum will teach you more than all your introductory science classes combined. This incredible museum presents you with the power of German engineering—prepare for everything from key mechanisms, musical instruments, and oil rigs to timekeeping microchips and the frontiers of nanotechnology. Reading all the explanations throughout the giant rooms, spread over eight floors, is impossible for us mere mortals, but anywhere you go, you're guaranteed to find something mindboggling. Before you think you've had enough knowledge for the day, be sure to check out the claustrophobic mining exhibit, which is appropriately situated in the basement.

i S1, S2, S3, S4, S5, S6, S7, S8: Isartor. On the island between the city center and the Au neighborhood. From the metro, head toward the river, cross onto the island, and turn right. €11, students €4, children under 6 free. Cash only. ☎ Open daily 9am-5pm.

Neuhausen

SCHLOSS NYMPHENBURG
PALACE

Schloss Nymphenburg ☎089 17 90 80 www.schloss-nymphenburg.de

This palace was supposedly modeled after Versailles and built in 1675 for Bavarian royalty. The main building, the lavish, three-story Stone Hall, has all your typical, intricate frescoed ceilings and enormous dangling chandeliers, but the real charm of this property is the enormous, gorgeous garden. Few tourists venture beyond the space immediately behind the castle, so the area with four ornate pavilions (Amelienburg, Badenburg, Magdaleneklause, and Pagodenburg) remains peaceful. Highlights of the property include the bedroom in which King Ludwig II was born and the Gallery of Beauties, featuring portraits of the 36 women whom King Ludwig I considered to be the most beautiful in Bavaria (our favorite is Helene Sedlmeyr). Summertime brings classical concerts to the park grounds; check kiosks for details. At the end of your trip to the palace, drink like royalty at the Hirschgarten, the largest biergarten in the world (www.hirschgarten.com).

i *Tram 17: Schloss Nymphenburg. Palace €6, students €5. Porcelain and carriage museums €4.50, students €3.50; pavilions €4.50/3.50; combination ticket €11.50/9. Audio tour €3.50. Gardens free. Museum Mensch und Natur €3, students €2, Su €1. ☒ Complex open daily Apr-Oct 9am-6pm; Oct-Mar 10am-4pm. Badenburg, Pagodenburg, and Magdalenklause closed in winter. Museum Mensch und Natur open Tu-W 9am-5pm, Th 9am-8pm, F 9am-5pm, Sa-Su 10am-6pm.*

Outside Munich

◪ NEUSCHWANSTEIN CASTLE   CASTLE
Schwangau, near Füssen   ☎083 62 93 08 30 www.neuschwanstein.de

Depending on who you ask, Neuschwanstein Castle is either a gorgeous, fairy-tale fortress or a 19th-century, Disney-esque castle that borders walks a fine line between cool and kitschy. We definitely don't deny the charms of the white Neuschwanstein, or "New Swan Rock," castle, which was commissioned by King Ludwig II and is perched precariously on a hilltop in the beautiful Bavarian Alps. The only way to get inside the castle, which is almost completely covered in paintings of scenes from Wagner's operas, is with a 30min. guided tour. No visit to this castle is complete without a walk across Marienbrücke, a slightly rickety wooden bridge across a waterfall that leads to a stunning side view of Neuschwanstein.

i *We recommend splitting a rental car with friends from your hostel or friends you're traveling with as the easiest mode of transportation to Neuschwanstein, as public transportation generally is very complicated. If you must take public transit, take the 2hr. DB train to Füssen (every hr.; €21 for Bayern ticket, €50 round trip normal ticket). Walk right across the street and take either the #73 or #78 bus to the last stop, Schwangau (10min.; free with Bayern ticket or €1.90 1-way). To get to the castle from the bus stop, you can either walk up the hill (40min.), take a bus (10min.; up €1.80, down €1, round trip €2.60), or take a horse-drawn carriage (15min.; up €6, down €3). Check the schedule of buses going back to Füssen—they leave every hr., synchronized with train departures. The main ticket office is approximately 100m uphill from the #78 bus stop. English tours are frequent, but earlier tours sell out quickly; it's a good idea to book in advance €1.80 surcharge). Guided tours of Neuschwanstein €12, students €8, under 18 free; Hohenschwangau €10.50/8/ free; combined ticket €23, students €21. ☒ Castle open Apr-Sept daily 9am-6pm; Oct-Mar 10am-4pm. Ticket office open Apr-Sept daily 8am-5pm; Oct-Mar 9am-3pm.*

DACHAU CONCENTRATION CAMP MEMORIAL SITE   MEMORIAL SITE
Alte Römerstr. 75, Dachau   ☎081 31 66 99 70 www.kz-gedenkstaette-dachau.de

The first thing prisoners saw as they entered Dachau was the inscription *"Arbeit Macht Frei"* ("Work will set you free") on the camp's iron gate. One of the most moving parts of the memorial site is actually part of the audio guide: survivors tell their life stories and the unimaginably inhumane life in the camp. The barracks, originally designed for 5000 prisoners, once held 30,000 at a time—two have been reconstructed for visitors, and gravel-filled outlines of the others stand as haunting reminders. It is impossible to prepare yourself for the camp's crematorium, which has been restored to its original appearance. The museum at the Dachau Memorial Site examines pre-1930s anti-Semitism, the rise of Nazism, the establishment of the concentration camps, and the lives of prisoners.

i *S2 (dir.: Petershausen): Dachau (30min.; 4 stripes on the Streifenkarte, free with Munich XXL ticket). Then, take bus #726 (dir.: Saubachsiedlung): KZ-Gedenkstätte (1 stripe on the Streifenkarte; €1.20, or free with Munich XXL ticket). All displays have English translations. Museum and memorial grounds free. Audio tours €3.50, students €2.50. Tours €3 per person. ☒ Memorial grounds open daily 9am-5pm. Museum and information office open Tu-Su 9am-5pm. Tours 2½hr. in English daily 11am and 1pm; in German noon. Documentary 22min. in German 11am and 3pm; in English 11:30am, 2pm, and 3:30pm.*

surfing the eisbach

As the world of science and technology progress, surfing has begun to break free from its coastal constraints and penetrate parts of the world previously relegated for farming. In Munich, a structural anomaly has created a standing wave in the heart of the city and in the shallows of the Eisbach. Even more anomalous is the surf culture that has flocked to it. Just minutes from some of the busiest parts of the city, long-haired surfer dudes and shredding surfer chicks make a daily commute to get their surfing fix as if Munich were on the coast of California.

On either side of the river wave, surfers wait their turn to plunge into the water. Given the difficulty of staying on the wave itself, surfers only last an average of 20 seconds before they're swept away in the rapid current. What makes the wave unique for surfers is that it operates unconditionally; 365 days a year and 24 hours a day, the Eisbach wave is flowing as usual.

For the traveler visiting Munich, the experience of viewing this city-wave and experiencing the culture is a must. For those who are more courageous, there are two other standing waves in the city that are much more manageable for beginners. One is in the Englischer Garten and the other is by the Zoo. Talk to the surfers at Santoloco Surf Shop and get yourself a board, wetsuit, and instructions. It's an experience you won't forget.

FOOD

TIMBALLO FOOD LOUNGE
CAFE $

Gabelsbergerstr. 9

TimBallo is located conveniently next to the Pinakotheken and makes for a perfect break from your museum explorations. In addition to providing some respite from the masses of portraits staring at you inside the Alte Pinakothek, it also is the antidote to much of German cuisine, offering salads and pasta dishes as opposed to more fried meat and potatoes. Some of the pasta dishes are so sought after that they will run out in the later afternoon, so head there before the rush to get the best they have to offer.

i Food €5-10. ☼ Open M-F 10am-4pm.

HANS IM GLUCK
BURGERS $$

Nymphenburger Str. 69

This place is decorated with floor to ceiling tree trunks giving the dining experience a foresty vibe The meals are far from green, though, with proper burgers being served with a modern twist. Like many of the American style burger places smattered around Germany, Hans Im Gluck takes America to school on turning burgers into artwork. The Hans Im Gluck burger is particularly thrilling.

i Entrees €10-15. ☼ Open daily 11am-11pm.

STEINHEIL 16
GERMAN $$

Steinheilstr. 16

When in Rome, do as the Romans do. When in Germany, drink beer and eat schnitzel. And Steinheil 16 is just the place to do it. With seriously large schnitzel pounded, battered, breaded, and fried to perfection, you can't go wrong. Order yourself a barrel-sized beer, enjoy the welcoming atmosphere, and watch the hours fly by.

i Food €10-15. ☼ Open daily 10am-1am.

RINGLER'S

Sendlinger Str 45

GERMAN $

This must be Bavarian soul food, because there is serious love put into every slice in every sandwich they make. That is just our way of saying if we could eat lunch at Ringler's every day, we would. Their meat is incredibly fresh, their sand-wiches are crafted with the utmost care, their gelato is the perfect digestif, and their employees will greet you with a smile. There's a reason the line stretches out of the door daily, and there's even more reason it's worth the wait. Go. You won't regret it.

i Food €5-10. ⏰ Open M-F 8am-6pm, Sa 10am-6pm; closed Sundays.

ZWICKL

Dreifaltigkeitspl. 2

GERMAN $$

Zwickl throws a contemporary spin on Bavarian classics. Didn't think schnit-zel could be bedazzled? Well it can, and Zwickl does it. With a menu that still revolves around the German staples of beer and meat, you'll get to taste the local cuisine but with a bit more style than many of the beer factories Munich is famous for. Whatever you do, make sure you try some of their homemade mustard. You'll never look at yellow mustard the same again. Our only issue with Zwickl is that it isn't the friendliest place for budget travelers and should only be visited if you're willing to splurge.

i Food €15-20. ⏰ Open daily 11am-11pm.

NIGHTLIFE

▦ HOFBRÄUHAUS

Platzl 9

BEER HALL

☎089 29 01 36 100 www.hofbraeuhaus.de

We could easily list this place under Sights—no trip to Munich is complete without a visit to its most famous beer hall. This is "das original" Hofbräuhaus beer hall that gave rise to dozens more around the world. Figures like Lenin, Hitler, and Mozart are mere footnotes in the long history of the place, which was royalty-only until King Ludwig I opened it to the public in 1828. Beer here comes in liters (€8); if you ask for anything less, they'll chortle and probably bring you a Maß anyway. By the end of the night you'll either be singing at the top of your lungs or singing a different tune at the famous vomitorium.

i S1, S2, S3, S4, S5, S6, S7, S8, U3, or U6: Marienpl. Take a left before the Altes Rathaus onto Burgstr. Then walk past the A ter Hof courtyard and take a right onto Pfisterstr. Arrive early to guarantee a spot, especially for large groups. Entrees €9.50-17. ⏰ Open daily 9am-11:30pm. Shows at 7pm.

▦ MUFFATWERK

Zellstr. 4

CONCERT VENUE

☎089 45 87 50 10 www.muffatwerk.de

This converted power plant hosts all kinds of concerts, from hip hop to jazz, and has hosted such names as Santana and Smashing Pumpkins. On Fridays and Saturdays, crowds storm the massive performance hall to hear live DJs. The attached beer garden, bar, and cafe all provide a more relaxed venue during the afternoon or evening. On your way here, check out the beach with a view of the dam.

i Tram 18: Deutsches Museum. Cross the bridge and turn left (follow the signs). Cover F-S €7-12. Concerts €15-35. Cash only. ⏰ Shows generally start 8:30-9:30pm; the hall opens 1hr. earlier. Check website for events. Beer garden open M-F 5pm-midnight, Sa 2pm-midnight, Su noon-midnight.

▦ KULTFABRIK AND OPTIMOLWERKE

Friedenstr. 10

CLUB

☎089 450 69 20 www.optimolwerke.de

Kultfabrik and Optimolwerke are amusement parks, except these ones will take you on a different kind of wild ride (one that may result in a technicolor yawn).

The two establishments, or rather collections of establishments, lie in adjacent lots, each containing enormous assortments of smaller bars and clubs. Hours, covers, and themes vary among the individual venues, which range from the fun-in-the-sun Bamboo Beach (Kultfabrik), complete with imported sand, to the darker Drei Turme (Optimolwerke), with its castle-like interior. Also within Kultfabrik is Kalinka, where you can fill up on vodka and party against a giant, seven-foot bust of Lenin. Kultfabrik prints a monthly magazine with the club schedules.

i *S1, S2, S3, S4, S5, S6, S7, or S8: Ostbahnhof. Walk through the underground tunnels past all the tracks to the back of the station and follow the crowds. On F, a single cover of €5 gets you inside many of Kultfabrik's clubs. Covers vary; generally around €5. Cash only. ☒ Hours vary, but most parties start 10-11pm; check schedule online.*

▨ BACKSTAGE

BAR, CLUB

Wilhelm-Hale-Str. 38 ☎089 126 61 00 www.backstage.eu

Backstage may be a converted gas station, but the abundance of trees and plants (lit up with vibrating green lights) makes this venue totally awesome, without the touch of scary-abandoned-factory feeling. The complex features live music from the indie underground scene. The local crowd varies depending on the act, but during the summer, you can always expect a crowded Biergarten with one of the best beer deals in town (Maß €4.80) and cheap shots (Th-Sa €1). The entire area includes three performance venues and multiple outdoor seating areas.

i *Trams 16, 17: Steubenpl. Walk south on Wilhelm-Hale-Str. and take the 3rd left, before the bridge. Follow the road as it curves until you reach Backstage. Freakout Party on Sa. Check the website for more events. Concert €15-30. Sa cover €7.50; includes 2 drinks. Shots €2.50. ☒ Summer beer garden open M-Th 5pm-1am, F-Sa 5pm-5am, Su 5pm-1am.*

CAFÉ KOSMOS

BAR

Dachauer Str. 7

We didn't expect Café Kosmos to have this much character (especially given its proximity to the central station), but it did and we loved it. With its signature spiral staircase, run down walls, and burning Vodkarellas, Kosmos took us right back to Berlin just seconds after we arrived in Munich. We're not talking techno music from dusk 'til dawn; we're talking about the 1950's era lounge with smoke stained couches and sexy patrons. Especially given how expensive Munich can be, Café Kosmos is surprisingly cheap. Oh, and grab an Astra beer as a preview of Hamburg.

i *Beer €2. Cocktails €5. ☒ Open M-F noon-1am, Sa-Su 2pm-3am.*

ALTER SIMPL

BAR

Türkenstr. 57 ☎089 272 30 83 www.eggerlokale.de

The gothic letters, wooden tables, hundreds of old posters, liters of beer, and great Bavarian food make Alter Simpl a genuinely awesome place to have a traditional meal or a beer at any time of the day. However, Alter Simpl stands out from its simpler cousins in a number of ways. Founded in 1903, the bar takes its name from an old satirical magazine called "Simplicissimus," with the magazine's iconic logo of a dog breaking the chains of censorship reworked into a dog breaking open a champagne bottle. There's even a statue of this red dog inside the establishment. Although the bar was once a second home to Munich's artists and intellectuals, it is now a lively hangout packed with students and a young crowd.

i *U3 or U6: Universität. Turn right onto Schellingstr. and then right onto Türkenstr. Beer €3.80. Snacks and entrees €5.60-15. Cash only. ☒ Open M-Th 11am-3am, F-Sa 11am-4am, Su 11am-3am. Kitchen open M-Th 11am-2am, F-Sa 11am-3am, Su 11am-2am.*

LÖWENBRÄUKELLER BEER HALL

Nymphenburgerstr. 2 ☎089 54 72 66 90 www.loewenbraeukeller.com

Marienplatz has Hofbräuhaus, Neuhausen has Löwenbräukeller, and we don't want to hear complaining about how similar beer gardens and halls can get. That's part of the magic. After all, you go for the beer, the company, and the waitresses in the Bavarian dresses. This beer garden may look like the other famous ones, but the entrance of Löwenbräukeller is easily identifiable thanks to its green tower and the characteristic Löwenbräu lion on the terrace.

i U1: Stiglmaierpl. English menu available. Maß €8.40. Entrees €5-14. Open daily 10am-midnight. Kitchen closes 11pm.

ESSENTIALS
Practicalities

- **TOURIST OFFICES:** English-speaking staff books rooms for free with a 10% deposit. München Ticket, a booking agency for concerts, theater, and other events, has locations at each tourist office. (Bahnhofspl. 2 ☎089 23 39 65 00 www.muenchen.de *i* Outside the train station. Map €0.40. Open M-Sa 9am-8pm, Su 10am-6pm.) 2nd location. (Marienpl. 2 ☎089 23 39 65 00 www.muenchen.de *i* Inside Neues Rathaus. Open M-F 10am-7pm, Sa 10am-5pm, Su 10am-2pm.)

- **CURRENCY EXCHANGE:** ReiseBank has decent rates, and Western Union will cash traveler's checks at a 1.5% commission. (Hauptbahnhof ☎089 55 10 80www.reisebank.de Open daily 7am-10pm.)

- **LUGGAGE STORAGE:** Lockers are in the main hall of the Hauptbahnhof. (☎089 13 08 50 36 *i* Max. 3 days €5 per day. Open M-F 7am-8pm, Sa-Su 8am-6pm.)

- **GLBT RESOURCES:** Bavarian queer publications include Leo, Blu (www.blu-magazin.de), and Rosa Muenchen (www.rosamuenchen.de). Gay & Lesbian Information Line. (Men ☎089 260 30 56; women ☎089 725 42 72 Open F 6-10pm.) LeTra is a resource for lesbians. (Angertorstr. 3 ☎089 725 42 72 www.letra.de Hotline M 2:30-5pm, Tu 10:30am-1pm, W 2:30-5pm.) Schwules Kommunikations und Kulturzentrum has resources, counselors, a small cafe, and a library for gay men. (Müllerstr. 43 ☎089 260 30 56 www.subonline.org Open M-Th 7-11pm, F 7pm-midnight, Sa 8pm-1am, Su 7-11pm.)

- **WOMEN'S RESOURCES:** Kofra offers job advice, books, and magazines and has a small cafe. (Baaderstr. 30 ☎089 201 04 50 www.kofra.de Open M-Th 4-10pm, F 2-6pm.) Frauentreffpunkt Neuperlach offers services for women, including an international coffee house and English conversation nights. (Oskar-Maria-Graf-Ring 20 ☎089 670 64 63 www.frauentreffpunkt-neuperlach.de Open Tu 11am-noon, Th 11am-noon, and by appointment).

- **INTERNET:** San Francisco Coffee Company has locations throughout the city. (Tal 15 www.sfcc.de *i* Free Wi-Fi with any purchase. Open M-F 7:30am-9pm, Sa 8am-10pm, Su 9am-8pm.) Coffee Fellows Cafe has an internet cafe and printers on the 2nd floor. (Schuetzenstr. 14 *i* Wi-Fi or computer use €1.50 per 30min.; €2.50 per hr. Free Wi-Fi 1hr. with any €5 purchase. Open M-F 7am-11:30pm, Sa-Su 8am-11:30pm).

- **POST OFFICE:** Hauptbahnhof Post Office. (Bahnhofpl. 1; www.deutschepost.de *i* The yellow building opposite the train station. Open M-F 8am-8pm, Sa 9am-4pm.)

- **POSTAL CODES:** Munich postal codes begin with 80 or 81. The Hauptbahnhof postal code is 80335.

Emergency

- **EMERGENCY NUMBERS:** ☎112. Police: ☎110. Ambulance: ☎089 19 222.

- **CRISIS LINES:** Frauennotruf Muenchen operates a rape crisis hotline. (Saarstr. 5 ☎089 76 37 37 www.frauennotrufmuenchen.de ✆ Available M-F 10am-midnight, Sa-Su 6pm-midnight.) Munich AIDS Help. (☎089 54 33 30.)

- **PHARMACIES:** (Bahnhofpl. 2 ☎089 59 98 90 40 www.hauptbahnhofapo.de *i* Exit the train station and take a right. ✆ Open M-F 7am-8pm, Sa 8am-8pm.)

- **HOSPITALS/MEDICAL SERVICES:** Klinikum Schwabing (Kölner Pl. 1 ☎089 30 680 www.klinikum-muenchen.de) and Red Cross Hospital Neuhausen (Nymphenburgerstr. 163 ☎089 12 78 97 90 www.swmbrk.de) both provide 24hr. emergency medical services.

Getting There

By Plane

Munich's international airport, Flughafen München (Nordalee 25 ☎089 975 00 www.munich-airport.de) is a 45min. train ride from the city center. Take S1 or S8 to Flughafen. (€9.80 on a Streifenkarte. ✆ Every 10-20min. 4am-1:30am). A cab ride to the airport from the city center cost €60.

By Train

Munich's central train station, München Hauptbahnhof (Hauptbahnhof 1 ☎089 130 81 05 55 www.hauptbahnhof-muenchen.de *i* S1, S2, S3, S4, S6, S7, S8, U1, U2, U4, or U5: Hauptbahnhof), has arrivals and departures to a host of European cities. Connected cities include **Berlin** (€120 ✆ 6hr., 2 per hr.); **Dresden** (€100 ✆ 6hr., 2 per hr.); **Frankfurt** (€91 ✆ 3hr., 2 per hr.); **Hamburg** (€129 ✆ 6hr., every hr.); **Köln** (€129 ✆ 5hr., 2 per hr.); **Amsterdam,**NHE (€150 ✆ 6hr., every 2hr.); **Paris,** FRA (€150 ✆ 6hr., every 2hr.); **Prague,** CZR (€60 ✆ 6hr., 2 per day.); **Zurich,** CHE. (€70 ✆ 4hr., 3 per day.) These prices are the official ones if you purchase the day of departure; you can often get heavy discounts (30-40%) by buying a ticket between three months and three days in advance.

Getting Around

By Deutsche Bahn

The S-Bahn is under the operation of the Deutsche Bahn (DB) network, which means that Eurail, InterRail, and German rail passes are all valid. Before beginning your journey, validate your ticket by getting it stamped in the blue boxes. DB officers often check for validation, and those without properly validated tickets are charged a heft €40 fine. The S-Bahn generally runs between 3:30am and 1:30am.

By Public Transportation

The U-Bahn, trams, and buses are all part of the city's MVV network (☎089 41 42 43 44 www.mvvv-muenchen.de) and require separate ticket purchases. Pick up maps at the tourist office or at the MVV Infopoint office in the Hauptbahnhof. Transportation schedules vary, but the U-Bahn opens around 4:30am and closes around 1am during the week (2am on weekends). Nachtlinien (night trams) run every 30min. and cover most of the city. Tickets come in multiple forms based on how far you're traveling and how long the pass is valid. The simplest form is the single Einzelfahrkarte (€2.50), which is good for 2hr. for a trip in one direction. All other trips depend on the distance, for which the Munich area is split into 16 different zones of concentric circles around the city center. For short trips (within the same zone), get a Kurzstrecke (€1.20). For multiple rides, buy a Streifenkarte (stripe ticket; €12), which usually comes with 10 stripes. The zones are further grouped into four different colors (white, yellow, green, and red), for which you can get one-day or three-day passes. For the most part, tourists will stay within the white zone, for which a one-day pass costs €5.40 and a three-day €13.30. Partner tickets can save you money if you're traveling in a group. There are several cards available:

- **ISARCARDS:** An IsarCard is a week- or month-long pass that can be even cheaper than the three-day pass. One-week passes cost €12.30-17.60, depending on whether you pick two, three, or four zones. IsarCards, however, are only valid during the week or the month proper (e.g., a weekly pass will only work from Su to Su, and 1-month passes work for specific months), so plan accordingly.

- **CITY TOUR CARDS:** This card gets you transportation, along with some tiny discounts to attractions in Munich. That said, these attractions are not always the most popular ones in town. The City Tour card probably isn't worth it if you're not getting the partner ticket.

- **BAYERN TICKET:** The Bayern Ticket gets you access to any public transportation within Bavaria for an entire day. (€21. ⏰ Valid M-F 9am-3am, Sa-Su midnight-3am.) The ticket also covers neighboring cities, including Ulm and Salzburg, making it perfect for day trips. The greatest savings can be achieved by getting a group Bayern Ticket, which covers up to five people for just €29.

By Taxi

Taxi-München-Zentrale (☎089 216 10 or ☎089 19 410 www.taxizentrale-muenchen. de) is a large taxi stand just outside the Hauptbahnhof. Taxi stands are located all around the city. The pricing algorithm is complicated, but there is a flat fee of €3.30, and shorter distances generally cost €1.70 per km.

By Bike

Munich is extremely bike-friendly. There are paths on nearly every street, and many locals use bikes as their primary mode of transportation. Renting a bike can be a great way to see a lot of the city in just a few days. Remember to stay within the bike lanes and that many lanes are one-way.

germany essentials

MONEY

Tipping

Service staff are paid by the hour, and a service charge is included in an item's unit price. Cheap customers typically just round up to the nearest whole euro, but it's customary and polite to tip 5-10% if you are satisfied with the service. If the service was poor, you don't have to tip at all. To tip, mention the total to your waiter while paying. If he states that the bill is €20, respond "€22," and he will include the tip. Do not leave the tip on the table; hand it directly to the server. It is standard to tip a taxi driver at least €1, housekeepers €1-2 a day, bellhops €1 per piece of luggage, and public toilet attendants around €0.50.

Taxes

Most goods in Germany are subject to a value added tax—or mehrwertsteuer (MwSt)—of 19%, which is included in the purchase price of goods (a reduced tax of 7% is applied to books and magazines, food, and agricultural products). Non-EU visitors who are taking these goods home unused may be refunded this tax for purchases totaling over €25 per store. When making purchases, request a MwSt form and present it at a Tax Free Shopping Office, found at most airports, road borders, and ferry stations, or by mail. Refunds must be claimed within six months. For more information, contact the German VAT refund hotline (☎0228 406 2880 www.bzst.de).

SAFETY AND HEALTH

Local Laws and Police

Certain regulations might seem harsh and unusual (practice some self-control city-slickers, jaywalking is €5 fine), but abide by all local laws while in Germany; your embassy will not necessarily get you off the hook.

Drugs and Alcohol

The drinking age in Germany is 16 for beer and wine and 18 for spirits. The maximum blood alcohol content level for drivers is 0.05%. Avoid public drunkenness; it can jeopardize your safety and earn the disdain of locals.

Needless to say, illegal drugs are best avoided. While possession of marijuana or hashish is illegal, possession of small quantities for personal consumption is decriminalized in Germany. Each region has interpreted "small quantities" differently (anywhere from 5 to 30 grams). Carrying drugs across an international border—drug trafficking—is a serious offense that could land you in prison.

Prescription Drugs

Common drugs such as aspirin (Kopfschmerztablette or Aspirin), acetaminophen or Tylenol (Paracetamol), ibuprofen or Advil, antihistamines (Antihistaminika), and penicillin (Penizillin) are available at German pharmacies. Some drugs—like pseudoephedrine (Sudafed) and diphenhydramine (Benadryl)—are not available in Germany, or are only available with a prescription, so plan accordingly.

germany

GREAT BRITAIN

What is the coolest country in the world? Everyone will have his or her own answer to this question—Hollywood wannabes will say America, sappy romantics will say France, and bold (possibly crazy) adventurers will say Nepal. But the answer just might be Britain. Name anything you love, and Britain has it. Music? The Beatles. The arts? The Edinburgh Festival. Learning? Oxford and Cambridge. History? On every street corner. Sports? "Football." Literature? Shakespeare. Celebrity gossip? The royal family.

Britain has everything a traveler could want, and it's one of the most accessible countries in the world. There's no language barrier, the waiters aren't judging you, and everything is crammed into a convenient island-sized package. But don't think Britain is resting on its laurels. This country continually invents and inspires, as musicians create new beats, modern-art museums deliver mind-blowing spectacles, and boy wizards save the world. In 2012, the Olympic Games even came to London for a record third time. Whether you spend your trip touring all of London's free museums or curled up in front of the BBC with a cuppa, you'll be experiencing British culture at its best. Forget about Nepal, get over France, and bid good day to the USA, because Britain is where it's at.

greatest hits

- **GOOD WILL PUNTING.** Need a break from all the colleges at Cambridge University? Rent a punt from **Scudamore's** (p. 411) and cruise down the River Cam.

- **GO ASK ALICE.** Visit **Christ Church College** (p. 400) in Oxford to see where Lewis Carroll first met the real Alice, before she headed off to Wonderland.

- **DRINKING WHISKEY AND RYE.** You'll have to shell out for a pricier ticket to get more than one sample, but visit the **Scotch Whiskey Experience** (p. 417) to get a healthy dose of Alcohol 101.

GREAT BRITAIN

SHETLAND ISLANDS
Lerwick

N LG

0   100 kilometers
0   100 miles

ORKNEY ISLANDS
Stromness
Kirkwall

Thurso

Lewis

OUTER HEBRIDES

Ullapool

Uig
The Uists
Skye

Inverness

Aberdeen

INNER HEBRIDES

Fort William

Mull
Oban

S C O T L A N D

St. Andrews

Glasgow   Edinburgh

Arran

N O R T H E R N I R E L A N D

Dumfries

Stranraer   Newcastle-upon-Tyne

Belfast

Carlisle   Durham

Isle of Man   Douglas

I S L E O F M A N

I R E L A N D

York

Isle of Anglesey   Manchester   Leeds

Liverpool

Bangor   Chester   Sheffield

Llangollen   Lincoln
Nottingham

E N G L A N D   King's Lynn

Aberystwyth   Birmingham   Norwich

Stratford-upon-Avon   Cambridge

Fishguard   **W A L E S**

Cheltenham

Pembroke   Swansea   Cardiff   Oxford   **LONDON**

Bristol   Bath   Canterbury

Salisbury   Dover

Portsmouth   Brighton

Exeter   *Isle of Wight*

Plymouth

Penzance

Channel Islands

F R A N C E

london

A screaming comes across the sky: the sound you make, realizing, as jet plummets into unfussed sprawl of the Big Smoke, you don't have a clue what to expect now the anticipation's frenzy rushes in past your continent, the ocean, its transitioning air, the unfamiliar molecules scattering and Europe's gravitational tug—tweed and tea? pubs, prowling flanges of wanton party bros pirouetting madly within the wee English night? the perpetual loosing of the river around and again around the land's fang? walking, grayscale, along the cement and loaded sky, to library, museum, cathedral, across a churchyard, the wet fingers of British rain flexing along the pavement like the living roots? towers and apartments this blond brick, this food that tastes like blond brick? the handsome strangers of the open road, the secret, sacred cross-pollination of two souls in stuffed isolation? then the wintry gush of Death's own parted lips, beckoning, lingering in the lap of July?

Well, stop yelling, dude. We wrote this book for you.

London (see above) is busy. Each of its 32 boroughs have distinctive characters and are themselves filled with distinctive characters, making the so-called city feel more like a conglomerate of neighborhoods and villages. The feisty independence and unceasing currents in and around each haul the London "buzz" in a new direction every few years, with the city's epicenter for groovy scenes and freaky happenings constantly on the move—previously disregarded neighborhoods are always on the verge of bursting into prominence.

There are, of course, many mainstays as well, and even the top sights' resigned touristiness is navigable if you know how and where to get in line, pay less, cut corners, avoid clichés, and, broadly, live it up. Every day in London brings something new, so finish your pint and Lets Go!

ACCOMMODATIONS

City of London

YHA LONDON ST. PAUL'S
HOSTEL $$

36 Carter Ln.   ☎01629 592 700 www.yha.org.uk/hostel/london-st-pauls

Less a hostel, more a self-contained summer camp, this massive accommodation features more than 200 beds, a restaurant/bar for mom and pop, and a prime location around the corner from its namesake, God's favorite hang. As such, its appeal is largely to families and travel groups, though YHA pledges its hospitality to all ages of traveler. If you don't mind (or would prefer, though that's a little weird) kicking it amid kidcies, book well in advance for a terrific deal.

i Dorms £17-25. ☼ Reception 24hr.

THE FOX AND THE ANCHOR
HOTEL $$$

115 Charterhouse St.   ☎020 7250 1300 www.foxandanchor.com

The well-worn grubby pub/afterthought hotel combo is thrown on its miserly ass here. "Luxury" is the key word, followed closely by "foxy," though "anchor" ranks near the bottom of the list. Let's Go is not sure what the anchor is emblematic of. Certainly not the wall-mounted flatscreen TV or Egyptian linen; perhaps the sinking feeling in our stomachs as we spent £200 per night—but the bed is so cozy and the pub food so yummy, yet, again, curiously un-nautical, theme-wise.

i Rooms £200.

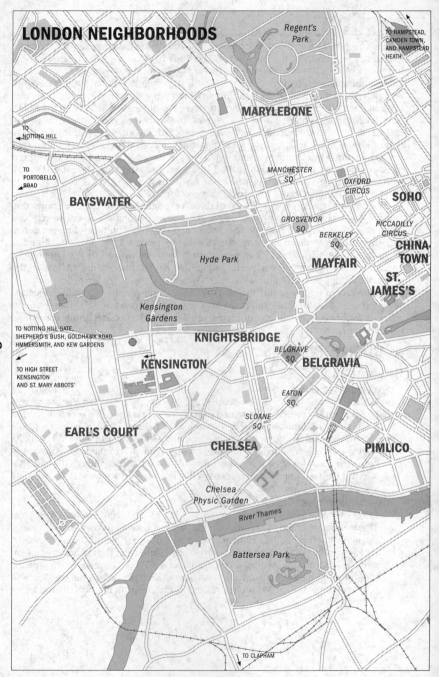

LONDON NEIGHBORHOODS

Regent's Park

TO HAMPSTEAD,
CAMDEN TOWN,
AND HAMPSTEAD
HEATH

MARYLEBONE

TO
NOTTING HILL

TO
PORTOBELLO
ROAD

MANCHESTER
SQ.

OXFORD
CIRCUS

SOHO

BAYSWATER

GROSVENOR
SQ.

PICCADILLY
CIRCUS

BERKELEY
SQ.

CHINA-
TOWN

Hyde Park

MAYFAIR

ST.
JAMES'S

Kensington
Gardens

TO NOTTING HILL GATE,
SHEPHERD'S BUSH, GOLDHAWK ROAD,
HMMERSMITH, AND KEW GARDENS

KNIGHTSBRIDGE

BELGRAVE
SQ.

BELGRAVIA

TO HIGH STREET
KENSINGTON
AND ST. MARY ABBOTS'

KENSINGTON

EATON
SQ.

SLOANE
SQ.

EARL'S COURT

CHELSEA

PIMLICO

Chelsea
Physic Garden

River Thames

Battersea Park

TO CLAPHAM

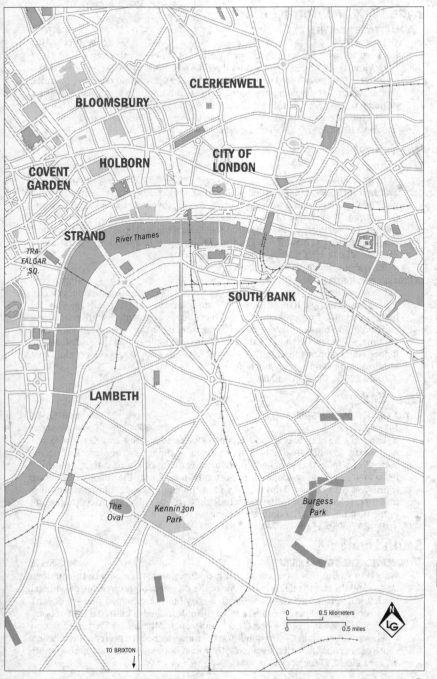

london

Hyde Park and Notting Hill

SMART HYDE PARK VIEW
HOSTEL $

16 Leinster Terr. ☎20 7402 4101

It's hard to say what exactly is supposed to be so cerebral about Smart Hyde Park View, but with clean, uncramped rooms (the beds in the larger ones are innovatively curtain-covered to afford extra privacy), you could certainly do much worse for a place to sleep. Just don't expect to bump into any Isaac Newtons, or much of anyone else, for that matter, as the pop-radio-booming lobby/bar and underutilized common room provide little in the way of social space.

i Dorms £16-24. Doubles £80-100. ☼ Reception 24hr.

Westminster

⬛ ASTOR VICTORIA
HOSTEL $$

71 Belgrave Rd. ☎020 7834 3077 www.astorhostels.com

This is a very good hostel: excellent location, gregarious staff who instantly call you "bro" and belt along with the lobby's Top 40, lovely bedrooms, and a strong friend vibe. There's less of an established clan—and less alcohol—here than at the Astor Hyde Park across town, but deep hangs can still be achieved if you puff out your touristy chest and make friends (however that works). More private than most hostels of its size, this is a very good deal.

i Dorms £20-27. ☼ Reception 24hr.

⬛ TRAVEL JOY HOSTELS
HOSTEL $$

111 Grosvenor Rd. ☎0207 834 9689 www.traveljoyhostels.com

Travel Joy is happy, happy, happy, and they want to do the same for you. Be happy, dammit: free breakfast in the morning is augmented with smoothies, pancakes, and omelets; free soda and juice from a bar that does good Thai food, anytime you want between 10am and 11pm; open-mic nights on Friday; movie nights', etc. What's the catch? You must give up your sooooooooooooul. Just kidding, there is no catch. Stay here.

i Dorms £25-30. ☼ Reception 24hr.

West End

YHA LONDON OXFORD STREET
HOSTEL $$

14 Noel St. ☎0800 0191 700 www.yha.org.uk

If London's hostels had a food chain—which, poor tasty traveler, we're not necessarily saying they don't—YHA would be at the apex. The variety of accessories here, including excellent kitchen, assortment of board games, colorfully festooned common space, and, importantly, location in the thick of London's touristiest district, are definitely aimed at the clan, though solo travelers may find themselves drawn to the menagerie; in terms of value for price, this is one of the best hostels in London. A hip hang it's not.

i Dorms £20-25. ☼ Reception 24hr.

South London

⬛ PUBLOVE @ THE STEAM ENGINE
HOSTEL $

Who is to say, in this futuristic age of machinery and space, where the publove begins and the steam engine ends? One of the very best of the growing pub/hostel market, this place is comfortable, with a cozy but not cramped feel—it doesn't skimp on the hostel part in order to favor the pub; indeed, it takes the best of both, with the pub itself, like the hostel reception, open 24hr. a day. That means food whenever you want it. Clean rooms, forthcoming staff, and a pretty good location south of Southbank, with transit close by, round out a very solid accommodation.

i Dorms £10-12. ☼ Reception 24hr.

Southbank

ST. CHRISTOPHER'S INNS - LONDON BRIDGE: THE VILLAGE
HOSTEL $

161-165 Borough High St. ☎020 7939 9710 www.st-christophers.co.uk

A stalwart of the London party-rocking scene, and singularly unabashed about its "Gonna Make You Lose Your Mind" intentions, The Village is the hostel equivalent of an LMFAO song. As underscored by the comparatively shrug-worthy common room, the venue's energy is dominated by the open-to-the-public karaoke bar downstairs, atop which is set a winding hallway of bedrooms and abandoned wine bottles. Accommodations are quite spacious, with even the cavernous 24-bed rooms affording some breathing room (if not a ton of privacy). Come here to smang or be smung.

i Dorms £17-20. 🕐 Reception 24hr.

THE WALRUS
HOSTEL $

172 Westminster Bridge Rd. ☎020 7928 4368

A funky little hostel perched atop a funky little pub in a funky little neighborhood. The sheer Englishness of this place (complete with framed Beatles artwork—we'll let you guess which song—presumably to offset, or augment, the mounting Funk Factor) will ceaselessly charm you. Do not be afeared of the fab overtures, though: the Funk halts at the hallway, with bathrooms and lodgings delightfully clean. Free Wi-Fi, lockers, padlocks, adapters, and towels, along with a good location and convenient Tube access, make this one of the best deals in town.

i Dorms £26-28. 🕐 Reception 7:30am-11:30pm.

Marylebone and Bloomsbury

CLINK 78
HOSTEL $

78 Kings Cross Rd.

In the era before the decision to just ship them all to Australia, England tried and imprisoned her criminals in two-for-one courthouse-jails like the one now converted into the popular hostel known as Clink 78. The theme has stuck around to cute effect—the TV and computer spaces, each a former courtroom, retain their bench, bar, jury box, and signposts for defendant and press, though we assume the plush padding has been added more recently. In the larger dorms, though, the tightly stacked bunks recall the building's original purpose with a little too much gusto. Of particular note is the basement's Clash Bar, where ubiquitous backpacker party bros shoot pool and pool their shots; DJs, karaoke, and beer pong are among the frequent diversions.

i Dorms £17-26. ☉ Reception 24hr.

CLINK 261 HOSTEL $

261-265 Grays Inn Rd.

Barless and several hundred beds smaller, Clink 261 is Clink 78's meeker little sister. Every night is movie night, with films chosen democratically by hostelgoers, and you're welcome to drink in the recently remodeled downstairs kitchen (open until 3am). Less exciting than the bigger Clink up the street, 216'll still meet your needs.

i Dorms £17-23. ☉ Reception 24hr.

ASTORS MUSEUM HOSTEL HOSTEL $

27 Montague St.

There are hostels that smell like feet and hostels that don't; Astors ["It's-Not-A"] Museum ["It's-A"] Hostel does not at all. Take that as a ringing endorsement of this homey hostel situated across the street from the British Museum. A few hostelgoers may be seen to chill their weary asses in the ground-floor TV lounge, watching British standup comics say British jokes in British accents. (It's very funny, Let's Go is informed.) Downstairs, the recently revamped kitchen is equipped for culinary sorcery, though you'll have to provide your own ingredients. Less rowdy than its cousins in the bar-hostel clan, though by extension also less communal, Astors offers a cheap, clean, classy place for trekkers to crash.

i Dorms £18-26. ☉ Reception 24hr.

South Kensington and Chelsea

ASTOR HYDE PARK HOSTEL $

191 Queen's Gate ☎020 7581 0103 www.astorhostels.com/our-hostels/hyde-park/

Your days of summer camp in a Victorian mansion a block from Hyde Park are over, but you can relive the glory days at this incredible hostel. True, Shauncy the Manservant won't be returning from his retirement in the Dutch Antilles, but the staff here are better anyway: gregarious, familial, and oozing international charm—many are backpackers themselves—they scrub bathrooms during the day and pubcrawl amongst you at night. Wi-Fi, padlocks, lockers, and (most importantly) the cozy vibe of a tight-knit community are all free.

i Dorms £18-24. ☉ Reception 24hr.

BARMY BADGER BACKPACKERS HOSTEL $

17 Longridge Rd. ☎020 7370 5213 www.barmybadger.com

A strong contender for the coveted Let's Go Most British Name Award, this homey hostel, run by the marmiest mum around and her faithful arthritic pooch, is also in the running for best accommodation in the area. Clean, spacious rooms make even the triple bunks comfortable (each level bedecked with hella memory foam and power outlet), and everything—from Wi-Fi to a personal locker and safe—is free except laundry. The drably upscale neighborhood's nothing to wave a weasel at hangout-wise, but the Earl's Court Tube stop is within spitting distance for a good-sized polecat.

i Dorms £25-27. ☉ Reception M-Sa 7:30am-5am, Su 9am-8pm.

ST. JAMES HOSTEL $

21-23 Longridge Rd. ☎074 5064 5573 www.saint-james-hostel.co.uk

Up the street from Barmy Badger, though lacking its neighbor's homey charm, St. James is a totally par-for-the-course nonparty backpacking destination. Its hallways clean to the point of pervasive Clorox odor, this hostel offers almost all the typical amenities—free Wi-Fi and morning breakfast as well as a well-

equipped, if subdued, common room (though there's no laundry). It has a convenient location close to the Earl's Court Tube stop, if not our heart.

i Dorms £15-22. Reception 24hr.

West London

MONKEYS IN THE TREES
HOSTEL $

49 Becklow Rd. ☎020 8749 9197 www.monkeysinthetrees.co.uk

The kitchen's first-aid kit expired in 2014, the Wi-Fi resets every half-hour, and
the wooden-frame bunks are cramped and cramping, but Monkeys in the Trees
has one significant ace in its hole: the people you'll meet here. Its distance from
central London means the backpackers who come here are getting set for the
longer haul, finding jobs, writing screenplays, and taking breaks from school,
making the downstairs pub a solid hang during the day. In terms of cozy, unique
community, it's second to none.

i Dorms £9.50-16.50. Check-in 2-11pm. Check-out noon.

ST. CHRISTOPHER'S INN SHEPHERD'S BUSH HOSTEL
HOSTEL $

13-15 Shepherd's Bush Green ☎020 8735 0270 www.st-christophers.co.uk

The St. Christopher's chain, in its attempt to corner the "cheap, sticky, 'n'
party-rockin'" market, gets one step closer with its Shepherd's Bush location.
The key differences here are the slighter number of rooms (only 19, with about
80 beds, making this less a party-rockin'-opolis than a party-rockin' parish), a
comfier common room festooned with pirouetting Blues Brothers statuettes,
and the location (next to the mall). Other than that, it's the same amenities you'll
find elsewhere: cozy beds, free Wi-Fi, and a downstairs pub that's definitely the
main reason everyone's there.

i Dorms £15.90-18.90. Reception 24hr.

East London

THE DICTIONARY HOSTEL
HOSTEL $$

20 Kingsland Rd. ☎207 613 2784 www.thedictionaryhostel.com

If you're a certain type of elaborate-facial-hair-sportin' bro or ripped-tights-
bleached-hair chicka, Shoreditch is where you're gonna want to be in London,
and The Dictionary is where you're gonna want to be within where you're gonna
want to be. Tube access isn't great, but you'll barely want to leave the neigh-
borhood—well-amenitied, pretty well-cleaned, and oozing vibe, The Dictionary
will make you feel like you never left Brooklyn(/Portland/Austin)—and all with
a helpful wall-size lobby map and directions about where to eat, drink, listen,
watch, and party in the here and now's happenin'est hood.

i Dorms £17-27. Reception 24hr.

THE BIRDS NEST
HOSTEL $

32 Deptford Church St. ☎020 8692 1928 www.thebirdsnestpub.com

Comfortable like your eccentric aunt's house, The Birds Nest pulls off a fairly
successful pub/music venue/hostel combo. Its location, a solid distance from
and without much in the way of access to central London, means that its main
occupants are residents and professional hopefuls, not sightseers. Accordingly,
you can only book stays here for a week at a time—though the per-night rate is
shockingly cheap. The lack of on-site laundry (not to mention the bedrooms,
cluttered with the belongings of longer-term inhabitants) might be a little too
funky for some, but if you don't mind a little funk, they'll give you the funk: free
live music goes 'til 11pm almost every night.

i Beds available only by the week. £55 per week.

london

North London

ST. CHRISTOPHER'S INN, CAMDEN
HOSTEL $$

48-50 Camden High St. ☎0208 600 7500 www.st-christophers.co.uk

Like the other St. Christopher's hostels, the Camden branch thrives on its conjoined Belushi's Bar, which is where the action takes place. Decor-wise it's the best in faux-artiness (like Camden itself), including motivate-you-to-travel wall slogans (like, guys—we're already here, you don't have to convince us) and a huge mural, inexplicably featuring American blues singer Robert Johnson alongside English mainstays Brian Jones and Amy Winehouse, which serves as a terrific metaphor for the St. Christopher's philosophy of "good times without thinking too hard."

i Dorms £18-20. ☾ Reception 24hr.

SIGHTS

City of London

ST. PAUL'S CATHEDRAL
CHURCH

St Paul's Churchyard ☎0207 246 8350 www.stpauls.co.uk

Sweet Christ of the Hay and Reaper, this is one of the few A-listers in London where our parsimonious Let's Go penny-pinchers have to admit the elaborate site is worth the elaborate price: the interior combines the best of London's museums, churches, towers, and pretty buildings, with every angle of sight, facing in, out, or up, worthy of long-standing contemplation. That the grounds have been churchland for nearly 1500 years comes across in the myriad styles and forms, from Henry Moore's futuristic neo-sculpture *Mother and Child* to the frankly terrifying Greek-style statues of British war heroes (of which there are many—aside from, you know, Jesus, the ground floor's perimeter mostly evokes commanders of military campaigns who met unfortunate ends at the hands of commanders of other military campaigns). There's an equally all-star cast memorialized in the crypt, including the cathedral's architect, Christopher Wren, visionary poet/artist William Blake, and, our favorite, Sir Arthur Sullivan, musical partner to comic lyricist W. S. Gilbert. Midway up the inner dome (there are a bunch, we're told, a bit over-proudly) is the Whispering Gallery, where it's very rude to shout, and for one of the city's best views, keep walking upstairs (and keep walking, and keep walking). A pretty sweet audioguide is covered in your ticket fee—curmudgeonly as we are re: electronics in the House of God, we suggest you make good use of it.

i *£18, online tickets £15.50. Students £16, online tickets £13.50. ☉ Open M-Sa 8:30am-4:30pm.*

COURTAULD GALLERY
MUSEUM

Strand   ☎020 7848 2526 www.courtauld.ac.uk/gallery

The Courtauld Gallery shares the National Gallery's predilections for historical Christian art and well-known Impressionists and is free for students, but the similarities end there: forgoing the bustle of London's more popular museums, this is one of the best and most underrated collections in the area. Set in cool stone within the magnificent Somerset House, its spiral staircases lead to a few quiet rooms of fantastic beauty. You'll be glad you came.

i *£7, students free. ☉ Open daily 10am-6pm.*

THE TEMPLE
CHURCH

2 King's Bench Walk   ☎020 7353 8559 www.templechurch.com

Interestingly enough, Dan Brown wasn't the first author to feature this formerly obscure church complex in the climactic scene of a European thriller named for the secret messages of a famous Renaissance artist—our own *The Michelangelo Cipher* beat him to the punch by about four months. Not that we care or anything. We are legally obliged to assert that the Knights Templar, who founded the original church in 1185, have since "disbanded." Nowadays the Temple is a combination of law offices, gardens, ancient churchspace, and soaring ceilings—an unholy blend of divine allure and savvy management that explains the church's recent adoption of a £5 ticket fee. Check online before you go, as the opening hours fluctuate with what seems like almost deliberate wildness.

i *£5, unless you just want to pray, in which case it's free. But do you really want to tempt a wrathful Lord? ☉ Hours often vary, so check the website for the most up-to-date schedule.*

TOWER BRIDGE
BRIDGE

Tower Bridge Rd.   ☎020 7403 3761 www.towerbridge.org.uk

If missed your chance to order service from our on-call Let's Go Bridge Mechanics Correspondent, you'll have to make do with this engaging exhibit perched atop one of London's more out-of-the-way river crossings. The bridge's history is explored in several installments, some with flashy animation and some a little more old-school, all of which gives way to the vertigo-inducing glass floor. For best results, plan your visit to coincide with a bridge lift, the times for which are listed on the website. Furthermore, tickets cross over that indefinable line between too expensive and within reason if you purchase them online.

i *£9, students £6.30. ☉ Open daily Apr-Sept 10am-5:30pm; Oct-Mar 9:30am-5pm.*

TOWER OF LONDON
CASTLE

        ☎844 482 7777 www.hrp.org.uk/TowerOfLondon

Legend has it that if you wait until deep into the blackest night, you may hear issuing forth from high atop the hoariest parapet a ghastly choir of tortured voices—the song of the many tourists fooled into spending nearly £20 to get into this old-ass castle. (Don't be tricked by the name—there is definitely more than one tower going on here, each with a distinct history, which we'll save you the aforementioned fee and summarize forthwith: the oldest pylon, White Tower, was built by William the Conqueror; the Bloody Tower is where the least fun king in English history, Richard III, killed off his competitors, Edward V and his brother ["Li'l"] Richard, possibly proceeding to stuff their bodies in a closet; the Wakefield Tower is allegedly infested with mythologically significant crows; and the Jewel House, interestingly, houses the jewels.) All in all, if you're very keen on masonry, lapidary, or the strange, slightly sexual tension arising from standoffs with ubiquitous beefeaters, make this a high priority.

i £24.50, online ticket £23.10; students £18.70, online ticket £17.70. ⏰ Open Mar-Oct M 10am-5:30pm, Tu-Sa 9am-5:30pm, Su 10am-5:30pm; Nov-Feb M 10am-4:30pm, Tu-Sa 9am-4:30pm, Su 10am-4:30pm.

MUSEUM OF LONDON
MUSEUM

150 London Wall   ☎020 7001 9844 www.museumoflondon.org.uk/london-wall

This oddly catch-all museum isn't exactly boring, covering a solid 10,000 years of area history, but for all its Roman burial pits, 18th-century pox-ridden longhorn cattle skulls, weirdly "middle school video book report"-esque clips of ancient terrain and gladiatorial fistfights, and ubiquitous references to the Thames as a "sacred stream," it's not altogether that exciting, either. Let's Go enjoys dioramas explaining the Black Plague, Great Fire, execution of Charles I, and reinstatement of Charles II like 10 years later (the populace was having trouble making up its mind at that point) as much as the next student budget travel guide, but for all the wealth of information represented here, it could do with some paring down and reorganization. Totally free, so there's that—best to come here, hit a few highlights, and be on your way without delving too deep into the geological past. Though that rocks too.

i Free. ⏰ Open daily 10am-6pm.

Hyde Park and Notting Hill

HYDE PARK
PARK

It's big and it's a park. Got it. Bigger and more jungley than the majestic Regent's Park to the north, Hyde Park consists of miles of tangled pathways meandering through small forests, along water features, and across enchanted prairies, though it should be noted that all trails inexorably lead into the dens of malevolent gremlins. We recommend the spaces least-overrun with faeries and other sprites, such as the Kensington Gardens, which is strictly flowers and statuettes, and the Round Lake, from which all merfolk were peaceably eradicated beginning in the 1950s. The whole park is bisected vertically by West Carriage Dr. (technically, everything west of this is Kensington Gardens, though you'd never know and we suspect this is just the Brits having a laugh at us again), which runs parallel to the picturesque and boat-friendly Long Water. There are no herons, and the utter lack of reed vegetation makes this an unlikely site for the future settlement of herons.

i Free. ⏰ Open 5am-midnight.

SPEAKERS' CORNER
LANDMARK

Hyde Park

"Komrades!" hissed the Voice of Insurrection as Let's Go approached the northeast corner of Hyde Park. "The blood of our revolution was for naught. Hark my doomful tale!" As explained to us, Let's Go discovered London's strongest bastion of free public discourse to be the site of aggressive cyclists and an even more aggressive pair of 15-year-old co-fondlers. Where the likes of Marx, Lenin, and Orwell once pontificated, glazed-over tourists now stare into smartphones. "Blood alone moves the wheels of history!" wheezed the Voice. "Also, don't forget to visit the Speaker's Corner Café for an assortment of espresso and pastries before you go!"

i Free. ⏰ Open 5am-midnight.

West End

NATIONAL GALLERY
Trafalgar Sq.
MUSEUM
☎020 7747 2885 www.nationalgallery.org.uk

Christ may have only wept twice, but here, you can relive those moments hundreds of times—if the contents seem surprisingly Jesus-y, bear in mind that the collection mostly spans the centuries when there wasn't much else to paint, and that to do so was to beg for allegations of witchery. To balance out the assorted diptychs, panels, nativity scenes, and frescos of the Lord and his chums sprawled on outcroppings, the wide-ranging collection includes an engaging array of pagan sex rites and antiquated divine assault. The elusive wing of Very Famous Impressionists deserves a whole visit to itself.

i Free. ◘ Open M-Th 10am-6pm, F 10am-9pm, Sa-Su 10am-6pm.

TRAFALGAR SQUARE
SQUARE

Let's Go is impressed by the gumption of our home country, which direct-mailed a statue of George "Let's Kick Some Redcoat Ass" Washington to the British government in 1924, which, sighing and shaking their heads, installed him along the back edge of Trafalgar Sq. a few years later. The rest of the square is less passive-aggressive, featuring a variety of fountains, stone beasts, tourists, and street entertainers, the latest generation of whom seem to have gained powers of levitation through selective inbreeding and/or Force-awareness. The corners of the park are decorated with four "plinths," three of which bear statues of famous British men, while the northwesternmost plinth features a changing exhibition spotlighting contemporary sculptors, which (sort of) explains the skeletal were-dog currently presiding from the column, gazing impassively, its eyeless stare frozen as Death's.

i Free. ◘ Open 24hr.

NATIONAL PORTRAIT GALLERY
St. Martin's Pl.
MUSEUM
☎20 7306 0055 www.npg.org.uk

We know, we know: this is not the most compelling museum. Almost entirely devoted to illustrations of centuries-old British aristocrats you've never heard of, this gallery's central location and free admission make it worth a quick stop early in your trip—you can blaze through the interesting parts (the oldest portraits, circa 1200s, and the newest, circa 1960s-present) in 45min. or less, and you'll pick up a little Albion history through osmosis while you're at it. Keep an eye out for the hidden gem, a grandly disinterested description of the American Revolution next to some familiar-looking former Brits.

i Free. ◘ Open M-W 10am-6pm, Th-F 10am-9pm, Sa-Su 10am-6pm.

ST. MARTIN-IN-THE-FIELDS
Trafalgar Sq.
CHURCH
☎020 7766 1100 www.stmartin-in-the-fields.org

OK, sure, ancient Anglican church with beautiful internal stone- and glasswork, sanctuary of regal tranquility, an intriguing loop of underlying tombs purportedly built on the site of pre-Christian (i.e., devil-related?) ceremonies just a couple steps off the main hubbub of Trafalgar Sq.—but honestly, the most practical reason you should keep this place in the back of your mind is that its subterranean bathroom is the cleanest and most convenient in the area. Call us crass, but that's important to know. Check the website for upcoming performances, or just wander on over for some quiet—it's the kind of place where you can spend five minutes or two hours. (The crypts are not extensive, especially compared to the adjoining Crypt Café and gift shop.)

i Free. ◘ Open M-Tu 8:30am-1pm and 2-6pm, W 8:30am-1:15pm and 2-5pm, Th 8.30am-1pm and 2-6pm, F 8:30am-1pm and 2-6pm, Sa 9:30am-6pm, Su 3:30-5pm.

great britain

Westminster

WESTMINSTER ABBEY
CHURCH

20 Dean's Yard

☎020 7222 5152 www.westminster-abbey.org

We've been hoping for a spectacularly God-tier throwdown between this and St. Paul's Cathedral for a long time (imagine the breakdowns: St. Paul's claims the Magnificence of Vaulted Ceilings round, Westminster comes storming back in the Memorials, Effigies, and Burials category, then wins the Pomp & Circumstance and Proximity to Large Bell contests, but St. Paul's retaliates with some brutal moves in the Just Sheer View inning, takes the Quietude Bonus, and is poised for victory before Westminster gets scrappy and manages a bloody draw in the final History of Knights matchup) but so far, neither has shown an inclination to do anything but be stately churches.

More Gothic than its crosstown rival, Westminster Abbey was built in the 11th century by Edward the Confessor, whose resplendent tomb is featured alongside countless sepulchers of fellow English royalty. Bedecked accordingly, the whole abbey drips tradition. Its welcoming layout, free audio tour, and all-star cast of memorials encourage you to weave in and out of the history without knocking anything over. (Don't be fooled by the Poet's Corner, though—a few greats, like Chaucer and Dickens, are buried here, but 90% of the busts and inscriptions are for writers whose remains lie elsewhere.) And it's not just a tourist trap—Westminster Abbey is still a place of worship: its hourly intercom-broadcasted prayers are introduced with messages of welcome to sightseers and pilgrims alike. You can skip the pricier daytime and come to a free Evensong instead.

i £20, students £17. ☾ Open M-Tu 9:30am-3:30pm, W 9:30am-6pm, Th-Sa 9:30am-3:30pm.

CHURCHILL MUSEUM/CABINET WAR ROOMS
MUSEUM

King Charles St.

☎020 7930 6961 www.iwm.org.uk

If you're like Let's Go—and good gracious, are we relying on that to sell these books—there's a small but vocal part of you still disappointed you never got to kick Hitler's ass. While only dreams can satisfy your deepest caprices, the adjoined Churchill Museum and Cabinet War Rooms are the next-closest you'll get. Used as the British strategic headquarters beginning in 1939, the current installations do an incredible job of blending the contemporary with the retrospective, including wartime memorabilia and recordings, and a preserved Map Room at the museums' heart; the Churchill wing explores the man with microscopic focus (all the better for clueless Americans who think FDR won the war. Pfah! we say).

i £16.35, students £14.40. ☾ Open daily 9:30am-6pm.

HOUSES OF PARLIAMENT
HISTORIC SITE

Parliament Sq.

☎20 7219 3000 www.parliament.uk

Man, didn't we fight a war with these guys so we didn't have to deal with their government anymore? In the years since the American Revolution (in Britain, the "IDGAF We Still Have Canada Conflict"), the singularly English balance between the elite and the salt of the earth has shifted again and again, from monarchs and ministers to Lords and Commons to the current proportionally elected three parties. Parliament has been at the core of every step along this grand democratic experiment, and its layout—a thoroughly modern administration housed within an extraordinarily ornate edifice—demonstrates the best of modernity and history. To get your gummint on, we recommend attending a debate, committee meeting or Question Time (though, as an non-UK citizen, you get bottom priority for tickets). Tours are also available but, again, aren't aimed

abbey road studios

While it's easy to get caught up in the mindless thrill of cat-and-mouse, many of the clueless tourists haphazardly dodging pissed-off drivers miss the real significance of Abbey Road—the studio itself. While still a functioning recording workspace and therefore not open to the public, Abbey Road Studios (or, as it was known before the iconic album cover catapulted it to global fame, EMI Studios) is, of course, best-known for being the site where The Beatles produced virtually all of their songs. In fact, the studio was briefly a kind of mecca for cosmic musical freaks, with the Fab Four's psychedelic peers, including Pink Floyd, The Zombies, and The Hollies, recording a cluster of significant albums in the 1960s. So, yes, click a quick pic before traffic kicks your dick, but Let's Go encourages you to blow your mind in other ways, too: bring your iPod and DJ your own summer of love.

at foreigners, who can only attend when Parliament isn't in session on Saturdays or over the summer. (What are they hiding?)

i *Tours available on Saturdays or on weekdays when Parliament is on recess. Check the website for more visiting and booking information. Audio tours £18, students £15.50. Guided tours £25, students £20.*

BUCKINGHAM PALACE
PALACE

☎020 7766 7300 www.royalcollection.org.uk

Dang. Queens have it made. Surrounded by guards (some with sweet hats, some AK-47s), brimming with porcelain, furniture, paintings, and miscellaneous treasure, and comprising a variety of stables and regal tearooms, Buckingham Palace is the place to be, especially if you are royalty and get to live here. Everyone else will have to make do with the attractions: the vivaciously decorated State Rooms, where the Queen hosts formal events; the Royal Mews, where horses (not Pokémon) and associated carriages are kept; and the Queen's Gallery, where the treasure—from photos of the first Antarctic expeditions to original da Vincis—is. Out front is where the famous Changing of the Guard ceremony takes place, albeit at a distance—arrive before 11:30am to get a good spot for viewing the 40min. spectacle, and as with everything else in London, the weekends are busiest, so we recommend the less-crowded middle of the week.

i *Combined ticket for the State Rooms, Buckingham Palace, the Queen's Gallery, and the Royal Mews £35.60, students £32.50. ☼ Open daily Jul-Aug 9:30am-7:30pm; Sept 9:30am-6:30pm. Hours vary monthly, so check website for most up-to-date schedule.*

BIG BEN
LANDMARK

While we hate to have to correct the pedants who insist that "Big Ben" refers not to the tower or clock on the north end of Parliament, but the 8ft., 13½-ton bell inside it—our Let's Go Temporal Mechanics Correspondent has recently unearthed evidence that "Big Ben" refers to the 600-year-old man whose godforsaken task it is to ring said chime every 15min. (the ironic thing being measuring in at only 6'1", Ben is by modern standards no longer the giant he once was).

i *Tours only open to UK residents.*

South London

SOUTH LONDON GALLERY
MUSEUM

65-67 Peckham Rd. ☎020 7703 6120 www.southlondongallery.org

Sprawling galleries like the Tate Modern force time-sensitive visitors to flit indecisively between their thousands of masterpieces as the perennially undiscovered ghost beckons from the next room. The more modestly ambitious South

London Gallery, by contrast, with its couple of installation pieces, practically begs unhurried stretches of meditation from languid viewers. Remarkably casual and inviting, you may be your only company during your visit, which makes the immersive experience so much the better. Complete with lovely adjoining cafe and niche shop, this is a must for the open-minded.

i *Free. 🕐 Open Tu 11am-6pm, W 11am-9pm, Th-Su 11am-6pm; closed Mondays.*

Southbank

▓ TATE MODERN   MUSEUM
Bankside   ☎020 7887 8888 www.tate.org.uk

Millennia later, galactic historians still wonder at the year 2115: the onset of humanity's pure symbiosis with machine, their subsequent colonization of the Milky Way's western spiral arm, and the rapid spiritual evolution of these motorized demigods as they became one with the very fabric of the cosmos. They needn't speculate; indicators of coming transcendence were right before our eyes at the Tate Modern. Freaky dreamscapes, distorted nudes, fleetingly recognizable industrial structures, and some of the biggest names in 20th-century art are all here, totally for free. If you don't "get" modern art—screw you, for one—go anyway; everyone could use some time spent in quiet reflection at this temple to the playful, fantastic, and nightmarish.

i *Free. 🕐 Open daily 10am-6pm.*

▓ IMPERIAL WAR MUSEUM   MUSEUM
Lambeth Rd.   ☎020 7416 5000 www.iwm.org.uk

At the other end of the spectrum is the brutally real Imperial War Museum. Its five floors contain artifacts spanning more than a century's worth of conflict, including World War II-era machinery, wreckage from the Twin Towers, and exhibitions of anti-war protest art. Deeply moving without descending to moralization, this is one of the most underrated museums in London.

i *Free. 🕐 Open daily 10am-6pm (last entry 5:30pm).*

SHAKESPEARE'S GLOBE   THEATER
21 New Globe Walk   ☎020 7902 1400 www.shakespearesglobe.com

All the world's a stage, but this playhouse arguably a little more so. The original Globe Theatre burned to the ground in 1613—something involving cannon fire and a thatched roof—but was rebuilt twice, once the following year and once more in 1997. Though the tour guides and subterranean exhibition space are cool, you'll enjoy seeing a real play even more, and feel marginally less touristy besides. (Standing tickets are only £5 and totally worth it.)

i *Tickets for performances vary but standing tickets are typically £5. Tickets for exhibition and tour £13.50, students £11. 🕐 Exhibition open daily 9am-5:30pm. Tours leave every 30min. M 9am-5pm, Tu-Sa 9:30am-12:30pm, Su 9:30am-11:30am.*

DESIGN MUSEUM   MUSEUM
28 Shad Thames   ☎020 7403 6933 www.designmuseum.org

Things look good here. Rotating exhibits feature beautiful examples of the ubiquitous (when we were there, an entire floor of designer shoes) and ubiquitous examples of the beautiful (a room of furniture arranged just so). But the real gem is the Design of the Year awards, in which mind-boggling innovations, from ocean cleanup infrastructure to rebooted feminist magazines to the next inexorable step toward the manufacture of our robot to-be overlords, are displayed in the top floor gallery. Prices are a little steep, but if you like pretty, they got pretty. (Sketchbooks encouraged.)

i *Note: relocating to the former Commonwealth Institute Building in Kensington in 2016. £13, students £9.75. 🕐 Open daily 10am-5:45pm (last entry 5:15pm).*

london

Marylebone and Bloomsbury

BRITISH MUSEUM
Great Russell St.

MUSEUM
☎20 7323 8299 www.britishmuseum.org

The jaw-dropping scale of the British Museum will be impressed upon you from the instant you enter. A Euclideanly weird checkered-glass ceiling ripples above the yawning marble interior, the whole dazzling rotunda raising an unsubtle middle finger to the faraway and Euclideanly pretty straightforward Louvre, whose checkered-glass triangles are comparatively tiny. (Unfazed, the Louvre rolls its eyes and lights a cig.)

Seen one way, the British Museum is a jarring reminder of the colonialist agenda that ransacked the globe for hundreds of years. Seen another, this is where all gods and men come to prove their mettle or die. The museum pits the best against the best in one beautiful, badass building: here are the primo depictions of ancient Mesopotamian military strategists, the best busts of early Buddhist transcendental beings, the cream of the crop of Cyprian messenger deities, the top Athenian funeral adornments, and the finest mausoleum you'll ever see indoors on a Tuesday afternoon. The whole thing is totally free, though donation bins beseech you like Dickens indigents at seemingly every turn. ("Please, sah, a bit more for the imperialist regime?")

As if the standard collections' opulence weren't enough, the British Museum is bedecked with two cafes, bookshops, and rotating ticketed exhibitions. Friendly staff swarm to answer your queries. Finally, whatever your mission, Let's Go encourages you to learn as much as possible while you still can about the top floor's Egyptian Mystery Cults—you never know.

i Free. Suggested donation €5. Audio guides £5, students £4.50. Maps £2 suggested donation. ☒ Open M-Th 10am-5:30pm, F 10am-8:30pm, Sa-Su 10am-5:30pm.

REGENT'S PARK
Chester Rd.

PARK
☎300 061 2300

In the early 19th century, throngs of insufficiently damp Londoners found it impossible to further their acquaintance with the English rain. Alarmed at the prospect of so many citizens remaining so dry, the desperate Prince Regent turned to architect John Nash, whose park-shaped solution has been exposing the umbrella-less to the elements since 1835. It's a beautiful, sprawling scene: the middle section of the park is dotted with athletic fields ("pitches," Let's Go is informed), three children's playgrounds deliver significant frolicking potential, and the southwesterly boating lake has no confirmed deaths since 1867. A triumph both of sporting and shrubbery, 10,000 wildflowers bloom among the park's 50 beautiful acres, while, not to be outdone, royal gardeners have produced more than 30,000 roses in Queen Mary's Garden. (O, the hubris of Man!) There's also the London Zoo to the park's northern end, and not to be missed is the open-air theater, which hosts a wide array of performances (tickets: www.openairtheatre.com). The Regent's Park also offers a thoroughly satisfying array of herons.

i Free. ☒ Open daily 5am-9pm.

BRITISH LIBRARY
96 Euston Rd.

MUSEUM, LIBRARY
☎30 333 1144 www.bl.uk

Sure, Leonardo's notebook, Shakespeare's First Folio, and Handel's handwritten *Messiah* are impressive, but what really makes the British Library so fascinating are the gems hiding in plain sight—here, a 15th-century Italian astrological guide (Capricorn, and everyone else: beware diseased rats); there, the first collection of female biographies (though it's not exactly an antique treatise of feminism—the 104 subjects are represented by only 56 images, many of which the author unashamedly reuses); and there, the handwritten lyrics to early Beatles songs (from before their post-White Album phase in which Yoko instructed the entire fab quartet to scream incoherently).

The Sir John Ritblat (!) Gallery, home to all these treasures and much more, is wonderfully free and worthy of hours of perusal all on its own. Beyond the gallery's gilded confines, the rest of the British Library is basically a research facility, with hundreds of hunched scholars nestled among its six floors, engaging in whatever scholars do. (Fantasize about books and vengeance? Let's Go is not sure.) To access the reading rooms, you'll need two pieces of ID (one with signature, one with home address) and a nerd drive that goes above and beyond. The library also hosts various exhibitions, which, though lavish, can cost upward of £10. Our advice: Skip the exhibition, soak up the Ritblat Gallery's peerless wow factor, then sip espresso like an intellectual on the first-floor cafe.

i Free. Special exhibition prices vary. ☼ Open M-Th 9:30am-8pm, F 9:30am-6pm, Sa 9:30am-5pm, Su 11am-5pm.

South Kensington and Chelsea

VICTORIA AND ALBERT MUSEUM
MUSEUM
Cromwell Rd.   ☎020 7942 2000 www.vam.ac.uk

We understand: the British Museum's a tease. If you crawled away from its collections all hot and bothered, begging for release, it's time you turned yourself over to the V and A's loving embrace. This is as intimate as museums get, though it still covers a surprising breadth of cultures and times; wander betwixt massive sculptures of naked dudes carrying off wives as they see fit and just murdering the hell out of every Philistine, but stumble into the next room and you might find Middle Eastern ruggery or the clothing of South Asia. Upstairs, there's a huge room where you can familiarize yourself with Raphael's cartooning phase. If you try you just might get what you need.

i Free. Special exhibit prices vary. ☼ Open M-Th 10am-5:45pm, F 10am-10pm, Sa-Su 10am-5:45pm.

NATURAL HISTORY MUSEUM
MUSEUM
Cromwell Rd.   ☎020 7942 5000 www.nhm.ac.uk

Though pitched at wide-eyed kids more than sexually frustrated 20-somethings (oh, how we know our readership), the Natural History Museum has one trump card: dinosaurs were raw as hell. ROAWRRWHRHGHHG. Laid out in a sprawl of color-coded zones so you can hone in on a particular pursuit—"Volcanoes and Earthquakes"; "Fishes, Amphibians and Reptiles" (though not "Oxford Commas")—it's worth a peek regardless of your age. Try not to spend too much on stegosauruses in the gift shop.

i Free. Special exhibit prices vary. ☼ Open daily 10am-4:50pm (last entry 4:30pm).

SAATCHI GALLERY
MUSEUM
Duke Of York's HQ, King's Rd.   ☎020 7811 3070 www.saatchigallery.com

When Let's Go visited this spiffy gallery, there were thousands of gleaming watches on display. (We kept expecting the staff to all start laughing, pull down a curtain, and go "Just kidding! Here's the real art gallery!" But it was all just watches. Everywhere we looked, more watches. Spooky effing watches.) You never know for sure what you'll find at Saatchi, unless you check its website or whatever; overflowing with helpful, snappily dressed staff, it's the best free modern gallery in the area.

i Free. ☼ Open daily 10am-6pm (last entry 5:30pm).

CHELSEA PHYSIC GARDEN
GARDEN
66 Royal Hospital Rd.   ☎020 7352 5646 www.chelseaphysicgarden.co.uk

Definitely the Physic Garden, and not the Psychic Garden, this is where you can come to see all manner of plants used in medicine, not mind-control. Founded in

portabello road

This charming street fronts shitty tourist shops at its southern end before a gradual northwesterly slope transforms it into a valley of paradise for the vintage shopper, bar crawler, or coffee fiend. Say a fervent prayer against temptation before embarking, as enticements—from Belgian waffles to made-before-your-eyes crepes, from secondhand clothing to umpteenth-hand soul records—will do their best to seduce you from all sides. (Some of it's cheap, some of it's not.) It's not all indie heaven, either, as the odd American Apparel or burger chain has crept in to sully the alt mix, and a few white-haired gents roam around calling each other "Reg." A calculatedly easy place to spend an afternoon, not to mention the carefully-budgeted contents of your coffers, Portobello Road is a definite don't-miss of the Hyde Park-Notting Hill region.

1673 by the Worshipful Society of Apothecaries, the site is home to about 5,000 plants of curative, comestible, or beneficial purpose. The Garden's features, including an after-hours Secret Garden (definitely not Secret Powers) tour and historical talks, are beyond the mind's comprehension.

i Free. ☼ Open Apr-June Tu-F and Su 11am-6pm; Jul-Sept Tu-W 11am-10pm, Th-F and Su 11am-6pm; Oct Tu-F and Su 11am-6pm; Nov-Mar M-F 9:30am-4pm.

West London

ROYAL BOTANIC GARDENS, KEW
GARDENS

Kew Rd.   ☎020 8332 5655 www.kew.org

But sweet damn are there a solid deal of gardens, parks, greeneries, clearings, commons, meadows, floral arenas, and summery anti-tundras in and around this city. Make no mistake: despite its regal claims, this is indeed another park, albeit a more dedicatedly pruned specimen than its more popular neighbors to the north. With this identification in mind, the winding paths, bridged lake, Japanese garden, and greenhouse jungle (with its uninspiring subterranean floor of fish tanks) might not merit the £14 student entry fee—unless you are extremely keen on hipster flowers or paintings thereof, hedges, and/or golf course grass. The herons at the gardens were haughty and aloof but authorized momentary glimpses.

i £15, online tickets £14; students £14, online tickets £13. ☼ Gardens open daily at 10am. Closing times vary depending on the day and season, so check the website for the most up-to-date information.

HAMPTON COURT PALACE
PALACE

East Molesey, Surrey   ☎020 3166 6000 www.hrp.org.uk/HamptonCourtPalace

There are two ways of looking at the one-stop catch-all funganza that is the Hampton Court Palace. One goes: Come on, dude. The royal family hasn't even lived here since King George II was busy spanking his grandkids. (True story; thanks, Wikipedia.) The other goes: This place is spooky as hell, with a maze, figurines of hella freaky animals, much architecture from a 500-year history of crazy anecdotes (another good one: King James hammered out the particulars of Bible production here), like a bazillion green acres, more stained glass and old-ass tapestry than Let's Go would know what to do with, and to top it all off, a mid-June festival featuring all manner of bardic hijinks. We say go.

i Tickets Mar-Oct £19.30, online £18.20; students £16, online £14.90. Tickets Nov-Feb: £18.20, online £17.10; students £15.40, online £14.30. Maze only £4.40. Garden only £5.80, students £4.90. ☼ Open daily Mar 29-Oct 24 10am-6pm; Oct 25-Mar 28 10am-4:30pm.

East London

ROYAL OBSERVATORY GREENWICH
OBSERVATORY

Blackheath Ave.   ☎020 8858 4422 www.rmg.co.uk

The hilltop Royal Observatory Greenwich, the best part of the parkwide conglomerate featuring the National Maritime Museum and the Queen's House Gallery, is a well-hyped but ultimately disappointingly earthbound destination. The best parts are the downstairs planetarium (which costs extra) and adjoining Astronomical Photographs of the Year gallery, which feature the best efforts of amateurs with their heads in the clouds. Also of note is the well-denoted Prime Meridian, where you can take your picture with like six other people as you all prove how very multihemispherical you are. Even our *Let's Go Astrophysics* Correspondent was a little underwhelmed by the "bang for the buck" ("pow for the pound"?) factor—we suggest doing the Astronomy Centre (free) and Planetarium (£6.50) by themselves if you're particularly stoked on stars, or just climb the hill for a nice view of eastern London.

i *Observatory £9.50, students £7.50. Planetarium shows £7.50, students £6.50. Combo ticket for both £12.50, students £9.50.* ☼ *Open daily 10am-5pm.*

WHITECHAPEL GALLERY
GALLERY

77-82 Whitechapel High St.   ☎020 7522 7888 www.whitechapelgallery.org

Carved into the sheer stone and ancient tombs of Whitechapel is this fabulous exhibition space, composed of several galleries and cinema rooms, themselves harboring a veritable "what is or soon will be up" of art, most of it modern, but with a terrific sense of the retrospective (with OG art films intermingled with the currently cutting-edge), itself produced by a variety of artists of a variety of nationalities and creeds, not to mention ages, and let's not even get into the political persuasions and disciplines, all of which can be sampled, even absorbed—we recommend blocking off a solid chunk of time to dig into the surprisingly voluminous gallery—for £0. Do.

i *Free.* ☼ *Open Tu-W 11am-6pm, Th 11am-9pm, F-Su 11am-6pm; closed Mondays*

North London

CAMDEN MARKET
MARKET

Camden High St.   www.camdenmarket.com

Markets walk a dangerous line once attaining self-awareness—recognizing with an instinctive buzz the droves of tourists descending like predatory birds, many onetime quaint farmers' outposts evolve to become kitschy in the extreme, replacing their tomatoes with stands hawking ever-more-desperate attempts to put the word "London" and associated hearts on bike seats, thongs, doilies, and sink-cleaning apparati.

Camden Market has veered ever closer to the mean clankings of commercial machinery in recent years, but the core of the bazaar remains relatively human, especially its central food stands, which deliver an incredible variety of meals at unbeatable prices. Other Camden Market goodies include a stand selling 100-year-old photography equipment (though we were disappointed by the way its seller assured us the contents would transfer easily to .jpegs), an all-neon clothing boutique, and miscellaneous CD shops of varying quality (go deeper to find the best ones).

☼ *Open daily 10am-6pm.*

HAMPSTEAD HEATH
PARK

Oh, dogg, but you know it is time for some strolling. You know this. Rural though it may seem, Hampstead Heath is only four miles from the heart of London, making its wild terrain of beauty easily accessible for wanderers who enjoy entrapping themselves in the illusion of nature. Its top feature is Parliament Hill, which has nothing to do with Parliament but is a commendable outcropping with a wide view of the whole city. Sprinkled throughout with patches of forest, walking paths, benches, and cafes, one could easily while the day away here. Hampstead Heath has achieved marked success where herons are concerned.

i Free. ☼ Open during daylight hours.

FOOD

City of London

✦ CITY CAPHE   SANDWICHES $
17 Ironmonger Ln.   www.citycaphe.com

"Sandwiches," mm-mm-mmmh—Let's Go may never have heard of this tasty bread-based dish before our arrival in London, but now we can't get enough of this little-known food genre. Near as we can tell, City Caphe makes some of the best and cheapest around—this no-frills (though colorfully decorated) French/Vietnamese sandwichery up an unassuming side street is sure to whet your appetite for the unfamiliar "sandwich"!

i Food £4-7. ☼ Open M-F 11:30am-4:30pm.

CEENA   KOREAN $$
13 St. Bride St.   ☎0207 936 4941 www.ceena.co

Frozen like a ghost town of the Ancient East in the early evening hours, this neo-Korean barbecue experiment is aimed at the area's capitalists—the main wall has a pleasantly "business school PowerPoint"-esque information display on the preparation of traditional victuals, etc.—but, we gotta say, it offers a tasty and filling meal. Not "budget" per se, this is a good deal for the area, and an interesting anomaly to boot.

i Food £2.70-16.30. ☼ Open M-F 11:30am-11pm.

CLERKENWELL KITCHEN   CAFE $
27-31 Clerkenwell Cl.   ☎20 7101 9959 www.theclerkenwellkitchen.co.uk

Lots of places will do you an English breakfast, but few will do it with the smiley zeal of this trendy pop-up. The coffee is best avoided, but the desserts are so fine and the soups luscious, providing a tantalizing diversion from the ultra-hip/yuppie-tastic neighborhood—it's a solid people-watching location, too.

i Food £4.50-11. ☼ Open M-F 8am-5pm.

Hyde Park and Notting Hill

SEE CAFÉ   JAPANESE $$
4d Praed St.   ☎20 7724 7358 www.seesushi.com/

If you're hankering for some Japanese cuisine, this restaurant will see to it that your desire is met. It's a little tricky to find, given its location behind a post office, but you'll see See Café as soon as you round the corner. Once you've had your seat, you'll see the towering metallic buildings reflected in the Paddington Basin, a curious waterway that must be seen to be believed. Well laid out and insightfully designed, See Café is a delight to the sight (not to mention taste); it's easy to see why so many hungry sightseers flock to see See. Seeing as See isn't seen by the sea, the scene's set with several selections of sustenance—some saltwater snacks, some slightly slippery sides; simultaneously sushi, sashimi, sake, satay, and Thai.

i Entrees £7-18. Bento boxes £9-12. Noodles £8-9.50. ☼ Open M-F noon-3pm and 6-11pm.

MULBERRY STREET PIZZA   PIZZA $
47 Moscow Rd.   ☎20 7313 6789 www.mulberrySt..co.uk

In the time before the Great Purge, an American city somewhat puzzlingly named New York, New York, gave rise to one of the most influential schools of the food subgenre known as "Za." Dense of crust and generous in sliceage, New York Za was thought to have perished along with the rest of the U.S. during the pre-Purge Continental Emetic; luckily for us, London chain Mulberry Pizza has dug determinedly through what was once Manhattan, even importing checkered walls and what appears to be an authentically stickered streetlamp from the rubble, all in the name of ensuring the prized Za's non-extinction. Also offering salads, Italian entrees, beer, wine, and desserts, this is perhaps your one chance while in London to remember the New York that once was (and could have been).

i *Slices £4-5. 10″ pizza £8.45-10.95. Entrees £8.95-11.45.* ☎ *Open daily noon-11:30pm.*

CRAZY HOMIES   MEXICAN $$
125 Westbourne Park Rd.   ☎020 7727 6771 www.crazyhomies.com

Imagining Mexican food in London is almost as difficult as saying the name of this restaurant with a straight face; luckily, Crazy Homies took our skepticism and punted it across the Atlantic like a deflating football. The ground floor, decorated with the, shall we say, imprecise perception Brits seem to have of Mexico—that is, camp movie posters in which sumptuously-breasted broads flee a grim reaper clutching halfheartedly at his motorcycle's ghostly handlebars—is pretty cramped, though this only encourages you to check out the cool bar area downstairs (dark, neon lights). The burritos are of the knife-and-fork variety, filling and intriguingly spiced. Not even our Let's Go Nautical Correspondent was brave enough to find out what a "wet burro" was—in part because it costs an extra £2 on a bill that already adds up quickly if drinks are involved.

i *Burritos, enchiladas, taco salads £7.75-14.95. 6 churros £5.50. Drinks £4-13.* ☎ *Open M-Th 6am-11pm, F 6am-11:30pm, Sa noon-10:30pm; closed Sundays.*

MIMO'S CAFÉ   ITALIAN, DELI $
19 London St.   ☎020 7706 7175

In all directions, expensive restaurants and grubby tourist shops scratch themselves and snicker at the same lackadaisical pranks. Fools! In the heart of squalor, Mimo's Café silently forges its empire. What seems on the outside like any of the innumerable delis dotting the area north of Hyde Park, Mimo's Café's ample room, homey air with cheerful regulars, and—most importantly—inexpensive menu of terrific food have earned it the coveted Let's Go Eat Breakfast There recognition. Options later in the day include a variety of dirt-cheap sandwiches, salads, and more significant pasta dishes.

i *Breakfast £3.50-4.50. Salads £4.75-6. Pasta £5.50-6.50. Sandwiches £4.* ☎ *Open daily 7am-10pm.*

West End

JUMBO EATS   WRAPS $
59 Brewer St.   ☎020 7494 2133

Long have we toiled and traversed, searching unsatisfied in our wicked and wandering ways: lore tells of a length of time, of utter upheaval and ubiquitous unrest, before the beginning of the bringer of the unbelievable: the wondrous, awesome, worthy wrap.

That time is now. We found the place where the wrap came from, the origin of the wrap, the setting of the wrap's creation myth, and it was right here in the West End all along. (Don't know how we could have missed it.) With amazing prices for about a billion options, veggie and meat and beyond, solid portions, fantastic service, extremely j-chilling of a vibe, they never run out of seating, and "Gangsta's Paradise" spits on the PA—though even Coolio doesn't know everything: this is no mere paradise. This is the birthplace of the wrap.

i *Wraps £4.50-5.50. Drinks £1-3.* ☎ *Open M-F 8am-8pm, Sa-Su 9am-8pm.*

NORDIC BAKERY BAKERY $
14a Golden Sq. ☎020 3230 1077 www.nordicbakery.com

The word's out—despite their website's self-promotion as a place where "visual clutter and noise is eliminated," our favorite hinterlandian transplant is no longer the temple of peace it alleges to have been. No matter: the food's good, and pretty damn Nordic, and with a prime location opposite Golden Sq. in Soho, there's plenty of room to escape the bustle. Prices are good for the neighborhood—OK for the billowing maelstrom of demand and satisfaction that is life in this age of machinery. Try the pancake, avoid the quiche.

i Food £1-6. Drinks £2-3. ☼ Open M-F 8am-8pm, Sa 9am-7pm, Su 10am-7pm.

Westminster

▨ POILÂNE BAKERY $
46 Elizabeth St. ☎0207 808 4910 www.poilane.fr

This first English iteration of the famous Parisian bakery chain set out to conquer new territories, Norman-style, in Pimlico, and we've never had Stockholm syndrome so bad. The bakers live above the shop, waking in the wee hours of each bready morning to go about their solemn craft, toiling in the dough, in the flour, in the heat of a thousand wood stoves. Everything from the pain au chocolat to the more complicated confections is to die for.

i Food £1.50-6. ☼ Open M-F 7am-7pm, Sa 7am-3:30pm.

▨ PIMLICO FRESH CAFE $
86-87 Wilton Rd. ☎020 7932 0030

Home of the mightiest croissant in the land, not to mention basically every other meal item you could want, timed to the hour of the day—salmon and avocado toast in the morning, lasagna in the afternoon, stews, omelets, curries, and damn near anything else at dinner. The variety doesn't hurt the taste one bit; its cooks cover some serious ground like a supercharged hurricane in the thick of summer. One of the true treasures of the Pimlico area.

i Coffee £2-2.50. Sandwiches £6-7. ☼ Open M-F 7:30am-7:30pm, Sa-Su 9am-6pm.

SPICY FOOD PLUS INDIAN $
83 Wilton Rd. ☎020 7834 8068

This might actually be the cheapest food in London—we're talking "no website" cheap, "served in a tin dish" cheap—but you wouldn't know it for the flavors involved. Filling portions of curry, rice, veggies, and some of the best naan in all of London make this hole in the wall a must for Pimlico's hungry.

i Drinks £1-3. Food £2-5.50. ☼ Open M-Sa noon-3pm and 4:30-11pm.

South London

▨ SNACKISTAN @ PERSEPOLIS MIDDLE EASTERN $
28-30 Peckham High St. ☎020 7639 8007 www.foratasteofpersia.co.uk

You know where those cookie-cutter "ethnic" stores like Urban Outfitters steal "authentic" rug designs from? This is what the whole industry aspires to be. Hang of the hippies and hip, home to cheap, delicious desserts, Snackistan doesn't give a damn about their posted hours—they'll stay open however long people are partying in their relaxed, sugary way. Only the occasional two seconds of shrill emergency exit alarm, ignored by everyone in the room, punctuates the ambience—yet somehow still adds to it. Bedecked with funny signs and with a staff ranging from friendly to Christ-like, this "Land of the Peckish" is a must for anyone in south London.

i Foods £3-5. Nonalcoholic drinks £1.50-3. ☼ Open daily 10:30am-9pm.

Nestled in the part of Covent Garden where wealthy people go to make their hands smell fragrant is the heptagoral death trap known as Seven Dials. Scores of lotus eaters are forever entombed in a waking half-life, not by choice, but due to the eerie arrangement of uneven cobblestone, perpetually cycling and darting traffic, the tourists' own recently-acquired confectionaries, and the ever-tested will not to die. Let's Go honors them.

For drivers, this is your fairly typical central statue-looping roundabout, albeit with several options beyond the norm for eventual de-circumvention. To pedestrians, Seven Dials is a polydimensional, perverted game of Frogger, with oncoming traffic subject to unfamiliar laws and irregular patterns as yet undescribed by the natural sciences or reason. Many unlucky or unwise enough to attempt an underprepared journey across the square's intermediate rings of desolation do not return; for even if the eye of the hurricane is breached in one direction, it may be weeks—twenty months, in the case of our erstwhile Let's Go Urban Planning Correspondent—before the vulturelike circulation of cabs and shipping vehicles realigns to allow safe passage, the poor interloper with only the dying heat of their overpriced pastry to warm them against a frigid moon hung amidst all the violence of space.

london

CAFÉ EAST

VIETNAMESE $

100 Redriff Rd. ☎20 7252 1212 www.cafeeastpho.co.uk

Tucked away along a sleepy stretch of southeast London asphalt—across the parking lot is a bowling alley and movie theater—Café East buzzes like a dining hall; you may have to wait up to 15 minutes for a table when they're at their busiest (they don't take reservations). The food is terrific, though, and in huge portions, and don't even think about asking for tap water—partly because the drinks are so tasty (the Che Ba Mau sweet drink is particularly fetching), and partly because they will not give you any.

i Entrees £8-9. Drinks £1.50-4. ☼ Open M and W-F 11am-3pm and 5:30pm-10:30pm; Sa 11am-10:30pm; Su noon-10pm; closed Tuesdays.

Southbank

PIE MINISTER

BAKERY $

Gabriel's Wharf, 56 Upper Ground ☎0207 928 5755 www.pieminister.co.uk

Surely, when Robert Plant sang "Ooh, your custard pie, yeah, sweet and nice / When you cut it, mama, save me a slice," he was referring to this quaint pie shop a stone's throw from the Thames. Quite cheap and utterly satisfying, with veggie and dessert options, this homey sanctuary is a must for travelers overwhelmed by the surrounding Southbank's weary commercialism. (Finding it can be slightly tricky—it's in there among the clothing boutiques.)

i Pies £4.50, with one side £6.50, with two sides £7.50. Drinks £1.60-2.30. ☼ Open daily 10am-6pm.

THE TABLE CAFÉ

CAFE $

83 Southwark St. ☎0207 401 2760 www.thetablecafe.com

Like a sci-fi Denny's from the hipster future where their food is really good and the furnishings are made from uncommon trees. Table isn't cheap, but, two Christs and half a Jesus, is this where we got the best lemon pancake we've ever had. The staff, led by one dude whose own mustache overwhelms him, are a well-heeled lot, knowledgeable and innovative. Bi-weekly Thursday Jazz Nights liven up an already friendly scene. Eat here and be glad you have done so.

i *Food £6-15. ☺ Open M 10am-4:30pm, Tu-F 7:30am-10:30pm, Sa-Su 8:30am-4pm.*

Marylebone and Bloomsbury

FORK DELI PATISSERIE
DELI, BAKERY $

85 Marchmont St. ☎020 7387 2680

Mother Earth is cruel to her soft-bellied children. Fork Deli Patisserie, an oasis of affordable pap, beckons. Much more than mere bean-toting cafe, FDP combines the best of coffeehouses (drinks are artisanal in every way but price), sandwich shops (with coveted vegetarian options, though sometimes in short supply), and dessert bar (have you ever had panini-pressed banana bread? YUM). The range of quality munchies, including various gluten-free sweets, outstrips most cafes and yielded a garbanzo salad our Let's Go correspondent called "absurdly tasty." FDP's location, midway between the British Library and Museum, allows even the raggedest of paupers a chance to refuel before once again attempting the ladder of high culture. Take note that it closes at 4pm on weekends.

i *Drinks £1.70-2.70. Pastries £1.70-3. ☺ Open M-F 7:30am-7pm, Sa 8:30am-4pm, Su 9am-4pm.*

THAI METRO
THAI $

38 Charlotte St. ☎020 7436 4201

Above all, Thai restaurants symbolize the beauty and breathtaking power of the natural world. The emergence of Thai Metro in central Bloomsbury has affordable Thai aficionados cheering on the inscrutable wisdom of natural selection with renewed fervor. Cheaper than the surrounding swarm, Thai Metro offers an extensive menu, with bang-up service to boot.

i *Starters £5. Stir fries £6-9. Noodles £6-7. ☺ Open M-F 5-10pm, Sa-Su 1-10pm.*

TAS RESTAURANT
TURKISH $$

22 Bloomsbury St. ☎020 7637 4555 www.tasrestaurants.co.uk

Don't be alarmed by the upscale decor (your emaciated Let's Go researcher, upon seeing white tablecloths for the first time in months, fell into a shadowy trance from which he's only just recovered); for being a location of much finery just outside spitting distance of the British Museum, Tas will keep you gorged without breaking the bank. A meal of compellingly prepared vegetables or assorted rices can be acquired with a juicy drink for just over £10, and this includes the free bread. In fact, it's worth coming here for the mouthwatering appetizer bread alone. If there were a way to eat only free bread, Let's Go would no doubt be writing travel books on it by now, but there you have it. Another day passes and we must purchase food to go along with our perfectly satisfying bread.

i *Meze £5-6. Entrees £9-12. Seafood £10-13. ☺ Open M-Sa noon-11:30pm, Su noon-10:30pm.*

MEAT LIQUOR
BURGERS $

74 Welbeck St. ☎20 7224 4239

This charmingly-named burger joint aims to win fans by overwhelming them with sheer 'tude. Lit dimly, splashed with graffiti, and crawling with 20-somethings (with whom you may end up sharing a table), it's the fast food equivalent of a rock concert—though "fast" may be putting it strongly, as lines spill out the main door frequently enough to merit the positioning of instructions-laden signposts. The food is good. Getchyer taste of America while in London, mate.

i *Burgers £7.50-8.50. Beer £3-4. Cocktails £7.50-10. ☺ Open M-Th noon-midnight, F-Sa 11am-2am, Su noon-10pm.*

South Kensington and Chelsea

KENSINGTON CREPERIE
CREPES $

2-6 Exhibition Rd.   ☎020 7589 8947 www.kensingtoncreperie.com

This chilling place is haunted by tortured souls who come in for the savory crepes, stay for the gelato then want sweet crepes to go with the gelato, need another savory crepe to cleanse their palate, follow it with a scoop of gelato, and so on. It took our Let's Go Aerospace Correspondent three full weeks to extradite herself from the Crepe Cycle, but the info she provided us was invaluable: while not inexpensive, the crepes are extensive and artfully crafted, and well worthy of a full meal—this ain't snack food. The gelato is, though, and yummy at that. A touristy location makes this a solid outpost for people-watching, too.

i *Crepes £4-10. Ice creams £3-6. Drinks £3-9. ☼ Open daily 8:30am-11:30pm.*

VQ CHELSEA
DINER $

325 Fulham Rd.   ☎020 7376 7224 www.vq24hours.com

Conveniently located a few blocks from Chelsea-Westminster Hospital, VQ Chelsea—the Diner That Does Not Close—has done its part to greasen up the community for close to two decades. Snug but not uncomfortable, it can get elbowy around dinnertime, but there's always the rest of the time that isn't dinnertime. Its 24hr. breakfast outdone only by its corresponding 24hr. alcohol license, this last holdout against the merciless conquest of time will be your go-to for diner food until your last breath.

i *Food £4-12 depending on extravagance. Beer £4-5.50. Nonalcoholic drinks £3.50. ☼ Open 24hr.*

RAISON D'ETRE
SANDWICHES $

18 Bute St.   ☎020 7582 5008 www.raisondetrecafe.com

Far be it from us to lay praise vociferously upon an anonymous Frenchman, let alone several in conjunction, but damn if Raison D isn't the reason to utilize saliva south of Hyde Park. As cheap as yer gonna get in South Ken, and with quick service besides, this unassuming sandwich shop rules the whole neighborhood from its quaint side street. Nab a baguette formed of only the sweetest Andalusian fixings, read the word "Californian" written by a French person, and guzzle a gigantic hot chocolate for like £7. Alright, France. You got us this time.

i *Coffee £1.90-2.70. Sandwiches £3-6. ☼ Open M-F 7am-6pm, Sa 7am-5pm, Su 11am-4pm.*

CAFÉ DECO + THE SANDWICH SHOP
CAFE $

54 and 62 Gloucester Rd.   ☎020 7225 3286

As people have said, London is truly the City of Great Questions. [Editor's note: This is not, strictly speaking, a thing people say.] How long can anyone endure on English breakfasts alone? Is there anything cheap to be eaten in South Kensington? Does this Aloe Vera Drink we've been unthinkingly swallowing contain the very nutrients a man needs to make the lonesome road his own home and find peace with his ego's foibles, or does its pulpy texture betray a more sinister agenda re: his tissues and structures? We hope you will investigate the answers to these queries at a little twofer we've discovered on Gloucester Rd., a few blocks south of Hyde Park. Café Deco will sell you a fine young breakfast baguette for a mean £2.25 and has better seating, while the Sandwich Shop's wide variety of pastas, breakfast items, and desserts provide further sweetenings for your DIY feast.

i *Entrees £4-5. Sandwiches £2-3.50. Coffee £1-2. ☼ Open M-F 5:30am-7pm, Sa-Su 6am-7pm.*

london

West London

SUFI RESTAURANT   PERSIAN $$
70 Askew Rd.

It's worth eating at this tucked-away Persian restaurant on the strength of the unbelievable naan bread alone. This is bread to die for, bread genuine as the tears of Christ, bread made in a kiln right before your child-stealin' eyes. The rest of the menu is delicious and filling and pretty middle of the road, price-wise; top it off with an authentic dessert and you've got one kickass meal in a classy venue.

i *Starters £3-4. Entrees £8-14. Drinks £1.50-3. Wines £4-6.* ☼ *Open M-Sa noon-11:30pm, Su noon-10:30pm.*

MR. FALAFEL   MIDDLE EASTERN $
New Shepherd's Bush Market, Uxbridge Rd.   ☎779 8906 668 www.mrfalafel.co.uk

Hey, Mr. Falafel man: Sing a song for me. Or give me a large falafel wrap plus drink (yummy salted yogurt, mm-hmm-mmm) at this friendly, no-frills restaurant for less than $8. Up to you, man. Bonus: visit the "Videos" tab on their website for some Tim-and-Eric-style throwback footage.

i *Wraps £4.50-6.80.* ☼ *Open M-Sa 11am-6pm.*

East London

▨ THE BIG RED PIZZA BUS   PIZZA $
30 Deptford Church St.   www.bigredpizza.co.uk

Straight-up, that's what this is. Seeing its next-door neighbor's "eccentric aunt" vibe and raising it a "sixties hippie bus," this pizzeria, bar, community space, and double-decker blast from your LSD-laden past is an absolute must in East London. Food and drink—yes, indeed, the bus serves you drinks; ohhh, yes—are reasonably priced, with a nice selection of desserts (the brownies are real fine). What makes this joint stand apart, aside from, you know, being a bus, is the entertainment: live comedy on Tuesdays, jazz on Fridays, and "busker night" on Wednesdays—strum a song, earn a pint.

i *Food £4-12. Drinks £1.50-4.50.* ☼ *Open Tu-Th 5-11pm, F-Sa noon-past midnight, Su noon-11pm.*

▨ THE LITTLE SQUARE OF FOOD TRUCKS OFF DRAY WALK   FOOD TRUCKS $

Rather than trying to choose just one of the excellent options we've sampled here, Let's Go invites you to do a little exploring, albeit within about 200 sq. ft. Tucked away amid chic boutiques and stalwart record store, Rough Trade, is this constellation of cheap and delicious eats: pizza, buffalo wings, BBQ, and much more. All of it is incredibly cheap, in generous portions, authentic—well, as authentic as buffalo wings get—and will make you feel cool as hell. Bonus: picnic tables for unabashed hipster-watching.

i *Prices vary, food usually £3-9. Drinks £1.50-4.* ☼ *Hours vary, generally daily 11am-midnight.*

North London

▨ YUMCHAA TEAS   TEASHOP $
35/37 Parkway   www.yumchaa.com

Cozy as can be, this loose-leaf tea gem is one of a micro-chain that's spread successfully throughout London. Spaciously designed and bedecked with an assortment of old-fashioned garden chairs, couches, and what appear to be dozens of different couples' wedding photographs (not sure what the story is there), Yumchaa is as wonderfully British as it gets, though with an unplaceable exotic tang. We cannot recommend the raspberry vanilla tea highly enough, and the chocolate velvet cake is not of this world.

i *Teas £5-8.* ☼ *Open M-F 8am-8pm, Sa-Su 9:30am-8pm.*

LALIBELA

ETHOPIAN $$

137 Fortress Rd.   ☎020 7284 0600 www.lalibelarestaurant.co.uk

If you've never had Ethiopian food before, we kindly, but firmly, demand that you go here. Arguably the best in the city at what it does, it isn't cheap, but won't break the bank, either—and portions are generous; you can stuff yourself for as little as £8 for veggie options and a little more for various meats.

i Food £4-15. Drinks £2. ☑ Open M-Th 6-11pm, F-Su noon-3pm and 6-11pm.

MARIO'S CAFÉ

CAFE $

6 Kelly St.   ☎020 7284 2066 www.marioscafe.com

This classic cafe hasn't yet descended into the dark bowels of tourist fancy, and you shouldn't feel too bad for helping it do so—the food is amazing, particularly the breakfasts, which are a notch above the competition. Mario himself bounces around the corners of this tight establishment gleefully, and the coffee is terrific.

i Food £3-7. Drinks £1.20-2.49. ☑ Open M-Sa 7:30am-4pm.

NIGHTLIFE

City of London

YE OLDE CHESHIRE CHEESE

BAR

145 Fleet St.   ☎020 7353 6170 www.cheshirecheeselondon.co.uk

This is one of those fairly typical-seeming homey London bars with a fantastic history: Great Fire notwithstanding, there's been a pub at this location since 1538, when, to be fair, there wasn't much else to name your pub after besides dairy products. Charles Dickens alludes to it in *A Tale of Two Cities*, regulars at various points include Mark Twain, PG Wodehouse, Alfred Tennyson, and Sir Arthur Conan Doyle, and, for four decades, an African gray parrot named Polly. Prices on food aren't amazing—we wouldn't be surprised if Polly died crackerless—but there are (fast-food-esque) combo deals to be had.

i Food £5.75-10.95. Drinks £4-19.95. ☑ Open M-F 10am-11pm, Sa noon-11pm; closed Sundays.

JAMAICA WINE HOUSE

BAR

St. Michaels Alley   ☎020 7929 6972

Another City mainstay (since circa 1652) with a friendly vibe, this relaxed saloon gets solid daps for its downstairs wine bar, which serves mysterious appetizers (what are fritters?) alongside pub classics and mouth-cidering ciders. The prices are nothing amazing compared to what you'll find elsewhere in the city, but for the City itself, they're pretty good.

i Wines £3-6. Beers £2-4. ☑ Open M-F 11am-11pm.

Hyde Park and Notting Hill

NOTTING HILL ARTS CLUB

CLUB

21 Notting Hill Gate   ☎020 7460 4459 www.nottinghillartsclub.com

Underground in the first, second, third-part-A, and third-part-B definitions of the word (Merriam-Webster, 2011), this deep bohemian hang lies behind a set of massive warehouse doors and two huge dudes possibly named Leroy. If you can find it—the unmarked entrance, wedged in between a Tex-Mex joint and several banks, easily escapes detection—descend the steep staircase into a hella chill lair of hipness. The club is live almost every evening of the week, hosting everything from straightforward DJ-steered dances to more exotic happenings like Funk Night and '90s garage revivals, so it's worth checking the online schedule to find something to match your taste.

i Cover varies depending on show, usually between £5-12. You can pay at the door or get tickets ahead of time (latter option is cheaper—check website for guestlist options). Beers £3.80-5.50. Wine £4.30-4.60. Shots £4. ☑ Open M-Th 7pm-2am, F 6pm-2am, Sa 4pm-2am, Su 6pm-1am.

PIX PINTXOS
BAR

185 Portobello Rd. ☎0207 727 6978 www.pix-bar.com

Though it may sound like a more appropriate method for pricing male prostitutes, Pix Pintxos has produced an ingenious method for keeping its customers
satisfied: grab as you go and pay later according to the size of the wooden knob
sticking out. The gimmick is cool, and portions are big enough that you don't
have to run up a massive bill to get stuffed. Spanish in vibe and cozy in feel, "PP"
sports a live DJ on some weekends and a convivial staff; aim for the very limited
open-air seating in the back for a bit of privacy and quietude.

i Wine by glass £5-9. Beers £4.50. Cocktails £9. ☒ Open M noon-10:30pm, Tu-Th noon-11pm,
F-Sa noon-midnight, Su noon-10:30pm.

THE PORTOBELLO GOLD
PUB

95-97 Portobello Rd. ☎020 7460 4910 www.portobellogold.com

Midway up what just hours ago was our favorite kitschy tourist boulevard, the
twilight transformation of Portobello Road into Portobello Pub Conglomerate
has produced at least one standout morph. The Portobello Gold doesn't deviate
too sharply from the typical pub archetype—here, too, you can find middle-aged
plaid-wearers belting (sometimes live) classic rock alongside a dash of young
people doing whatever young people do. Decor is prime here; there's a nice back
porch bedecked with what looks more or less like real palm trees depending on
the length of your stay, and we particularly enjoyed the fish tank here.

i Wine £3-5. ☒ Open Tu 1:30-5pm, W-Su 10am-midnight.

West End

LA BODEGA NEGRA
BAR

16 Moor St. ☎0207 758 4100 www.labodeganegra.com

The entrance to this subterranean spot is cleverly disguised as a sex dungeon,
for the purpose of, uh… well, we're not totally sure what the story is there, but
if you're brave enough to head downstairs, you'll be delighted to find a loud,
dark, mad groovy bar (or, at other times of day, restaurant; and, at the adjacent
location, cafe). Less "strip club," as it turns out, and more "old-school saloon
with modern touches," La Bodega Negra has an extensive cocktail menu and live
DJs at night, though there's no room to dance.

i Cocktails £8-9. ☒ Open M-Sa 6pm-1am, Su 6pm-midnight.

THE LOOP
BAR

19 Dering St. ☎020 7493 1003 www.theloopbar.co.uk

Everything about The Loop is massive, stirring a long-submerged claustrophobia
deep within Let's Go: three floors, four rooms, awesome decor, lots of things
that light up or go dark, ubiquitous stag and hen parties, dudes probably a bit
too comfortable in whipping out the rock horns, and a worthy menu—food is
amazingly enough pretty reasonable pricewise, with the appetizers even—dare
we say—cheap. We recommend checking their website, maybe even a few days
in advance, as therein you can find all manner of complex and pre-packaged
deals and loopholes for free drinks and fractioned drinks and entry of oscillating
prices before or after precise hours.

i Food £4-11. Drinks £2.75-9. ☒ Open M noon-11pm, Tu noon-midnight, W noon-1am, Th-Sa
noon-late; closed Sundays.

CELLAR DOOR
BAR

Aldwych ☎020 7248848 www.cellardoor.biz

Featuring everything from Monday drag queens to a Tuesday open mic (hosted
by an infamous gent known as "Champagne Charlie") to cabaret and burlesque,
this is one of the weirder nights out in London. Cellar Door brings an old-school

1930s New York vibe to London, with a wide-ranging drinks menu that includes absinthe and snuff. Not cheap, but worth the price.

i *Food £3-5. Drinks £4-9. ☺ Open M-Sa 4pm-midnight; closed Sundays*

THIRST   BAR
53 Greek St.   ☎020 7437 1977 www.thirstbar.com

Imagine IHOP, take away the breakfast, then strip the building to its sheer metallic frame, re-insert pink-red pleather couches, put up some seriously post-industrial lighting fixtures, slam a bar into the middle of it, and stop thinking about it as having anything to do with IHOP—you've pictured Thirst. Its patented "stupid hour" takes the place of "happy hour" and varies a little unpredictably night to night, but it makes drinks cheap and the cheap snacks yummier.

i *Drinks £8.50-12.50. ☺ Open M 4pm-1am, Tu-Sa 4pm-3am, Su 10am-4pm.*

Westminster

CASK   BAR
6 Charlwood St.   ☎0207 7630 7225 www.caskpubandkitchen.com

Beer, beer, beer; beer—beer, beer, beer; beerbeerbeer-beer (beer beer—beer!)… beer, beer. Discover all this and more at Cask. A great stop for tenderfoots and brew buffs alike, the spacious pub was established in 2009 to make a huge variety of pints available to everyone. The knowledgeable, friendly staff is happy to take the edge off the beer intimidation factor, shrugging off even the most incriminating mispronunciations with smiles. But do not step to these masters, ye beer trivia bros, for a bitter iciness borne of years of slow maturation lurks beneath their warm, frothy facades…. mmmm….

i *Pints start at £3.95. ☺ Open M-Sa noon-11pm, Su noon-10:30pm.*

THE RED LION   BAR
48 Parliament St.   ☎020 7930 5826 www.redlionwestminster.co.uk

Just up the road from 10 Downing St., generations of prime ministers downed keggers here until Edward Heath never showed in the '70s. Since his absence, you're unlikely to find the current PM, but The Red Lion's location across the way from Parliament ensures that some lesser politicos continue to trickle in. So do hordes of tourists, making its three-floor setup very necessary and often well used—but, steeped in tradition as it is, it's worthy of a stop, even if it doesn't become your go-to for your trip. The pies are extremely popular.

i *Pints start at £3.90. Food £5.25-14.*

South London

▩ MINISTRY OF SOUND   MUSIC VENUE
103 Gaunt St.   ☎0870 060 0010 www.ministryofsound.com

Among other artistic things (Shakespeare, etc.) London has been the land where freaky electronic wizards of the 1990s came to do battle. Their chief fortress was known as the Ministry of Sound. Stocked with what's said to be the "world's best sound system," on a sheer musical level this is perhaps the premier club in England; it's almost worth coming here just as a tourist for the musical history. Though catching those sonic sorcerers can cost a pretty penny, this venue makes it worthwhile.

i *Tickets generally £15-20. ☺ Open F 10:30pm-6am, Sa 11pm-7am.*

THE LOST HOUR   BAR
217-219 Greenwich High Rd.   ☎020 8269 1411 www.thelosthourgreenwich.co.uk

Are not all hours lost once gone by, irretrievable? Or does hope spring in the mewling of a newborn babe? Ruminate all night at this great pub: spacious and modern, the Lost Hour retains the traditional pub feel without descending into clichés. With excellent value for your pounds, both for food (all day breakfast:

yaasss) and drink, this makes a terrific destination on your night out—especially on Fridays, when live DJs help you lose time quicker—or as an early stop on your party train.

i Shots £1+. Beers 2 for £6-7. Cocktails £5+. Food £3-11. ☒ Open M-Sa 11am-11:30pm, Su 11am-11pm.

Southbank

THE HIDE
BAR

39-45 Bermondsey St.   ☎020 7403 6655 www.thehidebar.com

The Hide is a cocktail aficionado's paradise. Its stated goal: "not to get you drinking more, but better." While Let's Go does not believe these categories are mutually exclusive, it's nice to know such a place exists; here, it's all the perks of a classy night out without the need to actually be classy, and with a broad clientele besides (backpacking bums are slumped into leather couches alongside chic jazz cats).

i Beers £5 for a pint, £2.70 for a half-pint. Cocktails £9. Food £3-11. ☒ Open Tu 5pm-midnight, W-Th 5pm-1am, F-Sa 5pm-2am.

SOUTHWARK TAVERN
BAR

22 Southwark St.   ☎020 7403 0257 www.thesouthwarktavern.co.uk

London's really into its punitive institutions, and you should be, too. Rather than paying to go on the London Dungeon tour, though, you should chill in this former prison and drink beer while you're at it. You can relax in the main area or claim your own cell in the basement (choice seems pretty clear to us). The food's excellent, with the Sunday afternoon roasts particularly lauded for their selection and taste.

i Food £3.50-15. Drinks £4-10. ☒ Open M-Th 11am-midnight, F-Sa 11am-1am, Su noon-midnight.

Marylebone and Bloomsbury

THE SOCIAL
BAR

5 Little Portland St.   ☎0207 636 4992

By day, it's a Wi-Fi cafe, and by night, it is a bar. The upstairs section is shrug-worthy, though with above-average food—we're particularly delighted to see hot dogs catching on outside baseball stadiums—but things get more exciting as you move downstairs (don't they always?). Come to the club for its more fully fledged bar and themed nights, including a Wednesday new bands showcase and a Thursday hip-hop karaoke our Let's Go correspondent declared "scrupulously happenin'."

i Beers £4.50-6. Ciders £5-7. Food £3-12. ☒ Open M-W 11:30am-midnight, Th-F 11:30am-1am, Sa 6pm-1am; closed Sundays.

South Kensington and Chelsea

THE TROUBADOUR
BAR

263-267 Old Brompton Rd.   ☎0207 370 1434 www.troubadour.co.uk

Trust us; there will come a point in your stay when you'll long to hear a British Neil Young sing cheerful ballads of death. At such an occasion, look no further than this underground club (the top bit's a normal restaurant; just ask for the downstairs), where the genre formerly known as folk music has expanded its horizons to include soul, indie rock, and even forays into electronic gadgetry, six nights a week—hard to say if you'll peep the next James Taylor or James Blake. Also with a two-for-one happy hour on drinks 8-10pm and a broader-than-usual food menu.

i Cover £6-8. Cocktails £6-8. Burgers, salads, snacks £3.95-13.25. ☒ Open M-Th 9am-midnight, F-Sa 9am-2am, Su 9am-midnight.

great britain

royal albert hall

In 1861, Prince Albert, a real man of the people, died. This was a huge bummer for his bae slash first cousin, Queen Victoria, who in her mourning saw fit to open a gigantic concert hall ten years later. The hall's acoustics were terrible; the standard joke was that the RAH was the only place in Britain a composer could be sure to hear their concert twice. Renovated on and off during the remainder of its history, the Royal Albert Hall has become one of the most famous performance venues in Europe, holding concerts, ballets, operas, film screenings, circus shows, poetry recitals, and a variety of sporting events, including London's first-ever sumo wrestling tournament in 1991.

London is really into the "making people with less money stand whilst the upper classes gloat in their plump chairs" thing—see also Shakespeare's Globe—but if you see an ad for something that interests you, we urge you to take advantage of the offer and get tickets for the uppermost level of the Hall. Ad-hoc communities form in the jostling crowd peering down from the rafters as the pilgrims and pariahs of society merge; indeed, sometimes entire micro-civilizations rise and fall, Lord of the Flies-style, over the course of a three-hour concert. Besides, up here, there's more room to dance.

THE DRAYTON ARMS PUB

153 Old Brompton Rd. ☎020 7835 2301 www.thedraytonarmssw5.co.uk
Fairly typical as pubs go, the Arms is saved from anonymity by its inspired performances every night of the week in its black box theatre. Shows are a little pricey but are an intimate counterpoint to the scores of big-budget productions elsewhere in London. The bar area is comfortably laid out and homey, with elegant touches (it is Chelsea, after all).
i Drinks starting at £4. Food £6-8. ☑ Open M-F noon-midnight, Sa-Su 10am-midnight.

THE BLACKBIRD BAR

209 Earls Court Rd. ☎020 7835 1855 www.blackbirdearlscourt.co.uk
"Blackbird singing in the dead of night," warbles Paul. "There are no wings here, broken or otherwise, but the pies are great and the sandwiches cheaper than you'll find at other pubs in the area. All your life, live music by local musicians every Friday at 9pm, unassertive rock 'n' roll the rest of the time. You were only waiting for this pub to arrive in Kensington near Earls Court."
i Drinks starting at £3.50. Food £6.75. ☑ Open M-Sa 9am-11:30am and noon-10pm, Su 9am-11:30am and noon-9:30pm.

PIĀNO KENSINGTON BAR

106 Kensington High St. ☎207 938 4664 www.pianokensington.com
All the throwback factor and class of a piano bar, with a live trio on Sunday nights, but sans the massive cover charge and with relatively inexpensive food. Solid for an old-fashioned date, or just for some shadows to slink into and ruminate on God, Law, and/or Jazz. Dudes in fedoras may hang around, but as ever you can dispel them with some of our Let's Go Brand © Fedora Dude-Off (now in liquid and aerosol form).
i Food starting at £3-6. Wine £5-7. ☑ Open Tu-Sa 5pm-midnight, Su 6-11:30pm.

606 CLUB

MUSIC VENUE

90 Lots Rd. ☎020 7352 5953 www.606club.co.uk

On the more established, and therefore pricier, side of the live music club spectrum, this venue attracts a world-class roster of mostly jazz acts matched only by its crosstown rival, Ronnie Scott's. Booking using its online form (on an old-school Flash website) can be a bit of a hassle. So can getting your mind blown by the insane melodic wizardry of a traveling sax man who understands only the wordless aura of the blues. But that's life.

i *Cover and times are subject to change depending on the show. General cover £10, F-Sa nights £12. ☒ Shows M-Th 7-11:15pm, F-Sa 8pm-12:45am, Su 12:30-3:30pm and 7-11:15pm.*

West London

THE DOVE

BAR

19 Upper Mall ☎020 8748 9474 www.dovehammersmith.co.uk

Hit up this fine young (actually, apparently been around since forever—a list of famous diners includes Ernest Hemingway, Charles II, and James Thompson, writer of the Royal Navy's unofficial anthem "Rule Britannia!" in 1740) pub for its beautiful terraced riverside view and bang-up menu. That it features the Guinness Book-certified world's smallest bar-room gives you a sense of its slightly eccentric character—though there's plenty of room outside of that cell, and the outside's the best bit. Food is expensive, but the pub's worthwhile for the beer.

i *Drinks £4-10. Food £6-22. ☒ Open M-Sa 11am-11pm, Su noon-10:30pm.*

BUSH HALL

MUSIC VENUE

310 Uxbridge Rd. ☎020 8222 6955 www.bushhallmusic.co.uk

The British music scene's obsession with the young, glitzy, and attitudinal is a bit beyond Let's Go, but if you want to see a vicious young band of up-and-comers, this is certainly the place to do it. It's best to check online for whatever might tickle your fancy (and to make sure tix are still available, and that a wedding won't be going on that night). There's an affiliated dining room next door, with full and "pre-gig" menus for those in a rush to get musicked.

i *Ticket prices usually between £15-25. ☒ Hours vary based on the act. Check the website for the most up-to-date prices and times.*

East London

THE VANBRUGH

BAR

91 Colomb St. ☎20 8305 1007 www.thevanbrugh.co.uk

The website claims it's "Greenwich's Best Kept Secret," but there might be good reason for that—down an overlookable side street at the bottom of a long hill, you could be forgiven for mistaking this joint for a Miami villa garden. Once you're in the door, though, you'll dig the comfy couches, bumping soundtrack, and spacious outdoor seating. The food's a little spendy, but the desserts sublime and the drinks totally affordable.

i *Pints £3.50+. ☒ Open M-F noon-3:15pm and 6-9:45pm, Sa noon-4:45pm and 6-9:45pm, Su noon-8:45pm.*

93 FEET EAST

CLUB

150 Brick Ln. ☎20 7770 6006 www.93feeteast.co.uk

Wait, do they even use feet in England? It definitely originates from something about kings and the lengths of their sandals, right? These questions will not be resolved at this popular dance club, but it will, for at least a few moments, help you forget your units-of-measurement-related worries (or maybe just introduce new ones?). With a top-notch events calendar geared mostly toward DJs, you can also check the website for listings re: bands, film screenings, and poetry slams.

i *Pints £4. Burger and chips £4.90. ☒ Open M-Th 5-11pm, F-Sa 5pm-1am, Su 5-10:30pm.*

North London

🏛 SOUTHAMPTON ARMS
BAR

139 Highgate Rd.
www.thesouthamptonarms.co.uk

Its website, in icy Courier New, bitches out the alleged sign-design-thieves at a rival pub, the next page painstakingly delineating what does and does not constitute a "proper emergency" (i.e., the circumstances in which you are allowed to telephone them, basically limited to fires, floods, suicide bombers, and over-eager chimpanzees—we're not making this up). Desiccatedly dry British hipster pub wit aside, this is a delightful neighborhood pub. The challenging bit about blending in with the locals is finding a place to sit down.

i Pints £4. ☼ Open daily noon-midnight.

SPIRITUAL CAIPIRINHA BAR
BAR

4-6 Ferdinand St.
☎02 0748 56791

Ooooooh, spiiiiiiirituallllll. This bar/concert venue/record label's most prominent wall, or mosaic of Polaroids, dangles guitars behind the stage; weird art is to be found in just about every corner. Singer-songwriters strum earnestly most nights of the week, with open mics and happenings galore rounding out a very cool lineup. It's like being at the cool local music space your hometown never quite managed to get rolling—but it serves alcohol, too (caipirinhas are $4.50 during happy hour).

i Cocktails £7. ☼ Open M-Sa 6pm-1am, Su 6pm-midnight.

ESSENTIALS
Practicalities

For all the bombastic hostels, cafes, museums, and bars we list, we know some of the most important places you visit during your trip might actually be more mundane. Whether it's a tourist office, free Wi-Fi hotspot, or post office, these practicalities are vital to a successful trip, and you'll find all you need right here.

- **TOURIST OFFICES:** There are zillions of tourist information centers in London, and the visitlondon.com website can direct you to the nearest one (www.visitlondon.com/tag/tourist-information-centre); if you're thinking of exploring beyond the city, its sister site, visitbritain.com, offers droves of knowledge and will welcome you with a flattering quail. An easy place to start is by tracking down one of the blue- or magenta-shirted Team London Ambassadors loitering about in Trafalgar Sq.—they've volunteered to answer your questions about London, from travel advice to listings of "What's on" to bathroom directions.

- **LGBT RESOURCES:** The LGBT Tourist office near the Leicester Sq. Tube stop offers information on everything from saunas to theater discounts. (25 Frith St., www.gaytouristoffice.co.uk/). Boys (http://boyz.co.uk) lists gay events in London as well as an online version of its magazine. Gingerbeer (www.gingerbeer.co.uk) is a guide for lesbian and bisexual women with events listings. Time Out London's magazine and website (https://timeout.com/london) also provide a good overview of the city's LGBT establishments and the city in general.

- **INTERNET:** Wi-Fi abounds in this speed-of-tech city. Most cafes provide internet access. Chains like Starbucks and McDonald's almost always have free Wi-Fi, though you may pay a karmic debt or be reincarnated as a lesser being for consistent Wi-Fi squatting (though using these neo-corporatist freebees to plot the downfall of Western capitalism is encouraged). Other chains with Wi-Fi include The Coffee Republic (www.coffeerepublic.co.uk), Wetherspoon (i.e., the IHOP of pubs, www.jdwetherspoon.co.uk), and Pret a Manger (www.pret.com). Public areas also have Wi-Fi. The area between Upper St. and Holloway Rd., also known as The Technology Mile, is the longest stretch of free internet in the city.

- **POST OFFICES:** There are a lot of them, and they're easily Googled. Hostels also can point you in the right direction. Here's one, off the top of our heads: Trafalgar Sq. Post Office. (24-28 William IV St. ☎020 7484 9305. Charing Cross Tube stop. Open M 8:30am-6:30pm, Tu 9:15am-6:30pm, W-Th 8:30am-6:30pm, F 8:30am-6:30pm, Sa 9am-5:30pm, closed Su.)

- **BANKS/ATMS:** It's almost always cheaper to withdraw cash from ATMs than exchanging dollars for pounds via individual credit/debit transactions or at (heavens no!) tourist-manipulating money changers. ATMs also allow you to withdraw more dough in one go, meaning that you're only paying a single flat fee to take out large sums, rather than having a bank fee tacked on every time you swipe your plastic for a venti fat-free almond turtle mocha. Legend holds that there are as many ATMs in London as there are stars above the Albion sky—no matter where you are, there most likely will be a cash machine within a few blocks. Keep an eye out for free ATMs, though be aware that while the machine itself may not levy a few pounds for the transaction, your bank from home will probably still enact its standard debit withdrawal fees. You should be able to get by fine without ever setting foot in a London bank, but in case you do, keep an eye out for the larger ones, such as Barclay's, Natwest, Lloyd's, and the Royal Bank of Scotland. For tourist purposes, these are all essentially the same, unless your home bank has a special relationship with one of them.

Emergency

- **EMERGENCY NUMBER:** ☎999—that's for fire, medical, police, etc.

- **POLICE:** Emergency ☎999. Non-emergency ☎101. For hearing-impaired people using a Textphone, ☎18000.

- **RAPE CRISIS CENTER:** For women, with connections for organizations to help men as well: ☎0808 802 9999.

- **HOSPITAL:** University College Hospital (☎20 3456 7890), St. Thomas Hospital (☎20 7188 7188), St. Bartholomew's Hospital (☎20 7377 7000).

- **PHARMACY:** There are like 1000 pharmacies in London. "Boots" is a chain that's similar to an American Walgreens/CVS/etc. Zafash Pharmacy in Chelsea is one of the only 24hr. pharmacies. (☎20 7373 2798)

Getting There

By Plane

London's main airport is Heathrow (☎0844 335 1801 heathrowairport.com), and it's one of the busiest in the world. The cheapest way to get from Heathrow to central London is on the Tube. The southwestern end of the Piccadilly Line arrives from central London and loops around Heathrow. (Time depends on where you're coming from, but takes about 1 hour, comes every 5min., M-Sa 5am-11:54pm, Su 5:46am-10:37pm). Heathrow Express (☎084 5600 1515 www.heathrowexpress.com) runs between Heathrow and Paddington station four times per hour. The trip is significantly shorter (though comparably pricier) than many of the alternatives, clocking in around 15-20min. (£21.50 when purchased online or from station, £26.50 on board. 1st train departs daily around 5:10am.) The Heathrow Connect (www.heathrowconnect.com) also runs to Paddington but is cheaper and takes longer, since it makes five stops on the way to and from the airport. There are two trains per hour, and the trip takes about 25min.

The National Express (☎08717 818 178 www.nationalexpress.com) bus runs between Victoria Coach Station and Heathrow three times per hour. Though cheap and often simpler than convoluted Underground trips, the buses are subject to the slings and arrows of outrageous London traffic. Posing a similar traffic threat, taxis from the airport to Victoria cost around £60 and take around 45min.—in short, they aren't worth it.

Getting to Gatwick Airport (LDW; ☎0844 335 1802) takes around 30min., making it less convenient than Heathrow but less hectic, too. The swift and affordable train services that connect Gatwick to the city make the trip a little easier. The Gatwick Express train runs nonstop service to Victoria station, leaving approximately every 15min. (less frequently in the middle of the night). You can buy tickets in terminals, at the station, or on the train itself. (☎0845 850 1530 www.gatwickexpress.com. 1-way £17.70; round trip £31.05—round-trip ticket valid for a month).

National Express runs buses from the North and South terminals of Gatwick to London. The National Express bus (☎0871 781 8178 nationalexpress.com) takes approximately 90min., and buses depart for London Victoria hourly. Taxis take about 1hr. to reach central London. EasyBus (☎084 4800 4411 easybus.co.uk) runs every 15min. from North and South terminals to Earls Court and West Brompton.

By Train

Europe has left the one-time railroad-obsessed States far behind—London in particular offers several ways to easily reach other European destinations via train. Multiple companies pass through the city; the biggest are Eurostar (☎08432 186 186 www.eurostar.com), which travels to Paris and Brussels (and, thereby, beyond), and National Rail (☎08457 48 49 50 www.nationalrail.co.uk), which oversees lines running throughout the United Kingdom. Train travel in Britain is generally reliable but can be unreasonably expensive. Booking tickets weeks in advance can lead to large savings, but spur-of-the-moment train trips to northern cities can cost upward of £100.

By Bus

Bus travel is another, frequently cheaper, option. Eurolines (☎08717 818 181 www. eurolines.co.uk ☑ Phone lines open daily 8am-8pm) is Europe's largest coach network, servicing 500 destinations throughout Europe. Many buses leave from Victoria Coach Station, at the mouth of Elizabeth St. just off Buckingham Palace Rd. Many coach companies, including National Express, Eurolines, and Megabus, operate from Victoria Coach. National Express is the only scheduled coach network in Britain and can be used for most intercity travel and for travel to and from various airports. It can also be used to reach Scotland and Wales.

Getting Around

There's nothing quite so smug as the sound of a Transport for London operator using the intercom to intercom everyone in the station that there is "good service" on a particular line—and even when there are interruptions to service, TFL does a good job of keeping travelers aware. Each station will have posters listing interruptions to service, and you can check service online at www.tfl.gov.uk or the 24hr. travel information service (☎08432 22 12 34). The website also has a journey planner that can plot your route using any public transport service. Memorize that website. Love that website. Though many people in the city stay out into the wee hours, the Tube doesn't have the same sort of stamina; when it closes around midnight, night owls have two options: cabs or night buses.

Travel Passes

Travel passes are almost guaranteed to save you money. The passes are priced based on the number of zones they service (the more zones, the more expensive), but zone 1 encompasses central London and you'll probably seldom need to get past zone 2. If someone offers you a secondhand ticket, don't take it. There's no real way to verify if it's valid—plus, it's illegal. (Utilizing a complex succession of logical proofs, our *Let's Go Philosophy* Correspondent has informed us that illegality is bad.) Under-16s get free travel on buses, passengers ages 11-15 reduced fare on the Tube with an Oyster photocard. Students 18 and older must study full time (at least 15hr. per week over

14 weeks) in London to quality for the Student Photocard, which enables users to save 30% on adult travel cards and bus passes. It's worth it if you're staying for an extended period of time (study-abroad-sters, we're looking at you).

Oyster cards enable you to pay in a variety of ways, and you should get one if you plan on being in London for any decent length of time. Fares come in peak (M-F 6:30-9:30am and 4-7pm) and off-peak varieties and are, again, distinguished by zone. Oysters let you "pay as you go," meaning that you can store credit on an as-needed basis. Using an Oyster card will save you up to 50% off a single ticket. Remember to tap your card both on entering and exiting the station. You can use your card to add Travelcards, which allow unlimited travel on one day. This will only be cost-effective if you plan to use the Tube a lot; they cost ₤6.40 for day travel (on- or off-peak, doesn't matter) within zones 1 and 2. You can top up your Oyster at one of the ubiquitous off-licenses, marked by the Oyster logo, scattered throughout the city.

Season tickets are weekly, monthly, and annual Travelcards that work on all public transport and can be purchased inside Tube stations. They yield unlimited (within zone) use for their duration. (Weekly rates for zones 1-2 ₤32.10.)

By Underground

Most stations have Tube maps on the walls (though they may be placed in frustratingly out-of-the-way corners) and free pocket maps. The Tube map in no way reflects an above-ground scale, though, and should not be used for even the roughest estimation of walking directions. (Seriously.) Platforms are organized by line and will have the colors of the lines serviced and their names on the wall. The colors of the poles inside the trains correspond with the line, and trains will often have their end destination displayed on the front. This is an essential service when your line splits. Many platforms will have a digital panel indicating ETAs for the trains and sometimes type and final destination. When transferring within a station, just follow the clearly marked routes.

The Tube runs from Monday to Saturday from approximately 5:30am (though it depends on station and line) until around midnight, and less frequently on Sundays, with many lines starting service after 6am. If you're taking a train within 30min. of these times (before or after), you'll want to check the signs in the ticket hall for times of the first and last train. Around 6pm on weekdays, many of the trains running out of central London are packed with the after-work crowd, so if you don't want to wait for train after train before one with enough room for you finally arrives, it's best to avoid these lines at this time of day.

You can buy tickets from ticket counters (though these often have lines at bigger stations) or at machines in the stations. You need to swipe your ticket at the beginning of the journey and then again to exit the Tube. Random on-train checks will ask you to present a valid ticket to avoid the ₤50 penalty fee (reduced to ₤25 if you pay in under 21 days).

The Overground is a newish addition to the London public transportation scene. It services parts of the city past zone 1 where Tube lines are sparse and is particularly useful in East London. Fares and rules are the same as the Tube; you can just think of it as another line, except with a better view.

By Bus

While slower than the Tube for long journeys (thanks to traffic and more frequent stops), the buses that crawl antlike over London's every inch are useful for traveling short distances covered by a few stops (and several transfers) on the Tube. Bus stops frequently post lists of buses serving the stop as well as route maps and maps of the area indicating nearby stops. These maps are also very helpful for finding your way around a neighborhood. Buses display route numbers. The highest-traffic buses are being installed with LED signs which display the arrival times of incoming buses.

Every route and stop is different, but buses generally run every 5-15min. beginning around 5:30am and ending around midnight. After day bus routes have closed, night buses take over. These typically operate similar routes to their daytime equivalents, and their numbers are prefixed with an N (N13, for instance). Some buses run 24hr. services. If you're staying out past the Tube's closing time, you should plan your night-bus route or bring cab fare (single rides £2.20).

oxford

Oxford has prestige written all over it. This city is home to the oldest university in the English-speaking world, and over the course of nearly 1,000 years, it has educated some of the most influential players in Western civilization. Students around the globe aspire to join the ranks of Adam Smith, Oscar Wilde, Stephen Hawking, and Bill Clinton—not to mention 26 British prime ministers and 12 saints.

But if you can't join them, you might as well visit them. The city has plenty to entertain travelers of all persuasions: stunning college courtyards, centuries-old pubs, leafy river paths, occasionally rowdy clubs, and shops aplenty. During term time, rub shoulders with Oxford's thousands of students; in the summer, the colleges empty, and the city fills with photo-hungry tourists and eager summer-school imports. Either way, you can expect to be in the comradely company of students and budget travelers—don't panic if one or two of them actually refer to you as "comrade."

Unlike Cambridge, though, Oxford does not hold its time-resistant bubble for long. Once you get outside of the center's ancient streets and medieval architecture, the city comes (surprisingly) close to a modern metropolis. Don't limit yourself to the sights you've seen on postcards—the town rewards those willing to take the short trek to the outlying neighborhoods or venture down its tiny, twisting side streets.

ORIENTATION

Carfax, at the crossroads of Oxford's main shopping district, is the pulsing heart of the city. **High Street, St. Aldate's, Cornmarket Street,** and **Queen Street** all converge by the Town Hall to create a tourist-mobbed area—beware of the stampede of gaping cameras and more-than-over-eager parents who will callously trample you as potential competition.

get a room!

Compared to Cambridge, Oxford has a surprisingly good selection of budget accommodations. Establishments are clustered around the train station and on **Iffley Road;** the former are closer to town and the city's nightlife, but the latter are in a quieter and more sedate area near the shops and cafes on Cowley Rd. You can also visit **www.letsgo.com** for more Let's Go recommendations.

🏠 CENTRAL BACKPACKERS   HOSTEL $
13 Park End St.   ☎01865 242 288 www.centralbackpackers.co.uk
True to its name, this hostel is not only central but also filled with friendly backpackers excited to experience the latter part of Oxford's "think and drink" culture. The rooftop garden is a lovely anomaly in the hostel scene, and the rooms are clean and not cramped. The clubs on the street level don't stop believing until 3am. However, you can usually find a group to tag along with and partake in the libations yourself.

i From the train station, follow Botley Rd. east toward the town cente; 12-bed dorms £20; 8-bed £21; 6-bed women-on y £22; 4-bed £24. 🕘 Reception open 8am-11pm.

Most of the university's best-known colleges are located along High St. and the parallel roads to the north and south, with **Christ Church** around the corner on St. Aldate's. The bus station is in the eastern corner of Carfax, following the direction of **Queen Street,** while the train station is a bit farther in the same direction, across the river.

If you walk north up **Saint Giles** (Cornmarket St. becomes Magdalen St., which then turns into St. Giles), then make a left onto **Little Clarendon Street,** you'll reach **Jericho.** Home to the Oxford Canal, the Oxford University Press, and vibrant nightlife, this is Oxford's up-and-coming bohemian neighborhood. The main Jericho drag, **Walton Street,** runs off of Little Clarendon.

On the other side of the city center, down the hill and across Magdalen Bridge, is the **Cowley Road** neighborhood, centered around the eponymous street and home to numerous ethnic eateries and local pubs, which offer a nice change of pace from blue-blooded, tourist-jammed Oxford.

SIGHTS

Most people come to admire Oxford's dozen or so aesthetically pleasing colleges, and we advise you to look at the university's free info booklet, which details all of the colleges' opening hours and admission fees. You can find it on the university's website (www.ox.ac.uk) under "Visiting the University." However, due to conferences, graduations, and general eccentricity, the hours open to tourists might change without further notice, like your favorite bureaucratic Kafka novel. If you're traveling by yourself, you shouldn't have a problem getting admitted, but as a tour group size increases, you might have to book a Blue Badge tour through the Tourist Information Centre (TIC). One of the best ways to get into the colleges for free—especially during termtime—is to attend a church service in the college chapels. Show up 15min. before a service starts and tell the people at the gate that you'd like to attend; they'll usually let you in for free.

Attractions

ASHMOLEAN MUSEUM

MUSEUM

Beaumont St. ☎01865 278 000 www.ashmolean.org

The Ashmolean befits its dual honors of being the oldest university museum in the world and the most smorgasbordy collection in the UK (that's just our own award). While the British Museum is great for a survey of colonialism, the Ashmolean tries to work within a world narrative by organizing their collection into equal parts "Eastern," "Western," and "West meets East." As befits a university museum, the exhibits are highly educational; well-organized displays teach you about everything from the consolidation of northern European tribes to the decipherment of ancient Aegean scripts. As you feast on knowledge in this ivory tower, you can also feast on food, as the Ashmolean has Oxford's only rooftop restaurant.

i From Carfax (at the west end of High St.), head up Cornmarket St., then turn left onto Beaumont St. Free lunchtime gallery talks for 1st 12 who express interest Tu-F 1:15-2pm; pick up tokens at the information desk. Special exhibits £5-6. ☒ *Open Tu-Su 10am-6pm.*

BODLEIAN LIBRARY

LIBRARY

Broad St. ☎01865 277 162 www.bodleian.ox.ac.uk

The Bodleian is one of the greatest libraries in the world, holding millions of volumes, including the normal trifecta of rare manuscripts (Shakespeare's First Folio, the Gutenberg Bible, and the Magna Carta). However, there are also some neat deep cuts, like the oldest copy of The Song of Roland, the earliest surviving work of French Literature, and the Huntington MS 17, which is not a type of rifle but rather the oldest printing of the gospels in the West Nile dialect of Bohairic. The complex of 17th-century buildings surrounding the courtyard are impressive enough to justify the visit, but if you want to experience some inevitable Harry Potter déjà vu, you can take a tour. All tours go to the Divinity School, the oldest teaching room in the university; longer ones take you to the gorgeously ancient Reading Room and by the rotund Radcliffe Camera (a vital part of every TV serial that takes place in the city).

i Entrances on Broad St., Catte St., and Radcliffe St.; take Catte St. off High St. Entrance to the courtyard free. Entrance to Divinity Hall £1. 30min. tour of Library and Divinity Hall £5, 1hr. tour £7, extended tour £13. Audio tour £2.50. ☼ Open M-F 9am-5pm, Sa 9am-4:30pm, Su 11am-5pm.

THE PITT RIVERS MUSEUM

Park Rd.

MUSEUM

☎01865 270 927 www.prm.ox.ac.uk

There's no such thing as referencing colonialism too many times, so we're going to breach it once more. While not every one of the thousands of artifacts in Oxford's archaeological and anthropological museum was acquired by colonial shopping at a 1000% discount, at least they're not exploiting the items that were (admission is free). From macabre shrunken heads to provocative fertility statues, razor-like samurai swords to practical Maori spears, real Inuit furs to golden feathered cloaks, every shelf in every glass case teems with fresh wonders of the creativity and ingenuity of the human species. In classic Victorian style, every case is arranged not by culture, as is now the norm, but by theme, which brings the wonderfully stark comparisons to the dim, somber light around you. Giving you just enough information to whet your appetite for travel, understanding, and worldly experience, this is a must for any globetrotter.

i From High St., take Catte St. which becomes Parks Rd. Walk through the Museum of Natural History on the right. Tours W 2:30 and 3:15pm. Audio tour £2. Free. ☼ Open M noon-4:30pm, Tu-Su 10am-4:30pm.

MODERN ART OXFORD

30 Pembroke St.

GALLERY

☎1865 722 733 www.modernartoxford.org.uk

Oxford's entire appeal is founded on the fact that it is not modern *at all*. It's such a creature of the past that you can barely go for a meal, drink, or piss without finding out that Tolkien ate, drank, and pissed there, too. That's why this is your antidote to leaving the town covered in a thin film of historical dust. The museum rotates exhibits that are equal parts bizarre and incomprehensible: documentary films on things you didn't even know you were interested in, strange series of short film collages, sculptures without plaques. Unlike the other Oxford museums, which justify their exhibits by over-explaining, the Modern Art museum justifies itself by not, and thus allows the visitor's mind to wander creatively.

i From Carfax, walk down Queen St. Turn left onto St. Ebbe's St. Turn left onto Pembroke St. The gallery is on the left. Check online for current exhibits and night events. Bar open on event nights. Free. ☼ Open Tu-W 10am-5pm, Th-Sa 10am-7pm, Su noon-5pm.

CARFAX TOWER

Junction of St. Aldate's, Cornmarket, High, and Queen St.

TOWER

☎01865 792 653

This was the site of the former City Church of Oxford (St. Martin's Church). However, in 1896, university leaders decided that the bulk of the church needed to be demolished in order to make room for more traffic in the downtown area. Given the stagnant mass of tourist crowds that now mill around it below, that was probably a bad move. Despite its name sounding like an auto insurance price quote company, it actually comes from the French *carrefour*, or "crossroads," which makes sense, as the tower marks the official center of Oxford. To prevent the Tower of Babel II (and thus more linguistic majors), no building in the city center may be taller; this means that from the top, you get an extraordinary view over the university's spires.

i £2.20, under 16 £1.10. ☼ Open daily Apr-Sept 10am-5:30pm; Oct 10am-4:30pm; Nov-Mar 10am-3:30pm.

oxford

OXFORD CASTLE
CASTLE

44-46 Oxford Castle   ☎01865 260 666 www.oxfordcastleunlocked.co.uk

Sometimes disappearing down a dark passageway while following an underpaid, faux-torch-bearing actor is exactly what the doctor ordered. Oxford Castle will remind you that this hasn't always been the safe student haven it is today. A shot of medieval intrigue and a sudden understanding of the immense past behind every street corner can finely tune your appreciation for Oxford (even if it is done in costume and outrageously overacted bits). Life was tough, no question. People were thrown into dungeons, hanged, murdered, tortured, and even brought back from the dead—all slightly more fun than clubbing in Cambridge.

i Directly behind the Castle St. bus stop. Tours approximately every 20min. £9.25, students £7.25. ☼ Open daily 10am-5pm; last tour 4:20pm.

Colleges

■ CHRIST CHURCH
COLLEGE

St. Aldate's   ☎01865 276 150 www.chch.ox.ac.uk/college

Oxford's most famous college has the university's grandest quad and some of its most distinguished alumni. During the English Civil War, "The House" was home to Charles I and the royal family, who retreated to the Royalist-friendly university during Cromwell's advance (and, when the city came under threat, escaped dressed as servants). Speaking of "Off with their heads," the college is also notable as the place where Lewis Carroll first met Alice—the young daughter of the college dean. More recently, exploits in fantasy include the *Harry Potter* films, as some of the scenes were shot in the dining hall and central quad. For the Dark Ages version of magic, come here for Evensong to take a gander at the college for free and to experience the wonderful choir. Later on in the evening, listen for Great Tom, the seven-ton bell that has been rung 101 times (the original number of students/dalmatians) every evening since 1682 at 9:05pm to mark the original undergraduate curfew. And they say we live in an over-personalized age now. Today, it merely ushers in the beginning of an all-nighter sponsored by Red Bull, the internet, and shame.

i Down St. Aldate's from Carfax (at the west end of High St.). Depending on season £7-8.50, concessions £5.50-7. ☼ Open M-Sa 10am-4:30pm, Su 2-4:30pm. Evensong daily 6pm.

MAGDALEN COLLEGE
COLLEGE

High St.   ☎01865 276 000 www.magd.ox.ac.uk

Magdalen is spelled differently from its Cambridge counterpart, but pronounced in the same manner (MAUD-lin). With its winding riverbanks, flower-filled quads, and 100-acre grounds, Magdalen is possibly Oxford's most attractive college. The contrast between the medieval quad and the 18th-century New Building (where C.S. Lewis lived) also makes for some impressive architectural observations. Magdalen boys have traditionally been quite a catch—the college has housed seven Nobel Prize winners, Dudley Moore, and Oscar Wilde—so put your wooing cap on. The college also has a pleasant deer park, where equally attractive deer have grazed aimlessly for centuries.

i At the east end of High St., by the river. £5, concessions £4. ☼ Open Jul-Sept daily noon-7pm; Oct-Jun 1-6pm or dusk.

BALLIOL COLLEGE
COLLEGE

Broad St.   ☎01865 277 777 www.balliol.ox.ac.uk

Along with Merton and University, Balliol, founded in the 1260s, has a legitimate claim to being the oldest college in Oxford. Renowned for its PPE subject (Politics, Philosophy, and Economics), Adam Smith, Aldous Huxley, Christopher Hitchens, three British prime ministers, and six members of the Obama administration were produced from Balliol's mismatched spires. Its grounds feel impressively medieval, complete with crenellated parapets surrounding the first court (for a less intimidating view, go through the hedges on the right-hand side, past the first court, for a picturesque garden).

i From Carfax (at the west end of High St.,, take Cornmarket St., then turn right onto Broad St. £2, students £1. ☉ Open daily 10am-5pm or dusk.

MERTON COLLEGE
COLLEGE

Merton St.   ☎01865 276 310 www.merton.ox.ac.uk

Though Balliol and University were endowed before it, Merton has the earliest formal college statutes (1274), which helps to legitimize its boast of being the oldest college. Its traditions and high-achieving student body also give it a nerdy reputation. For example, the annual Time Ceremony has students dance around the Fellows Quad in full regalia, drinking port in celebration of the end of British Summer Time. JRR Tolkien was the Merton Professor of English here and spent his time casually inventing the Elvish language and writing a well-received minor trilogy on the side. The college's 14th-century Mob Quad is Oxford's oldest and one of its least impressive, while the nearby St. Alban's Quad is home to some of the university's best gargoyles.

i From High St., turn down Magpie Ln., then take a left onto Merton St. £3. ☉ Open M-F 2-5pm, Sa-Su 10am-5pm.

ALL SOULS COLLEGE
COLLEGE

Corner of High St. and Catte St.   ☎01865 279 379 www.all-souls.ox.ac.uk

Despite its misleadingly inclusive name, this is the most exclusive school of the Oxford lot, and its entrance exam is considered to be the world's hardest (although the Kobayashi Maru is the universe's). Only a few dozen rise to the annual challenge; one past prompt was "Does the moral character of an orgy change when the participants wear Nazi uniforms?" Answer: if Prince Harry is there, no. Finalists are then invited to a dinner, where the dons confirm that they are "well-born, well-bred, and only moderately learned." Ultimately, anywhere from zero to two graduate fellowships are offered each year (and include the great state architect T.E. Lawrence and great architect Christopher Wren). A walk around the college itself is one of quiet beauty and regality.

i Entrance to the right of Catte St. from High St. Free. ☉ Open Sept-Jul M-F 2-4pm.

FOOD

Here's one major perk of visiting a student town: **kebab trucks.** These student favorites line High St., Queen St., and Broad St. (we recommend Hassan's on Broad St.), and stay open until 3am during the week and 4 or 4:30am on weekends.

▧ THE VAULTS AND GARDEN
CAFE $$

St. Mary's Church, Radcliffe Sq.   ☎01865 279 112 www.vaultsandgarden.com

In the summer, this garden is hands-down the best place for lunch in the entire city. Based out of the University Church of St. Mary the Virgin, the large garden offers picturesque views of the Bodleian Library, Radcliffe Camera, and nearby colleges. You can even stretch out and soak up the sun on picnic blankets while enjoying the Brideshead life (although the emphasis is less on champagne and strawberries than on scones and tea). Notwithstanding, the eponymous vaults are a worthy consolation prize if rain reigns. The organic, locally sourced menu charges daily, with fresh salads, sandwiches, and soups, as well as coffee, yogurt, and pastries.

i Turn up St. Mary's Passage off Queen St. or High St. 10% student discount. Lunch entrees £7-10. Tea items £2.20 each. ☉ Open daily 8:30am-6:30pm.

GEORGINA'S
CAFE $

Avenue 3, The Covered Market   ☎01865 249 527

Hiding above the furor of the Covered Market sits this fantastically unpretentious coffee shop. The old movie posters papering the ceiling and the cluttered seating arrangements ensure that you can lounge here comfortably while tackling a large-portioned meal. If you need a solid breakfast after a regrettable late-night kebab run, their custom omelettes ($4.75) are a solid victory in the eternal struggle against hangover.

i From Carfax, walk down High St. Turn right and enter the Covered Market. Go onto Avenue 3 and look for a staircase about halfway down. Tends to be full or nearly full from noon-1pm.Bagels, ciabatta, and panini £3.20-3.95. ☼ Open M-Sa 8:30am-5pm.

THE EAGLE AND CHILD
PUB $

49 St. Giles'   ☎01865 302 925

This pub was a favorite watering hole of JRR Tolkien, C.S. Lewis, and the group of writers who dubbed themselves the"Inklings." However, while visiting a bar that a serial alcoholic like George Orwell or Charles Bukowski frequented is a legitimate chance to channel their energy, it's harder to link the author of "Mere Christianity" with a drinking establishment. This brick and wood pub is now more of a tourist destination than a charming bar, although the booths at the front can shield you from cameras and hushed awe.

i From Carfax (west end of High St.), follow Cornmarket St., which becomes St. Giles'. Sandwiches £5.75-9.75. Burgers £8-11.50. ☼ Open M-Th 11am-11pm, F-Sa 11am-midnight, Su noon-10:30pm.

ATOMIC BURGER
BURGERS $$

96 Cowley Rd.   ☎01865 790 855 www.atomicburger.co.uk

This funky, outer space-themed restaurant offers a pop culture laden litany of delicious burgers, sides, shakes, and drinks. You can blow out your brain's capacity *Hitchhiker's Guide*-style with Zaphod's Flaming Gargleblaster Margherita (tequila, triple sec, and absinthe; $7.50) or *Pulp Fiction*-style with a Big Kahuna burger. The inside of the restaurant looks like the bedroom of a child yearning to be an astronaut (or that of an adult with arrested development), but the joint is so earnestly not self-conscious that it makes you forget the heavy use of Comic Sans.

i Follow High St. past Magdalen College and across Magdalen Bridge and head down Cowley Rd. All burgers come with a free side. 10% discount on takeout. Gluten-free options, vegetarian options. Burger with 1 side £6.75-9.25. ☼ Open M-F noon-10:30pm, Sa-Su 10am-10:30pm.

FREUD
CAFE, BAR $

119 Walton St.   ☎020 7240 1100 www.freud.eu

We're pretty sure there's nothing in *Interpretation of Dreams* that explains what drinking and dancing in a cathedral means. Regardless of the inexplicable premise, Freud inhabits the vaulted interior of a 19th-century Greek Revival church, stained glass and all—if it wasn't for the cafe tables on the portico outside, you'd never guess that this place serves food. The cafe progresses into a cocktail bar at night, with a DJ on the weekends. That may explain the disco ball, but it doesn't make the presence of a cocktail menu above a church pew any more comprehensible.

i From the train station, follow Botley Rd. toward the town center, bear left onto Hythe Bridge St., then left onto Worcester St., which becomes Walton St. Freud is on the right, next to Radcliffe Infirmary. Sandwiches and pizza £5.50-8. Appetizers and snacks £1.75-4.50. Cocktails £6-7. ☼ Open M 5pm-midnight, Tu 5pm-1am, W 10:30am-1am, Th-Sa 10:30am-2am, Su 10:30am-midnight. Kitchen open daily until 10pm.

NIGHTLIFE

If the London clubbing scene is a nice Talisker, Oxford is a fair glass of Pinot Blanco, and Cambridge is a paper bag that once had Rubinoff and now has piss in it. Point being, nightlife here doesn't incur the excitement of London, but it could be much, much worse. The main clubbing area in Oxford is near the train station, on **Park End** and **Hythe Bridge Streets.** Both of these split off from **Botley Road** (the train station's home). The center of town has little in the way of dancing, but its many excellent pubs are perfect for a more laid-back evening.

◪ PURPLE TURTLE UNION BAR
BAR, CLUB

Fewin Ct. ☎01865 247 007 www.purpleturtlebar.com

Prepare yourself for claustrophobic tunnel vision as you consume enough flaming absinthe shots to become the green fairy incarnate. This underground bar is directly under the Oxford Union Debating Society, and true to form, you're probably going to host the largest internal debate of your life when trying to decide which one of the 40 shooter options (based on the personalities of the different colleges) is really you. We're going to put on our Sorting Hat and recommend the Slytherin shooter (green absinthe, apple sours) regardless. The dance floor can get a bit insanely cramped, but the DJs spin with a deft hand.

i From Carfax, walk down Cornmarket St. Turn left onto Frewin Ct. Beer from £2. Shooters £2.50. Shots from £1.50. ◪ Open M-Sa 8pm-3am, Su 8pm-2am.

◪ THE BEAR INN
PUB

6 Alfred St. ☎018 6572 8164 www.bearoxford.co.uk

The Bear may be the oldest pub in Oxford—the current building was built in the 18th century, but previous incarnations go all the way back to 1242 (and since bears in Oxford went extinct in the 10th century, who knows?). Anyway, the pub does show its age with low ceilings and rickety stairs that make it slightly perilous for the tall and/or clumsy patron. But don't let this put you off; the Bear is a great, unfussy place to enjoy a pint. The ties in the display cases have been given in exchange for half pints and hail from clubs and colleges around the world.

i Off High St., just behind Christ Church. Pub quiz Tu 8:30pm. Live music W 9pm. Pints £3.50. ◪ Open M-Th 11am-11pm, F-Sa 11am-midnight, Su 11:30am-10:30pm.

THE KING'S ARMS
PUB

40 Holywell St. ☎018 6524 2369 www.kingsarmsoxford.co.uk

The King's Arms embraced only men from 1607-1973, and as befits an old-guard vestige of the patriarchy, there are enough leather-bound booths and pervasive whiffs of mahogany to sufficiently prove its masculinity. However, the various traditional rooms don't ooze the fabricated pubbiness of the chains, and it's no surprise that professors sometimes hold office hours here. Brass tacks, it's on students' list of reliable pubs to hit when a Royal Baby is born, when Andy Murray wins Wimbledon, or when anything that will make day-drinking more excusable occurs.

i Across the street from the Bodleian Library. On the corner between Holywell St. and Park St. Beer from £3.40. ◪ Open daily 10:30am-midnight. Kitchen open until 9:30pm.

JERICHO TAVERN
PUB, LIVE MUSIC

56 Walton St. ☎018 6531 1775 www.thejerichooxford.co.uk

Radiohead debuted here back in 1984; since then, Jericho Tavern has been sold and bought, remodeled and rebranded, but has always remained an indie favorite and a good spot to find live music in Oxford. The heated outdoor beer garden is also a plus, especially if you get a Fruli Strawberry Beer (or, you know, something less girly) to enjoy out there. There's live acoustic at 8pm on Sundays, and board games are available for further entertainment.

oxford

i From Carfax, walk north on Cornmarket St., which becomes Magdalen St. Turn left onto Beaumont St., then right onto Walton St. The tavern is near the Phoenix Picturehouse. Pints around £3.50. ✪ Open M-F noon-midnight, Sa 11am-midnight, Su noon-midnight. Kitchen closes at 10pm.

THE CELLAR   LIVE MUSIC

Frewin Ct.   ☎018 6524 4761 www.cellaroxford.co.uk

"Underground" music is one of those phrases that is immediately coded as"furtive," "obscure," and "authentic." But the Cellar brings it back to its roots by being very obviously underground, with tunnels echoing the newest, boldest rock groups and alternative DJs. Going through phases of greatness and less-than-greatness over the last few years, the Cellar is on the upswing again, clinging to its independent identity and subterranean culture. In other words, it has not sold out like the Bridge (which joins artists to corporations, obviously).

i From the Town Center, walk down Cornmarket St. Turn left onto Frewin Ct. Check events online. Cover £5-12. ✪ Open M-Sa 10pm-3am, Su 10pm-2am.

ARTS AND CULTURE

OXFORD PLAYHOUSE   THEATER

11-12 Beaumont St.   ☎01865 305 305 www.oxfordplayhouse.com

Known to locals as "The Playhouse," this independent theater hosts student and amateur dramas, contemporary dance and music, comedy, lectures, and poetry. Whether it's Philip Pullman and Neil Gaiman chatting or a production staged completely in the dark, whatever event is on will not be your average sit-and-pretend-to-appreciate-theater experience. In the summer, the theater puts on Shakespeare performances in the quad in front of the Bodleian Library (and also hosts Globe Theatre touring companies, meaning a trip to London is not necessary).

i Down Beaumont St. from the Ashmolean Musem. Ticket prices vary. Advance concessions £2 off. Student standbys available day of show for £9.50. ✪ Box office open M-Sa 10am-6pm or until 30min. after curtain, Su from 2hr. before curtain to 30min. after (performance days only). Cafe open 10am-11pm (closes at 5:30pm on non-performance nights).

ESSENTIALS

Practicalities

- **TOURIST OFFICES:** The Tourist Information Centre (TIC) provides the free "What's On In Oxford" guide, sells discounted tickets to local attractions, and books rooms with a 10% deposit. (15-16 Broad St. *i* From Carfax, take Cornmarket St., then turn right onto Broad St. ☎01865 252 200 www.visitoxford.org ✪ Open M-Sa 9:30am-5pm, Su 10am-4pm. Closes 30min. earlier in winter.)

- **STUDENT TRAVEL OFFICES:** STA Travel. (Threeways House, 36 George St. *i* From Carfax, take Cornmarket St. Turn left onto George St. The office is on the right. ☎0871 702 9839 www.statravel.co.uk ✪ Open M 10am-6pm, Tu-Th 9am-7pm, F 10am-7pm, Sa 10am-6pm, Su 11am-5pm.)

- **TOURS** :The official Oxford University Walking Tour leaves from the TIC and provides access to some colleges otherwise closed to visitors. The 2hr. tours are capped at 19 people and are booked on a first-come, first-served basis. You can get tickets up to 48hr. in advance at the TIC, by phone,or online. (☎01852 726 871, ☎01865 252 200 to book tickets www.visitoxford. org *i* £8, children £4.50. ✪ Tours daily in summer 11am and 1pm (additionally 10:45am and 2pm on Sa). Themed tours, like the C.S. Lewis, Harry Potter and J.R.R. Tolkien Tours run on a varied schedule; check with the TIC. (*i* £15, concessions £10.)

- **CURRENCY EXCHANGE:** Banks line Cornmarket St. Marks and Spencer has a bureau de change with no commission. (13-18 Queen St. *i* From Carfax, walk down Cornmarket St. M&S is on the right. ☎01865 248 075 ☒ Open M-W 8:30am-6:30pm, Th 8:30am-7:30pm, F 8:30am-6:30pm, Sa 8:30am-6:30pm, Su 11am-4:30pm.) There is also a bureau de change with no commission attached to (but not affiliated with) the TIC.

- **INTERNET:** Free at Oxford Central Library; however, there is often a wait during prime hours. Some stations are open to pre-booking if you know exactly when you'd like to use it. (Westgate *i* From Carfax, walk down Queen St. The library is ahead. ☒ Open M-Th 9am-7pm, F-Sa 9am-5:30pm.) Offered for free at most cafes in the area.

- **POST OFFICE:** 102-104 St. Aldate's. (☎01865 513 25 postoffice.co.uk *i* From Carfax, take St. Aldate's. Bureau de change inside. ☒ Open M-Sa 9am-5:30pm.

Emergency

- **EMERGENCY SERVICES:** In any emergency, dial ☎999.

- **POLICE:** On the corner of St. Aldates and Speedwell St. (St. Aldates ☎08458 505 505 ☒ Open 24hr.)

- **HOSPITALS/MEDICAL SERVICES:** John Radcliffe Hospital. (Headley Way ☎01852 741 166 *i* Bus #13 or 14.)

Getting There

Botley Road Station (Botley Rd., down Park End St. ☎01865 484 950 ☒ Ticket office open M-F 5:45am-8pm, Sa 7:30am-8pm, Su 7:15am-8pm) receives trains from: **Birmingham** (£34 ☒ 1hr., every 30min.) **Glasgow** (£116 ☒ 5-6hr., every hr.); **London Paddington** (£23.40 ☒ 1hr., 2-4 per hr.); and **Manchester** (£62.80 ☒ 3hr., 2 per hr.).

By Bus

Gloucester Green Station is the city's main bus station. The Oxford Bus Company (☎01865 785 400 www.oxfordbus.co.uk) runs the **Oxford Express** (*i* Free Wi-Fi. £14, students £11 ☒ 1½hr., every 15-30min.) and the **X70 Airline** runs from Heathrow Airport. (*i* Free Wi-Fi. £23. ☒ 1½hr., every 30min.) It also runs the **X80 service** from Gatwick Airport. (*i* Free Wi-Fi. £28 ☒ 2½hr., every hr.) It's best to book tickets in advance on the Oxford Bus website. The **X5 bus** connects Oxford with Cambridge. (*i* Free Wi-Fi. £12.50 ☒ 3¼hr., every 30min.)

Getting Around

By Bus

Oxford Bus Company (☎01865 785 400 www.oxfordbus.co.uk) provides service throughout the city. Fares vary depending on distance traveled. (*i* Day Pass £4, weekly pass £14.) Weekly passes can be purchased at the Oxford Bus Company Travel Shop. (*i* 3rd fl. of Debenham's department store, on the corner of George St. and Magdalen St. ☒ Open M-W 9:30am-6pm, Th 9:30am-8pm, F 9:30am-6pm, Sa 9am-6pm, Su noon-4pm.) **Stagecoach** (☎01865 772 250 www.stagecoachbus.com) also runs buses in the city and to some surrounding villages. One-way tickets within the city usually cost £1.80. Buy a pass for a week of riding within Oxford for £16. Be careful when buying Day Passes because they don't apply to both companies. For real-time information on buses in Oxford, use www.oxontime.com, which will also text you the schedule.

By Taxi

Call **Radio Taxi**(☎01865 242 424) or **ABC** (☎01865 770 077) for taxis. There are taxi ranks at Oxford Station, Saint Giles, Gloucester Green, and in the evening at Carfax. Taxis may be hailed in the street.

By Bike

You can rent some wheels at **Cyclo Analysts**. (150 Cowley Rd. ☎01865 424 444 www.oxfordcycles.com *i* Includes lock. £10, 2 days £18, 3 days £24, every additional day £3. ☼ Open M-Sa 9am-6pm, Su 10am-4pm.)

cambridge

Eight centuries of history, 31 colleges, and the energy of a living university town, all in one easily accessible package. It was here that James Watson and Francis Crick (with the oft-forgotten Rosalind Franklin's help) discovered the double helix, Sir Isaac Newton deduced gravity, Lord Byron and John Milton wrote their famous poetry, and **Winnie-the-Pooh** was born. The city is dominated by its eponymous university; the school's medieval buildings line the winding streets, and every pub, club, and cafe seems to exist to serve students. If you're looking for the definitive Cambridge experience, try the "P and P" formula: Punting and Pimm's—in American, boating and boozing. This is best done in the summer, when the banks of the Cam turn green and flowers bloom in the college gardens, but to get a sense of the real Cambridge, you'll have to come during term-time, when the town fills with its 18,000 students.

ORIENTATION

With just two avenues—and helpful maps galore—Cambridge is relatively easy to navigate. The main shopping street starts at **Magdalene Bridge,** north of the River Cam, and appears alternatively as Bridge St., Sidney St., St. Andrew's St., Regent St., and Hills Rd. The other principal thoroughfare begins at **Saint John's Street** (just off Bridge St.), and becomes Trinity St., King's Parade, and Trumpington St. To get into town from the Drummer St. bus station, take **Emmanuel Road,** which leads to St. Andrew's St. and a bank-heavy block with loads of ATMs. To get to the center of town from the train station, follow **Station Road,** turn right onto Hills Rd., then follow it straight until it becomes St. Andrew's St. in the town center. The River Cam runs along the northern and western edges of the city center.

SIGHTS

Cambridge is quite different from Oxford—its "peer institution"—in that the colleges are more homely, with a few grandiose exceptions like King's and Trinity. We've listed our favorites below, but all the city-center colleges are beautiful (the "new," 20th-century colleges can be skipped), but if you're only in town for a few days,you can take a punt and see six or seven of them from behind in one go. The town itself—which is a sight in its own right—has the close-to-the-ground feel of an agricultural market (quite a contrast from Oxford's warren of gothic castles). As for the museums, most showcase what Cambridge is famous for: excellence in the sciences, from the poles of botany to engineering.

KING'S COLLEGE   COLLEGE
King's Parade   ☎01223 331 100 www.kings.cam.ac.uk

Founded by Henry VI in 1441, King's College was the feeder school for Eton until it relaxed its admission policy in 1873 and reluctantly began to accept students from vastly inferior schools like Harrow. These days, King's draws more students from state schools than any other Cambridge college, and it has gained a reputation as the most socially liberal of the institutions. Still, you wouldn't guess that from the massive buildings and the rolling grounds that scream privilege. Catch a look from the other side of the river to see the college in all its glory, then come visit the Gothic King's College Chapel, where spidering arches and stunning stained glass will wow even the most church-weary tourist. King's alumni include John Maynard Keynes, E.M. Forster, and Salman Rushdie.

i *King's Parade is the western of the city center's 2 main avenues, the northern continuation of Trumpington St. £7.50, concessions and ages 12-18 £5, under 12 free. ☎ Open during term time M-F 9:45am-3:30pm, Sa 9:30am-3:15pm; outside of term time M 9:45am-4:30pm, Tu-Su 9:30am-5pm. During term time, Evensong in chapel M-Sa 5:30pm; Su Eucharist 10:30am, Evensong 3:30pm.*

▨ TRINITY COLLEGE COLLEGE

Trinity Ln.   ☎01223 338 400 www.trin.cam.ac.uk

Welcome to the largest and richest college in Cambridge. Glib descriptions attribute its founding to Henry VIII, but it was really Catherine Parr who persuaded the ornery king to create a new college instead of destroying the whole Oxbridge system monastery-style. Now, Trinity is famous for its illustrious alumni, which include literati Dryden, Byron, Tennyson, and Nabokov; atom-splitter Ernest Rutherford; philosopher Ludwig Wittgenstein; and Indian statesman Jawaharlal Nehru. The epically beautiful Great Court is the world's largest enclosed courtyard—and also the track for young runners who attempt to beat the 12 strikes of the clock in under 43 seconds as shown in Chariots of Fire (even though it was filmed at Eton). The supposed great-great grandchild of the apple tree that inspired Issac Newton's theory of gravity stands near the gate; in the north cloister of nearby Neville's Court, Newton calculated the speed of sound by stamping his foot and timing the echo. In less practical exercises, Lord Byron used to bathe nude in the college's fountain and kept a pet bear because college rules forbade cats and dogs. The Wren Library houses alumnus A.A. Milne's handwritten copies of Winnie-the-Pooh and Newton's personal copy of his Principia. Trinity also has punts, available for rent by the river near Garret Hostel Ln.

i *Turn left off Trinity St. onto Trinity Ln. £3, children £1.50. Punts £14 per hr. with £40 deposit. ☎ Courtyard open daily 10am-4:30pm. Wren Library open M-F noon-2pm. Hall open 3-5pm. Punts available spring-summer M-F 11am-5:30pm, Sa-Su 10am-5:30pm.*

▨ THE FITZWILLIAM MUSEUM MUSEUM

Trumpington St.   ☎01223 332 900 www.fitzmuseum.cam.ac.uk

This grandiose revivalist museum has the variety of the British Museum without the crushing realization that all of the exhibits came about directly via colonialism (then again, an argument can be made for structural violence in the case of the absurdly wealthy British collector who started the museum). Loosely centered around "art and antiquities," the collection hosts a fearsome selection of Italian and French painters; Greek and Middle Eastern pottery; Egyptian sarcophagi; and illustrated medieval manuscripts. On the more modern side of things, there are some excellently preserved works by Thomas Hardy and Virginia Woolf as well.

i *Free. Audio tours £3, students £2. Guided tours £4. ☎ Open Tu-Sa 10am-5pm, Su noon-5pm. Guided tours depart from the courtyard entrance Sa at 2:30pm.*

ST. JOHN'S COLLEGE COLLEGE

St. John's St.   ☎01223 338 600 www.joh.cam.ac.uk

The motto of St. John's—*"souvent me souvient"*—is a triple pun, and none of them have to do with souvenirs. One meaning is "Often I remember," which is appropriate given that the college celebrated its quincentennial in 2011. William Wilberforce, William Wordsworth, Sir Cecil Beaton, and Douglas Adams are only a few of the students that have studied here through its history. A second meaning of the slogan is "Think of me often"—not difficult when considering the gorgeous chapel, Bridge of Sighs, or the 93ft.-long Fellows' Room where some of the D-Day planning happened. St. John's is also associated with its choir, which has been singing Evensong for over 300 years. The final pun is "I often pass

Budget lodging options in Cambridge are notoriously bad, as people who come to visit or live here either fall into the categories of "student with pre-arranged dorm room" or "parent with some dough to burn." There are few affordable rooms near the town center, and overpriced, occasionally sketchy bed and breakfasts fill the area to the north and south of town. In particular, B&Bs cluster on **Arbury Road** and **Chesterton Road** to the north; several can be found close to the station on **Tenison Road.** Bus #1 goes between Tenison Rd. and the town center, while bus #2 serves Chesterton Rd. When the university is not in session, many of the colleges offer their rooms (generally called "digs") at competitive prices (usually £30-70 for a single); check www.cambridgerooms.co.uk for more information. For more recommendations, visit **www.letsgo.com.**

LYNWOOD HOUSE
B&B $$$$
217 Chesterton Rd.   ☎01223 500 776 www.lynwood-house.co.uk

This recently renovated B&B traded in predictable floral motifs that commonly grace Victorian hotels for a bolder, modern theme. The rooms are nice, large, and well designed, with rich, tasteful color combinations and great furnishings. Though Lynwood House is a bit to the north of the city center, there's a convenient cluster of pubs and stores nearby.

i *From the town center, take either Victoria Ave. or Bridge St., then turn right onto Chesterton Rd. Free Wi-Fi and ethernet. Breakfast included. Ensuite bathrooms. Often 2-night min. stay. Check website for details. Singles £65-85; doubles £85-120.*

beneath it," which could possibly be interpreted now as snooty Trinity College rivals passing by while humming "We'd Rather Be at Oxford than St. John's" (sung to the tune of "She'll Be Coming 'Round the Mountain").

i *Head north on Sidney St., which becomes Bridge St. Take a left onto St. John's St. £5, ages 12-17 £3.50, under 12 free. ☒ Open daily Mar-Oct 10am-5:30pm; Nov-Feb 10am-3:30pm.*

MAGDALENE COLLEGE
COLLEGE
Magdalene St.   ☎01223 332 100 www.magd.cam.ac.uk

Magdalene College (pronounced MAUD-lin) was not only purposely built on the other side of the river in order to protect its Benedictine monks from the town's licentious crowd, but it was also the last Oxbridge college to admit women in 1988 (students protested vigorously by wearing black armbands). This is all a bit strange given the college's namesake, Mary Magdalene, and the fact that they host the most lavish May Ball every year (it's also the only college that insists on a white tie dress code). Academically, it's famous for the Pepys Library, which holds some of the diaries of C.S. Lewis, who, though an Oxford man, occasionally lived in Magdalene. The long riverfront area behind the main courtyards is technically closed to visitors, but some travelers report that if you look like a student—and act like you know what you're doing—it's possible to stroll unbothered along the willow-lined path.

i *Walk south down Huntington Rd. as it changes into Castle St., then into Magdalene St. Free. ☒ Open daily until 6pm. Library open daily Apr 20-Aug 31 11:30am-12:30pm and 2:30-3:30pm; Oct 6-Dec 5 2:30-3:30pm; Jan 12-Mar 13 2:30-3:30pm.*

WHIPPLE MUSEUM OF THE HISTORY OF SCIENCE
MUSEUM
Free School Ln.   ☎01223 330 906 www.hps.cam.ac.uk/whipple

The trope of "Oxford for humanities, Cambridge for sciences" goes a long way to explain the focus of this museum. Robert Whipple donated a collection of 1000 scientific devices to the university, and many of these are on display here. Newer additions include the Gömböc (a mathematically precise object that rolls to the same resting position no matter where you place it) and Fred, a 19th-century anatomical model whose parts have been mercilessly scattered across the museum. Several intriguing planetariums, some microscopes and telescopes, and a wealth of pocket calculators round out the quirkily fascinating collection.

i Turn left off St. Andrew's St. onto Downing St. Follow it until it becomes Pembroke and turn right onto Free School Ln.Free. ☒ Open M-F 12:30-4:30pm.

CHRIST'S COLLEGE COLLEGE

St. Andrews St. ☎01223 334 900 www.christs.cam.ac.uk

"Tempered to the Oaten Flute / Rough Satyrs danced and fauns with cloven heel" would be an epic testimonial on the "Is Christ's College Right For You?" admissions page. And indeed, that was how John Milton—called by his friends "The Lady of Christ's"—described the college in *Lycidas*. A portrait and bust in the Great Hall pay homage to Milton and another of Christ's famous alums: Charles Darwin, who didn't lionize the college nearly as much. Sacha Baron Cohen also graduated from Christ's, so we all look forward to the day when a picture of Borat will adorn the wall.

i Continue north on Hills Rd. until it turns into Regent St., then into St. Andrew's St. Free. ☒ Open daily 9:30am-noon.

JESUS COLLEGE COLLEGE

Jesus Ln. ☎01223 339 339 www.jesus.cam.ac.uk

Yes, it's hard to keep all of the colleges straight when the names are only variations on a New Testament theme. A good memory aide is to think of Jesus being tempted to stay hours in this college's 25 acres of lovely gardens and courts. Keep an eye out for some strange art installations that include the annual Sculpture in the Close (when we visited, it was 10 mannequins re-enacting a crime scene). Attracting an eclectic set, the college's alumni include Thomas Cranmer, Samuel Taylor Coleridge, and Nick Hornby.

i Go north on Sidney St. and turn right onto Jesus Ln. Free. ☒ Open daily 8am-dusk.

FOOD

For a "college town," Cambridge has more upscale dining options than off-licenses and supermarkets. However, there are a number of cheap cafes that can set you up with a meal for less than £5. The summer months see students camping out on one of the "Pieces" with wine and sandwiches or strolling the streets with ice cream cones.

▨ THE EAGLE PUB $$

8 Bene't St. ☎01223 505 020

Even though Cambridge students might roll their eyes at this pub's high tourist profile, it remains genuine enough to still draw crowds of locals. Why the fame? It's a veritable monument to life and death. On February 28, 1953, Francis Crick and James Watson burst into the Eagle to announce their discovery of the "secret to life"—the double helix. And toward the back, look for the messages and squad numbers that RAF men scorched into the ceiling on the evenings before piloting missions during World War II. For your hopefully less dramatic purposes, the bar adds to its storied charm with affordable alcohol and classics of the pub food genre—sausage and mash, a slab of a burger and chips, or a steaming steak and ale pie.

i Heading south on King's Parade, turn left onto Bene't St. Entrees £8-14. Pints around £3.50. Credit card min. £5. ☒ Open M-Sa 10am-11pm, Su 11am-10:30pm.

▨ STICKYBEAKS CAFE $

42 Hobson St. ☎01223 359 397 www.stickybeakscafe.co.uk

There's something beautiful about a cafe that provides all of the white, blinding modern vibe of a gallery while serving you gourmet food as well. The menu items here are a bit fancier than your average ham and cheese toast (think more continental, like bruschetta and olives), but you can nab some heartier breakfast staples for cheap if you're not satisfied with hostel corn flakes and toast.

i Hobson St. splits off to the right of Sidney St., next to Christ's College. Breakfast dishes £1.50-3. Lunch dishes £4.50-7. ☼ Open M-F 8am-5:30pm, Sa 9am-5:30pm, Su 10am-5pm.

DOJO'S NOODLE BAR
ASIAN $

1-2 Millers Yard ☎01223 363 471

The closest a dignified Cambridge student is going to come to a real dojo is in a Pokémon game, but the only thing getting beaten to death in this establishment are noodle puns (place settings are bordered with "Noodfucius," little words of wisdom). Every imaginable Asian noodle dish is served here: Japanese, Chinese, Thai, and Malaysian are all fair game. The quick service, large portions, and low prices make this a popular and worthy student haunt.

i Turn onto Mill Ln. off Trumpington St., then left onto Millers Yard. Entrees from £7-9. ☼ Open M-F noon-2:30pm and 5:30-11pm, Sa-Su noon-11pm.

INDIGO COFFEE HOUSE
CAFE $

8 St. Edward's Passage ☎01223 295 688

A student favorite, the Indigo Coffee House has two tiny floors of British charm tucked off an equally cute alley. Plentiful sandwich options (available on sliced bread, baguette, or bagel) extend from the standard ham and cheese to chorizo and tomato. They also serve up a host of cakes, croissants, and salads. Note the sign that threatens to levy a £1 fine for incorrect usage of the word "literally."

i Head toward Trinity on King's Parade and turn right onto St. Edward's Passage. It's 1 street to the right of St. Mary's Church when you're facing it. Sandwiches £3-5. Coffee from £1.50. Cash only. ☼ Open M-F 10am-6pm, Sa 9am-6pm, Su 10am-5pm.

NIGHTLIFE

Nightlife in Cambridge is split between pubs that close at 11pm and clubs that don't get going until midnight. Clubs are generally reserved for drunken student nights out, which, depending on what you're looking for, can either make for a great time or a total nightmare. The pubs tend to be of an extremely high quality—full of good beer (almost universally £3.50-4) and even better conversation. Keep in mind that, during term-time, colleges run their own bars, some of which are open to the public.

■ THE MAYPOLE
PUB

20A Portugal Pl. ☎01223 352 999 www.maypolefreehouse.co.uk

This lively pub is known affectionately as"The Staypole" thanks to it being one of the few bars in Cambridge with a late-night license. It takes advantage of its status as a "free house" (meaning that it's independent from any brewery and can serve whatever beers it wants) by stocking a selection of a dozen rotating beers on draft and many more in bottles. It's a tremendously popular spot, where students drink pints and pitchers of cocktails late into the night.

i When walking toward the river on Sidney St., turn right onto Portugal Pl. Pints from £3.50; pitchers £12-14. ☼ Open M-Th 11:30am-midnight, F-Sa 11:30am-1am, Su noon-11:30pm.

THE ELM TREE
PUB

16A Orchard St. ☎01223 502 632 www.theelmtreecambridge.co.uk

The pub may look very English, but its specialty is Belgian beer. Over 50 brews are represented here, and as you step inside, you'll be offered an incredibly helpful menu. The two rooms hold dusty bottles and tables filled with locals, while pictures of drinking customers cover the walls. Outside, the smoking crowd spills out as the only acknowledgment there's a pub in the quiet area. Occasionally, the space hosts live music.

i Walking south on Parker St., make a left onto Clarendon St. The pub is on the corner with Orchard St. Beer from £3.50. Cash only. ☼ Open daily 11am-11pm.

HIDDEN ROOMS

BAR

7A Jesus Ln.   ☎01223 514 777 www.hiddenthing.com

The curtained booths and leather upholstery of this cocktail bar recall the days when Churchill and de Gaulle would meet in this underground lounge. Even if state-making isn't on the evening's agenda, you'll feel sufficiently sophisticated as you sip on one of the dozens of classic and unclassic cocktails twirled and poured behind the glamorous bar. When the ol' peripheral vision inevitably starts to go, make a beeline to the club room, which offers a darker, louder section with quickly changing tracks and dazzling light shows.

i With the ADC Theater on your right, head to the end of Park St. Turn right onto Jesus Ln. It's on the right. 2-for-1 cocktails M-W.Cocktails £6.80-9.20. ☼ Open M-Sa 3pm-12:30am, Su 3-10:30pm.

ARTS AND CULTURE

▨ ADC THEATRE

THEATER, COMEDY, DANCE

Park St.   ☎01223 300 085 www.adctheatre.com

"It was grown-up and polished, yet at the same time bashful and friendly; it was sophisticated and intelligent but never pretentious or pleased with itself; it had authority, finish, and quality without any hint of self-regard, vanity, or slickness," wrote Stephen Fry of the first Cambridge Footlights show he saw. The "Arts Dramatic Club" is the student-run theater that hosts the Footlights, which launched the comedic careers of Hugh Laurie, Fry, and half of Monty Python. Many other famous actors who attended Cambridge—including Ian McKellen, Emma Thompson, and Rachel Weisz—performed here as well. During term-time, there are usually two performances per day, while out of term there are still shows most days. There are occasional dance shows in addition to the usual theater and comedy.

i Head away from town center and take a left off Jesus Ln. to get to Park St. Tickets £5-10, concessions sometimes available. ☼ Box office open Tu 12:30-7pm, W-Th 3-7pm, F 12:30-7pm, Sa 3-7pm.

▨ SCUDAMORE'S

PUNTING

Quayside   ☎01223 359 750 www.scudamores.com

For North Americans, punting is solely related to kicking a football across half a stadium. For Cantabrigians (excluding the Boston variety), it is glamorously sticking a pole in mud and vaulting your way along the river Cam. Unless you're an old hand or an idiot, it's best to avoid the self-hire option and get a tour guide to regale you with over-the-top accounts of alumni and their youthful exploits. Scudamore's is the gold standard, with a small kiosk on the river and a fleet of attractive men roaming around the banks aggressively advertising the punting experience.

i Underneath Magdalene Bridge. Take a right off Bridge St. Another location is at the end of Mill St. Self-hire £22 per hr., students £16; plus £90 deposit taken in the form of an imprint of your credit or debit card. Guided tours £16, concessions £14.50, under 12 £8. Discounts if you buy tickets online. Private and specialty tours can be pre-booked. ☼ Open daily 9am-dusk.

CAMBRIDGE CORN EXCHANGE

LIVE MUSIC

Wheeler St.   ☎01223 357 851 www.cornex.co.uk

Probably the largest music venue in Cambridge, the Corn Exchange has hosted most of the big-name musical acts that come through Cambridge, from the Beatles and Pink Floyd to The Smiths and Oasis. It also presents musicals, dance performances, and opera. The 19th-century building was established as a space for merchants to trade grain; nowadays, it serves as an exam room for the university when it's not being used for concerts (sadly, they don't play "School's Out" when you finish).

i Heading south on King's Parade, turn left onto Bene't St. and go straight until it becomes Wheeler St. Prices vary. Occasional student discounts. ☼ Open M-Sa 10am-5pm.

ESSENTIALS

Practicalities

- **TOURIST OFFICES:** The Tourist Information Centre at Peas Hill has National Express tickets, discounted punting tickets, and sightseeing bus tickets and also offers accommodations bookings and an access guide to the city for disabled visitors. (☎0871 226 8006 www.visitcambridge. org ✦ Open M-Sa 10am-5pm, Su 11am-3pm.)

- **STUDENT TRAVEL OFFICES:** STA Travel (38 Sidney St. ☎0871 702 9809 www.statravel.co.uk ✦ Open M-Th 10am-7pm, F-Sa 10am-6pm, Su 11am-5pm.)

- **TOURS:** Several walking tours leave from the Tourist Information Centre. The Guided Tour features King's College and Queens' College. (*i* £17.50, concessions £15.50, children £8. ✦ Tours leave daily at 1 and 2pm.)

- **INTERNET:** Jaffa Net Cafe. (22 Mill Rd. ☎01223 308 380 *i* £1 per hr. ✦ Open daily noon-midnight.)

- **POST OFFICES:** Bureau de Change. (9-11 St. Andrew's St. ✦ Open M 9am-5:30pm, Tu 9:30am-5:30pm, W-Sa 9am-5:30pm.)

Emergency

- **POLICE:** on Parkside. (☎0345 456 4564 ✦Open daily 8am-10pm.)

- **HOSPITALS/MEDICAL SERVICES:** Addenbrookes Hospital. (Hills Rd., by the intersection of Hills Rd. and Long Rd. ☎01223 245 151)

Getting There

By Train

The only significant starting point for trains to Cambridge is London. Trains arrive at **Station Road.** (*i* 20min. walk southeast from the town center. ✦ Ticket office open M-Sa 5:10am-11pm, Su 7am-10:55pm.) You can catch trains at London King's Cross (£22. ✦ 50min., 2 per hr.) and **London Liverpool St.** (£15.30. *i* 1¼hr., 2 per hr.)

By Bus

The bus station, mostly for short-distance buses, is on **Drummer Street.** (✦ Ticket office open M-Sa 9am-5:30pm.) Airport shuttles and buses to more distant destinations run from **Parkside.** Buses arrive from: London Victoria (*i* Transfer at Stansted. £12.70. ✦ 3hr., every hr.); Gatwick (£34. ✦ 4hr., every 2hr.); Heathrow (£28.60. ✦ 3hr., every hr.); Stansted (£10.50. ✦ 50min., every 2hr.); Oxford. (*i* Take the X5 bus. £12.50. ✦ 3¼hr., every 30min.)

Getting Around

By Bus

CitiBus runs from stops throughout town, including some on **Saint Andrew's Street, Emmanuel Street,** and at the train station. The most useful routes are C1 (from the station) and C2 (goes out along Chesterton Rd.). Single rides cost £2.20. **Dayrider Tickets** (unlimited travel for 1 day; £3.90) can be purchased on the bus; for longer stays, you can buy a **Megarider** ticket (unlimited travel for weeks; £13 per week).

By Taxi

For a taxi, call **Cabco.** (☎01223 312 444 ✦ Open 24hr.)

By Bike

You'll see students on bikes everywhere in Cambridge. To fit in, go to **City Cycle Hire.** (61 Newnham Rd. ☎01223 365 629 www.citycyclehire.com *i* £7 for 4hr., £10 for 8hr., £12 for 24hr., £17 for 2-3 days, £25 for 4-7 days, £35 for 2 weeks, £80 for up to 3

stonehenge

As the Stonehenge audio tour will explain, Stonehenge is not only an enigma, but a mystery (jury's out on whether either one is wrapped in the other). But the question remains: what is it all for? Is it a calendar? A status symbol? A sacrificial altar? Proof of extra-terrestrials? We're sad to inform you that merely visiting will not leave you with one definitive answer. However, whatever its purpose or maker, the stone circle really does inspire a sense of wonder—and that's enough of a reason for 21st-century tourists to visit.

◪ **STONEHENGE** MONUMENT
Amesbury ☎019 8062 2833 www.english-heritage.org.uk

A trip to Stonehenge paired with a stop in Salisbury—the nearest major city—is a full-day event that basically repeats the message of Ken Follett's *The Pillars of the Earth*: building stuff is hard. Stonehenge itself is a tricky customer. While only 30 years ago, the place was an out-of-the-way tourist spot that only very thorough travelers would attempt to visit, there are now bus tours that drop thousands of visitors next to the highway that Stonehenge overlooks. For casual appreciation of pagan architecture, an hour is all you need; the audio tour will walk you through the materials, construction, layout, and purpose of the pi-shaped masonry. Surprisingly, even though you'll share your magical experience with hundreds of people, the design of the walkway is expertly shaped so that you can get as many mystical selfies as your heart deigns without someone in a red windbreaker wandering into the shot. If you have more time and money saved up, traveling here via Salisbury instead of via the A303 is a nice way to get a more rounded survey of British history (and pre-history).

i By train: take the National Rail from Waterloo to Salisbury (around £40). Once in Salisbury, the Stonehenge Bus leaves from the train station for the site every 30min. from about 9:30am-6pm in summer and 10am-2pm in winter (£12). By bus: tours leave the city (£30 with price of admission). Adult £8, concessions £7.20. By large, with 50-ton rocks: leave that to the pagans. 🕑 Open daily Jan-Mar 15 9:30am-4pm; March 15-May 9:30am-6pm; Jun-Aug 9am-7pm; Sept-Oct 15 9:30am-6pm; Oct 15-Dec 9:30am-4pm.

edinburgh

Edinburgh is many things—a well-preserved medieval city, a college town, a cultural center—but it doesn't feel defined by any of those narrow labels. It feels more like something out of a fairy tale—some mystical place where all the homes are town-houses, all the streets are cobblestoned, and vast cliffs and forests jut into the city center. Indeed, to go for a walk in Edinburgh—whether it's through the stunning valleys of Princes Street Park or the awe-inspiring peaks of Calton Hill—is to be astonished. The locals are blasé but prideful. "Everything here is old and magnificent," one says. "People will say 'oh, that's only 600 years old.'"

Your sense of amazement will likely continue whether you're quaffing a pint in an eccentric pub or visiting one of the city's many museums. There's a reason this is the UK's most popular tourist destination after London.

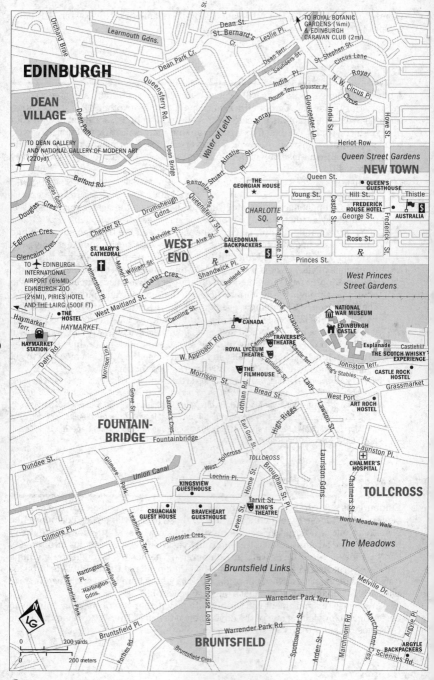

great britain

EDINBURGH

DEAN VILLAGE

WEST END

NEW TOWN

HAYMARKET

FOUNTAIN-BRIDGE

TOLLCROSS

BRUNTSFIELD

The Meadows

Bruntsfield Links

West Princes Street Gardens

Queen Street Gardens

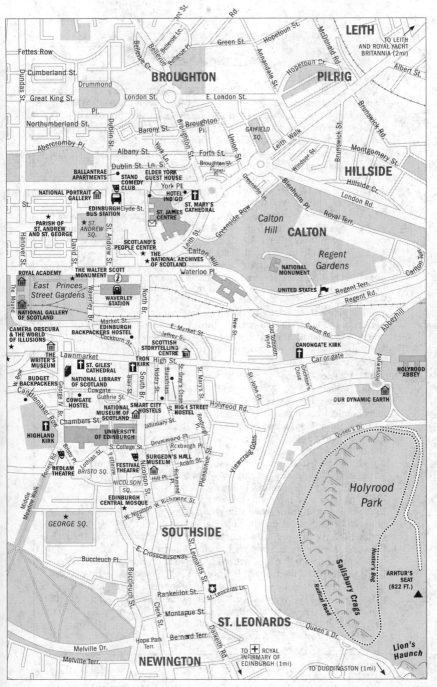

CALEDONIAN BACKPACKERS

HOSTEL $

3 Queensferry St. ☎131 226 2939 www.caledonianbackpackers.com

Caledonian Backpackers is a bit removed from Edinburgh's Old Town, where it can seem like there's a hostel on every corner. But that doesn't mean you're far from where the action is. Princes Street Gardens, Stockbridge, and the old town itself are all within walking distance. And if the thought of not being surrounded with fellow travelers terrifies you, the size of Caledonian Backpackers will put your fears to rest easily.

Despite its close proximity to many of Edinburgh's famous sites, you may be tempted to just stay at the hostel during your stay. Breakfast is available until noon, which basically eliminates the need for lunch. There's a bar on the premises, and the amount of additional social space is overwhelming. Be sure to check out the Cucumber Room, which might be more accurately titled "The Big, Shoes-Optional Room with a Lot of Couches and a Guitar," as well as the Beanbag Cinema.

Bathrooms are not ensuite for some of the larger rooms, but there are enough showers dispensed throughout the hostel so that you won't be left waiting. Towels, shampoo, and other toiletries can be purchased or rented.

The space itself is large, eccentric, and resolutely colorful—a lot of vintage molding and other architectural details have been left in, and colorful murals of different rock stars pepper the walls. And while the large size of your hostel means getting to your room might be something

i Dorms from £13. 🕐 Reception open 24hr.

BUDGET BACKPACKERS

HOSTEL $

37-39 Cowgate ☎131 226 6351 www.budgetbackpackers.com

Usually, great location comes with an obscene price tag. Think of the astronomical costs people pay for beachfront property. But that tried-and-true formula is turned on its head by Budget Backpackers, a hostel minutes away from Edinburgh Castle, the University of Edinburgh, and the Scotch Whisky Experience. Here, you can easily book a bed for £9 a night (provided it's not during the Edinburgh Festival Fringe, where prices skyrocket around the city). "We beat the pants off everyone else for value," the hostel proudly proclaims.

While you may have a tad more company than you're accustomed to (the biggest dorm holds a staggering 30 people), the rooms are big enough for you to keep your personal space intact. And they're clean enough for you to forget the number of people who circulate through here on a weekly basis. Sorry for bringing that up.

Though the hopping area will likely tire you out, Budget Backpackers has a number of attractions in the hostel itself. Spend some time in the chill out room, which features views of Edinburgh Castle and a large plasma screen TV. Breakfast isn't included, but the large kitchens will allow you to cook up whatever you like. And the food provided by the cafe is worth shelling out a few pounds for.

i Dorms from £9 a night. 🕐 Reception open 24hr.

SIGHTS

THE SCOTCH WHISKEY EXPERIENCE

DISTILLERY

354 Castlehill ☎131 220 0441 www.scotchwhiskyexperience.co.uk

Perhaps because it's not affiliated with a specific brand, the Scotch Whisky Experience doesn't beat you over the head the same way the Guinness Brewery and the Old Jameson Distillery do (both of those Dublin attractions, while certainly worth visiting, are not intended for those who want a fair and balanced appraisal of Guinness and/or Jameson). Make no mistake—these guys love everything about whisky—its history, its taste, and, most visibly, its color. The in-house restaurant is called "Amber," the staffers all wear amber ties, and there's even a light yellow glow in some rooms. But they also recognize that some people may not know very much about whisky, and that others might not even like it all that much. For that reason, the tour is a primarily educational experience, albeit one that will appeal to the novice and to the seasoned drinker who's looking to find out more.

You start by getting strapped into a barrel and undergoing a process designed to teach replicate the process of making whisky—it's kind of like a Disney ride combined with an unnatural fascination with alcohol. And while parts of this ride are cheesy, other segments are just plain nuts. Get excited for the yeast room.

The meat of the tour, however, is the whisky tasting. Unless you spring for a pricier ticket (the costliest option includes a three-course meal), you'll only be able to sample one of the four major types of Scotch whisky. This can be a fear-inducing choice, especially since the wrong whisky might well be nausea-inducing. Thankfully, the guides will provide you with a scratch and sniff card, allowing you some insight into the four major flavors. To top it all off, they've got the world's largest collection of Scotch whisky upstairs, seemingly rivaled only by the gift shop's selection.

i Silver tour £13.50, £10.50 for students and seniors, £6.75 for children. Golden tour £23.50, £20 for students and seniors. Platinum tour £27. ☺ Open daily 10am-6pm.

NATIONAL GALLERY OF SCOTLAND

MUSEUM

The Mound ☎131 624 6200 www.nationalgalleries.org

The Scottish National Galleries are beautiful. The buildings themselves are models of neoclassicism, all situated on pristine grounds, be it Princes Street Park or an old estate. And the art inside's pretty good too.

The flagship museum is the National Gallery of Scotland, located in the city center, close to Edinburgh Castle, the Scott Monument, and other frequent tourist destinations. Here, you'll see masterpieces by Rubens, Memling, Titian, and some Scottish artists who have been inexplicably confined to the basement. How's that for national pride?

Though the building is on the smaller side, don't be fooled when you think you've gone through the whole thing in an hour—certain galleries can only be reached through less-than-central passages. Although there's free Wi-Fi in the building, Google Maps can't help you find your way to the early Netherlandish painting room—you'll have to pick up one of the free maps to navigate the space.

If one of the works appeals to you (you'll probably find at least one that really catches your eye), the downstairs gift shop has a truly massive selection of postcards and prints to choose from. It's a cheap, easy-to-transport souvenir (if you get the postcard—prints can get a fair bit pricier).

i Free. ☺ Open M-W, F-Su 10am-5pm. Th 10am-7pm.

edinburgh

SURGEON'S HALL MUSEUM
Nicolson St. ☎131 527 1711 www.museum.rcsed.ac.uk

No one wants to visit a hospital while they're on vacation, but there's nothing wrong with checking out a museum of medical history and curiosities. That's just what you'll get at Edinburgh's Surgeon's Hall, which houses the Royal College of Surgeons of Edinburgh as well as a museum that dates back to 1699.

The collections range from the grisly (check out the Greig Collection of deformed skeletons) to the historic (they've got an original Squire inhaler, which was used to knock patients out with ether in the early days of anesthesia). You'll see plenty of organs and the like in jars (aortas, lymph vessels, and cranial nerves all pop up). Again, the emphasis is on the unusual—one heart has a massive hole caused by a bullet that went straight through it. Cue "You Give Love a Bad Name" by Bon Jovi. The strangest exhibit might well be the Dental History Collection, which traces dentistry back to ancient times. If you think getting your wisdom teeth out stinks, wait 'til you see what they did for toothaches in the Middle Ages.

If all this medical history inspires you, the museum has an interactive exhibit where you get to take on the task of keyhole surgery. After trying your hand at that, marvelous at the bizarre case of Robert Penma, who grew a 72 ounce tumor in his mouth that had to be removed without anesthetic. Really puts your appendix operation into perspective.

i Closed until Summer 2015.

EDINBURGH CASTLE
Castlehill ☎131 225 9846 www.edinburghcastle.gov.uk

You can't miss Edinburgh Castle. Located at the end of the Royal Mile, this immensely popular tourist attraction (1.2 million visitors in 2011) is visible from most points in Edinburgh's City Centre, especially from Old Town or Princes Street. You may do a double take when you first catch sight of the castle, which looks like some rural fortress dropped into the heart of cosmopolitan Edinburgh.

And you might keep doing double takes once you get inside. This is where the Crown Jewels of Scotland are kept, and as you might expect of crown jewels, they're pretty darned opulent. If you like your royal artifacts to be considerably less photogenic, check out the Stone of Destiny, a giant, gray stone used during coronations of Scottish kings. Though it kicked around England for 700 years, it was finally returned to Scotland in 1996.

The Castle's also home to the National War Museum, and for good reason—this site has arguably more importance as a military fortress than as a residential castle. Being at the top of a steep hill helps a lot. Though the National War Museum places understandable emphasis on history, it's also startlingly modern at times—you'll see things like chemical warfare suits right alongside 18th century uniforms. The army had a lot more style back then.

i £16, students and seniors £12.80, children £9.60. ☑ Open daily 9:30am-6pm.

FOOD

TANJORE
6-8 Clerk St. ☎131 478 6518 www.tanjore.co.uk

Edinburgh, for all its charms, can get slightly dreary sometimes. If the gray buildings, gray streets, and gray weather gets you down (an unholy trinity if there ever was one), a spicy meal at Tanjore will get you right back on track. This South Indian restaurant, located a few blocks past the University of Edinburgh, features some of the liveliest cuisine in the city. Go nuts with one of their famous curries, all helpfully labelled with a spice level. Be daring.

Edinburgh attracts artists all year round—the university and museums tend to do that—but what really brings creative types to Scotland's capital are the festivals.

The most famous, of course, is the Edinburgh Festival Fringe, an arts festival held at the end of July and beginning of August. It's the world's largest, and today regularly features over 2000 different performances. There's no selection process, so it's somewhat of a mixed bag—still, the diversity is totally unparalleled. Great for theater and comedy—Tom Stoppard's famous play *Rosencrantz and Guildenstern are Dead* premiered at the Fringe in 1966, and Steve Coogan, Flight of the Conchords, and Demetri Martin have all performed here.

Lesser-known but up-and-coming is the Edinburgh International Film Festival, which occurs at the end of every June. It lacks the red carpet glamour of Cannes and the indie chic of Sundance, but it does have an impressive stock of independent films from around the world, many of which you'll likely have trouble finding again. Be sure to check out a screener or three—when the director makes it big, you'll be able to tell your friends you got in on the ground floor.

Most of the films are followed by question-and-answer sessions, which feature not only obscure directors but TV stars like Parks and Recreation's Aubrey Plaza. What's not to like?

If you're looking for variety, you can't do much better than thali, a South Indian feast of 10 courses served on a giant metal platter. During the weekday, you pack pick one of these babies up for just £8 at lunch; you'll be set for dinner with this amazing deal.

The restaurant's BYOB (no corkage charge, so go crazy on that front) but their non-alcoholic drink menu's no slouch. Try their homemade lime soda or a refreshing mango lassis.

During the day, you'll see a lot of families or older couples. The low-key atmosphere isn't especially amenable to rowdier, younger crowds. Still, the food will provide all the excitement you need—especially if you spring for one of the spicier platters. And with prices like the £8-for-thali special, you really can't go wrong with Tanjore.

i Starters about £3. Mains from £7-10. ⏰ Open weekdays noon-2:30pm, 5-10pm. Weekends noon-3:30pm, 5-10pm.

ROAMIN' NOSE   ITALIAN $$
14 Eyre Place   ☎131 629 3135 www.theroaminnose.com

Given the weird name, the small menu, and the paintings of Bill Murray that fill up the wall, you could easily be forgiven for thinking that the Roamin' Nose is a joint primarily for hipsters, and that the food plays a secondary role to the cooler-than-thou atmosphere. Well, not only is the Roamin' Nose refreshingly devoid of bearded scenesters who will criticize your style and music taste, the hearty food is some of the best you'll find in Edinburgh. With a focus on pasta and other Italian dishes, the small menu is still chock-full of delicious items like spaghetti and clams. The specials list is nearly as long as the menu—go for the venison burger if it's available.

While you'll have to trust the staff when it comes to the menu—don't worry, it pays off—you'll have your pick of drinks. The selection of wines and beers is remarkably exhaustive, and they've got quite a few house cocktails as well. These are particularly worth taking note of, as they're seriously well-priced for

Edinburgh. You can expect to pay as much as £10 for the drinks at hot bars around town. But you don't need to order a drink for the Roamin' Nose to be worth it (even if it's a seriously well-priced drink). Just sink your teeth into one of their delicious meals—after taking a whiff, of course.

i Starters £3-4, Mains £10-14. ☒ Open M 9:30am-5pm, Tu-F 9:30am-10pm, Sa 10am-10pm, Su 10am-5pm.

OINK
PORK $

34 Victoria St.   ☎777 196 8233 www.oinkhogroast.co.uk

There's absolutely no ambiguity about what OINK is selling. If the name didn't tip you off, the giant roasted hog in the window sure will. This tiny restaurant sure knows how to make a pulled pork sandwich. And with all prices under £5 (even for the largest roll), the price is right.

Even if you're not a vegetarian, OINK might be slightly off-putting. The smallest sandwich, after all, is named "piglet." Winnie the Pooh fans, visit at your peril. And the fact that you can get your sandwich with haggis may not be appealing to most. As a side note, this is a great opportunity to try the infamous haggis without committing to a full plate of the stuff.

But if you do go in and get a nice and toasty hog roll, your taste buds will be thanking you all the way home. The impressive speed of the servers belies the exceptional care put into these flavorful sandwiches. Try it with some apple relish to add sweetness.

Somewhat curiously for a sandwich joint, OINK sells souvenir postcards, and that's a testament to just how much of a local fixture it is. Located on Victoria Street, near Grassmarket, OINK is surrounded by tourist hotspots but maintains a staunchly local flavor. Maybe the pig in the window scares off outsiders.

i Sandwiches £1.80-4.50. ☒ Open daily 11am-5pm.

NIGHTLIFE

BREWDOG
BAR

143 Cowgate   ☎131 220 6517 www.brewdog.com/bars/edinburgh

There are a number of hostels up and down Cowgate, and consequently there are a lot of Cowgate Bars that cater to the international party going crowd. BrewDog Edinburgh is not one of those bars. The first thing you see is a giant sign that reads "NO LIVE SPORT, NO FOOTBALL, NO SHOTS, NO STELLA." Under that, in smaller font: "but we do have board games!"

That they do. If you want a good pub quiz but can't find one, why not come here and play a round of Trivial Pursuit? They've got tons of games, along with a remarkable selection of beers on draught and in bottles. With guest beers like Mikkeler Black (16.8% ABV), who needs shots? And with numerous booths and large tables, you'll actually be able to sit down and play some of these board games. If for some reason you're carrying around old boxes of Monopoly or Candyland, bring them here—you'll get a pint for every board game you turn in. Relatedly, there are more than a few thrift stores in the area, some of which stock board games. Use that as you will.

But despite the lack of shots and the older crowd that populates BrewDog during the day, the atmosphere gets admirably rowdy at night. Craft beer gets the crowd just as wild as normal brews do—and since their motto is Beer for Punks, they're not opposed to thinks getting a little loud.

i Pints are generally from £3-5, but specialty brews can cost as much as £8. The wide selection of bottles is also highly variable in terms of price. Nearby: Budget Backpackers, OINK. ☒ M-Sa noon-1am, Su 12:30-1am.

HOLYROOD 9A

BAR

9a Holyrood ☎131 556 5044 www.theholyrood.co.uk

Holyrood 9a looks like a fairly traditional pub; wood paneled walls, amber-tinged lighting, old beer signs on the walls, all that jazz. Then you see the area behind the bar. This gleaming array of metal, glass, and mirrors looks like a space-ship has crash-landed in a typical Edinburgh pub, bringing with it a host of obscure spirits and over 20 varieties of beer.

From another planet or not, the variety of beers available at Holyrood 9a will certainly overwhelm you. They've even been known to commission special brews for special events; for their fifth birthday party, they served "Hollyrood" ale.

Moreover, the large space and big tables mean this is a social space, and not just a place for beer geeks to bug out over rare brews. It also means that if all your friends are beer geeks, you should grab a table as soon as you get to Edinburgh.

The food menu is no slouch either—the burgers are known as being some of the best of Edinburgh. Whether you stop by for an early afternoon drink or just want a few calories in your system before last call, ask to see the menu. You'll be pleasantly surprised.

Given the quality of the food and liquor, it's no surprise that Holyrood 9a gets pretty busy in the evening. You'll need to come early to snag a table, but if you get there during a busier hour, the attentive staff will make sure you're not without a drink for long. Best of all, finding the place couldn't be easier—the name is the address.

i *Pints £3-£5.* ☼ *Open M-Th, Su 9am-midnight, F-Sa 9am-1am.*

52 CANOES

BAR

13 Melville Place ☎131 226 4732 www.facebook.com/52canoes

Edinburgh's drink of choice will always be scotch, but 52 Canoes is proof that the city can branch out in a big way. This tiki bar boasts many varieties of rum, available to sample by themselves or in one of the many fruity cocktails on the menu (52 in total). Edinburgh's a long way from Polynesia, but the tropical decor and exotic soundtrack make this the perfect place to grab a Mai Tai or a Zombie (both of which are set aflame before being served to you) And if the weather outside's got you down, check out one of their warmers—cocktails made with hot tea, coffee, or other substances guaranteed to raise your body temperature. But the menu isn't limited to Polynesian drinks—you can also get Caribbean classics like the piña colada or daiquiri. Every Thursday from 6pm onwards, they host a reggae night. If you're enjoying Edinburgh but can't help but be dismayed by the lack of Bob Marley, this is the place to go.

Perhaps the most surprising thing about 52 Canoes, however, is the quality and variety of the food. You'll be able to order anything from beef skewers to Belgian waffles. Whatever you drunkenly crave will probably be available on the menu in some capacity, and the staff will be happy to cook it up for you. At heart, this outrageous tiki bar is just a friendly neighborhood pub, albeit one with leis and tiny umbrellas everywhere.

i *Cocktails £7-9, warmers £4-6. Nearby: Caledonian Backpackers, The Roamin' Nose.* ☼ *Open M-F 11am-1am, Sa-Su 9am-1am.*

ESSENTIALS

Practicalities

- **CASH:** There are ATMs up and down Princes Street, including a number of Royal Bank of Scotland ATMs located near the end of Princes Street and the beginning of Queensferry Road. There is also a Royal Bank of Scotland building with several ATMs.
- **INTERNET CAFÉ:** Here! Internet (23 Leven Street. M-F 10am-7:30, Sa 10-6, Su 10-5.) Filament Coffee (5 India Buildings, Victoria Street. Open daily 8am-7pm.)
- **POST OFFICE:** The post office at 40 Frederick Street has a 24 hour ATM. The post office is open M 9-5:30pm, T 9:30-5:30, W-F 9-5:30, and Sa 9-12:30. The post office on 33 Forrest Road offers currency exchange. Open M-F 8:30-6, Sa 9-5:30.

Emergency

- **EMERGENCY NUMBER:** 999
- **HOSPITALS:** Royal Edinburgh Hospital, Morningside Place. ☎131 537 6000.
- **PHARMACY:** Boots Pharmacy (40-44 North Bridge, Edinburgh. M-F 8-7pm, Sa 8:3-6:30pm, Su 10-6pm.)

Getting Around

Edinburgh has a bus and tram system. Tram tickets cost £1.50 for city zone travel—the main line runs along Princes Street and terminates at Haymarket. The bus system, Lothian Buses, has several routes; the 24 is easiest for getting from the North Town to the Old Town (and thus avoiding the numerous hills in between).

york

York is an unabashedly medieval city; expect tiny streets, crumbling buildings, and those famous city walls. But it's by no means a museum piece. It's go some of the best bars in the UK, a hopping restaurant scene, and one of the largest cathedrals in Europe. Even though it's no longer England's second city, that's no reason to believe it's been consigned to history's dustbin. Get in that York state of mind—you'll be pleasantly surprised.

SIGHTS

YORK CASTLE MUSEUM
MUSEUM

Eye of York ☎190 468 7687 www.yorkcastlemuseum.org.uk

Sure, the York Castle Museum is a hodgepodge—exhibits range from overviews of '60s fashion to restored prison cells from the 19th century—but that doesn't diminish the fun. This museum is all about the weirder side of history, whether that means showcasing a Victorian arcade machine depicting a public execution or showing old clips from Dr. Who.

The heart of the museum lies in its meticulous reconstructions of bygone environments. Here, you can gawk at 16th century dining rooms, '60s bars, and Victorian candy shops. In some, you can even walk around and explore the scene. It makes for some great tourist photography. If you really want to freak your parents out, send them a picture of you in one of the jail cells. Be sure to look extra forlorn—there were more than a few executions here in the 19th century. When it comes to depressing scenes, however, it's hard to beat the 1980s kitchen. Who knew corn flakes could look so tragic?

HOSTEL IN YORK
HOSTEL $$

88-90 Micklegate   ☎190 462 7720   http://safestayyork.co.uk

If there was ever a five-star hostel, this is it. Housed in the historic Micklegate House, the Hostel in York is so posh and aristocratic that it feels like an unused set for Downton Abbey. The rooms have exposed beams and old fireplaces, the common area is full of aged leather couches, and nearly every room is accompanied by a small caption explaining what historic event took place inside. Maybe this is something other hostels could do—"in 2007, three frat bros took numerous shots of Fireball in this room" and stuff like that.

With all that history to live up to, the staff doesn't skip on the amenities: the beds are especially large, continental breakfast is served from 7-9, and nearly all the rooms have bathrooms ensuite. And while you can't set those fireplaces roaring on a winter night, they're sure nice to look at. Of course, the feel of staying in a luxury hostel comes with a cost—literally. The price of staying in the Hostel in York is noticeably more expensive than that of other hostels in the area, particularly during the weekend and the summer months. If you're willing to spurge, however, you can't do much better than this joint. And if you're looking for a place to film an old British murder mystery, this is also the place to do it.

i Dorms from £16 on weekdays, from £27.50 during the weekend. Privates from £60 per room on weekdays, from £72 during the weekend. ☾ Reception open 24hr.

FORT BOUTIQUE HOSTEL
HOSTEL $

1 Little Stonegate   ☎190 463 9573   www.thefortyork.co.uk

Location-wise, you can't do much better than York's Fort Boutique Hostel. Located on Little Stonegate, a small street just off of Stonegate (surprise!), the hostel is minutes away from the Yorkshire Museum, world class bars like the House of Trembling Madness, and, of course, York Minstr. And if you really can't bear to go far, the hostel has its own restaurant, Kennedy's. Hotel residents get 20% off their bill there.

In fact, most of the hostel's business activities are conducted at Kennedy's; so much that when you get to the actual living area, it's so divorced from the reception desk that it feels like you're own personal apartment. The new wooden beds help on that front—it's like you've just gone to IKEA.

Breakfast is not included, but there's always that discount at Kennedy's. Wi-Fi is available throughout the hostel, and they also provide blow-dryers in every bathroom. There are also four blow-dryers in a hallway, just in case the bathrooms are occupied and you can't deal with towel-dried hair. It happens to the best of us.

i Dorms from £16. ☾ Reception until 11pm M-Tu, until 12am W-Th & Su, until 2am F-Sa.

york

In addition to these regular displays, the museum has begun mounting large temporary exhibits about historic events like World War I and its effect on England. If one of these larger events is on display while you're in town, it's worth shelling out a few extra pounds for; the same level of detail and seriousness in the regular exhibits is carried over to these ones. As a warning, any exhibit about World War I won't be half as lighthearted as the sixties room.

i Adult £9.50, students/seniors £8.50, children under 16 free. ☾ Open M-Su 9:30am-5pm.

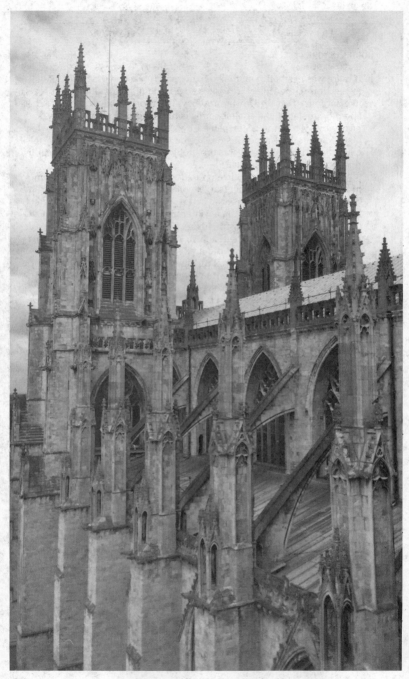

FOOD

1331
RESTAURANT $

13 Grape Ln.   ☎190 466 1130 www.1331-york.co.uk

Outside of 1331, there's a sign that lists its various roles. "Restaurant." Fine. "Bar." Yawn. "Venue." Slightly intriguing, but places that serve food and host live bands are a dime a dozen. "Cinema." Now we're talking. In fact, 1331 is downplaying their many faces here; in addition to a top floor restaurant and a basement movie theater (seats 24), they've got two bars, two outdoor seating areas (including their evocatively named "Secret Garden"), and a private room done up in Art Deco style that's available for private parties.

1331, in short, is the most versatile establishment in York. Part of its success stems from how it doesn't take any of its roles overly seriously. The restaurant offers a variety of specials and deals. The movie house doesn't confine itself to art house fare, but instead shows sports broadcasts and other crowd-pleasers. The bar has a number of local beers, but also highlights quirkier brews like the Belgian Kwåk (look out for the bizarrely shaped glass). And then there are those two for one cocktail specials on Saturday.

That's not to say, of course, that the food or drink is an afterthought. The menu features a carefully curated selection of British classics—you'll see revved-up editions of bangers and mash, ploughman's lunch, and other such delicacies.

i 2 courses for £9.95 from 11am-7pm. Starters £4-5, mains £10-14. Nearby: Barley Hall. ☼ Open daily 8am-2am.

SHAMBLES KITCHEN
SANDWICHES $

28 Shambles   ☎190 467 4648 www.shambleskitchen.co.uk

Given York's small size, you might expect your visit to be a fairly sleepy affair. But there's a lot to do in York—so much that it's easy to get overwhelmed, particularly if you've only planned to stop for a few days. If you're desperately trying to find the time to climb to the top of York Minster and complete a cycle on the Wheel of York, don't worry about finding a meal—Shambles Kitchen will provide a quick and tasty delight in the heart of York.

Located on the Shambles, a small street crammed with distinctive stores, Shambles Kitchen has a remarkably small menu: a daily special, a few wraps, and some salads. You're not going to waste a lot of time ordering, particularly if you take our advice and spring for the special, whatever it may be. Most likely it's a sandwich or a burrito, packed with pork and overflowing with tangy sauce. The portions aren't small, but you'll be able to scarf this bad boy down quickly, whether you do it on the run or while sitting at one of Shambles Kitchen's comically small tables.

If you get thirsty (salty meat can have that effect from time to time), Shambles Kitchen has a marvelous smoothie menu and a juice-cleanse-cycle thingamabob. Perfect if you're worried about the healthfulness of pulled pork sandwiches (at least they've got protein).

i Sandwiches £5-6. Smoothies £3-4. Nearby: Jorvik Viking Centre. ☼ Open M-Sa 9am-4pm, Su 10am-4pm.

NIGHTLIFE

HOUSE OF THE TREMBLING MADNESS
PUB

48 Stonegate   ☎190 464 0009 www.tremblingsmadness.co.uk

This notorious pub is named after delirium tremens, a common symptom of alcohol withdrawal. With the stuff they've got available, the name makes a lot of sense. This place is all about the beer—if you don't like the tons of cask ales or bottles they've got upstairs, you can pick up any of the bottles they have downstairs in their massive off-licence. If a bottle doesn't quite do it for you, you can get a yard of ale (the glass sis a yard long, if that wasn't clear) for £9. And if spirits are more your thing, why not try one of the strongest beers in the world? They've got four of them, ranging from BrewDog's Tactical Nuclear Penguin (32%) to the infamous Mystery of Beer, which clocks in at a whopping 70%. And no, you can't get a yard of that.

With all that craziness behind the counter, you might not register just how crazy the actual space is. This is a fairly well-preserved medieval building, and the general interior doesn't look to have changed since 1500 or so (it is up to fire code, however). The decor is strictly limited to dead animals, whether it's a taxidermied head, a bear skin, or a box full of spiders, butterflies, and beetles. PETA won't be holding mixers here anytime soon.

i Pints from £3-5. Yard of ale for £9. Shots of exceptionally strong beer from £4-8. Nearby: Barley Hall, 1313. ⏰ M-Sa 10am-midnight, Su 11am-midnight.

THE MALTINGS   BAR

Postern Tower, Tanner's Moat   ☎190 465 5387 www.maltings.co.uk

You'll likely arrive at York via train or bus, which means that the Maltings will likely be the first bar you see as you walk to town. That impression will likely put you off—the bar's exterior is all black, it's near a busy road, and it's immediately surrounded by a large parking lot. Ignore all that—once you step inside the Maltings, you'll be treated to a grown-up pub, one with all the character, warmth, and hardwood floors you could possibly want. And if you dig that all black feel, just step outside onto the terrace, which features nondescript black walls and tables composed of stones bound in metal wire. It seems more suited to a modern art show than a neighborhood bar, but who's complaining when you get some fresh air?

But the more traditional interior isn't a slouch of a space by any means. Enjoy live music in the bar area, or saunter over to the space near the kitchen (food is served from 12-2 on weekdays and from 12-4 during the weekends) and stretch out in a comfy chair.

The chief attraction, of course, is the generous selection of cask ales. You'll find some of Yorkshire's finest brews here, making this bar a near-perfect introduction to the region's beer scene. Now you'll understand why it's the first bar you see.

i Pints from £3-5. Nearby: Yorkshire Castle Museum, The Wheel of York/ ⏰ M-Sa 11am-11pm, Su noon-10:30pm.

ESSENTIALS
Practicalities

- **CASH:** There are a number of ATMs on Piccadilly, particularly on the end where it meets with Parliament Street. There are several ATMs up and down Parliament Street as well. **York Bureau de Change.** (3 Church Street, M-Sa 8:30-5, Su 10-4)

- **INTERNET:** Evil Eye Lounge, 42 Stonegate, York. (190 464 0002. M-W 10am-midnight, Th-F 10am-1am, Sa-Su 10am-midnight. Internet usage £1. You're unlikely to find another internet cafe that serves cocktails.)

- **POST OFFICE:** The main post office is on Lendal, off of Museum Street. There is an ATM, but it can only be used during post office hours. M-Sa 9-5:30pm.

Emergency

- **EMERGENCY NUMBER:** 999.

- **HOSPITAL:** York District Hospital, Wigginton Road, York. (☎190 463 1313)

- **POLICE:** Yorkshire Police Station. (☎0845 60 60 247).
- **PHARMACIES:** Monkbar Pharmacy (3 Goodramgate ☎190 462 6181 Open M-Sa 7:30-10:30, Su 8:30-6:30.)

Getting Around

There are five buses: the White Line, which goes to Askham Bar; the Yellow Line, which goes to Grimston Bar; the Red Line, which goes to York Designer Outlet; the Silver Line, which goes to Monks Cross; and the Green Line, which goes to Rawcliffe Bar. Single fares start at £1. A weeks pass can be purchased for £12. However, if you plan on sticking within the city centre (that is, within the old city walls), buses shouldn't be necessary. The city is highly walkable, being highly compact and having many pedestrian-only streets. While the medieval layout may require careful attention to your map, it doesn't mean you need a bus to shuttle you around. Bus information: ☎019 04 55 14 00 or ☎014 82 22 22 22.

manchester

After London, Manchester is the English settlement that feels most like a city—it's urban, cosmopolitan, and in-your-face. And that's a good thing. Don't be fooled by the remnants of industrial grit—this is a city with a thriving music scene, a penchant for independent film, and a collection of bars hipper than most of us can ever hope to be. But it's also the birthplace of modern industry, the place where the atom was first split, and the place where the first stored-program computer was built. Confused yet? Grab a pint and come along for the ride.

SIGHTS

NATIONAL FOOTBALL MUSEUM

MUSEUM

Urbis Building, Cathedral Gardens ☎161 605 8200 www.nationalfootballmuseum.com

The National Football Museum looks like a giant shard of glass from the outside and an airport from the inside, but a quick glance at any of the exhibits will very quickly remind you just what this museum is about. There are archival clips playing everywhere, sounds from famous games on the speakers, and enough vintage photos to last a lifetime. The sole exception: an inexplicable life-size statue of Michael Jackson, which used to stand outside Craven Cottage, a football stadium that's home to Fulham F.C.

Despite the name, there's a fair bit of attention paid to football's role on the international stage, with information about everything from Joan Míro's poster for the 1982 World Cup to why Brazil hates Uruguay for beating them in the 1950 world cup (some fans were so distraught they had to be hospitalized).

As one might expect, there's plenty of hero worship going on here, but the curators don't get too carried away either; they humorously note that a George Best-themed jigsaw puzzle failed miserably in the British marketplace when he started playing for the Northern Irish football team. The inclusion of sculptured caricatures from satirical TV show Spitting Image also lighten the mood.

Admission is free, and maybe that's for the best considering some of the items in the gift shop. The typical jerseys and football merchandise is priced as usual, but they offer have some signed items that are somewhat pricier; one with Péle's autograph sells for £399. The museum is just a few blocks from Exchange Square; if you're coming from the town centre, walk down Market Street and then north on Corporation Street. Once you get to Exchange Square, take a right.

i Free. ⏰ Open M-Sa 10-5pm, Su 11-5pm.

HATTERS MANCHESTER NEWTON STREET
HOSTEL $

50 Newton Street ☎161 236 9500 www.hattersgroup.com

Despite the name, there's nothing mad about Hatters Newton Street. One of two hostels the Hatters Group operates in Manchester (they also have locations in Liverpool and Birmingham, Newton Street stands apart from the rest with its large rooms, generous staff, and unpretentious atmosphere. Just above the sink in the kitchen, there's a sign with an angry baby on it: "Leave your dishes in the sink. I dare you" it reads. On every floor, there are blurbs about different Manchester bands and singers, ranging from the semi-famous (like Morrissey) to the not-quite-semi-famous (the Charlatans).

Though there are some privates, the emphasis is on dorms. These are generally quite large, meaning you won't be stepping on someone else's toes even if you're in a ten or eight person room. The bathrooms, while not always en suite, are quite clean and have a lot of showers; you won't be kept waiting. If you're looking for a more intimate experience, Hatters Hilton Chambers, in keeping with their name, offer a more hotel-style experience: there are far more doubles and other such private rooms.

Continental breakfast and Wi-Fi are available (though the Wi-Fi is only accessible on the ground floor). Other amenities include a range of guided pub crawls: you can opt for a more traditional night out or explore the stranger establishments in the Northern Quarter.

i Dorms from £13, privates from £20. ② Reception open 24hr.

THE WHEEL OF MANCHESTER
FERRIS WHEEL

Piccadilly Gardens ☎161 236 6512 www.freijwheels.com/our-wheels.php?city=manchester

The London Eye is definitely England's most famous ferris wheel (and probably its most famous eye, unless you count David Bowie's discolored one). But at 173 feet, the Wheel of Manchester is no slouch either. The current incarnation (it's been built three times at this point, at one point reaching a height of 180 feet) is located in Piccadilly Gardens, close to the National Football Museum and Manchester Cathedral. Given the number of tall buildings around Piccadilly Gardens, your view of greater Manchester may be somewhat limited, but you'll certainly still get thrills from looking down.

Though the Wheel of Manchester is currently located in Piccadilly Gardens, it stood in nearby Exchange Square until 2012. Some contend that the wheel was moved because people got tired of how it looked in Exchange Square, which means we can count on another move in about five years. We'll keep you posted.

The elephant in the room, of course, is that the Wheel of Manchester is currently closed until further notice. There have been no shortage of problems affecting the wheel—fountain leakage underneath necessitated the latest close, but just a couple weeks earlier it was scaled by a prominent gangster making a political protest. This never happened in Lock, Stock, and Two Smoking Barrels. For now, you'll have to content yourself with the thrills you get from looking up at the darned thing. Currently located in Piccadilly Gardens, the Wheel is just a few blocks away from Piccadilly Station.

i £9, seniors £7.50, children £6.50, under 3 £2.

CORNERHOUSE

70 Oxford St.

GALLERY

☎161 200 1500 www.cornerhouse.org

Manchester's city center is already compact, but in terms of sheer convenience you can't improve on the Cornerhouse. Imagine meeting a boy or girl in a bookstore. You have a coffee date, then check out an art gallery. You meet up again for dinner and a movie, then have drinks afterwards. All of those activities could take place in one building: the Cornerhouse. At the very least, you'll save big money on taxis.

Simply put, the Cornerhouse is a cultural juggernaut. The ground floor bookstore specializes in hyper obscure periodicals and texts on film theory. The movies shown are strictly independent. The coffee is only available black. Kidding about the last one. In fact, the atmosphere is far from alienating. The restaurant is staffed by a friendly group that's happy to tell you about the many beers and ciders they have on draught; they've got ten on tap, plus a few cask ales. And when you stop by on a quiet afternoon, you'll have no problem grabbing a table, whipping out your computer, and starting to work—the Wi-Fi's free.

Of course, the restaurant isn't why people are coming here (though they do have some great sandwiches, including a croque-monsier with pesto). The movies really are the main attraction. Here, you'll find all the latest independent hits.

i Gallery admission free. Tickets £6 before 5pm (£4.50 for students and seniors); £8 after 5pm (£6 for students and seniors). ☉ Galleries open Tu-Sa 12-8, Su 12-6, M closed. Film schedule variable.

FOOD

TERRACE

43 Thomas Street

RESTAURANT, BAR $

☎161 819 2345 twitter.com/nqterrace

Located in the swinging Northern Quarter district, Terrace cultivates a hip, detached atmosphere. The soundtrack is eclectic (everything from the Magnetic Fields to Serge Gainsbourg) but always rock snob approved. Most of the lighting comes from the floor length windows at the front and back, leaving much of the interior dim. There's exposed brick everywhere—some seats are nearly inside an old fireplace—and small red Christmas lights hang from the ceiling. Part of this is just keeping up appearances in the Northern Quarter—they're surrounded by vintage stores, hipster bars, and record shops, so they have to look the part. Can you imagine the fallout if they turned some more lights on?

Luckily, Terrace doesn't skimp on the most important part: its food and drink. With a big selection of beers on tap and a delicious array of sandwiches, burgers, and pizzas, Terrace excels with what seems like a very limited palette. The burgers and sandwiches are fairly traditional, but look out for the pizza's varied toppings: goat cheese, lamb meatballs, and duck have all popped up on various pies.

The bar crowd may get rowdy later in the evening (dancing's popular here), but a low-key atmosphere prevails during the day, aided by the mellow yet hip soundtrack.

i Pizzas, sandwiches, and burgers £7-11. ☉ Open Su-W 10am-midnight. Th 10am-12:30am. F 10am-1am. Sa 9am-1am.

KITCHENETTE

60 Oxford St.

RESTAURANT $$

☎161 228 6633 www.mudcrabindustries.co.uk/manchester

"High class junk food" is the Kitchenette's motto, and their menu certainly includes high-calorie classics like bacon cheeseburgers, mac'n'cheese, and nachos. But they're really known for their hirata buns, which they describe as "a New York version of Taiwanese street food with a Japanese name." It's a little confusing, and so is the way they serve it: the buns come in a thatched basket, the filling comes in porcelain containers, and everything's placed on top of a rough board of wood. Oh, and it also comes with your personal bottle of Sriracha. Though it may be hard to wrap your head around this (and even harder to wrap the filling into the bun), the taste is all the explanation you need. Two buns are hardly enough to fit all the meat and vegetables they give you (the goal is to get something that looks like "Pac-Man on steroids," if that helps) but you can get another 2 for £3. The fillings range from chargrilled steak to salmon teriyaki. There's even something to satisfy the vegetarians, who can rest assured that the "fried oyster mushroom" filling doesn't actually have oysters.

While you're stuffing Pac-Man and then stuffing your face, treat yourself to views of the Bridgewater Canal, visible through the large floor-to-ceiling windows in the lower area. Though the restaurant looks small from Oxford Street, there are sizable rooms downstairs, with tables and booths able to seat very large groups. Maybe they should call it Kitchenpalooza.

The beer menu isn't huge (3 on draught and a couple bottles), but the cocktails run the gamut from old school mouth-puckerers like the Americano to sweeter drinks like daiquiris and bellinis.

i Entrees £11-14. ☼ Open daily noon-11pm.

NIGHTLIFE

DUSK TIL PAWN
BAR

Stevenson Square, Northern Quarter ☎161 236 5355 www.facebook.com/dusktilpawn

Yes, From Dusk til Pawn is designed to look like a pawn shop from the exterior. There's no sign of it being a bar—just a couple old TVs, guitars, and a neon sign that says "PAWN SHOP." If you're looking for a bar, you might very well miss it; the ultra-hip Northern Quarter has enough vintage stores that a pawn shop doesn't merit a second look. If you're looking for a pawn shop (maybe you're a big fan of Pawn Stars and want to see how the Brits do it), you'll be pleasantly surprised with one of the coolest cocktail bars in Manchester.

Part Dusk til Pawn's success comes from its versatility. During the low-key early hours, the bartenders are eager to strike up conversation and might even take a shot with you. As the night heats up, the fairly large space fills up without seeming too crowded. You could easily end up spending a good portion of your evening here.

The liquor cabinet itself is pretty no-frills (metal and wood shelves), but the number of bottles has to be seen to be believed. Take special heed of the various bitters (look for all the tiny bottles) and marvel at the collection of gin, which includes more varieties than you knew existed (one is titled "Bathtub Gin").

Their selection of bottled beers isn't shabby, but those truly looking to stray from the beaten path should sample a pickleback (a shot of whiskey followed by a shot of pickle juice) or a backbeet (gin then beet juice). The first one may make you grimace, but the second one is a great way to get some beta-carotene in your system. Now that's drinking responsibly.

i Cocktails about £6.50; picklebacks/backbeets £3. ☼ Open Tu-Th 5pm-1am, F-Sa 5pm-3am, Su 5pm-1am. Closed Mondays.

THE TEMPLE
BAR

100 Great Bridgewater Street ☎161 278 1610

If you're walking down Oxford Street and hear a roar of voices coming from underground, don't freak out about mole-people planning a revolt. You're just passing by the Temple, a tiny but energetic bar located in a former public toilet. Yes, you read that correctly. And yes, it's been cleaned since then (the space has been a bar since the early '90s).

Any doubts you have while walking down the well-preserved staircase will be eradicated when you step into the actual bar, with its funky leather couches, old school jukebox, and generous beer and liquor selection. There are only a couple of beers on tap, but the large refrigerator has everything from light Mexican beers like Pacifico to Belgian heavy-hitters like Chimay. Given the small space, you'll probably be outed as a tourist pretty quickly—that is, if locals can believe you even found the place.

Rock and roll will be playing throughout the night, and while you won't see any dancing, the right song will get people yelling and singing along. If you need a bit of air, plenty of people hang on the steps to smoke (that won't help you with fresh air, but it's a nice respite from the interior nonetheless).

i Beers £3-5. ☼ Open M-Th 11:30am-1am, F-Sa 11:30am-2am. Su closed.

ESSENTIALS
Practicalities

- **CASH:** There are Lloyds ATMs located on 42-46 Market Street and at 324-326 Oxford Road, in the University District. There is a 24 hour ATM at the Atherton Post Office on 116-118 Market Street.
- **POST OFFICE:** Atherton Post Office, 116-118 Market Street. Open M-Sa 8:30am-6pm. Features include currency exchange and a 24 hour ATM.
- **INTERNET CAFES:** L2K Internet Gaming Café. (32 Princess Street. www.l2k.co.uk. ☎61 244 5566. Open daily 11am-10pm. £2 per hour. Printing costs 10p per page.)

Emergency

- **EMERGENCY NUMBERS:** 999 or 112.
- **PHARMACIES:** Boots Manchester Piccadilly (11-13 Piccadilly, Manchester. Open M-F 7:30am-8pm, Sa 9am-6:30pm, Su noon-5:30pm. ☎161 834 8244.)
- **HOSPITALS:** Manchester Royal Infirmary (Oxford Road. ☎161 276 1234.

Getting Around

Manchester's Metrolink is a tram system with six different routes. There are several stops within the city zones, including those at Piccadilly Station, Deansgate, and Market Street; however, you can also get out to suburbs like Rochdale. Singles are £1.20 within the city center.

liverpool

Liverpool may never again be as cool as it was in the early sixties, when Lilipudlian bands topped the charts worldwide (despite names like "The Swinging Blue Jeans."). But let's face it—most cities never attain that level of coolness anyway, and the city on the Mersey still has plenty to recommend it. From the staggering museums in the Cultural Quarter to the beautiful canals of Albert Dock, Liverpool is a city filled with vibrant attractions, most of which emphasize the city's varied history. As a major port, it imported items from all over the world; as a major pop music producer, it started exporting hits.

Whether you're having a pint at one of the city's many craft beer bars or sampling some great grub in the small but electrifying Chinatown, you'll soon discover that there's much more to this place than the Beatles—though if that's all you're interested in, you won't lack for places to visit.

get a room!

HOAX

54 Stanley Street   ☎151 909 4810 www.hoaxliverpool.com

If you are not the sort of person who likes to walk around very much, Hoax might be the hostel you're looking for. There is a restaurant on the premises. There is a bar in the basement. There is live music on Wednesdays, Fridays, and Saturdays. You can see a lot while moving very little. Hoax, of course, is not just for couch potatoes. Located near the Cavern Quarter and Albert Dock, it's a quick walk to many of Liverpool's most famous sites, making it a perfect home base for your touristic excursions into the city centre.

Regardless of your traveling habits, the rooms at Hoax will make you happy you stayed there. All bathrooms are ensuite, regardless of whether you're in a double, quad, or six or eight person dorm. Most of the rooms boast views of Liverpool's shopping district.

Breakfast is not included, but you can get discounted meals at Hopskotch, the aforementioned restaurant. The food is high-quality but not the healthiest (hotdogs and ribs abound).

All in all, the friendly staff, great accomodations, and surplus of activities make this a great place to stay. And that's no hoax.

i Dorms about £15, privates about £15 per person. ⏰ Reception open 24hr.

SIGHTS

THE BEATLES STORY   MUSEUM

Brittania Vaults, Kings Dock St.   ☎252 709 1963 www.beatlesstory.com

"Welcome to the story of the best band in the world, ever" reads a sign at the beginning of the Beatles Story. They're not pulling any punches here. Is this the best museum in the world, ever? No, but it's fun to visit nonetheless. As you walk through the exhibit, you'll encounter reproductions of various environments where the Fab Four played and worked: the Kaiserkeller in Hamburg, the Cavern Club in Liverpool, a Brian Epstein's office and record store, just to name a few. All this is interspersed with archival photos and, of course, a nonstop Beatles soundtrack. Many viewers make use of the free audio guide, as the wall text can be somewhat lacking. The post-Liverpool years go by a little more quickly, but there's still a lot to savor, including a Pan Am jet interior (for when they went to the States in 1964), a scaled up diorama of the Sergeant Pepper's Lonely Hearts Club Band cover (complete with a listing of every darned person who appears on it), and, of course, a yellow submarine. At the end, there are mini-exhibits about each member's life afterwards. You probably know what happened to John, Paul, and George, but this is your opportunity to learn all about Ringo Starr's ill-fated film career. Representative titles: Son of Dracula, Blindman, Caveman. And of course there's the gift shop, where you can finally get what you've always needed: rain boots that say "the Beatles."

The museum is located on Albert Dock, near the Maritime Museum, the Museum of Liverpool, and Tate Liverpool. Walk towards the Mersey from the City Centre.

i £12.95 adults, £9.50 students and seniors, £7 children. ⏰ Open daily: 10-5pm November-March, 9-5pm April-October

MUSEUM OF LIVERPOOL

Pier Head   ☎151 478 4545 www.liverpoolmuseums.org.uk/mol/

MUSEUM

James Joyce wrote that his goal with Ulysses was to provide a perfect image of Dublin, so that if the city was somehow destroyed it could be reconstituted from his novel. If Liverpool were to disappear, you could probably pull a similar trick with the Museum of Liverpool, which documents just about every aspect of the English city's history. The archival material contained here is tremendous—they've got everything from commemorative key-chains to a reconstruction of an overheard train car. Walk through the museum once and you'd ace a quiz about the city and its history.

The most energetic exhibit is the one devoted to Liverpool's musical heritage. The Beatles loom large here (obviously), but other Liverpool hit-makers like Frankie Goes to Hollywood, Cilla Black, and the Swinging Blue Jeans also get their fair share. You can test your knowledge with an interactive Liverpool music quiz and marvel at the collarless gray suits worn by the Beatles when they struck it big.

Still, other exhibits have plenty to offer as well—there's information about Liverpool's political history, its role as a global city, and numerous rotating exhibits highlighting specific figures or movements. The one complaint: a few too many creepy wax dummies, especially in the aforementioned train car. The museum is located on Pier Head, near Albert Dock. Walk towards the Mersey from the City Centre.

i Free. ☾ Open daily 10am-5pm.

INTERNATIONAL SLAVERY MUSEUM

Albert Dock, 3rd floor of Mersey Maritime Museum   ☎151 478 4499
www.liverpoolmuseums.org/ism

MUSEUM

Most of the Maritime Museum, where the International Slavery Museum is located, is upbeat and joyful. Look at these awesome boats! Revel in our shipbuilding history! Even the Titanic exhibit is tinged with nostalgia for a lost era.

If you have brains in your head, you have probably gathered that the International Slavery Museum has a very different tone, and that's to its credit. Though the exhibit doesn't shy away from depicting the horrors of slavery—you'll see shackles, iron muzzles, and torture devices, along with one darkened room with audio meant to approximate the experience of being on a slave ship—its larger focus is on Liverpool's complicity in the industry. And that turns out to be darned unsettling too. For maximum impact, make this one of your last stops in Liverpool.

One interactive portion features the names of several famous Liverpool streets, including the Beatles-inspiring Penny Lane. Flip the signs over, and you'll see which vicious slave trader or opponent of abolitionism the street was made for. This is Liverpool's history, the exhibit is saying, and we have to face it. Equally important is a window that allows the viewer to look out on the docks below. There's a simple text besides the window, reminding them that slave ships were built here.

Right in the middle of the exhibit, there's a staircase leading to the Maritime Dining Rooms, the upscale restaurant housed in the museum. We wonder if that's good for anyone's appetites. The museum is located in the Maritime Museum, near the Museum of Liverpool, the Beatles Story, and Tate Liverpool. Walk towards the Mersey from the City Centre.

i Free. ☾ Open daily 10am-5pm.

FOOD

LUCHA LIBRE
MEXICAN $$

96 Wood St. ☎151 329 0200 www.lucha-libre.co.uk

Yes, this Mexican street food restaurant is named after the weirdest sport in the world: Mexican wrestling. Can you think of another sport where the athletes star in films about fighting vampires? Didn't think so. But while the restaurant's decor traffics in that slightly goofy atmosphere, the attitude that Lucha Libre's staff has towards the food is 100% serious. Want burritos? Tacos? Enchiladas? They've got them all here, and they can fill them with whatever you like. Almost as long as their food menu is their list of available tequilas—the knowledgeable wait staff can help you pair a particular blend with your selected meals. They can also recommend which of the many appetizers and sides pairs best with your main choice. It's almost as if they want you to buy more food or something.

Despite the English reputation for mild flavors, these guys actually know how to pile on the spice. Water's served in carafes, and you may find yourself reaching for a refill or three after a whiff of the entrees.

Given the restaurant's proximity to cultural center FACT and the left-wing shops on Bold Street, the crowd is largely young and hip. You might find them heading to spots like the Shipping News or Santa Chupitos afterwards. But you don't need to be gearing up for a night on the town to enjoy Lucha Libre—all you need are some taste buds.

i Burritos £6-7, entrees £10-12.

NIGHTLIFE

SANTA CHUPITOS
BAR

41 Slater St. ☎151 707 6527 www.santachupitos.com

There are more than a few derelict shops on Slater Street, and at first glance Santa Chupitos looks like one of them. With an all black exterior, closed shades, and slim signage (there's a small plaque that reads "SANTAS CHUPITOS" in small letters), it's the kind of place you don't look at twice. But then you realize the door is open, there's music playing, and the bartender is mixing some delicious cocktails. You'll be glad you took a second look.

Inside, the decor is similarly muted—the walls are black and red, a couple red lights, and something that looks like a stuffed squirrel. Your eyes gravitate to the imposing bar, with a truly awe-inspiring collection of liquor, and the cocktail menu, written near the ceiling and decorated with numerous skulls. Despite the macho death wish decor, the cocktails consist of more than malt whisky and sweat. Many are frozen or involve copious amounts of mixers. Try the five dollar shake: blueberries, vodka, raspberry liqueur, and ice cream. Unfortunately, it costs more than five dollars. If you need something a little more manly, we recommend the Bacon and Maple Old Fashioned, which includes both bacon and maple syrup. Sounds like the Ron Swanson special. Out back there's a small seating area.

Bartenders will serve you complimentary snacks (pretzels, popcorn, and the like) in metal mugs. Given the high salt content of these snacks, it's not impossible that they want to get you thirsty so you'll buy more drinks. We're not complaining.

i Cocktails from £5-9. ☼ Open M-W 5pm-2am, Th 5pm-3am, F-Sa 5pm-4am, Su 5pm-3am.

THE PHILHARMONIC DINING ROOMS
BAR

36 Hope St. ☎151 707 2837 www.nicholsonspub.co.uk

The Philharmonic Dining Rooms constitute one of the nicest bars you will ever go to. Sure, there are bars with fancier cocktails, bars on the top of fifty-floor hotels, bars where you can't get in unless your great-great-great-great-grandfather signed the Magna Carta. But in terms of restrained yet pure classiness, it's hard to beat the Philharmonic, named for its proximity to Liverpool's concert hall. And the beer selection is pretty damn good too.

How nice is the Phil? Imagine wood paneled walls, marble fireplaces, stained glass windows, paintings on the ceiling—and that's only one room. The building is a Grade II listed site, having been recognized as an exceptional example of a Victorian pub. It feels almost unnatural to discuss contemporary events in this time capsule—you feel as if you should be debating Disraeli's foreign policy.

Still, that won't impede you and your friends for knocking back a few delicious pints in one of the bar's various rooms: choose from the main bar area, the Brahms room, the Liszt room, or the Grandé Lounge. With an ever-rotating selection of cask ales, this is where you go to enjoy great beer without having to endure a hipster crowd.

And then there are the men's urinals. Contrary to popular belief, they are not Grade I listed. They are, however, made of marble. Male readers, this is unquestionably the nicest thing you'll ever pee in. Female readers, don't fret: you can get a tour led by the management, though male patrons might be a little shocked.

i Pints £3-5. 🕐 Open M-Su 11am-12am.

ESSENTIALS
Practicalities

- **CASH:** There are Halifax ATMs located on 2 Paradise Street and 30 Bold Street. There is a Lloyds ATM located at 26 Broadway.
- **POST OFFICE:** 1-3 South John Street, Liverpool. Open M-Sa 9-5:30pm and Su 11-3pm. Features include currency exchange.
- **INTERNET CAFES:** Le Boulevard Internet Café, 39 Clayton Square Shopping Centre, Liverpool. ☎151 709 6247. Open daily from 9:15am-5pm.

Emergency

- **PHARMACIES:** Boots Pharmacy, Clayton Square Shopping Center. Open M-Sa 8:15am-7pm, Su 11am-5pm. ☎151 709 4711
- **HOSPITALS:** Royal Liverpool University Hospital, Prescot Street, Liverpool. ☎151 706 2000 In an emergency, dial 112 or 999.

Getting Around

Bus is the main form of public transport in Liverpool. Major bus stations in the city center are Liverpool ONE and the Queen Square Bus Station. Ticket fares depending on bus company; one of the cheapest is Arriva, with fares of £2.10 for adults and £1.70 for students with valid ID.

great britain essentials

VISAS

Britain is not a signatory of the Schengen Agreement, which means it is not a member of the freedom of movement zone that covers most of continental Europe. Fortunately, its visa policies are fairly simple (for casual travelers, at least). EU citizens do not need a visa to visit Britain. Citizens of Australia, Canada, New Zealand, the US, and many other non-EU countries do not need a visa for stays of up to six months. Those staying longer than six months may apply for a longer-term visa; consult an embassy or consulate for more information. Because Britain is not a part of the Schengen zone, time spent here does not count toward the 90-day limit on travel within that area. Entering to study or work will require a visa. Check www.ukvisas.gov.uk for more information.

MONEY

Tipping and Bargaining

Tips in restaurants are sometimes included in the bill (it will appear as a"service charge"). If gratuity is not included, you should tip your server about 10%. Taxi drivers should receive a 10% tip, and bellhops and chambermaids usually expect £1-3 per night. To the great relief of many budget travelers, tipping is not expected at pubs and bars in Britain (unless you are trying to get jiggy with the bartender). Bargaining is practically unheard of in the upscale shops that overrun London. Don't try it (unless you happen to be at a street market or feel particularly belligerent).

Taxes

The UK has a 20% value added tax (VAT), a sales tax applied to everything but food, books, medicine, and children's clothing. The tax is included in the amount indicated on the price tag. The prices stated in Let's Go include VAT unless otherwise mentioned. Upon exiting Britain, non-EU citizens can reclaim VAT (minus an administrative fee) through the Retail Export Scheme, although the process is time-consuming, annoying, and may not be worth it, except for large purchases. You can obtain refunds only for goods you take out of the country (not for accommodations or noms). Participating shops display a "Tax-Free Shopping" sign and may have a minimum purchase of £50-100 before they offer refunds. To claim a refund, fill out the form you are given in the shop and present it with the goods and receipts at customs upon departure (look for the Tax-Free Refund desk at the airport). At peak times, this process can take up to an hour. You must leave the country within three months of your purchase in order to claim a refund, and you must apply before leaving the UK.

SAFETY AND HEALTH

Police

Police are a common presence in Britain and there are many police stations scattered throughout the city. There are two types of police officers in Britain: regular officers with full police powers, and police community support officers (PCSO), who have limited police power and focus on community maintenance and safety. The national emergency number is ☎999.

Drugs and Alcohol

The Brits love to drink, so the presence of alcohol is unavoidable. In trying to keep up with the locals, remember that the Imperial pint is 20oz., as opposed to the 16oz. US pint. The legal age at which you can buy alcohol in the UK is 18 (16 for buying beer and wine with food at a restaurant).

Despite what you may have seen on Skins, use and possession of hard drugs is illegal throughout the United Kingdom. Do not test this—Britain has been cracking down on drug use amongst young people in particular over the past few years. Smoking is banned in enclosed public spaces in Britain, including pubs and restaurants.

Terrorism

The bombings of July 7, 2005 in the London Underground revealed the vulnerability of large European cities to terrorist attacks and resulted in the enforcement of stringent safety measures at airports and major tourist sights throughout British cities. Though eight years have passed, security checks are still as thorough as ever. Allow

extra time for airport security and do not pack sharp objects in your carry-on luggage—they will be confiscated. Unattended luggage is always considered suspicious and is also liable for confiscation. Check your home country's foreign affairs office for travel information and advisories, and be sure to follow the local news while in the UK.

MEASUREMENTS

Britain uses a thoroughly confusing and illogical mix of standard and metric measurement units. Road distances are always measured in miles, and many Brits will be clueless if you give them distances in kilometers. For weights, don't be surprised to see grams and ounces used side-by-side. There's also a measurement called a "stone," equal to 14lb., that is regularly used for giving body weights. Paradoxically, meters and centimeters are the most common way to give body heights. How the British ever accomplished anything in this world when they can't settle on a consistent system of measurements, we'll never know.

GREECE

Greece is a land where marble comes standard issue, circle-dancing and drinking until daybreak are time-tested rites of summer, and the past is inescapable. Tourists flock to hear the whispers of long-dead statesmen and playwrights echoing off the magnificent ruins of ancient civilizations. At the center of Greece's past and present is Athens. Though hemp-wearing backpackers and fanny pack-laden tourists have replaced the chiton-robed philosophers of the past, Athens maintains its position as a cultural hub of the Mediterranean. After centuries of foreign domination, Athens is now a world-class international capital, where the past and present sit comfortably side by side. It is also the gateway to the sun-drenched Cyclades, defined by white and blue stucco buildings, notorious nightlife, and fabulous beaches. Mix some hangovers with all your history by heading to Mykonos and Ios, then check in on Santorini's world-famous sunsets and peaceful mountain villages. They're just a short ferry ride away. Even with all those thousands of years of history, Greece remains constantly dynamic, and you'll always find something new to discover in this ancient land.

greatest hits

- **CHEAP EATS.** Eat souvlaki in **Monastiraki Square** (p. 445) in Athens. It's the most touristy fun you'll have for less than €2.
- **LIFE'S A BEACH.** Party until dawn at the beach clubs in **Mykonos** (#someregrets when taking a ferry the next morning; p. 448).
- **KICKIN' IT OLD SCHOOL.** Explore Ano Poli in **Thessaloniki** (p. 455). So vintage.

athens

Welcome to Athens, a city as old as Western Civilization but where the Acropolis towers over streets claimed by the youth and covered with graffiti. With so much history, so many ruins, and so many sculptures that can be seen just about everywhere (including the train stations), it's easy to get lost in the vastness of time and space in Athens. But you—you lucky bastard—have us as a guide. Don't let the ruins build up your entire trip. Athens is full of history, but it's a bustling city that's very much part of this century as well. Be sure to check out the Agora, the ancient marketplace of the Athenians, but don't forget about Monastiraki, the marketplace for today's locals. A vibrant cultural city, the symbolic and literal center of Athens stands at Syntagma Square. Leading straight into it is Ermou, the main crowded shopping street with a pretty cool Byzantine church, too. Walk west and you'll stumble into the old city of Plaka, Acropolis included. Head down Adrianou, and you'll get to Athens's flea market and souvlaki heaven of Monastiraki. On the other side of Syntagma is high society (literally and figuratively) in Kolonaki, the poshest neighborhood in Athens. Keep heading that way, though, and you'll reach the young, gritty, and raw Exarhia. The furthest neighborhood is Pagrati, with far more residential leanings. You'll have a hard time finding a map that covers it all and a harder time embracing it all yourself. But it's a city where Socrates and Aristotle strolled, democracy was born, and you've just arrived. So let's go.

SIGHTS

All things ancient. With a cool mountain and flea market thrown in.

ACROPOLIS
Entrance on Dionysiou Areopagitou ☎210 321 41 72 http://odysseus.culture.gr

HISTORICAL SITE

It's the Acropolis. Of course you're going to stumble across it. Whether on a Parthenon T-shirt in a Plaka souvenir store or from the rooftop lounge of your hostel, this is the image that defines Athens.

So what exactly is the Acropolis? A rocky hill. Okay, it's more than that. Originally a political center during the Mycenaean times (15-12th centuries BCE), in the 8th century, the Athenians got a grand ol' idea to build a temple to their patron goddess (and namesake), Athena, there. Thus, the Hekatompedon was made. Never heard of it? No worries. It wasn't that great. So they built a new temple to Athena, now known as the Old Temple, 50 years later. In 500 BCE though, the Persians came through (think 300 except less homophobic) and sacked Athens, burning down the city and the Acropolis. But have no fear, in Athens's Golden Age under Pericles (450-429 BCE), the Acropolis was remade starting with work on the gorgeous Parthenon, which is, yes, another temple to Athena.

After the 4th century CE, though, the Parthenon underwent a wild phase of promiscuity. Becoming everything from a Christian Orthodox church to a Catholic church to a mosque to storage for gunpowder (classy!), in 1687, it blew up. No one saw that coming. In the carnage left, Lord Elgin, a British ambassador, did whatever it is ambassadors do, which in this case was help himself to some gorgeous sculptures from the Parthenon, which are currently in the British Museum. What's left is the Parthenon today.

But enough history. It's time to get up close and personal with the Acropolis. Bring good walking shoes if you're heading up. You don't see the Acropolis from everywhere just because it's famous. It's also kinda high up and slippery as all get out in some places. Way to go, marble. Still, hike up to the tickets office, pay that €12 entrance fee, and prepare to be amazed.

The most prominent feature is, of course, the Parthenon. But don't forget to check out the gorgeous panoramas of Athens as you climb up. Under extreme renovation right now, the Parthenon has seen better days but still stands to impress. Built under the guidance of Phidias and designed by Iktinos, it took nine years to complete this masterpiece. Though Doric in structure, it still has Ionic features. The Doric metopes, or friezes, along the outer colonnade depict showdowns between humans and centaurs, Amazons, and giants (oh my!). The Ionic pediments showed the birth of Athena and the contest between Athena and Poseidon. Though the Parthenon may seem like a perfectly straight and strict building, approach it and you'll notice the curves of the columns that give the building more movement, more life.

If you look to the left of the Parthenon, you'll see the Erechtheion, which turns heads thanks to its lovely lady columns, or if you wanna talk nerdy, caryatid columns. Built during the Peloponnesian War, it's named after a hero Poseidon done effed up after he lost the contest for Athens. So naturally, it is a temple dedicated to Athena and Poseidon. It seems to have been appeasing enough.

As you walked in to see the showstopper Parthenon, you may have noticed some columns and a pile of rubble. Typical Athens. But this here was the Propylaea, or the gateway to the Acropolis. Never really completed, it's doomed to

athens

be an unfinished symphony here. On its right stands the Temple of Athena Nike, which is a temple to… Athena! Shocking.

After you leave such great heights, head down to the right of the Acropolis's main entrance to check out the Theater of Dionysus. God of drunkenness, revelry, and last Friday nights throughout history, Dionysus also happens to be the god of theater. Many greats like Sophocles and Euripides had plays performed here, and it continues to function as a theater.

And there you have it. The Acropolis. As you descend, don't feel sad. You'll see it about 100 more times before you leave Athens. And somehow, you'll never get tired of it. Love works in mysterious ways.

i Admission €12, EU students and seniors €6. ◷ Open daily 8am-8pm.

ACROPOLIS MUSEUM
MUSEUM

15 Dionysiou Areopagitou St. ☎21 0900 0900 www.theacropolismuseum.gr/en

Sleek, modern, air-conditioned. Not the first words that come to mind when you're thinking about the Acropolis (and really, when are you not thinking about it?). But head over to the Acropolis Museum and all that can be changed. A gorgeous new museum dedicated to all things Acropolesque, this may or may not be a huge middle finger to the British wankers who refused to return the "borrowed" Elgin Marbles until Athens had a proper place to exhibit them. But regardless, it stands as an impressive sight on its own.

The metallic black and silver color scheme, the enormous TVs, and the just-for-kicks iPads don't exactly scream, "Everything here existed before the last time you got laid!" but don't let that deceive you. Even as you make your way to the entrance, take a look down at the transparent floors that reveal the archaeological excavation happening below your feet. Admire the parts that are completely exposed and gaze at the wealth of coins in an ancient wishing well.

After the excitement of getting your ticket, you'll walk into a lobby of small-scale reconstructions of the Parthenon and a large TV screen showing whimsical animations of ancient Greek sculptures dancing around. Though probably meant for children, it will certainly also amuse easily distracted Let's Go writers and visitors who are high for a good 10min. The first floor of the museum is dedicated mainly to beautiful works of pottery and other votive offerings to the slopes of the Acropolis, where temples to Asclepius (the god of fixing your health after one too many amphorae of wine) and the nymphs used to exist. Head up to the second floor and you'll see gorgeous reconstructions of pediment structures that are a prime example of why Greek statues stopped having archaic smiles. Walk through the columned halls that make you feel like you're actually somewhere ancient and spend some time looking at the wealth of sculptures here. Shout outs go to a votive plaque by Megakles, which humbly says, "Megakles is good looking," and to the *kouroi* and *korai*, statues of young men and women that have some of the finest asses to be seen.

Reach the third floor, and your difficult escalator climb will be rewarded with a gorgeous panorama of Athens and the Acropolis itself. All around are marble reliefs from the Parthenon (note the spaces reserved for the Elgin Marbles should the Brits ever return them…). Here you can witness all the different ways centaurs can kick your ass while the Lapiths endure real #struggles. Watch a short documentary about the Parthenon, take a look at the reconstructions of the gorgeous Parthenon pediments, and there you have it. You've climbed the Acropolis Museum. So go forth, leave the modern marvels of air-conditioning and learn to carry the weight of the knowledge and culture you now bear after visiting this fine establishment.

i Admission €5, EU students and seniors €3. ◷ Open Apr-Oct M 8am-4pm, Tu-Th 8am-8pm, F 8am-10pm, Sa-Su 8am-8pm; Nov-Mar Tu-Th 9am- 5pm, F 9am-10pm, Sa-Su 9am-8pm.

ATHENS BACKPACKERS
HOSTEL $$

12 Makri Street   ☎21 0922 4044 www.backpackers.gr

Not called Athens's party hostel for nothing. With Daft Punk blasting at reception on a Wednesday night and a free ouzo shot when you first arrive, anyone staying here will remember it fondly.

The rooms are fairly standard. As with most hostels, there are beds. There are bathrooms. The location is right by the Acropolis metro stop, and yes, right by the Acropolis. It makes for great rooftop selfies, but the area can get touristy. What really sets this hostel apart is the lively, young crowd that gathers. Full of college students, recent grads, and the occasional young at heart, the beds in this hostel are not used until 4am on many nights. But paying the affordable €25 a night for a bed is still worth it.

If you can make it to breakfast from 7:30-9:30am, there are bread rolls and eggs to be had in the kitchen. With no lockout and no curfew, though, there's no shame in sleeping the hell out of that morning. You can spend your evenings trying to turn up at the gorgeous Sky Bar which offers a beautiful view of the Acropolis ...but only until 11pm when it closes. Afterwards, make your way out to Plaka and try to find Athens's nightlife, or since you're already surrounded by a party crowd, make your own.

Apart from offering great company, Athens Backpackers also has daily walking tours of the cities and relatively cheap excursions to surrounding cities and ancient sites such as Delphi, Marathon, and Mycenae. So whether you're looking for a bed right by the Parthenon or just want to get wasted, let your backpacks spend the night here. You won't regret it.

i Dorms €25-28. Doubles €40-45. Triples €30. ☒ Check in 2pm. Check out 10am. Reception 24hr.

STUDENT AND TRAVELLER'S INN
INN $$

16 Kydathineon   ☎21 0324 4808 www.studenttravellersinn.com

Are you a student? Are you a traveller? Then goddamn you are so inn here. Student and Travellers Inn is a great place to stay if you want decently priced rooms in the heart of Plaka and only Wi-Fi in select areas near reception.

Okay, but Wi-Fi issues aside, it's a clean, friendly dorm. Rooms are a little cramped but the air conditioning keeps everything pretty chill. Bathrooms are mostly not ensuite but kept spotless and the showers have enough water pressure that you might actually be able to wash your hair which is pretty ballin. The staff are kind here, there are plenty of mirrors in the hallways so you can always check yourself out, and it's only a few minutes walk from Syntagma and the Acropolis.

Though not the party hostel that Athens Backpackers has a reputation for, this is another young, social hostel with great people. The garden area not only has Wi-Fi but a lively social scene with a TV playing terribly wonderful movies, students throwing back a couple beers, and a stray cat who knows no boundaries and will jump up on your lap. So in theory it's the ideal place to get some pussy. And we can't say that about every hostel, so stay here and you won't regret it.

i Dorms €16-22. Doubles €30. Triples €24. Quad €22. ☒ Check in noon. Check out 11am. Reception 24hr.

athens

NATIONAL ARCHAEOLOGICAL MUSEUM

MUSEUM

44 Patission St. ☎213 214 4800 www.namuseum.gr

You're in Greece. You should spend your days staring at gorgeous, sculpted naked bodies. So go to the National Archaeological Museum. With its enormous collection of Greek (and some Egyptian!) art, there's no shortage of muscular frames and nude bods here. Oh, and some great art as well.

The museum is a bit difficult to navigate, with numerous halls and doors that just look so inviting. Chronologically, the first stop should be in Mycenaean and Cycladic art. Gaze into the mask of definitely-not-Agamemnon but an equally regal Mycenaean king. And see why the Mycenaeans were known for being rich in gold.

Next, wander through the *kouros/kore* galleries, with their beautiful sculptures of young men and women. Take your time here because there are some rather large ones... if you know what we mean. Continue with the sculptures into the Classical section, where a more naturalistic depiction arises. See how the gorgeous Artemision Bronze of Zeus or Poseidon steals the show.

But don't get lost in the abs of these sculptures. Turn into some of the galleries filled with glass cases along the way and see everything from ancient bridles for horses to hand mirrors to musical instruments. When you reach the enormous red room with a coy Aphrodite, take the stairs up to see the second floor.

Here, you'll find plenty of ancient pottery, along with surprise skeletons. Be prepared. Head back down and appreciate some more Hellenistic artwork. If everything is looking too Greek for you, head into the Egyptian gallery, which has plenty of boats and even some mummies.

Continue you walk through this museum. A thorough look will take several hours at least. And then if you ever get out of its labyrinth (so Greek!), you'll be rewarded with free Wi-Fi in the internet corner right by the tickets office. And also rewarded by having had the chance to see some of the most beautiful artifacts in Athens. That's cool, too.

i Admission €7, EU students and seniors €3. ⏰ Open daily 8am-8pm.

MT. LYCABETTUS

MOUNTAIN

Kolonaki. Funicular entrance at intersection of Kloutarchou and Aristippou St. ☎210 721 07 01

Forget Amsterdam—Athens is another great city if you want to get high. With plenty of hills that seem to keep popping up whenever you've got your backpack on, it's not hard to find amazing panoramas of the city. But sometimes amazing just isn't good enough. Always striving for excellence, head to the highest point in Athens: Mt Lycabettus.

Located in Kolonaki, the poshest neighborhood in Athens, Mt. Lycabettus provides endless fodder for bad jokes about high society and how, at 900ft above sea level, it's still easier to climb than the social ladder. If you're into hiking, it's about a 30min. climb up stone steps. If you're into sitting, you'll still need to climb up some steps of stairs until you get to the intersection of Ploutarchou and Aristippou St., where you can take the funicular up to the top.

Once you reach the top, prepare your eyes for one of the most gorgeous views of Athens. The whole city sprawls out in front of you with the oceans and the mountains in the distance. Take it in. Take some selfies. Accept that you are too high to actually get a good look at the Parthenon. And then take a romantic walk around with your phone (because iPhones over girlfriends any day of the week). And then switch from front cam and get an equally gorgeous view. Not bad, Athens.

i Funicular €7. ⏰ Funicular runs every 30min. 9am-3am.

ANCIENT AGORA OF ATHENS

Entrance at 24 Adrianou ☎210 321 01 85 http://odysseus.culture.gr

MARKET

The center of Athenian life. Political, communal, and economic. A place where Socrates, Aristotle, and Demosthenes all walked and argued. The main marketplace and the meeting place of the 500-men Boule which helped define Athenian democracy. And a place for a pretty nice walk, too. The Ancient Agora is kind of everything you ever wanted in Athens.

Not as crowded as the Acropolis because it's far more spread out, with plenty of gardens in between, the once bustling Agora is now a lovely little respite to take your boo to while getting a healthy dose of history. There are plenty of buildings and piles of rubble to admire. Here are some highlights.

Start with the completely renovated **Stoa of Attalos.** Once filled with shops and philosophers, only the museum shop and plenty of busts remain. A gorgeous building that now houses the Agora Museum, take some time looking at the pottery and sculptures here.

Head to the right to make a pilgrimage to the **Church of the Holy Apostles.** A beautiful medieval church from 1000 CE, let its quaint old design and beautiful frescoes inside charm you with the awesome might of God or something.

You love odeons, even if you're not exactly sure what they are (concert halls, pretty much). The passage of time is currently playing in the **Odeon of Agrippa,** but it's still some of the more intact ruins in the Agora, with towering statues standing starkly against the empty building. It's one of those postmodern art places now, we suppose.

Built to everyone's favorite god of lameness (getting thrown off Mt. Olympus builds character, at least), the **Temple of Hephaestus** is large and gorgeous and the best-preserved in all of Greece. Take a look at the friezes featuring Theseus battling the Pallantids on the side. Currently, instead of Hephaestus's thundering hammer, it's full of chirping now, making it a temple for the birds. Because Hephaestus must have enjoyed lame jokes.

i *Admission €4, EU students and seniors €2. ◙ Open daily 8am-8pm.*

MONASTIRAKI

SQUARE

Monastiraki metro stop. Ermou, Adrianou, Athinas, and Mitropoleos St. all converge here, too.

A region famous for housing Athens's flea market, souvlaki row, and some great street dancers (because sometimes white guys got game), Monastiraki should definitely be a place you hit up during your stay in Athens. In the shadow of the Acropolis, Monastiraki opens up to a giant square that's always crowded with locals and tourists alike. Take a seat anywhere you can and take it in for a moment.

If you're feeling hungry, this is by far the best place to get gyros and souvlaki at really cheap prices. There are also decent coffee and gelato places around and a Beneth right in the square, so you can get some great baklava, too.

Once you've gotten your fill of all this awesomeness, get ready to pop them tags with €20 in your pocket. It's time to check out the Athens flea market. Take any of the small side streets and find rows of stores and vendors with anything from Converses to hookahs to "THIS IS SPARTA" shirts (even though you're in Athens—minor plot point). Walk around and take a look at these stores because they're a good place to get some pretty cool stuff. Everything is fairly cheap, and there's no guarantee that you'll leave empty handed. Just save around €2 for more souvlaki in Monastiraki at sunset, and life will be practically complete.

athens

FOOD

KOSTAS · GREEK $

5 Pentelis · ☎210 322 85 02

Souvlaki is one of the surest signs that someone out there loves us. Warm pita bread, tender meat, fresh tomatoes, and French fries—it's the Elysian Fields in your mouth. A popular Greek speciality, finding *souvlaki* in Athens is like finding a Starbucks in New York.

But for some of the best *souvlaki* you'll ever have, walk a couple blocks away from Monastiraki and come to Kostos. It's easy to walk by Kostos unless you notice the line of people outside. Walk in and you'll find a cozy *souvlaki* heaven with toasting pita breads, plenty of pictures and newspaper clippings on the walls, and old Greek men taking shots of ouzo at the wooden bar. Welcome home.

The staff is incredibly friendly, the prices are cheap (€2.20 for *souvlaki*), and the food is incredible. Not traditional street souvlaki, there are usually only beef or pork kebab cut options instead of gyros and no French fries (difficult to accept, but stay strong). Bite into the *souvlaki*, though, and you'll fall in love. Warm, fresh, and with a spicy kick. Just when you thought *souvlaki* couldn't get better, Kostos will give you something new to swear by.

i Souvlaki €2.20. ☑ Open M-Sa 9am-3pm.

MONO · RESTAURANT $$

4C Benizelou Palaiologou · ☎210 322 850 · www.monorestaurant.gr

Don't let the name scare you off. If the low-quality tourist options in Plaka just aren't cutting it anymore, head down the small P. Benizelou to dine in this gem. Modern and sleek, with nature-inspired accents that give it a rustic tone, Mono is everything you wanted and more from a sketchily-named restaurant.

The food here is certainly worth its weight in euro coins. Appetizers range from mussels to cheese to flavored mushrooms. The seafood options are always delectable, and since you are in a port city after all, go for that swordfish and red tuna. Other meat options are limited to chicken or lamb, but you'll probably survive. The pasta here is exciting (which one rarely says about pasta), but squid ink or smoked pancetta make everything even more fun.

i Appetizers €6-12. Pasta €13-14. Entrees €13-24. ☑ Open daily 1pm-1am.

OPOS PALIA · GREEK $$

2 Veikou

A hidden treasure in the Plaka region. For some real, non-touristy, so-Greek-that-you-don't-really-know-what's-going-on food, come here. No sign, no menu, but plenty of Greeks playing backgammon and smoking cigarettes at the few tables outside.

There's no set menu, so every time you come in it's an adventure. But you can be sure that whatever they've got cooking today is going to be delicious. The food is very reasonably priced, with entrees around and always traditional and authentic. Relax, listen to all the Greek conversations around you, eat some amazing food, and for once, imagine what it's like to not be a tourist.

i Entrees €5-10. ☑ Seems to depend on food. Usually 10am-10pm.

AVOCADO · VEGETARIAN $$

30 Nikis · ☎210 323 78 78 · www.avocadoathens.com

You know what's great? Vegetables. A new vegetarian restaurant on a quiet street near Syntagma Sq., Avocado is the cool, hip place to go for delicious vegetarian meals. With a young staff, a clean and modern aesthetic, and John Lennon's "Imagine" playing on the radio, this could be the answer to all your vegetarian dreams. And that's before you even look at the menu.

Avocado has an extensive tea selection and even some kombucha if you want to get a little hipster. The appetizers range from good ol' nachos to "Mother Earth," a spinach tart with the works. Anyone dearly missing their meat can go on to order vegetarian or vegan burgers, or perhaps if you're feeling adventurous, a fancier Greek salad. The pastas are delicious, there are macrobiotic options, and we recommend anything with, well, avocados. Can't go wrong with that.

i Appetizers €5-7. Entrees €8-12. ☼ Open M-Sa 11am-10pm, Su 11am-7pm.

BENETH DESSERTS $
97 Adrianou ☎210 323 88 22

Just because you can't describe your love life as sweet and sticky doesn't mean your diet should follow suit. So while you're in Greece, say yassas to baklava. A delicious dessert made of filo pastry, honey, and chopped nuts, if you only eat one meal a day, make it baklava—it probably has enough calories anyway.

The best place to sink your teeth into these flaky layers of sweetness? Beneth on Adrianou. It's a storefront that's hard to pass up, with plates filled with chocolate-covered cookies, creamy cakes, and fresh fruit tarts. As you wander in the narrow bakery, prepare your eyes for the feast of baked breads, pies, and ice cream treats that will sing their siren song. But hold fast and save your dessert virginity (of the hour, of course) for some baklava (€1.95).

Beneth also offers a variety of sandwiches. Get your fill of tomato and mozzarella on fresh bread and then stay for dessert. If you're lucky, snag one of the two high tables out front.

i Baklava €1.95. Pastries and bread €1-4. ☼ Open daily 7am-10pm.

NIGHTLIFE

Athens is a decent city for nightlife. But to get really turnt up, head to the islands.

Athens

Athens isn't known for it's nightlife. Many Athenians hit up islands like Mykonos if they're looking for a good time in the summer. But it's not impossible to turn up in this sleepy city. Your best bet for getting shitfaced and dancing all night is in a region known as Gazi. Clubs and bars line the street here, and though drinks are expensive, most places don't have a cover.

Socilista at **Triptolemou 33** is a popular local nightclub where they play almost exclusively Greek house music, so you can feel the shame when the DJ stops the music—everyone sings the next lyrics, and you just take a long sip of your drink. Confetti and sparklers make up for it, though. If your ears are craving Pitbull, 1) welcome to planet Earth, and 2) you won't like it here. To get to Gazi, either take the metro to **Kerameikos** or take a taxi. Protip: always take a taxi with a meter. Acropolis area to Gazi costs about €5-6, and unmetered taxis may try to charge you up to €20.

Apart from Gazi, there are plenty of bars in the Plaka and Psiri regions if you want to drink and have a good time. Walk around here to see what's the most happening place, but don't expect anything too crazy, Some of these regions do get kinda sketch at night, so bring company or take a cab.

Go with friends, dance even if people start giving you weird looks, and have an awesome time. Because even if nightlife isn't Athens's specialty, it sure is yours.

Mykonos

If you remember Mykonos, you didn't do Mykonos right. (Just kidding—please drink responsibly.) Famous for being paradise (if your idea of paradise doesn't include sleep or Wi-Fi), Mykonos is where all the pretty young Athenians go on the weekends to get sloshed.

Take the ferry from Athens, and after 5hr (or 2.5hr. if you got money to blow on the fast ferry), welcome to paradise. The two big hostels here are **Paradise Camping**, which is right on **Paradise Beach** where all the action happens, and **Paraga Camping**, which is about a 5min. trek through some rocks from Paradise but is quieter and has a pool. In the end, it shouldn't matter which hostel you stay at unless your backpack is super picky. Nobody comes here for the beds. Our advice:

- **AFTERNOON-7PM:** Sleep on the beach or by the pool (careful: some beach chairs cost a surprise €5, either bring a towel or relax by the pool). Get some ice cream to keep you cool.

- **7-10PM:** Eat dinner and chill with friends at one of the many cafes that line the beaches. Souvlaki for €3 will probably be your best bet for a cheap eat.

- **10PM-MIDNIGHT:** Pregame. Apologize to your liver, then hit up the liquor store by the Paradise Mini Mart. It's ridiculously cheaper than drinks at bars.

- **MIDNIGHT-TOMORROW AFTERNOON:** TURN DOWN FOR WHAT? Party, bitches.

The big clubs by Paradise Beach alternate what days they're open, so ask around first. Covers are steep at €20, but if you play your cards right, you might be able to manipulate someone into paying for you. Most clubs don't get going until 1am or later, and then they keep going until morning. Earlier clubs and bars like **Tropicana** and **Guapaloca on Paradise** keep music going all day, and you might be able to find a crazy party at 5pm, too.

If you're looking for incredible nightlife that takes you into the morning, get the hell out of Athens and come here. Meet crazy people. Wait for the sunrise by drinking Grey Goose and smoking cigarettes on the beach. And have some of the most unbelievable stories to tell, all from one weekend. You'll only regret it in the late afternoon.

ESSENTIALS

Practicalities

- **VISAS:** If you're an EU citizen, feel free to skip this part because you don't need a visa. Citizens of the US, most of North and South America, and Australia as well as many other countries (be sure to check online) do not require a visa for stays up until 90 days. If you're going to be in Europe for more than 90 days, contact an embassy or consulate to hook you up.

- **WORK PERMITS:** You're allowed to work it but not work in Greece with a visa. Work permits take time and money to obtain, so contact the Greek consulate for more information.

- **MONEY:** Eurochange is one of the biggest chains where you can exchange other currencies for the euro. They're most commonly found in the airport but also throughout Athens. To withdraw money, make sure your debit or credit card has a four-digit pin, as that's most commonly accepted. Finding ATMs isn't hard. The most common banks are Alpha Bank, Eurobank, and Piraeus Bank. And they're often all right next to each other, so you get your pick of ATM color scheme.

- **INTERNET:** Thankfully, there are many free hotspots for Wi-Fi in Athens. Places to connect to the free athensWi-Fi are at Thisseio, Syntagma, and Kerameikou. For a comprehensive list including restaurants, cafes, and such, check out http://free-Wi-Fi.gr/en.

- **POST OFFICES:** Mail is handled by the Greek National Post Office (ELTA). Postcards and letters from Greece to outside Europe will cost €0.85. Some central post offices are at Dionisiou Areopagitou 7 by the Acropolis (open M-F 7:30am-8:30pm, Sa 7:30am-2:30pm), at the intersection of Mitropoleos and Syntagma Square (open M-F 7:30am-8:30pm, Sa 7:30am-2:30pm, Su 9am-1:30pm), and in Exarhia at Zaimi 36-38 (open M-F 7:30am-2:30pm).

Emergency

- **POLICE & FIRE:** ☎112
- **AMBULANCES:** ☎112 and 166
- **TOURIST POLICE:** ☎210 920 07 267 (Veikou St.)
- **PHARMACIES:** Look for a big green "+" sign anywhere, and you'll find a pharmacy. Late-night pharmacies stay open on a rotating basis. If you find a pharmacy that's closed, look at the sheet posted on the door that will tell you where the closest open pharmacy is.

Getting There

If you're coming into Greece, you'll probably be flying. Eleftherios Venizelos (ATH) is Athens's international airport. To get from the airport to Syntagma Square, the center of town, you can take the metro (the blue line) and get on any train you see. The airport's the last stop, so any train from here is going back into Athens. The metro ticket will cost you €8. Alternatively, you can take the airport bus, X95, which will take you into Syntagma Square and cost €5. Taking a taxi can cost you around €30-35 during the day and around €50 after midnight. Be sure to take a cab with a fare machine so you don't get ripped off.

If you're coming in by train, Larissa is the central train station. From here you can take the red line on the metro to Acropoli, then switch to the blue line and get off after one stop at Syntagma.

If you're coming in by ferry, the main port is Piraeus. From here you can take the green line on the metro to Monastiraki, then switch to the blue line to get to Syntagma.

Getting Around

Athens by foot is very doable, especially around all the touristy areas. Plaka, Monastiraki, and Syntagma Square are all within 10min. or so of each other. Thanks to the Olympics, the metro is efficient and reliable as well. Buy one ticket for €1.40, which is valid for 90min. A full day pass is €4, and a weekly pass is €14. Be sure to validate your ticket at one of the machines, or you'll have to pay a hefty fine. If you only want to take a bus, it's €1.20 at a bus station or on board. Tickets can be purchased at any station, any yellow box by a bus stop, or most kiosks.

Taxis are very affordable in Athens. Just make sure you don't get screwed over. Always take a taxi with a fare machine. Those without will always overcharge. There are usually two pricings: one before midnight and one after midnight, which is more expensive. For a good estimate of prices, from Plaka to Gazi should cost around €6. Make sure you're not being overcharged.

volos

Tucked away between the mountains and the sea, Volos is a gorgeous, small city where you can relax, look out over the water, and college party it up. Home to most of the University of Thessaly, Volos is a vibrant young town. Though on the more petite side, it packs in all the charm of a portside city while bursting with student culture. Clear blue waters, the looming Mt. Pelion, music concerts in the streets, and crowded tables where everyone's taking shots of tsipouro—whether you want a peaceful walk to the beach or a bar where you'll be taking in something other than water, there's no shortage of fun to be had in Volos. Try to befriend the local students, since they usually major in finding the parties, and there's not a lot of tourist infra-

AEGLI HOTEL
Argonafton 24

☎2421 024 471 www.aegli.gr

Sleek, modern, clean. Clearly not where the college students live. But if you'd like your own room with a view out over the port, come to Aegli Hotel. It's located right by the water and minutes away from the center of Volos. Ask for a port-side room if you want a look out over the water. Then prepare yourself for luxury.

Walk in, and let the classic wooden panels and marble entrance impress you. Reception is friendly, and the bedrooms are standard, with the same white and wooden panel aesthetic as you found at reception. Someone's taken their interior design courses here. You might feel bad dragging in the dirt and soil sample collection that has gathered on your backpack, but don't worry about it. You'll add some gritty touches to the impeccably white sheets on the bed.

Breakfast is served in a dining room. After breakfast, you'll always be faced with the difficult decision of if you want to explore the seaside or downtown first. Sucks to suck. But take your pick. And after coming back in the evening, head up to your room and get a beautiful view of Volos lit up and night. #flawless

i Singles €65. Doubles €60. Triples €75. ☒ Reception 24hr.

PARK HOTEL
Deligiorgi 2

☎2421 036 511 www.parkhotel-volos.gr/len

No, it's not just a classy name. This hotel is in fact directly in front of a beautiful seaside park in Volos. From the rooftop garden in this hotel, you get a lovely panorama of Volos and the mountains.

All the businessmen who use this hotel might make you tone down the racket a little bit. Keep that for the private rooms. The rooms are clean and if you're lucky you might even get a plant to love and cherish. It's like they brought the park to you! Apart from that, it's a fairly standard hotel. The rooftop garden is the most impressive part, with a gorgeous view over the sea.

The city center is within walking distance but still isolated enough to be in a quieter part of town, making it a decent place to park yourself for a night or two.

i Singles €60. Doubles €80. ☒ Reception open 7am-midnight. Check-in 2pm-midnight.

structure (or hostels) here yet. So if you're ready to rock this small joint, grab some tsipouro, guiltily water it down a little, and get ready to party all night by the beach.

FOOD

TA FILARAKIA
Antonopoulou 96-100

☎242 102 20 26

Tsipouro. Learn that word. It'll become your best friend in Volos. Where in Athens, ouzo is all the rage, come up to Thessaly, and it's all about the tsipouro. A tsipouradiko, if you're good with derivations, is a place that serves tsipouro. And so much more.

In an incredible tradition that should really just exist everywhere, it's very common in Volos for people to go to a tsipouradiko, order some tsipouro for each person, and as if by some alcoholic magic, the waiters bring the drinks and then several plates of delicious seafood.

Ta Filarakia is among the best *tsipouradika*. A favorite among the locals, it's tucked away from the busy, expensive ones by the seaside. Here, charming green wooden chairs and green-and-white-checkered tablecloths give a very homey, comforting feel. The perfect place to turn up. Prices are cheap, and the plates of food are plentiful.

Start with a tiny personal bottle of tsipouro for each person. Then watch your table fill up with calamari, shrimp, and maybe like five other kinds of fish that you can't really recognize. But they're all delicious and the perfect lemony, salty meal to go along with your drink. Finish your drink, order another, and watch your table be filled up with completely new dishes.

i Tsipouro €4 per glass. ☼ Open M-Sa 10am-2am.

LA MAMMA
PIZZA $

29 Metamorfoseos ☎242 103 33 38 www.pizzalamamma.gr

No college town is complete without some damn good pizza. And maybe your local Pizza Hut isn't cutting it anymore. Well welcome to the Mediterranean. La Mamma is a delicious pizza (sorry, redundant) place located in a more residential area of Volos. Specializing in deliveries, you can call to have a cute Greek guy bring you some mouthwatering pizza. Or go to the small store with a giant picture of a pizza as its sign, order a pizza, anxiously wait 10min., then take it home or eat it by the port. There's no place to sit inside, but a quick walk to Ermou and back should be enough time to make sure every topping has found its rightful spot on your pizza.

Staff is amazingly friendly and willing to offer you an English menu with 36 different varieties of pizza that could be stuffed in your mouth. Choose wisely because they're all delicious and freshly made with cheese and sauce that are like "whaaat how is this so good" good.

Apart from pizza, La Mamma also has a decent selection of pasta, salads, and appetizers ranging from garlic bread to cheesy fries to a club sandwich (which still counts as an appetizer, guys). Well-priced drinks include sodas, beers, and sangria in a bottle. Which along with the pizza pretty much sums up every college experience ever.

i Small pizza €6.50. Large pizza €8.50. Pasta €4-5. ☼ Open daily 12:30pm-12:30am.

METRO CREPE STATION
CREPES $

193 Dimitriados ☎242 102 75 50 www.metrocrepestation.gr

You don't need to be able to read the menu. If you perfect your pointing skills and just keep saying chocolate, you're guaranteed to come out with an amazing crepe. Trust us, we're experts.

Metro Crepe Station is your #1 stop for all your light, sweet, savory, crepey needs. Either order one of the predestined crepes on the menu or exercise some free will by building your own, which is always more fun.

Fillings include everything from cheese and salami to Nutella, merenda, and Oreo bits. All the fruit options are made with fresh fruit cut right in front of you. And with more varieties of chocolate than you could ever dream of, don't be ashamed to stand in awe for several moments before blindly asking for one.

All crepes are made on the spot, so after you order you can watch your crepe go from batter to light, tasty goodness and then get filled up with some sweet Nutella loving. Mmm. Then either sit at one of the tables inside or take it on the go in the main shopping district of Volos. Chocolate stains on your shirt are so in right now.

i Crepes €3-5. ☼ Open daily noon-5pm.

NIGHTLIFE

WHITE
Pirassou & Laxana

CLUB
☎695 165 94 45

The sleek white bar and couches give White its name, but the crowds of young students, the loud music, and the smoke and confetti are what make White the most popular summer club in Volos, where everyone comes to drink and dance from Wednesday to Friday. White's popular among the students and recent grads in the area, giving it a great young vibe. The DJs blast top 40 music under bright purple lights. There are usually themes for most of the nights, ranging from '90s Night to Greek Night.

This club fills up fairly fast on weekend nights, but parties really get going late. As the music blasts, people spend a fair amount of time talking and drinking. At least the club is so beautiful that you're guaranteed to have something to talk about.

So when in Volos, do as the students do. Come to a poolside bar, sip a mojito, and then get ready to listen to great music and fist bump all night long.

i Drinks €7-10. ☼ Open W-Sa 11pm-late.

TOY STORIES
Taki Ikonomaki 26

CLUB
☎242 103 30 34

It's all fun and games until someone gets wasted. Then it's even better. That's why God invented Toy Stories. It's more than just a bar. Consider this concept: drinks + board games. Yes? Oh god, yes. Instead of following that good ol' American idea of getting drunk as efficiently as possible, come here for a more casual night out. Grab a beer, choose a game, and let the fun begin.

The red wall right next to the bar is lined with boxes of everything from Ticket to Ride to Jungle Speed to "figure out that Greek board game," which seems to be a popular one. Take a look through the menu of board games, choose something that hopefully has English directions, and then prepare for the most fun you've had sitting down in a while.

Popular among many college students in the area, it attracts a young crowd but not a particularly turnt up one. It's a great place to start or end a night or just the place to go when you want to get with your friends and ask them questions about the stupid card on your forehead that you can't freaking figure out. Relive that childhood competitive board game spirit, get drunk off victory, and feel the frustration every time your jackass friends screws you over.

i Drinks €3-5. ☼ Open pretty much all the time. They start closing down when people start leaving.

O BAR
Leoforos Dimokratias

BAR
☎242 809 20 00

Don't let the rustic stone exterior scare you off. This place is as vibrant and young as any of the bars in Volos, with loud music, plenty of alcohol, and crowds of students. Enter and head toward the large white bar in the center, which is where all them alcohol-lovers flock, filling its four sides.

Guest DJs often play at this place, or you can come to the allegedly original Greek Night here where your ears will hear so much Greek pop and techno that maybe you'll actually learn some of this language.

This place can get rather crowded, but students in Volos like most students can't really be bothered with doing things in a timely manner, so most places around here turn up after 1am. Come in, grab a cocktail (or if you're smart, pregame with some tsipouro before), and then watch the room full up, listen to the beats play, and party until the early hours of the morning.

i Drinks €7-10. ☼ Open M-Th 11pm-5am, F-Sa 11pm-8am, Su 11pm-5am.

VOLOS

ESSENTIALS
Practicalities

- **POST OFFICES:** Mail is handled by the Greek National Post Office (ELTA). Postcards and letters from Greece to outside Europe will cost €0.85. Some central post offices are at Dimitriados and Ag. Nikolaou (open M-F 7:30am-8:30pm) and at 3 Chatzimichali (open M-F 7:30am-2:30pm).

- **INTERNET:** Wi-Fi can be hard to find outside of your hotel. Check for cafes or restaurants that offer complimentary Wi-Fi. The area by the main yellow building of the University of Thessaly also offers free Wi-Fi.

Emergency

- **EMERGENCY NUMBERS:** The emergency number in Greece is ☎112 for police, fire department, and ambulances.

- **AMBULANCE SERVICE:** ☎166

- **TOURIST POLICE:** ☎24210 39057, located at 179, 28th October St.

- **PHARMACIES:** Look for a big green "+" sign anywhere, and you'll find a pharmacy. Late night pharmacies stay open on a rotating basis. If you find a pharmacy that's closed, look at the sheet posted on the door that will tell you where the closest open pharmacy is.

Getting There

If you're coming from within Europe, RyanAir does offer some flights that fly directly into Volos Airport from Frankfurt, Milan, Rome, and Brussels. Other plane companies also offer flights in, but they are infrequent.

Your best bet for coming into Volos will be by bus. KTEL operates fairly frequent service between Athens, Volos, and Thessaloniki. The bus ride is 4hr. from Athens and about 2.5hr. from Thessaloniki.

From Athens

Buses leave from the Liosion station in Athens, which is known as Terminal B. A little outside the city, take bus 024 from outside the National Gardens and get off at the Praktoria KTEL stop. A taxi from Syntagma should cost you less than €10. Tickets can be reserved online in advance. Buses don't usually sell out. A ticket will cost you around €30 depending on when you're traveling.

From Thessaloniki

KTEL buses leave from the main bus station, KTEL Macedonia. To get here, take bus number 8 from the train station, Neos Sidirodromikos Stathmos, and get off at the KTEL Macedonia stop. Tickets to Volos from here will cost you around €18.

There are also trains going between Athens and Volos and Thessaloniki and Volos. Though they may move faster, they both stop at Larissa, and you'll have to switch trains to Volos, so most people prefer taking the bus.

Getting Around

Most people in Volos get around by bike. Tourists can certainly get by on foot. The city isn't very, big and you can walk around the main parts fairly easily. Buses do exist if you want to take them. Tickets are €1.10 for a bus ride. No underground metro exists for Volos. If you want to take a taxi to go anywhere in the city, it should cost you less than €6-7. Note that taxis have two fares: one for before midnight and the double fare from midnight-5am.

thessaloniki

Looking out from the castle in Ano Polis, Thessaloniki sprawls out in front of you. From the horizon meeting the ocean to the bustling city streets to the quiet village of the old city, every bit of this 2300-year-old city will charm you. The streets are filled with more Byzantine ruins and churches than you will be able to visit, and the Roman arches will be great landmarks to get you home. Among the castles and towers, a young population fills Thessaloniki with life. In the evening, the city fills up with all the cool kids drinking on the streets and a nightlife sector that is sometimes too crowded to walk through on Friday and Saturday nights at 3am.

get a room!

LITTLE BIG HOUSE
HOTEL $

Andokidou 24 ☎231 301 4323 www.littlebighouse.gr

Located in the beautiful Ano Polis, Little Big House might be a little uphill from the rest of the city, but you'll get the chance to explore life in this old-fashioned area while being only 15min. away from more central Thessaloniki.

Vicky who is just the nicest and most helpful person ever, will make sure you feel at home by answering every stupid question you have and welcoming you with a cold frappe, a traditional drink in Thessaloniki. The brightly colored rooms are incredibly spacious and probably some of the best you'll come across in your backpacking travels. Equipped with air conditioning, kitchens, ensuite bathrooms, plenty of mirrors, and even a balcony with a gorgeous view out over Ano Polis if you're up on the fourth floor, part of you won't want to leave your bed (and it won't be for lack of sleep).

The bar area offers complimentary tea and coffee and a decent €2 breakfast, though we recommend ordering a more substantial meal from the bar for €2-2.50, which could get you some toasted bread with Greece cheese spread and nuts. Coffee and alcoholic drinks are also reasonably priced, and there's seating on a rooftop patio as well. The bar, being one of the few in this part of the city, even attracts locals in the evenings.

i Dorms €17-19. Doubles €24. ✆ Reception open 8am-midnight.

STUDIOS ARABAS
HOSTEL $

Sachtouri 28 ☎694 446 6897 www.hostelarabas.gr

Also located in Ano Poli is Studios Arabas. Here you get all the charm of the old city, the 19th-century houses, and the not-from-this-century atmosphere.

In a quiet, unassuming yellow and orange building protected by copious amounts of foliage, you'll find this hostel. The staff and the people living here are very friendly and willing to help you out. The beds are very comfortable, and the rooms are spacious and clean.

Outside, you'll find a beautiful garden which has become a central social hub in this hostel. Occasional barbecues bring together everyone, and this is where you'll be able to meet anyone to take you out clubbing in Thessaloniki. Because nothing unites people like plastic chairs and good food. And a couple of bottles of wine. That'll do the trick, too.

i Dorms €15. ✆ Check-in and check-out at 11am. Reception open until 1am.

Aristotelous Square marks the central area in Thessaloniki. A large open plaza connects major streets like Nikis, which hugs the coastline; Tsimiski and Ermou make up two of the main shopping streets. To the west of the square lies the clubbing and bars district where you can go get crazy any day of the week. To the east lies the Rotunda and the student and university centers of the city. To the south is the ocean and plenty of bars facing out to the sea. Follow Nikis to the east and get to the lively area of the White Tower with music concerts, drinking by the port, and a pedal bar which is just the best idea ever. Go north (and up the not so gentle slopes), and you'll get to the old city of Ana Poli which is practically its own small town full of old houses and winding streets. Altogether you have the city of Thessaloniki. It will swallow you up with ouzo and history and Greek techno and the sea, and somewhere along the way, you'll fall in love.

FOOD

TO IGGLIS
GREEK $

Irodotou 32 ☎231 301 19 67

If you hike up to Ano Poli, you deserve a treat. Come up to To Igglis. A favorite of locals, it can be hard to grab a table here late at night, but if you snag one, prepare your taste buds. Take a seat outside under the leafy canopy and appreciate the charm of old buildings and cobblestone streets and listen to all the Greek conversations happening around you.

The waiters will welcome you to the old fashioned restaurant (complete with 1920s political posters on the fading red and yellow walls) with what you wished everyone welcomed you with: a shot of some really strong liquor.

The menu has charming English mistakes, but the food is flawless. Appetizers include delicious dishes, from everyone's favorite garlic bread to Greek salad to some smoked mackerel. The main dishes are mostly meat with Greek meatballs or lamb. Ask for the daily specials. They always have something delicious in the oven. The food is cooked by one guy behind a counter, and you can watch him work his magic.

Service can be a little brusque, and the food is brought out as it is ready instead of all at once. But once you start eating, you can't complain. Prices are very reasonable and the portions are huge.

i Appetizers €3-4. Entrees €7. 🕓 Usually noon-late.

MAGEIRES
BUFFET, RESTAURANT $

Basileos Irakleiou 42 ☎231 027 23 79

Eat food to save the world? Guess you could make that sacrifice. Mageires is at the beautiful intersection of eating cheap food and helping people in need. Hiring only those people who are disadvantaged, old, and in need, this restaurant does not discriminate based on skill or experience but offers jobs to anyone who needs one. Furthermore, any food leftover is given to the church and distributed among more people in need.

There is an incredibly cheap buffet where you can get a main course, a drink, a salad, fruit, and dessert for only €7. Main courses vary depending on what was cooked that day range from delicious meats like chicken or lamb served with rice and then a selection of cheeses, fruits, and salads to complement any meal. Grab a beer or some wine, and you're all set. There's a reason why young locals line up along here to grab lunch. The food is great and cheap.

All the food is lined up on a buffet on one side of the modern restaurant. Grab a plate and fill it up with everything you can. Then take a seat either outside where high tables face the wooden exterior, or stay in and sit at the white or wooden tables in the sleek marble restaurant.

i Buffet €7. 🕓 Open daily noon-7pm.

KATSAMAKA

GREEK $

1 Athonos Sq.

☎231 023 41 77 katsamaka gr

The sign has a chicken, a pig, and a goat on it. How could you not love it? Located right along the small Athonos Square, Katsamaka specializes in meat dishes, and it's pretty damn good at what it does.

Traditional Greek music plays, and inside you can watch delicious hunks of meat rotating on a spit. Appetizers include salads or some aged cheese. The main dishes are almost all meat, however. The menu offers both sandwiches and portions with various meat options. Choose either chicken, pork, beef, or some of the untranslatable options on the menu, and you'll be pleasantly surprised.

The food is served on wooden plates and baskets, so you know that this shit is the real deal. Try the meat and you'll understand why people come here. It's tender, well cooked, and really good. Portions are served with fresh vegetables, magically healthy tasting French fries, and some pita bread, meaning you could in theory make a sandwich. Or just go for the sandwich option, which is also delicious. Tourists and locals alike come here for a good lunch or dinner.

i Sandwiches €3-4. Entrees €7 ☑ Open daily noon-5pm.

NIGHTLIFE

HOME 9-11

BAR

Syngrou, entrance next to to Mauro Probato (take the stairs up)　☎698 625 00 53

Located on the top floor of an old 19th-century mansion, Home 9-11 is the perfect mix of classy, progressive, and turn down for whaaaat. As you're walking around this crowded nightlife district in Thessaloniki, you'll probably hear really loud music and at least once try to figure out where it's coming from. Look up. Right above a selection of other bars, you'll see the bright flashing lights and feel the deep basses of Home 9-11.

If you come in with a group, you'll be led to your own standing table and drinks will be brought to you. If you don't want anything, make sure to say so or you'll be charged for the not-so-complimentary water.

The DJs blast everything from Avicii to Katy Perry to plenty of Greek techno. Every now and then confetti falls from the ceiling and no one is surprised. The DJs are high energy and are all set to party with fog horns. The crowd is young and attractive but prefer to stand and drink with their friends rather than twerk.

i Drinks €4-10. ☑ Open M-F 9am-midnight, Sa 1-10pm, Su noon-2am.

TO MAURO PROBATO

CLUB

Syngrou 11

☎231 062 65 71

If the fuzzy sheep mascot doesn't win you over, the loud music and impressive DJ sets will. To Mauro Probato, which translates to "The Black Sheep," is a popular bar and disco. Walk in and you'll immediately know their specialty: rock. Giant rock posters line the back side of the room. On the right is the sleek purple bar which presents an impressive selection of alcohols behind it.

The crowd is everyone from student passersby in this busy district to some diehard rock fans who come with great mullets and cut off Sons of Anarchy bro tanks to tear this place apart.

This club gets a little more dance-y than some of the other ones, and considering the type of music, all you'll really need to do is jump up and down while yelling out all the words to your favorite Blink-182 song.

i Drinks €4-10. ☑ Open daily 8pm-6am.

Restaurant by day, crazy nightclub once the clock strikes midnight. Find crowds of people standing outside smoking cigarettes, feel your heart beat change to match the overwhelming bass drops, and you've made it to Piccadilly.

Stenciled signs and old wooden beams give this place an old-fashioned charm. The lights by the bar are all library-esque lamps, and the barstools feature various beer caps. Outside there are plenty of seats and tables where people flock to get away from the heat and throw back a cold drink. Inside, the music blasts louder than most of the surrounding clubs, but it can be hard to motivate this crowd to dance.

It shouldn't come as a surprise that people here prefer to drink and talk to the backdrop of loud EDM but will still refuse to dance. Come by late, around 1am, and this place will be filled up on weekend nights.

i Drinks €5-10. ✪ Open 24hr.

ESSENTIALS

Practicalities

- **POST OFFICES:** Mail is handled by the Greek National Post Office (ELTA). Postcards and letters from Greece to outside Europe will cost €0.85. Some central post offices are at 98 Agiou Dimitriou (open M-F 7:30am-2:30pm) and at 24 Eleftherias (open M-F 7:30am-2:30pm).

- **INTERNET:** Wi-Fi can be hard to find outside of your hotel or hostel. Check for cafes or restaurants that offer complimentary Wi-Fi. There are also many hot spots, but most of these charge money for internet access.

Emergency

- **TOURIST POLICE:** ☎23 105 54 870-1, located at 4, Dodekanissou St.

Getting There

If you're flying into Thessaloniki's Macedonia Airport, you'll need to take the bus line 78 to get into the city center. The bus also makes stops at the bus station, train station, and IKEA where there are several bus connections you can make. A one-way ticket is €0.90. If you want to take a taxi, it shouldn't cost you much more than €15 to the city center.

You can also come in by bus or train from Athens. KTEL operates a bus line from Athens to Thessaloniki that lasts 6hr. 30min. Or take the train run by OSE from Athens, which takes about 5hr. Both will cost you between €30-40.

To get to the city center from the train station, take one of the several buses that stop at the station. If you're at the bus station, take line number 8 to get to the train station and go from there.

Getting Around

Buses are the most common form of transportation in Thessaloniki and will take you almost anywhere. Fare is €0.90 for one way or €1 for two buses. There is no metro system. That being said, Thessaloniki is extremely walkable. To get from Ano Poli to the port takes about 15-20min. Just beware that this is a fairly hilly city, especially up near the old city.

greece essentials

MONEY

Tipping

In Greece, it's normal to include around a 10% gratuity to the bill if the service warrants it. More than that is just showing off your elevated social class. With revolutionary times in Athens and surrounding areas, revealing bourgeois sympathies is not a good idea. There is no need to tip for other services, although rounding up the price to the nearest euro is not unusual.

Taxes

With the EU continually bailing Greece out of its tar pit of debt, the value-added-tax (VAT), applied to all consumer goods, will increase to a maximum 23%. Also, Greece introduced a 10% excise tax on tobacco, fuel, and alcohol. The Greek inflation rate is currently the second highest in the European Union, but rates seem to be on the path to leveling out.

SAFETY AND HEALTH

Local Laws and Police

Greek police are used to having foreigners around, but that does not mean they allow them to break the law. The purchase of pirated goods (including CDs and DVDs) is illegal; keep your receipts for proof of purchase. Taking objects or rocks from ancient sites is forbidden and can lead to fines or prison sentences. Drunk driving and indecent behavior can also result in heavy fines, arrest, and imprisonment. Although legal in Greece since 1951, homosexuality is still frowned upon socially. GLBT individuals are not legally protected from discrimination. That said, destinations like Athens, Ios, and especially Mykonos offer gay and lesbian hotels, bars, and clubs.

Drugs and Alcohol

Visitors of all ages generally have very little difficulty obtaining alcohol in Greece. In contrast, drug laws are very strict. Conviction for possession, use, or trafficking of drugs, including marijuana, will result in imprisonment and fines. Authorities are particularly vigilant at the Turkish and Albanian borders.

Natural Disasters

In one of the world's most seismically active areas, Greece experiences frequent and occasionally large **earthquakes.** The most recent serious quake, in 1999, wreaked an estimated US$3 billion worth of damage and caused nearly 150 deaths and 2000 injuries in Athens. Earthquakes are unpredictable and can occur at any time of day. If there is a strong earthquake, it will probably only last one or two minutes. Protect yourself by moving under a sturdy doorway, table, or desk, and open a door to provide an escape route.

Demonastrations and Political Gatherings

Strikes and demonstrations occur frequently in Greece, especially during the never-ending economic crisis. Although generally orderly and lawful, they frequently spiral out of control: most recently, May 2011 riots and violent demonstrations involving destructive vandalism, fire, stun-grenades, tear gas, and forceful clashes between civilians and the police rocked Athens. The protests continued into summer 2011, ranging from violent, concentrated protests to city-wide strikes. Disruption of public services, such as public transportation and air traffic control, occur unexpectedly due to union strikes. Common areas for protest include the Polytechnic University area, Exharia, Omonia, Syntagma Sq. and Mavii Sq. in Athens. If a demonstration does occur during your trip, you should avoid these areas and stick to the quieter parts of the city. The islands are generally more peaceful.

HUNGARY

Throughout Hungary, the vestiges of Ottoman and communist rules can be found on the same block. Castles stand staunchly and thermal baths pool beside concrete Soviet monuments, overlooking the graves of 20th-century writers and medieval poets. Döner kebabs, bockwurst, and cheeses are peddled side by side, while Budapest locals frequent Turkish bathhouses.

But Hungary's real draw may be the freewheeling youth and a relentless drive toward the modern. Streets are packed with hip hangouts and their patrons exude a vehemently chill attitude, making this city one of the best student urban destinations in Europe. And even though the locals might be too cool for school, they do appreciate a tenacity to learn about their culture. So make the effort and immerse yourself in all that is Hungary, with endless plates of goulash, sleepless nights at ruin pubs, and countless cups of coffee with some newfound friends.

greatest hits

- **INSTAFAN.** Hipsters will appreciate the chill vibe and kooky décor at **Szimpla Kert** (p. 474), Budapest's original ruin pub.

- **FRESH TO DEATH.** Learn proper hummus-and-pita-eating techniques at **Hummus Bár** (p. 473).

- **BURN BABY BURN.** For an authentic, old-world Hungary experience, head northwest out of Budapest to **Győr** (p. 477), which means "burnt city."

budapest

From its river to its ruins, Budapest has a magnificence that is impossible to escape. The lush Buda hills, as well as the gushing thermal springs on which the city stands, suggest that Budapest was formed by a god with a taste for the luxurious. Man then robed the land in stunning artifices, like the impressive Parliament of Pest and the grand Buda Castle. These gems don't bandage the city's bloody, war-filled history but instead stand as testaments to them—reminders of what once was and as the city compasses toward a bright future. On top of the city's rich past is a unique lifestyle. The relaxed pace of daily life along the Danube that divides the city is juxtaposed with a vibrant, fast-paced nightlife full of Budapest's famous ruin clubs and Hungary's infamous shots of palinka. International travelers young and old come to Budapest en masse to explore one of Europe's most beautiful cities, giving its streets and dance floors a language of their own.

SIGHTS

Historic, beautiful, scenic, artsy, quirky: Istanbul has many personalities. Each sight has a history (often a very long one), and as a rule of thumb, the older the building, the more likely it's had at least one makeover. You'll see many mosques where Muslims covered or destroyed Christian symbols to make way for their own faith. Even contemporary spaces like the Istanbul Modern Art Museum have used the old (in this case, an abandoned warehouse) to create something new (a showcase for the country's contemporary art scene). Sometimes, however, renovation wasn't enough. The sprawling home of the sultans, Topkapı Palace, was abandoned for the more ornate and European-style Dolmabahçe. Go beyond art and architecture, too: you'll find culture and history everywhere. Remember to step back and take in the big picture. Revel in the sensation of crossing between continents like it's no big deal, float into the sky on the Turk Balon for an aerial view, or make your way up Çamlıca Hill for a 360-degree panorama. Whether you have your nose pressed against the glass or your neck craned back to take in the magnificence of the Blue Mosque, Istanbul has an incredible number of things to see.

hungary

⬛ BUDA CASTLE

1014 Budapest, Szent György tér 2   ☎(20) 439 7325 www.mng.hu/

PALACE

Buda Castle has undergone more facelifts than Bruce Jenner, and while the royal palace hasn't had to put up with a Kardashian cat fight, it too has seen its fair share of war. Built between the 12th and 14th centuries, the original castle was occupied by the Ottoman invaders, who turned it into barracks and then left it to decay. During the campaign to retake Buda by the allied Christian forces, much of the palace was destroyed by heavy artillery bombardment—almost as fierce as pregnant Kim K. It wasn't until the middle of the 18th century that the palace was completely rebuilt, only to be destroyed again less than a century later when the Hungarian revolutionary army laid siege to it during the 1848 revolution.

Finally Buda Castle caught a break towards the end of the 19th century, like Bruce at the finale of Season 2, but just as Season 3 brought a whole slew of new drama to poor Bruce, the end of WWII brought heavy artillery back to the palace when Axis forces used it as the best place to stage a last-ditch defense. The castle was reduced to smoldering wreckage.

Today Buda Castle 4.0 closely resembles its Habsburg incarnation with flowery courtyards, statues, and panoramic views of the Pest side of the Danube. Inside the palace are some of Hungary's great museums including the Budapest History Museum as well as the National Szechenyi Library. Although it has a rough past, Buda Castle is now as flourishing and beautiful as ever. If only we could say the same about poor old Bruce...but there is always Season 10.

i Free. ⏱ Buda Castle 24/7; Hungarian National Gallery T-Su 10am-6pm; Budapest Historical Museum T-F 10am-4pm and Sa-Su 10am-6cm; Szechenyi Library Tu-Sa 9am-8pm.

MATTHIAS CHURCH

1014 Budapest, Szentháromság tér 2   ☎(1) 355 5657 www.matyas-templom.hu/

CHURCH

If more churches looked like Matthias Church on Castle Hill, every Sunday would be as celebratory as Christmas and Easter. With its colorful roof and palace-like steeples, the church is one of Budapest's most photographed sights. Not only is a picture of Matthias Church a must, but once at the top, the incredible view overlooking the Pest side of the Danube is the perfect setting for a travel selfie that'll rake in the likes.

Sensing the potential 3-digit worth of thumbs up social media value, the Ottomans took over the church in 1541, converting it to a mosque, but years later, the Hasburgs needed a new cover photo, defeated the Turks, sacked the city, and renovated the building to fit into the perfect little rectangle above their profile photo. Okay, so the motivation may be a bit off, but the point is that Matthias Church has seen its fair share of change.

While the exterior of the church no longer reflects its original state, the inside is a mix of old and new. Facing the altar, turn left and you will find the tombs of King Bela III and his first wife, the only tombs in the church to survive the Ottoman occupation. However their corpses are no longer quite so grand as archeologists stripped the bodies of their royal jewelry in order to display them in the National Museum. Royal wrath resulting from the dejeweling has yet to be felt, so make sure to speak only words of admiration in Matthias Church, especially while viewing the replica of the Hungarian crown upstairs in the church's Museum of Ecclesiastical Art. You don't want to be in good favor with the spirit of Hungarian royalty when he arises to steal back his beloved jewels. But more importantly, if you have a negative thing to say about the breathtaking building, get out.

i Adults 1000 HUF; students and pensioners 700 HUF; children (up to 6 years of age) Free; family ticket (1-2 adults +children) 2500 HUF, 10% discount with Budapest Card. ⏱ M-Sa 9am5pm; Su 1-5pm.

budapest

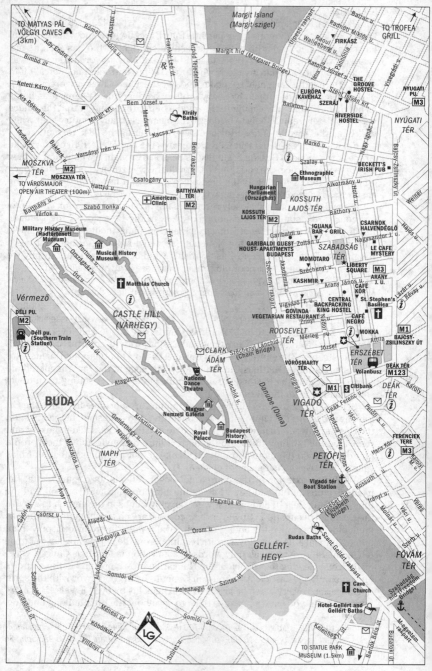

TO MATYAS PÁL VÖLGYI CAVES (3km)

TO TROFEA GRILL

Margit Island (Margit-sziget)

Margit híd (Margaret Bridge)

RX

Király Baths

Keteti Károly u.

Kis Rókus u.

Bem József u.

MOSZKVA TÉR

M2

MOSZKVA TÉR M2

TO VÁROSMAJOR OPEN AIR THEATER (100m)

BATTHYÁNY TÉR M2

American Clinic

Military History Museum (Hadtörténeti Múzeum)

Musical History Museum

Matthias Church

Vérmező

DÉLI PU. M2

Déli pu. (Southern Train Station)

CASTLE HILL (VÁRHEGY)

BUDA

National Dance Theatre

Magyar Nemzeti Galéria

Royal Palace

Budapest History Museum

NAPH TÉR

CLARK ÁDÁM TÉR

Széchenyi Lánchíd (Chain Bridge)

Danube (Duna)

FIRKÁSZ

THE GROOVE HOSTEL

NYÚGATI PU. M3

EURÓPA KÁVEHÁZ

SZERÁJ

RIVERSIDE HOSTEL

NYÚGATI TÉR

BECKETT'S IRISH PUB

Ethnographic Museum

Hungarian Parliament (Országház)

KOSSUTH LAJOS TÉR

KOSSUTH LAJOS TÉR M2

CSARNOK HALVENDÉGLŐ

IGUANA BAR + GRILL

GARIBALDI GUEST HOUST-APARTMENTS BUDAPEST

SZABADSÁG TÉR

LE CAFE MYSTERY

MOMOTARO

LIBERTY SQUARE M3

KASHMIR

ARANY J. U.

CAFÉ KÖR

GOVINDA VEGETARIAN RESTAURANT

CENTRAL BACKPACKING KING HOSTEL

St. Stephen's Basilica

CAFÉ NEGRO

ROOSEVELT TÉR

MOKKA

ERSZÉBET TÉR

BAJCSY-ZSILINSZKY ÚT M1

DEÁK TÉR M123

VÖRÖSMARTY TÉR

Volanbusz

Citibank

DEÁK TÉR

VIGADÓ TÉR

PETŐFI TÉR

FERENCIEK TERE M3

Vigadó tér Boat Station

Erzsébet híd (Elizabeth Bridge)

FŐVÁM TÉR

GELLÉRT-HEGY

Rudas Baths

Cave Church

Hotel Gellért and Gellért Baths

Szabadság híd (Freedom Bridge)

TO STATUE PARK MUSEUM (1.5km)

hungary

N

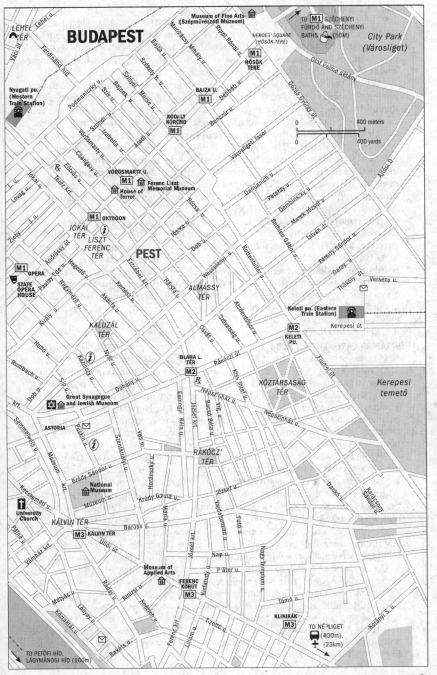

HOUSE OF TERROR

1062 Budapest, Andrássy út 60

MUSEUM

☎(1) 374 2600 www.terrorhaza.hu/

With its cheap beer, strong shots, and never ending nights, you may find yourself waking up in Budapest still drunk. Believe it or not, there comes a time to sober up and that is for Budapest's historical museum, House of Terror, which reminds even the wildest that Budapest was not always a party.

"Terror" reads out in a looming shadow when the sun hits Budapest's famous museum just right. The cold, ominous exterior is only a warning of what lies inside the museum on fascism and communism in Hungary that once served as the headquarters of the Hungarian Nazis. Although to say anyone "enjoys" the House of Terror's three floor exhibit would feel wrong, the museum is a must-see in Budapest. The rooms on the top two floors of the stone building are filled with video accounts from survivors of the terrors its named after. With informational sheets in both Hungarian and English at each room entrance, even the most historically challenged can follow along as the museum moves throughout the 20th century. If reading isn't your thing, the museum also offers an audio tour for a fee of 1300 HUF.

The true terror does not strike, however, until you descend the elevator to the basement. A short film is shown reminding you that before this building was a museum, it truly was a house of terror, housing prisoners to be tortured in its basement. Stepping into the small cells after exiting the elevator hits this point home, sending shivers down the spine. The museum turns from a lesson in history to an emotional journey ending with the Hall of Tears that stands as a symbolic cemetery to those whose bodies were never found. Give yourself about two hours to take this journey away from the party of a tourist in present-day Budapest and into the past.

i *Full price 2.000 HUF; Discount Price 1.000 HUF.* 🕑 *M-Sun 10am-6pm*

HUNGARIAN PARLIAMENT BUILDING

1055 Budapest, Kossuth Lajos tér 1-3

GOVERNMENT BUILDING

☎(1) 441 4000 www.parlament.hu/

"The motherland does not have a house," lamented Hungarian poet Milhaly Corosmarty in 1846. In response to the growing sense of Hungarian nationalism during the period, the palatial Gothic building looks more like a cathedral than a seat of government. The building is the largest in Hungary and third largest parliament in the world, towering at 96m—a number symbolizing the date of Hungary's millennial anniversary. A view of Parliament can be found every few blocks, a constant reminder of just how superior Budapest is to your local city.

While Parliament's exterior is more than enough to get a good eyegasm, tours are offered everyday in Hungarian and English that take you inside Parliament, whose sheer size and beauty making it a lover that FABIO could not even write. With 692 rooms, the building is so large, it once required more electricity than the rest of the city combined to supply it with enough power. Decked in gold and marble, the interior shines proudly on the original Holy Crown of Hungary.

Seeing Parliament during construction on one of the building's corners is not bad timing, but rather unavoidable as renovation is infinite. By the time it takes builders to renovate the whole building, a new wall is ripe for work. Similar to the readings of a college student, except workers on Parliament are actually being productive. As with a sexy exchange student, spend as much time with Parliament as possible, viewing it during the day and admiring its stone molding and from the Danube at night when it is illuminated. Because while your romance might be short, it is better to have loved and lost than never to have loved at all.

i *Full price 4000 HUF; Students (ages 6-24) 2000 HUF; EU adult citizens 2000 HUF; EU student citizens (ages 6-24) 1000 HUF; Free for Visitors under 6 years of age.* 🕑 *Apr-Oct M-F 8am-6pm, Sa-Su 8am-4pm; Nov-Mar M-Su 8am-4pm.*

get a room!

Although the majority of Budapest's hostels and hotels are within a tight radius of City Centre, your time in the city can vary greatly based solely on which roof you sleep under. From traditional hotels to tiny party hostels, determining what is the right establishment for you is essential to whether you get a good night's sleep or a great day out...or vice versa!

▨ MAVERICK HOSTEL
Ferenciek tere 2

HOSTEL $
☎1 267 3166

www.mavericklodges.com/eng/maverick_hostel_ensuites.php

With its marble walls, wrought iron stairs, and most importantly, extremely clean facilities, it's no wonder why the Maverick Hostel is top rated on hostelworld.com. Even in a 10-bed mixed dormitory, each traveler and his or her backpack have room to spread out. On top of this, four bathrooms with full shower facilities allow for one to take care of business whenever necessary. The hostel offers lockers to keep valuables in, although the familial atmosphere of Maverick feels safe and secure. Its location only a block from the Danube makes it easy for even the drunkest of customers to find their way home—just head to the Elizabeth Bridge.

Maverick is located right next to Budapest's major tourist streets, where hats and purses reading "Budapest" in fonts and color combinations worthy of the dollar store cost a small fortune and stand in front of equally overpriced restaurants advertising Hungarian specialties. If Maverick Hostel is your first or only stop, it is easy to fall into the trap of thinking that this is the heart of Budapest when in reality it is more like a fake limb. Fortunately, the real Budapest is only a wander away, and Maverick Hostel's small size, professionalism, and beauty make it well worth a stay.

i Dorms €6-10; doubles €30-34. ☑ Reception 24hr.

▨ CARPE NOCTEM
Szobi utca 5

HOSTEL $
☎70 670 0384 http://budapestpartyhostels.com

If you have any desire to get a good night's rest and have a productive early morning, 1) Why are you in Budapest? and 2) Do not stay at Carpe Noctem Hostel. This party hostel lives up to its name, seizing every night out at one of Budapest's ruin pubs or clubs. The staff at Carpe Noctem are young and international, serving as friends that clean your bathroom and show you where to go to have the best nights out. Hipster indie songs are constantly playing in the common room, where you'll find a number of guests and workers chilling all day long either recovering from a hangover or with a beer in hand. The sense of community forged at Carpe Noctem is due in part to their policy of allowing no group bigger than three to stay at the hostel, meaning that most of the guests are young solo travelers looking to meet new people and create lifelong friendships. And intimacy is easy to establish at this 20-bed hostel. Although Carpe Noctem's motto is "Fuck the day; seize the night," the location of Carpe Noctem is ideal for daytime adventures, too, and is just a short walk from Pest's beautiful Hero's Square, Szechenyi Baths, and main road Andrassy.

i Dorms €24. ☑ Reception 24 hr.

budapest

PALACE OF ARTS

1095 Budapest, Komor Marcell utca 1   ☎01 555 3301 www.mupa.hu/?secure

In a city full of ruins and buildings that are far older than the United States, Palace of the Arts stands out. Opened in 2005, the huge hall along the Danube is new to Budapest's stage, but its sleek modern architecture and large theater put it front and center in the music scene. The palace is every stage mom's fantasy: a triple threat. In it lies the Bartok National Concert Hall for music, the Ludwig Museum of contemporary art, and the Festival Theater for just about anything else.

50 years of research was put into the Bartok National Concert Hall to ensure it had heavenly acoustics. Appropriately, the huge hall looks like a Gothic cathedral, oval-shaped with 40 tons of canopy hanging overhead and one of Europe's largest organs against the back wall. Despite the way old school interior of Bartok, don't expect to see only the traditional operas and orchestras. A high-tech audio-visual system creates fantastic light shows and displays experimental film, ensuring that a visit to the symphony Bartok National Concert Hall will be a far cry from your fifth grade field trips.

If you're more into visual art than music, head on over to the left wing of Palace of the Arts to the Ludwig Museum. Here you'll find contemporary painters like Picasso and Tom Wesselman, modern Hungarian artists, and even a few creations by Yoko Ono, but please, Beatles Fans, mind your manners.

Dance, music, acting, and the inexplicable "performance art" all find homes on Palace of the Art's Festival Theater. At just under 500 seats, a show at the Festival Theater is far more intimate than the Bartok National Concert Hall, yet possesses the same state-of-the-art technology so that your dreams of getting up close and personal with The Naked Clown may be realized.

i *Students 500 HUF. 🗓 Check the website calendar for dates and times of upcoming events.*

MUSEUM OF FINE ARTS

1146 Budapest, Dózsa György út 41   ☎01 469 7100 www.szepmuveszeti.hu/

To the side of Hero's Square lies a house of heroes in the arts: The Museum of Fine Arts Budapest. While no Hungarian art is featured, the museum, which houses over 100,000 pieces, is made up of the work of international artists. Its works trace back farther than the family tree your great aunt dedicated the past 20 years of her life to cultivating. This is because its six departments include: Egyptian, Antique, Old Sculpture Gallery, and Old Painter Gallery on top of its more contemporary Modern and Graphics collections. So unless that great aunt brought it all the way back to the BC, Museum of Fine Arts has her beat.

And the museum has more than just your aunt beat. It holds the second largest collection of Egyptian art in all of Central Europe. Most of its claim to Egyptian fame was brought together by Hungarian Egyptologist Eduard Mahler in the 1930s. A favorite of the museum is its collection of painted mummy sarcophagi.

If you have a thing for gold—which, who doesn't?—the Ancient Gallery is for you. Objects mainly Greek and Roman sparkle throughout the exhibit. Further into the museum are the Sculpture and Painting Galleries in which you can spot a few da Vinci's, and tens of thousands of prints representing more periods of European graphic art than you probably knew existed.

The museum will transport you away from Hungary for hours with rooms full of paintings by Italian, Spanish, German, Dutch, English, and Flemish artists. (Flemish people come from Dutch-speaking Belgium.) (You're welcome.) However when you exit outside into the bright Hero Square and look back at the steps you've just descended, you'll finally see some of Hungary's finest art: the building of the Museum of Fine Arts Budapest.

i *1800Ft. Children and seniors in European Union free. 🗓 Tu-Su 10am-6pm.*

hungary

HUNGARIAN NATIONAL GALLERY

1014 Budapest, Szent György tér 2

MUSEUM

☎01 201 9082 www.mng.hu/en

Living in the Buda Castle, the Hungarian National Gallery is the king of Budapest, and unlike many before its time, its rule is just about perfect. The remarkable paintings and sculptures displayed by Hungarian artists from as early as the 10th century—the crucial era when soulmates hops and beer brewing found each other—live up to the magnificence of the castle. And with either an interest in history or a little imagination, the large gallery can provide for hours of entertainment.

Unless you're one of the three Hungarian Arts Scholars out there, you'll probably want to pay the extra 400Ft (less than $2) for the audio guide. It'll talk you through each exhibit, tell you why exactly there's a sculpture of a baby with missing arms, and fill you with facts to insure you kill the "History of Hungary" category on Jeopardy...which with such prime alliteration, they must have at some point.

But if you aren't really looking for a history lesson, that doesn't mean you should discount the gallery. The museum can be up to your own artistic interpretation. Its pieces on the second floor, famous paintings from the 19th century, look like excerpts from a movie with overly expressive actors. On top of this, their names like "The Bride," or "Harvesters" are so generic that they're just calling for back stories. You could spend minutes at each one, picturing things like how crunk the "Girls the Morning after the Ball" must've gotten the night before they were captured on canvas. The bro who snagged the one with the huge dorky smile and dreamy look in her eyes must've been a real fox.

While the historical Baroque section is full of figures that most of us probably don't recognize and wars that we're happy we didn't live through, the Hungarian National Gallery displays each painting and statue beautifully. Taking pictures of the works is not off limits, however it does cost an extra 250Ft...and don't try to be sneaky, museum workers are patrolling each corridor.

The third floor of the gallery reveals modern works of the 20th Century. Paintings from artists such as Lajos and Béla line the walls with fantastical, sharper strokes. Some of the works get a bit abstract, ending your time in the Hungarian National Gallery with the perfect taste of "wtf" that only art can produce.

i 1400Ft. Special exhibits generally around 1400Ft. Children and seniors in European Union free. Audio guide 400Ft. ⊠ Tu-Su 10am-6pm.

⊠ SHOES ON THE DANUBE

Bank of the Danube, Budapest 1052

MONUMENT

Whilst strolling along the Pest side of the Danube, it's easy to get caught up in the beauty of the city, and miss the small bronze shoes on the bank a little past the chain bridge, in front Parliament. But educate yourself; be aware, because here lies one of Budapest's most moving memorials: Shoes on the Danube Bank. The rather literal named memorial was designed to honor the Jews killed by the Arrow Cross militia, a fascist regimen during WWII. The bronze shoes symbolize those of the victims pulled from their homes in the Jewish ghetto the winter of 1944, taken by the river, stripped naked, and shot by a firing squad. Their bodies disappeared into the Danube, but thanks to sculptors Gyula Pauer and Can Togay, the memory of them will not. Just like each man, woman, and child had a story and life of their own, the now rusty shoes are of different styles and sizes. Deep. Behind the shoes is a bench with signs in Hungarian, English, and Hebrew reading "To the memory of the victims shot into the Danube by Arrow Cross militiamen in 1944–45. Erected 16 April 2005."

Although the hills, grand buildings, and warm welcome all make Budapest spectacular, one of the most beautiful things about the city is the way it embrac-

budapest

es its ugly past. And it manages to do this, while keeping its hipster off-beat ways, through the unique Shoes on the Danube Bank.

i Free. ⊘ Open daily.

◩ GRESHAM PALACE

PALACE

1051 Budapest, Széchenyi István tér 5-6 ☎01 268 6000
www.fourseasons.com/budapest/?source=tagreshampalacebudapestblhotel

If it's always been your dream to live in castle, then you're in luck because the Four Seasons Hotel took over the gorgeous Gresham Palace in 2001. However, if you're not a millionaire, you're screwed, because a room could cost you over $3000 a night. Still, you can pretend you're ridiculously wealthy or better yet, royalty for a few minutes and take a trip to the castle-like hotel.

Okay so Gresham Palace has never really housed queens and kings (except maybe for the occasional guest). In fact it was commissioned by the London based company Gresham Life Assurance Company in 1904 as a grand onsite foreign headquarters. How posh. The extravagant palace of marble was completed in 1907 and served as the offices and homes of the company's workers. Smart as they were, these playboys left sensing the danger of WWII, leaving the palace to be overtaken by Soviet soldiers. The once beautiful palace was left in a shambled state. It remained this way until finally breaking into the hotel business.

So what good is this to you, poor boy with big dreams? Well with it's prime real estate on the Pest side of the Chain Bridge, near Parliament, you are sure to get a big glimpse and a few pics by the breathtaking palace. If you feel so inclined, you can even step inside, and get one of the most luxurious meals the city has to offer in the Four Seasons Restaurant. Who knows, maybe this peak is the push you need to take your get rich quick scheme out of the backpack.

i Free. ⊘ Open 24/7.

MEMENTO PARK

PARK

1223 Budapest, Balatoni út - Szabadkai utca sarok ☎01 424 7500 www.mementopark.hu/

A ways outside Budapest's bustling metropolis lies a graveyard of stone. The ghosts that haunt the Memento Park are scarier than the ones of your childhood sleepovers, because their stories are all too real. While communism ruled Hungary, statues of communist dictators stood tall in the streets, reminding its citizens of the laws and leaders under which they lived. When Hungary embraced a free market economy in 1989, these statues were moved to the city outskirts faster than you can say Mátyás Rákosi—pretty easy for Hungarian!

It wasn't until architect Ákos Eleőd designed the open Memento Park in 1991 that these outcasts were put to use. While the majority of the park is the original statues of communist Hungary, one of its most famous is the copy of the Stalin monument...but not the whole thing. Rather, Eleőd's recreation is of when the original monument was pulled from the Grandstand, leaving only Stalin's giant bronze boots. So don't be confused by the missing body. It's history. And anyways, what is art without some thought-provoking simplicity?

Apart from sculptures of Marx, Lenin, and enough Hungarian dictators to build a small city with their bronze and marble bodies, the "park," which is now much more museum-like, includes a cinema that plays a short film with English subtitles about being a spy in communist Hungary called "The Life of an Agent." It also has Trabant—the car most commonly driven during the communist bloc—on display. Its powdered blue sides look oddly cheerful next to the dark statues.

For those who only need one hand to count all the communist dictators they know (not even including their thumb), there is a guided tour in English or Hungarian that runs a few times a day until the park's sunset close. The sad

stories and histories told in a Hungarian accent, paired with the cold eyes of the statues make the guided experience well worth the extra 7 bucks.

Although not so conveniently located, Memento Park is a sight you'll truly never forget...something you can't guarantee about the inside of a ruin pub!

i *1500Ft. English tour 1200Ft.* 🕐 *Open daily 10am-6pm.*

FOOD

A land once ruled by heavy dumplings, Budapest now offers a host of food selections from all over the globe. From its many Thai and Indian étterems (or restaurants) to its classic taco bars, burger joints, and even the occasional Michelin Star restaurant, Budapest is a welcoming place for the finest of foodies or those of us on the tightest of budgets. So do us all a favor, put your Big Mac down, and go out for some goulash soup and chicken paprika at least once—you're hungry in Hungary, after all!

🍴 TAJ MAHAL INDIAN RESTAURANT   INDIAN $

Szondi utca 40   ☎1 301 0447 www.tajmahal.hu/

If the richly colored tapestries and soft music of the sitar do not transport you straight from Hungary to India, then you must've had a sad childhood because your imagination sucks. On top of the authentic ambience of the Taj Mahal Indian Restaurant, the food can cure even the most serious of curry cravings. Even with the extra cost of naan and rice (complete necessities), the overall excellent experience at Taj Mahal is well worth each euro. The waitstaff goes above and beyond to ensure that your experience is personal. The chef himself may even make an appearance to discuss the meal—or to get his daily self-esteem boost, as the feedback is sure to be nothing but complimentary. Indian staples, from the basic naan and basmati rice to the more complex Taj Mahal Curry house special, are about as perfect as the geometry of the actual Taj Mahal. When looking to take a break from kebabs and goulash soup while maintaining enough dignity to avoid good ole Mickey D's, take a trip to Hungary's own Taj Mahal.

i *Appetizers €5-10. Entrees €15-20.* 🕐 *Open daily noon-11pm.*

🍴 TÖRÖK ÉTTEREM   KEBAB $

Six locations in districts V, VI, VII, VIII, IX, XIII.   ☎13541756 www.istanbuletterem.hu

While one considers many questions when traveling to foreign countries, the most pressing is perhaps, "Without Taco Bell, where will I satisfy my late night munchies?" Never fear, because Budapest offers an even better answer than Doritos-shelled beef: the kebab. Kebab stands decorate every corner of Budapest (kind of like Starbucks in Seattle), and Török Étterem stands above the rest. At just €3-4 per beef or chicken kebab, Török Étterem will thrill your taste buds and tickle your wallet, too. What separates Török Étterem from the millions of other kebab stands is the freshness of its ingredients. The meat is sliced from a large revolving cooker and is prepared to order so that it is in peak juiciness when served. Török Étterem also has an outdoor seating area, allowing you to take a proper pit stop in between bar hopping.

i *Kebabs €3-4. Pizza €1-2 per slice.* 🕐 *Open daily 11am-5am. Delivery 11am-10:45pm.*

🍴 BOOKCAFE (LOTZ ÉTTEREM)   SANDWICHES, SALADS $

Andrassy ut 39   ☎1 461 5830

www.facebook.com/pages/Book-Cafe-Lotz-Terem/

Although located right on Andrassy, Budapest's busiest shopping street, Lottz Étterem or the Bookcafe, may be missed by the average tourist but is a must-see—even if you aren't keen on buying the overpriced food. Hidden away on the second floor of Alexandra Bookstore, the ballroomesque interior, masterfully painted walls, and ceilings lined with gold molding will make you feel as though you're dining in a Fabergé egg. Unfortunately, you can't judge the food of Bookcafe by its spectacular cover. The sandwich and salad menu is small, simple, and expensive. Items such as goat cheese and fig salad in salt quiche are dressed to excess and run about €8 for a few bites. Compared to the entree menu, the desserts at Bookcafe feel like a steal, ranging between €2-4. Somehow, the comfortable seating and friendly waitstaff make the not super memorable food worth a trip to this hidden away cafe. So head over to Bookcafe with a camera (not an appetite), pick up a book from downstairs, and settle in with a nice cappuccino.

i *Drinks €2-8. Entrees €6-10. Desserts €2-4. ⏰ Open daily 10am-10pm.*

CYRANO   TRADITIONAL $$

Kristóf tér 7   ☎1 266 4747 http://cyrano.hu/

For the average backpacker, a Michelin recommended restaurant is out of the question, but a badass backpacker knows when it's worth it to say screw you, practicality, and splurge. Cyrano is worth it. At prices like this, a meal at Cyrano will probably be your only food of the day. However, you won't have to worry about fulfilling your daily calorie count thanks to the rich, cheesy, and creamy Hungarian-style cuisine. Take your time savoring every bite of the three-course lunch special and think of each small, gourmet serving as its own meal. With seating outside in the heart of Budapest's shopping district, there's no shortage of things to look at, so take a moment between filtering the pictures you just snapped of your Instagram-worthy plate and observe. The sidewalk feels more like an international runway than a strip of cement. Watch ladies who could be in Vogue and tweens who are surely featured on Pinterest pass by. Regardless, the service here will make you feel like royalty, too. The friendly and attentive waitstaff add to the glamour of Cyrano, and their experience dealing with clueless foreigners may be your lifesaver as you navigate the menu full of "Hungary's Culinary Adventure!"

i *Three-course lunch special €20. Entrees €20-50. ⏰ Open daily 8am-midnight.*

MANGA COWBOY   SANDWICHES $

Ráday utca 31   ☎1 215 8079 www.mangacowboy.hu/en/home

Let's be real, who can pass up a restaurant called Manga Cowboy? Even if you're a vegetarian with a distaste for Asian food, this American-Asian fusion burger stop is a must.

Although Manga Cowboy! produces delicious, high quality food, it's menu is a little bit all over the place. Manga Cowboy! offers everything from an assortment of huge "Sumo" sandwiches to American, Asian, and Bavarian (?!) burgers, ramen soups, matzo ball soups, wasabi tuna, ribs, something ambiguously called "Elvis," and to top it all off Oreo cheesecake. If you have no clue what you're hungry for, you might spend hours just gawking at the menu. If you're struggling, close your eyes and select one of their burgers. You won't be disappointed, as this silly little cowboy boasts some of the best patties in Budapest.

For the health conscious, Manga Cowboy! has you covered...almost. Its "Almost Healthy" menu has a couple of salads to keep your diet in check. But c'mon, if you've already committed to going to a place called Manga Cowboy! in Budapest, your diet can take a hit.

i *Burgers €8-12. ⏰ Open daily 9am-midnight.*

HUMMUS BAR   MEDITERRANEAN $

Október 6 utca 19   ☎1 354 0108 www.hummusbar.hu/

"Believe you can achieve the impossible" is written on the wall of Hummus Bar in Budapest. This may sound a little pretentious for a restaurant that just makes hummus and falafel. But the great achievement comes in how this place makes hummus and falafel so damn sexy.

Hummus Bar Budapest may just be one of the hippest, small fast food joints in all of Europe. Although the restaurant itself is not much to look at (takeout is

budapest

just as popular as eating in house), its menu has a wide range of hummus, from classic Hummus Tahini to extravagant Hummus ShakShuka Merguez, which includes tomato sauce, peppers, onions, spices, a poached egg, and a beef and lamb sausage. If you're aiming to achieve your own impossible by finishing that bad boy, make sure to go to the Hummus Bar's main location on Oktober St., as its menu is the most complete (some Hummus Bars serve only vegetarian menus). Whether simple or off the wall, each hummus meal is served with delicious laffa bread.

On top of badass hummuses, the Hummus Bar serves falafel that they claim to be the best ever. Their reports may be a bit biased, but regardless, you won't regret testing it out for yourself.

i Falafel €3.50-€5.50. Hummus €4.50-€8. ☒ Open daily 11:30am-11pm.

NIGHTLIFE

You know that crazy uncle who always somehow manages to bring the party to the most boring of family reunions? Maybe not, but if Central Europe is one big family reunion, Budapest is the uncle with the alcohol. With everything from your standard nightclub to parties in baths, on boats, and in ruins, this wild city offers a chance for you to strike out in your highest heels or get your boogie on in your Chuck Taylor's every night of the week.

▨ INSTANT

VENUE, BAR

Nagymező utca 38 ☎1 311 0704 http://instant.co.hu/en

Instant is a psychedelic maze full of optical illusions, flashing lights, and animal heads whose eyes may or may not be following its drunk inhabitants. While that may sound like a nightmare straight out of That 70s Show, Instant is a must-go if you want to experience the best of Budapest's nightlife. So first, close your air passages while crossing the barrier of smoke that serves as Instant's greeting—it's long entryway is the only smoker-friendly room in the joint—and then open your mind to Budapest's adult funhouse. With over 20 rooms and four stories, everyone is guaranteed a spot on one of Instant's many dance floors, each with its own DJ and bar. The music ranges based on room. Anything from the ultimate American "turn up" jams to techno remixes blasts through the halls of this ruin pub. While very popular amongst tourists, Instant is also a go-to for locals, a testament to the quality of the bar.

i Beer €2-4. Mixed Drinks €5-10.

SZIMPLA KERT

BAR

Kazinczy utca 14 ☎20 261 8669 www.szimpla.hu/

Budapest's first and most famous ruin pub, Szimpla Kert, is possibly the most poppin' and certainly the most trippy spot to be on any summer night in the city. While smoking cigarettes is not permitted in the central area of the bar, fruit flavored smoke from Hookah will assault your nose before you even step within Szimpla's graffitied arches. The drinks are on the expensive side for Budapest, but with no entrance charge, think of the extra dollar as going toward entertainment ranging from the experimental film being played in the pub's very own cinema-themed room to the screaming girls spraying whipped cream on each other and singing in every language they know. The bar fills up fairly early with an international crowd. However, if you're looking to really throw down on the dance floor, Szimpla may not be the spot. Instead, chill with everyone else in one of Szimpla's many cave-like rooms decorated by monitors flashing patterned lights that make you feel wavy in more ways than one. With its relaxed, low energy, Szimpla is an ideal first stop on a night of bar hopping.

i Beer €2-4. Mixed Drinks €5-10. ☒ Open daily noon-4am.

AKVARIUM

VENUE, BAR

Erzsébet tér 2 ☎30 506 2632 akvariumklub.hu

In the heart of the city center and right of Budapest's busiest road, Akvarium is impossible to miss. Akvarium is a hot spot in Budapest because of its versatility. Outside its terraced bar are huge pieces of local Hungarian art, while shirtless hipsters with cutoff jeans (or homeless people—the difference not always obvious) lounge around the pool, cooling off in the hot summer sun.

At night, these hipsters put on shirts and head to Akvarium's outdoor bar. Oftentimes an up-and-coming Hungarian band will play in the early evening, warming up the audience for nighttime festivities. The atmosphere changes from organic to funky as colored lights illuminate the pool and steps of the bar. Inside, you'll find another bar and a dance floor where locals and travelers alike come to party rock, while outside films or big sporting events are sometimes projected in the open air cinema.

Akvarium's sleek, fresh vibe is a nice contrast to the ruin pubs of Budapest but is just as hip. And if you're burning up on the dance floor, you can go back to the club's grassy roof and watch Budapest's very own big wheel, Sziget Eye, turn over your head.

i Cover €5-10, includes 1 drink. ☒ Open M-W 6pm-2am, Th-Sa 6pm-5am, Su 4pm-2am.

FOGASHAZ

CLUB, PUB

Akácfa utca 51 ☎1 783 8820 www.fogashaz.hu/

Although Fogasház ("house of teeth") was originally a dentist's office, its toothy logo and name are the only remaining traces of the misery the building once served. A last stop on many pub crawls, Fogasház is the perfect late-night place for those looking to burn off the calories of the previous hours' worth of drinking. Like any standard ruin pub, Fogasház has trendy decor, cheap alcohol, and an international, primarily tourist crowd. Unlike its peers, however, Fogasház boasts its versatility, housing a theater, art gallery, exit game, restaurant, and, of course, a bar. Though it has many unique facets, what separates Fogasház from just another pub or club is its mind boggling energy. Take this example: at just about anywhere in Fogasház, you can chat with someone from just about anywhere on the globe at just about any level of functioning. Then you can escape to the next room where you can show off your twerking skills to the beats of live Hungarian rappers. After that, you can can take a right and dance to some throwback American jams in a wild mob, where you might just crowd surf thanks to an Irish stag party (at least that was one particular researcher's experience). When your body can no longer take the high impact workout, Fogasház's convenient location in downtown Pest makes the walk to the night bus or back to your hostel manageable no matter how anaerobic your dancing was.

i Beer and wine €2-4. Mixed drinks €5-10. Pizza €1-2. ☒ Open M-Sa 2pm-4am, Su 4pm-4am.

ESSENTIALS

Practicalities

- **TOURIST OFFICES:** Tourinform arranges tours and accommodations (V, Suto utca 2, 01 429 97 51, open M-F 9-6:30pm, Sa 9am-2:30pm). The Budapest Card provides discounts, unlimited public transportation, and admission to most museums.

- **ATMS:** English-language ATMs (*bankamatik, bankomat*) can be found on almost every corner. If your account is at a foreign bank, cash withdrawal will cost you extra. Most ATMs dispense Turkish lire. If you want to withdraw American dollars or euro, try the banks around Sirkeci Train Station and İstiklal Cad.

budapest

- **LUGGAGE STORAGE:** 24hr. luggage storage *(Emanet Bagaj)* is available at **Atatürk International Airport** (☎0212 465 3442 10-20 TL per day) and **Sirkeci Train Station** (☎0539 885 2105 *i* 4-7 TL for 4hr., 0.50 TL per hr. thereafter; max. 4 days).

- **GLBT RESOURCES:** **Time Out Istanbul** magazine provides a good overview of the city's GLBT establishments. Some other organizations of interest are **Lambda** (Tel Sok. 28/5, 4th fl., Beyoğlu ☎0212 245 7068, advice line ☎0212 244 5762 www.lambdaistanbul.org ☑ Open F-Su 3-8pm; hotline open M-Tu 5-7pm and F-Su 5-7pm), trans-focused **Istanbul LGBTT** (Atıf Yılmaz Cad. Öğüt Sok. 18/4, Beyoğlu ☎0212 252 1088 www.istanbul-lgbtt.org), and Ankara-based **Kaos GL** (☎0312 230 0358 http://news.kaosgl.com).

- **LAUNDROMATS:** Most hostels will do your laundry for a small fee. If you'd prefer a laundromat, try **Beybuz** (Topçekerler Sok. 7A ☎0212 249 5900 *i* Wash 3 TL per kg. Dry cleaning 10 TL. ☑ Open 24hr.) or **Şık Çamaşır Yıkama.** (Güneşli Sok. 1A ☎0212 245 4375 *i* 15 TL per load. ☑ Open M-Sa 8:30am-8pm.)

- **INTERNET:** **Sultanahmet Square** offers free Wi-Fi. **İstiklal Caddesi** supposedly has free Wi-Fi as well, but coverage is spotty. One of the best internet cafes in town is **Net Club** (Büyükparmakkapı Sok. 8/6, 3rd fl. *i* Just off Istiklal Cad., a few blocks from Taksim Sq. 1.25 TL per hr. ☑ Open 24hr.), but there are many others around İstiklal and a few near the Sultanahmet tram stop. In most cafes, expect to pay about 2 TL per hr.

- **POST OFFICES:** Post offices in Budapest are generally open from M-F 8am-6pm, though some hours vary. To inquire about specific hours call 06 40 46 46 46. Postal services in Budapest are run by Maygar Post. Their website is all in Hungarian, so to find the post office nearest you, your best bet is use Google Maps. The main office is on Petöfi Sandor St., though there are many post offices in Budapest in each of its districts, all offering the same services.

Emergency

- **GENERAL MEDICAL EMERGENCY:** ☎112.

- **DOMESTIC INQUIRIES:** ☎198.

- **INTERNATIONAL INQUIRIES :** ☎199.

- **IN CASE OF FIRE:** ☎112.

- **24HR. MEDICAL ASSISTANCE IN ENGLISH (FALCK SOS HUNGARY):** ☎06 1 2000 100.

- **POLICE:** ☎01 438 80 80. The office for tourist police is located inside the Tourinform office at V, Suto utca 2. You can get here through the metro lines: M1, M2, or M3 at the Deak ter stop. Or you can reach them by phone at 01 438 80 80. The office is open 24hr.

- **LATE-NIGHT PHARMACIES:** Look for green signs labeled Apotheke, Gyogyszertar, or Pharmacie. Many pharmacies and drugstores are not open 24hr. Déli Pharmacy (XII district, Alkotás út 1/b), Óbuda Pharmacy (II district, Vörösvári út 84), Szent Margit Pharmacy (II district, Frankel Leó út 22), and Teréz Pharmacy (VI district, Teréz krt. 41) are all 24hr. pharmacies. The website budapest-moms.com also has a full list of 24hr. pharmacies.

- **MEDICAL SERVICES:** The majority of hospitals and clinics in Budapest are English speaking. Two sure bet 24hr. clinics are FirstMed Center (06 1 224 9090) and Rózsakert Medical Center (06 1 391 5903). The US embassy also maintains a list of English-speaking doctors. Call 112 if faced with a serious emergency. You should not hesitate to contact the police in Budapest if you are the victim of a crime. Be sure to carry a valid passport, as police have the right to ask for identification. Police can sometimes be unhelpful if you are the victim of a currency exchange scam; in this instance, it may be better to seek advice from your country's embassy or consulate.

Getting There

The Budapest international airport, Budapest Ferihegy Airport, is 16km southeast of downtown Budapest. For general information regarding the airport, call 36 1 296 9696. For information regarding flight details, call 36 1 296 7000. The airport has ATMs and many exchange bureaus, but avoid exchanging currency at the airport as nearly every block in downtown Budapest has an exchange station that offers far better rates.

There are many ways to get into the city from the airport. All major car rental companies have stations inside the airport. The airport also offers a minibus service that will take you to your final destination in the city. Prices range depending on address, but the minibus is guaranteed to be less than a taxi, but more than a standard bus.

The airport also provides a public bus, BKV number 200E, that goes to M3 station Kőbánya-Kispest (blue line), about 20min. away. You'll need to transfer from here to the metro, which will take you straight into the city center.

Then there are the infamous taxis, the fastest way of getting to the center of Budapest but also the most expensive.

Getting Around

By Taxi

Of course, taxis are also widely available in Budapest. Note that taxi rates are not government regulated. Therefore, using taxis runs quite a risk of emptying your pocketbook. Independent taxis are especially dangerous but not always easy to spot. Ask your hostel or hotel for the number of a reliable taxi company, which you should call if you need a taxi's services. While it may look glamorous to flag down a cab, in Budapest, this may just be your bank account's swan song.

Public Transportation

Almost no sight or activity is a far walk in Budapest. However, Budapest's public transportation company, BKV, offers bus, trolley bus, tram, and metro services, making it easy to maneuver the city for the time or movement impaired. BKV's services run daily from 4:30am-11pm. Tickets must be bought and presented before entering the bus or station. Tickets are cheap at 300 Ft (€1) per trip. If you plan on using public transportation a lot, look for deals like 24hr. or 72hr. unlimited or 10-ticket passes. These can be found at all metro stations where regular tickets are sold. Maps are at each metro station. The main station is Deák tér Station, where all lines interconnect. Budapest also offers a night bus, which runs every 15min-1hr. from 11pm-4am. Tickets are bought on board the night bus, and security officers now stand guard to make sure every party animal pays. All information on public transportation, specific pricing, and schedules can be found at www.bkv.hu/en.Ici.

győr

The charming, Italian Renaissance-style Győr that exists today is the sequel its predecessor, which was burnt down in the 16th century by its own commander, Kristóf Lamberg, during the Ottoman occupation in order to keep it from the claws of the invading Turks (fittingly, Győr means "burnt city"). While the cobblestone streets and decoratively molded buildings of the Győr you see today—most still over 400 years old—may not be the original, the feel of the city certainly is. The culture of Győr is rather homogenous. Here, English is rarely spoken as small-town Hungarians come together for a weekend getaway or trip to the theater. Here, friends recognize each other on the streets or in one of Győr's popular pubs. Here is a strong community based on familiarity and trust. For the outsider, Győr's intimacy may seem intimidating, but its beautiful Raba river, many statues, and old world charm are undeniable.

SIGHTS

◼ RADO HOLM   PARK
Hid street 12

If the peaceful yet charming alleyways and back roads of Gyor are not tranquil enough for you, 1) check your pulse, but 2) Gyor has an even more quiet, hidden getaway. In the middle of the Raba double bridge lies this small island. Don't read the world "island" and go looking for Hawaii. If you wanted a real tropical paradise, you should've gone to the Bahamas. Instead Rado Holm is a small park. It is lush, green, and has enough weeping willows for a whole soccer team of girls to play Pocahontas. Locals are oftentimes seen in this park sunbathing, picnicking, or just sitting and daydreaming. On top of the profound is a lot of PDA as Gyor's youth bring wine, cheese, and hormones to the park throughout summer days. So bring your own lover and a bottle of wine (if the two are synonymous, even better!) and escape the already chill city for its Antarctica of relaxed at Rado Holm.

i Free. ◷ Open 24hr.

FOOD

◼ PÁLFFY'TÁLIA   ITALIAN $
Széchenyi tér 3   ☎96 524680 www.palffyetterem.hu/hun/

Full of family gatherings, parties, and ladies who lunch, Palffy Italia hosts possibly half of downtown Győr on any given sunny day. And Palffy deserves its popularity. Not only is the decor and location of the large restaurant prime, but Palffy Italia's food is also on par. Its chicken may even be a birdie.

Palffy Italia is not a place for a quick bite. It offers many delicious courses. Try one of its soups, ranging from a deliciously classic Tuscan Tomato to one featuring coffee lamb. While perhaps most popular for its thin, family-size gourmet pizzas, the menu at Palffy Italia offers a range of pastas, salads, and meats—most featuring everyone's favorite artery blocker, mozzarella cheese. And if your meal isn't creamy enough already, Palffy's specialty desserts, like Nutella Cake, are sure to do you in.

Although the waitstaff may not perfectly understand English—and most certainly won't comprehend your horrid attempts at sounding out Hungarian—they are patient and excellent hosts. Most dishes at Palffy's Italia range from €10-20, making the classy deliciousness less of a splurge than you were expecting.

i Entrees €10-15. ◷ Open M-W 5-11:30pm, F-Su noon-11:30pm.

◼ JOHN BULL PUB   BAR $
Aradi vértanúk útja 3   ☎96 618 320 www.johnbullpub.hu/

When you think of pub food, the first thing that comes to mind is probably greasy burgers, greasier fries, and, if possible, a waiter with the greasiet hair. Fortunately, that's just not the case at "John Bull Pub" in Győr. Maybe it's the language barrier, maybe it's just that the chef at John Bull is damn good, but this restaurant's pub food is a whole lot of gourmet.

While the corner John Bull Pub sits on is not so busy, its dining room and outdoor seating are as bustling as the heart of Győr's city center (which is only a few blocks away). The menu has a wide assortment of savory gourmet goodies, like an A-Z option of pastas, salads, chicken, veal, and its most famous steak. And if perusing the menu like it's your favorite board on Pinterest isn't enough, John Bull Pub has classic sports bar entertainment: TV.

get a room!

GRÓF CZIRÁKY PANZIÓ GYŐR

HOTEL $$

Bécsi kapu tér 8   ☎96 528 466 www.hotelcziraky.hu/?lang=en

A 3min. walk from Széchenyi tér, Győr's main square, but tucked away in a secluded corner of the city center, Gróf Cziráky Panzió Győr is the perfect blend of peace and proximity. The moment you see the quaint yellow building of Gróf Cziráky Panzió, you'll be in love. It embodies the best of the old world feel that Győr has to offer. And your love will prove more than skin deep, as Gróf Cziráky Panzió's staff and rooms are equally charming.

The small hotel is three floors of rooms, each with a small private bath and television. If you've been staying in hostels, Gróf Cziráky Panzió's cozy rooms will feel like your own home...except with a maid to bring you fresh towels and make your bed each day. On top of the luxuries of having your own shower, Gróf Cziráky Panzió serves a complimentary breakfast spread each morning down in its basement, which operates as a restaurant at night.

Being as small as it is, there are some things Gróf Cziráky Panzió isn't able to offer. Good Wi-Fi and a public computer are two...but c'mon, you're in Hungary, get off Facebook and go see some stuff. There also isn't air-conditioning. Fortunately, while laying naked and exposed until you eventually fall asleep is always an option when dealing with the heat, the previously-mentioned charming staff would be more than willing to supply you with a fan, so just ask.

i Dorms €35; doubles €48. ☒ Reception open 6am-7pm.

BAROSS BOUTIQUE APARTMAN

APARTMENT $$

Baross Gábor u. 28   ☎70 232 1971 https://hu-hu.facebook.com/barossboutique

While the old world feel of Győr is probably what drew you to this small Hungarian city (if not, then what are you doing here?!), it's sometimes a relief to relax with some modern friends: namely, cable TV and a big, comfy couch. At Baross Boutique Apartman, you and your two special friends get your own space above one of Győr's most popular streets in city center. And not only do you get to crash with these two homies, but Baross Boutique Apartman studio apartments include a private entrance, small kitchen and dining table, a bathroom, and even your very own bed. If walls could talk, the ones at Baross Boutique Apartman would probably discuss indie music, Thoreau, and cappuccinos with skim milk—that's how hip they are. This trendy interior is a surprisingly nice contrast with the crown molded, stone buildings outside the apartment windows. Lean your head a little farther out the window and you'll find a host of shops and cafes along the cobblestone road. The location is ideal: the apartments are only a 5min walk from the train station and Győr National Theatre, and 2min from the central square. The only danger with such prime real estate is the ease at which you could get gelato—you wouldn't even have to change out of your boxers! But if slippered gelato runs sound like a dream, then book a few nights in a Baross Boutique Apartman studio apartment.

i Studio apartment €65-95. ☒ Reception 24 hr.

győr

The waitstaff, while they may not speak English, are still helpful with the menu. Through a series of gestures, they'll point you in a delicious direction. But if you are a bit nervous to engage in a salivating game of charades, splurge a little and try one of the pub's juicy steaks.

i *Entrees €10-20.* ☼ *Open M 10am-10pm, Tu-Sat 10am-midnight, Su 10am-10pm.*

NIGHTLIFE

◙ YOLO PUB   BAR

Baross Gábor út 5   ☎30 252 0100 https://hu-hu.facebook.com/yolopubgyor
When was the last time you heard someone say "YOLO" without any irony? Probably never. Well, in Gyor all of your ironic lingo can be taken a little too serious at the Yolo Pub.

While essentially just a dark basement with a black light, Yolo Pub is the hip hangout for Győr's youth. Hungarians stand outside the hole-in-the wall entrance in gaggles, ready to "turn up." And with a name like "Yolo," you know the turn up can't involve just your standard chill pub with a bit of dancing. Instead, Yolo Pub often hosts giant beer pong tournaments. Not to rain on anyone's parade, but in Hungary, the cups are usually white, although the cheap beer and ridiculous drinking games hosted by Yolo Pub are sure to make you feel all dormy regardless. So if you're above the age of 25, you may want to reconsider Yolo Pub. While not many in the local pub are able to speak English, pong tends to be a universal language, so if you think you have what it takes to show Hungary's youth the superiority of your red cup trained toss, hit up Yolo club.

i *Entry fee varies based on planned entertainment. Beer and wine €2-4. Mixed drinks €5-10. Cash only.* ☼ *Hours vary.*

ESSENTIALS
Practicalities

- **TOURIST OFFICES:** Tourinform arranges tours and accomodations. The Tourinform in Győr is between the train station and downtown at Baross Gábor út 21 (96 336 817).

- **ATMS:** English-language ATMs *(bankamatik, bankomat)* can be found on almost every corner. If your account is at a foreign bank, cash withdrawal will cost you extra. Most ATMs dispense Turkish lire. If you want to withdraw American dollars or euro, try the banks around Sirkeci Train Station and İstiklal Cad.

- **LUGGAGE STORAGE:** 24hr. luggage storage *(Emanet Bagaj)* is available at **Atatürk International Airport** (☎0212 465 3442 10-20 TL per day) and **Sirkeci Train Station** (☎0539 885 2105 *i* 4-7 TL for 4hr., 0.50 TL per hr. thereafter; max. 4 days).

- **GLBT RESOURCES: Time Out Istanbul** magazine provides a good overview of the city's GLBT establishments. Some other organizations of interest are **Lambda** (Tel Sok. 28/5, 4th fl., Beyoğlu ☎0212 245 7068, advice line ☎0212 244 5762 www.lambdaistanbul.org ☼ Open F-Su 3-8pm; hotline open M-Tu 5-7pm and F-Su 5-7pm), trans-focused **Istanbul LGBTT** (Atıf Yılmaz Cad. Öğüt Sok. 18/4, Beyoğlu ☎0212 252 1088 www.istanbul-lgbtt.org), and Ankara-based **Kaos GL** (☎0312 230 0358 http://news.kaosgl.com).

- **LAUNDROMATS:** Most hostels will do your laundry for a small fee. If you'd prefer a laundromat, try **Beybuz** (Topçekerler Sok. 7A ☎0212 249 5900 *i* Wash 3 TL per kg. Dry cleaning 10 TL. ☼ Open 24hr.) or **Şık Çamaşır Yıkama.** (Güneşli Sok. 1A ☎0212 245 4375 *i* 15 TL per load. ☼ Open M-Sa 8:30am-8pm.)

- **INTERNET: Sultanahmet Square** offers free Wi-Fi. **İstiklal Caddesi** supposedly has free Wi-Fi as well, but coverage is spotty. One of the best internet cafes in town is **Net Club** (Büyükparmakkapı Sok. 8/6, 3rd fl. *i* Just off Istiklal Cad., a few blocks from Taksim Sq. 1.25 TL per hr.

🕐 Open 24hr.), but there are many others around İstiklal and a few near the Sultanahmet tram stop. In most cafes, expect to pay about 2 TL per hr.

- **POST OFFICES:** The main post office in Győr can be found at Bajcsy-Zsilinszky út 46, right across from the Győr National Theatre. It's open M-F 8am-6pm.

Emergency

- **GENERAL MEDICAL EMERGENCY:** ☎112
- **HUNGARIAN POLICE DEPARTMENT:** ☎107
- **INTERNATIONAL COUNTRY CODE :** ☎+36
- **IN CASE OF FIRE:** ☎105
- **24HR. MEDICAL ASSISTANCE IN ENGLISH (FALCK SOS HUNGARY):** ☎06 1 2000 100.
- **TOURIST POLICE:** There is no tourist police office in Győr, but the Győr City Police are ready to assist in an emergency. The Győr City Police office can be found at Zrínyi utca 54 and can be telephoned at 96 520 000.
- **PHARMACY:** Look for green signs labeled Apotheke, Gyogyszertar, or Pharmacie. There are six pharmacies in Győr, three of them all clustered around Győr National Theatre. Aranyhajó gyógyszertár (Jedlik Ányos utca 16) has a selection of medicines and is open M-F 7am-6pm and Sa 7am-2pm. Most pharmacies are not open on weekends, and none are open 24hr. For serious medical emergencies, call 112.
- **MEDICAL SERVICES:** Because English is not widely spoken in Győr, the Petz-Aladár Teaching Hospital, which offers all services besides open-heart and transplant surgery, is recommended for tourists. It is one of the biggest hospitals in Hungary and located at Zrínyi utca 13 (96 418 244.
- **LOCAL LAWS AND POLICE:** You should not hesitate to contact the police in Budapest if you are the victim of a crime. Be sure to carry a valid passport, as police have the right to ask for identification. Police can sometimes be unhelpful if you are the victim of a currency exchange scam; in this instance, it may be better to seek advice from your country's embassy or consulate.

Getting There

The Győr International Airport, Győr-Pér Airport, has not been in use since December 2013. Therefore the closest airport is the Budapest international airport, Budapest Ferihegy Airport 16km southeast of downtown Budapest. For general information regarding the airport call 1 296 9696; for information regarding flight details call 1 296 7000. Győr is about a 1hr. 30min. drive from Budapest. Highway M1 connects the city with the capital. Check out www.elvira.hu to see train listings from Budapest to Győr. Trains between the two cities depart fairly regularly from one of Budapest's major train stations, the Keleti, Nyugati, or Déli. Győr's train station is about a two block walk from the city center.

Getting Around

All tourist attractions, hotels, and restaurants are located in Győr's city center. Anything can be reached by foot in under 15min.

hungary essentials

MONEY

Although part of the European Union, Hungary's official currency is the forint (Ft).

Currency Exchange

Hungary is part of the European Union, so euro are widely accepted, though its official current is the forint (Ft). Tipping: a 10% tip is customary in all situations where the customers and service workers come face to face. Most tips, however, are already added on to the bill. Taxes: goods, products, and services in Hungary are subject to a value-added tax of 25% (a reduced tax of 12% is applied to basic consumer goods). Ask for a VAT return form at points of purchase to enjoy tax-free shopping. Present it at customs upon leaving the country along with your receipts and the unused goods. Refunds can be claimed at Tax Free Shopping Offices, found at most airports, road borders, and ferry stations, or by mail.

Tipping and Taxes

Tipping is customary in all situations where the customers and service workers— waiters, taxi drivers, and hotel porters—come face to face. Depending upon how satisfied you are with the service, plan to tip 10-15%. Goods, products, and services in Hungary are subject to a value added tax (VAT) of 27% (a reduced tax of 18% is applied to basic consumer goods). Non-EU visitors who are taking these goods home unused may be refunded this tax for purchases totaling over 48,000Ft per store. When making purchases, request a VAT form and present it at a Tax Free Shopping Office, found at most airports, road borders, and ferry stations, or by mail. Refunds must be claimed within six months.

SAFETY AND HEALTH

Local Laws and Police

You should not hesitate to contact the police in Budapest if you are the victim of a crime. Be sure to carry a valid passport, as police have the right to ask for identification. Police can sometimes be unhelpful if you are the victim of a currency exchange scam; in this instance, it may be better to seek advice from your country's embassy or consulate.

Drugs and Alcohol

Avoid public drunkenness as it will jeopardize your safety. In Hungary, drinking is permitted at age 18. Marijuana is entirely illegal throughout the country. Carrying drugs across an international border—considered to be drug trafficking—is a serious offense that could land you in prison.

Smoking is incredibly popular in Budapest. If you are sensitive to cigarette smoke, ask for a non-smoking room in a hotel or hostel, or to be seated in the non-smoking area of restaurants.

IRELAND

If you haven't yet heard that Ireland is the land of shamrocks, shillelaghs, and 40 shades of green, you should probably purchase a television, a copy of Darby O'Gill and the Little People, or a guide to Western culture since 1855. Surprisingly prominent in the international imagination for an island of six million people, Ireland is a place that the rest of the world feels it understands very well, and the Irish themselves find much more complex. Their native country was originally chopped up into several dozen regional kingships, and today it's still split between two different countries, two different religions, and 11 different Wikipedia disambiguations. (Eight-seven percent of native Irish find that last division to be the most contentious.)

OK, we made that last statistic up. It's still no wonder, though, that Ireland and "Irishness" can be difficult to categorize. Its two capitals—Belfast in the North, and Dublin in the Republic—are at once the least and most "Irish" cities on the island. Belfast, home to the island's largest Orangemen parade and some its strongest pro-British sympathies, is Ireland's second-largest city and the one-time centerpiece of the iconic, tragic Troubles. Dublin, capital of the Republic and site of the Easter Rising, is increasingly urban and international, making it feel more like modern London than magical Glocca Morra. However, these cities' entanglement with issues of national identity, history, and globalization is a lot more Irish than that Claddagh ring your friend paid €50 for. Like pouring a perfect stout, dancing with Michael Flatley, or spelling a one-syllable word in Gaelic, visiting Ireland should be a wonderfully complicated experience—otherwise you're not doing it right.

greatest hits

- **REJOYCE.** At the **James Joyce Centre** (p. 491), pay homage to one of the fathers of literary Modernism.
- **CLUBLIN.** When you're fully saturated with Guinness and want to abandon the pubs for the clubs, look no further than **The Workman's Club** (p. 497), one of the best ways to end a night in Dublin.
- **PRIDE OF BELFAST.** Immerse yourself in the history of the *Titanic* in Belfast's **Titanic Quarter** (p. 501). As they proudly say, "It was fine when it left us."

dublin

It's all too easy to think you've figured Dublin out. All the major landmarks are within 15min. of each other. The National Gallery took you an hour to walk through. The first pub you went to served a great pint of Guinness. Pat yourself on the back, but sooner or later Dublin's going to impress you. Maybe you'll stumble upon the enormous Phoenix Park and get lost for a couple hours (for such a massive park, it only seems to have three exits). Maybe you'll realize that Dublin has two renowned modern art galleries, or that the pub you went to is one of thousands—and no, it wouldn't be a productive use of your time to have a pint of Guinness in all of them (at least try one of the craft brews). Maybe you'll have a deliriously good meal in an up-and-coming neighborhood like Smithfield or Stoneybatter. Point is, you'll learn your lesson. Dublin's been around for millennia, but it's not a museum piece like other European cities—the cityscape is changing (especially down by the quays), new bars and restaurants pop up daily, and the warhorse attractions still hold up pretty damn well (with the exception of the Natural History Museum, which is almost as endangered as the species it exhibits).

SIGHTS

Vikings, beer, and prisons. Dublin's attractions are a motley crew.

TRINITY COLLEGE
COLLEGE

College Green, Dublin 2   ☎1 896 1000 www.tcd.ie

With its enormous library and host of distinguished alumni including Jonathan Swift (although who knows why they're proud of that, he was a psychopath who advocated eating Irish children [see "A Modest Proposal"]), Trinity College might very well be the intellectual center of Dublin. But even if you're not in the mood for deep thought or glorifying cannibalism, a short stroll around the picturesque grounds is always appealing unless you hate fun. The most beautiful thing on campus, aside from the majestic Irishmen in kilts (Editor's note: Those aren't kilts...Maybe we shouldn't have subsidized all that Guinness in the name of research), might be the Book of Kells, a ninth-century illuminated manuscript renowned for its elaborate and striking designs. Attempting to read it, however, will not be very illuminating, as it appears to be written in Pig Latin and there's all these annoying illustrations instead of actual words. It's permanently on display in the Old Library, though you'll have to wait in line for at least half an hour before you see it. Located a few blocks away from the River Liffey, Trinity College is easily accessible by bus (13, 40, 49, and 65 all stop at College Green).

i Tours for £10. Admission to the Old Library: £9 for adults, £8 for students and seniors, free for children under 12. ☼ Tours of the campus begin at 10:15am and end at 3:40pm every day except Sunday, when they end at 3:10pm. Book of Kells ~ Open May-Sept M-Sa 9:30am-5pm, Su 9:30am-4:30pm, Oct-Apr M-Sa 9:30am-5pm, Su noon-4:30pm.

ST. STEPHEN'S GREEN
PARK

St. Stephen's Green, Dublin 2   ☎1 475 7816 www.heritageireland.ie

Though it's not the largest park in Dublin, St. Stephen's Green is still a sizable piece of greenery in the heart of Dublin. Tired of walking, sightseeing, or shopping in the neighboring Stephen's Green Shopping Center? Plop down on one of the Green's many benches and take in the lush scenery. If you notice strange smells, you're probably in the garden for the blind, where specially scented plants are on display. Getting there is easy—it's a short walk from Trinity College, and the end point of the Green Line tram.

i Free. ☼ Open M-Sa 8am. Closes 20min. before dark.

ireland

NATIONAL LIBRARY OF IRELAND
LIBRARY

Kildare Street, Dublin 2 ☎1 603 0200 www.nli.ie

If you ever needed to consult Irish governmental documents, this is the place for you. But even if tax records from the 1930s aren't your jam, the National Library of Ireland is certainly worth checking out. Stop by the striking reading room, and, if you have roots in Ireland, drop by the genealogy office to check up on that family history. Also notable: the exhibits honoring Irish writers like James Joyce and William Butler Yeats. Their Yeats collection is the biggest in the world, with a total of over 2000 items: everything from drafts of poems to his glasses. Like the National Gallery and the Museum of Archaeology and Ethnography, it's a block away from Trinity College.

i Free. ☼ Open M-W 9:30am-7:45pm, Th-F 9:30am-4:45pm, Sa 9:30am-4:30pm (reading room closes at 12:45pm), Su 1-5pm (exhibitions only).

NATIONAL GALLERY OF IRELAND
GALLERY

Entrance is on Clare Street ☎1 661 5133 www.nationalgallery.ie

The Hugh Lane and the Irish Museum of Modern Art may be more hip, but the National Gallery of Ireland is still an art world heavyweight. With works by such luminaries as Velasquez, Vermeer, and Caravaggio, this museum is the perfect way to spend a rainy afternoon—and believe us, Dublin has more than a few of those.

i Entrance is adjacent to Merrion Square West. Free. ☼ Open M-W 9:30am-5:30pm, Th 9:30am-8pm, F-Sa 9:30am-5:30pm, Su 12:30-5:30pm.

NATIONAL MUSEUM OF IRELAND — ARCHAEOLOGY AND ETHNOGRAPHY
MUSEUM

Kildare Street, Dublin 2 ☎1 677 7444 www.museum.ie

Dublin's other National Museums are all well and good, but this one is perhaps the most memorable—likely due to the four big bodies, remarkably well-preserved human specimens from the Iron Age. Details like their hair and fingers are especially lifelike and uncanny. If looking at likely victims of human sacrifice makes your stomach turn, there's loads more to see and do. The sprawling collection of medieval jewelry is particularly impressive.

i Free. ☼ Tu-Sa 10am-5pm, Su noon-5pm.

DUBLIN CASTLE
CASTLE

Dame Street, Dublin 2 ☎1 645 8800 www.dublincastle.ie

Like the White House, Dublin Castle is a governmental building that also doubles as a tourist attraction. Unlike the White House, Dublin Castle features a medieval tower that once housed many prisoners, one of whom escaped through the toilet. That's just one tidbit of Dublin Castle's storied history; it's been everything from a Norman fort to an Irish presidential inauguration location. Explore the incredibly opulent state rooms (Dublin Castle has been used to fill in for the Vatican in some television shows) before taking a relaxing walk in the garden out back. If the castle on its own isn't enough for you, check out the website (listed below) for information on special events. There's a bit of everything, ranging from performances of "A Midsummer Night's Dream" on the gardens to scavenger hunts.

i £5. Students £3. Children and seniors free. ☼ Open M-F 9am-midnight, Sa 1-10pm, Su noon-2am.

JAMESON DISTILLERY
DISTILLERY

Bow Street, Smithfield Village, Dublin 7 ☎1 807 2355 www.jamesonwhiskey.com

The actual whiskey is produced in Midleton, Ireland, but this tour still offers a detailed and fascinating look at how the stuff you get drunk on gets made. A sample of whiskey is included in the ticket cost. If you're still not satisfied, the large bar at the tour's conclusion offers a great selection of whiskey varietals and cocktails. If that's still not enough Jameson for you, you can proceed directly to

dublin

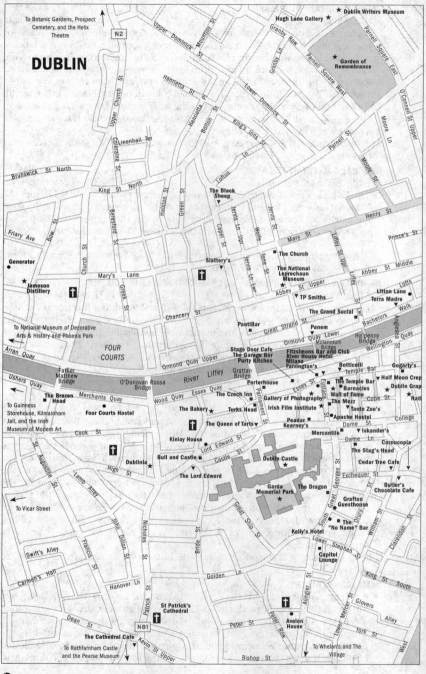

DUBLIN

To Botanic Gardens, Prospect
Cemetery, and the Helix
Theatre

N2

Upper Dominick St
Mountjoy St
Granby Row

★ Dublin Writers Museum
Hugh Lane Gallery ■

Granby Ln
Parnell Square East
Parnell Square West

★ Garden of
Remembrance

Henrietta St
Henrietta Pl
Lower Dominick St

Parnell St
Moore Ln
Moore St
O'Connell St Upper

King's Inns St
Bolton St
Linenhall Ter
Coleraine St

Brunswick St North

King St North

Lotus Ln
The Black
Sheep

Green St
Halston St
Jervis Ln Upr
Jervis St

Henry St

Mary St

Friary Ave
Bow St
Beresford St
Church St

Liffey St Upr
Abbey St Middle
Prince's St

Generator ●

Mary's Lane

Greek St

Slattery's
✝

Wolfe Tone St
Jervis Ln Lwr

★ The Church

The National
Leprechaun
Museum

Abbey St Upper

Lotts
Litton Lane
Terra Madre

Jameson ★
Distillery ✝

To National Museum of Decorative
Arts & History and Phoenix Park

Chancery St

PantiBar ■

▼ TP Smiths

The Grand Social ●

Bachelors Walk

Panem ●

Ormond Quay Lower

Great Strand St

Ha'penny
Bridge
Millennium
Bridge
Wellington Quay

Arran Quay

FOUR
COURTS

Ormond Quay Upper

River Liffey

Father
Matthew
Bridge

O'Donovan Rossa
Bridge

Stage Door Cafe
The Garage Bar
Purty Kitchen

Fitzsimons Bar and Club
River House Hotel
Milano
Farrington's

Botticelli ●

Gogarty's ●

Ushers Quay

Wood Quay

Grattan
Bridge

Porterhouse ●

Temple Bar
The Temple Bar
Barnacles ●
Wall of Fame
The Mezz

Half Moon Crep

To Guinness
Storehouse, Kilmainham
Jail, and the Irish
Museum of Modern Art

The Brazen
Head ●
Four Courts Hostel

Merchants Quay

Essex Quay

The Czech Inn ■

Gallery of Photography ●

Tante Zoe's ●

Dublin Grap ●

Nat ●

Essex St
Eustace St

Parliament St

Turks Head ★

The Bakery ●

Irish Film Institute ●

Apache Hostel ●

College

Cook St

The Queen of Tarts ■

Peadar
Kearney's ●

Dame St

Iskander's ●

Dublinia ★

Kinlay House ●

Lord Edward St

Mercantile ●

Cornucopia ●

High St

Bull and Castle ■

Castle St

The Stag's Head ●

Cedar Tree Cafe ●

The Lord Edward ■

Dublin Castle ★

The Dragon ●

Butler's
Chocolate Cafe ●

Lamb Alley

Garda
Memorial Park

Grafton
Guesthouse ●

John Dillon St

Nicholas St

Great Ship St

Kelly's Hotel ●

The
"No Name" Bar ●

Drury St
South Great Georges St
William St

Clarendon St

To Vicar Street

Swift's Alley

Francis St

Bride St

Golden Ln

Lower Stephen St

Capitol
Lounge ●

King St South

Carmen's Hall

Hanover Ln

Patrick St

Glovers
Alley

York St

Aungier St
Peter Row
Lower Mercer St

Dean St

St Patrick's
Cathedral ✝

N81

Peter St

Avalon
House ✝

To Rathfarnham Castle
and the Pearse Museum

The Cathedral Cafe ●

Kevin St Upper

Bishop St

To Whelan's and The
Village

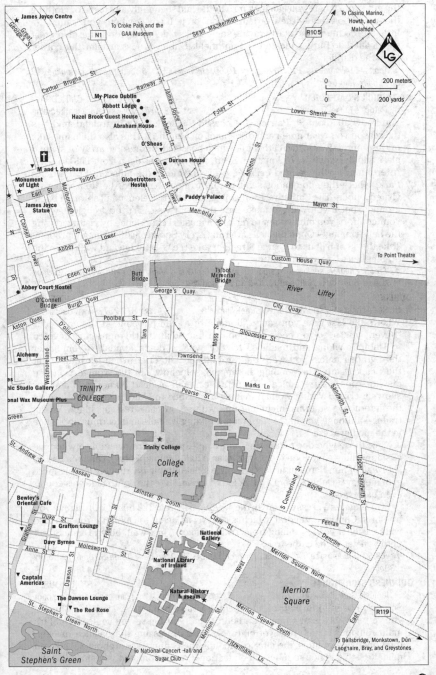

dublin

the gift shop, where you can pick up a bottle and seemingly any piece of clothing that could possibly fit the word "Jameson" on it. If (read: when) you "sample" a little bit too much and start craving some greasy, delicious food, there's a great spot called Jo'Burger located at Smithfield, Dublin 7, just around the corner from the distillery.

i Adults £14, students £10.60, seniors £9.60, children £7.70. Discounts available online. 🕐 Open daily 9am-6pm.

ST. PATRICK'S CATHEDRAL
CATHEDRAL

St. Patrick's Close, Dublin 8 ☎1 453 9472 www.stpatrickscathedral.ie

You know all about St. Patrick—he chased the snakes out of Ireland, and he's the reason you wear green and drink a lot on March 17. He's also the namesake of this impressive Gothic cathedral, which boasts an impressive array of stained glass and the gravesite of Jonathan Swift, who served as dean from 1713 to 1745. After admiring the vaulted ceilings, walk outside to the adjacent St. Patrick's Park, where the eponymous saint is said to have baptized the Irish when he visited Dublin. The Cathedral is, of course, open to travelers of all spiritual backgrounds, but if you want to make sure that your visit isn't too "religious-y" for your comfort, you might want to make it a musical experience by visiting during the bells-ringing ~ Open the bells are rung every Sunday at 10:30am and 2:30pm. Take the 49 or 54 bus to Pearse Street, or take the Green Line and walk from the St. Stephen's Green tram station.

i £5.50. Children, seniors, and students £4.50. Group and family discounts available. 🕐 Open M-Sa 9am-5pm, Su 9-10:30am, 12:30-2:30pm, and 4:30-5pm.

DUBLINIA
MUSEUM

On St. Michael's Hill and Winetavern Street, Dublin 8 ☎1 872 2077 www.dublinia.ie

When's the last time you saw a diorama of a man pooping? If the answer is "never," you need to check out Dublinia immediately. This museum, devoted to Dublin's Viking and medieval history, will no doubt appeal to your inner third-grader, unless you were the third-grader who cried when learning about the Black Death. The pooping diorama is, somehow, not the strangest one on display—one bizarre tableaux depicts a cart full of dead bodies, and another shows a crazed Viking woman making a sacrifice to Odin. Even more fun are the interactive stations, including one where you can dress up like a Viking trader—although you might regret it after going upstairs and learning about lice in the medieval era.

For those who don't want their museum experience to resemble a whoopee cushion (did we mention the poop diorama has sound effects?), Dublinia has no shortage of non-flatulent attractions. The most notable is probably a scale-model of medieval Dublin. From a quick look, it seems like the South Side was cooler even back then.

Getting there is easy enough; the 49, 49A, 54A, and 123 buses will all take you by Christ Church Cathedral, which is directly adjacent to Dublinia. You can also walk easily; if you're coming from Trinity College, just walk down Dame Street until you get to the cathedral.

i £8.50. Students/seniors £7.50. Children £6.50. 🕐 Open daily 10am-6:30pm; last entry 5:30pm.

GUINNESS STOREHOUSE
STOREHOUSE

St. James's Gate, Dublin 8 ☎1 408 4800 www.guinness-storehouse.com

So you've been to St. Patrick's Cathedral, you've been to St. Michan's Church, you've been to Christ Church Cathedral, and you figure you've seen Dublin's main religious structures. Not quite. You're still missing the basilica of beer, the holy place of hops, the altar of alcohol: the Guinness Storehouse. Make no mistake—this is not so much an educational attraction as it is a shrine to the

Dublin shuts down early—"LATE NIGHT PHARMACY—OPEN UNTIL 9PM" reads the sign on one store—so it's even more crucial to have a space you can call your own, sort of. Here are our picks for the best places to stay in Dublin.

BARNACLES DUBLIN   HOSTEL $

19 Temple Lane South, Dublin 2   ☎1 671 6277 www.barnacles.ie/dublin

There are 171 beds in this hostel, located in the heart of the Temple Bar district, and the enthusiastic, inclusive staff will make sure that by the end of your stay, you'll be buddies with every last guest—as well as staff members themselves! Hostel-wide pasta dinners, movie nights, game nights, and (for the livelier occupants) planned pub crawls abound. The dorms, each of which have between one and 11 beds, are similarly high-quality, but be warned: there are two classes of private rooms, one of which is miles better than the other. You're going to want those big windows and the beautiful view, not the skylight, so be sure to specify your preference for the top floor when booking.

i Dorms from £12, doubles and singles from £60. ☼ Reception open daily 24hr.

ISAACS HOSTEL   HOSTEL $$

2-5 Frenchmans Lane, Dublin 1   ☎1 855 6215 www.isaacs.ie

There seem to be a million hostels near Gardiner Street, but this is the one that you want to stay at. Why? Because the Isaacs Hostel is, by far, the most unique amongst the entire pack, complete with off-the-charts amenities like book exchanges, TVs, ping pong, and even a free sauna. The rooms aren't huge but they're sufficient, and the big windows make up for the room size. The bathrooms are generally spotless and are separated by gender. You'll be able to get to your gender-specific business without freaking out about an attractive member of the opposite sex walking in! The decorations in the residential areas are rather unimaginative, but there are actually some pretty cool arched stone vaults in the basement that show off the hostel's history as a wine shoppe.

i Dorms starting at £14, £48-60 for private rooms. ☼ Reception open daily 24hr.

KINLAY HOUSE HOSTEL   HOSTEL $$

2-12 Lord Edward Street, Dublin 2   ☎1 679 6644 www.kinlaydublin.ie

Littered with different movie posters (everything from The Philadelphia Story to Pulp Fiction), this massive hostel has an absurdly complex layout that could cause some confusion. However, if you're willing to potentially get lost wearing just a post-shower towel at least once (don't worry, it'll make for a great story and you may even make a new friend or two, wink, wink ,nudge, nudge), the Kinlay House Hostel offers some of the best cheap rooms in all of Dublin. The doubles and singles feature large windows that light the space nicely, and the wooden beds are very crafty. If you dig communal experiences, be sure to book a bed in the Kinlay Room, a massive dorm with a beautiful vaulted wooden ceiling that holds 24 people—you may not get all 8hr. of beauty sleep, but you'll be sure to have an unforgettable experience with some interesting fellow travelers.

i Dorms from £17, doubles from £25, singles from £30 (extra £5 to guarantee a shower in the room). ☼ Reception open daily 24hr.

dublin

acclaimed stout. Thankfully, there are no virgin sacrifices—just an admission fee.

Dubious? Consider the wall text in one room: "Centuries ago, many people were convinced that somehow, lead could be transformed into gold. In a way, Arthur Guinness was such a man. But where others failed, he succeeded." Consider the monolithic sculpture of a Guinness pint on one floor. Consider the fact that this bizarre museum is housed in a seven-story reproduction of a Guinness glass (the website proudly notes that it could hold a whopping 14.3 million pints, which would probably put you over the legal limit). By the time you finish the tour, you half expect the bathroom faucets to spout Guinness.

Getting there is pretty easy, especially considering its location in another dimension. Just walk west past Christ Church Cathedral, onto Cornmarket and onto Thomas Street. Hang a left on Crane Street and you'll start seeing signs. You're in Guinness territory now (you already were, but now you're in the inner sanctum). Admission may seem a bit steep, but it's fairly reasonable if you factor in the complimentary pint you get at the end. You may not go home ready to spread the gospel of Guinness, but the Storehouse will certainly convince you that it's a damn good drink.

i £16.50 for adults, £13 for students and seniors, £6.50 for children (who presumably aren't enjoying the complimentary pint). ☼ Open daily 9:30am-5pm. Open until 7pm in Jul and Aug.

KILMAINHAM GAOL   PRISON
Inchicore Road, Kilmainham, Dublin 8   ☎1 453 2037 www.heritageireland.ie

Yes, we know that "jail" is spelled oddly in Ireland, and we know that the last thing you want to do on vacation is go to prison. But that doesn't change the fact that Kilmainham Gaol is one of the most electrifying attractions in Dublin—and don't worry, that's not an electric chair joke. Most of the executions here were carried out by hanging.

Indeed, Kilmainham Gaol is most famous for having housed many famous Irish revolutionaries—many of the central figures in the 1916 Easter Rising were taken here and killed. You'll see where political figures like Eamon de Valera were imprisoned by the British government. Many places in Dublin commemorate these figures (see: Garden of Remembrance, the National Library, the Collins Barracks) but this is your opportunity to get really close to them (unless you do some gravedigging in Glasnevin Cemetery). But be forewarned: the only way to get access to the jail is through a guided tour. If you wanted to case the joint to see if you could have broken out of it, this probably isn't the attraction for you. For all others, the informative tour should be a boon to their enjoyment, especially since the jail contains very few labels or identifying marks.

Getting there, however, is kind of a hike, albeit a scenic one. Walk west along the River Liffey until you get to Heuston Station—take a right onto Military Road and follow it to the Irish Museum of Modern Art. Walk straight through that museum's beautiful grounds—it used to be the Royal Hospital and has a formal garden—and you'll come out right by Kilmainham Gaol. If you don't like beautiful scenery and/or it's raining, take the 13 or 40 bus from O'Connell Street. Or you could just commit a crime and get a ride over in a police van.

i £6. Seniors £4. Children and students £2. ☼ Open Apr-Sept daily 9:30am-6pm, last admission at 5pm. Oct-Mar M-Sa 9:30am-5:30pm, last admission at 4:30; Su 10am-6pm, last admission at 5pm.

GARDEN OF REMEMBRANCE

Parnell Square East, Dublin 1   ☎1 821 3021   www.heritageireland.ie

GARDEN

Are you the type of person that's really into cathedral floor plans but also hates ceilings? We have just the place for you. The Garden of Remembrance, a park meant to commemorate those who died in the Irish struggle for freedom (apparently kind of a big deal over here), is laid out in the shape of a cross, much like most cathedrals. The nave is the longer passage in the center, and the transept crosses it… wait you're reading this?

But the Garden of Remembrance is also a somber place of reflection (surprise!), so don't go expecting the madhouse that is St. Stephen's Green during lunch hour (although there may be a few people eating sandwiches at the covered benches). At the far end of the garden, there's a large bronze statue and a poem inscribed on a wall, both of which celebrate—you guessed it—Irish independence and the men and women that fought for it. All in all, it's central location by Parnell Square makes it a fine place to pay your respects (especially if you don't want to walk all the way to Glasnevin Cemetery, where some famous revolutionaries are buried).

i Free. ☑ Open daily Apr-Sept 8:30am-6pm, Oct-Mar 9:30am-4pm.

JAMES JOYCE CENTRE

35 North Great George's Street   ☎1 878 8547   www.jamesjoyce.ie

MUSEUM

James Joyce's Ulysses is set in 1904, and the Dublin depicted in that novel is obviously quite different from the one that exists today. To really get a sense of Joyce's Dublin, you can't do much better than the James Joyce Centre, which is located in a gorgeous Georgian townhouse just a few blocks east of Parnell Square. The guys at this museum take Joyce seriously (don't try to bluff your way through a conversation with them), evidenced by the fact that they're the ones who organize the city's annual Bloomsday events. If you should happen to visit Dublin during a month that's not June, the Centre still delivers the goods—most impressively, they have the door from 7 Eccles Street, where Bloom lives in the novel. It's kind of like the Irish equivalent of the Smithsonian American History Museum, where you can see the puffy shirt that Jerry wore on Seinfeld. Slightly more highbrow, but you get the point.

The self-guided museum also includes numerous objects from Joyce's own life, including a copy of his death mask. Heavy stuff. On the top floor, you can view furniture from the apartment where Joyce wrote *Finnegans Wake*. Though you may be tired from walking up three flights of stairs, you can't sit on these chairs, which is fitting because you also can't understand *Finnegans Wake*. You can also see a recreation of one of the apartments in which he wrote *Ulysses*. The wall text says he prided himself on his ability to get work done in hectic environments. Alright, Jimmy, but could you have finished *Ulysses* if you had to contend with BuzzFeed?

Though it may not appear so at first glance, this museum is a great place to go on a sunny day. For one thing, the galleries, with their large windows, are stunning in the sunlight; for another, walking tours leave from the museum on Tuesday, Thursday, and Saturday.

i £5. Students and seniors £4. Children presumably don't attend. Walking tours £10, £8 for students and seniors. ☑ Open Apr-Sept M-Sa 10am-5pm, Su noon-5pm; Oct-Mar Tu-Sa 10am-5pm, Su noon-5pm. Walking tours Tu, Th, and Sa 11am and 2pm.

DUBLIN WRITERS MUSEUM

18 Parnell Square, Dublin 1   ☎1 872 2077   www.writersmuseum.com

MUSEUM

Also known as "The Trinity College Alumni Museum," the Dublin Writers Museum celebrates everyone from George Bernard Shaw to Joseph Thomas Sheridan Le Fanu. Who? Exactly. Already it's clear that you need to visit this museum.

dublin

Its central location means there's no excuse; you just walk north up O'Connell Street, past Parnell Square, and turn left at the Garden of Remembrance. Get there and get reading; there's enough wall text at this museum to fill a book. Luckily, audio guides are available.

You can probably guess some of the contents of the Dublin Writers Museum; stuff about Jonathan Swift being a pioneering satirist, stuff about Oscar Wilde's fall from grace, the legally mandated *Ulysses* showcase. But what really makes the Dublin Writers Museum stand out is its impressive collection of memorabilia; or, in common parlance, junk the writers used to own. The memorabilia falls into three categories: archival (a program for the original production of Oscar Wilde's "Lady Windermere's Fan"), bizarrely personal (a luggage label used by Frank O'Connor; you wouldn't believe the insight it allows into his work), and downright hilarious (Samuel Beckett's home telephone, which included a button to disable incoming calls.). If you're the type that always preferred pictures to words, you're almost certainly in the wrong museum, but the second floor does feature portraits of the various authors. If you hate both pictures and words, you might get some pleasure out of the house itself—it used to belong to the Jameson family, which gives you some idea of how lavish it is. In the back, there's a bookstore where you can actually buy the works of the authors on display (though the exhibit includes enough information for you to fake your way through a dinner party). Buy a pen and paper while you're at it: maybe it's time for your magnum opus.

i £7.50. Students & seniors £6.30. Children £4.70. ☑ Open M-Sa 10am-5pm, last admission 4:15pm; Su 11am-5pm, last admission 4:15pm.

IRISH FILM INSTITUTE
INSTITUTE

6 Eustace Street, Temple Bar, Dublin 2 ☎1 679 5744 www.ifi.ie

Odds are you don't know very much about Irish film. No, Boondock Saints doesn't count. Neither does The Departed or Gangs of New York. And Braveheart is set in Scotland. Maybe you've seen Once. Maybe. All the more reason to visit the Irish Film Institute, a combination of a film archive, a cafe, and several movie theaters. Unlike most academic film institutions, this is both welcoming to the general public and full of really comfortable seats. The film archive requires appointments to be made in advance, but otherwise you can just wander in. Take stock of what movies are showing this week—if you haven't heard of any of the movies, pick the one with the weirdest title. What's the worst that could happen? Or spend some time in the cafe, a gem of restraint in the rather gauche Temple Bar district. Delicious paninis, a glass ceiling (hopefully just a literal one), and drinks ranging from fine wine to bottles of O'Hara's craft beer make this a far classier affair than the concessions stand at your local movie house (the lack of popcorn, however, is unforgivable).

Visitors to the gift shop may mistakenly believe they've found the film archive; in reality, there's just a really impressive selection of DVDs for sale, alongside a number of books about film and some sick posters (but good luck fitting them in your suitcase). If the sky opens up (believe us, it will), there are few better ways to spend an afternoon. Just walk west along the south side of the Liffey and take a left onto Eustache Street—the IFI will be near the intersection with Dame Street.

i Entrance free; ticket prices vary by time of day, but range from £7.60 to £9 (£5.90- £7.60 for students/seniors/children). ☑ Open M-Th 10am-11pm F-Su 10am-11:30pm.

JAMES JOYCE STATUE
STATUE

North Earl Street, Dublin 1

More than a century ago, James Joyce walked the streets of Dublin, gathering the source material for his magnum opus, *Ulysses*. Much has changed since

dublin

then—the number of people who have actually read *Ulysses* has increased by five, possibly six—and the best way to appreciate that is to pay a visit to the James Joyce Statue, located just off O'Connell Street. Though certain landmarks in *Ulysses*, like Davy Byrne's Pub or Glasnevin Cemetery, still survive today, this bronze statue, made by artist Marjorie Fitzgibbon and installed in 1990, is located outside a Thai food joint and a cut-rate barbershop. If Joyce were to write *Ulysses* today, would these factor into Leopold Bloom's famous journey? Maybe they're already in *Ulysses* and we just can't tell. It's a very complex novel.

Though Dublin has plenty of attractions devoted to Joyce and his work, this statue stands above the fold for two reasons: it's free, and it's the perfect place for a photo op. Come on, you know you want a new profile picture that says "I'm artsy and sophisticated." Or maybe you want to convince your mother that you went to Ireland not to get drunk on Guinness or Jameson, but because you genuinely care about its literary and artistic heritage. There's no more convenient way to get this point across—there's rarely a line to gaze at the statue, and taking a picture takes less than a second. That leaves you plenty of time to go to the Old Jameson Distillery or the Guinness Storehouse. If you genuinely do care about its artistic and literary heritage (nerd alert), you'll have plenty of time to visit the nearby James Joyce Centre or the Dublin Writers Museum.

i Free. ⏰ Open daily 24hr.

FOOD

Irish cuisine isn't just meat and potatoes anymore. With everything from Middle Eastern brunches to curry-fried fish and chips, Dublin is filled with delicious grub. Read on for our picks.

BROTHER HUBBARD

RESTAURANT $$

153 Capel Street, Dublin 1 ☎1 441 1112 www.brotherhubbard.ie

Utensils are served in vintage cans. The most popular item is a vaguely Middle Eastern take on pulled pork. The tip jar is divided into two categories, allowing you to voice your preference for "Mad Men" or "Mad Max." Brother hubbard is almost unbearably hip, but that shouldn't detract from its friendly atmosphere or impeccable food. The brunch menu is worth waking up early for, but late risers should direct their attention to the deservedly lauded pulled pork sandwich. If you're there on a nice day, be sure to get a seat in the courtyard area. Nearby: The Black Sheep (61 Capel Street), Beerhouse (84.5 Capel Street).

i Brunch entrees about £9, breakfast about £5. Sandwiches £7-11. Credit cards accepted. ⏰ Open M-F 8am-5:30pm, Sa-Su 10am-5pm.

SUPER MISS SUE

SEAFOOD $$

Units 2-3 Drury Street Car park, Dublin 2 ☎1 679 9009 www.supermisssue.com

Seafood joint Super Miss Sue fuses high class dining with world class drunk food. Say it's 7pm and you're looking to impress a date. Enjoy some high quality fish in the cafe area, where black curtains and walls of Campari bottles set the stage for elegant romance. Now say it's 2am, the date didn't go so well, and you're way too drunk. Ease yourself over to SMS Cervi, where you'll get the best fish-and-chips in Dublin, served in a sleek, slim package that's closer to an Hermès box than anything you'll find at McDonald's. The romance with this food is all you need. Go on a Friday night, when you can get the fish, chips, and soda combo for £10. Nearby: The Bar With No Name (3 Fade Street), Murphy's Ice Cream (27 Wicklow Street).

i £11 for fish and chips at SMS Cervi. Appetizers £8, entrees £14-30 at cafe. Credit cards accepted. ⏰ Café open M-W noon-10pm, Th-Sa noon-11pm, Su noon-10pm. Cervi M-Th noon-midnight, F-Sa noon-3am, Su noon-midnight.

ireland

BUNSEN
BURGERS $

36 Wexford Street, Dublin 2 ☎1 552 5408

Bunsen's entire menu fits on their business card. You can get a burger or a cheeseburger, and that can have one patty or two. You can get fries. You can get soda or a milkshake. This ain't rocket science (or molecular gastronomy). But sometimes simplicity is all you need, especially when everything they're offering is delicious. A cracking selection of beers and a killer indie rock playlist make this the perfect place to chow down before hitting up some of the more alternative bars on Wexford and Camden Streets.

i Burger £6.95, cheeseburger £7.45. Fries £3. Credit cards accepted. ⏰ Open M-Tu 12:30-9pm, W 12:30-9:30pm, Th-F 12-10:30pm, Su 1-9pm.

CRACKBIRD
FRIED CHICKEN $$

60 Dame Street, Dublin 2 ☎1 616 9841 www.joburger.ie/crackbird

Odds are you don't associate Dublin with fried chicken. One visit to Crackbird will change that. This mirror-filled hipster hangout offers a variety of takes on this American staple, but the one to order is the soy garlic chicken; it's their most popular dish for a reason. Salads are available for vegetarians, and a small but carefully curated selection of beer and wines round out the menu. Nearby: Kinlay House Dublin (2-12 Lord Edward Street), Dublin Castle (Dame Street).

i Single orders of chicken (4 pieces) about £11; double orders (8 pieces) £20. Salads £10. Mastercard and Visa accepted. ⏰ Open M-W noon-10pm, Th-Sa noon-11pm, Su noon-9 pm.

WUFF
RESTAURANT $$

23 Benburb Street, Dublin 7 ☎1 532 0347 www.wuff.ie

Don't be put off by this restaurant's spare, modern aesthetics. The delicious food and friendly wait staff is sure to make you feel at home, even if the bare-bulb lighting doesn't exactly scream "cozy." No surprises on the breakfast, lunch, brunch, and dinner menus (unless you've never encountered a ham and cheese omelette before), but the hearty flavors and generous portions will keep you coming back for more. Nearby: Seven Social (76 Benburb Street), Dice Bar (79 Queen Street)

i Credit cards accepted. ⏰ Open M-W 7:30am-4pm, Th-F 7:30am-9:30pm, Sa 10am-9:30pm, Su 10am-4pm.

NIGHTLIFE

"Good puzzle would be cross Dublin without passing a pub," Leopold Blooms ponders in *Ulysses*. What was true in 1904 is even more true today—there are currently over 1,000 bars in the city of Dublin That amount of choice can be very overwhelming; luckily, Let's Go is here to help you separate the wheat (wheat beer?) from the chaff.

CASSIDY'S
BAR

27 Westmoreland Street, Dublin 2 ☎1 475 1429

Cassidy's, despite its unassuming exterior, is a lot like your weird cousin's house. The decor is inspired by Star Wars and comic books. Hard rock is blasting from the stereo. You eat microwave pizza and play board games. Who knew that your weird cousin had all the ingredients for one of Dublin's best bars? "I usually don't go for hipster places," laughs one local. "But this place kind of gets away with it." Indeed, with its vintage Street Fighter game, its graffiti-covered walls, its garage rock soundtrack, and its killer beer selection, Cassidy's is as trendy as they come; but it's also an expressly welcoming environment.

Friendly bartenders help you navigate the daunting craft beer menu, featuring local favorites as well as hot imports like Mikkeler. Cocktails are also available, though the selection of liquors is somewhat less impressive than those you'll see at other bars (Gordon's seems to be their only gin option, for instance).

Because this is so close to the tourist-heavy Temple Bar area, the crowd is a mix of locals and tourists—it's a great place to go when you first get to Dublin, as you'll likely meet a few people who are also trying to figure the city out.

If it seems crowded upstairs, grab your drink and head to the basement area, accessible by two large staircases. The big tables down here are perfect for eating the glorious instant pizza available upstairs—only £10 for an entire pie and a pint, and £20 for a pie and a pitcher. Even if you don't need to go, it's worth checking the bathrooms out—the comic book decor continues and it's lit solely by candles in beer bottles.

i Cocktails about £7, pints from £4.50-5.50. Open daily 1pm-12:30am.

THE BERNARD SHAW   BAR

11-12 South Richmond Street, Dublin 2   ☎85 712 8342 www.thebernardshaw.com

As its namesake might have written, there are bars, and then there are superbars. Though there are plenty of hip joints in the Portobello area, the Bernard Shaw stands above the rest. Maybe it's the cocktail deals (2 mojitos for £10). Maybe it's the adventurous bar food (when's the last time you had arrosticini?). Maybe it's the fact that there's a garden out back, and in that garden there's a massive bus that's been converted into a pizza oven.

Though the selection of beers isn't as extensive as some of its neighbors (still there are some nice bottles), the Bernard Shaw is one of the few places in Dublin where you can get a decent cocktail for a decent price. And even if the cocktails were bad, it would be one of the few places in Dublin where you can get a bad cocktail for a decent price. Bring a friend and get that 2 for 1 deal; bring two friends and get three bottles of Bavaria or other select beers for £10. The Bernard Shaw is a place for socializing with friends. If the upstairs area looks deserted, it's probably because everyone's partying it up downstairs, where the DJ plays the hits. Don't be the guy who sits at the bar counter nursing a beer by himself. The fiesta-themed decor makes you look even sadder than you'd be otherwise. And on your way home, be sure to stop at the Bernard Shaw birthplace, which is located a couple of blocks away—just make sure you don't drunkenly pee on it.

i Beer £5- £6. Cocktails £7-8. Select cocktails are £10 for 2; select beers are £10 for 3. Open daily M-Th 8am-midnight, F 8am-1am, Sa-Su 4pm-1am.

DICE BAR   BAR

79 Queen Street, Dublin 2   ☎1 633 3936 www.thatsitdublin.com

"DICE BAR—PHAT JOINT" reads the sign outside. Damn straight. This cooler-than-cool Smithfield bar boasts an all black exterior, a second wave ska soundtrack (think Madness and the Specials, not Reel Big Fish and Sublime), and its very own beer and liquor: the tasty Revolution Red and something called "BATHTUB GIN," respectively. But that relentless air of cool belies its status as a great spot to just hang out and have a few drinks. Massive black leather booths mean that you can come here with a group and be sure you can all sit together (if you show up early enough, that is; on Friday nights, the clientele spills out into the surrounding street).

Perhaps the strangest thing about the Dice Bar, however, is how it changes over the course of an evening. If you swing by at 4pm, an hour after it opens, you're likely to find a group of girls sipping Yellowtail and, at 5pm, you'll find businessmen letting off steam with a couple pints of Guinness. The bartenders may seem slightly aloof, but they're very attentive to what you're ordering and, if you strike up a conversation at a quiet moment, they'll be happy to talk with you. Despite the rock'n'roll vibe, this is a friendly spot.

i Beers £4- £6, Cocktails £7.50 or 2 for £12. Pitchers £11-14. Open M-Th 3pm-midnight, F-Sa 3pm-1am, Su 3-11:30pm.

THE BLACK SHEEP
BAR

61 Capel Street, Dublin 1 ☎1 873 0013 www.galwaybaybrewery.com/blacksheep

The first thing you notice about the Black Sheep is how open it feels. Some bars in Dublin feel less like a social space and more like the Black Hole of Calcutta. But even when the Black Sheep is crowded, you can make your way to the bathroom without bumping into 20 people; even better, the significant distance between tables means you can chat with your friends without getting a sore throat from yelling. But the second thing you'll probably notice—and the thing that will probably keep your attention for the rest of the night—is the bar, which is decorated with hundreds of beer bottles. This is a Galway Bay Bar, so it's got that noted craft brewery's various beers on draught. It's also got a worldwide selection of beers, including Belgium's Delirium Tremens, said by some to be the finest in the world. Some of these varieties will run you a pretty penny—especially if you go for one with a high ABV (alcohol by volume)—but the pints are pretty fairly priced. Those looking for stronger stuff should try a shot of poitín, an Irish alcoholic beverage based on—you guessed it—potatoes. If you're hungry and swing by at an earlier hour, food is served until 9 pm.

i *Beers on draught about £5.50 for a pint; bottled beers £5-10.* 🕐 *Open M-Th, noon-11:30pm. F-Sa noon-12:30am, Su noon-11.30pm.*

THE WORKMAN'S CLUB
CLUB

10 Wellington Quay, Dublin 2 ☎1 670 6692 www.theworkmansclub.com

The Workman's Club is not the place to start your night (like Twister, it's best enjoyed after a few drinks), but it's the perfect place to end it. Though there's a £5 cover charge on Wednesday nights, what you're paying for is access to the space. In many Dublin pubs, you'll get the urge to dance—you're drinking, the Jackson Five just came on the stereo, it's understandable. Normally you need to resist that urge, lest you knock a friendly Irishman's pint of Guinness off the counter and suddenly he isn't so friendly anymore. At the Workman's Club, the spacious rooms on multiple floors allow you to dance the night away—well, until 2:30 am, but that's later than most Dublin establishments stay open.

Be sure to check ahead on the calendar to see if a live band is playing—even if there's not, you can count on DJ sets seven nights a week. If you're looking for nothin' but a good time, classic rock takes center stage on Tuesday nights. If you can't dance to anything that hasn't been approved by Pitchfork, Indie takes precedence on Mondays and Thursdays. So whether you pregame at your hostel, hit up a casual bar, or surreptitiously drink straight whiskey in the streets, make sure your night concludes at the Workman's Club.

i *£5 cover on Wednesday nights. Cocktails £7-9, pints £5-7.* 🕐 *Open daily 5pm-2:30am.*

ESSENTIALS
Practicalities

- **ATMS:** There are a number of 24hr. ATMs near Trinity College Dublin, including two in the Bank of Ireland, adjacent to College Green, and at Ulster Bank, which is across the street from the Bank of Ireland.

- **CURRENCY EXCHANGE:** Dublin City Centre Currency Store. (1 Westmoreland Street, Dublin 1. ☎1 670 6724. Open M-W 9am-6pm, Th-Sa 9am-7pm, Su 10am-7pm.)

- **POST OFFICE:** General Post Office, O'Connell Street Lower, Dublin 1. Also home to the An Post Museum, a small museum devoted to letters and the postal service in Irish history (admission £2). ☎1 705 8833. ~ Open M-Sa 8:30am-6pm.

dublin

- **INTERNET:** Internet Café (8 Lower O'Connell Street, Dublin 1. Offers luggage storage, internet access, and printing capabilities. £1.40 for the first 20min. of surfing. ~ Open M-F 9am-9pm, Sa 9am-8pm, Su 10am-8pm.)

Emergency

Emergency Numbers

- **GENERAL EMERGENCY:** ☎112 or 999.

- **POLICE TRAFFIC HOTLINE:** For reporting aggressive drivers. }353 18 90 205 805.

Hospitals and Pharmacies

- **MATER MISERICORDAE UNIVERSITY HOSPITAL.**

- **MATER MISERICORDAE RAPID INJURY CLINIC. THE FORGE, SMITHFIELD MARKET, DUBLIN 7.** Walk-in service. Treatment provided for non-life-threatening injuries to people over 16. For serious injuries, dial }999 or 112. ☎1 657 9000. ~ Open M-F 8am-6pm.

- **HICKEY'S PHARMACY:** 55 O'Connell Street Lower, Dublin 1. ☎1 873 0427. ~ Open M-F 8am -10pm, Sa 8:30am-10pm, Su 10am-10pm.

- **HAMILTON LONG PHARMACY:** 5 O'Connell Street Lower, Dublin 1. ☎1 874 8456. ~ Open M-F 7:30am-9pm, Sa 9am-9pm, Su noon-9pm.

- **HICKEY'S PHARMACY:** 21 Grafton Street, Dublin 2. ☎1 679 0467. ~ Open M-W 8:30am-8pm, Th 8:30-8:30pm, F 8:30am-8pm, Sa 9:30am-7pm, Su 10:30am-6pm.

belfast

Belfast is in a state of transition. Walking around the city, you'll see vacant lots next to Vespa stores, boarded-up houses next to trendy bars, and derelict storefronts next to hipster restaurants. In other words, Belfast is standing on the verge of gentrification, which means it's one of the most exciting places to visit in the United Kingdom.

With two major universities (one of which boasts a distinguished art school), legions of art galleries, and tons of trendy restaurants and pubs, Belfast is a city where there's always something happening, no matter what the producer of Game of Thrones says. And that's without even mentioning its devotion to history (check out Titanic Belfast or go on a Black Taxi tour), its distinctive churches, or its beautiful tree-lined avenues. Belfast is having a moment, and if the luxury hotels springing up on every corner are any indication, we're not the only ones who think it's about to hit the big time.

SIGHTS

QUEENS FILM THEATRE
THEATER

20 University Square ☎28 9097 1097 www.queensfilmtheatre.com

From the outside, Queen's Film Theatre looks like just another townhouse on University Place, indistinguishable from the numerous academic departments that occupy the others. Step inside, however, and you'll be greeted with a sleek, modern interior. This place has undergone a few renovations since being renovated in 1968.

As an arthouse cinema, Queen's Film Theatre isn't in the business of showing the latest Hollywood blockbusters; get excited for worldwide independent film with a smattering of old classics. The screens aren't IMAX-sized, but are pretty big for theaters of this ilk (at some independent cinemas, you're left in doubt as to whether this is the theater or the owner's living room).

ireland

BELFAST INTERNATIONAL YOUTH HOSTEL
HOSTEL $

22-32 Donegal Road   ☎28 9031 5435   www.hini.org.uk

Belfast has no shortage of quirky small hostels, but it's also got this no-nonsense establishment. Need a cheap bed, a clean shower, and no surprises? Belfast International Youth Hostel has you covered. There's little to no decoration on the walls, there's no pool table or spa, but everything's clean, well-lit, and bland in a pleasant way. Belfast Youth Hostel is where you play it safe—despite the name, there are plenty of older budget travelers, many coming with a family.

The rooms are on the smaller side, but the beds and showers are fairly large—if you've got a guest (wink wink), it shouldn't be a problem. All the rooms have windows, but none of them have a particularly good view (Donegall Street isn't Belfast's most scenic). At least you have some control over the ventilation.

Price-wise, you're not likely to find anything better in Belfast. The low cost is somewhat deceptive, as breakfast is not included—however, the on-site cafe, the Causeway Café, is well-priced and open daily from 7:55am-noon. Eat there and you'll probably still come out on top. The kitchen is open until 11pm daily.

Wi-Fi is available, but only on the ground floor. Luckily, reception is open 24/7 and you'll be able to access the lobby whenever you need to.

i *Dorms start at £10.50, doubles start at £20 per person.* ☑ *Reception open daily 24hr..*

VAGABONDS
HOSTEL $

9 University Road   ☎28 9023 3017   www.vagabondsbelfast.com

The name suggests desperation, but life is sweet at Vagabonds. Situated in a renovated townhouse on University Road, this hostel boasts a beer garden in back, numerous picnic tables in front, and two large common rooms indoors. And the actual bedrooms aren't too small either. Rooms range from a 14 bed dorm (complete with two showers and doors opening directly onto the beer garden) to more intimate privates. Most of the bathrooms are located on the ground floor, meaning you might be walking around the space with your towel—if you track water on the stairs, expect some dirty looks.

While most other hostels end their continental breakfast at 9 or 9:30am, Vagabonds keeps it going until 11am. If you end up getting back late from a Belfast pub crawl, you won't be starving next morning. In addition, the hostel keeps a chef on staff; for an added fee, you can get Italian dinners there nightly (lasagna goes for $4.50). Given these amenities, the vast amount of common space, and the size of their TV and pool table, we're not entirely convinced that the staff of Vagabonds wants you to explore the city; there's so much fun stuff going on at the hostel! They do, of course, offer promotions for several of Belfast's most popular tours and day-trip buses.

While there's no curfew, the reception closes around 9. Someone will be in the office 24/7, but be sure to call ahead if you're going to be later than nine; they'll be happy to keep the office open for you.

i *Dorms start at £13; privates start at £40.* ☑ *Reception open daily 9am-9pm; call ahead if you need to check in later.*

Still, the Queen's Film Theatre isn't just a place to watch movies. Though alcohol's not allowed in the theater, be sure to enjoy a pre-show drink at the well-stocked bar—there are a variety of beers from the local Hilden Brewery, as well as several whiskeys and other spirits (Jameson is a sponsor). The cafe area is worth hanging out in if only to look at the tables, all of which are individually decorated. Of particular note is the *Twin Peaks* table, which features black-and-white drawings of all the various characters on David Lynch's cult TV show.

i The theatre is located in the Queen's Quarter, near the university. Walk south down Botanic Road and take a left onto University Square; the theatre will be on your left. £4 per ticket. ☒ Box office opens at 6pm nightly.

ST. MALACHY'S CHURCH
CHURCH
24 Alfred Street ☎28 9032 1713 www.saintmalachys.ie

You've never seen a church quite like Saint Malachy's. Built between 1841 and 1844 , this Tudor Revival marvel is as lavish as they come. With an altarpiece featuring three massive oil paintings, a ceiling inspired by Henry VII's chapel at Westminster Abbey, and the biggest belfry in Belfast (try saying that three times fast), Saint Malachy's will damned near knock your socks off. In fact, it was supposed to be even bigger, but it was decided that mounting such a big project wasn't a great idea while Irish people were suffering due to the potato famine. All things considered, this was probably the right call—the initial plans called for the church to be a massive cathedral that would seat 7,000.

Given its size, it's not surprising the bell caused a few headaches over the years (we mean that literally and figuratively). When it was first installed, Dunville's, a nearby whiskey distillery complained—apparently the peals of the bell were affecting the distilling process, which lead to the bell being muffled with fabric. Alternative theory: everyone who had been drinking whiskey on Saturday night had a massive headache and couldn't bear the sound.

The church is located in the Linen Quarter, just a few minutes from City Hall. Walk towards the waterfront on Donegal Square South, which will turn into May Street. Then take a right and walk down Alfred Street. The church will be on your left.

i Free.

ULSTER MUSEUM
MUSEUM
Botanic Gardens ☎845 608 0000 www.nmni.com/um

It's not ridiculous to assume that the Ulster Museum is a small institution devoted to local history, much like the Clare Museum or the Galway City Museum. There's certainly local history here—check out the harrowing exhibit about the Troubles—but the Ulster Museum is far broader and stranger than that. The ground floor includes an exhibit designed to showcase the museum's breadth; on display are butterfly specimens, dinosaur bones, tableware from the early 1800s, an Ancient Egyptian stone carving, and Louboutin shoes. It's like every branch of the Smithsonian—art, history, natural history, anthropology—rolled into one deeply eclectic museum.

But the museum doesn't just display weird objects and ask you to make sense of them (ok, maybe they do on the ground floor exhibit). The place is filled with televisions showing short films about the items on display, allowing you to contextualize everything from woolly mammoth tusks to medieval relics. There are also interactive portions—don't you want to construct your own megalithic tomb?

Highlights include a massive skeleton of the Irish giant deer, old cannonballs and cannons from the Spanish Armada, and Takabuti, a well-preserved mummy that was the first to be brought to Ireland. There are also tons of rotating exhibitions, which only serve to highlight the diverse nature of the exhibitions at the Ulster.

Just as strange as the museum is the gift shop, which features shirts designed by the THAW Factory. You'll find t-shirts depicting such imaginary food brands as "Padraig Pearse Pasta Sauce" and "Border Butter Beans," all laced with imagery of the Irish Civil War and the Troubles. Let's just say it's a one-of-a-kind souvenir.

If you're in Belfast's City Centre, just walk South towards Queen's University Belfast; walk on University Road, which goes in front of the college, and the Ulster Museum will be on your left, along with the Botanic Gardens.

i *Free, suggested donation £3.* ☼ *Open Tu-Su 10am-5pm.*

TITANIC BELFAST   MUSEUM

1 Queens Road, Titanic Quarter   ☎28 9076 6399 www.titanicbelfast.com

The Titanic was one of the biggest disasters of the 20th century, but when James Cameron made *Titanic* in 1997, it belatedly became one of the world's biggest moneymakers (the film has grossed over $2 billion, and that doesn't account for the effect it had on the tissue industry). Belfast, where the Titanic was built in the early 20th century, has cashed in on this trend with Titanic Belfast, a museum opened in 2012. If the £15 admission didn't tip you off, this is a wholly commercial venture; and in fact, the area surrounding the center has been designated "Titanic Quarter" to aid development.

All profit motives aside, the museum is a thrilling experience—the various galleries immerse you in Belfast's shipbuilding past, take you to the bottom of the ocean floor (the museum projects Dr. Robert Ballard's high-definition footage of the ship's wreck), and clear up numerous myths about the boat and its sinking. There's also a reproduction of the ship's famous staircase, so be sure to dress up and get a picture. Of course, there's also a massive gift shop, where you can get any sort of clothing or accessory with the word "TITANIC" emblazoned on it. We hope that's not a comment on its structural integrity. We just have one question about the commemorative glasses—is it safe to put ice in them?

The museum is slightly removed from Belfast's city center, though it's certainly walkable. If you're coming from Town Hall, walk East towards the Lagan, then walk along the river until you get to Queens Bridge. Take a left on the other bank and walk past the W5; you'll get to the Titanic eventually.

i *£15.50. £7.25 for children 5-16. Free for children under 5. £10 for students during the week, £11 during the weekend. £11 for seniors during the week, £13 during the weekend.* ☼ *Open daily Apr 9am-7pm, May 9am-6pm, Jun-Aug 9am-7pm, Nov-Mar 10am-5pm. Last admission is 1hr. 40min. before closing.*

FOOD

MADE IN BELFAST   RESTAURANT $$

23 Talbot Street   ☎28 9024 4107 www.madeinbelfastni.com

Walk into Made in Belfast on Talbot Street, and you might think you've stepped into one of Belfast's many thrift shops. With its artfully curated vintage furniture and bizarre decor (yes, those are men's hats hanging from the ceiling; and, yes, that's a giant statue of a pink ostrich), Made in Belfast looks like the set of a Wes Anderson movie. The food is served in a manner that's just as strange—order the pulled pork sandwich and you'll get three slices of bread plus a jar filled with pulled pork—but what's strangest of all is how darned good it is. Inventive yet traditional, the cuisine at Made in Belfast is as flavorful and delicious as you're likely to find in the entire city. There's a big emphasis on sustainability here—several items on the menu, such as the "sustainable seafood chowder," make a point of it—so don't feel bad about ordering any meat products. They were almost certainly raised humanely.

The downside to Made in Belfast being so good is that they know it—the meals aren't cheap, though the lunch menu is fairly reasonable. In addition, there are several promotions. If you go here and save your receipt, you can get 10% off at their sister restaurant, the fried chicken-centric "Le Coop" (we wonder if they have beef—or chicken, rather—with Crackbird, a similarly hipster fried chicken joint in Dublin). And if you go on any day between Sunday and Wednesday, the cocktails are only £3.50. Pick one of these babies up and take a selfie—you could win a dinner for two.

i £10-12 for lunch, £14-18 for dinner. ☺ Open M-W 11am-9:30pm, Th-F 11am-10pm, Sa 10am-10pm, Su 10am-9pm.

ROCKET & RELISH   RESTAURANT $$
479-481 Lisburn Road   ☎28 90 665 655 www.rocketandrelish.com

Lisburn Road can take you far away from Belfast City Centre, but Rocket & Relish is worth the trek. This gourmet burger joint isn't about simplicity—all of its burgers come with various toppings—but it never lets complexity get in the way of quality. Their cranberry and brie burger might be the best, but the myriad others are all worth a try. If you're a vegetarian or just don't relish (haha, relish—get it?) the thought of eating red meat, they have veggie and chicken burgers available. Pair one of these suckers with a big frothy milkshake and it's like you're getting geared up for the coolest sock hop of all time. No alcohol's served on the premises, but there's also no corkage charge. That means that you should take advantage of the numerous off-licences along Lisburn Road—grab a six-pack or a bottle of wine and you'll be set.

But even though it's a takeaway burger joint, Rocket & Relish allows for a dining experience far beyond that of McDonald's. If you're sitting in, expect full table service. You'll also get the chance to admire the artfully sleek dining area, complete with vintage red metal chairs and cult film posters on the wall: "This is Spinal Tap," "Bottle Rocket," that kind of thing (haha, rocket—get it?). Best of all, the outdoor seating area in front is filled with Astroturf—these so-called beer gardens need to step up their game.

It's a truly welcoming atmosphere; if you've ordered burgers for takeaway, they've got a little waiting room set up for you, complete with couches and magazines. Now that's customer service.

i Burgers about £7 for 6oz. patties, £10 for 12 oz patties. Open M-Th 11:30am-9pm, F-Sa 11:30am-10pm, Su 1-9pm.

ALLEYCAT   RESTAURANT $
Church Lane   ☎28 9023 3282 www.alleycatbelfast.com

It's located just a block away from the Victoria Square Shopping Centre, but Alleycat feels like it's in a different world. "Thick Shakes — Proper Burgers — Craft Beers — Bourbon" reads the sign outside, and that non-nonsense attitude carries over tho the interior. There are three main areas: the restaurant portion, where the seating is mainly in booths; the bar area, with a mix of stools, booths, and tables (don't worry, you can get food here too), and the upstairs lounge, fully equipped with tables and a bar of its own. If you're out on the town and need some grub (and it's before 11pm, when they stop serving food), you'd be well advised to check out the upstairs area. It's generally quieter than the rest of the join, which means you'll get to eat your mozzarella sticks in piece while enjoying their generous (if slightly pricy) craft beer selection.

But Alleycat is worth visiting at any time of day, namely for its energetic take on comfort food staples: burgers, chicken wings, hot dogs, chili fries, and shakes (virgin and alcoholic) are all on the menu. There are no reservations, but plenty of deals; if you opt for takeaway, it's 10% off, and students get 20% off on Monday, Tuesday, and Wednesday. The one problem? That darn cat (obsession). The menu is filled with cat puns ("not a cat person? try our hot dogs!"), there are pictures of cats all over, and one of the hard shakes is named "Cat Nip." On the plus side, there's free Wi-Fi—all the better to check out some "I Can Haz Cheezburger" memes. Come to think of it, we're shocked that's not their motto.

i Starters from £4-6, mains from £7-8. 🍽 Food served daily noon-11pm. Bar open until 1am.

FRENCH VILLAGE CAFÉ
RESTAURANT $$

99 Botanic Avenue ☎28 9031 3248 www.frenchvillagebakery.co.uk

The first thing you have to understand about the French Village Café is that it's a family business, and the family's name is French. In other words, this isn't a knockoff of a Parisian bistro—this is a 100% Belfast original, and has been since 1981. Whether you're looking for a sit down meal or a sandwich to take to the nearby Botanic Gardens, French Village Café has you covered.

The menu is unapologetically bread-centric—this was founded as a bakery—which means one thing above all else: they've got some great sandwiches. For £2, you can pair any of these bad boys with a mug of soup and your choice of French fries (of course they've got more than one variety). And the soups, which change regularly, go far beyond tomato, pea, and chicken noodle. Check out their hearty cauliflower and chorizo blend. And if a restaurant that doubles as a bakery strikes fear into the heart of coeliacs, let it be known that gluten-free options are readily available.

Though it's certainly not a flashy establishment, the French Village Café's low-key style makes it one of the most attractive restaurants in Belfast: brick exterior, wood and tile walls on the inside, rustic wooden tables. As always, it's the little things that make the difference—check out the cushions on the back booths, which are covered in burlap sacks.

The prettiest part of the whole place, however, might well be the outdoor seating area, with its views of the tree-lined Botanic Avenue. Enjoy your meal with some wine as the sun goes down—with a corkage charge of £1.50, the price is right.

i Breakfast £4-7, sandwiches about £5, entrees £7 for lunch, £10-12 for dinner. 🕐 Open M-F 7:30am-8pm, Sa-Su 9am-6pm.

BRIDGE HOUSE
RESTAURANT S$

35-43 Bedford Street ☎28 9072 7890

www.jdwetherspoon.co.uk/home/pubs/the-bridge-house

The Bridge House is where you go with a big group of friends. The meals are cheap, most of them come with a drink (alcoholic, no less), and the big tables can suit as big a group as you could like. It's also got a great location—just a couple of blocks away from City Hall, it's situated right in between many of Belfast's hostels and the cool bars north of City Hall—the late nightclub Limelight is also exceedingly close.

The food covers pub classics, Irish cuisine, burgers, salads, paninis, and even a few Indian dishes (if you count chicken tikka masala). Everything is ordered at the bar, so your relationship with the wait staff might be a little impersonal; still, the employees are friendly and willing to answer questions about the menu or beer list.

Those great prices carry over to the alcoholic options. Unlike most of Belfast's bars, the Bridge House will rarely charge more than £4 for a pint; most cost about £3. Even better are their pitcher deals; most go for about £12 or £11, but you can get any 2 for £15. Best of all: Pimm's, the classic British fruit cup, is sold in pitchers for £6.65. If strawberry daiquiris or mojitos are a little too wimpy for you, then spend an extra £3 and they'll add two additional shots of alcohol to your pitcher.

The space is fairly nondescript—you've got wall to wall carpeting, fairly low ceilings, and a small outdoor seating area—but it doesn't matter when you've got great company and cheap eats.

i *£5 for sandwiches and starters, £7-10 for mains. £3-4 for pints.* ☑ *Open M-Th 8am-midnight, F-Sa 8am-1am, Su 8am-midnight.*

NIGHTLIFE

APARTMENT
CLUB

2 Donegall Square West   ☎28 9050 9777 www.apartmentbelfast.com

Unlike Dublin's notorious Bar with No Name, Apartment doesn't resemble an actual apartment. Unless your apartment is a duplex with three bars and a restaurant area (zoning is a mess these days). But with its floor-to-ceiling window views of Belfast City Hall, you'll wish it was one and that you lived there. You'll find plenty of well-dressed young urban professionals sipping cocktails—the list is quite extensive—and chilling out after a long day's work. And let's face it—there's no better place to kick back. With big couches, dark wooden walls, and a surprisingly well-priced food menu, the Apartment is both classy and relaxed. And those views of City Hall sure don't hurt.

The music is loud but not overpowering. Despite the size, there's no space for dancing, but if you hear a song you love (the soundtrack is generally '80s-themed) you can definitely hold a singalong at your table. Still, the Apartment is generally not the place to go crazy on the dance floor (namely because it doesn't even have a dance floor). Stop by on a late afternoon or before you hit up some other pubs—you'll have some great conversation before going crazy elsewhere.

i *Cocktails £6; pints £4.*

LOVE & DEATH INC.
BAR

10a Anne Street   ☎28 9024 7222 www.loveanddeathinc.com

If you think cocktails are for old fogeys and the girls on "Sex and the City" (Cosmopolitans, anyone?), then one visit to the ultra-cool Love and Death Inc. will change your opinion. In this self-proclaimed "cocktail speakeasy, eatery, music hall," the list of drinks comes in a comic book-style menu and covers everything from classics like gin and tonics to more extravagant drinks like the Devil in a Red Gown (vodka, berry cordial, lemon juice, raspberry and kumquat jelly, egg white, and balsamic vinegar; don't knock it until you try it!). On Friday or Saturday nights, you might find yourself having to wait a few minutes before you order, but the talented staff will whip up your cocktail ridiculously quickly.

They'll also be happy to send food orders down to their kitchen. Though it'll be difficult to grab a table during peak hours, the menu is served all day—stop by for lunch or in the late afternoon and you'll have no problem. The mac and cheese is especially worth checking out.

Once you've got your drink and your grub, take a step back and appreciate the shabby-chic decor. The walls and tables are covered with bright turquoise tiles, while the wooden floors are charmingly rustic. On the walls, you've got posters of Johnny Cash, the Beatles, and Led Zeppelin; from the ceiling hang old records, action figures, and a bicycle.

If you like cocktails and hate comic books—hate everything that's happened since the 1920s, in fact—then head on over to Love & Death Inc's sister bar, Aether & Echo, a prohibition-inspired joint. And don't worry—the gin wasn't made in a bathtub.

i *£6-10 for cocktails, £3-5 for pints.* ☑ *Open M-W noon-1am, Th-Sa noon-3am, Su 1pm-midnight.*

THE HUDSON

10-14 Gresham Street   ☎28 9023 2322 www.hudsonbelfast.com

BAR

You'll find a lot of places in Belfast that cater to beer geeks (the words "craft beer" seem to pop up on every third bar), but the best of them is the Hudson. The beers on draught are always changing, there are always promotions (they give discounts on Belgian beer during the World Cup), and the knowledgeable staff is quick to provide samples of unfamiliar brews. Trust us—there will be quite a few of these. Don't be swayed by the Guinness ads on the walls; it's far from the best thing on tap, sacrilegious as that may sound.

During the weekends, you'll also find a few spirits nerds: on Fridays and Saturdays, the bar offers 99 different whiskeys, taken from all around the world. Now this is globalization that we can get behind.

The atmosphere inside is decidedly laid back: floral wallpaper and Tiffany-style lamps will do that. The mood is mellow even during Thursday's weekly trad sessions—no drunker rave-ups to be found here, though that means you'll actually get to listen to the music.

Outside, the feel palpably changes: the Hudson has a massive beer garden, and the fact that it's surrounded by residential apartments doesn't seem to stop people from having a rowdily good time. Make sure you've got a few pounds on you, however—the outdoor bar is cash only.

i £4-£5.50 for pints. ☒ Open M-W 11:30-1am, Th-Sa 11:30-2am, Su noon-midnight.

CUCKOO

149 Lisburn Road   ☎28 9066 7776 www.facebook.com/cuckoobelfast

CLUB

To put it lightly, Cuckoo is over the top. There are three main floors and what seems like multitudes of mezzanines. There are chairs made from barrels (surprisingly comfortable) and couches with Egyptian hieroglyphs on them. Its dance floor has more disco balls than it knows what to do with. There's a giant statue of an angry ostrich, a television that's always showing movies like *Fear and Loathing in Las Vegas*, and a cocktail menu based on bizarre movie characters (try the "Ace Ventura" or the "Stifler's Mom"). But when that self-consciously weird vibe is combined with a kick-ass selection of beers and liquor, the result is unstoppable. So it is with Cuckoo.

Given its massive space, this is the place to go with a large group. But if you're traveling alone or with only one or two friends, Cuckoo is still the place to get down—there's always something going on here. This place has more events than college orientation week. There's a pub quiz Monday nights, open mics on Wednesdays (performers get two free beers, so keep this in mind if you're trying to save cash), ping pong tournaments on Thursdays… the list goes on and on. And no matter what night of the week you swing by, you'll be able to enjoy a great beer and check out their vast collection of games: air hockey, foosball, pinball, and the early arcade game Space Invaders are all up for grabs. And, of course, there's the main selling point: the ping pong tables on the uppermost level. If you grew up playing beer pong in some suburban basement, this will really bring you back; however, the craft beers available at Cuckoo surely trump whatever swill you were underage drinking back then.

i £3-4 for pints and shots. £2 drinks on "Cheapskate Tuesdays." ☒ Open M-Th 2pm-midnight, F-Sa noon-1am, Su 2pm-midnight.

THE DIRTY ONION

3 Hill Street   ☎28 9024 3712 www.thedirtyonion.com

BAR

The Dirty Onion proudly notes that they're housed in one of Belfast's oldest buildings (18th century ain't nothing to scoff at; for all you geniuses out there, that means the 1700s). But tradition isn't their main selling point—this is a bar, not a museum. And a party bar at that. The outdoor space is perhaps the

belfast

biggest in Belfast, and it's surely one of the most distinctive. Hemmed in by big, concrete walls, the beer garden is so shabby-chic that you might think people are throwing a party in a vacant lot. Muscle through the crowds and you'll see the bar; you'll also catch a glimpse of the second part of the beer garden, which exists under the original wooden frame of a 19th-century structure. Be careful where you drop your cigarettes—if you don't smoke, you'll think that you do after walking through the nicotine-happy crowd.

Inside, the atmosphere is much more traditional. The lighting's dim, the tables are long, Guinness is on draught, and there are posters for Luis Buñuel's surrealist film "Un Chien Andalou" on the walls. OK, maybe that last part's a little different. But in a good way, of course.

Also on the premises is Yardbird, a roast chicken restaurant just a staircase away from the action. You may want to scarf a few wings down before you hit the bar—it's never safe to drink on an empty stomach. Also, the chicken's delicious.

i £3-4 for a pint. ☼ Open M-Sa noon-1am, Su noon-midnight.

ESSENTIALS
Practicalities

- **CASH:** There are ATMs left and right in Belfast. There are two in Europa Bus Centre, accessible M-Sa 5am-10:45pm, Su 6am-10:30pm. If your bus gets in outside of those hours and you need cash, there's a Danske Bank directly outside Europa Bus Centre, on Great Victoria Street; this is open 24/7. There is also an Ulster Bank ATM at the Botanic Road train station. While others are scattered throughout town, one central locale with a lot of ATMs is Donegal Square; you'll find cash machines on the North, South, East, and West sides.

- **POST OFFICE:** The main one is at 12-16 Bridge Street; amenities include foreign currency exchange. Open from 9-5:30 M, W-Sa; open from 9:30-5:30 T.

- **INTERNET CAFES:** Browsers Internet Cafe, 77 Dublin Road, M-Sa 10am-9pm, Su 10am-8pm. ☎28 9032 2272.

Emergency

- **PHARMACIES:** Urban Pharmacy, 56 Dublin Road, M-F 8am-8pm, Sa 9am-5:30pm, Su 1-5:30pm. ☎28 9024 6336. Boots Pharmacy, 35-47 Donegal Place, M-W, F 8am-7pm, Th 8am-9pm, Sa 8:30-7pm, Su 1-6pm. ☎28 9024 2332.

- **HOSPITALS:** Belfast City Hospital, 51 Lisburn Road, ☎28 9032 9241. In an emergency, dial 112 or 999.

Getting Around

Somewhat confusingly, Belfast's main bus system is called the Metro. Don't think about it too much. Tickets can be purchased at the Donegall Square West Metro kiosk, which is where many of the routes begin. If you want a taxi, your best bet is Fona Cab (fonacab.com; ☎28 9033 3333). The lowest rates is £2.50 for the first 0.1 miles, then £1.25 per every additional mile. You won't want to take a road trip, but if your pub crawl ended way too far from your hostel, this is the way to go.

galway

A river runs through Galway. That's not so significant, you think. What European city doesn't have a river? Didn't they found these old places specifically because of where the river was? But Galway is really defined by the river—the city is located where the Corrib feeds into Galway Bay, and certain portions are carved up by canals, dams, and water locks. Because of this, Galway feels more maritime than most Irish port cities.

It also feels a lot more bohemian than most Irish cities—that's thanks to the large student population (NUI Galway has its campus here). There's lots to explore, from craft beer bars to daunting secondhand bookshops. And if exploring's your thing, be sure to take a day trip out to the more rural regions of County Galway. All in all, this college town is worth visiting even if it wasn't your alma mater. You'll be just as fond after a weekend.

SIGHTS

CONNEMARA NATIONAL PARK

PARK

☎7 610 0252 www.connemaranationalpark.ie

Galway City lacks open spaces on the order of Dublin's massive Phoenix Park, but County Galway is home to the sprawling Connemara National Park, which covers over 7,000 acres. If you feel like you need to get away from it all, this is where you head. The main attraction are the four hiking trails, one of which takes you to the very top of Diamond Hill (400m up, and with a view to match anything you've seen in).

If you're the sort who always thought views looked better on postcards, Connemara National Park has more to offer than just scenery. The park is home to many different kinds of wildlife, including the striking Connemara ponies; resist the urge to ride one. You can also retire to the tea rooms and enjoy some drinks and pastries; shelter has its perks, you know?

Getting there, however is kind of a hassle. You'll most likely need to take a tour bus (it'll run you about £20), as the public transportation is limited and infrequent. If you've rented a car or somehow have access to one (no, we are not endorsing grand theft auto), the route is fairly straightforward. Take the N59 to Recess, then take a right and drive down the Inagh Valley, then turn left for Letterfrack. Drive through Letterfrack and you'll come to the visitor center. And to top it all off, there's free parking. If only that was enough to justify the cost of the rental car.

i *Free—even parking!* 🕐 *Visitor center is open daily Mar-May 10am-5:30pm, 9:30am-6:30pm Jun-Aug, Sept-Oct 10am-5:30pm.*

QUAY STREET

STREET

Quay Street

With its cobblestoned streets, traditional pubs, and hostels, Quay Street is Galway's equivalent of Temple Bar. But don't let that association with Dublin's infamous district keep you away; Quay Street is one of the most charming alleys in Galway. Despite its small size—you can walk up and down its entirely in about five minutes—it's got tons of restaurants, bars, and unique stores.

One of the most popular establishment is the Quays, a bar with an interior designed to look like a ship. If you take a visit and start feeling seasick, it's probably time to lay off the Guinness.

Other highlights include McDonagh's, a restaurant that's been serving unbelievable fish and chips since 1902; Fat Freddy's, a pizza joint that's known as a date spot; and Martine's, a restaurant with the coveted domain name of "winebar.ie."

KINLAY HOUSE HOSTEL GALWAY

HOSTEL $

Merchants Road, Eyre Square ☎91 565 244 www.kinlaygalway.ie

Height makes a big difference. Kinlay Galway would be a good hostel even if it wasn't three flights off the ground, but the simple fact of having to climb up a giant staircase or taking an elevator ride (the staircase is truly massive; we highly recommend you take the elevator) lends it an air of elegance. It doesn't hurt that every room has a great view, be it of the surrounding street or of the hostel's courtyard.

Kinlay Galway doesn't offer anything truly out of the ordinary, but its rendition of the usual amenities is always more than just the usual. Galway's pubs might close early, but the Kinlay Galway lobby is open until four a.m., and the staff is perfectly happy to let you drink beer with your friends—just as long as you're not too rowdy or loud. Like a lot of hostels, they have computers you can use to access your email and such; unlike a lot of hostels, they have Macs. The continental breakfast is much bigger than most (scones, muesli, and different varieties of jam are all up for grabs), which is all the better for your lunch (not that we'd ever suggest you stuff a few slices of bread in your pocket).

Ensuite bathrooms aren't guaranteed, but the hall bathrooms are large and usually have more showers, meaning you won't be standing in your towel waiting for strangers to finish cleaning themselves. The dorms aren't the largest, but a ten-man that just opened provides a lot of living space; don't fear the thought of living with nine strangers in a room like this.

i £17 a night for dorms, £20 for weekends. £26 for privates. ☺ Reception open 24/7.

SAVOY HOSTEL

HOSTEL $$

Eglinton Street, across from the main post office ☎91 375 421 www.galwayhostel.ie

The wall-to-wall carpeting in this hostel may remind you of *The Shining*, but the Savoy Hostel offers a lot more "play" than the Overlook Hotel (though if you need to work, they do offer Wi-Fi and computer access). The basement common space could conceivably fit all the hostel guests at once (we haven't double-checked this with the fire department) and makes space for numerous tables, couches, and a large kitchen. The one downside: no windows, which sort of puts a damper on the bright color scheme.

The rooms, however, are well-lit and exceptionally clean. With their abundance of space furniture (there's a chair for each bed in the room, just in case you all need to sit down and have a roommate talk or something), they feel more like hotel rooms than your average hostel dorm. Hotel rooms with multiple beds and big lockers, but hotel rooms nonetheless. The best part are the ensuite bathrooms—these are some of the nicest (and biggest) showers that you'll encounter in Irish hostels. If you forget your towel, you can rent one from reception for €2. Rooms go up to six beds, and privates are also available.

Like most hostels, they offer a free continental breakfast. If you want something more filling (what, you got a problem with corn flakes or something?), they've got a deal with a local hotel that allows you to get a full Irish breakfast for €5. Not too shabby.

i Dorms £18 on weekdays, £23 on weekends; privates from £28. ☺ Reception 24hr.

Since this portion of Galway is closed to cars, pedestrians flood Quay Street most days. Many restaurants and pubs offer outdoor seating, so grab a table and check out the human parade. You'll also have a great spot for listening to Galway's many buskers. If the weather's not ideal, many of the pubs have trad sessions regularly (surprise, surprise), so you'll still be able to take in some live music.

Quay Street is located just a couple blocks from Galway's city centre; the surrounding districts are also worth checking out. Walking towards the bay, you'll come to the Spanish Arch section of Galway, named after a surviving portion of Galway's city walls. Here, you'll find the Galway City Museum.

GALWAY CATHEDRAL
CHURCH

☎9 156 3577 www.galwaycathedral.ie

You'll be able to see the Galway Cathedral's distinctive green dome from a lot of places in Galway, and maybe that's why they decided to build it in 1965; a prison stood there previously, and it must have gotten awful depressing to stare at that all day.

Since it was built in the '60s, Galway Cathedral isn't exactly a medieval artifact (one look at the stylized stained glass windows will tell you that), but that doesn't mean it's not an intriguing piece of architecture. The space inside is vast and cavernous—you'll be resisting the urge to yell "echo." If you're wearing rain boots, they will almost certainly squeak on the marble floors. As big as the cathedral is, there's only one bathroom—and it's specifically designated for those attending services.

Masses, which occur fairly regularly, are the one obstacle to viewing the cathedral; you're not supposed to circulate while they're in progress. If you end up doing so anyway, the church also offers regular confession hours.

Over the summer, the Cathedral hosts concerts that make use of its massive organ, installed in the '60s and renovated just a few years ago. Unlike the experience of viewing the cathedral, these are not free; £12 for regular tickets, and £10 for students, seniors, and the like. You can also check out their bookshop, which sells religious books alongside other souvenirs.

Getting there is pretty easy—just look for the dome and walk towards it!

i Free, suggested donation £2. Open daily 8:30am-6:30pm.

GALWAY CITY MUSEUM
MUSEUM

Spanish Parade ☎9 153 2460 www.galwaycitymuseum.ie

When you get to Galway, you may have a couple questions. What exactly is a Galway Hooker? What were those giant stones we saw on the drive into the city? And what's this Spanish Arch everyone keeps talking about? All these questions (and many more) can be answered at the Galway City Museum, which is devoted to...ok, do we really need to spell it out for you? Yes, it's about the history of Galway. If all the talk about Galway's fishing industry makes you hungry, you can get a meal at the museum's restaurant, the Kitchen, which is located on the ground floor.

Though there are plenty of artifacts from neolithic times (most of them on loan from the National Museum of Ireland), the exhibits on more recent history are also worth checking out. The room about Galway's musical history is particularly interesting. Here you can see such artifacts as a 1980 U2 poster, old dresses worn to dance-halls, and suits worn by the Royal Showband. The dresses are all right, but you'll be hard pressed to believe these guys actually wore the suits. Luckily, there are vintage pictures (and record covers!) to prove it. In addition to these historical exhibits, the museum features rotating art exhibits; works are generally by local artists, though there are occasional loans from the other museums in Ireland.

galway

Getting there is a piece of cake; just walk down Quay Street, then take a left instead of crossing the Corrib via Father Griffin Road. Walk through the Spanish Arch and the museum will be on your left.

i Free. ☼ Open Tu-Sa 10am-5pm, Su noon-5pm.

FOOD

MCDONAGH'S
22 Quay Street

SEAFOOD $

☎9 156 5001 www.mcdonaghs.net

If you happen to stumble into McDonagh's without knowing what they serve, you won't be in the dark for long. There's a swordfish head sticking out of the wall, there's a fake lobster in a lobster trap, there are paintings of ships every way you turn, and there seem to be barnacles everywhere. This is a seafood joint, one where you can order anything from cod to stingray. Dubious about the latter option? McDonagh's has been in business since 1902; they know exactly what they're doing. They wouldn't be able to sell commemorative t-shirts if they didn't.

Indeed, the fish and chips is renowned for being some of the best in Galway, if not all in Ireland. Since it's just a few minutes away from the docks of Galway Bay, you'd be hard-pressed to find fresher specimens. And the chips ain't half bad either.

If you've got time for a full meal, grab a seat in the restaurant area. The menu is predictably seafood-centric (baked cod, roast scallops, smoked salmon, grilled mackerel), but you can also order a steak if you've got some weird anti-pescatarian thing going on. Rest assured that you can get fish and chips in this area too.

If it's a nice day, be sure to grab one of the tables outside. McDonagh's is located at the very end of pedestrian-heavy Quay Street, giving you the perfect opportunity to people watch while you chow down on some chowder. These tables go quickly, however, so come by early if you want to beat the rush.

i £6-7 for fish, £2.70 for chips. ☼ Open M-Sa noon-11pm, Su 2-10pm.

UPSTAIRS AT MCCAMBRIDGE'S
38-39 Shop Street

RESTAURANT $$

☎9 156 2259 www.mccambridges.com

Most general stores don't have high-quality restaurants attached to them, but McCambridge's isn't your typical general store. The shop was founded in 1925, and has become a Galway institution in the time since; though the restaurant was only opened a couple years back, it's quickly approaching a similar status. On any given afternoon, you're likely to see people waiting on the stairs leading up to McCambridge's, as if they're waiting for St. Peter to open the door to heaven. Okay, maybe it's not that good, but the food at Upstairs at McCambridge's is definitely good enough to wait for.

The menu is eclectic, featuring everything from venison to quesadillas. Dish for dish, the most appealing is the Sunday brunch menu, which features a wide variety of omelets and pancakes (not to mention prawns).

The large windows give you a great view of Galway's streets, though you might be more captivated by the awe-inspiring wine cabinet. And if the bar looks familiar, that's probably because it's taken from the set of the film "Titanic." And you thought Belfast had a monopoly on that kind of thing.

The general store is worth checking out for its beer and liquor selection alone; the wines are global, and the beer fridge includes bottles by revered brewers like Mikkeller. If you don't have time for a sit-down meal, grab a sandwich at the takeaway bar downstairs.

i Entrees £10-11; brunch £6-7. ☼ Open M-W 9am-5:30pm, Th-Sa 9am-10pm, Su 10:30am-6pm.

CREOLE

49 Lower Dominick Street   ☎9 189 5926 www.creole.ie

Lower Dominick Street is full of trendy and upscale restaurants (and then, somewhat confusingly, there's Apache Pizza, possibly the worst chain in Ireland), but Creole stands out from the pack with its hearty take on Cajun classics—you're not going to find another place like this in Galway. Steak, baby back ribs, and gumbo are all on the menu, along with more Irish staples like baked potatoes. Get excited to chow down with some seriously flavorful food, whether you're going for dinner or Sunday brunch. The idea of a Cajun-themed restaurant in Galway is unlikely, but the strength of the food erases any doubts you might have. Just as good as the main courses are the desserts—key lime pie, donuts, and mud pie may not be great for your heart, but they'll certainly make your stomach feel good.

The decor is spare but sets the tone well—there are masks and brass band instruments on the walls, and each table has a miniature cactus. The sole misstep is the gaudy chandelier—just don't look up and it'll be fine. The music is mellow but funky; expect to hear jazz and classic soul instrumentals. The beer and wine selection is small but tastefully curated. Somewhat improbably, the venue hosts hen and stag parties; we're sure they don't get too out of hand.

i *Lunch £8-9, dinner £16-20. ☑ Open M-Sa noon-10pm, Su 1-10pm.*

NIGHTLIFE

THE SALTHOUSE

Ravens Terrace   ☎9 144 1550 www.galwaybaybrewery.com/salthouse

Like many pubs in Ireland, the Salthouse has an Irish flag on its ceiling. Alongside it are two other flags: one for Brooklyn Brewery, and one for Sierra Nevada. If the 23 beers on tap didn't tip you off, this is a place for people who care about beer. Spend a little bit of time here, and you'll quickly become one of those people.

Even though the Salthouse is owned by the Galway Bay Brewery (all of their beers are on tap), its range reaches far beyond the burgeoning Irish craft beer scene. The selection is truly international: Belgium, the United States, Germany, and other brewing stalwarts are well represented. Despite the small size of the bar—there's only room for about eight or nine people to sit at the counter—there are several bartenders working at all times, which may seem excessive until you realize these people aren't just here to serve you drinks, they're here to help you navigate the imposing selection. Ask them what's good and they'll respond "well, what do you like? Ales, lagers, stouts?" You're in good hands here. Keep an eye out for the specials, many of which actually offer a deal: a bottle of Mikkeler for £5, for instance, which is better than you'll see in some off-licences.

The space itself is fairly small, but a stone fireplace and eclectic decorations add to the homey atmosphere. Unlike many pubs in Ireland, you won't hear any music—just the happy roar of conversation. On a Friday night, people will spill out underneath the small awning in front, having a smoke or just getting some fresh air as they enjoy their beers.

i *Most pints are between £4 and £5, though certain brews can cost up to £9.*

THE BLUE NOTE

3 William Street   ☎9 158 9116 twitter.com/BlueNoteGalway

Though Galway doesn't lack for clubs, this is where the serious dancing goes on. With real DJ's on hand (yes, the type that actually spin vinyl records), the Blue Note serves up a potent mix of vintage soul, funk, and R&B tracks. There might be some vague antipathy towards modern music (the tip jar is labelled "Justin Bieber Assassination Fund), but that hardly matters when the DJ's playing classic Motown tracks. The dance floor isn't massive, but there's ample space for you to strut your stuff. Even if you don't go for the dancing, you might find yourself grooving after a pint or two; after all, who can resist songs like "I Want You Back" or "I Got You (I Feel Good)"?

Away from the floor, the Blue Note keeps the cool factor going strong. There are paintings of Wonder Woman and Walter White on the brick walls inside, and the large outdoor area is lit with Christmas lights. At the bar, there's a healthy selection of local and craft brews, as well as the regulars like Guinness. If you prefer harder stuff, they've got a generous selection of liquors and spirits—shots go for about £5—and know that they've got Jägermeister on tap.

The Blue Note also has an off-licence that's open until 11, which means you can buy bottles of beer or liquor to take home with you. Perfect if you want to keep the party going back at your hostel.

THE CRANE BAR   BAR

2 Sea Road   ☎9 158 7419 www.thecranebar.com

Travel can be wearying. Spending time in anonymous airports, train stations, and hostels can take a toll; haven't you seen "Up in the Air"? If those bad vibes should happen to strike you in Galway, there's only one place to go: a tiny neighborhood joint called the Crane Bar. Here, you'll find families or groups of old friends gathered together in a corner, fathers and sons sharing pints of Guinness, and local musicians playing traditional music. Truly heartwarming. It's what so many "traditional-style" pubs aspire to be—a genuine neighborhood staple. The little bits of cheesiness (exhibit A: their collection of novelty mugs, emblazoned with slogans like "I'll be mature if you will") just add to the Crane Bar's endearing nature.

The walls are decorated with sketches, black and white photos, and old beer advertisements for Guinness, Budweiser, and Heineken. All of these are also on draught, which is a pretty spooky coincidence. The liquor selection isn't huge, but you're not here for fancy cocktails: you're here for company, music, and a creamy pint. If you get a bit nippish, they have chips (crisps, rather) and peanuts available for sale. The traditional music happens on a nightly basis—share a few friendly words of conversation downstairs, then head to the second floor (first floor, rather) to hear some great Irish tunes (and no, that doesn't mean U2 songs).

i Pints £4.30, spirits £4.20.

ESSENTIALS

Practicalities

- **CASH:** ATMs in central locales include the Bank of Ireland ATM at 43 Eyre Square, the Ulster Bank ATM at 33 Eyre Square, the Bank of Ireland ATM at 22 Mainguard Street, and the Bank of Ireland ATM in the Quays Bar and Restaurant. All of these except the last are accessible 24 hours.

- **POST OFFICE:** Galway Post Office, 3 Eglinton Street (🕐 Open M 9am-5:30pm, Tu 9:30am-5:30pm, W-Sa 9am-5:30. Foreign exchange available here. ☎91 534 727.)

- **INTERNET CAFÉS:** Netcafe Galway, 9 Eyre Square (🕐 Open M-F 9am-10pm, Sa 10am-10pm, Su noon-9pm. Cash only. ☎91 393 750.)

Emergency

- **PHARMACIES:** Boots Pharmacy, 35 Shop Street (~Open M-W 9am-7pm, Th-F 9am-9pm, Sa 9am-7pm, Su 11:30am-6pm. ☎91 561 022.) University Late Night Pharmacy, 1-2 University Halls, Newcastle Road (🕐 Open M-F 9am-9pm, Sa 9:30am-6:30pm, Su noon-6pm.)

- **HOSPITALS:** University Hospital Galway, Newcastle Road, Galway City. In an emergency, dial ☎112 or 999.

Getting Around

Galway is a very walkable city (though be sure to bring a map, as there are numerous small side streets), but if it starts raining or you can't bear another step, the city is served by Bus Eireann. The most popular and frequently running route is the 401, which goes from Eyre Square to Salthill every 20 minutes. The 402, which also leaves at Eyre Square, has a number of popular destinations on its route, including the Galway Cathedral and NUI Galway. Bus fares are generally about £2.

kilkenny

When you arrive in Kilkenny, many questions will occur to you. Why are all the restaurants just as expensive as they are in Dublin? Why are there so many really nice hotels? What's up with all the craft galleries? Why does it feel like you can't turn around without seeing a health food store? And what's this about an internationally renowned comedy festival?

Kilkenny, with its influx of vacationers, gorgeous scenery, and cultural heritage, occupies a very special place in the Emerald Isle—it's basically the Irish Hamptons. But Long Island doesn't have anything to compare to the Kilkenny's history. Much of the town still looks as it did back in the 1600s. There's much to treasure in the so-called Marble City, from excellent Italian food to hundred-foot medieval towers—that you can still climb.

SIGHTS

KILKENNY CASTLE

CASTLE

The Parade   ☎56 770 4100 www.kilkennycastle.ie

On first glance, Kilkenny is a sleepy little town. Sure, it's got some medieval remnants, but what town in Ireland doesn't? But Kilkenny was actually a site of tremendous importance in Irish history, and there's no better place to learn that importance than at Kilkenny Castle. Today, the site looks like the beautiful country residence it is, but the tours remind you of the history that literally rocked this castle to its foundations. Most castles fell into disrepair because of simple neglect. Kilkenny Castle was partially destroyed during the Irish Civil War, when Irish Republicans were under siege in the structure.

In the 1640s, the castle became the home of the Irish confederate parliament, a short-lived Catholic government that was eradicated by Oliver Cromwell. After staying for years in the Butler Family, the castle was sold to the public for £50 in 1967. Talk about a steal.

If the tour only appeals to you in the same way an open house for an expensive mansion does, then you should know that the Long Gallery is in fact available to rent out for private events. Sadly, that incredible opportunity comes with a stipulation: it's only for classy events, like "classical music recitals, poetry readings and pre-dinner drinks receptions." In other words, you probably can't use it to play beer pong.

Getting here is easy; if you walk down John Street from the train station, you'll see it on your left as you cross the River Nore. If the line to get in gives you pause, spend a bit of time admiring Kilkenny Castle Park.

i £6, seniors £4, students/children £2.50. ☑ Open daily Mar 9:30am-5pm, Apr-May 9:30am-5:30pm, Jun-Aug 9am-5:30pm, Sept 9:30am-5:30pm, Oct-Feb 9:30am-4:30pm.

kilkenny

MACGABHAINNS HOSTEL
HOSTEL $

24 Vicar Street   ☎56 777 0970 http://macgabhainnsbackpackers.com

This family-run hostel may not be the place to rage with your frat bros—there's a baby living here—but you're unlikely to find a hostel that feels more like home. Granted, it's a home where you'll share a room with at least three other people, but it's a home nonetheless.

With its charming familial atmosphere, MacGabhainns is the perfect place to go after you've stayed in a few hostels. The familiar amenities are there—free WiFi, DIY breakfast in the mornings, a room to sit and watch TV—but there's none of the commercial sheen that you might find in other hostels. Best of all are the bathrooms, which feature real bathtubs and showers that actually feature water pressure—you'll be tempted to take off your flip-flops.

There are two types of rooms: four-bed dorms and six-bed dorms. Not the utmost in privacy, but the bunk beds and the rooms are pretty large. The rooms are a little dark (the windows are small), but clean and well-kept. It also has a great location (not that anything in Kilkenny has a truly bad location), being right next to the Cathedral Church of St. Canice and within two blocks of a post office.

i Dorms from £15-20. ⌂ Reception open daily 24hr. No curfew.

LANIGAN'S
HOSTEL $

28/29 Rose Inn Street   ☎56 772 1718 http://www.lanigans.ie

The fact that it's affiliated with a bar might give you pause. That won't be helped by the fact that you check in at the bar. "Are the rooms beneath the counter?", you wonder. But don't worry—though you're close enough to the bar to grab a pint in 10 seconds flat, the living quarters are actually separated from the bar by a narrow alley, meaning your slumber won't be interrupted by any drunken singalongs. There's also a night watchman on weekends, so the chances of any drunken pub-goers trying to sneak into the room are nil.

Inside the actual hostel, the rooms are large and labyrinthine; they're configured like suites, with a hallway leading to a bathroom, a closet, and a gigantic bedroom. The beds are nested into the wall, leaving the room with a ton of space in the middle; the twelve-man, the biggest room, is especially big, though the other rooms (the smallest is the 4-person room) aren't too shabby either. There's no food or drink allowed in the rooms, but if you're hungry you can always make your way to the bar; for an extra fee, you can have breakfast there daily, which is sure to be more filling and convenient than the DIY continental breakfast offered at most hostels.

i Dorms from £16. ⌂ Reception open daily 24hr.

BLACK ABBEY
CHURCH

Abbey Street   ☎56 772 1279 www.blackabbey.ie

Black Abbey was founded in the 13th century as a Dominican abbey and that's the role it still fills today. But it's had a pretty bizarre history in the meantime, largely due to the religious conflicts that are seen so often in Irish history (at one point it served as a courthouse and there was also a time when the Dominicans were allowed to practice but had to rent out the space). But since the 1860s, it's been a functioning church, and today a solemn attitude reigns in the place; there are still monks here, after all. That means you'll have to keep your voice down. Try not to get into any heated arguments about medieval architecture. While the nearby Canice Cathedral is also a functioning church, it's much more geared towards the casual tourist; in fact, they even charge admission.

Regardless, there's a lot worth seeing at the Black Abbey, even if you'll have to wait until the walk home to talk about it. None of the stained glass is medieval—most of it is self-consciously modern—but it's all very pleasant to look at. The eclectic architecture (though it was originally built in the 13th century, sections were added in the 14th and 16th as well) might just inspire a bit of debate.

i Walk down High Street, wait until it turns into Parliament Street, then take a right on—you guessed it—Abbey Street. Free. ⏱ No real hours, per se, but the first church event is at 10:15am and the last is at 6:45pm. Visiting between these times is probably best.

CASTLECOMER DISCOVERY PARK
PARK

The Estate Yard, Castlecomer, Co.   ☎56 444 0707 www.discoverypark.ie

Kilkenny Castle Park is all well and good, but Castlecomer Discovery Park is the place to really experience nature in County Kilkenny. Somewhat improbably founded in a failed mining town, Castlecomer Discovery Park features over 80 acres of forest for you to traipse around in, along with exhibits on the mining history, two massive lakes, and a rock-climbing wall. Be warned, however, that while admission to the park is free, some of the special attractions do have costs attached. Renting a boat for half an hour will set you back £10, while the astonishing Tree Top Walk (you'll be walking along a rope bridge nearly 10m off the ground) will cost you £12.50 (and you have to book in advance).

This being Kilkenny, there are of course multiple craft galleries and workshops on site. If you get caught in the rain, these establishments are the perfect place to wait out a quick shower. Castlecomer has a stone-carver, a ceramicist, and even some interior designers! After a particularly long hike has left you bereft of calories, stop by the cafe or, even better, the candy shop.

It's a 20-minute drive from Kilkenny City, but you can also take public transportation; just take the 717 or 7 from the Ormonde Street stop. This will take about an hour, so make sure you have something to read on the way there. You'll definitely be tired enough to nap on the way back.

i Free admission, £2 for parking. Some attractions have additional costs. ⏱ Open M-F 10am-5pm, Sa-Su 10:30am-5pm.

THE BLACKBIRD GALLERY
GALLERY

The Castle Yard   ☎87 784 3015 www.theblackbirdgallery.ie

Unless you have an extra couple hundred euro that you just can't bear the thought of not spending, most of what's for sale at the Blackbird Gallery will be out of our price range. Let's just say that you can buy someone a gift card for up to £1000. You'll also probably need an extra suitcase, and a big one at that (you can't really fold art). Still, don't let that dissuade you from paying a visit to the Blackbird, which brings together some of Ireland's most talented artists. Think of it as the "Now That's What I Call Music!" of Irish craft and design. But crafts aren't the only things on display, though the bowls and glasswork are certainly of note. The gallery also highlights contemporary artists like Louis Le Brocquy, whose work appears in the Guggenheim Museum and the Tate Modern (his work retails for at least £5000).

The gallery itself has a low-key beauty—it's located in the Kilkenny Design Centre complex, alongside some studios and directly in front of the Butler House and Gardens. Big windows add plenty of natural light. But the focus, as it should be, is on the art. Take a look around, and be sure to buy a lottery ticket when you head back to Kilkenny proper—maybe you'll get a little extra cash to take home a souvenir.

i *Free. ☺ Open W-F 11am-4pm, Sa 11am-5pm.*

FOOD

RISTORANTE RINUCCINI   ITALIAN $$$
1 The Parade   ☎56 776 1575 www.rinuccini.com

Step into Restaurant Rinuccini and you'll swear you've been transported to Italy—an Italy that exclusively uses Irish meat products, sure, but Italy none-theless. Breadsticks are on the table. Opera's on the soundtrack. The waiter says something you don't quite understand—oops, he just has an exceptionally thick Irish accent.

Still, Ristorante Rinuccini offers some of the best Italian food you're likely to get in Ireland. With tasteful decoration (dig those reproductions of Renaissance paintings), an adventurous menu, and a generous wine list, it's also the place to go for a classy meal in Kilkenny. A greenhouse-type area towards the front offers some spectacular views of Kilkenny Castle. For those who don't appreciate their meal being interrupted by people continually coming and going, try to nab a table in the intimate back room, where stone walls and red carpets set an even classier tone.

The restaurant boasts an extensive menu that shies away from the well-worn classics (instead of chicken parm, try some porchetta) in favor of more adventurous dishes, most of which are heavy on the meat—and, unfortunately, the cost. It's neither a place for vegetarians nor tightwads, but if you've been spending money wisely (i.e., grabbing lunch from your hostel's continental breakfast), Ristorante Rinuccini is definitely worth visiting. And surprisingly enough, it offers one of the best takeaway deals you're likely to find in all of Ireland: a pound of homemade lasagna for £6.

i *Lunch £10-12, pasta £16-18, entrees £24-27. Nearby: Kilkenny Castle, The Hole in the Wall. ☺ Open M-F noon-3pm and 5-10pm, Sa noon-3:30 and 5-10pm, Su noon-3:30 and 5-9:30pm.*

BLAA BLAA BLAA SANDWICHES   SANDWICHES $
3 Canal Square   ☎56 775 2212 www.facebook.com/blaablaablaasandwiches

The name of this takeout joint is sarcastic, of course. These people really care about sandwiches—despite the fact that they rarely charge more than £5 for one. Step inside the tiny space and you'll be confronted with a massive menu. The bacon, brie, and cranberry jam combination has to be tasted to be believed, but there are some more traditional choices if you can't bring yourself to try anything beyond a ham and cheese (it's hard, we know).

Don't let the cheap prices make you think these sandwiches are good for a snack. Get one of these bad boys and you'll be set for most of the day—as a follow-up, we suggest going to one of Kilkenny's many tapas places and ordering only one dish (you'll get a couple dirty looks, but you'll also avoid indigestion).

There are a few tables and benches outside, giving you the perfect oppor-tunity to admire the River Nore as you scarf down some delicious eats. If river views give you the chills, then take a short walk to Kilkenny Castle Park, where you can lounge around on the grass. The friendly staff will be sure to carefully pack your sandwich in a paper bag, so transporting it is a non-issue.

i *Between £4-6 for a sandwich. Nearby: Bridie's Bar & General Store, The Hole in the Wall, Brew-ery Corner, Kilkenny Castle, Lanigan's. ☺ Open M-F 8:30am-3:30pm, Sa 9am-4pm.*

NIGHTLIFE

THE HOLE IN THE WALL
WINE BAR

17 High Street ☎87 807 5650 www.holeinthewall.ie

The Hole in the Wall, a wine bar off of High Street, is a time machine. Much of the Kilkenny you see today was built in the early 17th century, but the Hole in the Wall is one of the few places where the interior remains unchanged. "You get to see what the houses were really like," says Michael Conway, the local doctor who owns and operates the bar. Indeed, stepping into the Hole in the Wall is a powerful antidote to the so-called "traditional" pubs; the walls and floor are bare stone, the room is cramped, and there's a bit of a draft. Yet the atmosphere is electrifying—this is nearly exactly what the place would have looked like in the 1580s, when the house was built by the Archer family. Conway also takes inspiration from the actual bar that existed here during the 1780s, when the space had its heyday.

The Hole in the Wall may not be for people who like their history during the daytime, but the variety of wines and bottled beers mean it's not just a museum piece. The selection is small but on point; let Conway recommend a wine or beer for you if you're not familiar with any of the names behind the counter. You're not going to come across a vintage from 1783, but there are some fine wines nonetheless.

i £5-6 for a glass of wine. Nearby: Brewery Corner, Blaa Blaa Blaa Sandwiches, Ristorante Rinuccini. ☒ Open M 7-11pm, Tu 3-7pm, W-Th 7-11pm, F 4pm-1am, Sa 11am-1am, Su 11am-11pm.

BREWERY CORNER
BAR

29 Parliament Street ☎56 780 5081 www.facebook.com/brewerycorner

Now that you're outside of the thriving urban centers of Galway or Dublin, you might think that you'll be drinking Guinness until you get home. Not so! You'll be able to get Smithwick's in a lot of places (not to mention Coors Light). And if none of those tickle your fancy, rest assured that there are craft beer joints out in the boonies. Case in point: the Brewery Corner in Kilkenny, a bar operated by the Carlow Brewing Company (Bottles of O'Hara's, one of their brands, are a common sight in Ireland). The number of beers on draught is in the double digits, and they have legions more in bottles behind the counter. They've even got a beer brewed specially for the bar—the Widow's Retro Pale Ale, named in honor of the Widow McGrath, a bar that used to occupy the space. If you're not into beer, there's a vast selection of whiskeys and other liquors to choose from—most cost about £5 or £6.

But though the Brewery Corner may make your beer geek friend salivate, it's not just a place for people to discuss the phenomenology of hops. The long bar and plentiful tables mean it's a great place to go with a group of friends, and the surprisingly cheap pints (well, cheap compared to Dublin) mean that you can all knock a few back.

i Pints between £4 and £5, whiskeys between £5 and £6. Nearby: Macgabhainn's Hostel, The Hole in the Wall. ☒ Open M-Th noon-11:30pm, F-Sa noon-12:30am, Su noon-11pm.

BRIDIE'S BAR & GENERAL STORE
BAR

72 John Street ☎56 776 5133 www.langton.ie/bars/bridies

When you get to the above address, you'll see a general store, and a rather bizarre one at that. Pay no heed to the whoopee cushions, lunchboxes, and goose fat for sale—we told you this was a bizarre store—and walk to the back, where Bridie's Bar awaits. There's still a bit of quirkiness—behind the bar, six painted teacups spell out BRIDIE—but the general tone is one of relaxation. You're not going to find anyone ripping Jägerbombs here (although Jägermeister is available). It's a quiet, wood-paneled space, lit by candles, windows, and the occasional electric

kilkenny

light. In short, this is the place to quietly sip a glass of whisky, and they've got a quite a few varieties behind the bar (most are between £4 and £7, though you can certainly splurge and get some Midleton Very Rare for £16). With its small tables, it's also the place to go with smaller groups—there's only one large table indoors, though the beer garden has a few more options.

It also boasts one of the better beer selections in Kilkenny—plenty of Carlow Brewing Company beers are on tap, as well as several from McGargles, a family brewery that claims it was "never established."

i Between £4 and £5 for a pint, between £4 and £7 for spirits. Nearby: Matt the Miller's, Blaa Blaa Blaa Sandwiches. ☒ M-W 11am-10pm, Th-Sa 6pm-2am, Su 11am-10pm.

ESSENTIALS
Practicalities

- **MAIN POST OFFICE:** between 72 and 74 High Street. (☒ Open M 9am-5:30pm, Tu 9:30am-5:30pm, W-F 9-5:30pm, Sa 9am-1pm.
- **ATMS:** There are two 24hr. ATMs at the Bank of Ireland, located at the junction between High Street and St. Kieran's Street (right by the giant sculpture of St. Canice's head). This is also approximately where High Street becomes Parliament Street.

Emergency

- **EMERGENCY NUMBERS:** ☎112 and 999.
- **HOSPITAL:** St. Luke's General Hospital: Freshford Road, Kilkenny. ☎56 778 5000.
- **PHARMACY:** Boots Pharmacy: ☒ M-Sa 8:30am-6pm, Su 10am-6pm. Heavy on the beauty products, but has the essentials too. Open later than the other pharmacies on High/Parliament Streets, of which there are several.

Getting Around

Getting around the city of Kilkenny is a breeze. There's no bus system, but the city itself is so small that you certainly don't need one. The train and bus station is five minutes away from the city center.

ireland essentials

VISAS

Citizens of almost all major developed countries (including Australia, Canada, New Zealand, the UK, and the US) do not need visas to enter the Republic of Ireland. Citizens of these countries can stay for up to 90 days without a visa, but after this period will have to apply for a longer-term visa. Note that the Republic of Ireland is not a signatory of the Schengen Agreement, which means it is not a part of the free movement zone that covers most of the EU. The advantage of this is that non-EU citizens can visit Ireland without eating into the 90-day limit on travel within the Schengen area. Some travelers have been known to use Ireland as a convenient location for "stopping the Schengen clock" and extending their Eurotrip. The only real disadvantage of Ireland's non-Schengen status is that you will be subject to border controls on entry, so don't forget your passport.

Those hoping to study or work in Ireland will have to obtain special visas to do so; consult your nearest Irish embassy or consulate for information on applying. You will generally need a letter of acceptance from a university or company in order to

apply. You can find more information on all visa questions at the website of the Irish Department of Foreign Affairs and Trade (www.dfa.ie).

Since Northern Ireland is in the United Kingdom, its visa rules are the same as for Britain. For information on these policies, see the Great Britain chapter.

MONEY

Tipping and Bargaining

Some restaurants in Ireland figure a service charge into the bill; some even calculate it into the cost of the dishes themselves. The menu often indicates whether or not service is included. If gratuity is not included, consider leaving 10-15%, depending upon the quality of the service. Tipping is not necessary for most other services, such as taxis and concierge assistance, especially in rural areas. In most cases, people are usually happy if you simply round up the bill to the nearest euro. But if a driver is particularly courteous and helpful, consider tipping 5-10%. Hairdressers, at least for women, are typically tipped 10% of the bill. Never tip in pubs—it's considered condescending. In general, do not tip bartenders, though some bartenders at hip urban bars may expect a tip; watch and learn from other customers.

Taxes

The Republic of Ireland has a 23% value added tax (VAT), although some goods are subject to a lower rate of 13%. Northern Ireland edges its southern neighbor with the UK VAT rate of 20%. The prices stated in *Let's Go* include VAT unless otherwise noted. Given the Irish government's serious cashflow problems, don't be surprised if the rates increase even more.

SAFETY AND HEALTH

Although Ireland has a long history of serious sectarian violence and terrorism, the situation has improved considerably in the last 15 years. It is still probably best to avoid incendiary discussions with strong opinions on the Northern Ireland question or by stating your undying love for Oliver Cromwell (this will not go down well). Always be aware of your surroundings and don't assume that the Troubles are completely over: there are still many fringe groups who are prepared to commit acts of terrorism.

Drugs and Alcohol

The Republic of Ireland and Northern Ireland both regulate the possession of recreational drugs, with penalties ranging from a warning to lengthy prison sentences. Possession of marijuana results in a fine, though repeated offenses can result in prosecution. Harder substances are treated with severity. If you carry prescription drugs with you, have a copy of the prescription and a note from a doctor readily accessible at country borders. The drinking age, 18 in both the Republic of Ireland and Northern Ireland, is more strictly enforced in urban areas. While there is no national legislation prohibiting drinking in public, local authorities may pass by-laws enforcing such a policy. Drinking is banned in many public places in Northern Ireland. Contact the local authority for more information.

ITALY

For the home of the papacy, Italy certainly knows how to do sensual pleasures right: stylish Vespas, intoxicating vino, vibrant piazze, and crackling pizzas covered in garden-fresh produce will light up your eyes, ears, nose, and taste buds as you make your way across the Mediterranean's favorite boot. In a country where la dolce far niente ("the sweetness of doing nothing") is a national pastime, you will nonetheless find yourself with a wealth of opportunities to pursue la dolce vita. And as a student traveler, you are uniquely situated to experience Italia in all its ridiculousness and sublimity. Striking out on your own, likely on a budget, you will open yourself up to what someone who stays in the swankiest hotels and eats at all the five-star restaurants will miss: making connections with the people and the way of life in Italy's many storied cities and towns. Wander your way along the canals in Venice and marvel at the famed mosaics of Ravenna. Try to dodge the sharp glances of the fashionistas in Milan and discover the moving stories of the flood-ravaged Ligurian Coast as you make your way along the Cinque Terre. Eat pizza in Naples, climb the Duomo in Florence, and explore ruins in Sicily. With its Renaissance art, Roman grandeur, and religious relics, Italy presents curious and intrepid travelers with an experience that is at once cultural, historical, and truly divine.

greatest hits

- **ANCIENT ANTIQUES.** The relics of ancient Rome pop up all over the place. **Rome** (p. 524) is obviously the place to start, but even cities like **Verona** (p. 588) and **Milan** (p. 562) share this fascinating history.

- **WHERE REBIRTH WAS BORN.** Thanks to the Renaissance, there's more art in Italy than even a Medici can handle. Get the best possible primer at the king of Italian museums: Florence's **Uffizi Gallery** (p. 616).

- **GIVE THE MAINLAND THE BOOT.** Once you've made it down the Mediterranean coast, hop on a ferry to see a whole other side of Italy in Sicily, including the Byzantine-influenced **Palermo** (p. 671) and the ruins of **Syracuse** (p. 679).

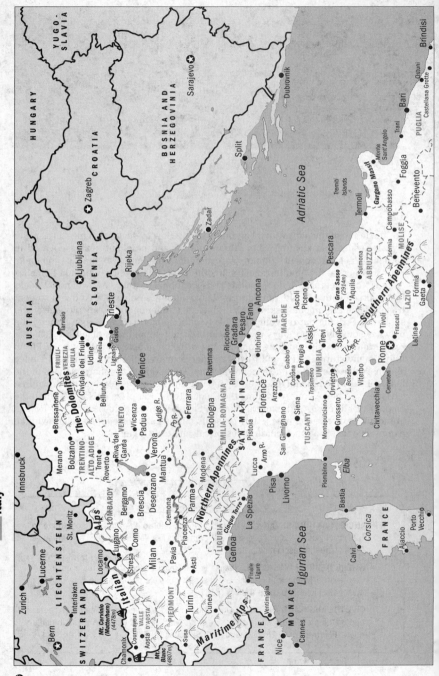

italy

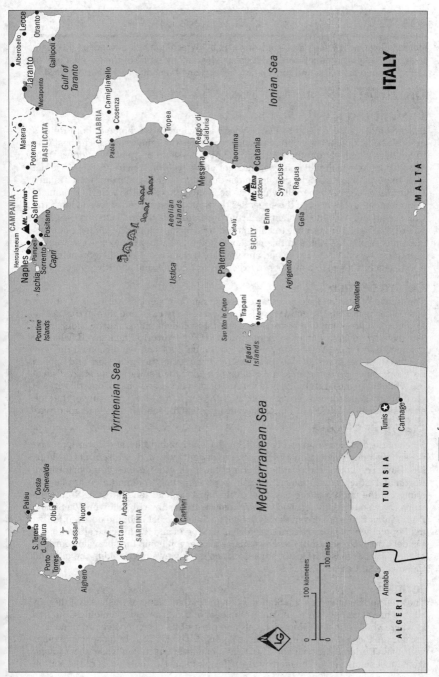

ITALY

Ionian Sea

Lecce
Otranto
Alberobello
Gallipoli
Taranto
Gulf of
Taranto
Metaponto
Matera
BASILICATA
Potenza
CAMPANIA
Mt. Vesuvius
Salerno
Positano
Sorrento
Capri
Ischia
Naples
Herculaneum
Pompeii
Camigliatello
Cosenza
CALABRIA
Paola
Tropea
Reggio di
Calabria
Taormina
Mt. Etna
(3350m)
Catania
Syracuse
Ragusa
Messina
Cefalù
Enna
SICILY
Palermo
Gela
Agrigento
San Vito lo Capo
Trapani
Marsala
Egadi
Islands
Pantelleria
Aeolian
Islands
Ustica
Pontine
Islands
Tyrrhenian Sea
Palau
S. Teresa
d. Gallura
Costa
Smeralda
Olbia
Arbatax
Nuoro
SARDINIA
Sassari
Oristano
Cagliari
Porto
Torres
Alghero

Mediterranean Sea

Tunis
Carthage
TUNISIA
Annaba
ALGERIA

MALTA

100 kilometers
100 miles
0
0

italy

rome

When in Rome, "If it ain't Ba-roque, don't fix it." Which is why Rome won't be cleaning up its streets anytime soon, but it's also why the city is one of the greatest places to experience the relics and ruins of art, history, and humanity in the entire world.

ORIENTATION

Ancient City

Situated just south and east of Piazza Venezia, Ancient City is home to both Rome's greatest collection of ancient ruins and its most overwhelming crowds. The best way to get here is either from the metro stop at M Colosseum or by walking down from Via Nazionale, which will spit you out right at the foot of Trajan's Column. Via dei Fori Imperiali runs straight through most of the sights here, starting with Trajan's Column and the Fori Imperiali, which can be found just east of the Vittorio Emanuele II Monument; to the west of the street lies the Roman Forum, and at its end loom the Colosseum and Arch of Constantine. From the arch, walk down Via di San Gregorio, where you'll find the entrance to Palatine Hill and, farther along, the far end of Circus Maximus. While the sights in this neighborhood are the area's major draw, wander into the streets just off Via Cavour, and you'll find Rome's delightful Monti neighborhood, which is home to a number of excellent restaurants and aperitivo spots.

Centro Storico

The tangle of vias and vicolos that comprise much of Centro Storico isn't always easy to navigate, but the good news is that nearly every twist and turn in this neighborhood will lead you to a historic church or down a charming, narrow side street. The main thoroughfare in this neighborhood is Corso Vittorio Emanuele II, which is connected to Piazza Venezia in the east via Via del Plebiscito and runs all the way west to the Tiber River. Just south of this road you'll find the Area Sacra and Campo de' Fiori; wander a bit north and you'll happen upon the Pantheon and Piazza Navona. While the sights and churches here are worth a visit at any time of day, this area is particularly good for an evening stroll, as both Campo de' Fiori and many of the side streets immediately west of Piazza Navona are great for food, drinks, and aperitivo.

Piazza di Spagna

Much of the area surrounding Piazza di Spagna is all ritz and glitz, and if you approach the square along Via dei Condotti, you can feast your eyes on the storefronts of shops like Burberry, Louis Vuitton, Gucci, and a bunch of other places you can't afford. Fortunately, the piazza's famed Spanish Steps are totally free and a great place to lounge in the middle of the day. One of the most popular landmarks in Rome, the steps can also be easily reached via M Spagna or from above by following Via Sistina from Piazza Barberini. From Piazza di Spagna, follow V. del Babuino north to Piazza del Popolo, which is also a terminus for Via di Ripetta and the massive artery that is Via del Corso. Northeast of these two major piazze, you'll find the sprawling gardens of the Villa Borghese, which is home to some great views overlooking the city and the must-visit Galleria Borghese.

Termini

The area surrounding Termini Station is, on the surface, kind of trash. As in, there is a lot of literal garbage here, and not a whole lot of sights or pretty buildings. But this is where you'll find a lot Rome's hotels and most of its cheap hostels. A number of hostels are located east of the station, so if you're staying in one of those, get familiar with Viale Enrico De Nicola and Piazza Indipendenza, which you'll use to get to and from most sights and/or the metro stop at Termini Station. To the west of the station you'll find a lot of kebab shops, but wander a little farther and you'll happen upon Basilica di Santa Maria Maggiore, the gem of the neighborhood. Walk north from here, and you'll hit Piazza della Repubblica, which is home to the Basilica di Santa Maria degli Angeli and one end of the Baths of Diocletian. Don't eat too many dinners in and around Termini if you can help it, but if you're in a pinch and are looking for good food close to your hostel, wander up to Via Venti Settembre and some of the streets farther north for better options. And while you're up there, absolutely do get gelato at Gelateria La Romana. And while buses #40 and #64 will become your best friend if you're staying near Termini, it's also perfectly safe to walk back to your hostel here at night as long as you keep your wits about you.

Vatican City

Besides the crowds that flood and wind their way around the walls of the Vatican and St. Peter's Square during the day, the neighborhood surrounding the Vatican is relatively quiet, local, and residential compared to some other areas of Rome. Accessible by both M Ottaviano and M Lepanto, the streets of this neighborhood lie on what could almost count as a grid, and some of the area's wide boulevards include Viale Giulio Cesare, Via Candia, and Via Cola di Rienzo. In many cases in this area, all roads lead to the Vatican and St. Peter's, and even if they don't, just look for the basilica's massive dome or the daunting, slanted walls of the Vatican if you need to orient yourself. Although the area gets a bit quieter after the major sights close in the evening, you can still find some great, understated food if you're willing to look hard enough (be sure to check out Pizzarium for lunch, Sciascia for coffee, and Fa Bio for sandwiches). The eastern perimeter of the neighborhood is marked by the Tiber and its many impressive bridges—you'll find a number of Bernini sculptures adorning the Ponte Sant'Angelo, across from which sits the Museo di Castel Sant'Angelo—and if you follow Lungotevere south along the river, you'll eventually reach Trastevere.

Trastevere

Tucked into a bend just west of the Tiber, Trastevere's name is derived from the Latin Trans Tiberim, which literally means "beyond the Tiber." This little neighborhood is a charming mix of twisting streets, yellowed buildings, stray cats, and crawling ivy. The busy, beating heart of the neighborhood is Piazza Santa Maria in Trastevere, where tourists sit on the steps of the square's central fountain and musicians riff on guitars late into the night. From here, you can wander the narrow side streets and discover many good, affordable restaurants. Home to John Cabot University and a number of college students, Trastevere also boasts Rome's largest concentration of trendy bars and hip hangout spots, many of which are centered around Piazza Trilussa. Trastevere is bisected by the busy Viale di Trastevere, and while the area to the west is often busy with tourists, to the east you'll find quieter streets and quainter, more authentic Roman restaurants nestled into a number of hidden piazze. And if you've had enough of all the eating and drinking (which is, admittedly, the main draw of the area), you can head up Via Garibaldi to Gianicolo Hill or take a breather under the palm trees of the Orto Botanico.

ACCOMMODATIONS

Ancient City

CESARE BALBO INN
V. Cesare Balbo 43   ☎06 98 38 60 81 www.cesarebalboinn.com   HOTEL $$

Given its unique location, reasonable rates, and some of the friendliest service you're likely to encounter in Rome, Cesare Balbo Inn might just be the best value accommodation the city has to offer. Tucked away on the quiet V. Cesare Balbo, the inn is just down the road from the stunning Basilica di Santa Maria Maggiore

rome

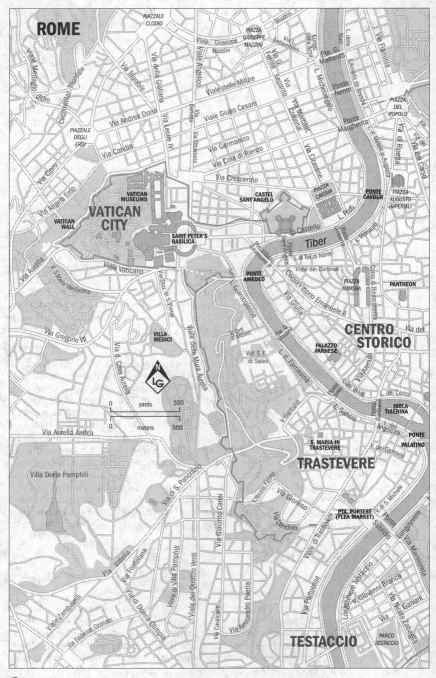

ROME

PIAZZALE
CLODIO

PIAZZA
GIUSEPPE
MAZZINI

Viale Giuseppe Mazzini

PIAZZA
DEL
POPOLO

Viale delle Milizie

PIAZZALE
DEGLI
EROI

Viale Giulio Cesare

Via Germanico

Via Cola di Rienzo

Via Candia

Via Crescenzio

VATICAN
MUSEUMS

PIAZZA
CAVOUR

PONTE
CAVOUR

PIAZZA
AUGUSTO
IMPERIALE

VATICAN
CITY

CASTEL
SANT'ANGELO

VATICAN
WALL

SAINT PETER'S
BASILICA

Tiber

Viale Vaticano

PONTE
AMEDEO

PIAZZA
NAVONA

PANTHEON

VILLA
MEDICI

CENTRO
STORICO

PALAZZO
FARNESE

ISOLA
TIBERINA

Via Aurelia Antica

S. MARIA IN
TRASTEVERE

PONTE
PALATINO

Villa Doria Pamphili

TRASTEVERE

PTA. PORTESE
(FLEA MARKET)

TESTACCIO

PARCO
TESTACCIO

italy

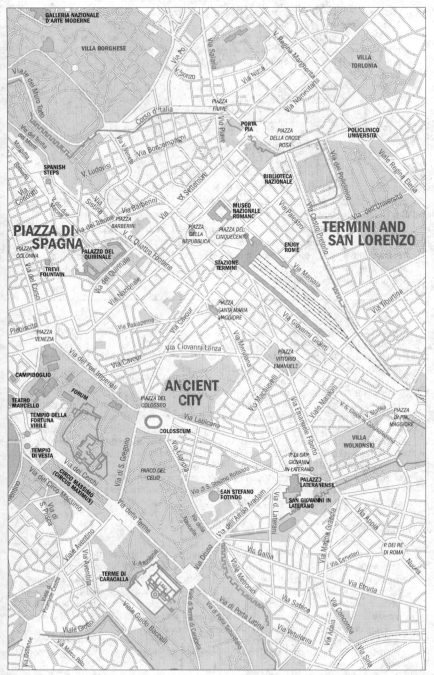

GALLERIA NAZIONALE
D'ARTE MODERNE

VILLA BORGHESE

VILLA
TORLONIA

Viale del Muro Torto

Via Po

Via Salaria

V. Sonzo

Via Nizza

Via Nomentana

Via Regina Margherita

Corso d'Italia

PIAZZA
FIUME

Via Piave

PORTA
PIA

PIAZZA
DELLA CROCE
ROSA

POLICLINICO
UNIVERSITÀ

Via del Policlinico

Viale Regina Elena

Via del Tritone
dei Monti

Magutta

Via Veneto

Via Boncompagni

V. Ludovisi

SPANISH
STEPS

Babuino

Via
Condotti

V. delle Mercedi

Via
Sistina

Via Barberini

IX Settembre

BIBLIOTECA
NAZIONALE

Via Palestro

Via Castro Pretorio

Via dell'Università

PIAZZA DI
SPAGNA

PIAZZA
COLONNA

Via del Tritone

PIAZZA
BARBERINI

V. d. Quattro Fontane

MUSEO
NAZIONALE
ROMANO

PIAZZA
DELLA
REPUBBLICA

PIAZZA DEL
CINQUECENTO

ENJOY
ROME

TERMINI AND
SAN LORENZO

PALAZZO DEL
QUIRINALE

Via del Quirinale

STAZIONE
TERMINI

Via Marsala

TREVI
FOUNTAIN

Via del Corso

Via Nazionale

Via Giovanni Giolitti

Via Tiburtina

Plebiscito

PIAZZA
VENEZIA

Via Panisperna

Via Cavour

PIAZZA
SANTA MARIA
MAGGIORE

Via Merulana

Via Cavour

Via Giovanni Lanza

PIAZZA
VITTORIO
EMANUELE

CAMPIDOGLIO

Via dei Fori Imperiali

ANCIENT
CITY

PIAZZA DEL
COLOSSEO

Via Machiavelli

Viale Manzoni

V. S. Croce V. Statilia

PIAZZA
DI PTA.
MAGGIORE

TEATRO
MARCELLO

FORUM

Via Labicana

Via Emanuele Filiberto

TEMPIO DELLA
FORTUNA
VIRILE

COLOSSEUM

VILLA
WOLKONSKI

TEMPIO
DI VESTA

Via di S. Gregorio

Via Gloria

P. DI SAN
GIOVANNI
IN LATERANO

CIRCO MASSIMO
(CIRCUS MAXIMUS)

Via del Cerchi

PARCO DEL
CELIO

Via di S. Stefano Rotondo

SAN STEFANO
ROTONDO

PALAZZO
LATERANENSE

SAN GIOVANNI IN
LATERANO

Via dei Circo Massimo

Aventino

Via di
S. Prisca

Viale Aventino

Via Aventina

Via delle Terme

Via dell'Amba Aradam

Via di S. Lateran

Via Gallia

Via Magna Grecia

Via Appia

P. DEI RE
DI ROMA

Via Cerveteri

Nuova

TERME DI
CARACALLA

V. Annonina

Via Druso

Viale Metronio

Via Etruria

Viale di
Pramigrada Cesta

Viale Aventino

Viale delle Terme di Caracalla

Via di Porta Latina

Via Satrice

Via Concordia

Via Magia

Via Sura

Viale Giotto

Viale Guido Baccelli

Via di Foro Sebastiano

Via Vetulonia

Via Ostiense

Via Marco Polo

and even closer to the charming streets and stylish aperitivo spots of Rome's Monti neighborhood (which also situates guests a short walk from Via Cavour, the Forum, and the Colosseum). Rooms are clean, colorful, and spacious, with high ceilings and bright red and orange bedspreads. Plus, the charming, chipper guys at the front desk are more than ready to answer any questions you may have.

i *From Termini Station, exit onto V. Giovanni Giolitti and proceed down V. Cavour. Turn right onto V. di Santa Maria Maggiore, which becomes V. Panisperna, then turn right onto V. Cesare Balbo. The inn is on the right. Singles €60. Doubles €70. Quads €80. Breakfast included. ☒ Reception 8:30am-6pm. Guests arriving later than 6pm must pay a small fee.*

lungo il tevere

You should really take a walk along the Tiber sometime during your time in Rome, and why not do it when there's also a lot of beer available for purchase along the way? From June-August, the city sets up a long stretch of tents on the west side of the river where you can booze and cruise all night long. Sure, it's touristy, but as Death Cab for Cutie said so eloquently, "You Are a Tourist." So have at it. Eat *al fresco*, drink *al fresco*, buy overpriced skirts *al fresco*. Alternately, just wander along and take in the spectacle after grabbing more quality food and drinks up the stairs and across Lungotevere in Trastevere.

CASA DI SANTA PUDENZIANA
V. Urbana 158

CONVENT $

If you're looking for a temporary taste of the monastic life, make like Ophelia and get thee to Casa di Santa Pudenziana. Despite those threats your mom made when you were a rebellious teen, your stay here is probably the closest you'll ever come to living in an actual convent. (Bonus: The *casa*'s women-only policy means you won't even have to deal with any whiny, existentially frustrated Hamlets during your stay here!) And don't worry if you haven't prayed the rosary recently—this *casa* is a perfect, welcome retreat for saints and sinners alike, complete with a homey breakfast room and courtyard. The elderly woman who runs this place might not speak a lot of English, but if you're staying here, you probably prefer things on the quiet side anyway.

i *From Termini Station, exit onto V. Giovanni Giolitti and proceed down V. Cavour. Turn right into P. dell'Esquilino, then turn left down V. Urbana. The casa is on the right. Dorms €26. Singles €40. Doubles €52. Breakfast included. ☒ Curfew M-F 10:30pm, Sa midnight, Su 10:30pm. Reception 7am-10:30pm.*

HOTEL ROSETTA
V. Cavour 295 B/1

HOTEL $$

☎06 47 82 30 69 www.rosettahotel.com

The courtyard where you'll find the stairs leading to Hotel Rosetta, with its yellow walls and laundry hanging from various windows, is surprisingly charming and quiet, especially given the noisy and bustling V. Cavour that rushes by just beyond its walls. The hotel itself is small and quaint, with a cabinet of trinkets behind the front desk and clean, basic rooms. Breakfast is not included, but Rosetta's central location (just a few minutes' walk from major sites like the Colosseum) will make it easy to find plenty of good food nearby.

i *M: Colosseum. Walk down V. dei Fori Imperiali and turn right onto V. Cavour. Hotel Rosetta is on the left. Singles €60. Doubles €80. Email info@rosettahotel.com for reservations. ☒ Reception 24hr.*

Centro Storico

◪ ALBERGO DEL SOLE AL BISCIONE   HOTEL $$$
V. del Biscione 76   ☎06 68 80 68 73 www.solealbiscione.it

Just a few feet from the bustling market stalls of Campo de' Fiori, Albergo del
Sole offers guests a stellar location right in the heart of Centro Storico while
also serving as its own kind of private retreat from the city. Although finding
your room may send you twisting up staircases and around several corners, the
maze-like hallways of this hotel open at several turns onto study rooms, pleasant
seating areas, and airy windows that overlook a tranquil courtyard. And while
the rooms are clean but very standard, these unexpected bonuses will add value
and charm to your stay.

i *From Campo de' Fiori, exit onto V. del Biscione. The hotel is on the right. Breakfast can be
purchased at the bar across the street or brought up to your room. Singles €100. Doubles €130.*
🕑 *Reception 24hr.*

ALBERGO POMEZIA   HOTEL $$
V. dei Chiavari 13   ☎06 686 13 71 www.hotelpomezia.it

Situated on the charming Via dei Chiavari, Albergo Pomezia's biggest selling
point is clearly its real estate, although a breakfast room and bar add extra value
to the convenience of this hotel's location. Reception and the clean, basic rooms
radiate a warm yellow light that you can wander back to after an evening spent
exploring the wine bars in and around Campo de' Fiori. Although breakfast is
included, consider popping downstairs one morning for some fresh bread from
Forno Marco Roscioli, a neighborhood favorite located just across the street.

i *From Campo de' Fiori, walk down V. dei Giubbonari and turn left onto V. dei Chiavari. The hotel is
on the right. Singles €80. Doubles €120. Breakfast included.* 🕑 *Reception 24hr.*

Piazza di Spagna

◪ HOTEL PANDA   HOTEL $$
V. della Croce 35   ☎06 678 01 79 www.hotelpanda.it

Sure, a single with a shared bathroom at Hotel Panda will run you about double
the price of a night in a hostel dorm, but given this hotel's excellent location
amid the glitz and ritz of the streets surrounding Piazza di Spagna, the rates
here are actually quite reasonable. Rooms are sometimes small but have a real
European, boutiquey feel about them, with rosy bedspreads, stone sinks, and
dark wood fixtures. If you're looking for the convenience of its prime location, a
break from the hostel life, or the simple privacy of a night to yourself (#nonew-
friends), Hotel Panda is a great option.

i *From P. di Spagna, walk down V. della Croce. Hotel Panda is on the left. Buzz for entry. Singles
from €65. Doubles from €95. Triples from €125.* 🕑 *Reception 24hr.*

Termini

◪ THE BEEHIVE HOTEL   HOSTEL $
V. Marghera 8   ☎06 44 70 45 53 www.the-beehive.com

Tucked in behind the walls of a colorful courtyard on Via Marghera, the Beehive
Hotel is the epitome of cute and offers a quiet alternative to the bumpin' party
hostel scene that surrounds much of Termini Station. And while the place isn't
exactly buzzin', the Hive (the hotel's eight-bed, mixed-gender dorm room) offers
a chance to get to know your fellow travelers while enjoying the comfort, amenities, and stellar service of a smaller and more intimate hostel. Although hostelers
don't have access to a kitchen or fridge while staying in the Hive, breakfast (made
with fresh, organic ingredients €2-7) is available in the morning, and snacks and
drinks (whether coffee, wine, or beer) can be enjoyed al fresco in the secluded

rome

peace of the front courtyard at any time. Who needs drunk Eurotrippers when you can hang out under a banyan tree all day?

i *From Termini Station, exit on o P. dei Cinquecento and turn right onto Vle. Enrico De Nicola, then right onto V. Marsala. Turn left onto V. Marghera and the Beehive is on the left (look for the sign under some leaves and vines). Dorms €25. Privates with shared bath €70. Privates with ensuite bath €80. Book early to secure a spot in the dorm.* ☒ *Reception 7am-11pm. Check-in 2pm.*

ALESSANDRO DOWNTOWN
HOSTEL $

V. Carlo Cattaneo 23 ☎06 44 34 01 47 www.hostelsalessandro.com

Despite being located closer to the bustle of Termini Station than its sister hostel, Alessandro Palace, Alessandro Downtown is actually the less rowdy of the two establishments. But with splashes of color on the walls and plenty of seating and vending machines in the large common area, the Downtown is still a great place to meet fellow globetrotters. Tailored specifically to the needs of young budget travelers, the hostel offers great nightly rates (exempt from the Rome tourist tax!) and opportunities to book discounted tours of all the city's major sights. Its central location right around the corner from the Basilica di Santa Maria Maggiore also puts you within striking distance of most of the city's main attractions. And perhaps most importantly, if your clean underwear supply is reaching critical levels, there are laundry facilities available for guest use.

i *From Termini Station, exit on o V. Giovanni Giolitti and walk down V. Gioberti. Then turn left onto V. Principe Amedeo, then right onto V. Carlo Cattaneo. Alessandro Downtown is on the left. Dorms €24-30. Private doubles from €38. Breakfast tickets €4. Laundry €4 wash, €4 dry, €1 detergent.* ☒ *Reception 24hr.*

THE YELLOW
HOSTEL $$

V. Palestro 49 ☎06 49 38 26 82 www.the-yellow.com

The Yellow is certainly a favorite among many 20-something Eurotrippers. But if you remove the beer goggles, you might realize that the Yellow isn't as cute as everyone thinks it is. The rooms are plain and perfectly serviceable (although both ensuite and hallway bathrooms are tiny and might leave you waiting for shower time), and the general tone of the entire hostel is something along the lines of, "Let's get wasted, man!" Almost everyone who works here is a young international staying in Rome on a holiday work visa for a few months, so don't expect any killer insights or local expertise from the staff. The hostel has an adjoining bar and restaurant where you can grab breakfast, lunch, and dinner (and drinks at all hours), and although that's where you'll find most of your hostel-mates eating and drinking, you're better off walking around the corner to the Bramble Bar & Kitchen. TL;DR: If you're in Rome to do more than just get drunk with a bunch of backpackers every night, maybe try staying somewhere else. If you're into that sort of thing, though, you're guaranteed to have a bitchin' time, brah.

i *From Termini Station, exit onto P. dei Cinquecento and turn right onto Vle. Enrico De Nicola. Walk through P. dell'Indipendenza and continue straight down V. San Martino della Battaglia, then turn right onto V. Palestro. Reception is on the right, across the street from the Yellow Bar. Dorms €30-37. Doubles from €90. Triples from €110.* ☒ *Reception 24hr.*

ALESSANDRO PALACE
HOSTEL $

V. Vicenza 42 ☎06 44 6 19 58 www.hostelsalessandro.com

Located on the other side of Termini Station, Alessandro Palace is very similar to its sister hostel—you'll find all the same beds, vending machines, and decor here. What you won't find at the Palace, however, are the laundry facilities, breakfast option, and exemption from Rome's nightly tourist tax that are a few of the perks of Alessandro Downtown. But the Palace does have an in-house bar and close proximity to the Yellow Bar, which may be game-changers for you. Otherwise, try to book a bed at the Downtown hostel before coming to the Palace.

i Directions: From Termini Station, exit onto P. dei Cinquecento and turn right onto Vle. Enrico De Nicola. Walk through P. dell'Indipendenza and turn right onto V. Vittorio Bachelet, then left onto V. Vicenza. The hostel is on the left. Dorms starting from €30. ☎ Reception 24hr.

Vatican City

COLORS HOTEL
HOTEL, HOSTEL

V. Boezio 31   ☎06 686 79 47 www.colorshotel.com

The distinguishing principle of this hotel isn't exactly high concept, but Colors certainly commits to its titular bit and delivers with green walls, orange bathrooms, pink bedspreads, and a yellow breakfast room. One of the few hotels with dorm rooms that you'll find this close to the Vatican, Colors is a little bit like living inside a crayon box, and it's all so sunny and bright that you might be distracted from the fact that the dorms don't have lockers and the breakfast is a bit expensive at €6.50. Still, bunking up here means you'll enjoy the amenities of a hotel (the cleaning staff will remake your bed, change out your towel, and leave a fresh bottle of water on your pillow every day), and rooms and bathrooms are incredibly clean. The hotel also has a common room and very pleasant terrace on the third floor where you can enjoy a beer, cigarette, or the sounds of Italians yelling and honking their cars horns in the street below.

i M: Ottaviano. Walk down V. Ottaviano and turn left onto V. Cola di Rienzo, then right onto V. Terenzio. Colors is on the corner of V. Terenzio and V. Boezio. Less than a 10min. walk to both St. Peter's and the Vatican Museums. Dorms from €28. ☎ Reception 24hr.

HOTEL AL SAN PIETRINO
HOTEL $$

V. Giovanni Bettolo 43   ☎06 370 01 32 www.sanpietrino.it

Located on a quiet street between two of the neighborhood's busier thoroughfares, Hotel Al San Pietrino offers some respite from the Vatican crowds while also placing you within striking distance of the area's major attractions (namely, the Vatican Museums, St. Peter's, and Old Bridge Gelateria). Rooms are large and airy, with tall windows and dramatic red curtains, while the corners of the tiled hallways are home to some friendly and otherwise pointless ceramic frogs. The hotel also has a breakfast nook where guests can relax, and although there is no actual breakfast to speak of (except for croissants on Sundays!), San Pietrino's cappuccino machine is available for use 24/7.

i M: Ottaviano. Exit onto V. Barletta and turn left onto V. Giovanni Bettolo. San Pietrino is on the right (look for the sign advertising it out front). Singles €50-70. Doubles €65-90. ☎ Reception 24hr.

PENSIONE PARADISE
PENSIONE $

Vle. Giulio Cesare 47   ☎06 36 00 43 31 www.pensioneparadise.com

Conveniently located just across the street from the Lepanto metro station, Pensione Paradise is tucked into its quiet, charming courtyard almost as tightly as you'll be tucked into its tiny rooms. And even though the wooden bed frames and close walls might make you feel like a Borrower living in a cupboard for a few days, it's all very cozy and comfortable. Reception is friendly and helpful, and all rooms (even those with shared bathrooms) come equipped with stone sinks that add to the boutique feel of the pensione.

i M: Lepanto. Pensione Paradise is across the street on Vle. Giulio Cesare. Singles from €50. Doubles from €70. ☎ Reception 8am-9pm. Check-in 2pm.

HOTEL NAUTILUS
HOTEL $$

V. Germanico 198   ☎06 45 49 31 39 www.hotelnautilusroma.com

Hotel Nautilus is probably the closest you'll come to staying in an American-style chain hotel while in Rome (unless, of course, you stay at the

Hilton by the airport). That means modern technology (a flatscreen TV at reception!), large rooms (the square footage accommodates more than just the bed!), and hotel "art" on the walls (don't miss that faux-trendy print of some of Rome's famous sights in the hallway!). It's all very airy, clean, and comfortable, and best of all, the rooms also feature green, life-giving views of the bright courtyard outside.

i M: Lepanto. Walk down V. Ezio and turn right onto Vle. Pompeo Magno, which turns into V. Germanico. Hotel Nautilus is on the right. Singles from €70. Doubles from €80. ☎ Reception 24hr.

Trastevere

Despite the many tourists who wander the picturesque streets of Trastevere at all hours of the day, the neighborhood has remained largely devoid of more traditional accommodation establishments like big hostels and hotels. And while this may be aesthetically advantageous—you won't come across any garish "HOTEL" signs here—it can make finding a place to stay a little bit trickier. What Trastevere does have in abundance is very small guest houses, bed and breakfasts, and apartments travelers can reserve for their stay. Often, these places only have a handful of rooms available and require you to set up your arrival time and arrangements in advance; this can usually be done online over the phone, or through websites like Airbnb. So if you aren't one of the many university students who live on this side of the river or a bad bitch staying at Orsa Maggiore Female Only Hostel, hop online and pick out one of the several centrally located spots.

🏠 ORSA MAGGIORE FEMALE ONLY HOSTEL HOSTEL $
V. di San Francesco di Sales 1a www.foresteriaorsa.altervista.org

Orsa Maggiore is basically your mom (or domestically minded dad! we here are Let's Go are gender-inclusive!): it feeds you breakfast free of charge, makes your bed for you every morning, and even does your laundry (alas, that last one will cost you €7, but it sure is an upgrade from turning your underwear inside and calling it clean). Adding to these comfort-of-home amenities, the dormitories at this female-only hostel also provide guests with personal nightstands and nightlights, along with lockers that are really more like very secure closets. Basically, you never need to go home! The only downside may be the hostel's lack of air-conditioning and in-room Wi-Fi, but with its abundant and Wi-Fi-equipped common areas (from the large breakfast room to the couch- and bookshelf-lined hallways to the courtyard filled with tables and benches), Orsa Maggiore provides plenty of options for lounging, loitering, and Snap Story backdrops. And while it's not necessarily the most social of hostels, Orsa Maggiore does have some black and white pictures of Sofia Loren, Audrey Hepburn, and other cool chicks on the walls. What other friends do you need?

i From Ponte Sisto, cross Lungotevere della Farnesina and walk left down the stairs to V. della Lungara, then turn right onto V. d. San Francesco di Sales. Orsa Maggiore is on the left. Dorms from €28. Breakfast included. ☎ Reception 24hr.

SIGHTS

Ancient City

🏠 COLOSSEUM ANCIENT ROME
P. del Colosseo

The first thought that'll cross your mind when you walk up to the Colosseum will be something along the lines of, "Oh my god," followed shortly by, "Oh, the humanity." While the towering arches of this magnificent colossus stand as Rome's most prominent testament to its ancient and fantastic history, the flood of 21st-century humans with selfie sticks surrounding the monument are likely to keep you firmly rooted in the present. And while the sheer mass of bodies that pour into the Colosseum each day might leave you feeling a little overwhelmed, at least it will give you some idea of what the stadium looked like on the day of a gladiator fight nearly 2000 years ago, when more than 70,000 Roman citizens crowded into the building to watch the Russell Crowes of antiquity fight it out for box office glory (or something like that).

Start your visit on the second level, where you can wander through the exhibition space set up in the building's outermost hallway and brief yourself on all the history of the Colosseum. What, you don't like history? You think artifacts are boring? Just look at those ancient toothpicks that Romans used to use after chowing down on hot dogs in between gladiator fights! Are you not entertained?! Once you've oriented and educated yourself, walk around the circumference of the upper level. Look down at the stage where spectacles of all varieties took place, the grand arches through which gladiators, prisoners, and other performers entered the arena, and the cross that marks where the emperors and important people of Ancient Rome used to sit. Then look up at the nosebleed seats where you would have sat with the rest of the plebs. Make your way downstairs and take another half-turn around the stadium, and keep an eye out for some of the marble that made up the original floor.

The more you wander around Rome and its ruins, the more impressive the preservation of the Colosseum will seem. Up close, the stadium certainly doesn't fail to impress. What's perhaps even more breathtaking, however, is those moments when you glimpse it from farther off, unexpectedly, looming in the distance like the mammoth and enduring ghost of Ancient Rome that it is.

i M: Colosseum. *The line for the Colosseum is almost more shocking than the thing itself, but if you buy your ticket at either the Roman Forum or Palatine Hill, you can enter through the left queue and bypass half a mile's worth of sorry suckers on your way inside. €12 combined with the Roman Forum and Palatine Hill. Ticket is valid for entrance to the Colosseum and the Forum/Palatine Hill for two consecutive days. Audio guide €5.50. Video guide €6.* ⌚ *Open daily 8:30am to one hour before sunset.*

PALATINE HILL   ANCIENT ROME
Perhaps the least popular site of the three included in the Colosseum-Forum-Palatine Hill ticket, Palatine Hill deserves a little more recognition. Mostly because, you know, this is where the city of Rome was born (according to legend, the cave where Romulus and Remus were nursed by the she-wolf was located on this hill, and the hill's Casa Romuli is allegedly where Romulus made his home after founding the city). And although people lived on Palatine Hill as early as 1000 BCE, if you were a citizen during the hill's later years, you likely would have been willing to kill somebody Caesar-style for a piece of real estate up here. As the Beverly Hills of the Republican and Imperial periods, Palatine Hill (from which we get the word "palace") was home to all the city's hottest property, and today you can see the ruins of centuries' worth of temples, the houses of Augustus and Livia, and the Imperial Palace, whose apartments once overlooked Circus Maximus. Stop by the Palatine Museum to brush up on a little history and then wander over to the beautiful Farnese Gardens and have a look out over the entire city before making your way down to the Forum.

i M Colosseum. Entrance on V. San Gregorio. You can also reach Palatine Hill from the Roman Forum. €12 combined with the Roman Forum and the Colosseum. Ticket is valid for entrance to the Colosseum and the Forum/Palatine Hill for two consecutive days.* ⌚ *Open daily 8:30am to one hour before sunset.*

THE ROMAN FORUM   ANCIENT ROME
Your visit to the Roman Forum will probably leave you thinking, "Wow, this city is really falling to pieces." But by this point, you've probably realized that that's

Rome's calling card: making tourists pay too many euro to see a bunch of dirt and old bricks. Still, what was once the center of Roman public life has become the center of Roman tourism, and a walk through the Forum is an essential part of any first visit to this city. The ends of the Forum are marked by the Arch of Titus (near the entrance) and the Arch of Septimius Severus (near the far exit at the foot of Capitoline Hill), and in between you'll find other highlights that include the Tempio di Romolo, the Tempio di Antonino e Faustina, and the House of the Vestal Virgins.

i M: Colosseum. Entrance to the Forum is on V. dei Fori Imperiali or V. San Gregorio (directly opposite the Colosseum). You can also enter the Forum from Palatine Hill. €12 combined with Palatine Hill and the Colosseum. Ticket is valid for entrance to the Colosseum and the Forum/Palatine Hill for two consecutive days. ☼ Open daily 8:30am to one hour before sunset.

FORI IMPERIALI
ANCIENT ROME

V. dei Fori Imperiali

A funny thing happened on the way to the forum—namely, you probably stumbled across a whole other set of fora. And while they might not be The Forum, you will probably come to know Fori Imperali as The Free Fora, which is almost better. Lining the V. dei Fori Imperiali between the Vittorio Emanuele II Monument and the Colosseum, these fora once served as the business district of Rome and are now home to many a ruin and lingering column, all of which can be admired from the various spots along the street. Overshadowing it all, however, is Trajan's Column, located at the far end of the Trajan Forum. Built to commemorate the emperor's victories in the Dacian Wars (and to tell the world, "Hey, guys, I have a big dick!"), Trajan's Column stands 98 ft. tall and is decorated with a single continuous frieze magnificent enough to distract you from all the phallic overcompensation.

i M: Colosseum. Walk down V. dei Fori Imperiali; the ruins and Trajan's Column are on the right. Free.

ARCH OF CONSTANTINE
MONUMENT, ANCIENT ROME

V. San Gregorio

Standing just across the street from the Colosseum, the Arch of Constantine is a bit dwarfed by its mammoth neighbor. In fairness, it's hard for any structure to compete with the Colosseum for people's attention, but we're pretty sure the Arch of Constantine is sitting there thinking, "At least I still have my youth and all my marble, god." The arch straddles the Via Triumphalis, the road used by emperors when they returned home after totally slaughtering the competition at away games. It was dedicated in 315 CE to celebrate Constantine's victory (and complete inability to work well with other people) over his co-emperor Maxentius in 312 CE. An architectural wonder in its own right, the arch is often admired in passing as everyone makes his or her way over to the Colosseum, but take a moment to pause and marvel at the friezes depicted on nearly every surface of the structure.

i M: Colosseum. The arch is right across from the Colosseum; you can't miss it. Free.

CAPITOLINE HILL
ANCIENT ROME

Tucked around the back side of the Vittorio Emanuele II Monument, Capitoline Hill converges around Piazza di Campidoglio, which was designed by Michelangelo and is punctuated by an equestrian statue of Marcus Aurelius. If you mount the hill from the central stairs on the west side Piazza Venezia, you'll be welcomed by two naked guys and their horses (alas, statues, although they do make you reconsider the logistics of bareback riding). Surrounding the piazza are the Capitoline Museums, which are home to the world's oldest public collection of ancient art. The back end of Capitoline Hill overlooks the Roman Forum, so wander around and take in the view of the ruins and the Arch of Septimius

take me to church

"But all Italian churches look the same!" said the beleaguered, world-weary American tourist after seeing one too many fancy gilded ceilings. Fair enough: if you're one of those travelers who can't appreciate the finer details of fine art, here are a few churches in Rome that house artwork famous enough for you to actually give a damn about.

- **CHIESA DI SAN LUIGI DEI FRANCESI:** The understated facade of this church belies the fact that it is home to three of Caravaggio's most celebrated paintings, including *The Calling of Saint Matthew.*

- **BASILICA DI SAN PIETRO IN VINCOLI:** Located near V. Cavour in Rome's Monti neighborhood, this church houses Michelangelo's famous High Renaissance sculpture of Moses.

- **CHIESA DI SANTA MARIA DELLA VITTORIA:** Although Bernini's fingerprints are all over St. Peter's Basilica, the artist's moving *Ecstasy of Saint Teresa* can be found in this church, tucked just up the road from P. Barberini.

- **BASILICA DI SANTA MARIA DEL POPOLO:** Often overlooked by tourists who visit Piazza del Popolo, this church houses two works by Caravaggio and also features gold frescoes painted by none other than Raphael.

Severus from that vantage point, then seek out one of the hill's shady retreats to rehydrate before heading back out into the sun.

i From P. Venezia, facing the Vittorio Emanuele II Monument, walk right down V. Teatro Marcello, then look for the stairs on the left and head up the hill. Free.

THE VELABRUM ANCIENT ROME

This sunken section of the ancient city lies in a valley between Palatine Hill, Circus Maximus, and the Tiber and features the lesser-known ruins of the Teatro di Marcello and the Arco di Giano, among others. The only reason most people wander down here, however, is to visit the Chiesa di Santa Maria in Cosmedin. If you're wondering what the giant line outside this otherwise random church is for, it's a crowd of people who are trying to capture the lingering essence of Audrey Hepburn and Gregory Peck, who famously visited the church's Bocca della Verita ("Mouth of Truth") in *Roman Holiday.* Although entrance to the actual church is free, most people just come here for a picture with the mouth (which, according to legend, will bite off the hand of a liar). So proceed with caution, prepare for a long wait, and just remember: you are not secretly a princess, and the sweaty guy in front of you in line is most definitely not Gregory Peck. Mostly, you stood in line for 30min. and all you got was a photo with the Bocca's ugly mug.

i From P. Venezia, facing the Vittorio Emanuele II Monument, walk right down V. del Teatro Marcello and continue as it turns into V. Petroselli. The Velabrum and its sights are in the flat region as the base of the hill. Church located in P. Bocca della Verita. Free. ☉ Church open daily 9:30am-5:50pm.

Centro Storico

⬚ PANTHEON
P. della Rotonda

ANCIENT ROME

You've probably heard excellent things about the Pantheon and its legendary unsupported dome—the largest of its kind 1889 years running. And man, this

italy

church really holds up to all the hype (and, you know, to gravity and time). Built in the second century CE, this temple to the gods (all of them) remains one of Rome's most impressive and best-preserved relics from the ancient period. While the building's 16 Corinthian columns are shocking enough in their size and girth, it is the Pantheon's richly colored interior and rotunda that will truly leave you dumbfounded. Try to preserve for yourself that moment when you first walked inside and caught of glimpse of the rotunda's central oculus and the blue sky beyond—try to remember the awe and smallness that you felt in that moment because it's pretty singular. And in case you need to be brought back down to earth, wander over to the left side of the church and look for the tomb of Raphael, whose inscription reads, "Here lies Raphael, by whom Nature feared to be outdone while he lived and, when he died, feared that she herself would die."

i *From P. Navona, exit onto Corsia Agonale, then turn left onto Piazza Madama, then take a quick right onto V. dei Salvatore. Turn right onto V. Della Dogana Vecchia, then left onto Salita de Crescenzi and proceed to P. Della Rotonda. Free. ☼ Open M-Sa 8:30am-7:30pm, Su 9am-6pm.*

PIAZZA NAVONA PIAZZA

If you're not looking for a selfie stick or an overpriced watercolor of the Colosseum, the main draw for the swarm of tourists who congregate in Piazza Navona is Bernini's famous Fontana dei Quattro Fiumi, which depicts personified versions of each major river of the four continents that were under papal control when fountain was constructed in 1651. Look for the Danube (Europe), the Ganges (Asia), the Rio de la Plata (America), and the Nile (Africa). Overlooking the fountain, you'll find the Chiesa di Sant'Agnese in Agone, a magnificent Baroque church designed by Bernini's rival, Francesco Borromini (take time to pop inside and admire the frescoes and gold leaf of the church's domed interior). The piazza is certainly popular among tourists, but after you've taken the time to admire the Bernini and the Borromini, make your way to the more charming side streets, where you'll find plenty of restaurants, wine bars, and gelaterias lining the narrow cobblestones.

i *From Corso Vittorio Emanuele II, turn into P. San Pantaleo and turn right into V. della Cuccagna and walk through Palazzo Braschi to P. Navona. Piazza and church free.*

VITTORIO EMANUELE II MONUMENT MONUMENT

P. Venezia

The Vittorio Emanuele II Monument is also known as Italy's "Altar to the Fatherland," and from its position overlooking the busy traffic circle of Piazza Venezia, everything about it seems to be saying, "Bow down, tourists." And you will, because its sprawling steps, enormous white columns, and imposing equestrian statue of V-Manny himself are just that impressive. Constructed in 1885 to celebrate nationalism and unification, the monument also features Italian flags that are almost as big as the American ones you'll find outside most Hummer dealerships. And even if most Italians refer to it as "The White Typewriter" or "The Wedding Cake," damn if it isn't a tasty slice. You can catch glimpses of the monument from almost every spot in Rome, and while each stolen glance never ceases to impress, nothing quite rivals walking right up to it. Don't forget to climb up the many steps on the west side of the monument to take in all of Rome from its panoramic terrace. The exhibits inside are only worthwhile if you're a Vittorio Emanuele II fanboy/fangirl. They have his trousers. What more convincing do you need?

i *P. Venezia. You can't miss it. Free. ☼ Monument open daily 9:30am-5:30pm.*

rome

CHIESA SAN LUIGI DEI FRANCESI   CHURCH
P. San Luigi dei Francesi 5

When you walk up to this 16th-century church and consider its relatively generic gray exterior, you might wonder, "Haven't I walked past this before?" Probably not, although the Chiesa San Luigi dei Francesi and its understated facade do look pretty run-of-the-mill (at least by Roman standards). And although the church distinguishes itself by being French, its real draw is entirely Italian: namely, the three famous works by Caravaggio that can be found here. Interestingly, the church's magnificent, gilded altar and intricate ceiling sculptures (turn around and check out the angels holding up the massive organ) take center stage here, while Caravaggio's *The Calling of Saint Matthew*, *Saint Matthew and the Angel*, and *The Crucifixion* are all crammed into the same corner chapel. Still, these Baroque masterpieces won't be hard to find—just look for the crowd of eager-beaver art students gathered in the upper-left-hand corner of the church. While admiring Caravaggio's supreme mastery of chiaroscuro, you can consider the play of light and shadow in more ways than one, as the church turns its chapel lights on and off every few minutes. Life imitates art, ya know?

i From P. Navona, exit onto Corsia Agonale, then turn left onto C. del Rinascimento, then right onto V. Santa Giovanna d'Arco. Free. ⊠ Open daily 10am-12:30pm and 3-7pm.

AREA SACRA   ANCIENT ROME
Bordered by V. di Torre Argentina, V. Florida, and Largo di Torre Argentina

Some people might say that the Area Sacra has really gone to the dogs in recent years. Or maybe to the cats—as in, part of this ancient ruin is literally a cat sanctuary. A tribute, perhaps, to some dangerously catty politicians? Because lo—this is also the place where a bunch of senators decided, in the immortal words of Gretchen Wieners, to "totally just stab Caesar" on the Ides of March, 44 BCE. The tall tree near the ruins of the Theatre of Pompey mark the place where Caesar's blood was spilled and the trope of stabbing your friend in the back (yes, you, Brutus) was born. Admire the ruins from the street and reflect on all the CW show plotlines that owe so much to this place.

i From P. Venezia, walk west down V. Plebiscito, which turns into Corso Vittorio Emanuele II; walk until the street meets Largo di Torre Argentina. Free.

PALAZZO VENEZIA   MUSEUM
V. del Plebiscito 118   ☎06 678 01 31 www.museopalazzovenezia.benicultural.it

The Palazzo Venezia could have been called "The House of Creepy Babies," or perhaps the "Let's Normalize Public Breastfeeding Museum." Indeed, much of the 14th-to-18th-century artwork you'll find here features plenty of wooden mothers and questionable interpretations of what infants look like. (You know how all parents think their babies are adorable even if they actually look like a squashed melon? That's also a symptom of a lot of the artists whose little darlings are housed here. Maybe these tots could grow into their weird, bulbous heads, but in this case, time will not tell.) Be aware: a lot of this museum is religious panel painting, plus some ceramics and one incongruous room of 18th-century portraits that are all pink cheeks and powdered wigs. Constructed during the Renaissance, the building itself features a dimly lit but imposing staircase and encompasses an impressive garden of palm trees, where it's easy to picture Mussolini dreamin' and schemin' his way to infamy (the palace once housed his offices, and its balcony served as stump for many of his speeches).

i From P. Venezia, walk down V. del Plebiscito. The museum entrance is on the left. €5, reduced €2.50. ⊠ Open Tu-Su 8:30am-7:30pm.

Piazza di Spagna

BORGHESE GALLERY

Ple. Scipione Borghese 5

MUSEUM

☎06 84 13 979 www.galleriaborghese.it

Cardinal Scipione Borghese knew a thing or two about how to pimp out a villa. An early patron of Gian Lorenzo Bernini and a devoted Caravaggio fanboy, Scipione sketched out plans for this gallery as a place to house his extensive art collection. Constructed in the 17th century and opened to the public in 1903, the Borghese Gallery is now home to some of the greatest Bernini sculptures in existence and the world's largest concentration of works by Caravaggio. Bernini highlights include everything from the masterful *Apollo and Daphne* to the mythic and moving *Aeneas, Anchises, and Ascanius* to the heartbreaking *The Rape of Proserpina*; the museum also houses Bernini's *David*, a more dynamic and Baroque take on the myth that Michelangelo so immortalized in his own famous statue. Give yourself plenty of time to circle each sculpture a few times—every angle reveals a new detail and serves as testament to Bernini's supreme skill (it's really no wonder he was such an egomaniac). Among the collection of Caravaggio paintings housed here, you'll find *David with the Head of Goliath, Sick Bacchus,* and *Boy with a Basket of Fruit* (who, if you think about it, is really kind of a tart). The 20 rooms of the gallery, spread out across two floors (sculptures on the first floor, paintings on the second), are a marvel in themselves, stuffed to the brim with statues and columns, adorned with intricate molding and gold leaf, and splashed with staggering ceiling frescoes.

After the magnificence of the first floor (where you'll find the majority of the works by Bernini and Caravaggio), the second level is a bit of a letdown, although it does feature a collection of paintings that includes works by Titian, Raphael, and Peter Paul Rubens, along with a couple Bernini self-portraits (because apparently even masterclass sculptors took time for a little #self-iesunday back in the day). Audio guides are available for a fee, but there are also informational cards (in both English and Italian) located in each room. Pro tip: After everyone has circled through the rooms on the first floor and headed upstairs to the paintings, take another spin through the sculptures; the rooms will likely be much emptier, and you might just find yourself one on one with a Bernini sculpture and nothing but the chirping of birds through the open window to disturb you.

i Located in the Villa Borghese Gardens, at the crossroads of Vle. dell'Uccelliera and Vle. del Museo Borghese. Reservations required. Book online or in person up to two weeks in advance. Bags of all sizes must be checked downstairs before you enter the gallery. €11, EU citizens 18-25 €6.50. Audio guides €5. ♿ Open Tu-Su 8:30am-7.30pm. Ticket office closes at 6:30pm.

VILLA BORGHESE GARDENS

GARDENS

The Borghese Gardens are no Central Park. For one thing, they're a lot older and more legit than Central Park, having been first built up by Scipione Borghese starting in 1605 and later restyled and perfected in the English taste in the 19th century. And perhaps that's why, in some ways, they look a little worse for the wear. But what this 148-acre park lacks in manicured lawns and frisbee-tossing yuppies it makes up for in purple wildflowers, fountains on fountains, the occasional horse track (casual), and long grass and towering trees that seem to defy the urban insanity of the surrounding metropolis. Located just above Piazza del Popolo, the sprawling gardens are crisscrossed by gravel trails and paved paths, and it seems like all roads lead to some pond or statue or obelisk (or, you know, the Galleria Borghese). As usual, when in Rome, no opportunity goes unexploited to try to sell stuff to tourists; said

rome

stuff here includes gelato carts, bike and *bici pincio* rentals, and overpriced cafes and restaurants within the grounds of the park.

i M Flamino or M Spagna. There are multiple entrances to the park: Porta Pinciana, Ple. Flaminio, Vle. Belle Arti, V. Mercadante, and V. Pinciana. Free. 🕐 Open 24hr.

PIAZZA DI SPAGNA AND THE SPANISH STEPS   MONUMENT, PIAZZA
P. di Spagna

If we're going to boil things down to their most basic elements, Piazza di Spagna is one big celebration of all the stuff rich people can buy, plus a Bernini fountain and a Keats museum that probably no one ever visits. And yeah sure, the Spanish Steps are historic (all 135 of them) leading to a sparse church, but they're also a giant audience of people looking out at a bunch of stores they can't afford. But don't worry—if you didn't factor Gucci and Prada into your backpacking budget, you can always console yourself with a selfie stick. At least Bernini's Fontana della Barcaccia (literally, "Fountain of the Ugly Boat") provides an opportunity to contemplate whether Bernini was being unduly hard on himself or if he was a just an egotistical bastard who knew that even if he made a shitty statue, people would still be taking pictures of it hundreds of years later. Hard to say, but probably the latter.

i M: Spagna. Free. 🕐 Open 24hr.

TREVI FOUNTAIN   FOUNTAIN
P. di Trevi

The only time to really see Trevi Fountain is at 4am, when the moonlight hits the water just right and you can fawn over its majesty while ignoring the guy reading a newspaper next to you. Because yes, it's always crowded. Full of tourists, shop vendors, or policemen making sure you don't pull a *La Dolce Vita* and hop in, Trevi is one of those iconic Roman places you have to see. Nicola Salvi's beautiful fountain cut from rock and stone depicts an enormous Neptune surrounded by the goddesses of abundance and good health, as well as two brawny horsemen chilling out just because. Do as the Roman tourists do and save up on those one-cent coins to toss in here: one ensures a prompt return to Rome, two will bring you love in the Eternal City, and three will bring about your wedding.

i From P. di Trevi, walk down V. Propaganda (right if facing the Spanish Steps) and veer right as it turns into Largo del Nazareno. Turn left onto V. Poli and continue on to where High Expectations meet Supreme Disappointment at P. di Trevi. Free. Unless you toss a coin into it.

PIAZZA DEL POPOLO   PIAZZA
P. del Popolo

Piazza del Popolo is ostensibly the "People's Square," but really, this place belongs to the massive Egyptian obelisk of Ramses II that dominates its center (the structure was first brought to Rome in 10 BCE and erected, like the giant phallic symbol that it is, in this square in 1589). Home to the church of Santa Maria del Popolo (worth a look), the piazza is also centrally located near Piazza di Spagna and the Villa Borghese Gardens, both a short walk away, and is situated at the opposite end of V. del Corso from Piazza Venezia—look straight down the street to catch a glimpse of the Vittorio Emanuele II Monument at the other end.

i M: Flamino. Or from P. di Spagna, proceed down V. del Babuino (left if facing the Spanish Steps). Free.

MUSEO DELL'ARA PACIS   MUSEUM
V. della Frezza 43   ☎06 06 08 www.arapacis.it

Consecrated on January 30, 9 BCE, and ostensibly dedicated to the Roman goddess of peace (but mostly to Augustus, to commemorate some of his not-so-peaceful conquests in Spain and Gaul), the Ara Pacis was buried underground for several centuries before being rediscovered and excavated in the early 20th century. (Because, you know, that kind of thing can happen in a city that's literally older than dirt.) Today, the Ara Pacis is the main (and nearly the only) attraction in this museum, which you might not have realized until after you paid €10.50 for the ticket. If you're particularly familiar with the reign of Augustus or can appreciate a nice frieze or two (the ones adorning the altar are quite stunning and well preserved), then this museum certainly warrants a look. For everyone else, it might not be worth the entrance fee, although the juxtaposition of ancient and modern architecture is a sight to see (made all the more intense by the fact that both the altar and its museum radiate varying shades of stunning white). If you're feeling ambivalent about whether or not it's worth your while (or your euro), the good news is that you can still catch a glimpse of the altar through the museum's large glass windows and sit for a spell next to the fountain outside the main entrance.

i From P. di Spagna, walk down V. del Babuino (left if facing the Spanish Steps) and turn left onto V. Vittorio. Continue several blocks as V. Vittorio turns into V. dei Pontefici, then turn left onto V. di Ripetta. The museum is on the right. €10.50, reduced €8.50. ☑ Open Tu-Su 9am-7pm.

Termini

BASILICA DI SANTA MARIA MAGGIORE   CHURCH
P. di Santa Maria Maggiore 28

Basilica di Santa Maria Maggiore is really feelin' itself. Forget about charity and humility, man: this church is all about the gold leaf life and, true to its Baroque style, architectural gluttony. Originally constructed in the fifth century as one of the first churches dedicated to the Virgin Mary (because apparently it took 500 years for this chick and her magic womb to finally get some recognition #yesallwomen), the basilica has undergone several restorations since then, including an interior renovation in the late 1500s. Located just a few blocks from Termini Station, the basilica is a must-see for anyone who possesses even the most basic appreciation of pretty stuff. The church also has an adjoining museum that you can visit for a fee, but once you've seen the altar and the columns and the ceiling (and, come to think of it, even the floor) of the church's interior, you've already seen the best part for free.

i From Termini Station, exit onto V. Giovanni Giolitti and turn right down V. Gioberti. Continue to P. di Santa Maria Maggiore. Modest dress required. Basilica free. Museum €4, reduced €2. ☑ Museum open daily 9:30am-6:30pm. Basilica open daily 7am-7pm.

CHIESA DI SANTA MARIA DEGLI ANGELI   CHURCH
P. della Repubblica

This famous church isn't fronting. Granted, that's mostly because it doesn't have a facade with which to front. Its less-than-impressive exterior and location amid the hustle of Piazza della Repubblica, however, doesn't mean you should overlook the Chiesa di Santa Maria Degli Angeli, because—spoiler alert—it was designed by Michelangelo (yeah, that guy). The vaulted ceilings and red granite columns of this shockingly large "theater of light" were designed by the master himself in 1563 after he was recruited to adapt part of the ruins of the ancient Baths of Diocletian (the basilica was built into what was formerly the frigidarium of the baths). Don't forget to check out the meridian line that runs from the east transept to the altar and the signs of the Zodiac that surround it.

i M Repubblica. Located on the northeast side of Piazza della Repubblica. Modest dress required. Free. Shawls available for €1. ☑ Open daily May-Sept 7:30am-7pm; Oct-Apr 7:30am-6:30pm.

BATHS OF DIOCLETIAN   MUSEUM
Vle. Enrico De Nicola 79   www.archeoroma.beniculturali.it

For a sight as old and as cool as the Baths of Diocletian, the city of Rome sure makes it hard for you to figure out where the hell they are. Do you see those signs for the baths in Piazza della Repubblica? Nope, the baths aren't actually here. Did you make it as far as buying a ticket to the National Museum and are now lost somewhere in Michelangelo's Cloister? Nope, no baths here, either. Although the cloister and its many sculptures are worth a stroll (note: the rest of the museums are not), the ruins of the ancient baths are what you came here to see, so upon leaving the ticket counter, hightail it through the bookshop and proceed through a door on the left, and you'll eventually find the towering walls of the age-old baths. You'll be rewarded with a nearly private viewing (congrats: no one else could figure out how to get here, either!). Indeed, the baths are shockingly quiet and empty, which only serves to accentuate the gravity of the massive ruins; the lack of other tourists also makes it a little easier to imagine ancient Romans flocking to these sumptuous pools nearly 2000 years ago (the baths were first dedicated in 306 CE).

i From Termini Station, exit onto P. dei Cinquecento and cross the street to Vle. Enrico De Nicola. Look for the signs for the Museo Nazionale Romana; the entrance for the museum and the baths is on Vle. Enrico De Nicola. €7, €3.50 EU students 18-25. Ticket provides entry to the Baths of Diocletian, Museo Nazionale Romano, Palazzo Altemps, and Crypta Balbi; valid for 3 days. ⌚ Open Tu-Su 9am-7:45pm.

Vatican City

THE VATICAN MUSEUMS
MUSEUM

Vle. Vaticano 97 ☎06 69 88 38 60 www.museivaticani.va

A visit to the Vatican Museums is a real test in avoiding oversaturation and, perhaps more critically, in maintaining your sanity and affection for humankind in general. Because you will be tested, both by the museums' more than 7km of galleries and by the hundreds of swarming tour groups, all of whom have determined to either elbow you in the kidney, step on your toes, or form one giant unmoving mass that will trap you in a corner of the Raphael Rooms.

But avoid the herds if possible and take your time as you make your way through the Vatican's sprawling and truly astounding collection of some of the greatest art in the world. The museum is one continuous loop, so you won't miss anything if you just follow the crowds (it certainly won't be hard to spot them). Try to take in the sculptural spread that is the Galleria Chiaramonti, with its concentration of more than 1000 statues collected in a single corridor. Admire the Belvedere Torso (a true butterface if there ever was one) in the Sala delle Muse and the giant, gilded bronze statue of Hercules in the red Sala Rotunda. Perhaps the most famous rooms here, however, are the Raphael Rooms, where you can see the legendary School of Athens (which is basically just the Raphael's Renaissance take on celebrity photobombing) and several of the master's other incredible frescoes. You'll then have to walk through some contemporary art galleries to reach to the climactic Sistine Chapel, where you'll be overwhelmed by bodies on all sides and in all dimensions: bodies on the walls, bodies on the ceiling, bodies all around you and up in your personal space. Marvel at this monsoon of humanity, remember to keep things "Silencio!," and reflect on Michelangelo's masterpiece, which contains more pasty white people than a Republican National Convention, before retreating out the back door.

i M: Ottaviano. Walk down V. Ottaviano, turn right onto V. dei Bastioni di Michelangelo, and follow the wall until you see the end of the line for the museums. Entrance on Vle. Vaticano. Make a reservation online in advance if you want to skip the lines. €16. Free last Su of each month. Audio guides with map €7. ⌚ Museums open Mar-Oct M-F 10am-6pm, Sa 10am-4pm; Nov-Feb M-F 10am-3pm. Museums open last Su of every month 9am-2pm for free. Last entry 1hr. 15min. before close.

the pope's general audience

Every Wednesday when the Pope is in town, he holds a general audience that anyone with a ticket can attend. And in a surprise twist, the Catholic Church won't even charge you for it, which is an especially good deal now that we finally have a pope that people can get excited about. Indeed, seeing Pope Francis (or as we like to call him, Dope Francis) is almost like seeing a celebrity, so pick up a ticket. You can reserve tickets in advance online, or you can just walk up to one of the Swiss guards at the Bronze Doors of St. Peter's and ask for one (Tu 3-7pm, W 7-10am). And no need to feel awkward if you're not Catholic—that just means you're one of those lost sheep who are extra welcome.

ST. PETER'S BASILICA
CHURCH

At the end of V. della Conciliazione ☎06 69 88 16 62 www.vaticanstate.va

Citizens of Renaissance-era Rome certainly didn't have to wonder where all their taxpayer tithes were being spent. Just one look up at St. Peter's ornate, mind-blowingly intricate ceiling and you can almost hear the coins in the coffer ringing and a thousand souls from purgatory springing. And while the Catholic Church's historical excess and overindulgences of more than one variety may be a little gross, fortunately for you, the price of admission to the basilica today will cost you little more than some time spent in line (which, in fairness, could be upward of 2hr. if you don't plan well).

The church itself, which was constructed over a period of more than 100 years during the late Renaissance, is so cavernous, sprawling, and richly decorated that it'll be hard to know where to look. Generally speaking, "anywhere" is a pretty foolproof strategy, although be sure to take note of Bernini's twisted baldacchino, which dominates the center of church and marks both the pope's altar and the spot just above St. Peter's tomb. To the right of the basilica's entrance, you'll also find Michelangelo's Pietà—the artist's famous, moving rendition of the Virgin Mary and Jesus shortly after the Crucifixion. (Since the dawn of the smartphone, Mary and her son have basically become the Beatles of St. Peter's, so try to make your way through the dense crowd of tour groups and iPhones held eagerly aloft to get a closer, more intimate look at Mary's mournful visage through the bulletproof glass.) And while a few of the chapels here are reserved for prayer, don't expect to find much peace or time for spiritual reflection while wandering through the rest of the basilica: this place is crawling with tour groups. But even these tour groups get swallowed up by the sheer size of this enormous basilica.

If you're not afraid of heights and don't get claustrophobic easily, take a trip up to the top of the basilica's dome—the views from the cupola are certainly worth the €5 fee (€7 if you want to take the elevator part of the way up). The trip up (which involves 551 steps, 320 with the lift) gives you a chance to walk around the inside of the dome and offers a bird's-eye view of the altar and the baldacchino below. Keep climbing (and don't worry when the walls begin to slant—it means you're inside the actual curve of the dome) and you'll reach the very top of the cupola and one of the most breathtaking views of the city. Look out across St. Peter's Square on one side and the Vatican and its manicured gardens on the other. On the way down, you can stop on a lower roof of the church and get a close-up look at the dome from below. Pro tip: if you plan

rome

to climb the cupola, do that first—the route back down will spit you out right inside the basilica.

i M: Ottaviano. Walk down V. Ottaviano and follow the walls of the Vatican to the square. Or walk down V. della Conciliazione. Knees and shoulders must be covered. Arrive early in the morning (before 8am) to avoid the crowds. And if you're not oversaturated after visiting the church, you can also pay a visit to St. Peter's Tomb and the Vatican Grottoes during your trip to St. Peter's. Basilica free. Cupola €5. ☉ Basilica open daily Apr-Sept 7am-7pm; Oct-Mar 7am-6pm. Cupola open daily Apr-Sept 8am-6pm; Oct-Mar 8am-5pm.

PIAZZA DI SAN PIETRO PIAZZA

At the end of V. della Conciliazione ☎06 69 88 16 62 www.vaticanstate.va

St. Peter's Square sits in front of St. Peter's Basilica (of all things) and can be approached from a number of different directions, although the most dramatic is certainly walking up to it along V. della Conciliazione. Designed by Bernini, the sweeping elliptical piazza is encompassed by enormous Tuscan colonnades topped with 140 statues of saints that, in the artist's own words, were intended to welcome visitors into "the maternal arms of Mother Church." (Kind of ironic syntax for an institution full of a bunch of dudes wearing funny hats.) The columns stand four rows deep, and if you look on either side of the square's central obelisk (yes, another one of those—Rome was even more into Egypt than you were in third grade), you'll find a circle marked "Centro del Colonnato" where, if you stand directly on it, all the columns line up perfectly. Because Bernini was artsy and good at math! The piazza is best visited at night, when the fountains and basilica are all lit up and when the line of people and sunbrellas waiting to get into the church has dissipated.

i M: Ottaviano. Walk down V. Ottaviano and follow the walls of the Vatican to the square. Or walk down V. della Conciliazione. Free. ☉ Piazza open 24hr.

MUSEO NAZIONALE DI CASTEL SANT'ANGELO MUSEUM

Lungotevere Castello 50 ☎06 68 19 111 www.castelsantangelo.com

Rome isn't exactly known for its old-school castles, but in case you've gotten sick of ancient ruins, Renaissance churches, or the overindulgence of Baroque art in general, this one's for you. Originally built as a mausoleum for Hadrian's super-important ashes (pardon his dust), the Castel Sant'Angelo was repurposed as a military fortress in the fifth century and later used as a papal castle and refuge starting in the 14th century. As a result, the current structure is composed of distinct levels that include the mausoleum, prisons and warehouses, military patios, papal apartments, and a panoramic terrace. So make like Bowser and roam the halls of this seemingly endless castle. Don't miss the Hall of Urns in the center of the castle (the room that is believed to have held Hadrian's ashes) or the winding, cavernous Rampa Diametrale in the dungeon-like inner halls (the lights along the passageways aren't quite torches, but the effect is close enough). Then contrast the dark, chilly vibe of the castle's bowels with the stunning sunlight and sweeping vistas you'll encounter with each new level of the structure, from the parapet walk (keep an eye out for the Borgo Passetto, the protected papal passageway that leads to St. Peter's) to the upper terrace to the final exposed roof of the fortress, from which you can look out over St. Peter's, Ponte Sant'Angelo, and all of Rome.

i The castle is at the end of V. della Conciliazione, at the intersection with Ponte Sant'Angelo. €10.50, reduced €7. ☉ Open Tu-Su 9am-7:30pm. Last entry 6:30pm.

Trastevere

GIANICOLO HILL HILL

Fun fact: Gianicolo Hill isn't actually one of the seven hills of Rome. Not that you were going to scale all of them anyway (it's too damn hot for that nonsense).

But as the second-tallest hilltop in the modern city, Gianicolo (alternatively Janiculum) is worth the relatively quick climb up V. Garibaldi from the west side of Trastevere. Wind your way up the road, or take a shortcut up a steep flight of stone steps; either way, fee_ free to refresh yourself after the climb at the rushing waters of the Fontana dell'Acqua Paola, where you can also enjoy a preliminary view of the city. Then make your way down Passeggiata del Gianicolo along a leisurely avenue of sycamores to P. Giuseppe Garibaldi, where you can perch yourself on a ledge and look out over nearly all of Rome (from the other side of the piazza, you can see St. Peter's Basilica through the trees). Relax and enjoy the view: the foreground may be littered with empty beer bottles, but the backdrop is harder to sniff at.

i *From P. San Egidio, turn left onto Vicolo del Cedro and climb the stairs, then take a left onto V. Garibaldi. Free.*

ORTO BOTANICO (BOTANICAL GARDENS) GARDENS
Largo Cristina di Svezia 24 ☎06 49 91 71 07 web.uniroma1.it/ortobotanico

Bordering the lower perimeter of Gianicolo Hill, Trastevere's Botanical Garden is a 30-acre sanctuary of paths, park benches, and more than 7000 species of plants, all of which are protected from the traffic, crowds, and litterbugs of Rome. It sounds different here: the quietude, and the sound of your own feet shuffling along the gravel paths, is almost unsettling. And while you can never fully escape the sounds of city police sirens and mopeds ripping down the surrounding streets, the chorus of birds in the trees and wind tossing the leaves creates a calmer kind of uproar here. The entire garden is a loop, so start at one end, make your way around the main pathway, and feel free to take detours along the meandering side trails. Wander through the garden's grand palm trees and admire its shady ginkgos, wind your way up to the Japanese garden and into a thicket of bamboo, and tiptoe your way down the different levels of the rose garden. There are plenty of benches along the way, so if you want to make an afternoon of it, bring a book or some music and spend a couple hours under the cover of the dense flora. Every now and then, look out through the trees to see the domes and rooftops of Rome peeping through breaks in the branches.

i *Walk to the end of V. Corsini until you reach Largo Cristina di Svezia. €8, reduced €4. ☒ Open May-June Tu-Su 9am-6:30pm; July-Aug Tu-Sa 9am-6:30pm; Sept-Oct Tu-Su 9am-6:30pm; Nov-Apr Tu-Sa 9am-6:30pm.*

FOOD
Ancient City

PIZZERIA DA MILVIO PIZZA $
V. dei Serpenti 7 ☎06 77 20 13 61

If you're starting to feel hangry after hours of sightseeing in the hot Roman sun, up your spirits and your blood sugar with a quick stop at Milvio. Located just off V. Cavour near the Colosseum, Milvio offers an assortment of pizzas, panini, and pastas whose quality far exceeds their budget prices. Order at the counter and then grab an orange, Jetson-esque plastic seat at one of the many tables at the back of the pizzeria. It's not the fanciest food you'll find in the city, but at this point in the day, you're probably a sweaty mess who's just looking for some carbs and a bathroom, dammit. For a cheap, fast, and satisfying meal in the middle of the day, Milvio fits the bill on all fronts.

i *M: Colosseum. Walk down V. dei Fori Imperiali and turn right onto V. Cavour, then left onto V. Serpenti. Milvio is on the left. Pizza €9-15 per kg. Panini €7. Pasta €5. ☒ Open daily 8am-midnight or later.*

LA CARBONARA

V. Panisperna 214

RISTORANTE $

☎06 48 25 176 www.lacarbonara.it

At La Carbonara, the writing's on the walls—and that's a good thing. With more than a decade's worth of notes and dedications scrawled on the walls from fans all over the world, La Carbonara certainly doesn't need TripAdvisor to assure you that you're going to have a good meal (they reinforce this point with the anti-TripAdvisor signs in the window—bold move, La Carbonara). Service is brusque but friendly, and the random assortment of posters, horse busts, and glass orbs scattered around the walls give the restaurant a cluttered, lived-in feel. You get the sense that La Carbonara isn't trying to impress you; rather, it sets the tone and makes the rules (one of which is "People with good taste talk in a low voice"—they even spelled it out in English for all you loud, ugly Americans). In return, you order some of their delicious pasta (classics like the *cacio e pepe* are foolproof) and go home happy.

i *From Basilica di Santa Maria Maggiore, proceed down V. di Santa Maria Maggiore, which becomes V. Panisperna. La Carbonara is on the left. Get here right when the restaurant opens if you don't have a reservation and want to get a table. Antipasti €5-10. Primi €6-10. Secondi €9-22. Drinks €3-5.* ⏰ *Open M-Sa noon-3:30pm and 7-11pm.*

LA TAVERNA DEI FORI IMPERIALI

V. della Madonna dei Monti 9

RISTORANTE $

☎06 679 86 43 www.latavernadeiforiimperiali.com

Squirreled away down the quiet, quaint V. della Madonna dei Monti in Rome's hip Monti neighborhood, La Taverna dei Fori Imperiali is the place to go if you feel like treating yourself. (Or if you found a €20 bill in the street or something.) Although the limited outdoor seating offers you views of the Fori Imperiali down the street, the warmly lit interior, with its yellow tablecloths and wine bottles lined up on the wall, is just as cozy and has views to match (this time of the restaurant's chefs, whom you can see whipping up dishes through a glass window at the back of the restaurant). And we know you're super hip and spontaneous and down for anything that's not going to "tie you down," but for a nice meal here, you will have to take the initiative of making a reservation a couple days ahead of time (we promise it will be an obligation you won't resent).

i *M: Colosseum. Walk down V. dei Fori Imperiali, then turn right onto V. Cavour, then left onto V. della Madonna dei Monti. Reservations most definitely required. Antipasti €9-16. Primi €9-12. Secondi €12-18. Dessert €6-7.* ⏰ *Open M 12:30-3pm and 7:30-10:30pm, W-Su 12:30-3pm and 7:30-10:30pm.*

Centro Storico

IL FORNO CAMPO DE' FIORI

Vicolo del Gallo 14

PIZZA, BAKERY $

www.fornocampodefiori.com

Forno means "oven" in Italian, and chances are you've seen a lot of these signs all over the city (and not because Italy is really into its appliances). Perhaps no *forno* pronounces itself so boldly as this one, but besides the giant lettering over the entrance, that's pretty much where the bakery/pizzeria's self-marketing ends. Despite being located in the northwest corner of Campo de' Fiori, it stands a bit aloof from the many mediocre restaurants lining the square and has no designated guy out front trying to pimp out the bakery; instead, it lets business come to its door. And with good reason. The baked goods, pizza, and focaccia here are fresh, fantastic, and shockingly cheap. Even if you're just passing through the Campo, stop for a bag of precious, perfect little pieces of biscotti that will run you just over €1.

i *Located in the northern corner of Campo de' Fiori. Pizza €10-17 per kg.* ⏰ *Open M-Sa 7:30am-2:30pm and 4:45-8pm.*

GELATERIA DEL TEATRO

GELATERIA $$

V. dei Coronari 65 ☎06 45 47 48 80 www.gelateriadelteatro.it

In contrast to Frigidarium, Gelateria del Teatro aims for more subtle flavors and carefully selected ingredients when whipping up its fresh, homemade gelato. And although it's incredibly popular and busy, this place takes its time, so grab a ticket at the front door and feast your eyes on all the options—you'll need some time to wrap your head around artisanal flavors like cherry and cheese, white chocolate and basil, and yogurt al lemon grass, and fortunately for you, there's no rush. Then take your milky, refreshing cup of *pistacchio di bronte* outside and enjoy it from one of the ceramic tables tucked just off the charming V. dei Coronari. It all might seem a little bougie to you (it's prices certainly are), but after a few bites, you might also realize that you don't care—because you're sophisticated, dammit.

i From P. Navona, turn left onto V. dei Coronari and walk a few blocks. The gelateria is on the left. Gelato €2.50-8. ☒ Open M-Th 10:30am-11pm, F-Sa 10:30am-11:30pm, Su 10:30am-11pm.

FORNO MARCO ROSCIOLI

BAKERY $

V. dei Chiavari 34 ☎06 686 40 45 www.anticofornoroscioli.it

One of the most popular bakeries in the neighborhood, Marco Roscioli is yet another *forno* near Campo de' Fiori that makes for a great lunch spot (even though once you walk inside, all you might want for lunch is a pastry of some sort). Order panini on the right and pizza on the left, where the guy behind the counter will serve up your slice with a sound thwack of his knife. Take your lunch to go and walk around the corner to San Carlo ai Catinari, where you can enjoy your lunch from the steps of the church.

i From Campo de' Fiori, exit onto V. dei Giubbonari and turn left onto V. dei Chiavari. Marco Roscioli is on the left. Pizza €10-18 per kg. ☒ Open M-Sa 7am-7:30pm.

FRIGIDARIUM

GELATERIA $

V. del Governo Vecchio 112 ☎33 81 80 02 20 www.frigidarium-gelateria.com

If you were starting to feel homesick for the U.S., just head to Frigidarium where you'll find pretty much every American in Rome congregated at all hours of the day. Allegedly the best gelato in Rome (although you might not have guessed it from the kitschy-looking red menus and storefront), you'll just have to swing by and decide for yourself—a task of Herculean proportions, we know. There's always a line here, and by the time you get to the front of it, you won't have much time to contemplate the flavors; fortunately, they're all thick, rich, and pack a punch to your taste buds, so try their namesake flavor or just point anywhere. As if that wasn't enough, you can choose to either have your gelato dipped in chocolate or topped off with whipped cream and a cookie.

i From P. Navona, exit onto V. Pasquino and continue through P. Pasquino to V. del Governo Vecchio. Frigidarium is on the left. Gelato €2-4. ☒ Open daily 10am-2am.

L'ANTICA SALUMERIA

ITALIAN $

P. della Rotunda 4

We're not exactly sure how this place has (allegedly) held up since 1375, but who knows—its direct view of the Pantheon may have provided some divine inspiration. And given that most of the food you'll find just outside the Pantheon is trash, Salumeria is a surprising find and a solid place to grab a midday panino. Although the penis pasta for sale might scream tourist trap, the smell of fresh baked goods and pistachio cookies wafting from Salumeria's open door should be enough to persuade you (and may even distract you momentarily from the square's main attraction). Get a panino to go and eat it from the steps facing the Pantheon and wonder how your life ended up so great.

i P. della Rotunda; on the right when facing the Pantheon. Pizza €2-4 per etto. Panini around €5. Pastries €1.80-4. ☒ Open daily 3:30am-2am.

rome

DAR FILETTARO A SANTA BARBARA

SEAFOOD $

Largo dei Librari 88   ☎06 686 4018

Flying in the face of Italian tradition and history in more ways than one (no pasta or pizza to be found here!), Dar Filettaro is something of an anti-Renaissance man. It does one thing and does it to perfection—and doesn't waste time trying to build dumb flying machines. So if Dar Filettaro's menu looks a little fishy to you, that might be because its sole entree is just a piece of fried fish. And if you feel a little underwhelmed when your single portion of golden brown cod arrives ungarnished on a white plate, that's totally normal. We thought the same thing. But beauty, as it turns out, is skin deep and then some—take a taste, and you might find yourself wondering why you've been eating pasta all week when Dar Filettaro has been just down the street from Campo de' Fiori the whole time. Service is brisk and bare-bones (ask for a napkin and you shall receive a piece of paper), and the small collection of tables here are crammed in tight, so either arrive early or take it to go.

i From Campo de' Fiori, walk down V. dei Giubbonari and turn left onto Largo dei Librari; Dar Filettaro is on the right. Cod €5. Antipasti €5. Salad €4.50-5. Dessert €3.50. ☼ Open M-Sa 5:30-11:30pm.

PIZZERIA BAFFETTO

PIZZA $$

V. del Governo Vecchio 114   ☎06 686 16 17 www.pizzeriabaffeto.it

Waiting your turn is all part of the experience at Pizzeria Baffetto. At least that's what you should tell yourself because you'll definitely find yourself queuing up outside. (But wait, didn't we already do this at the Vatican? And the Colosseum? And goddamn Frigidarium next door??) Fortunately, the red-shirted men who work at Pizzeria Baffetto know how to keep things moving along, filing groups in and out of the crammed restaurant and turning over tables with marvelous efficiency. From the crowded line on the street to the clattering of forks and knives inside to the chefs who are busy rolling dough in the middle of it all, there's a lot going on at Pizzeria Baffetto, perhaps even enough to distract from the fact that their pies might not actually be the best you'll find in Rome. Still, it's incredibly popular among tourists and celebrities alike, so you might just have to decide for yourself.

i From P. Navona, exit onto V. Pasquino and continue through P. Pasquino to V. del Governo Vecchio. Pizzeria Baffetto is on the left. Pizza €6-14. ☼ Open daily noon-3:30pm and 6:30pm-1am.

Piazza di Spagna

▣ PASTIFICIA

PASTA $

V. della Croce 8

It is a truth universally acknowledged that most of the food surrounding the Spanish Steps is a scam. Pastificio, however, is another (almost) age-old Roman institution that will make a visit to P. di Spagna worth your while. Cooking up unbelievably cheap, fresh pasta daily since 1918, Pastificio makes up for its lack of variety (only two types of pasta are available every day) with its absolute mastery of the craft. Just close your eyes and point—seriously, you really can't go wrong here. There's no seating (only a little counter space), so get your pasta in a box to go and enjoy the al dente noodles al fresco.

i From P. di Spagna, walk down V. della Croce. Pastificio is on the first block on the left. Fresh pasta €4. Dry bags of pasta starting at €6. ☼ Open daily 10am-9pm. Fresh pasta ready at 1pm.

CIAMPINI

ITALIAN $

P. di San Lorenzo in Lucina 29   ☎06 68 76 606 www.ciampini.com

Ciampini's uniformed waiters, marble countertops, and gold placards listing all its gelato flavors may have you thinking, "I'm so fancy," but you should know that a small cone (which is actually a pretty big cone and entitles you to three

aperetivo

With its evening tradition of aperitivo, Italy has basically found an excuse for its citizens to pregame dinner every single night. Not really, but this pre-dinner period is still a great way to get the fermented juices flowing before sitting down for a later meal (Italians normally don't eat dinner until 8:30 or 9pm, so aperitivo is a good way to tide yourself over between lunch and the last meal of the day). Although the tradition originated in northern Italy, aperitivo has made its way to Rome and trickled all the way down to the lowly tourists who frequently enjoy aperitivo in and around Campo de' Fiori, Piazza Navona, and Trastevere. Usually enjoyed anytime between 7 and 10pm, aperitivo is a great time to sample Italy's incredible cheeses, cured meats, and, of course, wine. Traditionally, patrons are expected to order one round of drinks per dish of food, so don't go ham on the vino unless you're planning on ordering more proscuitto, too.

scoops) will only run you €2.50. Life in the fast lane has never been so cheap (can't you taste this gold?). Lunch sandwiches are equally affordable and worth the slight walk from P. di Spagna for quality food in the middle of a long day of sightseeing. If you're interested in resting your dogs for a bit longer, Ciampini also has a full, sit-down menu and plenty of outdoor seating in the middle of Piazza di San Lorenzo.

i From P. di Spagna, walk down down V. del Condotti and turn left onto V. del Leoncino. Gelato €2.50-6.50. Sandwiches €4. Primi €10-13. Secondi €13-20. ⏰ Open M-Sa 7:30am-10pm, Su 9:30am-10pm.

CAFFETERIA CAMBI
PIZZA $

V. del Leoncino 30 ☎06 687 80 81

Located just around the corner from the busy shoppers and bustling mopeds of V. Tomacelli, this understated gem of a caffeteria is tucked under a nondescript awning that doesn't actually even say "Cambi." (C'mon, Cambi, have some self respect! You're worth it!) A short walk from P. di Spagna, Cambi is a great place to stop for a quick, authentic, and shockingly cheap piece of fold-up pizza. A variety of tarts, pastries, and panini are also available, but with more than a dozen varieties of white and red pizzas to choose from on any given day, the slices of pie here might be too good to pass up.

i From P. di Spagna, walk down V. del Condotti, take a slight right onto V. Tomacelli, and turn left onto V. del Leoncino. Caffeteria Cambi is on the right. Cash only. Very limited counter seating. Pizza priced by weight (approximately €2.50 per piece). ⏰ Open M-Sa 8am-8pm.

Termini

▣ ✦ GELATERIA LA ROMANA
GELATERIA $

V. Venti Settembre 60 ☎06 42 02 08 28 www.gelateriaromana.com

Despite its clean lines, light wood, and modern aesthetic, La Romana has actually been serving up incredible gelato since 1947 and now boasts several locations through Italy. And given its history (and, perhaps more importantly, the line of young Italians that spills out the door after dinner hours), La Romana is really the only gelato you should be eating on this side of town. Especially because a small cone (which includes two flavors and a finishing dollop of whipped cream) only costs €2. Flavors are listed on the wall in Italian, so if you're flummoxed and don't know what to order (note: you will be, and it's all amazing), just tell the girl at the counter to give you the two best flavors, and goddammit, she will. And as

rome

if that wasn't enough, she'll fill the bottom of your cone with melted chocolate (!!). So if you've ever had a hard time finishing your gelato, a) wut and b) soldier on, dear friend, because at La Romana, they save the best for last.

i From P. della Repubblica, continue down V. Vittorio Emanuele Orlando and turn right onto V. Venti Settembre. La Romana is located on the left, on the corner of V. Venti Settembre and V. Piave. Gelato from €2. ☯ Open M-Th 11am-midnight, F-Sa 11am-1am, Su 11am-midnight.

RISTORANTE DA GIOVANNI
RISTORANTE $

V. Antonio Salandra 1

Ristorante da Giovanni has been ahead of the game for a while, serving up simple and delicious Italian meals since 1948. Tucked in the basement of a building just off V. Venti Settembre, da Giovanni's white wood walls, plaid tablecloths, and old-fashioned Coca-Cola signs provide a quiet retreat from the city outside. The dishes here are understated but authentic (you can't go wrong with a classic like *cacio e pepe*), and the waiters' limited English will only add to your conviction that this place is the real deal.

i From P. della Repubblica, continue down V. Vittorio Emanuele Orlando and turn right onto V. Venti Settembre. Continue several blocks and turn left onto V. Antonio Salandra. Ristorante da Giovanni is on the right. Primi €6-7.50. Secondi €5.50-14. Dessert €4. ☯ Open daily noon-3pm and 7-10:30pm.

THE BRAMBLE BAR & KITCHEN
INTERNATIONAL $

V. Vicenza 40 ☎06 44 70 21 62 www.bramblebar.com

If you're staying near Termini Station and are looking for solid food close to home, skip the restaurant portion of the Yellow Hostel and Bar and head around the corner to the Bramble; prices for breakfast, lunch, and dinner are comparable, and the food is astronomically better. The Bramble services a mostly tourist crowd, and while the food isn't the best you'll have in the city, it's actually quite good. And because the mysteries of Italian breakfast (does it even exist??) remain opaque to many a tourist throughout their time in Rome, the Bramble is a particularly good option for travelers who can't get hip to the "espresso and go" style of most Italian mornings and just want some sit-down coffee and toast.

i From Termini Station, exit onto P. dei Cinquecento and turn right onto Vle. Enrico De Nicola. Walk through P. dell'Indipendenza and turn right onto V. Vittorio Bachelet, then left onto V. Vicenza. The Bramble is on the left. Free Wi-Fi. Guests staying at Alessandro Palace or Downtown get discounts. Primi €7.50-10. Secondi €9-18. Pizzas €7-9.50. Hamburgers €9-11. Breakfast €3-7. ☯ Open M-Sa 7am-midnight, Su 6pm-midnight in summer. Lunch menu available starting at noon.

FASSINO
CAFE $

V. Bergamo 24 ☎06 854 91 17

This creperie and gelateria is located a bit farther into Northern Rome than you're likely to be wandering, but if you want a chance to explore a less touristy area of the city, head for Piazza Fiume and enjoy cappuccino and gelato al fresco at Fassino. The staff here will be lookin' swanky (hello, bow ties), as will the granite table tops, vintage black-and-white photos on the walls, and piles upon piles of fancy pastries, but the prices here don't lie: this place is dirt cheap and has been since 1880. And that, we think, is worth the walk.

i From P. della Repubblica, continue down V. Vittorio Emanuele Orlando and turn right onto V. Venti Settembre. Continue several blocks and turn left onto V. Piave to P. Fiume. From the piazza, turn right onto V. Bergamo. Fassino is on the right. Gelato €1.80-3.50. Pastries from €2. Aperitivo €6.50. ☯ Open daily 7:30am-12:30am.

ANTICA PIZZERIA DE ROMA
PIZZA $

V. Venti Settembre 41 ☎06 42 01 01 20

Antica Pizzeria ain't much, but it is a great place for a grab 'n' go slice of pizza if you're walking down V. Venti Settembre on your way to or from a day of sightseeing. The margherita pizza is always a solid bet, and if you really want to fit in with the locals who frequent this place, learn to perfect the art of the "fold and go." There is some counter seating opposite a wall-length mirror—a nice opportunity to rest your feet and contemplate what your #selfie looks like without all the filters.

i From P. della Repubblica, continue down V. Vittorio Emanuele Orlando and turn right onto V. Venti Settembre. Continue several blocks. Antica Pizzeria is on the left. Pizza €0.90-1.60 per slice, €5-6 per individual pizza. Calzones €3.50. Beer €3. Wine €5. Cash only. ☼ Open M-Sa 9:30am-9:30pm.

MEID IN NEPOLS
ITALIAN $$

V. Varese 54   ☎06 44 70 41 31 www.meidinnepols.com

Whether or not the city of Naples gave this restaurant permission to use its name is unclear, but the giant wood-fired oven that greets customers when they walk in makes it pretty obvious that the pizza here definitely was not made in Naples. Not that the pizza here is bad, but it's about as authentic Neapolitan as all those knockoff Louis Vuitton handbags you can buy in Piazza Navona. Fortunately, the tourists who frequent this place don't seem to know the difference. (And as Joseph P. Kennedy told his sons, "It's not what you are, but what people think you are that is important." Yeah, think about it.) At least what Meid in Nepols lacks in true quality it makes up for with a wide, affordable variety of pizzas, pastas, and salads, along with tourist-friendly service (i.e., English speakers—English speakers everywhere!).

i From Termini Station, exit onto P. dei Cinquecento and turn right onto Vle. Enrico De Nicola. Walk through P. dell'Indipendenza and turn right onto V. Vittorio Bachelet, which turns into V. Varese. Meid in Nepols is at the end of the street, on the left. Pizzas €7-9.50. Antipasti €6.5-16.50. Primi €9.50-16.50. Secondi €9.50-16.50. ☼ Open M-F 12:30-3pm and 7:30-11pm, Sa 12:30-3pm and 7:30-11:30pm.

Vatican City

▨ PIZZARIUM
PIZZA $

V. della Meloria 43   ☎06 39 74 54 16

After a whole morning of walking through the Vatican Museums, the idea of eating your lunch standing up might not sound particularly appealing, but prioritize your stomach over your feet, and Pizzarium will make it worth your aching arches. Because while the high tables at this white-walled, open-doored pizza counter don't come furnished with any actual chairs, Pizzarium does have some of the best, crispiest square pizza in the city. And it's pretty gourmet, too: you'll find everything from giant peppers to dollops of ricotta cheese to fold upon fold of freshly sliced meat piled high on these slices of pie. Pick out a couple varieties and wait while the staff pops them back into the piping oven for a few minutes. And while the Catholic Church may have pinched a pretty penny out of you earlier today, Pizzarium is a total steal—a couple slices will generally run you less than the price of the Vatican Museums' €7 audio guide.

i From the Vatican Museum, walk down the steps to V. Tunisi and turn left onto V. Candia. Veer left onto V. Angelo Elmo and turn right onto V. della Meloria 43. Pizzarium is on the left. Pizza €17.50-30.50 per kg. ☼ Open M-Sa 11am-10pm, Su noon-4pm and 6-10pm.

▨ OLD BRIDGE GELATERIA
GELATERIA $

Vle. dei Bastioni di Michelangelo 5   ☎32 84 11 94 78 www.gelateriaoldbridge.com

The only bridge you'll find here is the one that spans the gap between your dreams and reality. Located just across the street from the slanting, defensive walls of the Vatican, Old Bridge serves up gelato that's almost as divine as the Holy See itself. There's almost always a line, and you won't have a lot of time to decide what flavors you want once you get up to the counter, but don't stress too much—you really can't go wrong with any of the options here. Seriously, this stuff is so good, it should probably be taken as a daily sacrament (also, it might be made out of the

Body of Christ). And as a final touch, Old Bridge's light, not overly sweet whipped cream is heavenly enough to have been blessed by Pope Francis himself.

i *Just off P. Risorgimento, across the street from the line for the Vatican Museums. Gelato €2-5.* 🕐 *Open M-Sa 9am-2am, Su 2:30pm-2am.*

SCIASCIA CAFFÈ
CAFE $

V. Fabio Massimo 80/A ☎06 32 11 580

Little known to tourists, Sciascia is a super local coffee shop that takes pride in its *caffè con cioccolato* (espresso with chocolate) and, probably, in its lack of foreigners. Not much English is spoken here, but the guys in bow ties at the counter will still serve you up one of the best cups of coffee you'll have in Rome (and they already know you're a stupid American, so have no shame—go ahead and order that post-11am cappuccino!). Then settle in at a table with your perfectly foamy cup of cultural faux pas and watch the local Italians file in, toss a euro to the girl at the counter, down their shot of espresso, and then head back out into the world. It's like all the tables and chairs in here are just for show (and for you, because you're a tourist who finally found a place in Italy where you can sit down with a cup of coffee).

i *M: Ottaviano. Walk down Vle. Giulio Cesare and turn right down V. Fabio Massimo. Sciascia is on the left. Espresso and cappuccino €1-3.50.* 🕐 *Open M-Sa 7am-8pm.*

FA BIO
SANDWICHES $

V. Germanico 43 ☎06 64 52 58 10 www.fa-bio.com

Sandwiches and smoothies? Fresh fruit and organic ingredients? Pressed juice? Did you take a wrong turn out of the Sistine Chapel and somehow end up in L.A.? No, you just found your way to Fa Bio. It's like your favorite American sandwich shop (complete with a modern interior, green and orange color scheme, and faux-blackboard menus on the wall), except these sammies come with fresh mozzarella and Italian pesto in addition to your standard summer tomatoes and avocados. Just a few minutes' walk from the Vatican, Fa Bio is a surprisingly hip hole in the wall (there a couple small tables in back, plus a few more seats at the counter), and although you'll have to wait a while for your food, it's because everything here is made entirely from scratch. So add a smoothie to your order because it's fresh and delicious (and you probably need some more Vitamin C in your life anyway).

i *M: Ottaviano. Walk down V. Ottaviano and turn left onto V. Germanico. Fa Bio is on the right. Ingredients run out later in the day, so arrive earlier if you want a full selection of all it has to offer. Sandwiches €4-5.50. Salads €5. Juice and smoothies €2.50-5.* 🕐 *Open M-F 11am-5:30pm, Sa 11am-4pm.*

SU E GIU CUCINA ROMANA
ITALIAN $

V. Tactio 42 ☎06 32 65 03 52 www.suegiucucinaromana.blogspot.com

Su e Giu Cucina Romana is proof positive that not all of the area surrounding the Vatican is a culinary wasteland. Located on a less than scenic stretch of Via Tacito, this restaurant may not look like much, but the simple, straightforward Roman dishes here speak for themselves. Served on basic white earthenware with paper napkins, the fare here is kind of like the delicious but unshowy comfort food that somebody's mom would serve when you visited her at home (if you actually had cool friends from Italy, that is). Try the bruschetta with sausage or the fried artichokes when they're in season, and you certainly can't go wrong with a classic plate of spaghetti carbonara. Tourists in the know tend to flock here around dinnertime, so arrive early if you're hoping to get one of the few tables outside.

i *M: Lepanto. Walk down V. Ezio, which turns into V. Tacito. Su e Giu Cucina is a few blocks down on the left. Antipasti €2-14. Primi €8-11. Secondi €9-15. Dessert €5-8.* 🕐 *Open M-Sa 12:30-2:30pm and 7:30-11:50pm.*

Trastevere

LA RENELLA
PIZZA $

V. del Moro 15   ☎06 581 72 65

La Renella doesn't mess around. This *forno* is fairly basic: just a countertop full of pizza and panini and a row of dark wood stools along the wall, but with sandwiches and biscotti this good, it doesn't really need to pander to customers with anything fancier (or with overly friendly service for that matter). Tourists and local Italians alike swing by for a panino on the go, and you should, too. Savor the perfectly salted bread and fresh mozzarella of a caprese panino, or go for something a little more adventurous—either way, you won't be paying much more than a few euro for a really sizable sandwich. Then stop by after dinner for a late-night piece of biscotti.

i From P. Trilussa, walk down V. del Moro. La Renella is on the left. Panini €3-3.50. Pizza €12-14 per kg. ☒ Open M-Th 7am-10pm, F-Sa 7am-3am, Su 7am-10pm.

FRUTTERIA ER CIMOTTO
MARKET

P. di San Giovanni della Malva 6   ☎06 580 64 60 www.fruterriaercimotto.com

Just because all those negronis you've been drinking are garnished with an orange wedge doesn't mean your Italian diet of pizza, pasta, and little else will prevent you from developing a nice case of scurvy while abroad. Fortunately, Frutteria Er Cimotto is here to help keep your teeth from falling out. Not your average mini-market, Er Cimotto has been providing Trastevere with fresh fruit and vegetables of all varieties since 1890. And while you can brown-bag it and load up on some much-needed fresh produce, you can also order fresh-pressed juices, homemade soups, and robust salads here. Pop in in the afternoon and walk away with a small bag of perfectly plump peaches for just a couple euro—a nice, healthy alternative for your midday snack (or maybe just a palette cleanser between rounds of gelato).

i From P. Trilussa, walk up V. Benedetta to P. di San Giovanni della Malva. Frutteria Er Cimotto is on the left. Fruit €3-20 per kg. ☒ Open M 7:20am-9pm, Tu-Sa 7:20am-10pm, Su 8:30am-9pm.

BISCOTTIFICIO ARTIGIANO INNOCENTI
BAKERY

V. della Luce 21   ☎06 580 39 26

Tucked away on the quieter side of Trastevere, this bakery is pretty inconspicuous and doesn't look like much. But pass through the strips of old plastic in the doorway into the plain white interior and let the scents and taste of fresh-baked cookies stimulate your other senses. The woman who works here is incredibly friendly, so swing by for a sweet pick-me-up as you wind your way through the rest of the neighborhood.

i From Ponte Garibaldi, walk into P. Sidney Sonnino and turn left onto V. della Lungaretta, then right onto V. della Luce. The bakery is on the left. Prices vary; everything here is generally very inexpensive and will only run you a few euro. ☒ Open daily 8am-8pm.

LA BOCCACCIA
PIZZA $

V. di Santa Dorotea 2   www.pizzerialaboccaccia.it

La Bocaccio is more than just a hole-in-the-wall. It's a hole in the wall tucked into a corner that's easy to miss if you're not looking for it. As a result, however, this pizzeria has a little square of Trastevere all to itself and serves square pizza that's worth seeking out. Fresh, perfectly crisp, and cheap, the pizza here can be enjoyed at all hours of the day. Pop in late at night and grab a slice, a beer, and a seat at one of the mismatched tables outside.

i From Ponte Sisto, walk down V. Ponte Sisto to P. di San Giovanni della Malva and turn right onto V. di Santa Dorotea. La Boccaccia is tucked into a corner on the left. Pizza €12-18 per kg. ☒ Open daily 10am-12:30am.

DAR POETA

ITALIAN $

Vicolo del Bologna 45 ☎06 588 05 16 www.darpoeta.com

This restaurant provides a perfect setting in which to write a sonnet to your one true love: complex carbohydrates. How do you love bruschetta and pizza? Let Dar Poeta help you count the ways—it offers dozens of varieties of both, from blue cheese and honey bruschetta to pizza with swordfish carpaccio and potatoes. And while the pies here aren't particularly gourmet, they do come out fresh and piping hot, and the light, flavorful crust is perfectly Roman. But consider your pizza the primi to Dar Poeta's main event: the legendary Nutella ricotta calzone, which is mammoth (and the most expensive thing on the menu) but worth the caloric and monetary splurge. This place gets popular in the evenings, so try to arrive on the early side of dinnertime if you want to get a table right away.

i From P. San Egidio, walk down Vicolo del Bologna. Dar Poeta is on the left. Bruschetta €2-3. Pizza €5-9.50. ☼ Open daily noon-1am.

DA ENZO

ITALIAN $$

V. dei Vascellari 29 ☎06 581 2 260

For a more local taste of the tourist-heavy Trastevere, head away from the crowds in Santa Maria, across Vle. di Trastevere, and over to the quieter side of the neighborhood, where you'll find Da Enzo. From the outside, this small restaurant may look like just another Italian eatery: all plaid tablecloths, cramped seating, canvas umbrellas, and wine bottles on the wall. But Da Enzo is a lot harder to get into than your average Trastevere tourist trap, mostly because this place cooks up classic Roman cuisine that's more than worth a reservation (or a long wait for a table at dinnertime). Try their fried artichokes and spaghetti alla carbonara. And if you want to beat the rush, either come early for dinner and try to get a table when the restaurant opens at 7:30pm or swing by for a late lunch.

i From Ponte Garibaldi, cross Lungotevere and walk through P. Sidney Sonnino down Vle. di Trastevere, then turn left down V. dei Genovesi. Turn left onto V. dei Vascellari; Da Enzo is on the right. Primi €9-11. Secondi €9-15. ☼ Open M-Sa 12:30-3pm and 7:30-11pm.

ROMA SPARITA

ITALIAN $$

P. di Santa Cecilia 24 ☎06 580 07 57 www.romasparita.com

Cheesy pasta served in a cup made out of even more cheese? This is the stuff of dreams, and this restaurant is your greatest gastronomical fantasies realized. If you feel like gathering the energy required to make an actual reservation, you can't do much better than Roma Sparita. Hidden away from the center of Trastevere in the quiet Piazza di Santa Cecilia, this restaurant is a bit more expensive than a typical budget eatery, but the quality of the food here makes those few extra euro really worth it. Sit at one of the many checkered tables outside and let the brusque but friendly waiters guide you through the menu: consider starting out with some fresh cantaloupe and prosciutto, and absolutely order the *cacio e pepe*, which will arrive in a fancy little parmesan cup and is some of the best you'll have in Rome.

i From Ponte Garibaldi, cross Lungotevere and walk through P. Sidney Sonnino down Vle. di Trastevere, then turn left down V. dei Genovesi. Continue several blocks and turn right onto V. di Santa Cecilia, then right into P. di Santa Cecilia. Antipasti €7-11. Primi €10-12. Secondi €10-12. ☼ Open M 7:30-11:30pm, Tu-Sa 12:30-2:30pm and 7:30-11:30pm.

PIZZERIA NERONE

PIZZA $

V. del Moro 43 ☎06 58 30 17 56 www.pizzerianerone.com

Pizzeria Nerone is kind of like Rome's version of a greasy pizza place, but in this case, "greasy" really just means more olive oil and more flavor. So stop by this underrated pizzeria and try to ignore all the touristy kitsch on the walls (although if you didn't have the patience to wait in line and stick

italy

your hand in the real Mouth of Truth, you can stick your finger in a miniature version here). Sure, the Roman statues in the corners may not be legit, but the woodfired oven in the middle of the restaurant certainly is. Your pizza will arrive still steaming, with plenty of gooey cheese and a chewy crust cooked to perfection. And while you'll find plenty of tourists here, there's also a steady flow of locals who stop by to take away a pizza or sit in the "regulars" section of the restaurant in back.

i From P. Trilussa, walk down V. del Moro. Pizzeria Nerone is on the right. Antipasti €3-8. Pizza €6.50-10. Calzones €8. ⏰ Open daily 7pm-12:30am.

NIGHTLIFE

Ancient City

AI TRE SCALINI
BAR

V. Panisperna 251 ☎06 48 90 74 95 www.aitrescalini.org

Perfectly placed in the dip of Via Panisperna (if you're having trouble finding it, just look for the wire of hanging ivy just outside the door), Ai Tre Scalini is a popular aperitivo spot for tourists and locals alike. "Snacks" start at just €3, so enjoy some olives or truffles with a pre-dinner drink in the dimly lit interior and sit back as your conversation mingles with the soft notes of the bar's jazzy background music. The bar is open until late (1am), and although a lot of hip locals and businessmen may be chilling outside with beers and glasses of wine, you're probably not cool enough for that, so look for a table inside instead.

i From Basilica di Santa Maria Maggiore, proceed down V. di Santa Maria Maggiore, which becomes V. Panisperna. Ai Tre Scalini is located at the dip in the road. Snacks €3-5. Aperitivo €7-16. Primi €7-8. Secondi €7-10. ⏰ Open daily 12:30pm-1am.

LIBERIA CAFFÈ BOHÈMIEN
BAR

V. degli Zingari 36 ☎33 97 22 46 22 www.caffebohemier.it

What looks like hipster gentrification in most American cities is actually a pretty unique find in Rome, which has yet to fully embrace the coffee-, cafe-, and "I just can't listen to anything that's not vinyl"-culture of places like Bushwick. And while the aperitivo and wine still make this a very Italian hangout spot, at least you'll probably recognize the moody couches, the collection of unread books on the shelves (who's reading those, anyway?), and the "I don't give a damn" punks hanging outside smoking cigs and sipping beers. Monti is chill, and this place is almost too chill for Monti, so come by after dinner to decompress with a cocktail or glass of wine.

i From Basilica di Santa Maria Maggiore, proceed down V. di Santa Maria Maggiore and veer left onto V. Urbana. Continue through P. degii Zingari and onto V. degli Zingari. Liberia is on the left. Aperitivo €8. ⏰ Open M 6pm-2am, W-Th 12:30-4pm and 6pm-2am, F-Su 6pm-2am.

SCHOLARS LOUNGE
IRISH PUB

V. del Plebiscito 101 ☎06 69 20 22 08 www.scholarsloungerome.com

Just down the road from Italy's altar to itself is a small corner of town where you can swap out the Eternal City for the Emerald Isle. A traditional Irish sports pub transplanted to the heart of Italy, Scholars Lounge offers Guinness on tap and over 250 varieties of whiskey (which, the last time we checked, was definitely a Scottish thing, but in this case, cultural appropriation works in your favor). The staff is mostly young internationals from the UK, and the dark wood interior, meat pies, and pictures of Samuel Beckett on the wall will have you thinking and drinking like a real Irishman (that is to say, a lot). A popular spot situated on a busy street, Scholars Lounge is a great place to wander into as you're making

rome

your way home on Corso Emanuele late at night or if you just need a break from sightseeing in the middle of the day.

i From P. Venezia, walk west down V. del Plebiscito. Scholars Lounge is on the right. Free Wi-Fi. Live music M, Th, F. Karaoke Tu, W, Su. Pints €6-7. Half-pints €4.50-5.50. Wine €4.50-5.50. Cocktails €8. Shots €5. Irish pie of the day €10.50. ☼ Open daily 11am-3:30am.

Centro Storico

CUL DE SAC
BAR

P. Pasquino 73   ☎06 68 80 10 94 www.enotecaculdesac.com

Cul de Sac is part gastronomical delight, part circus spectacle. Watch the guys at this incredibly narrow wine bar partake in a grand balancing act as they pluck bottles down from the ceiling with long instruments that could only be classified as wine claws. Then go back to your plate of freshly sliced cured meat and cheese because, despite the waiters' unending juggling act, the wine and aperitivo here is the real star of the hour. Select a glass or bottle from a list of more than 1,500 available every day and tuck in.

i From P. Navona, exit onto V. Pasquino and proceed to P. Pasquino; Cul de Sac is on the left. Cold cut meat €7-13. Cheese €7-9. Primi €8-10. Secondi €7-11. Wine starting at €4 per glass. ☼ Open daily noon-4pm and 6pm-12:30am.

LA BOTTICELLI
BAR

V. di Tor Millina 32   ☎06 686 11 07

Just because La Botticelli has been around for more than 100 years doesn't mean it's not hip enough to figure out how to project a Red Sox game on the back wall of the bar. You wouldn't have guessed it from the fancy Italian name, but La Botticelli is Rome's spin on an American sports bar, which means you'll find statues of saints wearing football helmets and Steelers pennants hanging from the towering antique bar here. So if you're looking for the comfort of home (or just need to see how your favorite team is doing), grab a table in the dimly lit interior, a stool at the bar, or a seat at one of the tables outside.

i From P. Navona, exit onto V. di Tor Millina. La Botticelli is on the left. Beer €5. Cocktails €6. Shots €3.50. ☼ Open daily 5pm-2am.

ABBEY THEATRE
IRISH PUB

V. del Governo Vecchio 51   ☎06 686 13 41 www.abbey-rome.com

How an Irish bar managed to secure such prime real estate just beyond the reach of Piazza Navona is a mystery. That being said, Abbey Theatre certainly makes the most of it. With its six rooms, multiple bars, and 16 immense television screens showing everything from women's FIFA to curling, Abbey Theatre is a great tourist pub for sports- and beer-loving internationals of all varieties (although it certainly keeps things green with the Guinness on tap, €11 Irish specials, and pictures of famous Irishmen painted on the walls). People often spill out the door and hang out on the street later in the evening, mingling with the crowd that gathers around Frigidarium across the street, Take advantage of the company, the free Wi-Fi, and the €5 summer drinks.

i From P. Navona, exit onto V. Pasquino and continue through P. Pasquino to V. del Governo Vecchio. Abbey Theatre is on the right. Summer drinks €5. Irish specials €11-15. ☼ Open M noon-2am, F noon-3am, Sa 11am-3am, Su 11am-2am.

FLUID
BAR

V. del Governo Vecchio 46   ☎06 683 23 61

Of all the fluids in your life (cleaning, lighter, bodily, etc.), this one is probably the hippest you've come across. Amid all the restaurants and Italian wine bars surrounding Piazza Navona, this self-consciously trendy cocktail lounge is a bit incongruous and looks like it got lost somewhere on its way from Tokyo to New York. That being said, if you're a hip millennial in search of a cocktail in a sea of

red wine and prosecco (you're young, and sometimes you just need to get hard...
at least with your liquor), this place might be the spot for you. If the glowing
white cubes in the front window aren't enough to entice you, just walk toward
the purple light at the back of the bar.

i From P. Navona, exit onto V. Pasquino and continue through P. Pasquino to V. del Governo Vecchio. Fluid is on the right. Cocktails starting at €8. ⟡ Open daily 7pm-2am.

THE DRUNKEN SHIP   BAR
P. Campo de' Fiori 20   ☎06 68 30 05 35 www.drunkenship.com

Although a college freshman might have been responsible for naming all
the drinks at the Drunken Ship (Blow Job, anyone? How about a Cum in my
Mouth?), anyone who is young at heart or doesn't understand American slang
will love this place. The Drunken Ship's dark interior may, in fact, remind you of
the lower quarters of a pirate ship (because you've spent so much time in those),
so set sail on the many wine-dark seas presented here. If you're not into Sex on
the Beach, you can always go for a Shit On the Grass, and then play some beer
pong with your fellow Eurotrippers.

i Located in the western corner of Campo de' Fiori. Beer €4-8. Long drinks €6. Cocktails €7. ⟡
Open daily 3pm-3am.

Piazza di Spagna

The area surrounding Piazza di Spagna isn't an ideal location for cheap nightlife
(most of the hip lounges, wine bars, and enotecas in this neighborhood will run your
backpacker budget into the ground). Fortunately, Italy's open attitude toward open
containers makes it possible for you to make your own kind of late-night fun even
in the priciest piazzas. Grab some cheap beers or a bottle of wine and hit up the
Spanish Steps just before sunset, where you and your friends can continue boozin'
and bummin' around as evening sets in.

Termini

THE YELLOW BAR   BAR
V. Palestro 40   ☎06 49 38 26 82 www.the-yellow.com

The Yellow Bar is here to remind you that getting blitzed in Europe has gotten
a lot more fun since World War II. This bar is like that frat bro you've seen at
parties who tries a little too hard to let everyone know that PBR is the best time
he's ever had. Swap the PBR for Carlsberg and Poretti, and you've got yourself
a night at the Yellow. So what is the difference between the Yellow and every
loud, sloppy American college party you've ever been to? Besides the currency
and the international crowd, not a whole lot. Alcohol flows continuously here,
mostly because it's so goddamn cheap (even the cocktails that run upward of
€7 and boast cheeky names like "Adios Motherfucker" contain more than your
money's worth of liquor). While there's plenty of seating both inside and out, the
bar area itself is small and always crowded, as is the dance floor downstairs, so
cozy on up to your fellow travelers, make some new friends, and see if you can
remember any of it in the morning.

i From Termini Station, exit onto P. dei Cinquecento and turn right onto Vle. Enrico De Nicola. Walk
through P. dell'Indipendenza and continue straight down V. San Martino della Battaglia, then turn
right onto V. Palestro. The Yellow Bar is on the left. Beer €2.50-4. Cocktails €4-7. ⟡ Open 24hr.
Happy hour daily noon-9pm.

TRIMANI WINE BAR   ENOTECA
V. Cernaia 37/B   ☎06 446 96 30 www.trimani.com

You're probably not going to make many new acquaintances at the quiet
Trimani Wine Bar, but who needs friends when you have a nearly endless selection of wines by the glass to keep you company? (You, Andre, and Franzia

rome

may go way back, but now that you're in Rome, it might be time to reevaluate your relationships and upgrade to a more sophisticated crowd.) In the wine business since 1821, Trimani will help you achieve your most ambitious #squadgoals. And if you're a bad judge of character and have no clue what to order, the helpful waitstaff can point you in the right direction. At the very least, you can always pair one of the fancy desserts with a nice, friendly glass of Moscato.

i From Termini Station, exit onto P. dei Cinquecento and turn right onto Vle. Enrico De Nicola. Cross the street to the left side of P. dell'Indipendenza and turn left onto V. Goito, then right onto V. Cernaia. Trimani is on the right. Wine by the glass €5-18. Primi, secondi, and antipasti €5-24. Dessert €8. ☒ Open M-Sa 11:30am-3pm and 5:30pm-12:30am.

BAR OASIES
BAR

V. Villafranca 1/A

Bar Oasies is a low-key, local alternative to the international Eurotripping that's going on at nearby hostels. And while there's nothing particularly special about the food or drinks here, there is a strange, stripped-down charm to this bar's total lack of self-promotion. It's just sitting there, doing its thing—green walls and red tablecloths and generic menu and all—and so is Dominico, one of the Italian bartenders who will happily use you as a specimen upon which to practice his English. Grab a seat outside and relax with a beer before reentering the fray at the Yellow Bar around the corner.

i From Termini Station, exit onto P. dei Cinquecento and turn right onto Vle. Enrico De Nicola. Walk through P. dell'Indipendenza and continue straight down V. San Martino della Battaglia, then turn right onto V. Villafranca. Bar Oasies is on the right. Wine €3-5. Beer €3-5. Cocktails €6. Primi €6-7. Secondi €5-8. Pizza €3-8. ☒ Open daily 7am-late (after 1am).

Trastevere

FRENI E FRIZIONI
BAR

V. del Politeama 4-6 ☎06 45 49 74 99 www.freniefrizioni.com

Who knew chandeliers and mason jars looked so good together? Freni e Frizioni did, but then again, this repurposed auto body shop seems to know a thing or two about design and hipster shit. From its high industrial ceiling to its movie-poster-inspired menu to the carefully curated clutter on its walls, Freni e Frizioni is about as hipster as Rome gets. Fortunately, it's so popular and such a good deal that you won't even have time to roll your eyes at its self-conscious trendiness while you make a beeline for the buffet table. Come by for aperitivo, when the crowd of young travelers and students spills out onto the patio and, more importantly, when the purchase of one drink gives you free range over a spread of unlimited bread, pasta salad, hummus, carrots, vegetables, and rice dishes.

i From P. Trilussa, walk down the tiny V. del Politeama and look for the steps (and the crowd) on the left. Beer €6. Long drinks €7. Cocktails €10. Lower prices after 10pm. ☒ Open daily 6:30pm-2am. Aperitivo 7-10pm.

MECCANISMO ROMA (CAFE FRIENDS)
BAR

P. Trilussa 34 ☎06 581 61 11 www.meccanismoroma.com

It's a youthful hangout spot in Trastevere, which means it must be—you guessed it—modern and trendy! Meccanismo will be your friend at all hours, but especially during aperitivo, when you can get a drink and some finger food for just €8 (even if you don't opt for the food, the waitstaff here will still bring you some potato chips in a hip little brown paper bag). There's plenty of outdoor seating here, so enjoy your drinks al fresco along the edge of Piazza Trilussa. And if you're feeling a little tender the next day, Meccanismo is open early and has coffee, tea, and a full American breakfast to help you soak up the hangover.

i From Ponte Sisto, walk across the street and into P. Trilussa. Meccanismo is on the left. Wine €3.50-4. Beer €4.50-7. Cocktails €7-9. Aperitivo €8. ⏰ Open daily 7:30am-2am. Aperitivo 6:30-9pm.

PIMM'S GOOD
BAR

V. di Santa Dorotea 8   ☎06 97 27 79 79 www.pimmsgood.it

The sun may have set on the British Empire, but a few redcoats have still managed to stake out a claim along V. di Santa Dorotea in Trastevere. "Anyone for Pimm's?" asks a mirror (embellished with an outline of the Union Jack) at the back of this modern bar and restaurant. The answer would appear to be "yes," although a lot of the people sitting outside here have actually opted for a negroni. Although the crowd relaxing under some canvas umbrellas and twinkly lights may be a little on the older side, Pimm's has live music multiple times each week, a great deal on aperitivo, and free Wi-Fi to boot. Stop by before 2pm, and you can even enjoy a traditional English breakfast.

i From Ponte Sisto, walk down V. Ponte Sisto to P. di San Giovanni della Malva and turn right onto V. di Santa Dorotea. Pimm's Good is on the left. Live music M, Th, Su. Aperitivo (drink and food) €8. Antipasti €5-12. Primi €8-12 Secondi €12-18. English breakfast €8. ⏰ Open daily 10am-2am.

BIR E FUD
BAR

V. Benedetta 23   ☎06 589 40 16 www.birefud.it

Beer lovers rejoice: you won't be drinking any more red wine or spritzers tonight. Instead, you can add even more carbs to your Italian diet by sampling the many yeast-y offerings of Bir e Fud. In keeping with the modern design of the many hip hangouts in Trastevere, this bar has clean lines, a sleek bar with a row of impressive bronze taps, and some kind of modern art on the wall that looks like a metallic version of those plastic six-pack rings that dolphins get their noses stuck in. Fortunately (or unfortunately), you'll be thinking more about wheat than wildlife conservation when your beer is served to you with a full, perfectly foamy head. Enjoy it outside, at a stool along the bar, or with some bruschetta at a table in back.

i From P. Trilussa, turn right onto V. Benedetta. Bir e Fud is on the left. Draught beer €5-6. Bruschetta €3-6. Pizza €6-12. ⏰ Open daily noon-2am. Kitchen closes at 1am.

ESSENTIALS

Practicalities

- **TOURIST OFFICES:** Comune di Roma is Rome's official source for tourist information. Green PIT info booths, located near most major sights, have English-speaking staff and sell bus and metro maps and the Roma pass. (V. Giovanni Giolitti 34 in Termini, P. delle Cinque Lune near Piazza Navona, P. Sidney Sonnino in Trastevere, and V. dei Fori Imperiali. ☎06 06 08 www.turismoroma.it. ⏰ Most locations open daily 9:30am-7pm; Termini location open daily 8am-8:30pm.)

- **LUGGAGE STORAGE:** Termini Luggage Deposit. (☎06 47 44 777 www.romatermini.com. Below Track 24 in the Ala Termini wing. Storage for bags up to 20kg. Max. 5 days. 1st 5hr. €6, €0.90 per hr. for 6th-12th hr., €0.40 per hr. thereafter. ⏰ Open daily 6am-11pm.)

- **POST OFFICES:** Poste Italiane are located through the city. (☎800 160 000 www.poste.it) The main office is located at Piazza San Silvestro 19. (☎06 69 73 72 16 ⏰ Open M-F 8:20am-7pm, Sa 8:20am-12:35pm.)

rome

Emergency

- **POLICE:** Police Headquarters. (V. di San Vitale 15 ☎06 46 861; M Repubblica.) Carabinieri have offices at V. Mentana 6 (Near Termini ☎06 44 74 19 00) and at P. Venezia 6 (☎06 67 58 28 00) City Police. (P. del Collegio Romano 3 ☎06 46 86)

- **LATE-NIGHT PHARMACIES:** The following pharmacies are open 24hr.: Farmacia Internazionale (P. Barberini 49 ☎06 4871195); Farmacia Risorgimento (P. del Risorgimento 44 ☎06 39738166); Farmacia Fargion (V. Cola di Rienzo ☎06 3244476)

- **HOSPITALS/MEDICAL SERVICES:** Policlinico Umberto I. (Vle. del Policlinico 155 ☎06 49971 www.policlinicoumberto1.it M Policlinico or bus #649 to Policlinico. Emergency treatment free. Open 24hr.) International Medical Center is a private hospital and clinic. (V. Firenze 47 ☎06 48 82 371 or ☎06 0862 441 111 www.imc84.com M Repubblica. Call ahead for appointments.) Rome-American Hospital. (V. Emilio Longoni 69 ☎06 22 551 for emergencies, ☎06 22 55 290 for appointments www.hcir.it. Well to the east of the city; consider taking a cab. To get a little closer, take bus $409 from Tiburtina to Ple. Prenestina or tram #14 from Termini. English speaking. Private emergency and laboratory services. ⌚ 24hr. emergency care.)

Getting There

If you're traveling to Rome from an international destination, you'll probably arrive at Da Vinci International Airport and take a train into the center of Rome. Trains from the airport arrive at Termini Station during the day, although if you're traveling by night you may have to transfer to a bus. For travelers on a budget, Rome Ciampino Airport is the closest budget airport, although getting to Rome will be a bit slower, as no trains run from here to the city center. If you're heading to Rome from elsewhere in Italy, take advantage of the train network that runs throughout the country.

By Plane

Commonly known as Fiumicino, **Da Vinci International Airport** (30km southwest of the city ☎06 65 951 www.adr.it/fiumicino) oversees most international flights. To get from the airport, which is located right on the Mediterranean coast, to central Rome, take the Leonardo Express train to Termini Station. After leaving the airport's customs, follow signs to the Stazione Trenitalia/Railway Station, where you can buy a train ticket to Termini Station at an automated machine or from the ticket office. (€14. 30min. every half hour.) The FL1 rail line runs regional trains to and from other stations in Rome, including Rome Tiburtina and has departures every 15min. Don't buy a ticket from individuals who approach you, as they may be scammers. If you arrive after the ticket windows have closed, you'll have to use an automated machine. Before boarding the train, make sure to validate the ticket in a yellow box on the platform; failure to do so may result in a fine of €50-100. To get to Fiumicino before 6:30am or after 11:30pm, the easiest option is to catch a taxi.

    Rome Ciampino Airport (CIA; 15km southeast of the city ☎06 65 951 www.adr.it/ciampino) is a rapidly growing airport that serve budget airlines like Ryanair and EasyJet. There are no trains connecting the airport to the city center, but there are some buses. The SIT Bus Shuttle (€4, 40min.) and Terravision Shuttle (€4, 40min.) run from the airport to V. Marsala, outside Termini Stations. For easy and cheap access to the Metro, the COTRAL bus runs to M Anagnina.

By Train

Trenitalia (www.trenitalia.com) trains run through Termini Station, central Rome's main transport hub. International and overnight trains also run to Termini. City buses C2, H, M, 36, 38, 40, 64, 86, 90, 92, 105, 170, 175, 217, 310, 714, and 910 stop outside in P. del Cinquecento, so you definitely aren't short on options for the next leg of your journey. The station is open 4:30am-1:30am; if you arrive in Rome outside this time frame, you will likely arrive in Stazione Tiburtina or Stazione Ostiense, both of which connect to Termini by the night bus #175. Trains run from: Bologna (€35-55, 2-4hr.); Florence (€20-50, 2-5hr.); Naples (€12-40, 1-3hr.); Venice (€50-80, 3hr. 30min.-6hr.); and Milan (€67-79, 2hr. 40min-3hr. 30min.).

Getting Around

By Bus

The best way to get around the city other than walking is by bus. Dozens of routes cover the entire city center as well as the outskirts. Bus stops are marked by yellow poles and display a route map for all lines (regular and night lines) that pass through the stop. Useful lines include #40 (Termini, P. Venezia, Argentina, P. Pia), #64 (Termini, P. Venezia, Argentina, Vatican), #62 (Repubblica, Spanish Steps, P. Venezia, Argentina, Vatican), and #81 (Vatican Museums, Spanish Steps, P. Colonna, P. Venezia, Circo Maximo, Colosseum). Tickets cost €1.50 for 75min. and can be purchased at tabaccherie, bars, or vending machines at metro stations. Although Let's Go does not condone freeloading, inside sources tell us that inspectors don't check tickets after 9pm.

By Metro

Rome's Metro system consists of two lines: Line A, which runs from Battistini to Anagnina (passing through P. di Spagna and Ottaviano near the Vatican) and Line B, which runs from Laurentina to Rebibbia (passing through the Colosseum, Ostiense, and southern Rome). The lines intersect at Termini Station. While the Metro is fast, it doesn't reach many areas of the central city and is best used when trying to get from one end of the city to the other. Stations are marked by poles with a red square and a white "M". Tickets can be purchased with cash at machines or sometimes with cards at ticket windows (€1.50 for 1 60min. ride). Validate your ticket at turnstiles upon entering the station. The Metro usually operates 5:30am-11:30pm (until 1:30am on Saturdays).

By Tram

Trams make many stops but are still an efficient means of getting around. A few useful lines include #3 (Trastevere, Piramide, Aventine, P. San Giovanni, Villa Borghese, P. Thorwaldsen), #8 (Trastevere to Largo Argentina),#9 (P. Venezia, Argentina, Trastevere), and #19 (Ottaviano, Villa Borghese, San Lorenzo, Prenestina, P. dei Gerani).

By Bike

ATAC runs Bikesharing. Purchase a card at any ATAC ticket office (06 57 003 M A: Anagnina, Spagna, Lepanto, Ottaviano, Cornelia, or Battistini or M B: Termini, Laurentina, EUR Fermi, or Ponte Mammolo. Bikes can be parked at stations around the city. Cards are rechargeable Initial charge €5, €.050 per 30min. thereafter. Bikes available max. 24hr.) Other companies also rent bikes, including Bici and Baci.

By Taxi

Given the scope of Rome's bus system, taxis should only be reserved for desperate or time-sensitive affairs. Legally, you may not hail a cab on the street–either call RadioTaxi (06 3570 www.3570.it) or head to a cab stand (near most major sights). Ride only in yellow or white cars and look for a meter or settle on a price before the ride. If the cost of your ride seems especially high, write down the license number and contact the company. Tips are not expected.

milan

Milan is a major city, a sea of asphalt punctuated by breathtaking strips of green where the bustle of daily life sometimes overshadows la dolce far niente. But beneath the industrial, fashion-focused lifestyle of Milan is a beautiful, historic district that can easily be overlooked. Whether it's €2000 Gucci shoes or Da Vinci's breathtaking Last Supper, here you will be intimidated. This city earns its cultural megatron status from the Renaissance works, awe-inspiring churches, and medieval castles. The Piazza del Duomo alone is built on the four great pillars of the Milanese lifestyle: the church (Duomo), art (Museo Novecento), commerce (La Rinascente), and rich Renaissance people (Palazzo Reale).

Milan is a city where all the women wear heels, where even the least fashion conscious can pick out the knock-off, where art is free and plentiful, and where it's normal to save up for one €60 meal instead of several crappy ones. The Italian ideal of la bella figura, an aesthetically conscious lifestyle includes everything from food to fashion sense to social prowess, reigns supreme in this sophisticated city.

With opera notes trilling from the famous La Scala and Renaissance artwork hiding around every corner, Milan is a rich well of culture from which to draw. It's evident in everything from the delicate Lombardian culinary specialties to the even more delicate (and expensive) clothing in the windows of what was once called Quadrilatero d'Oro (the Fashion District). Milan has a cultural energy that pulses to the beats of the elite discos, vibrates in the crowds cheering on the AC and Inter Milan soccer teams, and glows in the city's edgy and vibrant contemporary art scene. Milan is as fast and fierce as a cherry-red Ferrari, so grab your stilettos, throw on some hot-pink lipstick, and hop in.

SIGHTS

MILAN CATHEDRAL (DUOMO)
CHURCH

P. del Duomo ☎02 72 02 33 75 www.duomomilano.it

It is no wonder why this 350 ft tall Gothic church took 600 years to complete. Red, white, and black marble rigid, geometric patterns serve as the base for the two rows of statue-embedded columns reaching to the heavens. All light enters through floor to ceiling stained glass windows illuminating the lace-like ceiling, and portrayals of Jesus and other liturgical figures throughout the house of God. Enjoy, but restrain from shooting pics unless you have some weird "church guard chasing you through a tranquil church" fetish. To avoid the drama, if you are a photographer at heart and want to show mom that you have been a good Christian visiting churches, buy a bracelet or work on your sly game.

Though extremely impressive, much of the church is roped off, providing only a few rows of seats halfway down the cathedral for visitors to sit, overcome the overwhelming sense of intimidation, and ponder the genius craftsmanship and engineering intuition required to erect this brilliant house of prayer. Descend below the altar to see the resting place of Cardinal Arcivscoso of Milan whose silver encapsulated corpse is visible through a glass tomb. Most people do not enjoy being stared at; now imagine, being glared at for centuries after your death—the whole set up is a bit creepy if you ask us. And to add to the morbid theme gaze up at the statue of a man with protruding bones and spider-like veins, something you would expect to find in a medieval torture museum or at Party City for your Halloween yard decorations, but not in one of the world's greatest churches.

Before you leave the Piazza del Duomo, perhaps you would like to climb the Duomo for views of the city. Pay €7 to work off your cotoletta Milanese while climbing up the stairs or opt for the €12 lazy route via elevator. The highest

As a large, fast paced city Milan has its fair share of accommodations though many are oriented towards the rich fashionistas and business executives. However, there are some excellent hostel choices for your stay though most are a bit of a walk or metro ride away from the historic district. Compared to the rest of Italy, the best Milan hostels are relatively less expensive, but often fill up quickly, so be sure to book in advance.

GOGOL' OSTELLO
HOTEL $$

Via Chieti, 1 ☎02 36 75 55 22 www.gogolostello.it

As you enter, you will likely smell the aromatic meal being prepared upstairs by the owner and her mother. Patrons of this new hostel say that if you are lucky, she may even invite you to dinner after check-in. If not, many of our dining recommendations are just a short walk away. Dinosaur and sci-fi posters decorate the vibrant green and white walls of this supposed book-sharing hostel. The rooms are extremely clean, spacious, and have a home-y feeling despite the fact that you may be sharing the room with five others. The room atmosphere varies as people come and go; you may be bunking with an older gentlemen who needs your help with Skype or you may be lucky enough to share the room with two college backpackers. There is no lift so be prepared to trudge up three flights of stairs with your pack, but that should not be a problem for travelers like you. And for a nice rest, if not strangely in use for a children's birthday party or formal business meeting, relax on a couch in one of the turf-floored common spaces that will have you wishing there was a ball to kick around. The breakfast is minimal, but a good cup of joe in the morning is all you need after getting shwasted at a nearby club. With an extremely friendly staff in a fine neighborhood, just a 15 minute walk from the city center, the Gogol' Ostello is our favorite Milano hostel.

i 6-Bed mixed dorm €28. 4-Bed mixed dorm €30. Double room private €40. ☼ Reception M- F 8:30am-9:30pm, Sa 8:30am-11:30pm, and Su 9:30am-9:30pm. Checkout at 11am.

point accessible is far from the top of the main tower and the views of Milan are rather unspectacular. Our advice: pocket the cash, take the escalator seven flights up the neighboring designer department store, La Rinascente, and sip on a cappuccino while gazing at the Duomo's spires. At the same height without the burdensome steps, this terrace viewpoint is way more breathtaking than the pricey lookout from the Duomo. Check out the Museo del Duomo to further educate yourself about Milan's artistic and religious history. Entrance to the Duomo is free, but be sure to wear garments that cover the shoulders and the knees. The guards are very strict about proper attire.

i Free. €2 to take photos inside. ☼ Open daily 7am-6:40pm.

SFORZA CASTLE
CASTLE

P. Castello ☎02 88 46 37 00 www.milanocastello.it

At the crossroads of historical and modern Milan stands the pinnacle monument of Parco Sempione, the grand Sforza Castle. Encircled by a water-less moat, now a haven for stray cats, the majority of the castle has been transformed from the former Sforza residency into a castle showcasing century-old art, weaponry, and home decor. Full wall tapestries that could wrap around your freshman dorm walls three times over as intricate as many of the paintings were once used to

milan

insulate the palace. Though the Sforzas did not have to pay a monthly electric bill, the cost to commission such tapestries surely made for expensive heating.

The exhibit is so large that there is an entire wing dedicated to antique pianos and yet others, for armory to see how feuding knights duked it out. Just in case you have not seen enough Madonna col Bambino renditions, the castle has its fair share. Francesco Galli's is one of the best in the world, with emphasis on facial proportions reflecting the same perfection as the works of Leonardo da Vinci, Galli's mentor who dreamt up a fantastic room in the castle currently under renovation. But da Vinci is not the only heavy hitter highlighted in the castle. A circuitous walkway builds tension and curiosity as you are led to Michelangelo's "Pieta Rondanini," an unfinished sculpture, which the master worked on until his death. Moving on you will find yourself walking forwards in history from 1200 to the 1900s, where beautiful paintings are strangely juxtaposed across from furniture you would think you could by from Crate and Barrel. For the $1.50 student price, Sforza Castle's collection of museums is a must, a great way to immerse yourself in medieval culture and kill a few hours before heading to Navigli for your evening date with your trusty alcoholic friends, Peroni and Morretti.

i Castle free. Castle museums €5; €3 student. ☒ Castle open daily 7am-7pm in the summer, 7am-6pm in the winter. Castle museums open Tu-Su 9am-5:30pm, last entrance at 5pm.

GALLERIA VITTORIO EMANUELE II   MALL
P. del Duomo   ☎02 77 40 43 43

A purchase in the Quadrilatero D'Oro (Rectangle of Gold) will send any budget traveler deep into debt. Adjacent to the Duomo, the Galleria Vittorio Emmanuelle II was constructed between 1865 and 1877 as a four story shopping mall with both a glass dome and glass arched ceilings extending in all four directions. Marble inlay floors leading to one Gucci, a Versace, and two Pradas seperated for men and women. Rent here is at a premium, which is one of the reasons why a simple Gucci bag sells for €800. But if you have the money, why not indulge. As one of the Prada representatives told us, "quality lasts." So imagine the €2800 "leopard print calf hair top handle bag" as an investment rather than a waste of money enough to buy two MacBooks, cover three months of your mortgage, or pay for half a semester of school. Rationalizing is not the way to go in this mall, one of the world's oldest, where you feel like you have to pay to even breathe the air. Away from the epicenter of this goldmine are designer stores just as absurdly expensive, namely Luis Vuitton and Armani adding to the extraordinary concentration of swankiness. Well, for all the fashionistas out there, this beautiful structure is the dream.

i Entrance free. Everything else costs a little more. ☒ Most shops open from 9:30am-7:30pm.

BELLAGIO   FOUNTAIN
Bellagio, located on Lake Como

The fountain erupts with water as drunken gamblers publicly carrying boots filled with punch or straight-up bourbon stand at the pools edge, reveling at the glory of the Bellagio Hotel. Though they are not the least bit similar, something must have inspired Steve Wynn to name his Vegas casino after the small, charming Italian town on Lake Como. Do not come here expecting to find any resemblance or you will be seriously disappointed. For those who do not care about slots, Bellagio is objectively better. Settled at the crotch of Lake Como (no we did not make that up) where the two legs of the lake separate, this quaint village is built up into a small beautiful hill, providing views of both Menaggio and Varenna on either side of the lake. At night, lights shimmer all around the lake, creating the illusion of a vast open sky littered with large yellow stars -- it's quite magical if we may say so ourselves.

Though a night the Grand Hotel Villa Serbelloni would probably set you back 10 days of food and lodging, the Lake Como Youth Hostel in Menaggio is cheap and only a 10-min ferry ride away. Walk beside the waterfront parade of palm trees on Bellagio's colorful main street, more resemblant of a tropical paradise than Italian lake village. Burn the calories trudging up the steep hills through less traveled streets underneath canopy topped bridges and above incredible hotel villas before reaching the crotch where you gloriously stand, titanic-ing on the stone walkway reaching into the lake, excited to be at the balls of one of richest lakes in the world—that is the life. On the face looking out onto Varenna lies the Bellagio Rockefeller Residency, housing famous fellows for a month at a time while they write and research in the mountains (we would find the beauty distracting). Keep your eyes peeled in town—perhaps you may find Australia's former Prime Minister, Kevin Rudd (no not Paul Rudd—though that would be way cooler). And while you are here, why not stroll along the waterfront pebble paths to find perfection in landscape and architecture at Giardini di Villa Melzi.

PINCOTECA DI BRERA
MUSEUM

V. Brera 28 ☎02 72 26 32 64 www.brera.beniculturali.it

It is not uncommon to enter a deep inquisitive state when visiting the Pinoteca di Brera. You may wonder: Why do we so value Renaissance paintings? What is so special about Madonna col Bambino? Wasn't idealism a major focus for Renaissance artists? Then why did they not attempt to make Christ the child remotely attractive? Such questions may be inspired by both the paintings on the walls of the Pinoteca and the remarkable insight into the art restoration process. For a museum originally designed for art students' studies, the collection is extremely impressive. The astounding heavy hitters include Raphael's Marriage of the Virgin, Carvaggio's Supper at Emmaus, and Francesco Hayez's Il Bacio (you will know it when you see it). To freshen things up, the museum also boasts an interesting collection of 20th-century works. If all this meta art has inspired you, make your way downstairs and wander through the hallways of the school, where you can peek into classrooms and courtyards to witness sculpture sessions or impromptu performance art. Perhaps you may even catch a glimpse of the next modern master of the arts. If you are bold and hungry, strike up a conversation with some of the students picnicking in the courtyard, and before you leave, you may very well have had your initial inquiries completely answered.

i €9. Students €6. 🕐 Open Tu-Su 8:30am-7:15pm, closed Mon

PINOTECA AMBROSIANA
MUSEUM

Piazza Pio XI 2 ☎02 80 69 21 www.ambrosiana.it

The art is not the only impressive aspect of this exhibit housing the works of Renaissance greats including the likes of Botticelli, Luini, Tiziano Viecellio, Jacopo Bassano, Carvaggio, and the heavy hitter, Leonardo da Vinci. The awe-inspiring lineup is complemented by the rectangular light frames delicately suspended from the ceiling, illuminating the works in such a way that surreal figures achieve human perfection when viewed from any angle.

Aimlessly wandering through the maze of rooms that are most large Italian museums can be rather stressful and confusing—you constantly wonder if you have missed anything spectacular. To alleviate the frustrating pressures and enhance your viewing pleasures, the Pinoteca Ambrosiana provides a complementary map and guide to the exhibit. The tension builds as you enter the gray carpeted room housing a Carvaggio on red velvet walls. Sink into the comfy red chairs designed as if for a home theater facing the black and white Raphael spanning the entire wall below the frosted glass ceiling. Gaze at the several scenes, wondering what Raphael was thinking, or just take a nap—you surely cannot find a more impressive space in which to nap in all of Milan.

milan

After your afternoon siesta and before exploring the world of da Vinci, check out Paul Bril and Jan Brughel's paintings seemingly depicting Disney fairytale wonderlands minus Mickey and Minnie. Descend upon the ancient biblioteca, passing mosaics containing inscriptions of Virgil's Aeneid, taking you through a strange combination of Roman, Renaissance, and modern times. Strike up a conversation with the guards for the ultimate experience. Use this opportunity to exercise your broken Italian and better understand the historical context of the art. Listen to Heart of Courage by Invincible to pump you up and mentally prepare yourself for the largest collection of Leonardo's drawings in the world. His innovative brilliance depicts hydraulic water lifting, Euclidean geometry, toothed wheels, and a deep curiosity for the human eye. After absorbing the two-story Codex Atlanticus, exit through the weighty curtains right back into the hot, sweaty city center.

i €15. Students €10. ⏲ Open Tu-Su 10am-6pm, closed Mon

MUSEO POLDI PEZZOLI
MUSEUM

Via Alessandro Manzoni 12 ☎02 79 48 89 www.museopoldipezzoli.it/en

An unsuspecting museum blended in with the bustling designer shops and expensive hotels, the Museo Poldi Pezzoli is quite different inside. After you save €3 (almost enough to buy a beer in Milan) purchasing the reduced €6 student ticket, ascend the red-velvet banister staircase spiraling around a stone carved statue strangely home to goldfish of all things. As with many Italian museums, the collection is diverse comprising both Renaissance paintings and historical artifacts including glass cases of compasses and other navigational tools. Though potentially fascinating to the viewer, the dim lighting and comfortable seating propels the guard into a deep sleep. Try to find a reason for why the museum designers decided to set an entire room aside for Ippolito Costa's version of "Maddonna col Bambino," a scene more spectacularly depicted in some of the other thousand Renaissance versions. The paintings are beautiful, but this could not be a Milan museum without a touch of fashion, which can be found in the Sala Degli Ori, the best presented room in the museum. Set in glass cases on rising pedestals are intricate gold, silver, and ivory necklaces lying beside knives, bowls, crosses, and other material possessions necessary to throw a fabulous dinner party for the doge. The Portrait of a Man by Andrea Previtalli is a testament to the importance of presentation, with a gold frame propped upon glass in a mirrored case jutting out from the wall, transforming what may normally be perceived by unknowledgeable art viewers as an unimpressive work into a masterpiece. For a comfortable break from the luxuriate in modernity, sink into the anachronistic, vibrant, neon upholstered couches providing an alternative perspective of the works painted 500 years earlier. Once rested, to end your visit check out the Sala D'Armi to get face-to-face with fully armored knights grasping spears below the arched ceilings. One can only imagine how many lives the glass, encased weapons have taken.

i €9 for regular ticket; €6 for students. ⏲ Open M 10am-6pm, W-Su 10am-6pm, closed Tu.

COMO-BRUNATE FUNICOLARE
FUNICULAR

Piazza Alcide de Gasperi 4 ☎031 30 36 08 funicolarecomo.it

To experience the stunning Lake Como scenery without following the shoreline for hours, we suggest the funicular to Brunate. The nearly vertical trip triggers cringes from the feint of heart, but provides brilliant views of Como and the lake's southernmost leg. Those who desire to catch a glimpse of the wider northern half of the lake should leave the heart of Bruanate for a 15-min walk to the "panoramic" vista indicated on road signs. Walks extend elsewhere from Brunate, passing charming homes and mountaintop churches on the ascending road. Hikers may opt for one of the trails leading either up towards Monte Boletto or down towards the emerald water. If the concept of escaping the luxuries of civilization for nature sounds insufferable, choose one of the many trattoria in town to do what Americans do best: eat. Restaurant owners attentively keep post at the doorstep, menus in hand as they attempt to fend off competition in luring hungry tourists. In case the carbohydrate meal wasn't satiating, indulge in a creamy gelato or tart lemon soda to last you the 3-min descent back to opulence. Though there is an information booth in Brunate it is often inconveniently unmanned, so ask any questions you anticipate at the base of the funicular in Como.

i One way ticket €3. Return ticket €5.50. 🕑 Open daily 6am-10:30pm with departures roughly every 15-30min.

FOOD

Food here takes the word "expensive" to a new level. A fine dining experience at a famed restaurants will cost you a pretty penny, surely exceeding the €80 range. But since the majority of the world cannot afford such extravagant meals, Milan has more affordable traditional Lombardi-Milanese cuisine as well. The cotoletta (chicken cutlet) is a must, serving as a welcoming break from the carb lifestyle. Aperitivo unlimited buffets, though not the best quality, are the way to go if you are starved. As in all of Italy, the pasta is delicious and the cheapest option as a primi piatti after pizza, which is soupy and scrumptious as well. After a day of shopping, why not add to the expenses by indulging in a great Milanese meal.

RENDEZ VOUS UNO RISTORANTE PIZZERIA   PIZZA S$
Via Losanna, 11   ☎02 34 93 20 87

Away from the Duomo in the largely residential neighborhoods are the more affordable dining options. Choosing where to grab your meal can be quite difficult. For those who want to sit out on a beautiful street and people watch under the setting sun, Rendez Vous is the perfect place. The jocular wait staff and calm, cool atmosphere will certainly sow the seeds of love if you have found una donna bellissima. Watch as the neighborhood socialite takes his usual seat in the corner, sets aside his specs, and miraculously attracts locals and waiters alike for a communal smoke. Navigating the Italian menu may be difficult, but the animated waiters are surprisingly excited to attempt a translation! If you are adventurous, arbitrarily point and pick an item on the menu. Not knowing what you are about to consume will certainly intensify your meal. The pasta is gastronomically great, the gnocchi even better, and the decadent Tiramisu is a fattening delight. Don't succumb to your post-meal Grappa desires (not that anyone enjoys the putrid taste of Grappa). Instead, to top off your meal you will be handed a free glass of limoncello, which the waiter calls "a drink to ensure your return." Though we may not have been back ourselves, we certainly recommend Rendez Vous as a cheap, scrumptious meal after a tiresome day of exploring Milan.

i Primi piatti €7-15. Secondi piatti €10-25.

LA SALSAMENTERIA   SANDWICHES $
Via G. Chizzolini, 2

If buying round after round for your hostelmates each night is quickly shrinking your budget, try this inexpensive, ultra-modern deli for lunch-on-the-go. Skipping meals is not an intelligent move. Why waste €5 on a refrigerated, supermarket panino, when for about €3, you can order a sandwich on a variety of fresh, crispy rolls with your choice of sliced meats and creamy cheeses? Add some marinated vegetables for a tangy twist. La Salsamenteria is one of the only places in Milan where cheap and quality are not paradoxical concepts. Though €18/kilogram for capricola and €24/kilogram for a specialty fontina may have you regretting your choice of lunch spots, the sandwiches are priced by weight. English is a rarity here, so pointing at meats and just saying "si, si, si" is your best bet. The salamis are soft as a baby's skin and the locally produced taleggio cheese will melt in your mouth with welcoming sharp, flavorful explosions. And if the sandwich wasn't enough, crack a piece off of the homemade breadsticks included in your meal. Sure, this is not New York City's Zabars, nor a fancy butcher shop, but we officially deem this 3-month old deli an unnoticed Milano treasure. Stop on by before this piccolo place becomes the Katz's Deli of Milan. Have a sandwich for lunch, another for dinner, and with all the money saved, why not another for a midnight snack—delizioso, delizioso, delizioso!

i Less than €3 for a sandwich. ⟰ Open M-Sa 9am-8pm, closed Su.

OSTERIA DELLA STAZIONE
ITALIAN $$

Via Piero Della Francesca 68 ☎02 34 93 01 87 www.osteriastazione.it

Located in what appears to be a vivacious neighborhood boasting exorbitantly priced restaurants and a bumping disco club soon to be featured in the Italian film Alaska, Osteria Della Stazione is the place to be. Since we assume that a €100+ meal that you could get at Il Marchesino or Ristorante Cracco is out of your budget, this low key restaurant is a fine replacement. Though the red and white checkered table may remind you of a midwestern diner, you would never be provided with a complimentary glass of sparkling vino rosso in the States. The pastas are rather petite in size, but delicious nonetheless, and we highly recommend the trofie al pesto. But if you have been in Italy for a while consuming pasta night after night, it's understandable if you need a break. Unfortunately steak is not a Milano specialty. Go to Florence for the juicy bistecca and order a pizza here. Upon ordering, watch the chef toss the dough in the air, which will soon be transformed into a flavorful, soupy pizza. And just to ensure that you have had your fair share of alcohol, the waiter will prop down a freezing bottle of limoncello for you to pour yourself. If you chug quickly, this could be the start of a cheap, drunk night out in Milan.

i Primi piatti €9-10. Secondi €9-25. Pizza €5-12. ⟰ Open Tu-F 12:30pm-3pm and 7pm-midnight, M-Sa 7pm-midnight.

ANEMA E COZZE
VENETIAN $$

Via Palermo, 11; Corso Sempione, 41; Via Orseolo, 1; Via Casale, 7 ☎02 83 75 459

www.anemaecozze.com

Nostalgic for Venetian frutti di mare, yet salivating for Napolitano pizza? Well, it just can't be the same, because you're in.....Milan, not Venice or Naples. Lucky for you, we're only joking. Anema e Cozze offers the best of both worlds, Lombardi style. Sink you teeth into a sea of sauce and cheese, with a crisp sea floor, and shrimp floating atop. Or try a bowl of the succulent, parsley-studded clams swimming in bright lemon and tangy wine. To avoid looking like an amateur, avoid immediately cutting the pie or else risk an embarrassing soupy catastrophe. In the mean time gaze out at the canal, creepily watch young couples hooking up, and relish in Italian life. Though more pricey than the average pizzeria, here there is gourmet food, quality service and Mediterranean minimalist decor. The white tiles, sleek chairs, aqua accents, and mermaid emblem are fresh and tight. Though not quite the buffet, aperitivo Navigli style, the flavors are incomparable. The interior is so bright and popular that there are four locations dispersed across Milan proper—a high class chain, much better than Italian fast food chains. However, we suggest trekking over to the Via Casale branch in the evening overlooking the bumping nightlife before drinking away at the Old Fashion Cafe or one of Milans other 100 night clubs.

i Dishes range from €6-15. ⟰ Open daily 12:30-3pm and 7:30pm-midnight.

BREK   MARKET $

San Babila, Corso Venezia   ☎02 76 02 33 79 www.brek.com

Halfway between a supermarket and a specialty store, Brek is a popular chain
that offers delicatessen options for the grab-and-go crowd, but the best option
here is the buffet. Brek's primi prices are perfect for the budget traveler. The
food is freshly prepared in front of you, offering a wide variety of Italian delicacies from risottos to pastas, cheeses, meats, seafood, vegetables, and dessert.
The lasagnas are delicious but the gnochetti di patate pesto di zucchine e ricotta
affumicata is heavenly. For the same quality and quantity anywhere else in Milan
you would have to pay a fortune plus the obnoxious *coperto* cover charge. Here
you pay for what you eat, and what you eat is perfetto.

i €7-14. ⊙ *Open daily noon-3pm and 6:30-11:30pm.*

NIGHTLIFE

Milan not only boasts a cosmopolitan center of fashion and industry, but it also
offers a thriving nightlife for people of all ages and income brackets. Nightlife here
can be categorized many different ways according to price, atmosphere, location,
crowd, etc. But for simplicity, we will keep to two: the club scene and the bar scene.
Whether you are donning a classy Armani suit or faded shorts and a t-shirt will de-
termine where the night takes you. For obvious reasons, the two types of nightlife
are drastically different.

The Bar Scene

Behind fashion-oriented shops, bars appear to pull a close second in the competition
to take up as much property as possible in Milan. The heart of the historic district
where most tourists spend their days is littered with bars and restaurants on side
streets and small squares. The sheer quantity of places to grab a drink along Corso
Sempione northwest of the Arco della Pace is quite shocking. Luckily, this means
there is no shortage of alcohol in this city. You can quench your thirst anywhere with
a birra, limoncello, or whatever alcoholic beverage your liver desires.

Though we are sure that you can have a good night at one of the scattered bars
throughout the city, whether it be the rich Roialto or laid-back Offside Pub, there
is only one area in the city always brimming with students and cocktails. Bar after
bar lining both sides of the Naviglio Grande Canal, a beautiful strip of water in a
sea of pavement, bring students out every night of the week. With classy bars and
legal drinking, we are not sure how students manage to get any work done. Even
during finals period, when many college campuses in the United States are dull and
depressing, the bars are bumping.

The evenings are special as well as budget travelers and students capitalize on
ability to save a couple euros by enjoying aperitivo. This unique Italian traditions
combines two things, which Americans and Italians both love: alcohol and food. For
one price (usually around €8) you get an alcoholic beverage and are treated to a
buffet. Though the plastic plates are rather small to prevent diners from consuming
too much, aperitivo is an Americans dream—the buffet is unlimited. The amount
of dishes to choose from can be a bit overwhelming, which is why we suggest you
take small scoops of each before deciding what you like most in the unlimited buffet
(sounds American, not Italian right?). Salads, grilled vegetables, traditional American finger food, and pastas are all on the menu, which is ideal for the picky eater. Just
about every bar offers this aperitif option from about €6-10. The bars are completely
accepting, serving anyone from the guy with faded shorts and a Nirvana t-shirt to the
stylish woman wearing a slim cut Zara dress. Either sit and dine over a beer as an
aperitif or arrive later to join the young adult crowd flooding the streets lining the
Navigli Grande.

Though there is little to distinguish between the 30+ choices, here are two of our favorites:

- **BOND:** Various genres of live music play here whether it be a DJ bumping EDM or a bassist rocking softer beats. Combined with the sleek, bright, modern decor and open space to get up and move. this place would be fit for 007 himself, though we are not sure that inspired the design. Grab a drink and spill out onto the street to join the massive student party. *i* Pasquale Paoli, 2.

- **MAG CAFE:** Anyone who's someone frequents this classy bar boasting bulb-like chandeliers and chocolate wood decor. Always crowded and popping, Mag is the place to make some friends before hitting the clubs. *i* Ripa di Porta Ticinese, 43.

Club Life

The high life can be rough and full of rejection. It's a bit like the college process. You work extremely hard to find the perfect outfit to make you stand out in the crowd. Your plan for the night is to hit six of Milan's 100 clubs. Armani, Gucci, and Alcatraz are your reach clubs; Hollywood is your target; Old Fashioned and La Banque are your safeties. Is that enough? Will you get in or is your clubbing future destined for failure? You consult a group of Italian men donning Louis and Burberry—they must know the scene! "What is the key to getting in?" you plead with your mundane American accent. The guys smile and reply, "It's a game. The bouncers decide and it depends on who you know" in broken English. The lipstick is on, the button-down shirts are ironed, you've pre-gamed at one of the Navigli bars, and you're ready to hit the clubs. Armani: rejection. Gucci: rejection. Perhaps Alcatraz you will get lucky... after waiting 45 min in line. The overarching theme of the Milano club scene is that it is not rational. But that isn't really surprising given the zebra leather couches and absurdly expensive decor at the top notch clubs. Leave with a plan—check out the websites to examine the nightly sets and ask around for advice. Your decision depends on the genre of music you are looking for and the amount you are willing to shell out. Each club has a unique personality.One thing is for sure, your night will be expensive. Between the taxis, club cover charges, and drinks it can be difficult to stay under €100.

ESSENTIALS

Practicalities

- **TOURIST INFORMATION:** There are a few different tourist information spots in Milan. Milano Centrale Station: Open M-F alongside track 21 from 9am-5pm, Sa-Su 9am-12:30pm. Piazza Castello: Located at Piazza Castello on the corner of Via Beltrami. Open M-F 9am-6pm, Sa 9am-1:30pm and 2-6pm, Su and holidays 9am-1:30pm and 2-5pm. (www.visitamilano.it. ☎02 77 40 43 43)

- **POST OFFICES:** Go to www.posteitaliane.it to search for your closest branch. There is post office in Milano Centrale Station, which is fairly convenient, and others are scattered throughout the city.

Emergency

- **AMBULANCE:** ☎118
- **POLICE:** ☎113
- **CARABINIERI:** ☎112
- **FIRE DEPARTMENT:** ☎115

italy

- **PHARMACIES:** Pharmacies Hotline: ☎800 801185. All pharmacies have the green crosses on their stores.
- **HOSPITALS:** Ospedale Fatebenefratelli (C.so di Porta Nuova, 23. ☎02 63 631). San Giuseppe (Via S. Vittore, 12. ☎02 85 991). Istituto Europeo Di Oncologia – Eurpean Institute of Oncology (Via Ripamonti, 435. ☎02 57 48 91). San Carlo Borromeo (Via Pio II, 3. ☎02 40 45 4C4). San Paolo (Via A di Rudini, 8. ☎02 81841)

Getting Around

Tickets can be bought at Metro Underground stations or at tabbachi shops. One-way tickets are €1.50. Passes are €4.50 for 24hrs or €8.25 for 48hrs. The Milano Card is €13 and provides free transport, free medical service, and discounts (usually 10-20%) on certain museums, shopping, restaurants, etc. for a given period of time (24 or 72hrs).

venice

It's the city on water, a bastion of art, culture, and seafood, a mystical, well-preserved, tourist-transformed shell of century-old grandeur. Venice is well-visited for a reason: it's magical. Both in the glimmering interior of the Basilica di San Marco and at the edge of the city where you find yourself alone with sky and sea, Venice has an enchantment all its own that proves its place in the pantheon of Italian cities. Sure the overpriced gelato, crowds of ignorant tourists, and endless parades of fake Prada bags may make you sick and remind you of modern world realities. But as you meander along the maze of streets with a willingness to get lost, you will find that the old museum-turned palaces, 16th-century bridges, and unexplored alleyways built on 118 wood-piled islands truly make Venice unlike any other place in the world. Whether it is the myth of gorgeous gondoliers or the allure of a future Atlantis, Venice is undeniably a must on your journey through Italy.

SIGHTS

BASILICA DI SAN MARCO

CHURCH

Piazza San Marco 328   ☎041 27 08 311 www.basilicasanmarco.it

Italian churches are famed for their extravagant ceilings and domes commissioned by the Church, which at the time had no limit to its spending spree. Golden domes, frescoes by the Renaissance masters, and endless rows of marble statues all have tourists craning their heads back in awe, which makes for some of the least flattering poses with jaws dropped, tongues hanging out, and hair gravitating to the floor as if just shot with a tranquilizer. Basilica di San Marco (Saint Mark's Basilica for those with the ethnocentric intuition to ignore any writing not in English—there are a lot of those in Italy), which overlooks the water and is Venice's most renowned church, is perhaps an exception to the zombie-esque tourist phenomenon. Instead of growing entranced by the still-beautiful five domes dominating the golden ceiling of saints, visitors drop their heads to the floor and stare at the intricate, colorful mosaics, making for a crowd of tour groups and students like yourself bumping into each other left and right like teenage girls texting and walking.

Nonetheless, St. Mark's Basilica started in 828 and, according to the doge's order, is most definitely a must-see as long you avoid the multitude of little fees you can acquire inside. But don't worry, there is a silent space dominated by its red hues set aside for praying if you're inspired to be at one with Jesus. And most importantly, confessions are free. So you can go right in and liberate yourself from the sins of premarital sex and binge drinking that was your Venetian experience the night before. To top things off, this is probably the only time on

venice

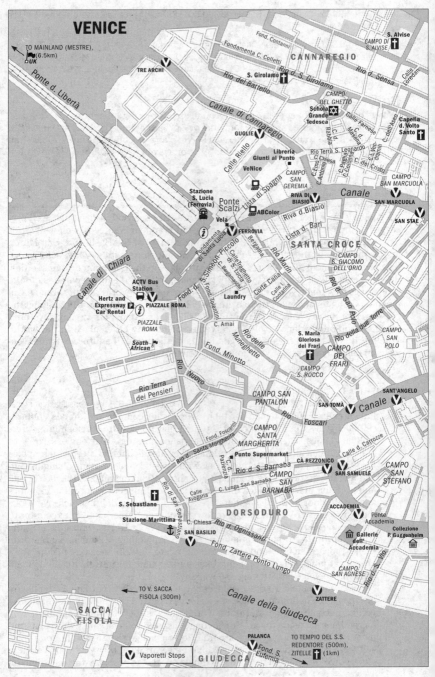

VENICE

TO MAINLAND (MESTRE),
UK (6.5km)

Ponte d. Libertà

TRE ARCHI

Fond. Contarini

Fondamenta C. Colletti

S. Girolamo

Rio del Battello

Rio d. S. Girolamo

CANNAREGIO

Rio d. Sensa

Calle loredan

S. Alvise

CAMPO DI
S. ALVISE

Canale di Cannaregio

CAMPO
DEL GHETTO

Schola
Grande
Tedesca

Capella
d. Volto
Santo

GUGLIE

Calle Riello

Libreria
Giunti al Punto

VeNice

Calle farnese

C. d. Ghetto

Calle Masena

Rio Terra S. Leonardo

C. d. Rabbia

C. Ferau

C. di S. Antonio

C. Pesaro

C.Colombo

C. Vergola

C. del Cristo

C. Chiesa

CAMPO
SAN
GEREMIA

CAMPO
SAN MARCUOLA

Stazione
S. Lucia
(Ferrovia)

Ponte
Scalzi

Lista di Spagna

ABColor

Vela

RIVA DI
BIASIO

Canale

SAN MARCUOLA

Riva d.Biasio

SAN STAE

FERROVIA

Lista d. Bari

Fondamenta
di Santa Lucia

Fond. d. S. Simeon Piccolo

Fond. d. S. Lucia

Fond. Tolentini

Calle Tolentini
di S. Lucia

Bergama

Rio Marin

SANTA CROCE

CAMPO
S. GIACOMO
DELL'ORIO

Rio di San Polo

ACTV Bus
Station

Calle Pegloggetto
di S. Lucia

Calle Bagamasco

Corte Canal

Calle
Contarina

CAMPO
SAN
POLO

Hertz and
Expressway
Car Rental

PIAZZALE ROMA

Laundry

Rio della due Torre

PIAZZALE
ROMA

C. Amai

Rio delle

Muneghette

Fond. Minotto

S. Maria
Gloriosa
del Frari

CAMPO
DEL
FRARI

Rio Nuovo

CAMPO
S. ROCCO

South
African

Rio Terra
dei Pensieri

Fond. Foscarini

Rio d. Santa Margherita

CAMPO SAN
PANTALON

Rio
Foscari

Canale

SAN TOMA

SANT'ANGELO

CAMPO
SANTA
MARGHERITA

Punto Supermarket

Rio d. S. Barnaba

Calle d. Carrozze

CÀ REZZONICO

CAMPO
SAN
STEFANO

Calle
di
Padenza

CAMPO
SAN
BARNABA

C. Lunga San Barnaba

SAN SAMUELE

S. Sebastiano

Calle
Avogaria

Rio d. San Sebastiano

DORSODURO

ACCADEMIA

Ponte
Accademia

Stazione Marittima

C. Chiesa

Rio d. Ognissand.

Collezione
P. Guggenheim

SAN BASILIO

Fond. Zattere Ponto Lungo

Gallerie
dell'
Accademia

CAMPO
SAN AGNESE

Rio d. S. Vio

TO V. SACCA
FISOLA (300m)

ZATTERE

SACCA
FISOLA

Canale della Giudecca

PALANCA

Fond. S.
Eufemia

TO TEMPIO DEL S.S.
REDENTORE (500m),
ZITELLE (1km)

Vaporetti Stops

GIUDECCA

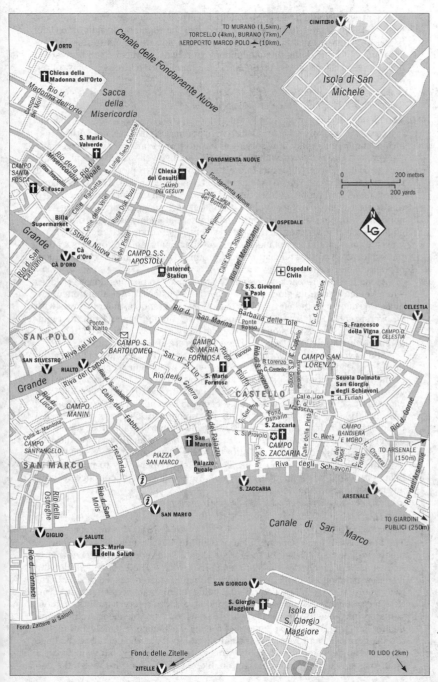

milan

your journey that you'll be happy you lugged around your heavy pack. Walk just past the Basilica away from the corner and veer the slightest bit right onto Calle S. Basso, where you can drop off your bag and skip the line into the Basilica (#winning)! And with the time and money you saved, dish out €8 to burn some beer carbs on the 98 meters up St. Mark's Campanile for a bird's eye view of the sinking lagoon city.

i Basilica free; San Marco Museum €5; Treasury €3; Golden Altarpiece €2. ⏰ Easter-Nov M-Sa 9:45am-5pm, Su 2-5pm; Nov to Easter 9:45am-5pm, Su 2-4pm.

GRAND CANAL
CANAL

That canal in Venice. No, not that one. Or that one. The enormous, grand one. Yes. With an alluring, diaphanous, silky flow serving as a tourist and commercial passageway, the Grand Canal is the weaving spine of this sinking, well-preserved, cultural time capsule. Without the canal there is no Venice, and ironically with the canal there soon will be no Venice as water levels rise. Perhaps one of the only places where heavy pollution and trash-littered shores yield a vibrant turquoise hue, this waterway ferries all that comes in and out of this lagoon city. Overpriced gondolas with couples hoping for the quintessential cuddly, twilight romance glide along as the vaporetti ferry lazy travelers, water taxis carry rich folk, noise-polluting water ambulances transport ill patients, and motorboats traffic rushed locals. And they all disrupt what promised to be an intimate experience of solitude under the stars.

Along the canal's banks are shells of what used to be splendorous palaces when Venice was in its glory days. Today these palaces, if not abandoned, are museums allowing student travelers to explore the grandeur that once was with an oversized backpack and cargo shorts—a welcoming change from the requisites a century ago. Names on the guest list, designer shawls, collared tuxedoes, and portfolios valued at a couple billion dollars are no longer required.

And as you wind your way from the uninteresting Piazzale Roma bus station under the Rialto and Accademia bridges while being pinned against the side of the mobbed vaporetto between the shoving elbows of two sweaty tourists, you may wonder why you paid €7 for this catastrophic ride or even why you came to this city at all. But when you escape the boat and the hordes of tourists swarming Piazza San Marco, head for the unmapped alleyways and tranquil peripheries branching off the Grand Canal where you will realize that Venice has its fair share of secrets. Vaporettos #1 and #2, though sometimes unpredictable and slow, span the canal from P.le Roma to San Marco and extend even farther to Lido. Water taxis, though expensive, are a convenient way to navigate this behemoth canal while gondolas provide a rare, enjoyable experience without any transportation function at all.

i Canal free. Vaporetto ride on canal (aka the poor man's gondola) €7.

TEATRO LA FENICE
THEATER

Campo St. Fantin 1965 ☎041 78 66 72 www.teatrolafenice.it

The opera is not most students' idea of nightlife, but if you love shrilling arias, the tuxedo life, and €250+ tickets, go right ahead. This Venetian theater, formerly known as San Benedetto, was christened La Fenice ("The Phoenix") following its reconstruction after a 1773 fire left it in rubble. The star-crossed theater burnt twice more in a city full of water before being rebuilt in its present, grand form.

That's all very fascinating and marvelous, but you'll forget it all the minute you step inside, as historical knowledge is swept away by sheer architectural beauty. Like many of the splendors of Venice, La Fenice resembles a big, historical, gorgeous, and way-too-expensive wedding cake: the ceiling of the huge theater is so decked-out with gold beams and pastel paint, you'll want to eat it like frosting, one layer at a time. If you, like many of us, aspire to see the cul-

get a room!

Staying in the heart of Venice can be rather tricky and very expensive. Unless you are willing to dish out a couple grand on the Danieli or a €200 3-star hotel, living the hostel life nearby the six sestiere (districts) is probably your best bet. However, we have compiled a list of the best places to stay in and near Venice, to help give you the best Venetian, budget experience. Though Hostelworld is an invaluable tool, check out individual hotel websites for deals that may include 10% discounts, free breakfasts, or both! Who knows? The possible permutations are infinite. The number one thing to keep in mind is not to be discouraged by the prices. Though nothing in Venice is cheap, the city is most definitely worth a visit even if it is just for a night or two! Here are your best bets for a bed that won't break your budget.

HOTEL TIZIANO   HOTEL $$$

Dorsoduro 1873   ☎041 27 50 071 www.hoteltizianovenezia.it

There are few places in Venice where you can find a single room during high season that won't require you pleading mom for money. Hotel Tiziano, in a quiet, university neighborhood, is just a 5 minute walk from the center of nightlife in Venice proper. Joke around and talk soccer with Ricardo or have a long conversation with Claudia. The entire staff is eager to help and always willing to strike up a conversation. The soft salami, cheeses, and rolls will melt in your mouth during the free breakfast in the main dining room. The fact that this hotel does not specialize in budget travel, with more expensive rooms rising up to €300 means that the facilities are clean and beautiful. The apartment is basic with a small bed and bathroom, but unfortunately no air conditioning. However, the location, serenity and personal space means you can don your birthday suit in the heart of the lagoon city.

i €80 for a single apartment. Breakfast included. Make reservations in advance, rooms are limited. ⚁ Check in at 2:30pm though storage is available for early arrivals. Check out at 11am.

GENERATOR HOSTEL VENICE   HOSTEL $$$

Fondamenta della Croce 86   ☎041 87 78 288 generatorhostels.com

A one-stop vaporetto ride away, this hostel on the island of Giudecca competes with 5-star hotels for the best hotel view in all of Venice. The best part is that a bed costs one tenth of the price. With a nice bar, incredible lounge area, restaurant, five televisions, and a massive projector screen, this is the place to save and meet travelers from around the world, while living in style. Though showers are a bit tight and the 16-bed dorms aren't massive, the facilities are safe and clean. You will not need more than a bed to pass out once in once the San Margherita bars are done with you and the hostelmates you met earlier in the day. And if a European football game is on, the party is in the hostel, with parties thrown by the staff and a DJ who loves playing your jams. Hands down, if you can get a bed here it is a 100% worth it. Enjoy Venice in what many backpackers have called "the best hostel in Europe."

i Dorms, €20-30; doubles €120; 5-person rooms €135. Breakfast not included. ⚁ Check in at 2pm though storage is available for early arrivals. Check out at 10am. No curfew so stay out partying all night (though the real party may be here in the Generator!)

venice

tural grandeur of La Fenice's stellar performances but lack the funds for equally stellar seats, the tour is a fine option. The 45-minute audio tour will provide the history and a look at a few scores that may be impressive, but for around €15 (€7 more than the tour price) you can get obstructed-vision seats. Visual deprivation may even make it easier to be swept up in the music of the opera and orchestral pieces.

i €9 for entrance and audio guide; €6.50 for students up to 26 years old. Opera tickets cost a little more. ☼ Open daily 9:30am-6pm.

PEGGY GUGGENHEIM COLLECTION
MUSEUM

Dorsoduro 701 ☎041 24 05 411 www.guggenheim-venice.it

While most of us go from country to country collecting ticket stubs, magnets and backpacking pains, Peggy Guggenheim chose a more sophisticated route by meeting artists and promoting their works. Her collect-as-you-go lifestyle led her to acquire works of just about every 20th century great. When you enter the main exhibition in this beautiful palazzo on the Grand Canal that you wish you could call home, Calder's Arc of Petals mobile and Picasso's La Baignade will drive you deep into air-conditioned paradise. This collection of modern art with an entire room dedicated to Jackson Pollack's expressionist splatter-paintings, several of Salvador Dali's melting scenes, vibrant Kandinsky's, the morphing figures of Max Ernst, and other great works by the likes of Miro, Magritte, Metzinger, Modrian, Chagall, Rothko, Ernst, and Bacon is rather small and lacks the intimidation factor of many larger museums of its kind. But still houses an impressive collection. One of the only places in Venice where you'll feel propelled forward in history, the Peggy Guggenheim Collection (€8 for students and just a couple minute walk following signs from the Accademia Bridge) is a refuge from the heat and a must even for those fortunate enough to have New York City as their artistic playground.

i €14; students under 25 €8. ☼ Open 10am-6pm; closed Tu.

CA' D'ORO
MUSEUM

Cannaregio 3932 ☎041 52 22 349 www.cadoro.org

If your first impression is that this palazzo will have a grand interior ornate with gold walls, ceilings, and floors as its name ("House of Gold") implies, you are sorely mistaken. Though the bottom floor just down the steps past the ticket office leads to a courtyard with a few statues and intricate mosaic floors know as Il Pavimento the rest of the house looks just like another museum.

The Giorgio Franchetti collection housed in this once thriving shell of a mansion boasts four large wall-sized tapestries and partially preserved frescoes along with many Renaissance paintings and sculptures. Our favorite is a paneled, nativity scene by Gaudenzio Ferrari (no, not the carmaker, though that'd be exciting). Bonus points if you can pick out the painting of two strong men standing like two teenage girls posing for a photo with their butts sticking out, a sight that even bleeding Jesus finds disgusting. For a break from the art, step through the glass doors onto the balcony, towering over the happening Grand Canal, though your best views will definitely be from the vaporetto down below.

As you walk up the stairs to the first floor and wonder if you successfully beat the crowds, don't flatter yourself—there's a reason this museum isn't crowded. Though beautiful pieces, the art sticks to the same Renaissance theme seen in larger, more impressive museums elsewhere. If you're headed to Florence, Rome, or even the Gallerie dell'Accademia, we recommend pocketing those €6 for barhopping at night instead. 3132 Calle Ca' D'Ora on the street to the Ca' D'Oro vaporetto stop.

i €6. ☼ M 8:15am-2pm; Tu-Su 8:15am-7pm.

CAFFÈ FLORIAN

P. San Marco   ☎041 52 05 641 www.caffeflorian.com

CAFE

The oldest cafe in Italy, Caffè Florian has continued to thrive in the magical Piazza San Marco since before the colonies declared independence from Great Britain. If you're the kind of person who would buy a €500 pair of shoes when you could get a pair of comparable quality for €50, Caffè Florian just may be your kind of place. For €38 you could get a cappuccino, fresh orange juice, fresh fruit salad, a croissant, toasted white bread, butter, jam or honey, dark chocolate cake, and yogurt. There you have it, the same continental breakfast served free at your hotel for a small fortune.

But for a more modest €19, you can indulge yourself in heavenly Coppa Caffè Florian gelato. Our recommendation: walk past the dapper dukes of Italy donning white tuxedos and black bow ties, imagine the never-ending grandiose that Florian has sustained, and make your way through the maze of white cloth tables lining the square as the eargasmic sound of the piano, accordion, and violin of the orchestra lead you away to flirt with the mass of pigeons that is San Marco Square.

i From the #1 (slower) or #2 San Marco (express - only stops at P.le Roma, Ferrovia, Rialto, Academia) vaporetto stop, walk right into the square and follow the music to your left under the shade of the Procuratie Nuove facade. Gelato €15-19 is probably one of the cheapest eats you can get at this caffè. ☒ The lavish cafe is open daily 9am-12am.

GALLERIE DELL'ACCADEMIA

Campo della Carità 1050   ☎041 52 00 345 www.gallerieaccademia.org

GALLERY

It's time for I Spy: Accademia Edition. How many Madonna and Child scenes can you find? We counted over 50. Oh and for a nice twist, how many different titles can you find for this same scene? We counted over five variations of Madonna col Bambino—if you have any interest in looking at chubby baby after chubby baby we're sure you can find some more. Not to throw shade at the beauty of the works, but once you've been to one Renaissance museum in Italy, it seems like you've been to them all.

There's an unsurprising theme of huge, precariously mounted masterpieces that look like they're about to fall on your head mixed in with small gold-painted, wooden depictions of martyrdom. Venice's prime museum for pre-19th century art, it's the place to be if you've got a hankering for huge paintings of Renaissance dudes adoring Jesus. Our favorite was Lorenzo Venziano's Polittico Lion con l'Annuncio, perhaps because it was the first "Madonna and Child" of the day or that we still weren't exhausted having only checked out the first room. Only 300 people are allowed in the museum at once so come early or late to avoid the dreaded crowds.

i €15, also includes admission to Palazzo Grimani. ☒ Open M 8:15am-2pm and Tu-Su 8:15am-7:15pm.

SAN GIORGIO MAGGIORE

San Giorgio Maggiore, across from St. Mark's Square

CHURCH

Are you dying for picturesque views of Venice to show mom and grandma why their help funding your trip was worth it? Then take the quick, one-stop vaporetto ride (#2) from the San Zaccaria stop located between the yachts you wish you owned in Piazza San Marco to this gorgeous little island across the way. When you are done taking shots—the camera kind—of one of the most picturesque locations in Venice, pay the €6 you saved from skipping Ca' D'Oro to ride the elevator up to the top of the famous Campanile (Bell Tower) here for remarkable views of Venice. The church is free and worth a peek. Designed by Palladio, the dome's intimidating height will astonish you, yet the simplicity of the structure will calm you in this cool refuge from the heat. A quick walk outside will take

venice

you past a locked garden, a private marina, and a simple cafe with service and seating.

i Church free. €6 for elevator to the top of the bell tower. ☒ Church is open daily Apr-Oct M-Sa 9am-7pm, Su 9am-11am and noon-7pm. Nov-Mar daily 9am-5:30pm.

MUSEO CORRER
MUSEUM

P. San Marco   ☎041 24 05 211 correr.visitmuve.it

Are you a history buff, art fanatic, or student suffering from FOMO syndrome ("fear of missing out")? This museum housing the Teodoro Correr collection leads you through the Royal Palace rooms of the Napoleonic Wing in San Marco Square, recreating the history of what once was a thriving, trading Venetian Republic—a shocking and welcoming reminder that the tourists have not always been the driving force behind this northern provincial economy.

It's too bad you can't simply relax on the red velvet and golden silk chairs overlooking the piazza that stand out throughout this fantastic display of wealth. For all the fans of Antonio Canova's statues (and who isn't a fan?) the museum's first floor is a paradise. Or if you're more like us you can walk quickly through wondering why the plaster sculptures had black dots and holes in the penis. And to continue with the unintentional phallic theme that this museum lends itself to, our favorite piece is the 7-foot pointed "Unicorn: The Tree of Jesse" rod carved out of Sea-Unicorn tooth from "Venezia?" as the description on the plaque reads, which is encased towards the end of the first floor. The sizable collection of golden coins and the two intricate model ships are nothing to scoff at.

Once you have ascended to the second floor of the grandiose building that quietly overlooks Piazza San Marco, get excited to speed through what appears to be room after room of "Madonna and Child" variates, leaving those who pick up on this glaring repetition unsurprised about what the next room has in store. Most stunning in our opinion are the numerous antiquated globes and the two Murano glass chandeliers in the Sala delle Quattro Porte from which blue, pink, and white blossom.

For a student discount price of €10 from the standard €16 entry fee you are admitted to the Museo Correr and granted free skip-the-line access to Doge's Palace. In addition to the impressive collection of swords and large-barreled guns in the Doge's apartment, the Sala del Maggior Consiglio is the closest thing to Michelangelo's Sistine Chapel you will see in Venice. The room is well preserved with massive gold frames embedded in the ceiling and a wall painting that achieves the paradoxical complexity that Raphael perfected in the Vatican. It's not nearly as famous and perhaps not as grand, but there's a case to be made that this room is not far off. This uncrowded chronicle of the splendorous Venetian history is worth a peek.

i €16; students under 25 €10. Also includes admission to the Doge's Palace. ☒ Open daily Apr-Oct 10am-7pm; Nov-Mar 10am-5pm.

CA'REZZONICO
PALACE

Dorsoduro 3136   ☎041 24 10 100 carezzonico.visitmuve.it

This grand palace took over a century to complete (1649-1756), and with the winning combination of a walk through the now 18th-century museum and your imagination, you'll have no doubt why that is. From the large, canal-level courtyard showcasing fresh pigeon poop, an antiquated gondola, and a small fountain crowded by enthralled tourists watching pigeons bathe and turtles bask, head up to where the fun begins.

From red velvet walls to gold frames and Murano glass chandeliers, everything stylistically works (coming from the home decor fashionistas that we are). All rooms on each floor branch off the portego, the large, mostly empty spine of the palazzo. The famed Giambattista Tiepolo is responsible for four magnificent canvas ceilings throughout the house. The work of Lazzarini, Tiepolo's mentor, is also highlighted in the house. Whether the student surpassed his teacher in grandeur and style is something we'll leave you to decide.

Moving through the rooms you'll find scenes by Francesco Guardi, which serve as a comforting verification that the masks sold in shops on just about every Venetian street corner are not simply a tourist scam, but a historical tradition of the Carnevale di Venezia. Further on, you'll find a small piano situated amongst glass cases of china—mix music with fine dining and you get 18th-century Venetian class. Keep your eyes peeled for both the paintings of an anachronistic parrot and an emaciated dog whose owners donning red jackets and long, elegant gowns apparently could not afford to feed. And as you enter the Egidio Martini Picture Gallery, you'll be greeted by paintings of strong, intelligent babies. One is walking a hyena-cougar morph on a leash, another is playing a trumpet bigger than him, and others are examining mind-boggling instruments fit for the great minds of Aristotle and Sophocles (future Harvard freshmen right here). And when you turn the corner thinking you've escaped the strangeness, you'll find works of babies flying, blowing bubbles, and nursing— all the things you did as a baby (well at least some of them). Ca' Rezzonico is overall an impressive, pallazzo-turned-museum to add to your list.

i €8; students under 25 €5.50 ⏰ Open Apr-Oct 10am-6pm. Nov-Mar 10am-5pm.

FOOD

Nothing in Venice is cheap, especially not the food. We realize that budget travel is hard, but if there is a place to splurge it's here. Dig a little deeper into your wallet to afford the unsurprisingly, pesce-driven Venetian cuisine. Everything that comes into city must do so by boat, jacking up the prices of all goods (inflation alert!). You can find the tourist-oriented pizzerias and cheaper cafes serving mediocre food for decent prices as well. But how can you pass up scallops and squid purchased daily at the Rialto fish market and served up fresh for you later that evening. As long as you'll eat just about any sea creature from shark to crustaceans, non-English menus shouldn't be a problem. Just employ our point-and-choose method for the true experience. Antipasto misti, black-ink squid, and risotto di pesce are popular dishes, and spritzes are the drink of choice! Rule of thumb: if you don't know what you are ordering, have a friend order something simpler so if things go horribly wrong and it turns out you fancy shark, at least you'll have a little nibble. The pizza is good, calzones are better, but fish is best, so try it! We know you can pick out the tourist-catered restaurants, which are more or less the same so we picked some special restaurants serving up traditional Venetian cuisine for a delicious, dining experience.

OSTERIA AL MASCARON
OSTERIA $$$

Calle Lunga Santa Maria Formosa 5225   ☎041 52 30 744 www.osteriamascaron.it

Escape the Piazza San Marco crowds and tourist trap restaurants where locals would never set foot by heading up north to Campo S. Maria Formosa where after-school giochi di calcio and locals sipping on spritzes is more the style. Off a narrow side street (as most streets in Venice tend to be), resides this small, lively restaurant proud of its history, where as you make your reservation, two older men will repeatedly practice your name with their thick accents for all on the street to hear. Though pricey (just like everywhere else in Venice), use this meal to experiment with what this Venetian ristorante ironically specializes in given the pig painting and statues: forget bacon, it's all about the pesce.

Thank god for the translated menus, unless you enjoy being surprised by unfamiliar, tentacled sea-creatures in your spaghetti. For the daring, splurge on the €16 antipasto misto with an assortment of scaly fish and crustaceans and share a pasta for two with your hostelmate. With a few glasses of the fine house

Venice

wine and an exceptional display of your outgoing personality, engage in humorous conversation with the artists, painters, and tourists that frequent this fun restaurant. Then afterwards you'll be set for the walk to the bars of Campo Santa Margherita for some more quality time with Bacchus (the Roman god of wine) and your hostelmate (or soon-to-be girlfriend/boyfriend after treating them to all this).

i Primi mainly for 2 €26-46. Secondi €16-19. ☺ Open M-Sa noon-3pm and 7-11pm.

GAM GAM
KOSHER $$

Ghetto Vecchio 1122 ☎041 27 59 256 www.gamgamkosher.com

"Great food. Great Prices. Great Time." is the English motto atop the menu. We agree! The realization that Italian-Kosher fusion exists is life-changing. While you're trying out the Italian version of gefilte fish feeling a bit nostalgic for your usual seder, don't be surprised if a friendly waiter pulls up a chair and sits down across from you to make this more like Grandma's Passover shindig. Don't let the pigeons who have been known to hop up on tables contribute to the communal atmosphere. Shoo them away and relish as the lapping waves, vaporetti and Hasidic Jews pass by, all adding to the lively Jewish Ghetto experience. If homemade matzahball soup doesn't quell your homesickness woes, perhaps the delicious couscous, homemade hummus, or schnitzel will do the job. If you plan to break from the traditional Italian cuisine for a night please don't settle for cheap kebabs at places that also sell pizza (not a promising sign). Opt for Gam Gam ("Also, Also") and enjoy the communal atmosphere on the banks of the Cannaregio Canal.

i Antipasti €8-10. Entrees €9-22. ☺ Open Su-Th noon-10pm; F noon-two hours before sundown; Sa (excluding summer) one hour after sundown-11pm.

RISTORANTE DA ALVISE
RISTORANTE $$$

Sestiere Cannaregio 5045a ☎041 52 01 515 www.ristorantedaalvise.it

If you find yourself lost in the north side of Venice, which is a residential neighborhood separated from the comforting sounds of English speakers dominating touristy Venice, don't freak out! This is the real experience. Follow the maps or just get lost using the navigational skills you cultivated as a Cub Scout, and make your way to scary northern waters looking out towards the morbid, gated island of S. Michele (a massive cemetery) and beyond. You'll find bustling civilization as you are used to once again right past the Fondamente Nove vaporetto stops. Right here, you'll find Ristorante Da Alvise, a great place to share gigantic calzones, dig into risotto di pesce, and pop open a bottle of Venetian prosecco. Enjoy as the waves of water ambulances booking it to the nearby Ospedale splash against the shore. Don't worry, the umbrella-covered patio will provide the perfect escape from the relentless sun without the need for a dip in the polluted, murky Venetian waters.

i Antipasti €9-25. Pizza €7-11. Primi €8-15. Secondi €15-25. ☺ Open daily noon-2:30pm and 7pm-10:30pm. Closed Mondays in the winter.

HOSTARIA DA BARBARIGO
SEAFOOD $$

Fondamenta Barbarigo 2344 ☎33 98 66 55 59

If you love seafood and are dying for a truly home-cooked meal, get away from the S. Margherita bar scene and pay a visit to Antonella and Michele's family-run ristorante. This is the perfect place to practice your Italian ordering skills. Though Michele speaks very little English, Antonella will take a break from frying up the fried squid and preparing the crostini with stockfish she bought at Rialto market that morning to tell you the menu. Your meal will run you about €15-20 depending on what you order, but don't hold back. For the pastas, try the shark or the swordfish carbonara. The scampi with cherry tomatoes is a safe play, but for the adventurous try the black squid ink. But don't order the

venice

squid if a romantic evening under the stars on the quiet nearby lawn is in the works; the ink will turn both her lipstick and his teeth black. This meal is an epicure's fantasy. While you wait for Antonella to prepare your meal, showcase your artistic prowess on the paper placemat and Michele will put it up with the other masterpieces. The only thing we wish were different is the Inter flag on the wall; they support the wrong Milan. Oh well, we're forgiving!

i *Antipasti €2-12. Primi €12.* ☼ *Hours vary. Generally open Tu-Sa 11:30am-3:30pm and 6pm-11:30pm and the kitchen closes at 10pm. Closed Sundays and Mondays.*

6342 A LE TOLE
RISTORANTE **$$**

Castello 6342
☎041 52 00 474

Take a peek through the windows and watch the chef roll out the dough for homemade artichoke ravioli as his sous-chef tosses the long fettuccine in flour. Food is an art form in this country, but the opportunity to watch the masters at work is relatively rare. If the allure of fresh pasta is not enticing enough, perhaps the array of delicious low-priced pizzas will seal the deal. The massive fork on the wall, the orange draped windows, and dim lighting illuminating the scenes of Venice hanging on the walls set a lively vibe for this air-conditioned restaurant. The fairly priced menu allows the well-to-do and the students to enjoy a quality, homemade meal not far from Piazza San Marco.

i *Pizza €6. Pasta €12.* ☼ *Open Tu-Sa 11:30am-3:30pm and 7-10:30pm, but the kitchen closes at 9pm and it is smart to stop by to see when chef Antonella will get things cooking.*

NIGHTLIFE

Venice is certainly not your club hub, but if you know where to look, you may be able to find some atmosphere to satisfy your post-midnight desires. As you wander the streets it may appear that Venice is devoid of youth—local youth that is. Opera, Vivaldi concerts, and strolls through the city are Venice's most popular "nightlife activities". But don't fret; students and alcohol do go hand-in-hand at Campo Santa Margherita. Bars line the square and Ca' Foscari college students litter the streets, which makes for an exciting night if you are willing to bud into conversations with your poor Italian skills. Though bars do exist in other places, C. S. Margherita is the place where the youth go to find a good time. Though we cannot confirm, word has it that there is a €15 bar run lap around Campo Santa Margherita that will have you feeling pretty damn good.

MARGARET DUCHAMP
BAR

Campo Santa Margherita 3019
☎041 52 86 255

The sleek black chairs outside this blue and magenta, colorfully lit bar set the raging vibe that deems it the king of Santa Margherita. There are booths inside for the lovie-dovies who would rather sit in seclusion than interact with the regulars. But don't miss out! Absorb the energetic atmosphere to build courage for a body shot on the blue, neon lit bar, the easiest way in all of Venice to get four free shots. When the interior fills up, people flood the square hoping to catch a glimpse of the soccer game. But you will also find socialites and classy gondoliers by the Heiniken pillars who changed from their blue and white striped attire into their "I'm here to drink and get the ladies" look. The lively atmosphere earns Margaret Duchamp the #1 for our list of top nightlife spots in Venice.

i *Beer €4. Mixed drinks €3-7.* ☼ *Open M 10am-2am, W-Su 10am-2am.*

ORANGE BAR
BAR

Campo Santa Margherita 3054A
☎041 52 34 740 www.orangebar.it

As the name suggests, everything is orange here. After you order your orange Aperol spritz inside the orange-walled room with the Picasso-esque painting (classy), head outside to one of the most lively student bars in Campo Santa Margherita. Take a seat in a woven orange chair with a clique of college students or if you are sick of the orange theme, burn some calories huddling around the perimeter as many people do. Whether MTV is your jam or watching Juventus is more appealing to you, the 42" television in the window has it all, from Kardashians whining to Pirlo taking the pitch. Local cappuccino stop by day, lively alcohol-fest by night, Orange Bar is a good bet for a fun time.

i Most drinks €3-5. Cocktails on list €7. ☻ Open daily 9am-2am.

CAFFE AL FONTEGO
CAFE

Campo Santa Margherita, 3426 ☎041 39 90 444 www.cafealfontegovenice.com

In a small brick building at the corner of Campo Santa Margherita is this small bar with lots of character. To preserve history, the owners left the washing area of the former laundromat in the basement below. Though you may need to do a wash as you get sloppy with your drinking, we highly doubt the machines are intended for public use. The party here is often quick—buy your drinks, down your shots, and move on. Though there's a small side room for indoor seating, Venetian students prefer standing outside, shouting and shaking their heads vigorously as they throw back the €1 shots. Caffe al Fontego is a great place to grab your drinks, but lacks outdoor seating so don't be that drunkard here who's too hammered to stand.

i €1 shots. €3-3.50 apertivi. €5-6 cocktails. ☻ Open daily 7am-1am.

BACARO JAZZ RISTORANTE COCKTAIL BAR
JAZZ BAR

San Marco 5546 ☎041 52 85 249 www.bacarojazz.com

Pricey drinks! Who doesn't love that? After a night at this bar you will know exactly why: location, jazz, and decor Just two minutes from the Rialto Bridge, you can immediately switch from enjoying Grand Canal views to enjoying a cold, fruity spritz. Do not expect live jazz performances as the name suggests. Instead, the bar cycles through an eargasmic selection of jazz greats including the likes of Miles Davis, John Coltrane, and Billy Holiday. And that decor! Italian flags hang from the awning, abstract jazz scenes cover the walls, and a Fender Stratocaster guitar hangs above the padded bar stools. But the real stunner is how the owners decided to decorate the ceiling. Bacaro calls it "warm decor"—we call it hot. Several Victoria's Secrets must have been bought in order to fill the ceiling with bras of all colors and sizes.

i Drinks €4-13. Buy one drink, get one free during Happy hour will leave you happy indeed. ☻ Open daily 11am-2am. Happy hour daily 4-6pm.

PICCOLO MONDO DISCO BAR
BAR

Dorsoduro 1056a ☎041 52 00 371 www.piccolomondo.biz

Once you make it past Franco, the owner, through the iron doors, you will be transported back to the 1980s when disco was nightlife. Though nations have moved on to hip-hop, rap, and dubstep over the past 30 years, this club has yet to change. Dance through the night with well-dressed clubbers and hipsters alike, all nostalgic for the beats of the past. Founded in 1963 (which must be when the website was made as well) Franco used to welcome world-renowned artists to this hospitable space, a place Peggy Guggenheim suggested calling "El Souk". When the space became a nightclub in 1978, who knew that though disco would die, Piccolo Mondo would survive, preserving the same popping vibe and comfy couches enjoyed by partiers decades ago.

i Cover charge €10. Drinks €8-13. ☻ Open daily 10pm-4am.

venice

ESSENTIALS
Practicalities

- **TOURIST OFFICES:** Head to one of the four main tourist information branches in Venice for the Venice Card, maps (€2.50), museum passes and more. Though the tourist information booths can at times be helpful especially for buying more prolonged vaporetto passes the website should answer most of your questions (info@turismovenezia.it, www.turismovenezia.it). **Venezia San Lucia Train Station Tourist Office** (☎041 52 98 711 for Tourist Contact Center) is open daily 9am-1:30pm in front of the station overlooking the Grand Canal in a white kiosk and 1:30pm-7pm alongside Track 1. **Ple. Roma Tourist Office** (☎041 24 11 499) is open daily 9:30am-2:30pm. Additional offices are near P. San Marco (San Marco 71) and San Marco Giardinetti.

- **DISABILITY SERVICES:** Città per tutti provides information and advice to travelers with disabilities. (Ca' Farsetti, S. Marco 4136 on ground floor, ☎041 274 8144, V: Rialto, on Riva del Carbon, 2-3 min. southwest of Rialto Bridge. Open Th 9am-1pm.)

- **LUGGAGE STORAGE:** Stazione Santa Lucia located alongside track 1 just past the tourist information booth (☎041 78 55 31). Fee/luggage item (20 kilo max weight): €6 for first 5 hr; €0.90 for every following hour up to 12 hr; €0.40/hr after 13+ hr.

- **LAUNDROMATS:** Orange Self-Service Lavanderia. (Santa Croce 665 ☎346 97 25 446) Open daily 7:30am-10:30pm.

Emergency

In Venezia San Lucia Station there is a red SOS machine that will connect you to medical, police, or fire aid with the press of a red button (located by the passage near tracks 2 and 3).

- **POLICE:** Polizia di Stato. (Santa Croce 500, 041 27 15 511, www.questure.poliziadistato. it, near Ple. Roma.) Carabinieri. Provincial Command Venice (Campo San Zaccaria, Castello 4693A, 041 27 411, V: San Zaccaria. Walk straight and follow the signs.) Other locations on Burano (V. San Martino 16), Lido (Riviera San Nicolo 33), and Murano (Fondamenta Riva Longa 1).

- **LATE-NIGHT PHARMACIES:** Late night pharmacies are open on a rotating basis. Visit www.farmacistivenezia.it/turni2.php and click on "Asl 12 Venezia e isole" for an up-to-date late night pharmacy schedule.

- **HOSPITALS/MEDICAL SERVICES:** Ospedale Civile. (Campo Giovanni e Paolo Santissimi, Castello 6777, 041 53 94 111, www.ulss12.ve.it, Fondamenta Nuove. Walk east and turn right after the 1st bridge. The hospital has limited hours and is likely to direct you elsewhere for further treatment.)

Getting Around

For information about vaporetto transportation and mainland buses go to www.actv. it/en. There are special tourist travel cards for unlimited travel during the given time period: €7 for one way up to 60 minutes; €20 for 24 hours; €20 for 72 hour youth card (for ages 14-29); €50 for 7 days.

italy

padua

As the oldest city in northern Italy and the home to the 800-year-old University of Padua where Galileo Galilei himself once taught, Padua doesn't hide in the shadow of its waterlogged sister, Venice. Bitch, please. Padua is a bustling, vibrant young town and an economic capital in its own right. During the school year, almost 60,000 students descend upon this town and fill the piazzas with clinking glasses, songs, and loud laughter. Wander through the markets in Piazza della Frutta and Piazza delle Erbe, all in the shadow of the enormous Palazzo della Ragione. Stroll down the shops on Corso Umberto I and eventually find yourself in Prato della Valle, an enormous park and the largest piazza in all of Italy. Head east and you'll get to the famously beautiful Basilica of St. Antony where many come on pilgrimage. Much like ourselves, if we had to describe Padua in three words, it would be young, educated, and beautiful. Don't let the small cobblestone streets deceive you—this city is larger than you'd expect and holds none of that tourist trash dumped upon Venice every summer. And there's even a river if you sorely miss waterworks. Charming yet modern, vibrant yet historic, and a city not to miss in northern Italy. Let's go to Padua.

SIGHTS

PALAZZO DELLA RAGIONE
PALACE
P. delle Erbe ☎049 820 5006

So large and imposing that it takes up the attention in two piazze, the Palazzo dei Ragione is not a sight to miss in Padua. It's iconic for its long arcades that have become home to the meat markets during the day and its enormous roof, which is believed to be the largest unsupported roof in Europe. Sure, from the outside the palace is impressive, especially when it's all lit up and purdy at night, but if you have some time and a couple euro to spare, be sure to climb up and see this palace inside, in all its glory.

Work started on the "Palace of Reason" in 1172, and this bad bitch was completed in 1219. Originally built with three roofs, in 1306, the whole palace was united under one roof under God, and so it was good. The palace was built as the seat of parliament in Padua, so what visitors are allowed to see is the enormous assembly hall which now displays exhibitions and art installations.

Even if there is nothing snazzy happening at the time of your visit, this palazzo is well worth a visit. The inner hall is enormous, coming in at nearly 100m long. All around the hall are gorgeous allegorical frescoes. On one end is the sculpture of a giant horse that some attribute to Donatello, but many art historians cry neigh.

i €4; more when special exhibirs are being displayed. ☒ Open daily 9am-7pm in summer. Open daily 9am-6pm in winter.

PRATO DELLA VALLE
SQUARE
At the end of V. Umberto I

Your middle school self's heart will probably reach out to Prato della Valle—it's not easy being one of the biggest squares in Europe. But the biggest squares sometimes end up being the most beautiful. Don't worry, your day will come. Maybe.

The cobblestone streets in Padua are all full of small town charm. But follow C. Umberto I for a little bit longer, and bam. Welcome to Prato della Valle. The largest piazza in Italy (and one of the largest in Europe), this 90,000 sq. m piazza is a sight to see. An enormous ellipse of green grass and trees, with a beautiful river and fountain and 78 gorgeous white statues surrounding it all. Damn.

padua

Housing options are limited in Padua. To avoid paying too much or staying too far in the suburbs, either opt for the only hostel in town or (to be a little better off) look up places to stay on Airbnb.

CITTÀ DI PADOVA HOSTEL

HOSTEL $

V. Aleardo Aleardi, 30 ☎049 875 2219 www.ostellopadova.it

That "If it ain't on hostelworld.com, it doesn't exist" attitude won't help you much in Padua. The main hostel in town is sadly not on our favorite hostel site, but don't worry. Last time we checked, it very much does exist.

A member of HI, the Città di Padova Hostel knows what it's doing. A very clean and standard hostel, if you're on a budget, this is the place to stay. Just minutes away from Prato della Valle, the location is about as perfect as you can get (the city part in this hostel's name ain't no lie).

The dorms are fairly standard, with bunk beds and spacious rooms that are never overcrowded with guests, so you can make some cool young friends without getting too overwhelmed (we get it, social interactions are hard). All the rooms and bathrooms are kept immaculately clean, which is the least they can do with an obnoxiously long lockout from 9:30am-3:30pm.

A colorful building with flowers at reception and a large common area, this place will give you a friendly enough vibe. Free breakfast is decent, with some bread and juice to start the day bright and early. Lockout is a little annoying, but the prices can't be beat in Padua. Enjoy a crazy stay here (until the 11:30pm curfew, after which you have to request a night key) with the fun young crowd that shows up, and be thankful you're not off living in the suburbs like some other visitors. You're totally winning.

i Dorms €19-23. ☑ Reception open 7-9:30am and 3:30-11:30pm.

This piazza is a favorite of locals who come by to study in the grass, work on that tan, or sit on some of the benches by the fountain with their romantic partner and practice some of that famous Italian PDA.

Walk around, admire the half-naked tanning Italians, and take a look at some of the statues. Not all of them will ring a bell, but some famous subjects include Galileo, the Roman author Livy, painter Andrea Mantegna, and sculptor Canova.

Festivals are often held in here, especially during New Years, when this large square is graced with fireworks. A popular hangout spot for the youth, the best way to enjoy the Prato is to grab some gelato from C. Umberto I, stroll down to the green, and sit and enjoy some delicious sweetness in one of the most beautiful squares in Italy. Be there or be square.

FOOD

IL GHIOTTONE

PIZZA $

V. Dante 20

A literal hole in the wall, Il Ghiottone is that storefront on V. Dante that you might pass every day where all those young college punks are constantly lining up. And with good reason, too. Serving up hot, delicious panzerotti for only €2-3, this is the perfect place to go for a cheap, filling lunch or dinner. So get your ass in line with them.

What is this food that the angels call panzerotto, you may ask? Think calzone, but smaller. A wrapped-up, toasted pocket filled with gooey cheese and tomato sauce and prosciutto or speck or vegetables or whatever else your heart happens to desire. Sound delicious? Perfect. Because panzerotti are Il Giottone's specialty.

This fast-food stop is really just a window looking out into the street. Inside is the smiling face of a slightly tired guy who has been throwing delicious, warm panzerotti out all day. Check out the options of the pieces of paper taped up on the outside counter and the walls. Pick what you want and then wait in line.

Don't worry. By sheer willpower of wanting food, the line moves fast. Soon you'll be able to exchange some euro coins for a cold drink and a warm, toasty panzerotto. There's no seating around here, so take that bad boy down to P. dei Signori and grab a seat on some steps and bite into the warm, melty goodness of Italian food.

i Panzerotto €2-4. 🕐 Open M-Sa 10am-11pm.

LA ROMANA
GELATERIA $
C. Milano, 83 ☎049 799 5625 www.gelateriaromana.com
With three geleterias in P. dei Signori alone, there's no shortage of this classic Italian treat in Padua. But for some of the best gelato in town, head to Geleteria La Romana. With lines that will remind you of Florence, locals and tourists alike gather at this famous gelato shop to get a couple scoops of the tastiest (and cheapest!) gelato around.

Sure, the line may go out the door and down the street. But hey—it's gelato. If there were ever a cause worth waiting for, forget marriage. We're waiting for gelato. Since 1947, this place has been serving out cups and cones of their famously good gelato. Inside the automatic glass doors is a fusion of classic and modern to satisfy all tastes. Comfy white couches, bar stools, and cute little tables fill up the large interior, so you can be all comfy while experiencing a foodgasm.

Vintage touches, like all the flavors written in cursive on little chalkboards behind the counter, give this place its charm. But no one waits 15min. for just charm. It's all about the gelato. Delicious flavors include the classic crema dal 1947, which is thankfully still fresh, and biscotto della nonna, a scrumptious gelato with cookie bits. For wild nights, go for the mascarpone al caffè con cioccolato fondente. All the flavors are delicious, and all the servings are generous.

i Gelato €2-4. Granita €3. 🕐 Open M-Th noon-midnight, F noon-1am, Sa 11am-1am, Su 11am-midnight.

NIGHTLIFE

BAR NAZIONALE
BAR
P. delle Erbe 41 ☎049 65 79 15
By no means your wild, late-night college bar (the doors close here at a modest 11:30pm), Bar Nazionale is still the go-to place to grab a drink in the evening. Famous for its tramezzini, little triangular sandwiches that are so delicious you'll have to eat about 10 to feel satisfied, come here during lunchtime and snacktime hours to devour these, then wander back later for a drink or two.

Boasting one of the most beautiful locations in Padua, this bar is right in P. delle Erbe next to the Palazzo della Ragione, which is the piazza's beautiful fountain and stunningly gorgeous at night. With the lit-up arcades of the palace and the soothing rush of the fountain, you'll be able to take in the cobblestone while still appreciating the regal feel of Padua right here at this bar.

Inside is a rather small space where you can check out the tramezzini and order at the wooden bar. But if you're planning on staying a while, grab one of the many umbrella'd tables outside. Be warned: this place gets super busy during the evening, so you may have to deal with slow waitstaff. But you're in Italy. Relax. Your drink will come. And then when that Spritz does arrive at the table, chat away with friends, order some sandwiches (did we mention we love the sandwiches?), and enjoy a relaxing, calm night in the beautiful city of Padua. La bella vita, anyone?

i Drinks €4-10. Tramezzini €1.50-2. ⏰ Open M 7am-10:30pm, Tu-, 7am-11:30pm, Sa 7am-10:30pm, Su 9am-9:30pm.

ESSENTIALS
Practicalities
- **TOURIST OFFICE:** Office located in Galleria Pedrocchi. M-Sa 9am-7pm.
- **TOURIST INFORMATION:** ☎049 20 10 080
- **ATMS:** P. delle Erbe

Emergency
- **EMERGENCY TELEPHONE:** 112
- **FIRE:** 115
- **POLICE:** 113
- **HOSPITALS:** Azienda Ospedaliera di Padova (V. Aristide Gabelli, 61)
- **PHARMACIES:** Pharmacy located at V. Gorizia, 1 near P. della Frutta

Getting There
Padua is easily reached by train. Trenitalia runs frequent service between Venice and Padua at least once every hour and sometimes as frequently as every 10-15min.

Getting Around
By Bus
The buses run through Padua and service its suburbs. If you're staying in the suburbs, you'll need to rely on buses far more, but the center of Padua is mostly pedestrian only and very walkable.

By Foot
Padua is a very walkable city, so your feet will probably be your main means of transport in this city.

verona

Fair Verona will charm you faster than Romeo decided he was totally over Rosaline and super into some new chick named Juliet. Although the city's history stretches back to ancient times, as the setting for William Shakespeare's *Romeo and Juliet* (along with *The Taming of the Shrew* and *The Two Gentlemen of Verona*), Verona is today best known as the hometown of literature's most famous doomed lovers. Now a popular destination among European families, literary nerds, and new generations of young lovers, Verona both embraces its ties to the Shakespeare (tourists can take a picture of themselves on Juliet's balcony, visit her tomb, and enjoy summer performances of the Bard's most famous tragedy at the city's ancient Arena) while also offering visitors so much more. Veer away from the kitschy, heart-filled T-shirt shops and discover the real Verona, with its beautiful squares, centuries-old churches, and magnificent bridges that straddle the twisting Adige River. Nestled in the hills of the Veneto region, Verona's unique mix of ancient and medieval history is what will really have you falling head over heels, although its inescapable association with the two star-crossed lovers does add a tinge of wistful romance and tragedy to the already beautiful city. And if all goes well, your weekend love affair with Verona will probably end better than Romeo and Juliet's did. (Too soon?)

ORIENTATION

From the train station, you will approach Verona's *centro* along the wide Corso Porta Nuova, which runs all the way to the massive clock of Portoni della Bra and Piazza Bra, the first of Verona's two major squares. Here you'll find several restaurants, a charming green park and fountain, and the Arena di Verona. From the far end of Piazza Bra, the glitzy, shop-lined marble Via Mazzini runs north to the bustling Piazza delle Erbe; Verona's busiest and most central square, Piazza delle Erbe is packed with restaurants, bars, and market stalls and is also home to the looming Torre dei Lamberti. Farther north lies the Adige River, which cuts a horseshoe-like bend across the city; while the majority of Verona's most popular sights lie south of the Adige's banks, a visit to the Teatro Romano and Castel San Pietro will require you to trek over the Ponte di Pietra, while Castelvecchio and its stunning defensive bridge are nestled along a bend in the river a bit farther to the south and west of the major sights.

ACCOMMODATIONS

BED AND BREAKFAST CITTADELLA   B&B $$
Vicolo Volto Cittadella 16   ☎045 485 92 17 www.cittadellavr.it

This cozy little bed and breakfast just off Corso Porta Nuova is a great spot to tuck in for a couple days in Verona. The handful of rooms here are bright, beautifully decorated, and air-conditioned. If the feast of options at breakfast isn't enough to satisfy your appetite, the staff here will leave fresh snacks for you in your room every afternoon. A message painted in the hallway hopes that "may all who enter as guests leave as friends," and although you probably won't be staying in Verona long enough for that to actually happen, B&B Cittadella does promise a friendly stay.

i Walking north down Corso Porta Nuova, turn right onto Vicolo Volto Cittadella. The B&B is on the right. Singles from €60. Doubles from €90. ☒ Reception 7am-9pm.

SIGHTS

If you're planning to see most of the sights in town, consider purchasing the Verona Card, which grants access to almost all the monuments, churches, and museums in Verona (along with a little balcony you might have heard about). Passes can be purchased at the tourist office or at most of the major sights. A 24hr. pass costs €18, while a 48hr. pass is €22; considering that the Arena alone will run you €10, the Verona Card is probably worth the upfront investment.

◪ ARENA DI VERONA   ANCIENT ROME
Piazza Bra 1   ☎045 800 51 51 www.arena.it

Constructed in 30 CE and once able to seat 30,000 spectators, Verona's Arena isn't quite the Colosseum, although it did play host to its fair share of gladiator fights back in the day. It's also the third-largest ancient Roman amphitheater in the world, so give it a little bit of credit. Since the 18th century, the Arena has become renowned for a slightly more sophisticated and humane form of entertainment, replacing dramatic fights to the death with the drama of opera. If you're in town on the night of a summer performance, you should try your best to purchase last-minute tickets; while an afternoon romp up and down the stadium seats and through the cavernous bowels of the amphitheater might keep you entertained for about 20min., the true glory of the Arena can be better appreciated in the evening, when the stage is set and the seats are filled to capacity.

i *Located on the north end of P. Bra. Hard to miss. €10, reduced €7.50. Free with Verona Card.* ⚄ *Open M 1:30-7:30pm, Tu-Su 8:30am-7:30pm.*

▨ TORRE DEI LAMBERTI   TOWER
V. della Costa 1   ☎045 927 30 27

Part of a group of towers constructed near the Palazzo della Ragione, the Torre dei Lamberti is the only one of the original four that remains standing at full height today. The climb up the 300+ steps here will take you right into the heart of the bell tower, where you can stop on the first landing and look out over the entire city before scaling the final twisting staircase to the tippy top. Way up here, lovers linger as they look out over the city through some netting while tangled in each others' arms. Adding to the romance already in the air, the walls of this topmost level are covered in the names of couples who have probably already broken up by now.

i *From P. delle Erbe, walk down V. della Costa. The ticket office is on the right (enter the tower through the giftshop). Elevator available for part of the climb. €5. Free with Verona Card.* ⚄ *Open M-F 10am-6pm, Sa-Su 11am-7pm. Last entry 45min. before close.*

▨ CASTEL SAN PIETRO   CASTLE
Regaste Redentore

You can't actually go inside the castle that lies at the top of this hill, but the views of Verona and the Adige River from San Pietro make it more than worth the climb up here. After crossing the river over the Ponte di Pietro, scale the many steps that lead you winding your way up to the tree-lined terrace where you sit and admire the entirety of Verona from a sunny bench or ledge. The gates remain open until midnight, so you can take in the beauty of the city lit up at night, although we recommend visiting during the day if you want to avoid all the Romeos and Juliets who hike up here after dinner to "let lips do what hands do" under the cover of darkness.

i *From Ponte di Pietro, cross the street and climb the set of stairs directly across from the bridge. Free.* ⚄ *Open daily 6:30am-midnight.*

PIAZZA DELLE ERBE   PIAZZA
At the end Via Mazzini and its many upscale shops lies Piazza delle Erbe, Verona's most popular square and once the site of its forum during the Roman Empire. Today, the piazza is still stuffed with plenty of market stalls that sell everything from fruit cups to party masks, although amid all the bartering going on, you'll also find a white marble column topped off with St. Mark's Lion and a fountain featuring a statue of Madonna Verona. The other major focal point of the piazza is the Torre dei Lamberti, whose massive clock tower looms over the whole square. And although Juliet's famous balcony may be located just down the street, the beautiful buildings of Piazza delle Erbe boast their own collection of iron-wrought balconies and Baroque decorations that adds to the timeless charm of the square.

i *From P. Bra, walk down V. Mazzini to the piazza, on the left. Free.*

CASA DI GIULIETTA   LANDMARK
V. Cappello 23   ☎045 803 43 03 www.casadigiulietta.verona.it

Allegedly the home of Juliet Capulet, Literary Character Who Didn't Actually Exist, the Casa di Giulietta is a popular stop for tourists who seem to have forgotten that Romeo and Juliet is a work of fiction. Still, you should probably drop by and see her balcony just for the ritual of it. If you've already paid for the Verona Card, a quick turn through the rooms here isn't a complete waste of your time; in addition to snapping a picture of yourself standing out on Juliet's balcony,

Although Shakespeare laid the scene for three of his plays in fair Verona, it remains unclear whether the Bard ever actually visited the now celebrated city. It is believed that Shakespeare based his tragedy on Luigi da Porto's *La Giulietta*, which detailed an allegedly true tale of 14th-century star-crossed lovers from the rival Cappelletti and Montecchi families of northern Italy. And sure, mentions of sycamore groves and romantic balconies may match up with what you'll see in Verona today, but other than that, there's little proof that any actual Romeos and Juliets ever roamed the streets of this city or stabbed themselves to death in any of the churches here. And that balcony that everyone's losing their damn minds over? That's also almost definitely a bunch of BS, but you'll probably go check it out anyway just because *you never know.*

you can also admire multiple artists' rendition of Romeo, Home Intruder, along with the bed where cinematic love was consummated in the 1968 film version of the play. Other than that, just stick to the ivy-covered courtyard, where you'll find vandals of all varieties leaving letters to Juliet on the walls of the archway leading to the house. In the far corner of the courtyard, there's also a statue of young Juliet whose right boob has been groped by way too many tourists (she's 13, you guys!).

i From P. delle Erbe, walk down V. Cappello. The archway leading to Juliet's house is on the left. €6, reduced €4.50. Free with Verona Card. ☑ Open M 1:30-7:30pm, Tu-Su 8:30am-7:30pm.

DUOMO
CHURCH

P. Duomo 21   ☎045 59 28 13 www.cattedralediverona.it

Although the striking white bell tower of Verona's Duomo is probably the first thing you'll notice about this church (that and the fact that it's basically located in a parking lot), its exterior also features two Romanesque porches and a charming little statue of an angel robed in blue. Inside, there's even more going on, from the large orange columns lining the central nave to the black tiling on the floor to the curved marble surrounding the central altar. Thanks to a great deal of restoration work, the frescoes surrounding the church's many chapels are remarkably intact. Don't leave without making a quick pass through the baptistry and a second church that now serves as an interesting archaeological site.

i From P. delle Erbe, walk down Corso Sant'Anastasia to Chiesa di Sant'Anastasia, then turn left onto V. Duomo. €2.50. Combined admission to Duomo, S. Anastasia, S. Zeno, and S. Fermo €6. Free with Verona Card. ☑ Open M-F 10am-5:30pm, Sa 10am-4pm, Su 1:30-5:30pm.

CHIESA DI SANT'ANASTASIA
CHURCH

P. Sant'Anastasia   ☎045 800 43 25

Most visitors flock to Verona's Duomo first, but the Chiesa di Sant'Anastasia is, in fact, the largest church in town. With its red marble pillars and vaulted ceilings, the church, which was designed by Dominican friars in the 13th century, stands as one of the most beautiful examples of Italian Gothic architecture in all of Italy. Although the facade was never completed, the interior more than makes up for it with its intricately painted ceiling, whose every inch is covered in handpainted flowers and crawling vines, plus a few saints here and there. Stop by in the late afternoon, when low sunlight glancing in through the windows creates a warm, rosy glow in the nave of the church.

i From P. delle Erbe, walk down Corso Sant'Anastasia to the church. €2.50. Combined admission to Duomo, S. Anastasia, S. Zeno, and S. Fermo €6. Free with Verona Card. ☑ Open M-Sa 9am-5:30pm, Su 1-6pm.

verona

PIAZZA BRA

PIAZZA

You won't come across any lingerie shops or people running around in their skivvies here (it's not that kind of bra, dummy). Instead, you'll find plenty of restaurants and bars lining one side of this circular piazza, which is also home to Palazzo della Gran Guardia, Palazzo Barbieri (Verona's town hall), and the magnificent ancient Arena. In the center of the square lies an immensely charming garden, where you can sit in the shade of pine and cedar trees while watching little kids run around the central fountain. And depending on when you visit, the piazza might also be cluttered with piles of set pieces waiting to be used for performances inside the Arena.

i At the end of Corso Porta Nuova. Free.

CASTELVECCHIO

CASTLE

Corso Castelvecchio 2 ☎045 806 26 11 www.comune.verona.it/castelvecchio

Constructed in the Middle Ages as a fortress for the ruling Scaliger dynasty, Castelvecchio sits on the banks of the Adige River and now houses the Museo di Castelvecchio. The ratio of guards to visitors at the museum is about 1:1, so you will probably find yourself saddled with a new security-minded shadow as you wander among the statues and partially finished frescoes housed here. We recommend that you pass through the art galleries fairly quickly, pause for a hot second in the weapons room, and move on to what's actually cool here, which is roaming the battlements on the upper level of the castle. From these lookouts, you can gaze upon the streets of Verona on one side of the fortress and out over the impressive, red-brick Ponte di Castelvecchio (also known as Ponte Scaligero) from the other.

i From P. Bra, walk west down V. Roma to Corso Castelvecchio. €6, reduced €4.50. Free with Verona Card. ☒ Open M 1:30-7:30pm, Tu-Su 8:30am-7:30pm.

TEATRO ROMANO E MUSEO ARCHEOLOGICO

ANCIENT ROME, MUSEUM

Regaste Redentore ☎045 800 03 60 www.museoarcheologico.comune.verona.it

The Teatro Romano is slightly less impressive than Verona's other ancient theater, but here the stage and stone stadium seats are charmingly secluded within clusters of cedar trees and other flora. Climb up to the top of the theater and look out over the ruins and the city before passing through the archeological museum on your way out (provided it's open—the museum houses the city's largest collection of Roman artifacts but has been closed for construction since 2013).

i Cross Ponte di Pietro and turn left onto Regaste Redentore. The theater is across the street, on the left. While the Museo Archeologico is under construction, entry to the theater is reduced to €1. Free with Verona Card. ☒ Open M 1:30-7:30pm, Tu-Su 8:30am-7:30pm.

FOOD

🖼 GELATERIA AMORINO

GELATERIA $

Corso Sant'Anastasia 1 ☎045 208 02 94 www.amorino.com

By this point, you're probably no stranger to gelato, but have you ever tried gelato that's shaped like a flower? Order a cone at Amorino, and you can learn to pluck the petals off an ice cream cone faster than Romeo deflowered Juliet. There's almost always a line here, and it moves a little slowly, but hey, that's just because they're taking the time to handcraft everyone's cone into a perfect rose. You can technically order as many flavors as you'd like regardless of what size cone you purchase, but you know what they say—the bigger the scoops, the better the bloom.

i On the far left end of P. delle Erbe when facing the clock tower. Cones €2.70-4.50. Cups €2.70-8.50. ☒ Open daily 11:30am-11pm.

OSTERIA AL DUCA
V. Arche Scaligere 2   ☎045 59 44 74 www.osteriaalduca.it

ITALIAN $$

Let the red neon lights of Osteria al Duca draw you into its cozy interior, where you can settle in under the low wooden beams and sample some traditional dishes of the Veneto region. The restaurant's set €17 menu includes one *primo* and one *secondo*, which means you can enjoy both fresh pasta and your first taste of horsemeat (it's a local specialty, so don't think about Seabiscuit too much and just try it). The osteria's staff doesn't speak much English but is incredibly friendly and won't even turn their noses up at you if you can't clean your plate.

i From P. delle Erbe, walk down V. della Costa and turn right onto V. Arche Scaligere. Osteria al Duca is on the left. Two-course menu €17. ☾ Open M-Sa noon-2:30pm and 6:30-10:30pm.

TRATTORIA AL POMPIERE
Vicolo Regina D'Ungheria 5   ☎045 803 05 37 www.alpompiere.com

ITALIAN $$

If you feel like treating yourself to a particularly excellent meal in Verona, head to Al Pompiere, which occupies a tiny side street all to itself just around the corner from Piazza delle Erbe. Prices here are on the slightly more expensive side, but that's because the food is pure poetry (and not the tragic Shakespearean kind). After a pasta *primo*, treat yourself to a rich meat *secondo* like calf liver or beef cheek—or maybe just some roasted lamb. The green tablecloths, black-and-white framed photos on the wall, and puppets hanging from the ceiling add even more charm to an already memorable meal.

i From P. delle Erbe, walk down V. Cappella and turn right onto Vicolo Regina D'Ungheria. Primi €11-14. Secondi €12-19. Dessert €3-8. ☾ Open daily 12:30-2:30pm and 7:30-10:30pm.

NIGHTLIFE

Verona isn't a particularly poppin' place late into the night, but its sizable student population does mean that travelers will usually be able to find a place to kick back and relax with fellow young people on a weekend night. And while we can't promise any masked balls where you might meet the super hot offspring of your father's enemy, we can recommend a few bars to check out. Piazza delle Erbe is usually a good bet while the restaurants in the square start folding up their umbrellas after dinner; the three bars in the northwest corner of the piazza (including Casa Mazzanti Caffè) are usually buzzing into the early hours of the morning.

CASA MAZZANTI CAFFÈ
P. delle Erbe 32   ☎045 800 32 17 www.ristorantemazzant .it

BAR

Throbbing music and blue light emanates from the dark interior of this hip bar in the corner of Piazza delle Erbe. Pull up a sleek white chair and join the crowd of young travelers and Italians gathered here for late-night drinks. And if the outdoor tables look too full or the crowd too glitzy for your taste, you can always hop over to one of the more dressed-down bars next door.

i Located in the northwest corner of the piazza (upperleft-hand corner when facing the tower). Drinks €4-10. ☾ Open daily 8am-2am.

ACCADEMIA CAFFÈ
V. Roma 4a   ☎345 701 7323

BAR

For a quieter drinking scene, veer away from the sprawling patio seating of the bars and restaurants lining Piazza Bra and seek out Accademia Caffè. Settle into the black wicker chairs outside this small bar and relax—despite the name, the only thing you'll be studying here is the cocktail list and the people wandering by along V. Roma.

i From P. Bra, walk west down V. Roma. Accademia is on the right. Beer €3-5. Wine €2.50-6. Cocktails €5-6. ☾ Open until late.

verona

ESSENTIALS
Practicalities

- **TOURIST OFFICES:** Central Tourist Office. (V. degli Alpini 9 ☎045 80 68 680. Walk south from Arena di Verona into P. Bra. The tourist office is on the left. ☼ Open M-Sa 9am-7pm, Su 10am-4pm.)
- **LUGGAGE STORAGE:** Porta Nuova Station. (Located on the ground floor of the station. 1st 5hr. €6, 6-12th hr. €0.90, €0.40 per hr. thereafter. ☼ Open daily 8am-8pm.)
- **CURRENCY EXCHANGE:** There is a Forexchange currency exchange point near Piazza delle Erbe on V. Cappello. (V. Cappello 4. ☼ Open M-Sa 11am-7pm.)
- **ATMS:** There is a Unicredit ATM located in the corner of Piazza Bra, near V. Roma. (P. Bra 26/E ☎045 487 1304.)
- **POST OFFICES:** Poste Italiane. (V. Carlo Cattaneo 23. From P. Ba, take V. Fratta and turn left onto V. Carlo Cattaneo. ☼ Open M 8:30am-1:30pm, Tu-F 8:30am-7pm, Sa 8:30am-12:30pm.)

Emergency

- **POLICE:** Polizia di Stato. (Lungadige Antonio Galtarossa 11 ☎045 80 90 411. From P. Bra, continue as it becomes V. Pallone. Cross over the river and turn right onto Lungadige Antonio Galtarossa.) Carabinieri. (V. Salvo D'Acquisto 6 ☎045 80 561. From the city center, walk along Corso Porta Nuova and turn right onto V. Antonio Locatelli.)
- **HOSPITALS/MEDICAL SERVICES:** Ospedale Civile Maggiore. (Ple. Aristide Stefani 1 ☎045 81 21 111. www.ospedaleuniverona.it.)

Getting There

Aeroporto Valerio Catullo Villafranca (VRN; ☎045 80 95 666 www.aeroportoverona. it) is Venice's small international airport. Flights are available through smaller airlines such as Ryanair and Vueling from many cities in Italy, including Rome and Naples, along with other major European cities. An Aerobus shuttle runs from the airport to the train station every 20min. (€6). Verona Porta Nuova station (Ple. 25 Aprile. ☎199 89 20 21 www.grandistazioni.it) is where most travelers arrive in Verona. You can get to Verona by bus, but the train is by far the best and most common option. Trains arrive from Padua (€7-18, 45min.-1hr.), Milan (€13-22, 90min.-2hr.), Venice (€9-22, 1-2hr.), and Rome (€60-100, 3hr.).

Getting Around

Verona is an incredibly walkable city, and it is unlikely that you will need anything but your own two feet to get around town. That being said, city buses operated by ATV are available and run all across the center of Verona and through the surrounding area (☎045 80 57 811 www.atv.verona.it). Tickets can be purchased from tobacco shops or onboard (buying a ticket on board will cost you €0.80 extra, and you must pay with exact change). Lines and routes are posted outside each bus stop; pay attention to the schedules, as Sunday, holiday, and night service have different bus numbers and routes. Most buses run from Verona Porta Nuova, where you can catch the regional bus to Lago di Garda. RadioTaxi also has 24hr. taxi service (☎045 53 26 66 www.radiotaxiverona.it) clustered around P. delle Erbe and P. Bra. Bike shares are another option, and stations are scattered throughout the city (☎800 89 69 48 www.bikeverona.it).

italy

bologna

La dotta, la grassa, la rossa. To spend any time in the capital of Emilia-Romagna is to understand the three defining characteristics of the city's identity. *La dotta*: the learned. Bologna is, first and foremost, a university town (and by first and foremost, we really mean it—the University of Bologna is the oldest in the world still in operation, having been founded way back in 1088). Where other Italian cities teem with tourists and their beloved selfie sticks, Bologna's streets are animated by a more vital and local spirit—all those people reading newspapers outside cafes in the middle of the afternoon are actual residents of Bologna, and those kids sitting along the curbs of bar-filled streets every night are students from the university. *La grassa*: the fat. While the people of Bologna aren't actually packing on a lot of extra pounds, they do know how to indulge in excellent, rich food at all hours of the day. The city is known for its tortellini, lasagna, and, of course, tagliatelle bolognese (which, heads up, ain't your mama's Chef Boyardee ragu). Sample as many traditional dishes as you can during your stay here because, as one local told us, to know the cuisine of Bologna is to understand the city. *La rossa*: the red. Bologna's final distinctive trait may refer to the anti-Fascist spirit and communist sympathies you'll find among many of its residents, but it also reflects, quite literally, the color and character of the city and its streets. Indeed, the endless maze of portico-lined medieval streets here will have you seeing new shades of red (and orange and rust and umber) with every twist and turn. Bologna truly is a city unlike any other, and to visit here is to abandon the usual rhythms of the tourist life and surrender yourself to the food, the architecture, the friendly people, the park benches, and the slower pace of real Italian life that you will discover under Bologna's many covered archways.

ORIENTATION

With a population of over 375,000, Bologna is actually a fairly large and sprawling modern city. Most of the places you'll be visiting during your stay, however, are located within the historic *centro*. The focal point of the city center is Piazza Maggiore, where you'll find the massive Basilica di San Petronio, several of the city's palazzos, and the popular Fontana del Nettuno. Directly to the north, the wide, commercial street of Ugo Bassi runs through the center of town to the Two Towers, the other major (if slightly off-kilter) landmarks with which to orient yourself. From here, Via Zamboni stretches northeast to the university area of town, while Via Castiglione runs south to the Giardini Margherita, just outside the city center, and also forms one perimeter of the Quadrilatero, a site of medieval markets that is now home to a concentration of bakeries, jewelers, and other shops (Piazza Maggiore, V. Rizzoli, and Piazza della Mercanzia constitute the other boundaries of the district). While you can find good food throughout the city, Via Pratello and Via Mascarella are filled with restaurants and bars that particularly popular among Bologna's younger crowds. West of the city center, the Portico di San Luca begins at the Arco del Meloncello and runs 3.5km uphill to the magnificent Santuario della Madonna di San Luca.

ACCOMMODATIONS

ALBERGO PANORAMA

HOTEL $

V. Giovanni Livraghi 1   ☎051 22 18 02 www.hotelpanoramabologna.it

With singles starting at just €40 per night, you can't do much better than Albergo Panorama, whose central location just off Ugo Bassi makes it a comfortable and convenient place to spend your time in Bologna. Breakfast here is served on a tray every morning, and although you'll be the one dishing it up and carrying it back to your room, the abundance of croissants and fresh fruit make it more than worth the self-service (and hey, breakfast in bed is still breakfast in bed).

The sign downstairs may say that Albergo Panorama is located on the fourth floor, but if you're good at counting, you'll soon realize that it's actually on what Americans would call the sixth (we recommend that you take the lift and skip the 120 steps it takes to get up to your room). Fortunately, the high altitude at this *albergo* means that, although the views in each room aren't quite panoramic, they do feature a beautiful backdrop of rooftop gardens and the yellows and oranges of Bologna's colorful buildings.

i Walk down Ugo Bassi away from the Two Towers and turn left onto V. Giovanni Livraghi. The hotel is on the right. Singles with shared bath €40. Doubles from €55. ⏰ Check-in noon-9pm.

ALBERGO CENTRALE HOTEL $

V. della Zecca 2 ☎051 22 51 14 www.albergocentralebologna.it

At Albergo Centrale, the name says it all: rooms here are a few minutes' walk from the heart of Bologna and start at just €45 per night. And while the prime location and cheap rates are the primary draw here (rooms themselves are clean and comfortable but fairly basic), Albergo Centrale has the added draw of incredibly friendly reception and a couple of nooks and seating areas where you can enjoy the hotel's complimentary breakfast.

i Walk down Ugo Bassi away from the Two Towers and turn left onto V. della Zecca. The hotel is on the left. Singles with shared bath €45. Double with shared bath €65, private bath €72. ⏰ Reception 24hr.

ART HOTEL OROLOGIO HOTEL $$

V. IV Novembre 10 ☎051 745 74 11 www.bolognarthotels.it

There's nothing particularly artsy about this slightly more upscale hotel just down the street from Piazza Maggiore, although the primary colors of the hallways here may remind you of craft projects of days past. Inside the actual rooms, the heavy curtains and fancy bedspreads will have you feeling a little more grown up. All the rooms here are pretty plush, but if you throw in an extra €10 and splurge on the deluxe option, you'll get a little breakfast nook to sit in during your down time (although the dining room on the first floor still offers plenty of relaxation space for all the plebs staying in classic singles).

i From P. Maggiore, walk down V. IV Novembre 10. The hotel is on the left. For cheaper rates, call or email instead of booking online. Singles €80 classic, €90 deluxe. Doubles €85 classic, €95 deluxe. ⏰ Reception 24hr.

SIGHTS

Enjoy the many towers, churches, and palazzos of Bologna's historic *centro*, but venture outside the old city walls to add a little greenery to *la rossa*'s landscape of red roofs and endless maze of orange porticos.

▨ SANTUARIO DELLA MADONNA DI SAN LUCA CHURCH

V. di San Luca 36 ☎051 614 23 39 www.sanlucabo.org

If there are two things you need in your life right now, it's probably a little more exercise and a little more Jesus. (Well, maybe not the last one—you have seen your fair share of Madonna and Childs lately.) But regardless of your current level of physical fitness and/or the present state of your soul, make the pilgrimage up to the Santuario della Madonna di San Luca, a massive basilica that dominates a hilltop on the outskirts of Bologna. You may be escaping the city, but you can never escape its distinctive penchant for porticos; indeed, the real draw here, almost more than the basilica itself, is the 3.5km continuous portico that leads up to the church. The longest of its kind in the world, the Portico di San Luca is composed of 666 arches that ambitious tourists, locals in exercise gear, and little old ladies with swinging rosary beads pass under on their way up the hill.

On the way, the portico twists and turns its way uphill at a generally forgiving grade, although the gentle slope does give way at points to stacks of stairs. When you finally reach the top, you'll find yourself in the midst of the church in all its magnificent orange glory (are you even surprised?). The basilica boasts more moisture-wicking outfits than you'll find in most churches, along with an icon of the Virgin Mary that has plenty of pilgrims down their knees and fiddling with their rosary beads. And while the church and altar are worth a pass through, the views here are what will really make you feel religious, with glimpses down onto Bologna far below in one direction and more sweeping views of distant, hazy blue mountaintops in the other. If you have a free afternoon, this is certainly a highlight—just make sure you have the hours and energy to commit to it.

i *The portico begins at Porta Saragozza, outside the city center. Walk all the way up the portico to the church at the top of V. di San Luca. Free. ☒ Open daily 7am-12:30pm and 2:30-7:30pm.*

BASILICA DI SANTO STEFANO CHURCH
V. Santo Stefano 24 ☎051 22 32 56

At the Basilica di Santo Stefano, you get seven churches for the price of one (which, in Bologna, is still blessedly "free"). A Russian nesting doll of a Catholic church, the basilica was constructed over many centuries and is composed (in the order that you will likely walk through them) of the Church of St. John the Baptist (constructed in the eighth century and still the primary place of worship in the church today), the dark and haunting Church of the Holy Sepulcher (fifth century), the Church of the Saints Vitale and Agricola (first built in the fourth century but reconstructed in the 12th), the Courtyard of Pilate (13th century), the Church of the Trinity (13th century), the Cloister, and the Chapel of the Bandage (which now also houses a free museum). The entire complex, with its quiet brick courtyards and gloomy old altars, is quite striking and unlike most churches you'll come across in Italy—take a turn through its many component parts before admiring the beauty of the sum total from the piazza outside.

i *From the Two Towers, walk down V. Santo Stefano to the piazza. Free. ☒ Open daily 7am-noon and 3:30-6:45pm.*

PIAZZA MAGGIORE PIAZZA
As Bologna's main square, Piazza Maggiore is a good place to orient yourself within the *centro* and is also home to many of the city's most magnificent buildings, including the Basilica di San Petronio and Palazzo Comunale. In the summer months, the piazza hosts a series of free outdoor film screenings. Adjoining the main piazza is Piazza del Nettuno, named after its popular fountain that depicts Neptune lording over a bevy of fat water babies and a bunch of maidens who are quite literally feelin' themselves by the water's edge.

i *From the crossroads of Ugo Bassi and V. dell'Indipendenza, walk across P. del Nettuno to P. Maggiore. Free.*

BASILICA DI SAN PETRONIO CHURCH
P. Galvani 5 ☎051 23 14 15 www.basilicadisanpetronio.it

With its towering rows of brown stone stacked on top of pink and white marble, the unfinished facade of San Petronio certainly makes a strong statement as the focal point of Piazza Maggiore and might leave you with a hankering for some Neapolitan ice cream. Inside, this Gothic church adheres to what we're now assuming must be the Official Color Scheme of Bologna, with long, striking reddish-orange columns that line the three naves of this absolutely cavernous church (and it would have been even bigger—the city originally had plans to build a church that would surpass St. Peter's in size, but then the po-pope shut that shit down). Still, this church comes in at a respectable 15th largest in the world and is impressive in its own right. Soak it up and remember how stunning it all looks, because a Kodak moment here will cost you €2.

i *It's the bigass church in P. Maggiore. Free. If you want to take pictures, a pass costs €2. ☒ Open daily 7:45am-1:30pm and 3-6:30pm.*

bologna

TWO TOWERS
TOWER

P. di Porta Ravegnana
☎051 647 21 13

You might be surprised to learn that Pisa isn't the only town in Italy with a leaning tower. Technically, Bologna has two, although the majorly off-kilter Garisenda (which once stood at 60m but had to be cut down to 48m in the 14th century to prevent it from completely falling to pieces) makes the taller Asinelli look fairly straight by comparison. Scale the 97.2m of the Torre Asinelli, however, and you might get a sense of its tipsiness from the narrow and often slanted wooden steps (497 total) that lead up to the top of the tower. After the seemingly endless climb, you'll be rewarded with breezes from the surrounding hills and great views of the city, which will give you a better sense of the *centro*'s layout. Note the five long, straight streets that run, like spokes in a wheel, from the towers out to the five gates of the old city walls. Fun fact: University of Bologna students never climb the tower due to an urban legend that those who do won't graduate (even more superstitiously—and impractically—they also never cross Piazza Maggiore on its diagonal).

i Located at the far end of Ugo Bassi. Torre Asinelli €3. ☑ Torre Asinelli open daily 9am-7pm.

PINACOTECA NAZIONALE
MUSEUM

V. delle Belle Arti 56
☎051 42 09 411 www.pinacotecabologna.it

It really should come as no surprise that a university town as old and storied as Bologna would have a great art museum. But still—the overachieving collection of work at the Pinacoteca Nazionale is really gunning for that A. And with its collection featuring works by greats such as Giotto, Raphael, Titian, and others, it definitely earns it. The 29 rooms of this excellently curated museum will carry you through the rich history of Italian (and often specifically Bolognese) art history, starting in the 13th century with a number of ornate, gilded altarpieces and working its way through the Renaissance and all the way up to the powdered wigs of the 18th century. The collection is certainly worth an hour or two of your time, and the walk down to the museum will also take you through the university area of town.

i From the Two Towers, walk down V. Zamboni until it meets with V. delle Belle Arti; the art museum is right near the intersection of the two streets. €4, reduced €2. ☑ Open Tu-W 9am-1:30pm, Th-Su 11am-7pm.

GIARDINI MARGHERITA
GARDEN

P. di Porta Santo Stefano

The Giardini Margherita perfectly exemplifies the local vitality of Bologna. While this 64-acre park located just south of the centro is certainly a nice place for tourists to take a stroll, it is primarily filled and buzzing with locals. From the joggers who make their way along the curving roads and paths to the vast, grassy field where teenagers kick around soccer balls to the tiny go-carts and swings where little kids bump around under the eyes of watchful parents, the park is a locus for Bolognese of all ages, sizes, and activity levels. And it's large enough to accommodate everyone's choice of afternoon diversion (even yours, which will probably involve buying some gelato at one of the stands in the park and engaging in an aggressively un-aerobic sprawl underneath a shady tree).

i From the city center, walk all the way down V. Castiglione; entrance to the gardens is located through Porta Castiglione and across Vle. Giovanni Gozzadini. Free.

PALAZZO DELL'ARCHIGINNASIO
PALACE

P. Galvani 1
☎051 27 68 11 www.archiginnasio.it

This 16th-century palace once served as the seat of the University of Bologna from 1563 to 1805 and now houses the more than 800,000 volumes of the Biblioteca dell'Archiginnasio. Although the library is not open to tourists, you can come here and admire the coats of arms of more than 5000 former university

mortadella: it ain't no baloney

Forget Oscar Mayer. In Bologna, our baloney has a first name, and it's *m-o-r-t-a-d-e-l-l-a*. But the pink American lunch meat that you're probably most familiar with does, indeed, descend from a popular Bologna sausage called mortadella. Made from finely ground pork, mortacella is a cold cut meat that looks a lot like its bastardized American cousin, save for its distinctive white squares of pork fat and, occasionally, pieces of green olive that add a little texture to the mix. The meat is flavored with black pepper and myrtle berries, which give it its unique flavor, and although the little pieces of lard may have scared off the U.S. government (American baloney is not allowed to have any chunks of pork fat visible in the sandwich meat), don't let it freak you out because it's really good. Try mortadella in a sandwich or as an appetizer with some crostini.

teachers and students that cover the walls and ceilings of the central courtyard and stairwells here. You should also consider throwing down the €3 it costs to visit the Anatomical Theatre upstairs where medical classes were once held. The entirely wooden interior of this small lecture hall features bodies crawling on the ceiling (look, there's Apollo suspended among the creepy crawlers) and rows of benches where we can only assume students once took copious notes during dissections (because back in the day there wasn't any Facebook to browse when they should have been paying attention). And unlike the buff, totally swole statues you find throughout the rest of Italy, the skinless statues that flank the lectern here know it's (literally) what's on the inside that counts (namely, your tendons and ligaments).

i *From P. Maggiore, walk down V. Archiginnasio (to the left of San Petronio when facing the church). The palazzo is on the left. Courtyard free. Anatomical Theatre €3.* ⏰ *Anatomical Theatre open M-F 10am-6pm, Sa 10am-7pm, Su 10am-2pm.*

FOOD

As locals will tell you, pick any trattoria or osteria in Bologna, and you're guaranteed an excellent meal. Absolutely order a platter of cheese or meat (or both) and a basket of crostini (thin, flaky, and flavorful, it's like bread but even better), then dig into one of Bologna's renowned pasta dishes—don't leave town without trying the tortellini, lasagna, or, of course, tagliatelle bolognese.

LA SORBETTERIA DI CASTIGLIONE   GELATO
V. Castiglione 44   ☎051 58 21 78 www.lasorbetteria.it

For the best gelato in Bologna, walk a little farther out from the center of town to La Sorbetteria Castiglione, whose silver canisters of gelato gleam in the lavender interior of this adorable pasticceria. Flavors here are listed in Italian, and although the place is frequented by locals, the friendly guys and gals behind the counter will still flash a winning smile at bumbling tourists like yourself. And good news for all you people who have trouble deciding between cones and cups—at La Sorbetteria, they're one in the same, so you can have your coppetta and eat it, too.

i *From the city center, walk down V. Castiglione. La Sorbetteria is a few blocks down on the left. Additional location at V. Saragozza 83. Gelato from €2.50.* ⏰ *Open daily 11am-midnight.*

bologna

OSTERIA AL 15
V. Mirasole 15

ITALIAN $

☎051 33 18 06

A bit of a trek from Bologna's more central eateries, the walk over to Osteria al 15 will take you winding through portico after portico to this quieter side of town. Tucked under an archway on an otherwise empty street, it's not easy to find this restaurant if you're not looking for it, which means you'll likely be one of the few tourists here. Indeed, step into this cozy, cluttered osteria, and you'll find yourself among tables crowded with Italian families chattering away animatedly while passing around plates of pasta. The homestyle food and friendly manager here add to the sense of comfort and family, so order some traditional Bolognese ragu and settle in among the pots and pans hanging from the walls, the cabinets full of colorful owls, and the old brown magazine pages plastered on the ceiling.

i From P. Maggiore, walk down V. Massimo D'Azeglio several blocks, turn left onto V. delle Tovaglie, right onto V. Paglietta, then left onto V. Mirasole. The restaurant is on the right. Primi €8-9. Secondi €9-10. ☼ Open M-Sa 7:30pm-1am.

MOUSTACHE
V. Mascarella 5

ITALIAN $

☎051 23 54 24 www.moustachebologna.com

To eat among some real Italians, head over to Moustache on V. Mascarella. This laid-back restaurant and bar serves up authentic Bolognese dishes at student-friendly prices. Come here and eat the way Italians do—pass around a basket of crostini and a plate of cheese and meat, relax, eat slowly, tuck into some richy, meaty pasta, and just hang out for a while as you make your way through a couple bottles of wine. On weekends in the summer, sit outside and enjoy live street music late into the night.

i From V. Marsala, turn onto V. Mentana, then veer right onto V. delle Belle Arti, then left onto V. Mascarella. Moustache is on the right. Primi €6-9. Secondi from €7. ☼ Open M 6pm-midnight, Tu-Th 6pm-1am, F-Sa 8pm-1:30am.

PIZZERIA DA CIRO
V. De Gessi 5

PIZZA $

☎051 22 69 17

If you've had enough ragu to satisfy your craving for a while and are looking for a cheap, familiar slice of pizza, head to Pizzeria da Ciro, where the thin-crust pies are made fresh, hot, and crispy. The plain white walls and pale green tablecloths here don't make much of a first impression, but what this pizzeria lacks in interior design it makes up for in the warm chatter of Italian families and couples that crowd in here for simple, no-fuss plates of pizza and pasta. The waiters don't speak much English, but luckily for you, the point-and-smile method of ordering goes over pretty well here.

i From Ugo Bassi walking away from the Two Towers, turn right onto V. Calcavinazzi and continue onto V. de Gessi. The pizzeria is on the right. Pizza €6.50-8. Primi €7-8. Secondi €9-16.

NIGHTLIFE

Unlike most cities, the summer months in Bologna are actually on the quieter side, as the drain of students from the city leaves its streets and bars emptier in July and August than they are during the school year. That being said, there's still plenty happening all year round, and visiting in the summer does mean you might have a chance to catch the live music lineup that plays in V. Mascarella on weekends. In addition to the street music, V. Mascarella is also lined with a number of restaurants, bars, and jazz clubs (check out Cantina Bentivoglio and Bravo Caffè). For more popular late-night options, head down to V. del Pratello, where young people gather under the porticos with drinks and cigarettes in hand outside the many bars on this street. At the end of the night, make your way to one of the squares in town, where you're guaranteed to find young locals hanging out on the curbs and under archways as dusk bleeds into dawn.

🏨 PUB MUTENYE
BAR

V. del Pratello 44

The wooden furniture and warmly lit interior of this bar is a welcoming variation from the dark walls and green lights you find in so many Italian pubs. Although Mutenye's cozy front bar and back room provide plenty of space for patrons to mill about, on warm summer nights, most of the locals who frequent this pub enjoy pints at tables or under the porticos outside. And if the many varieties of beer available here aren't enough, there's always the pinball machine in the corner to help keep you entertained throughout the night.

i Walk down Ugo Bassi away from the Two Towers to where it ends, then cross the street and veer slightly left onto V. Pratello. Pub Mutenye is a few blocks down on the left. Beer from €3. Wine from €3. ☼ Open daily 5pm-3am.

OSTERIA L'INFEDELE
BAR

V. Gerusalemme 5   ☎051 23 94 56

The walls here may display a few famous international names and faces (hey look, there's Obama in full red-white-and-blue "Hope" mode, right under a poster of his BFF, Vladimir Putin) but the crowd here is mostly local Italians who greet the bartenders and each other upon entry and then proceed to hang around until the wee hours of the morning. Tuck into a seat at one of the wooden tables and let your eyes flicker over the bar's assortment of old magazine covers and black-and-white photos on the walls, or step outside and enjoy some fresh night air with the crowd gathered out on the curb.

i From P. Santo Stefano, walk down V. Gerusalemme. The bar is on the left. Beer €3.50-4.50. Cocktails €6-7. Whiskey and rum €5-7. Shots €2. ☼ Open M-Sa noon-3am, Su noon-midnight.

BARAZZO
BAR

V. del Pratello 66b   ☎328 796 73 13 www.barazzo.it

If you find yourself far from V. Mascarella and are looking for some live music to go with your Saturday-night spritzers, stop in at Barazzo, whose main stage hosts a variety of musical acts throughout the week. While the bar also offers a full menu, the tunes and atmosphere here are the main draw, so pop in after dinner for a beer or cocktail and get ready to sit back, relax, and face the music (in a literal, totally non-ominous kind of way).

i Walk down Ugo Bassi away from the Two Towers to where it ends, then cross the street and veer slightly left onto V. Pratello. Barazzo is a few blocks down on the left. ☼ Open Tu-Su 6pm-3am.

ESSENTIALS
Practicalities

- **TOURIST OFFICES:** IAT provides information and is the starting point for walking and bus tours. (P. Maggiore 1E ☎051 23 96 60. ☼ Open M-Sa 9am-7pm, Su 10am-5pm.)

- **LUGGAGE STORAGE:** Stazione Centrale. (Located on the ground floor. ☼ Open daily 7am-9pm. 1st 5hr. €6, 6-12th hr. €0.90, €0.40 per hr. thereafter.)

- **ATMS:** There is a Unicredit ATM located at V. dell'Indipendenza 11.

- **POST OFFICE:** Poste Italiane. (P. Minghetti 4 ☎051 275 67 36. ☼ Open M-F 8am-6:30pm, Sa 8am-12:30pm.)

Emergency

- **POLICE:** Polizia di Stato. (V. degl Agresti 3 ☎051 23 76 32)

- **HOSPITALS/MEDICAL SERVICES:** Policlinico Sant'Orsola Malpighi. (V. Pietro Albertoni 15 ☎051 63 62 111. www.aosp.bo.it. Follow V. San Vitale to V. Giuseppe Massarenti and turn right. ☼ Open 24hr.)

bologna

get a room!

OSTELLO DANTE HOSTEL $

V. Nicolodi, 12 ☎0544 42 11 64 www.hostelravenna.com

Though a 20min. walk from the city center may seem like Hell, have no fear—the descent to Hell is easy, right? Located in a more residential part of town, Ostello Dante is still the place for backpackers to stay. This is a colorful, fully-equipped, music-blasting hostel with a large surfboard outside that will welcome you in. The bright, fun atmosphere and €20 a night price tag will make it a hard place to leave.

The floors here are divided by gender, and the rooms are fairly standard. Comfy beds, plenty of outlets, and painted Dante quotes will make you happy. But the lack of Wi-Fi in the rooms and air conditioning in the summer might make you feel like you're in an inferno. Sleep in your room, but spend most of your time either in the enormous common rooms downstairs or out enjoying the wonders of Ravenna.

With a full bar, a big breakfast in a spacious dining room, a game room, and a cool TV lounge with plenty of ornaments and throws on the couches, there's no shortage of space here. You'll be sure to find somewhere to lounge about during the summer nights.

This hostel might not be the prime location in Ravenna, but it is right across from a supermarket, which will become necessary, since dining options are very limited in this area and almost nonexistent after 9pm. A wander into town takes 20min. by foot, and there are also buses. Or rent one of the bikes this hostel offers. Unlike Dante, it's thankfully not an epic journey out of here.

i Dorms €20. ☼ Reception open 7-11am and 2:30-11:30pm. No curfew, main door locked after 11:30pm. Key available from reception upon request.

A CASA DI PAOLA B&B $$$

V. Paolo Costa 31 www.acasadipaola.it

A charming little residence that's just a 5min. walk from San Vitale (and pretty much any other sight you'll want to see in Ravenna), A Casa di Paola is the perfect place to stay if you're looking for a bit more of an intimate experience with you and your backpack.

Friendly staff, eccentric wooden furniture, those pretty landscape paintings—it feels just like home here. Mixing modern furniture with classic wooden floors and gorgeous frescoed ceilings, the rooms here will provide you with some of the most fun you've ever had in bed (sorry, that's not saying much). If you're bored, take a stroll down to the adorable little library and enjoy some time lounging about with a book on the terrace.

If you're going to be on the go in Ravenna, have no fear. Bikes are available for free from here, though everything is within walking distance from this amazing location (though a ride down to the beach may be worthwhile if you're insistent on working on that tan in the north of Italy). A Casa di Paola also a short walk from the train station, making life oh so nice.

i Singles €60. Doubles €42.50. Triples €30. ☼ Check in from 2pm. Check out by 10:30am.

Getting There

For those arriving by plane, Aeroporto Guglielmo Marconi (BLQ; V. Triumvirato 84 ☎051 64 79 615 www.bologna-airport.it) is northwest of the city center. ATC operates the Aerobus, which runs from the airport to Stazione Centrale (€6, every 15min.). For those arriving by train, Stazione Centrale services Florence (€19-24, 35min.), Milan (€17-40, 1-3hr.), Venice (€12-30, 90min.-2hr.), and Rome (€49-56, 2hr. 15min.), among other smaller cities.

Getting Around

Bologna is most easily navigated on foot, although ATC does operate a comprehensive bus system throughout the city. Tickets cost €1.30 if purchased before getting on the bus or €1.50 if purchased on board.

ravenna

Capital of the Western Roman Empire, major city during the Byzantine Empire, and home to some of the most famous mosaics in the world, there might not be too many epic movies and shows about Ravenna, but there sure should be. This city is overflowing with history, artwork, and fame. Renowned for its Byzantine mosaics, every turn in this beautiful city will bring you to another gorgeous church or baptistery that would be the showstopper in any other city. But nah, that's just another place with some sixth-century sheep mosaics that took up a couple pages in your art history textbook. No big deal. Home to plenty of Jesuses and heavenly ceilings, along with some famous descerts to Hell—be sure to pay your respects to Dante's tomb here—Ravenna's got it all. And free city Wi-Fi, too. If you're not allowed into churches anymore, there are beaches and a large urban sprawl just a bus ride away, but at least spend a little time in the historical center. Where else can you gain the approval of the Virgin Mary and the powerful former brothel worker, Empress Theodora, at the same time?

SIGHTS

BASILICA OF SAN VITALE   CHURCH
V. San Vitale   ☎0544 54 16 88 www.ravennamosaici.it

You call yourself a history buff. Your girlfriend just thinks you can't let go of the past. Either way, you should go see the Basilica of San Vitale in Ravenna. In a city with eight UNESCO World Heritage sights, if you only have time to see one of them (which you really shouldn't...they're all super close to each other), make sure you go see this basilica.

One of the most famous early Christian churches in the world, it may not look like much from the outside. You're in Italy—you may be used to flashier churches than this brown, octagonal one. But the Byzantines had a few tricks up their sleeves. Walk in, and you'll say what every early Christian wanted you to say: "OMFG."

A stunning interior decorated almost from floor to ceiling with colorful, intricate mosaics, this basilica will leave you speechless. Take in the gorgeous dome, the beautifully decorated apse, the stern Jesus staring at you, and the magic enlightened sheep. It's really not baaaaad.

Beautiful stars, peacocks, golden expanses of space—everything inside here shines. You'll be torn between wanting to wander around and see everything and taking a seat to just let your eyes feast on this magnificent structure. Do both.

The most famous mosaics are probably the ones inside the apse on the left and right, just below the purple-clad Jesus. Here, you'll see the mosaics of Emperor Justinian I in purple with his attendants and the regal Empress Theodora with her attendants. If you've ever cracked open an art history textbook, they'll seem familiar. Note the formality and regality given to Theodora, a famously powerful woman and one of few empresses who can say she got her humble beginnings in a brothel. Which makes the real question: What were you doing last Friday night, Justinian? Spend as much time as you can in this incredible church. But don't get tired of mosaics just yet. Step outside and walk on over to the Mausoleum of Galla Placidia.

i Inclusive ticket €9.50, reduced (student with ID) €8.50. Valid for 7 days and allows entrance to Archiepiscopal Museum, Chapel of Sant'Andrea and the Ivory Throne, Neonian Baptistery, Basilica of Sant'Apollinare Nuovo, Basilica of San Vitale, Mausoleum of Galla Placidia. ⏱ Open Apr-Sept 9am-7pm; Mar-Oct 9:30am-5:30pm; Jan 11-Feb 10am-5pm.

THE MAUSOLEUM OF GALLA PLACIDIA

MUSEUM

V. Giuliano Argentario, 22 ☎0544 54 16 88 www.ravennamosaici.it

The Mausoleum of Galla Placidia will probably be the UNESCO sight that requires the least amount of time to visit. This might or might not be due to the alleged 5min. time limit everyone is allowed inside (but don't worry, no one will put your body in the mausoleum if you stay a couple extra minutes).

Compared to San Vitale, this structure is tiny. But it's also home the oldest and best preserved Byzantine mosaics in the world. Way to go, Ravenna. Galla Placida was the daughter of the Roman Emperor Theodosius I. (Strange names ran in the family.) She died in 450 CE and was believed to be in the largest sarcophagus. The other two sarcophagi once held her husband, Emperor Constantius III, and either her brother, Emperor Honorius, or her son, Emperor Valentinian III. If being in tight spaces with dead bodies creeps you out, don't worry. There are no more remains here. Only gorgeous mosaics.

Admire the deep blue of the night sky inside here. The lighting may not be great since the museum has chosen to use those strange dorm room standing lamps that really help no one get homework done. But still, the beautiful floral mosaics and the animal ones are worth taking a good look at.

Most famously, this mausoleum is home to the Lunette of Christ as Good Shepherd. This gorgeous mosaic shows Jesus as the iconic shepherd tending to his sheep. It's a beautiful piece in its own right. But our favorite part is the anatomically incorrect, absurdly long tails on the sheep. The Lord works in mysterious ways.

i It's the building on the right when you exit the back of the Basilica of San Vitale. Inclusive ticket €9.50; reduced (student with ID) €8.50. Valid for 7 days and allows entrance to Archiepiscopal Museum, Chapel of Sant'Andrea and the Ivory Throne, Neonian Baptistery, Basilica of Sant'Apollinare Nuovo, Basilica of San Vitale, Mausoleum of Galla Placidia. ⏱ Open Apr-Sept daily 9am-7pm; Mar-Oct daily 9:30am-5:30pm; Jan 11-Feb daily 10am-5pm.

FOOD

PROFUMO DI PIADINA

PIADINI $

V. Cairoli 24

If there's one thing Let's Go loves, it's holes-in-the-wall. Unless they're in the hostels, in which case you should get that checked out. But for some of the best piadinas in Ravenna, you've just gotta go to this little hole-in-the-wall piadineria: Prufumo di Piadina.

"This isn't pizza! What Italian food is this?" you may cry out. Calm down. But here in Romagna region, it's all about the piadina, an Italian flatbread sandwich that's usually made with fresh toasted bread and then filled with tomatoes, cheese, prosciutto, smoked ham, salami and other delectable choices. In short, it's delicious.

The lines outside this piadineria can get a little long during lunch time, so take this bonus time to scan the chalkboards outside and decide what you'd like in your tummy today. The restaurant itself is actually just a kitchen in the back and a tiny, tiny waiting area in the front where a beaming staff member will gladly take your order, give you a number, and then tell you to wait.

Take your warm toasty piadina and then walk out the cobblestone streets of Ravenna to P. del Popolo, where you can grab a bench and bite into a delicious, gooey lunch. Ravenna's truly a place of religious experiences.

i Piadina €3-4. Rotoli €4-6. Porchetta €6. ☼ Open M-Sa 9am-3pm.

SORBETTERIA DEGLI ESARCHI   GELATERIA $
V. IV Novembre 11   ☎0544 36 315

There are few words that go better with gelato than "artisan." Every perfectionist in the world should just go out and open an artisan gelato shop. Because it literally is perfection. That's why if you're in Ravenna, you have to stop by Sorbetteria degli Esarchi for some deliciously kickass artisan gelato.

Inside, there's not much other than a counter full of gelato. And that's all you really need. The friendly staff will wait while you narrow down on some pistachio, or maybe you're craving dark chocolate and cookies today. Decisions are always difficult. The gelato here is fresh, delicious, and extremely reasonably priced. While surrounding areas may expect you to pay big bucks for their organic gelato, this place is the real deal. Try some amazing gelato (the smile from the staff comes for free), and then walk out of the tiny storefront outside to the seating area. The little white metal chairs and tables are the perfect place to people watch all the tourists on V. IV Novembre. Sure, the mosaics they're seeing are going to be great. But you've got gelato. So life is good.

i Gelato €2-4. ☼ Open daily 11am-9pm.

ESSENTIALS

Getting There

The easiest way to get to Ravenna is by train. Trenitalia runs frequent service to Ravenna from all surrounding major cities.

Getting Around

By Bus

Buses are run by START and are frequent and reliable. They're the easiest way to get from the city center to the suburbs to the beach. Tickets cost €1.30.

By Foot

Ravenna is easily navigated by foot. The city center is small and no cars are allowed in most of it. Still, beware of bikes and Vespas in pedestrian areas.

Practicalities

- **TOURIST OFFICE:** Office located at V. Salara 8/12
- **TOURIST INFORMATION:** ☎0544 35 75 53 54 04
- **ATMS:** P. del Popolo

Emergency

- **EMERGENCY TELEPHONE:** 112
- **FIRE:** 115
- **POLICE:** 113
- **HOSPITALS:** The main hospital is Domus Nova Spa Ospedale (V. P. Pavirani, 44).

ravenna

rimini

Rimini is affectionately called the Ibiza of Italy, so if you're looking to party it up at some of the hottest nightclubs in the region, this is the place to be. The small city center of Rimini is where your train will drop you off, and this is a nice area to daytrip to if you want to check out some churches or museums. But if you're coming during the summer, hop on that bus 11, and let's go to the beach. As the throbbing pulse of Rimini during the summer, the beach is where all the action is. After midnight, of course. During the day, spend some time at the beaches (though they aren't the nicest in the Adriatic) or working off that hangover. Once the sun goes down, let the fun begin. Hostels here are all ready to cater to the crazy partying youth, with music blasting, full bars, and nightly trips out to the clubs in the area. If you aren't at a disco dancing away to Calvin Harris every night while you're here, you're doing Rimini wrong. All the clubs are incredible, with at least several floors, flashing lights, and occasionally brilliant DJs like Afrojack and David Guetta who stop by. If you can make the trek out, Baia Imperiale here is the largest club in all of Europe. So break out the short shorts, the bro tanks, and that wild party animal that makes the youth so great. Let's go get turnt up in Rimini.

SIGHTS

THE BEACH
BEACH

Along the coast, one street down from Vle. Regina Margherita

If you're looking for something to do during the sunlight hours in Rimini, just walk one street down from the clubs. Rimini's other main attraction is, yes, being a coastal town. If you've been waiting your whole life to dip your toes in the Adriatic, now's your chance. A short disclaimer: Rimini is no Mykonos. Don't expect any pristine white sand and clear blue waters here. Rimini is famous in Italy for its parties, not so much for the beaches. But that shouldn't deter you. A beach is a beach, and soaking in the sun while listening to the waves rolling in will still be enjoyable here.

To find a beach, take a walk along the water (or as close as you can get to the water). Lining the entire beach, except for the occasional free public beaches, are strings of companies who own a part of the beach and are willing to share it with you for a price. Don't worry, they're usually not too exorbitant, and if you walk past a few, you can check out what deals are happening.

Beaches are numbered from 1 up past 150. A lot of them are largely the same and offer amenities like chairs, umbrellas, changing areas, hot showers, kids' fun parks (yaaas!), and beach volleyball courts, just to name a few. Settle for a number, head on in, and enjoy the beach life. Sip some cocktails from the bar while watching young Italian hunks spike that volleyball over the net all while working on that gorgeous tan. Who knew Rimini could be so much fun in the sun, too?

i Prices vary, some beaches free. ☼ Hours vary, dawn to dusk.

MUSEO DELLA CITTA
MUSEUM

V. L. Tonini, 1 ☎0541 79 38 51 www.museicomunalirimini.it

You know what's better than crazy nightclubs and soaking in the sun on the beach? Museums! We're not even joking. Okay, so maybe you didn't come all the way to Rimini for an education. But if you have even a slight interest in history and cool archaeological finds, Rimini's actually got quite a few of them. So to make up for all those brain cells you've been losing at the bar, take a stroll into the city center of Rimini and check out the excitingly named Museo della Citta.

Located on a small alleyway in the city, this gorgeous museum with lovely and friendly curators doesn't usually get a lot of attention. But the exhibits are

italy

get a room!

SUNFLOWER BEACH BACKPACKER HOSTEL
HOSTEL $

Vle. Siracusa, 25 ☎0541 37 34 32 www.sunflowerhostel.com

Really the only place you should consider staying in Rimini. Unless you wanna be lame and sleep. But who comes here for that? A top-tier party hostel, Sunflower Beach has it all. Full bar, loud speakers, disco ball, young staff, and comfy beds for you to sleep in, too! Not that you'll be using those until the morning.

Located right off Rimini's main drag near the beach, this hostel has spacious dorms, colorful halls, comfy common rooms, and Wi-Fi that's really good in the stairwell. It might not be luxury, but it'll do. Free breakfast is served in the mornings, where you get your choice of chocolate cereals and toast with Nutella. Because the fact that you're eating breakfast is healthy enough.

Sunflower Beach is not only great for its accommodations, but it's also the place to stay if you want to party. With amazing organized party nights pretty much every goddamn evening, you'll have a blast even if you're traveling solo. Pub and disco crawl? Check. Outings with transportation included to the largest disco in Europe? Yup. Be able to check out all the great clubs in Rimini (even the ones that are far away) and get to go with an incredible group of people. Resident party king Roberto leads the group every night, and his twerking skills will make sure every party gets started right.

So if you want to have fun in Rimini and remember about 60 percent of it, stay here.

i Dorms €18-25. ⏰ Reception 24hr.

---

pretty ballin'. Start all the way on the bottom floor and get a long look at prehistoric Rimini. After your fair share of Etruscan remains and quotes on the walls, you'll be able to head into the most spectacular part of the museum, where you'll find monumental work by Augustus and then one of the best mosaic collections you'll ever see.

Sure, Ravenna might be known for its mosaics, but Rimini's no measly second place. Gorgeous and enormous mosaics showing ships and gods and goats take up a majority of the second floor. Spend your time walking through them and be sure to also check out a recreation of some rooms from the surgeon's house where some of these mosaics were found.

The top floor is home to more medieval and Renaissance work. This small city happens to house a Ghirlandaio up here as well. Plenty of pretty paintings and tapestries here will get your mind off Rimini's other attractions for at least a little bit. Bump into fellow likeminded tourists and laugh about those silly people who are too busy partying to care about high art. And then, later that night, become one of those said people. But for now, bask in culture and get drunk off amazing brushstrokes, you classy bitch.

i €6, students €2. ⏰ Oct-Apr 11 Tu-Sa 8:30am-1pm and 4-7pm, Su 10am-12:30pm and 3-7pm; Apr 12-June 8 Tu-Sa 4-10:30pm, Su 10am-11:00pm; June 9-Sept Tu-Sa 2-11pm, Su 5pm-11:00pm.

rimini

FOOD

CASINA DEL BOSCO
PIADINI $

Vle. Antonio Beccadelli, 15   ☎0541 56 295 www.casinadelbosco.it

Tucked on a curve full of busy restaurants between the beach and the city center is this charming and crowded restaurant. A favorite among locals coming in to carry out some food back to the city or tourists who have ventured a little up from the clubbing zone, Casina del Bosco never disappoints. It can be hard to snag one of the cute wooden tables with umbrellas lined up on the sidewalk here, but if you do, prepare for an amazing meal.

Casina del Bosco's specialty? Piadina. A type of Italian flatbread sandwich typical in the Romagna region, you might as well get a little taste of culture in Rimini along with all that house music. These flatbreads can be filled with anything from roast beef to prosciutto crudo and tomato. The salami or tuna are delicious; otherwise, go a little crazy with a wurstel hot dog. If you're in the mood for a sweeter piadina, Nutella options are also available. These warm, toasted sandwiches are deliciously crispy to bite into with fresh meats and vegetables inside that make the perfect sandwich.

Food is served quickly, so despite the crowds you'll never have to wait too long. Enjoy the rustic charm of wicker plates and this quieter and slightly older part of Rimini, where you're more likely to see families.

For dessert, there are delicious gelato options. The meringue one is ice cream heaven. Or finish up this lunch with a glass of wine, then head out back into the city or back out to start drinking in Rimini. It's five o'clock somewhere.

i *Piadina €4-6.* ☼ *Open daily 11:30am-2am.*

NIGHTLIFE

COCORICO
CLUB

Vle. Chieti, 44   ☎0541 60 51 83 www.cocorico.it

If you wub wub wub EDM, no trip to Rimini is complete without a visit to the famous Cocorico. A club located slightly outside Rimini in Riccione, strap that bright green foreigner bus bracelet on your wrist, and let's go turn up with some of the hottest DJs in the world. A major concert venue in this area, famous DJs who have graced this club include Skrillex, Afrojack, deadmau5, and Alesso. Come any week of the summer, and chances are you'll be able to see some amazing act to live-Tweet home about.

Cocorico is located in an iconic and enormous glass pyramid. Futuristic and archaic, deafening then silent right before the beat drops, and always an unforgettable experience, this disco has it all. Divided into three parts, you get your pick of what kind of night you want. In the main pyramid stage are the enormous crowds of people, the smoky atmosphere, and the bright lasers that all say "Main act here, bitches!" This is where you'll be able to rave to the headliners of the weekend and see those David Guetta songs performed live.

Too bass-heavy for you? Head out into the garden, and you'll find more commercial pop hits from all decades being played. Occasional paid dancers make this a great place to go to if you want to see something that isn't bright, flashing lights for a little bit. Head even further in from the garden, and you'll get to the alternative stage, which is where all the cool cats hang out and sit around and listen to music that's…alternative. You've probably never heard of it before.

Regardless of what you come to Cocorico to do, you'll end up talking about it all the way back to your hostel on the Foreigner Bus and for a while after that. Because it's not every night you get to rave with world class DJs in a glass pyramid. Oh, Rimini.

i *Varies depending on show. Around €20-40.* ☼ *Varies depending on show. Usually 10pm-late.*

CARNABY

Vle. Brindisi, 20 ☎0541 37 32 04 www.carnaby.it

CLUB

Carnaby holds the prestigous position as one of Rimini's most popular night-clubs. Considering the vibrant nightlife scene in this party city, that's really saying something. With its classic three floors and three atmospheres slogan, this nightclub is hoppin' any day of the week and has been doing so since 1968.

Walk into this crazy club, and you'll get to choose your own adventure. The ground floor is usually the most happening of the three, where DJs spin hip hop music so you can twerk the night away to greats like Kanye and Jay-Z. Because sometimes you got 99 problems but not knowing how to werk that stripper pole ain't one.

If you're feeling more rave-y, head up to the second floor. EDM and hard techno play here, meaning not a lot of David Guetta but plenty of fist pumping and jumping up and down. The very top floor has an extensive lounge area where you can sit and smoke (because this is Italy). There's a full bar up here, and if you want to collect your free drink with cover ASAP, head up here first. There is a much smaller dance area here, where live musicians sometimes come to play. For the rest of the night, there's a strange mix of Latin and oldies and boy bands.

Dance the night away and then be thankful that unlike many great clubs in Rimini, this one is right off the main street, so your drunken walk home won't be too embarrassing. That counts as a win.

i Around €15 cover charge. ☼ Open M-Sa 10pm-4:30am, Su 10pm-12am.

ALTROMONDO STUDIOS

V. Flaminia 358 ☎335 564 5740 www.altromondo.com

CLUB

Spaceship-esque automatic doors, bright spinning lights, barely clothed dancers, and a guy dressed in mesh and a studded Roman helmet who comes out of the ceiling and shouts "ALTROMONDO!" You could say that this club has an other-worldly feel to it. So, welcome to ALTROMONDO.

When the bus drops you off in the middle of nowhere, don't fret. You're probably in the right place. If you walk out and see a futuristic building decked-out in silver with funky doors, you're here. Altromondo is more than a club. It's a whole damn experience. The club itself is impressive and large enough for you to lose your frenemies in. Along the walls are plenty of super comfy black leather couches and seats where you can take a seat and sip your overpriced bar drink instead of risking spilling any of it on the dance floor.

The music here is great and so is the dancing scene. EDM and house music blast all night. The lights are incredible, but keep an eye out for a robot guy in stilts and an LED suit who comes out and shoots lasers into the crowd. Prepare to be stunned by this club and then play it off by dancing. Watch out for Sunday and Wednesday foam parties, and fall in love with this journey to another world.

i Prices and hours vary based on show and DJ.

ESSENTIALS
Practicalities

- **TOURIST OFFICES:** Office located in Ple. Fellini. (☎541 56 902)
- **TOURIST INFORMATION:** 5415 69 02
- **ATMS:** Along Vle. Regina Margherita.

Emergency

- **EMERGENCY TELEPHONE:** 112

rimini

- **FIRE:** 115
- **POLICE:** 113
- **HOSPITALS:** Rimini's main hospital is Ospedale Infermi (Vle. Luigi Settembrini, 2)
- **PHARMACIES:** Vle. Regina Margherita, 261

Getting There

Rimini is best reached by train. The train station is in the city center. To get to the beach where most hostels and summer life are, take Bus 11 from the train station. It goes right down Vle. Regina Margherita, Rimini's main drag.

Getting Around

By Bus

The main bus to know is Bus 11. This goes from the city center and train station all the way down Vle. Regina Margherita, which it follows to the end of town. Bus stops don't have names but numbers. For example, Sunflower Beach Backpacker Hostel is at stop 26. Tickets cost €1.30.

By Taxi

Taxis are fairly inexpensive in Rimini, but if you're trying to catch a ride home from the club, try to rely more on the foreigner bus, which your hostel owners can arrange.

By Foot

Rimini is easily walkable, especially if you want to stick around the beach and clubbing scene. To get into the city, hop on the bus 11. The city center is very walkable, too.

florence

The capital of Tuscany and birthplace of the Italian Renaissance, Florence may not be able to lay claim to the thousands of years' worth of ruins and ancient history that you can wander through in Rome, but its legacy is something else entirely. Ruled by the storied Medici family and home to many great artists and thinkers, Florence boasts a history both Shakespearean in its political drama and unparalleled in the wealth of art that it created. Just as the city's artistic giants—from Michelangelo to Botticelli to Donatello—mastered space, lines, and geometry to create some of the greatest buildings, paintings, and sculptures in human history, so, too, does the city itself seem to be a purposeful work of art, with its bright palette of yellow and orange buildings, its cohesive architecture, and its clean, tourist-friendly streets. In every respect, Florence is a city of high culture—from the masterpieces of the Uffizi and the Galleria dell'Accademia to the dresses and trousers on display in the windows of fashion houses to the DOCG-stamped bottles of Chianti that you can sample in the vineyards that surround the city. The spell of Florence's perfection can very occasionally be broken by the crush of tourists flooding Piazza del Duomo or snaking along the walls of the city's museums—and sitting low in a valley surrounded by the far off Apennine mountains, Florence is particularly susceptible to hot summer days that leave tourists and their cones of gelato dripping under the Tuscan sun. It is this same cradled position, however, that makes the city so stunning when viewed from the high perches of spots like Piazzale Michelangelo or the Forte di Belvedere. When the sun begins to retreat behind the distant peaks and the pink haze of the sunset envelopes the low-lying city, the iconic orange Duomo and the bridges of the Arno take on new hues and new beauty—and despite its feast of towers, cathedrals, and Renaissance treasures, the entire spread of the city itself is perhaps Florence's greatest marvel.

ORIENTATION

The heart of the city and its most popular sights are concentrated in Piazza del Duomo. Slightly to the north in San Lorenzo lies the Basilica di San Lorenzo, the San Lorenzo outdoor market, and the many food stalls and eateries of Mercato Centrale. From this neighborhood, Stazione Santa Maria Novella is easily reached via the busy Via Nazionale. Wander farther south to Santa Croce, a popular nightlife neighborhood that surrounds the basilica from which it takes its name. The second-busiest square in the city is Piazza della Signoria, where you'll find plenty of statues, stringed orchestras, and the towering Palazzo Vecchio. Just around the corner sits the Uffizi Gallery and the distinctive gray architecture and long galleries of Piazza degli Uffizi. From here, cross the famed Ponte Vecchio (or any of the city's lesser bridges) to the Oltrarno (literally "beyond the Arno"). On this side of the river, you'll find Palazzo Pitti, the sprawling Boboli Gardens, and the popular restaurants and bars of Piazza Santo Spirito to the west and Piazzale Michelangelo and San Miniato al Monte looming high above the rest of the neighborhood in the east.

ACCOMMODATIONS

▦ OSTELLO GALLO D'ORO   HOSTEL $$
V. Cavour 104   ☎055 552 2964 www.ostellogalldoro.com

This may be the hostel of the "golden cockerel," but the only roosters you'll find here are the ones in the Wi-Fi passwords. One of Florence's smaller hostels, Gallo D'Oro comprises just one floor, but its single, twisting green hallway is decorated with letters from and pictures of happy hostel guests, all of whom proclaim their collective love of cock (sorry—it was too easy!). The close quarters here means that you'll get to know both your fellow travelers and the wonderful staff quite well (shoutout to the awesome Matteo and Martina!). Adding to the family feel of this hostel are the omnipresent snacks in the common area, the books available to browse on the shelves in the hallways, and a bountiful breakfast spread featuring fresh, homemade breads and tarts.

i From the Duomo, walk down V. Cavour several blocks. The hostel is a 10min. walk down the street, on the right. Dorms from €30. Breakfast included. Laundry machine available. ◨ Reception 24hr.

WOW FLORENCE HOSTEL   HOSTEL $$
V. Venezia 18/b   ☎055 579 603 www.wowflorence.com

You always wanted to be a superhero, and WOW Florence Hostel just might be your chance. At the very least, the color blocking and countless posters of comic book heroes at this hostel will make you feel like you're living inside the pages of a Marvel (or DC!) comic book. The rooms here are just as colorful as reception, and the hostel offers plenty of spaces to hang out with your fellow travel avengers (whether it be the high-ceilinged common room, breakfast area, or sunny smoking patio). WOW is located all the way up on the fifth floor, so either whip out those Spidey web-slinging powers or, you know, just take the elevator.

i From the Duomo, walk down V. Cavour several blocks and turn right onto V. Venezia. The hostel is on the left. Dorms €29. Singles €50. Breakfast €5. ◨ Check-in 2pm.

ACADEMY HOSTEL   HOSTEL $$
V. Ricasoli 9   ☎055 265 4581 www.academyhostel.eu

If all goes well, the only thing you'll be studying at this hostel is the inside of your eyelids—and maybe some of the inspirational quotes plastered throughout reception and above the beds in the dorm rooms. (One of these adages is "Keep Calm and Let Reception Handle It," so you know you'll be in good hands here.)

florence

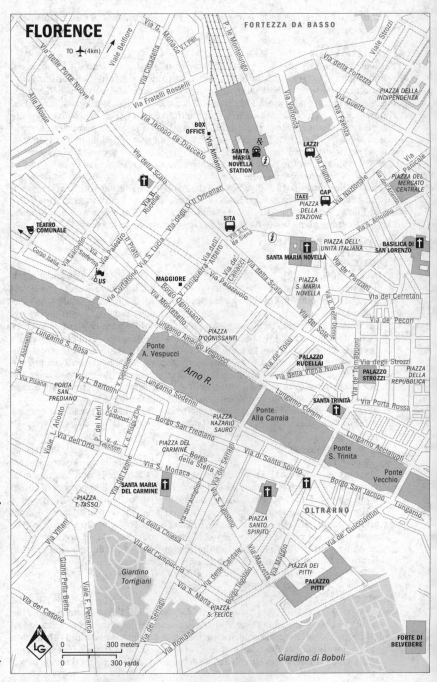

FLORENCE

TO ✈ (4km)

FORTEZZA DA BASSO

italy

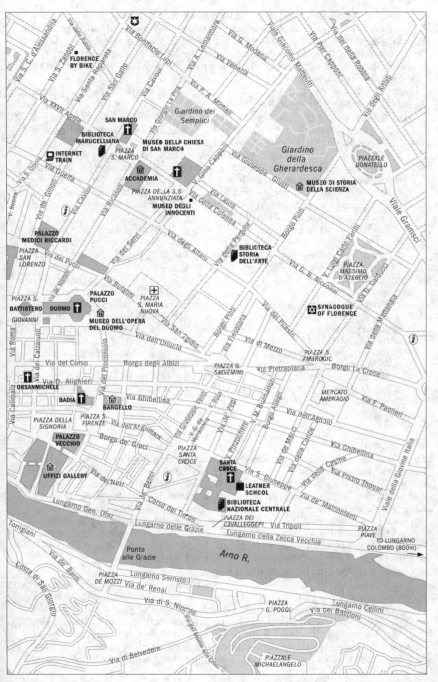

florence

Rooms here are clean and basic, while the cluttered, homey reception area is a bit more colorful and offers guests plenty of space to lounge and hang about—as long as it's not during the 11am-2:30pm lockout. A few of the dorms have white partitions between the beds, which makes the whole thing feel a little bit like a hospital room, but it really just means more privacy in which to dress your blistery sandal wounds.

i From the Duomo, walk a short way down V. Ricasoli. The hostel is on the left. Dorms €34. Quads €45. ☒ Reception 24hr. Lockout daily 11am-2:30pm.

PLUS FLORENCE HOSTEL
HOSTEL $

V. Santa Caterina D'Alessandria 15 ☎055 628 6347 www.plushostels.com

The giant lettering and sliding doors that usher you into the cool, sprawling lobby of this massive hostel makes Plus feel more like a giant corporate hotel (or maybe even a convention center) than a youth hostel. With multiple locations throughout Europe, this behemoth of a hostel features an internet cafe, fitness center, restaurant, and even an outdoor swimming pool and bar. And if that wasn't enough, it has beds and toilets, too! Now you know where the "plus" in the name comes from.

i From the Santa Maria Novella train station, walk through P. Adua onto V. Bernardo Cennini, then turn left onto V. Faenza, then right onto V. Pratello. Continue a ways before curving right on V. Cosimo Ridolfi, walk through P. dell'Indipendenza, and turn left onto V. Santa Caterina D'Alessandria. Dorms from €25. ☒ Reception 24hr. Check-in 2:30pm.

HOSTEL ARCHI ROSSI
HOSTEL $$

V. Faenza 94r ☎055 290 804 www.hostelarchirossi.com

The cool-colored murals that cover the walls of reception might make you feel like you're living inside a full-sleeve biker tattoo, but fortunately for you, this hostel is a little bit cozier than an easy rider's bicep. In addition to the chill guys at the front desk, the lobby will also greet you with vending machines and a full breakfast buffet every morning. And while rooms are comfortable but basic, they do glitz things up a bit with gold metal bunk frames.

i From Santa Maria Novella train station, walk through P. Adua and onto V. Bernardo Cennini, then turn right onto V. Faena. The hostel is just a few steps away, on the left. Dorms €28-30. ☒ Reception 24hr. Check-in 2:30pm.

SIGHTS

The Duomo

The Duomo sights include the Cathedral of Santa Maria del Fiore, Brunelleschi's Dome, the Campanile (Giotto's Bell Tower), the Baptistery of San Giovanni, the Crypt of Santa Reparata, and the Museo dell'Opera. Entrance to the church is free, and entry to the other sights can be purchased through a combined ticket (€15); after your ticket is activated upon visiting your first sight, you have 24hr. to visit the remaining sights until your ticket expires, so plan your sightseeing accordingly. Tickets can be activated at any point within the first six days after purchase. Purchase tickets at the ticket office (across the street from the entrance to the Baptistery in P. San Giovanni) or directly at the entrance to the Bell Tower.

DUOMO (CATHEDRAL OF SANTA MARIA DEL FIORE)

P. del Duomo ☎055 23 02 885 www.operaduomo.firenze.it

Constructed from 1296 to 1436, the Duomo was basically Florence's version of a giant, Renaissance foam finger intended to tell the rest of Tuscany, "Hey, guys—we're #1! Also, Siena, you suck!" As the heart of Florence and the focal point of the cityscape, the church is certainly unlike any other you'll find in Italy—at least from the outside. Compared to its exterior—which is a veritable feast of pink, green, and white marble, all leading up to its stunning and iconic orange dome—the interior of the Duomo is often regarded by travelers as something of a letdown. And certainly, in comparison to the absolute gluttony of most Baroque Roman churches, this basilica is much more modest and restrained, with simple white walls, understated tiles, and just a few stained-glass windows looming above the central altar. At the same time, its massive, cavernous, and solemn interior is impressive in its own right—indeed, as opposed to the sensory overload that is Rome's St. Peter's, what's impressive here is simply the mammoth size of the church. And hey, the fresco on the ceiling of the dome is certainly nothing to sniff at—for a closer look at the dome itself (which, spoiler alert, contains a few very large, very disconcerting cracks) and a bird's-eye view of the church's tiling below, take time to climb the cupola. On your way out of the church, pop down into the Crypt of Santa Reparata in the basement.

i *P. del Duomo. Entrance is through the left door when facing the facade. Free.* ⏰ *Open M-Sa 10am-5pm, Su 1:30-4:45pm.*

CAMPANILE AND DOME

P. del Duomo   ☎055 23 02 885 www.operaduomo.firenze.it

For your own up-close, bird's-eye view of both the Duomo and the Bell Tower, you'll need to climb each structure in order to get a good look at the other one. So kick your glutes into gear—you've got some stairs to scale. Although the Campanile features two-lane traffic all the way up and down the tower (tuck into those corners!), its 414 steps are still slightly less strenuous than the Dome's 463. The Bell Tower is also separated into several levels, which means you can stop every 100 steps or so to have a seat, take a breather, and look out over the city through some grated windows. At the top of the tower, you might find yourself fully exposed to the merciless summer sun, but you'll also be looking right in the face of the basilica's magnificent orange Dome.

The climb up the Dome itself is a little less straightforward—you'll find yourself walking up some stone steps, then twisting up spiral staircases and winding your way up dark, narrow, slanted hallways as you rise higher and higher in the dome—but its views, both of the interior of the basilica's dome and of the entirety of Florence, are pretty unparalleled. Take your time, squeeze through some narrow passages, and be patient if traffic seems to be moving slowly—although you may be sweating your brains out and developing rapid onset claustrophobia, it will all be worth it (unless you actually have claustrophobia, in which case you should probably skip this one). The ticket to the Duomo sights only lasts 24hr. after first validation, so either plan your time wisely and climb one of these bad boys in the afternoon and the other one the next morning, or prepare for some burning calves and do the whole thing in the same day.

Note to travelers: Don't be a dick and draw a bunch of dicks (or even something less offensive like your initials) on the walls of the Dome or the Campanile. No one else cares when you were here (or that you were here at all), so just keep your pen in your pants, please.

i *Entrance to the Dome is on the north side of the Cathedral (via the Porta della Mandorla). Entrance to the Bell Tower is pretty easy to spot. €15 with Duomo sights ticket. Dome open M-F 8:30am-7pm, Sa 8:30am-5:40pm (last entry 40min. before close). Bell Tower open daily 8:15am-6:50pm.*

BAPTISTERY OF SAN GIOVANNI

P. San Giovanni   ☎055 23 02 885 www.operaduomo.firenze.it

Sitting just opposite the doors of the Duomo, the Baptistery of San Giovanni is perhaps most famous for its doors, which were commissioned through a series of competitions during which a number of great artists fought for the honor of designing the doors. Of the three sets of doors, the most famous are the golden Gates of Paradise (also known as the East Doors, directly facing the cathedral), which were designed by Lorenzo Ghiberti and include a number of panels depicting the life of Christ. Inside, the dark, cave-like interior of the Baptistery provides a shocking contrast to the building's white marble facade, although if you crane your neck upward and have a look at the ceiling mosaics, you'll discover a brighter array of colors (including more gold!) and the looming visage of an enormous Christ at the Last Judgment.

i *Entrance on the north side of the Baptistery in P. San Giovanni. €10 with combined ticket for Dome, Campanile, Baptistery, and Reparata. ☒ Open M-F 8:15-10:15am and 11:15am-6:30pm, Sa 8:15am-6:30pm, Su 8:15am-1:30pm.*

Piazza della Signoria

THE UFFIZI GALLERY

Piazzale degli Uffizi 6

MUSEUM

www.uffizi.org

The Uffizi Gallery comprises two U-shaped floors that house some of the greatest artwork in all of Italy and the world. After you make your way through the infamous line outside, you'll begin your visit upstairs on the first floor, where the numbered rooms of the gallery begin just off the First Corridor, which is lined with busts and portraits of famous Florentines and plenty of Medicis (in case you forgot who they were). From here, make your way into Room 2, where you'll find a lot of large gilded altarpieces whose main theme seems to be "Madonna and Child" (what else?). Rooms 3-4 features Gothic artwork from Siena (which rival Florence seems to have reluctantly let slip into the collection). Starting in Room 7 (which features the debut of perspective!), watch as the Renaissance unfolds before your eyes. In Room 8, you'll see the familiar profiles of Piero della Francesca's *Portraits of the Grand Dukes of Urbino*. Room 15 features early works by Leonardo da Vinci (including his *Annunciation*), while Room 35 (with red walls that denote 16th-century artwork) houses pieces by Michelangelo. Farther along, the stunning Room of Niobe is lined with a collection of statues depicting the mother's tragedy. The museum's main event, however, happens rather early on in Rooms 10-14. Here you'll find the famous works of Botticelli, including his iconic *Birth of Venus* and his perhaps even more detailed and beautiful *Allegory of Spring* (which features a slightly more clothed depiction of the goddess of love).

After all the Botticelli and masterpieces of the main floor, most tourists tend to file quickly through the rooms on the ground floor (which, to be fair, are not laid out quite as nicely as the ones above). But if you follow the crowds like a mindless lemming, you'll be missing out on entire rooms dedicated to the likes of Caravaggio (Rooms 90-93), Raphael (Room 66), and Titian (Rooms 83). Note that here paintings are labeled with their artist's Italian names, which is partly why so many people pass by Raffaello Sanzio da Urbino and Tiziano Vecelli without even noticing. There are also plenty of works by Rembrandt, Peter Paul Rubens, Goya, and others in the blue rooms dedicated to foreign artists on the ground floor.

Depending on the time of year (and time of day) that you visit the Uffizi, the line for entry can take quite a while. If you haven't made a reservation before you arrive, check the electronic sign outside entrance #2 that displays the current average wait time. If the wait is only 60-90min. and you have a good book or podcast with you, it's worth standing in line (don't worry if it seems like the line isn't moving very quickly—that's because they only let new batches of people in every 30min. or so). Going later in the day sometimes means that you'll encounter shorter lines, but make sure that the wait will still leave you at least two hours to tour the museum before it closes. And if you want to avoid all that stress entirely, you can make a reservation ahead of time; if you go this route, take your booking number to door #3 (across the piazzale from the main entrances) to retrieve your actual ticket and then proceed to door #1 (skipping all the non-reservation people waiting to enter through door #2). The Uffizi is large enough and its informational cards sparse enough that it is worth it to invest €6 in the audioguide (just make sure you bring a passport or driver's license, as you'll need to turn in some form of identification in order to rent out the guide).

i Right around the corner from P. della Signoria. €12.50, with reservation €16.50. ☒ Open Tu-Su 8:15am-6:50pm. Ticket office closes at 6:05pm, museum begins closing at 6:35pm.

THE BARGELLO
V. del Proconsolo 4

MUSEUM

☎055 23 88 606

A visit to the Bargello will require much less of your time than most other museums in Florence, and it will also demand a lot less of your money. For just a few euro, you can enter this palace and wander through one of the city's greatest collections of sculpture work and pieces by early Renaissance artists, including Brunelleschi and Ghiberti. While the inner courtyard is lined with impressive statues and coats of arms, some of the museum's most famous sculpture work is located upstairs. The largest and most impressive room here is the Salone di Donatello, which was inaugurated in 1886 on the 500th anniversary of the artist's birth and now houses several of his most celebrated statues. Watch as the Gothic influences of the early 15th century give way to the classically inspired stylings of the early Renaissance, a shift perfectly exemplified in Donatello's two statues of David. Downstairs, you can swing through another room of sculptures on your way out; this collection features statues from the later years of the Renaissance and includes four works by Michelangelo, including his *Apollo-David* and a decidedly tipsy Bacchus.

i From P. del Duomo, walk toward the river down V. del Proconsolo. Entrance to the museum is on the left. €4, reduced €2. ☒ Open daily 8:15am-4:50pm. Last entry 30min. before close. Closed 1st, 3rd, and 5th Monday and 2nd and 4th Sunday of each month.

PIAZZA DELLA SIGNORIA

PIAZZA

Known to most tourists as "that square with all the statues," Piazza della Signoria is home to a number of sculptures that you can see without having to pay any entrance fees or wait in any lines (imagine that!). You'll find most of these statues in the square's Loggia, which is home to Giambologna's impressive *Rape of the Sabine Women* and Benvenuto Cellini's *Perseus with the Head of Medusa*. Perhaps even more popular, however, is the square's famous statue of Poseidon, which is situated outside the Palazzo Vecchio just a few feet away from a reproduction of Michelangelo's *David* that stands in the exact spot where the original was once installed. You'll probably pass through this piazza without even trying to several times during your time in Florence, especially if you're planning to visit the palazzo, but try swinging by in the evening, when you can catch some live music in the square and see the statues all lit up at night.

i This is the main piazza north of the Uffizi. Free.

PALAZZO VECCHIO
P. della Signoria

PALACE

☎055 27 68 465

If you spent all morning and afternoon waiting in lines for the Uffizi and the Galleria, the good news is that you'll still have time in your day to visit the Palazzo Vecchio, which is one of the few museums in town that stays open after dark. The town hall of Florence, the Palazzo and its tower is the central fixture of Piazza della Signoria. Buy your tickets on the ground floor, drop your bags at the cloak room, and start your visit in the Tracce di Firenze where you can take a look at some paintings of Florence throughout the years, including some more contemporary ones depicting the damage inflicted on the city by WWII and the flood of 1966. After this brief visual history lesson, head upstairs

florence

to the rooms of the palace. Highlights include the Apartments of Leo X on the first floor and the Apartments of the Elements on the second floor; the floor plans of both levels line up perfectly, and the second-floor rooms dedicated to individual deities each correspond to a Medici family member whose room lies below (note, for example, how the Ceres Room is the room of Cosimo Il Vecchio—because just as Ceres provided for man by blessing him with the fruits of the earth, so did Cosimo bring prosperity to the city of Florence). Those Medicis and their God complexes, man. Farther along, the women of the Medici family get their due in the Apartments of Eleanor, which celebrate bad bitches like Esther, the Sabines, and Penelope of Ithaca. Don't miss the room covered floor to ceiling in gold lilies, and finish your tour with a trip up the tower, where you will find perhaps the least crowded stairs in Florence, along with a direct view of the Duomo.

i The huge building in P. della Signoria. Museum €10, reduced €8. Tower and battlements €10, reduced €8. Archaeological tour €4. Museum and tower combined ticket €14, reduced €12. ✆ Museum open Apr-Sept M-W 9am-11pm, Th 9am-2pm, F-Su 9am-11pm; Oct-Mar M-W 9am-7pm, Th 9am-2pm, F-Su 9am-7pm. Tower and battlements open Apr-Sept M-W 9am-9pm, Th 9am-2pm, F-Su 9am-9pm; Oct-Mar M-W 10am-5pm, Th 10am-2pm, F-Su 10am-5pm. Nighttime tour of the tower and battlements 9-10:30pm.

PONTE VECCHIO   BRIDGE

Try walking anywhere along the north side of the Arno, and you'll likely find yourself tangled up in throngs of tourists trying to capture a perfect selfie with this famous bridge. While the structure itself is impressive—it spans the narrowest section of the Arno river and is believed to have been first constructed by the Romans, although the current iteration dates back to the medieval period—what's less mesmerizing is the crush of tourist crowds that you'll encounter if you ever try to cross it. Where the bridge was once home to merchant stalls and butcher shops, it is now lined with gold shops and vendors selling everything from paintings to laser pointers. Still, the Ponte Vecchio is an iconic symbol of Florence and is the only bridge in the city to have survived the devastation of World War II and the Nazi occupation (according to local legend, the protection of the Ponte Vecchio was an express order from Hitler himself). Despite its history and enduring power, however, the bridge is still best seen and admired from afar.

i From the Uffizi, walk to the river and turn right. It's the bridge with all the shops on it.

Santa Maria Novella

🖼 MUSEO DI FERRAGAMO   MUSEUM
P. Santa Trinita 5r   ☎055 289 430 www.museoferragamo.it

If you can't afford any actual Ferragamo shoes and are too sweaty to even browse the store, you're still more than welcome to pay the €6 entrance fee to this museum (located in the basement of Palazzo Spini Feroni) and explore the history of Salvatore's much sought-after kicks. Each year, a different exhibit is featured in this museum, and you might be disappointed to find out that the majority of it has nothing to do with shoes. In 2015-16, the exhibit traced the history of the Palazzo Spini Feroni itself, and although the collections here are quite interesting and carefully curated, you came here to drool over heels you will never own. Fear not: regardless of the rest of the exhibition, the first couple rooms of the museum always focus on Ferragamo and feature shoes from his collection of dainty prototypes made throughout the first half of the 20th century. As you explore the delicate curves and decorative touches of these handmade shoes, you will gain a new appreciation for the true art that is good fashion. And if you're lucky, the museum might be displaying its collection of wooden casts used to make custom shoes for Ferragamo's most famous clients, including the likes of Ava Gardner, Audrey Hepburn, and Marilyn Monroe.

i Enter at P. Santa Trinita on the side of the building that faces away from the river. The museum is in the basement of Palazzo Spini Feroni. €6. ◷ Open daily 10am-7:30pm.

BASILICA DI SANTA MARIA NOVELLA CHURCH
P. Santa Maria Novella 18 ☎055 21 92 57 www.chiesasantamarianovella.it

Another gaping, white-walled Florentine church, the Basilica di Santa Maria Novella at least had the originality to add a little stripey pizazz to its ceiling. The huge frescoes covering the walls of the church's chapels also make up for its otherwise basic interior (you can even walk around the central chapel here and check out the intricate altar that features a miniature Duomo). For even more frescoes (in case you haven't had enough of those things), take a turn through the Chapter House and the Green Cloister, which also features scenic views of a lot of dead grass.

i From Santa Maria Novella train station, walk south through P. della Stazione and onto V. degli Avelli. The church is in P. Santa Maria Novella. €5, reduced €3.50. ◷ Open Apr-Oct M-Th 9am-7pm, F 11am-7pm; Nov-Mar M-Th 9am-5:30pm, F 11am-5:30pm.

San Lorenzo

▨ MEDICI CHAPEL CHAPEL
P. Madonna degli Aldobrandini 6 ☎055 238 86 02

The dome of this chapel is perhaps the second-most prominent in Florence's cityscape, but it's surprising how few tourists actually make it inside. Which is a shame because it's basically one giant vault of dead Medicis. Pass through security, and you'll find yourself right in the crypt of the building, where you can brush up on your Medici family tree and try to connect the dots between the artifacts on the walls and their owners buried in the ground below your feet. The real gem of the building, however, is the Chapel of Princes, whose decadent polychrome marble walls and semi-precious stone floor come in rich shades of greens, browns, blues, and maroon. In case you couldn't guess from the chapel's name (or from all the COSMVSes written in massive Latin letters on the walls), this extravagant mausoleum was constructed for the extra-special remains of the Medici grand dukes, six of whom are buried here in elaborate tombs that look kind of like giant bathtubs. After feasting your eyes on all this posthumous narcissism, finish your tour in the comparatively understated Sagrestia Nuova, whose white walls and Pantheon-esque dome were designed by Michelangelo (be sure to also take note of the artist's masterful sculptures of *Day and Night*, which adorn the tomb of Giuliano, the *Duke of Nemours*, on the right side of the room).

i Located just behind the Basilica di San Lorenzo. From the church, walk down P. di San Lorenzo and turn left onto V. del Canto de' Nelli. Entrance to the chapel is on the left. €8, reduced €4. ◷ Open daily 8:15am-5pm. Last entry 20min. before close. Closed on the 1st, 3rd, and 5th Monday and 2nd and 4th Sunday of each month.

BASILICA DI SAN LORENZO CHURCH
P. San Lorenzo 9 ☎055 21 66 34

First consecrated in 393 CE and later rebuilt during the 14th century, the Basilica di San Lorenzo was Florence's very first cathedral. It's also a pretty good place to start your sightseeing in the city. Not only will the white walls and slate-gray columns here introduce you to the restrained architecture and subdued aesthetics of many Florentine churches (a shocking contrast to the Baroque gluttony of Rome's basilicas), but the church also highlights the work of some of Florence's most celebrated artists: Brunelleschi's clean designs feature heavily here (although his sacristy is punctuated by flashier poly-

chrome contributions from Donatello, who is also buried in the crypt), while the Library of Cosimo Medici (also housed in this complex) was designed by none other than Michelangelo. You can either buy a ticket for just the church or for the church, library, and crypt; we recommend the latter ticket if you want to brush up on some of your Medici family history in addition to getting your prayer on.

i From the Duomo, walk up through P. San Giovanni (past the Baptistery) and turn right onto Borgo San Lorenzo. The church is on the left in P. San Lorenzo. €4.50, for basilica and library €7.50. ☉ Open M-Sa 10am-5pm, Su 1:30-5pm.

PALAZZO MEDICI RICCARDI PALACE
V. Cavour 1

Of all the Medici property in town (which is, admittedly, most of Florence), the Palazzo Medici Riccardi is probably the most skippable. That being said, if you have an extra 30min. in your day and a few euro in your pocket, take a swing through the palace where some of these ruling dukes actually lived. The highlights are the palace's central courtyard (which you can get a peek into from the street) and the beautiful Chapel of the Magi, whose colorful fresco is chock-full of Medici faces and looks like something straight out of a fairytale storybook.

i From P. di San Lorenzo, walk down V. Cavour. The palace is on the left; entrance is at V. Cavour 3. €7, reduced €4. ☉ Open M-Tu 9am-7pm, Th-Su 9am-7pm.

San Marco

GALLERIA DELL'ACCADEMIA MUSEUM
V. Ricasoli 58 ☎055 238 86 12 www.polomuseale.firenze.it

Visitors to Florence line up outside the Galleria dell'Accademia for hours to witness the glory of Italy's most famous Renaissance man (and his equally famous manhood). Michelangelo's *David*, however, is more than just the sum of his parts (although those parts are pretty impressive, too). There's a gravity and haunting magic to him that you'll get a taste of the moment you round the corner of the museum's introductory room and catch your very first glimpse of the world-famous statue standing in his own private tribuna at the end of a long gallery. For a slayer of giants, the 17 ft. *David* is a behemoth in his own right. Walk a little closer and gaze up his mammoth hands, his huge toe nails, and every curl of his giant head—then take a moment to consider the smaller details of this masterpiece, like the veins on *David*'s arms, the outlines of his ribs, and the dimple of a belly button in the ripple of his rock-hard abs. Indeed, it's hard to admire Michelangelo's unparalleled artistry without also taking time to admire *David*'s killer bod ("Holy V-lines, Batman!"). After you've circled the base of the statue and ogled his butt for a (dis)respectable amount of time, walk back through the gallery of Michelangelo's unfinished *Prisoners* statues and marvel at how *David*, like the slaves arrested in stone, was once little more than a vision trapped in a block of marble.

Besides Michelangelo's masterpiece, there's not a whole lot to the Galleria (your visit will likely not last more than an hour), although Giambologna's plaster for the *Rape of the Sabine Women* in the Sala del Colosseo is quite moving (the finished sculpture can be seen in Piazza della Signoria), and a room full of spotty busts down the hall from *David* once served as a 19th-century artists' workshop. The second floor is entirely 14th- and 15th-century religious altar pieces. Not to be outdone by the lesser biblical figure on the main floor, Jesus takes center stage here in a variety of ages, sizes, and poses (most of which are still "crucified"), as if to say, "Hey guys, I know David has a seriously hot bod, but I died for your sins, OK?" For all you heathens out there, this floor is pretty skippable.

i From P. del Duomo, walk down V. Ricasoli. Entrance to the museum is on the right; pick up reserved tickets at the office on the left. The length of the lines here, coupled with the relatively short amount of time you're likely to spend in the actual museum, make the Galleria a good place to splurge on a reservation. €8, with reservation €12. ☼ Open Tu-Su 8:15am-6:50pm. Ticket office closes at 6:20pm, museum begins closing at 6:40pm.

Santa Croce

GREAT SYNAGOGUE OF FLORENCE
V. Luigi Carlo Farini 6

SYNAGOGUE
☎055 234 66 54

Hozier may want to take you to church, but at this point in your trek through Italy, your own personal tune may have changed to something like "Please, God, don't take me to another church." So if you've had your fill of crucifixes, Madonna and Childs, and New Testament frescoes, seek out the Great Synagogue of Florence, whose oxidized copper dome stands out like a Gatsby-esque green light in a sea of Catholic churches and red Tuscan roofs. Constructed in the late 1800s, the synagogue's towering palm trees, pink pomato stone, and Moorish influences provide a welcome contrast to most of the church facades you've seen thus far. Inside, the synagogue takes on a different color scheme all together—the walls of the temple are entirely covered in hand-painted blue, red, and brown arabesques. Note the stars of David that adorn the tiled floor and, on the far right, the women's gallery, which is separated from the rest of the temple by a non-Beyoncé-approved partition. The beauty of the synagogue is even more remarkable when you consider that it was almost entirely lost during the German occupation of Italy during World War II, when the Fascists seized the synagogue and turned it into a garage, then rigged it with explosives during their evacuation of the city. The building remains standing thanks to the efforts of resistance fighters who were able to defuse most of the bombs. Even today, however, you can still see scars from Fascist bayonets on the doors of the Holy Ark. Don't miss a chance to get a closer look at the dome on the first floor of the museum upstairs; continue up one more floor to find a small and moving exhibit dedicated to the Jews of Florence who were murdered during the Holocaust.

i From P. del Duomo, walk down V. dell'Oriuolo, turn left onto Borgo Pinti, then right onto V. di Mezzo, left onto V. dei Pepi, right onto V. dei Pilastri, then left onto V. Luigi Carlo Farini. €6.50, reduced €5. ☼ Open June-Sept M-Th 10am-6:30pm, F 10am-5pm, Su 10am-6:30pm; Oct-May M-Th 10am-5:30pm, F 10am-3pm, Su 10am-5:30pm. Last entry 45min. before close.

BASILICA DI SANTA CROCE
P. Santa Croce 16

CHURCH
☎055 246 61 05 www.santacroceopera.it

At the Basilica di Santa Croce, it's never #toosoon to cash in on dead famous people. You'll find a lot of them here, and you'll have to drop a few euro if you want to see their final resting places. The walls of the cathedral are lined with a number of magnificent tombs, but it won't be too hard to spot the most famous ones (just look for the clusters of tourists huddled at various points along the perimeter of the church). Dante's tomb is massive (and, spoiler alert, contains no Dante—he rests in Ravenna), while Machiavelli's is a little less grand than you might expect for such a prince. The two most impressive tombs, however, are Michelangelo's and Galileo's (located on opposite sides of the nave near the front doors of the church). Both tombs feature polychrome marble and easily recognizable tributes to each titan: Michelangelo's is decorated with statues representing painting, sculpture, and architecture, as well as a bust of the artist himself, while Galileo's is adorned with a sculpture of the scientist with the world in his hand.

i Located on the far east end of P. di Santa Croce. €6, reduced €4. ☑ Open M-Sa 9:30am-5:30pm, Su 2-5:30pm. Last entry 30min. before close.

West Oltrarno

PALAZZO PITTI
P. de Pitti 1

PALACE

☎055 294 883 www.uffizi.firenze.it

The Palazzo Pitti certainly isn't shy about announcing itself—not only is the palace itself quite daunting in size, but the huge plaza out front will also give visitors plenty of time to admire the mammoth structure while they truck it across the bare expanse of asphalt on their way up to the ticket office. The palace, once the primary residence of the Grand Dukes of Tuscany and later a base used by Napoleon, now houses a number of museums and galleries: the Galleria Palatina, Galleria d'Arte Moderna, and Appartamenti Reali can all be visited by purchasing the palazzo's Ticket 1, while the Museo Degli Argenti, Galleria del Costume, and Museo della Porcellana are included in Ticket 2. The biggest draw of the palace complex, however, is actually its sprawling grounds, which comprise the enormous and beautiful Boboli Gardens. Entrance to the gardens is included in Ticket 2.

i Cross the Ponte Vecchio to Oltrarno and follow V. de' Guicciardini to P. de' Pitti. Ticket 1 €13, reduced €6.50. Ticket 2 €10, reduced €5. ☑ Open daily 8:15am-6:50pm. Last entry 45min. before close.

BOBOLI GARDENS
Palazzo Pitti

GARDENS

☎055 229 87 32 www.uffizi.firenze.it

Although there are a number of gates to the garden along its extensive perimeter, the easiest way to enter the Boboli Gardens is through the Palazzo Pitti (where you'll likely be purchasing your ticket anyway). From the courtyard of the palazzo, a left turn will lead you along a number of sunny paths and hedgerows; walk straight ahead, and you'll find yourself climbing up a set of steps to the central fountain of Neptune and some crisp brown lawns; continue farther up, and you'll reach the pretty gardens of the Porcelain Museum, which also provide some nice overlooks onto the surrounding Tuscan hills. Perhaps the nicest, shadiest paths of the park, however, are farther to the east (a right turn from the main entrance); here you'll find a number of green, canopied paths, hidden fountains and statues, and the garden's impressive, sloping Cypress Alley.

i Enter through Palazzo Pitti. €10 with Ticket 2. ☑ Open daily 8:15am-6:50pm. Last entry 45min. before close.

FORTE DI BELVEDERE
V. di San Leonardo 1

FORTRESS

For an incredible view of Florence from West Oltrarno that won't cost you €10 (looking at you, Boboli Gardens), hike your way up to Forte di Belvedere (where you can, quite literally, look down on the Boboli Gardens, as well as out over the entirety of the city). Constructed by order of the Medicis in the late 16th century, the fortress now hosts contemporary art exhibitions and the occasional celeb wedding (Kim + Kanye 4ever, y'all). Roam the grounds and walk around the fortress for views of the city and the Tuscan countryside in every direction.

i Cross the Ponte Vecchio to Oltrarno, then turn left onto V. de' Bardi. Veer right onto Costa dei' Magnoli and follow it uphill as it curves right becomes Costa San Giorgio. When the road forks, veer right onto V. del Forte di San Giorgio. Free.

florence

SANTA MARIA DEL CARMINE (BRANCACCI CHAPEL)
P. del Carmine

CHAPEL

☎055 21 23 31

The sole draw of the understated Santa Maria del Carmine, located in a quiet corner of West Oltrarno, is the church's famous Brancacci Chapel. It even acknowledges as much, roping off the entirety of the cathedral's beige interior save for the chapel and allowing visitors to enter this tight corner of the church through a single side door. Often regarded as the Sistine Chapel of the Early Renaissance, the Brancacci Chapel features a cycle of frescoes depicting stories from the life of St. Peter, including a depiction of the Temptation of Eve that you'll probably recognize from one of your high school history textbooks (you can check out the perpetuation of the "women ruin everything" trope on the far right wall).

i Cross Ponte alla Carraia to Oltrarno and continue straight along V. dei Serragli, then turn right onto V. Santa Monaca and follow it to P. del Carmine. €6, reduced €4.50. ☼ Open M 10am-5pm, W-Sa 10am-5pm, Su 1-5pm. Last entry 45min. before close.

East Oltrarno

▨ PIAZZALE MICHELANGELO

PANORAMA

Perched high above the city and across the river in East Oltrarno, this piazzale boasts some of the best views of Florence you're likely to find in the whole city. The only downside is that it's not exactly a well-kept secret. Throughout the day and well into the evening, tourists of all sorts make the long trek up the stairs to this square (the grade is gently sloping at first and then turns into flight upon flight of steps). Piazzale Michelangelo is particularly popular in the evenings, when countless tourists crowd along the edge of the square to watch the sun dip below the mountains. As night sets in, young people gather on the steps at the top of the square and listen to live musicians while nursing cheap bottles of beer and wine (you can either BYOB or purchase something from the bar or refreshment stands up here). Start trucking your way up here about 45min.-1hr. before sunset to get a good spot for the light show and the changing colors of Florence and the Arno at dusk. And if you can tear your eyes away from the cityscape for a moment or two, take note of the green David standing tall and proud in the center of the piazzale.

i From pretty much any bridge, bear east along the river until P. Giuseppe Poggi, where the base of the steps is located. If you're not wearing walking shoes, take bus #12 or 13. Free.

FOOD
The Duomo

MESOPOTAMIA

MIDDLE EASTERN $

P. Salvemini 14

This Mesopotamia is neither the cradle of human civilization nor the cradle of authentic Tuscan food. But everyone gets drunk sometimes, and this little kebab shop will do the trick when you get a case of the late-night drunchies. But if, fair reader, you fancy yourself a little classier than the Eurotrippers who stumble in here as late as 5am, Mesopotamia is also a nice place to stop for a quick lunch in the middle of a day of sightseeing (it's just down the street from the Duomo and professes to serve the best kebabs in Florence).

i Follow V. dell'Oriuolo from the southeast corner of P. del Duomo. Mesopotamia is on the left when the street opens onto a piazza. Kebabs €4-7.50. Falafel €4-5. ☼ Open daily 11am-5am.

italy

Piazza della Signoria

DA VINATTIERI
SANDWICHES $

V. Santa Margherita 4r   ☎055 29 47 03 www.davinattieri.it

The hot, toasted panini at Da Vinattieri get Let's Go's vote for the best sandwiches in the city. Located just down the road from Casa di Dante, this tiny shop just might be the ninth circle of Sandwich Heaven and is tucked far enough away from Piazza della Signoria that it escapes the crush of tourist crowds at more centrally located lunch spots. And with sandwiches ringing in at just €4 a pop, you won't be feeling salty about these prices—although you will be enjoying some sea salt sprinkled on Da Vinattieri's excellent, crusty bread. The long list of panini offered here includes options like lard, goat cheese, and walnuts and salami, gorgonzola, and sun-dried tomatoes.

i From P. della Signoria, walk down V. dei Magazzini (away from the river), turn right onto V. Dante Alighieri, then make a quick left onto V. Santa Margherita. Da Vinattieri is on the right. Sandwiches €4. Wine €3-6 per glass. ☒ Open daily 10am-5pm (although they stop serving sandwiches whenever they run out of bread).

'INO
SANDWICHES $

V. de' Georgofili 3   ☎055 21 92 08 www.inofirenze.com

What ends in "ino"? Panino and vino! Another great sandwich shop located near the Uffizi, 'Ino's paninis will run you a little bit more than your average lunch spot, but the high-quality ingredients and seating in the modern white interior here make the prices more than worth it. Paninis are hot and made to order, and 'Ino's crusty, floury bread is filled with thinly sliced meats and fresh cheeses. If you're having trouble deciding between options like the Anna (*salame rosa e pestato zucchine e zafferano*) and the Favoloso (*mortadella, gorgonzola e salsa Mediterranean*), you can always just go with their daily special. Pair your sandwich with some wine or lemonade and grab a seat at a table inside or along the counter (even during peak lunch hours, you can usually squeeze in somewhere).

i From the Uffizi, walk down V. Lambertesca and turn left onto V. de' Georgofili. 'Ino is on the right. Pay in exact change or with card. Panini €7-9. ☒ Open M-F noon-5pm, Sa-Su 11:30am-5pm.

PIZZERIA O'VESUVIO
PIZZA $

V. dei Cimatori 21r   ☎055 28 54 87 www.ovesuviofirenze.com

The only thing that might erupt here is your stomach, and if it does, it will be in the name of a worthy cause. O'Vesuvio serves up hot, perfectly thin Neapolitan pies out of the volcanic wood-fired oven in the middle of the restaurant, and you have the option to order your pizza with stuffed crust. And not the Domino's kind, either—these crusts come stuffed with creamy ricotta, which is pretty much what dreams are made of. And while the decor and ambience of this restaurant leave a little to be desired—what do some California Highway Patrol badges, a single *Scarface* poster, some soccer jerseys, and a lone hanging cluster of plastic grapes have in common, besides the fact that they're all here?—you'll probably be too distracted trying to finish your pizza to notice. (Yes, it will all fit in your stomach, so just keep going, and leave some room for the Nutella pizza dolce to top things off.)

i From P. della Signoria, walk down V. dei Calzaiuoli and turn right onto V. dei Cimatori. O'Vesuvio is on the right. Pizza €7-9.50. Calzones €6.50-9. ☒ Open daily 11:30am-4pm and 6:30-11:30pm.

ALL'ANTICO VINAIO
SANDWICHES $

V. dei Neri 74r   ☎055 238 27 23 www.allanticovinaio.com

All'Antico Vinaio isn't exactly a well-kept secret—the line of tourists here around lunchtime often rivals the one just around the corner at the Uffizi. But that's because the giant sandwiches here are so damn cheap—for just €5 euro, you'll get two floppy, floury pieces of focaccia stuffed with mozzarella, meat, and other fresh ingredients listed on the wall of this tiny sandwich shop. It's a good thing college parties taught you how to double fist like a pro because the giant square sandwiches here are so big you'll need to hold onto them with both hands. Order one of their popular panini (try the Summer Sandwich) or make your own. As the signs will remind you, "Don't mix meats! It's blasphemy!!" and "Don't mix cheeses, is not pizza!!" (Sure, the guys here are a little totalitarian about the whole sandwich-crafting thing, but if you're OK with your culinary creativity being stifled, All'Antico is worth it and knows what it's doing.)

i From the Uffizi, walk right down V. della Ninna and onto V. dei Neri. All'Antico is on the right. Panini €5. ☒ Open Tu-Sa 10am-4pm and 6-11pm, Su noon-8pm.

San Lorenzo

▓ FRUTTA SECCA (DRIED FRUIT AND NUTS)   MARKET $
Mercato Centrale

Your campfire gorp doesn't even come close to the kind of trail mix you could throw together at Frutta Secca. In addition to all your standard almonds, walnuts, peanuts, and cashews, this market stall of fruity dreams also has almost every variety of dried fruit you could think of: swing by and pick up some pineapple rings, banana chips, dried cherries, blueberries, or raspberries, or go out on a limb and throw in some ginger and dried kiwi into the mix. Just make sure your eyes aren't bigger than your pocketbook—the grams add up faster than you'd think.

i Located inside Mercato Centrale. From main entrance on V. dell'Ariento, turn left; the stall is in the far corner on the ground floor. Dried fruits €1-4 per 100g. Nuts €2-5 per 100g.

▓ TRATTORIA ZÀ ZÀ   ITALIAN $$
P. del Mercato Centrale 26r   ☎055 21 54 11 www.trattoriazaza.it

For some real, family-style Florentine cooking, head to Zà Zà in the square behind Mercato Centrale. The chairs, walls, and little dolls on the shelves here all pop with color, as do the Florentine-style dishes, the multitude of which might overwhelm you with the sheer number of options. Let us make it a little easier for you: order the Florentine steak and a nice glass of red wine. (If you're going to splurge on steak at any point during this trip—which you really should—this is a good and relatively affordable place to do just that, especially if you have friends with whom to split the 1kg+ of red meat.) This popular restaurant has seating in abundance—both on the sprawling patio and in the seemingly endless vaults of the interior—so you don't have to be too worried about snagging a spot here.

i Located behind Mercato Centrale. Look for all the patio seating. Antipasti €4-12. Primi €8-16. Secondi €9-23. Steak €38-44 per kg. ☒ Open daily 11am-11pm.

▓ L'BRINCELLO   ITALIAN $$
V. Nazionale 110   ☎055 28 26 45

The orange walls and rainbow-colored chairs of this osteria might remind you of an American Mexican restaurant, but the food at L'Brincello is authentic Florentine fare (you won't find any pizza on the menu here). Order one of the excellent pasta dishes (the gnocchi with sausage and gorgonzola is particularly rich and delicious), or really commit to the regional cuisine and try a deep red Tuscan steak. This restaurant doesn't get busy until much later in the evening, so if you arrive any time before 9pm, don't be surprised if it's just you and the couple guys hanging out behind the cash register. At least the many clusters of garlic cloves dangling from the ceiling will keep the vampires out.

i From the train station, walk down V. Nazionale several blocks. The osteria is on the right. Primi €9-18. Secondi €9-18. Dessert €5. ☒ Open daily noon-3pm and 7-11pm.

florence's secret bakeries

One reason to brave the wasteland that is Florence's clubbing scene is a chance to grab a 3am chocolate croissant from one of the city's "secret bakeries." Which aren't actually much of a secret among Florence's study abroad crowd. But that doesn't mean you shouldn't follow in the sorority girls' footsteps and make your way to one of the bakeries in town that will slip a few piping hot pastries to drunk travelers who stop by in the early hours of the morning (when the chefs are already awake and cooking up fresh batches of the day's baked goods). One such bakery is tucked into V. del Canto Rivolto; stop by around 2 or 3am, knock on the door, and slide a euro to the guy who answers it. Keep quiet and be respectful, and they should grant your requests for croissants, cannoli, or whatever else they happen to be baking up in the wee hours.

TRATTORIA MARIO ITALIAN $
V. Rosina 2r ☎055 21 85 50 www.trattoria-mario.com

Just because you can't see inside this restaurant doesn't mean it's a particularly hidden gem. Indeed, what's obscuring the front windows of this tiny but insanely popular lunch spot are all the "recommended by" stickers it has earned from countless critics and guidebooks over the years (including a few from yours truly). If you can even manage to open the door and push your way inside, you'll probably be looking at at least a little bit of a wait—fortunately, the traditional Tuscan dishes here are certainly worth the tight squeeze.

i Located behind Mercato Centrale (around the corner from Trattoria Zà Zà). Primi €5-6.50. Secondi €6.50-14. ☼ Open daily noon-3:30pm.

DA NERBONE ITALIAN $
Mercato Centrale

Amid the maze of meat counters and crates of fresh produce on the ground floor of Mercato Centrale sits Nerbone, a Florence institution since 1872. This permanent lunch stall serves up fresh pasta, risotto, and other specialities on ceramic plates that posted signs warn you not to take upstairs. Instead, place your order, grab a tray, collect your food, and find a seat at one of the marble tabletops just across from the counter. Enjoy your lunch amid the buzz and chatter of the market and under Nerbone's clusters of plastic hanging flowers.

i Located on the ground floor of Mercato Centrale. Look for its distinctive green wooden signs overhead. Panini €3.50-4. Primi €4. Secondi €7. ☼ Open M-Sa 7am-2pm.

ANTICA GELATERIA FIORENTINA GELATERIA $
V. Faenza 2A www.gelateriafiorentina.com

Piazza del Duomo is lined with plenty of either crappy or overpriced gelateria. Just a few blocks away, however, Antica Gelateria Fiorentina's cups and cones of creamy, high-quality gelato start at just €1.50. Try the deep, dark black chocolate ("a good choice," as the guy behind the counter will tell you) and park yourself outside on one of the wooden benches.

i Just around the corner from the Medici Chapel on V. Faenza. Gelato €1.50-5. ☼ Open daily noon-midnight.

florence

San Marco

ITIT IL SANDWICH CAFE
CAFE $

V. Cavour 45r
☎339 619 15 44

ITIT really wants you to review them on TripAdvisor (they appreciate every review—"especially 5 star reviews!"). And you might judge them for making their Wi-Fi password "tripadvisorplease" if you weren't so effing excited to find an Italian coffee shop with free working Wi-Fi, an abundance of outlets, and baristas who won't give you the stink eye if you pull out a laptop and decide to sit and work while finishing off your cup of Americano. They will definitely charge you for it—at ITIT, "for here" also means "that'll be an extra €0.50"—but at least they won't judge you openly. Grab a sandwich and order yourself an iced cappuccino, a latte macchiato, or something fun like the Shakerativo and settle in for a while.

i From the Duomo, walk down V. Cavour. The cafe is on the left. Drinks €1-4.50. ⏰ Open M-Sa 8am-8pm, Su 10am-8pm.

East Oltrarno

▨ GELATERIA LA STREGA NOCCIOLA
GELATERIA

V. de Bardi 51
☎055 238 2150 www.lastreganocciola.it

The best gelato in Florence is just a stone's throw from the Ponte Vecchio and flies shockingly under the radar. While tourists ogle the jewelry shops on the bridge and then wander starry-eyed into the overpriced gelaterias nearby, Strega Nocciola sits quietly by with its covered canisters of gelato waiting to be discovered by people in the know. With more exotic flavors like lavendar, blood orange, and Aztec (white chocolate cinnamon), along with classics like chocolate and pistachio, this is definitely the place to splurge on multiple scoops. If you vacillate long enough about how you will ever possibly decide, your scooper might even offer to let you sample a number of the options before you take your deep dive into an incredibly light and flavorful cup of Strega gelato.

i Cross the Ponte Vecchio and turn left onto V. de Bardi. Strega Nocciola is a few doors down on the right. Gelato €2.50-5. ⏰ Open M-F 11:30am-midnight, Sa-Su 11am-midnight.

I'PIZZACHIERE
PIZZA $

V. San Miniato 2
☎055 246 63 32

Sitting near the base of the long steps leading up to Piazzale Michelangelo, I'Pizzachiere is located right in the heart of East Oltrarno. It also really wants you to know that its Neapolitan pizzas are the real deal—just take a moment to read the broken English on the first page of the menu explaining why the pies here are awesome (or just wait until your pizza arrives and see for yourself). If you arrive early enough, grab a seat at one of the wooden tables outside and enjoy your bready, freshly made pizza while watching countless tourists pass by with wine bottles in hand on their way up to the piazzale. The cheese and toppings here are hot and gooey, so let your pizza sit for a few minutes before carving into it.

i Cross the Ponte alle Grazie over to Oltrarno, continue straight through P. de' Mozzi, then turn left onto V. di San Niccolo. Continue a ways until it curves right and turns into V. San Miniato. The pizzeria is on the right. Small pizzas €5.50-9.50. Big pizzas €10-16. Dessert €3.50-7. ⏰ Open 6-11:30pm (or whenever they "finish the mixture").

West Oltrarno

GUSTA PIZZA
PIZZA $

V. Maggio 46r
☎055 28 50 68

Some of the best pizza in Florence is also some of its most popular (who'd have thunk?). Come here around dinnertime, and you'll find this tiny pizzeria packed with tourists and buzzing with locals who drop by to pick up boxes of 'za to go.

chianti

You may have imbibed your fair share of red wine in college, but now that you're in Tuscany, it's time to swap out those boxes of Franzia for a more sophisticated bottle of Chianti. In addition to enjoying a nice glass with dinner every night, try to squeeze a wine tour into your visit to Florence, which is situated just north of the Chianti wine region that lies between the Florence and Siena. A visit to a winery and the vineyards of Chianti will not only give you a legitimate excuse to get tipsy in the afternoon but will also offer you a chance to see the beautiful Tuscan countryside that surrounds the city of Florence. A wine tour will also teach you how to sip vino like the classy broad that you aspire to be (hold that glass by the flute!) and recognize a nice bottle of Chianti (look for the black rooster and the DOCG label). If you're lucky, your tour will also include samples of aged cheese, balsamic vinegar, and grappa (a 60% alcohol Italian "digestive" that tastes something akin to gasoline). A popular and reliable company through which to book an afternoon in wine country is **My Tours**, which operates daily tours. (☎39 055 284770 www.mytours.it *i* Tours €42; include two tastings and transportation to and from Santa Maria Novella train station. ☼ Tours run 2:30-7:45pm) If you're interested in booking longer, fancier (read: more expensive) tours, book online or talk to your hostel or hotel for recommendations.

You won't find a lot of different varieties of pizza here, but that's because Gusta's pizza is so good that they don't need to get overly fancy with their toppings (stick to the classics and you'll do just fine). Crowd around the wooden barrels and glass tabletops inside if you can; alternatively, take your pizza to go and enjoy it from the steps of the Chiesa di Santo Spirito just down the road.

i From the Ponte Santa Trinita, walk straight down V. Maggio a few blocks. Pizza €4.50-8. ☼ Open Tu-Su 11:30am-3pm and 7-11pm.

OSTERIA SANTO SPIRITO
ITALIAN $

P. di Santo Spirito 16r ☎055 238 23 83 www.osteriasantospirito

For some excellent Tuscan fare in the quaint setting of Piazza Santo Spirito, wander across the river to this popular osteria in West Oltrarno. There are plenty of tables outside in the piazza, so have a seat on one of the pastel-colored chairs and people-watch while munching on bread served in a metal colander. The pastas here are excellent (we especially recommend the oven-baked gnocchi with truffle oil, which comes out hot enough to scald your fingers and your tongue). Dishes at this restaurant might be on the pricier side, but the good news is that you can order reduced portions of any primo for a few bucks less. (NB: Service can be pokey, so if it seems like your food is taking a while, don't be afraid to give your waitress a little nudge to help speed up the process.)

i From the Ponte Santa Trinita, walk through P. de' Frescobaldi and take a right onto V. di Santo Spirito, then a quick left onto V. del Presto di San Martino. Turn right into P. di Santo Spirito; the restaurant is in the corner of the piazza. Arrive early if you don't have a reservation. Antipasti €5-15. Primi €4-16. Secondi €8-25. Dessert €6. ☼ Open daily noon-11:30pm.

GELATERIA SANTA TRINITA
GELATERIA $

P. Frescobaldi 11/12r ☎055 238 11 30 www.gelateriasantatrinita.it

For thick, creamy, and cheap artisanal gelato, hop across the river to Oltrarno and Gelateria Santa Trinita. The rose-colored walls here may be a little brighter and warmer than the girl behind the counter, so take your gelato to go or step

florence

into the side room and eat it on a cushioned bench surrounded by bottles upon bottles of wine.

i Located just across the street from Ponte Santa Trinita in Oltrarno. Cones €2.50-8. Cups €1.90-6.90. ☉ Open daily 11am-midnight.

NIGHTLIFE

Despite its large population of study abroad students, Florence doesn't boast one of Italy's most bumpin' late-night scenes. At some point during your stay here, truck it up to Piazzale Michelangelo for drinks on the steps while watching the sunset. Piazza della Signoria is a good place to stop earlier in the evening for live music (enjoy a bottle of wine or two to the soundtrack of a live full-string orchestra). As the night wears on, the bars and streets surrounding Santa Croce and, on the other side of the Arno, Santo Spirito are generally Florence's most exciting nightlife spots.

▨ KING GRIZZLY BIRROTECA
BAR

P. dei Cimatori 5

For some really good draft beers or a wee dram of whiskey, seek out King Grizzly, which doesn't do much to announce itself on the corner of P. dei Cimatori. A rather small Irish bar, Grizzly manages to fit a few giant barrels into its dark wood interior, along with a collection of tables and barstools that line the floor-to-ceiling, open-air windows (which one might just call "no walls"). While a number of in-the-know Americans gather here for a pre-dinner drink, it's never overly crowded; if you really want to hang with the cool kids, head for the tiny back patio, where a number of Italians lounge about with pints and cigarettes.

i From P. della Signoria, walk down V. dei Calzaiuoli and turn right onto V. dei Cimatori. King Grizzly is in the corner of P. dei Cimatori, on the right. Beer from €3. Rum and whiskey €5-7. ☉ Open daily 6pm-2am.

▨ CAFFE SANT'AMBROGIO
BAR

P. Sant'Ambrogio 7r ☎055 247 72 77

On first glance, Caffe Sant'Ambrogio might just look like a collection of packed tables and chairs outside a pharmacy in an otherwise empty piazza. But the actual bar is there, too, just across the street. But if you're visiting Florence in the summer, you won't be spending much time in the sleek, blue-lit interior; instead, ask to be seated outside and settle in for a few drinks with the young travelers and Italians who flock here late into the evening. Alternatively, enjoy your drink and a cigarette on the steps of the Chiesa Sant'Ambrogio (we're pretty sure God won't judge you for it).

i The cafe is in the piazza at the end of V. Pietrapiana. Wine from €4. Mixed drinks from €6. ☉ Open daily 10:30am-2am. Aperitivo 6-9pm.

▨ RED GARTER
BAR

V. de' Benci 33r ☎055 248 09 09 www.redgarteritaly.com

If a sorority girl falls off the karaoke stage, but it's too loud in the bar for anyone to hear it, does she make a sound? The kids at Red Garter will never know, and everyone is probably too drunk to remember it in the morning anyway. But that's what makes the Red Garter the perfect place to let go of your inhibitions and bust out that karaoke rendition of "Party in the U.S.A." that you've had in your back pocket this whole trip. Full of young, English-speaking travelers and college students passing around pitchers of beer and mixed drinks, Red Garter is one of the best spots to have a decidedly non-local experience and turn up in Florence (because isn't that what #Eurotripping is really all about?). Crowd into a table downstairs, try to find a seat up on the balcony, or claim your rightful place up on the karaoke stage.

i From P. di Santa Croce, walk down V. de' Benci. Red Garter is on the right. Beer €4-6, pitchers €18-21. Cocktails €7.50, pitchers €36. ☉ Open M-Sa 4pm-4am, Su 11:30am-4am.

italy

LION'S FOUNTAIN

BAR

Borgo degli Albizi 34r   ☎055 234 44 12 www.thelionsfountain.com

In case you couldn't tell from all the "I <3 Lion's Fountain" signs everywhere, this bar really wants you to love it. And even if you may not fall head over heels for this fairly standard Irish pub, you will appreciate its wide variety of cheap drinks, its outdoor seating in a little piazza, and its free Wi-Fi. Sports fans in particular might even develop a little crush on its collection of large television screens, which broadcast football matches every day (check the schedule outside to see who's playing whom).

i From the back of the Duomo walk south down V. Proconsolo, then turn left onto Borgo degli Albizi. Lion's Fountain is near the end of the street, on the left. Beer €4-7. Cocktails €6-8. Whiskey €6.50. Shots €4. ☼ Open daily 10am-2:30am

MOYO

BAR

V. de' Benci 23   ☎055 247 97 38 www.moyo.it

Apparently, an elaborate chandelier hanging in the middle of the bar wasn't quite enough for Moyo, so they upped the ante and added a disco ball. While all the study abroad kids get plastered just a few doors down at the Red Garter, a more mature crowd gathers at Moyo to enjoy sophisticated cocktails on the patio. If the stylish decor and throbbing background beats here aren't too hip for you, settle in for a fancy drink and maybe even a few puffs of a hookah.

i From P. di Santa Croce, walk down V. de' Benci. Moyo is on the right. Cocktails €7-9. Shots €4. ☼ Open daily 8am-3am. Aperitivo 7-10:30pm.

DOLCE VITA

BAR

P. del Carmine 5   ☎055 28 45 95 www.dolcevitafirenze.it

Life really is sweet when you're sipping spritzers al fresco with a full view of the Chiesa di Santa Maria del Carmine just across the piazza. With a sleek white design both inside and out, throbbing, moody music, and bartenders in button-down shirts, Dolce Vita is a more grown-up option for aperitivo or late-night drinks in Florence. Come for the cocktails and stay for the sophisticated crowd and secluded setting in Piazza del Carmine.

i Cross Ponte alla Carraia and walk straight down P. Nazario Sauro, then turn right onto Borgo San Frediano and left into P. del Carmine. Dolce Vita is on the left side of the piazza when facing the church. Cocktails from €7. ☼ Open M-W 7pm-1:30am, Th-Sa 7pm-2am, Su 7pm-1:30am.

THE WILLIAM

BAR

V. Antonio Magliabechi 7/9/11/13   ☎055 263 83 57 www.thewilliampubflorence.com

For a more relaxed evening in Santa Croce, walk down the street from the church and grab a few pints at the William. While the bar has great deals on cocktails and shots, the real draw here is its extensive beer menu, which divides the numerous brews offered by country of origin. (NB: Belgium's Delirium Tremens is certainly a step up from the PBR you've been drinking at American frat parties.)

i From the steps of the Basilica di Santa Croce (facing the church), walk right down V. Antonio Magliabechi. The William is on the right. Beer from €3. Wine €3-7. Cocktails €5-7. Liquor €5-8. Shots €3-5. ☼ Open daily 11:30am-3am.

EASY LIVING

BAR

P. Poggi   ☎335 663 03 41 www.easylivingfirenze.it

Let's go to the beach—or at least to the banks of the Arno. At Easy Living, an outdoor bar and restaurant that overlooks the river in East Oltrarno, you can crowd in with fellow travelers and young Italians for aperitivo, provided you can find a seat amid the sea of packed plastic tables and chairs here. Alternatively, you can saddle up to the bar, grabs a few drinks, and find a place to perch on the ledge overlooking the river. The food here isn't anything to write home about, but the atmosphere is more than worth the trek—it's also a good place to land after you make your way down from watching the sunset up at Piazzale Michelangelo.

i Cross Ponte alle Grazie and turn left onto Lungarno Serristori. Easy Living is located along the river in P. Poggi. Drinks from €5. ☺ Open daily 10am-1:30am.

ESSENTIALS
Practicalities

- **TOURIST OFFICES:** Uffici Informazione Turistica (www.firenzeturismo.it) has its primary office at V. Manzoni 16. (☎055 23 320 ☺ Open M-F 9am-1pm.) Other locations include P. Stazione 4 (☎05 21 22 45 ☺ Open M-Sa 8:30am-7pm, Su 8:30am-2pm), V. Cavour 1r (☎055 29 08 32 ☺ Open M-Sa 8:15am-7:15pm, Su 8:30am-1:30pm), and Borgo Santa Croce 29r (☎055 23 40 444).

- **CURRENCY EXCHANGE:** There are a number of currency exchange points in and around P. del Duomo. Look for offices at the corner of V. Cavour and P. del Duomo and the corner of V. Roma and P. di San Giovanni. There are also a currency exchange offices on V. di San Lorenzo and V. dei Calzaiuoli.

- **ATMS:** BNL has locations at V. Giuseppe Giusti 2, V. dei Cerretani 28, and V. le Spartaco Lavagnini 27. You can also find ATMs on V. Cavour and in P. di San Lorenzo.

- **LUGGAGE STORAGE:** At Stazione di Santa Maria Novella. (Near platform 16 on the ground floor. 1st 5hr. €6, 6th-12th hr. €0.90 per hr., €0.40 per hr. thereafter. ☺ Open daily 6am-11pm.)

- **POST OFFICES:** Florence's main post office is located at V. Pellicceria 3, south of P. della Repubblica. (☎055 27 36 481 ☺ Open M-F 8:30am-7pm, Sa 8:30am-12:30pm.) There are additional post offices around town, including one office at V. Pietrapiana 53.

- **POSTAL CODE:** 50100

Emergency

- **EMERGENCY NUMBER:** ☎118

- **POLICE:** There is a police station at V. Pietrapiana 50r (In P. dei Ciompi ☎055 203911 ☺ Open M-F 8am-2pm). Urban Police Helpline is available 24hr. at ☎055 32 83 333. The emergency Carabinieri number is ☎112.

- **LATE-NIGHT PHARMACIES:** Farmacia Comunale. (P. Stazione Santa Maria Novella 13 ☎055 21 67 61 ☺ Open 24hr.) Farmacia Molteni. (V. dei Calzaiuoli 7r, just north of P. della Signoriav ☎055 215472 ☺ Open 24hr.)

- **HOSPITALS/MEDICAL SERVICES:** Ospedale Santa Maria Nuova is northeast of the Duomo and has a 24hr. emergency room (P. Santa Maria Nuova 1 ☎055 27 581). Tourist medical services can be found at Via Lorenzo II Magnifico 59, in the north of the city, near P. Liberta. (☎055 47 54 11 ☺ Open M-F 11am-noon and 5-6pm.)

Getting There

How you arrive in Florence will be dictated by where you come from. Florence may have named its Amerigo Vespucci airport after the guy who in turn gave the Americas their name, but that doesn't mean the city has any flights from the USA. Those flying across the Atlantic will have to transfer at another European airport. If flying from within Europe, it will probably be cheaper for you to fly into the budget-airline hub that is Pisa Airport. Buses run regularly from Pisa Airport to Florence; they take just over 1hr. and cost about €10. If coming from within Italy, you will most likely catch a train, which will bring you into Santa Maria Novella station. If traveling locally, buses may be useful.

By Plane

Aeroporto Amerigo Vespucci is Florence's main airport. (V. del Termine 11 ☎055 30 615 www.aeroporto.firenze.it) From the airport, the city can be reached via the VolainBus shuttle. You can pick up the shuttle on the Departures side. (Exit the airport to the right and pass the taxi stand. Dropoff is at Santa Maria Novella station. €6. 20-30min., every 30min. 6am-8:30pm and every hour 8:30-11:30pm.) A cab from the airport to the city center costs around €25.

By Train

Santa Maria Novella train station dominates the northwest of the city. (www.grandistazioni.it ☑ Open daily 6am-midnight.) You can purchase tickets from the fast ticket kiosks or from tellers. There are daily trains from Bologna (€19, 40min.), Milan (€44-55, 2hr.), Rome (€34-39, 1hr. 30min.), Siena (€9, 1hr. 45min.), and Venice (€39-45, 2hr.). For precise schedules and prices, check www.trenitalia.com.

By Bus

Three major intercity bus companies run out of Florence's bus station. From Santa Maria Novella train station, turn left onto V. Alamanni—the station is on the left by a long driveway. SITA (www.sitabus.it) runs buses to and from Siena, San Gimignano, Chianti, and other Tuscan destinations. LAZZI buses connect to Lucca, Pisa, and many other regional towns. CAP-COPIT (www.capautolinee.it) runs to regional towns. Timetables for all three companies change regularly, so check online for schedules.

Getting Around

The main thing you should know is that Florence is a small city. Most visitors simply walk everywhere without any need for public transportation. This is ideal for the budget traveler, as you won't rack up any metro or bus fares like you would in many other European cities. That being said, if you're looking to avoid the hike up to Piazzale Michelangelo or are planning to venture elsewhere outside the compact city center, Florence has got you covered.

By Bus

As the city's only form of public transportation, Florence's orange buses are surprisingly clean, reliable, and organized. Operated by ATAF and LI-NEA, the extensive bus network includes several night-owl buses that take over regular routes in the late evenings. The schedule for every passing line is posted on the pole of each well-marked bus stop, complete with the direction the bus is going and a list of every stop in order. Most buses originate at P. Stazione or P. San Marco. Buses #12 and #13 run to Ple. Michelangelo; bus #7 runs to Fiesole. You're unlikely to need to use the buses unless you're leaving the city center. You can buy tickets from most newsstands, ticket vending machines, *tabaccherie*, or the ATAF kiosk in P. Stazione (☎800 42 45 00; 90min. ticket €1.20). You can also sometimes buy tickets directly from the bus driver, but they cost more and there is no guarantee the driver will have tickets. Stamp your ticket when you board the bus; you then have the length of time denoted by the ticket to re-use it. Be careful—if you forget to time-stamp your ticket when you board the bus (and can't successfully play the "confused foreigner" card), it's a €50 fine.

By Taxi

To call a cab, call Radio Taxi (☎055 4390, ☎055 4499, ☎055 4242, or ☎055 4798). Tell the operator your location and when you want the cab and the nearest available care will be sent to you. Each cab has a rate card in full view, and the meter displays the running fare. If you're traveling far or are nervous, it never hurts to ask for an estimate before boarding. There are surcharges for Sundays, holidays, luggage, and late nights. Unless you have a lot of baggage, you probably won't want to take a taxi during the day, when traffic will make the meter tick up mercilessly. Nevertheless,

florence

top 5 foods to try in tuscany

Tuscany doesn't specialize in Pisa pizzas, so when you find yourself in the Italian Hillz, head for a local trattoria and try some of these regional specialties.

1. TORTELLI LUCCHESE. It may look like standard meat ravioli, but this egg-based pasta primi isn't your average Chef Boyardee. In addition to being served in a meat sauce, this pasta is also stuffed with even more meat and can be served in a variety of fashions. Try one of them at Anne e Leo (Lucca).

2. CECINA. Cecina is basically a chickpea pancake that's often served up in triangular, pizza-like slices. Hummus lovers will wonder why the hell they didn't think of this before. Give it a go at Pizzeria Il Montino (Pisa) or Pizzeria Da Felice (Lucca).

3. WILD BOAR. Siena doesn't mess around with hot dogs and lunchmeat and pulled pork. Instead, you'll find wild boar on the menu at pretty much every sandwich shop and restaurant in town.

4. BUCCELLATO. A Lucchese speciality, this lightly sweetened bread is made with currants and anise seeds and can be found at every bakery in town. Pick up a piece at Pasticceria Pasquinelli (Lucca).

5. WINE. You're in Italian wine country! So grab yourself a nice Chianti and some fava beans and enjoy.

cabs are a manageable late-night option if you're outside the city, and especially if you're in a group and can split the fare with friends. Designated cab stands can be found at P. Stazione, Fortezza da Basso, and P. della Repubblica. Cabs can also often be found at Santa Maria Novella and in P. del Duomo.

By Bike

It takes some confidence to bike in the crowded parts of central Florence, but cycling is a great way to check out a longer stretch of the Arno or to cover a lot of territory in one day. Bikes can be rented from Florence By Bike (V. San Zanobi 54r ☎055 488 992 www.florencebybike.it ☒ Open Apr-Oct M-F 9am-1pm and 3:30-7:30pm, Sa 9am-7pm, Su 9am-5pm; Nov-Mar M-Sa 9am-1pm and 3:30-7:30pm). The company rents out a range of bikes, including city bikes (€3 for 1hr., €9 for 5hr., €14 for 1 day) and mountain bikes (€4 for 1hr., €18 for 5hr., and €23 for 1 day) and also offers guided tours.

pisa

Given Pisa's rich ancient history and charming modern cityscape, it's almost a shame that this thriving university town is so thoroughly overshadowed by its slightly off-kilter tower. An important port city since the days of Ancient Rome, Pisa became a preeminent maritime capital and commercial center during the Middle Ages. Indeed, its medieval history is evident in its imposing city walls and the architecture of its central monuments in Piazza dei Miracoli (which have, collectively, been named an UNESCO World Heritage Site). And while the Arno River that bisects the city is no longer the central artery of Italian trade and commerce that it once was, it remains lined with the colorful pink, yellow, and orange pillbox buildings that are so characteristic of Pisa. Certainly, those who keep their visit to Pisa limited to a photocall with the Leaning Tower might leave the city convinced that it's little more than a stomping ground for flocks of tourists, but visitors who delve a little deeper will discover that Pisa is, in actuality, a college town. Once the site of studies by hometown hero Galileo, who attended the University of Pisa and allegedly used the Leaning Tower as a means of studying gravity, the city is today home to more than 50,000 students whose presence has resulted in a rather vibrant (if not raucous) collection of local eateries and late-night bars. So spend your morning in Pisa taking obligatory selfies with that cattywampus tower before heading south to the Arno and its surrounding streets to explore what else the city has to offer.

ORIENTATION

Although you'll likely arrive in Pisa via the train station, which is located on the south side of town, the city's most famous sights are located across the Arno River and farther north in P. dei Miracoli. Here you'll find the Duomo, the Battistero, Camposanto, and the famous (infamous?) Leaning Tower. You can approach this piazza and its sweep of shockingly green lawns along the wide, pedestrian V. Santa Maria, which is lined with a number of touristy restaurants and hotels. For better culinary options, veer off this well-beaten path to the charming P. dei Cavalieri and the winding, criss-crossed streets beyond. For after-dinner activities, look to the north shore of the Arno, just across from Ponte di Mezzo; here you'll find a lot of nightlife and restaurants centered around P. Garibaldi, Borgo Stretto, and the surrounding *piazze* and side streets. And once you've taken enough terrible pictures of yourself with the Leaning Tower, head to the riverfront and the little streets that run parallel and perpendicular to it; a walk along the water, criss-crossing bridges and wandering down adjacent alleyways, makes for a surprisingly beautiful and relaxing afternoon after a morning of more hardcore sightseeing.

ACCOMMODATIONS

🏨 HOSTEL PISA TOWER
HOSTEL $

V. Piave 4 ☎050 520 2454 www.hostelpisatower.it

From the random guitar in the living room to the faded flowery sheets in the dorms to the endless supply of Twinings tea in the kitchen, this place often feels more like a house than a hostel. And who knows, by the end of your short stay here, the nice people who run this place—including the guy at the front desk who might offer you apricots one afternoon and the white-haired man who'll ask you to turn off the lights in the living room whenever you decide to go to bed—just might feel like a weird little family. But if bonding with strangers isn't your thing, a) why are you traveling? and b) walk out the front door, and one look at the Leaning Tower looming over the city walls just down the road should be enough to convince you that this is a supremely convenient place to shack up for a night or two.

i From the monuments, walk east and turn left down V. San Ranierino. Walk through the archway and turn left onto V. Contessa Matilde, then right onto V. Piave at the traffic light. Hostel Pisa Tower is on the right. Breakfast not available, although there are vending machines and an espresso machine available for 24hr. use. Dorms from €23. ⚥ Check-in 2pm-12:30am. Check-out 10:30am.

HOTEL HELVETIA
HOTEL $

V. Don G. Boschi 31 ☎050 553 084

When you consider how close a bed here will position you to P. dei Miracoli, Hotel Helvetia's rates for single rooms are almost as mind-boggling as the physics of the Leaning Tower itself. Tucked around a corner just off V. Santa Maria, rooms here are basic but clean—and really, who cares about interior design when you're paying this little to sleep in a room where you're guaranteed to be the only person snoring? If the privacy and prime location weren't enough, the staff here is also very helpful and friendly. And although breakfast is not provid-

ed, there is a courtyard and common area whose painted walls will remind you to go see Pisa's Keith Haring mural at some point during your stay.

i From the monuments, walk down V. Santa Maria and turn left onto V. Collegio Ricci, then right onto V. Don G. Boschi. Singles with shared bath €45, with ensuite €54. Doubles with shared bath €54, with ensuite €64. ⏰ Reception 8:30am-midnight.

IL CAMPANILE BED AND BREAKFAST
P. Arcivescovado 15

B&B $$

☎050 563 040 www.ilcampanile.it

If you're willing to pay a few extra bucks to stay in the shadow of the Leaning Tower, blow your budget at Il Campanile. Because in addition to the ideal location, you'll also be paying for a stunning breakfast spread that gets wheeled up to your room on a tray every morning. (Remember when you thought about doing that for your mom on Mother's Day? Lucky for you, Il Campanile actually follows up on its shit.) And while this bed and breakfast isn't so swanky that you'll feel like actual royalty staying here, the surprisingly large rooms, marble foyer, and garden and gazebo area will at least have you feeling like a second cousin once removed (and for a pleb like you, that's pretty freakin' fancy).

i From the monuments, cross V. Santa Maria to P. Arcivescovado. Il Campanile is on the left side of the piazza. Doubles €70-75. Breakfast included. ⏰ Check-in 2pm. Check-out 10:30am.

SIGHTS

PIAZZA DEI MIRACOLI

PIAZZA

Most of Pisa's major sights are centered in the P. dei Miracoli (literally, the Square of Miracles), whose monuments include the Leaning Tower, the Duomo, Camposanto, and the Battistero. And while the tower is forever flooded with throngs of posers, the rest of the piazza and its clean, perfectly manicured grounds take on an almost university-like feel, with plenty of students and tourists seeking out patches of grass in the shade of the monuments or the city's walls. After the sun sets, groups continue to lounge and loiter on the lawns, while couples retreat to the crooks and crevices of the various monuments under the cover of night.

i Free. ⏰ Open 24hr.

LEANING TOWER

TOWER

You may have seen the Leaning Tower on hundreds of pizza boxes throughout your life, but nothing quite compares to seeing it in its pearly marble flesh, looming over the buildings and walls of Pisa in its charmingly off-kilter way. Indeed, the tower's famous, fantastic tilt is a marvel that might have you wishing you had brought your protractor to Italy (or at least wishing you remembered how to use a protractor). Fun fact: the Leaning Tower is also the site of the highest incidents of accidental photobombing in the world—walking around the tower, you will be ruining or in the background of somebody else's cheesy photo at pretty much any given moment. And although this tower may be the tipsiest in Italy, it hasn't quite reached the point of falling-down-drunk, which means you can climb it if you so desire. Just keep in mind that scaling these slanted, slippery steps is likely the most expensive thing you'll do in Pisa (it'll run you €18 and requires a reservation that you can make at the ticket office), while a corny picture outside the tower is priceless in more ways than one.

i P. dei Miracoli. Just follow the crowds. Reservations to climb the tower must be made in advance. Steps are narrow and slippery, and those under the age of 18 must be accompanied by an adult. €18. ⏰ Open daily Apr-Sept 8am-8pm; Oct 9am-7pm; Nov-Feb 10am-5pm; Mar 9am-6pm. Last entry 30min. before close.

CAMPOSANTO

CEMETERY

It is perhaps fitting that this quiet, relatively empty cemetery is the least visited of the monuments in P. dei Miracoli. The wide, rectangular hallways of the structure are lined with tombs (both on the walls and underfoot) and form the perimeter of a grassy central courtyard. Apart from the occasional tomb that protrudes from the ground (watch where you're walking), the most interesting parts of Camposanto are the faded frescoes that cover its walls; be sure to stop in and see the room that explains their history and long process of restoration, which was at one point severely jeopardized by the Nazis during World War II.

i *P. dei Miracoli. Camposanto is behind the cathedral. €5. Combined ticket with 1 other monument/Museo delle Sinopie 7. Combined ticket with 2 other monuments/Museo delle Sinopie €8.* ☎ *Open daily Apr-Sept 8am-8pm; Oct 9am-7pm; Nov-Feb 10am-5pm; Mar 9am-6pm. Last entry 30min. before close.*

BATTISTERO   BAPTISTERY

We would nominate Pisa's Battistero as the actual best-looking monument in Piazza dei Miracoli. If you take a second to tear your eyes away from the Leaning Tower, let them come to rest on this bulbous little baptistery. Constructed in 1152, the marble structure looks almost like the dome of a great cathedral, minus the actual church (because everyone knows that, just like muffins, the best part of a church is the top). And although the Battistero's interior is a little plain, its circular geometry makes for perfect acoustics. Be sure to stop inside and catch a demonstration of the building's flawless resonance once every 30min., when a guard closes all the doors, orders everyone to shut the hell up, and sings a few long notes that continue to reverberate and echo throughout the Battistero for the next several minutes. The guards themselves are pretty nonchalant about the whole thing, but the lingering echoes of the simple song are quite beautiful and haunting for visitors.

i *P. dei Miracoli. €5. Combined ticket with 1 other monument/Museo delle Sinopie €7. Combined ticket with 2 other monuments/Museo delle Sinopie €8.* ☎ *Open daily Apr-Sept 8am-8pm; Oct 9am-7pm; Nov-Feb 10am-5pm; Mar 9am-6pm. Last entry 30min. before close.*

DUOMO   CHURCH

If you're quickly approaching the "every goddamn church looks the same" quota of your Italian sojourn, Pisa's Duomo just might push you past your breaking point. While its interior houses some richly colored Renaissance paintings and its altar offers a large, lively depiction of Jesus that might catch your eye, the rest of the cathedral is the same massive columns, gilded ceilings, and antiquated "cover those blasphemous bare shoulders" rules that you'll find in most other churches in Italy. That being said, entry is free, so you really should take a turn through the Duomo's shady interior at some point between photo ops with the tower outside. The most impressive views of the church, however, are really from outside; stand back and admire its intricate and impressive facade, which, when paired with the complementary white exteriors of the Leaning Tower, the Battistero, and Camposanto, is truly stunning against the backdrop of the verdant, manicured lawns of P. dei Miracoli.

i *P. dei Miracoli. Free.* ☎ *Open daily Apr-Sept 10am-8pm; Oct 10am-7pm; Nov-Feb 10am-5pm; Mar 10am-6pm. Last entry 30min. before close.*

MUSEO DELLE SINOPIE   MUSEUM

There's not a whole lot to see at the Museo delle Sinopie besides some faded biblical frescoes, a little bit of the history of P. dei Miracoli, and a 3D virtual tour of the monuments that looks like it was made sometime in the late '90s. Still, entry to the museum is included in most tickets for the monuments, so take a pass through here whenever you find yourself most in need a spot of A/C in the middle of your day of sightseeing. And depending on the exhibit, the contemporary art displayed on the second level might be worth a visit.

i *Located on the south end of P. dei Miracoli, across from the lawns. €5. Combined ticket with 1 other monument €7. Combined ticket with 2 other monuments €8.* ☎ *Open daily Apr-Sept 8am-8pm; Oct 9am-7pm; Nov-Feb 10am-5pm; Mar 9am-6pm. Last entry 30min. before close.*

GIARDINO SCOTTO
Lungarno Leonardo Fibonacci

GARDEN
☎050 910 111

For a little green space free of leaning tourists, stroll east down the Arno and take a turn through the Giardino Scotto, a local park where you'll find some shady paths, park benches, playground equipment, and palm trees, along with the occasional amorous couple finding a little splendor in the grass. Enclosed on one side by some old Roman walls, the park is now home to more modern attractions, like a permanent outdoor movie theater and some in-ground trampolines that you're definitely too old to jump on.

i Located on the south side of the Arno, across from Ponte della Fortezza. Free. ☼ Open daily May-June 9am-8pm, July-Aug 8am-8:30pm, Sept 9am-8pm, Oct 9am-7pm, Nov-Jan 9:30am-4:30pm, Feb-Mar 9am-6pm, Apr 9am-7pm.

ORTO BOTANICO DI PISA
V. Luca Ghini 5

GARDEN
☎050 221 1310 www.biologia.unipi.it/ortobotanico

There's not much to this botanical garden that you haven't already seen, but there's also not much in the way of an entrance fee, so for a quick return to nature, have a stroll through the garden's palm trees, around its lilypad-covered fish pond, and between its impressive thickets of bamboo. We would say have a seat and enjoy the shade of the trees for a while, but the mosquitoes here will probably suck you dry before your bum hits the park bench.

i From the monuments, walk down V. Santa Maria and turn right onto V. Luca Ghini. The entrance to the gardens is through the building on the left. €2.50, reduced €1.50. ☼ Open M-F 8:30am-5:30pm, Sa 8:30am-1pm.

FOOD

PIZZERIA IL MONTINO
Vicolo del Monte 1

PIZZA $
☎050 598 695 www.pizzeriailmontino.com

Il Montino occupies a little street all to itself, which can make it a bit hard to find, so just look for the neon signs perched high up on either corner of the restaurant. Below them, you'll find a collection of tourists who have done their research and zig-zagged over here for the best piece of Pisa in pizza. Or something like that. The cheese practically drips off these hot, fresh pies when they land on your table, and the subtle crunch of the thick crust adds nice contrast to the gooier toppings. If you're eating outside at one of the many wooden tables, you might find yourself squished in side-by-side with your neighbors—but just think of it as an opportunity to make some new friends and salivate over all the other varieties of pizza you couldn't order in one go. Do yourself a favor and order the *torta di ceci*—it's a little chickpea pie that's one of Il Montino's specialities.

i Pizza €5.50-8. Torta di ceci €1.50. ☼ Open M-Sa 10:30am-3pm and 5:30-10:30pm.

ANTICA TRATTORIA IL CAMPANO
V. Domenico Cavalca 19

ITALIAN $$
☎050 580 585 www.ilcampano.com

You might have heard a thing or two about Pisa pizza, but for some genuinely authentic regional cuisine, stop by Trattoria Il Campano. The waiters here don't speak much English, and you won't find any pizza on the menu, but that's how you know you're in for a real deal Tuscan meal. Order some of the fresh pasta and indulge in the simple, understated flavors of the local specialties. The lunch and dinner menu might be a little more than you're used to spending, but if you're planning to indulge anywhere in Pisa, it should be here (and not, let's be honest, on the €18 that it costs to climb the Leaning Tower). Sit outside against the brick walls of this secluded restaurant and enjoy a late lunch under a dark canopy of hanging plants.

i Antipasti €5-10. Primi €7-9. Secondi €15-18. Light lunch menu €15. Dinner menu €30. ☼ Open M-Tu 12:30-3pm and 7:30-10:45pm, Th 7:30-10:45pm, F-Su 12:30-3pm and 7:30-10:45pm.

pisa

FILTER COFFEE HOUSE
COFFEEHOUSE $

V. Santa Maria 47 ☎349 648 3414 www.filtercoffeelab.com

Were you starting to forget what iced coffee in a giant, disposable cup looked like? Lucky for you, Filter is here to fill that Venti-sized Starbucks hole in your life. Primarily serving Pisa's student population, Filter looks like it could have been imported straight from Seattle (modern industrial decor, barista nose rings, and all). The only difference is that there are no green straws, and the coffee here is actually a lot better than the corporate stuff you're used to. Still, Filter's menu is populated with plenty of recognizable favorites, including iced lattes, flat whites, and macchiatos, along with the rare sight of (could it be?) Italians sitting and lingering with with their caffeinated drinks. Sit down and study for a while, or order your croissant and coffee to go. Because you can, dammit—walk around with that sucker all day! Or at least until all the ice melts in the unreal summer heat (the plastic cup might make you feel like an American, but you're still very much in Tuscany).

i *From the monuments, walk down V. Santa Maria; Filter is on the right. Drinks €2-4. Pastries €1-3.* ⏰ *Open M-F 7:30am-6pm, Su 8:30am-6pm.*

PIZZERIA LE MURA
PIZZA $

Largo del Parlascio 33/34 ☎393 225 7773 www.pizzerialemura-pisa.it

For a simple and satisfying slice of pizza near the Leaning Tower, head down to Pizzeria Le Mura, where Mrs. Elena and her family have been serving up hot, fresh, bready pies for more than 40 years. Cute little instructions on walls and the menu will show you how to order (spoiler alert: order your pizza at the counter, then grab a seat either inside in the A/C or outside on the patio and wait for your food to arrive). The charming cartoons of Mrs. Elena and her beloved pizza oven are almost as charming as Elena herself, whom you'll find behind the counter, still running the show more than four decades after she rolled her first dough.

i *From the monuments, walk down V. Cardinale Maffi Pietro to Largo del Parlascio. Le Mura is on the right. Pizzas €5-12. Individual slices also available.* ⏰ *Open for lunch and dinner Tu-Su.*

LA BOTTEGA DEL GELATO
GELATERIA

P. Garibaldi ☎050 575 467

Plopped down just north of the river in P. Garibaldi, La Bottega Del Gelato serves up smooth, creamy gelato at all hours of the day, making it a perfect spot for a mid-afternoon pick-me-up or a late-night treat (or both, let's be honest). With its flavors listed outside, La Bottega gives you some time to contemplate your flavor choices before you get up to the crowded counter. The gelateria has a few tables outside, but there's also seating under the statue in the center of the piazza; you could also take your gelato for a nice little walk along the Arno, but then again, that would be healthy and unnecessarily aerobic, so maybe not.

i *On the west side of P. Garibaldi, across the street from Ponte di Mezzo. Gelato €1.50-3.* ⏰ *Open daily 11am-1am.*

PANINERIA L'OSTELLINO
SANDWICHES $

P. Cavallotti 1 ☎050 00 000 www.lostellinopisa.com

For a fast lunch just down the road from the Leaning Tower, this panineria does the job. In case you couldn't tell from all the pigs and pork paraphernalia cluttering up the walls, you should probably order a sandwich that features L'Ostellino's special Tuscan ham. You also can't go wrong with some of the spicy salami or any of the many cheeses here. Sandwiches are served on thick, crunchy bread and wrapped in yellow paper, so if you can't grab a spot at one of the handful of tables in the tiny interior, you can always walk back down the road to Piazza del Duomo and pop a squat in the shade outside the cathedral.

i *From the monuments, walk down V. Santa Maria and turn left onto P. Cavallotti. The panineria is on the left. Sandwiches €3.50-5.50.* ⏰ *Open daily noon-10pm.*

NIGHTLIFE

BAZEEL
BAR

Lungarno Pacinotti 1   ☎340 288 1113 www.bazeel.it

You may not fully realize the meaning of a crowd "spilling into the street" until you come to Bazeel during aperitivo. Indeed, the throngs that gather here for cheap drinks and a buffet of fried finger food certainly spill (and in more than just the "sorry my wine is now all over your shirt" sense). As the evening progresses, young folks pour out the doors of the bar, into p. Garibaldi next door, and all the way across the street, where they sit along the walls of the Arno with drinks and cigarettes in hand. Maybe it's because they're not into the cat videos being projected onto the back wall of the bar's large, open interior, or maybe it's just that Bazeel offers so much outdoor seating that it's hard to resist frozen cocktails outside on a warm summer night.

i *On the west side of P. Garibaldi, across the street from Ponte ai Mezzo. Beer €3-6. Wine €3.50. Cocktails €5.50. Frozen cocktails €6.50. ☺ Open M-Th 7:30am-1am, F-Sa 7:30am-2am, Su 8am-1am. Aperitivo 7-9:30pm.*

SUD
BAR

V. delle Case Dipinte 21/23   ☎347 889 0864 www.senzaunadirezione.it

Sud is a hip and happening little gem that's particularly popular with 20-somethings looking for a good deal on aperitivo. And while the name might imply that this place is primarily for foamy suds-lovers, you might consider skipping your standard beer for a taste of one of the bar's many varieties of Italian liqueurs. (Or do both and just remember that beer before liquor, never sicker...or is it beer after liquor? Either way, you're young and don't get really bad hangovers yet, so just dive in.) Order through the walk-up window outside (it's like a drive thru without the cars!) and try to land a seat under one of the umbrellas or squeeze in on the wooden benches near the front door.

i *From P. Garibaldi, walk down Borgo Stretto and turn right onto V. Mercanti, then left onto V. delle Case Dipinte. Sud is on the left. Drinks €1-4.50. Panini €4. ☺ Open M-Th 7pm-12:45am, F-Sa 7pm-1:45am, Su 7pm-12:45am. Aperitivo 7-9pm.*

ORZO BRUNO
BAR

V. delle Case Dipinte 6   ☎050 578 802 www.orzobruno.it

Beers lovers can't do much better than Orzo Bruno, whose yellow walls and cartoons of beer pints painted on its glass windows help it stand out from the crowd of other bars along V. delle Case Dipinte. Wooden blocks on the walls provide the details of the many varieties of beer you can sample here, which will delight connoisseurs and overwhelm and confound college students who thought a Corona with lime was the apex of the fermented yeast experience. The crowd here is a little older, but grab a spot at one of the many dark wood tables and relax with a pint while staring out the floor-to-ceiling glass windows at all the youths drinking spritzers and shitty beer across the street.

i *From P. Garibaldi, walk down Borgo Stretto and turn right onto V. Mercanti, then left onto V. delle Case Dipinte. Orzo Bruno is on the right. Beer €3-4. Cocktails €4.50. Whiskey and rum €4-6. Bruschetta €3. Panini €4.50-5.50. ☺ Open M-Th 7pm-1am, F-Sa 7pm-2am, Su 7pm-1am.*

ESSENTIALS

Practicalities

- **TOURIST OFFICES:** The office in P. Vittorio Emanuele II provides maps, an events calendar, and other assistance (P. Vittorio Emanuele II 16 ☎050 42 291 www.pisaunicaterra.it ☺ Open daily 10am-1pm and 2-4pm.). Second office in Piazza del Duomo (☎050 550100 www.pisaunicaterra.it ☺ Open daily 9:30am-5:30pm.).

- **ATMS:** To withdraw cash near the monuments, there are two ATMs on V. Santa Maria next to the Hotel Duomo, as well as other cash machines around town.

- **LUGGAGE STORAGE:** In the train station. At the left end of Binario 1.

- **POST OFFICES:** P. Vittorio Emanuele II 7/9, on the right side of the *piazza* (☎050 51 95 14 ☒ Open M-Sa 8:15am-7pm.).

- **POSTAL CODE:** 56100

Emergency

- **POLICE:** Polizia Municipale (V. Cesare Battisti 71/72 ☎050 91 01 11).

- **LATE-NIGHT PHARMACIES:** Lungarno Mediceo 51. On the north shore of the river, so the east (☎050 54 40 02 ☒ Open 24hr.).

- **HOSPITALS/MEDICAL SERVICES:** Santa Chiara. V. Roma 67, near P. dei Miracoli; entrance is adjacent to V. Bonanno Pisano (☎050 99 21 11).

Getting There

By Plane

Galileo Galilei Airport (☎050 84 93 00 www.pisa-airport.com) is practically within walking distance of the city, but the train shuttle takes only 5min. The shuttle arrives at platform 14 in Pisa Centrale (€1.10). The airport is a major budget airline hub for all of Tuscany, including Florence. Apart from a few flights to Morocco and northern Africa, no intercontinental flights serve Galileo Galilei, but you can fly directly to Pisa from most European cities.

By Train

Pisa Centrale will be your main port of entry from other Italian destinations (P. della Stazione, South of P. Vittorio Emanuele II ☎050 41 385 ☒ Ticket office open 6am-9pm, but there is always a long line; check out the 24hr. self-service machines.) Trains run to and from Florence (€9, 1hr. 15min.), Rome (€30-50, 3hr.), and Lucca (€4, 30min.). If leaving from San Rossore, Pisa's secondary station is in the northwest part of town; buy tickets at a local *tabaccheria*.

By Bus

SITA (☎043 62 28 048 www.sitabus.it) and Terravision (☎44 68 94 239 www.terravision.eu) run buses betweens Pisa's airport and Florence, while Lassi (☎058 35 84 876 www.lazzi.it) and CPT (☎050 50 55 11 www.cpt.pisa) run buses that leave from and arrive in P. Sant'Antonio. Buses leave from Florence's Santa Maria Novella bus station. (From the train station, take a left onto V. Alamanni; the station is on the left by a long driveway. €10, 1hr. 15min.) Buses to Lucca leave from Pisa Airport and run to and from P. Giuseppe Verdi in Lucca (30min.).

Getting Around

On Foot

There's little need for anything but your feet while you're in Pisa. From the train station to P. dei Miracoli—the longest diameter of the city and also the route you're most likely to take—is about a 20-25min. walk.

By Bus

LAM Rossa runs a loop between the airport, train station, tower, and several other points in Pisa every 20min. Most buses stop at P. Sant'Antonio, just west of P. Vittorio Emanuele II. You can purchase bus tickets (€1 for 1hr.) at a *tabaccheria* or at ticket machines at Pisa Centrale and Galileo Galilei Airport.

lucca

On the train ride into Lucca, watch as the hills of Tuscany give way to full-fledged mountains. Nestled within the green folds of these rising slopes lies Lucca, a closely guarded pocket of meandering streets where foot travelers roam and bikers pedal around with baskets on their handlebars, while most cars and motorized vehicles keep to the busier streets outside the city's ancient walls. While no one attraction in particular draws visitors to Lucca, its cumulative collection of churches, bell towers, trattorias, and shops that sell everything from ceramics to stilettos make it a relaxed and thoroughly charming retreat from the camera phones, selfie sticks, and Leaning Tower key chains that taint other popular Tuscan destinations. The city's famous walls are in themselves a worthwhile destination—for while they now form an infinite park stretching 4.2km around the old city and have become a site of recreation and relaxation for locals and tourists alike, they also stand as testament to Lucca's centuries-old history. So grab a bike and storm the walls—this is Tuscan vacationing at its finest and most breezy.

ORIENTATION

Lucca is small and (literally) contained enough that you can make your way around the city center quite easily on foot. From the train station south of the city walls, you can reach the center by making your way through Porta San Pietro. From here, P. Nazionale and P. San Michele, two of the city's major squares, are both situated along the busy V. Vittorio Veneto, where you'll also find many of the city's bars and eateries. To the east, the very commercial, shop-lined avenue that is Via Fillungo runs north to P. Anfiteatro, an elliptical plaza that was once the site of a Roman amphitheater and is now home to a number of bars and restaurants. Walk far enough in any direction and you'll hit the city's famous walls; there are paths and steps leading up to the elevated park at various points along the perimeter of the city center.

ACCOMMODATIONS

HOSTEL SAN FREDIANO
HOSTEL $

V. della Cavallerizza 12   ☎0583 48 477 www.ostellolucca.it

The wide stairways, gaping ceilings, and gilded mirrors at Hostel San Frediano don't feel very hostel-y, although the hallways' many posters of other popular international destinations will remind you that you are, in fact, staying at a Hostelling International establishment (they'll also remind you, for better or for worse, of all the other places you could be right now). Still, the many couples and families staying in the private rooms here give this place the atmosphere of a sprawling hotel. What the hostel does have to offer its more youthful guests are common areas in abundance: from a downstairs lounge filled with beanbags to a room of tables and chairs to another one lined with floral couches, you won't have any trouble finding a place to hunker down and chill for a while. Just down the road from P. San Frediano, the hostel is centrally located and also offers quick access to the north side of the city walls, in case you're interested in a little morning exercise (or watching other people partake in morning exercise while you eat your breakfast from the sedentary comfort of the hostel's back garden).

i Walking north down V. Fillungo, turn left into P. San Frediano, then right down V. della Cavallerizza. The hostel is on the left. Dorms from €26. ☾ Reception 24hr.

ALBERGO LA LUNA
HOTEL $$

V. Fillungo, Corte Compagni 12   ☎0583 493 634 www.hotellaluna.com

Step out the doors of Albergo La Luna, and you'll find yourself right in the thick of Lucca's crowds, street vendors, and abundant al fresco restaurant seating. Just off the main thoroughfare that is V. Fillungo, this hotel certainly boasts

lucca

prime real estate, although its winding staircases and quiet, cozy rooms will still give you the feeling of being tucked away from the busy-ness of the outside world. With wood-beamed ceilings and floral bedspreads, rooms here are quaint and comfy, while the breakfast spread downstairs will have you feeling like a queen. Reception is friendly and helpful and offers such services as bike rental from the comfort of your hotel.

i *Just off V. Fillungo in Corte Compagni (on the right when walking north). Singles €70. Doubles €80-120.* ☺ *Reception 24hr.*

ALBERGO SAN MARTINO
HOTEL $$
V. della Dogana 9 ☎0583 469 181 www.albergosanmartino.it

Hidden just around the corner from the Lucca Cathedral and tucked between the yellow walls of a secluded alleyway, Albergo San Martino offers an ideal combination of prime location and quiet retreat. Moreover, its rooms are large and bright, with colorful paintings on the walls and long, airy windows, while the crocheted blanket on the couch outside reception and the round wicker chairs on the patio add touches of homey comfort to this otherwise slick, impeccably run hotel.

i *From the Lucca Cathedral, walk down V. Duomo and turn left onto V. del Molinetto, then right onto V. della Dogana. The hotel is around the corner. Rooms in hotel from €80. Rooms in annex from €70.* ☺ *Reception 7am-11pm.*

HOTEL DIANA
HOTEL $$
V. del Molinetto 11 ☎0583 492 202 www.albergosanmartino.it

Owned by the same people who run Albergo San Martino, Hotel Diana makes for a slightly edgier, more modern hotel experience. Or at least more colorful: rooms here come in shades of red, purple, lime green, and gray, and although breakfast is not provided, beds here will run you about €20 less than the rooms on the other side of the alley at San Martino.

i *From the Lucca Cathedral, walk down V. Duomo and turn left onto V. del Molinetto. Hotel Diana is on the right. Rooms from €60.* ☺ *Reception 7am-11pm.*

SIGHTS

THE WALLS
CITY WALLS

Lucca's city walls are kind of like the Wall from *Game of Thrones*—just replace the snow with sunshine and all the sad bastards with happy bikers. Comprising a 4.2km loop that encompasses Lucca's city center, the walls date back to the third century CE (although the current iteration was completed in the 1600s) and now form one continuous park around the city where locals and tourists alike picnic, jog, bike, and loiter. A nice contrast to the meandering streets of the *centro*, the path offers views down onto Lucca's rooftops and narrow roads from its elevated perch. Feel free to wander along the various ramparts for better views of the city below and the mountains beyond, although straying from the main path may lead you across various teenagers making out at the edges of the park.

i *There are steps and paths leading up to the walls at various points along the perimeter of the park. Free.* ☺ *Open 24hr.*

TORRE GUINIGI
TOWER

V. Sant'Andrea

If you've been in Italy for more than a couple of days, chances are you've already climbed your fair share of towers. But this one ups the ante by putting a garden on top of all the hundreds of stairs. Torre Guinigi—known to tourists as "that tower with a bunch of trees on top of it"—does, in fact, have trees on top of it. It also boasts some stunning views of Lucca's rooftops, the city's several other towers, and, if you look closely, tiny little pedestrians making their way around the city walls. Catch a breeze and some shade up here and take in the sweep of the surrounding mountains, whose size and scope can't be fully grasped even from the elevated heights of the city's walls. The blue of the sky, the dark green of the mountains, and the red of the rooftops are, collectively, worth the climb.

i *From P. San Michele, walk north down V. Calderia, turn right onto V. Buia, and continue until it turns into V. Sant'Andrea. The tower is on the left. €4, reduced €3. ☒ Open daily June-Sept 9:30am-7:30pm; Oct 9:30am-5:30pm; Nov-Feb 9:30am-4:30pm; Mar 9:30am-5:30pm.*

LUCCA CATHEDRAL
CHURCH

P. Antelminelli ☎0583 490 530 www.museocattedralelucca.it

Lucca has its fair share of incredible churches—round any corner in the city and you're bound to stumble onto one of them—but perhaps none is as grand as the Lucca Cathedral (it's also the only church in the city you'll have to pay to see). But cough up the €3 entrance fee and have a look inside at the church's starry blue ceiling, the celestial fresco above its altar, and the pretty pockets of stained glass that cast patches of rainbow-colored light on the floor. And to distinguish itself from Lucca's many other churches, this overachieving cathedral boasts two additional marble altars on either side of its central altar and not one, but two organs. On the way out, take note of all the lions and little men who have watched over the doors of the cathedral for centuries.

i *From P. Nazionale, walk down V. Duomo; the cathedral is on the right. €3. ☒ Open M-F 9:30am-5:45pm, Sa 9:30am-6:45pm, Su 11:30am-6pm.*

PALAZZO PFANNER
GARDENS, MUSEUM

V. degli Asili 33 ☎0583 954 029 www.palazzopfanner.it

Although you can see most of this palace's gardens from the top of the city walls that loom above the hedgerows, it's still worth a visit if you want to spend a little while pretending you're a member of the 17th-century Lucchese aristocracy. Originally constructed in 1660, the palace was later repurposed as the famous Pfanner Brewery until it shut its doors in 1929 (too bad for you). But you know what they say: when life takes away your beer, it gives you lemons. Because instead of a nice frosty pint, what you'll find here today are lemon trees, a pleasant fountain, a few Baroque statues, and some thickets of bamboo. The mansion itself is less charming than the gardens, unless you're particularly interested in understated frescoes or finding out what 19th-century vaginal irrigators looked like (somewhat incongruously, the main display of the palace's grand rooms is a collection of Dr. Pietro Pfanner's old medical textbooks and instruments).

i *From P. San Frediano, walk down V. San Frediano and turn left onto V. Cesare Battisti, then right onto V. degli Asili. €6, reduced €5. ☒ Open daily Apr-Nov 10am-6pm.*

PUCCINI MUSEUM
MUSEUM

Corte San Lorenzo 9 ☎0583 584 028 www.puccinimuseum.org

In case you couldn't tell from the blue Birth Room at the Puccini Museum, Lucca is indeed the birthplace of Giacomo Puccini, the Italian opera composer whose most famous works include *Madame Butterfly* and *La Boheme*. The museum itself is housed in Puccini's restored childhood home in Corte San Lorenzo. Highlights include the Steinway piano where the artist composed several of his pieces, a number of original documents and letters, and a trophy room boasting many of Puccini's honors and awards. While *Madame Butterfly* fanboys will certainly enjoy the opportunity to root through his drawers (you can open up a few of them to discover letters from Richard Wagner and original autographed scores), visitors less familiar with the artist and his work won't be missing much if they skip this museum.

i *From P. San Michele, walk down V. di Poggio Seconda and turn right into Corte San Lorenzo. Ticket office located around the corner at P. Cittadella 5. €7, reduced €5. ☒ Open May-Oct daily 10am-7pm; Nov-Mar M 10am-1pm, W-Th 10am-1pm, F 10am-4pm, Sa-Su 10am-6pm; Apr daily 10am-6pm.*

lucca

FOOD

PIZZERIA DA FELICE
PIZZA $

V. Buia 12 ☎0583 494 986 www.pizzeriafelice.it

One of the best spots in the city to stop for a grab-and-go slice, the large, floppy pieces here are the epitome of well-made greasy pizza. There's some seating at a couple tables and the counters along the walls, so either squeeze into the cramped interior or take your pizza to go. A single, satisfying slice will only run you about €1.40, and you'd do well to pair a piece of margherita pizza with a slice of Da Felice's *cecina*—fried chickpea pie (just trust us—it's basically pizza made out of hummus, and you don't even need to eat any carrots or celery to enjoy it).

i From P. San Michele, walk north down V. Calderia and turn right into P. del Salvatore. Continue down the right side of the piazza; Da Felice is on the right. Pizza €1.40 per etto. ☼ Open M 11am-8:30pm, Tu-F 10am-8:30pm, Sa 10am-9pm.

LA BOTTEGA DI ANNA E LEO
ITALIAN $

V. San Frediano 16 ☎393 577 9910

For authentic Tuscan cuisine in a quiet, local setting, round the corner from San Frediano and sit outside at one of the yellow tables of the small, easygoing Anna e Leo. Enjoy a glass of wine with your back to the setting sun while your waitresses do the same from behind the deli counter inside. Dishes here are simple and traditional, so try one of the two varieties of *tortelli Lucchesi* or one of the nightly specials. Compared to other popular trattorias in Lucca, the pace of this bottega is slower and more relaxed, so feel free to linger and sip a cup of coffee after your meal while local Italians stop in to take away a panino or call "Ciao!" to the waitstaff on their way by.

i From P. San Frediano, walk around the left side of the church. Anna e Leo is on the left. Antipasti €4-8. Primi €6-9. Secondi €8-12. ☼ Open Tu-Su 9am-3pm and 6-10:30pm. Wine and salumi 6-8pm.

TRATTORIA DA LEO
ITALIAN $

V. Tegrimi 1 ☎0583 492 236 www.trattoriadaleo.it

If you're feeling hungry like a lion and are hankering for some Tuscan comfort food, Trattoria Da Leo will do the trick. A primo and secondo at this bustling trattoria won't run up the bill too much, and the meat dishes here are hearty (and have protein in them—remember what that tastes like?). The restaurant is extremely popular in the evening, especially among families, and as a result service can be a bit distracted and brusque; don't take it personally if the manager rushes you out the second you've licked your bowl of tiramisu clean. Come early if you want a seat outside, although on a hot summer evening, you might prefer a spot in the air conditioning indoors, where you can dine surrounded by orange walls and a rather large religious painting of a mother suckling her infant child (#freethenipple).

i From P. San Michele, walk north up V. Calderia, which turns into V. Tegrimi. Da Leo is on the left. Cash only. Primi €7-7.50. Secondi €9.50-20. ☼ Open daily noon-2:30pm and 7:30-10:30pm.

OSTERIA BARALLA
ITALIAN $

V. Anfiteatro 5 ☎0583 440 240 www.osteriabaralla.it

With a number of outdoor tables clustered along two walls of this restaurant, Osteria Baralla is a perfect spot for an evening meal. Order yourself a glass of wine, enjoy people watching along the charming side street, and indulge in local Tuscan specialties (if you're having trouble making up your mind, the friendly waiters will offer a few suggestions). This osteria has been in business since 1860, and the simple, reliable dishes here make it easy to see why. But that isn't to say that Barello is behind on the times: in addition to their old-school, authentic cuisine, they also offer complimentary Wi-Fi in case you want to Instagram a picture of your stewed rabbit in real time.

i From V. Fillungo, turn onto V. Anfiteatro; Osteria Baralla is on the left. Primi €8-12. Secondi €12-25. ✆ Open M-Sa 12:30-2:20pm and 7-10:20pm.

PASTICCERIA PASQUINELLI   BAKERY $
V. San Paolino 38

For a local taste of the Lucchese specialty *buccellato* (bread with currants and anise seeds), stop by Pasquinelli on your way through P. San Michele. Half a small loaf of this bread will run you less than €3, and you can pair it with an equally cheap cappuccino or cup of Pasquinelli's *cioccomarocco*. Service may be a bit bristly toward tourists, but that's how you know it's good.

i From P. San Michele, walk down V. San Paolino; Pasquinelli is on the right. Half a small loaf €3. ✆ Open daily 7:30am-7:30pm.

NIGHTLIFE

Just because Lucca is a vacation destination for families (many of them young, even more of them blonde) during the summer months doesn't mean that you can't find some good places for your very 18+ adult self to find a drink after dinner. And although you won't be staying out especially late in Lucca, here are some areas of town to hit up for a nightcap.

Piazza San Michele

As dusk sets in, P. San Michele livens up. Students sit on the steps of the square surrounding the Chiesa di San Michele, eating from budget boxes of Da Felice pizza while a slightly older crowd fills the outdoor seating of the bars and restaurants that line the square. Walk around the perimeter of the piazza anytime after dinner, and you'll find plenty of travelers enjoying a late night espresso and live music al fresco; we recommend joining their ranks at Caffe del Mercato (P. San Michele 17). Or for something even sweeter, sit outside Gelati di Piero (P. San Michele 14) with a cocktail, a cappuccino, or a cup of gelato (or all three) with one of its signature waffles and people watch from a bustling corner of the square.

Via Vittorio Veneto

The main drag of Lucca's nightlife, here you'll find a number of bars where you can sip wine for a little while before wandering down to Piazza Nazionale and Corso Garibaldi for round two. And if you're feeling responsible and want to practice your alternating, stop at Gelateria Vereta for a cup of gelato between bars.

Via Michele Rosi

For a younger crowd, head down to the far end of V. Fillungo to V. Michele Rosi, where you'll find large crowds of younger folks smoking and drinking on the curbsides just outside the archway that separates the two streets. Grab a drink at Ciclo DiVino wine bar (V. Michele Rosi 7) or De Cervesia Pub just across the street (V. Michele Rosi 20) and join the mingling and lingering crowds outside. Although neither bar is open much past 10 or 11pm most nights, the area makes for a nice, laid-back retreat from the families and little kids you'll find riding bikes through the more central streets of Lucca in the after-dinner hours.

Piazza Anfiteatro

While the late-night crowd you'll find here is more likely to be finishing up dinner than the people who are already downing cocktails in Piazza San Michele, Piazza Anfiteatro is still a great place to come for a glass of wine in the evening. Wander around the outer ring of the oval piazza to find the more secluded venues, or try the nearby Vinarkia wine bar (V. Fillungo 188).

lucca

ESSENTIALS
Practicalities

- **TOURIST OFFICES:** Centro Accoglienza Turistica, the main branch of the Lucca's primary tourist office, schedules guided tours and provides audio tours, information about events, and internet access. (Ple. Verdi ☎0583 58 31 50 www.comune.lucca.it/turismo. Look for "i" sign on the left.)
- **CURRENCY EXCHANGE:** Available at the Forexchange. (V. Calderia 3. ☺ Open M-Sa 10am-1:30pm and 2:30-5:30pm.)
- **ATMS:** Available at the Forexchange (V. Calderia 3 ☺ Open M-Sa 10am-1:30pm and 2:30-5:30pm) and several other locations throughout the centro.
- **LAUNDROMATS:** Lavanderia Self-Service. (V. Borgo Giannotti 529 ☎347 482 39 74. ☺ Open daily 7am-10pm.)

Emergency

- **POLICE:** Polizia Municipale, in the westernmost point inside the walls. (Ple. San Donato 12 ☎0583 44 27 27) Carabinieri, in the southwest of the *centro*. (Cortile degli Svizzeri 4 ☎0583 4751)
- **LATE-NIGHT PHARMACIES:** Farmacia Comunale, outside the city walls, opposite Baluardo San Colombano. (P. Curatone 7 ☺ Open 24hr.)
- **HOSPITALS/MEDICAL SERVICES:** Campo di Marte, outside the city walls, northeast of the city. (V. dell'Ospedale ☎0583 9701 ☺ Open 24hr.)

Getting There
By Train

To get to Lucca from Florence, the train is your most reliable option. Take the Viareggio train—Luca's the third-to-last stop before Viareggio (€8, 90min.). You can order your ticket from the self-service kiosk or window. Trains arrive at the station in Ple. Ricasoli, just south of the city walls. (☺ Ticket office open daily 6:30am-8:10pm.) Direct trains run back to Florence (€8, 90min.) and Pisa (€4, 30min.).

By Bus

Because of the several trains that run between Lucca and Florence, it doesn't make much sense to take the bus. However, if you do, you can take the blue VAI bus R002 (www.lucca.cttnord.it) from the Florence bus terminal (From the left side of the train station facing the trains, take the first left and walk up the block. The terminal is on the left.) You'll arrive in Ple. Verdi (1hr. 15min.).

Getting Around
By Taxi

Taxi stands (marked with codes identifying the pickup point) can be found at the train station, P. Napoleone, P. Santa Maria, and Ple. Verdi.

By Bus

Lucca offers both suburban buses and seven town buses around the city, run by the company CLAP (☎0583 541 239 www.lucca.cttnord.it). You can catch pretty much any bus at Ple. Verdi, just inside the west side of the city walls. Buses stop running around 8pm.

By Bike

You'll find the same rates and hours at each of the major rental places around town. Street bikes, mountain bikes, and tandem bikes can be rented by the hour, by the day, or for longer periods. Try Poli Antonio Biciclette, Berutto Cicli, Promo Tourist, or the tourist office in Ple. Verdi.

siena

Siena is, in many ways, Tuscany at its finest and most essential. Climb up to the top of the Torre della Mangia (or scale any street in the city center, really) to see what we mean: while the highest peaks and towers of the city reveal sweeping views of red roofs, stacks of tan Tuscan buildings, and an unrelenting patchwork of hills and fields in every direction, the narrow streets of the city itself are also built directly into the dips, slopes, and steep grades of the region's difficult topography. But Siena is worthy of the sweat you'll sacrifice to it. Once a thriving republic of the Middle Ages before being devastated by the Black Death, Siena today retains a charming mix of medieval heritage and modern Tuscan culture, from the winding layout of its historic centro (which has been designated an UNESCO World Heritage Site) to the green of its surrounding hillsides to its penchant for panini packed with boar meat. While the bars and restaurants stacked and teetering along steep Siena streets are in themselves a sight to see, the city's actual historic and artistic landmarks (you know, the ones you have to pay to see) are flat-out staggering, particularly in the case of its Duomo, whose striped, geometrically-intricate interior makes it one of the most stunning churches in all of Italy. The true spirit of Siena is most palpable twice a year each summer, when Il Palio di Siena—the city's historic medieval horse race—is held on July 2 and August 16 in Piazza del Campo. The days leading up to the race sees Siena's streets decorated in the flags of the city's 17 neighborhoods (*contrade*, singular *contrada*), while locals and tourists alike take part in the traditional ceremonies and spectacles of the centuries-old race. Even outsiders who can never fully grasp the magnitude of the race and the intense meaning it holds for the Sienese will still find themselves powerfully moved by the excitement, despair, and insanity that the Palio brings out in the city's passionate people.

ORIENTATION

The sloping streets of Siena are built directly into the hills and dips of its Tuscan setting, and you can feel it everywhere, whether you're racing around a steep bend on one of the city's free-flying buses or dragging your way up and down the narrow streets of the centro on stiff calves. Most of Siena's buses pass through P. Gramsci, which is located just north of the city's stadium and east of the Fortezza Medicea. An easy way to get from bus stops to the city center is to find V. Montanini and follow it south to Il Campo, the thriving heart of the old city. Here you'll find not only the race track that hosts Siena's Palio twice a year but also the Palazzo Pubblico and its Torre del Mangia—perhaps the city's most iconic and recognizable structure. The campo is lined with restaurants and bars and gives way to a number of tiny *vicoli* that boast even more tucked-away eateries. From Il Campo, follow the many signs to the fantastic, striped Duomo and its accompanying sights. Nearby, V. Fontebranda leads down to the city's medieval fountain, while a bit farther north, V. Sapienza will drop you off at the doors of San Domenico. Siena's centro, which is confined within the city's medieval walls, is closed off to cars, making things a little easier for foot-travelers; that being said, the twists and turns and steep grades of these streets can get confusing, so bring a well-marked map and don't be surprised if you make a

il palio

On two days in the middle of the hot Tuscan summer, the city of Siena comes alive as horses, men in medieval tights, and thousands of overheated spectators flood Piazza del Campo during the Palio di Siena. Held twice a year—first on July 2 in honor of Madonna of Provenzano and again on August 16 to celebrate to the Assumption of Mary—Siena's historic medieval horse race sees the city's 17 districts battle it out for local glory in a sporting event that dates back to the Middle Ages. While the week leading up to the race sees the horses paraded through Il Campo and members of the various *contrade* gathered together for neighborhood dinners, the day of the Palio itself is unparalleled in the emotions, intensity, and fanaticism it stirs up in the passionate Sienese. And then, after nearly two hours of parades in which members of each contrada march around Il Campo in traditional medieval garb, the cannons sound, and 10 of the 17 *contrade* thunder around the Campo's track in a blistering, exhilarating bareback race that often sees jockeys fall off their horses and thoroughbreds crash on their way around the tight bends in the track. For days after the race, you can hear members of the winning *contrada* celebrating their victory throughout the streets of the city, and the parades, dinners, and victory banquets continue as long as six months after the race.

wrong turn that sends you traipsing down a steep hill only to realize you've made a terrible mistake and have to turn around and climb back up.

ACCOMMODATIONS

HOTEL ALMA DOMUS
HOTEL $$

V. Camporegio 37 ☎0577 44 177 www.hotelalmadomus.it

Sitting quietly along a set of sloping stairs just down the road from San Domenico, Hotel Alma Domus offers a surprisingly varied range of rooms and rates. Decide whether or not you're Covergirl worth it and consider your many options, from sparse economy singles, which provide a neat and tidy place to sleep but little else, to superior doubles whose balconies and pillowy beds make for a cloud-like retreat from which to gaze out onto some incredible views of the city. Whether you choose to live like a deity or a dormouse, all guests are free to enjoy the complimentary breakfast, plentiful common spaces, and sunny courtyard dotted with clusters of red flowers. Popular among students, the economy singles are a great way to snag a cheap room in the middle of Siena's city center.

i From Basilica San Domenico, walk down V. Camporegio; Hotel Alma Domus is around the bend in the road, on the left. Economy singles €51. Classic singles €55. Superior doubles €80-90. Breakfast included. ☼ Reception 24hr.

ALBERGO BERNINI
HOTEL $$

V. della Sapienza 15 ☎0577 289 047 www.albergobernini.com

Located just a few twists and turns from the heart of Siena's centro, Albergo Bernini boasts the antique furniture, rustic tiled floors, and flowery bedspreads that you'll find in many a boutique hotel. The only difference here is that the quaint, homey decor doesn't translate to pint-sized living space. Instead, the rooms and beds here are enormous (at least by Italian standards). And although you might not be in the company any actual Baroque masterpieces while staying at Bernini, the abundance of space (bolstered by the hotel's breakfast room, courtyard, and several seating areas) means you'll have plenty of room to get splashy, flashy, and dynamic (and, you know, sculpturally exquisite) all on your own. You may not be in Florence yet, but ask for a room with a view and wake up to the Siena skyline and its towering Duomo every morning.

i From the city center, walk down V. d. Terme and turn left onto V. della Sapienza. Albergo Bernini is on the left. Doubles with shared bath €65, with ensuite €85. Breakfast €5. ☒ Reception 8am-11pm.

SIENA HOSTEL HOSTEL $
V. Fiorentina 89 ☎0577 169 8177 www.sienahostel.it

For the cheapest private bedrooms in Siena, strap on your backpack, pack an extra water bottle, and strike out for the Siena Hostel—it's going to be a bit of a hike. Because although staying here technically situates you "in Siena," you won't be anywhere near the actual city center (or the train station, for that matter). Located a 10-15min. bus ride from the center of town and all the major sights, eateries, and points of interest, this hostel will, at the very least, give you a taste of Sienese residential life and easy access to local grocery stores (there's one just around the corner). That being said, the hostel does post comprehensive bus schedules in reception and makes up for its inconvenient location with plenty of pleasant outdoor seating, lounge chairs, a ping-pong table, vending machines, and lots of private rooms (this place may be called a hostel, but it's really more like a very youthful hotel). And who knows—you might be willing to forgive and forget the terrible location after a few mornings of the incredible complimentary breakfast spread (which is basically an all-you-can eat buffet of multigrain cereal, croissants, donuts, rolls, espresso, and Nutella).

i From the train station, take Bus #4 to Fontebecci or Bus #10, 35, or 36 to Antiporto. Dorms from €22. Singles from €35. Doubles from €48. Breakfast included. ☒ Reception 24hr.

SIGHTS

DUOMO CHURCH
P. Duomo ☎0577 283 048 www.operaduomo.siena.it

And you thought all churches in Italy looked the same. Sure, this Duomo has the cavernous ceilings, mammoth columns, and decorative floors of your standard over-the-top Catholic church, but just when you thought a leopard can't change its spots, Siena's Duomo surprises with an abundance of stripes and goes straight zebra. Moreover, its aforementioned ceiling is a deep blue and spotted with gold stars, its dichromatic columns aren't your standard Corinthian, and its floors, rather than being covered in familiar mosaics, are decorated with cartoon-like drawings that will remind you more of a comic book than Bible stories of old. The entire church is truly a marvel, mostly because of its dense layers of atypical geometry: the interior is an optical illusion of steps, curves, and lines, and some of the tiling on the floor is very proto-Escher in style. Follow the suggested itinerary around the perimeter of the church (and stay inside the red ropes!) and take note of works by Donatello and Bernini. On your way out, swing through the Piccolomini Library, on the right, for an equally overwhelming sensory experience: the colors here are of a slightly more vibrant palette and are just as visually engrossing.

i Follow the signs in the city center to P. Duomo. You can't miss it. €7. Opa Si Pass Mar-Oct €12; Nov-Feb €8. Pass is valid for three days and includes entry to the Duomo, the Crypt, the Baptistery, and the Museo dell'Opera and Facciatone. ☒ Open daily Mar-Oct 10:30am-7pm; Nov-Feb 10:30am-5:30pm.

PIAZZA DEL CAMPO PIAZZA
Siena's most central and celebrated square, Piazza del Campo is impossible to miss—pretty much the second you get off the bus in the city center, you'll see signs on every corner pointing toward Il Campo. Twice a year, it becomes the pulsating center of Italy's most famous horse race, the Palio di Siena. And while

the square is decidedly less exciting for the other 363 days of the year, it is where you'll find plenty of restaurants, bars, and side streets to explore in the evening. And if you're not here when the Palio is happening, you can always walk around the racetrack and imagine what it feels like when the horses and their jockeys come thundering around the corners of the piazza in pursuit of local glory.

i Follow the ubiquitous signs that point to Il Campo. Free.

PALAZZO PUBBLICO AND TORRE DEL MANGIA   MUSEUM, TOWER
P. del Campo 1   ☎0577 292 614

If the ticket booth smells a little bit like horses, that's because this is where Siena's prized thoroughbreds storm out into Il Campo on the day of the Palio. Every other day of the year, however, the palace and its Civic Museum (which can be visited for a fee of €9) are a little less showstopping. The highlight here is truly the Torre del Mangia, which dominates Il Campo from below and, from above, offers the absolute best views of Siena's rooftops, the Duomo, and the surrounding Tuscan hills. The trip up to the crown of the tower itself will be one of simultaneous splendor and Hitchcockian horror; wind your way up the narrow staircase like the Jimmy Stewart that you wish you were and prepare to redefine your definition of vertigo upon reaching the very top and getting a glimpse of the tiny Il Campo below. And to make the whole thing even more classically cinematic, enjoy the shrieking, swooping birds that circle the tower tirelessly.

i It's that tall thing at the bottom of Piazza del Campo. Tower €10. Civic Museum €9, reduced €8.
🕐 Tower open daily Mar 16-Oct 10am-7pm; Nov-Mar 15 10am-4pm. Civic Museum open daily Mar 16-Oct 10am-7pm; Nov-Mar 15 10am-6pm. Ticket office closes 45min. early.

CRYPT   MUSEUM
P. Duomo   ☎0577 283 048 www.operaduomo.siena.it

Although these subterranean rooms are called the Crypt, you won't be seeing any dead people here. Unless you count Jesus, who is depicted on the walls of this cavern in a series of frescoes that capture the moments before, during, and after the Passion. For a series of cave paintings that were completely forgotten until just recently, when they were accidentally discovered during excavations under the Duomo in 1999, the frescoes here are remarkably well preserved and shockingly vibrant in hue. Despite the bright reds and rich blues of these frescoes, however, their mournful subject matter is actually quite somber and moving if considered in the right mood. Note, in particular, the depiction of Joseph of Arimathea removing the nails from Jesus's feet after the Crucifixion and Mary holding her lifeless son in her arms after his painful sacrifice. Although a visit here won't take up much of your time, the crypt is included in the Opa Si Pass and is worth a stop.

i Just past the Duomo sights ticket office, on the left. €6. Opa Si Pass Mar-Oct €12, Nov-Feb €8. Pass is valid for three days and includes entry to the Duomo, the Crypt, the Baptistery, and the Museo dell'Opera and Facciatone. 🕐 Open daily Mar-Oct 10:30am-7pm; Nov-Feb 10:30am-5:30pm.

MUSEO DELL'OPERA AND PANORAMIC FACCIATONE   MUSEUM
P. Duomo   ☎0577 283 048 www.operaduomo.siena.it

The Museo dell'Opera is a whole lot of wooden sculptures and panel painting (along with the super old throw pillow here and there), and none of it will be of much interest for non-art-history students (hey, it's OK—you're a student of life, man). Still, most of the rooms here are air-conditioned, so maybe take a little while to ponder those dusty pillows while giving all that back sweat some time to dry. Even more critically, you'll need to wind your way up through the museum to reach the Facciatone, which you'll find at the end of the Hall of Vestments. Wait your turn to climb up to this panoramic overlook and take in a sweep of

siena

Siena and Tuscany that rivals that of the Torre del Mangia. Heads up for people who are afraid of heights—the guardrail at the top isn't particularly high.

i To the right of the Duomo sights ticket office. €7. Opa Si Pass Mar-Oct €12, Nov-Feb €8. Pass is valid for three days and includes entry to the Duomo, the Crypt, the Baptistery, and the Museo dell'Opera and Facciatone. ☒ Open daily Mar-Oct 10:30am-7pm; Nov-Feb 10:30am-5:30pm.

BAPTISTERY
BAPTISTERY

P. San Giovanni   ☎0577 283 048 www.operaduomo.siena.it

Located at the bottom of a steep flight of stone steps at the back of the Duomo, the Baptistery is almost like a miniature version of the church itself, complete with the signature stripes, cool colors, and even more ceiling frescoes. It's also much smaller and easier to take in than the cathedral, so have a seat and look heavenward (for insights, answers, God's grace...or just a nice view). Despite the rich, dense detail of the frescoes and the ornate baptismal fount, the whole thing is a bit dark and chilly for a place meant for welcoming/dunking babies into the Kingdom of God.

i At the bottom of the steep steps behind the Duomo. €4. Opa Si Pass Mar-Oct €12, Nov-Feb €8. Pass is valid for three days and includes entry to the Duomo, the Crypt, the Baptistery, and the Museo dell'Opera and Facciatone. ☒ Open daily Mar-Oct 10:30am-7pm; Nov-Feb 10:30am-5:30pm.

BASILICA CATERINIANA SAN DOMENICO
CHURCH

P. San Domenico 1   www.basilicacateriniana.com

If you look out over Siena from any high point in the city, you'll likely see San Domenico looming in the distance, a giant brick block of a church located farther west and north of the more central sights. And while the Gothic basilica, built in the 13th century and later enlarged, is most impressive when viewed from afar, if you find yourself nearby, it doesn't hurt to pop your head inside and have a look at the church's massive, gaping interior. Quite sparse in comparison to many Italian churches, San Domenico does boast the remains of some frescoes on its walls and some more recent stained glass behind its altar.

i From the city center, walk west down V. della Sapienza to P. San Domenico. Free. ☒ Open daily Mar-Oct 7am-6:30pm, Nov-Feb 9am-6pm.

FONTEBRANDA
FOUNTAIN

V. di Fontebranda

Fontebranda is less of a fountain in the modern (or even Renaissance) sense and more of a random watery cave that you might happen upon while looking for something a little grander. But lo, this is it! Constructed in 1081 and rebuilt in 1246, the three basins of this medieval watering hole were once used to supply good old H2O for animals, mills, and the local Sienese, but now, like your great-aunt in a nursing home, they pretty much just sit here being old. The Fontebranda may look like something out of the *Chamber of Secrets* (don't look the fish directly in the eyes!) but was, in fact, featured in Dante's *Inferno*.

i From P. del Campo, cross V. di Citta and follow V. di Fontebranda down to the fountain. Free.

FORTEZZA MEDICEA
FORTRESS

P. della Liberta

You might end up wandering around this fortress's high, mossy walls wondering where the hell the entrance is. Just keep walking and eventually you'll find it. Although this structure was once used to fight off invading forces from Siena's archrival Florence, today the biggest spats the city has to deal with are the ones between its own *contrade*, and so the Fortezza Medicea is now mostly a bunch of hot gravel surrounded by some high walls. Still, the upper perimeter of the fortress offers some shady trees, purple flowers, and park benches, so have a stroll around and look out on Siena from a variety of angles. The fortress also hosts outdoor movies in the summer as part of Siena's Cinema in Fortezza program, and if you're visiting in the afternoon, consider stopping at Antica Enoteca Italiano for a glass of real Italian wine.

i From P. Gramsci, walk west down Vle. C. Maccari to the fortress. The entrance to Fortezza Medicea is on the left. Free.

FOOD

GINO CACINO DI ANGELO
DELI $

P. Mercato 31 ☎0577 223 076 www.ginocacinodiangelo.blogspot.it

For a fast, affordable, and delicious lunch near Il Campo, veer away from the overpriced V. Citta and head for the square hidden just behind Palazzo Pubblico; here, in the corner of P. Mercato, under a canopy of purple flowers, you'll find Gino Cacino. Step inside and the floral scents will be quickly replaced by the rich aromas of the aged cheese and freshly sliced meat that crowd the counter of this small and cluttered deli. If you can, find a stool and order a plate of cheese and meat, which will be brought out on a wooden board. Otherwise, you can't go wrong with one of its panini, made fresh and served hot on a crusty bun (yes, that is cheese rind in your sandwich, and it's awesome); take it to go and eat it in the shade on one of the benches in the center of the piazza.

i From P. del Campo, walk to the back of the square (behind Palazzo Pubblico) to P. Mercato. Gino Cacino is on the left under the purple flowers. Panini €3.50-7. Cheese and meat plates €6-9. ☒ Open daily 7:30am-8pm.

OSTERIA LA CHIACCHERA
ITALIAN $

V. Costa Sant'Antonio 4 ☎0577 280 631 www.osterialachiacchera.it

For simple, authentic, and memorable Tuscan dishes, wander through Siena's winding streets to Osteria La Chiacchera, which sits nestled into the side of the steep V. Costa Sant'Antonio. Seating here can get tight when the restaurant is busy, but the closeness, combined with the brick-walled interior and friendly warmth of the waiters, makes for a cozy atmosphere in which to enjoy the homestyle Italian cuisine. And if you get here early enough, try to snag a seat outside—the tables are staggered on the hillside, so you can spend your evening looking down onto V. Costa Sant'Antonio as it dips and falls away from the restaurant (like eating your meal at the top of a rollercoaster, but without the nausea).

i From the city center, walk down V. d. Terme and turn left onto V. della Sapienza, then left down V. Costa Sant'Antonio. The osteria is on the right. Antipasti €3.50-9.50. Primi €6-8. Secondi €7.50-9.50. Dessert €4-4.50. ☒ Open M noon-3pm and 6:30-10pm, W-Su noon-3pm and 6:30-10pm.

GROM
GELATERIA $

V. Banchi di Sopra 11 ☎0577 289 303

Sitting amid the many clothing stores that line V. Banchi di Sopra, on first glance, Grom's tall glass storefront and gaping, white-walled interior looks less like an ice cream shop and more like just another shopping outlet. But slow down and stop in for a cup of Grom's cheap and ethical gelato (and its perhaps even more ethical and humane A/C). Part of an Italian chain, Grom makes its gelato with exclusively all-natural ingredients and uses only Carrubba flour as its primary thickening ingredient. And if you don't really know what that means, just know that it tastes great.

i From P. del Campo, walk up to V. Banchi di Sopra. Grom is on the left. Gelato €2.50-3.50. ☒ Open M-Th 11:30am-midnight, F-Sa 11:30am-1am, Su 11am-midnight.

IL POMODORINO
PIZZA $

V. Camporegio 13 ☎0577 286 811 www.ilpomodorino.it

Just down the road from San Domenico, Il Pomodorino is a perfect place for a late-afternoon lunch or an inexpensive dinner. Or an afternoon snack or late-night munchies—it doesn't really matter when you get your next hankering for

siena

carbs, because this restaurant serves up pizza of all varieties at all hours of the day. And with its white wicker patio seating tucked along the curving, hilly Via Camporegio, Il Pomodorino also offers a unique spot from which to enjoy a Tuscan afternoon and a truly incredible view out onto the whole city.

i From Basilica San Domenico, walk down V. Camporegio. Il Pomodorino is on the left. Salads €8-10. Pizza €7.50-11. ☼ Open M-Sa noon-1am, Su 7pm-1am.

LA FONTANA DELLA FRUTTA
V. delle Terme 65-67

MARKET $
☎0577 40 422

In addition to its many overpriced eateries, Siena's centro is also home to a number of little markets, deli counters, and produce shops. Of the latter, La Fontana Della Frutta just might be the best. Stop in for some lasagna and pasta salad, or just to stock up on some much-needed fruits and vegetables (you know, for all those vitamins and minerals you haven't been consuming). And if you're a thirsty bitch, order your fruits and veggies juiced—La Fontana will slice, dice, and press its produce for you in a number of different combinations, including grapefruit-apple-papaya and avocado-celery-lime.

i From the city center, walk down V. delle Terme. La Fontana Della Frutta is on the left. ☼ Open daily 8am-7:30pm.

SAVINI
V. de Montanini 9

BAKERY $
www.dolcezzesavini.it

A bakery with a number of other locations in Italy, Savini is just down the road from Il Campo and is a great place to pop in for an afternoon pick-me-up, whether it be a panini, an iced donut, or a bite of their popular *panforte*. Don't let the fact that it's part of a chain dissuade you: prices here are low and ingredients are fresh, so let Savini be your refuge from the many overpriced bakeries you'll find just outside Il Campo and along V. Citta.

i From P. del Campo, walk down V. Banchi di Sopra, which turns into V. de Montanini. Savini is on the left. Panini €3. Pastries €1-3. ☼ Open daily 7:30am-7:30pm.

NIGHTLIFE

CAFFE DEL CORSO
V. Banchi di Sopra 25

BAR
☎0577 226 656

Skip the restaurant upstairs and go straight for Caffe del Corso's comprehensive cocktail list. Divided into easily consumable categories, this mixed drink menu allows you to browse lists of short drinks, long drinks, and after-dinner drinks, all of which could be grouped together under the single umbrella of "cheap drinks" (because that's the one you really care about). And with Caffe del Corso's open-air windows and plentiful outdoor seating in an alley just off V. Banchi di Sopra, you can drink in both your frozen daiquiri and the Siena summer night, all to the tune of Justin Timberlake and other top pop hitmakers.

i From P. del Campo, walk down V. Banchi di Sopra. Caffe del Corso is on the left. Cocktails €5. ☼ Open Tu-Su 8:30am-3am.

SAN PAOLO PUB
Vicolo San Paolo 2

BAR
☎0577 226 622 www.sanpaolopub.it

Tucked into a small *vicolo* just off Il Campo, San Paolo Pub is something like a cross between a speakeasy and a man cave (in charming Tuscany, of all places). It's also everything you could want in a sports bar, from the red leather booths inside to the dark tables and barstools on the patio to the wide selection of cheap beer and panini that you can keep pounding into the wee hours of the morning. And if all that wasn't enough, there's even some AstroTurf on the patio outside (all the better for you to play the field upon).

i Vicolo San Paolo is one of the little streets just off the northwest side of P. del Campo. Beer €3.50-6.50. Cocktails and liquor €4.50-7. Panini €5. ☼ Open daily 10:30am-2am.

ANTICA ENOTECA ITALIANA ENOTECA

P. della Liberta 1   ☎0577 228 811 www.enoteca-italiana.it

Built into the walls of the Fortezza Medicea, Enoteca Italiana offers an Italian wine-tasting experience that couldn't get more Tuscan if a lovelorn Diane Lane showed up. With its curved brick archways, dim lighting, and wine bottles displayed carefully on its walls, Antica Enoteca Italiana is worth the trek it will take to get over here, as visitors can enjoy the unique experience of sampling authentic Italian wine from a collection of more than 1500 varieties. While you can certainly make a reservation for a wine tasting, you can also keep things low-key and just stop by and sip a glass on the terrace. And if you get the munchies with your drunchies, the enoteca also has a restaurant where you can enjoy a full meal or the rotating tasting menu in addition to your *vino*.

i From P. Gramsci, walk west down Vle. C. Maccari. Antica Enoteca Italiana is inside the entrance to the Fortezza Medicea, on the left. Wine by the glass starting at €1.50. Antipasti €10-12. Primi €10-12. Secondi €13-18. ☼ Enoteca open Tu-Sa 3-8pm. Restaurant open M-Sa noon-midnight.

ESSENTIALS

Practicalities

- **TOURIST OFFICES:** APT Siena provides maps for a small fee. It also has brochures and a bookstore. Facing the tower in P. del Campo, it's on the left side of the piazza. (P. del Campo 56 ☎0577 28 05 51 www.terresiena.it ☼ Open daily 9am-7pm.)

- **CURRENCY EXCHANGE:** Forexchange (V. di Citta 80).

- **ATMS:** Monte dei Paschi at V. Banchi di Sopra 84 near Il Campo.

- **LUGGAGE STORAGE:** The underground bus station in P. Gramsci has luggage storage.

- **POST OFFICES:** Poste Italiane (P. Matteotti 37 ☎0577 21 42 95). Just past the main bus stops. Additionally, stamps can be purchased and letters posted at a number of the tobacco shops in the city center.

Emergency

- **POLICE:** V. del Castoro. ☎0577 201 111. Near the Duomo.

- **LATE-NIGHT PHARMACIES:** Several pharmacies in the centro share a late-night rotation. Visit any one of them to check the schedule outside and get the number of the pharmacy on duty. The easiest to find is Farmacia del Campo (P. del Campo 260 ☎0577 28 02 34). Facing the Torre del Mangia, it's on the right side of the Campo, nestled between some restaurants.

- **HOSPITALS/MEDICAL SERVICES:** Santa Maria alle Scotte; take bus #3 or 77 from P. Gramsci (Vle. Mario Bracci 16 ☎0577 58 51 11 ☼ Open 24hr.).

Getting There

Traveling to Siena from Florence is easy enough, but if you're arriving in the city from elsewhere, you'll likely have to transfer trains or buses at least once.

By Bus

Although traveling to Siena by rail is a popular option, the bus station is significantly closer to the center of Siena than its far-flung train station. The TRA-IN/SITA bus is also faster than the train and runs directly to Siena's P. Gramsci from Florence. From Florence, the #131 bus will take you to Siena; you can catch either the #131O regular bus (€8, 1hr. 35min.) or the #131R rapid bus (€8, 1hr. 15min.).

siena

OSTELLO DI PERUGIA CENTRO
HOSTEL $

V. Bontempi, 13   ☎075 57 22 880 www.ostello.perugia.it

And then sometimes your hostel is a former Borgia Palace. It's Italy. It happens. Located right in the center of town and a minute away from P. IV Novembre, the "centro" part of this hostel's name doesn't lie—you'll have plenty to do outside your hostel.

But for the hours that you do spend in here, don't squander them all in your relatively plain dorm, mercilessly segregated from the opposite sex by a door that must always remain closed (so much for some Borgia-style debauchery). Head down to the spacious common room area. An enormous kitchen waiting to be cooked in has plenty of picnic-style tables and benches where you can enjoy a nice meal. The TV room is also large and has plenty of comfy couches.

What really steals the show, however, is the common room with all the tables and chairs. Exciting! But then look up. Those gorgeous ceiling frescoes? Yeah, you should take some pictures. Those are originals that the Borgias also admired. If that's not enough, walk out onto the terrace, and you'll get one of the most beautiful views of Perugia. The Borgias knew what was up.

i Dorms €17. ⏲ Reception 7:30-11am, 3:30pm-midnight. Lockout 11am-3:30pm.

PERUGIA FARMHOUSE BACKPACKER HOSTEL
HOSTEL $

V. Settevalli,, 760   ☎339 562 0005 www.perugia-farmhouse.it

Not so surprisingly, this hostel is a farmhouse. Didn't see that coming. But no, it's like a legit farmhouse. Complete with barn animal friends. This place takes the word "rustic" and doesn't even try. It just is rustic. Brick stone, goats, chickens, donkeys, and some good farmer hospitality—this place definitely has more of a cozy feel than most sterile hostels you might stay at. Take your bag off, and welcome home.

This place is for people who don't really need to be in the city center. Stay here if you're okay with spending your vacation on a farm and then taking occasional excursions into the city (but not after 9:30pm, when you should catch the last bus). It all adds up to not too many wild nights but plenty of wilderness nights.

There's a cute, close community here, and if that doesn't do it for you, there's a drop-dead gorgeous pool and beautiful scenery. Being in the middle of nowhere has some perks when you want to explore the lovely Umbrian geography.

People living here tend to make their own fun with pizza nights, s'mores nights, BBQs, and nearby wine and beer tasting areas. So even if you're not right in the city, some wine, pool time, and farm friend comfort might make it all worth it.

i Dorms €18-23.

By Train

If bumpy roads make you feel like you're trapped in a popcorn bag, the train may be a better option for you. Trains arrive at the Siena train station in P. Rosselli, a 15min. walk outside Siena's centro or a 10min. ride via bus #3, 4, 7, 8, 10, 17, or 77. Trains arrive from Florence (€9, 90min.), Poggibonsi (€4, 30min.), and Chiusi-Chianciano (€9, 90min.). Those traveling from Rome will need to transfer at Chiusi-Chianciano.

italy

Getting Around

Once you're within the walls of Siena's historic centro, the best and virtually only way to get around is on foot (unless you really enjoy biking up and down steep hills). Siena's extensive bus system will only really be useful for travelers who are staying far outside the city center (i.e., at the Siena Hostel). Bus tickets cost €1.20 per ride and must be validated on the bus. Nearly all buses end their routes in P. Gramsci, northwest of the centro, and its underground station sells tickets for bus trips to other towns. Many buses also pass through the Siena train station. In the evenings, Siena switches over to a night bus system. Check the schedules outside the bus stops or in P. Gramsci.

perugia

Chocolate, jazz, breathtaking views: it seems unfair that Perugia gets it all. But it does. Perugia is the host city for Umbria Jazz and Eurochocolate, so you'll be sure to find something here, whether it's the largest Baci chocolate in the world or some cool cats having a jam sesh in a local bar During the school year, you can to pretend to be one of the 34,000 students who attend the University of Perugia. Otherwise, feel free to explore Perugia by living in a former Borgia palace, walking on an aqueduct, or eating all the free samples after a tour of a chocolate factory. Living it up amid the medieval architecture and modern population of this city isn't hard. The city is built among hills and sometimes has gravity-defying slopes and stairs upwards. What this means, though, is that Perugia is filled with breathtaking panoramas of Umbria, with rolling green hills and distant mountains, all of which can be enjoyed with some smooth jazz playing in the background as you bite into delicious artisan chocolates. Mmm, right on.

SIGHTS

GALLERIA NAZIONALE DELL'UMBRIA   MUSEUM
C. Pietro Vannucci, 19   ☎075 5866 8410 www.gallerianazionaleumbria.it

Modern, sleek, well-curated (!), and with a Jesus to die for every one of your many, many sins, the National Gallery of Umbria is not a place to miss. For the well-curated part alone. See what can be done with the help of our Lord, all you other bad regional museums? Housed in the beautifully medieval Palazzo dei Priori, the guarding lions and decorated archways leading to the door may not have screamed "cutting edge in a couple thousand years," but the exhibits are still something to see.

After a long flight of stairs, emerge in the beautifully sleek opening exhibit with high vaulted arches and specially designed panels that fit all the lovely painted 13th century crosses this place has, meaning you can view them from all sides. The museum progresses through early paintings of Jesus, going all the way into the Renaissance so you can see how, over time, painters were finally able to paint baby Jesus without making him look like a creepy little man. Also keep an eye out for the room in which Mary decides to have a little more fun as a virgin and goes blonde.

As you walk around, be sure to peek into the corridors as well as the rooms. Lovely gems like some enormous bronze contraptions with the description "wafer makers await." Some rooms also have beautiful frescoed walls, which have nothing to do with the museum. Just a consequence of being in a former palace, we guess.

Once you enter into the Renaissance work, admire how well everyone can draw arches. And Jesus. The museum continues downstairs as well, so don't miss the Renaissance happenings there. You'll get to see the famous Perugino, who as you might've guessed, gets his name from this fair city. Mannerism follows, and then many Caravaggio wannabes pop up. You could be described as one of them as well, seeing as backpacking will leave you pretty ba-roque! But aside from that joke, it is a gorgeous museum.

i €6.50. ☺ Open Tu-Su 9am-7pm.

PERUGINA CHOCOLATE FACTORY
CHOCOLATE FACTORY

V. San Sisto 207   ☎075 527 67 96 www.perugina.it

It's a Chocolate Factory. Unless you've been scarred and are terrified that you'll turn into a giant blueberry, we couldn't stop you from coming here. Perugina, a division of Nestle Italy, is a famous chocolate brand that you've probably seen during your travels in Italy. If not, you've been doing traveling wrong and should go have their famous Baci chocolate or try some Baci gelato right now. Even better: come on this chocolate factory tour and then eat enough Perugina chocolate in the tasting part of the tour to last you at least a week. Don't feel bad. This factory produces two million Baci chocolates—per day.

Located in San Sisto, about 15min. by bus from Fontivegge, this enormous chocolate factory runs tours Mondays to Fridays. Call ahead to make a reservation and figure out when English tours are given. The tour starts out with a fun for the whole family short film that describes the history of Perugina, which started as a small family business and then, through the help of Nestle, went hella corporate (which is pretty much the American dream). Watch some of the chocolates being made in detail here. During the summer, the factory is in low season and you watch most of it from above, so seeing all the chocolates being made just ain't possible sometimes.

The tour continues into the museum, where you'll be given a thorough debrief on what exactly chocolate is and important questions like "What's the difference between dark and white chocolate?" will be explained. Afterwards, watch another short movie about the Il Bacione, the largest single piece of chocolate ever made, which was displayed at Eurochocolate 2012. It gets eaten to the soundtrack of some Enya at the end of the movie. After this, it's the moment you've been waiting for: free samples. Try 10 different types of Perugina chocolate, ranging from 70% dark bars to the famous Baci. Eat as much as you can, feel a little sick, then walk through the wondrous chocolate factory itself from above. See enormous machines pump out little delicious bits of chocolate then wrap them up in foil and package them under the watchful eyes of some workers. The two million Baci comment isn't an exaggeration. As the only factory able to produce Baci, they're all made here. After a walk through the factory, walk by the tasting room, stuff your mouth and pockets again, and then end at the gift shop. Because sometimes you just need to buy more chocolate.

i High season €9. Low season €5. ☺ Call to ask about tour times.

CHURCH OF SAN DOMENICO
CHURCH

V. del Castellano, 4   ☎075 572 4136

As the largest church in Umbria, San Domenico looms out over most scenic panoramas of Perugia. Go big or go home. It's time to get up close and personal with this church. Built in a rather austere Gothic style, the walls here don't need frescoes and intricate decorations to impress. They do that by sheer size alone. The apse window is the largest in Italy, coming in at 21 x 8.5m. Which all sounds fine as a number. But walk in, and you'll realize what "largest church in Umbria" really means.

Even when filled with people, walking around here will still feel like a lonely experience. Cavernous, echoing, and starkly empty. To get a true perception of size, take a look at a person walking in this church. Then look at the size of the column next to him. Yeah, this place is big. Plain white walls, a beautiful stained glass window, and some worn frescoes on some of the walls are all there is to see now. It once used to house the Perugia Altarpiece by Fra Angelico, but this is now housed in the National Gallery of Umbria.

Still wanna see some cool shit, though? Head into the cloisters next to this church. It's currently home to the National Archaeological Museum in Perugia. Even if urns aren't your jam, a walk in these cloisters is still beautiful. The halls in the museum are lined with Etruscan statues and funerary monuments. A bizarre amulet room contains all the weird things people used to carry for good luck. Because sometimes a wine cork is super lucky. The museum goes way, way back into Neanderthal era at one point, too. Head down and see the Cutu tomb, a completely intact Etruscan tomb which will give you the shivers. To calm down, head back up to the cloisters and enjoy some fast, complimentary Wi-Fi. History's always looking out for you.

i Free. ☒ Open daily 7am-noon and 4-7pm.

FOOD

AL MANGIAR BENE
ITALIAN $$
V. della Luna
☎075 573 1047

Italian food is great. But sometimes you just want to know the cow that gave the milk that was used in the cheese that's now the Parmesan on the table. For days like this, go to Al Mangiar Bene. Where American hipsters have made healthy, local food a pretentious occasion, this eco-conscious restaurant still has all the rustic charm of a small Italian eatery, with wooden tables, vaulted arches, and a cozy locale down an unassuming alleyway.

Locals and tourists alike flock to this place during lunch and dinner times (just be warned that if you're craving pizza, it's only served during dinner). Nevertheless, everything you eat here is delicious. From the fresh, purified water to the bread that for some reason just tastes so damn good...and your food hasn't even arrived yet.

For pasta, you get to play the fun game of "match the best type of pasta with the best type of sauce." Our suggestion? The umbricelli with the wild boar sauce. Because you can't leave Umbria without trying some wild boar. The steaks and meat options may get a little pricey, but knowing the restaurant's commitment to organic and healthy, you'll feel good eating these animal friends. Come during dinner, and you'll be able to try the delicious pizza options ranging from classic margherita to something more exciting like spicy sausage.

Enjoy the homey feeling of this restaurant and then eat as much as you possibly can. It's the healthy thing to do.

i Appetizers €6-12. Pizza €5-8. Pasta €6-10. Meats €10-18. ☒ Open M 7:30-10:45pm, Tu-Sa 12:302:45 pm and 7:30-10:45 pm, Su 7:30-10:45pm.

PIZZERIA MEDITERRANEA
PIZZA $
P. Piccinino 11/12
☎075 572 1322

The long lines outside this restaurant at lunchtime? Yeah, that should tip you off. The pizza here is ballin'. Located steps outside P. IV Novembre, if you want to snag a seat here, come close to opening at 12:30pm. Even if you don't make it in time, don't worry. Much like your pro-abstinence health teacher might have told you, some things are worth the wait.

This rustic little gem of a restaurant opens up to two large dining rooms that fill up during peak hours. The two-man pizza team working the dough and the oven whip out delicious, fresh pizzas like nobody's business, so even if you have to wait outside, the wait for pizza is never more than 5min.

perugia

Delicious options range from classic cheese and tomato sauce to some great prosciutto options. In trouble? Go for the Pizza Emergency made with delicious ricotta, eggplant, cherry tomatoes, and mozzarella. It'll be sure to cure whatever pizza problems you may be having or will ever have. The prices are very reasonable, service is fast, and despite the growing lines outside, you'll never feel rushed. That doesn't mean you won't devour your generous portions in a couple minutes (because you will), but stick around for some wine or a nice chat while letting that pizza become one with you. Then be ambitious and order seconds.

i Pizza €5-10. ☑ Open daily 12:30-2:30pm and 7:30-11:30pm.

CAFFÈ DELLA PENNA
C. Cavour 24

CAFE $

Mornings suck. Some great, cheap coffee and friendly, boisterous staff can make them suck a little less. To start your day right, head to Caffe delle Penne on V. Cavour. The workout along the steps leading down to this street will put you in the mood for some sweet, sweet pastries. You'll find them in this cafe once recommended with the rave review "They're the only place I know in Perugia that doesn't burn their coffee." This cute, colorful cafe holds true to that and so much more.

With a mixture of jazz and '60s Beach Boys music, you can appreciate really good cappuccinos and chocolate-filled cornetti here while listening to some Surf City. Plenty of fun, high tables decorated with photographs and newspaper clippings stand across from the bar. If you're still missing your bed, take one of the couches in the lounge area. Around the bar, which is also filled with liquors if you want to come by again after noon, are also love notes to jazz and vintage posters.

A favorite among locals, you'll often see old men reading the morning papers here, and the waitress can often greet many customers by name as they walk in the door. Come here enough, and maybe you'll even get this honor. If not, just enjoy the great espresso and chill ambience while preparing for a hike around Perugia.

i Coffee €1-1.10. Pastries €0.70-1. ☑ Open M-F 7:30am-midnight, Sa-Su 8am-midnight.

NIGHTLIFE

PIAZZA IV NOVEMBRE

SQUARE

In Perugia, people love going out. But sometimes, it's as if they forgot to go anywhere. With public drinking being totes okay, a popular youth pastime at night is grabbing some beers or mixed drinks served from one of the small bars on Vanvucci and then just sitting on the steps of the Duomo in Piazza IV Novembre and chatting the night away. There are no glass bottles allowed, so be prepared to see all those cool cats with plastic cups. But hey, they aren't red Solo cups, so the Italians are probably still winning.

The square and surrounding areas become packed with people walking back and forth (but not really going in anywhere) with their friends and stopping to get a mojito every now and then. To fit in, grab some friends and walk around this area on Friday and Saturday nights. It's the cool thing to do, and you'll see all sorts of people, from tourists to jazz bands to elderly couples, enjoying their literal nights out in Perugia.

If you're looking for wild bars or discos, they're further away, but this is a great place to start the night or just spend an entire chill evening. People stay out late, so grab that cup on Saturday night and keep drinking till communion starts on Sunday.

ELFO PUB

V. Sant'Agata

PUB

☎347 078 5981

Famously the unofficial pub of the Umbria Jazz Festival, all the cool cats of jazz gather here at Elfo Pub. Tucked away down some winding streets outside of P. IV Novembre, if you can't find this almost hidden joint, follow the guys with saxophones on their backs. They'll probably know the way. Or just follow the music as you clamber down some steep streets in Perugia.

The only bar on this lonely street, it fills up quite fast on weekend nights and pretty much every day during Umbria Jazz. A bright green light bathes the entrance in an eerie haze. Walk in and you'll be transported to some jazzy heaven. Spontaneous jam sessions inside this cavernous little bar fill the room with vaulted arches with life. From the ceiling by the bar hangs the famous lucky bike. Rub its wheel for good luck. No one really knows why it's lucky, but some rubbing never hurt anybody.

With great beer, wooden seats and tables, and a small cozy location, when this bar can't hold its clientele, they all spill onto the steps and into the streets, so amateur (and some really good professional) jazz music can spread all throughout Perugia. Snaps to you, Elfo.

i Drinks €3-8. ☼ Open daily 8am-2:30am.

LA TERRAZZA

Mercato Coperto

BAR

Bright pink and purple chairs, umbrellas, drinks, and a drop dead gorgeous panorama of the city of Perugia. Nightlife just got an upgrade. La Terrazza is a beautiful outdoor bar open during the earlier hours for coffee and snacks and then fills up after midnight on busy nights when people who want to drink in the beautiful nighttime view and a couple shots of tequila stop by.

Located in Mercato Coperto, this lively area has all the souvenirs you could ever need but never once feels to cliche because every time you sigh at being in Perugia, look out and you'll catch a glimpse of the preserved medieval city with its high hills, beautiful churches, and distant mountains that you're staying in. So it can't be too bad.

The bar itself isn't incredibly remarkable but probably boasts one of the best spots in Perugia. When to come can be tricky. For the best view possible, come around sunset. This place will be rather sleepy, but the city itself lights up in the sun's glow. For a more rockin' time, come by on weekend nights after 10pm and, for a safe bet, after midnight. Then you can live it up next to the glowing lights of the city below you.

i Drinks €3-10. ☼ Open daily 11am-2am.

ESSENTIALS

Practicalities

- **TOURIST OFFICE:** The Tourist Information Center is in P. Matteoti. The hours are M-Sa 8:30am-1:30pm and 3:30-6:30pm and Su 9am-1pm. Here you can purchase a thorough map of historical Perugia for 50 cents.

- **TOURIST INFORMATION:** ☎075 573 6458

- **ATM MACHINES:** Along Corso Vannucci

Emergency

- **EMERGENCY TELEPHONE:** 112

- **FIRE:** 115

perugia

- **POLICE:** 113
- **HOSPITALS:** Hospital Santa Maria della Misericordia (V. Brunamonti, 51)
- **PHARMACIES:** Farmacia Lemmi at Corso Vannucci 57

Getting There

By Metro

Trenitalia runs regular trains to Perugia from Rome and Florence as well as many other surrounding large cities. You'll need to make a transfer or two if you're coming from somewhere further like Naples or Milan. The main station is known simply as Perugia or Fontivegge. From the train station, either take the Minimetro to Pincetto or a bus to P. Italia to get to the city center.

By Bus

The main bus station in Perugia is at P. Partigiani. Sulga offers transportation between Perugia and Florence. Other bus companies such as APM, SSIT, and ATC Terni offer transport throughout Umbria and beyond.

Getting Around

By Minimetro

The minimetro will become your adorable, futuristic best friend if you need to get from the train station to the city center often. Running from Pian di Massiano through Fontivegge to Pincetto, you can catch the minimetro from M-Sa 7am-9:20pm and Su 8:30am-8:20pm. Tickets cost €1.50. Hold on to your ticket after entering; you'll need it to exit the station.

By Bus

Buses will take you anywhere you don't feel like walking. The main places to catch a bus are at P. Italia and Stazione Fontivegge. Tickets cost €1.50.

By Taxi

Taxis in Perugia are expensive, and unless you're going hella far, you probably won't need one. P. Italia is a good place to find a cab, however.

By Foot

A lot of Perugia is walkable if you don't mind the occasional stairs or sharp inclines.

assisi

italy

A breathtakingly beautiful town built in the mountains, Assisi possesses the kind of natural beauty that will make you want to renounce all your worldly goods. Famous for being the birthplace of St. Francis of Assisi (shocker, we know), the founder of the Franciscan order of monks, don't be surprised to find monks in full regalia wandering around in the pizzerias here. The occasional barefoot pilgrim, complete with rags and walking staff, graces this religious center, too. There are no shortage of churches in Assisi, the most famous of course being the Basilica of San Francesco d'Assisi, with its beautiful mosaics and picturesque views from all around. Pretty much any of the small cobblestone streets will give you a workout by sending you ever upward (you are on a mountain, after all) to churches or beautiful historical sights. Assisi can easily be seen in a daytrip, but if you can, stay overnight and watch the sunset behind the basilica turn the sky gorgeous shades of pink and purple and enjoy some flavor of the ecstasy that made the monks give up their iPhones. Maybe these sunsets make it worth it.

BED AND BREAKFAST NEW DAY

B&B $$

V. San Francesco, 18   ☎075 81 37 39   www.bandbnewdayassisi.it

There aren't any good hostel-priced accommodations right in Assisi, but Bed and Breakfast New Day offers great rooms in the city at reasonable prices. And oh yeah, it's down the street from the Basilica of San Francesco. Is there anything else you really need in Assisi?

Located in a renovated 13th-century building, you'll get the full rustic charm of the city here. Be sure to book here in advance, as there are only two rooms, a single and a double, so plan ahead by a couple weeks. Once you snag a room, however, prepare for a friendly welcome from the staff. The street is a quiet one, so you'll have plenty of quiet time to sleep or meditate and let go of worldly goods and such. The bathrooms are large, and the rooms are clean and comfortable, with cute wooden accents and floral decor.

A great breakfast is served in the morning with warm pastries and coffee and tea, so try to wake up early for that. Assisi isn't a huge town, and since you probably won't be staying here for more than a night or two, spending the big bucks to get St. Francis at your doorstep is worth every euro penny.

i Singles €45. Doubles €90.

SIGHTS

BASILICA OF SAN FRANCESCO

CHURCH

P. San Francesco   ☎075 81 90 01   www.sanfrancescoassisi.org

For a man who renounced all his worldly goods, St. Francis sure did get an amazingly glamorous basilica in Assisi. As the main sight to see in this mountain town, this church has been visited by monks, pilgrims, and tourists for centuries. And seeing its beauty after a rugged climb up the mountain (or rugged bus ride up) will make the effort to get to Assisi so worth it.

Enormous and difficult to miss, from first sight, it's a masterpiece. With beautiful arched colonnades leading to the lower entrance, you'll just have to walk in to see the honors bestowed upon this man. St. Francis, back when he was just Francis, was a man who saw the true way and decided to live as a beggar and eventually founded the Franciscan order. Making him kind of a big deal. Now plenty of monks grace this basilica, wearing their iconic brown robes throughout the aisles and out into the city and the pizzerias too. It's pretty awesome.

Walk into the church and let the lower basilica amaze you. With enormous arches and a ceiling painted dark blue and with stars like the night sky, it's like a whole new world down here. Every inch in covered by frescoes, and all of them are beautiful. Giotto might steal the show upstairs, but take a look at all these masterpieces.

Walk down the aisle and you'll get to the tomb of St. Francis himself, surrounded by even more ceiling frescoes. The tomb is elaborate, decked out in gold, with bright green lanterns and tiny little columns surrounding it. If you want to get closer to St. Francis, you can take a walk down below the tomb, which is an area reserved for quiet prayer. Another relic room is also downstairs and features some great finds, like the robes and (our personal favorite) slippers of St. Francis himself.

Take the stairs up to the upper basilica, which is just as impressive. Giotto's frescoes take up much of this high-ceilinged basilica. Admire the stained glass windows as well. Then walk out, and you'll get the most iconic view of the basilica, complete with the hedges outside that spell out PAX, or peace. Snap some pictures, maybe a selfie, and then leave feeling #blessed.

i *Free.* ✪ *Open daily 6am-7pm.*

DUOMO DI SAN RUFINO
P. San Rufino   ☎075 81 22 83   www.assisimuseodiocesano.com   CHURCH

Where the Basilica of San Francesco will make you look up at beautiful night skies and ceiling frescoes, the Duomo of Assisi will make you look down. Underneath this church are the ruins of the old church that it was built upon, and open green glass floors at some points in the cathedral allow you to look down and see it.

Once you look up at the actual church itself, come face to face with a dramatic suspended Christ hanging from the altar. Shock value points. This church may not be as elaborate as some other important ones you may see in Assisi, but it is one of their most important ones, being the Duomo and all. Walk around the rather stark white walls and look at the gorgeous statues of St. Francis, among other saints who stand around this church.

The whole cathedral is made with beautiful marble. There is an area reserved for praying, and though you're usually not allowed in, take a peek at the pretty pastel paintings in the room. If you come at the right time, the choir might be practicing, filling the entire Duomo with angelic singing voices.

On your way out, take a look down at the ruins again (the effect never gets old), and then prepare to leave the cool church to pilgrimage through the rest of Assisi.

i *Free.* ✪ *Open daily 7am-noon and 2pm-sunset.*

ROCCA MAGGIORE
Ple. della Libertà Comunali   ☎075 815 52 34   www.comune.assisi.pg.it/indirizzi-e-contatti   CASTLE

If Assisi isn't high up enough for you, climb up to Rocca Maggiore. An ancient castle and fortress, this place has survived because of its great defenses. And also for being hella high up. Take the steps up and prepare for an uphill battle. Once you get up here, though, you'll find some amazing views of Assisi from above.

This impressive castle that dominates the skyline was built in the 1100s and to this day presents the might of a former great fort. And if you choose to make it up here, you get to pay it a visit! Largely unguided, a wander through here is exactly that—a wander. Check out the fortifications all around it. Enter some rooms and find the creepiest exhibits known to mankind, where curators have felt the need to do banquet table recreations with faceless mannequins dressed up all old-timey style. We're not saying that they move when you don't look, but try not to spend too much time with these mannequins if you can.

As you make your way around the fort, try to find the least sketchy flight of stairs and take it up. Any of these flights will offer you more rooms with temporary exhibits but also even higher views of rolling hills and mountains and the precious Assisi down below. After you've had enough of stone walls, impenetrable fortifications, and creeptastic rooms, head down to the gift shop where you can buy medieval props that were definitely not meant for five-year-olds. They were made for you.

i *€5. Students and over 65 €3.50.* ✪ *Open daily in summer 9am-8pm.*

FOOD

PIZZERIA IL DUOMO   PIZZA
V. Porta Perlici, 11   ☎075 81 63 26 www.assisiduomo.com

You'll need to do some praying to find cheap eats in Assisi. Overrun by monks
and tourists, this city has become a little too filled with souvenir shops instead of
Jesus. So if you're really craving a meal but don't feel like asking for alms, head
to Pizzeria Il Duomo.

So maybe it's not the best pizza in all of Italy. But it sure is cheap by Assisi
standards. A backpacker's and student's haven, this pizzeria serves up fast and
decent pizza with great menu deals. Walk into this seemingly small pizzeria by
the gorgeous Duomo and realize that the small door opens up to a Duomo-sized
restaurant. Two large rooms accommodating large groups and tavola-per-unos
pretty well, this restaurant is prepared for the hordes of tourists waiting to descend. Maybe even an occasional monk. Anything is possible with the help of the
Lord.

The menu is that of a fairly standard pizzeria. Cheese, tomatoes, prosciutto—whatever you want, it's probably here. What makes this place stand out are
the great deals. Choose from any combination of drinks, French fries, and pizza
in the special menus, and then let it all be served in front of you in the cute
wooden and brick restaurant.

i Pizza €4-7. Special menus €5-10. ⏰ Open daily noon-3pm and 7-10pm.

ESSENTIALS

Practicalities

- **TOURIST OFFICE:** There's a tourist office right by the Basilica di San Francesco. Closed during
  lunchtime.
- **ATMS:** Located mostly by the bus station.

Emergency

- **EMERGENCY TELEPHONE:** 112
- **FIRE:** 115
- **POLICE:** 113
- **HOSPITALS:** Ospedale Civile di Assisi (V. Fuori Porta Nuova)
- **PHARMACIES:** Located in and surrounding P. del Comune.

Getting There

By Metro
Frequent Trenitalia service runs between Perugia (Stazione Fontivegge) and Assisi.
Tickets cost around €2-7. From the Assisi station, take one of the buses running Line
C (€1.30) that stop outside up to the city center of Assisi. Buses run every 40min.

By Bus
Buses run from Perugia's Piazza Partigiani straight into the center of Assisi. Tickets
cost €3-4.

Getting Around
Do as the Franciscans do. But no need to be barefoot. All of Assisi is walkable if you
don't mind some steep inclines.

pompeii

If Rome isn't Roman enough for you, take a daytrip to Pompeii, the city buried in time. Sailing around the Bay of Naples, you'll see Mt. Vesuvius lurking formidably over nearly all vistas. On August 24, 79 CE, the volcano erupted, blanketing Pompeii in a cloud of ash. Though tragic for the residents of this ancient metropolis, the eruption created a gold mine for archaeologists and a historical playground for tourists. Streets covered in stone blocks, fading frescoes, chipped mosaics, and a labyrinth of small rooms may get repetitive after a few hours but nonetheless inspire thoughts about how different life was nearly two millennia ago.

ORIENTATION

The ruins cover 66 hectares of land, although only 45 are accessible to the public. The area around the Circumvesuviana, the Porta Marina entrance, and Piazza Esedra is full of expensive restaurants and souvenir shops. A 20-25min. walk down V. Plirio and then V. Roma leads to the modern city's centro. From here, the Trenitalia train station is down V. Sacra in P. XXVIII Marzo. Inside the ruins, the most important sights are located on the western side, closer to the Porta Marina entrance. These sights include the Forum and the House of the Faun. A little to the east is the old city's brothel, and at the far eastern corner, you'll find Pompeii's amphitheater. Working your way back from there toward the entrance, you'll pass the Great Theater on the southern edge of the ruins.

SIGHTS

One ticket gives you the run of an entire ancient city. But touring the ruins is no simple undertaking—Pompeii was a true metropolis, complete with basilicas, bars, and brothels, and that kind of scope can be intimidating. Plenty of tour guides will try to coerce you into joining their group, which will cost €10-20. Rather than shelling out to become one of the crowd, opt for an informative audio tour (€6.50, 2 for €10). While both options will teach you a lot, one of the most fun ways to experience Pompeii is to navigate its maze-like streets solo—even with a map, you're likely to get lost. Of course, the pleasure of going at it alone can be mitigated when the city is packed, and at times, it's hard to walk down one of Pompeii's cobbled streets without running into another visitor. Come in the early summer or the fall for a slightly less crowded experience. If you plan on seeing more sites, a combined ticket allows entry to Herculaneum, Oplontis, Stabia, Boscoreale, and Pompeii over the course of 3 days. (*i* €11, EU citizens ages 18-24 €5.50, EU citizens under 18 and over 65 free; combined ticket €20/10/free. Cash only. ☑ Open daily Apr-Oct 8:30am-7:30pm; Nov-Mar 8:30am-5pm. Last entry 1½hr. before close.)

Near the Forum

As soon as you enter through Porta Marina, you can get down to business at the main market district in Pompeii, complete with the Basilica, Temple of Venere, and Forum. Stand in the middle of the Forum and look left, and you'll get a beautiful view of Mt. Vesuvius looming above the city. Next, wander into the Granai del Foro, which has plaster body casts, including the famous one of the dog. But if these are all too mortal for your divine tastes, walk into the Tempio di Apollo, which has copies of the statues of Apollo and Artemis that once dominated the area (the OG versions are at the Naples's Museo Archeologico Nazionale). If you're feeling dirty (because the showers in your hostel are always full), check out the well-preserved baths in the Terme del Foro. It can count as your proper hygiene care for the week.

pompeii

Near the House of the Faun

To see more luxuries than you're getting at your one-star hostel, invite yourself over to the Casa del Fauno, an enormous and impressive ancient Roman home. With a bronze faun statue explaining the name and various mosaics, the lack of the famous Alexander Mosaic may be heartbreaking, but it's still a spacious, luxurious old home. For more tastes of wealth, go to the House of the Small Fountain, which has a fountain (no plot twist there). But also take a look at the frescoes, mosaics, and small sculptures while you're here. To see things on a larger scale, go to the House of the Vettii, where you'll find the famous frescoes of a well-endowed Priapus, who holds his place as the elephant in the otherwise gorgeous red room.

Near the Brothel

If ruins and an ancient city haven't left you all hot and bothered, you're probably just hard to please. But go to the ancient brothel, the Lupanare, and try to not be a little turned on (by history, of course). The explicit frescoes on the wall displaying various sex positions were either used to get the clientele excited or to give them a list of services provided. Various stone beds (which were covered with mattresses) occupy the surrounding rooms that were once sprinkled with graffiti about the ladies (and their various) there. Nearby, the Stabian Baths have a body cast and more mosaics for those who prefer non-pornographic images.

Near the Great Theater

To make your visit to Pompeii even more dramatic, head to the Great Theater, where rowdy Romans once gathered to watch bawdy plays and summer rock and roll concerts. Or something like that. Nearby, the Small Theater was built for the hipsters in the city to gather and listen to poetry readings in an acoustically impressive structure. The Botanical Garden next door offers some natural wonders of the area (because nature isn't all explosions and volcanoes).

Near the Amphitheater

To see what Pompeii residents did for fun when they weren't dying, check out the massive amphitheater where they gathered to watch others die. Holding 20,000 spectators during gladiator battles, it's almost large enough to accommodate all the tourists getting in your personal space. The Great Palaestra nearby is a lovely place for respite where you can sit under some trees and feel one with nature before you head to the Garden of the Fugitives to dampen your mood with some more plaster casts of the less-than-fortunate Pompeii-ers. But if you're set on ending things on a happier note, walk through the House of Octavius Quartio and House of Venus before you leave, where horticulture will give you some symbolic understanding of man's control over nature. And maybe convince you to take up gardening. (Your mom will be so proud.)

ESSENTIALS

Practicalities

- **TOURIST OFFICES:** Offices at P. Porta Marina Inferiore 12 (☎081 53 63 293) and at V. Sacra 1 (☎081 85 07 255) offer free maps of Pompeii, tickets for sightseeing buses around Campania, and pamphlets about area museums. (www.pompeiturismo.it ☒ Open daily 8:30am-6:30pm.)
- **LUGGAGE STORAGE:** Bag check at the archaeological site is free and mandatory for large bags.

Emergency

- **POLICE:** Carabinieri in Pompei Centro at V. Lepanto 61. (☎081 85 06 163)

Italy

Getting There

The best way to get to Pompeii's archaeological site is to take a train to Naples's Stazione Centrale from Termini Station. (€11-45. ☒ 1-3hr., 50 per day 4:52am-9:50pm.) Once in Naples, go to the lower level to catch the Circumvesuviana train (€2.90. ☒ 20-30min., every 15min.) toward Sorrento. Get off at Pompei Scavi. From the train, the ruins' main entrance, Porta Marina, is to the right. If you proceed down V. Villa dei Misteri, you can head through the less crowded entrance at P. Esedra (although audio tours are not available here). Alternatively, you can take a Trenitalia train from Naples. (€2.90. ☒ 20-40min., every 30min.) The train drops you off in modern Pompeii's centro. From the station, walk up V. Sacra until you reach P. Bartolo Longo. Turn left down V. Colle San Bartolomeo. It's a 20-25min. walk to the archaeological site's main entrance; it's better to enter at the less crowded P. Anfiteatro, a short way down V. Plinio.

palermo

Gritty, bustling, historic, and real. Palermo takes thousands of years of history under Greek, Byzantine, Norman, and Spanish influence, fills its streets with gorgeous theaters and churches, and then walks by them all without looking twice. Though a popular tourist city, it never feels like one. The famous buildings all look worn, and the cobblestone streets by the markets are littered with shrimp tails. Palermo is not a historic relic. It's still a living, thriving city full of fishermen, immigrants, students, and businessmen all going about their days in the shadow of breathtaking Byzantine cathedrals. At night, the city comes alive with huge crowds gathering at bars and discos, filling open squares with chatter and street food, and dancing until the early hours of the morning.

Palermo is the kind of city that could swallow you up with its slightly grimy building facades and winding narrow streets. To situate yourself, know the three main streets: Via Roma, Via Vittorio Emmanule and Via Maqueda, which will take you pretty much anywhere you want to go. Palermo's famous street markets, which fill up old streets with everything from swordfish heads to sassy Italian t-shirts, are at Ballaro, Vucciria, and Capo. Head down Via Maqueda and you'll get to the famous Teatro Massimo, the second largest theater in Europe that could house operas with elephants. Head down Via Roma and you'll reach the Politeama, an enormous piazza with another large theater. Along the way, numerous churches with golden Byzantine mosaics covering every inch or spiraling Baroque columns or Arab style roofs done by master craftsmen line the streets, so always be sure to peek in. In between all the culture and history and zooming Vespas, you'll catch a glimpse of Palermo in all its raw, gorgeous glory.

SIGHTS

CAPPELLA PALATINA AND PALAZZO REALE   PALACE

P. Indipendenza   ☎091 626 2833 www.federicosecondc.org/en/norman-palace
Sometimes having a palace just isn't enough. If you're like the Norman kings in Sicily, you'll want a drop dead gorgeous chapel as well. A visit to the Palazzo dei Normanni, also known as the Royal Palace, will make you feel lowly in more way than one. It's like the building form of middle school, but with its beautiful architecture and mosaics, it's well worth a visit.

The main attraction of the entire palace is the Palatine Chapel. Built in the 1100s, this chapel is one of the most beautiful you will see in all of Sicily. Every inch is covered with Byzantine-style mosaics, leaving all the walls a shimmering gold in the light. Every arch and every corner is filled with brightness and beau-

AI QUATTRO CANTI
HOSTEL $

P. del Ponticello, 1 ☎339 266 0963 www.aiquattrocanti.hostel.com

Ai Quattro Canti, named after the nearby baroque square of the same name, is an adorable little hostel with bright colors, comfy couches, and boards advertising past crazy tequila parties. Which captures everything anyone ever wanted from a hostel.

It's rather small, with only two rooms and two bathrooms, but if you can snag a room here, take it. The prices are cheap, the beds are comfy, and the hostel owner, Giuseppe, is amazing. He fosters a close environment, encouraging new people and old to go out to dinner or grab really cheap beers together, and he is always willing to make you an espresso. Take it. Then go out with a bunch of your new hostel friends and relish in that backpacking life.

The hostel also has a decently-sized kitchen and enough utensils to cook your own food. The hostel is steps away from V. Maqueda and V. Vittorio Emanuele, too, so good cheap food isn't hard to find in this area. The great location right in the center of everything will make you want to walk everywhere in Palermo, but the kitchen walls lined with possible excursion destinations and information about how to get there might give you enough wanderlust to head to more gorgeous beach resorts for a day. So if you're looking for a fun, social place to stay with pink couches, flowery '70s curtains in some doorways, and blue waves on the walls, come here.

i Dorms €16. ⏰ No curfew. Reception hours vary.

A CASA DI AMICI
HOSTEL $

V. Dante 57 ☎091 765 4650 www.acasadiamici.com

Who doesn't like houses and who doesn't like friends? That's why the concept behind A Casa di Amici is brilliant. Add in squeaky clean rooms, comfortable beds, air conditioning, and a great social atmosphere, and you've got a winner.

Bright, spacious rooms, hardwood floors, and a sleek, artsy aesthetic make this hostel an ideal place to stay. The large common areas and social atmosphere also make this an ideal place to have a kickass time in Palermo. The facilities are great. Free breakfast and access to musical instruments? We feel like that's something every hostel should start to offer. Because after some drumming lessons, you'll finally find an appropriate way to beat it in a hostel, thus solving an age old problem.

Located a little off V. della Liberta, you'll still be within walking distance of the main streets and sights in Palermo. Add to that free Wi-Fi, free towels, and free TV, and you might be so overwhelmed that you'll have to use the yoga and meditation room. This hostel is always prepared. Once you've collected yourself, head out into Palermo, which isn't as clean as your hostel, but it's still got that fun charm.

i Dorms €16-20. ⏰ Reception 24hr.

tiful artistry. The mosaics represent everything from the Signore, Jesus Christ himself, to acts of the apostles to beautiful flora and fauna.

The most beautiful aspect of this chapel, however, is its seamless integration of Norman, Byzantine, and Arab works. Built in a Norman palace with Norman

italy

architecture and doors with Latin inscriptions, the chapel opens up to gorgeous Byzantine mosaics and Greek text; then, as you look up, you'll see the Arabic arches and roof with Arabic script. Multiculturalism, bitches.

As you walk out of the chapel, be sure to check on the chapel's left, where there's an inscription written in Latin, Greek, and Arabic, capturing all the styles represented here. Afterwards, head up to the more palace-y part of this palace. Walk through some beautiful halls and rooms filled with paintings of everything from Hercules and his labors in parliament (damn that bureaucracy) to portraits of the viceroys. Though the palace part may pale in comparison to the shimmery chapel, it's still worth a look. It's all higher society, after all.

i €8 M, €7 Tu-Th, €8 F-Su. ☎ Open M-Sa 8:15am-5:40pm, Su 8:15am-1pm.

MONREALE
MEDIEVAL CITY

About 15km south of Palermo lies the beautiful medieval city of Monreale. Serviced regularly by Palermo city buses 389 and 309, which drop you off steps away from a free shuttle into Monreale proper, make the trip down here if you have a couple hours to spare.

Located high up on a mountain, this city offers stunning views of Palermo and the sea below. It's also full of winding cobblestone streets that eventually give way to a small, pulsing city that exists apart from the tourist world. Small bakeries and pizzerias line all parts of town. Find somewhere a little off the beaten road for a good meal. Some of the "fast food" options are surprisingly delicious in this city.

Take some time wandering around Monreale, then go off to see the main attraction itself. Impossible to miss (kinda because the bus drops you off right there) is the enormous cathedral. As one of the greatest examples of Norman architecture, this Duomo is a breathtaking sight. Inside, everything is shimmering gold. Beautifully crafted Byzantine mosaics cover every part of the ceiling, making sure you spend a lot of time looking up. Gilded, shining figures float in golden backgrounds. A famous and large Christ Pantocrator stares severely from the apse. Scenes from the Bible, such as Noah's Ark, surround the rest of the interior.

It's one of those rare creations where everything is pretty. The blue and gold ceilings, the Corinthian columns, the back door which is so high it almost opens up the entire church. If you time your visit here, you might be able to wedding crash one of the many lucky couples who get to be married in this marvelous cathedral. During these adorable moments, maybe you can even catch stern Jesus looking a little happier. He practically glows.

i Cathedral entrance free. ☎ Open M-Sa 8:30am-12:45pm and 2:30-5pm, Su 8-10am and 2:30-5pm.

SAN GIUSEPPE DEI TEATINI
CHURCH

C. Vittorio Emanuele, at Quattro Canti

One of the churches in the beautiful baroque square of Quattro Canti, San Giuseppe del Teatini is a hidden gem in the midst of the loud, gritty city. The weathered facade gives way to a gorgeous and untouched Sicilian Baroque church from the 17th century.

Step inside and be taken aback first by how beautiful the red and green marbles and twisting columns are, and then by the fact that there's practically no one here. Every corner is decorated with rich marbles and stunning frescoes. Take a look up at the elaborate ceiling painted with soft pastels. Then look down at the lovely marble floor. The statues decorating the church are masterfully made, and some, like the Virgin Mary, are done in a flowered marble.

The altar is breathtaking and will make you keep looking up as cherubs and angels peer out in high relief. The twisted baroque columns and cherub'd columns and bright marbles all give the building itself a sort of movement. But then the interior is silent. Here is a ruin kept in perfect condition, in all its grandeur, with very few people to come admire it. And within all that, it captures an essence of the forgotten beauty in Palermo. It's enough to make you start writing poetry or something. We can respect that.

i Free. ◌ Open daily 8:30-11am and 6-8pm.

PALAZZO CHIARAMONTE
MUSEUM

P. Marina, 61 ☎091 607 5306

One of the more unusual sights in Palermo, this historical castle turned Spanish Inquisition prison turned museum is a somber and eye-opening look into the past. Once home to the powerful Sicilian lord, Chiaramonte, this castle built in the 14th century has had quite the life beyond that. During the late-15th century to early 16th, this castle fell under the rule of the Spanish, who destroyed many of the symbols of Chiaramonte. Then from 1600 to 1782, it was the home to the tribunal and many prisons for the Spanish Inquisition. Now both the prisons and a few rooms of the palace are open to the public as a museum that can only be visited along with a guide.

First, a guide will take you into the archaeological site where artisans quarters from the 10th century have been dug up (i.e., this is where you can check out some cool pots—no museum in Sicily is complete without those). Next is the Interrogation room where a Spanish inquisitor was killed, which seems super badass. Unfortunately, now it's just a room.

After this introduction, the tour takes a turn for the dark and twisted. It heads into the prisons where much graffiti from the prisoners remains. The Poet's Cell is famous for having verses scribbled on the walls. Other sections have elaborate sketches and drawings of wide-eyed saints and slightly inaccurate maps of Sicily. The walk through the cells is like a walk through an intellectual asylum. Terrifying, heartbreaking, beautiful. Many write on the walls asking for death. Other create gorgeous human figures. One of the last rooms may pull some heartstrings, since it was home to an Englishman who wrote his graffiti in English.

Following the prisons, turn into the palace. All the symbols of Chiaramonte were destroyed by the Spanish, but the two visible rooms here are still beautiful. Note the Arab influences in the doors and take a look at the gorgeous painted ceilings. The palace is a short visit with looks only into two large rooms, but it's also home to Renato Guttuso's painting, Vucciria. Then let the guide lead you back out into the sunset and take a couple moments to figure out what the hell just happened. History, that's what.

i €5. ◌ Open Tu-Sa 9am-6:30pm, Su 10am-2pm.

DUOMO
CHURCH

P. di Cattedrale ☎091 33 43 73 www.cattedrale.palermo.it

As the most important church in Palermo, we guess this is worth a visit. As you're walking down V. Vittorio Emanuele, stop at the Duomo to go see a building undergoing an intense architectural identity crisis while also embodying in stone the confusing history of the city.

To get the true scope of the Duomo's rich architectural diversity, we'll have to start way, way back. In 1184, the Archbishop of Palermo had this grand old idea to build a cathedral. Perché, non? He chose the site where it stands today because there used to stand an old mosque from the ninth century which itself had been built over an old Christian basilica. This place was just ripe for some more building. The story goes that the archbishop wanted to build a cathedral that would rival the one in Monreale. Well, he failed. Sorry, Palermo. Monreale is widely recognized as a more beautiful church. But all is not lost—the Duomo still stands as quite the masterpiece.

Starting in 1184, the Duomo was built in a Norman style. In the 13th and 14th centuries, however, like any good angsty teen, the facade started its Gothification. In the 15th century, the Spanish brought their Catalan style to mix with the Gothic. In the 18th century, the cathedral underwent a neoclassical phase. So now as you walk in, the main facade is Gothic. Step in and you'll enter a scavenger hunt for history. Look out for columns inscribed with Qur'an verses and the south porch done in the Catalan style. The interior has a stark neoclassical appearance, which is quite different from the bedazzled interiors of the Duomo at Monreale. Still, the sheer size, history, and self ascribed-importance make this Duomo incredible.

Inside are also the tombs of past Italian kings. For a modest fee, you can go see the royal pantheon and some impressive tombs, including that of Roger II, the first king of Sicily. If bling's your thing, also stop by the treasury full of gold and crowns. Take that, Monreale. You don't have to be the prettiest when you've got the bling.

i Free. €2 for crypts. €3 for crypts and treasury. €7 for crypts, treasury, and roof. ◷ Open M-Sa 9am-5:30pm, Su 7:30am-1:30pm and 4pm-7pm.

FOOD

ANTICA FOCACCERIA DEL MASSIMO ITALIAN $
V. Bara all'Olivella 76 ☎091 33 56 28

Want to know where all the locals eat? Look no further than Antica Focacceria del Massimo. Don't let its proximity to Teatro Massimo fool you. Authentic local food, authentic locals, and some of the best food around can be found here.

Let your counter-cultural personality rejoice at the lack of tourist menus here. This large restaurant has a cafeteria-esque feel with tables scattered everywhere and everyone from workers to students trying to get a glimpse of what's on today's menu. This busy restaurant specializes in pasta. Walk in and head toward the counter in the back where there's a menu posted. Delicious meals range from ravioli to spaghetti to probably some of the best lasagna in Palermo. All for around €3-4.

Head to the cash register, pay for your meal, and then go to the back counter of pastas, give your receipt to the chef, and wait around 5min. for your freshly-made pasta to come to the table where you sit down. Oh, and then breathe. It's not that complicated. Trust us.

The pasta comes in large portions, so one plate could easily fill you for lunch and keep your wallet filled for the rest of the day. The al dente is perfect, the sauces are fresh, and after you take one bite, you, too, will realize why locals flock here for lunch at all hours.

i Pasta €3-4. Panini €2.50-4. ◷ Open daily 8am-4pm.

MOUNIR PIZZA $
V. Giovanni da Procida 19 ☎091 77 30 005

Most of the time, you really shouldn't wander into small alleyways in Palermo. But make an exception for Mounir. For some incredible (and incredibly cheap) pizza in Palermo, veer a little off your trusted V. Roma and go to Mounir. A small pizzeria with plenty of outdoor seating, this is a popular venue among the young crowd thanks to its delicious food, large servings, and bargain prices.

Walk into the storefront, and you'll see Mounir himself tossing pizza dough and ceremoniously dumping delicious toppings like prosciutto and tomatoes on fresh-baked pizza. There's a modest menu hanging up on the wall where you can choose which pizza you'd like to be made right on the spot. If pizza isn't what

palermo

you're craving, you should really get that checked out, but there's also a decent kebab menu. Can't decide? Go for a kebab pizza.

Delicious choices include prosciutto and cheese, quattro formaggi, or capricciosa when you're feeling a little gluttonous and just want it all. Order, then grab a table outside. Not enough tables? One of the waiters will set one up for you. There is usually a wait because all the pizzas are made fresh, and it can take some time on a busy Friday night. But it's always worth it.

i Pizza €4-8. ☼ Open daily 7pm-1am.

PASTICCERIA CAPPELLO
V. Colonna Rotta, 68

BAKERY $
☎091 48 96 01

There are a lot of words to describe Palermo. Sweet isn't usually one of them. That's until you decide to haul ass up to Pasticceria Cappello, at which point Palermo is just a slightly more Mafia-riddled version of Candyland.

Walk into this pastry shop and you'll be surrounded on all sides by pastries, tarts, cannoli, gelato, and pretty much anything else one could need to satisfy every desire behind glass counters. If you're in the mood for gelato or granita, head to the right, where a counter of smooth, fresh gelato will parade a rainbow of flavors in front of your eyes. If your dreams are a little more solid, take your pick of pastries everywhere else in the shop.

Delicious cannoli with sweet ricotta, tart pastries made with fresh berries, and delicious cream cakes topped with fresh and exotic fruits like kiwi, mango, and pineapple—you really can't go wrong here. And with most of the small pastries costing less than €0.50, it would just be wrong not to try almost all of them.

i Pastries €0.20-2.50. ☼ Open M-Tu 7am-9:30pm, Th-Su 7am-9:30pm.

AL GELONE
V. Giuseppe Puglisi Bertolino, 23

GELATO $
☎091 36 36 04

You know what you need? Gelato. Obviously. So go to Al Gelone. Venture a little beyond P. Sturzo, and you'll be rewarded with some fresh, delicious (and cheap!) gelato. Modern quirkiness at its finest, the bright colors, neon spoon decor, and tables in the shape of giant spoons are something to look at. If you can bear to look away from the large selection of gelato, that is.

On the right wall as you enter, there's a giant picture of a chef magically pointing with his finger as fresh ingredients swirl about. Which, okay, is a little weird, but this gelato is pretty damn magical. We think that's the message of the mural.

Flavors range from fresh pistachio to coffee where you can still taste the grounds to anise because why the hell not. Cones are cheap, at €2 for a medium, so don't be afraid to ask for two flavors. If you want something a little lighter and more refreshing, head to the counter on the far end for some granita, which is like ice cream but made with water instead of cream, meaning it will quench your thirst a little better. So we think you should just have both. Order, pay, then take your gelato, sit on one of the white stools filled with sand (really, don't ask questions—it's modern art) and enjoy the loveliness of smooth, cold gelato that you just have to devour before it melts all over you. The brain freeze is worth it.

i Gelato €1.50-3. ☼ Open daily 11am-1am.

ANTICA FOCACCERIA SAN FRANCESCO
V. Alessandro Paternostro 58

STREET FOOD, RISTORANTE $$
☎091 32 02 64 www.anticafocacceria.it

Since 1834, Antica Focacceria San Francesco has been serving up delicious street food in a charming little cobblestone piazza next to a church. For five generations, this restaurant has seen everyone from weary travelers to hungry locals to mob bosses to carabinieri at its doorstep. But nothing has stopped this family from making some of the best food in Palermo.

Enjoy the rustic charm of the enormous brown and gold doors, walk by the kitchen where all the magic happens, and take a seat outside where you can admire the prettiness of old Sicilian buildings and churches outside. Then get ready to feast.

The menu is divided into two parts: the street food and the food for fancy shmancy travelers (which is still reasonably priced). As far as street food goes, try some of the delicious and filling arancini, fried rice balls filled with meat and cheese in a way that will almost make you never want to eat regular off-the-street arancini again. There's also unsurprisingly focaccia at this focacceria, which is a type of Italian flatbread that can be filled with tomatoes and cheeses.

If eating street food in a sit down restaurant is a little too crazy, there's also a great selection of pastas and seafood. Try the rigatoni, which is al dente at its perfection. You also can't go wrong with anything plus sardines in Palermo.

i Street food €3-4. Entrees €8-15. 🕐 Open daily 11am-12am.

NIGHTLIFE

NOGA WINE BAR
V. dei Chiavettieri

WINE BAR

Located on the popular V. dei Chiavettieri, which is lined with bars, Noga Wine Bar stands out. Walk by during aperitivo hours and you'll see that this place has the perfect mixture of ambient street seating and delicious, generous portions of aperitivo food. How could you pass it up?

The waiters are the perfect mixture of helpful and sassy. If you ask for a menu, they'll probably inform you that they are the menu. Know some good aperitvo drinks off the back of your hand. Can't decide? Spritz is always a safe option. Or if you're feeling a little classier, this is a wine bar. Ask a waiter for their recommendations on the best wine.

After you buy your drink, congratulations. You've gained entrance to an amazing aperitvo buffet. Try delicacies ranging from rice with salmon to those little rolled up hot dogs that Italians seem to love so much. The food is very well done and much better than the chips and peanuts you might get in America. Chickpeas and bread, grilled eggplants, salads with olives—if you aren't careful, this place turns into dinner. Call it a chiusitivo instead.

The drinks are delicious, the aperitivo is reasonably priced, and the seating on V. dei Chiavettieri (since there isn't much room inside the actual bar) will give you the perfect chance to people watch. And laugh at how measly everyone else's aperitivo seems. You are so winning right now.

i Drinks €5-8. 🕐 M-F 6pm-2am, Sa 6pm-3am, Su 6pm-2am.

AI BOTTAI
V. Bottai, 62

PUB

☎091 774 67 86

As you cross V. dei Chiavettieri onto V. Bottai in your late night Palermo adventures where crossing streets is a life threatening sport, you'll stumble into an enormous crowd sitting, talking, and singing in the streets. Welcome to Ai Bottai.

A lively pub in Palermo, there's always something happening here. Football game, live music, wild Tuesday night—everything's a reason to celebrate. This place is popular, so crowds usually fill the area on Friday and Saturday nights. Try to snag a table to meet some of the friendliest bartenders in the area while downing delicious drinks. If that's as impossible as getting laid in Palermo (… not your best odds), just stand.

Most of the time, you won't even see the bar inside, since everyone prefers to hang out on the pedestrian-only road here. TVs are set up outside during game days; otherwise some jazzy music may blast. Either way, the traffic here is always astonishing. Try one of the drinks, and you'll begin to understand why. With

palermo

good beers, great cocktails (some even colored to look like the Italian flag!), and reasonable prices, this is one of the go-to pubs in Palermo. Ravers will be disappointed, but if you just crave some company and crowds, wiggle yourself in here. Because everyone needs some close human contact + alcohol every now and then.

i Drinks €4-8. ☾ Open daily 4pm-3am.

VUCCIRIA
MARKETPLACE

Off V. Roma, near V. Argenteria area.

As bustling as the vucciria, or marketplaces, are in the morning, a different sort of crowd fills them up on weekend nights. Fish stands give way to burgers and beer stands, and the shoppers leave to make room for students looking to turn up. Popular among the youth in Palermo for their large open spaces, loud music, and, of course, cheap, cheap beer, if you're looking for a fun night out with your friends, hit up a marketplace

For some good fun, head to the aptly-named marketplace, Vucciria. Here, crowds gather for late-night food as stands pop up and cook meat right in front of you, filling the streets with a hazy, delicious smoke. Get at us, smoke machines in discos. Plenty of bars line this area, so as the night progresses, the crowd gets rowdier and takes up much of the square behind the marketplace as well. Everyone mingles as music blasts, and no one really knows what bar they're at, but that just sounds like an ideal Friday night.

LA CHAMPAGNERIA DEL MASSIMO
WINE BAR

V. Salvatore Spinuzza, 59 ☎091 33 57 30

For a wild night of drama, intrigue, and fun fun fun, go to Teatro Massimo. Then take a sharp turn and head straight for the bars. In case operas don't seem like your ideal wild night out, Palermo's got you covered. Right outside the theater are plenty of bars filled with people who have found a different kind of entertainment: good alcohol. Now that's where the party starts.

Head to La Champagneria Del Massimo, which is steps outside the theater, and welcome to a boozy haven. You just have to try to act a little classy. As a wine bar, there's always an incredible selection of wine (and other, stronger drinks) lining the walls inside. Bottles on bottles on bottles. On almost every wall. Challenge accepted.

If you wanna be a champagne master, you've gotta catch 'em all (or something like that). Come here and walk inside, where you'll be met by a classy wooden bar surrounded by wine bottles and wine glasses hanging from the ceiling. If you come in the evening, you'll make aperitivo hours. Grab a glass of something (it'll probably be good) and enjoy the wonders of free food with any alcohol purchase. Come by at night, and you'll see a little more fun. A popular place to come and drink, people fill up these tables, bathe in the kindness and generosity of the owners and servers, and drink away. Though a quieter, calmer place to spend the night, it's in the area of some rowdier bars and clubs if your wine tasting adventure goes a little crazy. It happens.

i Drinks €6-10. ☾ Open M-Sa 9am-3am.

DON CHISCIOTTE
CLUB

V. Candelai 52/54 ☎349 59 23 650

Plenty of places have loud music blasting on V. Candelai. Don Chisciotte actually has a dance floor to go along with it. Success. Walk into a bright, neon-lit room with an enormous bar on the left. You can grab a drink of anything that you need to get you to start dancing. The art here will be trying to get the bartender to hear you over the bar's own deafening music.

After a couple shots, turn your attention to the right. The doorway opens up to one of the larger dance floors in Palermo. There's no lighting except for some

italy

strobe lights, which are covered up by the smoke machine. Is there anyone else here? Nobody really knows.

If you come by too early (i.e., midnight), the dance floor is still prepared for you, with benches along the sidelines where you can sit and check out the sexy shadows coming and going into the room until the place turns a little rowdier. Twerking might not be everyone's favorite activity at this bar, but since it is one of the few places in Palermo with a legitimate dance floor, if any young Italians want to dance, they'll probably end up here by the end of the night. So take a seat, go slightly deaf from all the electronic beats, and when the party gets a little more turnt up (or you get a little more turnt up), do that smoke and neon light some justice and hit the dance floor with some sweet moves that no one will ever really see.

i Drinks €5-8. ☼ Open daily 6pm-2am.

ESSENTIALS
Practicalities

- **POST OFFICE:** Mail is handled by Poste Italia. The central post office is at V. Roma 320 (open M-Sa 8:20am-7:05pm).

- **INTERNET:** Wi-Fi can be hard to find outside of your hotel. Check for cafes or restaurants that offer complimentary Wi-Fi.

Emergency

- **EMERGENCY NUMBERS:** The emergency number in Italy is 112 for police, fire department, and ambulances.

- **PHARMACIES:** Look for a big green "+" sign anywhere, and you'll find a pharmacy. Late-night pharmacies can be a little difficult to find. Closed pharmacies will usually list where the nearest open pharmacies are.

Getting There

Falcone–Borsellino Airport is the airport in Palermo. Transport from the airport to the city is easily done by the Prestia Comandé bus, which costs around €6-7 and departs from the airport every 30min. and goes to Stazione Centrale, the main train station in Palermo. If you arrive by ferry, the bus 139, which stops right outside the port, will take you from the port to Stazione Centrale.

Getting Around

Palermo is a mammoth of a city, but the main tourist area between the train station and Politeama is walkable. The main bus stations are at Stazione Centrale (where you can also catch trains heading to other cities), Piazza Independenzia, and Piazza Sturzo. Bus tickets cost €1.40 and can be bought in Tabaccherie.

syracuse

From the tiny cobblestone streets in the island of Ortigia to the sprawling ruins in the archaeological park to gorgeous sunsets by the ocean, Syracuse has all the charm you could ask for in a small Italian town. And then there's the food. All the delicious cannoli, gelato, and signature pizzolo will keep your stomach satisfied. Should you hunger for some knowledge and history, this ancient town of Archimedes will take care of you with its museums and sites.

get a room!

LOLHOSTEL HOSTEL $
V. Francesco Crispi 92-96 ☎0931 465 088 www.lolhostel.com

Stay at LolHostel, and you can ROTFLOL at the prices everyone else is paying to stay in Syracuse. This is the only hostel in town, and if you're a world weary backpacker, you'll probably be staying here. But you can be assured that you won't be complaining.

Located on the V. Crispi, you'll be a minute away from the bus and train station that'll bring you in and only 10-12min. away from the archaeological park and the city center in Ortigia, so you can #brb quite often. And it's also right off Corso Umberto, which is full of delicious and cheap noms.

Walk in, and you'll be greeted by friendly reception and given a map with more recommendations than you'll be able to cope with. On the ground floor is a fully functional IKEA-esque kitchen where you'll assure yourself you'll cook once you get the motivation to go to a supermarket (so probably never). There's also a lounge with fluorescent colored chairs and a full bar next to the kitchen that serves the cheapest drinks around. Complimentary breakfast is served every morning, and if you're up before 11am, make sure you go because delicious pastries. Take some marmalade-filled cornetti out to the garden, and it will be one of your better morning experiences.

All the bedrooms are located upstairs. The 20-bed loft is an impressive feat, but the eight-bed rooms are also large and spacious. With windows on the ceiling, the rooms can be a little dimly lit, but everyone looks better in dim lighting. The beds are standard, but the blankets are ridiculously soft.

The hostel caters to a young student crowd but isn't much of a party hostel, so you might have to be the party sometimes. But still, after a busy night in Ortigia, the walk back will never be bad, and you'll <3 being able to stay here. Maybe even <4.

i Dorms €20-23. 🕐 Reception 24hr. May-Aug.

To orient yourself, start at the train and bus station, where you'll probably be arriving. From here, always head east. (There's nothing but sunsets and cowboys in the west.) The main street, Corso Umberto, will take you anywhere you'd like to go. Follow it to Corso Gelone to get to the archaeological park or keep heading straight and to get to the bridge that leads to the island of Ortigia and the old part of the city. Here, the winding narrow roads lead into beautiful open piazze like Piazza del Archimede and the famous Piazza del Duomo. Walk in any direction long enough and you'll reach the bluest water over which you can watch breathtaking sunsets.

SIGHTS

DUOMO DI SIRACUSA CHURCH
Piazza Duomo ☎093 16 53 28

Enter the Piazza Duomo and its namesake will steal the scene. Always surrounded by paparazzi and always looking flawless, this celebrity cathedral is famous for a reason. First of all, it's drop dead gorgeous. Soaring white Corinthian columns, large arched windows, towering statues. Could it be any more of a cathedral? Built in two different periods, this cathedral displays both Baroque and Rococo styles which come together in a gorgeous fluid façade that's full of fun movement.

The statues outside start with St. Peter on the lower left, St. Paul on the lower right, San Marciano, the first bishop of Syracuse on the upper left, Santa Lucia, the patron saint of Syracuse on the upper right, and everyone's favorite virgin who isn't you in the center. Take a walk through the columns to see the inside. Remember to be modestly dressed and then pay a modest fee – it's all about the modesty in here. Except for the ridiculously elaborate doors with their swirling columns. Did we mention that this cathedral has got some good moves?

Once you step in, however, you'll see the Duomo's most famous secret: it was once an ancient Greek temple. Large stone arches line both sides of the nave giving it an ancient feel. Probably because it is ancient. The Duomo is built on an ancient doric temple to Athena. According to Cicero, this used to be a gorgeous marble and gold temple to the virgin goddess (still not you). Athena's shield once graced the doors in bright gold and helped ships navigating from afar. Good goddess Athena.

Much like many ancient temples, it became repurposed as a Christian church and this one now celebrates another virgin. The old columns of the temple were reused providing quite a physical link between the past and the present. The main altar displays more beautiful white Corinthian columns and a painting of the Virgin with child. Walk around the main nave then take a look inside the little chapels. There is small but beautiful one dedicated to Santa Lucia. And before you leave, be sure to look down as you're walking around as well. There are some great mosaics that might even floor you.

i Admission €2. ☼ Open daily 7:30am-7:30pm.

THE ARCHAEOLOGICAL PARK OF SYRACUSE   ARCHAEOLOGY
Entrance at intersection of Corso Gelone and Via Paolo Orsi

If you like old shit, you're in the right country. And if you're in Syracuse, get your ass over to the Archaeological Park. A vast area filled with ancient Greek and Roman ruins, this is a place no history buff or saw-300-and-got-really-excited-kind-of-person can miss.

About a 10-min walk from the new city or 20-min if you're posh enough to stay in Ortigia, head up and once you start seeing wheat fields and such you're either stuck in the Gladiator movie, or you've arrived. The strangely difficult to find ticket office is located past all the souvenir shops by the bus parking area. It may cost you a pretty penny, but if you plan on visiting the Archaeological Museum as well, buy a combined ticket and save some euros.

The entrance to the park is right across the street. The first couple stops are actually free and open to the public. Turn left after entering through the main gate and you'll get to the ruins of a Roman amphitheater. See the giant stone ruins pop up through the overgrown field and try to imagine what it would be like to watch people fight to the death here. Yeah, gladiator battles were weird. Walk down and as you avoid the large tour groups, you'll see the Ara di Lerone on your left, which was used by the Greeks for animal sacrifices. Now largely in ruins, it's still a pretty cool sight before you head into the ticketed area of the park.

Once you're in, head down and the stone ruins will give way into a lush jungle of palm trees. Also the temperature will drop by like five degrees which is nice too. This is the Latomia del Paradiso. Once an ancient quarry site, it's been filled with trees ever since and is now a beautiful paradise. Inside here you'll find the Ear of Dionysus. Before you cry out that's the strangest thing you've heard, calm down. It's only a cave. A very pretty cave at that. In the shape of a very big ear and with incredible acoustics that you can try out for yourself, legend has it that the tyrant king Dionysus used to keep prisoners here so he could hear everything they said. We don't know how the prisoners didn't see it coming since they were being kept in a giant ear.

Head back up and out of the gardens and you'll see the steps leading to the Greek theater. As one of the world's largest, this is still indeed a functional theater where dramas are performed in the summer. An impressive 455 feet in diameter, it's still surprisingly in tact. Used for plays in ancient days, the Romans weren't always willing to put up with your drama so it was sometimes filled with water for mock sea battles. On a hot day, filling the theater with water doesn't seem like a bad idea. Just saying.

i €10. Combined ticket with museum €13.50. ⟁ Open daily 9am until 2 hours before sunset

PAOLO ORSI REGIONAL ARCHAEOLOGICAL MUSEUM   MUSEUM
Viale Teocrito, 66   ☎093 14 89 511 www.regione.sicilia.it/beniculturali/museopaoloorsi/
If the archaeological park wasn't able to convince you of how much history Syracuse has, hit up the museum for a more air-conditioned tour of the past. Located about five minutes away from the park, the museum is in a beautiful little garden with swaying palm trees and all about dat Mediterranean life.

Walk in to a pretty modern museum with plenty of windows looking out at the funky Sanctuary of the Madonna of Tears and get ready to see more history than you'll ever be ready for. The museum itself is divided into four major sections which like your grades go from A to D. The first section takes you way way back. Start with a geological foundation of Syracuse. Various rocks and some fossils of pygmy elephants make sure you realize what kind of island climate you're dealing with. Also pygmy elephants are just fun. The section begins to challenge you when you claim how much you love pot, because holy shit there are a lot of pots here. Everything from potsherds to pots big enough that you could sit in them, you're bound to find one pot you like.

Section B will take you a little further into history with the Greek colonies. Plenty of kouroi and korai, statues of young men and women, as well as beautiful remains from Greek temples. Along with a very silly gorgon. Section S is home to findings from Hellenized subcolonies aka more pots and some pretty statues. Section D will take you up and towards the height of sculpture in this museum.

Admire some flowing beards, expressive faces, and of course the beautiful Landolina Venus which apart from boobs is a very beautiful and delicate statue. While you're up in D, be sure to walk around on the second floor to see the famous Sarcophagus of Adelphia. A marble sarcophagus that is a great example of art from late antiquity, this sarcophagus shows plenty of Biblical scenes using adorable little figures in the sarcophagus, and with Christianity wraps up our long trek through the ancient world in this museum that has proved to you that history is cool. And that people used a shit ton of pots.

i €8. Combined ticket with park €13.50. ⟁ Tu-Sa 9am-6pm, Su 9am-1pm.

PIAZZA DUOMO   SQUARE
Piazza Duomo
There's nothing quite like being lost in the tiny alleys and streets in Ortigia only to have the road open up to the breathtaking Piazza del Duomo. Considered one of the more beautiful piazze in Italy by, well, anyone who has actually visited it, Piazza del Duomo will take you in with its irregular but fascinating semioval shape filled with twisting Baroque buildings and of course the Duomo itself and make you fall in love with a square that isn't your first boyfriend.

The most eye-catching building of all is the Duomo, a stunning cathedral built out of a Greek temple to Athena. High Corinthian columns, large arched windows, gorgeous statues, and great steps to sit on and watch Syracuse pass you by.

Next to the Duomo on the left is the Archbishop's Palace, which is sadly not open to the public. Thanks a lot, archbishop. Across on the right is the Palazzo Beneventano dal Bosco, a rather boxish but still beautiful baroque palace with large rectangular windows. In the furthest end of the piazza is the Church of Santa Lucia alla Badia which, with its high white façade and columns is yes, also baroque (with a touch of rococo). You might be seeing a trend here. There are many restaurants and bars in this area as well, but as a well-travelled backpacker you'll realize that famous piazza aren't the best places to get deals.

So grab some gelato from the side streets and then come sit here. Enjoy the over the top whimsy, the not quite straight up and down, and the large arches and windows of the baroque and rococo. Huzzah.

FOOD

LA VOGLIA MATTA
C. Umberto I, 34

GELATO $

☎093 16 71 18

Let's be real. The #1 reason you've come to Italy? History, beaches, the gorgeous men? Nope. Even better: gelato. So when you're in Syracuse, be sure to hit up one of the best gelaterias in town...like, a couple times a day. La Voglia Matta: translated as "The Crazy Desire," it pretty much sums up all your feelings about gelato. Come in and let your dreams be realized.

Located right on Corso Umberto and just minutes before the bridge to Ortigia, stop here for a cone to make your entrance onto the beautiful island even sweeter. You'll probably have tp walk by the counter a couple times before you can come up with the winning combination of the many flavors on hand. With everything from classic lemon and pistachio to Kinder, all these are artisanal and handmade gelati. To act like a true Italian, get the ricotta penne and ciocolato nero, which is ricotta with sweet fruit and dark chocolate (it's a specialty of this gelateria).

La Voglia Matta also sells delicious espresso if you need a wake up shot. There aren't a whole lot of places to sit in the small shop, but try to snag one from the collection of white tables inside. Otherwise, take your gelato and go. Walk across the bridge to Ortigia, take look at the water below, and enjoy the beauty of gelato. And Syracuse, too.

i *Gelato €2-5. ☼ Open daily 9am-2pm, 4pm-midnight.*

BAR MIDOLO
C. Umberto I, 86

BAR $

☎093 16 80 46

Pizza. Arancini. Cannoli. All in one place? With everything you've ever wanted from Italy under the same roof, we're pretty sure Bar Midolo is some small bar form of heaven. In an unassuming storefront on a corner of Corso Umberto, at Bar Midolo you'll find a line of locals waiting for anything from morning coffee to a fast lunch to some delicious pastries. Join them. Take a walk inside and browse the counters lined with delicious Italian treats, like various kinds of arancini—little but surprisingly filling rice balls stuffed with ragu, cheese, and all other kinds of savory goodness. We recommend the arancini prosciutto.

Though known for its arancini, Bar Midolo also sells various types of delicious pizza and other bready treats, all for extremely reasonable prices. If you have more of a sweet tooth, go to the counter right by the pizzas and find a delectable selection of dolce: small fruit tarts, little pies with nuts, and, of course, cannoli.

Bar Midolo has some of the best and cheapest cannolis in all of Syracuse. As if you needed an excuse to buy a cannoli here. Try the little ones. They're like two bites of pure deliciousness, and you can pop them in your mouth as you walk around Ortigia. And so, for a quick lunch and dessert, be sure to do

syracuse

as the locals do and pop into Bar Midolo. Then come back here for your three mandatory afternoon snacks. You need that energy, after all.

i *Pizza and arancine €1-2.50. Pastries €0.50-1. ☼ Open daily 6am-11pm.*

NIGHTLIFE

IL SALE
BAR

V. Amalfitania 56 ☎093 14 83 666

In a small alley off a small alley in Syracuse, Il Sale is about as Ortigia as you can get. Look for the chalkboard advertising drinks and live music on V. Amalfitania and take the narrow path leading you up. You'll emerge victorious in a gorgeous, cavernous bar.

Rock hewn and more stoned than you'll ever be (hopefully), this large bar charms with its cave-like appearance. There's outdoor seating on a rocky platform and plenty of locals gather here to sit at tables, grab a drink, and talk the night away.

The lights are low while jazzy music plays, and it's casual and peaceful here, tucked away from the busy P. del Duomo.

The interior is swanky, with a shiny bar and an eye-catching display of liquors. Cocktails here are a little on the pricier side, which might be why people here don't drink to get tipsy. Though full of people, this isn't a wild bar but is instead a charming, ambient place to stop by with a friend or two and talk about how much you love Syracuse. Because, really, what else is there to talk about in Syracuse?

i *Drinks €5-10. ☼ Open M-Th 7pm-3am, F-Sa 7pm-4am, Su 7pm-3am.*

PUB LES CREPES
PUB

9 V. Maniace www.lescrepespub.altervista.org

Hungry? Of course you are. This Saturday night, combine your two favorite things—beer and chocolate—by coming to Pub Les Crepes. Bright orange walls, wooden tables, and Nutella. Perfection. A quiet but delicious place to start the night, take a seat on a bar stool and ogle the crepe choices. Anything from a sweet Nutella and Baileys to a more savory Salmon and Philadelphia cream cheese, we never said choices on wild nights out were going to be easy.

Service is friendly, the food is great, and the cozy and casual atmosphere will make you feel no shame as you get melted chocolate gooeyness all over your turn-down-for-what clothes. No one will notice in the dark anyway. And the prices? Mmm—delectable.

So after you finish your third crepe, turn your attention to the adorable wooden bar with teapots on it. Oh, and it's also lined with liquor. As one of the cheaper places to get a shot or a cocktail, we recommend you spend a decent amount of time here before heading out to some of the classier places in Ortigia. If you're feeling brave, go for the tequila shots. Otherwise a small beer will run you up €3 or so.

Come with your friends, eat crepes, drink some €5 cocktails. If you're feeling adventurous, ask about table games like Taboo that you can rent out (in Italian, of course—it'll be a learning experience). And after you've had your fill of delicious food, bright walls, and wooden tables, head out for the night to somewhere grungier. Or maybe somewhere with more late night food. Pick your own adventure.

i *Crepes €4.50. Shots €3-5. Beer €2.50-4. Cocktails €5. ☼ Open Tu-Su 9pm-2am. Open for lunch M-F 12:30-3pm.*

DAIQUIRI LOUNGE

BAR

Piazza Duomo

☎320 785 71 29

And sometimes, when you're by the Duomo on a Saturday night, you just need a little advance on your Eucharist. Come to Daiquiri. A wine and cocktail bar right in P. Duomo, this swanky bar will make drinking on some steps look downright classy.

If you haven't noticed yet, Taormina's kind of on a mountain. Steep inclines and rock hewn stairs make up most of the side streets. While you might be sure that this geography stands to screw you over, Daiquiri uses it to its advantage. Located on some large stone steps leading up from P. Duomo, to get a seat, you'll have to back that ass up onto one of the luxurious white cushioned chairs or couches with sleek white tables set out on the stairs themselves.

The interior of the bar is pretty much just the bar itself. Most people who come here find a table outside and enjoy the beautiful view of the Duomo at night. Catering to a slightly posh crowd (i.e., everyone in Taormina), you'll have to wear a dress or put on some slacks if you want to come here. Don't worry, drinks here are relatively cheap by local standards, so trying to look nice will pay off.

Listen to jazzy music, enjoy the comfy white chairs, and try some of the delicious drinks. This place never gets crazy, but it's a good place to chill after a day at the beach.

i Drinks €4-8. 🕐 Open daily 7pm-3am.

ESSENTIALS

Practicalities

- **POST OFFICES:** Mail is handled by Poste Italia. Postcards and letters from Greece to outside Europe cost €0.85. The centra post office is at P. Riva della Posta right across the bridge into Ortigia (open M-F 8:20am-7:05pm, Sa 8:20am-12:35pm).

- **INTERNET:** Wi-Fi can be hard to find outside of your hotel. Check for cafes or restaurants that offer complimentary Wi-Fi. There is free Wi-Fi from the city available outside the Tempio di Apollo in Ortigia.

Emergency

- **EMERGENCY NUMBERS:** The emergency number in Italy is 112 for police, fire department, and ambulances. More specific numbers are listed below.

- **POLICE:** 113

- **AMBULANCE SERVICE:** 118

- **FIRE BRIGADE:** 115

- **PHARMACIES:** Look for a big green "+" sign anywhere, and you'll find a pharmacy. Late night pharmacies stay open on a rotating basis. Check www.comune.siracusa.it/index.php/it/farmacie to find out which ones are open overnight.

Getting There

The closest airport to Syracuse is Catania. From Catania, you can take an AST or Interbus regional bus that will take you from the airport to Syracuse for around €6.

Getting Around

Luckily for you, Syracuse is not a big town. From the bus station to the island of Ortigia takes about 15min. walking, and the Archaeological Park to Ortigia takes about 20min. There are no cars allowed on Ortigia, so your best bet in Syracuse all around will be walking.

italy essentials

MONEY

To use a debit or credit card to withdraw money from an ATM (*Bancomat* in Italian), you must have a four-digit Personal Identification Number (PIN). If your PIN is longer than four digits, ask your bank whether you can use the first four or if they'll issue you a new one. If you intend to hit up ATMs in Europe with a credit card, call your credit card company before your departure to request a PIN.

The use of ATM cards is widespread in Italy. The two major international money networks are MasterCard/Maestro/Cirrus and Visa/PLUS. Most ATMs charge a transaction fee, but some Italian banks waive the withdrawal surcharge.

In Italy, a 5% tip is customary, particularly in restaurants (10% if you especially liked the service). Italian waiters won't cry if you don't leave a tip; just be ready to ignore the pangs of your conscience later on. Taxi drivers expect tips as well, but luckily for oenophiles, it is unusual to tip in bars. Bargaining is appropriate in markets and other informal settings, though in regular shops it is inappropriate. Hotels will often offer lower prices to people looking for a room that night, so you will often be able to find a bed cheaper than what is officially quoted.

SAFETY AND HEALTH

Local Laws and Police

In Italy, you will mainly encounter two types of boys in blue: the *polizia* (☎113) and the *carabinieri* (☎112). The *polizia* are a civil force under the command of the Ministry of the Interior, whereas the *carabinieri* fall under the auspices of the Ministry of Defense and are considered a military force. Both, however, generally serve the same purpose, to maintain security and order in the country. In the case of attack or robbery, both will respond to inquiries or desperate pleas for help.

Drugs and Alcohol

The legal drinking age in Italy is (drumroll please) 16. Remember to drink responsibly and to **never drink and drive.** Doing so is illegal and can result in a prison sentence, not to mention early death. The legal blood alcohol content (BAC) for driving in Italy is under 0.05%, significantly lower than the US limit of 0.08%.

Travelers with Disabilities

Travelers in wheelchairs should be aware that getting around in Italy will sometimes be extremely difficult. This country predates the wheelchair—sometimes it seems even the wheel—by several centuries and thus poses unique challenges to disabled travelers. **Accessible Italy** (☎378 941 111 www.accessibleitaly.com) offers advice to tourists of limited mobility heading to Italy, with tips on subjects ranging from finding accessible accommodations to wheelchair rental.

italy

THE NETHERLANDS

There are few places in the world that can pull off the Netherlands's unique combination of reefer-clouded progressiveness and folksy, earnest charm. This part of Europe somehow manages to appeal both to tulip-loving grandmas and ganga-crazy, Red-Light-ready students. So, like everyother college student, come to Amsterdam to gawk at the coffeeshops and prostitutes, but don't leave thinking that's all there is to this quirky country. Take some time to cultivate an appreciation for the Dutch masters. Obviously, most Dutch people aren't pot-heads—they'll tell you that if marijuana was legalized in the states, 700,000 fewer people would need to be incarcerated annually. Consider what it would be like to live in a place where hookers are unionized and public works like windmills, canals, and bike lanes define the national character, and get ready to go Dutch!

greatest hits

- **LET'S (VAN) GOGH:** The area around Museumplein in Amsterdam features not one, but two of Europe's greatest art museums. Savor the Dutch Golden Age at the **Rijksmuseum** or *Sunflowers* at the **Van Gogh Museum** (p. 693).

- **DAM GOOD BARS: Leidseplein** is a nightlife haven, with laidback and musical bars littering the streets (see Nightlife, p. 700).

- **IT'S ELECTRIC!: Electric Ladyland** (p. 698) the world's "First Museum of Fluorescent Art," will take you on an unforgettably weird trip into the world of glowing rocks and "participatory art."

amsterdam

"Quit smirking!" is your unfortunate follow-up every time you tell someone you're going to Amsterdam. "I mean, sure there are hookers and weed, but the city's got so much more to it! Like—like—like history. And. . . um. . . canals, a-and bikes! And the Anne Frank house!"

Relax, fidgeting traveler. We wrote this chapter for you.

The Netherlands' shall-we-say-permissive attitudes are the product of a long tradition of liberalism and tolerance that dates back far before the advent of drug tourism and prostitutes' unions. One of the few areas in Europe to fall outside the influence of the all-powerful Vatican, Amsterdam was for centuries a refuge for Protestants and Jews, with the wealth of its tremendous trading empire—stretching from New York (er, New Amsterdam) to Indonesia—incubating the artistic achievements of the Dutch Golden Age and nurturing the political and economic birth of modern Europe. Nowadays, this diverse and progressive city is as famous for its art museums and quaint canal-side cafes as for its coffee shops and women of the night.

The most subtly satisfying aspect of your trip will be strolling the streets, every route bringing unpredictable glimpses of this pretty city's culture and vitality. Quite compact for all its riches, Amsterdam can be biked or even walked in a day, rambling from the peaceful canals of the Jordaan to the gaudy peepshows of the Red Light— though to plow directly through would be to miss out on all the density's offerings. So drop that J, pack along this book, and Let's Go!

ACCOMMODATIONS

COCOMAMA
HOSTEL $$

Westeinde 18 ☎020 627 2454 www.cocomama.nl

It's all about decadence here at the award-winning Cocomama: check-in is accompanied by your choice of water, tea, or champagne, and the triple-tiered bunks feel fit for Dutch royalty (those flower-flaunting fools). A lavishly-decorated basement kitchen, with garden-y backyard, lends the whole thing a communal feel that's cozier than a Dutch monarch is to his tulips.

i Dorms €40-50. ✆ Reception open 9am-9pm.

STAYOKAY STADSDOELEN
HOSTEL $$

Kloveniersburgwal 97 ☎020 624 68 32 www.stayokay.com

With "only" 200 beds, this Stayokay is less than half the size of its less centrally-located sibling, and feels like a correspondingly more friendly and relaxing place to hang out. Less of an emphasis is placed on groups and families, meaning that individual backpackers can come here and dip into the social scene. A friendly staff and clean rooms round out this very worthy accommodation.

i Dorms €30-35. ✆ Reception 24hr.

SHELTER CITY
HOSTEL $

Barndesteeg 21 ☎020 625 3230 www.shelterhostelamsterdam.com

Just a short drunken swerve from the Red Light District is this outpost of godliness, where even ye, sinner that ye are, have a chance to repent—it's the larger and more centrally-located of the two Christian hostels known as Shelter, although its increased size won't make you anonymous in the eyes of staff (or God). With good rooms and a koi fish pond to boot, this is a wonderful sanctuary for people of all, or no, faiths.

i Dorms €20-30. ✆ Reception 24hr.

THE NETHERLANDS

North Sea

0 — 25 miles
0 — 25 kilometers

TO NEWCASTLE, ENGLAND

TO HARWICH, ENGLAND AND HULL, ENGLAND

Schiermonnikoog
Ameland
Terschelling
Vlieland
Wadden Islands
Waddenzee
Texel
Den Helder
Leeuwarden
Harlingen
Heerenveen
Groningen
Assen
Hoogeveen
Meppel
Vecht R.
IJsselmeer
Hoorn
Alkmaar
Zaanse Schans
IJmuiden
Edam
Zwolle
Haarlem
Amsterdam
IJssel R.
Zandvoort aan Zee
Aalsmeer
Noordwijk aan Zee
Lisse
Scheveningen
Leiden
Utrecht
Apeldoorn
The Hague
Delft
Amersfoort
DE HOGE VELUWE NATIONAL PARK
Hoek van Holland
Gouda
Pijn R.
Arnhem
Rotterdam
Waal R.
Nijmegen
Maas R.
Rhine R.
Breda
Maas R.
GERMANY
Eindhoven
Antwerp
Roermond
Cologne
BELGIUM
Brussels
Maastricht

FLYING PIG DOWNTOWN
HOSTEL $$

Nieuwendijk   ☎100 020 420 6822 www.flyingpig.nl

EDM thrums in the main common room/bar of this classic party hostel. A notch above the surrounding competition in terms of staff, cleanliness, and décor, the Flying Pig Downtown offers a safe place to crash, and its welcoming atmosphere ensures you'll meet some cool compatriots.

i Dorms €30-45. ☼ Reception 24hr.

FLYING PIG UPTOWN
HOSTEL $$

Vossiusstraat 46/47   ☎020 400 4187 www.flyingpig.nl

Well-staffed and -décor'd—the common room/bar looks handsome with its warm woodiness. Paintings of (non-Amsterdammer 27-Clubbers) Jimi Hendrix, Kurt Cobain, and Amy Winehouse adorn the walls. The Flying Pig Uptown's massive size, with more than 200 beds, can be a little overwhelming for those who're looking for a cozy relaxing place to make cozy relaxing friends. If your goal is partyrockin', however, look no further.

i Dorms €30-45. ☼ Reception 24hr.

SHELTER JORDAN
HOSTEL $

Bloemstraat   ☎179 020 624 4717 www.shelterhostelamsterdam.com

If your time in Amsterdam leaves you feeling morally and spiritually bankrupt, look no further than this Christ-tastic outpost in the middle of one of the city's hipper areas. Well-cleaned, comfortable, and our-smiles-never-skip-a-beat

amsterdam

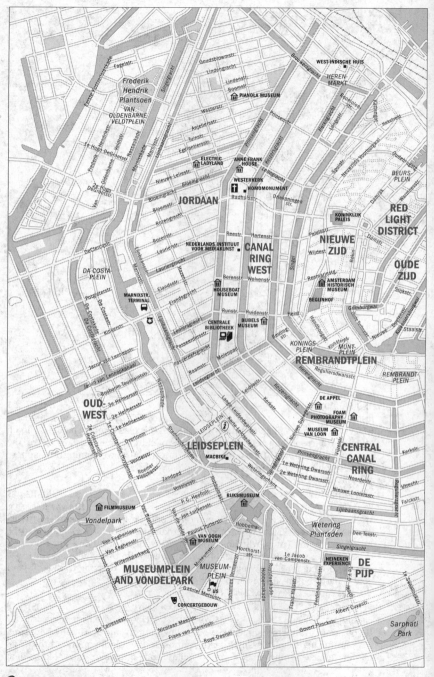

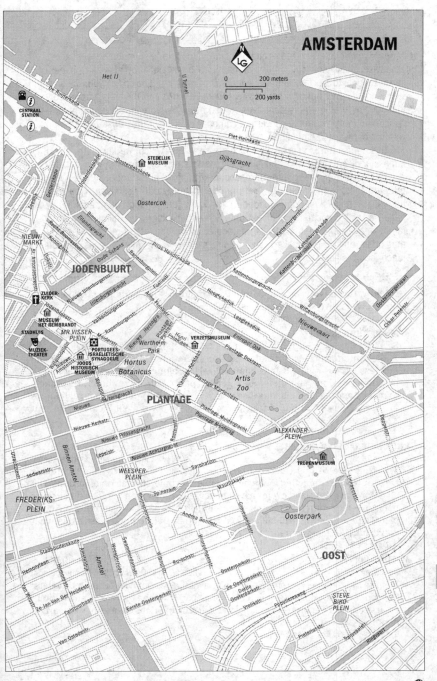

AMSTERDAM

Het IJ

UJ Tunnel

0   200 meters
0   200 yards

N
LG

CENTRAAL
STATION

De Ruijterkade

Piet Heinkade

STEDELIJK
MUSEUM

Oosterdokskade

Dijksgracht

Oostercok

NIEUW-
MARKT

Binnenkant
Eilandsgracht

Oosterdokskade

Kattenburgerstr.

Kattenburgerkade

St. Antoniesbreestraat
Kloveniersburgwal
Geldersekade
Koningstr.

Oude Schans
Rapenburgerstraat

JODENBUURT

Nieuwe Uilenburgerstr.
Uilenburgergracht

Prins Hendrikkade
Foeliestr.

Hoogte Kadijk

Kattenburgergracht

Kattenburgerkade

Wittenburgergracht

Oosterburgervaart

Obbr. Pelerstr.

ZUIDER-
KERK

Jodenbreestr.

MUSEUM
HET REMBRANDT

STADHUIS

MR VISSER-
PLEIN

MUZIEK-
THEATER

JOODS
HISTORISCH
MUSEUM

PORTUGEES-
ISRAELIETISCHE
SYNAGOGE

Valkenburgerstr.

Nieuwe Herengracht
Nieuwe Prinsengracht

Anne Frankstr.

Plantage Kerklaan

Henri Polaklaan

VERZETSMUSEUM

Entrepot Dok

Plantage Doklaan

Nieuwevaart

Laagtekadijk

Hortus
Botanicus

Wertheim
Park

Artis
Zoo

Plantage Middenlaan

Nieuwe Amstel
Waterlooplein
Weesperstr.
Keizersgracht

PLANTAGE

Plantage Muidergracht

Plantage Kerklaan

Nieuwe
Nieuwe Kerkstr.

Plantage Muidergracht

ALEXANDER-
PLEIN

Nieuwe Prinsengracht

Lepelstr.

Nieuwe Achtergracht

Binnen Amstel

Sarphatistr.

TROPENMUSEUM

WEESPER-
PLEIN

Mauritskade

Utrechtsestr.

sedwarsstr.

Swammerdamstr.

Wibautstraat

Linneausstraat

FREDERIKS-
PLEIN

Sarphatistr.

Roetersstr.

Andrea Boninstr.

Oosterpark

Stadhouderskade

Amstel

Weesperzijde

OOST

Hemonylaan

2e Jan v Der Heijdestr.

Hemonystr.

Ceintuurbaan

Oosterparkstr.

2e Oosterparkstr.

Derde
Oosterparkstr.

Vrolikstr.

STEVE
BIKO
PLEIN

Jan Wolkerspl.
2e Jan Van Der Heijdestr.

Eerste Oosterparkstr.

Populierenweg

Pretoriusstr.

Transvaalpl.

Van Ostadestr.

Ringdijk

amsterdam

hagelslag

Though your hostel's austere complimentary toast-jam situation may suggest otherwise, the Dutch don't mess around with breakfast. They also dig on desserts—though to be fair, name a culture that doesn't. (Lookin' at you, Iceland. Just kidding—their national pastry, the *snuour,* is kingly.) In the '30s, supposedly in response to a very persistent five-year-old boy who wrote letters pleading for a chocolate breakfast item, an inventive company of plucky Dutch upstarts came up with a great way to combine the two: *hagelslag.*

This confection is essentially chocolate sprinkles—which, we know, are kinda lame since ten years ago. But seriously, don't sleep on this—it's your socially acceptable way of eating a ton of chocolate first thing in the morning. Take your buttered toast, add *hagelslag.* Take unbuttered toast, add *hagelslag.* (You may not eat just *hagelslag.* Come on, dude.) And know your product: don't accept any *hagelslag* with a cacao rating of less than 35%—that's known in Holland as "cacao fantasy *hagelslag.*" As in, *hagelslag* unmoored to the tenants of reality, *hagelslag* that exists only in dreamlike wisps, a mirage deep in the mind's recesses: you reach, but it is gone.

friendly, this is your best opportunity to build in some structured Bible study between massive sinning sessions.

i Dorms €20-30. ✆ Reception 24hr.

AIVENGO YOUTH HOSTEL
HOSTEL $

Spuistraat 6 ☎020 421 3670 www.aivengoyouthhostel.com

A slick interior design, including the incorporation of forest-like columns and quintessential Rothko posters, comes close to making up for the fact that there's no common room, and therefore no hang space, and you're therefore unlikely to make amazing hostel buddies here. If you've packed your own hostel buddies in your suitcase, and y'all wanna party, Aivengo's convenient location makes it a pretty good deal.

i Dorms €18. ✆ Reception 24hr.

INTERNATIONAL BUDGET HOSTEL
HOSTEL $$

Leidsegracht 76 ☎020 624 2784 www.internationalbudgethostel.com

The chill vibe of this canalside hostel is best emblemized by the 2nd floor's aerosol wall art depicting a curvaceous naked women toking on a fat doob like all nature's patterns and cycles have converged calmly upon her. The downstairs hangzone-reception may remind some a little too strongly of a coffee shop, complete with a menu of grill-made breakfast food—but be honest, isn't this what you came to Amsterdam for?

i Dorms €30. ✆ Reception 24hr.

MEETING POINT
HOSTEL $

De Wallen ☎020 627 7499 www.hostel-meetingpoint.nl

In spite of its name, Meeting Point isn't particularly convivial for solo travelers; the common area consists of a fairly typical bar, smoking room, and small kitchen. Its central, boisterous location and fixed, cheap prices ensure its well-earned popularity.

i Dorms €18. ✆ Reception 24hr.

AROZA   HOSTEL $$

Burgwallen Nieuwe Zijde   ☎020 620 9123 www.aroza.nl

This hostel doesn't seem quite sure what it wants its feel to be—some of its labyrinthine walls are graffitied by previous tenants, some bedecked with cool old early-1900s flower sketches. Like many of the other hostels in the area, the bar is the common room, and that's where the socializing emanates from. Bonus: all rooms include a bathroom.

i *Dorms €35-40.* ☼ *Receptions 24hr.*

SIGHTS

▧ RIJKSMUSEUM   MUSEUM

Museumstraat 1   ☎0900 07 45 www.rijksmuseum.nl

You won't forget the first time you see the Rijksmuseum's soaring gothic façade: the commanding exterior of Amsterdam's flagship art museum bespeaks the centuries of history within. With an excellent array of Dutch works, from frankly stunning medieval and religious compositions (don't miss the painted allegories of saints and martyrs) to the basement-level collection of weaponry and model ships; from 17th century landscapes and portraits from the Dutch Golden Age to the top floor's contemporary and experimental art (we don't want to spoil anything, but the phrase "vagina bed" will be bandied about). Air conditioned and immaculately laid out, this is a must-see for your trip.

i *€17.50. Free with Museumkaart (€59.90, valid for one year).* ☼ *Open daily 9am-5pm.*

▧ VAN GOGH MUSEUM   MUSEUM

Paulus Potterstraat 7   ☎020 570 5200 www.vangoghmuseum.nl

It's hard to imagine a museum dedicated to a single artist, especially one who painted for less than a decade, offering enough variety and depth. But while the works of everyone's favorite bad boy painter/facial surgeon are indeed on display at this gorgeous museum, the famous paintings are just one dimension of what's offered here: different exhibits examine the artist's correspondence and letters, shed light on his fascinating biography, or contemplate his complicated personal life. Interspersed with the van Goghs are paintings by the artists who influenced him, and others by those he influenced. We think it's the best museum in Amsterdam, but unfortunately, so does everyone else; discouragingly busy at peak hours, it's worth the wait, so get here early.

i *€17. Free with Museumkaart (€59.90, valid for one year).* ☼ *Open M-Th 9am-6pm, F-Sa 9am-10pm, Su 9am-6pm.*

EYE FILM INSTITUTE   FILM INSTITUTE

IJpromenade 1   ☎020 589 1400 www.eyefilm.nl/en

Like Sauron of old does this futuristic white building turn its vengeful socket upon the city and towards all we hold dear. Only a minute's ferry ride from Centraal Station, the Institute screens a wide breadth of artful programming, from cinematic retrospectives to up-and-coming docu-makers (and, with the student discount, often for cheaper than seeing a current release in downtown Amsterdam). The in-institute bar-restaurant will seduce you with its quaint view of the IJ, but will take all your money and leave you waiting, wanting, lusting for more—hit up an eatery up the street if you're looking to nibble before a film.

i *Movie tickets €10, students €8.5. Exhibition €9, students €7.5. Exhibition free with Museumkaart (€59.90, valid for one year).* ☼ *Exhibition open M-Th 11am-7pm, F-Sa 11am-9pm, Su 11am-7pm.*

TASSEN MUSEUM OF BAGS & PURSES   MUSEUM

Herengracht 573   ☎020 524 6452 www.tassenmuseum.nl

An entire museum comprised of pouches, sacks, satchels, briefcases, luggage, and the forlorn-looking boyfriends who have been dragged along to look at it all (poor souls: their journey is over, their battle fought and lost)—if this sounds up your alley, and God help you if it does, you won't be let down. Yes, signs on the wall will try to frame it in terms of the fundamentally human quest for beauty, or the twin axis of style (Minimalist vs Maximalist; Classicist vs Eccentrist), or the surprisingly interesting historical evolution of the bag, but don't be fooled: this is, in the end, about purses, purses, and more purses, to say nothing of the collections of the "vanity cases and minaudières" section, nor the variety of folding trunks and suitcases waiting, forever, upstairs.

i €12.50; students €9.50. Free with Museumkaart (€59.90, valid for one year). 🕐 Open daily 10am-5pm.

FOTOGRAPHIEMUSEUM AMSTERDAM (FOAM) · MUSEUM
Keizersgracht 609 · ☎020 551 6500 www.foam.org

One of the best-curated museums in Amsterdam, the "FOAM" offers terrific breadth, from showcases of up-and-coming talents to revivals of famous works from the past. Its twisting white halls and chambers go on for a deceptively long time (you could easily spend a whole afternoon here), and it's all set inside an understated exterior that blends right in with the surrounding apartments, making this truly a treasure of the city—nowhere else could you find such aloof elegance.

i €10, students €7.50. Free with Museumkaart (€59.90, valid for one year). 🕐 Open M-Th 10am-6pm, F-Sa 10am-9pm, Su 10am-6pm.

PIANOLA MUSEUM · MUSEUM
Westerstraat 106 · ☎20 627 9624 www.pianola.nl

This was about the point where we went, "Come on, how many museums does this city have, anyway?" But for all the furrowedness of our brooding eyebrows, this turned out to be one of the most enchanting museums in Amsterdam. Dedicated to the player piano, or pianola, a little-remembered playback instrument from wayyy back even before records (do ya know what a record is, sonny? Heh heh, well, back in my day...) which beginning at around 1900 automatically played paper "rolls" containing different songs, kind of like the hand-cranked cylindrically-operated miniature gift shop harps so beloved by the youths of today. The museum archives contain over 25,000 of such rolls, so browse around for your favorite prewar jingle and let the entertainment-machines do the rest.

i €5. 🕐 Open July-Aug Th-Su 2pm-5pm; Sept-June Su 2pm-5pm.

HUIS MARSEILLE, MUSEUM FOR PHOTOGRAPHY · · · · · · · · · · · · · · · · MUSEUM
Keizersgracht 401 · ☎0 20 531 8989 www.huismarseille.nl

Presenting a homier, quirkier feel than the nearby FOAM, the Huis Marseille absolutely holds its own in terms of sheer excellence of artwork—you can get lost here amidst the six exhibition spaces, each with its own distinct feel, and interconnected by old school Dutch passages. One of the lesser-frequented spots for tourists, this museum is a great place to immerse yourself.

i €8, students €4. 🕐 Open Tu-Su 11am-6pm.

HOMOMONUMENT · MUSEUM
Westermarkt · www.homomonument.nl

The Homomonument is the culmination of a movement to erect a memorial honoring homosexual victims of Nazi persecution—but it's also meant to stand for all people, past and present, who've been oppressed for their sexuality. Designed by Karin Daan and opened in 1987, the monument consists of three connecting pink granite triangles—in remembrance of the symbol the Nazis forced homosexuals to wear—which represent the past (one triangle points toward the Anne Frank House), the present (another is perched gently over the water and points toward the National War Monument in Dam Square), and the future (pointing toward the headquarters of the COC, a Dutch gay rights group,

which, founded in 1946, is the oldest continuously operating gay and lesbian organization in the world). Look for the engraved words "Naar Vriendschap Zulk een Mateloos Verlangen" ("such an endless desire for friendship"), a line from the poem "To a Young Fisherman" by the gay Dutch Jewish poet Jacob Israel de Haan (1881 - 1924).

i *Free.* ⏱ *Open 24/7.*

ONS' LIEVE HEER OP SOLDER
CHURCH

Oudezijds Voorburgwal 40   ☎020 624 6604 www.opsolder.nl

When Catholicism was banned in Holland in the 17th century, a merchant built this secret church (English: "Our Lord in the Attic") in the top floor of his building; to this day, it stands in muted contrast to the lavishness of Oude Kerk around the corner. Its interior décor mostly confined to the organ and elegant altarpiece, this is one of those "come for the history, stay for the history" destinations you won't find anywhere else.

i *€9. Free with Museumkaart (€59.90, valid for one year).* ⏱ *Open daily M-Sa 10am-5pm, Su 1pm-5pm.*

AMSTERDAM SEX MUSEUM
MUSEUM

Damrak 18   ☎020 622 8376 www.sexmuseumamsterdam.nl

Unless you were previously unaware of sex—like, as a concept—there's not that much new information in this museum. (The brief "Sex Through the Ages" presentation is hilariously simplistic, though the elegant British-accented narration is priceless.) But perhaps we're missing the point: who needs information when you've got smut? Museumgoers' reactions differ widely to the contents; some leave slightly offended by the hardcore porn-and-fetish room, some find the farting dolls titillating, and others inexplicably insist on having their picture taken with one of the giant model penises. If you really want to see a parade of pictures of people having sex, you could just visit a sex shop in the Red Light District. Or, you know, use Incognito Mode on Chrome.

i *€4.* ⏱ *Open daily 9:30am-11:30pm.*

ANNE FRANK HOUSE
MUSEUM

Prinsengracht 263-267   www.annefrank.org

Don't balk at the two-plus hours you'll spend waiting outside—this could very well be the most meaningful thing you do on your trip. After World War II, Anne's father Otto, the sole Frank family member to survive the Holocaust, published the now-famous diary and helped establish a foundation to prevent the house's demolition. The modern museum preserves the building's amazing history, augmenting excerpts from Anne's diary with interviews with Otto and the Franks' helpers—non-Jewish coworkers who hid and supplied the family during their years in the secret annex. The meditative journey through the museum is perfectly designed and deeply moving without a trace of heavy-handedness.

i *€9. Free with Museumkaart (€59.90, valid for one year).* ⏱ *Open Apr-June M-F 9am-9pm, Sa 9am-10pm, Su 9am-9pm; Jul-Aug daily 9am-10pm; Sept-Oct M-F 9am-9pm, Sa 9am-10pm, Su M-F 9am-9pm; Nov-Mar M-F 9am-7pm, Sa 9am-9pm, Su 9am-7pm.*

WESTERKERK
TOWER

Prinsengracht 281   ☎20 624 7766 www.westerkerk.nl

B-b-big towers! Cool, man! Way up there above the rest of the city, it'll take you half an hour just to scale the thing, which might've been the whole idea back when Europeans were invading each other's churches with more consistency. A bombastic selection of bells in the tower belfry—we've been looking forward to using that word for the whole book: belfry—is just icing on the cake; the best view in Amsterdam is really what's waiting at the top. Somewhere down below the church, Rembrandt is buried, though due to oversights, no one's totally clear just where. The tower tour is a must, but you can also come for free at any point, and a calendar of upcoming concerts is on their web site.

i Free. Tours €7. ☑ Open M-Sa 10am-3pm.

STEDELIJK MUSEUM BUREAU AMSTERDAM (SMBA)
MUSEUM

Museumplein 100   ☎20 5732 911 www.stedelijk.nl

There's no telling what you'll stumble across here, except that it'll probably be "art." Local artists use the space to showcase artwork in rotating exhibitions; past features included "The Marx Lounge" (red room with a tableful of books on critical theory) and "ZERO: Let Us Explore the Stars." Special lectures and movie screenings are also sponsored occasionally.

i €15, students €7.50. ☑ Open M-W 10am-6pm, Th 10am-10pm, F-Su 10am-6pm.

VONDELPARK
PARK

Vondelpark, Vondelpark, we long for your greens. Dubbed by everyone around the "Central Park of Amsterdam," the comparison's understandable if not totally apt—while it is indeed the citizenry's favorite parkspace, and on summer days the whole town seems to descend upon it, the park's actually located decently far from the center of things (though thanks to Amsterdam's compactness, none of the city's destinations are that remote from each other). Besides, you can't toke a doob in the middle of Manhattan. Named for 17th-century poet and playwright Joost van den Vondel, a.k.a. the "Dutch Shakespeare" (competitive much? what is it with these comparisons?), the park boasts an open-air theater, which puts on free concerts in the summer, and should that not prove entertainment enough, as of 2008 it is legal to have sex [thumbs up] in the park, provided you stay away from the playgrounds (duh, perv) and dispose of condoms.

i Free.

what's up with the tulips, anway?

Chances are, you'll meet some tulips in Amsterdam, and—getchyer mind outta the gutter—we mean the plant specimen. The bulb has a complex history in Amsterdam: introduced to Europe as a gift from the Ottoman Empire in the mid-1500s, tulips became especially popular in the Netherlands for their hardiness in the famously low-lying area. As Holland gained independence and stoked its economic prospects, citizens clamored for the exotic-looking flower, which came to be a powerful status symbol. Prices for individual bulbs skyrocketed, with local taverns becoming the epicenter of what the Dutch came to term *windhandel*, or "wind trade." As the wanton whims of the tulip bubble thrashed ever onward, after a certain point no flowers were actually changing hands—it became more lucrative just to resell the tulips one had recently "acquired" on paper. Even people who had never seen tulips with their own eyes were getting in on the action.

Eventually—some speculate due to a particularly nasty outbreak of the Bubonic Plague, which kept death-fearing auction-goers from participating—prices crashed and the bubble burst spectacularly, though not before ten acres of land had been offered in exchange for a single bulb. "Tulip mania" remains a figure of speech for the self-perpetuating insanity of unrestrained economics, seen recently in accounts of the dot-com bubble and 2008 subprime mortgage crisis. The moral of the story, of course, is to get in early, play the market born seemingly overnight around the craze for a little-understood foreign import, wait until the last possible second, leap out, resettle in South America with your fortune, and live out your days in luxury.

amsterdam

ELECTRIC LADYLAND

MUSEUM

Tweede Leliedwarsstraat 5 ☎0 20 420 3776

The "First Museum of Fluorescent Art" begs many questions (namely, what was the second?); its passionate and eccentric owner, Nick Padalino, will gladly spend hours explaining the history, science, and culture of fluorescence to each and every in-the-dark visitor crossing the doorstep into his one-room basement, which is where the museum is located. We promise it's way better than we're making it sound: the true spirit of Amsterdam is alive and well here, from the globally-harvested collection of glowing rocks to the hands- and feet-on brightly-colored stalactites. (Though all the psychedelia raises another question—how'd this dude dodge Jimi's copyright lawyers?)

i €5. ☑ Open Tu-Sa 1pm-6pm.

FOOD

▨ EETSALON VAN DOBBEN

CAFE $

Korte Reguliersdwarsstraat 5-7-9 ☎020-6244200 www.eetsalonvandobben.nl

If you're on the prowl to "eet" the cheapest meals in the entire city, put this on your list—most sandwiches are in the €2.50-4 range, and frankly you wouldn't know it for their taste, and the traditional croquette is a delicacy. Smallish and friendly, with purported historical ties dating back to the 1950s, the place's vibe is pleasantly neighborhoody. And did we mention €3 sandwiches?

i Sandwiches €2.50-5. ☑ Open M-W 10am-9pm, Th 10am-1am, F-Sa 10am-2am, Su 10am-8pm.

▨ LOUIS

CAFE $

Singel 43

For your hardworking Let's Go team, the question with places like this one is always whether to call it a bar, a restaurant, or a cafe: Louis combines the best of all food and drink categories, serving up ravishing (yet affordable) sandwiches to compliment the long list of brews and mixed drinks. The décor is perfectly laid-back, with framed photographs of rusting automobiles and a wide selection of Dutch-edition Dan Brown novels alongside the old wooden tables. (Be aware that facing out the window near the back end of the venue makes it likely that you'll be locking eyes with a hooker all day/night. Which is a plus or a minus, depending on your tastes.)

i Sandwiches and salads €4-11. Drinks €2.50. ☑ Open M-Th 11am-1am, F-Sa 11am-2am, Su 11am-11pm.

NOORDERLICHT CAFÉ

RESTAURANT $$

NDSM Plein 102 ☎020 4922 770 noorderlichtcafe.nl

Poised bustlingly to the north of Amsterdam, this utterly charming greenhouse-cafe feels removed from the city's downtown area by miles and years. Offering seasonal dishes, freaky sculpture art, and a beautiful look at Lake IJ, everything here is futuristic and upscale—come for lunch to avoid the more exorbitant dinner pricing.

i Lunch €4.50-11.50. Dinner €5.50-28.50. ☑ Open daily 11am-10pm.

IJSSALON TOFANI

CAFE, ICE CREAM $

Kloveniersburgwal 16 ☎0 20 624 3073

You heard it here first—roll through for some of the city's top gelato. As you'll no doubt notice in your gamboling and wayfaring, not every two-bit self-proclaimed dessert server in the downtown is worth stopping by, but this place absolutely is. A nice array of flavors ranges from the classic to the esoteric. Outdoor seating seals the deal.

i Sandwiches €4.50-7. Drinks €2-5. ☑ Open daily noon-midnight.

ZUIVERE KOFFIE
CAFE $

Utrechtsestraat 39

The wonderfully Dutch expression "dat is geen zuivere koffie" translates literally to "that's no pure coffee," but really means something like "I smell a rat," or "something's fishy," or "there's fungus among us." This cozy store is the opposite of all those things, submitting croissants and sandwiches for your deep pleasure (and don't get us started on the apple pie). And the coffee itself is, indeed, pure.

i Sandwiches €5. Drinks €2-4. Ⓩ Open M-F 8am-5pm, Sa 9am-5pm.

PLLEK
CAFE $

Tt. Neveritaweg 59 ☎020 290 0020 www.pllek.nl

We have no idea how it's pronounced, either, but Pllek offers a dash of industrial/ rustic beauty up north of the city and the Lake IJ. A variety of programming makes the trek totally worthwhile—Movie Nights by the water on Tuesdays are particularly charming, and while a dish involving squid can never be described as "charming," we enjoyed it (although the specialty here is definitely drink-grabbing, not extensive meals). Busy on nice days.

i Sandwiches €6.50-8.50. Ⓩ Open M-Th 9:30am-1am, F-Sa 9:30am-3am, Su 9:30am-1am.

WINKEL 43
BAKERY $

Noordermarkt 43 ☎020 623 022 www.winkel43.nl

Pie, pie, pie. Is that all anyone cares about anymore? Get outta here, old man! At Winkel, the answer's obviously yes: don't be surprised if everyone here has a slice, along with an (un)healthy dollop of whipped cream. There's food here, too, but that's a little beside the point.

i Slices €4.50-7.50. Ⓩ Open M 7am-1am, Tu-Th 8am-1am, F 8am-3am, Sa 7am-3am, Su 10am-1am.

CAFÉ CHRIS
PUB $

Bloemstraat 42 ☎020 624 5942 www.cafechris.nl

The oldest pub in Jordaan (opened 1624) remains a perennial favorite for its relaxed and welcoming air—free from tourist swarms, the staff will treat you like one of Amsterdam's own, even instructing you on how to order your drink in Dutch. The jukebox goes and goes.

Ⓩ Open M-Th 3pm-1am, F-Sa 3pm-2am, Su 3pm-9pm.

'T KUYLTJE
CAFE $

Gasthuismolensteeg 9 HS ☎020 6201045 www.kuyltje.nl

This avocado-colored cafe will serve you some of the best "broodjes" (sammie rolls), hot or cold, in Holland. Humming with cheerful banter and activity most days, 't Kuyltje, in spite of its edgy use of punctuation, provides further evidence that family-run cafes are the friendliest places wherever in the world you're traveling.

i Sandwiches €4.50. Ⓩ Open M-F 7am-4pm, Sa 10am-4pm; closed Sundays.

LITTLE SAIGON
VIETNAMESE $

1012 BB Amsterdam ☎020 737 249 www.littlesaigon.nl

Either of the two locations of this Vietnamese joint will stand out from the surrounding riffraff on the grounds of price, quality, and tight-shipness. The interior's compact, but to great effect—if you listen closely, you can hear the sizzles of your food being prepared, awaiting you. The menu arcs toward the pricier end, but it's possible to get a bowl of delicious ban mi for as little as €6.

i Ban mi €6-10. Ⓩ Open daily noon-11:30pm.

BAKKERIJ EETHUIS LAVINA
BAKERY $

Van Woustraat 32 ☎684 821 417

This bakery is a vestige of unreachable Old Europe, with friendly-eyed service and a variety of unbelievably tasty bready/cheesy/meaty/veggie-y creations,

amsterdam

inscrutable to the uninitiated, baked right before your eyes. The late hours make this a prime stop for midnight (and beyond) munchies, and its location along the main drag of Van Woustraat gives it killer proximity to a number of watering holes. Not that you have to drink water.

i *Bread roll €1.50-2.50.* ⏰ *Open daily noon-1am.*

BLACKGOLD
COFEE HOUSE $

Korte Koningsstraat 13
www.blackgoldamsterdam.com

For further proof that the Dutch are the planet's most culturally advanced civilization, look no further than this coffee shop/record store. Simultaneously oozing cool and caffeine, you can at once get wired and mellow out with the latest beats. Vinyl might be a little hard to store in your luggage, but holy shit, man, look what I just found. . . [pulls a record so obscure it lacks even a name]

i *Espresso €2.50.* ⏰ *Open M 9am-5pm, Th-F 9am-5pm, Sa 10am-5pm, Su 11am-5pm. Closed Tu-W.*

TOMATILLO
MEXICAN $

Overtoom 261
☎020 683 3086 www.tomatillo.nl

Tacos in Holland? Strange as it may seem, it's a thing, and for years now Tomatillo's been pulling of their Tex-Mex trick with aplomb, avoiding the overcheesiness synonymous with many Gringo attempts at the cuisine. Reasonably priced and quite clean in its small, open space, this'll do ya right.

i *Burritos €9-12. Beer €4.* ⏰ *Open M-Th 4pm-10pm, F-Su noon-10pm.*

NIGHTLIFE

▨ BITTERZOET
CLUB

Spuistraat 2
☎020 42 123 18 www.bitterzoet.com

The area immediately around Centraal Station isn't exactly known for being the epicenter of cool, but maybe it's the low expectations that came together to form something unpretentiously rad here at Bitterzoet. Sometimes DJ'd, sometimes with live acts, this is a dependable party close enough to city center for you to eventually stagger back to your nearby hostel.

i *Tickets vary €8-18.* ⏰ *Open M-Th 8pm-3am, F-Sa 8pm-4am, Su 8pm-3am.*

▨ CAFÉ BRECHT
BAR

Weteringschans 157
☎020-6272211 www.cafebrecht.nl

The cozy and AC'd cool Café Brecht (named for German writer, poet, and thespian Eugen Berthold Friedrich Brecht) drops you straight into a relaxed Berlin-style "living room cafe" from prewar decades of yore—frumpy regulars vape in the back as table lamps glow. The drink menu is a little pricey, but not terribly so, and offers a mouth-watering assortment of exotic brews, from Czech beers to intriguing fruit/cider combinations to Italian coffee to harder liquors. It's equally easy to while away an afternoon or an evening (or both) here in the company of pals or a good book.

i *Drinks €2-7+.* ⏰ *Open Su-Tu noon-1am, F-Sa noon-3am.*

COFFEESHOP EN MUZIEKSTUDIO DE GRAAL
COFFEE SHOP

Albert Cuypstraat 25
☎20 471 1791

Tucked sneakily between restaurants and cafes, this truly dank coffee shop has just the right combination of old chairs, slow rap, and reptile tanks to keep you occupied for hours. The shopkeepers are chill as all get, happy to instruct, and help maintain the place's lovable calm—you'll always have a place to sit here. There's a cat, too. Nice.

i *Marijuana €7-12 per gram.* ⏰ *Open daily 10am-1am.*

1. Road Where a Canal Would've Done Just as Well

2. Street Where Van Gogh Went One Time For a Beer, Though He Swore He'd Never Do It Again

3. Alleyway Where the City's Reptilian Citizenry Go to Shed Their Beautiful, Blonde Skin

4. Cursed Overpass Where Only Tourists Who Stop at at Least Five Canalside Cafes May Pass Safely

5. Street Wherein Famed Early Dutch City Planner Johannes Hans Van Shnockleck Designed the Bulk of His Streets

---

PRIK
CLUB

Spuistraat 109 ☎0 20 320 0002 www.prikamsterdam.nl

"Amsterdam's favorite gay bar," which just celebrated its 9th birthday, is actually named for the Dutch word for "bubble," you naughty-minded traveler, and features cocktail specials all day on Thursday, not to mention cock specials basically always. Service is great, DJs spin the night away on weekends, and a variety of special and themed nights are advertised on the web site.

i Beers €3.50. ◙ Open M-Th 4pm-1am, F-Sa 4pm-3am, Su 4pm-1am.

LA TERTULIA
COFFEE SHOP

312 Prinsengracht ☎0 20 623 8503 www.coffeeshoptertulia.com

Remember, Let's Go never recommends drug use—all we're saying is, while you totally could come all the way to Amsterdam and not try a "Ganja Shake," what will the cool rebel kids back home you're trying to impress think? Better enjoy this not-that-unlikely-seeming combination at La Tertulia, a split-level coffee shop that's a cut above for its attention to the non-weed things (yes, a real category): friendly service, leafy ambiance, bang-up food, and outdoor, canal-side seating.

i Marijuana €8-12 per gram. ◙ Open Tu-Sa 11am-7pm

HILL STREET BLUES BAR
COFFEE SHOP

Warmoesstraat 52 A ☎020 638 7922 www.hill-street-blues.nl

A favorite amongst the tourist crowd for its ambiance, including a soundtrack that specializes in drum & bass and jungle music, Hill Street Blues Bar is nothing to turn your hip young nose up at—they know their cannabis. Like virtually every other coffee shop in Amsterdam, seating can be limited, so try to think not like a stoner (for once) and show up when the others aren't around. Or be content to stand for a bit.

i Marijuana €7-12 per gram. ◙ Open M-Th 9am-1am, F-Sa 9am-3am, Su 9am-1am.

HANNEKES BOOM
BAR

Dijksgracht 4 ☎020 419 9820 www.hannekesboom.nl

This derelict-looking shack ain't frontin' when it claims to be in the "best place in Amsterdam"—perched on an outcropping with a beautiful view of the Oosterdok canal, this is where the city's young and handsome descend on hot summer days, plop their flirty selves down on benches, stools, and tree branches, and dangle their smooth/hairy legs from the wharf. Pleasantly busy without feeling chaotic, Hannekes Boom provides ever-flowing drinks at reasonable prices on through afternoon and evening.

i Drinks €4+. Food €11-20. ◙ Open M-Th 10am-1am, F-Sa 10am-3am, Su 10am-1am.

amsterdam

DULAC

Haarlemmerstraat 118   ☎020 624 4265 www.restaurantdulac.nl

Bizarre sculptures crowd in among the world-weary students congregating at this bar; as it's some of the only nightlife in the area, you might have to put up with some inanimate company (though if you happen to make a friend here, chances are he'll not made of stone). A 50% student discount on food helps seal the eating deal.

i *Beer €2.50. Food €10+.* ☒ *Open M-Th 3pm-1am, F 3pm-3am, Sa noon-3am, Su noon-1am.*

BIMHUIS

MUSIC VENUE

Piet Heinkade 3   ☎020 788 2188 www.bimhuis.com

Up north of the city, this imposing black skyward cube doesn't exactly call to mind the jazz of your grandparents' youth, but that's because that bland shit is dead, cat, dig? Tickets can be expensive, but if you treat yourself, you'll get to hear some of the leading innovators in the unstoppable artform—as an already-up and still-coming cultural magnet, Amsterdam attracts all the biggest names, and venues like Bimguis are why.

i *Hours and tickets vary (usually between €20-30) depending on the show.* ☒ *Check website for schedule.*

DURTY NELLY'S PUB

PUB

Warmoesstraat 115   ☎020 0 638 0125 www.durtynellys.nl

The riproarin' 'n' rough 'n' rowdy crowd congregating here aren't all backpacking scallywags who'll successively wander to the upstairs hostel to sleep; the thick atmosphere swirls travelers and tourists together for what'll no doubt be an unforgettably forgotten night. The Irish theme is there—it's named after an original pub back on the island—but not in an in-yer-face way.

i *Beer €4.70-6.* ☒ *Open M-Th 9am-1am, F-Sa 9am-3am, Su 9am-1am.*

ESSENTIALS

Emergency

- **EMERGENCY NUMBER:** ☎112

- **EMERGENCY DOCTOR:** ☎088 003 0600

- **POLICE (NON-EMERGENCY):** ☎0900 8844

- **RAPE CRISIS CENTER:** ☎31 887 555 588

- **HOSPITAL:** Academisch Medisch Centrum (Meibergdreef 9 ☎20 566 9111; tourist medical service: ☎020 592 33 55.)

- **PHARMACIES:** There isn't a single pharmacy open 24-hours all the time, but each night, there should be at least one that is open. Call ☎020 694 8709 for information about what's open.

Practicalities

- **TOURIST OFFICES:** VVV is the main tourist office in Amsterdam (Zeestraat 37. ☒ Open March-Sept M-Sa 10am-5pm, Su 11am-4pm; Oct M-Sa 10am-5pm; Nov-March M-Sa 10am-3pm.)

- **MUSEUMKAART:** This Museum Card allows entrance to over 400 museums in Amsterdam including the Anne Frank House, Van Gogh Museum, and Rijksmuseum. It costs €59.90 for adults and €32.45 for youth up to 18. The card is valid for one year.

- **BANKS/ATMS:** There are so, so, so many ATMs in Amsterdam. You can't walk down the street without tripping over like three. And a lot of them are feeless, too. It's almost like they want you to take out money so you can spend it. You can also pay for most things with a debit/credit card (i.e. without drawing cash), especially at stores, though some restaurant/cafe places have a minimum or don't accept plastic.

- **GLBT:** GAYtic is a resource center endorsed by VVV. (Spuistraat 44 ☎020 330 1461; www. gaytic.nl. ☑ Open M-Sa 11am-8pm, Su noon-8pm.)
- **INTERNET:** Openbare Bibliotheek Amsterdam has free Wi-Fi and computer access (☑ Open daily 10am-10pm). The Mad Processor, a favorite of gamers, also offers Wi-Fi for €1 per 30min (open daily noon-2am, ☎020 612 1818; www.madprocessor.nl).
- **POST OFFICE:** The main branch of the post office is located at Singel 250 (☎020 556 3311. ☑ Open M-F 7:30am-6:30pm, Sa 7:30am-5pm.)

Getting There

By Plane

Schiphol Airport is the major airport. The train from the airport to Centraal station costs €4.40. A train leaves 4-10 times per hour except between 1am and 6am, when it leaves once per hour. It's a 15-20 minute ride.

By Train

Taking the train is a good way of getting around within the continent. Trains arrive from all over and almost always end up at Centraal station. Rail Europe can be a good resource for comparing prices.

By Bus

Taking the bus is another way of getting around the continent and the UK. Eurolines (020 560 87 88) is the best choice.

Getting Around

While the tram and buses exist for those who are in a rush, Amsterdam's small size makes it very easily walkable if you have time to spare. In short, the Metro isn't that useful. A single journey costs €2.90, which can be paid in cash or by using a chipkaart—just make sure to tap your card on and off or you'll be charged hella euro. Trams run 5am-midnight, and night buses fill in the intermediate hours.

the netherlands essentials

SAFETY AND HEALTH

Drugs and Alcohol

It hardly needs to be stated that attitudes toward conscience-altering substances are quite different in Amsterdam than in other areas of the world, though the city is taking active measures to change this image. The Dutch take a fairly liberal attitude toward alcohol, with the drinking age set at 16 for beer and wine and at 18 for hard liquor. Public drunkenness, however, is frowned upon and is a sure way to mark yourself as a tourist.

When it comes to drugs other than alcohol, things get a little more interesting. Whatever anyone standing outside of a club at 4am might tell you, hard drugs are completely illegal and possession or consumption of substances like heroin and cocaine will be harshly punished. Soft drugs, such as marijuana, are tolerated, but consumption is confined to certain legalized zones, namely coffeeshops (for marijuana) and smartshops (for herbal drugs). However, the age of the coffeeshop is, in some ways, coming to a close. Under new laws passed by the Dutch government, only Dutch residents over the age of 18 will be allowed to enter coffeeshops. As of 2012, customers will have to sign up for a one-year membership, or "dope pass," in order to use the shops, which have been blamed in recent years for encouraging drug trafficking and criminal activity.

Prostitution

The "world's oldest profession" has flourished in the Netherlands, particularly in Amsterdam's famous Red Light District. Legal prostitution comes in two main forms. Window prostitution, which involves scantily clad women tempting passersby from small chambers fronted by a plate-glass window, is by far the most visible. Another option is legalized brothels. The term usually refers to an establishment centered around a bar. Women, or men, will make your acquaintance—and are then available for hour-long sessions.

The best place to go for information about prostitution in Amsterdam is the Prostitution Information Centre. (Enge Kerksteeg 3, in the Red Light District behind the Oude Kerk ☎020 420 7328 www.pic-amsterdam.com ☒ Open Sa 4-7pm. Available at other times for group bookings, call ahead.) Founded in 1994 by Mariska Majoor (once a prostitute herself), the center fills a niche, connecting the Red Light District with its eager visitors.

GLBT Travelers

In terms of sexual diversity, in Amsterdam, anything goes—and goes often. Dark-rooms and dungeons rub elbows with saunas and sex clubs, though much more subdued options are the standard. Despite this openness, certain travelers—including drag queens and kings, other cross-dressers, and transgendered visitors more generally—should take extra caution walking the streets at night, especially in and around the Red Light District. All GLBT visitors to Amsterdam should also be aware that, though the city is a haven of homosexual tolerance, the recent infusion of fundamentalist religiosity into the Dutch political dialogue has created an environment detrimental to complete acceptance of GLBT behaviors and visibility.

Minority Travelers

Despite Amsterdam being known for its openness, there's a lot of hullabaloo about ethnic minorities coming into the Netherlands. Immigrants aren't always welcomed with open arms. Although foreign tourists of all stripes are sometimes treated with suspicion, it's mostly non-white visitors who occasionally encounter hostility. Muslims, or those who appear Muslim, seem to run into the most problems. The city is still generally tolerant, but sadly racism is not unheard of.

the netherlands

NORWAY

Norway's rugged countryside and remote mountain farms gave birth to one of the most feared seafaring civilizations of pre-medieval Europe: the Vikings. Modern-day Norwegians have inherited their ancestors' independent streak, voting against joining the EU in 1994. Currently, Norway enjoys one of the highest standards of living in the world. Its stunning fjords and miles of coastline make the country a truly worthwhile destination—but sky-high prices may challenge even the best-prepared budget traveler.

greatest hits

- **GET CULTURED:** Pay a visit to Oslo's **National Art Gallery** (p. 709) to see classics like Edvard Munch's Scream and works by your boys Picasso and van Gogh.

- **BEER WITH US HERE:** Though the name may sound like something you got by banging your keyboard, **Schouskjelleren Mikrobryggeri** (p. 714) is easily the best microbrewery in Oslo.

- **PINING FOR THE FJORDS:** No trip to Norway is complete without some fjords. Hop on a boat in **Bergen** (p. 719) to see these natural wonders.

oslo

Oslo might not be a cultural capital in the style of Paris, London, or Berlin, but it has a unique identity as an international city smack in the middle of nature. A short train ride can often bring you from bustling, modern shopping centers to wilderness so pristine Columbus would claim it for the Spanish Crown. It's a place where nightclubs spill out into botanical gardens, and kebab, Thai, and gourmet burgers are all available five minutes from your camping site.

The streets have a clean—some might say sterilized—feel, but the 20+ hours of sunlight during the summer mean that you have all the time in the world to explore them. The main tourist attractions can all be covered in a few days, but spots off the beaten path—microbreweries, student neighborhoods, and tasty ethnic eats—make spending extra time here certainly worth the trouble.

Due to high taxes, high incomes, and a high standard of living, there's no cheap anything in Oslo; it vies with Tokyo and London every year for the title of world's most expensive city. Even the stingiest backpackers will find it hard to get by on less than $100 a day if they want to eat full meals and experience everything, but we hope the tips and tricks in this book help guide you in the right direction. Oslo is a place with such a collage of identities—young, Nordic, punk, American, European, African, and more—that it would be a real shame to miss blowing through some money here while you're in Europe.

ACCOMMODATIONS

OSLO CENTRAL HOSTEL
HOSTEL $$

Kongensgate 7 ☎231 00 801 hihostels.no/en/hostel/oslo-central-hostel

This place is like a hostel on steroids. It has a new, modern building with every service a traveler could need: among them, laundry, breakfast, and heated bathrooms (that last one may not sound impressive, but after you use it, you'll find our own bathrooms barbaric by comparison). Each room comes with sockets by the beds, ensuite bathrooms, and free Wi-Fi—short of reading you a bedtime story, this place does it all. The price alone should convince you to stay, but if not, know that HI members get a 10% discount and there's always a colorful cast of characters in the rooms.

i From Oslo S, walk three blocks south to Radhusgata. Walk west until building #7. Dorms 395-445 NOK. 🕐 Reception 24hr.

ANKER APARTMENTS
HOTEL $

København gata 10 ☎229 93 000 www.ankerapartment.no

Hopping hostels is a hit-or-miss situation, and our researcher was so down on his luck when he entered Anker Apartments that the most articulate thing he could say was, "Wow!" Indeed, the apartments might be the best money you spend while in Oslo, as 220 NOK gets you a spot in a spacious four-bed unit with a kitchen and bathroom in one of Oslo's coolest neighborhoods. The lobby is massive and nicely furnished, with a TV, foosball tables, and IKEA furniture so artsy it'd make Andy Warhol throw up. If that's not enough, the building is connected to a cheap, fully stocked grocery store, making it the perfect base of operations as you head out to explore Grünerløkka or simply kick back with some canned reindeer and Netflix on sad Saturdays.

i Take Bus 30 to Daelenenga. Walk down Københavngata. The apartments are on the left. Dorms 220-250 NOK. Singles 500 NOK. Doubles 700 NOK. 🕐 Reception 24hr.

SENTRUM HOSTEL
HOSTEL $

Tollbugata 8 ☎223 35 580 www.sentrumhostel.no

Sentrum is three short blocks from Karl Johans Gate, which means there's no need for a cab at the end of your late-night boozing and kebab-ing. Towels and linens are included in the price, and the communal kitchen and rec room make it easy to meet other hostelers. All the rooms come equipped with comfortable single mattresses, but know that this place is a bit of a labyrinth: bathrooms and showers are communal and on different floors. For the area and the price you're paying, though, it's as good a bargain as the Louisiana Purchase.

i Oslo S. Walk down Karl Johans gate. Turn left onto Skippergata, then right onto Tollbugata. Dorms 260 NOK. ☒ Reception 10am-midnight.

ANKER HOSTEL
HOSTEL $

Storgata 55 ☎229 97 200 www.ankerhostel.no

Short of sleeping on a bench, this is one of the cheapest accommodations you'll find in Oslo (though only slightly more comfortable). It's located 10 minutes away from Oslo Sentralstasjon and offers four- and six-room deals for around 250 NOK per night. If that doesn't sell you, then maybe the bar will: at 35 NOK a pop, the staff sells what may be the cheapest beer in Norway. For a bare-bones price, you're getting bare-bones accommodations—replete with graffiti in the hallways and elevator. Seeing as the hostel charges extra for sheets, towels, and kitchenware, Lord knows you could use a drink. On another booze-themed note, youthful revelers and thirsty businessmen alike may enjoy the famous Oslo Pub Crawl, which leaves from Anker's lobby every Saturday during the summer.

i Tram 12, 13, 17 or bus 31 from Jernbanetorget/Oslo S to Hausmannsgata (Haussmans Gate). Walk 100 feet forward. The hostel is on the left. Dorms 230-290 NOK. ☒ Reception 24hr.

CITYBOX OSLO
HOTEL $$$

Prinsens Gate 6 ☎214 20 480 www.citybox.no

If you're looking for a brief respite from sticky showers and odiously squeaking bunkbeds, this is the perfect place to decompress. The title "CityBox" is surprisingly accurate: your reservation gets you one bathroom, one bed, and one fold-out desk. It's the kind of place slightly older people would refer to as "nifty" and "kitsch." While those words taste like battery acid in our mouths, we will say that the hotel's proximity to Karl Johans nightlife is a definite plus. It may be out of the price range for many backpackers, but prices tend to be lower on Sundays or if you book in advance.

i Oslo S. Walk down the parade street Karl Johans Gate. Turn left onto Skippergata, then right onto Prinsens Gate. Singles 830-900 NOK. ☒ Reception 24hr.

OSLO VANDRERHJEM HARALDSHEIM
HOSTEL $

Haraldsheimveien 4 ☎222 22 965 www.haraldsheim.no

Though Haraldsheim is only 20 minutes from downtown Oslo, it feels like it's located somewhere between Narnia and the Shire. Its outdoorsy environment attracts a different clientele—at the time of Let's Go's visit, the majority of hostelers seemed to be adults on a hiking trip—but the kitchen, views, and rooms are just as good as what you'll find in hipper neighborhoods. With prices the same between here and downtown, the choice comes down to your preferences: if you'd like to hike and play backgammon with a kind soul, this is the place for you; if you want the college frat boy life, book closer to Karl Johans (or possibly Cancun).

i Take bus 31 to Sinsenkrysset. Walk through the underpass. Turn right and walk until you come to a hill. The hostel is on top of the hill. Dorms 250-300 NOK. 10% discount for HI members. ☒ Reception 24hr.

OSLO

PERMINALEN HOTEL

HOTEL $$

Øvre Slottsgate 2 ☎240 05 500 www.perminalen.no

Though it's advertised on sites like Hostelworld, Perminalen is very much not a hostel; it's a hotel that offers shared rooms at hostel-level rates. While this does mean you get a pretty sweet setup—private bathroom, work desks, TV, Wi-Fi, and more—it also means that there's no hostel atmosphere and no shared kitchens to use. This place has essentially all the same services as Oslo Hostel Central down the block and is roughly the same price, so it really comes down to a matter of personal preference.

i Oslo S. Walk south along Skippergata until you reach Tollbugata. Turn right onto Tollbugata. After four blocks, turn left onto Øvre Slottsgate. The hotel is on the left. Shared rooms 380 NOK. Singles 620 NOK. Doubles 860 NOK. ☺ Reception 24hr.

SCANDIC OSLO AIRPORT

HOTEL $$$

Ravinevegen 15 ☎231 55 900

We think "Scandic" would make a pretty bitchin' name for a Pokémon, but it's actually a hotel a stone's throw away from the airport (Note: figure of speech. Do not throw anything near an airport unless you want a free ticket to Guantanamo.) Rooms are admittedly pricey by backpackers' standards, but they have all the clean, modern, angular charm you've come to associate with Scandinavia. The obvious reason for staying here is location (for 70 NOK, you can hop on a bus and be at the airport in ten minutes) but an extra plus while staying here is the breakfast—while most hostels give you some pitiful helpings of cucumber and toast, Scandic is sure to stoke the fire in your American loins with its copious offerings of bacon, eggs, and more.

i Take the shuttle from Oslo Airport that goes directly to the hotel. Singles 1400-1500 NOK. ☺ Reception 24hr.

CAMPING

Even Oslo's cheapest accommodations are at least 250 NOK a night. Think for a second what you could do if you saved that money. You could save up for college, you could pay off your debt...you could even afford a real Norwegian beer! So give your wallet and mental health a break and make the smart choice—sleep in the great outdoors!

LANGØYENE CAMPING

CAMPING

Langøyene Island

Head to Langøyene Island in the Oslofjord and you'll find a nude beach, volleyball courts, and enough campground to lie back and sleep without the person next to you causing a fuss! Cost of entry is free (though you have to bring your own tent) and as long as you don't scream, murder, or litter, you can stay here as long as you want. Bathrooms, hiking, and a coffee shop on the island make it a convenient place to spend the night, but be sure to check the ferry schedule so you don't get stranded.

i Take the B4 ferry from Radhusbrygge/behind City Hall to Langøyene Island (requires a valid NSB metro pass or the Oslo Pass). Free. ☺ Ferries leave for the island about every 15 min during the summer, but be sure to check the schedule. You must bring your own tent. Quiet hours 11pm-7am.

EKEBERG CAMPING

CAMPING

Ekebergveien 65 ☎221 98 568 www.ekebergcamping.no

As opposed to the free-for-all of Langøyene, Ekeberg is a structured, professional camping site that charges for everything it provides. It has room for about 600 "units" and specializes in accommodating mobile homes, though visitors are also welcome to use tents (they're just not as likely to get a spot near a power outlet for the night). The amazing view and proximity to Oslo's downtown (about 15min. by bus) is a huge advantage, but when you add up the price of entrance, showers, and any snacks you buy on site, you're likely to find that this place costs roughly the same as a hostel, but with a higher chance of bug bites. Our recommendation: if you're the kind of person who cries at the beauty of the Grand Canyon, spend a night here; if you're only pitching a tent because your wallet is empty, head to Lar.gøyene and camp for free instead.

i Take bus 34 to the Ekeberg Camping stop. Tent or caravan with car 270 NOK. Tent (up to 2 people) 185 NOK. Motorhome 255 NOK. Shower (6min.) 15 NOK.

SIGHTS

KON-TIKI MUSEUM

MUSEUM

Bygdøynesveien 36 ☎230 86 767 www.kon-tiki.no

As the descendants of Vikings, it's no surprise that Norwegians are crazy about boats—but that thalassomania (look it up; it's a real word!) pushes its own limits at Bygdøy's Kon-Tiki museum. Erected in honor of Thor Heyerdahl, the intrepid, shirtless Norwegian who sailed a balsa raft across the Pacific in 1947, the museum hosts the original Kon-Tiki boat and enough memorabilia to make you want to dive overboard. For just 60 NOK, you can uncover the story of Heyerdahl's raft, which beat the odds to sail on for 101 miraculous days; watch our hero go from scientist to seafarer to environmentalist; or just revel in the man's John Stamos-level sex appeal.

i Take bus 30 directly to the museum. 90 NOK, students with ID 60 NOK. ⏲ Open daily June-Aug 9:30am-6pm; Sept-Oct 10am-5pm; Nov-Feb 10am-4pm; Mar-May 10am-5pm.

NATIONAL ART GALLERY (NASJONALGALLERIET)

MUSEUM

Universitetsgata 13 ☎219 82 000 www.nasjonalmuseet.no

Wherever they go in Europe, most people feel the need to visit at least one institution of higher culture. What's Paris without the Louvre, after all, or London without its famed British Museum? Lucky for you, Oslo has one of the most impressive art collections in Europe. Located right off Karl Johans Gate, the National Gallery is home to such classics as Edvard Munch's *Scream* (no photographs allowed) and a number of impressive works by Picasso and Van Gogh. There's something for everyone, whether portraits, landscapes, or pieces that draw a fine line between modern art and vomit on a canvas. More importantly, its student price of 30 NOK makes it a steal. Just don't make it into an art heist.

i Oslo S. Walk down Karl Johans gate. Turn right onto Universitetsgata. The museum is on the left. 50 NOK, students 30 NOK. Free on Sundays. Backpacks and purses must be checked in lockers for a fee of 20 NOK. ⏲ Open Tu-W 10am-6pm, Th 10am-7pm, F 10am-6pm, Sa-Su 11am-5pm, closed Mondays.

NORWAY'S RESISTANCE MUSEUM (NORGES HJEMMEFRONTMUSEUM)

MUSEUM

Bygning 21, Akershus Festning ☎230 93 138

Like much of Europe during World War II, Norway was forced to play host to the worst guests of the century when the Nazis invaded in 1940. As the museum imparts, that five-year saga involved painful collaboration, starvation, and murder—but also *Avengers*-level resistance. Visitors may be surprised to learn that Norwegian crack troops stopped Hitler from building an atomic bomb, or that they saved over half the country's Jewish population by smuggling them into Sweden. The exhibit is well planned and remarkably honest in its presentation of the facts. For any with an interest in World War II or just general badassery, it's well worth the trip. (Best done in conjunction with the Kon-Tiki museum, as the ferry to the Bygdøy area departs from Aker Brygge, five minutes away from where the Resistance Museum is.)

i Tram 12 to Aker Brygge. Walk east toward the medieval fortress overlooking the harbor (Akershus). Follow the signs to the museum once there. 50 NOK, students 25 NOK. ⏲ Open Jun-Aug M-Sa 10am-5pm, Su 11am-5pm; Sept-May M-F 10am-4pm, Sa-Su 11am-4pm.

BOTANICAL GARDENS
GARDEN

Sars Gate 1

This park is a massive open space with greenhouses, arboretums, and gardens—each with its contents meticulously labeled and displayed to the public. Sure, *lobivia ferox* and *psilotum nudum* sound more like *Star Wars* characters than plant species, but you don't have to be a botanist to enjoy the scenery! The gardens are a quick tram ride from the Anker Hostel and located near a number of cheap Middle Eastern restaurants in the trendy Grünløkka district. If you wish to wax poetic to a date about how much you "really get" Henry David Thoreau, this is the place to do it!

i Bus 31 to Lakkegata skole. From the station, turn left onto Trondheimsveien, then right onto Sofienberggata. Turn right onto Sars Gate. The entrance to the gardens is on the left. Gardens free. Museums 50 NOK, students 25 NOK. ☼ Gardens open daily 7am-9pm. Museums open Tu-Su 11am-4pm, closed Mondays.

FROGNER PARK AND VIGELAND SCULPTURES
PARK

Kirkeveien/Middelthuns Gate

If you have a secret Freudian fantasy of being trampled by tourists, Frogner is the place for you. The park looks like Norway's take on Versailles, though with more sculptures and less decapitating the monarchy. The main path takes you through a number of fountains and gates until you reach the "Monolith" sculpture installation; to both the left and right are grassy fields where you can sit back with a book and wonder how there are 150 different species of roses in one park but you're still single. As long as you're not suffering from irritable bowel syndrome (in which case, have fun paying money to use the toilets here) there's really no reason not to visit.

i Tram 12 to Frogner Park (Frognerparken). Free. ☼ Open 24hr.

VIKING SHIP MUSEUM
MUSEUM

Huk aveny 35 ☎221 35 280

The Vikings were like the Danny Zucco of the Middle Ages, though instead of smoking cigarettes and singing "Grease Lightning" they were plundering Europe and exploring the boundaries of the known world. If you're craving a taste of their swashbuckling exploits, head to the Viking Ship Museum and marvel at the three massive ships on display. Though you may leave wondering if they were built to compensate for something, the sheer size of these puppies will have you going berserk. Ha. (Best done in conjunction with the other Bygdøy museums like Kon-Tiki or the Norwegian Folk Museum, as all are within walking distance of one another.)

i Take the B4 ferry from Aker Brygge Harbor (55 NOK roundtrip) to the Viking Museum stop in Bygdøy. Alternatively, take bus 30 to the Vikingskipshuset stop. 80 NOK, students 50 NOK. ☼ Open daily May-Sept 9am-6pm; Oct-Apr 10am-4pm.

OPERA HOUSE
LANDMARK

Kirsten Flagstads Plass 1 ☎214 22 121 www.operaen.no

The Opera House rises aggressively out of Oslo Harbor to throw a giant middle finger to indie music and traditional architecture. It's massive, shiny, and tilted at a 45-degree angle. The outside is a good place for a picnic or hanging with friends, while those with a bit more cash on their hands can venture inside to see the very blonde (and very talented) Norwegian Opera and Ballet.

i Oslo S. Turn left onto Langkaia. Turn left onto Operagata. The opera house is impossible to miss. Tickets from 100 NOK. ☼ Box office open M-F 10am-8pm, Sa 11am-6pm, Su noon-6pm.

HOLMENKOLLEN
MUSEUM

Kongeveien 5 ☎229 23 200 www.skiforeningen.no

If Norwegians are slaves to a cult of skiing, then Holmenkollen is their high temple—literally. It's over 1000 ft. above sea level and hosts one of the world's

OSLO

largest ski jumps. If heights aren't your thing, visitors can set foot in the Ski Museum or step into the ski simulator to experience nausea in 3D. If you're willing to shell out some serious bank—we're talkin' 50 Cent-style "In Da Club" bank—then try your hand at Holmenkollen's 1200-foot zipline. To clarify, that's the height of the Empire State Building. On a zipline. All you need is 120 NOK for museum entrance, 590 NOK for the ride, and an extra pair of underwear just to be safe.

i Take the 1 train from Oslo S to the Holmenkollen stop. Walk down Holmenkollveien for about 15min. Turn left onto Kongeveien. Ski Museum 120 NOK, students 100 NOK. Ski simulator 50 NOK. Overwhelming sense of vertigo: priceless. ☎ Ski Museum open daily June-Aug 9am-8pm; Sept 10am-5pm; Oct-Apr 10am-4pm; May 10am-5pm.

EKEBERG SCULPTURE PARK
Kongsveien 23

PARK
www.ekebergparken.com

If Oslo's cars and buildings have you shuddering like a Luddite and you just want some Mother Gaia, there's a place for that: Ekeberg Park. Though it bears an eerie resemblance to the set of *Friday the 13th*, the chances you will be killed by Freddy Krueger here are astronomically low; it's much more likely you'll run across the dozens of sculptures that give the place its name, or the pristine forests that make it one of Norway's national heritage parks. Be on the lookout for our favorite installations (*The Couple* and *The Cave*) but pack your own lunch—as an intrepid, broke backpacker, you don't want to be spending all your dough on an overpriced hamburger.

i Take Tram 18 from Oslo S/Jernbanetorget to the Ekebergparken stop. Free. ☎ Open 24hr.

NOBEL PEACE CENTER
Brynjulf Bulls plass 1

EXHIBIT
☎483 01 000 www.nobelpeacecenter.org

The Nobel Peace Center has rolling exhibits on recent recipients of the prize. There's an enormous amount you can learn about past winners and the organization itself if you spend a good 20 minutes walking around. Though it might not be as impressive as places like the National Gallery, the Nobel Peace Center's later hours and location near Oslo's main sights makes it an ideal spot to stop by at the end of a long day.

i Take bus 30/31 to Radhuset. The museum is directly next to Aker Brygge harbor. 90 NOK, students 60 NOK. ☎ Open May-Aug M-W 10am-6pm, Th 10am-8pm, F-Su 10am-6pm; Sept-May Tu-Su 10am-6pm, closed Mondays.

FOOD

🔖 MATHALLEN
Maridalsveien 17

INTERNATIONAL $$
☎400 02 409 www.mathallenoslo.no

This place might just be God's gift to Oslo. It's a collection of pop-up restaurants and stands directly below a culinary school, and even the stingiest of stingy travelers would be amiss if they didn't drop a little dough here. The selection is too big to count, but some wallet- and palate-pleasing choices would have to be Noodles, Obento Box, and French Bakery, while Hopyard has a big enough beer selection to put Germany to shame. Free Wi-Fi and an enormous amount of free cheese makes this Let's Go's favorite place to spend the day eating in Oslo.

i Take bus 34 to Telthusbakken. Walk down Maridalsveien. The restaurants are on the left. Prices vary. Cheaper options 100 NOK. Sit-down restaurants 200 NOK. ☎ Open Tu-F 8am-late, Sa-Su 10am-late.

ILLEGAL BURGER
Møllergata 23

BURGERS $$
☎222 03 302

"You miss 100% of the shots you don't take." We believe John Wilkes Booth said that, and he could not have been more correct. You may think a restaurant with a name like Illegal Burger is just another yuppie get-up trying to be edgy—the estranged cousin of bars named Pepto Bismol—but this is the kind of place God would have made on the third day and called "good." Though it's generally packed out the door, you won't be sorry you waited: burgers like the bacon and guac Hot Mama Deluxe, or the smokey Illegal Special, are so tasty they could make the Grinch love Christmas. The place might be slightly pricey, but you want to shell out for the fries with aioli; if your wallet's feeling light, though, maybe hold back on the Danish beer.

i Oslo S. Walk down Karl Johans Gate. Turn right onto Møllergata. Walk five blocks, and the restaurant is on your left. Burgers 95-200 NOK. ☎ Open M-Th 4-11pm, F-Sa 4pm-3am, Su 3-10pm.

CARMEL GRILL

MIDDLE EASTERN $

Dronningens gate 27 ☎224 16 769

For the cash-strapped traveler, Middle Eastern food is going to be your best friend while in Oslo. Even among the hundreds of kebab stores in Oslo, Carmel sets itself apart with the size of its portions (hint: they're huge) and the number of items available. The 70 NOK "kebab i pita" is one of the best deals in the area and may have the only vegetables you'll eat all day; the hummus and shish kebab are so authentically Middle Eastern they're on an FBI watch list (just kidding).

i Oslo S. Walk down Karl Johans gate. Turn right onto Dronningens gate. The restaurant is on a raised brick platform among other stores. Entrees 60-120 NOK. ☎ Open daily 9am-3:30pm.

HAI CAFÉ

VIETNAMESE $

Calmeyers gate 6 ☎222 03 872

Craving pho, banh mi, or other words you can't properly pronounce? Hai Café is about as cheap as it gets. With appetizers going for 60 NOK and entrees in the 120 NOK range, you can eat tasty food here without having to splurge. Hell, with the money you'll save, you can even order a bottle of its alcohol-free wine (and wonder where your life went so wrong). The place is generally packed, and the menu has numbers on it for the linguistically challenged.

i Oslo S. Walk down Lybekker gate. Turn right onto Calmeyers Gate. The restaurant is on the left. Entrees 120-300 NOK. ☎ Open M-Sa 11am-10pm, Su noon-10pm.

RICE BOWL THAI CAFÉ

THAI $

Youngs gate 4 ☎224 12 006 www.ricebowl.no

Authentic and tasty Thai in a restaurant that describes itself as having "an oriental feel." Questionable labels aside, the food here speaks for itself: main dishes might not be dirt cheap—averaging 120-145 NOK—but the portions are big enough to put you in a food coma for the entire day. If those prices are looking as feasible as Chris Christie's presidential run, though, go for a couple appetizers instead: at around 50-65 NOK each, they're cheap enough to stave off starvation until you can finally raid your hostel's kitchen later that night.

i Oslo S. Walk down Lybekker gate. Turn left onto Stor Gate then right onto Youngs gate. The restaurant is on your left. Entrees 120-300 NOK. ☎ Open M-Sa noon-9pm, Su 2-8pm.

MUNCHIES

BURGER $

Thorvald Meyers gate 36a www.munchiesoslo.no

Beneath the pretty exterior of scenic mountains and breathtaking vistas, there is a bitter and angry conflict simmering on Oslo's streets: who has the better burger, Munchies or Illegal? Out of respect for the natives we will remain silent on our ruling, but here are the facts: the Munchie Burger (112 NOK) is juicy and packs an incredible punch with its blue cheese and bacon. The veggie burger (98 NOK) is similarly large and comes with a delectable mango curry, while the fries with aioli dip might just be the best in town. The restaurant itself is in a slightly more hip locale than Illegal, though its interior—which strikes one as ironically McDonald's-themed—is about equally crowded. Ultimately we suggest you try both. But if you want to keep your head, be very careful who you tell your opinion to.

i Nybrua. Walk up Thorvald Meyers gate. The restaurant is on the right. Gluten-free and vegetarian options available. Burgers 96-150 NOK. ☎ Open M-W 11am-10pm, Th 11am-midnight, F-Sa 11am-3am, Su 11am-10pm.

BARI
MIDDLE EASTERN $

Torggata 23 ☎221 11 965

There are a million places to get Middle Eastern food in Oslo, but Bari has something special—it's either the creamy naan gyros, the curry and french fry pizzas, or the Dorian Gray-style paintings on the inside. The place tends to be packed (especially on weekends), but you will quickly forget the wait once you unwrap the foil on your greasy treat and realize that this is high art in culinary form. Can you find somewhere in Oslo with better taste and portions for the price? To quote Wallace Shawn in *The Princess Bride*, "Inconceivable!"

i Oslo S. Walk down Karl Johans gate. Turn left onto Torggata. The restaurant is on the right. Entrees 69-79 NOK. Pizza 75-110 NOK. ☎ Open M-Th noon-midnight, F-Sa noon-3am, Su noon-midnight.

CAFÉ SARA
INTERNATIONAL $$

Hausmanns gate 29 ☎220 34 000 www.cafesara.no

If an album drops in the woods and no one is there to hear it, will a hipster still claim it's his favorite? We all know the answer is yes, but just to be sure you can ask the clientele at Café Sara in Oslo's trendy Grünerløkka neighborhood. The restaurant has a young and vibrant feel, and its menu reflects that—it serves everything from kebabs and burritos to salads and tzatziki, with a great craft beer list on top of that. If we didn't know any better, we would say we'd teleported into Williamsburg, Brooklyn, only with fewer fedoras. Also like Williamsburg, this place is a bit pricey. Our favorite dish, the Iskender Kebab, seemed to be a cheaper option at 134 NOK, so consider it for drinks or snacks rather than a full-on meal if you're on a budget.

i Take bus 34 to Jakob Kirke. The cafe is right across from Kulturkirken Jakob. Appetizers 84 NOK. Entrees 130-160 NOK. Beer 10-60 NOK. ☎ Open M-Sa 11am-3:30am, Su 1pm-3:30am.

HEALTHY LIVING ASIAN EXPRESS
ASIAN $

Karl Johans gate 24

This place is cheap and big-portioned. If you're craving Chinese in Oslo, Asian Express serves quick, affordable, and (allegedly) healthy takeaway. The tasty noodles and fried rice come with large portions of meat, and the cheap price range means that you can add on an appetizer without having to ask for an IMF bailout. With its chic, box-like setup right in the middle of Karl Johans, this is the perfect place to fuel up before an afternoon at the National Gallery.

i Oslo S or Nationaltheatret. Pop-up stand in the middle of Eidsvolls plass. Appetizers 55-70 NOK. Entrees 89 NOK. ☎ Open M-F 11am-7:30pm, Sa noon-7pm, Su 1-7pm.

NIGHTLIFE

⬛ MIKROBRYGGERI
BREWERY $

Trondheimsveien 2 ☎213 83 930 www.schouskjelleren.no

Though the name may sound like something you got by banging your keyboard, Schouskjelleren is easily the best microbrewery in Oslo. The bartender is a zany, chatty Englishman with impeccable taste in the beer he brews. If you're looking for a suggestion, you can't go wrong with the James Blond or Empress of India, both 78 NOK. If that's not enough, it's in a vaulted cellar that looks like a Viking mead hall. You can't get more Scandinavian than that.

i Take bus 30/31 to Heimdalsgata. Turn left onto Trondheimsveien. The brewery is on the right. Beers 80 NOK. Imported beers 90-110 NOK. ☎ Open M-Tu 4pm-1am, W-Th 4pm-2am, F-Sa 4pm-3:30am, Su 4pm-midnight.

GUDRUNS

Karl Johans Gate 10

Gudruns is a hit with locals and tourists alike, so prepare for weekend waits of up to 30min. if you're trying to get in. The ground floor is stocked with dusty books and sofas straight out of a Victorian novel, as well as a bar about 30 ft. long. Keep walking and you'll reach the second bar, which has an exposed roof, dance floor, and smoke machines. If neither of those do it for you, there's also an awning overlooking the entire club where you can sit back and heap scorn on the plebeians below. Expect beers in the 75 NOK range (selection includes Brooklyn Lager, Pilsner, and Carlsberg) and mixed drinks or shots around 110 NOK.

i *Oslo S. Walk down Karl Johans Gate. Gudruns is on the left. Must be 20+. Cover 100 NOK. Beer 80 NOK. Mixed drinks 110 NOK. ☒ Open F-Sa 11pm-3am.*

JOHN'S BAR

BAR

Universitetsgata 26 ☎400 07 078 www.johnsbar.no

If you're craving cheap drinks and Top 10 hits from the '80s, John's Bar is the place for you. Located one block over from Oslo's main road, the bar is packed on weekends by a motley crew of tourists, students, and bewildered onlookers. Try to get there on the earlier side, as it fills up quickly, and know that if you go, you will dance and, more likely than not, you will have drinks spilled on you.

i *Oslo S. Walk down Karl Johans gate. Turn right onto Universitetsgata. The bar is on the right. Must be 20+. Beer 80 NOK. Mixed drinks 100 NOK. ☒ Open Th-Su 10pm-3am.*

BAR FLY

BAR

Stortingsgata 12 ☎224 14 011 www.barfly.no

Any bar that names itself after Bukowski's autobiography has got some big shoes to fill—but Bar Fly does just that, and it does it in style. The dimly lit interior, surrounded by wall-to-wall mahogany, allows for several dozen people to sit comfortably in booths and stools. The cocktail menu is enormous, and by Oslo's standards, the prices aren't bad. A shot of Jack Daniels fetches 78 NOK, which may not sound like a bargain, but it is significantly cheaper than the same shot at Dr. Jekyll's around the corner (116 NOK) or mixed drinks at nearby Lawo Terrasse (100-180 NOK). The crowd is often in its late 20s and older, but the laid-back atmosphere and central location make this an ideal stopover for anyone trying to get a taste of Oslo nightlife.

i *National Theater. Walk down Stortingsgata. The bar is on the right. Beers 90 NOK. Cocktails 75-180 NOK. ☒ Open M-Th 7pm-3am, F-Sa 6pm-3am, Su 9pm-3am.*

FYRHUSET

BAR

Maridalsveien 19 www.fyrhusetkuba.no

As the name might suggest, this bar looks like a fire house with a red brick exterior (the name actually means "lighthouse," but we're going to stick with our first impression). It has a standard selection of beers in the 80-95 NOK range—Ringnes on tap, a few IPAs and some foreign imports—but what really sets the place apart is its atmosphere. Play shuffleboard with burly Norsemen upstairs or challenge your table to a competitive game of Jenga on the ground level. The location on the edge of Kuba park and near a graphic design school makes Fyrhuset an excellent place for meeting locals and testing how much game you've got.

i *Take bus 54 to Telthusbakken. Walk into the park directly south and you'll see the bar. Beers 78-90 NOK. ☒ Open daily 3pm-midnight.*

CROWBAR

BAR

Torggata 32 ☎47 213 86 757

Despite the aggressive-sounding name, this place has nothing to do with armed robbery or segregation; it's a hip microbrewery in Grünerløkka just a few feet down the road from Café Sara. We would describe the environment as somewhere between a frat party and a Viking mead hall: on weekends it's packed wall to wall, and the scent of grilled meat and other partygoers fills the room with a musk and moisture that are hard to describe. The selection of beers is enormous, and the staff is very helpful with recommendations, but the real reason to come is the kebabs: part pork, part diet guilt, they're indescribably good after a couple brews and a game of ping pong upstairs. If you're looking for a fun, young environment in Oslo, this is your place.

i Take bus 54 to Jakob Kirke. Turn left onto Hausmanns gate. Turn right onto Torggata. The bar is on the right. Beers 72-90 NOK. Tasting samplers of 6 beers 250 NOK. ☼ Open F-Sa 8pm-3:30am.

INGENSTEDS BAR
Brenneriveien 9 ☎950 96 829 www.ingensteds.no
This place is a hipster's wet dream. To get there, you walk through an alleyway plastered with colorful street art and enter into a large open space with tables, a dance floor, and enough paintings and sculptures to make up for that day you skipped the National Gallery. The outdoor portion overlooks a river and is shaded by trees, while the upstairs gives you a spot to kick back and contemplate what the fat baby in that Victorian-style painting is thinking about. The place is often rented out for artistic events like book launches or poetry readings, but on weekends it is always open to the public after 11pm.

i Turn left onto Brenneriveien. Turn right onto Maridalsveien. The bar is on the right. Beers 72-82 NOK. Cocktails and mixed drinks 90-100 NOK. ☼ Open F-Sa 8pm-3:30pm.

ESSENTIALS
Practicalities
Tourist Offices
Oslo Visitor Center (Østbanehallen to the right of Oslo S's main entrance. Jernbanetorget 1 ☎815 30 555 www.visitoslo.com. ☼ Open daily 9am-6pm.) Services include booking the Oslo Pass, city bike rentals, free brochures ("The Oslo Guide"), and currency exchange.

Tours
Several tours are available in Oslo.

- **BÅTSERVICE:** Fjord Sightseeing (☎233 56 890) leaves from Rådhusbrygge port 3, directly in front of City Hall in Aker Brygge. This guided tour takes you around the islands of the Oslofjord, the Opera House, and a number of interesting architectural sites along the harbor. Longer tours, starting in the evening and offering complimentary shrimp snacks, leave from the same area. 270 NOK. Earliest tours start at 10:30am, latest at 4:30pm. Tours last 2 hrs.

- **VIKING BIKING TOURS:** Viking Biking Tours (☎412 66 496 vikingbikingoslo.com/tours) are tours conducted in English that take you around the major sights of Oslo, from Aker Brygge to Vigeland to Karl Johans and beyond. Smaller groups can select customized tours in various European languages as well. All tours leave from the shop, located at Nedre Slottsgate 4 (Oslo S is nearest station). 250 NOK. Bike rental 125-200 NOK. Leave at 1pm daily. Tours last 3hr.

Money
If you want to exchange hard currency rather than withdraw from an ATM, Oslo Airport Gardermoen has two DNB exchange offices (one in arrivals and one in departures) that take a 2.5% commision on the cash you trade in. Generally, most commercial banks exchange at a ratio of of 1NOK to 12 cents, meaning they're skimming off roughly 7% of your cash.

If you still want to trade in your cash, know that banks in Oslo will often add a transaction fee (roughly 50 NOK or $6.30) on top of whatever percentage they take from the money you exchange. Forex Bank (with locations in the Oslo S airport express terminal and on Karl Johans Gate) does not do this and is a particularly good option for those exchanging small amounts. (☎221 72 265, website (in English): www.visitoslo.com/en/produc./?TLp=181207. ☑ Open M-F 7am-11pm, Sa 9am-6pm, Su 10am-5pm.)

You can pay for almost everything in Norway with debit or credit cards, but most chain stores like 7-11 and Deli de Luca (located all around the Karl Johans/ Oslo S area) will have an ATM. Do note you will likely be charged an extra fee for withdrawing cash abroad. ATMs and currency exchange are also available at Oslo Airport Gardermoen.

Luggage Storage

You can hire out a 24hr. locker at Oslo Sentralstasjon for 40-80 NOK depending on luggage size. The station is closed daily 1:10-4:30am, so plan accordingly.

Most (if not all) hostels offer free luggage storage during the day. Do this at your own discretion, however, as all guests have access to the luggage rooms.

GLBT Services

Health Centre for LGBT Youth (Mailundveien 23 ☎481 13 013 lhbt@bga.oslo.kommune.no. ☑ Open Wednesdays 4-7pm.) Walk-in health center for LGBT youth (13-30) offering information, medical care, and professionals to speak to about emotional or mental health issues.

Laundromats

Laundromat Café (Underhaugsveien 2 ☎213 83 629 www.laundromat.no. 30 NOK for wash, 40 NOK for 30min dry. Machines only take 10 NOK pieces and you must bring your own detergent. ☑ Open M-F 7am-1am, Sa-Su 10am-1am.) Going to a laundromat is about as fun as passing a kidney stone: it's smelly, it's boring, and only the most curious among us get a sexual thrill out of it. Laundromat Café, however, seeks to tear down that wall of boredom by turning laundry into a full-fledged dining activity: as you wait for your clothes to dry, you can order pizza and ribs off their menu, or simply kick back with tequila and craft beer until the world becomes as dizzy as the washing cycle. If that doesn't suit you, there's also a library with some 4000 titles because why not? This is Europe.

Internet

Wi-Fi is available widely throughout Oslo, with places such as the Opera House, Mathallen Food Court, art museums, and most train stations offering free connectivity. All Oslo hostels listed here have free Wi-Fi, and some (such as Anker Hostel) do not require a password or username to log in.

Post Office

Oslo Sentralstasjon Postkontor (Jernbanetorget 1 inside Oslo S. ☑ Open M-F 9am-6pm, Sa 9am-3pm, closed Sundays.)

Emergency

Emergency Numbers

- **POLICE:** ☎112
- **FIRE:** ☎110
- **AMBULANCE:** ☎113
- **CONFIDENTIAL HELPLINES:** Mental Health Helpline (confidential): ☎810 30 030. The Social and Ambulatory First Aid Service (confidential, free suicide/abuse/sexual assault hotline): ☎234 87 090.

Medical Services

All of the following hospitals accept walk-ins from foreigners and speak English. Be sure to bring identification and relevant health insurance documentation for public hospitals.

- **OSLO EMERGENCY WARD:** (Storgata 40 ☎229 32 293. ☾ 24hr.) This is the recommended location for serious or life-threatening emergencies such as fractures, cuts, assault, etc.

- **OSLO AKUTTEN EMERGENCY WARD:** (Rosenkrantzgate 9 ☎220 08 160. ☾ Open M-W 8am-7pm, Th 8am-5pm, F 8am-4pm, Sa 9am-3pm, closed Sundays.) Private emergency ward that allows walk-ins. Specialist appointments can also be booked in advance by phone or email. Cost of evaluation by specialist (ENT, gynecologist, dermatologist, etc.) is 790 NOK, payable by card.

- **WALK-IN CLINIC:** Aker Brygge (Filipstad Brygge 1 ☎930 18 668 ☾ Open M-F 8am-8pm, Sa-Su 10am-6pm.) Walk-ins and scheduled appointments in a private hospital.

- **24HR. PHARMACIES:** Generally, you'll find an Apotek on every other block in Oslo. However, only two are open 24hr.: the Jernbanetorget Apotek directly opposite of Oslo S and Apotek 1 Emergency Room at Storgata 30, right next to the Oslo Emergency Ward. Both take credit cards.

Getting There

By Plane

Oslo Airport, Gardermoen (Oslo Lufthavn in Norwegian), is Norway's largest airport with roughly 23 million visitors a year. Located 47 km north of Oslo proper, it is the incoming destination for the majority of international flights into the country and operates 24hr per day. The cheapest way to get from the airport to Oslo is to take the Flytoget train directly from the airport. It leaves every 20 minutes and takes roughly 20 minutes to get to Oslo S (other stops include Lillehammer and Nationaltheatret). The cost of a one-way ticket to Oslo S is 180 NOK for adults and 90 NOK for students, seniors, and children. Tickets are available for purchase at the airport and at Oslo.

Flybussen offers cheap and convenient buses to and from the airport. Tickets can be bought (by card) on the bus or booked online. Adult tickets between the Oslo bus terminal (directly behind Oslo S) and the airport are 175 NOK, with student and senior tickets costing 100 NOK. (http://www.flybussen.no/en/Oslo/document/3448. Same service also available for airport-downtown transportation in other Norwegian cities.)

Taxis from Oslo Airport can be booked and quoted at the Taxi Information Desk. Most taxi companies will have a fixed price to and from the airport. Oslo Taxi, for example, charges between 590-610 NOK before 5pm and 720 NOK after, while metered taxis will generally charge between 10-12 NOK per kilometer and may add on an extra fee for not booking in advance. To book a cab, call ☎232 32 323 or contact the taxi companies themselves. Our advice, though, is to stick to the bus or the train unless you have a lot of people and/or a lot of luggage.

By Train

NSB (Norwegian State Railways) is Norway's main rail company and runs 15 different lines that criss-cross the country, making it a convenient choice if you're travelling to Flåm, the Arctic Circle, or practically anywhere else. National trains leave directly from the main departures hall of Oslo Sentralstasjon, better known as Oslo S. (www.nsb.no/en/our-destinations/stations/oslo-s. Luggage storage available. ☾ Open M-F 6:30am-11:15pm, Sa-Su 10am-6pm. Waiting room open daily 3:45am-1:30am). For NSB tickets, schedules and more, visit www.nsb.no, or call ☎815 00 888 (press 9 for information in English). Eurail passes can be used except on the NSB Flytoget train that travels to and from the airport.

Buses

Most buses coming from the airport or elsewhere in Norway and Europe will arrive at the Oslo Bus Terminal, at Schweigaards gate 10, directly behind Oslo S and connected to it. (Storage lockers available, including some that are accessible 24hr. per day. ☎47 23 00 24 00 akt.as. ⏰ Waiting room open 24hr. Ticket counter open M-F 7am-11pm, Sa-Su 8am-10pm.)

Getting Around

Public Transportation

Oslo is serviced by an extensive network of buses, trams, ferries and underground trains. To use public transport, you need to buy an NSB Card for a prepaid amount of time. (Single ticket 30 NOK; 24hr. 90 NOK; 7-day pass 240 NOK; 30-day pass 680 NOK. Prices cut in half for children, students, and seniors.) These can be purchased at Oslo S, most 7-11 stores, and a number of different public transportation stops.

Note: People will rarely check to see if your card is valid, but the fine for getting caught on transportation without one is between 950-1150 NOK. So buy a ticket. If you do not have a ticket, you can purchase a one-time ticket on board or on your phone, but the price goes up by about 20 NOK.

For those looking to pack a lot of traveling into a little amount of time, a good economic choice is to buy the Oslo Pass (24hr. 320 NOK; 48hr. 470 NOK; 72hr. 590 NOK). The pass allows you free use of public transportation in zones 1 and 2 of Oslo as well as free entrance to a number of museums and parking in municipal parks. It can be bought in Oslo S, the Oslo Visitor Center, and most hotels and hostels. For a full list of benefits, see www.visitoslo.com/en/activities-and-attractions/oslo-pass.

Taxis

Taxis are available in Oslo, but the cost and availability of public transportation make them a secondary option at best. Try Oslo Taxi (☎223 88 090). Prices increase over the course of the night and depend on whether you are hailing on the street or have pre-booked. For cars with four passengers or less, the minimum fare will be in the 109-170 NOK range and increase at a rate of around 8 NOK per minute.

Uber is also available in Oslo, with a base price of 65 NOK, a minimum fare of 100 NOK, and a cost of 5 NOK per minute. Surge pricing rates apply.

bergen

Bergen feels like Oslo's younger brother who quit the rat race years ago and decided to hike, fish, and sell organic glitter instead. Does organic glitter exist? We're not sure, but it's almost certainly available here if it does.

Though we may sound like a broken record, there really is something for everyone here. Bergen mixes the charm of a small town—with colorful wood houses and quaint mom-and-pop stores—with the bigger brands and buildings you'll find in any European metropolis. Surrounding everything are the Seven Mountains, which are not the newest craft beer out of Brooklyn but rather the tree-lined peaks covering the entire city. Visitors may also recognize the port as being the inspiration for the setting of *Frozen*, and while we can't promise you magic snowmen or hopelessly sheltered princesses, we can promise you the freshest and tastiest fish you've ever had (not really the same thing, but we needed a transition, so there you go).

Backpackers and budget travelers will be relieved to know that Bergen is not as expensive as Oslo, though you should still be prepared to spend $80-100 a day if you want to live comfortably (and leave aside some money for a fjord tour). There is a huge student population here and an even better food scene, so don't be afraid to spend a few extra nights as you explore this town.

ACCOMMODATIONS

MARKEN GJESTEHUS
HOSTEL $

Kong Oscars gate 45 ☎553 14 404 www.marken-gjestehus.com

Bergen is a small place, and Marken is one of your best options while you stay here: it offers shared rooms for cheap with amenities like a kitchen, ensuite lockers, and sockets by the beds. Individually, these may not seem important, but after a long day of traveling you might just be on your knees thanking the Good Lord Cthulhu that you don't have to shell out extra cash to keep your stuff safe. The location in the middle of downtown is a huge plus, and the common room has a chilled-out atmosphere that makes it easy to meet other travellers. Just be sure to book in advance—the rooms sell out quickly.

i Dorms 250-320 NOK. Singles 575 NOK. Doubles 870 NOK. ⏰ Reception May-Sept 9am-11pm; Oct-Apr 9:30am-4:30pm.

BERGEN YMCA HOSTEL
HOSTEL $

Nedre Korskirkeallmenningen 4 ☎556 06 055 www.bergenhostel.com

YMCA might have the most "hostel-ian" (hostile?) feeling of any place in Bergen, and that's both a godsend and a curse. On the one hand, it's very easy to meet people here: the TV lounge and dining room are always full, the rooms have ensuite bathrooms, and the hostel is five minutes away from the city's main attractions. On the other hand, though, the dim lighting, broken computers, and cramped kitchen give it a somewhat rough feel. It's a good place to go if you're on a budget and want good location, but know that you're not going to be pampered.

i Dorms 195 NOK. Singles 600 NOK. Doubles 850 NOK. ⏰ Reception June-Aug 7am-midnight; Sept-Oct 8am-9pm; Nov-Mar 8am-3:30pm; Apr-May 8am-9pm.

SIGHTS

FISH MARKET
MARKET

Bergen Harbor

Ever seen *Free Willy? The Little Mermaid? Finding Nemo?* At Bergen's Fish Market, you can finally discover what the favorite protagonists from all these movies taste like—and do it cheaply, too! Walking past the various stands, you'll come across everything from salmon to herring to massive crabs in vaguely sexual positions. Many of the vendors actually give away free samples. Our thrifty researcher-writer munched on whale, salmon, cod, caviar, and reindeer salami in one visit. It may feel like a touristy place, but you can't beat the scenery: it's in a harbor that looks exactly like the one from *Frozen.* Take your prejudice and just let it go when you visit.

i Entrance free. Prices at stands vary. ⏰ Open daily 7am-8pm.

LEPROSY MUSEUM
MUSEUM

Kong Oscars gate 59 ☎481 62 678 www.bymuseet.no

"I've got a hot date at the Leprosy Museum tonight!" said no one ever. There's a good reason for that: the museum, fascinating as it is, is seriously depressing. It tells the story of leprosy in Norway and is located on the site of a former leper hospital that operated for 500 years. Walking through the cramped rooms, you're exposed to the miserable conditions the lepers lived in, and the history of how we learned to beat the disease (spoiler alert: it involved a liberal interpretation of "patients' rights"). If you're interested in the history of medicine and have some extra time in Bergen, it's definitely worth a visit.

i 70 NOK, students 35 NOK. ⏰ Open daily 11am-4pm.

HAAKON'S HALL (BERGENHUS FORTRESS)
HALL

Bergenhus Festning   ☎555 46 387 www.bymuseet.no

Can you imagine any better place to be than a Viking mead hall (that is, if you weren't a woman, peasant, priest, pig, or prisoner)? We can't, so we suggest you head to Haakon's Hall and tour a joint that even Beowulf would've considered "hip." Unfortunately, much of the original building was destroyed by fire, neglect, and Nazis—basically everything besides Charlie Sheen—so what you're actually walking through is a recreation. Nonetheless, the architecture is astounding and, as an extra perk, your ticket gets you a free coffee and tea at the cafe. Now how's that for a taste of Valhalla?

i At the end of Bryggen road. 70 NOK, students 35 NOK. ⓩ Open daily 6:30am-11pm.

KODE 2: KUNSTMUSEUM
MUSEUM

Rasmus Meyers allé 3   ☎555 68 000 www.kodebergen.no

Even if you can't tell the difference between a porcupine and a painting, this museum has some serious mojo. When you buy your ticket and go upstairs, you have a choice of two exhibits: Monuments and Contemporary. The former is a collection of 3D pieces showcasing various themes (e.g. bloody cotton swabs that represent political violence; giant yellow blankets that represent…mustard?). The latter is more free-form, with exhibits ranging from an arts-and-crafts room and a naked mannequin with what looks like leprosy to a film of a woman describing all the creative ways she's trying to kill herself. If it all seems too meta for you, the museum also has an authentically "artsy" cafe and bookshop where you can try to forget all of the thinly veiled genitals you just saw.

i 100 NOK, students 50 NOK. ⓩ Open daily 11am-5pm.

ULRIKEN CABLE CAR
PANORAMIC VIEW

Ulriken 1   ☎536 43 643 www.ulriken643.no

Yes, this is listed in every tourist brochure, and yes, we're supposed to be the ones on the front lines of finding you cool off-the-beaten-path stuff to do, but give us a break! This one is mainstream but totally worth it. The cable car offers breathtaking views of all of Bergen and is a good compromise for those who can't make a full hike. The ride up—though it may trigger vertigo—is the most fun you'll ever have getting high (we think). Tickets can be booked from the Bergen Tourist Office, and buses to the cable car leave regularly from there.

i One-way tickets 95 NOK. Return tickets 155 NOK. Bus and cable car 245 NOK. ⓩ Open daily 9am-9pm.

FOOD

TREKRONEREN
NORWEGIAN $

Kong Oscars Gate 1

Much like a frat party before 8pm, this place is a total sausage fest. They've got lamb, frankfurter, bratwurst, and about 10 other kinds of delectably tubed meats—all smothered in nutmeg, chili, and garlic. Our personal favorite has to be the reindeer sausage, which comes with mustard, ketchup, fried onions, and juniper berry jam... because why not. The small portion (55 NOK) is enough to keep you full for a good couple of hours. It doesn't get cheaper or tastier than this.

i Directly off of Fish Market. 150g sausage 55 NOK. 250g sausage 85 NOK. ⓩ It's a pop-up stand so hours vary, but generally open in the morning until late.

HORN OF AFRICA
ETHIOPIAN $$

Strandgaten 212   ☎954 25 250

Horn of Africa encourages eaters to stick it to The Western Man by asking a fundamental question about modern society: why can't we eat with our hands? In here, there is no judgment or exclusion, only the piping hot sauces of the chili beef Tibbs, the buttery smoothness of the chicken wat, and the satisfaction of knowing you don't have to use a fork. For the uninitiated, Ethiopian food often includes scooping up spiced meats and veggies from a shared tray using a sour, spongy bread called injera—it's delicious, it's filling, and it's what Patrick Henry had in mind when he said "Give me liberty or give me death." The place is immaculately decorated, to say the least, and a welcome break from the endless fish and crab restaurants you'll find in this Frozen town. And the alcohol is cheap by Norway standards, so bottoms up!

i Entrees 160 NOK. Beers 60-70 NOK. ☒ Open Tu-Th 3-10pm, F-Sa 3-11pm, Su 3-10pm, closed Mondays.

GODT BROD
CAFE $

Vestre Torggaten 2   ☎555 63 310 www.godtbrod.no

This is not the newest rapper on a 2 Chainz tour but rather a cozy cafe with two locations in downtown Bergen. While most people use "cozy" liberally—employing it to describe $1200-a-month New York basements in order to justify their crumbling acting careers—we actually mean it here; Godt Brod is the kind of place where you feel comfortable wearing a tacky Christmas sweater as you waste away an hour over coffee and scones. The prices are reasonable: pastries and coffee are in the 30-40 NOK range, with some a little higher. And the mozzarella and herb spelt-bread sandwiches are surprisingly good for a chain store. Highly recommended, either for a quick caffeine boost or a mellow snacking afternoon.

i Coffee 30-40 NOK. Pastries 30-40 NOK. Sandwiches 80 NOK. ☒ Open M-F 7am-6pm, Sa 8am-5pm, Su 9am-5pm.

ICHIBAN SUSHI
SUSHI $$

Håkonsgaten 17   ☎559 00 460 www.ichibanbergen.no

You might think that Norway is an odd place for Japanese food, but you have to remember that this country invented salmon sushi (and, we might wager a guess, salmon itself). Among the dozens of restaurants serving sushi, though, Ichiban is still in a class of its own. While it's mostly a takeout place, dishes like the shrimp and halibut nigiri or salmon maki rolls are so fresh they taste like they were plucked from Nemo's classroom this morning (and probably were). The food is reasonably priced by Norway standards, and the nearby park makes an excellent place for lunch. It's certainly not a fancy place with a wild menu, but it's worth your time if you're craving some raw sea creatures in your gullet.

i 8pc. 69-99 NOK. 16pc. 165-200 NOK. ☒ Open Tu-Sa noon-9pm, Su 2-9pm, closed Mondays.

NABOEN
PUB $

Sigurds Gate 4   ☎559 00 290 www.grannen.no/naboen2

Though the entrance level at Naboen's is a full-blown restaurant, you want to head straight downstairs when you enter the place. The pub in the cellar—perhaps Bergen's best-kept secret—has what may be the best meatballs east of the Mississippi (west of the Mississippi? Does Mississippi have meatballs?). For 136 NOK, you get you an enormous plate of meat, cranberries, cauliflower and gravy so juicy it gives Gushers a run for their money. Sampled with a Lucky Jack beer (our recommendation; 78 NOK), this might be the closest humankind ever gets to achieving orgasm in gastrointestinal form.

i Entrees 90-160 NOK. Beer 90 NOK. ☒ Open M-Th 4pm-1am, F-Sa 4pm-2am, Su 4pm-1am.

PINGVINEN
NORWEGIAN $$

Vaskerelven 14   ☎556 04 646 www.pingvinen.no

As you might have noticed in your travels, Norway has a lot of ethnic food—kebab, noodles, sushi, etc.—but not a lot in the "Norwegian" department. Pingvinen is where that trend ends. This place has all the low-brow subtlety of a pub with food that could easily qualify for a four-star restaurant: meatballs, smoked

norway

fjord tours

A trip to Norway without seeing the fjords is like a night in Vegas, without the hookers and blackjack: it's certainly possible, but you can't really say you've had an authentic experience without them. Bergen proudly calls itself, "The Gateway to the Fjords" (new *Game of Thrones* title?) and a quick boat ride from here will send you past some of Europe's most dramatic scenery. Bergen is small enough to cover in a day or two, so we recommend you book one of these tours during your stay. Shorter trips, such as the **Skjerjehamn cruise** (465 NOK, students 365 NOK. ☒ 4hr.) will take you by boat through the mountainous coastline to offshore islands that are quaint, idyllic, and a dozen more great Instagram adjectives. Longer trips like the **Hardangerfjord cruise** (750 NOK, students 425 NOK) last 12 hours or more and often involve multi-step trips by bus and boat through terrain straight out of *The Lord of the Rings*. All tours can be booked at the Bergen Tourist Center the day before the trip; you can find a full listing of tours in the information pamphlets there. Once you try it, you'll be surprised how fun and *afjordable* the whole experience is. Stop cringing—it was cute.

herring, lamb stew, even horse meat all artfully concocted in a culinary celebration of the motherland. The space is small enough that you may need to wait for a table, but the staff seems particularly attentive to tourists and newcomers.
i Entrees 150-200 NOK. ☒ Open daily 11am-3am.

NIGHTLIFE

DICKENS KONTORET   BAR
Nygaardsgaten 2   ☎474 52 544 www.dickensbergen.no
Dickens is classy as shit. Wood paneling, a dimly lit interior, drink menu so decadent it may have come from a boozy pharaoh's tomb. This is the kind of place where you sip whiskey and talk about philosophy. So as you debate Lichtenstein's addendum to the Hamburger morality theorem—or, you know, whatever—consider the tangy burn of a Nikka from the barrel (98 NOK) or a cigar blend cognac (139 NOK). You can't go wrong with the menu here, though this place is probably best for dates or a quick drink to start the night before you move on to Bergen's cheaper, wilder locales.
i Drinks 100-150 NOK. ☒ Open M-Th 4pm-12:30am, F-Sa 4pm-2am, Su 4pm-12:30am.

KAOS   BAR
Nygaardsgaten 2   ☎452 60 706 www.kaos-bergen.no
Don't be that red squiggly line in a Word doc and try to grab a sharpie and write "Chaos" on the door of this student-run bar. No one likes a Grammar Nazi, and it's not likely to get you laid. What might get you laid (out) is the insanely cheap alcohol here: beers on tap go for 59 NOK, and shots of anything are 49 NOK. That's as cheap as the budget for *Leprechaun: Back 2 tha Hood* (look it up: it's a real thing), and every student in Bergen seems to know it. The place is often packed out the door, but squeeze into a booth in the cellar or upstairs area, and it's impossible not to make friends.
i Beers 59 NOK. Shots 49 NOK. ☒ Open M-F 3pm-3:30am, Sa 1pm-3:30am, Su 5pm-3:30am.

GARAGE   BAR
Christies gate 14   ☎553 21 980 www.garage.no
Garage is like Kaos's rougher, older brother from the wrong side of the tracks. Though it has a distinct heavy metal vibe, the clientele on any given night

includes students, musicians, and a few hopelessly out-of-place Germans in Hawaiian shirts. The bar has a larger selection than Kaos does, though beers are about the same price (64 NOK on tap; slightly higher for bottled and imported) and shots are in the 70-90 NOK range (e.g., Jack Daniels 86 NOK). If you're craving a peek at Norway's (in)famous metal scene, Garage also hosts shows every night. The beer, sweat, and fun from this place will have you smelling like Ozzy Osbourne for the next week.

i Beers 64 NOK. Shots 70-90 NOK. ☏ Open M-F 3pm-3:30am, Sa 1pm-3:30am, Su 5pm-3:30am.

ESSENTIALS
Practicalities

- **TOURIST OFFICE:** Bergen Tourist Information Center offers services like souvenirs, tour booking, free Wi-Fi, and currency exchange. (Strandkaien 3 ☎555 52 000 www.visitbergen.com. ☏ Open June-Aug daily 8:30am-10pm; Sept daily 9am-8pm; Oct-Apr M-Sa 9am-4pm; May daily 9am-8pm.)

- **TOURS:** Best booked from the Bergen Tourist Information center. Help desk and representatives are available to help book fjord tours, daily excursions, trips to the Ulriken Cable Car, and tours of Bergen itself.

- **CURRENCY EXCHANGE:** If you're not using an ATM, the Bergen Tourist Information Center offers currency exchange at rates more or less the same as what you'll find at banks and the airport.

- **ATMS:** You can pay for almost everything in Norway with debit or credit cards, but the Bergen train station and most chain stores like 7-11 and Deli de Luca (located all around the Fish Market area) will have an ATM (in Norwegian: Minibank). You will likely be charged an extra fee for withdrawing cash abroad. ATMs and currency exchange are also available at Bergen Airport.

- **LUGGAGE STORAGE:** Luggage storage is available at both the Bergen train station and the bus station (directly next to each other) for 20 NOK per locker (with slightly higher prices for bigger lockers).

- **INTERNET:** Wi-Fi is available widely throughout Bergen, with hostels, hospitals, the tourist center and many of the bars and restaurants in the area near Dickens Kontoret offering free connectivity (often with a password). Internet is also available at the Bergen Public Library. (Strømgt 6. ☏ Open M-Th 10am-8pm, F 10am-5pm, Sa 10am-4pm, Su noon-4pm.)

- **POST OFFICE:** Bergen Sentrum postkontor is inside the Xhibition shopping center. (Småstrandgaten 3 ☏ Open M-F 9am-6pm, Sa 10am-3pm, closed Sundays.)

Emergency Numbers

- **POLICE:** ☎112

- **FIRE:** ☎110

- **AMBULANCE:** ☎113

- **CRISIS HOTLINES:** Kirkens SOS i Bjorgvin suicide hotline. (Offices also available at Kalfarveien 79 ☎815 33 300 www.kirkens-sos.no. ☏ Open M-Tu 8am-3pm, Th 8am-11pm, F-Su 8am-3am, closed Wednesdays.)

- **LATE-NIGHT PHARMACIES:** Duty Pharmacy (Apoteket Nordstjernen) is located inside the Bergen bus station. (☎552 18 384. ☏ Open M-Sa 8am-11pm, Su 2pm-11pm.)

- **HOSPITALS:** Helse Bergen. (Haukelandsveien 22. For emergencies, call ☎113; for minor injuries, call ☎555 68 760. Open 24hr.) Bergen Legevakt. (Vestre Strømkaien 19 ☎555 68 700 ☏ Open 24hr.)

Getting There

By Plane

Bergen Airport (Bergen Lufthavn) is Bergen's main airport, located about 12 miles away from the city's main attractions. It operates a number of international flights, particularly between cities in the UK, Sweden, Germany, and other European capitals.

The easiest way from the airport to Bergen is the Flybussen (www.flybussen.no; 90 NOK, students 70 NOK). The buses stop at a number of places throughout Bergen, with the most popular being the Bergen bus station, every 15 minutes (trip lasts around 25 minutes).

Cab rates change depending on time of day and number of passengers, but there is a taxi desk at the airport where you can find contact information and price quotes. For example, a taxi from the Fish Market to airport with Bergentaxi, midday on a weekday, comes out to a little less than 500 NOK.

Trains

NSB railways operates all of the trains coming into and out of Bergen (the average price of a ticket from Oslo to Bergen, one of the most scenic rail trips in Europe, is around 699 NOK, students 634 NOK. The route takes around six-and-a-half hours). All trains drop off at Bergen train station (Strømgt 4. Luggage storage, cab stand, ATMs, and cafes on site. ☼ Waiting room open daily 6am-12:10am. Ticket booths and services open M-F 6:45am-7:15am, Sat-Sun 7:30am-4pm.)

By Bus

most buses between Bergen and other Norwegian cities are run through Bussekspress and cost about as much as the train—550-700 NOK for a one way ticket from Oslo, 12 hours in total. All buses drop off at the Bergen bus station (Stromgaten 8).

Getting Around

Public Transportation

The town of Bergen is incredibly compact, and all of the main sights are within walking distance. Taking public transportation is often less effective because of the wait times and dropoff locations.

Bergen's public transportation is called Skyss and includes all of the buses and trams in the Hordaland region (the municipality in which Bergen is located). Much like in Oslo, tickets can be bought for 24hr. (90 NOK), 7-day (235 NOK), or longer periods and are available for purchase at every transportation stop. If you find yourself without a pass, you can also buy one directly on the bus or tram, though the cost will be higher.

Much like the Oslo Pass, the Bergen Card gives you free access to public transportation and discounts at a number of museums, restaurants, and parking spaces. It's a smart purchase if you're trying to pack a lot into a short amount of time, but if you're in Bergen mainly for hiking or low-intensity sightseeing, it might not be worth it. The card can be purchased at the Tourist Information Center at the following prices: 24hr. 200 NOK; 48hr. 260 NOK; 72hr. 320 NOK.

For 999 NOK, the Fjord Card grants unlimited 5-day access to express boats leaving from Strandkai Terminal (next to the tourist center). If you're planning on seeing a lot of fjords or exploring Bergen's offshore islands, this is a good investment.

Taxis

One cab company is Bergen Taxi (☎559 97 050 www.bergentaxi.no). Prices vary dramatically depending on the time, day of the week, and number of passengers. For a sample, Friday nights for a cab with four people or less will start at 54 NOK if hailed on the street, and then go up by 9.30 NOK per minute, with a minimum fare of 136 NOK. For a full table of prices and times, see the website.

norway essentials

VISAS

Norway is not a member of the EU, but it is a member of the Schengen area. Citizens of Australia, Canada, New Zealand, the US, and many other non-EU countries do not need a visa for stays of up to 90 days. However, if you plan to spend time in other Schengen countries, note that the 90-day period of time you are allowed to visit without a visa applies cumulatively to all Schengen countries.

MONEY

Norway uses the Norwegian krone (NOK or kr.) as its currency.

Tipping is not usually expected in Norway. In restaurants, it is common to round up the bill to the nearest 10 or 100 NOK, or 6-10% of the bill if you have received exceptional service, but this is not required. Taxi drivers also do not expect tips, but if you wish to tip, round up the bill.

ATMs in Norway are common and convenient. They are often located in airports, train stations and major pedestrian areas. The two major international money networks are MasterCard/Maestro/Cirrus and Visa/PLUS. To find out what out-of-network or international fees you may be subject to by using ATMs, call your bank.

ALCOHOL

The minimum age to purchase alcohol in Norway is 18 for drinks below 22% ABV and 20 for drinks above 22% ABV. Selling alcohol to or buying alcohol for minors under 18 is illegal. Bars, clubs, and discos may have different age restrictions based on what they serve, but are usually either 18 or 20. Remember to drink responsibly and to never drink and drive. The legal blood alcohol content (BAC) for driving in Norway is under 0.02%, significantly lower than the US limit of 0.08%.

norway

POLAND

Poland is a sprawling country where history has cast a long shadow. Plains that stretch from the Tatras Mountains in the south to the Baltic Sea in the north have seen foreign invaders time and time again. Meanwhile, the contrast between western and eastern cities is a remnant of Poland's subjection to competing empires. Ravaged during WWII, and later, viciously suppressed by the USSR, Poland is finally self-governed, and the change is marked. Today's Poland is a haven for budget travelers, where the rich cultural treasures of medieval Krakow and bustling Warsaw are complemented by wide Baltic beaches, rugged Tatras peaks, and tranquil Mazury lakes.

greatest hits

- **HERE BE DRAGONS:** Be king or queen for a day and visit the **Wawel Castle** (p. 739) in Kraków. Just don't wake up the infamous Wawel Dragon.

- **COFFEE AND KAFKA:** Bookworms and coffee addicts come together at this coffee shop with a library and book exchange (p. 731).

- **AUSCHWITZ:** A visit to this well-known concentration camp is a sobering, poignant experience (p. 735).

"A provocation." "Offensive." Are these describing *Let's Go* reviews? No—these are actually quotes from politician Stanislaw Pieta regarding Tęcza, a rainbow sculpture that stands at the center of Plac Zbawiciela, otherwise known as Savior Square. The sculpture could itself use a savior, seeing as it has been attacked numerous times by those firmly opposed to the LGBTQ+ community. The work of Julita Wojcik, Wojcik insists that the sculpture isn't actually related to the LGBTQ+ movement at all—but that doesn't deter the haters. And it doesn't deter the lovers either. In protest of the arson the sculpture has repeatedly faced, LGBTQ+ advocates have taken it upon themselves to kiss in front of the sculpture. The rainbow has been rebuilt over and over, perhaps accidentally a symbol of hope for activists.

warsaw

The capital of Poland, Warsaw has lived through German and Soviet occupation, and counts the Holocaust and communism in its history. These experiences, combined with modernization, bring Warsaw to its current form: remnants of the Jewish ghetto, the Palace of Culture and Science, skyscrapers, parks, and the cobbled streets of Stare Miasto all meet. The city is complex, multi-dimensional, and cannot be reduced to a single word. Warsaw honors its history with sites like the Jewish Historical Institute, while welcoming the present with its towering skyscrapers. The rumble of cars borders the respite of parks, giving the air of New York smashed with Paris and Prague, topped off with Varsovian flair. The city was burned down during World War II and has since been rebuilt, giving it a mosaic feel of old and new. Warsaw is split by the Vistula River and counts mermaids as its symbol.

ACCOMMODATIONS

OKI DOKI HOSTEL

HOSTEL $$

plac Dąbrowskiego 3   ☎228 280 122 www.okidoki.pl

Hostel life can get ugly. Indulge in a touch of beauty with Oki Doki's rooms, each with a separate theme and decorated by a Warsaw artist. A snoring hostelmate or a snoring hostelmate and art? Oki Doki is recognized as a member of Europe's Famous Hostels, a group that only selected one hostel in Warsaw. The hostel is about a 9-minute walk from the Palace of Culture and Science and offers 24hr. reception for whatever ungodly hour you decide to return. There isn't a real need to go out late though. The hostel has its own bar, bringing fun even closer to you than it was before. As morning comes, hit up their 15 zł breakfast to refuel before hitting up sights.

i M1/M2: Świętokrzyska. From the station, take the stairs and turn left onto Świętokrzyska. Down two blocks, turn left onto Szkolna, and then right onto plac Dąbrowskiego, where the hostel is on your right. Dorms 67-72 zł. ⏰ Check-in 3pm. Check-out 11am. Reception 24hr.

PATCHWORK HOSTEL

HOSTEL $

Chmielna 5   ☎222 583 959 www.patchworkhostel.pl

As colorful as a quilt indeed, Patchwork Hostel finds itself in a very unique and lively part of town. One might even liken it to—a patchwork? The location is prime, though; close to the Palace of Culture and Science and to numerous stores, Patchwork keeps exercise to a minimum, enjoyment to a max. In a city as spread out as Warsaw, this is a real blessing. The new hostel on the block, the

poland

facilities are in great condition, and like any newbie, the staff is eager to please because if the staff is upbeat, so is the hostel.

i M2: Nowy Świat – Uniwersytet. From the station walk out and turn right onto owy Świat St. Walk about three blocks and turn right onto Chmielna, where the hostel will be on your left. Dorms 60-70 zł. ⏰ Check-in 3pm. Check-out 11am. Reception 24hr.

MISH MASH HOSTEL   HOSTEL $

Nowogrodzka 42   ☎512 951 446 www.mishmashhostel.pl

An artsy ambience greets you from the second you step in: gray patterned wallpaper and art reminiscent of Banksy. The rooms of Mish Mash are simple and minimalist, but they don't skimp on what's important: TV. You'll find one in each room, as well as in the common room. (We know how easy it is to slip into a soap opera obsession.) Mish Mash also offers a common kitchen and comfortable rooms. Mish Mash can be found in the Sródmiescie district, a little over 20 minutes away from Łazienki Park, and a nine minute walk from the Palace of Culture and Science.

i M1: Centrum. From the station, take the stairs and then turn right onto Marszałkowska. At the next block, turn right onto Nowogrodzka, where the hostel will be on the right. Dorms 50-80 zł. ⏰ Check-in 1pm. Check-out 11am. Reception 7am-midnight.

SIGHTS

ROYAL CASTLE   CASTLE

plac Zamkowy 4   ☎223 555 170 www.zamek-krolewski.pl

Originally built in the 14th century, the Royal Castle was produced by Italian architects, for Polish King Sigmund III, who descended from the royal Swedish Vasa family. Like a college brochure, this castle is the spitting image of diversity and pulls it off remarkably well. During World War II, the castle was completely destroyed by the Germans, and the version that stands today is a reconstruction of the original. As of now, the castle counts the King's Apartment, Deputies' Chamber, and Royal Library as part of its tour and also has a permanent exhibit in the basement about the reconstruction process of the castle. Europe's first constitution, while signed at the Presidential Palace, was written up here. The building has taken up many different functions, but it has consistently housed important political roles throughout the years. The Castle and Old Town have since been granted UNESCO World Heritage Site status. If the castle's just not doing it for you, you'll find a magnificent river view right behind.

i M1: Ratusz Arsenał. From the Metro station, get on the 26 tram toward Wiatraczna to Stare Miasto, where you can take the crosswalk to reach the Royal Castle. Castle tour 23 zł, reduced 15 zł. Entrance free on Sundays. ⏰ Open M-W 10am-6pm, Th 10am-8pm, F-Sa 10am-6pm, Su 11am-6pm. For more detailed prices and hours for individual exhibitions, please check the website for the most up-to-date information.

TOMB OF THE UNKNOWN SOLDIER (GROB NIEZNANEGO ZOLNIERZA)   TOMB

plac Pilsudskiego

A monument to Polish soldiers who died for their country, the Tomb of the Unknown Soldier holds the remains of a soldier who died in battle. As with any of the other tombs of unknowns found worldwide, the emphasis is not on the individual, but on what the individual represents. The soldier buried is a symbol of the sacrifice so many Poles made in defense of their country, and it is with that in mind that Warsaw honors this soldier fiercely. Guards are appointed to stand alongside the tomb every day, changing station every hour, every day of the year. The dedication the Varsovians show this monument is intense, but deservedly so, in light of the dedication these soldiers showed Poland. Found on plac Pilsudski, the monument is small but somber and poignant. The tomb lays at the center, flanked by guards and burning flames. The monument is not without its own story of turmoil—it has faced destruction, and its significance has transformed over time. As it stands today, however, the tomb is a beautiful-ly-executed memorial to heroes past.

i M1/M2: Świętokrzyska. From the Metro stop, ride the N44 tram toward Zajezdnia Żoliborz for 3 stops to Hotel Bristol. From here, turn left onto Generala Michała Tokarzewskiego-Karaszewicza and then take the crosswalk.

PRESIDENTIAL PALACE (PALAC PREZYDENCKI) PALACE

Krakowskie Przedmieście 48/50   ☎226 951 070 www.prezydent.pl

The name says it all—the Presidential Palace in Warsaw is the official seat of the President of Poland. Recognizable by the huge white building and the guards standing outside, the aesthetic of this place is "stay out." What do you mean the President doesn't want to see us? What do you mean you need an invitation? We came out to have a good time, and honestly, we're feeling so attacked right now. The palace dates back to the 1600s and has seen some serious history play out. Stanisław II August Poniatowski was coronated here, an affair that cost over 2,000,000 zł, and a statue of his brother, Józef Poniatowski, stands out front. Chopin once performed at the Presidential Palace, and Europe's first constitution was signed here. You won't get to see the site up close, but a selfie with the stone lions out front is almost the same thing, right? Swap a politician for a stone-cold carnivore, and who could even tell the difference?

i M2: Nowy Świat – Uniwersytet. From the station, turn left onto Nowy Świat St. Continue onto Krakowskie Przedmieście. The palace is on the right.

PALACE OF CULTURE AND SCIENCE PALACE

plac Defilad 1   ☎226 567 600 www.pkin.pl

Built between 1952 and 1955, the enormous structure was a "gift from the Soviet people," offered by Stalin himself to the Poles, and its construction still prompts passionately divided public reaction. Regardless of opinion, this 42-story build-ing looms over everything and there's no ignoring it at all. More than a palace though, the structure is a bit of a mini-village, with its own post office, shopping mall, a cinema with eight screens, four theaters, two museums, and an entire college spanned across two floors. Despite its size, the palace offers little to see, though it does have a stellar observation deck. With a panoramic view of the entire city, including the Vistula River, the deck is a prime date location, guaranteed to bring you plenty of class.

i M1: Centrum. From the station, walk onto plac Defilad. The palace is right ahead. Palace re-quires guided tour for admission.Tours for individuals available through CREATours (entrance on Marszałkowska). Admission 30 zł. ☼ Open M 10:30am-5:30pm, Tu-Th 10:30am-1:30pm, F-Su 10:30am-5:30pm.

JEWISH HISTORICAL INSTITUTE MUSEUM

Tłomackie 3/5   ☎228 279 221 www.jhi.pl

The Jewish Historical Institute of Warsaw stands as the only establishment in Poland that dedicates its collection entirely to the culture of Jews in Warsaw. Including exhibits of paintings, memoirs, and World War II testimonies from Jewish survivors of the Holocaust, the museum brings to life the vivid reality that Polish Jews faced in their everyday lives during the war. A key highlight of the museum is the Warsaw Ghetto exhibit, with photos and film footage from the ghetto itself, painting a troubling but accurate picture of the Jews' suffering. Many of the relevant Warsaw Ghetto sights, like boundary markers, still stand today, and are certainly worth a visit. The institute is located relatively far away from these, but for anyone interested in Jewish history, there is nothing like firsthand experience to make the facts salient. For those pressed for time, we suggest walking down Grzybowska street and seeing the ghetto boundary marker at Grzybowska 45, walking down the street to a remaining portion of the Ghetto Wall at Walicóv 11, and visiting the Nożyk synagogue and Prozna.

i M1: Ratusz Arsenał. *From the station, turn right onto aleja Solidarności/DW629, and then make a right onto Tłomackie. 10 zł, students 5 zł.* ☼ *Open M-F 10am-6pm, Su 10am-6pm, closed Saturdays.*

FOOD

SAM
INTERNATIONAL $$

Lipowa 7a
☎600 806 084

We all know a Sam. We all love a Sam. We love SAM. A restaurant, cafe, and bakery, SAM is the food trifecta, and it does each label justice. A relaxed and naturally lit open space, SAM is a breath of fresh air—particularly if you go for the outdoor seating. On the inside, a long table stands in the center with small ones to the side. Large windows let light flood in, ideal for the Vitamin D-deprived. The restaurant has your usual—ham and cheese sandwiches, omelets—but splits from the crowd with its vegan and vegetarian options and offerings like Thai rice, lime and chili ice cream, and saffron ice cream. Don't let the casually American name throw you. A meal at SAM can very much be an international experience.

i M2: Centrum Nauki Kopernik. *From the station, walk down Wybrzeże Kościuszkowskie. Turn left onto Lipowa. The restaurant is on the left. Salads 24-36 zł. Vegetarian and vegan meals 16-36 zł. Meat dishes 7-38 zł.* ☼ *Open M-F 8am-9:30pm, Sa-Su 9am-9:30pm.*

KAWIARNIA KAFKA
CAFE $

Obożna 3
☎228 260 822

On the edge of a park, Kawiarnia Kafka's layout invites customers to float in and out of the space, lounging on the grass, at the outside tables, or at the inside ones. Antlers decorate one wall, books another, but despite the name, Kawiarnia Kafka is anything but pretentious. The cafe boasts a book collection and book exchange, meaning patrons can get their fill of coffee, food, and words all in one stop. Buying a book is, much like us, cheap and easy—books are sold by weight, but reading in the cafe is our favorite: free. Kafka stands near the University of

a starbucks conspiracy?

If you spend enough time walking around Warsaw, you'll notice that the city's current coat of arms features a beautiful, topless mermaid (#freethenipple). This mermaid is Warsaw's mascot, but none of the legends can quite agree on why. As one legend goes, a merchant laid claim to a mermaid, kidnapping her and holding her against her will. A fisherman came to her rescue, releasing her and winning her trust. Since then, the mermaid has defended the city, ever loyal out of gratitude. Another legend claims that the mermaid instead guided and protected Prince Kazimierz, and was thus chosen as the emblem in honor of her kindness. Finally, another legend posits that the mermaid loved a griffin who protected the city (because if you're listening to tales about mermaids, can you really complain about logic?). Upon the griffin's death, she replaced him in his role, and was made the emblem of Warsaw as a thank you. Older versions of the coat of arms looked nothing like the current one; rather than a beautiful woman, at their center stood a stout man with a tail and scaly legs. Puberty hit, beauty standards changed, and these days the emblem now exhibits a beautiful woman, her tail curls up toward her shield, and her arm holding a sword above her head.

Warsaw; the cafe's extensive menu and 10% student discount draw the young intellectuals in. When Tinder inevitably disappoints, consider that you could probably do worse than the crowd here.

i M2: Nowy Świat – Uniwersytet. From the station, turn left onto Nowy Świat. At the next corner, turn right onto Mikołaja Kopernika and then take another right onto Obóźna. The cafe is on your right. Salads 17-25 zł. Kanapki 9-14 zł. Coffee drinks 6-14 zł. ☑ Open M-F 9am-10pm, Sa-Su 10am-10pm.

PAŃSTWOMIASTO
POLISH **$**

Generała Władysława Andersa 29 ☎224 009 464

High ceilings and neutral toned decoration punctuated with colorful art grant Państwomiasto the air of a Manhattan loft. (Like what we expect Taylor Swift's apartment looks like—she's got a blank space baby, but the rest of us don't have any space at all.) Państwomiasto, on the other hand, has large windows that let light flood in, and a wide floor space with scattered wooden tables. The cafe leads the pack by offering food options past sandwiches and salads. Protein and complex carbs join the menu, which features gems like tagliatelle with duck, and nachos.

i M1: Dworzec Gdański. From the station, walk onto Generała Władysława Andersa. Follow this road for 10min. Państwomiasto is on your right. Snacks 9-22 zł. Pasta dishes 25-27 zł. Salads 22-26 zł. Cocktails 15-22 zł. ☑ Open daily 9am-midnight. Kitchen closes at 10pm Su-Th, 11pm F-Sa.

COFFEE KARMA
CAFE **$**

Mokotowska 17 ☎228 758 709

Wooden tables, window benches, and colorful cushions fill the inside of Coffee Karma, a cafe found on plac Zbawiciela, a hipster home. The cafe has a clear view of the controversial rainbow structure that stands at the center of the square. Coffee Karma has a mix of seating, making it a good place to work, meet a date, or soak up some sun outdoors. Put another way, it's a good place to go, whether you're trying to get the A or the D. Karma's numerous outlets and food options mean it's easy to spend a day here. On the other side of the roundabout, Plan B comes to life as Coffee Karma closes.

i M1: Politechnika. From the station, turn left onto Ludwika Waryńskiego, heading toward Polna. Turn left onto Jaworzyńska. Turn left at the end of the road onto Mokotowska where the cafe is on your left. Kanapki 13-21 zł. Salads 23-29 zł. Coffee drinks 6.50-15 zł. ☑ Open M-F 7:30am-11pm, Sa 9:30am-11pm, Su 10am-11pm.

CHARLOTTE
BAKERY **$**

aleja Wyzwolenia 18 ☎226 284 459

Also on plac Zbawiciela, Charlotte is a taste of France just a few borders away. Casually Parisian—oxymoron?—the bistro sells items like pastries, *croquees monsieur*, and *croques madame*. If you think there's a better way to start the day than with a croissant…that's blasphemy. Charlotte is all class, and it's the best place in the square to enjoy a glass of wine. Recommended for breakfast or a brunch date, the space is somewhat small but bustling, and it's very popular. For those of us dedicated to the pursuit of carbs, the bakery sells fresh products to take home. Bread for now, bread for later. We about that life.

i M1: Politechnika. From the station, turn left onto Ludwika Waryńskiego, heading toward Polna, and turn right into Nowowiejska. The cafe is across the square. Salads 8-18 zł. Breakfast 8-25 zł. Hot beverages 2-9 zł. ☑ Open M-Th 7am-midnight, F 7am-1am, Sa 9am-1am, Su 9am-midnight.

NIGHTLIFE

PARDON TO TU
BAR

plac Grzybowski 12/16 ☎513 191 641

Pardon To Tu, a popular nightlife spot, celebrates words. A record store, bookstore, pub, and music joint, Pardon To Tu is effortlessly hip, hold the

"ster." Undoubtedly, this is a hipster hangout, but it swaps all of the tropes of hipsterdom for a genuine love for artistic expression. Pardon To Tu indulges in a contemporary and sleek look. One wall of the interior is covered in names of bands; the others hold assorted records and books for sale. In warm weather, the outside seating is the ideal place for a slow-paced, happy day. At night, the place hosts concerts for music aficionados who love to sip beer and say, "Right on."

i M1/M2: Świętokrzyska. From the station, turn left onto Bagno. Turn left onto plac Grzybowski. The bar is on your left. Nonalcoholic drinks 4-18 zł. Beer 6-12 zł. Cover for shows varies, usually between 20-80 zł. Often there is a student discount. ☑ Open daily 10am-late.

PLAN B
BAR

aleja Wyzwolenia 18
☎503 116 154

The name drips innuendo. Plan B pretty much invented plac Zbawiciela, the beloved youth hub of Warsaw. The pub occupies the upper level of a space decorated with graffiti, and is credited with giving the square its cool reputation. Graffiti and slouchy couches contribute to the pub's "too cool to try" air. But it's still definitely hot—Plan B hosts plenty of events, fills up regularly, and can be easily spotted by the crowd lounging outside the doors.

i M1: Politechnika. From the station, turn left onto Ludwika Waryńskiego, heading toward Polna. Turn right onto Nowowiejska. The pub is across the square. Beer 7-15 zł. Wine 10 zł. Cocktails 13-27 zł. Snacks 10-12 zł. ☑ Open daily noon-3am.

BAR STUDIO

plac Defilad 1

BAR

☎603 300 835

The Palace of Culture and Science, home to Bar Studio, inspires mixed emotions in Varsovians. The extensive structure is, to many, a reminder of Soviet domination and communist days. Others hold more positive perceptions, seeing it as an architectural gem that defines the city. At the heart of this controversial place, Bar Studio takes up residence in the Studio Theatre. A restaurant with a cafe atmosphere and a bar at night, Bar Studio is easily an all-day affair. The outdoor seating offers a view of the rest of the palace while the inside seating is a comfortable and sleek place to get work done. As your day turns from coffee to vodka (or vodka to more vodka?), Bar Studio transitions into a bar. Bar Studio hosts regular events in their large space, and caters to the nightlife crowd. A historical building, there's hardly a better place to indulge in beats and drinks in an authentic Varsovian experience.

i M1: Centrum. From the station, the bar is right out on the courtyard of the Palace of Culture and Science. Cocktails 15-25 zł. Beer 4-15 zł. Entrance to events 5-10 zł. ☼ Open 9am-late.

ESSENTIALS

Practicalities

- **TOURIST OFFICES:** Palace of Culture and Science (plac Defilad 1 ☼ Open daily May-Sept 8am-8pm; Oct-Apr 8am-6pm.). Old Town (Rynek Starego Miasta 19/21/21a ☼ Open daily May-Sept 9am-8pm; Oct-Apr 9am-6pm.).

- **BANKS/ATMS:** ATMs are readily found throughout the city at most banks as well as by the arrival terminal at the airport. Shopping malls that have ATM machines are also commonly found around the city.

- **INTERNET:** Warsaw has free public Wi-Fi available in Old Town, in areas such as the Powiśle district and Krakowskie Przedmieście. Free Wi-Fi is also available at Starbucks, Costa Coffee, Coffee Heaven, KFC, McDonald's, and most hostels and hotels. There are also internet cafes available throughout the city: Arena Internet Cafe (plac Konstytucji 5 ☼ Open 24hr.) and A2 Cafe (plac Konstytucji 5 ☼ Open 24hr.)

- **POST OFFICE:** FUP Warszawa 1 (aleja Jana Pawła II 82 ☎223 132 388 ☼ Open M-Sa 8am-8pm, Su 10am-4pm.)

Emergency

- **EMERGENCY NUMBER:** ☎112

- **EMERGENCY NUMBER FOR FOREIGNERS:** ☎608 599 999 or ☎222 787 777 ☼ Available June 1-Sept 30, daily 8am-10pm.

- **POLICE:** ☎997

- **CITY GUARD:** ☎986

- **FIRE:** ☎998

- **HOSPITAL:** Szpital Orłowskiego: Strona główna (ulica Czerniakowska 231 ☎226 283 011). Szpital Kliniczny im. Księżnej Anny Mazowieckiej (Karowa 2 ☎225 966 100). Samodzielny Publiczny Centralny Szpital Kliniczny (Stefana Banacha 1A ☎225 991 000).

- **24HR.PHARMACIES:** Apteka Franciszkańska (Fanciszkańska 14 ☎226 353 525 ☼ Open 24hr.). Apteka 24h PZF Cefarm (ulica Gagarina 6 ☎228 413 783 ☼ Open 24hr.).

poland

Getting There

From the airport, you can take the SKM S2 train to the city center. Tickets for the train can be purchased at the Passenger Information Point in the Arrivals hall, from ticket machines placed at bus stops and next to the train station entrance, from ticket machines in SKM trains and on some buses, or from bus drivers.

You can also use buses. Bus 175 runs daily 4:30am-11pm and will take you to the city center. Bus 188 runs daily 4:45am-11:20pm and will take you through the city center and to the Praga district.

Getting Around

Public Transportation

All public transportation tickets can be purchased at newspaper kiosks or ticket machines in the Metro stations. The price for a ticket for one trip is 4.40 zł. Tickets for one day (15 zł) or one weekend (24 zł) can also be purchased.

Taxi

Ubers are readily available in Warsaw. You can also use cabs throughout the city, in which fares will start at 8 zł and cost 3 zł per kilometer during the day. Taxis can be called through the following companies: Glob Cab Taxi (☎666 009 668 www. globcabtaxi.pl) and VIP Taxi Warsaw (☎791 550 525 www.viptaxiwarsaw.pl).

auschwitz

Auschwitz-Birkenau is located about an hour and a half outside Kraków by public transportation. The concentration camp is found in the city of Oświęcim, 50 kilometers west of Kraków. What is colloquially known as "Auschwitz" is divided into three parts: Auschwitz I, Auschwitz II-Birkenau, and Auschwitz III. The last part is not open for tours, and a shuttle bus runs regularly between Auschwitz I and II. If you

take a bus from Kraków, the bus will drop you off in front of the Auschwitz-Birkenau Memorial and Museum.

SIGHTS

Perhaps the best known of the concentration camps, Auschwitz-Birkenau was the largest of the Nazi concentration camps and understandably is taken by many as representative of one of the greatest tragedies in human history. A short distance from Kraków, the grounds offer visitors a sobering, poignant experience. The site witnessed some terrible crimes and as a result demands certain standards of respect. Certain blocks forbid camera usage out of respect for their specific exhibits, flash is forbidden indoors, and visitors are asked to remain silent inside of the gas chambers. While not forbidden, it is in poor taste to take selfies and questionable to chat loudly or pose for pictures with the blocks, crematoria, and ruins of warehouses. A visit to the concentration camp, or any concentration camp, is a deeply emotional lesson on humanity's capacity for both evil and compassion. Interspersed in the narrative of suffering, there remain many uplifting stories of courage and selflessness among the prisoners. To get as much out of the experience as possible, stay focused on the tour, and the gravity of what you are witnessing and, above all, prioritize respect for the area and its victims with your behavior. Guided tours are available and should be reserved online.

The Auschwitz-Birkenau Memorial and Museum tour covers Auschwitz I and Auschwitz II-Birkenau. Each site takes at least 90 minutes to fully visit, and a more thorough visit could easily take longer. Auschwitz III is not open for visitation. The tour includes exhibits of collections of prisoners' possessions, pictures of prisoners, a display of prison attire, cans of Zyklon B used in gas chambers, information on Josef Mengele's sadistic experiments, a visit to barracks and crematoriums, and a visit to a memorial enacted in Birkenau, among other elements. The tour begins at Auschwitz I and continues on at Auschwitz II-Birkenau with a shuttle bus taking visitors between the sites.

Three different tours exist. General tours last about 3½ hr. and visit both camps. One-day study tours last about 6 hr. and include the Central Sauna, a visit to different crematoria, and extra exhibits. While admission to the grounds is free, the tours are not.

i Admission free. General tour 40 zł, reduced 30 zł. 6 hr. study tour 65 zł, reduced admission 30 zł. ☒ Museum open daily Apr-May 8am-6pm; June-Aug 8am-7pm; Sept 8am-5pm; Oct 8am-4pm; Nov 8am-3pm; Dec 8am-2pm; Jan 8am-3pm; Feb 8am-4pm; Mar 8am-5pm.

ESSENTIALS

Emergency

- **EMERGENCY NUMBER:** ☎112

- **LOCAL POLICE:** ☎338 475 200

- **TOURIST INFORMATION:** Oświęcim Tourist Center. (12 St. Leszczyńskiej str. ☎33 843 00 91 www.it.oswiecim.pl ☒ Open May-Sept 8am-6pm; Oct 8am-5pm; Nov-Mar 8am-4pm; Apr 8am-5pm.) Auschwitz Jewish Center Tourist Information Point. (Pl. Ks. J. Skarbka 5, 32-600 Oświęcim. ☎338 447 002 www.ajcf.pl. ☒ Open Apr-Sept M-F 10am-6pm, Su 10am-6pm, closed Saturdays; Oct-Mar M-F 10am-5pm, S 10am-5pm, closed Saturdays.)

Getting There

There are many organized tours to Auschwitz, such as those run through SeeKrakow or Cracow Tours, and booking a tour through such agencies can save you the trouble of having to find transportation. However, it is also not difficult to make your way to Auschwitz independently. Buses leave regularly from Kraków main station, also called Kraków Główny railway station, or Dworzec Główn, and will drop you off in front of the Auschwitz-Birkenau State Museum. The station is conveniently located in the northeast side of Old Town, right by the Main Market Sq. and is within easy walking distance of most accommodations. You can purchase tickets online at www. lajkonikbus.pl by entering the departure station as Kraków and the destination as Oświęcim. This would reserve a seat for you, but, in a rush, tickets can be bought at the ticket offices in the bus station or on board the bus as well. The earliest bus leaves from Kraków at 5:30am, and the last bus leaves Auschwitz at 7:30pm; each way costs 13zł. Oświęcim and Kraków are on either ends of the bus route, and the trip will take 1hr. 25min. each way.

kraków

By our best unscientific estimates, Kraków is at least half fowl—but that's no foul. The Krakovians adore their pigeon friends, and some will even go as far as to let the birds rest on top of them. The touristy areas, Wawel Hill and Main Market Square in particular, are covered in the creatures, but the locals pay little attention to their fluttering. As legend has it, the animals are former knights, loyal to a prince past and transformed into avian form by the hand of a witch. There's much more to the city than its wildlife, however. Formerly the capital of Poland, the city is rife with historical buildings and noteworthy architecture, all wrapped up in legends and lore. The Wawel Castle on Wawel Hill, for example, served as the seat of Polish royalty for centuries—and the hill is said to have been the home of a dragon who demanded the sacrifice of young maidens. In Kraków you'll also find sights like the Main Market Square, St. Mary's Basilica, and Schindler's Factory. At a short distance from the city stands the Wieliczka Salt Mine, which hosts over a million tourists a year. The former concentration camp Auschwitz-Birkenau is also easily accessed from Kraków, though you don't have to leave the city to better understand Jewish history and culture. The Jewish Quarter of Kraków is well developed and culturally rich, an homage to the past influences of Jewish culture on the city, and an insight into contemporary Jewish culture. Much of the city feels medieval and historical, but places like the Museum of Contemporary Art in Kraków will jolt you back into this century.

ACCOMMODATIONS

CRACOW HOSTEL
HOSTEL $

Rynek Główny 18 ☎124 291 106 www.cracowhostel.com

Sitting smack in the middle of Main Market Square, Cracow Hostel boasts a great location, surrounded by the life and hype of Cloth Hall by day and clubs, pubs, and bars by night. In addition to typical hostel amenities—including laundry service, towels, and locks—Cracow also has a cozy shared living room featuring high ceilings and a winding staircase leading up to well-lit rooms and dorms. The hostel takes up residence in a building hailing from the 14th century, making a stay here basically like a history lesson. With its direct view of Cloth Hall and abundant sunlight in the rooms, Cracow Hostel presents the perfect selfie opportunity for those looking to change their social media pictures. After all, if a backpacker backpacks but the internet doesn't see it, did he really go backpacking?

i From Main Market Square, the hostel is at the southeast corner of the square, by the Church of St. Wojciech. Dorms 43-60 zł. ⚅ Check-in 1pm. Check-out 11am. Reception 24hr.

GREG & TOM BEER HOUSE HOSTEL
HOSTEL $$

Floriańska 43 ☎124 212 864 beerhouse.gregtomhostel.com

Weekly live music events and daily pub crawls give this hostel its bubbly atmosphere. Located 5min. away from Main Market Square, Greg and Tom's Beer Hostel stands on a busy street with plenty of bars and clubs around to check out. Don't feel like going out? Worry not, for the hostel is also equipped with its own pub, providing plenty of opportunities for people to meet, talk, and drop their guards and, if willing, their pants too. With a young, vibrant atmosphere, Greg and Tom's provides plugs by every bed, reliable Wi-Fi, and, to top it off, good food from its restaurant, proving to be a great option for anyone with respectable priorities.

i From Main Market Square, find plac Mariacki and walk toward it. Walk onto Floriańska. The hostel is on the right about three blocks down. Dorms 57-70 zł. Breakfast included. ⌚ Check-in 2pm. Check-out 10am. Reception 24hr.

MOSQUITO HOSTEL
HOSTEL $$

rynek Kleparski 4 ☎124 301 461 www.mosquitohostel.com

Despite what its name suggests, this hostel actually does not suck—blood, or anything else—at all. Located just off Main Market Square, Mosquito is the cool mom of hostels. With daily events ranging from shisha evenings to Polish shot tastings and homemade cookie nights, Mosquito will responsibly introduce you to the wonders and blunders of Mad Dogs (trademark Polish shots) while also filling you with baked love. The hostel won't do your taxes or help you move into college, but it'll support you non-stop with a nearby supermarket, a Polish restaurant, and an ATM all open 24hr., making sure even your jetlagged sleep schedules are accommodated. All that in addition to 24hr. reception adds up to a great deal, and Mosquito is sure to take care of most of your needs.

i From Main Market Square, walk down Szczenpańska. Turn right onto Basztowa and then turn left onto rynek Kleparski. The hostel is on the right. Dorms 65-80 zł. Laundry free. ⌚ Check-in 1pm. Check-out 11am. Reception 24hr.

FLAMINGO HOSTEL KRAKÓW
HOSTEL $

Szewska 4 ☎124 220 000 www.krakow.flamingo-hostel.com

Placed centrally in Old Town and right next to Cloth Hall, convenience in location makes this hostel a solid option. With towels, locks, and laundry offered at a small fee, the hostel also prides itself on its karaoke facilities and bar for those looking for music to raise their spirits or, alternatively, just spirits. With rooms housing between two to 12 guests, the beds are spaciously arranged. Warm mauve walls in the dark will make you dream of swimming in pools of wine, and the chocolate factory across the street makes this hostel a sweet, sweet deal indeed.

i From Main Market Square, walk down Szewska. Flamingo is on your left, half a block down. Dorms 35-55 zł. Breakfast included. ⌚ Check-in 2pm. Check-out noon. Reception 24hr.

TRAVELLERS INN HOSTEL
HOTEL $

plac Na Groblach 8 ☎124 294 723 www.travellersinn.pl

As the name directly states, Travellers is indeed a hostel for travelers. Located conveniently by the foothill of Wawel Castle, Travellers Inn is outside Old Town and five minutes away from Planty Park. It's perfect for those who have traveled enough or, alternatively, are old enough to realize you always need at least some distance, even from the things you love. That said, Travellers is by no means distant from the action. Five minutes away from Kazimierz, the Vistula River and Main Market Square, its location is still central, with a lower risk of running into drunken tourists on your way back from the town. For those wanting to remove themselves even farther from the city, the hostel offer six free bicycles and three suggested routes, all of them moving away from Old Town toward a calmer and less traveled part of Kraków. You did indeed come for the city, but sometimes you just need to not be near tourists and pigeons, and that's a sentiment that Travellers supports.

i From Main Market Square, head toward Szewska and walk onto Wiślna. Make a slight left to walk onto Karola Olszewskiego. Continue onto I obwodnica/Straszewskiego. Turn right onto plac Na Groblach, where the hostel`s on your right. Singles 110 zł, doubles 180 zł, triples 195 zł, quads 240 zł. ☒ Check-in 1pm. Check-out 11am.

SIGHTS

WAWEL CASTLE
CASTLE

Wawel 5   ☎124 225 155 www.wawel.krakow.pl

For centuries, Poland's royalty resided atop a hill in Kraków, calling home the medieval Wawel Castle. (It definitely sounds better in Polish—more of a V sound.) The site the Castle occupies, Wawel Hill, is itself remarkably old, settled in the Paleolithic Age. The hill carries its own lore, including that of the Wawel Dragon. Said to live in a cave in the hill, the dragon terrorized the town, demanding the regular sacrifice of young girls. Coronations have been held in Wawel Cathedral since that of Władysław the Short. Several generations of Polish rulers took residence in Wawel Castle until it was occupied by the Austrians. Once again in Polish possession, the Wawel Castle is a large complex with several exhibitions operating as a museum. Among them: the Wawel Cathedral, the State Rooms, the Royal Private Apartments, the Crown Treasury and Armory, Leonardo da Vinci's *Lady with an Ermine*, Oriental Art, Lost Wawel, the Dragon's Den, Sandomierska Tower, and Wawel Architecture and Gardens. The last three are seasonal exhibits.

i From Main Market Square, walk onto Grodzka and continue onto droga Do Zamku. The castle is on your right. State Rooms 18 zł. Royal Private Apartments 25 zł. Crown Treasure and Armory 18 zł. ☒ State Rooms and Royal Private Apartments open Tu-F 9:30am-5pm, Sa-Su 10am-5pm, closed Mondays. Crown Treasure and Armory open M 9:30am-1pm, Tu-F 9:30am-5pm, Sa-Su 10am-5pm. For more detailed prices and hours for individual exhibitions, please check the website for the most up-to-date information.

MUSEUM OF CONTEMPORARY ART IN KRAKÓW
MUSEUM

Lipowa 4   ☎122 634 000

A cafe, shop, and, of course, contemporary art exhibit, the MOCAK is one of the finest ways to spend an afternoon in Kraków. Highlighting the works of present-day artists, both Polish and foreign, the building itself, glass and concrete, is as interesting as the art it presents. The museum is quite new, having opened in 2010, and emphasizes Polish contemporary art that provokes social commentary. Within its walls, there's intellectual stimulation for the artistically inclined, whimsy for the artistically-disinclined. Have you seen art nowadays? Weird is good, and it's better than spending a day looking at portraits of constipated royalty. Six wives? Looking like that, Henry? Now that's just weird.

i From Main Market Square, walk onto Sienna, and continue onto Starowiślna. Continue onto most Powstańców Śląskich. Turn right onto Lipowa. The museum is on the right. 10 zł, students 5 zł. Free on Tuesdays. ☒ Open Tu-Su 11am-7pm, closed Mondays.

WIELICZKA SALT MINE
MINE

Daniłowicza 10, Wieliczka   ☎122 787 302 www.wieliczka-saltmine.com

Attracting over a million tourists a year, the Wieliczka Salt Mine is undoubtedly popular. Once fully operational, the mine was built in the 13th century and produced table salt back when the industry was lucrative. Now it serves as a source of national pride as one of the 12 UNESCO-listed sites in Poland. The mine is a beautiful collaboration between man and nature, proof that sometimes beauty isn't skin deep, but actually 135m under the ground. Among the works

józefa street

Bright colors of galleries juxtaposed against the walls of peeling paint give this street its uniquely artistic atmosphere. Nestled in the Kazimierz district, the street is home to the High Synagogue, which stands as a reminder of the Jewish history that the street was borne out of. Once the center of Jewish life in Kraków, Kazimierz became one of the most dangerous districts of the city during the Communist Era. But since then, the district, and with it, Józefa Street has been revived by a newfound air of youthful hipsters and artists. The art galleries that line the street show that while the street may not be young and fresh, the talent certainly is. The works, ranging from traditional to contemporary works and cups shaped like heads, will make you question the definition of art. Is this art? Don't let it get to you; definitions are too mainstream anyway. The street is home to a slew of old and new shops, boutiques as well as cafes, bars, and plenty of opportunities to update your Snapchat story. With its vibrant atmosphere, Józefa has become a great hub for tourists and artists alike, and a must-stop place for anyone with that unique friend you never know what to buy for. What do you mean you didn't like your 'I Love Kraków' mug?

exhibited you'll find a salt rendition of *The Last Supper*, plus altars and statues. The mine is also home to the Chapel of St Kinga, a majestic structure with a salt chandelier. The shortest guided route through the mine is about 2½hr. long, and they all include a lot of walking. It seems like a lot of effort, but considering this is as interesting as salt is probably going to get, it is well worth your time.

i The salt mine is accessible from Kraków by public bus 304, which can be boarded from the Jubilat station by the supermarket. Get off 8 stops later at Wieliczka Kościół. From here it is a 10-minute walk to the mines. 79 zł, students 64 zł. ☑ Open daily Apr-Oct 7:30am-7:30pm; Nov-Mar 8am-5pm.

MAIN MARKET SQUARE & CLOTH HALL
LANDMARK
Rynek Główny 1-3   ☎124 335 400

Originally designed in 1257, Main Market Square has been the centerpiece of Kraków's Old Town since medieval times, functioning as a central meeting place for Krakovians and pigeons. The pigeons aren't that special but appear special due to their seemingly infinite quantity. At the center of the square is Cloth Hall, built in the 14th century and one of the oldest shopping malls in the world. It wasn't exactly a great place for the cool kids to hang out around after school, but convenient for traveling merchants from foreign countries to trade goods. Since then, Cloth Hall has become less for traveling merchants, more for traveling tourists, with a multitude of stalls lining the inside walls, presenting prime souvenir opportunities. Overlooking the square is St. Mary's Basilica. Its colorful interior is even more impressive than its height. One of the largest medieval squares in Europe, Main Market Square is definitely a must-see.

i St. Mary's Basilica 10 zł, students 5 zł. ☑ Cloth Hall open Tu-Su 10am-6pm, closed Mondays. St. Mary's Basilica open M-Sa 11:30am-6pm, Su 2-6pm.

SCHINDLER'S FACTORY
MUSEUM
Lipowa 4   ☎122 571 017 www.mhk.pl/branches/oskar-schindlers-factory

In the small district of Podgórze, where the Jewish Ghetto was once centered during World War II, stands Schindler's Factory, which reopened in 2010 as a modern museum devoted to showcasing Kraków's daily struggles with war and its atrocities during the Nazi occupation. While currently an interactive museum, the factory was once home to an enamel factory run by Oskar Schindler, who hired Jewish employees from the ghetto, at first to reduce costs of production, but later on to prevent their persecution at great personal cost and risk. By the end of the war, Schindler had saved the lives of about 1200 Jewish workers at his factory. The museum has dedicated a portion of its space to features on Oskar Schindler's life and legacy but otherwise holds its main focus on the history of World War II and its influences on Kraków. The permanent exhibit called "Kraków under Nazi Occupation 1939-1945" features several multimedia installations with photos, recordings, and historical documents. Inside the museum is also a screening room for lectures, movies, and meetings. Kraków is otherwise a vibrant city, but Schindler's Factory serves as a somber reminder of Poland's more troubling history.

i From Main Market Square, walk onto Sienna and continue onto Starowiślna. Continue onto Most Powstańców Śląskich. Turn right onto Lipowa, where the factory is on the right. 21 zł, students 16 zł. Free on Mondays. ☒ Open Apr-Oct M 10am-4pm, Tu-Su 9am-8pm, first Monday of the month 10am-2pm; Nov-Mar 10am-2pm Tu-Su 10am-6pm.

FOOD

ALCHEMIA
PUB, RESTAURANT $$

Estery 5 ☎124 212 200 en.alchemia.com.pl

Part pub, part restaurant, part music venue, Alchemia dabbles in everything, and it's got the Midas touch. The music festival Kraków Jazz Autumn, organized by Alchemia in conjunction with other groups, has received great praise, including the title of "Event of the Year 2012" by Jazzarium. The pub and restaurant, located off of bustling plac Nowy in trendy Kazimierz, is one of the most popular in the square, and deservedly so. In recent years, Alchemia has become increasingly well known and fields a steady stream of patrons every night. Medieval meets quirky, the pub decor feels old but not outdated. Candles illuminate the space, optimal for those of us who look better in dim light anyway. On the other hand, the kitchen part of the establishment, Alchemia od Kuchni, is sleek, modern, and well lit. While vodka shots are best taken in the dark, Alchemia understands that food deserves to be experienced with all five senses.

i From Market Square, walk down Sienna toward Stolarska. Continue onto Starowiślna. Turn right onto Dietla. Turn left onto Świętego Sebastiana, and continue onto Brzozowa, and then Jakuba. Make a right onto Warszauera. Alchemia is on the left. Street food 15-19 zł. Burgers 22-25 zł. Entrees 22-36 zł. Draught beer 6-11 zł. Cider 11-13 zł. ☒ Restaurant open M-Th 9am-11pm, F-Sa 8am-midnight, Su 8am-11pm. Club open M 10am-4am, Tu-Su 9am-4am.

PASJO CAFÉ
BREAKFAST $

Wielopole 7 ☎782 101 201

A cozy Kraków cafe, Pasjo meets the highest standard we hold: the kind of place we'd want to see in the morning. Layered coffee sacks decorate the bar at the entrance; tables and armchairs fill the rest of the space. The overall ambiance is calming and pleasant, and Pasjo is one of the best places in the city for relaxing, indulgent cup of coffee. Their breakfast options are fresh and filling—we suggest opting for one of the simpler options like bread, butter, and scrambled eggs. However you like your eggs, Pasjo will come through.

i From Main Market Square, head down on Sienna toward Stolarska. Continue onto Wielopole. The cafe is on the right. Coffee drinks 6-15 zł. Egg breakfasts 9-16 zł. Burgers 17-28 zł. ☒ Open M-Th 8am-8pm, F 8am-10pm, Sa 9am-10pm, Su 9am-8pm.

CHEDER CAFÉ
JEWISH $

Józefa 36 ☎124 311 517

Hebrew for "room," Cheder is indeed that and more. Solidly in the Jewish Quarter of the city, the cafe occupies a former prayer house and bases its menu and decor off the culture. Armchairs, bookshelves, and a large carpet seating

area compose the main fixtures of the place, accented with Jewish elements like the image of a menorah. Mint tea and hummus grace the menu as universal favorites—in layman's terms: Good. Put in mouth. The cafe prides itself as a Jewish meeting point and cultural hub, hosting various educational events on topics such as the Hebrew alphabet. Regardless of whether you're Jewish, the cafe is worth a visit. Wi-Fi and good coffee? Universal.

i From Main Market Square, walk down Sienna, then continue onto Starowiślna. Turn right onto Dietla. Walk down a block, and then turn left onto Świętego Sebastiana, continuing onto Brzozowa and then Jakuba. About two blocks down, turn right onto Józefa, where Cheder is on the left. Coffee drinks 8-12 zł. Teas 5-12 zł. Pitas 13 zł. ☼ Open daily 10am-10pm.

MOABURGER
BURGERS $
Mikołajska 3
☎124 212 144

Thought by some to be the best burger joint in the city, it's definitely somewhere at the top of the list. Its meat comes on the most satisfying six inches (of bun) you've ever had and dips into unique flavors like mint yogurt and beetroot. Next to the Main Market Square, Moaburger is a Stare Miasto gem, close to many popular sights. The restaurant is slightly more upscale and quirky than your run-of-the-mill diner, but at the end of the day, it gives the people what they want: meat on bread. A New Zealand joint, Moaburger is the second-best thing to come from the land of the kiwis—Lorde is lord(e)—and a strong contender for the best-burger-in-Kraków debate that inexplicably rages on.

i From Main Market Square, walk onto Sienna toward Stolarska until turning left onto Mały Rynek. Beef burgers 17-27 zł. Vegetarian burgers 15-18 zł. Chicken burgers 17-22 zł. ☼ Open M-Sa 11am-11pm, Su noon-9pm.

MOSTOWA CAFÉ
CAFE $
Mostowa 8
☎730 480 477

The name says it all—art and coffee, a one-stop shop. Who's a bigger snob, an art lover or coffee lover? The answer is the guy who loves both. Art lines the walls of the inside part, where patrons can order coffee ranging from the plain (espresso) to the fancy (Aeropress). If you take a fancy to the pieces hanging, they're for sale, so take one home. Or at least to your hostel—no guarantees for getting it the rest of the way. If you find yourself close to the Wisła River, stop by for a drink or coffee at Mostowa. Its loungey chairs will keep you in place for a while, but limited snack options mean it's not an ideal place to spend the entire day. Food > inertia.

i From Main Market Square, walk down Grodzka. Turn left onto Świętego Idziego. Continue onto Stradomska and then Krakowska. Turn left toward plac Wolnica and stay on it until you take the 2nd exit on the roundabout onto Mostowa, where the cafe is. Coffee drinks 5-10 zł. Alcohol 5-35 zł. Snacks 5-8 zł. ☼ Open daily 10am-8pm.

NIGHTLIFE

MIEJSCE
BAR
Estery 1
☎783 096 016

Sharing a name and owners with a retro furniture store, this Kazimierz bar draws significant influence from its sibling establishment. Quirky and colorful pieces fill the place, a clean break from the dark, mysterious style of neighboring Alchemia. On the first day, God said "Let there be light," and only Miejsce listened. Another flavor of hipster in the Kazimierz 50 shades, Miejsce is a calm and comfortable place to grab a drink.

i From Main Market Square, walk down Sienna toward Stolarska. Continue onto Starowiślna. Turn right onto Dietla. Turn left onto Świętego Sebastiana, and continue onto Brzozowa, and then Jakuba. Make a right onto Miodowa, and left onto Estery. The bar is on the right. Alcoholic drinks 12-21 zł. Tea 6-8 zł. Wine 9 zł. ☼ Open M-Th 10am-midnight, F-Sa 10am-5am, Su 10am-midnight.

KLUB PIĘKNY PIES

BAR, CLUB

Bożego Ciała 9

Since it bears a name that translates to "Beautiful Dog," we are inclined to like this place. After all, we love all things doggy—pugs, pomeranians, hot dogs, doggy style. Hip posters adorn the walls, red, black, and grey, of Klub Piękny Pies. Another Jewish Quarter bar and club, Piękny Pies is a magnet for the creative Kraków crowd. The club changes location like Taylor Swift changes boyfriends. (That is, sensibly and with thoughtful deliberation to move on to better things.) At home now in the Kazimierz area, Piękny Pies remains as popular as it was elsewhere. The venue leans toward rock and indie music, often bringing in live artists as well. Fiercely loved, the place keeps full and chatty late into the night.

i From Main Market Square, walk on Sienna toward Stolarska and continue onto Starowiślna. Turn right onto Dietla and walk for about three blocks until turning left onto Bożego Ciała. Piekny Pies is on your right. Cover for events varies. Cocktails 11-30 zł. Wine 7 zł. Prosecco 4 zł. ☒ *Open daily 4pm-late.*

ESZEWERIA

BAR

Józefa 9 ☎122 920 458

If your grandma opened a pub. (The cooler one, though.) Considering its dark and antique-y vibe, it's mildly surprising prune juice isn't on the menu. Brooding and soulful, Eszeweria is the place to work on your Tumblr poetry. (Bet it's going great, Frost.) Old couches and lamps define Eszeweria, making for a dimly lit, romantic aesthetic. Enjoy your drink inside or outside in the garden seating. The place keeps full but not boisterous; time rambles on here in the tranquil space. In the Kazimierz district, it's easy to wander from pub to pub, and this is certainly one worth trying.

i From Main Market Square walk on Sienna toward Stolarska and continue onto Starowiślna. Turn right onto Dietla. Turn left onto Bożego Ciała, and then left onto Józefa. Eszeweria is on the right. Beer 6-11 zł. Wine 8-40 zł. Coffee 6-9 zł. ☒ *Open daily noon-late. Garden open noon-10pm.*

ESSENTIALS
Practicalities

- **TOURIST INFORMATION CENTERS:** InfoKrakow is the official city information network run by Kraków. There are 5 tourist centers run in Old Town, as well as a hotline (☎124 320 060 ☒ Open daily 9am-5pm) available to call. They are Cloth Hall (Sukiennice) Tourist Center (Rynku Glowny ☒ Open daily 9am-7pm), Wyspianski Pavillon (Pawilon Wyspianskiego) Tourist Center (2 plac Wszystkich Swietych Square, at Grodzka, open daily 9am-5pm). Tourist Information Center (2 Sw. Jana ☒ Open daily 9am-7pm). Tourist Information Center (Szpitalna 25 ☒ Open daily May-Oct 9am-7pm; Nov-Apr 9am-5pm). Tourist Service Centre (Powisle 11 ☒ Open daily 9am-7pm).

- **BANKS/ATMS:** ATMs can be found all around the city outside or inside banks that are readily available in the shopping centers, on campuses, or public spaces in the city, especially in central Old Town.

- **INTERNET:** Internet access is not difficult to find within the city. At the airport, free Wi-Fi is available for an hour, and most cafes and restaurants will have free Wi-Fi available. Public libraries (buildings that end with "Biblioteka Publiczna") will also have free Wi-Fi available, but otherwise there are also internet cafes around the city that offer fast Wi-Fi at a small price such as Planet Internet Cafe (Rynek Główny 24 ☒ Open daily 10am-10pm) or Internet Cafe Hetmańska (Bracka 4 ☒ Open 24hr.).

- **POST OFFICE:** Most Kraków shopping malls will have a post office. The main office is on the edge of Old Town, just outside Planty Park. (Westerplatte 20 ☎124 210 348 ☒ Open M-F 7:30am-8:30pm, Sa 8am-2pm)

the tale of the krakow dragon

There's nothing like a story of rags to riches, and this one starts with a dragon so it's got to be good. Legend has it that there once was a dragon that lived under Wawel Hill in Krakow, and every now and then it terrorized the village. In exchange for defeating the dragon, the King offered the throne after his death, and of course, because he could, his daughter's hand in marriage as well. One day, a young shoemaker named Krak challenged the dragon by placing a sulphur-soaked sheep in front of the dragon's lair, which it promptly gobbled up. The dragon was next seen roaring in pain and drinking half the Vistula River, after which is exploded and died. But how? Well, Young Krak would have been happy to tell you that sulphur is in fact flammable, and the dragon essentially died from its own flames. Because science. The moral of the story is, of course, that it does indeed pay to be a nerd, and sometimes payment comes in the form of royalty and a city named after you. Stay in school, kids.

Emergency

- **EMERGENCY NUMBER:** ☎112
- **POLICE:** ☎997
- **AMBULANCE:** ☎999
- **FIRE:** ☎998
- **HOSPITALS:** The following are 24hr. hospitals with emergency wards that are obliged to help anyone who turns up regardless of nationality or health insurance. University Hospital of Krakow (Mikołaja Kopernika 36 ☎124 247 000). The Hospital of the Ministry of Internal Affairs (ul. Kronikarza Galla 25 ☎126 151 734)
- **PHARMACIES:** Magiczna Pharmacy (ulica Ćwiklińskiej 10 ☎126 581 001 ⌚ Open 24hr.)

Getting There

It is easy to use public transportation to get from the airport to the city center. There are a total of three bus lines that run: the 292 bus runs during the day and comes every 20 minutes; the 208 bus also runs during the day and comes every hour; and the 902 bus runs during the night between 11pm and 4am every hour. The tickets cost 4 zł and can be purchased at the RELAY shop in Terminal 1, at the vending machine at the bus stop, or from the driver. The journey from the airport to the Kraków Glowny station, called "Dworzec Glowny Wschod," takes about 40 minutes.

Taxis are also available at the airport through Kraków Airport Taxi, Kraków airport's official taxi service. The taxi ride from the airport to the city center costs about 75 zł, and reservations can be made online: www.krktaxi.pl/en/order_a_taxi_online.

Getting Around

Public Transportation

There is no subway in Kraków, but there is a system of trams and buses that connect districts in Kraków with Old Town. A one-way ticket for both trams and buses is 3.80 zł, and a two-way ticket is 7.20 zł. You can also purchase tickets for 20 minutes (2.80 zł), 40 minutes (3.80 zł), 1hr. (5 zł), or 90 minutes (6 zł) as well. Tickets can be purchased in blue ticketing machines by several bus and tram stops, or you can purchase a 1hr. ticket from the driver. Once boarding the tram or bus, be sure to insert your tickets into the yellow validating machines to start using the ticket. Once it's been validated, the ticket no longer needs to be validated again unless it is for a round-trip journey.

There is no public transportation that runs within Old Town, but it is very walkable and the town can be crossed by foot in about 20 minutes.

Taxis

Taxis are readily available at a relatively small price in Kraków, and fares should not go over 120 zł within city boundaries. Maximum rates within the main urban zone are 2.80 zł per kilometer during daytime on weekdays, and taxi ranks can be found around the city in streets such as ul. Rzeźnicza, ul. Retoryka, and ul. Bernardyńska.

poland essentials

VISAS

Poland is a member of the EU, and also a member of the Schengen area. Citizens of Australia, Canada, New Zealand, the US, and many other non-EU countries do not need a visa for stays of up to 90 days. However, if you plan to spend time in other Schengen countries, note that the 90-day period of time you are allowed to visit without a visa applies cumulatively to all Schengen countries.

MONEY

Despite being a member of the EU, Poland is not in the Eurozone and uses the Polish złoty (PLN or zł.) as its currency.

In restaurants, it is customary to tip 10% of the bill, or 15% if the service was exceptional. Be careful with saying "Thank you" or "Dziękuję" to the waiter when he comes to pick up the bill, since it usually means you don't want any change back. For taxis, tipping is not expected, but you may round up the bill or tip around 10% for good service.

ATMs in Poland are common and convenient. They are often located in airports, train stations and major pedestrian areas. The two major international money networks are MasterCard/Maestro/Cirrus and Visa/PLUS. To find out what out-of-network or international fees you may be subject to by using ATMs, call your bank.

ALCOHOL

The minimum age to purchase alcohol in Poland is 18, though technically there is no minimum age to drink alcohol (woo!). Remember to drink responsibly and to never drink and drive. The legal blood alcohol content (BAC) for driving in Poland is under 0.02%, significantly lower than the US limit of 0.08%.

PORTUGAL

Portugal draws hordes of backpackers by fusing its timeless inland towns and majestic castles with industrialized cities like Lisbon, whose graffiti-covered walls separate bustling bars from posh fado restaurants. The original backpackers, Portuguese patriarchs like Vasco da Gama, pioneered the exploration of Asia, Africa, and South America, and the country continues to foster such discovery within its borders, with wine regions like the Douro Valley, immaculate forests and mountains in its wild northern region, and 2000km of coastline for tourists to traverse and travel.

greatest hits

- **MOMA MIA.** You'll need a lot of energy for Lisbon nights, so spend your days enjoying the tasty fare at **Moma** (p. 755).

- **BAIRRO ALTO NIGHTLIFE.** Don't fear crowd-induced pit stains in this neighborhood—everyone drinks on the sidewalks (p. 758).

- **ONCE UPON A TIME.** Get your crown ready: a visit to **Sintra** (p. 769) might make you forget you don't actually live in a fairytale.

PORTUGAL

MINHO

Vila Nova de Cerveira
Valença do Minho
Caminha
Viana do Castelo
Minho

Parque Nacional da Peneda-Gerês

Serra-Do Gerês
Caldas de Gerês

Parque Natural de Montesinho

TRÁS-OS-MONTES
Bragança

Costa Verde
Lima
Cávado
Barcelos
Braga
Guimarães
Amarante

Tâmega

Parque Natural do Alvão
Mirandela
Vila Real

Miranda do Douro

Parque Natural do Douro Internacional

Porto
DOURO LITORAL
Serra Do Marão
DOURO ALTO

Espinho

Douro

Ovar

Aveiro
Viseu

BEIRA ALTA

ATLANTIC OCEAN

BEIRA LITORAL

Luso
Buçaco

Mondego

Serra Da Estrêla
Guarda
Manteigas

Coimbra

Parque Natural da Serra dá Estrêla
Sabugal
Sortelha

Figueira da Foz

Costa Da Prata

Conímbriga

Zêzere

Serra Da Gardunha
Monsanto

BEIRA BAIXA

Leiria
Batalha
Nazaré
São Martinho do Porto
Alcobaça
Fátima
Tomar

Castelo Branco

Ilhas Berlengas
Cabo Carvoeiro
Peniche
Caldas da Rainha
Óbidos

Serra De Aire

Tejo

Castelo de Vide
Marvão

RIBATEJO
Santarém
Crato
Portalegre

ESTREMADURA

Ericeira
Vila Franca de Xira
Mafra
Sintra
Queluz

Serra De São Mamede

SPAIN

Cascais
Estoril
⊛ Lisboa

ALTO ALENTEJO
Estremoz
Elvas

Parque Natural de Arrábida
Setúbal

Évora Monte
Évora

Cabo Espichel
Trôia Peninsula
Sesimbra

Alcácer do Sal

Baía de Setúbal

Costa Azul

Sines
Santiago do Cacém
Beja

BAIXO ALENTEJO

Guadiana

Costa Dourada

Mira

Mértola

Lagos
Silves
ALGARVE
Cabo de São Vicente
Sagres
Portimão
Albufeira
Tavira
Vila Real de Santo António

Faro
Olhão

Golfo de Cádiz

0   50 kilometers
0   50 miles

portugal

lisbon

Portugal's capital is a mosaic, comprised of different neighborhoods that all come together to form the cohesive metropolis that is Lisbon. Each district has its own indelible character, from the graffiti-covered party that is Bairro Alto to chic Chiado and on to touristy Baixa and the crumbling tiles of Alfama—cross a single street or descend one steep staircase and you're someplace new. As is typical in Europe, the classic-to-the-point-of-cliché juxtaposition of ancient and modern holds here. But the true joy of Lisbon comes in peeling back the different layers of "old" that simultaneously exist. Pre-WWI tram cars run through the streets past buildings reconstructed after the earthquake of 1755. These are mixed in with remnants of the Renaissance, the Moorish invasion, and the Iron Age. Together, all of these layers form Lisbon, a city as full of surprises as it is of history. To experience its character to the fullest, get lost here. Let your nose lead you to *sardinhas assadas;* stumble through an alleyway to find an architectural marvel; talk to the locals at the hole-in-the-wall and take their advice. We promise you won't regret it.

ORIENTATION

Lisbon's historic center has four main neighborhoods: **Baixa,** where accommodations, shopping, and tourists abound; **Chiado,** where the shopping gets a bit ritzier; nightlife-rich **Bairro Alto,** still farther west; and ancient **Alfama,** on the east side of Baixa. The narrow, winding streets and stairways of Alfama and Bairro Alto can be confusing and difficult to navigate without a good map. The **Lisboa Mapa da Cidade e Guia Turístico** €3) has nearly every street in these neighborhoods labeled and is a good investment if you're going to be exploring Lisbon for a few days. Even so, expect to spend some time aimlessly wandering, as even the most detailed of maps will have a hard time effectively detailing these neighborhoods. The maps at the tourist offices are reliable but do not show the names of many streets, particularly in Alfama and Bairro Alto. **Tram #28E** runs east-west, parallel to the river, and connects all these neighborhoods, with its eastern terminus in the inexpensive and off-the-beaten-path neighborhood of **Graça.** The palm-tree-lined **Avenida da Liberdade** runs north from Baixa all the way to the business district around the Praça do Marquês de Pombal, and on the far western edge of the city lies **Belém,** a neighborhood full of magnificent sights and delicious treats.

Baixa

Baixa, Lisbon's old business hub, is the city's most centrally located neighborhood, and its streets are lined with accommodations and clothing stores. An oasis of order for travelers weary of getting lost in labyrinthine old cities, the entire neighborhood is flat and on a grid. The main pedestrian thoroughfare is the broad **Rua Augusta,** which runs from the massive riverside **Praça do Comércio** to Pr. de Dom Pedro IV, better known as **Rossio.** Ⓜ**Baixa-Chiado** has an entrance at the western end (to your right as you face the river) of R. da Vitória, which runs east to west and crosses Rua Augusta. Connected to Rossio's northwest corner is **Praça dos Restauradores,** a huge urban transit hub where the Rossio train station (for trains to Sintra) and tourist office can be found; it is also the main drop-off point for airport buses. From Pr. dos Restauradores, **Avenida da Liberdade** runs away from Baixa to the **Praça do Marquês do Pombal** and its surrounding business district.

Bairro Alto and Chiado

Bairro Alto (literally, "High Neighborhood") is a hilly stretch of narrow cobblestone streets with graffiti-covered walls and laundry-lined balconies, best known for its unique nightlife and its *fado* (the Portuguese equivalent of soul music, if soul music made you weep like a little girl). The best way to get there is to take the metro to Baixa-Chiado (Chiado exit), walk straight across Largo do Chiado, between the churches, and right up Rua da Misericórdia (it becomes R. de São Pedro de Alcântara) before heading left into Alto's daytime slumber or nighttime madness.

Chiado, slightly down the hill toward Baixa, is a little more clean-cut and cultured than its raucous neighbor to the west. The **Rua Garrett** cuts through the neighborhood, running between the **Largo do Chiado** and the stores and shopping center on R. do Carmo. The **Praça de Luís de Camões,** right next to Lg. do Chiado, connects the two neighborhoods.

Alfama

Alfama, Lisbon's hilly medieval quarter, was the only district to survive the 1755 earthquake, and those who have spent long, hot hours lost in its confusing maze of alleyways might sometimes wish it hadn't. Many alleys are unmarked and take confusing turns and bends; others are long, winding stairways known as *escadinhas;* still others are dead ends. Expect to get lost repeatedly—with or without a detailed map. The **Castelo de São Jorge** sits at the steep hill's peak, where you will find impressive views of all of Lisbon. The **Sé** (cathedral) is closer to the river and to Baixa. When in doubt, walk downhill to get closer to the river, where there is a flat, open area that will help you get your bearings. The **Mouraria** (the old Moorish quarter, more recently a multicultural neighborhood with immigrants from across the globe) is on the north and west slope of the hill, away from the river; and **Graça,** a slightly less confusing neighborhood, sits to the northeast.

Graça

Graça, a hilly, residential district, is one of Lisbon's oldest neighborhoods. An easy tram ride on **28E** to the end of the line drops you off in **Largo da Graça.** On one side of the square is **Igreja da Graça,** a shady park, and a spectacular *miradouro* (viewpoint); the other side (where the tram stops) is a busy intersection lined with cheap eateries. It's an easy walk downhill from Graça into Alfama, or a less confusing tram ride back.

Around Praça do Marquês de Pombal

The large Praça do Marquês de Pombal sits at the end of **Avenida da Liberdade,** opposite Pr. dos Restauradores. This is Lisbon's modern business district, full of department stores, shopping centers, office buildings, and some accommodations. But what space isn't taken up by commerce is lush and green, with multiple expansive parks. To the north of Praça do Marquês de Pombal is the **Parque Eduardo VII,** and to the northeast of that is the impressive **Museu Calouste Gulbenkian,** which is located in the **São Sebastião** district and has its own green space as well. Behind the shopping malls, the back streets of the area are quiet and contain small mom-and-pop shops where the prices tend to be a bit more reasonable than in more tourist-oriented areas.

SIGHTS

Bairro Alto and Chiado

▨ MUSEU ARQUEOLÓGICO DO CARMO
Lg. do Carmo

CHURCH, MUSEUM
☎213 47 86 29

Sick of those big, boring churches that all look the same? This archaeological museum is housed in a 14th-century Gothic church like any other, except it's missing its roof. The ruins became ruins in the 1755 earthquake and ensuing fire, and today they stand as an open courtyard under empty arches where the roof once stood. After you take in the cinematic setting, head inside to the museum— the collection spans four millennia and includes some pretty gruesome Peruvian

portugal

mummy children. But even the sight of potentially undead South American kiddies can't trump the view from beneath the vaulted arches of the church.

i Ⓜ*Baixa-Chiado (Chiado exit, or bus #758, or tram 28E. From Rossio, walk (steeply) up Cç. do Carmo to Lg. do Carmo. €3.50 students and seniors €2, under 14 free.* 🕐 *Open M-Sa Jun-Sept 10am-7pm; Oct-May 10am-6pm.*

IGREJA E MUSEU DE SÃO ROQUE
CHURCH, MUSEUM

Lg. Trindade Coelho ☎213 23 54 44 www.museu-saoroque.com

The Plague reached Lisbon in 1505, brought into the city on an infested ship from Venice. King Manuel I was not too happy about this and requested a relic of São Roque from the Venetians in return, as this saint was supposed to have powers that could ward off disease. That didn't work out, and thousands of Portuguese succumbed to the Black Death. Nevertheless, the Jesuits put up this church in the saint's honor in the 16th century. The alms box on the left side of the nave echoes the awestruck words of many who enter: "Jesus, Maria, Jose" ("Jesus, Mary, and Joseph"). The church is truly magnificent, with not a square inch untouched by the ornate decorations, so be sure to look up at the beautifully painted ceiling. The museum houses a collection of art and relics pertaining to the Jesuits as well as a collection of Eastern art that includes a dazzling chest with glimmering inlay from Macau.

i Ⓜ*Baixa-Chiado (Chiado exit. Bus #758 or tram 28. From Lg. do Chiado, head uphill on R. da Misericórdia; the church is at the far side of the plaza on the right. Museum €2.50, students, under 14, and over 65 free; Su before 2pm free.* 🕐 *Church open M 2-6pm, Tu-W 9am-6pm, Th 9am-5pm, F-Su 9am-6pm. Museum open Tu-W 10am-6pm, Th 2-9pm, F-Su 10am-6pm.*

MUSEU DO CHIADO AND MUSEU NACIONAL DE ARTE CONTEMPORÂNEA
ART MUSEUM

R. Serpa Pinto, 4 ☎213 43 21 48 www.museudochiado-ipmuseus.pt

This constantly updated museum has tons and tons of exhibition space but devotes only a small amount of it to its permanent collection (otherwise it wouldn't stay contemporary for very long, now would it?), which means the temporary exhibitions (four per year) get lots of room for full, comprehensive shows. Consequently, this museum is like a box of chocolates—you never know what you're gonna get. You might see abstract paintings or Portuguese photography or something completely different, but even if it's plastic containers (stacked artistically, rest assured), there will be something intriguing for you to ponder.

i Ⓜ*Baixa-Chiado (Chiado exit. Bus #758, or tram 28E. From Lg. do Chiado, head 1 block toward Baixa (behind you as you exit the metro station), then right down R. Serpa Pinto. €4, seniors €2, students €1.60, under 14 free; Su before 2pm free.* 🕐 *Open Tu-Su 10am-6pm.*

Alfama

🏛 CASTELO DE SÃO JORGE
CASTLE, HISTORIC SITE, VIEWS

Castelo de São Jorge ☎21 880 06 20 www.castelosaojorge.pt

Built by the Moors in the 11th century on the highest point in Lisbon, this hilltop fortress was captured by Dom Afonso Henriques, Portugal's first king, in 1147. With one of the best views in Lisbon, the castle also acts as a one-stop shop for the entire historical Lisbon experience. Walk along the ramparts, see live images of Lisbon fed from an ancient periscope, feel like Indiana Jones at archaeological ruins dating from the Iron Age to the Renaissance (whip optional), and gawk at the seemingly random, yet stunningly beautiful, peacocks that strut about. At night, "Lisboa Who Are You?," a show exclusively comprised of images and Portuguese music, tells the story of Lisbon from beginning to end (€15).

i *Bus #737, or trams #12E and 28E; follow signs to Castelo €7, students and seniors €3.50, under 10 free.* 🕐 *Open daily Mar-Oct 9am-9pm, Nov-Feb 9am-6pm. Last entry 30min. before close. Museum has guided tours daily at noon and 4pm. Periscope 10am-5pm.*

lisbon

LISBON LOUNGE HOSTEL/LIVING LOUNGE HOSTEL
HOSTEL $

R. do Crucifixo, 116 ☎213 46 10 78 www.lisbonloungehostel.com

These nearby hostels, under joint ownership, have large common spaces and spacious rooms with the best interior design around, hostel or not. While Living Lounge has individually decorated rooms, Lisbon Lounge features bright colors and amazing street art. Both offer breakfast, loads of tours and activities (some free), and a delicious, traditional nightly dinner €10) with endless wine.

i *Lisbon Lounge: From Ⓜ Baixa-Chiado, take R. da Vitória exit, then immediate right onto R. do Crucifixo, then 1st left onto R. de São Nicolau, and walk 4 blocks. Living Lounge: From Ⓜ Baixa-Chiado, take R. da Vitória exit, then immediate left onto R. do Crucifixo. Lisbon Lounge: June 1-Sep 15 dorms €22; doubles €60. Apr 15-May 31 and Sept 16-Oct 14 dorms €20; doubles €60. Oct 15-Apr 14 dorms €18; doubles €50. Living Lounge: dorms and doubles same rates as Lisbon Lounge. Apr 15-Oct 14 singles €35; Oct 15-Apr 14 singles €30. ☒ Reception 24hr.*

LISBON DESTINATION HOSTEL
HOSTEL $

R. Primeira de Dezembro, 141, 3rd fl. ☎213 46 64 57 www.rossiopatio.com

Set in the top of the stunningly beautiful Neo-Manueline behemoth that is the Rossio train station, Lisbon Destination Hostel takes the cake for best common area in Baixa, if not Lisbon. With astroturf, tropical music, and a soaring ceiling of glass windows, it feels like you are closer to the Caribbean than the Tejo.

i *Ⓜ Restauradores. Walk away from the giant statue as you exit. The Rossio train station will be on your right. On the 3rd fl. Dorms €18-23; singles €35-40; doubles €30-35. ☒ Reception 24hr.*

LISBON POETS HOSTEL
HOSTEL $

R. Nova da Trindade, 2, 5th fl. ☎213 46 12 41 www.lisbonpoetshostel.com

Not just for the literary snob, this cultured hostel is luxurious enough to satisfy even the least poetic of travelers. The dorm rooms, named for famous poets, are large and clean, and the common room has space for you to write your own couplets in comfort. Activities ranging from city tours to fado nights to cafe crawls take place daily and are free for guests.

i *Ⓜ Baixa-Chiado; take the Pr. do Chiado exit, and turn right up R. Nova da Trindade. Credit card min. €50. Dorms €18-22; private doubles €45-60. Discount with stay in Oporto Poets Hostel (min. 5 nights between the two). ☒ Reception 24hr.*

THE INDEPENDENTE HOSTEL AND SUITES
HOSTEL $

R. São Pedro de Alcântara, 81 ☎213 46 13 81 www.theindependente.pt

In an opulent white building right across from the gorgeous Miradouro de São Pedro, The Independente is quite luxurious for the price. A large staircase leads up to the generous common room looking out over the miradouro. Rooms are sizable and many have small balconies.

i *Ⓜ Baixa-Chiado (Chiado exit). Take R. da Misericórdia until it becomes R. São Pedro de Alcântara. The hostel is on your left and shares a building with a cafe. Breakfast and linens included. Towels €1.50. Lock and keycard €5 deposit. June-Sept dorms €17-20; suites €110. Oct-May dorms €13-18; suites €95. ☒ Reception 24hr.*

SÉ CATEDRAL DE LISBOA
CHURCH, MUSEUM

Lg. da Sé   ☎21 886 67 52

Lisbon's 12th-century cathedral is massive and intimidating, built to double as a fortress, if needed. Its austere Romanesque style makes the few brightly-colored stained glass windows leap out of the walls, where the same ornamentation would be lost in a busy Gothic or Baroque church. The cloisters, an archaeological site perpetually under scaffolding, are well worth the cash, giving visitors a glimpse of the remains of Moorish houses, Roman sewers, and more. The treasury boasts relics, manuscripts, and lots of other shiny valuables.

i *Bus #737, or tram #28E. From Baixa, follow R. Conceição east (to the left as you face the river) up past the church, then turn right onto R. Santo António da Sé and follow the tram tracks; it's the large, building that looks like a fortress. Free. Cloister €2.50. Treasury €2.50. ☒ Church open M 9am-5pm, Tu-Sa 9am-7pm, Su 9am-5pm. Treasury open M-Sa 10am-5pm. Cloister open May-Sept M 10am-5pm, Tu-Sa 10am-6pm; Oct-Apr M-Sa 10am-5pm. Mass Tu-Sa 6:30pm, Su 11:30am.*

Graça

PANTEÃO NACIONAL
TOMBS, HISTORIC SITE

Campo de Santa Clara   ☎21 885 48 39 www.igespar.pt

The Igreja de Santa Engrácia was started in the late 17th century, but once the architect died the king lost interest in the project and the funding dried up, leaving the church unfinished for some 250 years. The dictator Salazar rededicated the building as the National Pantheon, although it now, ironically, houses the remains of some of his staunchest opponents. Start at the ground level and see the tomb of the much beloved Amália Rodrigues, queen of fado, among others, then take the stairs leading all the way up to the top of the dome, a distinctive feature of the Lisbon skyline.

i Ⓜ*Santa Apolónia, bus #34, or tram #28E. Get off tram 28E at Voz do Operário stop in front of Igreja e Mosteiro de São Vicente de Fora, then follow Arco Grande de Cima (to the left of church), then take the 1st right, 1st left, and then another right. €3, students and under 14 free, seniors €1.50. Su before 2pm free for all. ☒ Open Tu-Su 10am-5pm.*

IGREJA E MOSTEIRO DE SÃO VICENTE DE FORA
CHURCH, MONASTERY

Lg. de São Vicente   ☎21 882 44 00

The Church and Monastery of St. Vincent is grandiose, with impressive architecture, vaulted ceilings, and an extremely intricate altar. However, the recorded classical music (to make sure you experience the proper amount of reverence) is a bit much. The attached monastery—a beautiful site in its own right—has a small museum dedicated to the church's history, as well as lots of great features, such as a tiny Baroque chapel, an extremely old cloister, and access to the roof with a magnificent view of the surrounding area.

i Ⓜ*Santa Apolónia, bus #34 or tram #28E. Get off tram 28E in front of the massive white church at the Voz do Operário stop. €4, students and seniors €2. ☒ Open Tu-Su 10am-6pm. Last entry 1hr. before close.*

MUSEU NACIONAL DO AZULEJO
MUSEUM

R. da Madre de Deus, 4   ☎21 810 03 40 mnazulejo.imc-ip.pt

Enter this museum via its tranquil courtyard, passing by the incredible Manueline doorway of the Convento da Madre de Deus. The museum is devoted to the art of the azulejo (glazed and painted tile), one of Portugal's most famous and most ubiquitous forms of art. Some of the tiles are whimsical, others saucy, and others just impressive: the early 18th-century (pre-earthquake) panorama of the city of Lisbon is one of the world's largest works of azulejo).

Ignore the tacky faux-azulejo boards with cut-outs to stick your face in for a photo-op, and move on to the incredible sanctuary to lift your spirits.

i Take bus #794 from Santa Apolónia station bus stop (side closest to the river) to Igreja da Madre de Deus. €5, seniors €2.50, under 14 free. Su before 2pm free for all. ⌚ Open Tu 2-6pm, W-Su 10am-6pm. Last entry 30min. before close.

Belém

The Belém waterfront, a couple of kilometers west of Lisbon's center, is a majestic tribute to Portugal's Age of Discovery and its legendary seafaring spirit. This is where history-changing explorers Vasco da Gama and Prince Henry the Navigator left for distant lands, and the opulence of the new worlds they opened up can be seen today just a short tram ride from Baixa, in Belém. Equally as famous and almost as important as the historic sights is ⓼Pasteis de Belém, a pastry shop with a reputation as rich as its pastries. (R. Belém, 84-92 21 363 74 23 Pastries €1.05 Open daily 9am-11pm.) The easiest way to get to Belém is to take tram 15E from Pr. do Comércio (dir.: Algés) to the Mosteiro dos Jerónimos stop, which is one stop beyond the one labeled Belém.

⓼ MOSTEIRO DOS JERÓNIMOS
CHURCH, MUSEUM

Pr. do Império ☎21 362 00 34 www.mosteirojeronimos.pt

The Hieronymite Monastery was established in 1502 to honor Vasco da Gama's expedition to India. We're guessing the explorer's spirit is pleased with this ornate tribute. The Manueline building has the detail of its Gothic predecessors and the sweeping elegance of the oncoming Renaissance. In the 1980s, the monastery was granted World Heritage Site status by UNESCO and remains in pristine condition, both inside and out. The church contains tombs (both symbolic and actual) of Portuguese kings and bishops. Symbolic tombs (cenotaphs) include areas of tribute to Vasco da Gama and Luís de Camões, Portugal's most celebrated poet. Entrance to the cloister is not cheap (€7), but free Su before 2pm), but it's worth it to see one of Lisbon's most beautiful spaces, which somehow retains its charm despite being filled with hordes of tourists. Those on a shoestring budget can see the chapel for free, but the cloister is the real sight here.

i Tram #15E or bus #28, 714, 727, 729, 743, 749, 751 to Mosteiro dos Jerónimos. Free. Cloister and museum €7, over 65 €3.50, under 14 free; Su before 2pm free. Combined ticket with Torre de Belém €10. ⌚ Open May-Sept Tu-Su 10am-6:30pm; Oct-Apr Tu-Su 10am-5:30pm. Last entry 30min. before close.

⓼ TORRE DE BELÉM
DEFENSE TOWER, VIEWS

Torre de Belém ☎21 362 00 34

Portugal's most famous tower has risen out of the water (except at low tide, when it's connected to the shore by a narrow, sandy isthmus) from the banks of the Tejo for nearly 500 years, gracing visitors' memories and souvenir stores' postcards since its completion in 1519. Be prepared to relive childhood games (no, not The Floor is Lava) as you pretend to fire cannons on two different levels. Then head downstairs and check out the prison cells and ammunition area (hopefully this doesn't also remind you of your childhood). It's worth going up all the way to the top to see breathtaking panoramic views of Belém and the Tejo. There is also a rhinoceros carving in homage to the real rhino the king tried to bring back for the pope, because nothing garners favor from the pope like a large, horned animal.

i From Mosteiro dos Jerónimos, take the unmarked underground walkway in front of the monastery (from entrance, head toward the river; it's a small stairway) to other side of road and tracks and walk west along the river (to the right as you face the water) about 15min. Alternatively, walk in the same direction on the monastery's side of the road and take the pedestrian walkway over the road at the tower. €5, over 65 €2.50, students and under 14 free. Su before 2pm free for all. Combined ticket with Mosteiro dos Jerónimos €10. ⌚ Open May-Sept Tu-Su 10am-6:30pm, Oct-Apr Tu-Su 10am-5:30pm. Last entry 30min. before close.

São Sebastião

MUSEU CALOUSTE GULBENKIAN
Av. de Berna, 45A

MUSEUM

☎21 782 30 00 www.museu.gulbenkian.pt

Want an art history survey course for under €5? This museum has a large and eclectic collection of works from the ancient Mesopotamians and Egyptians to the Impressionists and beyond. The collection belonged to native Armenian and oil tycoon Calouste Gulbenkian, who came to Portugal on vacation in 1942 and never left. When he died, he gave his massive art collection to the state, which, like any good state, decided to charge people to look at it. The building itself is hideous, but the treasures inside are not—in particular the illuminated manuscripts from the Middle East to France seem to have been dunked in molten gold, and the dark, quiet room with a garden view is a lovely place to unwind

i Ⓜ*São Sebastião, or buses #96, 205, 716, 726, 746, 756. Exit* Ⓜ*São Sebastião at Av. António Augusto de Aguiar (north exit) and go straight uphill along the avenue until you reach the massive Pr. Espanha, then turn right. It is NOT the building that looks like a castle in the park to the right; keep going along the avenue. €4, students under 25 and seniors €2, under 12 free. Temporary exhibits €3-5.* Ⓩ *Open Tu-Su 10am-6pm.*

FOOD

Lisbon has some of the best and most reasonably priced restaurants this side of the Rhine, and some of the finest wine to boot. Depending on the neighborhood, an average full dinner will usually run about €10-12 per person, with the *pratos do dia* often only €5-7. Some of the best and least expensive meals can be found in the ubiquitous **pastelarias.** Although the focus of these pastry shops are the counters, which contain mountains of treats, they also serve up tasty and well-priced meals. That said, don't skip the pastries: **pasteis de nata** are generally less than €1 and are the city's most popular sweet. The Portuguese love their coffee, but realize that when you order **cafe,** you are actually ordering a shot of espresso. You can order a "normal" coffee (*abatanado* or *americano*), but you might get some looks; many Portuguese think of it more as soup than real coffee. Local specialties include summertime *caracois* (small snails; look for a restaurant with a sign that says "Há caracois" in the window), *lombo de porco com amêijoas* (pork with clams, much tastier than it sounds), and the Portuguese staples *alheira* (smoked chicken sausage) and *sardinhas assadas* (grilled sardines). But the ultimate Portuguese food is **bacalhau** (codfish). Prepared in over 1000 different ways, cod is practically a religion here. A source of national pride, it can be found in almost any restaurant you visit. Some of the best deals, in terms of getting a lot for a little, are the *tostas,* large grilled sandwiches topped with melted butter that usually cost €2-3. The local traditional drink is **ginjinha** (pronounced "jee-JEE-nyah," also often called *ginja*), a sour cherry liqueur served ice-cold in a shot glass and meant to be sipped. If it's bad, it tastes like cough syrup, but if it's good, it's delicious and refreshing, particularly on hot Lisbon afternoons. It usually costs €1-1.50 and is sometimes served in a shot glass made of chocolate for a little extra dough.

Baixa

⬛ MOMA
R. de São Nicolau, 47

PORTUGUESE, ITALIAN $$

☎914 41 75 36

A white, simple, and clean aesthetic complements this delicious oasis of good food in the desert that is Baixa. Moma's chalk menu tells the story of Portuguese cuisine with an Italian twist. The dishes tend to be cool, light, and creative for the hot summer months, but heavier meals are here for the taking as well (the €9 veal filet is heaven on a plate). Outside is the best place to enjoy your meal; you will find yourself in the middle of the R. de São Nicolau but separated from the touristy madness by umbrellas and bamboo blinds.

i Ⓜ*Baixa-Chiado (Baixa exit). Exit metro station onto R. da Vitória, then right 1 block, and then left onto R. de São Nicolau. Entrees €6-9.* ⚑ *Open M-F noon-6pm.*

BONJARDIM GRILL $$$
Tv. de Santo Antão, 12 ☎213 42 74 24

A little bit past Rossio, this restaurant is just off the food-filled R. de Santo Antão and takes up almost an entire block to serve massive portions for animal lovers (i.e., not the PETA kind) to feast upon. Dine outside and enjoy your meal from the "king of chicken" while watching either crabs and lobsters duke it out in the window aquarium.

i Ⓜ*Restauradores or buses #36, 44, 709, 711, 732, 745, 759. Take Travessa de Santo Antão from the east side of Pr. dos Restauradores. Meals €10-30.* ⚑ *Open Tu 6-11:30pm, W-Su noon-11:30pm. Outdoor seating until 10pm.*

Bairro Alto and Chiado

⚑ **CERVEJARIA TRINDADE** PORTUGUESE $$$
R. Nova da Trindade, 20C ☎213 42 35 06 www.cervejariatrindade.pt

Cervejaria Trindade is famous all over Lisbon for its molhos, beer-based sauces that were invented here. These savory and buttery sauces taste incredible on just about any meat you can think of, and eateries throughout the city will often offer a course "à trindade," named for this establishment. The restaurant is also famous for its history, as it was occupied by a convent as far back as the 13th century (the pulpit is still in the main dining room) and became one of Lisbon's first breweries at the start of the 19th century (don't skip the beer). The enormous dining rooms are covered with azulejos from this period, and the cloister of the convent is used for dining as well.

i *From*Ⓜ*Baixa-Chiado, exit onto Lg. do Chiado, then take a sharp right up R. Nova da Trindade (to left of A Brasileira). Meat dishes à trindade €9-18. Pratos do dia M-F €7.50.* ⚑ *Open daily 10am-2am.*

⚑ **KAFFEEHAUS** AUSTRIAN $$
R. Anchieta, 3 ☎210 95 68 28 www.kaffeehaus-lisboa.com

It's understandable if you didn't come to Lisbon to order in German, but this neo-Bohemian cafe has outrageously good food at great prices. The outdoor seats are on the narrow (and thus shady and breezy) street outside, while the inside of the cafe is air-conditioned and contemporary, with angular lamps and a single wall covered in posters. There is a comprehensive bar, but the real treats are the several refreshing homemade lemonades with unexpected but tasty additions such as ginger. Come on Sunday morning for brunch (€6.50-10).

i *From*Ⓜ*Baixa-Chiado, exit onto Lg. do Chiado, take a very sharp right down R. Garrett 2 blocks, then head right down R. Anchieta. Sandwiches €4-6. Salads €5-10. Entrees €9-17. Vegetarian options €9-11. Coffees €1-3.* ⚑ *Open Tu-Sa 11am-midnight, Su 11am-8pm.*

O FOGAREIRO PORTUGUESE $$
R. da Atalaia, 92 ☎213 46 80 59

As a visitor to Lisbon, it can be difficult to get traditional Portuguese food without stooping to the level of insanely touristy or ridiculously expensive. Luckily, O Fogareiro is there for you, with its tasty plates, its many reasonable pratos do dia, and most importantly, its lack of pushy waiters trying to lure you inside or to their sketchy, nondescript van. It really depends on the place. Order a bottle of wine, some olives, and bacalhau (Portuguese cod), and you will finally have the picturesque dinner you have been waiting for.

i Ⓜ*Baixa-Chiado (Chiado exit), tram 28E, or bus #758 to Lg. do Luís Camões. From there, take R. do Loreto and turn right on R. da Atalaia. Entrees €9-12. Pratos do dia €7-9.* ⚑ *M-Sa 8pm-2am.*

portugal

Alfama

Alfama's maze of winding streets hides many small, traditional restaurants. The cheapest options tend to gather along Rua dos Bacalhoeiros, with the tastiest options located along Rua de São João da Praça.

⬛ POIS, CAFE
CAFE $$

R. de São João da Praça, 93 ☎21 886 24 97 www.poiscafe.com

This Austrian-run cafe is quite comfortable, with couches, book-lined walls, and even a toy corner. Don't worry if it looks crowded inside; tables are shared. Almost everything on the menu has something inventive in it (e.g. apple and pesto on a veggie sandwich), although some more traditional options are available. Don't skip out on the custom lemonades, even though the coffee is almost as good.

i Tram #28E to Sé. From plaza in front of cathedral, walk to the right of cathedral; the cafe is on the right. Lunch menu €5. Baked goods €2-7. ⊙ Open Tu-Su 11am-8pm.

⬛ TASCA BELA
TAPAS, PORTUGUESE $$

R. dos Remédios, 190 ☎96 467 09 64

Tasca Bela deals only in petiscos, the Portuguese version of tapas. Come with friends and enjoy a myriad of reasonably priced small dishes for everyone to share. The restaurant is covered with old-time photos and Portuguese guitars, and they have fado multiple times per week. They are also open late, so it's a great place to fill up when you feel those 2am munchies coming on. Order the chorizo assado (€6) and watch it come out flaming. But beware, you might leave without your eyebrows.

i Ⓜ Santa Apolónia. Head to the right of the Museu Militar, then left onto R. Remédios. Petiscos €1-6. ⊙ Open daily 8pm-4am.

TABERNA MODERNA
MODERN PORTUGUESE $$$

R. dos Bacalhoeiros, 18 ☎21 886 50 39

This restaurant sits close to the water, but that doesn't mean it's the same as all of its traditional Portuguese neighbors. As the name suggests, Taberna Moderna puts modern twists on Portuguese food by bringing in foreign influences, including Japanese and Italian. The dining room is wide open and minimalistic but gains personality from the giant nude painting adorning one of the walls.

i Ⓜ Terreiro do Paço. From the north end of Pr. Comércio with the river behind you, take a right onto R. da Alfândega, then take a left after 3 blocks. The restaurant is on your right. Entrees €9-14. ⊙ Open Tu-W 7:30pm-midnight, Th-Sa 7:30pm-2am.

ÓH CALDAS
PORTUGUESE $$$

R. de São Mamede, 22 ☎21 887 57 11

This traditional restaurant (with an untraditional honeycomb design on the wall) has favorites like sardinhas assadas (grilled sardines), alheira (smoked chicken sausage), and an ever-changing three-course daily menu (€12). Its location on the scenic route between the Sé (cathedral) and the Castelo de São Jorge makes it a convenient Alfama stop.

i From Baixa, follow R. Conceicao east toward Alfama (to left as you face the river), just past the Igreja da Madalena. Head left up Tv. Almada for 3 blocks, then left onto R. São Mamede. Daily menu €12. ⊙ Open daily noon-4pm and 8pm-midnight.

Graça

⬛ HAWELI TANDOORI
INDIAN $$

Tv. do Monte, 14 ☎21 886 77 13

A small island in a sea of pastelarias and other Portuguese cheap eats, Haweli Tandoori offers something that isn't found anywhere else in Graça: Indian food. Not only is it Indian, it's also delicious. The chicken tikka masala (€8) is savory, and the garlic naan (€1.50) is buttery and scrumptious. Naturally, plenty of vegetarian options are also available. And most surprisingly, the vast majority of the clientele is comprised of locals (everyone gets tired of codfish, eventually).

i *Take tram #28E to end of the line; walk down the street past the big church, and take a left onto Tv. do Monte. Naan €1-2. Entrees €6-10. ☾ Open M noon-3pm and 7-10:30pm; W-Su noon-3pm, 7-10:30pm.*

O VICENTINHO
PORTUGUESE $

R. da Voz do Operário, 1A

With a strikingly orange interior, O Vicentinho offers a comfortable place to sit down and enjoy a meal. Nice wooden tables give the ambience of a real restaurant at the prices of a pastelaria. Finally, you can enjoy your Sande Mista (ham and cheese sandwich; €2) without having to stand at a counter, staring at a blank, white, tile wall or pretending to text someone in order to avoid making awkward eye contact.

i Ⓜ*Santa Apolonia, bus #34 or tram #28E. Get off tram 28E in front of the massive white church at the Voz do Operário stop. Sandwiches €2. Pratos do dia €6. ☾ Open M-Sa 9am-7pm.*

NIGHTLIFE

Bairro Alto

▥ ASSOCIAÇÃO LOUCOS & SONHADORES
BAR

Tv. do Conde do Soure, 2 ☎213 47 82 50

A few minutes away from the craziness of the Bairro Alto scene, the Crazies' and Dreamers' Association sits quietly in a nondescript building, with only a small, mysterious yet welcoming wooden sign on the door. Once inside, you will be glad that this gem is a well-kept secret. Dimly lit, this smoky bar is filled with clutter, paintings, and books. The chatter of friends and the smooth sounds of jazz somehow allow it to be simultaneously gritty, sophisticated, and sincere. Beer is cheap, bar snacks are on the table, and cigs are available at the bar.

i Ⓜ*Restauradores. Cross the square and take a left onto Cç. da Gloria in the northwest corner, then take a right on R. São Pedro de Alcântara. Take a left onto R. Luisa Todi, which becomes Tv. do Conde do Soure. Beer €1.10. ☾ Open Tu-Su 10pm-3am.*

▥ PAVILHÃO CHINÊS
LOUNGE

R. de Dom Pedro V, 89 ☎213 42 47 29

A little north of the main Bairro Alto scene, this nightlife spot is a bit more laid-back (and indoors) than its raucous neighbors, but it's hardly boring. A massive labyrinth, Pavilhão Chinês feels like a clash of the Victorian and the absurd, with thousands of figurines and odd paintings covering the place from floor to ceiling, while men in fancy blue vests tend the ornate wooden bars. There is a huge menu of teas and classic drinks, like the Sidecar (they're bringin' it back, baby) presented in a 50-page menu-cum-graphic novel.

i *Bus #758. From Pr. de Luís de Camões, follow R. da Misericórdia up toward the miradouro, and keep following the same street as it bends to the left and becomes R. de Dom Pedro V. Beer €3. Tea €4. Drinks €6-9. ☾ Open M-Sa 6pm-2am, Su 9pm-2am.*

PORTAS LARGAS
BAR, MUSIC

R. da Atalaia, 105 ☎213 46 63 79

This staple of the Bairro Alto scene has live music every night (sometimes really good, other times unfortunate covers of '80s songs that are so bad they're good) and some of the biggest, strongest caipirinhas (the national cocktail of Brazil, made from sugar cane rum, sugar, and lime) and mojitos (around €5-7). True to its name, the large doors allow a good deal of traffic to make its way inside, but you can enjoy the music and drinks just outside if things get too crowded.

Just don't expect to be able to loiter inside and enjoy the music without buying a drink.

i ⓂBaixa-Chiado (Chiado exit). Bus #758 or tram 28E. Walk up R. da Misericórdia 3 blocks from Pr. de Luís de Camões, then left or 5 blocks. Beer €4. Cocktails €5-7. ⓉOpen Jul-Sept M-Th 7pm-2am, F-Sa 7pm-3am, Su 7pm-2am; Oct-Jun M-Th 8pm-2am, F-Sa 8pm-3am, Su 8pm-2am.

BICA ABAIXO
BAR

R. da Bica de Duarte Belo, 62 ☎213 47 70 14 www.bicaabaixo.blogspot.pt

This bar is located on the steep slope of the shiny, silver Elevador da Bica funicular, just to the south of the center of Bairro Alto. It's perfect for those making the trek down to the river or for those sick of Bairro Alto's cheaply made drinks—the native Brazilians who own and run this small bar make the best caipirinhas €3.50) in town, crushed, mashed and mixed together right in front of you.

i ⓂBaixa-Chiado (Chiado exit). Or tram 28E to Calhariz-Bica. From Pr. de Luís de Camões, follow R. do Loreto (far-right corner of plaza, with your back to the metro station) 3 blocks, then turn left down R. da Bica de Duarte Belo the bar is on the left. Beer €1.50. Mixed drinks €3-4. ⓉOpen daily 9pm-2am.

Alfama

🞖 LUX
CLUB

Av. do Infante Dom Henrique ☎21 882 08 90 www.luxfragil.com

This club is known far and wide as one of the best clubs in Western Europe; Lisboans abroad will tell you that if you visit one discoteca in Lisbon, it has to be this one. The enormous riverside complex has three stories of debauchery, though you'll leave with a few more of your own Chill on the calm rooftop with amazing views, start to get schwasty at a slightly more intense bar on the floor below that, then descend into the maelstrom on the lowest level to find a raging disco, howling and shrieking with electronic music. Drinks are pricey (cocktails €8-12) and everything is cutting edge. "We cannot escape from each other" is written all around the main bar, giving creepy single guys a great segue into awful pickup lines. The bouncers tend to be very selective, so just act cool and try to get on their good side by being polite and speaking Portuguese. Dress well—only wear jeans or sneakers if the jeans are super-skinny and the sneakers are canvas high-tops, since the stylin' hipster look tends to play well.

i ⓂSanta Apolónia, bus #28, 34, 706, 712, 735, 759, 781, 782, 794. Just east of Santa Apolónia train station, on the side of the tracks closest to the river. Cover usually €12. ⓉOpen Tu-Sa midnight-6am.

🞖 GINJA D'ALFAMA
GINJINHA

R. de São Pedro, 12

Hidden in the heart of Alfama, this tiny hole-in-the-ancient-wall bar specializes in ginjinha, Lisbon's native wild-cherry liqueur, and serves it up cheap and ice cold (€1). You can take it outside to the small tables around the corner, which are much cooler than the stifling bar itself. It's a great place to start the night, serving sandwiches for a good carbo-load before moving on to more raucous nightlife.

i Bus #28, 34, 706, 712, 735, 759, 781, 782, 794. Walk down R. São João da Praça, to the right of Sé Cathedral as you're facing it, and follow the same street (bear left at the fork 1 block past the cathedral) as it becomes R. São Pedro; it's a small store on the left side. Ginjinha €1. Sandwiches €1.50-2.50. ⓉOpen M 9:30am-midnight, W-Su 9:30am-midnight.

RESTÔ
BAR, CIRCUS

Costa do Castelo, 7 ☎21 885 55 50 www.chapito.org

This bar has amazing views over Alfama and the Tejo, though they are best enjoyed during the daytime. At night, the outside patio comes alive with a carnival feel, and not without reason—it's on the grounds of Chapitô, a gov-

lisbon

ernment-funded clown school. On most evenings, there are circus shows, with tightrope walkers and trapeze artists practicing aerial acrobatics over the party below. Go downstairs to enjoy the separate, dark and smoky bar that usually has live music, albeit fewer clowns.

i Bus #737 to Costa do Castelo. From Baixa, it's a long walk uphill: follow R. da Conceição east toward Alfama (left as you face the river), past Igreja da Madalena, and up Tv. Almada to the left to R. São Mamede. Go up the steep and windy Tv. Mata, then left up Cç. Conde de Penafiel to Costa do Castelo, then right. Beer €2. Cocktails €5-7. ☼ Open M-F noon-3pm and 7:30pm-1am, Sa-Su noon-1:30am.

Riverfront: Cais do Sodré, Santos, Alcântara, Docas

OP ART   CLUB
Doca de Santo Amaro   ☎936 24 09 81   www.opartcafe.com
During the daytime, this is a pleasant spot to sit by the water and watch the waves while listening to the hum of the cars passing over the bridge. On Friday and Saturday nights, it's a completely different story. Guest DJs rattle the panes of the all-glass structure, pumping hip hop, house beats, and more until the sun starts to rise over the Tejo. Stay all night and see the 25 de Abril Bridge (modeled after the Golden Gate Bridge) light up in the morning for the full experience.

i Buses #28, 201, 714, 720, 732, 738 or trams #15E and 18E. Head toward the bridge along the waterfront. Cove €5-10; includes 1 drink. Beer €2.50. Cocktails €5-7. ☼ Open Tu-Th 3pm-2am, F-Sa 3pm-6am, and Su 3pm-2am.

DOCK'S CLUB   CLUB
R. da Cintura do Porto de Lisboa, 226   ☎21 390 02 22
This disco near the bridge is famous for its Ladies' Nights on Tuesday (well, Wednesday morning), when women not only get in free but also get €14 in free drinks. Spare your friends the social commentary on this potentially sexist practice and enjoy the music blasting from the two different bars inside or the fresh air on the patio in back.

i Buses #28, 201, 714, 720, 732, 738 or trams #15E and 18E. Cove €10-15. Beer €3. Cocktails €6. ☼ Open Tu midnight-6am, Th-Sa midnight-6am.

MUSICBOX   CLUB, LIVE MUSIC
R. Nova do Carvalho, 24   ☎21 347 31 88   www.musicboxlisboa.com
This venue gets great indie and punk bands to play early in the night (sets usually start at 11pm), and the best local DJs spin from 2am until closing, which is shortly after dawn. The line is often so long you'll be surprised there's not a roller coaster waiting when you finally get to the door, but it's worth the wait. The space is small enough that 100 people will feel like a great crowd, but there will likely be even more than that.

i Ⓜ Cais do Sodré or bus #28, 35, 36, 44, 706, 714, 735, 758, 760, 781, 782, 794 to C. Sodré. From Pr. Luís de Camões, walk all the way down R. Alecrim, then take a sharp right once you get to the bottom to double back under the bridge. Cover €6-10; usually includes 1 drink. ☼ Open W-Sa 11pm-7am.

ARTS AND CULTURE

Fado

A mandatory experience for visitors, Lisbon's trademark form of entertainment is traditional fado, an art form combining music, song, and narrative poetry. Its roots lie in the Alfama neighborhood, where women whose husbands had gone to sea would lament their fado (fate). Singers of fado traditionally dress in black and sing mournful tunes of lost love, uncertainty, and the famous feelings of saudade (to translate saudade as "loneliness" would be a gruesome understatement). However, many fado venues will have less melancholic songs and even some comical crowd pleasers (if you understand Portuguese, at least). Many fado houses are located in Bairro Alto and in Alfama between the cathedral and the water, and finding one is not difficult, as you can hear snippets of songs drifting into the streets as you pass by (fadistas don't use microphones, but that doesn't mean you won't hear them). Almost all fado houses are rather touristy, but locals—especially older folk—still crowd in amongst the hordes of tourists. Expensive fado houses with mournfully high minimums include Café Luso (Tv. Queimada, 10 213 42 22 81 www.cafeluso.pt €16 min. Open daily 7:30pm-2am) and Adega Machado (R. Norte, 91 213 22 46 40 www.adegamachado.pt €16 min. Open Tu-Su 8pm-3am). There are also some well-marked and easy-to-find places on Rua de São João da Praça in Alfama, including Clube de Fado, with road signs pointing you in that direction all the way from Baixa. The places listed below are either free or truly worth the money.

A TASCA DO CHICO
BARRIO ALTO

R. do Diário de Notícias, 39
☎965 05 96 70

This Bairro Alto fado location is popular with locals and has no cover charge or drink minimum. You're going to want a cold drink, however, as everyone is packed in like sardinhas by the time the fado starts. Many choose to grab a spot at the open window and watch from the cool(er) street outside. Pretty much any amateur fadista who wants to take a turn can sing, so on any given night you can hear something you'd rather forget followed by the next big thing in fado.

i Ⓜ*Baixa-Chiado (Chiado exit). From Pr. Luís de Camões, head up R. Norte (to the right near the far side of the plaza if your back is to the metro station) for 1 block, then take a quick left. Next, turn right up R. Diário de Notícias. Beer €1.50.* Ⓩ *Open M-Sa 6pm-3:30am. Fado starts around 9:30pm, but arrive much earlier to get a seat.*

VOSSEMECÊ
ALFAMA

R. de Santo António da Sé, 18
☎218 88 30 56 www.vossemece.com

This fado joint, conveniently located near Baixa, is housed in a beautiful, if oddly shaped, stable; arched ceilings and heavy stone columns run farther than the eye can see into the darkness of the surprisingly spacious restaurant. The fadistas rotate, each singing a couple of songs ranging from lively and funny to mournful and heart-wrenching. There's no cover charge or drink minimum, and the drinks are reasonably priced (€3 50-6.50) and quite good; however, the environment lends itself more toward sitting down for a nice meal with a bottle of wine.

i Ⓜ*Baixa-Chiado (Baixa exit), or tram #28E. Follow R. Conceiçao east toward Alfama (to the left as you face the river) past Igreja da Madalena; it's on the corner across the street to the left. Drinks €3.50-6.50. Entrees €10-15.* Ⓩ *Open M-Tu noon-4pm and 8:30pm-midnight, Th-Su noon-4pm and 8:30pm-midnight. Fado performances 9pm-midnight.*

Feiras Markets

FEIRA DA LADRA
GRAÇA

Campo de Santa Clara

Held in Graça near the edge of Alfama, the so-called "thief's market" is Lisbon's best known feira. The stalls at this market, which takes place every Tuesday and Saturday, stretch from the Mosteiro de São Vicente da Fora to the Panteão Nacional, with vendors selling treasures (ornate antique silverware), junk (used tennis balls), and everything in between (bootlegged kung-fu action movies). Prices are flexible, and bargaining is encouraged, but initially posing too low of an offer can be taken as an insult. Hawk-like vision may be necessary to spot the diamonds in the rough, but if you want anything worth having, get there early before the tour groups pick the place clean.

i *Take tram #28E to Igreja e Mosteiro de São Vicente de Fora, then walk to the left of the big white church.* Ⓩ *Open Tu and Sa 7am-2pm.*

ESSENTIALS
Practicalities

- **TOURIST OFFICE: Main Tourist Office.** (Pr. Restauradores, 1250 ☎21 347 56 60 www.
  visitlisboa.com *i* ⓂRestauradores, or bus #36, 44, 91, 709, 711, 732, 745, or 759. On west
  side of Pr. Restauradores, in Palácio da Foz. ◫ Open daily 9am-8pm.) The **Welcome Center**
  is the city's main tourist office where you can buy tickets for sightseeing buses and the **Lisboa
  Card,** which includes transportation and discounted admission to most sights for a flat fee.
  (R. Arsenal, 15 ☎21 031 28 10) The **airport branch** is located near the terminal exit. (☎21
  845 06 60 ◫ Open daily 7am-midnight.) There are also information kiosks in Santa Apolónia,
  Belém, and on R. Augusta in Baixa.
- **CURRENCY EXCHANGE: NovaCâmbios** in Rossio. (Pr. Dom Pedro IV, 42 ☎21 324 25
  53 www.novacambios.com ⓂRossio. Bus #36, 44, 91, 709, 711, 732, 745, or 759. On west
  side of Rossio plaza. ◫ Open M-F 8:30am-3pm.)
- **INTERNET: Biblioteca Municipal Camões** has free internet access. (Lg. Calhariz, 17 ☎21 342
  21 57 www.blx.cm-lisboa.pt *i* ⓂBaixa-Chiado, tram 28E, or bus #58 or 100. From Pr. Luís
  de Camões, follow R. Loreto for 4 blocks. ◫ Open Jul 16-Sept 15 M-F 11am-6pm; Sept 16-Jul
  15 Tu-F 10:30am-6pm.)
- **POST OFFICE: Correios** main office is on Pr. Restauradores. (Pr. Restauradores, 58 ☎213 23
  89 71 www.ctt.pt *i* ⓂRestauradores. Bus #336, 44, 91, 709, 711, 732, 745, or 759. ◫
  Open M-F 8am-10pm, Sa-Su 9am-6pm.)

Emergency

- **POLICE: Tourism Police Station** provides police service for foreigners. (Pr. Restauradores,
  1250 ☎21 342 16 24 *i* ⓂRestauradores. Bus #36, 44, 91, 709, 711, 732, 745, or 759. On
  west side of Pr. Restauradores, in Palácio da Foz next to the tourist office.)
- **PHARMACY: Farmácia Azevedo and Filhos** in Rossio posts a schedule of pharmacies open
  late at night, as do most other pharmacies; or just look for a lighted, green cross. (Pr. Dom
  Pedro IV, 31 ☎21 343 04 82 *i* ⓂRossio. Bus #36, 44, 91, 709, 711, 732, 745, or 759.
  In front of metro stop at the side of Rossio closest to river. ◫ Open daily 8:30am-7:30pm.)
- **HOSPITAL/MEDICAL SERVICES:** Lisbon's main hospital is **Hospital de São José.** (R. José
  António Serrano ☎21 884 10 00 *i* ⓂMartim Moniz. Bus #34, 708, or 760. ◫ Open 24hr.)
  Hospital de São Luis is in Bairro Alto. (R. Luz Soriano, 182 *i* ⓂBaixa-Chiado. From Pr. Luís de
  Camões, follow R. Loreto 4 blocks, then turn right onto R. Luz Soriano. ◫ Open daily 9am-8pm.)

Getting There

BY PLANE

All flights land at **Aeroporto de Lisboa** (LIS; ☎21 841 35 00), near the northern edge of
the city. The cheapest way to get to town from the airport is by **bus.** To get to the bus
stop, walk out of the terminal, turn right, and cross the street to the bus stop, marked
by yellow metal posts with arrival times of incoming buses. Buses #44 and 745 (€1.75.
◫ 15-20min., daily every 25min., 6am-12:15am) run to Pr. Restauradores, where they
stop in front of the tourist office. The express AeroBus #1 runs to the same locations
(€3.50 ◫ 15min., daily every 20min., 7am-11pm) and is a much faster option during
rush hours. A **taxi** downtown costs €10-15, but fares are billed by time, not distance,
so watch out for drivers trying to take a longer route.

BY TRAIN

Those traveling in and out of Lisbon by train are regularly confused, as there are
multiple major train stations in Lisbon, all serving different destinations. The express
and inexpensive **Alfa Pendular** line runs between Braga, Porto, Coimbra, and Lisbon.

Regional trains are slow and can be crowded; buses are slightly more expensive but faster and more comfortable. **Urbanos** trains run from Lisbon to Sintra and to Cascais, with stops along the way, and are very cheap and reliable. Contact **Comboios de Portugal** for more information (☎80 820 82 08 www.cp.pt). Those who want to head south should go to the **Entrecampos** station. **Estação Cais do Sodré** is right at the river, a 5min. walk west from Baixa or a quick metro ride to the end of the green line. **Estação Rossio** is the gorgeous neo-Manueline building between Rossio and Pr. Restauradores and services almost all Lisbon suburbs, with lines ending in Sintra, Cascais, Azambuja, and Sado. **Estação Santa Apolónia** is one of the main international and inter-city train stations in Lisbon, running trains to the north and east. It is located on the river to the east of Baixa; to get there, take the blue metro line to the end of the line. Trains run between Santa Apolónia and: Aveiro (€26 ⏰ 2½hr., 16 per day 6am-9:30pm); Braga (€32.50 ⏰ 3½hr., 4 per day 7am-7pm); Coimbra (€22.50 ⏰ 2hr., 20 per day 6am-10pm); and Porto (€24-30 ⏰ 3hr., 16 per day 6am-11pm). **Estação Oriente** runs southbound trains. The station is near the Parque das Nações, up the river to the east of the center; take the red metro line to the end of the line. Trains run between Oriente and Faro (€21-22 ⏰ 3½-4hr., 5 per day 8am-8pm) with connections to other destinations in the Algarve.

BY BUS

Lisbon's bus station is close to Ⓜ Jardim Zoológico but can be hard to find. Once at the metro stop, follow exit signs to Av. C. Bordalo Pinheiro. Exit the metro, go around the corner, and walk straight ahead 100m; then cross left in front of Sete Rios station. The stairs to the bus station are on the left. **Rede Expressos** (☎70 722 33 44 www.rede-expressos.pt) runs buses between Lisbon and: Braga (€20 ⏰ 4-5hr., 14-16 per day 7am-12:15am); Coimbra (€14 ⏰ 2hr., 24-30 per day 7am-12:15am); and Lagos (€19.50 ⏰ 5hr., 14-16 per day 7:30am-1am).

Getting Around

Carris (☎21 361 30 00 www.carris.pt) is Lisbon's extensive, efficient, and relatively inexpensive transportation system and is the easiest way to get around the city, which is covered by an elaborate grid of subways, buses, trams, and *elevadores* (funiculars, useful for getting up the steep hills). Fares purchased on board buses, trams, or *elevadores* cost €1.75; the subway costs €1.15, but you must first purchase a rechargeable *viva viagem* card €0.50). The easiest and most cost- and time-effective option for those who will use a lot of public transportation is the unlimited 24hr. **bilhete combinado** (€5), which can be used on any Carris transport and means you don't have to go into a metro station to recharge your card before getting on a bus or tram. You can buy the *bilhete combinado* in any metro station, and you can fill it with up to seven days' worth of unlimited travel.

BY BUS

Carris buses (€1.75, €1.15 with *viva viagem* card) go to just about any place in the city, including those not served by the metro.

BY METRO

The metro (with €1.15 *viva viagem* card) has four lines that cross the center of Lisbon and go to the major train stations. metro stations are marked with a red "M" logo. Trains run daily 6:30am-1am.

BY TRAM

Trams (€1.75, €1.15 with *viva viagem* card) are used by tourists and locals alike to get around. Many vehicles predate WWI. Line 28E runs through Graça, Alfama, Baixa, Chiado, and Bairro Alto; line 15E goes from the Pr. Comércio to Belém, passing the clubs of Santos and Alcântara.

Lisbon

BY TAXI

Taxis in Lisbon can be hailed on the street throughout the center of town. Good places to find cabs include the train stations and main plazas. Bouncers will be happy to call you a cab after dark. **Rádio Táxis de Lisboa** (☎21 811 90 00) and **Teletáxis** (☎21 811 11 00) are the main companies.

coimbra

Welcome to Coimbra, one of the world's oldest college towns. Home to the 700-year-old University of Coimbra, this hilltop city caters to a unique cohort of people: college students, which is great news for you. In Coimbra, you will find cheap meals, cheap drinks, and plenty of secluded spots to read a book or gaze out across a sea of stucco walls and red roofs to the Mondego River. Party all night on Tuesdays and Thursdays during term, allegedly the best nights to go out, or any given weekend during the summer holidays, and during your days off, spend hours wandering through the ancient cobbled streets in search of the University's famous Joanina library. If you're visiting for only an afternoon, you're bound to see men dressed in Hogwarts-esque black robes, strumming guitars and trying to serenade pretty girls—these are the University's *fado* singers, who may very well try to serenade you, or at least give you a tour of one of the world's most picturesque universities. Even if you're visiting Portugal to get away from school, let yourself be a student for a day. The kids in Coimbra certainly know how to have a good time.

SIGHTS

FADO AO CENTRO   NEIGHBORHOOD

Rua Quebra Costas 7, 3000-340 Almedina   ☎239 837 060 www.fadoaocentro.com/en

Lisbon isn't the only city known for its traditional Fado music. Coimbra's Fado is slightly different than that of Lisbon, which is characterized by its melancholic *saudade* tones. Instead, Coimbra's Fado originates from the halls of its very university, where male students would serenade their female classmates on the streets or underneath their windows (classic). Wander through the avenues of Coimbra on any given afternoon and you may see them, dressed in black capes and carrying uniquely-fashioned guitars (Coimbra guitars, to be exact).

While many restaurants provide free Coimbra Fado while you dine, Fado ao Centro offers its visitors live shows with a bit of a history lesson and, to finish it all off, a refreshing glass of Port wine. Sure, the music costs €4.10, but despite being a popular tourist destination, all the music played at Fado ao Centro is authentic and charming. Even better, while tourists can listen and experience the music, the musicians explain the history of their music after every few songs or so, just to contextualize the experience for listeners. The performances last for 50min., during which the musicians sample several styles and song types, including the live serenade. Traditionally, in this form of serenading, a male university student goes to the street under the window of a woman he loves, and he sings her a song (accompanied by guitar). If she likes the song, she will switch on and off her light three times. If any passersby like the song, instead of clapping, they make a sound similar to clearing one's throat. At Fado ao Centro, you will have the opportunity to try the fun grunt yourself, in a group of other visitors.

Shows occur every night at 6pm. If you're visiting with a group, it's recommended that you reserve seats ahead of time, as there usually is a large stand-by crowd waiting outside the door. Once you're in, the ambiance is magical. The small room is shut only by red velvet curtains to make the room completely dark, old Fado musicians pictures litter the walls, and the communal spirit of the performance truly make for an outstanding experience.

The cultural center is also open daily to provide free information about Fado in Coimbra. Stop by from 4-5:30pm to hear musicians rehearse.

i Performances €10. ☼ Cultural center open daily 10am-7pm. Performances 6pm.

MUSEU NACIONAL DE MACHADO DE CASTRO
MUSEUM

Largo Dr. Jose Rodrigues   ☎239 853 070   www.museumachadocastro.pt

Not only does the Museu Nacional de Machado de Castro host an incredibly diverse array of items, it organizes them in such an enticing way that you'll learn more and enjoy the actual visit itself, in addition to the artifacts. Start on the bottom floor of the Roman Cryptoporticum, which was erected in the first century as a political, administrative, and religious center of Aeminium Roman Coimbra. You'll find yourself wandering through a labyrinth of arches and tunnels in a cool, dark space, which includes statues, busts of ancient Roman kings, and other figures. Once you complete the two levels of the ancient Roman ruins, head back upstairs to the museum's art gallery, which hosts a rich collection of Flemish and Portuguese mannerist work, particularly focusing on religious themes. This museum does a great job of organizing its materials, particularly its paintings and precious metals, as each are accompanied with an extensive description and analysis of the piece. In addition to the paintings, the museum boasts incredible views of the city from its crystal clear windows, and accompanying each view is a description of what the visitor sees through the window, such as ancient churches and old architectural features.

Just as cool as these awesome views is the museum's collection of precious metalworks, which are displayed in lit-up black cases that are almost like modern works of art themselves. Here, you'll find ruby-encrusted crowns, ornate golden chalices, and dozens of different reliquaries holding ancient bones (or, in the case of a small cross, teeth!). In the next set of rooms, you can admire original azulejos (Muslim wall tiles) imported from Sevilla, as well as rugs, carriages, and beautiful pottery work dating back to the 16th century.

Free to any passerby is the museum's courtyard, which overlooks Coimbra and is especially beautiful during sunset. Enjoy a meal on the museum's terrace (nope, you don't need to purchase a ticket to dine here!) or simply relax and enjoy the stunning views.

i €5, students €3. ☼ Open Apr-Sept Tu-Su 10am-6pm; Oct-Mar 10am-12:30pm, 2-6pm.

FOOD

COMPOSTU TAVERN
PORTUGUESE $$

Rua Capitao Luis Gonzaga, 27/29   ☎23 970 38 92

Are you willing to take a bit of a hike for your meal? If so, you'll find that Compostu Tavern is totally worth it, especially once you take your first bite into a francesinha, the restaurant's speciality. What is a francesinha, you may ask? Well, it's a typical Portuguese sandwich usually made from bread, cured ham, steak, tomato, cheese, and a special sauce. Sometimes, you'll find your francesinha will be made with French toast with an egg over easy cracked over the top. Trust us, it's quite filling. Compostu's francesinha is classic Portugal. Try Novilho, French toast with bacon, sausage, steak, cheese, French fries, and an egg, all drowned in a savory, slightly spicy and piping hot secret sauce (€10). If you're a vegetarian (and you're visiting Portugal?!), try the French toast with lettuce, corn, mushrooms, soybeans, tomato, onion, cheese, boiled egg, and French fries (€11). Try a few sides to curb your hunger even more, like fried eggs (€0.50), soup of the day (€1.50), or mixed salad (€2.50). You can also try small fish dishes to start, like shrimp patties (€1.50) or fried prawns in curry sauce (€8). Their starter

GRANDE HOSTEL COIMBRA

Rua Antero Quental 196   ☎239 108 212 www.grandehostelcoimbra.com

Situated on a quiet street corner just off Coimbra's main plaza and steps away from the city's world famous university, the Grande Hostel Coimbra has an excellent location for any traveler visiting the area. Its large facilities (and by large, we mean multiple stories) offer travelers a beautiful terrace/patio on which to dine, a large kitchen (free breakfast is included, as are coffee and tea all day), comfortable beds, rooms with lovely views of the historic old city, and comfortable common rooms, one that has a television set, a collection of movies, and a book exchange. While the facilities aren't squeaky clean like those of government-run hostels, you'll find the Grande Hostel cozy, sort of like home. Plenty of large windows allow natural lighting to flow into the rooms and showers are large—the perfect combination. Enjoy a drink from the hostel's mini bar (cheap beer and soda offered) on the patio as the sun sets, get to know the hostel staff, or stroll down to the old city for a night of jazz during the summer (recommended by the owner, who definitely knows a lot). The hostel staff can also direct you to a tip-based walking tour (only on weekdays) and other activities in the city.

When you first arrive, don't be afraid of the doodle-like paintings decorating the hostel's walls. One, which has a girl's body and a panda's head, swings eerily from a swingset while a man with a lion head photographs her. Instead of focusing on the weird painting thing (that doesn't match the style of the hostel at all), focus on climbing all of those stairs. Yep, there's a ton until you actually get to reception. Good workout though, right?

i Mixed dorms €13-18, privates €19. ☒ Check-in 2-10:30pm.

SERNATA HOSTEL

Largo da se Velha 21/23   ☎239 853 130 www.serenatahostel.com

Serenata is located in the heart of everything that is old in Coimbra, which means it's in the center of everything in Coimbra. Steps away from the old cathedral in the Largo se Velha plaza, you'll find yourself with quite a hike from the bus station, but you'll be seconds away from the university and, naturally, all of the hottest (and cheapest!) nightlife around. The hostel is housed in what was once the musical conservatory of the University of Coimbra, offers free traditional breakfast and a pub crawl (which you'll be hard pressed to find elsewhere in the city), two lovely terraces, and incredible views of Coimbra. The rooms are large and clean. Make sure to talk to the staff about where to eat and visit in the city; they know hidden gems and aren't afraid to spoil them!

If you're staying at Serenata during the university's academic term, even better. You'll rub elbows with typical party-crazy college students who find the best spots to drink and be merry (Muelas, for example), all of which seem to be located in the same square as the hostel. So follow the students!

One of the highlights of Serenata is its breakfast of teas, jams, honey, ham, marmalade, and cereals. You can fill yourself up without spending a buck downtown. Now, let's work on getting them to buy some Nutella...

i Mixed dorms €15-16, privates €17-22. ☒ Reception 24hr.

portugal

of diced pork in wine garlic (€5) is heavenly and a great way to start into that francesinha, although if you don't like the idea of eating French toast for dinner, you can always ask for a different plate, like beef, hamburgers, or omelettes. Take your friends or a significant other to the top floor of the restaurant for a beer, since the views from Compostu Tavern are beautiful and its rustic decor suitable for either occasion. Watch a game on the television, or sit by the window for some fresh air while digging in. And don't worry about the portion sizes—the hike back to your hostel will get you fit and digested in no time.

i *Francesinha €8.50-11. Sides €0.50-5. Starters €1-8. ② Open M-F 4pm-2am, Sa noon-2am.*

GALERIA BAR SANTA CLARA

BAR $

Rua António Augusto Gonçalves, 67   ☎965 877 055 http://galeriasantaclara.blogspot.pt

From the freshness of its food to the quirkiness of its decor, Galeria Bar Santa Clara is the perfect place to unwind and recharge after a day of trekking up and down the hills of Coimbra. Sit on its terrace, underneath a beautiful canopy of green, leafy vines, and enjoy a view of the city from the ground up. You can sit on a number of plush chairs, couches, or beanbags and sip sweet Moroccan mint tea, eat a bite of cake, and bask in the crisp Coimbra air.

The bar's decor is eclectic and artsy, with white, bulbous lamps dangling on the terrace and mismatched jaguar-spotted chairs in the interior. The food, too, is divine. Try an olive-oil dipped, rich vegetable wrap with sauteed spinach and grilled tomatoes. Also try the "Santa toast," which is made from a baguette, pesto, olive, pickles, dates, goat cheese, sliced sausage, and French fries (only €4.50!). Fresh fruit milkshakes, with strawberry, kiwi, or others, cost €2.50, and loose-leaf teas cost €2.20 before 10pm. Also try a plate of fresh, spongy, cinnamon-y scones and a pot of tea for only €3.70.

Come back a little later to enjoy the bar at its hottest time—night. The furniture and view are still the same, only it's nighttime, drinks are readily available, and everyone is mingling. If you come during the academic year, you'll meet dozens of university students sitting over bottles of green or rose wine, chatting about philosophy or art or physics—the usual stuff. You're a university student too, right? Why not join them. The ambience is much different than smoky, drink-to-get-drunk sorts of bars. Instead, Galeria Bar Santa Clara is a place to enjoy sophisticated drinks and lounge in the beautiful joys of studenthood.

i *Lunch €4-6. Desserts €2-4. Cocktails €4-6. Beer €1-3. ② M-Th 2pm-2am, F-Sa 2pm-3am, Su 2pm-2am.*

NIGHTLIFE

THE ROCK PLANET

CLUB

Rue Almeida Garrett, 1   www.facebook.com/rockplanetcoimbra

Upon first glance, Coimbra doesn't seem like the type of place to have a three-story nightclub. But didn't your parents ever teach you not to judge a book by its cover? This is a college town, after all. The Rock Planet is a wild and eccentric nightclub geared toward students, with funky decor, pretty cheap drinks (considering it's a nightclub), and, of course, good ol' rock and roll music. Climb up to the third floor and you'll see a hilarious upside-down piano (how did they do that?) and a tram for decor, while at the entrance, you'll see a model car. Behind the bars, you'll find model motorcycles and big electric guitars—the epitome of cool, right? The bottom floor is, of course, the main dance floor, but you can certainly mix and mingle on the upper floors as well. There are plenty of places to sit and relax while chatting with friends, or, on the other hand, dance the night away and, like a good college student, get totally wasted. Keep on the lookout for special deals and promotions as well as guest DJs and live performances, which are typically advertised on the club's Facebook page.

To enter, you'll get a voucher card on which you must spend a minimum of €3-10 worth of drinks, depending on the night and on your gender (per usual). Don't hit up the club until you're totally sure all the bars are closed down for the night (usually at 2am) because things don't start getting lively until around 2:30am.

i Drink vouchers €3-10. ◷ Open Tu-Sa 10pm-6am.

ESSENTIALS
Practicalities

- **COUNTRY CODE:** ☎351

- **TOURIST OFFICE INFORMATION:** Regional Tourist Office. (Largo da Portagem, ☎239 488 120) Municipal Tourist Office. (Edifício da Biblioteca Geral da Universidade de Coimbra Praça da Porta Férrea, ☎239 859 884) Tourist Support Line. (☎800 296 296)

- **ATM MACHINES:** ATM machines can be found in the offshoots of Praça 8 de Maio, especially on Rua Visconde Da Luz, the main road (which turns into Ferreira Borges). Also try Praça da República and the road Rua António Vasconcelos.

Emergency

- **EMERGENCY TELEPHONE:** }112

- **FIRE:** Bombeiros Sapadores de Coimbra Avenida Mendes da Silva, Quinta da Nora. (☎239 792 800, emergencies ☎239 792 808) Bombeiros Voluntários de Coimbra. (Avenida Fernão de Magalhães, 179 ☎239 823 383, emergencies ☎239 822 323)

- **POLICE:** Polícia de Segurança Pública, 1st Precinct. (av. Elísio de Moura, 155 ☎239 797 640) Polícia de Segurança Pública, 2nd Precinct (rua Olímpio Nicolau Rui Fernandes ☎239 851 300) Polícia Judiciária (Criminal Police). (rua Venâncio Rodrigues, 16/18 ☎239 863 000, 239 828 130)

- **HOSPITALS:** Hospitals of the University of Coimbra (av. Bissaya Barreto, Praceta Mota Pinto ☎239 400 400, Linha Azul ☎239 827 446) Hospital Centre of Coimbra, General Hospital. (Quinta dos Vales, 3041-801 S. Martinho do Bispo ☎239 800 100)

- **PHARMACIES:** Like most other places in Portugal, pharmacies are marked by large green crosses (that may be glowing). Farmácia Santa Isabel Lda Avenida Sá da Bandeira 28 (☎239 824 916) Farmácia Miranda. (Praça do Comércio 42)

Getting There

There are two train stations and one bus station in Coimbra. Estação Coimbra-A is located next to the river, and Estação Coimbra-B is about 3km northwest of the city itself. All trains stop at Coimbra-B, but long distance trains (like those from Lisbon) do not connect to Coimbra A, so you'll need to take a free train that connects to A in order to reach the city. Trains arrive from Lisbon's Santa Apolonia station, and rides last 1.5-2hr. and cost €22-24, depending on which train you catch. Trains run from 6am on weekdays and 7am weekends to 9:30pm daily.

Trains leave from Porto's Campanhã station to Coimbra, and the journey usually takes about 1hr. (If you take the fast train, which runs about every hour and costs either €14.80 or €18.30 depending on the train you catch.) Slow, urban trains take about 2hr. and come less often but are much cheaper (€8.55).

Alternatively, you can catch a coach bus from either of the two cities. All buses will arrive at the station located on Fernão de Magalhães, which is situated right next to a bus stop that offers multiple buses running into the city center and the Praça da República (look out for numbers 5, 19, 19T, 24, 25, 25T, 28, 30, and 30T—these numbers apply for the train stations, too).

Buses from Lisbon leave from the Sete Rios station, and cost €14.50, with a journey that takes 2hr. and 30min, generally. Buses run every 40-60min. Coimbra may not be the last stop on your bus, so make sure you're paying attention!

In Porto, buses depart from the Bathala bus station. A one-way fare is €12.80 and journeys last about 1hr. 30min. Buses depart once about every 2hr.

BY TAXI

You can call any of these taxi companies if you want a ride to your accommodations. Taxis can also usually be found near the train station. Ferrão & Irmão, Lda. (☎239 716 133) Gualter Nogueira Ramos, Lda. (☎239 713 338) Politáxis—Central de Rádio Táxis (☎239 715 445, 239 499 090, 239 826 622, 239 822 287) Táxis Antral de Coimbra (☎239 822 472, 239 822 008, 239 836 474) Táxis Lima & Ribeiro, Lda. (☎239 722 292).

Getting Around

Coimbra is by far easiest traversed by foot, since really all that travelers want to see are the university and the old city, which can be reached by bus from the stations (choose anything traveling toward Praça da República). If necessary, travelers can catch buses to and from most everywhere in the city (even the most rural and out-there suburbs of Coimbra).

sintra

Visit Sintra and be a king (or queen, or fairy princess) for a day. This small village situated just 15mi. north (or a 40min. train ride) of Lisbon, nestled in lush verdant hills and just a short drive away from the incredible beaches of central Portugal. The tall hills encompassing the village create a microclimate, capturing the mist and marine layer of the Atlantic Ocean and thus allowing a wider variety of forest plants to grow in the region. In this environment, you'll find a beautiful palace jutting from the lush mountainside, visible from Lisbon on a clear day. You'll trek to an ancient Moorish castle with a view of the Atlantic, through acres and acres of jungle-like parks, into deep wells and through dark grottoes. During your downtime, you'll munch on Queijadas and Travesseiros, traditional sweets of Sintra, watch the sunset in what seems like a million different colors from the westernmost point of the continental Europe, and contemplate whether or not you should actually climb to the mountain (just do it). Sintra truly is a magical place hidden in the depths of central Portugal. You're in for more than just a fairytale.

SIGHTS

PENA NATIONAL PALACE

PALACE

Estrada da Pena ☎21 923 73 00 www.parquesdesintra.pt

You'll see the Pena National Palace perched upon the mountainsides of Sintra as you drive along the roads below. The ornate, colorful palace had humble beginnings in the Middle Ages, beginning its Romanticist life as a small chapel dedicated to Our Lady of Pena. According to legend, construction began after an apparition of the Virgin Mary appeared in that spot. The palace is located on the second-tallest peak in Sintra, surpassed only by the Cruz Alta (the high cross), which is located to the south and is included in the palace's gardens.

In 1838, King Ferdinand II of Portugal acquired the former monastery and began to renovate it into a palace. At the time, the monastery included a chapel, a sacristy, a bell tower, and a cloister, which is today known as the "old Palace." Ferdinand enlarged the monastery and added rooms at his discretion, inducing bedrooms, a magnificent kitchen, and studies—all of which have incredible views of Sintra below, in addition to an ocean view to the west. Inspired by

German romanticism, Ferdinand had the exterior of his palace painted in soft pinks and yellows, which makes Pena even more noticeable and stark against the lush, verdant hillside. Additionally, he commissioned a series of gardens to be designed and planted in the region surrounding his palace. Like a classic scientist, Ferdinand took advantage of Sintra's microclimate (the hills block the sun and capture the mist, creating a cool, damp environment) to plant exotic new species from South America as well as some from Germany.

Today, there are more than five hundred species of trees in the park, many of which are marked with placards for visitors to read. Today, visitors can enjoy the natural beauty of the park as well as the architectural wonder of the palace itself, which has been named a UNESCO world heritage site and one of the seven wonders of Portugal. Pack some good walking shoes with you, because unless you plan on driving to the top (which you shouldn't, since the walk is gorgeous), you're in for quite a steep incline.

i Palace and park €14; park only €7.50. "Happy hour" (9:30-10:30am) €13. ⏰ Palace open 9:45am-7pm; last tickets 6:15pm. Terrace open 9:45am-7:30pm; last tickets 6:45pm.

MOORS CASTLE

CASTLE

Estrada da Pena ☎21 923 73 00 www.parquesdesintra.pt

It's almost like the Great Wall of China, or, at least, you'll feel that way after trekking up to and across the towers of the Moors Castle. Just a couple hundred meters away from the Pena Palace and perched atop one of Sintra's largest peaks, the castle is quite visible to anyone in the valley below. Just gazing at the castle from below conjures images of fairytales, from knights in shining armor to medieval dragons and fair princesses. You will probably even see a number of small children running up and down the towers (how on earth do they have the stamina for that?) waving plastic swords and capes around.

The castle was constructed by none other than the Moors in the 10th century, after their conquest of the Iberian peninsula, and was initially used as a lookout fortress for the nearby city of Lisbon. From its towers, which steadily grow steeper as you traverse the castle from its start to finish, visitors have a 180-degree view of the Atlantic Ocean (this is, of course, on a clear day, and Sintra's known for its fog). After King Afonso Henriques captured Lisbon in 1147, he began to make changes to the castle (which was captured along with Sintra). In 1744, an earthquake damaged much of the castle, and only recently have extensive refurbishments been made. In 2009, an initiative called "Conquering the Castle" began archeological work in partnership with the Universidade Nova de Lisboa. The work is intended to provide a better idea of how the castle was occupied under Muslim and Christian rule, and as a result, several new findings have been discovered, like a medieval Christian cemetery, foundations of Muslim houses, and various coins from the first Portuguese dynasty, among other artifacts and structures.

Besides the incredible history behind the castle, visitors should come for the beautiful views. Imagine yourself as a Moorish soldier, staring out into the Atlantic, protecting your nation. Then go buy a fake sword and battle with the kids.

i €7.50. See website for more information about combined ticket prices with other sights, like the Pena Palace. ⏰ Open 9:30am-8pm; last tickets 7pm.

FOOD

O APEADEIRO

PORTUGUESE $$

Avenida Dr. Miguel Bombarda, 3A ☎21 923 18 04 http://restauranteapeadeiro.pt/

If you're staying in Sintra for a night, a great place to eat out is O Apeadeiro, a small, family-style eatery by the rail station. In a town whose restaurants are

ALMÁA SINTRA HOSTEL

HOSTEL $$

Caminho dos Frades   ☎21 924 00 08 www.almaasintrahostel.com

It's not every day that you end up feeling better about yourself for being a tourist. Almáa Hostel in Sintra is an eco hostel dedicated to sustainable tourism practices and ensuring that its guests are comfortable while staying at the foot of the beautiful Sintra mountain range. All of its furniture is manufactured by local artists with recycled materials, and the hostel itself is situated on property that's been around since the 12th century, when the Moors ruled the land. Speaking of, Almáa means "water" in Arabic, and Alma means "soul" in Portuguese. Sound heavenly? There's more.

The hostel's water is fresh spring water, which also keeps its 3/4 acres of lush gardens alive. Almáa offers yoga classes every Monday, Wednesday, and Friday and Chi Kung classes on occasion as well. By appointment, visitors can book meditation sessions, acupuncture and shiatsu, walking and hiking tours, nature sketching tours, and healing workshops. Plus, its interior is one of the most calming, comfortable, and beautiful you will ever see in a hostel. Its living room floors are decorated with green ceramic tile and colorful rugs, while its walls are painted a warm orange, with sea shells and flowers pasted on here and there. The hostel has plenty of books housed in its four large, blue bookshelves, and a quaint, lovely kitchen offers amenities for guests who would prefer to do their own cooking.

The hostel is about a 10-15min. walk from the city center, but the walk itself is quite straightforward (as in, you just walk straight). It's also 5min. away from the Palácio da Regaleira, a sight you definitely don't want to miss when in Sintra. Free storage lockers are included, as is a breakfast of toast, jam, cereal, and coffee.

i From Quinta da Regaleira, go through the car park to the right and simply keep walking for about 500 yards. The hostel is on the left. 8-bed mixed dorm €20; 5-bed mixed dorm €22; 3-bed mixed dorm €24. Twin private with shared bath €28; twin private bath €32. ☑ Reception until midnight; if you plan on staying out later, make sure to notify the receptionist if possible and call them to let you back in.

otherwise primarily geared toward tourists, O Apeadeiro is somewhat of an oasis, a hidden gem frequented by locals and known for its friendly staff and great service. Its intimate, dim atmosphere makes for a great romantic spot, or, if you're dining alone, a nice place to sit and reflect on your travels. The blue mosaic tiles on the walls will remind you of azulejos from Lisbon, but the whole of the restaurant, and of course, of Sintra itself, has a smaller, charming feel to it, perfectly encapsulated by O Apeadeiro.

Here, you'll sample traditional Portuguese cuisine, from bifinho to Algarve tuna. Choose from several courses of meats, fish, and even vegetarian options (though if you're coming to Portugal, you should probably reconsider your diet choices). One of their specialities, *bife à cafe*, is a heart steak drown in a secret, savory coffee sauce and served with a platter of french fries to dip when the meat is gone (€12). Another, *lombinhos de porco à Madeira*, is a special pork tenderloin that hails from the Portuguese archipelago of Madeira (€8). For dessert, try *pudim flan, natas do céu,* or *taça do chefe* for €2.60-2.85. Not sure what those are? Just think cream. Lots of egg yolk custard, and cream.

After you pay your bill, and even after you drink a bottle of wine, the restaurant will serve you a complimentary glass of port. In fact, they bring a whole bottle out for you to drink in one of the traditional small port glasses, just to make you feel welcome, at home, and in love with the city and O Apeadeiro.

i Combo plates €6-7, meats €8.50-11.50, fish €11.50-14. Desserts €2.60-2.85. ☼ Open F-M 9am-midnight; closed Thursday

CAFE A PIRIQUITA
PORTUGUESE $
Rua das Padarias ☎21 923 06 26

It's one of Sintra's worst-kept secrets. A Piriquita is a bakery and cafe good for brunch, lunch, mid-afternoon coffee, and, of course, sweet desserts and pastries all around the clock. The shop is quite famous for a few menu items, including its queijadas, which are sweet cheese-filled bites made of eggs, milk, and sugar, as well as its *travesseiros* (literally translated as "pillows"), which are flaky egg-cream and almond-cream filled pastries. Also try a *pastel de Sintra*, a soft pastry with cinnamon and sugar or a sweet, roll-like *pastel de Cruz Alta*. All of these delicious pastries are actually owned, by title, by A Piriquita. Taste one and you'll see why.

Besides its sweet snacks, the restaurant also serves traditional, light Portuguese lunches, complete with toasts, croissants, sandwiches, and cheeses. You can eat heartily here without breaking your bank, too! The restaurant's famous pastries only cost around €1.30 each, and its toasts range from €1-3 each as well. Drinks also cost from €1-3.

The atmosphere of A Piriquita is so friendly, bustling, and intimate that the owners just had to open up a second location nearby. So if you can't find yourself a spot at the original, which often has very long lines both to sit down and take away, you can head over to the second spot just down the road and up the hill a bit– and this one has a terrace where you can enjoy views of the city center below. The cafe is always bustling and its staff are so friendly. Even though its menus do not have English or French translations, the waiters will guide you through the restaurant's selection and help whenever necessary. So if you're daytripping Sintra and are feeling a bit hungry after hiking all day, A Piriquita is definitely the place to go for a nice lunch.

i Toast €1-3, desserts/pastries €1-4, drinks €1-3. ☼ Open Th-M 8:30am-10pm; closed Wednesday.

NIGHTLIFE

ADEGA DAS CAVES
BAR
Rue Pendoa 2 ☎21 923 08 43 www.adegadascaves.com

Located in the heart of Sintra village, Adega das Caves is a classic nightlife destination for fun-seekers, both locals and travelers. Like most bars in the village, this one operates as a restaurant during the daytime and a bar at night, but while its restaurant is pretty average, the two-floor bar is a hot spot. Adega das Caves translates into "Wine Cellars" in English and has been serving quality Portuguese wine, for which the bar is most famous, since 1945. Its interior is quaint, if not a little small, and rustic, complete with a number of small tables decorated with checked clothes and a bar with stool seats. Travelers from all over the world tend to rendezvous and mingle here, so you never know what type of interesting people you will meet at the bar. Jsut check out the bar's Facebook page, and you'll see photos of people from Romania, Macau, Brazil, Denmark and more. Adega das Caves stays open until 2am each night, after which stragglers may slowly and subtly be kicked out from the bar.

i Beer €1.60-3. Mixed drinks €4-6. ☼ Open daily 10am-2am. Kitchen open until midnight.

Rua Consiglieri Pedroso 16 ☎21 923 43 55 www.facebook.com/EstradaVelha

Another bar with two floors! How much better can it get? This bar is more like a bar than a living room, and it is quite rustic, with polished redwood ceilings, gray stone walls, and a beautiful wine stock displayed just behind the bar. You may just find yourself staring at the wine bottles for a while, wondering which one to choose, before the bartender actually chooses for you.

The bar has been serving late-night Sintra wanderers since 1985, which is good for the few of them who actually still exist in the city. Estrada Velha is open until 2am, and although the bar will not admit new patrons after 2am, they will allow those already inside the bar to lounge around for a while until it's deemed too indecent to stick around much longer. So feel free to loiter! There are plenty of seats on the first floor (the bar serves as a restaurant during the daytime), and the second floor is posh and clean, with another bar and a few bench seats to serve large groups. Estrada Velha is also quite close to the world-famous Lawrence Hotel, which is known for having hosted Lord Byron during his trips to his beloved Sintra.

Stop by after a hard day of hiking to unwind with friends and enjoy a night out. You'll feel well rested and even a little cheerier afterwards.

i Beer €3-5. Mixed drinks €5-7. ✪ Open 11am-2am daily.

ESSENTIALS

Practicalities

- **TOURIST OFFICE:** The city's main tourist office is located in the center village, near the Sintra National Palace, and is open Jan-July and Sept-Dec from 9:30am-6pm. In August, it is open from 9:30am-7pm. (351 21 923 11 57, sintra@atlx.pt, 23 Praça da República). Another tourist office is located by the train station. Sintra Railway Station Information Office (Av. Miguel Bombarda Tel: 219 241 623 Open daily in summer 9am-8pm. Open daily in winter 9am-7pm.)
- **COUNTRY CODE:** 351
- **TOURIST INFORMATION:** 21 923 11 57
- **ATM MACHINES:** You'll find a number of ATM machines in Sintra, mostly in the center village and near the train station. It's best if you get your money from Lisbon, if possible, as lines at these ATMs in Sintra may be long.

Emergency

- **EMERGENCY TELEPHONE:** 112
- **FIRE:** 21 923 62 00
- **POLICE:** Municipal: 21 910 72 10. National Guard: 21 924 78 50. Policia Judiciaria: 21 864 10 00.
- **HOSPITALS:** Amadora Sintra Hospital: 21 434 82 00, 21 434 84 44. Cascais Hospital: 21 482 77 00

Getting There

Because Sintra is a popular day trip destination from Lisbon, it's easiest to catch a train from Lisbon. The fastest and cheapest way is from the Rossio Train Station in central Lisbon. Trains leave every 15min. from 6am-8pm, and then every 30min. until the last train at 1am. The train will stop at Estaç&ã;o Sintra, the Sintra train station, which is a 15min. walk or 10min. bus ride (435 or 434) from the city center

BY TAXI

Taxis are located at the train station or across from the Sintra-Vila post office. The taxis don't have meters, so if you don't want to get scammed, it's best to contact the tourist office ahead of time to ask about regular fares.

Getting Around

Most things are located within close proximity to each other, so it's easiest to walk in Sintra (even up to the Palace and the Moorish castle—the hike is lovely!). If you do need to take the bus up to the city center, you can take the 435 for €2.50, or the 434 for €5 for a single loop, which stops at many of the historic sights in the city, like the Pena Palace and the Moor Castle. Otherwise, you can purchase a day pass for the 434 for €12, or a single-route for €3. The 434 runs about every 20min., ending service at 5pm. To get to other sites outside of the main center of Sintra, like Cabo da Roca, take a bus from the train station. Lines 403 and 503 depart from the train station every 30min. or so until around 6pm. They depart from Cabo da Roca on the same time table, but their final bus leaves for Sintra at around 7pm. One-way tickets cost €2.25.

portugal essentials

MONEY

Tipping and Bargaining

Native Portuguese rarely tip more than their spare change, even at expensive restaurants. However, if you make it clear that you're a tourist, they might expect you to tip more. Don't feel obligated to tip; the servers' pay is almost never based on tips. No one will refuse your money, but you're a poor student so don't play the fool.

Bargaining is common and necessary in open-air and street markets. Haggling is also most effective when buying several items or in bulk. However, do not barter in malls or established shops.

Taxes

Portugal has a 13% **value added tax** (*imposto sobre* or *valor acrescentado*; IVA) on all meals and accommodations. The prices listed in *Let's Go* include IVA unless otherwise mentioned. Retail goods bear a much higher 23% IVA, although the listed prices generally include this tax. Non-EU citizens who have stayed in the EU fewer than 180 days can claim back the tax paid on purchases at the airport. Ask the shop where you have made the purchase to supply you with a tax return form, but stores will only provide them for purchases of more than €50-100. **Taxes**, presently 23%, are included in all prices in Portugal. Request a refund form, an *Insenção de IVA*, and present it to customs upon departure.

SAFETY AND HEALTH

Local Laws and Police

You should feel comfortable approaching the police in Portugal, although few officers speak English. The **Policía de Segurança Pública** is the police force in all major cities and towns. The **Guarda Nacional Republicana** polices more rural areas, while the **Brigada de Trânsito** is the traffic police, who sport red armbands. All three branches wear light blue uniforms.

Drugs and Alcohol

Recreational drugs are illegal in Portugal, and police take these laws seriously. However, recreational drug use has been decriminalized, so instead of jail time and fines, perpetrators face community service and government-imposed therapy. The legal minimum drinking age is 18. Portugal has one of the highest road mortality rates in Europe. Do not drive while intoxicated, and be cautious on the road.

SLOVENIA

The first and most prosperous of Yugoslavia's breakaway republics, tiny Slovenia revels in republicanism, peace, and independence. With a historically westward gazy, Slovenia's liberal politics and high GDP helped it gain early entry into the European Union. Fortunately, modernization has not adversely affected the tiny country's natural beauty and diversity: it is still possible to go skiing, explore Slovenia's stunning caves, bathe under the Mediterranean sun, and catch an opera—all in a single day.

greatest hits

- **HAPPILY EVER AFTER:** Whether you're looking to swim along the beaches or hike up some mountain trails, **Lake Bled** (p. 785) will be the perfect fairy tale setting for your next Instagram post.

- **BRINGING SAX-Y BACK:** Like jazz? Great, head to **Sax Pub** (p. 783) in Ljubljana. Don't like jazz? Have a liter of rosé for €10. Then you'll love jazz.

- **BIG SAUSAGE SURPRISE:** Klobasarna (p. 782) in Ljubljana is a tiny joint that specializes in delicious, cheap sausages. Try the half sausage which only goes for €3.50.

Ljubljana

Budapest is the new Prague. Bratislava is the new Budapest. Zagreb is the new Bratislava. Or maybe Prague is back in again? Keeping track of what's hot in Central Europe can be tricky. And that means it's easy to lose sight of Ljubljana—wait, how do you pronounce that? Is that in Slovenia or Slovakia?

Confusing spelling aside, Ljubljana is a charming city that should be a destination for anyone visiting Central Europe. Though the nightlife never rises to a fever pitch, the restaurants, classy bars, and stunning sights make it an attractive place for anyone looking for a more low-key vacation—or maybe you just need a scenic place to recover after raging in Prague. Check out the parks, the museums, the castle—or just sit alongside the meandering river with a can of Laško.

ACCOMMODATIONS

HOSTEL AVA
HOSTEL $

Trubarjeva Cesta 5 ☎01 425 50 06 www.hostel-ava.si

Obsessed with Ljubljana's contemporary art scene? Then stay in this unique hostel, which is affiliated with Ljubljana's Academy of Visual Art. Couldn't care less about art but want a hostel with big rooms, clean showers, and a great location? Then you should also stay at Hostel AVA. Located on the very hip Trubarjeva Cesta—look out for vegan restaurants and smoke shops—Hostel AVA offers large suites at cheap prices. Even if you're in an 8- or 12-bed dorm, you're sure to have your own space. Though it feels more like a real hostel than some of Ljubljana's more apartment-like setups (hall bathrooms, big rooms pack with showers—you get the idea), it's still plenty comfortable.

i *From the bus or train station, walk west on Trg Osvobodilne fronte, then take a right onto Resljeva Cesta. Take a left at Trubarjeva Cesta; the hostel is on your right. Dorms €13-15.* ⌚ *Reception open Jul-Sept 8am-midnight; Oct-June 9am-1pm.*

HOSTEL CELICA
HOSTEL $$

Metelkova 8. ☎01 230 97 00 www.hostelcelica.com

Obsessed with Ljubljana's contemporary art scene, but want something a little more structured than art school? Then why not stay in Hostel Celica, which for over a hundred years was used as a prison? It sounds like a hostel that would be perfect for, well, Hostel, but Hostel Celica is actually one of the most distinctive and exciting places to stay in all of Ljubljana. Located in the vibrant Metelkova City, Hostel Celica has the usual amenities (Wi-Fi, clean bathrooms, towels), but it also boasts eclectic room design and unique history. This is probably the only hostel dorm that you'll ever be tempted to Instagram for good reasons. However, that history comes at a cost—Hostel Celica charges a good three or four euros more than other hostels in the area. But hey, at least they don't charge bail when you want to leave.

i *Walk west from the bus or train station, then take a right onto Metelkova. Dorms €18-22. Private rooms €24-30. Breakfast €3.* ⌚ *Reception 24hr.*

ANA HOSTEL
HOSTEL $

Komenskega ulica 10 ☎01 292 7997 www.ana-hostel.com

Located midway between the train station and the Ljubljanica, Ana Hostel offers convenience as well as quiet—it's hard to get some sleep when there are rows of bars just feet from your room. Here, there's a decidedly classier vibe, part of which comes from the old townhouse it's housed in. The high-ceilinged rooms are filled with light as well as furniture: bookshelves and bedside tables abound. Some of the three-bedded rooms even have kitchens attached. Even the hall

Ljubljana gets warm over the summer—it's not uncommon to see temperatures rising to the high 80s or low 90s (Fahrenheit, not Celsius—it gets hot, but not that hot). And with the usual urban oases coming up short (air conditioning is sparse in Ljubljana's national museums), you may need to get creative.

1. Stand by the fountain in Novi Trg. It seems to be just a little too powerful—that is, the water comes out with such force that there's a lot of splashing. You'll get wet, but not too wet.

2. Indulge your longing for ice cream. Nearly every bar or café along the Ljubljana serves ice cream—go crazy and get five scoops.

3. Go swimming at Park Tivoli's swimming pool. Not to be confused with Tivoli Pond.

4. Get out of Ljubljana. Not only will the weather be cooler in the Julian Alps, but the bus there will probably be air-conditioned!

5. Go to the Ethnographic Museum. This one actually is air-conditioned!

bathrooms look swanky—although you still have to share them. Common spaces include a courtyard out back—yeah, this is the good life.
i *From the bus or train station, walk west on Trg Osvobodilne fronte, then take a right onto Resljeva Cesta. Take a left at Komenskega ulica; the hostel is on your left. Dorms €17. Privates €40.* ☒ *Reception 24hr.*

H2OSTEL
HOSTEL **$**
Petkovškovo nabrežje 47 ☎41 66 22 66 www.h2ohostel.com
H2Ostel is actually a few different hostels, including Hostel Most, arranged under one umbrella. The reason for that? Well, most of these hostel rooms are more like a studio apartment than anything else, complete with kitchenettes and en-suite bathrooms. Have you ever wanted to pretend you were living in Slovenia with 4 to 5 other roommates? Well, H2Ostel will give you that chance.
i *From the bus or train station, walk west on Trg Osvobodilne fronte, then take a right onto Resljeva Cesta. At the river, take a left; the hostel is on your left. Dorms €14.* ☒ *Reception open 8am-11pm.*

HOSTEL DRAGONDOSS
HOSTEL **$**
Prečna ulica 4 ☎07 043 70 03
Dragondoss is one of the smaller hostels in Ljubljana, but its central location and cozy interiors still guarantee a good time. They also have the best prices in all of Ljubljana, meaning they're also guaranteeing you a good time elsewhere—buy some fine Slovenian wine with your savings! A few amenities, such as towels and Wi-Fi, are included.
i *From the train/bus station, walk west and then take a right onto Kolodvorska ulica. When you come to the fork in the road, take the left onto Prečna Ulica. Dorms €12-16.* ☒ *Reception June-Oct 24hr. Nov-May 8am-10pm.*

SIGHTS

PARK TIVOLI
PARK
Main entrance at Cankarjeva Cesta
Don't have time for a day trip during your stay in Ljubljana? No need to fret—Park Tivoli, the largest of Ljubljana's many parks, is a perfectly acceptable substitute for frolicking in the Slovenian countryside. Though it features some gorgeously landscaped gardens, a manmade pond, and a stately castle, Park Tivoli can also feel startlingly rural. Dubious? Just take a hike up Šišenski Hill,

ljubljana

which divides the park from Ljubljana's zoo (worth a visit if you want to see horses that aren't on your dinner plate). If you're not really the nature type, pay a visit to Tivoli Castle, which regularly hosts art exhibits and also houses a cafe. If you're looking to exercise, the park has tennis, volleyball, and basketball courts, as well as soccer fields and a swimming pool.

i Admission free.

NATIONAL MUSEUM / NATURAL HISTORY MUSEUM

MUSEUM

Prešernova 20 ☎01 241 09 40 www.nms.si

It's not quite two museums for the price of one—the two institutions have separate admission prices—but you'll get to check out two of Slovenia's most famous museums without a lot of walking. The National Museum takes up all of the first floor, some of the second, and a bit of space outside; the Natural History Museum gets the rest of the second floor. This makes sense, since the history of Slovenia is slightly more important than that of the development of life on planet earth. You'll see such artifacts as the remains of a 10th century woman from Bled, Roman ruins from Ljubljana, and also an Egyptian mummy that doesn't really have that much to do with Slovenia. Upstairs at the Natural History Museum, a gigantic woolly mammoth skeleton holds sway over somewhat less impressive skeletons. The dioramas may be more dramatic than you're used to—one shows a big cat with a bird stuck in his mouth—but that just helps to liven things up.

i National Museum €6, students €4. Natural History Museum €4, students €3. Combined ticket €8.50, students €6. ☒ Open M-W 10am-6pm, Th 10am-8pm, F-Su 10am-6pm.

MODERNA GALERIJA LJUBLJANA

MUSEUM

Cankarjeva 15 ☎01 241 68 34

Odds are you've never heard of any of the artists in this museum. Zoran Musič? Misread Begi? Jakob Savinšek? Maybe you spotted Laibach in your goth cousin's industrial rock collection. But even if you know nothing about modern art in Slovenia, the Moderna Galerija still holds great appeal. Be warned, however, that this museum does not exactly give off good vibes—for proof of that, just see Savinšek's series of agonized sculptures with names like "Malice," "Nightmare," and "Falsehood." But if you can take a little moodiness, then walking through these galleries will give you an alternate history of modern art. As the decades pass by, the art gets louder and more aggressive—TV screens and jarring noises abound. If you're pooped from a walk in Tivoli Park, we recommend you start at this end—it's sure to wake you up.

i €5, students €2.50. Free on the first Sunday of every month. ☒ Open Tu-Su 10am-6pm.

LJUBLJANA CASTLE AND MUSEUM OF PUPPETRY

CASTLE, MUSEUM

Grajska planota 1 www.ljubljanskigrad.si

Yes, this is the building on Ljubljana's coat of arms, and no, there's no dragon crouching on top (though there are numerous dragon toys for sale in the gift shop). Ljubljana Castle, originally built in the 11th century and rebuilt several times since then, has served as a military outpost, an arsenal, a penitentiary, and a WWI prisoner of war camp. Today, it's a fascinating look into Slovenian history, as well as the absolute best spot from which to view the city—the castle's tower offers 360° views of Ljubljana and its surroundings. Elsewhere, you can check out old prison cells, take a virtual tour of the castle in its heyday, or grab a bite to eat at the castle's restaurant.

Also housed in the castle is the Museum of Puppetry, which is just as disturbing as you might expect—did you know that the first Slovenian puppet show proper was named "Dead Man in a Red Coat"? And it also lets you make your very own puppet show! If you're having violent thoughts about the dude in your hostel who snores really loudly, this is the place to work through it.

Given the lengthy, winding walk necessary to get up to the castle—there's no straight path up the hill—it's worth buying a ticket on the funicular, the inclined railway that makes getting up and down a breeze. Even if you're up for a bit of a hike, take the funicular one way and soak in the great view.

i €7.50, students €5.20. ⏱ *Open daily, though hours vary by season. Check online for a more complete schedule. June-September castle open 9am-11pm, museum open from 9am-9pm.*

SLOVENIAN ETHNOGRAPHIC MUSEUM   MUSEUM
Metelkova 2   ☎01 300 87 00 www.etno-muzej.si

Spend a couple of days in Ljubljana, and you'll start to wonder. You'll see people eating deer medallions and horse burgers, reading Slavoj Žižek, talking about their bachelor parties where they locked a friend in a dog cage and made him drink tequila, and you'll start to think—what is this country? No better place to find that out than at the Ethnographic Museum, which, in its exploration of the world's culture, also penetrates deep into Slovenian identity. They've got everything from traditional country garb to Slovenian pressings of Tom Jones records, and while not all the wall text is in English, the artifacts can often speak for themselves. Special attention is paid to the mundane; this is, after all, a museum that mounted a special exhibition about doors in Slovenia, complete with walls full of different keys, doorknobs, and knockers.

i €4.50, students €2.50. ⏱ *Open Tu-Sa 10am-6pm.*

FOOD

PIZZERIA FOCULUS   PIZZA $
Gregorčičeva ulica 3   ☎01 251 56 43. www.foculus.si

Scared of trying—gasp—Central European cuisine? First off, you shouldn't be. But if you're a picky eater or you're traveling with one, know that Slovenia, being close to Italy, is also home to some great pizza. One of the finest joints in town is the vaguely Roman-themed Pizzeria Foculus, located on the charming Gregorčičeva ulica. The staff proudly proclaims that theirs is the best in Slovenia, and they're certainly in the running: the thin-crust pizza is delicious with a variety of options for vegetarians and meat-lovers alike (ham, salami, pepperoni—pile it on!). The highlight may be the pizza bufala, topped with cherry tomatoes and chunks of mozzarella. If you're with a friend or are just absurdly hungry, go for the large size; otherwise, the so-called "small" is more than enough.

i Small pizzas €7-9. Large pizzas €8-10. Salads €6-8. ⏱ *Open daily 11am-12am.*

PIVNICA UNION   PUB $
Celovška Cesta 22   ☎01 471 73 35 www.pivnica-union.si

Here's the easiest way to explain Pivnica Union: imagine Budweiser opened a brewpub where you could get their classic lager, specially hopped and unfiltered versions of their flagship brew, and various one-offs made by expert brewers. Imagine they served food, and it was both really cheap and really good. So far, Budweiser has done nothing of the sort, but Pivovarna Union, Ljubljana's second largest brewery (it's affiliated with the largest, Pivovarna Laško) certainly has. Beer enthusiasts will enjoy the special brews, but the real attraction is the constantly changing daily special. You're not likely to find a better deal than the most basic option, which gives you a full meal for only €6: roast chicken, pork, baked trout, and veal shank have all appeared on the rotating menu. And yes, you can get Laško and Union everywhere in Ljubljana, but won't it taste best where it's made?

i Daily specials €6-12. Beer €2-4. ⏱ *Open M-Th 11am-12am, F-Sa 11am-1am, Su 12pm-5pm.*

ljubljana

KLOBASARNA

SLOVENIAN $

Ciril-Metodov Trg 15 ☎51 605 017 www.klobasarna.si

Ljubljana has tons of restaurants serving Slovenian delicacies, but most of them will set you back at least €15 or €20. For a more economical but still delicious take on Slovenian cuisine, check out Klobasarna, a tiny joint that specializes in big sausages. Ok, yes, sausages, double entendres, very funny. We can stop giggling now. The 1/2 sausage only goes for €3.50, and it comes with a big bun as well as generous helpings of mustard and horseradish. Before you know it, you'll be full and no one will want to talk to you until you eat an entire pack of Altoids. If you're still hungry for more, grab some štrukel, or rolled pastries—€1.50 for 1 or €4 for 3. Perfect for a quick bite before you make the long trek up to Ljubljana Castle.

i Sausage €3.50. Pastries €1.50-4. ⏱ Open M-Sa 10am-11pm, Su 10am-3pm.

NAMASTE

INDIAN $

Breg 8 ☎01 425 01 5 www.restavracija-namaste.si

You wouldn't necessarily expect Slovenia to have great Indian food, but it makes sense if you think about it: both cuisines do heavily feature both meat and potatoes. If that doesn't convince you, then a visit to Namaste, a North Indian restaurant located on the North bank of the Ljubljanica, will surely change your mind. Though Namaste, like many of Ljubljana's restaurants, offers outdoor seating, its stylishly yellow interior is just as inviting. Though there are tons of tables, carefully arranged screens allow for privacy no matter where you're sitting. In other words, if you get some mango lassi on your shirt, you won't be the laughingstock of the room. Until you get up to leave and everyone sees how you ruined your nice shirt. But we digress.

With a wide selection of chicken, lamb, and fish dishes, Namaste will easily satisfy your cravings for meat that's not spiced with horseradish or mustard. Vegetarians need not worry—there are copious veggie plates as well, something that's not always guaranteed in Ljubljana. If you're looking for something to wash all of that spicy food down (fun fact: water doesn't really help!) Namaste also has you covered. There's a wide selection of Slovenian wine, Slovenian and Indian beers alike, and variously flavored lassis if you need something to beat the summer heat. When you finish, take advantage of Namaste's location, perched just at the end of Ljubljana's main drag. If you're looking for a rowdy night, bars and clubs are just a short walk up along the river. If you're looking for a quieter night, just walk in the opposite direction. The river keeps going and the streets are well lit—what more could you ask for?

i Starters €5-7. Entrees €10-14. ⏱ Open M-Sa 11am-12am, Su 11am-10pm.

REPUBLICA PASTA

ITALIAN $

Slovenska Cesta 51 ☎40 151 705.

Slovenia has been inhabited since history began, and since then it's been ruled by a variety of different cultures: Austria-Hungary, Italy, Germany, Serbia, etc. Today, Slovenia is independent, but one of the ways it manifests its history is through its varied cuisine. Case in point: this tiny takeout joint on Slovenska Cesta. If you're down with pasta, then this is one of your best bets for quick, cheap, and delicious food in Ljubljana. Choose from a variety of toppings and sauces (beef with tomatoes, smoked salmon, and pesto are some of the highlights), then pick from one of their various pastas—which, incidentally, are also available for purchase if you want to bring them home (well, to your hostel) and cook them yourself.

i Small pasta €4. Large €5. ⏱ Open M-F 10am-8pm.

NIGHTLIFE

SIR WILLIAM'S PUB
BAR

Tavcarjeva ulica 8a ☎sirwilliamspub-eng.webs.com

Step inside Sir William's, and you might think you've been transported to a posh English pub. But though they have a powerful selection from the British Isles (everything from good old Guinness to double IPAs from the Scottish beer punks at BrewDog), Sir Williams is as devoted to Slovenian craft beer as they come. Human Fish beers are always on tap, and offerings from Reservoir Dogs, Pelican, Maister Brewery, and Pivovarna Mali Grad can be easily found to. And we haven't even gotten to the selection of Belgian, American, and German beers, as well as the many beer cocktails offered. Though Slovenia's well known for its wine (ok, maybe not that well-known), its beer scene has expanded in recent years. Sir William's bills itself as a "House of Beer," and it deserves that mantle. Most other bars in the city stick to Union and Laško, two macro lagers owned by the same conglomerate (is there any difference? Well, some Slovenians have this motto: drink Laško, piss Union), so to explore some new lands and beers, come here .

i Beers from €2.50-7 (although only rare bottles will reach the upper part of that range). ☑ Open M-F 8am-1am, Sa 10am-1am, Su 5pm-12am.

SAX PUB
BAR

Eipprova 7 ☎05 180 44 50

In case you thought the word "sax" meant something different in Slovenian ("I dunno, maybe it means "good times" or "everybody, drink now!), the drawing of an instrument on the menu will set you straight. Sax Pub is all about jazz. Well, kind of. They have jazz performances on a semi regular basis. Pictures of jazz legends hang on the wall. But even if you think Duke Ellington defeated Napoleon at Waterloo (it's the duke of Wellington, dude), you're still sure to enjoy this graffiti-covered bar. Like wine? Sax Pub is a place where you can get a liter of rosé for €10. Like weird spirits? Sax Pub distills their own—a shot of any of them goes for €2. "Some are good, some are less good," one bartender laughs. "There are a lot." Indeed—spruce, pear, regrat, and pelin are all on the menu. So grab a drink, be it beer (they have cult Austrian brewers Bevog on tap) or something harder (in addition to homemade spirits, they've got quite a few whiskeys, rums, and other such delights), and head outside. If it's sunny (day drinking on vacation is no capital crime, after all), then Sax Pub's four massive umbrellas will protect you from the heat. If it's night, a charming set of vintage lightbulbs will bathe you in a yellow glow. The cigarettes of fellow patrons will also provide some light. Inside, you've got what looks like a normal, homey Slovenian country bar, albeit one overrun by jazz hounds. Chill out and listen to the music while enjoying your drink—it's sure to be a good night at Sax Pub.

i Shots €2. 1 L of wine €10. ☑ Open daily 10am-1am.

TOZD
BAR

Gallusovo nabrežje 27 ☎04 06 99 453

The sleekly minimal signage signals upscale cocktail joint. The military green seat cushions, complete with the name TOZD in industrial lettering, screams boot camp. And the beakers they serve water in say "high school science fair." Confused yet? To put it bluntly, Tozd is a bit schizophrenic. But every element, no matter how disconnected it may seem, is geared towards ensuring your enjoyment. Of all the bars and cafes littered along the Ljubljanica, Tozd, located near Stari Trg is absolutely the finest. If it's alcohol you're looking for, they've got one of the strongest selections in Ljubljana. When it comes to beer, choose from Slovenian craft brewers Human Fish (on tap!), Reservoir Dogs, and Pelican,

Austrian brewers Bevog, or Serbian brewers Kabinet. But don't worry—they've also got Lasko, Union, and the other Slovenian macros. For wine, they've got tons of offerings from both Italy and Slovenia. And when it comes to harder stuff, they've got whiskey, cognac, bitters, gin, rum, vodka—the works, essentially. And they have cigarettes. Choose your vice wisely. If you're trying to take it easy, they've got soda, sandwiches, and tapas—if you're not trying to take it easy, come back the next morning (or early afternoon) for artisanal coffee.

i *Beers €3-4.50. ☼ Open daily 8:30 am-1am.*

VINOTEKA MOVIA
WINE BAR

Mestni trg 4 ☎01 425 54 48 www.movia.si/en/ljubljana-wine-bar-shop

So you're looking to learn about Slovenian wine. Good on you, expanding your horizons. But where to begin? Every bar has some Slovenian wine, but where can you really get the expert opinion? Why not start with a bar run by a family that's owned a winery since the 1820s? Vinoteka Movia, with its extensive selection of wines crafted by the Movia estate, is a perfect place to spend a low key evening (what else would you expect from a bar partially located in City Hall?). Occasionally music from the neighboring bar will bleed into your conversation, but usually there'll be nothing but olives to distract you from your glass of white or red.

i *Glasses of wine €2-6. Tastings €14-16. ☼ Open M-Sa 12pm-12am.*

BIKOFE
BAR

Zidovska steza 2 ☎05 016 88 04

Bikofe is located extremely close to the University of Ljubljana, and the low-key vibe inside makes it seem like this hipster hangout is the world's coolest dorm room. That doesn't mean you'll be greeted with solo cups and blaring dubstep—expect some craft cocktails and downtempo techno instead. Carefully selected beers and wines are also available; if you're not looking to imbibe, they've got homemade iced tea for €2.50. In other words, Bikofe is not populated by Slovenian frat boys. You'll find older couples, young men in drag, groups of girls smoking cigarettes, dudes by themselves drinking beer and staring into the distance. It's eclectic, just like the many colored bar stools, mirrors, birdcages, and paintings that decorate Bikofe's interior. But, as always in Slovenia, most of the action is outside. Located on the tiny Židovska steza, Bikofe has a fairly large deck with comfortable chairs. It's not uncommon to see the staff outside too, hanging on the stoop. You'll have all the comfort of the many bars along the Ljubljanica, but without all the hubbub. Unless, of course, someone gets into a loud argument about the validity of Marxist dialectic in today's day and age. Anything's possible at Bikofe.

i *Beers €2-3.50. ☼ Open M-F 8am-1am, Sa-Su 10am-1am.*

ESSENTIALS

Practicalities

- **MONEY:** ATMs are everywhere—just look for the Bankomat sign. If you need to exchange money, there is a bureau of exchange in the train station, Železniška postaja, located on Masarykova Cesta.

- **TOURIST INFO CENTER:** Adamič-Lundrovo nabrežje 2 (☎01 306 12 15)

- **POST OFFICE:** Slovenska cesta 32. ☼ Open M-F 8am-7pm, Sa 8am-12pm.

Emergency

- **POLICE:** ☎113

- **MEDICAL EMERGENCY OR FIRE:** ☎112

- **HOSPITAL:** University Medica Centre Ljubljana, Zaloška 2 ☎01 522 50 50.
- **PHARMACIES:** Ljubljana Central Pharmacy (Prešernov trg 5 ☎01 230 61 00. M-F 7:30-7:30pm, Sa 8-3pm. Closed Sunday.) Lekarna pri Polikliniki (Prisojna ulica 7 ☎01 230 62 30. ☑ Open 24/7.)

Getting Around

The city center is highly walkable. If you need to use a bus, buy an Urbana Card for €2 euro at a tourist information center. Single rides cost €1.20.

bled

Just over an hour away from Ljubljana, Bled is a great choice for a day trip, but that doesn't mean you'll be bored out of your mind if you stay longer than that. There's tons to do here, from paddleboarding to touring a glacial gorge. Slovenia is Europe's third-most forested country, and places like Bled are where you get to appreciate those rural qualities. Just sit back, enjoy the lake, and try not to become so carefree that you decide to start gambling at Casino Bled.

ACCOMODATIONS

BLED HOSTEL
HOSTEL $

Grajska cesta 17   ☎04 250 57 45 www.bledec.si

Located just meters from the bus station, Bled Hostel is perfect if you're only in Bled a short while—you can dump your things in one of their lockers and be at the lake in minutes But due to their comfortable beds, large kitchen and common area, and happening bar, you'd be just as happy if you stayed at Bled Hostel for a bit longer. The pub downstairs is often packed with locals, so be prepared to meet Slovenian friends as well as backpackers.

i *Walk uphill from the bus station; the hostel will be on your left. Dorms €18-20. ☑ Reception 24hr.*

HOSTEL BLEDEC
HOSTEL $

Grajska cesta 17   ☎04 250 57 45 www.bledec.si

Though it's a bit farther away than Bled Hostel, nothing is really that far away in Bled—besides, you'll be slightly closer to Vintgar Gorge if you want to visit that! This is a clean, decently sized hostel; look for lots of fellow backpackers.

i *Walk uphill from the bus station; the hostel will be on your left. Dorms €16. ☑ Reception 24hr.*

SIGHTS

LAKE BLED

Unless you have a weird and twisted obsession with Bled Cream Cake, there is one reason and one reason only that you're visiting Bled: the lake. Whether you're looking to swim or to enact your fantasies of living in a fairy tale (just look at that island with the church on it!), Lake Bled will satisfy you.

Though walking along its perimeter will only take about an hour and a half, there are a variety of ways to approach Lake Bled. The best views can be had from Bled Castle and Osojnica, an observation point on top of one of the neighboring mountains. Needless to say, it's easier to get up to Bled Castle; though the trek uphill to Osojnica is punishing, you'll also be far more prepared to jump in the water once you get back down.

Along the lake, there are several designated swimming areas (elsewhere, boats will be docking, or the water is too shallow). One of these areas requires payment, but they also have water slides; if you're bummed there's no Six Flags

Slovenia, maybe this spot is for you. If you don't want to swim, rent a boat or a paddle board—the hourly rates are reasonable, and some hostels will even give you a discount.

i Free. ☎ Open 24hr.

FOOD

GRILL BABJI ZOB
BURGERS $

Cesta svobode 8   ☎838 10584 grillbabjizob.si

This inviting joint (located just steps from the bus station and boasting a view of Lake Bled that's only slightly impeded by trees; hey, you can't win 'em all!) boasts that they have the best burger in town. Technically speaking, what they serve is not a burger but strips of meat accompanied by onions and chewy bread. But let's not quibble about semantics; it's still tasty, and as long as you don't go in expecting a quarter pounder with cheese you're in good hands. Why come all the way to Slovenia to get burgers anyway? In any case, the meat strips (now we see why they refer to them as burgers) are cheap—5 pieces cost just under €5, and probably kind of healthy. Onions are good for you!

i Burgers €5. ☎ Open daily 9:30am-11pm.

PIZZERIA RUSTIKA
PIZZA $

Riklijeva cesta 13   ☎04 5768 900 www.pizzeria-rustika.si

The crowded street (ok, crowded for Bled, a town with a population of 6,000) that Pizzeria Rustika is located on? Not exactly rustic. The wooden interiors, complete with fuzzy photos of cows? That's more like it. Same goes for the wooden deck on the second floor. As is often the case in Slovenia, the so-called "small" pizzas are more than satisfactory—that's especially true here, as the crust is slightly thicker than you'll find elsewhere. If you don't think you're up to such a big meal, then just opt for one of their salads—just as tasty.

i Small pizza €6-8. Larger €7-10. ☎ Open daily 12pm-11pm.

NIGHTLIFE

PUB BLED
BAR

Svobode 19a   ☎04 574 26 22

No, not Club Med—Pub Bled! Ok, our apologies. Let's start over. Pub Bled's got a fairly refined, old school look—wood panelling, old photographs, located just above a fine dining restaurant. But make no mistake—this is a joint where people go to get wild. You see those TVs above the bar? One's for sports, and one shows a slideshow of all the different cocktails they have. Frustrated with bars that give you small cocktails? Get 3 liters of select cocktails (cuba libres and mojitos, among others) for €35. And yes, they've got Laško and Union—this is Slovenia, after all.

i Beers €2-3. Cocktails €5-7. ☎ Open M-Th 9am-1am, F-Sa 9am-3am, Su 9am-1am.

ESSENTIALS

Practicalities

- **MONEY:** There are two ATMs in the town center—one located in the Hotel Park complex by Svobode Cesta, and one in the shopping complex by Ljubljanska Cesta.

- **INTERNET CAFÉ:** Apropos Cocktail Bar has free Wi-Fi and a computer. Ljubljanska 4 ☎04 574 40 44. ☎ Open daily from 8am-12am.

- **POST OFFICE:** Ljubljanska 10 ☎04 578 09 00. ☎ Open M-F 8am-7pm, Sa from 8am-12pm.

bled

Emergency

- **HOSPITAL:** Zdravstveni Dom Ble (☎04 575 40 00)
- **POLICE:** ☎113
- **MEDICAL EMERGENCIES, FIRE:** ☎112
- **PHARMACIES:** Bled Pharmacy, Ljubljanska 4.

Getting There

Buses leave from Ljubljana to Bled every hour. The journey takes a little over an hour and tickets cost €6.30. Tickets can be purchased at the bus station.

Getting Around

Bled is a small town and has no public transportation. Call Bled Taxi if you need a ride: ☎04 171 07 47.

slovenia essentials

VISAS

Slovenia is a member of the EU, and also a member of the Schengen area. Citizens of Australia, Canada, New Zealand, the US, and many other non-EU countries do not need a visa for stays of up to 90 days. However, if you plan to spend time in other Schengen countries, note that the 90-day period of time you are allowed to visit without a visa applies cumulatively to all Schengen countries.

MONEY

Slovenia uses the Euro (EUR, €) as its currency.

Tipping is not expected in Slovenia. In restaurants, it is common to round up the bill to the nearest euro, but this is not required. Taxi drivers also do not expect tips, but if you wish to tip, round up the bill.

ATMs in Slovenia are common and convenient. They are often located in airports, train stations and major pedestrian areas. The two major international money networks are MasterCard/Maestro/Cirrus and Visa/PLUS. To find out what out-of-network or international fees you may be subject to by using ATMs, call your bank.

ALCOHOL

The minimum age to purchase alcohol in Slovenia is 18, though technically there is no minimum age to drink alcohol. Remember to drink responsibly and to never drink and drive. The legal blood alcohol content (BAC) for driving in Slovenia is 0% for drivers with less than three years of experience, and 0.05% for everyone else, significantly lower than the US limit of 0.08%.

SPAIN

Spain is a single, unified nation—but you wouldn't know it from traveling there. Each region's culture is as distinct from that of the rest as another country's. Just as the landscape varies from sun-soaked olive orchards in Andalucía to rainy and verdant hills in Galicia to windswept plains along the Camino de Santiago to Europe's best beaches all along the Mediterranean coast, so, too, do the languages and cuisines and attitudes change. And, of course, the fierce identities of Spain's unique cities can hardly be ignored. Quirky Barcelona, bureaucratic Madrid, sunny and southern Sevilla, and up-and-coming Bilbao will all claim to be the country's best; decide for yourself whether you prefer Madrid's stuffy museums to Barcelona's beaches, or tour Andalucía to figure out which city has the best mosque-turned-cathedral.

Where are you going? Make sure you have the right language, cuisine, and culture going in (don't try to order a pintxo in Granada or a pa amb tomàquet in Santiago), and enjoy the best Spain has to offer.

greatest hits

- **PICASSO, SHMICASSO.** See his works at the **Reina Sofía** in Madrid (p. 800) and the **Museu Picasso** in Barcelona.

- **CITY AT YOUR FEET.** Climb the **Columbus Monument** (p. 840) at the end of Las Ramblas and gaze out over all Barcelona.

- **THE LONG AND WINDING ROAD.** Finish your pilgrimage at the **Catedral de Santiago de Compostela** (p. 894), the terminus of the Camino de Santiago. Then go out and go hard in the hot nightlife spots next door.

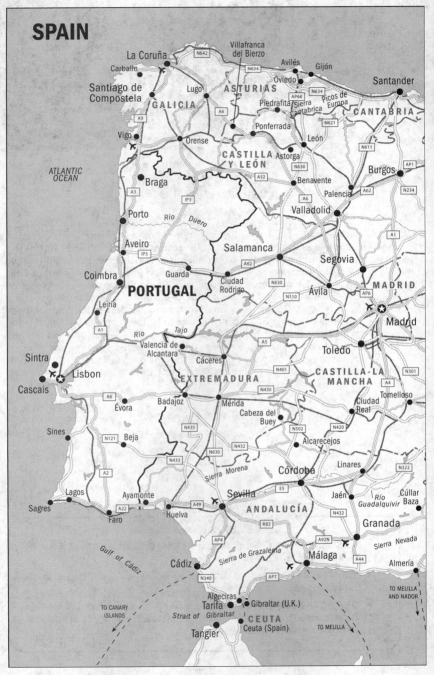

SPAIN

spain

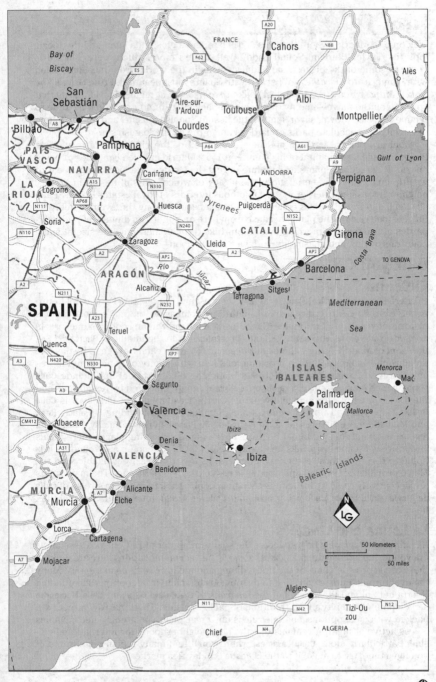

spain

madrid

Welcome to Madrid, where the days starts late, the nights ends later, and the locals look like Javier Bardem. Sound good? Well, there's more. Much more. Madrid is home to some of the biggest and baddest sights in the world, from museums filled with iconic art to *discotheques* packed with Spain's most beautiful. From Goya's *The Naked Maya* by day to the (almost) naked *madrileños* at night, Madrid insists that you stay on the move—in only the most laid-back style, of course. When it's time to recuperate, slow down, savor some of the best in Spanish cuisine, and lounge in one of the city's immaculate parks or gardens under the warm Spanish sun.

Madrid's plazas, gardens, and monuments tell of the city's rich history. After Philip II made it the capital of his empire in 1561, Madrid enjoyed centuries of being on top. It served as Spain's artistic hub during the Golden Age, becoming a seat of wealth, culture, and imperial glory, the legacy of which can still be felt in literary neighborhoods like Huertas, in the sumptuous interiors of royal estates like the Palacio Real, and in the badass collections of the museums along the Avenida del Arte. So get some rest on the plane, because from here on out, it's all dinners at midnight, parties at three in the morning, marathon treks through museums the size of small countries by day, and chasing down Javier at high noon.

ORIENTATION

El Centro

Bordered by the beautiful Palacio Real in the west and the relaxing Parque del Retiro in the east, El Centro, the heart of Madrid, encompasses the city's most famous historic sites and modern venues. Churches, plazas, and winding cobblestone streets are set beside clubs and countless tapas restaurants. In the middle is **Puerta del Sol,** the "soul of Madrid," where thousands descend to ring in each New Year. By day, the area around Puerta del Sol is a commercial hub with plenty of name-brand stores and fast-food chains. The eight streets branching off Puerta del Sol include **Calle Mayor,** which leads west to **Plaza Mayor,** a vibrant square bordered by restaurants and filled with street performers and vendors. On the western side of Pl. Mayor is **Calle Bailen.** Here you will find El Centro's most famous sights, including **El Palacio Real,** and Madrid's most picturesque formal gardens in **Plaza de Oriente.** Finally, **Plaza Santa Ana,** to the south of Puerta del Sol, provides a popular meeting place where locals and tourists escape for drinks and tapas. While El Centro can be a bit chaotic, it is home to the city's most essential landmarks. El Centro is easily walkable, and the Metro provides convenient and reliable access to the rest of the city. The main sights are deceptively close to one another. When in doubt, stick to the main streets of **Calle de Alcalá, Calle Mayor, Calle del Arsenal,** and **Calle de Atocha** for restaurants, nightlife, hostels, and cafes.

La Latina and Lavapiés

La Latina and Lavapiés lie just across the southern border of El Centro. These areas are young, hip, and distinctively *madrileño*. While accommodations here are limited, these areas provide some of the finest dining and nightlife options in the city. Many unadventurous tourists will stick to the obvious food and drink options surrounding Puerta del Sol and Pl. Mayor, but the *tabernas* of **Calle Cava Baja** and **Calle Alemendro** serve some of the city's best traditional Spanish cuisine. These narrow streets are packed with meal options, and one rule is universal: quality matters. While Lavapiés is less active at night, it remains one the best neighborhoods for international cuisine, particularly along **Calle Lavapiés,** where you'll find many Indian restaurants. If you have time, try to make it to the **El Rastro** Sunday flea market.

Las Huertas

Las Huertas' streets are lined with quotes from writers like Cervantes and Calderón de la Barca, who lived in this literary neighborhood during its Golden Age. But don't tell that to the other tourists. Most travelers are content with the commercialism of El Centro and miss out on the countless cafes, bars, pubs, and clubs lining the narrow streets of Huertas. Las Huertas feels like a playground for 20-somethings, with small independent shops, cafes, *cervecerías*, bars, and clubs in every direction. **Plaza Santa Ana** and **Plaza del Ángel** are the vital centers of the area, but you will find a greater diversity of food and drink venues as you move outward, especially east down **Calle de las Huertas** and to the north up **Calle de la Cruz**. Huertas is bounded in the north by C. Alcalá, in the south by C. Atocha, and in the east by Paseo del Prado. Despite being only a five minute walk from Sol, Huertas is very much its own world, particularly when Madrid's best nightlife scene (headlined by superclub **Kapital**) gets going.

Avenida del Arte

Avenida del Arte is a beautiful, canopied street that holds all of Madrid's world-class museums. While the city center is largely commercial (save for the odd cathedral or convent), Avenida del Arte protects Spain's most prized cultural artifacts, from Picasso's *Guernica* to Goya's *Second* and *Third of May*. While the **Museo Nacional del Prado**, the **Reina Sofía**, and the **Museo Thyssen** have become famous individually, it is their totality that makes the Avenida del Arte such a powerful showing of Spain's culture. The walk along the tree-lined **Paseo del Prado** has become a cultural phenomenon of its own, a celebration of the beauty and sophistication of this city. The avenue is also conveniently located next to the **Parque del Buen Retiro,** Madrid's Central Park, which borders the eastern edge of the city. This is where the fast pace of cosmopolitan life breaks down, where *madrileño* families come to spend time together, and where tourists can escape their hostel bunk beds.

Gran Vía

Calle Gran Vía is filled with all the stuff that tourists don't need to come to Europe to see: fast-food restaurants, chain stores, and traffic jams. It's like the Broadway of every big city in America. When wandering around Madrid for a few hours, you're bound to run into Gran Vía, the city's main commercial avenue. If its lavish architecture and sky-high buildings aren't enough to please any tourist, the street is home to a number of clubs, restaurants, and department stores unlike any other in the city. Completed in 1929, the street ends in the Plaza España, a large square surrounding a grandiose monument and fountain dedicated to *Don Quixote* author Miguel Cervantes (also a great place to sit and watch the hustling Madrileños rush past). While visitors should note that over the years, Gran Vía has transformed into a large tourist trap (you'll find menú del día and tapas prices here are more expensive than in other neighborhoods in the city like el Barrio de las Huertas or Chueca), the ornate and diverse architecture is worth the trip (plus, the street leads straight to Palacio Royal and the nightclub La Riviera).

While the main avenue tends to be crowded and commercial, the greater Gran Vía area should not be discounted. Spanning east to west from **Plaza de Cibeles** to **Plaza de España**, Gran Vía has a number of up-and-coming restaurants, bars, clubs, and live music venues—you just have to look hard (and be blessed with the handy guidance of *Let's Go*). On the southeastern boundary with Chueca, you will find the highest concentration of small restaurants, bars, and boutiques, particularly on **Calle de la Reina** and **Calle de las Infantas**. So get off the main road and discover local favorites, like the always-packed Spanish dive bar **El Tigre,** where a single beer comes with a free pile of deliciously greasy, doughy tapas.

madrid

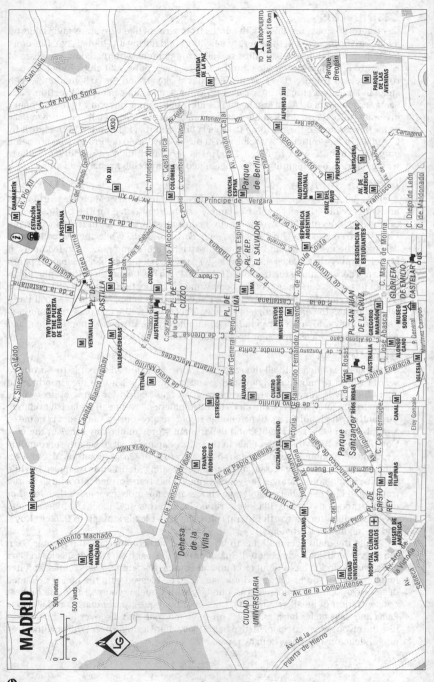

spain

MADRID

500 meters
500 yards

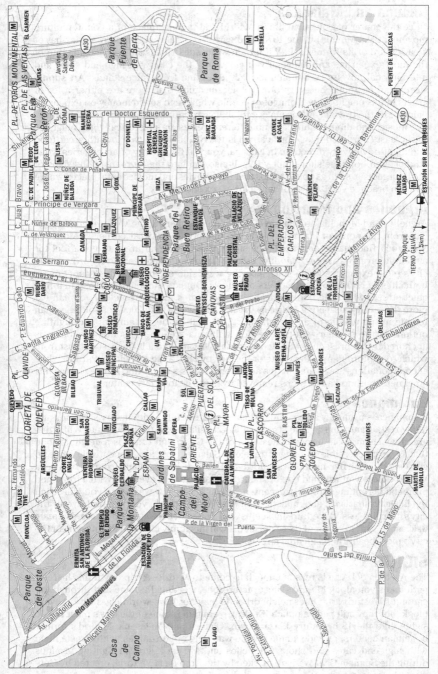

madrid

Chueca and Malasaña

Once the center of bohemian life in Madrid and the birthplace of a counterculture movement (La Movida) in the 1970s and early '80s, Malasaña is today somewhat of a caricature of its former self. Within a few decades, Malasaña has become one of the most expensive and image-driven *barrios* of the city, with high-end cafes and international novelty restaurants like creperies and fresh juice stands. Art supply stores can be found on every other block, meaning that there are either a lot of artists in this neighborhood or a lot of people who like to spend money on expensive paints. For the traveler, Malasaña is a total playground, with the city's best nightlife, live music, and dining. Chueca is no different. Malasaña's historically gay neighbor to the east (bordered by C. Fuencarral) is today a high-end *barrio* with great food and nightlife in every direction. In Chueca, you will find plenty of art galleries, yoga studios, and boutique shops, but you will also run into the more insidious signs of the bourgeoisie, such as yoga studios that rent movies and movie rental places where you can practice yoga. Oh yeah, and a lot of sex shops.

Argüelles and Moncloa

Argüelles and Moncloa are quiet residential areas spanning the western edge of the city from the north of Plaza de Espana to the city's northwest corner at Moncloa. You won't find many tourists here; instead, these are great areas to get a feel for authentic, everyday *madrileño* life. **Caso de Campo** and **Parque del Oeste** provide the city's most expansive green spaces on the west side of Madrid, which function as both sites of recreation and centers of culture. Outside the major parks, you'll find quiet streets with little bookstores, shops, and cafes. From Argüelles, you can explore the oddly captivating **Templo de Debod** to the west (it's a 2000-year-old Egyptian temple in the middle of a Spanish park) , as well as the restaurants and nightlife options in the popular-with-college-kids Malasaña area to the south. Monocloa is anchored by the presence of Franco's **Arco de la Victoria,** and it is the best outpost from which to explore Parque del Oeste or journey by bus to the Palacio El Pardo . While accommodations are limited in this area, some tourists might find refuge staying in a quiet neighborhood a few stops removed from the chaotic city center.

Salamanca

Salamanca is primarily a high-end residential district filled with luxury shopping and fancy restaurants on the side streets of C. Castellano and C. de Serrano. While this area may seem posh, buried beneath all of the Gucci and Prada is a neighborhood that is very accessible to budget travelers. Salamanca is also deceptively close to city center, just a five-minute walk north up Paseo de la Castellana from el Arco de la Victoria. Here you will find one of Madrid's most beautiful avenues, with a tree-lined promenade running through the center. As you make your way north you will reach the **Biblioteca Nacional,** and, making your way further north, you will find two of the city's terrific, less visited art museums: the **Museo Sorrola** and the **Museo de Lazaro Galdiano**. A visit to either of these museums will inevitably take you down some of the city's most beautiful residential streets.

SIGHTS

The Avenida del Arte is reason enough to come to Madrid. A trip down this historic path takes you along Madrid's most picturesque, tree-lined avenue and through the canon of Western art. Other neighborhoods may not have world-class art on every block, but they still pack a punch. El Centro contains some of the city's most iconic sights, like the 18th-century Plaza Mayor. Chueca and Malasaña, Madrid's former bohemian centers, provide ample people-watching opportunities, with streets lined with high-end cafes and shops. Argüelles and Moncloa, crucial fighting grounds during the Spanish Civil War, are marked by the Arco de la Victoria, erected by General Franco and perhaps the most visible remnant of his haunting legacy. The palace El Pardo, just north of Moncloa, offers a view into the dictator's private bunker. Argüelles and Moncloa are also home to the city's most anomalous historical sight, the Egyptian Templo de Debod.

El Centro

🏛 PALACIO REAL

PALACE

C. de Baillén ☎91 454 87 00 www.patrimonionacional.es

If you spent your childhood dreaming of princesses, knights, and dragons, the Palacio Real, Madrid's own royal palace, will be your dream come true. While the palace may not look as grand or as medieval as expected from the outside, its interior is ornately decorated with gold and porcelain in Rococo, Neoclassical, and Baroque styles. Grandiose Catholicism-inspired frescoes shade the ceilings of many rooms in the palace, thick velvet rugs and lavish tapestries color the floors and walls, and green and white marble-carved arches and columns make the voluminous space between the palace's many rooms sparkle. You should start looking for a knight in shining armor, since the sheer size and scale of the palace might make you faint.

Even with all of its grandeur, it may come as a surprise that the Palacio Real is the largest palace in all of Western Europe. With 135,000 square feet and 3,418 different rooms, the palace has enough space to accommodate some of Francisco de Goya's, Diego Velázquez's, and Juan de Flandes's most cherished works.

The palace was commissioned by King Philip V and built in 1734 on the site of Alcazar, an ancient ninth- or 10th-century Moorish fortress, which burned in a fire that same year. Originally, the palace was intended to be a place for the monarch and his family to live, which they did up until the end of Alfonso III's reign. Today, the building is the official residence of the royal family, but they do not in fact stay there. Instead, it functions as a site for official celebrations and banquets for the state, and often passersby will find the street leading to the palace's entrance closed off by the police and the national guard due to some such ceremony.

Finish up a visit to the palace with a trip to the armory, a two-floor building that holds centuries-old lances, shields, and armor. Check out the old suits men going to battle for the King of Spain used to wear, along with their deadly swords, horse's (and children's!) armor, and sabers. It's hard not to imagine a thousand clunking Spaniards going to war against Britain or Austria when walking around this dark, dungeon-like room.

The palace and its exterior gardens are open to the public nearly every day of the year, except for special ceremonies and occasions (which can occur very last minute). Whip out your student ID for a half-off discount, or visit the palace on weeknights from 6-8pm for free admission. Beware: lines are like those at an amusement park. They can take an hour or more to get through, so plan ahead. Backpacks are not allowed in the palace (you can use a deposit-based storage locker).

i Ⓜ*Opera. Walk west down C. de Arrieta. Palacio Real is at the end of the road. Come early to avoid long lines. €10, with tour €17; ages 5-16, students, and seniors €5. ☑ Open daily Apr-Sept 10am-8pm; Oct-Mar 10am-6pm.*

PLAZA MAYOR

PLAZA

Pl. Mayor

As you'll soon learn, Madrid has a lot of plazas. Each comes with its own statue or fountain, a number of restaurants, and, of course, a gaggle of tourists.

Why is La Plaza Mayor different? Well, in English, La Plaza Mayor means "the main square." The plaza, located in the heart of el Centro (otherwise, located in the heart of the heart of Madrid—or better, the heart of the heart of the heart of Spain), is by far one of the city's most popular hubs. Flanked by Madrid's most famous and historical attractions like Chocolatería San Gines and Botin, La Plaza Mayor is the perfect starting point from which to begin a day of sightseeing. Meet a friend near dusk (10pm) at the 400-year-old statue of Philip III, who ruled over Spain during the plaza's construction and revel at the square's simple, yet regal architecture and design.

Three mostly residential buildings surround the plaza, which first opened in 1620. The two prominent buildings are la Casa de la Panadería and la Casa de la Carnicería (bakery house and butcher house, respectively), the former of which housed a bakery in its earlier days and now functions as a municipal and cultural center. Initially, the building was constructed with wood, but after suffering demolition from several fires, architects finally decided to build it from stone. Historically, the plaza has been a center for bullfights, royal coronations, and during the Spanish Inquisition, the location of public executions for heretics or transgressors of "fe," the Catholic faith.

After admiring the colorful, allegoric facades on la Casa de la Panadería, wander down one of the offshoot streets (after avoiding street vendors) for a light dinner or a round of tapas. Because the plaza is such a hotspot for tourists, many of the restaurants directly inside the plaza will sell more expensive food, and according to some locals, the meals these restaurants serve aren't of the best quality. Walk in the direction of Puerta del Sol, the plaza's neighboring square (and home of Oso y el Madroño, part of Madrid's coat of arms) or in the direction of Las Huertas and find a few authentic bars there instead.

i Ⓜ*Sol or* Ⓜ*Opera. From Puerta del Sol, walk 2min. down C. Mayor toward the Palacio Real. Pl. Mayor is on the left.*

PUERTA DEL SOL   PLAZA
Puerta del Sol

Spain's *Kilometre Zero*, the point from which all distances in Spain are measured, is located in Puerta del Sol. You certainly can't get more *"el centro"* than the center of the Spanish kingdom itself, but unfortunately, that's pretty much the most distinctive part about "Sol." It's a geographic reference point, but there's not much to see here other than two statues (the one depicting a bear climbing up a tree is supposed to be famous, but it's hard to see why), chain stores, and hordes of tourists. It's like Times Square, minus the pretty lights and cool stores. In fact, the huge space it spans is actually where locals gather to ring in the New Year. The tradition is to drunkenly eat 12 grapes at midnight and make 12 wishes for each of the upcoming 12 months. The plaza, memorialized in Goya's *The Third* and *Second of May*, is today overrun by newsstands, billboards, scam artists, and street performers dressed like Mickey Mouse and Spongebob. You're better off walking either north, south, east, or west of *Kilometre Zero* if you're looking for a more authentic Madrid. With the regional government situated on the southern end of the plaza, the Puerta del Sol has also been the site of major protests and political rallies.

i Ⓜ*Sol.*

CATEDRAL DE LA ALMUDENA   CATHEDRAL
C. Bailen   ☎91 542 22 00

Catedral de la Almudena is an anomaly. Big cathedral in major European city—must be hundreds of years old, right? Nope. While Madrid became the official capital of the Spanish Kingdom during the reign of Philip II, it took many years for the Spanish Catholic Church to recognize the city as a worthy religious center, preferring the former capital of Toledo. Because of this, the Church was resistant to the idea of building a new central cathedral in Spain. While

get a room!

Madrid has a range of affordable housing options in almost every neighborhood. For more listings, visit **www.letsgo.com**

🛏 LAS MUSAS HOSTEL
HOSTAL $$$

C. Jesús y María, 12 ☎915 39 49 84 www.lasmusashostel.com

Las Musas hostel is an epicenter for young people looking to discover all that is Madrid—nightlife, flamenco, tapas, and of course, booze. Situated in a quaint apartment just off the plaza Tirso de Molina and blocks away from the Plaza Mayor, Puerta del Sol, and Gran Via, Las Musas offers its travelers eight different types of rooms. With ridiculously comfortable beds, in-suite bathrooms, a free breakfast of churros (yum) and fruit, and a multi-purpose kitchen, the hostel strives to provide a home away from home. Tip filled walking tours of the area, discounted flamenco nights, tapas tours, nightly bar crawls, and inexpensive day trips to Toledo are also offered to guests who want a taste of Madrid before diving in by themselves. Storage lockers are provided, but small padlocks cost €3. Wi-Fi is also only available in the lobby, and the hostel has a 48hr. cancellation policy.

i Mixed rooms €15-20. Singles and doubles starting around €45. ☼ Reception 24hr. Check in 3:30pm; check out by 10:30am.

🛏 ALBERGUE JUVENIL MADRID
HOSTEL $

C. Meija Lequerica, 21 ☎91 593 96 88 www.ajmadrid.es

Located just minutes away from el Paseo del Prado and the Golden Triangle of Art (a.k.a the Prado, Reina Sofía, and Thyssen-Bornemisza) and in close proximity to three metro stops, this hostel allows travelers to explore the most exciting sights in Madrid with little hassle or confusion. An English speaking staff, free breakfast, spacious rooms, storage lockers, free and reliable Wi-Fi, and a social coordinator delegated to take you and fellow travelers out to bars are all added pluses. With 25 rooms that host from four to six people each, you will undoubtedly be able to find a bed at this hostel, even when booking last minute.

i Laundry €3. Towels €3. 4- to 6-bed co-ed dorms. Book at least 5 days in advance. Under 25 starting at €18.50, 25 and over starting at €21. ☼ Reception 24hr. Check in by 3pm, check out by 11am.

🛏 LA POSADA DE LAS HUERTAS
HOSTAL $

Huertas, 21 ☎914 295 526 www.posadadehuertas.com

Even La Posada de Las Huertas's name is poetic. Translated to "Orchard Inn," this hostel is burrowed in the heart (in fact, on the central road) of el Barrio de Las Letras, a neighborhood in Madrid famous for hosting some of the most prolific writers of the Spanish Golden Age, like Miguel Cervantes and Lope de Vega. Travelers looking for a place with easy access to the dynamic nightlife of La Latina and a relaxing environment for nights off will find this hostel very suitable. Travelers are provided with free Wi-Fi, free breakfast, linens, a full kitchen, and, storage lockers. Make sure to check out the hostel's bar crawls, free sangria nights, and walking tours for a chance to bond with fellow hostel-goers and learn more about the city's literary barrio.

i Rooms €13-20; free cancellation up to a day before the reservation. ☼ Check in 1:30pm, check out before 10:30am.

madrid

Catedral de la Almudena was conceived in the 16th century, construction did not begin until 1879 and was only just completed in 1999 (meaning this towering European cathedral is younger than you are). Located next to El Palacio Real, this monumental cathedral is a happy accident: the Catholic Church's love child with the city of Madrid. The architectural style reflects this precarious past: the roof is painted in bright, bold patterns that resemble the work of Henri Matisse, while the panes of stained glass recall Picasso and the Cubist tradition. In this way, Catedral de la Almudena separates itself from run-of-the-mill European cathedrals in which you walk into a cavernous space, note that it looks cool, feels impressive, makes you feel insignificant, and then you leave. If you look hard, you'll find little hints of Modernism that you won't find in any other cathedral.

i *Right next to Palacio Real. Free. ⚅ Open daily 10am-2pm and 5-8pm.*

CONVENTO DE LA ENCARNACIÓN
CONVENT

Pl. de la Encarnación, 1   ☎91 454 88 00

Every July 27, it is said that the blood of St. Panthalon, held in a crystal orb, visibly liquefies. It is not entirely clear that St. Panthalon was in fact a living, breathing (and bleeding) person, but a crystal orb containing his alleged blood is on display at the Convento de la Encarnación. Convents are normally incredibly exclusive: it doesn't matter how hot your friends are, you still aren't getting in (that bouncer, Sister Martha, is such a witch!). This convent is a little different. While it was founded as an exclusive center of monastic life nearly 400 years ago, today it is accessible to the general public for a small entrance fee. Self-guided tours aren't allowed; the only way into the chapel is to pay for the group tour, which generally runs every 30min. The tour takes you through the formerly secluded chapel, filled with artwork by European masters, and into the famous reliquary, which contains thousands of Christian relics, most notably those blood-filled crystal orbs. It's 5min. away from the Catedral de Almudena, and while Almudena is bigger and prettier, the convent has more history and authenticity behind it. And some mean nuns, if getting yelled at by old ladies is your thing.

i *ⓜOpera. Take Pl. de Isabel II northwest to C. de Arietta and turn right onto Pl. de la Encarnación. Tours conducted in Spanish every 30min. €3.60. ⚅ Open Tu-Sa 10am-2pm, Su 10am-3pm.*

Avenida del Arte

▣ MUSEO NACIONAL CENTRO DE ARTE REINA SOFÍA
MUSEUM

C. Santa Isabel, 52   ☎91 774 10 00   www.museoreinasofia.es

The Reina Sofía, the Golden Triangle of Art's southernmost leg, offers visitors a refreshing break from Madrid's neoclassical artistic tradition. Its four floors of collections and exhibitions are stocked with 20,000 pieces of 20th-century art from around the world, with a special emphasis on the modern Spanish canon. The museum owns some of the most widely celebrated works from Spanish powerhouses like Pablo Picasso and Salvador Dalí, including Picasso's 349cm × 776cm "Guernica," which is guarded by two officials in a room the museum specifically commissioned to house the painting. Much of the art, which spans a variety of mediums like sculpture and videography, is abstract (think squiggly lines and colleges), so don't spend too much time contemplating the meaning of one painting. The labyrinthine system of galleries and rooms in the Reina Sofía can sometimes prevent efficient museum going, and a time-crunch is particularly pressing if you choose to attend the museum for free from 7-9pm on a weeknight. Most importantly, do not forget to use the elevators that face the square in front of the museum.

i *ⓜAtocha €8. Temporary exhibits €4. Weeknights 7-9pm free. ⚅ Open M 10am-9pm, W-Sa 10am-9pm, Su 10am-2:30pm.*

MUSEO NACIONAL DEL PRADO   MUSEUM

C. Ruiz de Alarcón, 23   ☎91 330 28 00 www.museodelprado.es

Located in the heart of central Madrid, the Museo Nacional del Prado, Spain's largest art museum, is a symbol of national pride and a relic of the nation's rich artistic history. El Prado's ornate and ionic column-laden building was originally designed in 1785 to house the National History cabinet, but at the request of King Ferdinand VII and Maria Isabel de Braganza it was converted into a national museum of painting and sculptures. Today, the royal family's collection comprises the foundation of the museum's expansive assemblage of some of the most important pieces of Western and Spanish Renaissance art, including Diego Velázquez's "Las Meninas" (located in room 12 on the first floor of the building), Bosch's "The Garden of Earthly Delights" (room 56A, floor 0), and Rubens's "The Three Graces" (room 29, floor 1). Also impressive is del Prado's wide repertoire of Francisco Goya's paintings; the museum owns more than 140 of his works, including his famed (and creepy) black painting "Saturn Devouring one of His Sons" and his "Third of May" piece that somberly depicts the aftermath of the dos de Mayo uprising.

If trying to find these famous works sounds overwhelming, luckily for you, the museum's information booklet provides the names and locations of each of its fifty "masterpieces" from the Western canon. The museum itself can be somewhat difficult to navigate (its main entrance is on floor zero, whose "salas," or galleries, number 45-75, and there is a separate building housing the museum's special temporary exhibitions), but follow this booklet and you should find your way around the museum's 100-plus galleries without too much trouble. Museum officials speak broken English, which may or may not be helpful when trying to locate a piece of art or inquiring about temporary exhibitions. Museum officials recommend visiting between the hours of 1pm and 3pm, when most locals are eating lunch, and say that, not surprisingly, Saturday is the museum's busiest day.

i Ⓜ*Banco de España and* Ⓜ*Atocha. From* Ⓜ*Atocha, walk north up Paseo del Prado; the museum is on the right, just past the gardens. General Admission with a museum guidebook €23, general admission €14, €7 reduced fee 65+, large families, and 6-8pm M-Sa. students 18-25 free (ID required).* Ⓩ *Open M-Sa 10am-8pm, Su and public holidays 10am-7pm.*

MUSEO THYSSEN-BORNEMISZA   MUSEUM

Paseo del Prado, 8   ☎91 369 01 51 www.museothyssen.org

It's easy to forget about the Thyssen-Bornemisza when hopping between the juggernaut that is the Reina Sofía and Prado museums. But that's good news for you—the crowds for this world-class museum are short and sweet. The museum is housed in the 19th-century Palacio de Villahermosa and contains the donated collection of the late Baron Henrich Thyssen-Bornemisza. Today, the museum, with the world's most extensive private showcase, with items ranging from 14th-century Flemish altarpieces to an impressive collection of German avant-garde canvases from the early 20th century. This museum is particularly sweet for tourists; whereas Prado and Reina Sofía have exhibits focusing on very particular Spanish art, there's a more diverse selection of art here, including the likes of Edward Hopper.

i From the Prado, walk north up the Paseo del Prado. The museum is at the corner of Carrera de San Jeronimo and Paseo del Prado €7, children under 12 free. Ⓩ *Open Tu-Su 10am-7pm.*

CAIXAFORUM   MUSEUM

Paseo del Prado, 36   ☎91 389 65 45

The most striking feature of the Caixaforum is the vertical garden on the exterior of the building—it looks like someone planted a forest on the side of a modern building. Other than that, this museum is surprisingly uninspiring for having been designed by the same architects as London's legendary Tate Modern. There's not much of a focus at Caixaforum; there are only two floors of monochromatic, tinny gallery space for various art, design, and architecture exhibits. The basement auditorium hosts miscellaneous events, from architecture lectures to dance performances to film screenings.

i ⓂAtocha. *From the metro, walk north up Paseo del Prado; the Caixaforum is on the left €4.* ☒ *Open daily 10am-8pm. Closed Dec 25, Jan 1, and Jan 6.*

PARQUE DEL BUEN RETIRO
PARK

Pl. de la Independencia, 7 ☎915 30 00 41 www.esmadrid.com/es/retiro

Every large city needs a pedestrian-friendly park to diversify its otherwise concrete and statue-ridden landscape. Madrid, although an unusually green city already, is no exception. Buen Retiro Park, a 350-acre plot of grass, trees, and walking trails, sits tranquilly between Calle Alfonso XII and Avenue de Menéndez Pelayo. The park, commissioned by the Count Duke of Olivares in the 1630s, is nearly 400 years old and saw the blossoming of Hapsburg court life, mock naval battles in its grand pond, and even Italian operas performed on its grounds.

While lush, meandering gardens and grassy lawns dotted with trees comprise the majority of the park, there are other attractions, like a large monument to Alfonso XII, the historic Casita del Pescador, and number of quaint ponds. Plenty of food vendors, fortune tellers, and portrait-sketchers linger close to high traffic areas like the monument or the Crystal Palace, but these places bear the only sign of tourism. Otherwise, the park is peaceful and quiet—the perfect escape from the hustle and bustle of downtown Madrid.

Pack a picnic lunch and walk underneath the vine-covered Rosadela in the park's main garden or go boating on the majestic lake in front of Alfonso XII's monument. Even go for a short stroll through the park or join hundreds of other runners on a warm, breezy day. The park seems a world away from Spain's lively capital. Also check out Madrid's literary festival, also located on Paseo de Carruajes, which runs from late May to mid-June each year.

i ⓂRetiro. *Or, from*ⓂAtocha, *pass the roundabout north onto Calle de Alfonso XII. The park is on the right. Free. Row boats M-F until 2pm; €1.40, Sa-Su and holidays €4.55.* ☒ *Open in summer daily 6am-midnight; in winter 6am-10pm. Estanque pier open 10am to 45min. before sunset; Jul-Aug 10am-11pm.*

Las Huertas

REAL ACADEMIA DE BELLAS ARTES DE SAN FERNANDO
MUSEUM

C. de Alcalá, 13 rabasf.insde.es ☎91 524 08 64

The oldest permanent art institute in Madrid, the Royal Academy of Fine Arts of San Fernando was created in 1752 and was the premier center for Spanish arts up until the mid-20th century. Since then, it has been transformed into a low-key, badass museum, often forgotten among the museum titans of the Prado and Reina Sofia. This place is great because there are little to no tourists or crowds, it's free all the time for students (and only €5 for everyone else), and it's located in an amazing Baroque palace, where you can imagine 19th-century Spanish students once chilled while making art and other hipster stuff. The museum contains three main floors and features a permanent collection of Spanish, Italian, and Flemish art—particularly notable are the Goya paintings in Room 13, including two rare self-portraits. The third floor is primarily 20th-century contemporary art, which follows the trajectory of post-Cubism Spanish art. Even if you don't like art at all, you get free entry to a baller palace—on Wednesdays.

i *From Puerta del Sol, walk east down C. de Alcalá. Real Academia de Bellas Artes is on the left. €5; groups of 15-25, university students, teachers, under 18 and over 65 free. Free for everyone on W.* ☒ *Open Tu-Su 10am-3pm.*

La Latina and Lavapiés

BASILICA DE SAN FRANCISCO EL GRANDE
CATHEDRAL

C. de San Buenaventura ☎91 365 38 00

One of the grandest and most distinctive structures in Madrid is often overlooked by most tourists. While everyone visits the Catedral Almudena just up the road, many end up missing out on this basilica, which comes to life in stunning fashion when lit up at night. The cathedral has three chapels, including the Chapel of San Bernardino de Siena, where Goya's magnificent painting of the chapel's namesake rests. Pay close attention to the picture, and you will see that the figure looking down on the right is Goya himself. Don't forget to check out the adjacent gardens, which have spectacular views of the rolling edges of Madrid.

i *From Ⓜ La Latina, walk straight west down Carrera San Francisco. Free. Guided tour €3. ◯ Open Tu-Su 10:30am-1pm and 4-6:30pm.*

LA IGLESIA DE SAN ANDRÉS
CHURCH

Pl. de San Andrés

One of the oldest parishes in Madrid, La Iglesia de San Andrés used to be *the* go-to church for La Latina local and patron saint of Madrid, San Isidro Labrador. Much of the original interior was destroyed during the Spanish Civil War, but the structure still showcases a Baroque style crafted by designer José de Villarreal. The large domed ceiling and colorful stained glass make for a pretty, if not particularly daring, aesthetic. It's not a must-see, but it's definitely worth stopping by if you're in the area.

i *Ⓜ La Latina. Make a left onto C. de la Cava. Free.*

Chueca and Malasaña

PALACIO LONGORIA
BUILDING

C. de Fernando VI, 6

This just might be the ugliest building in the city. Depending on who you are, you will either find Palacio Longoria to be an eyesore or a beautiful relic of Neo-classical revivalist architecture. Whether you like it or not, you will probably run into this monochromatic, bombastic building during your time in Chueca—it is worth noting its peculiarity as the only true example of Catalan *modernismo* (à la Gaudí) in Madrid. Palacio Longoria was built in the early 20th century as a private residence for banker Javier González Longoria. In 1950 it was converted into a private office building for the General Society of Spanish Authors and Editors. As such, the building is rarely open to the public, but its intricately embellished façade is a sight to behold as you make your way through Chueca.

i *From Ⓜ Chueca, take C. Gravina 1 block west to C. Pelayo and continue 2 blocks north. The building is on the left. The interior is only open to the public during National Architecture Week (2nd week of Oct).*

CONVENTO DE LAS SALESAS REALES
CATHEDRAL

C. Barbara de Braganza, 1 ☎91 319 48 11 www.parroquiadesantabarbara.es

Conceived in 1748 by Barbara of Portugal, this monastery continues to function as a church, but it's a great place to get away from the irony and trendiness of Malasaña and Chueca and experience some Centro-esque tourism. Right next to the Supreme Court of Spain and some lovely green Spanish plazas, this area has a surprisingly small tourist crowd (tourists' greatest fear seems to be hipsters). The interior of the church is pretty standard, but the clean and peaceful exterior area is a must-see.

i *Ⓜ Colon. From Pl. Colon, go down Paseode Recoletos and take a right onto C. de Barbara de Braganza. Free. ◯ Open M-F 9:30am-1pm and 5:30-8pm, Sa 9:30am-2pm and 5-9pm, Su 9:30am-2pm and 6-9pm. Closed to tourists during mass.*

madrid

MUSEO DE HISTORIA
C. Fuencarral, 78 ☎91 701 18 63 www.munimadrid.es/museodehistoria

MUSEUM

This renovated 18th-century building constructed under Philip V now holds small collection of models, illustrations, and documents that showcase the history of Madrid. While it's mildly interesting to see how Gran Vía and Pl. Mayor looked back in the day, it's quite a small exhibit and doesn't justify going out of your way to visit this museum. The building itself is a historical relic, one of Madrid's few lasting examples of Baroque architecture. The facade is currently being renovated, and upon completion, the museum will have a totally new state-of-the-art facility.

i ⓂTribunal. Walk straight north up C. Fuencarral. The large pink building is on the right. Free. ⓐ Open Tu-Sa 10am-9pm, Su 11am-2:30pm.

Gran Vía

▨ PLAZA DE ESPAÑA
PLAZA

In a city filled with statues of Spanish royalty and Roman deities, Pl. de España is something of an anomaly. Located on the western edge of Gran Vía, Pl. de España is a monument to the father of Spanish literature, **Miguel de Cervantes.** The stone statue of Cervantes at the center of the plaza is surrounded by characters from his most celebrated work, *Don Quixote.* The bronze statues immediately below Cervantes depict the hero Alonso Quixano and his chubby and slightly less heroic sidekick, Sancho Panza. To the right and left are Quixano's two love interests, the peasant lady Aldonza Lorenzo and the woman of his dreams, Dulcinea Del Toboso. Plazade España is less touristy and more lively than other plazas (like Pl. Mayor). More than just a place to gawk at a statue, this plaza also has a fountain that shoots up "Old Faithful"-style on the hour, with lots of seating around it for people who want to read or make out. In addition, there are hordes of vendors selling items like jewelry, souvenirs, and sunflower seeds. Also, it seems to be the only plaza with park-like grassy lawns for lounging (and, fine, for making out).

i The western end of C. Gran Vía, also accessible by ⓂPlaza de España. Free.

▨ PLAZA DE CIBELES
PLAZA

One of Madrid's many plazas, la Plaza de Cibeles is probably its most famous—and most photographed. The plaza sits at the intersection of three different districts of Madrid—Salamanca, Centro, and Retiro—and symbolically acts as a central converging point in the city. In the middle of the plaza is a fountain named after Cybele, an ancient Anatolian mother goddess who gathered a significant cult following in Greece. The nearly 250-year-old fountain depicts her likeness sitting atop a chariot pulled by two lions.

Four prominent buildings surround the plaza: Palacio de Cibeles, Palacio de Linares, Palacio de Buenavista, and the Bank of Spain. Right behind the plaza is the Cibeles Palace, or the former Palace of Communication (as in, it used to be a post office). Constructed in a fusion of neo-Gothic, neo-Plateresque, and Catalan art nouveau styles, the palace is not a sight to miss, especially at night when the building lights up against the black Spanish sky. Today, the building functions as Madrid's city hall, the setting in which city council meetings take place.

Because of the plaza's prominent and visible location in the city, fans of Madrid's fútbol team, Real Madrid, have taken to draping its flag across the fountain whenever the team wins La Liga (their soccer league), Copa del Rey, or the Champions League. Basically, the flag is there a lot.

The plaza's center is located at the hub of a roundabout, so be careful when crossing the road to visit (be warned, many Madrileño drivers are reckless).

i Intersection of C. de Alcalá, Paseo de Recoletos and Paseo del Prado.

spain

Argüelles and Moncloa

🏛 TEMPLO DE DEBOD
TEMPLE, PARK

Paseo del Pintor Rosales, 2 ☎91 366 74 15 www.munimadrid.es/templodebod

The Templo de Debod is the centerpiece of the Jardinez Ferraz, a favorite park among locals. It's a 10min walk north from the Palacio Real, and you'll be hard-pressed to find many tourists among the sun-lounging park goers. It looks out of place, and that's because it is. It's an Egyptian temple, originally built in the second century BCE, but it was donated to Madrid by Egypt in 1968 for the Spanish government's role in saving the temples of Abu Simbel. So there's literally a 2000-year-old Egyptian temple in the heart of Madrid. On top of that, the park is on high ground, offering a great view of Madrid landmarks (such as Palacio Real) as well as the rolling green countryside. Good luck finding a better place to watch the sunset.

i Ⓜ*Plaza de España. Walk to the far side of Pl. de España, cross the street, and walk a couple of blocks right; the temple is on the left. Free. ☒ Open Apr-Sept Tu-F 10am-2pm and 6-8pm, Sa-Su 10am-2pm; Oct-Mar Tu-F 9:45am-1:45pm and 4:15-6:15pm, Sa-Su 10am-2pm. Rose garden open daily 10am-8pm.*

🏛 EL PARDO
PALACE

C. de Manuel Alonso s/n ☎91 376 15 00

A 20min. bus ride out of Moncloa, El Pardo is Palacio Real's more rural, less tourist-packed, and less grandiose little brother. Originally built in the 15th century as a hunting lodge for Henry IV, El Pardo is now most famous as the private residence of General Franco during his military dictatorship. The mandatory guided tour (45min.) takes you through regal rooms covered with frescoes of royal figures and hunts as well as Franco's private quarters, which have remained largely untouched since his death in 1975. His wardrobe, prayer room, personal study, and bedroom (where he kept his most treasured personal possession, a relic of St. Teresa's silver-encrusted petrified arm) are all on display. The tour even takes you into Franco's bathroom, and yes—he had a bidet. Nowadays, in addition to its function as a tourist attraction, El Pardo is used to host state galas and functions and is the official hotel for foreign dignitaries.

i Ⓜ*Moncloa. Take bus #601 from the underground bus station (terminal 3) adjacent to Moncloa. Mandatory 45min. guided tour in Spanish/English; last tour leaves 1hr. before close €9, students and over 65 €4 ☒ Open Oct-Mar M-Sa 10:30am-4:45pm, Su 10am-1:30pm; Apr-Sept M-Sa 10:30am-5:45pm, Su 9:30am-1:30pm.*

CASA DE CAMPO
PARK

Zoo Madrid ☎91 512 37 70 www.zoomadrid.com

If Parque del Oeste or Retiro Park are too tame for you, Casa de Campo offers a more sprawling experience. You won't find well-kept, lawn-ready grass to lounge on here; the fauna of Casa de Campo is more wild, rough, and untamed. For a pedestrian traveler, it's easy to get lost in the vast winding paths, so make sure you have a nice map, a good sense of direction, and a love of walking. Bike trails crisscross the park, and kayaks and canoes are available for rent at the park lagoon. If you are looking for something more than a tranquil afternoon in the park, **Parque de Atracciones** (an amusement park) has rides that will jack your heart rate up without fail. No need to commit yourself to the all-day pass (€24); single- and double-ride tickets can be purchased on the cheap (single €7; double €12). The park also has Madrid's only zoo and aquarium, but be prepared to shell out for an entrance pass (€19), and don't expect any particular Castillian flair from the monkeys; they're just regular monkeys. Make sure you know what metro station to get off at to avoid walk-

madrid

ing long distances: Lago for the lagoon, Batan for the amusement park, and Casa de Campo for the zoo/aquarium.

i Ⓜ*Lago, Batan, and Casa de Campo are all within the park. To get there from the city center:* Ⓜ*Batan or bus #33 or 65. Let's Go does not advise walking here after dark. Entrance to the park is free; venues and rentals are ticketed.* ☑ *Parque de Atracciones open M-Sa 9am-7pm. Zoo Madrid open daily, but check website for hours and schedule changes.*

MUSEO DE AMÉRICA   MUSEUM
Av. de los Reyes Catolicos, 6   ☎91 549 26 41 www.museodeamerica.mcu.es

Gotta love Spain; they know what's up and have created a whole museum dedicated to the greatness of (as the Spanish say) "'Murica!" Just kidding. In 1771, Carlos III started a collection that brought together ethnographic objects from scientific expeditions and pieces from the first archaeological excavations carried out in the Americas. So instead of seeing bald eagles, monster trucks, and Big Macs, you can see old maps and conquistador memorabilia. Today, the modern Museo de América holds a collection that encompasses mainly South American cultures. Some of the most interesting artifacts are treasures from the pre-Columbian cultures conquered by Spain, including some Mayan hieroglyphic documents. This museum isn't nearly as popular as the Prado, so you don't have to worry about crowds. Be warned that all the exhibit descriptions are in Spanish, with no English translation.

i Ⓜ*Moncloa. Cross the street, make a left, and walk straight €3; reduced €1.50; under 18, over 65, and students free.* ☑ *Open M-Sa 9:30am-6:30pm, Su 10am-3pm.*

Salamanca

🏛 MUSEO SOROLLA   MUSEUM
C. General Martinez Campos, 47 http://museosorolla.mcu.es/   ☎91 310 15 84

Museo Sorolla is a must-see for art lovers; prior knowledge of Joaquim Sorolla not necessary. It's an important counterpoint to the impersonal big museums like Prado or Reina Sofia—where we often forget that there's a human being behind each painting. Focusing on a single artist and inhabiting Sorolla's former residence and studio, Museo Sorolla gives you a sense of the deeply personal nature of art. It helps that Sorolla is also one of Spain's most talented painters. You get a sense of the story of Sorolla's artistic career, starting with the realism of his teachers, turning to impressionism, and then finally pioneering the beautiful luminist movement. The beach scenes are gorgeous: broad swaths of blue-green paint that boldly reflect the play of light on the water. More importantly, you get a sense of the Sorolla the family man, who captured his love in countless portraits such as *Mi Mujer y Mis Hijos* ("My Wife and Kids"). Come to Museo Sorolla and witness the power of art to immortalize love.

i Ⓜ*Iglesia. Turn right on C. General Martinez Campos €3. Free on Su.* ☑ *Open Tu-Sa 9:30am-8pm, Su 10am-3pm.*

MUSEO LAZARO GALDIANO   MUSEUM
C. Serrano, 122   ☎91 561 60 84 www.fig.es

Mueso Lazaro Galdiano calls itself "probably the best private art collection." It puts the word "probably" in there because we all know that title actually belongs to Museo Thyssen in Avenida del Arte. Don't be mistaken, Jose Lazaro Galdiano—one of Spain's most influential patron of arts and literature in the early 20th century—amassed quite an impressive collection (13,000 pieces on display). But it lacks the breadth of the Thyssen collection. While it includes a number of significant works, such as Goya's *Witch's Sabbath*, and *El Greco's Portrait of St. Francis of Assis*, the vast majority of his collection consists of stiff 16th- to 18th-century religious portraits and scenes. If you loved Prado and Palacio Real, you'll probably enjoy this too. Much like the Royal Palace, each room is decked out in fancy woodwork and usually an impossibly intricate ceiling fresco. Worth checking out is the top fifth floor, which includes the miscellaneous items of his collection, such as ivory-coated muskets and fancy sabers.

i ⓂGregorio Maranon €4, students €3, EU citizens free. ⓩ Open Su 10am-3pm Tu-Sa 10am-4:30pm.

FOOD

The 2-5pm siesta commonly practiced by restaurants and stores across Madrid can make finding a place to eat lunch after a morning of touring difficult. But while many restaurants close their doors for siesta, working men and women throughout the city often do not have time to go home for lunch and then return to their offices. To accommodate these men and women, many restaurants that stay open during siesta offer menús del día, cheap two-course meals that can be eaten relatively quickly. As one Madrileño commented, these meals are not advertised to tourists, who often fall prey to the poor quality, expensive food sold around major attractions like the Plaza Mayor. So here's your Let's Go tip: if you want a filling, cheap meal that can fuel you even on the hottest of summer days, look for these menús del día. Typically priced at €9-12, these meals give you bread, a starter course, a main course, a drink (sangria, anyone?), dessert, and a cup of coffee or tea.

Also important to note: meal pricing depends on where you sit in the restaurant. For your cheapest option, eat at the bar. Your most expensive meal will be on the terrace or the patio outside of the restaurant.

🗌 ENRIQUE TOMAS

RESTAURANT $

C. Tetuan, 19 ☎912 99 20 70 www.enriquetomas.com/en

It's hard to be a vegetarian if you live in Madrid. All across the city, butcher shops and restaurants advertise their Jamon Iberico—Iberian ham—and assortments of dried meats. One such butcher shop/restaurant fusion, Enrique Tomas, offers cheap late-night, meaty snacks (similar to tapas) with refreshing wine and beer. Pay only €5.90 for a grande plate of Madrid's famous Iberian Ham—enough to feed four ravenous tourists—or a plate of acorn-fed pork loin. Check the restaurant out around 10pm—this is when all the young (or old!) locals gather in the shop to snack before another night of partying 'til dawn. Plus, if you're extra nice to your server, he or she may give you a free plate of snacks (tomato-paste and bread, gratis, sounds nice). Beware: this is NOT a place for vegetarians or anyone averse to thick legs of meat hanging around the walls and windows.

i Large plates of meat €5.90. Drinks €1-4. Plates of cheese €2-4. ⓩ Open M-F 9am-midnight, Sa-Su 9am-1am.

🗌 LAS BRASAS DE VULCANO

TAPAS $$

C. Álvarez Gato, 7 ☎915 22 36 05 www.lasbrasasdevulcano.com

Tapas, tapas, tapas! This lively, loco (sometimes the waiters try to dance with customers) restaurant is at its best when the sun goes down and hungry gatos are out. Here's a spot you'll find yourself surrounded by Spanish speakers (and therefore no English waiters)—but that's a sign of authenticity, right? Sit by the large, open window, watch pub-crawlers pass by, and share hour-long conversations and a €10 bottle of wine with your friends. The food's great too. Enjoy a plate of hot pimento peppers for €4.50 or half a barbequed chicken for the same price. Drinks (wine, sangria, beer) go for €2 a glass, while bottles of wine to share cost €9-11, and a liter jar of sangria costs €8. Las Brasas's raciones (full meals) are popular too; try their Iberian ham or manchego cheese—to share, of course.

i Entrees €10-30. Tapas €2-8. Drinks €2. ⓩ Open daily noon-2am.

madrid

ALBUR
RESTAURANT $$$

C. de Manuela Malasaña, 15 ☎915 94 27 33 www.restaurantealbur.com

Looking for a classy night out? Still want a taste of traditional Spanish flavors? Try Albur, a renaissance restaurant (in terms of its offerings) that specializes in fish and paella Valenciana, that savory rice and seafood dish that traces its origins back to a lagoon in nearby Valencia, Spain. How perfect—Albur translates to "dace," or a type of freshwater fish, in English. Located in the heart of Madrid's alternative neighborhood (and by alternative, we mean hipster) Malasaña and just off the main road Fuencarral, Albur is easy to find but still far away enough from the traditional tourist and commercial avenues in el Centro that you'll find yourself chowing down on an authentic dish. The price range of this restaurant is a little higher than the usual cheap menús del día offered at other off-the-beaten-path restaurants, but only slightly, which speaks to the quality—and quantity—of food served. The restaurant itself has plenty of seats including a bar, and if you sit here your check will be cheaper than had you sat at a regular table. Although the kitchen closes on late weekday afternoons, if you're out of late lunch/early options on the weekends, Albur keeps a *cocina abierta* ("open kitchen") from 1pm. Join the party later at night when the rest of the late-night-snack crowd shows up. Try a glass of Albur's fine wine (blanco, tinto, or Rosado) for €2-4 (or a full bottle for only €14) and a few seafood-inspired tapas from €6 and up.

i Entrees €5-15. Menú del día €10. Desserts €2. ☼ Open M-Th 12:30pm-5pm and 7:30pm-midnight, F 12:30pm-5pm and 7:30pm-1:30am, Sa 1pm-1:30am, Su 1pm-midnight.

CAFETÍN LA QUIMERA
RESTAURANT, FLAMENCO $$

C. Sancho Dávila, 34 ☎913 56 93 61 www.tablaoflamencolaquimera.com

Tablaos, or restaurants in which flamenco shows take place, are scattered throughout the nation's capital and promise one of the best meals you will have in Spain. One of the most famous in the city, Cafetín La Quimera, also offers one of the cheapest shows you'll be able to find, starting at €14.50 for a reservation and one drink of your choice. A full meal for two, plus the tickets, include a starter of cherry tomatoes and goat cheese with herbs as well as a Spanish omelet, and entrees range from cured beef from León to piquillo peppers stuffed with meat (sorry vegetarians, it's a tough ride from here on out. Better try another city, ASAP). If you chose the drink-only option and are feeling hungry during the show, menus, which offer Spanish omelettes for €12 and other entrees for an upwards of €16, are available. Although you can't probably predict your hunger in advance, it is recommended you purchase your meal with your show ticket. And let's not forget—the actual flamenco show. La Quimera prides itself on inviting the most authentic local and national talent (no imported foreigners, cough cough) to its stage, and if you've never been to a flamenco show before, you're in for a real treat. Even if you have, these guys are always good. Showcasing the fuerza (strength) of a cante (song), toque (guitar), baile (dance), and palmas (handclaps), this performance is bound to be loud. Better eat up fast—you'll be so transfixed by the flamenco that you won't have that much time to focus on the meal in front of you.

i With reservation: Show and drink €14.50; show, drink, and tasting menu €31. Without reservation: show and drink €30; show, drink, and tasting menu €62. ☼ Open M-Th 7pm-midnight, F-Su 6pm-3am.

TABERNA POMPEYANA
RESTAURANT $$

C. Álvarez Gato, 5 ☎915 22 93 75 www.lapompeyana.com

Enjoy a meal at Taberna Pompeyana and step back to classical Italian times—sort of. This restaurant has a penchant for corny jokes and fat Italian women (see their emblem as an example), which says nothing to the quality and rich flavor of its inexpensive meals. While chuckling at the faux-Classical busts and yellowing skull table weights, make sure to try out Pompeyana's €10 menú del día, whose options include mixed meat paella, savory, cheesy lasagna, and more. A cool, tall cerveza goes for €2, as does a tinto de verano or a sangria. True to its hilarious (and slightly off-putting) fat, naked donna, the restaurant also serves a lot of Italian (and surprisingly, it does a fine job). Pizzas cost €7, salads from €3-6.50. After a meal here, maybe you'll end up looking like that fat Greek woman—their portions are huge.

i *Entrees €5-15. Menú del día €10. Desserts €2. ☒ Open M-F noon-1:30am, Sa-Su noon-2pm.*

◪ EL SOBRINO DE BOTIN
TAPAS $$

C. de Cuchilleros, 17 ☎91 366 42 17 www.botin.es

The world's oldest restaurant according to *The Guinness Book of World Records*, El Sobrino de Botin reeks of roasted pig and illustrious history (it was founded in 1620). Goya was a waiter here, and it was one of Hemingway's favorite haunts thanks to its suckling pig (€24). He writes in *The Sun Also Rises*, "We lunched upstairs at Botin's. It is one of the best restaurants in the world. We had roast young suckling pig and drank rioja alta." This is a truly authentic historic landmark and protector of the *madrileño* culinary tradition, although there is a large crowd of tourists. From the *guildedoil* still-life paintings, antique revolvers, and porcelain-tiled walls, El Sobrino is what so many restaurants in the barren El Centro restaurant scene artificially aspire to be. As you approach the winding wooden staircase surrounded by craggy stone walls, you will notice *"el horno,"* the nearly 300-year-old wood-fired oven that continues to roast the same traditional dishes. While the food isn't cheap, even their simple dishes like the *sopa de oja* (garlic soup with egg; €7.90) are all premium authentic quality and far better than what you can expect from neighboring El Centro restaurants. Delicious food and an authentic time capsule of history: Botin is a must-eat in Madrid.

i *From ⓂSol, walk 6 blocks west down C. Mayor to C. Cava de San Miguel to C. de Cuchilleros. Prices rang €6-30. ☒ Open daily 1-4pm and 8pm-midnight.*

◪ CAFÉ DE CÍRCULO DE BELLAS ARTES
CAFE $$$

C. de Alcalá 42 ☎91 521 69 42 www.circulobellasartes.com

The 10min. walk out of Puerta del Sol to get to this cafe is worth it just to get away from the tourists. It's also good for a nice stroll through Madrid's more modern, Manhattan-esque side. This is a classic European sidewalk cafe, although the emphasis during lunch is more on a sit-down restaurant experience than grab-and-go tapas and coffee à la carte. The interior is decked-out with crystal chandeliers, columns stamped with Picasso-like figure drawings, and frescoed ceilings. The wicker chairs on the street side terrace make for a comfortable place to relax and people-watch amid the bustle of C. de Alcala. The lunch menu focuses on a two-course meal; €16 can get you Valencia-style *paella* and Iberian meat with potatoes. Included in all meals is an alcoholic beverage to begin with and a coffee as dessert. Consider it the Spanish version of a Four Loko. Dinner is a cheaper, more traditional tapas experience. After eating, pay €2 (student price) to see the sweeping city view at the top of the connected seven-story Circulo de Bellas building (there's restaurant seating up there during the non-scorching months).

i *From ⓂSevilla, walk 2 blocks west down C. Alcala. Coffee €3-6. Wine €3-6. Sandwiches €5-8. Lunch 2-course meal €16. ☒ Open M-Th 9:30am-1am, F-Sa 9:30am-3am, Su 9:30am-1am.*

◪ TABERNA MALASPINA
RESTAURANT $

C. Cadiz, 9 ☎34 915 234 024

It's hard to believe that just a block south of the Sol and all its overpriced, tourist-trap restaurants is Taberna Malaspina, an authentic, value-priced gem. The house special, *malaspina*, is a generous serving of melted cheese, oregano, to-

madrid

mato, and ham on an open-faced piece of toasted bread. This place also features a wide selection of wines for around €2 a glass (or €9 a bottle), and the friendly staff is quick to offer suggestions to help you navigate the menu. A few drinks with your meal enhances the restaurant's warm ambience. It's easy to imagine yourself as Hemingway during his time in Madrid while you sip your wine at the bar, surrounded by conversing locals at this cozy establishment. Good food, drink, and conversation: what else is there to want in life?

i From ⓂSol, walk south down Calle de Carretas. Turn left onto Calle Cadiz, Malaspina is on the left. Tapa €4-10. Beer and wine €2. ⓧ Open daily 10:30am-2am.

MERCADO DE SAN MIGUEL
MARKET $

Pl. de San Miguel   ☎915 42 49 36 www.mercadodesanmiguel.es

Feeling overwhelmed by the number of cafeterías, panaderías, cervecerías, chocolaterías, fruterías, and churrerías lining the streets of Madrid? Don't know what to choose? Check out El Mercado San Miguel for a sampling of each in a low-stress environment that will give you your best introduction to the many foods of Madrid. Open every day of the week, the market hosts dozens of vendors who sell a range of products like fresh fruit, cut meat, and tapas (and even lotion, though the majority of vendors here sell perishable items). Although the spot is a tourist target, surprisingly, prices aren't unreasonable. Try a meat paella and red wine for €5, or a delicate chocolate bonbon for €0.50. Though translucent glass walls surround the market, allowing it to stay open regardless of weather conditions, seating in the enclosed marketplace itself is limited. Instead, buy lunch and wander around nearby La Plaza Mayor or the beautiful cobblestone alleyways of el Centro. Often the market will feature live music in the evening, so make sure to stop by to catch a drink when the sun sets.

i At the Pl. de San Miguel, off the northwest corner of Pl. Mayor right beside the Cerveceria. Prices vary. ⓧ Open M-W 10am-midnight, Th-Sa 10am-2pm, Su 10am-midnight.

CHOCOLATERÍA SAN GINÉS
CHOCOLATERÍA $

Pl. de San Ginés, 5   ☎91 366 54 31

After spending all day looking at 500-year-old buildings and pretending to care, it's okay to let loose. Sometimes this means treating yourself to a good dinner; sometimes it means ingesting unconscionable amounts of deep-fried batter and melted dark chocolate. Popular among locals and tourists alike, the famous Chocolatería San Ginés has been serving the world's must gluttonous treat, *churros con chocolate* (churros dipped in warm melted chocolate, €4), since it was founded in 1894. San Ginés has the neat decor and service (waiters serve your churros and chocolate) of a fancy, date-ready cafe but is also open 24hr. for all your late-night, post-clubbing needs. Get the best of both worlds: find a hot date at the club, put a pair of churros on your tab, and then have some wicked, chocolate-fueled hostel sex afterward.

i From Puerta Del Sol, walk down C. Arenal until you get to Joy nightclub. Chocolatería San Ginés is tucked in the tiny Pl. de San Ginés. Chocolates from €4. ⓧ Open daily 24hr.

MUSEO DEL JAMÓN
TAPAS $$

C. Mayor, 7   ☎91 542 26 32 www.museodeljamon.com

You never forget the day you lose your *bocadillo* virginity in Madrid. The *bocadillo* is the simplest but most satisfying meal you will have in the city, and Museo Del Jamón (literally, "Museum of Ham") does right by this tradition: crispy Spanish baguettes, freshly sliced *jamón*, rich Manchego cheese, and dirt cheap prices (€1-2). Vegetarians beware: there is meat everywhere. Cured pig legs dangle from the ceiling, and the window display brims with sausages. Museo del Jamón is reliably packed with tourists drawn in by the hanging meats and the promise of authentic Spanish tapas. Fanny packs and cameras are plentiful, but nothing can take away from the satisfaction of an authentic and criminally cheap meal. The upstairs dining room also offers more substantial entrees like *paella* (€12) and full *raciones* (€10-15) of *jamón* and *queso*. However, as one local put it, "A sandwich for one euro, it's good. But a whole meal, you can find better elsewhere."

i From ⓂSol, walk 2 blocks west down C. Mayor. Several locations throughout El Centro. Sandwiches €1-3. Sit-down menu €10-20. ☒ Open daily 9am-midnight.

EL ANCIANO REY DE LOS VINOS
SPANISH $$

C. de Bailén, 19 ☎91 559 53 32 www.elancianoreydelosvinos.es

Right across the street from the Catedral de la Almudena, this is a pit stop for an afternoon drink and snack. Founded in 1909, El Anciano Rey de los Vinos is a granddaddy in the world of tapas bars in El Centro (maybe not a great-granddaddy, but a granddaddy nonetheless). There's noise and bustle from C. de Bailén, but the big draw of this place is its straight-shot view of the cathedral. So as people across the street enter to confess and pray away their sins, you can sit easy and comfortably drink away your own. It helps that the vermouth goes down cold and smooth and comes with a Spanish-style potato salad. While the menu is not particularly inventive, at a certain point, beer is beer and chairs are awesome—especially after a long day of museum-going.

i From the Catedral de la Almudena, walk across C. de Bailén. Tapas €6-13. Beer €2. Wine €3. ☒ Open daily 8:30am-midnight.

🏁 ALMENDRO 13
SPANISH $$

C. Almendro, 13 ☎91 365 42 52

The simple, woody interior of Almendro belies the fact that this is not your average Spanish restaurant. While many *madrileño* restaurants serve pre-made tapas at an uncomfortably lukewarm temperature, everything at Almendro 13 is made hot and fresh to order. The specialty here is definitely the *huevos rotos*—fried eggs served on top of a heaping pile of fries with a variety of toppings (€6-9.50). It's so gluttonous and guiltily delicious that it feels like it should belong in America (or on an episode of *Man v. Food*).

i ⓂLatina. Walk west on C. Plaza Cebada 1 block, take a right onto C. del Humilladero, walk 1 block to C. Almendro, and walk up 1 block. Sandwiches, tortillas, and salad €6-8. Entrees €6-9. Beer, wine, and vermouth €3. ☒ Open daily 1-4pm and 7:30pm-12:30am.

🏁 CAFE BAR MELO'S
BAR $

C. Ave María, 44 ☎91 527 50 54

Bread, cheese, and meat, cooked together to simple perfection. And for cheap. What else could you want? A Bentley? A fur coat? All you backpackers want all the same things, but Cafe Bar Melo's has mastered the art of the grilled *zapatilla* (grilled pork and cheese sandwich; €3). Don't expect glamorous decor: Cafe Bar Melo's looks something like a hot dog stand at a major league baseball park after seven innings of play, but that's all part of the magic.

i ⓂLavapiés. Walk up C. Ave María 1 block. Sandwiches €2-5. Beer €1-3. ☒ Open Tu-Sa 9pm-2am.

🏁 TABERNA DE ANTONIO SANCHEZ
TAPAS $$

C. del Mesón de Paredes, 13 ☎91 539 78 26

Founded in 1830 by legendary bullfighter Antonio Sanchez, this *taberna* is as traditional as it gets. The *taberna* features traditional, matador-worthy favorites like morcilla *a las pasas* (black pudding and raisins; €9), as well as gazpacho €4), *sopa de ajo* (garlic soup; €4), and plenty of Manchego cheese and *jamón ibérico* to keep you happy. If you squint your eyes through the darkness, you can see that the walls are covered with original murals by the 19th-century Spanish painter Ignacio Zuloaga and victory trophies from bullfights of centuries past.

i From ⓂTirso de Molina, walk past Pl. de Tirso de Molina until you get to C. del Mesón de Paredes. Take a left (south) onto C. del Mesón de Paredes. The taberna is on the left. Entrees €3-15. ☒ Open M-Sa noon-4pm and 8pm-midnight, Su noon-4pm.

madrid

NUEVO CAFE BARBIERI

CAFE $

C. Ave María, 45   ☎91 527 36 58

With high, molded ceilings and large windows, Nuevo Cafe Barbieri has a much more open and breezy feel than other cramped cafes. While this may be Lavapiés's finest traditional cafe during the late afternoon, it's also a buzzing nightlife hub on weekends. Although you won't find much of a food selection here, they have a Cadillac-sized espresso machine and a Jeep-size mixed drink menu to match. Barbieri specializes in mixed drinks like the Barbieri (coffee, Bailey's, cream; €4.50) and the Haitiano (coffee, rum, cream; €4.50).

i Ⓜ Lavapiés. Walk up C. Ave María 1 block. Desserts €4-7. Coffee drinks €2-5. Tea €2.50. ☼ Open M-W 4pm-12:30am, Th 4pm-1:30am, F-Su 4pm-2:30am.

🔲 CERVECERÍA LOS GATOS

TAPAS $$

C. Jesús, 2   ☎91 429 30 62

If you took one of the grandfather tapas bars of Las Huertas and gave it a healthy dose of Viagra, it would look and feel something like Cervecería Los Gatos. Sandwiched between the madness of Las Huertas and the more quiet museum district, Los Gatos is a local hangout that most tourists haven't yet discovered. At first glance, Los Gatos seems like a pretty typical Spanish tapas bar, but a closer look reveals that it actually has an oddball sense of humor. The decorations are a grab-bag of eclectic items: signed football jerseys, a painting of skeletons drinking at a bar, an antique motorcycle, mounted bull heads, and an actual gas pump. The *pièce de résistance* is the fresco: a version of Leonardo da Vinci's *The Creation of Man*, in which Adam gracefully holds beer. If ever there's a place to snack on traditional tapas, this is it.

i Ⓜ Antón Martín. Take C. Atocha southeast ½ block to C. de Moratin. Take C. de Moratin 4 blocks east to C. Jesús. Turn left (heading north) onto C. Jesús and walk 2 blocks. Pinchos €2-4. Racciones €8-18. Cash only. ☼ Open daily 1:30pm-2am.

🔲 LA BARDEMCILLA DE SANTA ANA

TRADITIONAL $$

C. de Augusto Figueroa, 47   ☎91 521 42 56

If you're wondering what made Javier Bardem the tall, strapping, dazzling Spanish beauty he is today, look no further than La Bardemecilla. Unfortunately, this Bardem family restaurant is actually unrelated to everyone's favorite, creepily handsome (fictional) killer. Fortunately, they serve Spanish family recipes like *huevos de oro estrellados* (eggs scrambled with *jamón iberico* and onions; €8.70). With two Madrid locations, Grandma and Grandpa Bardem are getting some long overdue street cred. This place sets itself apart from other traditional tapas bar in the same area with its more homey, less touristy vibe. It almost feels like your aunt's dining room, complete with warm orange paint, framed black and white pictures, and a piano.

i From Pl. Santa Ana, take C. Núñez de Arce, on the west side of the plaza, north toward Puerta del Sol. Follow C. Núñez de Arce 1 block. The restaurant is on the right just before C. de la Cruz. Pinchos €2-4. Entrees €8-10. ☼ Open Tu-F noon-5:30pm and 7pm-2am, Sa 8pm-2am, Su noon-5:30pm and 7pm-2am.

LATERAL

TAPAS $$

Pl. Santa Ana   ☎91 420 15 82   www.cadenalateral.es

Lateral stands apart form the other slightly boring, traditional Spanish cervecerias on Pl. Santa Ana. If the curators of the Reina Sofía were to make a modern tapas restaurant, it would look something like this, with a spacious interior, marble bar, and white leather bar stools. Menu items like the lamb crepe (€4.50), raspberry mango foam (€4), and the salmon sashimi with wasabi (€6.50) are a nice break from the traditional ox tails and butcher-meats of similar establishments. Bring one of your hostel friends to share the €16 sampler. And don't forget to try a hand-crafted berry mojito (€7)—it's so good, you'll be shaken from your everyday hellish malaise and learn to love again. One last thing: they don't offer substantial entrees, so either order a lot of tapas or have your mother pack you a mayonnaise sandwich to eat on the curb.

i Facing the ME Madrid Reina Victoria Hotel in Pl. Santa Ana, Lateral is on the left. Tapas €3-8. Mixed drinks €7. Combination platters €16. ⏰ Open daily noon-midnight.

CASA ALBERTO
TRADITIONAL $$

C. de las Huertas, 18 ☎91 429 93 56 www.casaalberto.es

Founded in 1827, Casa Alberto is one of Madrid's oldest taverns. Once upon a time, bullfighters came here for a "cup of courage" before they entered the bullring. Today it's a tourist favorite, and with good reason. The walls are lined with photographs of famous matadors and celebrities who have visited, and the charm hasn't entirely faded. Enter your own bullring of fear by trying tripe: what could be more carnivorous than putting another animal's stomach inside your own? Feeling even more daring? Eat a pig's ear. Damn, still hungry? How about snails and lamb hands? Your insatiable hunger howls for more. Have some beef cheek. Congratulations, you are a winner. If you're not feeling it, you can try less adventurous dishes like the Madrid-style veal meatballs or *huevos fritos* served with garlic lamb sweetbreads and roasted potatoes.

i From Pl. del Ángel, walk down C. de las Huertas toward the Prado. Casa Alberto is on the right. Entrees €5-20. ⏰ Open daily noon-1:30am.

FATIGAS DEL QUERER
TRADITIONAL $$

C. de la Cruz, 17 ☎91 523 21 31 www.fatigasdelquerer.es

While it doesn't have the "history" or institutional status of some of Las Huertas' other tapas bars, Fatigas del Querer still serves great traditional fare in a more central location. The spacious interior is a refreshing change-up from the many cramped taverns Madrid offers. Enjoy fairly standard (but still tasty) tapas beneath a fading fresco and mounted racks of wine bottles. The waitstaff is particularly attentive and keeps the turnaround quick.

i From Pl. del Ángel, go north up C. Espoz y Mina and bear right. The street becomes C. de la Cruz. Tapas €4-12. Cash only. ⏰ Open M-F 11am-1:30am, Sa-Su 11am-2:30am. Kitchen open until 1am.

LA FINCA DE SUSANA RESTAURANT
MEDITERRANEAN $$

C. de Arlabán, 4 ☎91 429 76 78 www.lafinca-restaurant.com

Despite its proximity to Sol, La Finca de Susana is largely untouched by the tourist hordes. Located down a smaller street, this restaurant is popular among locals for offering a gourmet, sit-down dining experience (think white tablecloths set with silverware and wine glasses) at a surprisingly reasonable price. Though the look and feel is relatively classy (don't worry, your T-shirt is fine), a meal here will only set you back around €10. The Mediterranean-inspired menu offers greater variety than the traditional *taberna*, with popular dishes like *arroz negro con sepia* (stewed rice with cuttlefish; €11) and *cordera al horno* (roasted lamb; €12). Come early or make a reservation.

i Ⓜ Sol. Follow C. de Alcalá east and take a right (south) onto C. de Seville. Follow C. de Seville to C. de Arlabál and take a left (east). Entrees €7-16. ⏰ Open M-W 1-3:45pm and 8:30-11:30pm, F-Sa 1-3:45pm and 8:30pm-midnight. Su 1-3:45pm and 8:30-11:30pm.

EL BRILLANTE
TAPAS $

Pl. Emperador Carlos V, 8 ☎91 539 28 06

El Brillante provides quality budget eating in the pricey Avenida del Arte. There's nothing flashy about the interior—the focus is on the wide selection of affordable Spanish food. While its claims that its *bocadillo de calamares* (fried calamari sandwich; €6) are the best in Madrid have not been substantiated by any awards or reviews, patrons don't seem to care, and they order the sandwich in abundance. Don't like the idea of putting suction cups in your mouth? There's something here for everyone (even Italian food, with pizzas and pasta for €6).

The restaurant has indoor bar seating and outdoor terrace seating with a prime view of Reina Sofia's towering glass architecture.

i Ⓜ*Atocha. Sandwiches €4-8.* 🕐 *Open daily 7am-1am.*

LA PLATERIA DEL MUSEO

TAPAS $$

C. Huertas, 82 ☎91 429 17 22

Roughly equidistant from the Prado, Reina Sofia, and Thyssen, La Plateria is in prime museum territory. And they know what customers want after a long day of pretending to appreciate art: booze, but in a sophisticated sense. You'll find a more middle-aged clientele sitting outside on the large terrace sipping sangria (€3.50), wine (€4), and mixed drinks (€7). Although they don't have a huge selection of meal-sized entrees, they do offer traditional tapas, with staples like *patatas bravas* (€6), *gazpacho andaluz* (€4.50), and *croqueta de jamon* (€3). More than anything, La Plateria del Museo stands out for its exceptional terrace seating and proximity to the three museums of Avenida del Arte.

i *From* Ⓜ*Atocha, follow Paseo del Prado 2 blocks to Las Huertas and turn left. Appetizer €2.50-8. Drinks €2-6.* 🕐 *Open daily 7am-1am.*

▨ [H]ARINA

CAFE $$

Pl. de la Independencia, 10 ☎91 522 87 85 www.harinamadrid.com

[H]arina is one of the best cafes in Madrid; it has a prime location, affordable prices, and delectable cafe fare. Its refreshingly modern, whitewashed decor (think Crate&Barrel) stands out among the many cafes that feel old and tired. Outside seating will give you an unobscured view of **Puerta de Alcala,** a Neoclassical arch built in 1778. Lots of restaurants exploit their prime location by offering expensive, mediocre food to compensate for the views. [H]arina, however, offers surprisingly affordable and delicious salads, pastries, sandwiches, and paper-thin pizzas (all looking like they've been pulled straight out of a food magazine). Indoor and outdoor seating are both generally packed, particularly on weekends, and many patrons take their food to go from the bakery.

i Ⓜ*Banco de España, walk 1 block east to Pl. de la Independencia; the restaurant is on the southwest corner. Coffee €2-4. Salads €8. Sandwiches €6. Pizzas €9-11. Terrace seating requires a €1 additional charge.* 🕐 *Open daily 9am-9pm.*

PIZZERÍA CASAVOSTRA

ITALIAN $$

C. Infantas, 13 ☎91 523 22 07 www.pizzacasavostra.com

Pizzería Casavostra was first opened five years ago, but it looks like it's here to stay. Locals dig the fact that everything on Casavostra's menu is fresh, from the brick-oven pizzas to the traditional appetizers. While many of the restaurants between Gran Vía and Chueca try hard to break out of the tapas mold, Casavostra keeps things simple with a traditional Italian menu. The pizzas (€8.50-14) are fired in the brick oven and topped with ingredients like arugula, fresh mozzarella, and cherry tomatoes. The appetizer salads come in huge portions and are great to share for a first round (€5-10). They also offer a full selection of *burrata* (unpasteurized mozzarella) appetizers that are so good, you'll never think twice about Louis Pasteur again. The atmosphere is clean and modern, with smooth wooden tables and bulbous, overhanging lamps that make the color of the food really pop.

i *From* Ⓜ*Gran Vía, walk east 1 block to C. Hortaleza, then 2 blocks north to C. de la Infantas. Follow C. de las Infantas. Drinks €2-4. Appetizers €4-12. Entrees €7-15.* 🕐 *Open daily noon-1am.*

EL BOCAITO

TAPAS $$

C. de la Libertad, 6 ☎91 521 31 98 www.bocaito.com

Ever since Spain's most well-known filmmaker, Pedro Almodóvar, cited El Bocaito as one of his favorites in Madrid, it has been all the rage. Founded in 1966, El Bocaito is as traditional as tapas bars get, from the matador paraphernalia on the walls to the platters of *pinchos*. El Bocaito sticks to tradition and does it well, and its back-to-back bars and four small dining rooms are packed nightly with locals. While drinks (€2-4) and tapas (€2-5) won't cost much, a full sit-down dinner with a bottle of wine and entrees (€12-20) is decently expensive.

i From ⓂGran Vía, walk E 1 block to C. Hortaleza, 2 blocks N to C. de la Infantas, and then follow C. de las Infantas 4 blocks west to C. de la Libertad. Drinks €2-4. Appetizers €2-5. Entrees €10-20.
🕐 *Open M-F 1-4pm and 8:30pm-midnight, Sa 8:30pm-midnight, Su 1-4pm and 8:30pm-midnight.*

▨ MERCADO DE SAN ANTON   MARKET $$
C. Augusto Figueroa, 24   ☎91 330 07 30 www.mercadosananton.com

This is Europe's fierce rebuttal to Whole Foods. What was once an open-air market in the middle of Chueca is now a modern glass building filled with fresh produce vendors, *charcuterías*, *bodegas*, and a rooftop restaurant. It's the bigger, four-story version of Centro's Mercado de San Miguel, a place to get a sweeping tour of Spain's culinary landscape, from tapas to sushi to burger sliders. Prices might be a bit steep, but it's free to just gape and drool over the gorgeous displays of food.

i Ⓜ Chueca. On the southern end of Pl. de Chueca. For the rooftop restaurant, make reservations in advance at 91 330 02 94. Visit www.laccocinadesananton.com for more on the restaurant. Varies greatly, but a full meal at the market costs around €10. Cash only. 🕐 *1st fl. market open M-Sa 10am-10pm. 2nd fl. restaurants and bars open Tu-Su 10am-midnight. Rooftop restaurant open M-Th 10am-midnight, F-Sa 10am-1:30am, Su 10am-midnight.*

▨ SAN WISH   BURGERS $
C. de Hortaleza, 78   ☎91 319 17 76 www.san-wish.com

The motto of this modern burger joint is "Because a good sandwich is right and necessary." From their language, these guys know that a perfect burger can be a religious experience. Luckily, they're doing God's work here, making juicy, affordable, one-of-a-kind burgers. Go for the *hamburguesa voladora* (chicken, tomato, lettuce, grilled cucumbers, melon chutney; €6.50), or, if you're feeling safe, the *clásica* (sweet pickle, tomato, and lettuce; €6.50). The young and hungry *madrileño* crowd can't seem to get enough of this place; the limited seats are nearly impossible to snag, especially during peak weekend hours.

i From Ⓜ Chueca, take C. Gravina 2 blocks east to C. de Hortaleza, then take a right onto C. de Hortaleza. The restaurant is on the right. Sandwiches €5.50-8.90. Beer €1.50-3.50. Wine €2.50.
🕐 *Open M 8pm-midnight, Tu-Sa 1-4pm and 8pm-midnight, Su 2-4pm.*

BAZAAR   MEDITERRANEAN $$
C. de la Libertad, 21   ☎91 523 39 05 www.restaurantbazaar.com

You're going on a date with that cute girl from the hostel, but you're trying not to break the bank (after all, who knows if you'll see this chica again after next week). Luckily, Bazaar offers an impressive, classy dining experience at a shockingly reasonable price. This expansive two-story restaurant has the look and feel of a high-end place, with white tablecloths and wine glasses waiting on the table, and they offer a full menu of fresh pasta, salads, and meat dishes. The upstairs and downstairs dining rooms are quite large but partitioned into smaller, more intimate seated spaces by shelves filled with artisanal food displays.

i Ⓜ Chueca. Make a left onto C. Augusto Figuroa and a right onto C. de la Libertad. Entree €7-10.
🕐 *Open M-W 1:15-4pm and 8:30-11:30pm, Th-Sa 1:15-4pm and 8:30-midnight, Su 1:15-4pm and 8:30-11:30pm.*

LO SIGUIENTE   TAPAS $$
C. Fernando VI, 11   ☎91 319 52 61 www.losiguiente.es

With high bar tables, metal stools, and silver columns, Lo Siguiente is a balance between a traditional tapas bar and a *nouveau* Chueca restaurant. While it may have a cool, polished aesthetic, Lo Siguiente is still an informal restaurant that *madrileños* come to for traditional Spanish staples (after all, all those Chueca sushi-burger fusion restaurants can get tiring and confusing). You can get all of

madrid

the staples, like the classic *huevos rotos* (a fried egg over pan-fried potatoes, garlic, and chorizo; €9.50), but don't be afraid to try the lighter Mediterranean items, like tomato and avocado salad and ceviche served atop grilled vegetables.

i From Ⓜ Chueca, head 2 blocks northeast on C. San Gregario and take a left onto C. Fernando VI. Lo Siguiente is on the right. Meal €10-15. ⌚ Open M-Th 8:30am-1am, F-Sa 8:30am-2:30am, Su 8:30am-1:30am.

🅼 LA DOMINGA
TABERNA $$
C. del Espíritu Santo, 15   ☎91 523 38 09 www.ladominga.com

Now with two locations (one in Chueca, one in Malasaña), La Dominga is quietly making a name for itself as a *taberna* that balances tradition with modernity. Although it offers traditional dishes like *rabo de toro* (oxtail stew; €14), it also caters to a younger Malasaña clientele with plenty of contemporary dishes. Dishes like the beef carpaccio (served with parmesan and arugula; €13) are more refined than the heavier stewed and grilled meats that dominate traditional Spanish cuisine. That said, the specialty here is still the very traditional *croquettas* (fried stuffed bread; €9.70) that Madrid publication *La Razon* calls the best in the city.

i Ⓜ Tribunal. Go west on C. de San Vincente Ferrer, make a left onto C. del Barco, then a right onto C. del Espíritu Santo. Entrees €10-15. ⌚ Open daily 1-4:30pm and 8:30pm-midnight.

🅼 LAMUCCA
INTERNATIONAL $$
Pl. Carlos Carbonero, 4   ☎91 521 00 00 www.lamucca.es

Start with an appetizer of Mexican quesadillas (€9.50). Enjoy a pizza "*la de pulpo gallega*" (octopus, potatoes, paprika; €15). Finish with a dessert of sticky rice with mango (€5). Lamucca has possibly the most eclectic, globe-trotting menu in Madrid. Dishes like Thai curried chicken with jasmine rice (€11) share the menu with Italian pizza and pasta, as well as contemporary Spanish dishes like beef carpaccio (€13). This is a hugely popular local favorite. There's not much seating inside, but the outside terrace offers a wide spread of tables on the cozy Pl. Carlos Carbonero.

i Ⓜ Tribunal. From the pack of restaurants on east C. del Espíritu, head south on C. de la Madera 2 blocks, turn left onto Calle el Escorial, then right onto Calle Molino de Viento. Appetizer €5-12. Entrees €12-20. Pizza €10-15. ⌚ Open daily 1pm-1am.

HOME BURGER BAR
BURGERS $$
Other locations: C. San Marcos, 25 and C. Silva, 25   ☎91 522 97 28

Home Burger Bar pays its respects to the classic 1950s American diner look but doesn't hit you over the head with it (looking at you, Johnny Rockets). For example, instead of overstated, cherry-red booths, you get plush, wine-colored stools. In addition to classic burgers (with the option of add-ons like thick cut bacon), they offer a number of vegetarian options, like the falafel burger (€11.25). All burgers are made from organic meat and come with a side of Caesar salad.

i Ⓜ Tribunal. Go west on C. de San Vincente Ferrer, make a left onto C. del Barco, and take a right onto C. del Espíritu Santo. Burgers €10-13. Sandwiches €8-15. ⌚ Open M-Sa 1:30-4pm and 8:30pm-midnight, Su 2-4:30pm and 8:30-11pm.

CAFÉ MAHÓN
CAFE $$
Pl. del 2 de Mayo, 4   ☎91 448 90 02

With a combination of international favorites, Mediterranean-inspired salads, and traditional Spanish entrees, Café Mahón has something for everyone—at a budget price. Located on the edge of one of Malasaña's most tranquil plazas, this cafe uses bright open space and simple kitchen furniture to create a casual vibe. International comfort foods spice up the menu next to traditional Spanish tapas. Try the nachos with cheese and guacamole (€7), the hummus appetizer (€6), or the moussaka (€8). A menu of specialty teas (€2-3.50) and coffees keeps people coming throughout the day to enjoy the terrace seating and watch little kids play on the local jungle gym.

i From ⓂTribunal, head west on C. de la Palma 2 blocks west to C. San Andres, take a right, and continue until you reach the plaza. Cafe Mahon is at the northwest corner. Appetizer €6-9. Salads €7. Entrees €7-12. ☑ Open daily Jul-Aug 3pm-2am; Sept-Jun noon-2am. Terrace open daily Jul-Aug 3pm-1am; Sept-Jun noon-1am.

EL RINCÓN CAFE $$

C. del Espíritu Santo, 26 ☎91 522 19 86

If you're looking for a classic, bohemian Malasaña cafe experience, look no further than El Rincón, which perfectly balances hip personality with accessibility. With its simple wooden tables, small Asian prints on the walls, and chalkboard menu, it's a thoughtful little cafe. For those consistently overwhelmed by the options at restaurants, El Rincón offers a refreshingly simple five-item entree menu, featuring dishes like rigatoni with truffles.

i ⓂTribunal. Go west on C. de San Vincente Ferrer, make a left onto C. del Barco, and take a right onto C. del Espíritu Santo. Sandwiches €5. Entrees €10. Cocktails €5-7. Wine €2.50. Coffee €2-3. ☑ Open daily 11am-2am.

LOLINA VINTAGE CAFÉ CAFE $

C. del Espíritu Santo, 9 ☎66 720 11 69 www.lolinacafe.com

Lolina looks like it was assembled from a shopping spree at a Brooklyn thrift store. Literally nothing matches—from the mismatched armchairs to the vintage lamps to the '60s green and white wallpaper. But in the context of trendy Malasaña, it all somehow works. The cozy space's bright natural light attracts people at all times of the day, whether for morning tea or late-night cocktails. The food options are simple but tasty, with a selection of salads (€8), bratwurst sandwiches (€5), and open-faced *tostas* (€4). Surprisingly one of the only places on C. del Espiritu Santo with Wi-Fi, this is the perfect place to hang out and soak in the hip Malasaña vibe without breaking the bank.

i ⓂTribunal. Go west on C. de San Vincente Ferrer, make a left onto C. del Barco, then make a right onto C. del Espíritu Santo. Free Wi-Fi. Salads €8. Cocktails €6. Coffee and tea €2-5. ☑ Open M-Tu 9:30am-1am, W-Th 9:30am-2am, F-Sa 9:30am-2:30am, Su 9:30am-1am.

OLOKUN CUBAN $$

C. Fuencarral, 105 ☎91 445 69 16

Olokun is an authentic Cuban restaurant that doesn't take itself too seriously. While in some senses a classic Cuban bar with a very tropical vibe (melon mojitos and kiwi daiquiris; €5), Olokun's dark walls are covered in the scribbles and signatures of all of its past customers. It also features a foosball table in the basement, just for kicks. Olokun takes its menu of hearty Cuban dishes seriously, from the dark mojito (made with black rum; €7) to the traditional platters like *Mi Vieja Havana* (pork, fried plantains, black beans; €14) and *soroa* (chili, fried plantains, rice; €15).

i From ⓂTribunal, walk straight north up C. Fuencarral. The restaurant is on the left. Entree €10-15. ☑ Open daily noon-5pm and 9pm-2am.

▨ LA TABERNA DE LIRIA SPANISH $$$

C. del Duque de Liria, 9 ☎91 541 45 19 www.latabernadeliria.com

You're in Spain, and you've already saved a lot of money staying at dirt-cheap hostels and eating €1 *bocadillos*—you owe yourself at least one nice, authentic Spanish meal. Look no further than La Taberna de Liria. Head Chef Miguel Lopez Castanier has led Taberna de Liria through a very successful 22 years in Madrid (and published a cookbook), establishing it as a local favorite for gourmet Spanish cuisine. The dishes aren't particularly experimental, which is good for us travelers who are just looking for authentic Spanish food. The unassuming, simple decor and atmosphere keeps the emphasis on the food. Try

madrid

the foie gras appetizers (€11-14), and be sure to call ahead to make reservations, particularly on weekends.

i ⓂVentura Rodriguez. Walk forward, take the left fork in the road (C. San Bernardino), and walk straight forward. Appetizer €8-15. Entrees €17-25. Full tasting menu €50. ☒ Open M-Sa 2-4pm and 9-11:45pm.

EL JARDÍN SECRETO
C. de Conde Duque, 2

CAFE $

☎91 541 80 23

Tucked away in a tiny street close to C. de la Princesa, El Jardín Secreto takes its secret garden theme very seriously. Even the entrance is hard to find (it literally looks like a normal wall with a window), but that doesn't seem to deter the locals from coming here. Enjoy a selection of affordable, classic cafe fare in a dark, lush, fairy tale environment, filled with beaded window coverings, wooden ceiling canopies, and crystal ball table lamps. For a real taste of what Secreto has to offer, try the chocolate El Jardín, served with chocolate Teddy Grahams and dark chocolate that pools at the bottom of your cup (€6) ,or the George Clooney cocktail with *horchata*, crème de cacao, and Cointreau (€7.25). Maybe it's a magical potion that makes you as pretty as George Clooney. More likely, you'll just get buzzed.

i ⓂVentura Rodriguez. Head left at the fork in the road (C. San Bernardino). Coffee and tea €3-6. Cocktails €7.25. Desserts €4.20. ☒ Open M-W 4:30pm-12:30am, Th-Sa 5:30pm-1:30am, Su 4:30pm-12:30am.

LAS CUEVAS DEL DUQUE
C. de la Princesa, 16

SPANISH $$$

☎91 559 50 37 www.cuevasdelduque.galeon.com

Eating at this restaurant is kind of like eating in a Neanderthal's den. The restaurant is located partially underground, in a cave-like interior that goes for the same kind of historic Spanish appeal as Sobrino de Botin. Food-wise, Cuevas emulates Botin as well, focusing on big-game dishes like the suckling pig with potatoes (€19). They offer a great selection of steaks and grilled fish; the filet mignon (€20) is particularly popular.

i ⓂVentura Rodriguez. Take the left fork in the road onto C. San Bernardino; the restaurant is on a tiny street to the right. Entree €15-30. ☒ Open daily 7-11pm.

LA ÚRSULA
C. López de Hoyos, 17

TAPAS $$

☎91 564 23 79 www.laursula.com

Across the street from the Museo Lazaro Galdiano, La Úrsula is an upscale tapas bar with terrace seating on a quiet side street off C. Serrano. The setting is fantastic (although limited), and like most places in Salamanca, it attracts a steady crowd of wealthy, well-dressed *madrileños*. La Úrsula offers particularly great lunch deals, including one of the city's best hamburger specials (€8)—a large burger with three tasty toppings of your choice (fried egg, manchego, sauteed peppers, etc.) and served with fries, a drink, and coffee or dessert. For the early-risers out there, Ursula offers an affordable breakfast menu (€2-5) until 12:30pm.

i ⓂGregorio Marañon. Cross C. Castella on C. de Maria de Molina. Follow C. de Maria de Molina for 3 blocks until you reach C. Serrano. Menú del día €7-11. Meals €14-20. Cash only. ☒ Open daily 8am-noon.

NIGHTLIFE

EL TIGRE
C. Infantas, 30

BAR, RESTAURANT

☎915 32 00 72

A bustling, macho restaurant, El Tigre lives up to its name. When you walk into the bar, you'll see animal heads stuck to the walls and a crowd of drunk Europeans standing around bars, sipping extra-large mojitos, beers, and sangrias. Drink at this rowdy bar for just €6, which gets you a cup of booze so big you'll have to hold it with two hands and for no extra cost you'll get a few plates of meaty tapas (apparently, they want to make sure you're not too drunk to function after hitting up their bar). El Tigre is the perfect first stop for a night out, and since it's only open until 1am, you'll get kicked out just as clubs across the city start to get lively. Make some new friends while standing around (no seating, folks), since this grisly bar is a local hotspot for college students.

i Large sangria, mojitos, beer, sidra €6. Meals €7-18. ☑ Open M-F noon-1am, Sa 1pm-2:30am.

KAPITAL
CLUB

C. Atocha, 125 ☎914 20 29 06 www.grupo-kapital.com/kapital

When you ask people in the know about Madrid's nightlife, they have one word for you: Kapital. This seven-floor mega club located in Huertas, the pulse of mainstream Madrid party culture, is sweaty, trashy, and electric—think of it as a huge frat party, only darker, with classier attire and more women. The renovated-theater dance club is known for attracting a diverse group of people—from local Madrileños to European college students to (allegedly) members of the Real Madrid soccer team. Each of its seven floors has a different character. While the first floor is the liveliest, complete with sugary-flavored smoke machines and house music, the second floor has a bustling karaoke stage, the fourth contains "the kissing room" (interpret that as you will), and the seventh has a hookah bar. Each floor is known for playing a different style of music as well, like reggae or hip-hop. Although the club opens at midnight, it isn't at its best until 2:30 or 3am. Dress up for this one (you'll thank us later).

i Cover €15-20. Drinks €10-15. ☑ Open Th-Sa midnight-6am.

TUPPERWARE
BAR, CLUB

Corredera Alta de San Pablo, 26 ☎625 52 35 61

Why is it called Tupperware? We don't know—but it doesn't sound too mainstream. Just how they want it. Tupperware is a, dare we say it, groovy bar/dance club nestled on a bustling side road in Malasaña (the hotspot for alternative—hipster—Madrileños). Painted bright with what looks like half graffiti, half urban art, the walls inside are brought alive by multi-colored, beady disco lights and the awesome hand-drawn murals they illuminate. In addition to one bar on the first floor, the bar also has a few comfy chairs and a table for leisurely chatting. Check out the upstairs when the bottom floor is too crowded for your own aloof preferences. Equipped with another bar, a dance space, and chairs and couches for more "leisurely talk" (because that's all couches are used for, nowadays). While leisurely talking, quietly jam out to some great American oldies and alternative rock—we're talking Red Hot Chili Peppers, Pixies, Nirvana. Or jam out not so quietly. That's what dance floors are for, right? An added plus to the already-rocking bar: drinks are cheap. Finally, when you're used to paying €6 for a small cup of beer or sangria, €3 for two San Miguels will definitely be welcome. Try sangria for €2, and most other mixed drinks and wines from €2-6 per copa (cup). And when you're standing at the bottom floor, make sure to look behind the bar. Here, you'll find some classic, childhood stuff—Barbie dolls, Batman comic books, plastic Santa Claus figurines. Only this time around, they're found behind the bar of a hipster dance club instead of under a Christmas tree.

i Drinks €2-6. ☑ Open Tu-Su 6pm-3:30am.

LA VÍA LÁCTEA
BAR, CLUB

C. Velarde, 18 ☎914 46 75 81 www.facebook.com/lavialacteab

This place has been around since your parents were in their 20s. And if they were a) Madrileño, b) into rock and roll and c) part of the youth counterculture movement La Movida Madrileña, they probably haunted this place every weekend. La Vía Láctea, or "Milky Way" in English, is one of the city's hippest bars. A relic of the Madrileño youth movement that emerged after Franco's death in

madrid

1975 (and, like most other countercultural movements in the world, involved drugs, sex, and guitars), La Vía Láctea hasn't aged a bit. Come inside at 1am or so on a Saturday night (well, Sunday morning) and find yourself surrounded by the coolest Madrileños the city has to offer, gathered around the bar or playing pool in the back room. You won't be hearing any Enrique Iglesias or Prince Royce (Billboard's hottest Latin singers, for those of you not in the know—and since you're visiting Madrid, you should get familiar soon). Instead, bob your head to some classic American rock and roll (seems to be a favorite motif here in Malasaña). For song titles, ask your Dad, he'd have probably listened to those songs at your age. There are two floors to the bar/dance club, the top being a lot quieter and more relaxed for those who need an escape from the crowded and sweaty floor below. For all its oldies glory, the alcohol prices are anything out of the ordinary for the pricy city of Madrid. Most drinks cost €6+ per cup, and that includes beers. But unlike some fancier (and more touristy) bars around el Centro and Sol, there's no cover charge to visit the Milky Way. (That may just be the first, and last, time anyone's ever said that before.)

i Drinks €6-10. ♋ Open M-Th 8pm-3:30am, F-Sa 8pm-3:30am, Su 8pm-3:30am.

DIPLODOCUS ROCK BAR
BAR

C. de Manuela Malasaña, 31 www.diplodocusrockbar.com

This place's mascot is a dinosaur, which perfectly symbolizes the whole place itself. Diplodocus, a North American beast from the Jurassic Period, apparently had the longest skeleton of any dinosaur thus far discovered. We guess this rock bar wanted to be the best—and the biggest.The bar is known for its heavy rock music (if you're not into that, or not willing to get totally trashed in a foreign country, this may not be the best place for you). At night, when the bar really livens up, the place starts to resemble a cave (maybe because of the dark lights and crowded space, maybe because of the drunk Madrileños—who knows?). In addition to its monster-sized drinks (check out the website for a few examples, most of which are larger than your head), the bar hosts parties with neighboring bars, like the with the infamous Tupperware in an event called Tuppersex. We'll let you decide what that means. When visiting the bar, share one (or more) of its specials with a group of friends, unless you're confident in your ability to drink up the volume of your head. Try a Hinojosaurio, a hearty mix of champagne, gin, vodka, lemon, and sugar, or a bright green Peranodonte, mixed with Geneva, rum, Limoncello, Whisky, infused with lemon and peppermint. Perhaps Diplodocus's most famous drink is its Leche de Brontosaurio (Brontosaurus Milk), which is a mix of rum, vodka, and sweet flavors like currants, cinnamon, sugar, and of course, milk. Try these drinks from an upwards of €7, or mini drinks (like normal beers) for €4-6. On Thursdays until 11pm is that bar's Happy Hour, in which it serves two "mini" drinks for €9 (but by their standard, they're already pretty monstrous). Classic Malasaña, this bar is a hub for locals. You may be hard-pressed to find English speakers here, but at least you'll be in one of the most authentic spots around!

i Drinks €4-6. ♋ Open W-Sa 9pm-3am.

PALACIO GAVIRIA
CLUB

C. del Arenal, 9 ☎91 526 60 69 www.palaciogaviria.com

Built in 1850 and inspired by the Italian Renaissance, Palacio Gaviria is a beautiful palace turned hot nightlife joint. Make your royal entrance by heading down the grand marble staircase to the dance floor, which is powered by techno beats and electric dance moves. Be on the lookout for promoters of Palacio Gaviria in Puerta del Sol, as they will often have vouchers for free entry or drinks.

i From Puerta del Sol, walk straight down C. del Arenal. Cover M-Th €10, F-Sa €15, Su €10. ♋ Open daily 11pm-late.

CAFE DEL PRÍNCIPE

Pl. de Canalejas, 5

BAR

☎91 531 81 83

As the name would suggest, this place is more of a restaurant with a large selection of drinks than a designated nightlife bar (no events or bands play here). However, they do advertise the "best mojitos in Madrid" (they're good, but that claim might be a stretch) as well as a variety of entrees and beverages. Only a block away from Sol, come here to take a tranquil break from the noise without venturing too far from all the clubs. This place is old-fashioned classy, with dark oak and a gold-trimmed bar that attracts an older clientele.

i Right at the corner of C. de la Cruz and C. de Príncipe. Mixed drinks €5-15. ☼ Open M-Th 9:30am-2am, F-Sa 9:30am-2:30am, Su 9:30am-2am. Kitchen open M-Th 9:30am-4pm and 8pm-2am, F-Sa 9:30am-4pm and 8pm-2am, Su 9:30am-4pm and 8pm-2am.

JOY ESLAVA

C. del Arenal, 11

CLUB

☎91 366 37 33 www.joy-eslava.com

Joy is a permanent fixture in the ever-changing Madrid nightlife scene. Located just two blocks west from Sol, Joy is an incredibly popular superclub, second in size only to the seven-story Kapital in the art district. Number one among study-abroad students and travelers, Joy Eslava plays an eclectic mix of music and features scantily clad models (of both genders) dancing on the theater stage. Balloons and confetti periodically fall New-Year's-Eve-style from the ceiling onto Joy's famously attractive clientele. Ask your hostel receptionist or promoter during the day for coupons for discounted admission or free drinks.

i Cover M- €12, Th €15, F-Su €18. ☼ Open M-Th 11:30pm-5:30am, F-Sa 11:30pm-6am, Su 11:30pm-5:30am.

REINA BRUJA

C. Jacometrezo, 6

CLUB

☎91 542 81 93 www.reinabruja.com

Reina Bruja is not just a club; it's a futuristic fantasy land. In Reina Bruja, the internationally renowned industrial designer Tomas Alia has created a world of endless light and sound. Every surface of this club, including the toilet seats, change color using cutting-edge LED technology. Reina Bruja is Madrid nightlife at its most creative and over-the-top. This subterranean world of phosphorescent lighting and stenciled pillars is popular with tourists (although less popular than Joy) but hasn't lost its edge in the *madrileño* scene. It's an edgier, more alternative club than the mainstream, super popular nightlife juggernauts of Joy and Kapital.

i Next to ⓜCallao. Cover €12; includes 1 drink. Wine €7. Mixed drinks €9. ☼ Open Th-Sa 11pm-6am.

POUSSE

C. de las Infantas, 19

BAR

☎91 521 63 01

With refurbished antique furniture alongside sleek leather loveseats and music from every decade, the ambience at Pousse is self-consciously eclectic. The cardboard and finger paint art on the walls was made by either avant-garde artists or kindergartners (you never know—there are some pretty pretentious kindergartners out there who really dig Abstract Expressionism). The drink menu is every bit as mixed as the decor, with everything from all-natural fresh fruit milkshakes (€6) to gourmet cocktails made with premium liqueurs (€9-13). Each cocktail has its own full-page entry in the lengthy drink menu and specials like Meet Johnny Black (Black Label whiskey, fresh OJ, sugar, and lemon; €12) are all made with fresh juices and top-dollar booze. Pousse attracts a loyal crowd of locals, but the tourists have caught on, too.

i From ⓜGran Vía, walk north up C. de Hortaleza, then make a right onto C. de las Infantas. Drinks €6-13. ☼ Open M-Sa 10pm-2am.

madrid

MUSEO CHICOTE

C. Gran Vía, 12

BAR

☎91 532 67 37 www.museo-chicote.com

After a cursory glance, Museo Chicote seems like an unadventurous, standard bar. But inside, once you see the walls covered in black-and-white photos of all the famous people who have come here since its creation in 1931, you'll realize this is one of Madrid's most historic bars. A longtime favorite of artists and writers (one of the many places Hemingway got drunk), this retro-chic cocktail bar maintains its original design. During the Spanish Civil War, the foreign press came here to wait out the various battles, and during the late Franco era, it became a haven for prostitutes. Today, it's a lounge with lots of dark leather seating for a diverse clientele. Museo Chicote offers one of the best happy hours on Gran Vía (cocktails €5; 5-11pm), but things shift pretty quickly at midnight, when the nightly DJ set starts. Well-known DJs playing everything from '80s American pop to European house.

i From ⓂGran Vía, walk east. Museo Chicote is on the left. Cocktails €10-15. ☼ Open daily 8am-3am.

◪ CASA LUCAS

C. Cava Baja, 30

BAR

☎91 365 08 04 www.casalucas.es

Props to Casa Lucas for making life seem simple and delicious. On a long block of successful restaurants, bars, and *tabernas* that thrive on gimmicks, Casa Lucas stands out by sticking to the basics: freshly prepared tapas and a premium, ever-changing wine list. With no gimmicks or hipness here, this no-frills spot attracts an older crowd. The tapas here are a notch above what you will find elsewhere, if slightly more expensive (starting around €5).

i ⓂLa Latina. Walk west down Pl. de la Cebada. Make a right onto C. de Humilladero and continue right onto C. Cava Baja. Wine by the glass €2-4, by the bottle €16-25. Raciones €7-15. ☼ Open M-Th 8pm-midnight, F-Sa 8pm-1am, Su 8pm-midnight.

LA PEREJILA

C. Cava Baja, 25

TAPAS, BAR

☎91 364 28 55

La Perejila is filled with beautiful antiques from the golden age of flamenco, vintage photographs, gold-leafed paintings, and vases of flowers that make this place come alive. Live parakeets greet you at the door, and finding a seat in this popular place is hard but well worth the effort. Come here for the titular *"La Perejila"* (veal meatballs served in a clay pot; €9). The wine selection changes daily, but their advertised "exquisite vermouth" is a favorite.

i ⓂLa Latina. Walk west down Pl. de la Cebada. Make a right onto C. de Humilladero and continue right onto C. Cava Baja. Cocktails €5-10. Tostados €5-7. Entrees €9-12. ☼ Open Tu-Sa 1-4pm and 8:15pm-12:30am, Su 1-4pm.

ANGELIKA COCKTAIL BAR

C. Cava Baja, 24

BAR

☎91 364 55 31 www.angelika.es

Angelika is notable for two things: the mojitos and the movies. You won't find a curated wine list here; instead, you'll find simple and well done €5 mojitos and daiquiris. In addition to that, the walls are lined with DVDs available for rental. Angelika has over 3000 titles and charges just €10 for 25 movies. We can't decide if this is the most cinema-friendly bar in Madrid or the world's bougiest Blockbuster.

i ⓂLa Latina. Walk west down Pl. de la Cebada. Make a right onto C. de Humilladero and continue right onto C. Cava Baja. Cocktails €5-10. ☼ Open M-W 9am-1pm and 3pm-1am, Th-Sa 6pm-2:30am, Su 5pm-1am.

EL BONANNO

Pl. del Humilladero, 4

BAR

☎91 366 68 86 www.elbonanno.com

Located at the southern end of the bustling C. Cava Baja, El Bonanno makes a great place for the first stop of the evening or a last-minute drink before you hit the club. Plaza del Humilladero is pure, delightful mayhem on popular nights, with tipsy Spaniards packing into every corner of the plaza. Unfortunately, El Bonanno doesn't have any terrace seating, which limits you to the nice but cramped interior and tempers your ability to partake in the mayhem.

i Ⓜ*La Latina. Walk 1 block west down Pl. de la Cabeza. Take a left onto Plaza del Humilladero. Beer and wine €1.50-3. Cocktails €3-10. ☼ Open daily 12:30pm-2:30am.*

SHOKO
DISCOTECA

C. de Toledo, 86 ☎91 354 16 91 www.shokomadrid.com

Shoko has one of the most distinctive club interiors in Madrid. It features bamboo shoots that reach to the ceiling, a spacious main floor for dancing, and a raised section that doubles as a stage for internationally acclaimed acts or as a swanky VIP section. It feels like a club out of *Kill Bill*. This place has killer feng-shui, but it's also a farther walk from Centro than other clubs (around 20min. south).

i Ⓜ*La Latina. Head south down C. de Toledo. Cover €10-15. ☼ Open daily 11:30pm-late.*

SOL Y SOMBRA
CLUB

C. de Echegaray, 18 ☎91 542 81 93 www.solysombra.name

With thousands of LED lights on every last surface, Sol y Sombra might be the closest you're going to get to *Tron* while clubbing in Madrid. Unlike the warehouse-style *discotecas* around the city, Sol y Sombra is surprisingly intimate, with the size and set-up of a typical bar. The walls shift in color to accent the bold patterns of the club, while the music shifts between techno, jazz, funk, and hip hop. This is not a sloppy Eurotrash *discoteca*; instead, it's a cool and innovative club. While you should expect a line out the door during prime weekend hours (midnight-3am), you won't be endlessly stranded: people tend to move in and out pretty quickly on their way to bigger *discotecas*. Find a mate on the dance floor and take advantage of the two for €12 mixed drink special.

i Ⓜ*Sol. From the metro, walk toward the museum district on Carrera de San Jeronimo and make a right onto C. de Echegaray. Cover €8 on weekend, includes 1 drink. Beer €5. Cocktails €7 ☼ Open Tu-Sa 1pm-3am.*

EL IMPERFECTO
BAR

Pl. de Matute, 2 ☎91 366 72 11

El Imperfecto is rocking the alternative vibe pretty hard (almost to the point of kitschy-ness). An orgasm of colors, hippie slogans, and American film and music icons, El Imperfecto has the feel of a counterculture bar from a decade you can't quite place your finger on. This shoebox interior is always fun and upbeat, with people sipping cocktails (€6-10) and milkshakes (€4-6). The special here is the two for €10 mojito special. While Imperfecto doesn't offer live music or a clubby dance floor, you should expect a crowd—and, on weekend nights, plenty of American study-abroaders, some friendly German accents, and fellas that might smell like cannabis. El Imperfecto is packed during weekend dinner hours (11pm-1am), so expect to stand at the bar.

i Ⓜ*Antón Martín. Walk uphill until you reach Pl. de Matute. Make a right toward C. de las Huertas. El Imperfecto is on the right. Drinks €4-10. Sangria €2 per glass, €11 per pitcher. ☼ Open M-Th 2:30pm-2am, F-Sa 2:30pm-2:30am, Su 2:30pm-2am.*

▨ BOGUI JAZZ CLUB
JAZZ CLUB

C. Barquillo, 29 ☎91 521 15 68 www.boguijazz.com

Bogui is Chueca's premier jazz venue and one of its most happening weekend clubs. Nightly sets of live jazz (9 and 11pm) are a fantastic way to get plugged into the local music scene. During weekend DJ sets (Th-Sa 1am), Bogui brings in some of Madrid's best-known jazz, funk, and soul DJs from Sala Barco. Bogui also caters to a Chueca crowd that likes to dance. The Wednesday midnight set (otherwise known as *La Descarga*, or "The Dump") is when musicians from around the city convene for a late-night jam session after a long night of gigs.

i *From Ⓜ Chueca, take C. Gravina 2 blocks west to C. Barquillo. The club is on the left. DJ sets Th-Sa free; concert €10. Beer €4. Cocktails €7. €1 surcharge on all beverages Th-Su. ⌚ Open Tu-Sa 10pm-5:30am.*

AREIA
BAR, TAPAS

C. de Hortaleza, 92 ☎91 310 03 07 www.areiachillout.com

Areia calls itself a "chillout zone," which must sound *so* cool to native Spanish speakers but a little lame to us Anglophones. Luckily, names aside, this is one of the coolest spots in Chueca thanks to its unbeatable beach theme. This bar and lounge is like a huge sandbox. In addition, it has a crimson-draped ceiling, low-lying tables, candles, and large cushion seats where people snack on international tapas. Relive your spring break glory (or infamy) with €5 daiquiris.

i *Ⓜ Chueca. Make a right onto C. Augusto Figuroa, then a right onto C. de Hortaleza. Cocktails €5-9. ⌚ Open daily 1pm-3am.*

DAME UN MOTIVO
BAR

C. Pelayo, 58 ☎91 319 74 98

The idea here is to do away with all of the excess of Chueca nightlife—cover charges, overpriced sugary drinks, flashing lights, and loud music—and offer an alternative environment for people who just want to hang out and converse. Locals seem to dig this minimalist take on nightlife in the otherwise maximalist Chueca scene. It's a popular destination at the start of the night. During the week, people come here to enjoy the film and book library.

i *From Ⓜ Chueca, take C. Gravina 1 block west to C. Pelayo and continue north½ a block. The bar is on the right. Check out Dame un Motivo's Facebook page for event listings. Beer €1.30-2.50. Cocktails €5.50. ⌚ Open W-Th 6pm-2am, F-Sa 4pm-2:30am, Su 4pm-2am.*

STUDIO 54
DISCOTECA

C. Barbieri, 7 ☎61 512 68 07 www.studio54madrid.com

You're going to see a lot of six packs at Studio 54, and we're not talking about beer. With pulsing Spanish pop and sculpted bartenders wearing nothing but bowties, Studio 54 tends to attract a crowd of predominantly gay *madrileños* and American and European tourists. This is one of the most popular young gay clubs in Chueca. If you haven't yet spent a night dancing to ridiculous pop music (think One Direction), this is the place to do it, with crystal chandeliers and disco balls hanging above a violet dance floor.

i *Ⓜ Chueca. Walk straight south down C. Barbieri toward Gran Vía. The discoteca is on the right. Cover €10 after 1am. Cocktails €8. ⌚ Open Th-Sa 11:30pm-3:30am.*

EL 51
COCKTAILS

C. de Hortaleza, 51 ☎91 521 25 64

If you're still stuck on a non-Spanish schedule (that is, getting drunk and going out before midnight), you should take advantage of El 51's happy hour, which runs until 11pm on Friday and Saturday. El 51 is a posh, single-room cocktail lounge with white leather chairs, crystal chandeliers, and mirrors lit with violet bulbs. Just steps from the center of Chueca's nightlife, this place tends to pack people in during prime hours (midnight-2am). Spanish pop plays in the background, but, they keep the volume low enough that you can still hold a conversation.

i *Ⓜ Chueca. Make a right onto C. Augusto Figueroa, then a right onto C. de Hortaleza. Cocktails €8-10. ⌚ Open Tu-Su daily 6pm-3am.*

LONG PLAY
DISCOTECA

Pl. de Vázquez de Mella, 2 ☎91 532 20 66

Clubs in Chueca come and go, but Long Play has been around for a long time. Once a venue of the early 1970s *madrileño* counterculture, today Long Play is the veteran of Chueca's gay clubs. While the younger locals prefer newer clubs to

spain

Long Play, it still manages to attract a solid crowd of older gay *madrileños*, European tourists, and American study abroaders. The downstairs DJ plays a variety of international pop, and things get pretty sweaty on the upstairs dance floor, which plays strictly European house.

i Ⓜ*Gran Vía. Head north up C. de Hortaleza, make a right onto C. de las Infantas, then a left into Pl. de Vázquez de Mella. Cover €10 Th-F after 1:30am (includes 1 drink), €10 Sa all night. Drinks €8. ☪ Open daily midnight-7am.*

🏴 LA VÍA LÁCTEA
BAR

C. Velarde, 18 ☎91 446 75 81 www.lavialactea.net

This is a Spanish temple dedicated to rock, grunge, and everything '70s counterculture. La Vía Láctea was founded in the early years of Movida Madrileña, a youth-propelled revolution of art, music, fashion, and literature. Today, it's more a relic of this past than a continuing force of change, with pop music memorabilia covering the walls from floor to ceiling and a fine perfume of stale beer lingering in the air. Every night, locals and tourists gather here to shoot pool and hang out under the warm neon glow.

i Ⓜ*Tribunal. Walk north up C. Fuencarral and make a left onto C. Velarde. Cover €10 after 1am, includes 1 drink. Beer €3-5. Cocktails €5-7. ☪ Open daily 7:30pm-3:30am.*

CLUB NASTI
DISCOTECA

C. de San Vicente Ferrer, 33 ☎91 521 76 05 www.nasti.es

Club Nasti is the polar opposite of big, touristy nightclubs that you'll find elsewhere in the city. This is the club of choice for Malasaña hipsters and club rats, who enjoy Club Nasti's curated repertoire of synth pop, electro beats, and punk jams. For a lighter touch, try Friday nights, when house DJs spin indie rock like the Strokes and the Arctic Monkeys. The small dance floor gets packed as the night progresses.

i Ⓜ*Tribunal. Walk south down C. de Fuencarral and make a right onto C. de San Vicente Ferrer. Cover €10 after 2am, includes 1 drink. Beer €4-5. Cocktails €8-9. ☪ Open Th-Sa 1-5:30am.*

BARCO
MUSIC, DISCOTECA

C. del Barco, 34 ☎91 521 24 47 www.barcobar.com

With a jam-packed program of nightly concerts, late-night DJ sets, and weekly jam sessions, this small venue covers a wide spread of musical terrain. BarCo has made itself a name as a stalwart venue for local acts, with most bands drawing heavily on funk, soul, rock, and jazz. While the concert schedule is continually changing, the nightly DJ sets are given to a handful of veteran European DJs who have been spinning in Madrid for years. The Sunday night jam session brings in some of the city's best contemporary jazz musicians. This is the nucleus of Malasaña's eclectic live music scene, and the bar's clientele changes nightly depending on who's playing.

i Ⓜ*Tribunal. Head south on C. de Fuencarral 3 blocks. Take a right onto C. Corredara Baja de San Pablo, walk 2 blocks, and take a left (south) onto C. del Barco. The bar is on the right. Cover €5-10. Beer €5. Cocktails €7. €1 drink surcharge F-Sa. Cash only. ☪ Open M-Th 10pm-5:30am, F-Sa 10pm-6am, Su 10pm-5:30am.*

🏴 TEMPO CLUB
MUSIC

C. Duque de Osuna 8 ☎91 547 75 18 www.tempoclub.net

Tempo Club proclaims that it focuses on "*musica negra*": funk, Afro, Latin, jazz, soul, and beats. Decorated with unorthodox dome chairs and bold, clean streaks of warm reds and oranges, Tempo's decor represents its mission statement: a modern take on '70's-style grooves. Even when the DJ takes over for the late night set, the rhythm section often sticks around. While Tempo thrives on rich instrumentals, most of the acts also involve talented vocalists. The venue is divided between a street-level cafe and cocktail area and the downstairs concert hall. This is a refreshing alternative to the hordes of countless clubs that all feel the same.

i ⓂVentura Rodriguez. From C. Princesa, follow C. del Duque de Liria south to the intersection with C. Duque de Osuna. Turn left onto C. Duque. Live performances Th-Sa. Cocktails €5-8. Cash only. ☒ Open daily 6pm-late.

CAFE LA PALMA
MUSIC

C. de la Palma 62   ☎91 522 50 31 www.cafelapalma.com

Cafe la Palma is in many ways a typical Malasaña rock club even though it's just outside the *barrio*. Like many clubs in the area, La Palma has a clean, versatile open space that strives to be a lot of different things—a cafe that people can enjoy during the day, a cocktail lounge at night, a concert venue in the late night, and a full club with a live DJ set in the early morning. The music acts La Palma attracts are every bit as eclectic as the venue itself, ranging from trance to heavy rock to open mic nights. While this place tries to accomplish a lot within the three small rooms of the cafe, it doesn't spread itself too thin. There is a drink minimum (€6) for some live sets, but this is a great alternative to forking over a fat cover charge.

i ⓂPl. de España, follow C. de Los Reyes northeast 2 blocks, take a left onto C. Amaniel, and walk 2 blocks to C. de La Palma. Drink min. for some events €6; check website for more info. Cocktails €6. Cash only. ☒ Open daily 5pm-3am.

ORANGE CAFÉ
BAR, CLUB

Serrano Jover, 5   ☎91 542 28 17 www.soyorangecafe.com

Orange Café is a venue for local rock acts in the evening and a packed dance club later at night. This is a pretty standard club, designed for easy consumption by college-age kids and American tourists. Orange Café isn't as popular as similar mainstream clubs Joy Eslava and Kapital because of its not-as-central location. Women should take advantage of free drinks and free entry on Wednesday nights until 1:30am. Check the website for a list of concerts and cover charges.

i ⓂArgüelles. Cover €10-15 depending on the night. ☒ Open M-Th midnight-5am, F-Sa 11pm-6am.

EL CHAPANDAZ
BAR

C. de Fernando, 77   ☎91 549 29 68 www.chapandaz.com

Ever wonder to yourself how you would spice up a typical night out at the bar? How about by adding some panther's milk and cave decorations? If that's your idea of fun, El Chapandaz is the place for you. During the day, it's just a funky-looking restaurant, but at night it transforms into the most ridiculous bar in Madrid. It is a fully functional, lactating cave with stalactites hanging from the ceiling that periodically drip milk into glass pitchers. The house drink, *Leche de Pantera* (panther's milk), is a combination of rum, cinnamon, and that special milk. If you are suspicious (for perfectly good reasons), it also offers standard fare and a full menu of sweet, fruity, and colorful drinks. The bar is generally quiet until 11pm but fills up with a mostly international, study-abroad crowd that stops in for the novelty before heading out to the clubs.

i From ⓂMoncloa, head to the intersection of C. de Fernando and C. de la Princesa and walk east down C. de Fernando. International night Tu. Drink €10. ☒ Open daily 1pm-3am.

ARTS AND CULTURE

With some of the best art museums, public festivals, and performing arts groups in the world, Madrid's arts and culture scene is thriving. From street performers in Parque del Buen Retiro to Broadway musicals, you can find anything you're looking for in this metropolis.

Corridas (Bullfights)

Whether you view it as animal cruelty or national sport, the spectacle of *la corrida* (bullfighting) is a cherished Spanish tradition. Although it has its origins in Roman gladiator practices, bullfighting is now a distinctly Spanish sport. The sport has been subject to continuing animal rights protest in recent years, in addition to suffering fading popularity with the younger generations. More a form of performance art than a sport (every bullfight has the same outcome of the bull "losing"), bullfighting draws hordes of tourists (in addition to lots of old Spanish men) who flock to see the tradition that Hemingway celebrated as "the only art in which the artist is in danger of death and in which the degree of brilliance in the performance is left to the fighter's honor." It's not for the faint of heart, of course—be prepared to see a bull suffer for 20-30min. before being killed.

If you choose to go, it is important to know a little bit about the rituals of the sport. The bullfight has three stages. First, the *picadores* (lancers on horseback), pierce the bull's neck muscles. Then, assistants thrust decorated darts called *banderillas* into the bull's back to injure and fatigue it. Finally, the *matador* kills his large opponent with a sword thrust between the bull's shoulder blades, killing it instantly. Animal rights activists call the rituals savage and cruel, but aficionados call it an art that requires quick thinking and skill.

The best place to see bullfighting in Madrid is at the country's biggest arena, **Plaza de las Ventas,** where you can buy tickets in *sol* (sun) or *sombra* (shade) sections. Get your tickets at the arena the Friday or Saturday leading up to the bullfight. (C. de Alcalá ☎237913 56 22 00 www.las-ventas.com *i* Ventas ticket office open 10am-2pm and 5-8pm.) You'll pay more to sit out of the sun, but either way, you'll have a good view of the feverish crowds that cheer on the matador and wave white handkerchiefs, called *pañuelos*, after a particularly good fight. Tickets range from €5 for nosebleeds to €80 for front-row seats. Each ticket includes usually around three bullfights, each of which lasts 20-30min. Rent a seat cushion at the stadium or bring your own for the stone seats. Bullfights are held Sundays and holidays throughout most of the year. During the **Fiesta de San Isidro** in May, fights are held almost every day, and the top bullfighters come face to face with the fiercest bulls. People across Spain are bitterly divided about the future of the sport, so visitors should approach the topic with sensitivity.

Flamenco

Many flamenco clubs offer overpriced dinners combined with overdone music and dance spectaculars geared toward tourists. There are some clubs in Madrid that offer more traditional and soulful flamenco. You'll still pay a decent amount to see it, but it's a great way to learn about the art form that is often described as Europe's counterpart to the blues.

▨ CASA PATAS
LAS HUERTAS

C. de los Cañizares, 10 ☎91 369 04 96 www.casapatas.com

Casa Patas is like the Sobrino de Botin of flamenco venues. It's the place to be if you want the authentic, traditional experience—but it's pricey and attracts a large tourist crowd. Throughout most of the day, it functions as a normal Spanish restaurant, but at night, Madrid's finest dancers perform the art of flamenco on the stage in the back of the restaurant. Tickets aren't cheap, but they're worth every penny if you're looking for a proper flamenco show. Shows sell out frequently, particularly in the summer months, so be sure to get your tickets in advance. The restaurant and tapas bar up front serves the usual suspects: platters of *jamón y queso* (€19), fried squid (€13), and *albondigas de la abuela*. *i* Ⓜ Antón Martín. From the metro, walk up C. de Atocha and turn left onto C. del Olivar. Casa Patas is on the right. Tickets €32; includes 1 drink. Entrees €10-25. ☒ Open M-Th 1-4pm and 8pm-midnight, F-Sa 7:30pm-2am. Flamenco M-Th 8:30pm, F-Sa 9pm and midnight.

madrid

CARDAMOMO

C. de Echegaray, 15 ☎91 369 07 57 www.cardamomo.es

Cardamomo advertises itself as the "only tablao flamenco recommended by *The New York Times.*" More importantly, Let's Go recommends Cardamomo for showcasing less touristy flamenco that features a raw, improvisational quality to it. The focus is more on rhythm and movement and less on the kitschy costumes that are usually synonymous with flamenco. You can expect syncopated guitars, soulful old men crooning flamenco verse, and swift choreography—all in an intimate space, with spectators packed table to table in the narrow interior. The nightly sets are short (50min.) but intense and a good way of seeing flamenco without dedicating an entire evening to it.

i Ⓜ*Sol. Walk east toward Pl. de las Cortes and make a right onto C. de Echegaray. Ticket €25; includes 1 drink. Check with your hostel for discounts.* Ⓩ *Shows daily 10:30pm.*

Fútbol

You might see churches in every city you visit in Spain, but the official national religion is *fútbol.* Matches are a beloved spectacle everywhere in Spain, but particularly in Madrid, which is home to **Real Madrid,** arguably the greatest soccer club the world has ever known (at least that's what the locals will tell you). On game days, which start around the end of August and run through the end of May, locals line the streets and pack bars to watch the matches. Celebrations after games are common in public plazas and squares, helped by the fact that most matches fall on Saturdays. For Real Madrid, the victory party always takes place in **Plaza Cibeles,** just outside the town hall. *Fútbol* doesn't just happen on the field in Spain—it takes over city life, particularly on big game days. The other two major teams in Madrid are **Atlético** and **Getafe.**

Seeing a game live with 80,000 other fans can be an incredible experience but is often logistically difficult to arrange. Tickets are expensive and hard to come by. All teams sell a number of tickets through their stadium box offices and release a limited number online through their club website. If you are intent on going to a game, research ticket availability at least two weeks in advance. Tickets are also available from vendors outside the stadium, but these are often counterfeited or marked up well above face value. Tickets for Atlético and Getafe tend to be cheaper and more available than tickets for Real Madrid. Regardless of whether you make it to the stadium or not, it's worth going to a local tapas bar to watch.

▓ ESTADIO SANTIAGO BERNABEU

Av. Cochina Espina, 1 ☎91 464 22 34 www.santiagobernabeu.com, www.realmadrid.com

Site of the 2010 European Final Cup, Estadio Santiago Bernabeu is also home to Real Madrid, named the greatest club of the 20th century by FIFA. Tours are a bit pricey (€19) but a must-do for soccer fans; they take you through the club's most hallowed grounds, from the trophy room to the visitors' dressing room to the pitch itself. If you can, try to see an actual game at the stadium, as tickets can start as low as €25. Advance tickets can be purchased at **www.servicaixa.com,** and remaining tickets are released on the club website at 11am the Monday before each game.

i Ⓜ*Santiago Bernabeu. The stadium is across the street from the metro. Ticket €30-300. Tours €19, under 14 €13.* Ⓩ *Season runs Sept-May. Check online for game schedules and tour times.*

ESTADIO VICENTE CALDERÓN

Paseo de la Virgen del Puerto, 67 ☎91 364 22 34 www.clubatleticodemadrid.com

Estadio Vicente Calderón is home to the Atlético Madrid *fútbol* club. With a storied past that includes European Cups and international recognition, this Madrid-based club participates in the esteemed Primera División of La Liga. While they've had some big wins in the past, Atlético Madrid is the perennial underdog in the city rivalry with Real Madrid. While this stadium may not be the city's biggest stage for football, tickets for games are more readily available and cheaper. Tickets can be purchased at www.servicaixa.com or on the club website.

i Ⓜ*Pirámides. From the metro, head west 1 block to C. de Toledo, follow 1 block south to Paseo de los Melancolicos. The stadium is on the left. Prices vary. Tours €10. ⚄ Check the website for schedule. Tours Tu-Su 11am-8pm.*

SHOPPING

El Rastro

Every Sunday from 9am-3pm, thousands of people from across Madrid and beyond flock to the Ribera de Curtidores. Packed like sardines on the avenue, pedestrians push and shove to move forward, gaping at the rainbow flags and kaleidoscopic stands lining the street. They haggle with vendors, pushing prices down, handle an eclectic range of objects—from medieval swords to fresh tulips—carry bags stuffed with dirt-cheap, second-hand clothing. "Precios bajos!" the vendors yell across the street, trying to outdo their neighboring competitors to attract more customers. Here, it is loud, crowded, dusty.

This is El Rastro, the capital city's largest flea market.

In English, "El Rastro" translates to "the trail." According to legend, pig slaughterhouses and tanneries once stood in the area now occupied by the marketplace. The market itself is one of the oldest in Western Europe, and in the 19th century, it was a setting for the rogues and crooks of Madrid to buy and sell a hodgepodge of items. Times have changed since then—but not by a long measure. Buyers can still purchase a random assortment of new and used items in the outdoor menagerie, but should be wary of the inevitable pickpockets who loiter in the area and prey on unaware pedestrians.

Buyers can choose from more than 3,000 colorful, diverse merchant stands to purchase goods in the market. Buried deep within the market—which is located on Ribera de Curtidores and Plaza de Cascorro—one can find a mixture of traditional and modern items, from rich red rugs to contemporary art mockups. It's no exaggeration to say there's something for everyone in this market.

Less visited, but perhaps home to even more hidden gems than El Rastro's main avenue, are the market's side streets, narrow offshoots bordering the market. Here, the quieter streets are clear of entertainers (statue men, women who crank eerie music boxes) and often can hold some incredible and unique collector's items, like old pieces of clocks, keys, and jewel-like stones.

After wandering up and down the streets of el Rastro, pedestrians will be grateful to see cafes offering cheap breakfasts of churros con chocolate or ice-cold beers. When visiting the market, make sure to check out the many tapas bars in the area or inexpensive menús del día to satiate a hungry stomach.

ESSENTIALS

Practicalities

- **TOURIST OFFICES:** The **Madrid Tourism Centre** in Pl. Mayor (☎91 588 16 36 www.esmadrid. com) is a good place to start; this is where you'll find city and transit maps as well as suggestions for activities, food, and accommodations. English is spoken at most tourist offices throughout the city. There are additional tourist offices and stands around town; look for large orange stands with exclamation marks. **Calle del Duque de Medinaceli 2.** (☎91 429 49 51 ⚄ Open M-Sa 9:30am-8:30pm, Su and holidays 9:30am-2pm.) **Estacion de Atocha.** (☎91 528 46 30 ⚄ Open M-Sa 9:30am-8:30pm, Su and holidays 9:30am-2pm) **Madrid-Barajas Airport Terminal 1.** (☎91 305 86 56) **Terminal 4.** (]90 210 00 07 ⚄ Open daily 9:30am-

8:30pm.) There is also a tourist office at the **airport train station**. (☎91 315 99 76 ⌚ Open M-Sa 8am-8pm, Su 9am-2pm.)

- **TOURS:** Different themed tours leave regularly from the **Madrid Tourism Centre.** For dates, times, and more info, visit www.esmadrid.com. Many youth hostels host tapas tours, pub crawls, and walking tours for reasonable prices. Check out www.toursnonstop.com. **LeTango Tours** is run by a Spanish-American husband-wife team, with tours that take you to local bars, provide fun city facts, and explain Spanish traditions. (☎91 369 47 52 www.letango.com). Run by historian and writer Stephen Drake-Jones, the **Wellington Society** (☎60 914 32 03 www.wellsoc.org) offers different themed tours of Madrid and daytrips to Toledo and Segovia. Another option is **Madrid Vision** (☎91 779 18 88 www.madridvision.es), which runs the double-decker red buses that you see throughout the city. Choose between the *historicó* and *moderno* routes. Each route makes 15-20 stops around the city. (*i* €17; discounts online.)

- **CURRENCY EXCHANGE:** The most convenient (although not always the cheapest) place to change your money is at the airport. There are also currency exchanges in Puerta Del Sol and Gran Vía (look for booths that say "change"), but try to use these as a last resort, as rates are bad and commission charges are high. Most *hostales* and hotels will also be able to change your money; rates vary by location. Another option is **Banco Santander Central Hispano,** which charges €12-15 commission on non-American Express Travelers Cheques (max. exchange €300). Wherever you go, be sure to bring your passport as identification.

- **LUGGAGE STORAGE:** Store your luggage at the **Aeropuerto Internacional de Barajas.** (☎91 393 68 05 *i* 1-day €3.70; 2-15 days €4.78 per day. ⌚ Open 24hr.) or at the **bus station.** (*i* €1.40 per bag per day. ⌚ Open M-F 6:30am-10:30pm, Sa 6:30am-3pm.)

- **POST OFFICES:** Buy **stamps** (*sellos*) from a post office or tobacco stand. Madrid's **central post office** is at Pl. de Cibeles. (☎91 523 06 94;90 219 71 97 ⌚ Open M-F 8:30am-9:30pm.) Mailboxes are usually yellow, with one slot for "Madrid" and another for everywhere else.

- **POSTAL CODE:** 28008.

Emergency

- **EMERGENCY NUMBERS: Medical emergency:** ☎061 or ☎112. For non-emergency medical concerns, go to **Unidad Medica Angloamericana,** which has English-speaking personnel on duty by appointment. (C. del Conde de Aranda, 1, 1st fl. ☎91 435 18 23 ⌚ Open M-F 9am-8pm, Sa 10am-1pm.)

- **POLICE: Servicio de Atención al Turista Extranjero (SATE)** are police who deal exclusively with tourists and help with contacting embassies, reporting crimes, and canceling credit cards. (C. Legantos, 19 ☎91 548 85 27; ☎90 210 21 12 ⌚ Open daily 9am-midnight.)

Getting There

By Plane

All flights come in through the **Aeropuerto Internacional de Barajas** (☎902 404 704 www.aena.es). The **Barajas** metro stop connects the airport to the rest of Madrid (€2). To take the subway into the city center, take the #8 toward Nuevo Ministerios, transfer to the #10 toward Puerta del Sur, get off at Tribunal (3 stops), transfer to the #1 toward Valdecarros, and get off at Sol. The journey should take 45-60min. By bus, the **Bus-Aeropeurto 200** leaves from the national terminal (T2) and runs to the city center through ⓜAvenida de America. (☎90 250 78 50 ⌚ Every 15min., 5:20am-11:30pm.) **Taxis** (€35. 30min.) are readily available outside of the airport. For more info on ground transport, visit **www.metromadrid.es.**

By Train

Trains (☎90 224 02 02 www.renfe.es) from northern Europe and France arrive on the north side of the city at **Chamartin**. (C. Augustin de Foxa ☎91 300 69 69, ☎91 506 63 29.) Trains to and from the south of Spain and Portugal use **Atocha;** buy tickets at the station or online. There is a **RENFE** information office at the main terminal. (☎90 224 02 02 ☑ Open daily 7am-7pm.) **AVE** trains offer high-speed service throughout Spain, including Barcelona, Salamanca, Segovia, Sevilla, and Toledo. Be sure to keep your ticket, or you won't be able to pass through the turnstiles. Call **RENFE** for both international destinations and domestic travel. (☎902 24 34 02 for international destinations; ☎90 224 02 02 for domestic.) Ticket windows are open daily 6:30am-9pm; when they're closed, you can buy tickets at vending machines.

By Bus

If you prefer four wheels, many private bus companies run through Madrid, and most pass through **Estación Sur de Autobuses.** (C. Mendez Alvaro ☎91 468 42 00 www.estacionautobusesmadrid.com ☑ Info booth open daily 6:30am-1am.) National destinations include Algeciras, Alicante, Oviedo, and Toledo, among others. Inquire at the station, online, or by phone for specific information on routes and schedules.

Getting Around

By Metro

The Madrid metro system is by far the easiest, cheapest way to get you almost anywhere you need to go in the city. It is clean, safe, and recently renovated. Service begins M-Sa at 6am, Su at 7am, and ends daily around 1:30am. Try to avoid rush hours (daily 8-10am, 1-2pm, and 4-6pm). You can buy either a one-way ticket (€1), or, if you're making multiple trips, you can save by purchasing a combined **10-trip metrobus ticket** (€9.30). Trains run frequently, and green timers above most platforms show the next approaching train times. Be sure to grab a free metro map (available at any ticket booth or tourist office). **Abonos mensuales,** or monthly passes, grant unlimited travel within the city proper for €47.60, while **abonos turísticos** (tourist passes) come in various increments (1, 2, 3, 4, or 7 days) and sell for €6-25 at the metro stations or online. For metro information, visit www.metromadrid.es or call ☎90 244 44 03.

By Bus

Buses cover areas that are inaccessible by the metro and are a great way to see the city. The pamphlet "Visiting the Downtown on Public Transport" lists routes and stops. (Free at any tourist office or downloadable at **www.madrid.org.**) Tickets for the bus and metro are interchangeable. The *Búho* (owl), or night bus, travels from Pl. de Cibeles and other marked routes along the outskirts of the city. (☑ M-Th every 30min. midnight-3am, every hr. 3-6am; F-Sa every 20min. midnight-6am; Su every 30 min. midnight-3am.) These buses, marked on the essential **Red de Autobuses Nocturnos** (available at any tourist office) run along 26 lines covering regular daytime routes. For info, call **Empresa Municipal de Transportes** (☎90 250 78 50 www.emtmadrid.es). **Estacion Sur** (C. Mendez Alvaro ☎91 468 42 00) covers mainly southern and southeastern destinations outside Madrid, such as **Granada, Malaga, Sevilla,** and **Valencia.** Visit www.avanzabus.com for timetables and routes.

By Taxi

Registered Madrid taxis are black or white and have red bands and small insignias of a bear and *madroño* tree (symbols of Madrid). Hail them on the street or at taxi stands all over the city. A green light means they're available. The fare starts at €1.75 and increases by €1 every kilometer thereafter. To call a city taxi, dial ☎91 447 51 80.

By Moped And Bike

Biking in the city is ill-advised, but Casa de Campo and Dehesa de la Villa both have easily navigable bike trails. You can rent a bike from **Karacol Sport.** (C. Tortosa 8 ☎91 539 96 33 www.karacol.com *i* Cash deposit or €50 and photocopy of your passport required. €18 per day. ⍉ Open M-W 10:30am-3pm and 5-8pm, Th 10:30am-3pm and 5-9:30pm, F-Su 10:30am-3pm and 5-8pm.) **Motocicletas Antonio Castro** rents mopeds for €23-95 per day, including unlimited mileage and insurance, but you'll need your own lock and helmet. You must be at least 25 years old and have a driver's license for motorcycles. (C. Clara del Rey, 17 ☎91 413 00 47 www.blafermotos.com ⍉ Open M-F 8am-6pm, Sa 10am-1:30pm.)

barcelona

Barcelona, a favorite travel destination for millions worldwide, is the second largest city in Spain and the capital city of Catalonia. The city is bustling and loud, and the first thing it will tell you is to get lost. Not in the "you don't belong here" sense, but because you can walk around aimlessly, with literally no idea where you are, and still have a good time. Around every corner there will be an alluring alleyway of stores, a museum of interest or beautiful building, or a tapas bar with a seat calling your name, and you genuinely need no directions to have a remarkable trip. This loudness also comes in a multitude of languages, and if you have come with the intention of practicing your Spanish, you'll need to make it known to the locals because they will talk to you in English if they are aware that you speak it. This is because Barcelona is an inherently social place. In many restaurants, there are more outdoor seats than indoor seats, because being integrated with the community is part of what makes the city so unique. With a thriving nightlife in front of a gorgeous beach, historical remnants of some of the world's most significant artists, and one of the best public transit systems of any global city, Barcelona has more than enough attractions to entertain travelers: young, old, single, or grouped.

ORIENTATION

Though a large and complex city, Barcelona's *barris* (neighborhoods) are fairly well-defined. The **Ciutat Vella** (old city) is the city's heart, comprised of **El Raval** (west of Las Ramblas), **Barri Gòtic** (between **Las Ramblas** and Via Laietana), **El Born** (between Via Laietana and Parc de la Ciutadella), and **La Barceloneta** (the peninsula south of El Born). Farther down the coast (to the left as you look at a map with the sea at the bottom) from the *Ciutat Vella* is the park-mountain **Montjuïc** and the small neighborhood of **Poble Sec** between Montjuïc and Avinguda Paral·lel. Farther inland from the *Ciutat Vella* is the large, central, rigidly gridded zone of **l'Eixample,** and still farther away from the sea is **Gràcia.** The **Plaça de Catalunya** is one of the city's most central points, located where Las Ramblas meets the Passeig de Gràcia; it is essentially the meeting point of El Raval, Barri Gòtic, and l'Eixample.

Barri Gòtic and Las Ramblas

You will get lost in Barri Gòtic. Knowing this, the best way to properly orient yourself in the confusing neighborhood, where streets still follow their medieval routes, is to take a day to learn your way around. **Las Ramblas** provides the western boundary of the neighborhood, stretching from the waterfront to **Plaça de Catalunya. Via Laietana** marks the eastern border, running nearly parallel to Las Ramblas. The primary east-west artery running between Las Ramblas and V. Laietana is known as **Carrer de Ferran** between Las Ramblas and the central **Plaça de Sant Jaume** and as **Carrer de Jaume I** between Pl. Sant Jaume and V. Laietana. Of the many plazas hiding in the

spain

Barri Gòtic, **Plaça Reial** (take the tiny C. de Colom off Las Ramblas) and Plaça de Sant Jaume are the grandest. The neighborhood is better known, though, for its more cramped spaces, like the narrow alleys covered with arches or miniature *placetas* in the shadows of parish churches. The **L3** and **L4** metro lines serve this neighborhood, with ⓂDrassanes, ⓂLiceu, and ⓂCatalunya along Las Ramblas (L3) and ⓂJaume I at the intersection of C. Jaume I and V. Laietana.

El Born

El Born, which makes up the eastern third of the **Ciutat Vella,** is celebrated for being slightly less touristy than the Barri Gòtic and slightly less prostitute-y than El Raval. The neighborhood is renowned for its confusing medieval streets, whose ancient bends hide fashionable boutiques and restaurants both traditional and modern. The **Passeig del Born,** the lively hub of this quirky *barri*, makes for a good bar- and restaurant-lined starting point.

El Raval

There's no point beating around the bush: El Raval is one of Barcelona's more dangerous neighborhoods. But this doesn't mean that you should avoid it. Just be careful and aware—even during the day—and be prepared to deal with persistent drug dealers and aggressive prostitutes. In particular, avoid **Carrer de Sant Ramon.** Clearly, El Raval does not lack character, and it is actually one of the city's most interesting neighborhoods. Everything tends to be significantly less expensive than on the other side of Las Ramblas, and a large student population supports a bevy of quirky restaurants and bars. Areas around the **Rambla del Raval** and the **Carrer de Joaquim Costa** hide small, unique bars and late-night cafes frequented by Barcelona's alternative crowd. For daytime shopping, check out **Riera Baixa**, a street lined entirely with secondhand shops that also hosts a flea market on Saturdays, or the ritzier neighborhood around **Carrer de Doctor Dou, Carrer del Pintor Fortuny,** and **Carrer Elisabets** for higher-end (though still reasonably priced) shops.

L'Eixample

In this posh neighborhood (pronounced leh-SHAM-plah), big blocks, wide avenues, and dazzling architecture mean lots of walking and lots of exciting storefronts. *Modernista* buildings line **Passeig de Gràcia** (first word pronounced pah-SAYCH), which runs from north to south through the neighborhood's center (ⓂDiagonal, ⓂPasseig de Gràcia, ⓂCatalunya). **L'Eixample Dreta** encompasses the area to the east around the **Sagrada Família,** and **Eixample Esquerra** comprises the area closer to the **University,** uphill from **Plaça de la Universitat.** Though the former contains some surprisingly cheap accommodations for those willing to make the hike, the Eixample Esquerra is somewhat more pedestrian-friendly and more interesting to walk around. While this neighborhood is notoriously expensive, there are some cheaper and more interesting options as you get closer to Pl. Universitat. The stretch of **Carrer del Consell de Cent** west of Pg. de Gràcia boasts vibrant nightlife, where many "hetero-friendly" bars, clubs, and hotels give it the nickname **Gaixample.**

Barceloneta

Barceloneta, the triangular peninsula that juts out into the Mediterranean, is a former mariners' and fishermen's neighborhood, built on a sandbank at the beginning of the 18th century to replace the homes destroyed by the construction of the *ciutadella*. The grid plan, a consequence of Enlightenment city planning, gives the neighborhood's narrow streets a distinct character, seasoned by the salty sea breezes that whip through the urban canyons. Tourists and locals are drawn to the unconventional Barceloneta by the restaurants and views along the **Passeig Joan de Borbó,** the renowned beaches along the **Passeig Marítim de la Barceloneta,** and the *discotecas* at the **Port Olímpic.**

Gràcia

Gràcia is hard to navigate by metro. While this may at first seem like a negative, the poor municipal planning is actually a bonus. Filled with artsy locals, quirky shops, and a few lost travelers, Gràcia is a quieter, more out-of-the-way neighborhood, best approached by foot. Ⓜ**Diagonal** will drop you off at the northern end of the Pg. de Gràcia; follow it across Avda. Diagonal as it becomes **Carrer Gran de Gràcia,** one of the neighborhood's main thoroughfares. Ⓜ**Fontana** lies farther up on C. Gran de Gràcia. If you're heading uphill on C. Grande Gràcia, any right turn will take you into the charmingly confusing grid of Gràcia's small streets, of which **Carrer de Verdi,** running parallel to C. Gran de Gràcia several blocks away, is probably the most scenic. For bustling *plaças* both day and night, your best bets are **Plaça de la Vila de Gràcia** (more commonly known as Pl. Rius i Taulet), **Plaça del Sol,** and **Plaça de la Revolució de Setembre de 1868,** off of C. de Ros de Olano.

Montjuïc and Poble Sec

Montjuïc, the mountain just down the coast from the old center of Barcelona, is one of the city's chief cultural centers. Its slopes are home to **public parks,** some of the city's best museums, theaters that host everything from classical music to pop, and a kick-ass **castle** on its peak. Montjuïc (old Catalan for "mountain of the Jews," possibly for the Jewish cemetery once located here) also has some of the most incredible views of the city. Many approach the mountain from the **Plaça de Espanya,** passing between the two towers to ascend toward the museums and other sights; others take the funicular from Ⓜ Paral·lel.

The small neighborhood of Poble **Sec** (Catalan for "dry village") lies at the foot of Montjuïc, between the mountain and **Avinguda del Paral·lel.** Tree-lined, sloping streets characterize the largely residential neighborhood, with the **Plaça del Sortidor** as its heart and the pedestrian-friendly, restaurant-lined **Carrer de Blai** as its commercial artery.

SIGHTS

Sights in Barcelona run the gamut from cathedrals to casas to museums and more. Here's a brief overview of what each neighborhood has to offer. El Gòtic is Barcelona's most tourist-ridden neighborhood; despite the crowds of foreigners, however, the Gothic Quarter is filled with alley after alley of medieval charm. Beginning along the sea and cutting straight through to Pl. de Catalunya, Las Ramblas is Barcelona's world-famous tree-lined pedestrian thoroughfare that attracts thousands of visitors daily. El Born is a sight in itself, with ancient streets surrounded by sloping buildings or crumbling arches suddenly opening onto secluded *placetes*. El Raval has its own beauties, from the medieval Hospital de la Santa Creu i Sant Pau to the present-day artwork housed in the modern buildings of MACBA and CCCB. L'Eixample's sights are mostly composed of marvelous examples of modernista architecture; the Sagrada Família, in particular, is a must-see. Barceloneta is filled with Catalan pride, from the red-and-yellow flags hanging on apartment balconies to the museum devoted to Catalonia and its history. Gràcia contains the epic mountain/modernista retreat, Parc Güell, as well as a few independent examples of this historic Barcelonan style. Finally, Montjuïc—you know, that big hill with the castle on it that you can see from just about anywhere in Barcelona—is home to some phenomenal museums, a model Spanish village, and, of course, that castle.

Barri Gòtic and Las Ramblas

Beginning along the famous seaside, tree-lined pedestrian thoroughfare that attracts thousands of visitors daily, the walkway demarcated as La Rambla funnels thousands of tourists every year through its course. Marked by shady trees, cafes galore, tourist traps, and a multifarious array of street performers, gorgeous edifices, animal vendors, and extremely adroit pickpockets, the five distinct promenades seamlessly mesh to create the most lively and exciting pedestrian bustle in Barcelona (and perhaps in all of Europe). The *ramblas*, in order from Pl. de Catalunya to the Columbus Monument are: **La Rambla des Canaletes, La Rambla dels Estudis, La Rambla de Sant Josep, La Rambla dels Caputxins,** and **La Rambla de Santa Mònica.**

◪ MUSEU D'HISTORIA DE LA CIUTAT   ROMAN RUINS

Pl. del Rei   ☎932 56 21 00 www.museuhistoria.bcn.es

If you thought the winding streets of the Barri Gòtic were old school, check out the Museu d'Història de la Ciutat's Roman ruins, hidden 20m underneath Pl. del Rei. Beneath the medieval plaza lies the excavation site of the long-gone predecessor of Barcelona: the Roman city of Barcino. Raised walkways allow passage through the site of the ruins beneath the plaza; regardless, watch your step, as some parts can be dark and uneven. You'll probably catch sight of huge ceramic wine flasks dotting the intricate ancient mosaics—surefire proof of Barcelona's revelrous ancestry. The second part of the museum features the (comparatively) newer Palacio **Real Major,** a 14th-century palace for Catalan-Aragonese monarchs. Inside the palace, the glorious and impressively empty **Saló de Tinell** (Throne Room) is the iconic seat where Ferdinand and Isabella welcomed Columbus after his journey to the New World. The **Capilla de Santa Àgata** uses its rotating exhibits to delve into the intricacies of the modern Catalonian's way of life.

i Ⓜ*Jaume I. Free multilingual audio tours. Museum and exhibition €7, students and ages 16-25 €5, under 16 free.* ◲ *Open Apr-Oct Tu-Sa 10am-7pm, Su 10am-8pm; Nov-Mar Tu-Sa 10am-5pm, Su 10am-8pm.*

◪ AJUNTAMENT DE BARCELONA (CITY HALL)   GOVERNMENT

Pl. de Sant Jaume, enter on C. Font de Sant Miquel   ☎934 02 70 00 www.bcn.es

The stolid, 18th-century Neoclassical façade facing the Pl. de Sant Jaume hides a more interesting, 15th-century one, located at the old entrance to the left of the building (where the tourist office is on C. Ciutat). You can only get into the City Hall building on Sundays or if you get voted in, but once you're inside, it's marvelous. The lower level of this bureaucratic palace is home to many pieces of sculpture from modern Catalan masters, while the upper level showcases elaborate architecture, vivid stained glass, and lavish rooms like the *Saló de Cent,* from which the *Consell de Cent* (Council of One Hundred) ruled the city from 1372-1714.

i Ⓜ*Jaume I. Follow C. de Jaume I to Pl. de Sant Jaume; City Hall is on the left. Tourist info available at entrance. To enter, take alley to the left of City Hall and take a right onto C. Font de Sant Miquel. Free.* ◲ *Open Su 10am-1:30pm. Tours every 30min. in Spanish or Catalan.*

CATEDRAL DE BARCELONA   CATHEDRAL

Pl. de la Seu   ☎933 15 15 54 www.catedralbcn.org

Located in the Gothic Quarter, the Cathedral of Santa Eulalia, or the Barcelona Cathedral, is a masterpiece architecturally and the seat of the archbishop of Barcelona. This beautiful gothic cathedral has 500 year old stained glass windows, a gorgeous garden, rooftop access by elevator, many naves and side rooms, and even roaming ducks. It is free to enter and there are no lines, but if you wish to tour the roof or see areas not free to the public such as the museum, the tour costs €6. It's not Sagrada Familia, but it's definitely worth a visit, even if only for an hour. You can get excellent views of the city from the top of the

barcelona

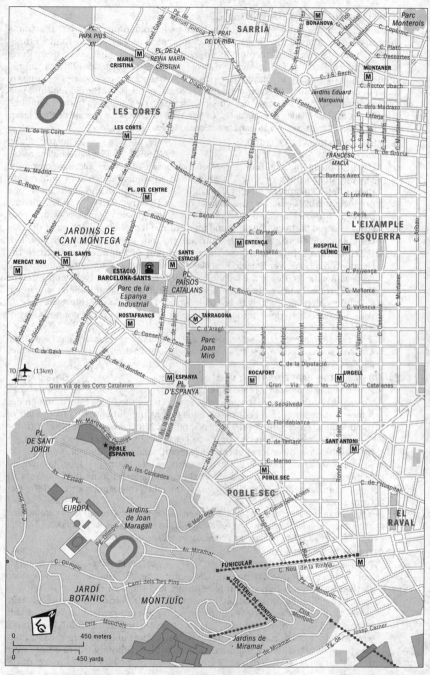

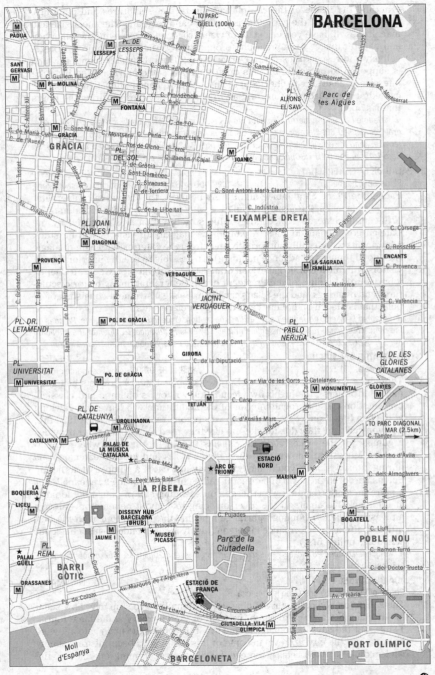

BARCELONA

barcelona

tour, and the inside of the church has spectacular sculptures and paintings. The atmosphere of the cathedral is peaceful and reverant. The sheer size and magnitude will have you in a state of wanderlust, and every window, chamber, and cloister makes for a great photo opportunity. Make sure to dress conservatively and respect those in prayer, and drink from the water fountain which is supposed to be good luck. It's open for mass some mornings, so if you're interested, make sure to check out the hours beforehand online. Otherwise, the cathedral is available for any and all to enter as they please during the hours that it's open.

i Ⓜ*Jaume I. From the metro, turn left onto V. Laietana, then left onto Av. de la Catedral. Cathedral free. Museu €3. Elevator to terrace €3. Inquire about guided visit to museum, choir, rooftop terraces, and towers, as hours vary. ☒ Catedral open M-Sa 8am-12:45pm and 5:15-7:30pm, Su 8am-1:45pm and 5:15-7:30pm. Entry with donation M-Sa 1pm-5pm, Su 2pm-5pm.*

PALAU DE LA GENERALITAT
Pl. de Sant Jaume   ☎934 02 46 00 www.gencat.cat/generalitat/eng
GOVERNMENT

Facing the Pl. de Sant Jaume and the Ajuntament, the Palau dela Generalitat is a big player in the plaza's popularity with protesters and petitioners. The 17th-century exterior conceals a Gothic structure that was obtained by the Catalan government in 1400. Although the majority of visitors will be stuck admiring its wonderfully authoritative feel from the exterior, with a bit of magic (i.e., good timing and advance planning), it's possible to see the interior. There, visitors will find a Gothic gallery, an orange tree courtyard, St. George's Chapel, a bridge to the house of the President of the Generalitat, many historic sculptures and paintings, and the **Palau's carillon,** a 4898kg instrument consisting of 49 bells that is played on holidays and during special events.

i Ⓜ*Jaume I. Take C. de Jaume I after exiting the station. Once in Pl. de Sant Jaume; Palau is on the right. Free. Make reservations online at least 2 weeks in advance. ☒ Open to the public on Apr 23, Sept 11, and Sept 24, and on the 2nd and 4th Su of each month from 10am-1:30pm.*

GRAN TEATRE DEL LICEU
Las Ramblas, 51-59   ☎934 85 99 00 www.liceubarcelona.cat
THEATER

Though La Rambla itself is one of Europe's grandest stages (tourists being the main performers), the highbrow Liceu is known for its operatic and classical presentations. The Baroque interior of the auditorium will leave you gawking at the fact that it only dates to 1999. It was reconstructed following a 1995 fire, and you can't say they don't make 'em like they used to. A 20min. tour provides a glimpse of the ornate *Sala de Espejos* (Room of Mirrors), where Apollo and the Muses look down with their divine gazes and judge theater patrons during intermission. If you're lucky, you may just catch a glimpse of authentic Spanish ardor in the form of a director yelling furiously during a rehearsal. For a more in-depth tour that won't leave you spending half of your time looking at the stackable chairs in the foyer or being told about benefactors (always a pleasure, Plácido Domingo), arrange a behind-the-scenes tour with the box office or attend a performance in person (highly recommended—just check out schedules online first).

i Ⓜ*Liceu. Discounted tickets available. Tours start every 20min. ☒ Box office open M-F 1:30pm-8pm.*

PLAÇA DE L'ÀNGEL
Corner of Via Laietana and C. de la Princesa
LANDMARK

The square immediately surrounding the Ⓜ*Jaume I* metro stop may now seem like nothing but a place to catch the train or grab a pastry and a lame tourist T-shirt, but the days of Roman Barcino saw this spot as the main gate allowing passage into the city. To revel in some of this seemingly absent history, simply walk parallel to **Via Laietana,** the ever-bustling street forming one side of the

You can find accommodations in any of the neighborhoods that *Let's Go* lists, and they will all have their pros and cons. For more recommendations visit, www.letsgo.com.

HOSTAL MALDÀ   HOSTAL $
C. Pi, 5   ☎933 17 30 02 www.hostalmalda.jimdo.com

Hostal Maldà provides a dirt-cheap home away from home, complete with kitschy clocks, ceramics, confusing knickknacks, and a kick-ass manager who could probably be your grandmother. She ensures that the multiple door keys, specific doorman procedures, and 24hr. reception will keep you and your valuables safe.

i Ⓜ Liceu. Begin walking away from Las Ramblas in front of the house with the **dragon** and take an immediate left onto C. Casañas. Stay on this road as it passes in front of the church and through the Pl. del Pi. Enter the Galerias Maldà (interior shopping mall) and follow the signs to the hostel. Singles €15, with shower €20; doubles €30; triples €45; quads €60. Cash only. ☒ Reception 24hr.

SANT JORDI: SAGRADA FAMÍLIA   HOSTEL $$
C. Freser, 5   ☎934 46 05 17 www.santjordihostels.com/apt-sagrada-familia/

From the fun staff to the hostel's apartment-style setup (and even a communal guitar in the main lobby), this place knows how to cater to the backpacking crowd. With rooms for one, two, or four people, you can pick your privacy without the isolation of a *pensión*. If closer quarters are more your style, they also have air-conditioned eight-, 10-, and 12-person dorms in the next building, whose common areas include Seussian wall niches and a small half-pipe on the terrace.

i Ⓜ Sant Pau/Dos de Maig Walk downhill on C. Dos de Maig toward C. Còrsega. Turn left onto C. Rosselló and stay left as the road splits to C. Freser. 4-bed dorms €16-28; 4-bed hostel rooms €16-28; 6-, 8-, 10-, and 12-bed hostel dorms €16-35 (triples are scarce); singles €18-40; doubles €30-45. ☒ Reception 24hr. Quiet hours after 10pm.

ALBERGUE-RESIDENCIA LA CIUTAT   HOSTEL $
C. ca l'Alegre de Dalt, 66   ☎932 13 03 00 www.laciutat.com

This hostel crams 180 beds into a quiet location that's still close to some popular pubs and bars. Relax between the large lobby decorated with some funky cartoon wall art or the common room. The dorms are simple and brightly painted. Consider asking for a discount rate that skips breakfast to save you a few bucks.

i Ⓜ Joanic. Walk along C. l'Escorial for 5-10min., passing through the plaza. Take a right onto C. Marti before the Clinic and take the 1st left onto C. ca l'Alegre de Dalt. 1- to 10-bed dorms €17-20; singles €35-50; doubles €52-60. 1st night deposit required for online booking. Visitors allowed only from 10am-11pm. ☒ Reception 24hr.

HELLO BCN HOSTEL   HOSTEL $$
C. Lafont, 8-10   ☎934 42 83 92 www.hellobcnhostel.com

Finally, a place where exercise junkies can pump some iron while on vacation. This hostel boasts a gym, a large, spacious common room where dozens of college kids congregate on nightly basis, and late-night excursions. There are several opportunities to go on daytrips, from tanning on Barceloneta's beaches to trekking at the towering Mt. Monserrat.

i Ⓜ Paral·lel. Follow C. Nou de la Rambla up into Poble Sec past Apolo Theater and turn left onto C. Vilà i Vilà, then right onto C. Lafont. Dorms €13-30; doubles €90-100; triples €110-120; quads €100-130. ☒ Reception 24hr.

barcelona

square's border. For a more contemporary piece of history (though it still dates from the triple digits CE), look no further than the statue of an angel pointing to her toe. This sculpture commemorates the event for which the plaza was named—according to legend, the caravan carrying the remains of St. Eulàlia from the church of Santa Maria del Mar stopped here; suddenly, the urn containing remains became too heavy to carry, and when the caravan members set them down, an angel appeared and pointed to her own toe, alerting the carriers that one of the procession's officials had stolen St. Eulàlia's pedal digit. With a shame equivalent to being published with a thumbs down symbol in a *Let's Go* travel guide, the church member returned the toe to its brethren and the remains miraculously reverted to their original weight.

i Ⓜ*Jaume I. Free.*

COLUMBUS MONUMENT
TOWER

Portal de la Pau
☎933 02 52 24

The *Mirador de Colom* at the coastal tip of La Rambla offers a phenomenal view of the city and an absolutely killer sunrise/sunset just a smidge farther down the coastline (sometimes also called the extra *Rambla del Mar*). This area features a 60m statue, constructed in the 1880s for Barcelona's World's Fair in order to commemorate Christopher Columbus meeting King Ferd and Queen Izzy in Barcelona upon his return from America. Though some say the 7.2m statue at the top of the tower points west to the Americas, it actually points east (fail, right?), supposedly to his hometown of Genoa. Reliefs around the base of the column depict the journey, as do bronze lions that are guaranteed to be mounted by tourists at any given moment. Just don't try to mount them if you're stumbling back home up Las Ramblas at dawn, especially if you don't have a buddy's camera documenting the whole incident.

i Ⓜ*Drassanes. Entrance located in base facing water €4, seniors and children €3.* Ⓧ *Open daily May-Oct 9am-7:30pm; Nov-Apr 9am-6:30pm.*

El Born

This part of the *ciutat vella* (ancient city) is a sight in itself, with ancient streets surrounded by sloping buildings and crumbling arches suddenly opening onto secluded *placetes*. In addition to the joys of just walking through the neighborhood, there are certain sights you just can't miss.

🎵 PALAU DE LA MÚSICA CATALANA
MUSIC HALL

C. Palau de la Música, 4-6
☎902 44 28 82 www.palaumusica.org

Home to both Barcelona's Orfeó Choir and the Catalan musical spirit, the Palau is Barcelona's most spectacular music venue (it became a UNESCO World Heritage Site in 1997). Lluís Domènech i Montaner, contemporary of Gaudí and architect of the **Hospital de Sant Pau, Casa Fuster,** and the Castell **dels Tres Dragons,** crafted this awe-inspiring *modernista* masterpiece from humble materials such as brick, ceramic, stone, iron, and glass in just a short three years. True to the *Art Nou* movement's principles, the building (1905-08) is covered inside and out with organic motifs. The breathtaking inverted dome of the stained glass ceiling and the tall stained glass windows make the luminous interior shimmer. Columns pose as abstract trees, while intricate ceramic flowers decorate the ceiling. In fact, the concert hall's designer packed the floral motif in just about every nook and cranny of the theater—see for yourself, it's rather eye-opening. Behind the stage, angelic muses emerge from the walls, which are part flat ceramic tiles, part stone sculpture. Above and around the stage, angels interact with trees, the riding Valkyries, and musicians such as Wagner and Beethoven. Back in commission after a 30-year hiatus, the Palau's glorious 3772-pipe organ stands front and center in the upper portion of the hall. Below it hangs the coat of arms of

Catalunya in all its splendor, comprised of the cross of St. George (patron saint of Spain) along with four stripes. The Palau offers reduced-admission concerts regularly, which is a nice break from the typical €17 price tag. After touring, you'll officially be able to declare how artsy and Euro-knowledgeable you are.

i Ⓜ*Jaume I. On Via Laietana, walk toward the cathedral for about 5min., then take a right onto C. Sant Pere Mas Alt. Palau de la Música Catalana is on the left. Schedule of events and ticketing info on website. Guided tours €17, students €11, under 10 free. 55min. tours daily 10am-3:30pm, in English every hr. and Catalan and Spanish every 30min.* Ⓒ *Guided tour schedules vary by season. Aug tours daily 9am-6pm, Easter week 10am-6pm. Box office open daily 9:30am-3:30pm; Jul and Aug 9am-8pm.*

🏛 MUSEU PICASSO

C. de Montcada, 15-23 ☎932 19 63 10 www.museupicasso.bcn.cat/en MUSEUM

The Picasso Museum has free admission to all students, but is a very popular tourist destination that usually has long lines and limited capacity. Regardless, it's worth waiting for because it is truly a treasure trove of art. Upon entering, there are a series of rooms that start from Picasso's earlier years and lead into his critical success. The museum has informational signs written in Catalan, Spanish, and English that introduce each series of paintings, and each series typically features one defining work of that time. In the rooms that capture his formative years, you can see the original First Communion and Science and Charity paintings, as well as sketches he made for them and a history of their context. As the chronology progresses, the museum takes you through his different periods as an artists and explains the people and places that influenced him. More interesting however may be the smaller paintings that were donated by his family which receive little to no attention beyond the museum. Many of these, such as "At the Sick Woman's Side" are beautiful masterpieces that fail to show up even through extensive internet searches. After viewing many of his famous works, the tour leads you to a section of art from the man who founded the museum (a friend and influence of Picasso's). After, you'll be sent to a gift shop where you can buy books, posters, and prints of many of the works in store. If you want something but can't take it around Barcelona with you, they also have a delivery service which might be of interest. The gift shop connects with the bottom of the museum, where you can either return to view more paintings, head to a limited time exhibition if they have it, or make your way out to explore the city.

i Ⓜ*Jaume I. Walk down C. de la Princesa and turn right onto Carrer de Montcada. Admission €11; ages 16-24 and over 65 €6; under 16, teachers, PinkCard cardholders, and ICOM members free. Audio tour €3. Accepts Mastercard and Visa. 1st Su of each month free, other Su free after 3pm.* Ⓒ *Open Tu-Su 10am-8pm. Last entry 30min. before close.*

PARC DE LA CIUTADELLA

Between Pg. de Picasso, C. Pujades, and C. Wellington PARK, MUSEUMS

The Parc de la Ciutdella is a open park in the Ribera district near the city port. It's free to access and open throughout the day. Historically, it started as a fortress and was later turned into a park in 1869. It has beautiful gardens, a large lake, enormous sculptures from the 19th and 20th centuries, the Barcelona Zoo and Zoological Museum, a geology museum, several aesthetically appealing buildings, and the enormous Arc de Triomf. Between the Arc and the Parc are usually tons of street performers trying to earn cash quickly for their dances, bubble blowing, or musical talents. The parc has many attractions, but it's also a great place to relax or jog when it's not in peak hours. Because there's so much to do, it can often be exceptionally crowded and if you're trying to unwind then it may cause you more trouble than good. If you're coming to see the attractions, you can visit the zoo, rent out a boat on the lake for half an hour, or have a picnic and people watch. The parc is rated exceptionally well online, and often regarded as an attraction that cannot be missed. However, despite it's beauty it is just a park, and should not be considered over other great sites like the Sagrada Família.

i Ⓜ*Arc de Triomf. Walk through the arch and down the boulevard to enter the park. Free Wi-Fi available at the Geological Museum, Parliament building, and Zoological Museum. Park free. Museum €4.10-7, Su 3-8pm free. Zoo €17. ☒ Park open daily 10am-dusk. Natural History Museum open Tu-F 10am-7pm, Sa-Su 10am-8pm. Zoo open daily May 16-Sept 15 10am-7pm; Sept 16-Oct 29 10am-6pm; Oct 30-Mar 26 10am-5pm; Mar 27-May 15 10am-6pm.*

CHURCH OF SANTA MARIA DEL MAR

CHURCH

C. Canvis Vells, 1 ☎933 10 23 90 933 10 23 90

El Born is dominated by this church's stoic presence, but it's nearly impossible to get a good glimpse from the outside. Nearby streets allow remotely satisfactory views of the exterior from the Fossar de les Moreres at the end of Pg. del Born. The Pl. de Santa Maria, located at the west entrance of the church, holds the best outside views of the church's impressive rose window (which dates to 1459) and the intricate relief and sculptural work of the main entrance. The best view of the stained glass, of course, is from inside on a sunny day. Constructed between 1329 and 1383, this church exemplifies the Catalan Gothic style—tough on the outside, light and airy on the inside. The inside is spacious and open, with tall, slim, octagonal pillars lining the main nave and no constructed boundaries between the nave and the altar. Despite the beautiful architecture, the interior has limited decoration (apart from the stained glass, of course) due to a fire that gutted the church in 1936 during the Spanish Civil War. Be sure to check the secret, miracle-holding treasure room of eternal light in the back—okay, it's just the chapel, but it goes largely unvisited and grants a close-up of some amazing artistry and friezes of God near the ceiling.

i Ⓜ*Jaume I. Walk down Carrer del'Argenteria to enter the plaça. Santa Maria del Mar is on the right. Free. ☒ Open M-Sa 9am-1:30pm and 5:30-8:30pm, Su 10am-1:30pm and 5:30-8:30pm.*

ARC DE TRIOMF

ARCHITECTURE

Between Pg. de Lluís Companys and Pg. de Sant Joan

For a proper greeting from the city of Barcelona, be sure to get off the metro at the **Arc de Triomf Station. At** first glance, you'll notice that this is most definitely not Paris's Arc de Triomphe (this one is actually reachable and not swimming in an ocean of tourists); the slight differences between the two encapsulate why Paris is Paris and Barcelona is awesome. Where else can you find such a relatively unoccupied attraction? People don't really come to Spain to see this, so it's pretty much as private as a massive, open historic site can be. Situated at the beginning of a wide, cinematic-like boulevard leading to the **Parc de la Ciutadella,** the arch not only frames the palm tree- and *modernista*-building-lined road and its incredible terminus but also literally embraces visitors with a sculptural frieze by Josep Reynés inscribed with the phrase *"Barcelona rep les nacions,"* or "Barcelona welcomes the nations." This declaration was made along with the arch's construction for the 1888 Universal Exhibition, when it served as the main entrance to the fair grounds in the Parc. Today, the arch serves as little more than a historical artifact, but it's worth a look if you're in the area. The triumphant bricks-on-bricks of the arch was designed by Josep Jilaseca i Cassanovas in the Moorish revival style. Its exterior is decked out with sculptures of 12 women representing fame and a relief by Josep Lllimona that depicts the award ceremony. Much the opposite of gargoyles atop the structure are several white angel sculptures and eight massive. The whole thing graces the surrounding area with its architectural superiority.

i Ⓜ*Arc de Triomf. Free.*

El Raval

PALAU GÜELL   PALACE

C. Nou de la Rambla, 3-5   ☎934 72 57 75 www.palauguell.cat

Commissioned by Eusebi Güell, the wealthy industrialist of Parc Güell fame, Güell Palace has stood tall since its 1888 completion as the master creation of none other than Antoni Gaudí. Being the only project that Gaudí himself directed until its debut, Palau Güell represents one of the artist's early works. Its roots in the Islamic-Hispanic architectural tradition are visible in the Moorish arched windows that have been elongated and smoothed out with a typical Gaudí twist. Be sure to look up in the Saló Central to see another example of this: tiny holes in the conical ceiling allow in rays of light, reminiscent of a combination of God's light piercing clouds and a nicely constructed Indian harem. You'll probably have someone snicker at you as you stare with your mouth agape at the ceiling's rainbow, typically Gaudían ceramic-tiled chimney, and impressive geometric conglomerations dotting the inside.

i ⓂLiceu. Walk toward the water on Las Ramblas and take a right onto C. Nou de la Rambla. Rooftop closed when raining. Group reservations need 48hr. advance call €12, reduced €8. Free 1st Su of month. Audio tour included in admission. ☒ Open Apr-Oct Tu-Su 10am-8pm; Nov-Mar Tu-Su 10am-5:30pm. Last entry 1hr. before close.

MUSEU D'ART CONTEMPORAN DE BARCELONA (MACBA)   MUSEUM

Pl.Àngels, 1   ☎934 12 08 10 www.macba.cat

Bursting out of the narrow streets and into its own spacious plaza, American architect Richard Meier's bright white edifice has sought to bring artistic enlightenment to the masses. The stark, simple interior displays an impressive collection of contemporary art, with particular emphasis on Spanish and Catalan artists, including a world-renowned collection of the interwar avant-garde and a selection of works by Miró and Tàpies. Found very near the CCCB, the Universitat, and a host of other sights around El Raval, MACBA is a must-see attraction for travelers, locals, and students alike. Be sure to check the website, as events, exhibitions, and even small concerts may occur within a week's notice. The museum completely transforms during Barcelona's Sónar music festival every year, converting into the Sónar Complex stage.

i ⓂUniversitat. Walk down C. Pelai, take the 1st right, and turn left onto C. Tallers. Take a right onto C. Valldonzella and a left onto C. Montalegre. Admission includes English-language tour. Entrance to all exhibit €9; children under 14, Tarjeta Rosa, over 65, the unemployed, teachers, members of the AAVC, and ICOM members free. ☒ Open M-F 11am-7:30pm, Sa 10am-9pm, Su and holidays 10am-7pm. Library open M-Th 10am-7pm. Last entry 30min. before close.

CENTRE DE CULTURA CONTEMPORÀNIA DE BARCELONA (CCCB)   EXHIBITION CENTER

C. Montalegre, 5   ☎933 06 41 00 www.cccb.org

The Centre de Cultura Contemporània de Barcelona boasts everything from art exhibits of old African sculptures to Shakespearean theater to Roman literature to open-air beer expos—the best potpourri of culture you'll ever see. Three exhibition galleries host large and involved temporary exhibits that vary in quality and quantity by month. Two lecture halls, an auditorium, and a bookstore fill out the architecturally wonderful (and award winning!) complex comprised of several upright glass and mirror structures. Paired with the thought-provoking collections of the nearby MACBA, the CCCB offers everything to help one become the epitome of a cultured character.

i ⓂUniversitat. Walk down C. Pelai, take the 1st right, and then turn left onto C. Tallers. Turn right onto C. Valldonzella and left onto C. Montalegre. General admission €6; seniors, under 25, large families, group visits, and single-parent households €4; 2 or more exhibitions €8/6. ☒ Exhibits open daily 11am-8pm. CCCB Archives open Tu-F 3-8pm, Sa-Su 11am-8pm. Guided tours in Spanish Sa 11:30am. Last entry 30min. before close.

barcelona

L'ANTIC HOSPITAL DE LA SANTA CREU I SANT PAU

C. l'Hospital, 54-56

Now the site of the Institue d'Estudis Catalans, the Escola Massana, and the 1.5 million volume Bibilioteca de Catalunya, l'Antic Hospital de la Santa Creu i Sant Peu (or the Old Hospital of the Holy Cross and St. Paul) is a 15th-century Gothic building located in the middle of El Raval. Although it no longer functions as the neighborhood hospital, the interior courtyard, complete with an orangery and romantic perching spots, will nicely pad your collection of Facebook pictures. The operating theater has a rotating marble dissection table for the non-squeamish, and the archives hold records of the admittance of famous Catalan architect Antoni Gaudí to the hospital before his death in 1926. At that time, the hospital was used to treat the poor, and Gaudí was mistaken for a homeless man and brought to the premises after a tram struck him. Try to stop by the Gothic chapel art museum, La Capella, as well—it hosts multiple monthly exhibitions.

i ⓂLiceu. Walk down C. l'Hospital. Free Wi-Fi in courtyard. Biblioteca (932 02 07 97 www.bnc. cat). La Capella(932 42 71 71 www.bcn.cat/lacapella). ⓘ Open M-F 9am-8pm, Sa 9am-2pm. Biblioteca open M-F 9am-8pm, Sa 9am-2pm. La Capella open Tu-Sa noon-2pm and 4-8pm, Su 11am-2pm.

L'Eixample

🏛 CASA BATLLÓ

ARCHITECTURE

Pg. de Gràcia, 43 ☎934 88 06 66 www.casabatllo.es

Built sometime between 1875 and 1877, the Casa Batlló was originally designed for a middle class family in the luxurious center l'Eixample. Take a peek at yet another of Gaudí's creations in all its visceral, organo-skeletal design sprinkled with the ever-present hints of Nouveau Art. From the spinal-column stairwell that holds together the scaly building's interior to the undulating **dragon's** back curve of the ceramic rooftop to the skull-like balconies on the facade, the Casa Batlló will have you wondering what kinds of drugs Gaudí was on and where one might go about acquiring them if they lead to such remarkable renovations (it was originally built by Emilio Salas Cortés). Much of the inside is lined with *trancadís*, or scatters of broken tile that lend to gorgeous color transitions and contrasts. The building has hardly a right angle inside or out; every surface— stone, wood, glass, anything—is soft and molten. This architectural wonderland was once an apartment complex for the fantastically rich and is now the busiest of the three *modernista* marvels in the **Manzana de la Discòrdia** on Pg. de Gràcia. A free audio tour lets you navigate the dream-like space at your own pace, so be sure to spend some time with the doors of wood and stained glass, the soft scaled pattern of the softly bowed walls, and the swirly light fixture that pulls at the entire ceiling, rippling into its center. Gaudí's design ranges from the incredibly rational to the seemingly insane, including a blue light well that passes from deep navy at the top to sky blue below in order to distribute light more evenly. Be sure to visit the rooftop where you can get a great view of Barcelona below.

i ⓂPasseig de Gràcia. Walk away from Pl. Catalunya on Pg. de Gràcia; Casa Batlló is on the left. Tickets available at box office or through TelEntrada. Admission includes audio tour. €20.35, students and BCN cardholders €16.30. ⓘ Open daily 9am-9pm. Last entry 40min. before close.

🏛 SAGRADA FAMÍLIA

ARCHITECTURE

C. Mallorca, 401 ☎935 13 20 60 www.sagradafamilia.cat

If there is one building that stands out in all of Catalonia, it's la Sagrada Familia. Featured in every panoramic shot of the city, it's the Eiffel Tower or Statue of Liberty of Barcelona. It was Gaudí's lifelong project that he died working on (he was tragically struck by a tram and confused for a bum because of how he dressed). Since his death, construction has stopped and resumed for years, and will continue to do so until the projected completion date around 2030. However, the cranes and construction crew have become part of the scene thanks to their mere presence for so long. In recent years, the inside of La Sagrada Família became open to the public to tour for a fee, and the church holds masses on a weekly basis inside. The view from the inside is as absolutely breathtaking as the view from the outside. The extremely tall ceilings are all adorned with incredibly intricate carvings and statues, and elaborately designed stained glass windows that let in and reflect the sun's light all throughout the basilica. Two sets of enormous doors on each side permit people to come and leave, and whenever a tourist steps in for the first time, they are temporarily paralyzed in wanderlust (and then they reach for their cameras). On the back end of the basilica is a wall with the Lord's Prayer written in hundreds of different languages, and on the opposite ends are televisions showing documentaries on the history and construction of the building, which lead to a private prayer area. Near the entrance doors are elevators which allow access to the top of the towers. Tickets for this cost extra, but are absolutely worth it because the towers are incredibly high above the city, and you can get an excellent view of the city, ocean, and horizon in the distance. Additionally, you can look down from the towers and see the rest of the construction from a different angle, as well as the hundreds of people that are touring around below you. Visiting La Sagrada Família is imperative for any body traveling to Barcelona. If you only have a few hours in the city, almost all of your time should be spent inside the basilica and above on the towers. The rest should be spent getting to and from there.

i Ⓜ*Sagrada Família. Towers closed during rain. Basilica €13.50, with audio tour €21.50; students €11.50; under 10 free. Elevator €4.50. Combined ticket with Casa-Museu Gaudí (in Parc Güell) €17. Online ticketing strongly recommended.* ☒ *Open Apr-Sept daily 9am-8pm; Oct-Mar 9am-6pm; Dec 25-Jan 6 9am-2pm. Visitors must leave by 30min. past ticket office closing. Last elevator to the tower Nativity Lift 15min. before close. Passion Lift 30min. before close. Guided tours in English May-Jun M-F 11am, noon, and 1pm; Jul-Aug M 5pm; Sept-Oct M-F 11am, noon, and 1pm; Nov-Apr M-F 11am, 1, and 3pm.*

CASA MILÀ (LA PEDRERA)   ARCHITECTURE

Pg. de Gràcia, 92 C. Provença, 261-265   ☎902 202 138 http://www.lapedrera.com/en/visitor-information

La Pedrera still functions as a home for the rich, famous, and patient—the waitlist for an apartment is over three decades long—as well as the offices of the Caixa Catalunya bank. Many portions of the building are open to the public, including an apartment decorated with period furniture (contemporary to the house, not designed by Gaudí) and the main floor. The attic, a space known as **Espai Gaudí**, boasts a mini-museum to the man himself, including helpful exhibits explaining the science behind his beloved caternary arches and what exactly it means for the architect to be "inspired by natural structures." It is complete with all his jargonistic models and Einsteinian mathematical formulas working behind the scenes to create his living oeuvres. Up top, a rooftop terrace gives light to what many a critic has called the perfect European Kodak moment, whether it be with the desert-like sculptural outcroppings part of the building or of the panorama overlooking Barcelona to the Sagrada Família. During the summer, the terrace lights up with jazz performances on Friday and Saturday nights in a series known as *Nits d'Estiu a La Pedrera.*

i Ⓜ*Diagonal. Walk down Pg. de Gràcia away from Avda. Diagonal; La Pedrera is on the right. Purchase tickets to Nits d'Estiu a La Pedrera online via TelEntrada at www.telentrada.com. €16.50, students and seniors €14.85, under 6 free. Audio tour €4. Nits d'Estiu a La Pedrera €30; includes access to Espai Gaudí. 10 language options available for tours.* ☒ *Open daily Mar-Oct 9am-8pm; Nov-Feb 9am-6:30pm. Last entry 30min. before close. Concerts mid-Jun-late-Aug, some F and Sa 8:30pm.*

barcelona

CASA AMATLLER

Pg. de Gràcia, 41

ARCHITECTURE

☎932 160 175 www.amatller.org

Finally another whimsical place that can rival some of Pg. de Gracia's other creations. Casa Amatller stands as the counterpart to Gaudí's neighboring acid-trip Casa Batlló, and it was the first in the trio of buildings now known as the **Manzana de la Discòrdia.** In 1898, chocolate industrialist Antoni Amatller became the rich hipster of his time by veering form the Gaudí-dominated expert architectural sweets and instead commissioned **Josep Puig i Cadafalch** to build his palatial home along Pg. de Gràcia, and out popped a mix of Catalan, Neo-Gothic, Islamic, and even Dutch architectural motifs all expertly overlapping on a strict gridline. A carving of Sant Jordi battling that pesky dragon appears over the front door, accompanied by four divinely artsy figures engaged in painting, sculpting, and architecture. Also at the foot of the principal entrance is a tile on the ground marking 0km of the **European Route de Modernisme.** The start of this invisible path is Barcelona's age-old endeavor to spread the *moderniste* movement throughout Spain as well as the rest of Europe. The building's entrance is free to see—note the ornate lamps and amazing stained-glass ceiling in the stairwell, created by the same artist that did the ceiling of the Palau de la Música Catalana. The rest of the building is even more spectacular and is well worth the €10 tour.

i Ⓜ*Passeig de Gràcia. Walk away from Pl. Catalunya on Pg. de Gràcia; Casa Amatller is a couple of blocks up on the left. Reservation by phone or email required for tour. Tours €10. Kid workshops €6 daily 10am-8pm.* Ⓩ *Guided tours M-F 10, 11am, noon, 1, 3, 4, 5, and 6pm.*

HOSPITAL DE LA SANTA CREU I SANT PAU

C. Sant Antoni Maria Claret, 167

ARCHITECTURE

☎933 177 652; guided visits 902 076 621

Considered one of the most important pieces of *modernista* public architecture, this hospital's practice challenges the meaning of "neouveau." Dating back to 1401 when six smaller hospitals merged, the Hospital de la Santa Creu i Sant Pau is the newer embodiment of the medical practice formerly housed in the **Antic Hospital de la Santa Creu** in El Raval. Wealthy benefactor Pau Gil bequested funds for the building with strict instructions, including the name appendage. Construction then began in 1902 under the direction of Lluís Domènech i Montaner (designer of the godly **Palau de Musica Catalana** in El Born), who in Gaudían fashion, died before its completion. His son saw the work to fruition, giving the hospital 48 large pavilions connected by underground tunnels and bedazzled with luxurious modern sculptures and paintings. Although the hospital ceased to function as a hospital in 2009, it has been named a UNESCO World Heritage Sight and ironically now welcomes even more visitors than it did as a hospital. Much of the complex is currently closed for renovation, but the little bits open around back are neat spots for a few selfies and snapchats (or 15).

i 8, over 65, and unemployed €5. Modernisme Route 50% discount. Bus Turístic 20% discount. *Barcelona City Tour 20% discount.* Ⓩ *Tours in English M-Su 10, 11am, noon, and 1pm. Tours in French M-Su 10:30am. Tours in Spanish M-Su 11:30am. Tours in Catalan M-Su 12:30pm. Follow the information boards for updated information.*

FUNDACIÓ ANTONI TÀPIES

C. Aragó, 255

ART, ARCHITECTURE

☎934 87 03 15 www.fundaciotapies.org

Housed in a building by *modernista* architect Lluís Domènech i Montaner, the Fundació Antoni Tàpies is unmissable thanks to the giant mess ball of wire and steel atop the low brick roofline. Made by the museum's namesake, Antoni Tàpies, it's actually a sculpture entitled *Núvol i Cadira* (Cloud and Chair; 1990) that supposedly shows a chair jutting out of a large cloud. Once inside, the lowest and highest levels are dedicated to temporary exhibitions on modern and contemporary artists and themes—recent shows have included work by

Eva Hesse and Steve McQueen—while the middle floors hold Tàpies' own work. Start upstairs and work your way down, watching the descent from surrealist-symbolist beauty into a misshapen chaos of not so well-seeming forms.

i ⓂPasseig de Gràcia. Walk uphill on Pg. de Gràcia and turn left onto C. Aragó. €7; reduced entrance €5.60. Articket free. ☑ Open Tu-Su 10am-7pm. Closed Dec 25, Jan 1, and Jan 6. Last entry 15min. before closing. Museum shop open Tu-F 10am-7pm, Sa-Su 10am-2:30pm and 3:30-7pm. Library open Tu-F 10am-2pm and 4-7pm. Admission to library by appointment.

FUNDACIÓ FRANCISCO GODIA ART
C. Diputació, 250 ☎932 72 31 80 www.fundacionfgodia.org

The next time you start making NASCAR the butt of a redneck joke, consider the Fundació Francisco Godia. Though Godia was a successful businessman by trade, his two true loves are the focus of this museum: art collecting and Formula One racing. The museum reflects these disparate interests—a front room filled with racing trophies and riding goggles amongst other racing paraphernalia. A man of exquisite taste and great artistic sensitivity, Francisco Godia gathered together an exceptional collection of paintings, medieval sculptures, and ceramics. Some of his favorite works are on display at the Francisco Godia Foundation, including many of his favorite 20th-century artifacts. Due to Godia's broad collecting interests, the permanent collection features everything from stunning 12th- and 13th-century wooden sculptures to medieval paintings to modern works by Santiago Rusiñol, Joaquím Mir, and Gutiérrez Solana. In fact, the foundation continues to acquire contemporary pieces, and temporary exhibits attempt to fit somewhere into the framework of the diverse collection.

i ⓂPasseig de Gràcia. Walk away from Pl. Catalunya on Pg. de Gràcia and take the 1st left onto C. Diputació. Guided tours in Spanish and Catalan free Sa-Su at noon. €6.50, students €3.50. Temporary exhibits €5-10. ☑ Open M-Sa 10am-8pm, Su 10am-3pm.

Gràcia

Some of the most defining features of Gràcia's cityscape are the cafe-lined **plaças** that seem to appear out of nowhere around every corner. The **Plaça de la Vila de Gràcia** (also known as Plaça de Rius i Taulet) is one of the largest and most beautiful, with a massive 19th-century clock tower (ⓂFontana; take a left down C. Gran de Gràcia, then a left onto C. Sant Domènec). With your back to the powder-blue municipal building, head up the street running along the right side of the plaza, and in a few blocks you'll get to the **Plaça del Sol**, the neighborhood's most lively square, especially at night. Two blocks east of that (follow C. Ramon i Cajal) is the **Plaça de la Revolució de Setembre de 1868**, a long, open square with the word "Revolució" engraved in the pavement. Head up C. Verdi from Pl. Revolució de Setembre 1868 and take a left at the third intersection, which will bring you to the shady **Plaça del Diamant**, while a right will bring you to the true gem that is the **Plaça de la Virreina**.

🖼 PARC GÜELL PARK, ARCHITECTURE
Main entrance on C. Clot

Park Guell is a garden, park, and housing complex that's located on the hill of El Carmel in the Gracia district. It was designed by Gaudi in the early 1900s as summer homes for really wealthy families in Barcelona, and now it's open for tourism as a UNESCO World Heritage Site. The tour used to be completely free, until recent years when the city added an €8 fee for entrance. The park outside the architectural site is still free, however. Getting to the park requires a long walk uphill, and you can get within 20 minutes of the site by taking the metro. The garden features several important Gaudi creations.

The first thing you'll see is the main terrace, which overlooks the park and has mosaic work along the benches along the perimeter. This offers the most complete view of Barcelona and the bay, where you can see other famous buildings like Sagrada Familia. You can walk down underneath it and see the unique dome shaped roofing. This eventually leads to the multicolored mosaic salamander known as "el drac" at the main enterence. You can take pictures with the salamander, but there's always a security guard watching it after it was vandalized in February 2007. After, you can continue down the stairs until the Gaudi House Museum, which shows several original works. Nearby is a restaurant and gift shop that are next to the street exit. Tickets are only for certain times, and make sure you arrive early because you're only supposed to stay in the park for a limited amount of time.

i Ⓜ*Lesseps. Walk uphill on Travessera Dalt and take a left to ride escalators. Or* Ⓜ*Vallcarca. Walk down Avda. República Argentina and take a right onto C. Agramunt, which becomes the partially be-escalatored Baixada Glòria. Bus #24 from Pl. Catalunya stops just downhill from the park. Free. Guardhouse €2, students €1.50. Free Su after 3pm and 1st Su of each month. Casa-Museu Gaudí €5.50, students €4.50.* ⏰ *Park open daily May-Aug 10am-9pm; Sept 10am-8pm; Oct 10am-7pm; Nov-Feb 10am-6pm; Mar 10am-7pm; Apr 10am-8pm. Guardhouse open daily Apr-Oct 10am-8pm; Nov-Mar 10am-4pm. Casa-Museu Gaudí open daily Apr-Sept 10am-8pm; Oct-Mar 10am-6pm.*

Montjuïc and Poble Sec

🔲 FUNDACIÓ MIRÓ

MUSEUM

Parc de Montjuïc ☎934 43 94 70 www.fundaciomiro-bcn.org

It's time to visit Fundació Miró. From the outside in, the museum serves as both a shrine to and a celebration of the life and work of Joan Miró, one of Catalonia and Spain's most beloved contemporary artists. The bright white angles and curves of the Lego-esque building were designed by Josep Lluís Sert, a close friend of Joan Miró.Since it first opened, the museum has expanded beyond Miró's original collection to include pieces inspired by the artist. A collection of over 14,000 works now fills the open galleries, which have views of the grassy exterior and adjacent **Sculpture Park.** The collection includes whimsical sculptures, epic paintings, and gargantuan *sobreteixims* (paintings on tapestry) by Miró, as well as works by Calder, Duchamp, Oldenburg, and Léger. Have fun gazing at Calder's politically charged **mercury fountain,** which was exhibited alongside Picasso's *Guernica* at the 1937 World's Fair in Paris. Like much of Barcelona, the foundation refuses to be stuck in its past—although an impressive relic of a previous era, Fundació Miró continues to support contemporary art. Temporary exhibitions have recently featured names such as Olafur Eliasson, Pipllotti Rist, and Kiki Smith, while the more experimental **Espai 13** houses exhibits by emerging artists selected by freelance curators. Overwhelmed? You should be. This is one of the few times we recommend paying for the audio tour (€4).

i Ⓜ*Paral·lel. From the metro, take the funicular to the museum. €11, students €6, under 14 free. Temporary exhibits €4, students €3. Espai 13 €2.50. Sculpture garden free.* ⏰ *Open Jul-Sept Tu-W 10am-8pm, Th 10am-9:30pm, F-Sa 10am-8pm, Su 10am-2:30pm; Oct-Jun Tu-W 10am-7pm, Th 10am-9:30pm, F-Sa 10am-7pm, Su 10am-2:30pm. Last entry 30min. before close.*

MUSEU NACIONAL D'ART DE CATALUNYA (MNAC)

MUSEUM

Palau Nacional, Parc de Montjuïc ☎936 22 03 76 www.mnac.cat

This majestic building perched atop Montjuïc isn't quite as royal as it first appears. Designed by Enric Catà and Pedro Cendoya for the 1929 International Exhibition, the Palau Nacional has housed the Museu Nacional d'art de Catalunya (MNAC) since 1934. The sculpture-framed view over Barcelona from outside the museum can't be beat,and more treasures await on the inside.

Upon entrance, you'll be dumped into the gargantuan, colonnaded **Oval Hall,** which, though empty, gets your jaw appropriately loose to prepare for its drop in the galleries. The wing to the right houses a collection of Catalan Gothic art, complete with paintings on wood panels and sculptures that Pier 1 would kill to replicate. To the left in the main hall is the museum's impressive collection of Catalan Romanesque art and frescoes, removed from their original settings in the 1920s and installed in the museum—a move that was probably for the best, considering the number of churches devastated in the civil war just a decade later. More modern attractions grace the upstairs, with modern art to the left and drawings, prints, and posters to the far right.

For those intoxicated by the quirky architecture of the city, Catalan *modernisme* and *noucentisme* works dot the galleries, from Gaudí-designed furniture to Picasso's Cubist *Woman in Fur Hat and Collar.* The collection, which spans the 19th and early 20th century, includes an impressive selection from the under-appreciated Joaquim Mir and a couple of large, fascinating works by the more renowned José Gutiérrez Solana. If art isn't your thing, check out the currency collection—though beauty may be in the eye of the beholder, this 140,000-piece brief in the history of Catalan coins will have hardly any detractors.

i ⓂEspanya. Walk through the towers and ride the escalators to the top; the museum is the palace-like structure. Permanent exhibit €12, students €6, under 16 and over 65 free. Annual subscription (permanent and temporary exhibits) €18. Combined ticket with Poble Espanyol €15. Articket €30. Audio tour €3.10. 1st Su of each month free. ☒ Open Tu-Sa 10am-7pm, Su 10am-2:30pm. Last entry 30min. before close.

POBLE ESPANYOL   ARCHITECTURE
Av. Francesc Ferrer i Guàrdia, 13   ☎935 08 63 00 www.poble-espanyol.com
One of the few original relics from the 1929 International Exhibition that still dots the mountain, the Poble Espanyol originally aimed to present a unified Spanish village. Inspired by *modernista* celebrity Josep Puig i Cadafalch, the four architects and artists in charge of its design visited over 1600 villages and towns throughout the country to find models to copy in constructing the village's 117 full-scale buildings, streets,and squares. Though intended simply as a temporary arts pavilion, the outdoor architectural museum was so popular that it was kept open as a shrine (or challenge) to the ideal of a united Spain that never was. It's perfect for those traveling only to Barcelona who want to get some idea of what the rest of the country looks like—the "Barri Andaluz" feels like a Sevilla street, with whitewashed walls and arches. Nowadays, artists' workshops peddle goods along the winding roads, spectacles take place during the day, and parties rage at night.

i ⓂEspanya. Walk through the towers, ride the escalators, and take a right €11, students €7.40, at night €6.50 (valid after 8pm) combined visit with National Art Museum of Catalonia €18. Audio tour €3. ☒ Open M 9am-8pm, Tu-Th 9am-midnight, F 9am-3am, Sa 9am-4am, Su 9am-midnight. Last entry 1hr. before close. Workshops and shops open daily in summer 10am-8pm; in fall 10am-7pm; in winter 10am-6pm; in spring 10am-7pm.

BARCELONA PAVILION   ARCHITECTURE
Av. Francesc Ferrer i Guàrdia, 7   ☎934 23 40 16 www.miesbcn.com
Though the original Barcelona Pavilion was dismantled when the International Exhibition ended in 1930, this faithful 1986 reconstruction recreates the original feel perfectly. **Ludwig Mies van der Rohe's** iconic 1929 structure of glass, steel, and marble reminds us that "less is more." The open interior is populated solely by the famous Barcelona chair and a reflecting pool with a bronze reproduction of Georg Kolbe's *Alba.* This pavilion—simple, tranquil, sleek—changed modern

architecture, modern design, and the way we look at both, whether we realize it or not.

i ⓜEspanya. Walk through the towers and take the escalators up Montjuïc. Barcelona Pavilion is on the 1st landing to the right; follow the signs. €5, students €2.60, under 16 free. Free 30min. guide service Sa 10am, English 11am, Spanish noon. Catalan Bus Turístic, Barcelona Card, Barcelona City Tour reduction 20%. Cash only at front entrance. ⓩ Open daily 10am-8pm.

CASTLE OF MONTJUÏC
CASTLE

Carretera Montjuïc, 66   ☎932 56 44 45 www.bcn.cat/castelldemontjuic

Built in 1640 during the revolt against Philip IV, this former fort and castle has been involved in its fair share of both Catalan and Spanish struggles. The fortress first saw action in 1641 against Castilian forces and continued its function as a military post until 1960, when it was ceded to the city and refurbished as a military museum by Franco (incidentally, this is the only place in Catalunya where one can find a statue of the narcissist). Despite being handed to the city, the fort was controlled by the army until 2007, when its direction was finally handed to the Barcelona City Council. The inside walkways offer mazes, incredible views of the harbor and city, as well as a moat-turned-beautifully-manicured-garden for those that make the hike (or shell out for the rather expensive, €11 cable car ride to the top). Once there, try to mount those massive steel juggernauts!

i ⓜEspanya. Montjuïc telefèric on Avda. Miramar. Free. ⓩ Open daily Apr 1-Sept 30 9am-9pm; Oct 1-Mar 31 9am-7pm.

FOOD

Given the cosmopolitan character of Barcelona, you can find just about any food you crave in this city. The cheapest options are chain supermarkets (Dia, Caprabo, and Spar, to name a few) and local groceries that tend to run a few cents cheaper still; in terms of prepared food, kebab restaurants are some of the cheapest and most plentiful. Local Catalan cuisine is varied and includes food from land and sea: some of the most traditional dishes are *botifarra amb mongetes* (Catalan pork sausage with beans), *esqueixada* (cod with tomato and onion), *llonganissa* (a kind of salami), and *coques* (somewhere between a pizza and an open-faced sandwich; singular *coca*). The simplest and most prevalent dish is *pa amb tomàquet* (bread smeared with tomato, garlic, olive oil, salt, and pepper). Note also that the Catalan for "salad" is *amanida;* this bears no relation to the word in English or Spanish, which confuses some travelers poring over a menu in search of *ensalada*.

Barri Gòtic and Las Ramblas

LA BOQUERIA (MERCAT DE SANT JOSEP)
MARKET

Las Ramblas, 89

If you're looking for ruby red tomatoes, leeks the size of a well-fed child's arm, or maybe just some nuts and a zumo smoothie, the Boqueria has you covered in the most beautiful way—quite literally. Just look for the stained-glass archway facing Las Ramblas that marks the entrance of this expansive tented open market. Though each neighborhood in Barcelona has its own *mercat*, the Mercat de Sant Josep is not only the biggest and most impressive in the city, it's the largest market in all of Spain. If filling your stomach from the glowing rows of perfectly arranged, perfectly ripened produce doesn't satisfy your gut, restaurants surrounding the market and dotting La Rambla offer meals made from produce directly from the nearby vendors.

i ⓜLiceu. Walk on Las Ramblas toward Pl. de Catalunya and take a left onto Pl. de Sant Josep. ⓩ Open M-Sa 8am-8pm, though certain vendors stay open later.

ATTIC

Las Ramblas, 120   ☎933 02 48 66 www.angrup.com

After a long day along Las Ramblas, Attic provides a soothing world away from the performers, pickpockets, and fanny-packing crowds. Attic has no dress code, but you should really consider changing out of that pit-stained T-shirt and cargo shorts. With over 10 menus of varied price tags to choose from, Attic provides its customers with everything from €29.95 *Ocells* and *Flors* menus to the hefty €65 *Festa* menu. Perch yourself on the rooftop terrace floor overlooking Las Ramblas at dinner for a truly memorable experience.

i ⓜLiceu. On Las Ramblas, toward Pl. Catalonia. Appetizer €4.50-12. Meat entrees €8-14. Fish €10-13. ⓩ Open M-Th 1-4:30pm and 7-11:30pm, F-Sa 1-4:30pm and 7pm-12:30am, Su 1-4:30pm and 7-11:30pm.

ESCRIBÀ

Las Ramblas, 83   ☎933 01 60 27 www.escriba.es

Grab a coffee and feast your eyes on any of the colorful and sugary oeuvres patiently awaiting passage to some lucky customer's mouth. With beckoning tarts, croissants, cakes, and rings made of caramel, Escribà tempts even the most devout sugar-avoiders from all four corners of its beautiful *modernista*-style store. If you're not in the mood for sweets or a mug of their killer raspberry hot chocolate, try a savory dish, such as the croissant with blue cheese, caramelized apple, and walnuts (€4.50) or the "bikini" bread mold with ham and brie (€4).

i ⓜLiceu. Walk toward Pl. Catalonia. Escribà is on the left. Sandwiches €3.50. Menú €5.90. Sweets €3-5. ⓩ Open M-Th 1-4pm and 8-11pm, F-Su 1-5pm and 8-11:30pm.

L'ANTIC BOCOI DEL GÒTIC

Baixada de Viladecols, 3   ☎933 10 50 67 www.bocoi.net

Enter the lair of L'Antic Bocoi del Gòtic, where walls of stone and exposed brick surround patrons with cave-like intimacy. The restaurant specializes in Catalan cuisine, with fresh, seasonal ingredients, and prides itself on bringing new ideas to traditional food. The amicable staff recommends the selection of cheeses and their own take on the *coques de recapte*, a regional dish made of a thin dough with fresh produce and thickly layered meats (€8.50-9).

i ⓜJaume I. Follow C. Jaume I toward Pl. Sant Jaume, then turn left onto C. Dagueria, which becomes C. dels Lledó, then Baixada de Viladecols. Reservations recommended. Appetizers €7-10. Entrees €10-21. ⓩ Open M-Sa 7:30pm-midnight.

CAFÉ VIENA

Las Ramblas, 115   ☎933 17 14 92 www.viena.es

This cafe has earned much renown for a fulsome 2006 *New York Times* article whose author raved for several paragraphs about Viena's *flauta ibèric* (Iberian ham sandwich; €6.60), calling it "the best sandwich I've ever had." The sandwich's secret, which the article's author almost figured out but couldn't quite discern, is that the *flauta* comes on *pa amb tomàquet*, the staple of the Catalan kitchen that involves smearing tomato on bread before seasoning it with salt, pepper, olive oil, and garlic. And it is a damn good sandwich, the sort that melts in your mouth with each bite. Munch away while the piano echoes its tunes from the veranda at this grandiose establishment.

i ⓜCatalunya. Follow Las Ramblas toward the sea. Sandwiches €2.40-9.30 (most under €4). Coffee €1.30-2.40. ⓩ Open M-Th 8am-11:30pm, F-Sa 8am-12:30am, Su 8am-11:30pm.

LA CLANDESTINA

Baixada de Viladecols, 2bis   ☎933 19 05 33

This is a hidden—dare we say, clandestine?—tea house with the most relaxed atmosphere in all the Barri Gòtic. With an interior of clutter and many-colored walls, this establishment will envelop you in its thick air, fragrant with freshly brewed tea and hookah. The cavernous *teteria* makes for a great place to take a

barcelona

short (or long, if you're feeling real Spanish) reprieve from the frenetic pace of the Gothic Quarter. Everyone from the neighborhood book club to young'uns in their 20s will meet you here.

i ⓜJaume I. Follow C. Jaume I toward Pl. Sant Jaume, then turn left onto C. Dagueria, which becomes C. dels Lledó, then Baixada de Viladecols. Free Wi-Fi. Sandwiches €4.20-4.40. Tea €2.50-6; pots €10-15. Juices €2.80-3.60. Cash only. ☒ Open M-Th 9am-10pm, F 9am-midnight, Sa 10am-midnight, Su 11am-10pm.

VEGETALIA
ORGANIC, VEGETARIAN $$

C. dels Escudellers, 54   ☎933 17 33 31 www.restaurantesvegetalia.com

Vegetalia delivers delicious, organic, natural, and environmentally conscious food at reasonable prices. Relax at the bar and chat with the easygoing staff about the ironic history of the Pl. de George Orwell or experience the square for yourself after ordering at the walk-up window. Try the popular bowl of nachos (€5.50) and wash it down a glass of fresh-squeezed lemonade or a soy drink (€2.20).

i ⓜLiceu. Walk down Las Ramblas toward the sea and take a left onto C. dels Escudellers. Organic store in the rear. Free Wi-Fi. Appetizer €5.50-12. Entrees €4-8.80. Desserts €2.50-4.50. ☒ Open daily 11am-11:30pm.

El Born

🏶 EL XAMPANYET
TAPAS $$

C. de Montcada, 22   ☎933 19 70 03

Since its founding in 1929, El Xampanyet is as authentic as it gets, with sheep-skin wine bags, an overwhelming selection of *cava*, and old locals spilling out the door and onto the street. Four generations of family ownership has lead to the museum of casks, blackened bottles, and kitschy bottle openers displayed against hand-painted ceramic tiles and topped by large, century-old barrels filled with vintage beer. We recommend that you try the cask-fresh *cerveza* (€3.50) or the house wine *xampanyet* (€2), and pad your stomach with some of the delicious tapas.

i ⓜJaume I. Walk down C. de la Princesa and take a right onto C. de Montcada, toward the Museu Picasso. Xampanyet is on the right before the Placeta Montcada. Tapa €1-13. Beer €3.50. Wine and cava from €2. ☒ Open daily noon-3:30pm and 7-11pm.

🏶 PETRA
RESTAURANT $$

C. dels Sombrerers, 13   ☎933 19 99 99

With dark wood, stained glass, Art Nouveau prints, menus pasted onto wine bottles, and chandeliers made of silverware, Petra's eccentric decor will have you expecting any meal to give your wallet liposuction. Luckily, the lively bohe-mian feel is matched by bohemian prices. Pasta dishes like the rich gnocchi with mushrooms and hazelnut oil (€5.20) and entrees such as the duck with lentils (€7.90) are easy on the wallet, as is the midday *menú* of a main course (varies daily), salad, and wine for €6.60—a true steal and a local favorite.

i ⓜJaume I. Walk down C. de la Princesa and take a right onto C. del Pou de la Cadena. Take an immediate left onto C. de la Barra de Ferro and a right onto C. dels Banys Vells. Petra is located where C. dels Banys Vells ends at C. dels Sombrerers. Menú €6.50. Appetizers €5-7. Entrees €8. ☒ Open Tu-Sa 1:30-4pm and 9-11:30pm, Su 1:30pm-4pm.

🏶 LA BÁSCULA
CAFE, VEGETARIAN $$

C. dels Flassaders, 30   ☎933 19 98 66

This working cooperative serves vegetarian sandwiches, *empanadas*, salads, and more—the menu changes daily. Doors laid flat serve as communal tables, and a mixture of art, environmentally-friendly sodas, and protest flyers set this restaurant apart. Though robed in the same antique exterior (complete with a large, warehouse-like entrance) as more expensive places, Báscula provides a more reasonably priced alternative to the upscale eateries. Hours and seating availability may change as the restaurant fights for its right to serve in-house, but takeout is available no matter the outcome. Try the daily special (€8-10) or one of their recommended plates, like the vegetable curry couscous with coconut milk (€8.50).

i ⓜJaume I. Walk down Carrer de la Princesa and take a right onto Carrer dels Flassaders. Entrees and salad €7-9. Sandwiches and soups €4-5. Piadinas €6. Cash only. ⓩ Open W-Sa 1pm-11pm, Su 1-8pm.

🏩 LA PARADETA
SEAFOOD $$$

C. Comercial, 7 ☎932 68 19 39 www.laparadeta.com

For the highest quality seafood, this hybrid fish market/restaurant is where Barcelona goes. The line often stretches down the ever-under-construction Carrer Comercial, but it's worth the wait to pick out a fresh fish to be cooked to your liking. When they call your number, head up and grab your meal, then sit back down and dig in. The authentic seaworthy feel of this establishment is worth of an ahoy or two, so drop by if you're feeling fresh (fish, that is).

i ⓜJaume I. Follow Carrer Princesa all the way to Carrer del Comerç, then turn right, then left at Carrer Fusina (just before the market). Turn right onto Carrer Comercial. Market prices fluctuate. ⓩ Open Tu-Su 1pm-4pm and 8pm-11:30pm.

El Raval

🏩 CAN LLUÍS
CATALAN $$$

C. Cera, 49 ☎934 41 11 87

Can Lluís? Yes he can! This crowded restaurant has been an El Raval staple since its founding in the 1920s, when this neighborhood was Barcelona's Chinatown. Don't be intimidated by the fact that everyone already knows each other or that you'll almost certainly be spoken to in traditional Catalan. Just remember: *"Què vols?"* ("What do you want?") is your cue to order. Respond with an order of tiny faba beans with cuttlefish (definitely worth the €13.90) for an appetizer and the Monkfish Rounds with Spanish ham (€18.90) for your main dish.

i ⓜSant Antoni. Follow Ronda Sant Antoni toward Mercat de Sant Antoni, bear left onto Ronda Sant Pau, and then head left onto C. Cera. Appetizers €7.40-16. Entrees €7.90-27. Desserts €3.20-5.50. ⓩ Open M-Sa 1:30-4pm and 8:30-11:30pm.

🏩 SOHO
PITA, HOOKAH $

C. Ramelleres, 26

A welcome recent addition to the neighborhood, Soho might be confused for an average eatery given it's lack of flashy interior design. No matter—try the €2 Moroccan tea or the cheap and simple meat and vegetarian options (€2). The whole place feels very impromptu, with menu items written by hand and plenty of exposed plywood, but at prices this low, you can't really complain. There are smaller, more intimate rooms which are perfect for test-driving a hookah (€10) from the set available on the counter at the entrance.

i ⓜUniversitat. Walk down C. Tallers and take a right onto C. Ramelleres. Pita and drink €3.50. Cash only. ⓩ Open M-Sa 1-10pm.

🏩 JUICY JONES
VEGETARIAN $$

C. l'Hospital, 74 ☎934 43 90 82 www.juicyjones.com

Very similar to the kindred Juicy Jones down in the Barri Gotic, this place will give you some great Indian *thali dahl* and curry options as well as an ever present assortment of zumos and smoothies. The liquid landscape of the menu offers one kickin' Banana GoGo smoothie you would be a fool not to try (cacao, banana, soy milk, cane sugar, ice, and coconut shavings (€3.95). If you've ever

barcelona

wondered what M.C. Escher's art would have looked like if he used more color and took more shrooms, the interior will satisfy your curiosity.

i Ⓜ*Liceu. Walk down C. l'Hospital. Juicy Jones is on the right at the corner of C. l'Hospital and C. En Roig, before Rambla del Raval. Tapas €2-4. Sandwiches €3-5. Daily thali plate €6. Menú €8.50.* ☾ *Open daily 1-11:30pm.*

NARIN
C. Tallers, 80

MEDITERRANEAN $

☎933 01 90 04

Sitting discreetly among the shops and cafes of C. Tallers, Narin is hiding the best baklava (€1) in Barcelona as well as equally scrumptious falafel, shawarma, kebabs, and pita bread combinations. You have to try the chicken and falafel pita, the perfect snack for a hot afternoon. Luckily, beers come cold and cheap (€1.80) for those looking to brave the bar. A tiled dining room provides a reprieve from the buzz of the electric shawarma shaver.

i Ⓜ*Universitat. Walk down C. Tallers. Pita €2.50-4. Durums €3.50-6.50. Main dishes €6-8.* ☾ *Open M-Sa 1pm-midnight, Su 6pm-midnight.*

L'Eixample

◪ LA RITA
C. Aragó, 279
la-rita-restaurantm

CATALAN $$

☎934 87 23 76 http://www.grupandilana.com/es/restaurantes/

La Rita serves traditional Catalan dishes with a twist; the duck with apples, raspberry *coulis*, and mango chutney—you will surely find—go great with just about everything. Though the price is dirt-cheap given the quality and quantity of food off the pricey C. Aragó, the interior is anything but—expect an upscale but relaxed ambience that will make you appreciate the dressy casual clothes you brought instead of the traveler's reusable T-shirt. Try an order of the exquisitely steamed black sausage croquettes with apple sauce (€3.95) or the veal meatballs with cuttlefish (€8.55).

i Ⓜ*Passeig de Gràcia. Walk up Pg. de Gràcia away from Pl. Catalunya and turn right onto C. Aragó. Appetizers €4.70-8.80. Entrees €7-12. Menu (two main courses and dessert) €19.* ☾ *Open daily 1-3:45pm and 8:30-11:30pm.*

◪ OMEÍA
C. Aragó, 211

SYRIAN $$

☎934 52 31 79 www.omeia.es

When you're tired of cheap shawarma stands, stop into Omeía for some authentic Middle Eastern fare. Devour an order of their lamb tagines with prunes and almonds (€13) or fill up with one of the traditional Jordanian dishes (€11-13). Pick something you haven't got a chance of pronouncing correctly and hope for the best! And remember that you can't ever go wrong by ordering yogurt with honey (€2.50).

i Ⓜ*Universitat. Walk up C. Aribau to the left of the University building and turn right onto C. Aragó. Appetizers €6-7. Salads €6-6.50. Entrees €7.50-18. Traditional specialties €11-13. Lunch menú €7.50. Coffee €1.10. Wine €1.80-2.* ☾ *Open daily 12:30pm-4:30pm and 8pm-midnight.*

Barceloneta

◪ BOMBETA
C. de la Maquinista, 3

TAPAS $$

☎933 19 94 45

A hardy, good old-fashioned tapas bar is personified in this local, nearly oceanfront establishment. Take heed of the warning scrawled above the bar, "*No hablamos inglés, pero hacemos unas bombas cojonudas*"—or, "We don't speak English, but we make ballsy *bombas*." The TV-aggrandized persona of the typical rough 'n' tough Spaniard finds its incarnation in the bar staff. Ask any question, and they will respond with rough Catalan accents and a trusty smile while doggedly assembling your order. Treat yourself to the house *pièce de résistance* known as *bombas* (scrumptious fried potato balls reminiscent of light garlic and onion scents stuffed with perfectly-seasoned, spicy ground beef and topped with an exquisite house sauce; €3.90 for 2).

i Ⓜ*Barceloneta. Walk down Pg. Juan de Borbó (toward the beach) and take a left onto C. Maquinista. Appetizers €3-9.50. Entrees €5-18. Cash only.* ☑ *Open daily M-Tu 11am-midnight, Th-Su 11am-midnight.*

▨ SOMORROSTRO
SEAFOOD $$$

C. Sant Carles, 11 ☎932 25 00 10 www.restaurantesomorrostro.com

This extraordinary restaurant assembles a new menu every day based on selections from the catch of the day that the young chefs, Jordi Limón and Andrés Gaspar, have selected. Somorrostro is not cheap—its rotating menu of seafood dishes, *paella*, curries, and other dishes runs about €13-20 per entree—but the nighttime *menú* (€15-17) of the chefs' gastronomical experiments is the real treat. Try to beat the lunch and dinner rush by showing up more near the start of each serving session. The *Mostaca Synera* (€5.40) is the perfect starting drink and can be enjoyed as one wistfully gazes at and interprets the old black-and-white French photographs spanning the back wall.

i Ⓜ*Barceloneta. Walk down Pà del Palau over Ronda Litoral, following the harbor. After crossing Litoral, take the 5th left onto C. Sant Carles. Free Wi-Fi. Appetizers €6-14. Entrees €13-20. Weekday lunch buffet €13 per kg. Dinner menu €15-17. Wine €3-6.* ☑ *Open M-Sa 8-11:30pm, Su 2-4pm and 8-11:30pm.*

L'ARRÒS
Paella $$$

Pg. Joan de Borbó, 12 ☎932 21 26 46 www.larros.es

At first glance, L'Arròs ('Rice') appears to be a typical tourist trap, complete with a striped, blue and white canopy beckoning weary travelers into the pleasant shade. Although it may be found along Barceloneta's main beach drag, don't let the uninspired decor and multilingual menu of this *arrocería* fool you. What the restaurant lacks in atmosphere, it wholeheartedly makes up for with its Spanish *paella*, which Barcelona natives claim is some of the best in town. Top if off with soothing Tahiti vanilla ice cream (€5.90) or Syrian Rose Cake with custard, raspberries, and mango sauce (€7.20). Even more reason to smile is the special-diet-friendly menu, which offers mindful options for those lactose/gluten/nut-allergy intolerant.

i Ⓜ*Barceloneta. Walk on Plà del Palau over Ronda Litoral and follow Pg. Joan de Borbó. Appetizers €8.75-19.50. Entrees €8.60-18.50.* ☑ *Open daily noon-11:30pm.*

BAR BITÁCORA
TAPAS $

C. Balboa, 1 ☎933 19 11 10

During the summer months, the seemingly quaint, relaxed aura of this establishment's main room peers into a vibrantly painted, terrace-like back room crammed full of young people who flock from the beach like pigeons for a crunchy chunk of bread. The 10% surcharge to sit amid the Rubik's-cube assortment of colors in the courtyard terrace will give you a more memorable experience. Your respite from the heat and bustle of Barceloneta will be made much more enjoyable by the groovy atmosphere of the terrace room. A cheap but filling daily *menú* (entree with salad and *patatas bravas*, bread, a drink, and dessert; €5) offers travelers a nice cash-saving option; however, should the heat make you super adventurous, you can order a tangy house *Mojito* or *Caipirinha* €5 each) and an order of refreshing and not too heavy *fresas con nata* (strawberries and cream; €3). Kick back with friends and listen to the varied music from all places international echoing throughout the bar's sound system.

i Ⓜ*Barceloneta. Walk down Pg. Joan de Borbó (toward the beach) and take the 1st left after Ronda del Litoral onto Carrer Balboa. Tapas €2.50-8. Sangria €3. Menú del día €5-7.* ☑ *Open M-W 10am-midnight, Th-F 10am-2am, Sa noon-2am, Su noon-5pm.*

barcelona

Gràcia

⊠ UN LUGAR DE GRÀCIA
C. Providència, 88

CATALAN $$
☎932 19 32 89

Un Lugar de Gràcia has the best-priced and most ample lunch special in the neighborhood by far: any two dishes from the midday *menú*—no distinction between first and second courses, so the very hungry may essentially order two main courses at no extra cost—bread, water or wine, and pudding/dessert for €11.20. The food may be a bit generic, with your typical assortment of pastas, meats, some fish options, and of course tapas; however, they come in great quantity for a steal of a price. For an ultra hearty meal, try the *bife ancho a la parilla de origen argentino*—that's grilled Argentinian flank steak.

i ⓂJoanic. From the metro, follow C. Escorial uphill and take a left onto C. Providència. Entrees €6-11. ⌚ Open M-Th noon-4pm, F-Sa noon-4pm and 8-11pm. Also open for F.C. Barcelona matches.

⊠ SAMSARA
C. Terol, 6

TAPAS $$
☎932 85 36 88

Samsara has a long regular menu with some of the best tapas in the neighborhood as well as about a half dozen *"novetats,"* which are daily tapas specials with international twists on customary Catalonian dishes. This restaurant also offers comfy cushions for its local and foreign customers; low rising communal tables and even lower cushioned ottomans will help you make new, hungry friends.

i ⓂFontana. Head downhill on C. Gran de Gràcia, then turn left onto C. Ros de Olano, which becomes C. Terol. Tapas €1-7.50. Beer €2.20. Wine €3.30-3.50. ⌚ Open M-W 8:30am-1:30am, Th 8:30pm-3am, F 8:30am-3pm, Su 7:30pm-1am.

LA NENA
C. Ramón y Cajal, 36

CAFE $
☎932 85 14 76

Welcome to grandma's house! But this was the cool grandma who used to feed you tons of sweets and spoil you as a kid. La Nena has an extensive menu of gourmet hot chocolate, crepes, *bocadillo* sandwiches, and quiches at unbeatable prices. Watch out, you party people—there's a hilarious banner displaying grandma's "no alcohol served here" declaration. This is a great place to slow down and have a *choco brasil* (hot chocolate with a ball of coffee ice cream inside; €4).

i ⓂFontana. Follow C. d'Astúries away from C. Gran de Gràcia and take a right onto C. Torrent de l'Olla. Walk a few blocks and take a left onto C. Ramón y Cajal. Sandwiches €2.50-6. Quiches €6. Pastries €1.20-4. Cash only. May call to reserve. ⌚ Open daily 9am-10pm.

GAVINA
C. Ros de Olano, 17

PIZZA $$
☎934 15 74 50

Gavina is Gràcia's most heavenly pizzeria. The gigantic hand coming out of the wall, or the parade of angels encircling the chandelier, are bound to make you feel super holy (and hopefully hungry). You'll probably forget about the rather bulky pope figurine watching the tables near the door once you try the strawberry cheesecake tart (€4.50). The big draw, though, is neither the impressive kitsch nor desserts but is instead the gigantic, delicious pizzas (€6.50-14). Try the namesake Gavina (potatoes, ham, onion, and mushrooms; €12) or the pizza of the day—but be sure to bring friends or an otherworldly appetite.

i ⓂFontana. From the metro, walk downhill on C. Gran de Gràcia and take a left onto C. Ros de Olano. Pizza €6.50-14. Midday menú W-F €10, includes pizza, dessert, and a drink. Chupitos €2. ⌚ Open M 1pm-4am and 8pm-1am, Tu 7pm-1am, W-Th 1pm-4am and 8pm-1am.

Montjuïc and Poble Sec

The neighborhood of **Poble Sec** hides a number of good, inexpensive restaurants and bars—perfect for those who don't feel like breaking the bank to eat at a museum cafe up on Montjuïc, or for those looking to explore a lovely neighborhood a bit off the beaten track.

✎ QUIMET I QUIMET
TAPAS, BAR S$

C. Poeta Cabanyes, 25 ☎934 42 31 42

With five generations and 100-plus years of service under its belt, Quimet i Quimet knows what's up. If you're lucky enough to visit this place when it isn't super busy, take a moment to be mesmerized by the massive liquor bottle display lining the establishment's walls. Try the salmon, yogurt, and truffle honey or the bleu cheese with baked red pepper sandwich.

i Ⓜ*Paral·lel. Follow Av. Paral·lel away from the water, past the small plaça on the left, then head left up C. Poeta Cabanyes. Tapas €2.50-3.25. Beer €5.75 per bottle. ⏰ Open M-F noon-4pm and 7-10:30pm, Sa and holidays noon-4pm. Closed Aug.*

NIGHTLIFE

Barri Gòtic and Las Ramblas

✎ BARCELONA PIPA CLUB
BAR, CLUB

Pl. Reial, 3 ☎933 02 47 32 www.bpipaclub.com

With pipes from six continents, smoking paraphernalia decorated by Dalí, and an "ethnological museum dedicated to the smoking accessory," the only pipe-related article missing from this club—albeit somewhat appropriately—is René Magritte's *Ceci n'est pas une pipe* ("This is not a pipe."). Despite its cryptic lack of signage and the furtive ambiance of a secret society, the low-lit, amber-colored bar, pool room, and music lounge has a surprisingly high amount of visitors. Take a few puffs as you listen to the retro blues and ragtime tunes.

i Ⓜ*Liceu. Walk on Las Ramblas toward the water and turn left onto C. Colom to enter Pl. Reial. Pipa Club is an unmarked door to the right of Glaciar Bar. To enter, ring the bottom bell. Rotating selection of tobacco available for sale. Special smoking events. Jazz jam session Su 8:30pm. Beer €4-5. Wine €4-5. Cocktails €7.50-9. Cash only. ⏰ Open daily 11pm-3am.*

✎ HARLEM JAZZ CLUB
JAZZ CLUB, BAR

C. Comtessa de Sobradiel, 8 ☎933 10 07 55 www.harlemjazzclub.es

With live performances nightly and a drink often included in the cover (check the schedule), this is a budget-conscious music lover's paradise. This sophisticated jazz house posts performance schedules on the door, letting you choose whether you'll drop in to hear lovesick English crooning or a saucier Latin flavor. Acts range from funk and soul to Latin jazz, and the crowd is just as varied.

i Ⓜ*Liceu. Walk toward the water on Las Ramblas and take a left onto C. Ferran, a right onto C. Avinyó, and a left onto C. Comtessa de Sobradiel. Live music usually begins at 10 or 11pm. Calendar of events available online or at the door. Cover €5-6; sometimes includes 1 drink. Beer €3.80. Cocktails €7.80. Cash only. ⏰ Open M 8pm-1am, Tu 8pm-12:30am, W-Th 8pm-1am, F-Sa 8pm-5am, Su 6pm-1am.*

✎ SINCOPA
BAR

C. Avinyò, 35

At night, this music-themed bar—rumored to have once been owned by none other than Manu Chao—plays host to as many nationalities and performers as it has currencies and secondhand instruments on its walls. Of Barri Gòtic's bars, Sincopa undoubtedly sports some of the most colorful decor and clientele. One night, the crowd might be on a chemically-induced "vacation" and chilling to *Dark Side of the Moon;* the next, everyone will be salsa dancing.

i Ⓜ*Liceu. Walk on Las Ramblas toward the water and take a left onto C. Ferran and a right onto C. d' Avinyò. Beer €2-4. Cocktails €7. Juices €2.50. Cash only. ⏰ Open M-Th 6pm-2:30am, F-Sa 6pm-3am, Su 6pm-2:30am.*

barcelona

MANCHESTER

BAR

C. Milans, 5

☎627 73 30 81 www.manchesterbar.com

The names of the drinks posted on the front door—Joy Division, The Cure, Arcade Fire, and many, many more—set a rockin' mood. After passing the spinning turntable at the entrance, you'll see intimate, perfectly dimmed red seating, and gleefully gabbing young people. The happy hour, with €1 Estrella Damms, will have you singing along to "Friday I'm in Love" before the evening's up.

i ⓂLiceu. Walk toward the water on Las Ramblas and head left onto C. Ferran, right onto C. d'Avinyó, and left onto C. Milans, before C. Ample. Manchester is at the bend in the street. Beer €2-4. Shots from €2.50. Cocktails €6. Cash only. ☑ Open M-Th 7pm-2:30am, F-Sa 7pm-3:30am, Su 7pm-2:30am. Happy hour daily 7-10pm.

LAS CUEVAS DEL SORTE

BAR

C. Gignàs, 2

☎932 95 40 15

The eponymous caves, with miniature stalactites on the ceiling, are filled with alcohol, partygoers, and a subtle earthy scent. Exquisite mosaics crop up in the most unexpected places, including the bathrooms. Seriously, though, it'll be the most aesthetically pleasing potty break you ever take. Downstairs, small tables and another bar surround a disco-balled dance floor, where revelers party on with cocktail in happy hand.

i ⓂLiceu. Walk toward the water on Las Ramblas and head left onto C. Ferran, right onto C. d'Avinyó, and left onto C. Gignàs. Cocktails €5-7. ☑ Open M 7pm-2am, W-Su 7pm-2am

El Born

⬛ EL CASO BORN

BAR

C. de Sant Antoni dels Sombrerers, 7

☎932 69 11 39

This is a quieter alternative for those too cool to bother with the packed houses and inflated prices of nearby Pg. del Born. Cheap drinks tempt travelers, while relaxed seating, a chill crowd, and a drinks menu with cocktails named for the Bourne movies (the name is a pun on *El Caso Bourne,* the Spanish title of *The Bourne Identity*) provide ample reason to start the night here.

i ⓂJaume I. Walk down C. de la Princesa and take a right onto C. de Montcada. Upon entering Pg. del Born, take a right onto C. dels Sombrerers and then take a right again onto the 1st street on your the, C. de Sant Antoni dels Sombrerers. Cava €1.80. Beer €2. Cocktails €5-7. ☑ Open Tu-Th 8pm-2am, F-Sa 8pm-3am.

⬛ LA LUNA

BAR

C. Abaixadors, 10

☎932 95 55 13 www.lalunabcn.com

Another of Barcelona's most beautiful bars, La Luna sits under timeless vaulted brick arches, with dim lighting and mirrors behind the bar making it seem even larger. Comfortable lounge seating in front makes for a good place to camp out and take in the bar's beauty. The tropical mojito (with coconut rum for €7) and the *mojito de fresa* (€7.30), which replaces the lime with strawberries, are both quite popular. Leather upholstery exudes class, so do your best not to show up in basketball shorts and flip-flops.

i Open M-W 6pm-1:30am, Th-F 6pm-2:30am, Sa 1pm-2:30am, Su 1pm-1:30am.

LA FIANNA

BAR

C. Manressa, 4

☎933 15 18 10 www.lafianna.com

A glass partition divides the restaurant and bar, but be prepared to push your way through on weekend nights no matter where you choose to wine or dine. Unlike at other places in the area, finding a seat at the bar is a distinct possibility; getting a spot on one of the comfy couches is another story altogether. Patience pays off with large mojitos (€7) made with special bitters as you gaze upon the Euro-rockin' interior design, super chic furniture, and just the right amount of dim lighting.

i Ⓜ*Jaume I. Walk down Via Laietana and take a left onto C. Manresa. The restaurant is on the right after passing C. de la Nau. All cocktails €4.50 M-Th 6-9pm. Discounted tapas M-Th 7pm-12:30am, F-Sa 7pm-11:30pm, Su 7pm-12:30am. Tapas €2-4.80. Beer €2.50-3.40. Shots €4. Cocktails €6-7.* ✪ *Open daily 6pm-midnight.*

EL BORN
BAR

Pg. del Born, 26 ☎933 19 53 33

Shed the themes and pretense and stop at El Born for a straight-up bar—no more, no less. Marble tables and green decor provide a simple, no games interior that nonetheless attracts burly jocks, retired dads, and everyone in between attempting who come here to watch the Champions League finals or the French Open (really, whatever's big in Euro sports at the time of your visit). With cheap beer (€2-2.50) and ambient music, it's no wonder this place is always full. Usual patrons are more of the male variety, so ladies should bear that in mind. Some filling options include the *empandas* (€2) or a *sandwich de Milanesa* (€2.90).

i Ⓜ*Jaume I. Walk down C. de la Princesa and take a right onto C. de Montcada. Follow until you hit Pg. del Born and take a left. Free Wi-Fi. Beer €2-2.50. Mixed drinks €6.* ✪ *Open Tu-Su 10am-2:30am.*

EL COPETÍN
LATIN BAR

Pg. del Born, 19 ☎607 20 21 76

This dance floor just won't quit: Latin beats blare all night long, attracting a laid-back, fun-loving crowd that knows how to move like Shakira. A narrow, tightly packed bar up front provides little reprieve for those who need a drink, as the waitstaff will probably be too busy shakin' anyway to tend to your every beck and call. Most people who come here come prepared to dance.

i Ⓜ*Jaume I. Walk down C. de la Princesa and take a right onto C. de Montcada. Follow to Pg. del Born. Mixed drink €7.* ✪ *Open M-Th 6pm-2:30am, F-Sa 6pm-3am, Su 6pm-2:30am.*

BERIMBAU
BRAZILIAN BAR

Pg. del Born, 17 ☎646 00 55 40

This *copas* bar, reportedly the oldest Brazilian bar in Spain (founded 1978), offers a range of drinks you won't easily find this side of the Atlantic. Try the *guaraná* with whiskey (€8), an orange and banana juice with vodka (€9.50), or the tried and true (and damn good) caipirinha (€8). Samba and Brazilian electronic music fill the room with a *brasileiro* feel as the wicker furniture and stifling heat complete the scene.

i Ⓜ*Jaume I. Walk down C. de la Princesa and take a right onto C. de Montcada. Follow to Pg. del Born, then turn left. Beer €2.50-3. Cocktails €7-10.* ✪ *Open daily 6pm-2:30am.*

CACTUS BAR
BAR

Pg. del Born, 30 ☎933 10 63 54 www.cactusbar.cat

Cactus Bar is renowned along Pg. del Born for its big, tasty, and potent mojitos (€8). If you can get a bartender's attention over the clamor, you generally don't need to specify which drink you want; just use your fingers to indicate how many mojitos it'll be. The constant stream—or devastating flood—of customers means the bartenders work as a team, creating a mojito assembly line that churns out over a dozen of the minty beverages at a time. Get your drink in a plastic cup to go instead of the weighty tall glasses and enjoy it on the (slightly) less crowded Pg. del Born right out front. If mainstream doesn't float your boat, try the house gin and tonic—it'll definitely wake you up (€7.50).

i Ⓜ*Jaume I. Walk down C. de la Princesa and take a right onto C. de Montcada. Continue until you hit Pg. del Born, then take a left. DJs M and W. Beer €3. Cocktails €8. Breakfast €3.50-4.50. Sandwiches €2.50-3.70. Tapas €1.80-6.50.* ✪ *Open M-Sa noon-2am, Su noon-midnight.*

barcelona

El Raval

MARSELLA BAR   BAR

C. Sant Pau, 65   ☎934 42 72 63

Enter this amber-colored establishment lined with antique mirrors, cabinets, old advertisements, and ancient liquor bottles that have likely been there since the *modernisme* art form was first invented. The easygoing crowd is loyal to Marsella even after a few absinthes (€5). It may be a bit crowded in here, but it'll be well worth your glass of greenish glow (really, everyone orders one) below the ridiculously ornate chandeliers. Maybe you can even catch a glimpse of some long-past customers' phantoms, like Hemingway, Gaudí, or Picasso.

i ⓂLiceu. Follow C. Sant Pau from Las Ramblas. Beer €3. Mixed drinks €5-6.50. Cash only. Ⓩ Open M-Th 11pm-2am, F-Sa 11pm-3am.

MOOG   CLUB

C. Arc del Teatre, 3   ☎933 19 17 89 www.masimas.com/moog

Buried in the heart of Old Chinatown and long changed since its days of flamenco bohemia, Moog still stands as one of Europe's most important dance clubs, renowned for its electronic music. This club has featured several big name DJs like Robert X, John Acquaviva, and many from the Berlin label Tresor-all. Come inside to experience musical flavors favored by everyone from electronica aficionados to lost souls just trying to find a place to dance and shed some Spanish cuisine-induced pounds the fun way.

i ⓂDrassanes. Walk away from the water on Las Ramblas and turn left onto C. Arc del Teatre. Discount flyers often available on Las Ramblas. Cover €10. Ⓩ Open daily midnight-5am.

BAR BIG BANG   BAR,

MUSIC CLUB C. Botella, 7   www.bigbangbcn.com

Sitting in the Ciutat Vella for over 20 years now, Big Bang features everything from jazz to blues to funky swing. Stand up and vaudeville-esque theater are other acts that the crowd can drink to. Out front, customers are serenaded by big band favorites—both local and national—from the stereo and projector screen that have entertained patrons for years.

i ⓂSant Antoni. Walk down C. Sant Antoni Abad and take a right onto C. Botella. Free Wi-Fi. Schedule of performances and special events on website. Shot €3. Beer €3-4. Ⓩ Open Tu-Th 10pm-2:30am, Su 10pm-2:30am.

BETTY FORD'S   BAR

C. Joaquin Costa, 56   ☎933 04 13 68

This ain't your dad's antique Ford, honey. During the earlier hours of the evening, this bar and restaurant stuffs local students with its relatively cheap and famously delicious burgers (€6.50). Happy hour (6-9pm) provides cheap drinks, and later in the night, the place gets packed with a young, noisy crowd that will actually overflow onto the street, so get here early!

i ⓂUniversitat. Walk down Ronda de Sant Antoni and take a slight left onto C. Joaquin Costa. Burger €6.50. Shakes €3.50. Mixed drinks €5-6; happy hour drinks €4. Cash only. Ⓩ Open M 6pm-1:30am, Tu-Th 11am-1:30am, F-Sa 11am-2:30am. Happy hour M-Sa 6-9pm.

LLETRAFERIT   BAR, BOOKSTORE

C. Joaquin Costa, 43   ☎933 17 81 30

A chillax oasis away from the hectic nightlife of C. Joaquin Costa, Lletraferit (Catalan for "bookworm") offers some respite in the form of cute, colorful drinks and a little bit of literature to accompany your liquid journey. Grab a cocktail (€6-8.50) and settle into a comfy leather armchair or head around to the back, where a cozy library and bookstore awaits you.

i ⓂUniversitat. Walk down Ronda de Sant Antoni and take a slight left onto C. Joaquin Costa.

Cocktails €5-8.50. Cash only. ☒ Open M-Th 4pm-2.30am, F-Sa 5pm-3am.

VALHALLA CLUB DE ROCK
BAR, MUSIC CLUB

C. Tallers, 68

Words to our metalhead *Let's Go* readers: get ready to bust out your screamo skills, air guitars, and '80s rock-on hand gestures. Step through the front entrance, and you'll see what is a concert hall some nights and an industrial nightclub on others. It's a haven for those who may gotten tired of the techno at Moog or the eccentricity of Sant Pau 68. Free entry on non-show nights means you can use the cash you save to try the entire selection of *chupitos del rock*, specialty shots named after rock bands from Elvis to Whitesnake (€1). It'll make you holla for Valhalla.

i Ⓜ*Universitat. Walk down C. Tallers. Search for Valhalla Club de Rock on Facebook to find a calendar of concerts and special events. Shot €1-2. Beer €1.50-5. Mixed drinks €6-7. Cash only.* ☒ *Open daily 6:30pm-2:30am.*

L'Eixample

⧫ LES GENTS QUE J'AIME
BAR

C. València, 286 bis ☎932 15 68 79

Start with a little red velvet. Then add in some sultry jazz and an environment redolent of gin and *modernisme*, and you'll be transported back some 100 years to a *fin-de-siècle* fiesta. Black-and-white photographs, cool R&B, and vintage chandeliers set the mood for you to partake in sinful pleasures. Not sure where to head for the rest of the night? Cozy up next to the palm reader or have your tarot cards read to avoid making the decision yourself.

i Ⓜ*Diagonal. Head downhill or Pg. de Gràcia and turn left onto C. València. Les Gents Que J'aime is downstairs, just past Campechano. Palm reading €25-35) and tarot €20-30) M-Sa. Beer €4.50. Wine €5-10. Cocktails €5-10.* ☒ *Open M-Th 6pm-2:30am, F-Sa 7pm-3am, Su 6pm-2:30am.*

⧫ LA FIRA
CLUB

C. Provença, 171 ☎933 23 72 71

Decorated entirely with pieces from the old Apolo Amusement Park in Barcelona and featuring a slightly Latin vibe, this club is like that creepy carnival from *Scooby Doo*, but with a bar instead of a g-g-g-ghooooost. Check out the upgraded Scooby Snax (mojitos €10) as you jam out to top 40 and Latin tracks along with happy club goers.

i Ⓜ*Hospital Clínic. Walk away from the engineering school along C. Rossello and take a right onto C. Villarroel. Take the 1st left onto C. Provença; La Fira is a few blocks down. Often hosts shows or parties, sometimes with entrance fee or 1 drink min. Cover sometimes €10, includes 1 drink. Beer €5. Cocktails €10.* ☒ *Open F-Sa 11pm-5am.*

LUZ DE GAS
CLUB, BAR

C. Muntaner, 246 ☎932 09 77 11 www.luzdegas.com

This is one of the most renowned clubs in the city, and with good reason. Imagine that George Clooney bought out the casino he and his crew robbed in *Ocean's 11* and then recruited hot, classy Spaniards to run it. That's Luz de Gas. Red velvet walls, gilded mirrors, and sparkling chandeliers will have you wondering how you possibly got past the bouncer, while the massive, purple-lit dance floor surrounded by multi-colored bars will remind you what you're here for. Big name jazz, blues, and soul performers occasionally take the stage during the evening hours, but after 1am, it turns into your typical *discoteca*. Ritzy youths dance to deafening pop in the lower area, while the upstairs lounge provides a much-needed break for both your feet and ears.

i Ⓜ*Diagonal. Take a left onto Avda. Diagonal and a right onto C. Muntaner. For show listings and times, check the Guía del Ocio or the club's website. Cover €18, includes 1 drink. Beer €7. Cocktails €10.* ☒ *Open Th-Sa 11:30pm-5am.*

barcelona

ANTILLA

CLUB

C. Aragó, 141   ☎934 51 45 64 www.antillasalsa.com

Be careful when entering—this Latin bar and dance club is so full of energy that dancers often turn into Shakira and J. Lo when getting down. You can do it, too, by attending salsa lessons from 10-11pm on Wednesdays at the Escuela de Baile Antilla. Enjoy it all between the palm trees painted on the walls and the Cuban *maracas*, bongos, and cowbells littering the sandy bar.

i Ⓜ*Urgell. Walk along Gran Via de les Corts Catalanes and take a right up C. Comte d'Urgell. Walk 3 blocks and take a left onto C. Aragó. Cover €10, includes 1 drink. Beer €5-10. Cocktails €5-12.* ✆ *Open W 9pm-2am, Th 11pm-5am, F-Sa 11pm-6am, Su 7pm-1am.*

ESPIT CHUPITOS (ARIBAU)

BAR

C. Aribau, 77

Shots, shots, shots—you know the rest. You can get your inner circus freak on here, as many shots involve spectacular sparks of pyromaniacal proportions. Try the Harry Potter, which might literally light up the night. For a good laugh, order the Monica Lewinsky for somebody else and thank us later. Crowd in with everyone who loves to test this location's 45 person max. capacity or grab your drinks and go.

i Ⓜ*Universitat. Walk up C. Aribau to the left of the university building; Espit Chupitos is 4 blocks uphill. Shot €2-4. Cocktails €8.50.* ✆ *Open M-Th 10:30pm-2:30am, F-Sa 10:30pm-3am.*

Barceloneta

🎏 ABSENTA

BAR

Carrer de Sant Carles, 36   ☎932 21 36 38 www.kukcomidas.com/absenta.html

Not for the easily spooked, Absenta is like an episode of *The Twilight Zone* if you were inside the TV looking out while also experiencing a touch of the absinthe-induced hallucination this establishment is so famous for. This local hangout spot is the original Spanish speakeasy. With funky light fixtures and vintage proscriptions against the consumption of the vivid green liquor scolding you from above the bar, you will naughtily sip away at the eponymous absinthe (shot for €4, glass for €7). If the overhanging, life-size pirate fairy statue with a glass of absinthe in one hand does not grab your attention, perhaps the static TV sets with flickering art will. If you're in the mood to munch while lounging at any one of the several tables shy of the bar's entrance, try a house panini with ham or *empanadas de carne* (classic meat turnovers). Maybe the country-style blues playing overhead will let you muster up the courage to order the head mixologist's special 50-60% alcohol house-brew of absinthe.

i Ⓜ*Barceloneta. Walk down Pg. Joan de Borbó toward the beach and take a left onto C. Sant Carles. Beer €2.30. Mixed drinks €7.* ✆ *Open M 11am-3am, Tu 6pm-3am, W-Sa 11am-3am, Su 11am-2am.*

¿KÉ?

BAR

Carrer del Baluard, 54   ☎932 24 15 88

This small bar attracts internationals and provides a calm alternative to the crowded beaches and throbbing basses of the *platja* (not to mention ridiculously comfy bar stools). A Spanish sign that reads "Barcelona's most well-known secret" entitles you to be part of the in-crowd should you make it to this establishment. Frequented by celebrities, artists, and production crews for movies, this bar speaks for itself in all its vivacious, colorful splendor. The clementine-colored chandeliers shed only enough light to see bottles of all hues stacked on the wall or the barrage of dangly trinkets poised throughout the locale. Shelves doubling as upside-down tables, fruit decals along the bar, and a playful group of semi-creepy faces peering down from overhead will have you wondering "¿*Ké?*" as well. Sip on an infusion drink (€1.50), sangria (€5), a

spain

cocktail (€6), or a cheap beer (€2.50) as you jeer at the running slideshow of past bar events displayed on the main parlor TV screen.

i ⓂBarceloneta. Walk down Pg Joan de Borbó toward the sea and take a left onto Carrer Sant Carles. Take a left onto Carrer del Baluart once you enter the plaça. Free Wi-Fi. ☒ Open M-Th 11am-2:30am, F 11am-3am, Sa noon-3am.

CATWALK
DISCOTECA

C. Ramón Trias Fargas, 2-4   ☎932 24 07 40 www.clubcatwalk.net

One of Barcelona's most famous clubs, Catwalk has two packed floors of *discoteca*. *Downstairs*, bikini-clad dancers gyrate to house and techno in neon-lit cages while a well-dressed crowd floods the dance floor. Upstairs, club-goers attempt to dance to American hip hop and pop in very close quarters. Dress well if you want to get in—really well if you want to try to get in without paying the cover (this mostly applies to the ladies). Don't bother trying to get the attention of a bartender at the first bar upon entering; there are about six others, and they're all less busy. Don't come before midnight or you'll find yourself awkwardly standing around semi-old people with those one or two guys on the dance floor who are always going a bit too ham.

i ⓂCiutadella/Vila Olímpica. No T-shirts, ripped jeans, or sneakers permitted. Events listed on website. Cover €15-20, includes 1 drink. Beer €7. Mixed drinks €12. ☒ Open Th midnight-5am, F-Sa midnight-6am, Su midnight-5am.

OPIUM MAR
CLUB, RESTAURANT

Pg. Marítim de la Barceloneta, 34   ☎902 26 74 86 www.opiummar.com

Slick restaurant by day and even slicker club by night, this lavish indoor and outdoor party spot is a favorite in the Barça nightlife scene. Renowned guest DJs spin every Wednesday, but the resident DJs every other night of the week keep the dance floor sweaty and packed, while six bars make sure the party maintains a base level of schwasty. Dress classy and be prepared to encounter the super rich, super sloppy, and super foreign internationals.

i ⓂCiutadella/Vila Olímpica. Events are listed on the website. Cover €20, includes 1 drink. ☒ Restaurant open daily 1pm-1am. Club open M-Th midnight-5am. F-Sa 1-6am, Su midnight-5am.

Gràcia

◾ EL RAÏM 1886
BAR

C. Progrès, 48   www.raimbcn.com

A few steps through the cluttered entrance reveals a calm buzz of chatting patrons who come here to unwind after a long week of work. This time capsule of an establishment is a mix of a Catalan bodega and '50s Cuban bar. Established in 1886, it is now a shrine to Cuban music and memorabilia that attracts down-to-earth locals with rum drinks like the incredible mojitos (€6).

i ⓂFontana. Walk downhill on C. Gran de Gràcia and make a left onto C. Ros de Olano. Walk for about 4 blocks and take a right onto C. Torrent de l'Olla. Take the 4th left onto Siracusa; El Raïm is on the corner at the intersection with C. Progrès. Wine €2. Beer €2.30-3. Shots €2-3.50. Mixed drinks €5.50-7. ☒ Open daily 8pm-2:30am.

◾ VINILO
BAR

C. Matilde, 2   ☎626 46 7 59

Join the locals on the comfy couches while you enjoy simple tapas and whatever is being played from the back monitor, whether it be movies, concerts, or F.C. Barcelona matches. Ponder at what would possess the interior designers to place such a big gramophone next to the bar and then marvel at the local works of art.

i ⓂFontana. Head downhill on C. Gran de Gràcia, turn left onto Trevassera Gràcia, and take the 2nd right onto C. Matilde. Beer €2.50-3.50. Mixed drinks €6.50-7. ☒ Open in summer M-Th 8pm-3am, F-Sa 8pm-3:30am, Su 8pm-3am; in winter M-Th 8pm-2am, F-Sa 8pm-3am, Su 8pm-2am.

EL CHATELET

C. Torrijos, 54 ☎932 84 95 90

El Chatelet features happens to dish out some of the biggest glasses of liquor *Let's Go* has ever seen. A cozy street corner setting with an adjacent room makes this a rather spacious environment that is nevertheless always crowded with chatty patrons. Big windows give you front row people watching seats that look onto C. Torrijos and C. Perla. Try the *sexopata* panini, composed of avocado, mayo, and that iconic Iberian ham.

i ⓂFontana. Head downhill on C. Gran de Gràcia and turn left onto C. Montseny. Follow it as it turns into C. Perla and turn right onto C. Torrijos. Beer €2-4. Mojitos €3.50, weekends €5.50. Mixed drinks €6. Panini €3.50-4.50. ☼ Open M-Th 6pm-2:30am, F-Sa 6pm-3am, Su 6pm-2:30am.

ASTROLABI

BAR, LIVE MUSIC

C. Martínez de la Rosa, 14

You will actually have fun cramming into this 38-person joint, as the live music this place features daily (starting around 9pm) is excellent. The neat, trinket-filled interior is a cozy scene in which to mingle with the happy patrons who frequent this place. Try the crowd pleasing *Great Estrella Galicia* (€2.80) as you merrily sing along with the mix of locals and internationals.

i ⓂDiagonal. Take a left onto Pg. de Gràcia, cross Avda. Diagonal, and turn right onto C. Bonavista before Pg. de Gràcia becomes C. Gran de Gràcia. Take a left onto C. Martínez de la Rosa. See Facebook group for special events. Beer €2.50-2.80. Wine from €2. Mixed drinks €6. Cash only. ☼ Open M-F 8pm-2:30am, Sa-Su 8pm-3am. Live music daily 10pm.

LA CERVERSERA ARTESANA

BAR, BREWERY

C. Sant Agustí, 14 ☎932 37 95 94 www.lacervesera.net

We must admit, it's pretty neat to drink in the only pub in Barcelona that brews its own beer on site. With a huge variety of brews—dark, amber, honey, spiced, chocolate, peppermint, fruit-flavored, and more—there's literally something for any beer-lover. Kick back with friends as F.C. takes on the world from any of the flat screen TVs in this never-too-crowded spot.

i ⓂDiagonal. Head uphill on Pg. de Gràcia and take a right onto C. Corsega, at the roundabout where Pg. de Gràcia meets Avda. Diagonal. C. Sant Agustí is the 3rd left. Beers €3.15-4.95. ☼ Open M-Th 5pm-2am, F 5pm-3am, Sa 6pm-3am, Su 5pm-2am.

OTTO ZUTZ

CLUB

C. Lincoln, 15 ☎932 38 07 22 www.ottozutz.com

Like a multilayered rum cake, this place has three levels of boogie throughout its interior. The levels host DJs of varying musical genres, blasted for all of C. Lincoln to feel until dawn. As you might expect, a crowd of young people jostles around this club at all hours of the night, and as a result, it tends to get pretty hot during the summer months.

i ⓂFontana. Walk along Rambla de Prat and take a left as it dead ends into Via Augusta. Take the 1st right onto C. Laforja and the 1st right again onto C. Lincoln. Cover €10-15; includes 1 drink. Beer €6. Mixed drinks €6-12. ☼ Open M midnight-6am, W-Sa midnight-6am.

THE SUTTON CLUB

CLUB

C. Tuset, 13 ☎934 14 42 17 www.thesuttonclub.com

Don't even think about showing up in your black gym shorts, Converse sneakers, or light-wash jeans—wear as fine of threads as a traveler can manage. Make your z's sound extra Catalonian when talking to the bouncers, and don't make any sudden movements at the door. Once you're in, though, all bets are off: four bars provide mass quantities of alcohol to a dance floor that gets sloppier as the night goes on. Check online for concerts or special events.

i ⓂDiagonal. Turn left onto Avda. Diagonal, walk about 4 blocks, and turn right onto C. Tuset. Cover €12-18; includes 1 drink. Beer €7. Mixed drinks €10-15. ☼ Open M-Th 11:30pm-5am.

KGB

CLUB

C. ca l'Alegre de Dalt, 55 ☎932 10 59 06

In Soviet Russia, the club hits you! But seriously folks, you'll be stunned by the varying music genres here, ranging from dubsteb and reggae all the way to top 40. It's small, but the overcrowding is what makes this place awesome. Entrance is free with a flyer; otherwise you'll have to pay €10-15 to join this Party.

i Ⓜ*Joanic. Walk along C. Pi i Maragall and take the 1st left. Cover with 1 drink €10-12, with 2 drinks until 3am €12-16, free with flyer. Beer €4. Mixed drinks €7-10. Cash only. Check online for concert listings. ☒ Open Th 1am-5am, F-Sa 1am-6am.*

CAFÉ DEL SOL

CAFE, BAR

Pl. Sol, 16 ☎932 37 14 48

One of the many tapas bars lining the Pl. del Sol, the Cafe del Sol offers cheap and delicious eats. Tune into the English pop rock sheltered by some subtle, dimmed lighting that makes for a fun soiree. Try the house recommended pumpkin ravioli and funghi sauce or the runny eggs with straw potatoes (€4.50).

i Ⓜ*Fontana. Walk downhill on C. Gran de Gràcia, turn left onto C. Ros de Olano, and right onto C. Virtut. Beer €2.80. Mixed drinks €6-7. Tapas €3.50-8.50. Entrees €4-8. ☒ Open daily 11pm-3am.*

Montjuïc and Poble Sec

⊠ BARCELONA ROUGE CAFÉ

BAR

C. Poeta Cabanyes, 21 ☎934 42 49 85

Just imagine walking into the newest chamber of the Playboy Mansion in all its lusty red glow. Throw in neat albums for sale and a kicking Moscow Mule (vodka, pickle, ginger, lime, and ginger ale), and you have Rouge. With a nice arrangement of leather chairs and a parade of vintage decor (like a shoddy copy of Jan van Eyck's *The Arnolfini Wedding*), this bar creates a sexy environment where a crowd of hip and friendly customers will party with you. If nothing else, you must try the signature Barcelona Rouge, comprised of vodka, berry liquor, lime juice, and shaved ice (€6.50).

i Ⓜ*Paral·lel. With Montjuïc to your left, walk along Avda. Paral·lel. Take a left onto C. Poeta Cabanyes. Rouge Café is on the left, before Mambo Tango Youth Hostel. Free Wi-Fi. Beer €1.50-3. Cocktails €5-7. ☒ Open Th-Sa 9pm-3am.*

⊠ MAUMAU

BAR

C. Fontrodona, 35 ☎934 41 80 15 www.maumaunderground.com

The epicenter of Barcelona's underground, Mau Mau is best known for its online guide to art, film, and other hip happenings around the city (quick tip for the pro partier), but this is very much worth the hike up C. Fontrodona. The mega loft graciously doles out upwards of 20 girls and dozens and dozens of mixed drinks with all sorts of funky names, from Dark and Stormy (€8) to the proletarian Moscow Mule (€8). At a place where only the suavest go to socialize in a cool, open space, there isn't even a cover charge to keep you out.

i Ⓜ*Paral·lel. Facing Montjuïc, walk right along Av. Paral·lel and take a left onto C. Fontrodona. Follow the street as it zig-zags; Mau Mau is just a few blocks down. 1-year membership (includes discounts at Mau Mau and at various clubs, bars, and cultural destinations around the city) €12. No cover for visitors. Beer €2-3. Mixed drinks from €6-11. Cocktails €6-8. ☒ Open Th-Sa and festivals 9pm-3am. Other days of the week for special events (see website for details).*

LA TERRRAZZA

CLUB

Avda. Marquès de Comillas, 13 ☎687 96 98 25 www.laterrrazza.com

One of the most popular clubs in Barcelona, La Terrrazza lights up the Poble Espanyol after the artisans and sunburned tourists call it a day. The open-air dance floor floods with many colored lights and humans as soon as the sun goes down. Try any of the mixed drinks (€8-12), all made quicker than you can twerk.

i Ⓜ*Espanya. Head through the Venetian towers and ride the escalators. Follow the signs to Poble Espanyol. Free bus from Pl. Catalunya to club every 20min. 12:20am-3:20am; free bus from Terrazza to Pl. Catalunya nonstop 5:30am-6:45am. Cover €18, with flyer €15; includes 1 drink. Beer €5-10.* ☒ *Open F-Sa 12:30am-6am.*

TINTA ROJA
BAR

C. Creu dels Molers, 17   ☎934 43 32 43   www.tintaroja.net

Resulting from an inventive and artsy couple who have perfected a mix of eccentric and authentic, this establishment was been named after the 1941 tango, "Tinta Roja." Out front, you can sample any of their fine alcoholic beverages that use Argentinian *legui* as the main mixing agent. Inside the buzzing grotto, you can observe many of the head manager's impressive artistic. Ten paces away is where his wife gives dance lessons on Wednesdays at 8:30pm. See how well you can bust out some Spanish groove while a tad under the influence.

i Ⓜ*Poble Sec. With Montjuïc to the right, walk along Avda. Paral·lel. Take a right onto C. Creu dels Molers; Tinta Roja is on the left. Tango classes W 8:30-10pm, dance from 10pm-1am. Wine €2.70-3.90. Beer €2.50-5.50. Argentine liqueurs €6.60-7.50. Mixed drinks €7.50.* ☒ *Open W 8:30am-midnight, Th 8:30pm-2am, F-Sa 8:30pm-3am. Hours may change to accommodate special events; check online.*

Tibidabo

Tibidabo—the mountain that rises behind Barcelona—is easily reached by a combination of FGC and tram during the day, but a seriously long uphill hike once trams stop running at 10pm. A cab from Pl. Lesseps to Pl. Doctor Andreu is about €8; from Pl. Catalunya, it's about €13. Once you figure out a safe way to get home, head here for a night of incredible views that seem to twinkle more with every drink.

🏅 MIRABLAU
BAR, CLUB

Pl. Doctor Andreu, S/N   ☎934 18 56 67   www.mirablaubcn.com

With easily the best view in Tibidabo—and arguably the best in Barcelona—Mirablau is a favorite with posh internationals and the younger crowd, so dress well. It also happens to be near the mountain's peak, so we only recommend walking up here if you prefer to sip your cocktails while drenched in sweat. The glimmering lights of the metropolis and the bar's quivering candles create a dreamlike aura that earns Mirablau a *Let's Go* thumbpick. If the club is more your style, head downstairs where pretty young things spill out onto the terrace to catch their breath from the crowded dance floor.

i *L7 to FGC: Avinguda de Tibidabo. Take the Tramvia Blau up Avda. Tibidabo to Pl. Doctor Andreu. Th-Sa credit card min €4.70. Drinks discounted M-Sa before 11pm, Su before 6pm. Beer and wine €1.80-6. Cocktails €7-9.50. 11am-5:30am.* ☒ *Open M-Th 11am-4:30am, F-Sa 11am-5:30am*

MERBEYÉ
BAR

Pl. Doctor Andreu, 2   ☎934 17 92 79   www.merbeye.net

Merbeyé provides a dim, romantic atmosphere on an outdoor terrace along the cliff. With the lights in the lounge so low that seeing your companion may be a problem, Merbeyé is the perfect place to bring an unattractive date. Smooth jazz serenades throughout, and with just one Merbeyé cocktail (cava, cherry brandy, and Cointreau (€9-10), you'll be buzzed real quick.

i *L7 to FGC: Avinguda de Tibidabo. Take the Tramvía Blau up Avda. Tibidabo to Pl. Doctor Andreu. Beer €2.50-4. Cocktails €9-10. Food €2-7.60. 11am-2am.* ☒ *Open Th 5pm-2am, F-Sa 11am-3am.*

ARTS AND CULTURE
Music and Dance

For comprehensive guides to large events and information on cultural activities, contact the **Guía del Ocio** (www.guiadelociobcn.com) or the **Institut de Cultura de Barcelona (ICUB)**. (Palau de la Virreina, La Rambla, ☎99933 16 10 00 www.bcn.cat/cultura. ☒ Open daily 10am-8pm.) Should you be super wary and wish to make good use of Spain's awful Wi-Fi services (and test your Catalan skills), check out **www.butxaca. com,** a comprehensive bimonthly calendar with film, music, theater, and art listings, or **www.maumaunderground.com,** which lists local music news, reviews, and events. The website **www.infoconcerts.cat/ca** (available in English) provides even more concert listings. For tickets, check out **ServiCaixa** (☎902 33 22 11 www.servicaixa.com. ☒Located at any branch of the Caixa Catalonia bank. ☒Open M-F 8am-2:30pm), **TelEntrada** (☎902 10 12 12 www.telentrada.com), or **Ticketmaster** (www.ticketmaster.es).

Although a music destination year-round, Barcelona especially perks up during the summer with an influx of touring bands and music festivals. The biggest and baddest of these is the three-day electronic music festival **Sónar** (www.sonar.es), which takes place in mid-June. Sónar attracts internationally renowned DJs, electronica fans, and partiers from all over the world. From mid-June to the end of July, the **Grec** summer festival (http://grec.bcn.cat) hosts international music, theater, and dance at multiple venues throughout the city, while the indie-centric **Primavera Sound** (www. primaverasound.com) at the end of May is also a regional must-see. *Mondo Sonoro* (www.mondosonoro.com) has more information and lists musical happenings across the Spanish-speaking world.

RAZZMATAZZ
POBLE NOU

C. Pamplona, 88 and Almogàvers, 122 ☎933 20 82 00 www.salarazzmatazz.com

This massive labyrinth of a converted warehouse hosts popular acts, from reggae to electropop and indie to metal. The massive nightclub complex spans multiple stories in two buildings connected by industrial stairwells and a rooftop walkway. The big room thumps with remixes of current and past top 40 hits, while the smaller rooms upstairs provide more intimate dance spaces. The open-air top floor could be mistaken for a low flying cloud due to the all the smokers bro-ing out here. If there isn't a concert going on, you can still find a young crowd doing the twist (read: grindage) to a DJ onstage.

i Ⓜ*Bogatell. Walk down C. Pere IV away from the plaza and take the 1st slight left onto C. Pamplona. Razzmatazz is on the right. Tickets available online through website, TelEntrada, or Ticketmaster. Ticket €10-25.*

SALA APOLO
POBLE SEC

C. Nou de la Rambla, 113 ☎934 41 40 01 www.sala-apolo.com

Looking to party but lamenting the fact that it's Monday? Sulk no more—for a number of years, Sala Apolo has been drawing locals to start the week off right with Nasty Mondays, featuring a mix of rock, pop, indie, garage, '80s, typical electro, and a special electronica dubbed "fidget house." In fact, the night is so popular that it has spawned Crappy Tuesdays (indie and electropop). Stop by later in the week when just about anybody and everybody is around, and check the website to see which of the latest indie groups may be rolling through. If you pop in on the right Sunday evening, you may even get to partake in Churros con Chocolate night, which is exactly what it sounds like, plus some dancing.

i Open daily midnight-6am, earlier for concerts and events; check website for event schedule.*

Festivals

Barcelona loves to party. Although *Let's Go* fully supports the city's festive agenda, we still need to include some nitty-gritty things like accommodations and, you know, food, so we can't possibly list all of the fun annual events. For a full list of what's going on during your visit, stop by the tourist information office. As a teaser, here are a few of the biggest, most student-relevant shindigs.

FESTA DE SANT JORDI
LAS RAMBLAS

Las Ramblas

A more intelligent, civil alternative to Valentine's Day, this festival celebrates both St. George (the **dragon**-slayer and patron saint of Barcelona) and commemorates the deaths of Shakespeare and Cervantes. On this day, Barcelona gathers along Las Ramblas in search of flowers and books to give to lovers.
🗓 *Apr 23.*

FESTA DE SANT JOAN
BARCELONETA, POBLENOU

The beachfront

These days light a special fire in every pyromaniac's heart as **fireworks,** bonfires, and torches light the city and waterfront in celebration of the coming of summer.
🗓 *Night of Jun 23-Jun 24.*

BARCELONA PRIDE
CITYWIDE, L'EIXAMPLE

Parade ends in Avda. Maria Cristina, behind Pl.Espanya

This week is the biggest GLBT celebration in the Mediterranean, and Catalunya is no exception. Multiple venues throughout the region take active part in the festival, which culminates with a parade through "Geixample" and a festival.
🗓 *Last week of Jun.*

FESTA MAJOR
GRÀCIA

Pl. Rius i Taulet (Pl. Vila de Gràcia)

Festa Major is a community festival in Gràcia during which artsy intellectuals put on performances and fun events in preparation for the Assumption of the Virgin. Expect parades, concerts, floats, arts and crafts, live music, dancing, and, of course, parties.
🗓 *End of Aug.*

LA DIADA
EL BORN

C. Fossar de les Moreres

Catalunya's national holiday celebrates the end of the Siege of Barcelona in 1714 as well as the reclaiming of national—whoops, we mean regional—identity after the death of Franco. Parties are thrown, flags are waved, and Estrella Damm is imbibed—lots of Estrella Damm.
🗓 *Sept 11.*

FESTA MERCÈ
CITYWIDE, EL BORN

Pl. Sant Jaume

This massive outpouring of joy for one of Barcelona's patron saints (Our Lady of Mercy) is the city's main annual celebration. More than 600 free performances take place in multiple venues. There is also a **castellers** competition in the Pl. Sant Jaume; competitors attempt to build *castells* (literally "castles," but in this case human towers) several humans high, which small children clad in helmets and courage then attempt to climb.
🗓 *Weeks before and after Sept 24.*

Fútbol

Although Barcelona technically has two *fútbol* teams, **Fútbol Club Barcelona (FCB)** and the **Real Club Deportiu Espanyol de Barcelona (RCD),** you can easily go weeks in the city without hearing mention of the latter. It's impossible to miss the former, though, and with good reason. Besides being a really incredible athletic team, FCB lives up to its motto as "more than a club."

During the years of Francisco Franco, FCB was forced to change its name and crest in order to avoid nationalistic references to Catalunya and thereafter became a rallying point for oppressed Catalan separatists. The original name and crest were reinstated after Franco's fall in 1974, and the team retained its symbolic importance; it's still seen as a sign of democracy, Catalan identity, and regional pride.

This passion is not merely patriotic or altruistic, though—FCB has been one of the best teams in the world in recent years. In 2009, they were the first team to win six out of six major competitions in a single year; in 2010, they won Spain's Super Cup trophy; in 2010 and in 2011, FCB took Spain's La Liga trophy; and in 2011, they beat Manchester United to win the UEFA Champion's League, cementing their status as the best club in the world. Their world-class training facilities (a legacy of the 1992 Olympics) supply many World Cup competitors each year, leaving some Barcelonans annoyed that Catalunya is not permitted to compete as its own nation, much like England, Wales, and Scotland do in the United Kingdom. In fact, Spain's 2010 World Cup victory disappointed much of the Catalonian populous and many die-hard FCB fanatics.

Because FCB fervor is so pervasive, you don't need to head to their stadium, the Camp Nou, to join in the festivities—almost every bar off the tourist track boasts a screen dedicated to their games. Kick back with a brew and be sure not to root for the competition.

ESSENTIALS

Practicalities

- **TOURIST OFFICES: Plaça de Catalunya** is the main office, offering free maps and brochures, last-minute booking service for accommodations, currency exchange, and box office. (Pl. de Catalunya, 17S. ☎93 285 38 34 www.barcelonaturisme.com *i* ⓂCatalunya, underground, across from El Corte Inglès. Look for the pillars with the letter "i" on top. ☒ Open daily 8:30am-8:30pm.) **Plaça de Sant Jaume.** (C. Ciutat. 2. ☎93 270 24 29 *i* ⓂJaume I. Follow C. Jaume I to Pl. Sant Jaume. Located in the Ajuntament building on the left. ☒ Open M-F 8:30am-8:30pm, Sa 9am-7pm, Su and holidays 9am-2pm.) **Oficina de Turisme de Barcelona** (Palau Robert, Pg. de Gràcia, 107. ☎93 238 80 91, toll-free in Catalunya ☎012 www.gencat.es/probert *i* ⓂDiagonal. ☒ Open M-Sa 10am-7pm, Su 10am-2:30pm.) **Institut de Cultura de Barcelona (ICUB)** (Palau de la Virreina, Las Ramblas, 99. ☎93 316 10 00 www.bcn.cat/cultura *i* ⓂLiceu. ☒ Open daily 10am-8pm.) **Estació Barcelona-Sants.** (Pl. Països Catalans. ☎90 224 02 02 *i* ⓂSants-Estació. ☒ Open Jun 24-Sept 24 daily 8am-8pm; Sept 25-Jun 23 M-F 8am-8pm, Sa-Su 8am-2pm.)
- **LUGGAGE STORAGE: Estació Barcelona-Sants.** (*i* ⓂSants-Estació. Lockers €3-4.50 per day. ☒ Open daily 5:30am-11pm.) **Estació Nord.** (*i* ⓂArc de Triomf. Max 90 days. Lockers €3.50-5 per day.) **El Prat Airport.** (*i* €3.80-4.90 per day.)
- **GLBT RESOURCES: GLBT tourist guide,** available at the Pl. de Catalunya tourist office, includes a section on GLBT bars, clubs, publications, and more. **GayBarcelona** (www.gaybarcelona.net) and **Infogai** (www.colectiugai.org) have up-to-date info. **Barcelona Pride** (www.pridebarcelona.org/en) has annual activities during the last week of June. **Antinous** specializes in gay and lesbian books and films. (C. Josep Anselm Clavé, 6. ☎93 301 90 70 www.antinouslibros.com *i* ⓂDrassanes. ☒ Open M-F 10:30am-2pm and 5-8:30pm, Sa noon-2pm and 5-8:30pm.)
- **INTERNET ACCESS:** The **Barcelona City Government** (www.bcn.es) offers free Wi-Fi at over 500 locations, including museums, parks, and beaches. **Easy Internet Café** has decent rates and around 300 terminals. (Las Ramblas, 31 ☎93 301 75 07 *i* ⓂLiceu. €2.10 per hr., min. €2; day unlimited pass €7, week €15, month €30. ☒ Open daily 8am-2:30am.) **Easy Internet**

Café. (Ronda Universitat, 35 *i* €2 per hr.; day pass €3, week €7, month €15. Open daily 8am-2:30am.) **Navegaweb.** (Las Ramblas, 88-94. ☎93 318 90 26 nevegabarcelona@terra. es *i* ⓂLiceu. Calls to US €0.20 per min. Internet €2 per hr. Open M-Th 9am-midnight, F 9am-1am, Sa 9am-2am, Su 9am-midnight.) **BCNet (Internet Gallery Café).** (C. Barra de Ferro, 3 ☎93 268 15 07 www.bornet-bcn.com. *i* ⓂJaume I. €1 per 15min., €3 per hr., 10hr. ticket €20. Open M-F 10am-11pm, Sa-Su noon-11pm.

- **POST OFFICE:** Pl. Antonio López. ☎93 486 83 02 www.correos.es. *i* ⓂJaume I or ⓂBarceloneta. Open M-F 8:30am-9:30pm, Sa 8:30am-2pm.

- **POSTAL CODE:** 08001.

Emergency

- **EMERGENCY NUMBERS:** ☎112. **Ambulance:** ☎061.

- **POLICE: Local police:** ☎092. **Mossos d'Esquadra (regional police):** ☎088. **National police:** ☎091. **Tourist police:** Las Ramblas, 43 ☎93 256 24 30 *i* ⓂLiceu. Open 24hr.

- **LATE-NIGHT PHARMACY:** Rotates. Check any pharmacy window for the nearest on duty or call **Informació de Farmàcies de Guàrdia** (☎010 or ☎93 481 00 60 www.farmaciesdeguardia. com).

- **MEDICAL SERVICES: Hospital Clínic i Provincial.** (C. Villarroel, 170. ☎93 227 54 00 *i* ⓂHospital Clínic. Main entrance at C. Roselló and C. Casanova.) **Hospital de la Santa Creu i Sant Pau.** (☎93 291 90 00; emergency ☎91 91 91 *i* ⓂGuinardó-Hospital de Sant Pau.) **Hospital del Mar.** (Pg. Marítim, 25-29. ☎93 248 30 00 *i* ⓂCiutadella-Vila Olímpica.)

Getting There

By Plane

There are two possible airports you may use to reach Barcelona. The first, **Aeroport del Prat de Llobregat** (BCN; Terminal 1 ☎93 478 47 04, Terminal 2 ☎93 478 05 65), is located slightly closer to the city, though both necessitate bus rides. To get to Pl. Catalunya from the airport, take the **Aérobus** in front of terminals 1 or 2. (☎92 415 60 20 www.aerobusbcn.com *i* €5.30, round-trip ticket valid for 9 days €9.15. 35-40min.; every 5-20min. to Pl. Catalunya daily 6am-1am; to airport 5:30am-12:10am.) To get to the airport, the **A1** bus goes to Terminal 1 and the **A2** goes to Terminal 2. For early morning flights, the NitBus **N17** runs from Pl. Catalunya to all terminals. (*i* €1.45. From Pl. Catalunya every 20min. daily 11pm-5am, from airport every 20min. 9:50pm-4:40am.) The **RENFE Rodalies** train is cheaper and usually a bit faster than the Aérobus if you're arriving at Terminal 2. (☎90 224 34 02 www.renfe.es *i* €1.45, free with T10 transfer from Metro. 20-25min. to Estació Sants, 25-30min. to Pg. de Gràcia; every 30min., from airport 5:40am-11:38pm, from Estació Sants to airport 5:10am-11:09pm.) To reach the train from Terminal 2, take the pedestrian overpass in front of the airport (with your back to the entrance, it's to the left). For those arriving at Terminal 1, there's a shuttle bus outside the terminal that goes to the train station.

The **Aeroport de Girona-Costa Brava** (GRO; ☎90 240 47 04 www.barcelona-girona-airport.com) is located just outside of Girona, a city about 85km to Barcelona's northeast. However, **Ryanair** flights arrive at this airport, so it may be your best bet for getting to Barcelona on the cheap. The **Barcelona Bus** goes from the airport in Girona to Estació d'Autobusos Barcelona Nord. (☎90 236 15 50 www.barcelonabus. com *i* Buses from the airport to Barcelona Nord are timed to match flight arrivals. Buses from Barcelona Nord arrive at Girona Airport approximately 3hr. before flight departures. €12, round-trip €21. 1hr. 10min.)

By Train

Depending on the destination, trains can be an economical choice. **Estació Barcelona-Sants** (Pl. Països Catalans *i* ⓂSants-Estació) serves most domestic and international traffic, while **Estació de França** (Av. Marqués de l'Argentera *i* ⓂBarceloneta) serves regional destinations and a few international locations. Note that trains often stop before the main stations; check the schedule. **RENFE** (reservations and info ☎90 224 02 02; international ☎90 224 34 02 www.renfe.es) runs to Bilbao (€65); Madrid (€118); Sevilla (€143); Valencia (€40-45); and many other destinations in Spain. Trains also travel to Milan (€135 via Girona, Figueres, Perpignan, and Turin); Montpellier (€60); Paris (€146); and Zurich (€136.) via Geneva and Bern. There's a 20% discount on roundtrip tickets, and domestic trains usually have discounts for reservations made more than two weeks in advance. Call or check website for schedules.

By Bus

Buses are often considerably cheaper than the train. The city's main bus terminal is **Estació d'Autobusos Barcelona Nord.** (☎90 226 06 06 www.barcelonanord.com *i* ⓂArc de Triomf or #54 bus.) Buses also depart from **Estació Barcelona-Sants** and the airport. **Sarfa** (ticket office at Ronda Sant Pere, 21 ☎90 230 20 25 www.sarfa.es) is the primary line for regional buses in Catalunya, but **Eurolines** (☎93 265 07 88 www.eurolines.es) also goes to Paris, France (€80) via Lyon and offers a 10% discount to travelers under 26 or over 60. **Alsa** (☎90 242 22 42 www.alsa.es) is Spain's main bus line. Buses go to Bilbao (€43); Madrid (€29-34); Sevilla (€79-90); Valencia (€26-31); and many other Spanish cities.

By Ferry

Ferries to the Balearic Islands (Ibiza, Mallorca, and Minorca) leave daily from the port of Barcelona at **Terminal Drassanes** (☎93 324 89 80) and **Terminal Ferry de Barcelona** (☎93 295 91 82 *i* ⓂDrassanes). The most popular ferries are run by **Trasmediterránea** (☎90 245 46 45 www.trasmediterrana.es) in Terminal Drassanes. They go to Ibiza (€90 ⌚ 9hr. 30min.) and Mallorca. (€83. ⌚ 8hr.)

Getting Around

By Metro

The most convenient mode of transportation in Barcelona is the **Metro.** The Metro is actually comprised of three main companies: **Transports Metropolitans de Barcelona** (TMB ☎93 318 70 74 www.tmb.cat), whose logo is an M in a red diamond; **Ferrocarrils de la Generalitat de Catalunya** (FGC ☎93 205 15 15 www.fgc.cat), whose logo is an orange square; and **Tramvia de Barcelona** (Tram ☎90 070 11 81 www.trambcn.com), whose logo is a green square with a white T. The TMB lines are likely the ones you will use most. Thankfully, all three companies are united, along with the bus system and Rodalies train system, under the **Autoritat del Transport Metropolità** (www.atm.cat), which means that you only need one card for all forms of transport, and that you get free transfers. Most Metro lines are identified with an L (L1, L2, etc.), though some FGC lines begin with S, and all Tram lines begin with T. (*i* 1 day €6.20, 10 rides €8.25, 50 rides €33.50, 1 month €51. ⌚ Trains run M-Th 5am-midnight, F 5am-2am, Sa 24hr., Su 5am-midnight.)

By Bus

For journeys to more remote places, the bus may be an important complement to the metro. The **NitBus** is the most important: it runs **all night long** after the Metro closes. Look for bus lines that begin with an N. Barcelona's tourist office also offers a **tourist bus** (http://bcnshop.barcelonaturisme.com *i* 1 day €23, 2 days €30) that hits major sights and allows riders to hop on and off. Depending on how much you plan to use the route (and how much you fear being spotted on a red double-decker labeled "Tourist Bus"), a pass may be a worthwhile investment.

By Bike, Motorcycle, And Scooter

Motocicletas (scooters, and less frequently motorcycles—*motos* for short) are a common sight in Barcelona, and **bicycles** are also becoming more popular. Many institutions rent *motos*, but you need a valid driver's license recognized in Spain (depends on the company, but this sometimes means an international driver's license as well as a license from your home country) in order to rent one. Many places also offer bike rental. If you will be staying in the city for an extended period, it is possible to buy a bike secondhand (try **www.loquo.com**) or register for **Bicing** (☎90 231 55 31 www.bicing.cat), the municipal red and white bikes located throughout the city.

By Taxi

When other cheaper and more exciting options fail, call **Radio Taxi** (☎93 225 00 00). Taxis generally cruise at all hours; when the green light is on, the cab is free.

toledo

Welcome to Toledo, the world's oldest proponent for coexistence. In this ancient city perched atop a massive hill and surrounded by its very own moat (actually the Tagus River, but we can pretend), wander down any street and you're likely to find a Star of David, Arabic script, and a cross, all within a few yards of each other. This is a city of cathedrals, synagogues, and mosques, of Moorish architecture and cross-shaped transepts. Before the Spanish conquered Toledo in 1085, Muslim Moors ruled the land. The city itself dates back to the Bronze Age (for those of you not in the know, around 600 BC) and was under Roman rule. While visiting, make sure to check out the ancient Roman ruins and city walls—thousand-year remnants of a time long since passed.

Today, you'll find yourself at the heart of Spain's Catholic pulse. Spain's greatest cathedral (or so we think) is located just blocks away from Toledo's central Plaza, Zocodover, and churches with sky-high, panoramic views cover the city. While this sleepy, medieval town is known for its sharp souvenirs (check the sign at the train station that warns you about pointy objects crossing customs), take a hike across the hills and find the city's hidden nooks, from ancient Roman military fortifications to fishing spots on the river. While the town may seem touristy at first, it's exploration, creativity, and a bit of marzapan that will make your trip anything but ordinary—or, for that matter, 21st-century.

SIGHTS

Everywhere you turn in Toledo there's another sight, another museum, another church. Don't let yourself be overwhelmed by all of it! Instead, check out the following major attractions, and buy yourself a wristband (pulsera turística) for €8, which will get you into the following attractions any time you want to visit, given that the wristband is still intact around your wrist. Check out la Iglesia Santo Tomé, which holds El Greco's masterpiece "The Burial of Count Orgaz" (a must see during your time in Toledo), Sinogoga (Synagogue) de Santa María la Blanca, Monasterio (monastery) de San Juan de los Reyes, Mezquita del Cristo de la Luz, Iglesia de los Jesuitas (which, if you climb to the top, is the highest point in the city), and la Iglesia del Salvador (a neat archeological site that lets you go underneath the church and climb up to its bell tower). If you don't purchase the wristband, one-time entrance to each of these sites is €2.50.

CATHEDRAL OF TOLEDO

C. Cardenal Cisneros, 1 ☎925 22 22 41 www.catedralprimada.es

It's hard to miss the Cathedral of Toledo. Standing at 146 feet tall, the cathedral towers over the red brick roofs of the city, a 500-year-old behemoth in an already-ancient town. It took builders 267 years to construct the giant structure (although a structure, which was initially used by the Moors, had been in place in the spot since the sixth century, and it's no wonder why). Step inside the holy space and revel at the diversity and complexity of its structures, from the ornate marble pilasters to the ancient, stained-glass rose window situated just outside the cathedral's nave. Though dimly lit (for effect, and to allow natural, consecrated lighting to flow into the vacuous space), the cathedral's walls seem alive with color. Deep red paintings, like El Greco's famous "Disrobing of Christ," remain in the sites in which they were originally intended. Golden gates, mosaic-like altars, and lavishly painted marble sculptures instill the Cathedral with a kind of brimming energy, one that—even if you aren't religious—will make you feel some sort of spiritual stirring.

Visiting one of Toledo's most iconic sites is a little pricy. General admission to the cathedral costs €8, while full admission, including access to the Cathedral's tower and Campana Gordo, Spain's largest bell, costs €11. Included within the prices of both tickets is a free audio guide, which offers listeners comprehensive historical and aesthetic analysis of the cathedral in English, Spanish, and French. Unfortunately, the cathedral is not one of the €8 wristband sites either. But, despite the cost of the ticket, a trip to Toledo's ancient cathedral is well worth your time. Photography is allowed, and if you're on Instagram, you may very well be glued to your phone the entire time, trying to capture the perfect shot of the awe-inspiring baroque altarpiece located at the back of the cathedral's main altar.

If you do visit, make sure to check the mass schedule ahead of time, since often portions of the cathedral can be closed in order to accommodate worshippers. Liturgy is held at every morning and evening—tourists and sightseers are welcome to participate.

i €8 general admission, €11 for access to tower and bell, free audio guide. ⌚ Open M-Sa 10am-6:30pm, Su and holidays 2-6:30pm.

MUSEO DE SANTA CRUZ

C. Miguel de Cervantes, 3 ☎925 22 10 36 www.turismocastillalamancha.es

In a town where tourism is the number one industry, you'll be hard-pressed to find a place that offers free entry. Look no further than Toledo's own Museo de Santa Cruz, a small body of art located just off the Plaza de Zocodover. Originally built as a charitable hospital in the 1490s to care for the poor and weak, the museum now holds collections of 17th-century ceramics, Classical sculptures, paintings by El Greco from his workshop, and works by Francisco Goya and José de Ribera. The building itself is a work of art too. With a plateresque façade, an incredible coffered ceiling, a tranquil courtyard garden, and an ornately designed and decorated staircase, the museum feels airy, light, and peaceful (just like how hospitals are supposed to feel, right?).

It's difficult to describe the museum's collection in just a few words, since there seems to be no rhyme or reason to its holdings. Though the museum is divided into sections—archeology, ceramics, and paintings from Toledo—its collection is eclectic. On one side of the museum, visitors can view ancient elephant tusks and animals bones; on another, decapitated and de-limbed Classical statues from the second and third centuries; and on another, El Greco's painting "Assumption of the Virgin," perhaps the museum's most famous work.

toledo

We know you do your booking online! View more listings at **www.letsgo.com.**

ALBERGUE LOS PASCUALES

HOSTEL $

Cuesta de Pascuales, 8 ☎925 28 24 22 www.alberguelospascuales.com

Similar to the Albergue Juvenil hostel in Madrid (and, for that matter, any of the hostels of the same namesake in Spain), Pascuales is clean, comfortable, and close to anything and everything you need in Toledo. When you arrive at the city center, la Plaza de Zocodover, you just need to walk straight and to the right, where you will find a set of stairs that lead directly down to the hostel. It couldn't get any easier to find. The hostel is quiet, probably because most travelers who spend a night in the city do just that—only one night, if that, since Toledo can easily be conquered in a day. Free Wi-Fi, free breakfast (if you'll take small pastries, muffins, and a cup of coffee or tea as breakfast) is provided, as are small storage lockers (no carry-ons will be able to fit), and linens. The hostel's managers are thoughtful and helpful, and if you don't speak much Spanish you should get along just fine, though you may not get the best restaurant tips. Make sure to check out the map that the hostel manager provides when you check in, on which they mark up and circle various points of interest that you'll want to look for while in the city.

i €14.30; privates and mixed rooms available. ☼ Reception open 8:30am-8:30pm. Check in after 1pm; check out by 10:30am. Breakfast from 8:30am-10am.

If you were lucky enough to be in the area in 2014, the museum celebrated the 400th anniversary of El Greco's death by collecting his works from around the world—including "View of Toledo," which is housed in New York City's Metropolitan Museum of Art, and "Knight with His Hand on His Breast," housed at the nearby Prado Museum in Madrid. While his works have returned to their international owners, the exhibition rejuvenated the Museo de Santa Cruz, perhaps paving the way for an even brighter (literally and figuratively) and more dynamic future.

i Free. ☼ Open M-Sa 9am-7pm, Su and holidays 10am-2pm.

ALCANTARA BRIDGE

BRIDGE

Toledo

As the saying goes, you'll be crossing a lot of bridges in life, but never one like the Alcántara. This ancient Roman bridge connects the steep hills of central Toledo to its northeastern edge and crosses over the tranquil Tagus River, just near a man-made rapid that provides the perfect tinkling water effect to complete the awe-inspiring experience. Built around 105 CE at the request of Roman Emperor Trajan, the bridge spans approximately 190 meters across the river and 45 above it. The archway over the central pier is inscribed with words supposedly from Trajan's reign: Pontem perpetui mansurum in saecula, "I have built a bridge that will last forever." Seems like he did a good job at that. The bridge has survived both the elements and a number of wars from pre-modern times, including partial destruction by the Moors in the 13th century and by the Spanish against the French in the 19th century—but even so, that which is left intact is nearly 2,000 years old. If you're visiting from the heart of Toledo—anywhere near Plaza Zocodover—you're in for quite a trek. Walk down what seems like a million flights of stairs to arrive at the foot of the bridge—and of course, to return, climb right back up. The positive side? It's a great leg workout. Plus,

spain

if you walk around the Huerta del Rey, or the King's botanical garden (read: the dirt, albeit beautiful, trails bordering the Tagus River), you can catch a view of the bridge from all sorts of different angles (Instagram, anyone?) in addition to catching another great workout.

MONASTERY OF SAN JUAN DE LOS REYES

C. Reyes Católicos, 17

MONASTERY

☎925 22 38 02 www.sanjuandelosreyes.org

This naturally lit monastery smells like fresh flowers. Inside the structure is a verdant, lush garden, surrounded by cool grey brick and spiraling arabesque towers. Visitors can view the garden, the upstairs patio, and the single nave, with seats, an altarpiece, and religious symbols—small spaces, sure, but beautiful and pristine nonetheless. With your €8 wristband you can find peace here as many times as needed, so long as you keep the band attached to your wrist and find reasons to need tranquility.

The Monastery of San Juan de Los Reyes was commissioned by the Catholic monarchs in Toledo in 1476 to honor the Castilian victory over the Portuguese in the Battle of Toro. Initially, the structure was designed to hold the monarchs' tombs, but eventually the monarchs gave the monastery to the Franciscan order. Designed by architect Juan Guas, the structure represents a fusion of Spanish-Flemish Gothic style, but a fire during the French invasion in 1808 destroyed the original altarpiece and other facets of the building. Thus, architect Arturo Mélida carried out a Neo-Gothic reconstruction with traces of Romanticism in the late 1800s (don't be disappointed when you learn some parts of the building are not, in fact, 500 years old).

The Monastery is a shady and, for Toledo, unfrequented spot (don't hold me to this on Saturdays) for tourists, so after a day of trekking up and down the many hills of the city, take a rest and enjoy a little bit of history. San Juan Los Reyes is within short walking distance of the Iglesia de Santo Tomé, a number of synagogues, and of course, a lot of food options like tabernas and bars to get your rejuvenated once more.

i €2.50. ⏰ Open Mar-Oct 15 daily 10am-6:45pm; Oct 16-Feb daily 10am-5:45pm.

FOOD

LIZARRAN

C. Toledo de Ohio, 3

BAR, CAFE $

☎914 90 28 05 www.lizarran.es

Stop in at Lizarran for three minutes or three hours. This lively bar, cafe, cafeteria, and whatever other type of Spanish restaurant exists, is a multipurpose space that accommodates people looking for a quick bite or those who seek a long conversation with friends over coffee and lunch. Peek in during the morning for a snappy cup of cafe con leche or at night for a full bar and a game of fútbol. Anyone who's hungry and looking for a pit stop is welcome.

Lizarran's menu is diverse, but perhaps its most popular dishes are its small (but filling, and inexpensive!) tapas sandwiches, like salmon quiche or bacon-chicken salad on bread. Sort of like a classy buffet, you can open up the sandwich display cases in the front of the restaurant and serve yourself a bit of finger food, for anywhere from €1-2 a pop. They also serves traditional Southern Spanish raciones for €5.90, a "doble cerveza" for €1.50, menús del día for €10—and even for those who don't need all of the food served in a menú del día, an "express" meal (one meal, as opposed to two, a drink, and a dessert) for €7.50.

The restaurant is part of a small Spanish chain that was founded in Barcelona in 1988. Since then, it has expanded internationally into other parts of Europe, Asia, and South America. But don't let its global presence dissuade you from eating here in favor of another "authentic" restaurant. The Toledo-based cafe caters its menu toward foods of the region, serving Toledo's tradition-al-style stew (a favorite among customers). Plus, its servers are so friendly, the atmosphere so upbeat and local, and the prices so cheap in a rather expensive town, that it's difficult to pass up on a few tapas here.

i Tapas €1-2. Café con leche €1.40. Raciones €5.90. Beer €1.50. ☼ Open daily 10:30am-midnight.

POSADA EL CRISTO DE LA LUZ
ARABIC $$

C. Cristo de La Luz ☎622 54 12 97 http://posadacristodelaluz.com

If Toledo's the city of three cultures, it must also be the city of three cuisines. That's your cue to go hunting for some good Arabic food, and it won't be too difficult here, because the Moors have had a foothold in Toledo since before the Spaniards even arrived. One such Arabic restaurant, Posada El Cristo de la Luz, looks like it hasn't changed a bit it since before the Spanish conquered Toledo in 1085 and tourists began flocking not soon after. Enter the restaurant up its stone stairs and through its terrace (don't eat there, more expensive!), where you'll enter what looks like your cool Grandma's attic—that is, if your Grandma smokes hookah. Plush blue, red, and golden cushions invite you to sit, while plenty of stone-rimmed mirrors and glinting reflective surfaces allow you to admire yourself while chowing down on that steamy platter of falafel and hummus. The restaurant is dimly lit, fragrant, and quite warm and comfortable. What's even better—they don't play that corny imitation "Arabic" music for which many Middle Eastern restaurants have a penchant. Instead, expect soft, contemporary string music and jazz.

Though this place may look like your cool Grandma's attic, no need to worry about her cooking. Everything at Posada El Cristo de la Luz is tender, savory, and flavorful mixed with rich spices and cool herbs. Crunchy falafel and cucumber cream costs €4, and fatair (a mix of cheese, meat, and spinach) costs €6.

Finally, for those of us unaccustomed to the concepts of siesta and "cocina abierta" (open kitchen), Posada El Cristo de la Luz will come as a refreshing exception, especially after an hour of hunting for restaurants from 4-6pm. Yes, Posada El Cristo de la Luz has an open kitchen all the time, and they even serve their €10 menú del día after 6pm (though they don't include a dessert, but no one's perfect).

i Menú del día €10. Entrees €3-7. ☼ Open M-Th 12:30pm-midnight, F-Su 12:30pm-2am.

NIGHTLIFE

DRAGOS
BAR

C. Sillerias, 11 ☎925 67 22 23 www.facebook.com/pages/Dragos-Night-Toledo

First things first: people don't come to Toledo to party. Sure, there are a number of bars and pubs in the area open later into the night, but most close anywhere from midnight-2am, significantly earlier than do any of the bars and clubs in neighboring Madrid. Dragos, one of these bars, is a great find in the sleepy town of Toledo. It's a hub for young students and travelers to meet with friends, grab a few drinks, and soak up the warm Toledo air after dinnertime, to relax after a day of climbing the steep city's hills, or just to catch up. Located right off la Plaza de Zocodover, Dragos it is easy to find, fairly inexpensive, and a nice, laid-back intimate bar that doubles as a restaurant during the daytime. Plus, with a television set in the corner of the bar for watching fútbol games, large windows apt for people watching, and an open terrace perfect for lounging in the warm evening breeze with a group of friends, this bar offers more than a few good drinks.

Try a tequila shot, complete with lime and salt, or other shots, for €1-2, a medium-sized beer for €1.50, a regular-sized beer for €2, or mixed drinks from €3-6. The bartender is a friendly, funny man who speaks broken Spanish (together, you may just have a primitive conversation) and encourages you to drink more, and more (that's right, the life of the party in Toledo). While Dragos's kitchen closes at nighttime, stop by during the day for a taste of its delicious, traditional *menús del día* offerings (€12). No matter what time you visit, you're sure to spot a person or two taking a break from the bright Toledo sun and hills to enjoy a meal and a drink at this hole-in-the wall bar.

i Shots €1-2. Beer €1.50-2. Mixed drinks €3-6. ⏰ Open M-Th 7:30am-1:30am, F-Su 7:30am-2:30am.

ESSENTIALS

Practicalities

- **TOURIST OFFICES:** There are a number of tourist information offices and checkpoints throughout the small city, but one of your best options is Castilla La Mancha, located on Puerta de Bisagra, (☎925 220 843), open M-F 9am-6pm, Sa 9am-7pm, Su 9am-3pm. Also try the Municipal Tourism Office in the Plaza del Consistorio, (☎925 254 030), open daily from 10am-6pm. Once you get into the Plaza de Zocodover, there's a tourist information spot just down the street called Casa de Mapa (yes, ask for a map here). (*i* Open daily from 11am-7pm.) They will also likely give you directions to your hostel, since the city is so small. Additionally, maps are available at the train station, and your hostel will likely give you a map outlining specific attractions in the city. Do make sure to take one with you. It will probably be more helpful than Google—for once in your life.

Emergency

- **EMERGENCY NUMBERS:** ☎112. **Ambulance:** ☎092.

- **POLICE: Local police:** ☎92 525 59 00. **Municipal Police** ☎092. **National police:** ☎091.

- **MEDICAL SERVICES:** There are a few hospitals inside of Toledo that still function today. Try the Hospital Virgen de la Salud, located at 30 Avenue de Barber (☎925 26 92 00).

Getting There and Getting Around

Outside of the main, hilly center of Toledo is Toledo's train station (Paseo de la Rosa), which serves Renfe trains and in front of which urban buses stop every few minutes. From Madrid, taking a high speed Renfe train to Toledo for €12.70 lasts about 30 minutes, whereas a bus from the Plaza Eliptica Bus Station can take about 1.5 hours, but can cost €9 or less. A car ride from Madrid to Toledo also takes about an hour, since the city is approximately 43 miles south of Madrid on the A-42 highway. Exits to Toledo are well posted along this highway.

From the train station, you can choose to walk to the city center (which is definitely doable, albeit an upward trek), catch a taxi, or take a €2.50 city bus just outside of the station to la Plaza de Zocodover, which takes around 10 minutes (probably your best option). Within the city, there is no public transportation besides the urban buses and taxis, which mainly stop on Cuesta del Alcázar and Cuesta de la Vega. Everything in Toledo is within walking distance. This will be your best, cheapest, and easiest option, since streets are often very narrow and cars cannot pass through.

Even if you're only staying in Toledo for one day or overnight, it's useful to know the ins-and-outs of the city's services, since constant heat and lots of climbing can prove particularly hazardous.

toledo

valencia

Valencia's a lot like Madrid—cultural, artistic, festive—only unlike Madrid, it's in the middle of somewhere: the beach. Make the four-hour bus trip southeast of Spain's capital and find yourself in a bustling beach town steeped with ancient culture, crazy nightlife, and of course, paella. From the impressive modern architecture of the city's behemoth entertainment complex, the City of Arts and Sciences, to the tallest (and one of the oldest) spots in town, the Cathedral (which purportedly holds the Holy Grail), Valencia combines the old and the new, a perfect fit for anyone who ventures over. When you're visiting, don't forget to stop by the central market (Mercat Central) for a famous Valencian orange, Horchateria Santa Catalina for the city's sweet drink orxata (horchata, only the original kind made of tiger nuts—you'll either love it or hate it), and any local bar for a taste of Agua de Valencia, the city's lifeblood alcoholic drink. And in case you're wondering, most everything in Valencia is written in Valencia, a dialect of Catalan. Most people speak Spanish and English too, though, so don't even bother learning the phrase "benvingut" (welcome).

SIGHTS

PALACIO DEL MARQUES DE DOS AGUAS
PALACE

C. del Poeta Querol, 2   ☎963 51 63 92 http://mnceramica.mcu.es

You've probably seen a lot of museums while traveling. Museums with lots of paintings by really famous people, or sculptures, or even piles of trash re-appropriated and labeled as "art." But have you seen an entire museum dedicated to ceramics? The former home of a family of Venetian nobles, the Palacio del Marques de Dos Aguas now functions as just that, hosting an impressive collection of pottery from the second century to the twentieth. The "palace"—or, a very fancy, very large house—dates back to the 18th century and was built in Baroque/Rococo style with alabaster.

Before you enter the museum, make sure to take a long look at the exterior facade. The two carved men on the front of the museum represent the two river mouths (dos aguas) of the city, while a "rotating Virgin" also graces the front of the palace. Yes, the family had a Virgin Mary placed on its outer facade complete with the ability to turn inwards to face the house dwellers when they were inside, or to face the street when they weren't home (great cue for robbers, right?).

The labyrinthine palace is lavish, to say in the least. Complete with crystal chandeliers, plush velvet couches, classical frescoes, and priceless jewelry (all on display or part of the architecture of the building itself), the museum holds a wide array of aristocratic objects that give viewers a taste of what life must have been like for the nobles of Valencia and Spain in the mid-18th century. Beautiful painted bowls and china from Asia and Europe can be viewed in the museum in additional to special exhibitions, like a history of fans (the waving kind, not the person kind—though both do wave, we suppose) from the 18th century onward.

The best news? Students get in free! If you've already graduated and don't have an old ID card, pay €3 to visit all four floors of painting, jewelry, and of course, ceramics.

i €3, students free. Free Sa after 4pm and Su. ⌚ Open Tu-Sa 10am-2pm and 4-8pm, Su 10am-2pm.

BIOPARC VALENCIA
ZOO

Pío Baroja, 3   ☎902 250 340 www.bioparcvalencia.es/en

Lions, tigers, bears—in central Valencia—oh my! The city is very (and by very, we mean VERY) proud of its in situ (a.k.a. no cages) zoo for animals of all shapes and sizes. The 10-hectare zoo is located at the west end of the city's Jardín del Turia—the giant, river-shaped series of parks and recreational centers that snakes through Valencia—and hosts a variety of animals from Africa. Biopark describes itself as "a zoological park of a new generation," implementing a new concept of "zoo immersion" by reconstructing animals' natural habitats and hiding the barriers between animals and the public. Instead of using railings and barricades to separate animals and people, the park uses "natural" barriers like streams and rocks, in order to immerse zoo-goers in the habitats of the animals while not endangering either. While partly intended to be educational, reconstructing the animals' natural habitats also emphasizes the park's dedication to conservation and preservation of endangered species.

During your visit, you'll completely forget that the zoo is located in the middle of an urban, bustling beach city. From its quaint ponds to its wide grassy landscapes, the zoo really does feel like a world away from city life. In addition to all-access day passes, Bioparc offers a number of events and special themed days for zoo goers to enjoy and learn more about the flora and fauna they are viewing. Try for World Wetlands Day, Africa Day, or World Environment Day.

On their website and at the front entrance the park also lists the times it feeds certain animals, like its elephants and monkeys.

While the price of a single-day visit is nothing to go bananas over, students under the age of 25 with a valid ID card do receive a 15-percent discount off an otherwise €23.80 ticket. Can you do math? That's €20.23 folks. Sometimes being a student has its perks.

i €23.80, students €20.23. ☑ Open Apr-June daily 10am-8pm; July-Aug daily 10am-9pm; Sept-Oct daily 10am-7pm; Nov-Mar daily 10am-6pm.

L'IBER MUSEO DE LOS SOLDADITOS DE PLOMO   MUSEUM
C. Caballeros, 20-22   ☎963 918 675 www.museoliber.org

Imagine if toys came to life, just as they do in the Toy Story movies. If that was the case, L'Iber Museo de Los Soldaditos de Plomo would be a frantic, bustling place. The Museum was opened to the public in 2007, after local Valencian Álvaro Noguera Giménez embarked on a project in the early 1980s to create a museum of historical miniature figures. His own toys constituted the early foundations of the museum, which now holds more than a million pieces and displays to the public approximately 85,000 of them—the most expansive and complex collection the world has ever seen. The museum is housed in an ancient Gothic palace that was originally the home of the Marquis of Malferit, and each of its rooms on the second floor that hold figurines feels quite homey—perfect for keeping toys.

Walk around the museum's rooms and view figurines of Russian soldiers, ancient Christians walking the Corpus Christi procession, Real Madrid CF and and FC Barcelona players facing off in the early 20th century. The figurines are incredibly detailed; so intricately carved and painted you may as well believe they truly are alive. Watch emotions unfold, actions begin to play out in these still, frozen scenes. The diorama settings the figurines dwell within are also extremely well done. Powdery snow dusts, battlefields, and leafy trees populate verdant meadows. Rooms are organized by theme—Napoleonic, Antiquity, Corpus Christi, Daily Life, and more.

Maybe visiting a miniatures museum doesn't sound like the most exciting thing to do during your stay in Valencia. You may think that, but don't be too quick to judge. It's an incredibly worthwhile and inexpensive museum, a sort of hole-in-the-wall many college students don't think about. The museum showcases a different type of art—miniatures—that provides a refreshing alternative to typical museum works like paintings and sculptures. So channel your inner wide-eyed-with-wonder child. The toys are waiting.

i €5, €3 students. ☑ Open W-Su 11am-2pm and 4-7pm.

CITY OF THE ARTS AND SCIENCES
Av. del Profesor López Piñero, 7

MUSEUM, AQUARIUM
☎902 10 0031 www.cac.es

Just when you thought Valencia couldn't get more diverse, you stumble upon the City of Arts and Sciences. A city within a city, Valencia's biggest tourist attraction. The entertainment complex holds multiple attractions, including a science museum, an aquarium, an Imax theatre, a botanical garden, an opera house, and more. Even if you don't have time to peek inside each of these attractions (and you won't, no one will, ever), it's worth a quick trip just to marvel at the architectural feat that is the complex. Its science museum was designed in the shape of a whale's skeleton; its aquarium takes the shape of a water lily. Thousands of liters of water compose shallow fountains and pools within the complex, within some of which people can ride in hamster wheels or go kayaking.

Just take it all in slowly, and choose wisely. The City of Arts and Sciences' aquarium, called L'Oceanogràfic, is definitely recommended, since it's the largest aquarium in all of Europe, clocking in at 10,000 square meters and 42 million liters of water. The aquarium is home to hundreds of different species, including walruses and turtles. Walk into one tunnel, look up at the ceiling, and try not to

get a room!

We know you do your booking online! View more listings at **www.letsgo.com**.

RED NEST
C. Paz, 36

HOSTEL $
☎963 42 71 68 www.nesthostelsvalencia.com

When you walk up Calle de La Paz to Red Nest's front door, you will see a sign advertising the hostel as the best in Valencia. With a full bar, a location right in the center of the city, and a vibrant social atmosphere, we don't doubt them. Come to Red Nest if you're looking to meet new people from around the world and remain close to the heart of Valencia's old city. The hostel mixes comfort with an energetic social scene, offering low-priced tapas and bar specials many nights a week, and also hosting a famous pub crawl (perhaps the best way to meet people) which stops at Valencia's best and most popular clubs, ending at the ultra cool L'umbracle terrace. Join Red Nest's staff for a tour of "Old" Valencia and "New Valencia" as well as an urban graffiti tour to see the best artwork in the city (for free!). The hostel has plenty of common spaces, especially its kitchen, where many people opt out of restaurant dining and instead come together to share a meal and conversation.

The staff is friendly and helpful, willingly pointing you in the direction of the beach, the market (a great place to grab cheap meals instead of eating out), and other sites in the city. Check out their restaurant and sightseeing recommendations. Included in the costs of the hostel are free Wi-Fi, clean linens, and storage lockers. Breakfast is not included. It's €8, but delicious, with pastries, orange juice, and other snacks. Tea and coffee (with milk and sugar on the side) are free and provided all day in the kitchen, which closes around midnight.

The hostel is so popular it even has a second location just around the corner, called the Purple Nest. Both are relatively the same (though apparently the Red Nest's bar is busier and better most nights). You get access to both of them, so your call—and your drinks.

i Dorms €14-16, privates €20-22. ☼ Reception 24hr. Check out by 10:30am. Breakfast from 8:30am-10am.

spain

scream when you realize sharks are swimming above your head. That's just part of the fun.

The city's science museum, called El Museu de les Ciències Príncipe Felipe, is also worth a full day trip. This interactive museum is home to a number of breathtaking exhibits that display, for example, the sequencing of the human chromosome, or a live electricity animation.

Besides its regular exhibits and activities, the City of Arts and Sciences hosts a number of concerts, fairs, and parties. One of Valencia's biggest clubs parties each night in the Umbracle, an open-air botanical garden of sorts. There's even a stage located in one of the complex's many pools—still waiting on that concert, but it's bound to be good.

i Sciencemuseum and IMAX cinema €12.60. Museum and aquarium €29.70. IMAX and aquarium €30.30. All three €36.25. Student discount of 15%. ☉ Open M-F 10am-6pm, Sa 10am-7pm, Su 10am-6pm.

FOOD

HORCHATERÍA SANTA CATALINA
RESTAURANT $$
Pl. de Santa Catalina, 6 ☎963 91 23 79 www.horchateriasantacatalina.com

If you've ever lived in Southern California or have visited Mexico, you're bound to have tried horchata, a sugary sweet cinnamon and rice drink perfect for summer days (and featured in a popular Vampire Weekend song of the same namesake). Thought the drink originated in Mexico too? Think again. Valencia's rendition of the drink—orxata—is made from small, wrinkly seeds called tiger nuts. The end result is a watery, semi-sweet drink. Some love it, some hate it, and others say it tastes like carrots. Try it to find out. The drink is rumored to have come into being when Muslims brought tiger nuts into Valencia, and one legend links the origins of orxata's name to King James I of Aragon. According to legend, he was given the drink by a local girl and apparently really liked it, exclaiming in Catalan "Açò és or, xata!" ("That's gold, darling!" Sound it out).

This small Horchatería offers its namesake drink for a cheap price, as well as chocolates, ice creams, pastries (try a classic farton with your horchata drink), coffees, and liquors. If you're feeling a bit hungrier than your typical cafe con leche and snack, try rice, ham salad, muscles, or soup. This place seems to have it all, and for being near the city center, offers its food and drink for a relatively cheap price. €2 for a cool cup of horchata, other food and courses cost from of €4-10.

Santa Catalina is located in historic central Valencia next to the church of Santa Catalina and near the city's cathedral. We suggest grabbing an ice-cold orxata to go on a breezy Valincian afternoon and strolling through the beautiful downtown district of the city. You can't beat leisure and good eats on vacation.

i Orxata (horchata) €2. Other food €4-10. ☉ Open daily 8:15am-9:30pm.

MERCAT CENTRAL
MARKET
Pl. Ciudad de Brujas ☎963 82 91 00 www.mercadocentralvalencia.es

What's the cheapest way a college student can eat in Valencia? The Mercat Central (in Spanish: Mercado Central), or Central Market of the city. Housed is a beautiful building covered in colorful yellow and blue ceramics and spiraling Arabesque style designs, the market is a near-daily hotspot for both locals and visitors to the city. In total, the market covers 8,160 square meters and hosts nearly 400 merchants who sell their fresh produce, fish, and other foods on a daily basis, with nearly 1500 people involved in the production and selling of these items. The central market is the largest of its kind in Europe, and with prices cheaper than any good menú del día, you're not going to want to miss out.

valencia

While eating at restaurants is one way to get a taste of local food and culture, many traveling students simply cannot afford eating out each night. Instead, try your hand at the market. Cooking up something in your hostel is both fun and rewarding, if you have the time and space to do so.

Get transported back to a fresh Valencia farm as you bite into a fresh apple, a delicious jamon iberico sandwich, or a cup of cool, rich yogurt. There's doubtless something for everyone here—meat lovers, vegans, even people who live solely off desserts (and what's so bad about that?). Eating at the market makes for a fun morning away from the heat and touristy crowds of central Valencia. Plus, if you play your cards right, you can grab a fresh bag of produce and other foods for under €10—and feed yourself for a week.

i Prices vary depending on vendor. ☒ Open M-Sa 8am-2:30pm.

LA RIUÀ
C. del Mar, 27

RESTAURANT $$
☎963 91 45 71 www.lariua.com

The napkins at La Riuà are thicker than your hostel's blankets—a sure sign of fancy, and definitely over budget. But fear not, broke college student! While you'll see a number of 40-year old European men in rolled shirt sleeves and Rolexes ordering copious amounts of rose wine, La Riuà offers hot, authentic paella starting only at €10. The wait to eat your meal can be an upwards of 30 minutes (they want to make sure you're REALLY hungry, right?), but when you see that simmering pan of soft yellow rice, potatoes, and meat heading in your direction, you'll forget everything else.

Try La Riuà's pork, potato, and garbanzo beans paella or its famous Paella Valenciana, complete with savory seafood and fresh rabbit, for only €10 for one or two people. Larger pans of the region's most famous dish are offered starting at €12 and can cost as much as €23, though when ordering these dishes most people eat with groups of friends or family. Fine wines, desserts, and that gaudy mineral water in its blue glass bottle are also served, again starting cheap and getting much more expensive as the quality and quantity of food and drink rise.

The atmosphere in which you will dine matches the quality of food served perfectly. The walls of La Riuà are covered with blue and white ceramic plates and tasteful Spanish flags and trinkets. Even its floors—adobe red tile with ceramic tile inserts—are beautiful. Dine alone or with friends; the restaurant accommodates both experiences. Sweet free white wine shots are also provided to diners at the end of each meal (probably one of the fanciest shots you will ever take). Just make sure not to eat the bread they tempt you with as you are agonizing over the long wait for your meal. As usual, no es gratis.

i Paella €10. Salads €10. Meats €12-18. Fish €15. Café con leche €1.40. Raciones €5.90. Beer €1.50. ☒ Open M 2-4:15pm, Tu-Sa 2-4:15pm and 9-11pm.

NIGHTLIFE

ESPIT CHUPITOS BAR
Dr. Chiarri, 8

BAR
☎649 19 61 65 www.espitchupitos.com

Have you ever seen a bar on fire? Taken a fiery shot of liquor and inhaled its fumes when you've finished? If you visit Espit Chupitos Bar in Valencia, you're in for one of the most exciting rounds of shots you've probably ever experienced. Walk into the bar after an early night of pub-crawling and stare at its chalkboard wall listing more than 600 different kinds of shots offered. Yes, 600. We didn't even know that many existed, but apparently creativity is one of Espit's best qualities.

If you name it, they have it. Jello shots, Girl Scout Cookie shots, orange cream shots, pop rocks, and even shots on fire—literally. You can actually choose to roast a marshmallow on your shot should you so desire. Yes, it's about the alcohol, but it's also about the experience of consuming the alcohol. Slurp up shots in straws, drink shots from a bowl, lick…. the Monica Lewinsky shot. The bar's a great place to pregame for Valencia's hottest clubs with friends. However, this bar is not at all for the faint hearted.

Espit charges €1-2 per shot, but you won't need too many to start feeling their effects. A dark, grimy, intimate atmosphere (everyone's crowded around the bar, everyone's rubbing up against one another) makes the shot-taking experience even better for the group. Don't expect too much mingling with strangers, though. Visiting the bar is a bonding experience for people already in groups together, not a place to meet new local friends.

For those who want to be the butt of a few jokes after visiting the bar, Espit offers other types of drinks, like beers and cocktails. But since you're at a Chupitos bar, it's kind of mandatory that you take at least one shot. Then you can mix in a few other drinks.

i Shots €1-2. Beer and mixed drinks €3-6. 🕐 Open W-Sa 11pm-3:30am.

UNIC DAILY GOODNESS
BAR

Jaume, 1 ☎963 92 05 70 http://unicdailygoodness.com

Ah, nothing like hearing a familiar Madonna song in a bar 3,000 miles from home. At Unic, the prices may be a little high, but the music, the atmosphere, and the dancing are worth a couple of euros. A retro, cosmopolitan, trendy/urban bar located in the popular Carmen neighborhood of the city, Unic is a hub for young people looking to start their night with a bit of energy and playfulness. Jam out to classic American '80s hits, and if you're not too drunk yet, take a bit of time to admire the bar's classy decor. Typewriters and old telephones decorate the walls (how they stay put, we have no idea), and an artsy cardboard deer head stands vigilant just behind the bar (thank you, Unic, for inadvertently supporting animal rights!). Find yourself in a happy mix of locals and recent European (or American) college graduates. You'll be able to understand some language while still enjoying a wholeheartedly "local" experience.

The bar is known for its cocktails and vodka tonics, so make sure to try one if you visit. Be cautioned: the drinks here are not cheap (but quality does improve with an increase in price, the world seems to have determined). Your least expensive mixed drink here is classic Agua de Valencia, for €7, and, if you somehow find yourself a rich European prince for the weekend to try out a champagne, your most expensive drink will be veuve clicquot for €120. Don't worry—there's not too much in between €7 and €120. The average price of a drink at Unic is €10.

Start your night laidback and fun with Unic. But if you're looking to save up some money for the clubs, it might be good to pregame before and take a sip of Agua later.

i Drinks €7-12.

L'UMBRACLE
BAR

Av. Del Saler, 5 ☎671 66 80 00 http://umbracleterraza.com

You visited the museum during the daytime, now it's time to party there at night. Check out this famous open-air club at 1am on a Saturday night—its busiest and craziest hour. Situated in the heart of the City of Arts and Sciences, L'Umbracle is loud, sweaty, and packed (luckily for you, the cool ocean air gives the place a nice breeze during its hottest nights). The live DJ plays fast-paced house music and bright lights color the floor and walls of the space, sort of like a 21st-century disco under the stars.

The cover price is a hefty €15, which is comparable to that at major clubs in Madrid like Kapital or Joy Eslava. The environment is also similar to these clubs. Dress your best (look your best), and come with girls. All problems will

valencia

be solved. Be warned: security guards are known to card people they don't deem "good enough" for their club, and will sometimes impose a 21+ age barrier toward entrance even though Spain's drinking age is 18. If you make it through, congratulations! If not, you're just too good for this city anyway.

Though L'Umbracle is party central, if you need to cool down for a minute after a long night of drinking and dancing, you'll find plenty of space and seats to mingle and chat with friends. As with any club, drink prices can be rather exorbitant, so you're better off pregaming at a bar or pub prior to visiting the club. Check out their website to see if any concerts or events will be going on during the time you're thinking of visiting.

i Cover €15. Mixed drinks starting at €8. Beer €4. ☼ Open Sa 1am-late.

ESSENTIALS
Practicalities

- **TOURIST OFFICES:** The city has a number of tourist offices, including one in the airport and several in the city center. Consider purchasing a Valencia Tourist Card that is available in 24, 48, or 72-hour increments. It offers free public transportation (bus, metro, etc.) throughout the city, including the journey to and from the Valencia airport, free entry to public museums and monuments, and various citywide discounts.

Emergency

- **EMERGENCY NUMBERS:** ☎112. **Ambulance:** ☎061.

- **POLICE: Local police:** ☎092. **Mossos d'Esquadra (regional police):** ☎088. **National police:** ☎091. **Tourist police:** Las Ramblas, 43 ☎93 256 24 30 *i* Ⓜ︎Liceu. ☼ Open 24hr.

- **PHARMACIES:** Like everywhere else in Spain, pharmacies are marked by lighted crosses, either green or blue. Most pharmacies close at 10pm and are closed for siesta time, from around 2-4pm.

- **MEDICAL SERVICES:** There are a number of hospitals and healthcare facilities in the city. Try Hospital de València al Mar for general services. Located at Rio Tajo 1. ☎34 963 352 500. The General Hospital is located at Avda. Tres Cruces and can be reached at ☎963 352 500.

Getting There
By Plane

Great news! Valencia has its own airport. It's located a few miles outside of the city, on Carretera del Aeropuerto, and connects about 15 different European countries to Valencia, Spain. Vueling, Turkish Airlines, Air France, and Air Berlin, among others, fly through Valencia. The city's metro line 3 runs between the airport and the city center, and a one-way ticket costs €1.50, while a return ticket costs €2.90. The metro station is on the ground floor of the regional flights terminal. A number of taxis also line up just outside of the airport and cost €1.08 per kilometer. Taxi trips from the airport cost €5.40+ the regular fares. A flat rate of €20 is applied to trips from the airport to the city center.

By Bus

Another great way to get to Valencia (and decidedly cheaper than flying) is by bus. From Madrid, a bus ride takes 4-5 hours and costs about €25. From the bus station, you can take a city bus (like number 8) to the city center (Av. Menéndez Pidal, 11).

Getting Around

By Bus

Valencia has a metro system, but it's not very useful for transportation in the city, as is used mainly by commuters from the suburbs. Instead, Valencia has a strong urban bus network (Valencia Municipal Transport Company, or EMT) with 52 different routes. This will be your best option for getting around the city, which is rather sprawling and often difficult to conquer by foot. Fares cost €1.50 per ride.

By Bike

Valencia's a flat city with tons of bike lanes ready for tourists! Try renting with one of several different companies, like Valencia Bikes or Valenbisi.

sevilla

Tell anyone in the South of Spain that you're visiting Sevilla and the typical response will be, "So lucky, I love that city." We're still waiting to hear from someone who does not love the beautiful Andalusian capital. Stroll through the twisting streets of the ancient port city and discover centuries of history within the architecture, from the mosaic, Moorish Real Alcázar in the heart of Sevilla to the verdant, colorful Plaza de España just a few steps away. In the summer months, head over to the river at sunset for brilliant, golden views, and wait a couple hours for some of Spain's most vibrant nightlife. The city is rich, in its history, diversity, and people, offering visitors authentic southern Spain experiences while also catering to a burgeoning youth population lookin' for a good night on the town.

Sevilla was the hub of the empire in the 16th century during Spain's conquest of the Americas, since all goods had to be regulated through the city before being redistributed throughout Spain. In later years, globetrotter Ferdinand Magellan would depart from the port to start his voyage around the world. In the 11th century, Muslims ruled the land, and in the 18th, the city established one of the world's most renowned bull rings, drawing the attention of royalty and celebrity fighters from across the globe. Spend a day wandering the city and imagine life back in the golden days of Spain. Stumble upon the tobacco factory, the university, and the hospital. Mysteries and secrets hide around every corner. In Sevilla, you might learn a thing or two about the world.

SIGHTS

ALCAZAR
PALACE

Patio de Banderas
☎954 50 23 24 www.alcazarsevilla.org

If you've been traveling around in Spain for a while, you've probably seen your fair share of castles, cathedrals, etc. Maybe you're a little tired of them by now. Sure, they're beautiful, grand, historical, but you can't help but feel that they all look a little bit the same. If this sounds like you, take a trip to the Alcázar of Sevilla, a former Moorish palace overrun by the Spanish Catholics that still retains its old age, Arabic feel. Because its upper rooms are still used by the Spanish royal family (how and why, we aren't really sure), the Alcázar is one of the oldest palaces still in use worldwide.

Enter the 11th-century palace and get lost in its maze of large gardens and ceramic rooms. There is little to no furniture in the palace's interior—instead, find breathtaking, colorful tile work dappled with shells and Hand of Fatima motifs, as well as arabesques. The rooms are voluminous and broken only by typical Mudéjar archways, like those found in many mosques, like the Great Mosque of Cordoba. Don't get us started about the gardens. Walk through a few rooms in the palace and out into its many courtyards, like the Mannerist Garden of Troy, and find sleepy trees, bright bougainvillea branches, and plenty of doves.

What's incredible about the Alcázar is that, from the outside, it's a very unassuming—if not drab—building. Only visitors who pay the €9.50 (€2 for students!) can truly see the manifestation of the phrase "don't judge a book by its cover"). One would never believe how many gardens and architectural masterpieces can fit inside the walls of this fortress. Additionally, the Alcázar saw centuries of architectural alteration that influenced its current form. If you're an art history buff, you'll drool over the mixture of styles, from Mudéjar Renaissance to Baroque. Some contemporary thinkers may even consider the interior minimalist, if that's the intention 11th-century Muslims had when constructing their castle.

Have we convinced you yet? This place is one of the most stunning in Spain, if not in the entire world. Yes, praise humanity for its architectural feats.

i €9.50, reduced €4.50 . ☒ Open Apr-Sept daily 9:30am-7pm, Oct-Mar daily 9:30am-5pm.

PLAZA DE TOROS DE LA REAL MAESTRANZA DE CABALLERÍA DE SEVILLA   BULLRING
Paseo de Cristóbal Colón, 12   www.realmaestranza.com

Plaza de toros de la Real Maestranza de Caballería de Sevilla. That's quite a mouthful. If something's got a name this long (and the word Real, which means Royal, in it), you know it's worth a visit. Such is the case with Sevilla's famed bullring, allegedly the second oldest in the world (slightly younger than that in Ronda). Its construction began in 1749 and wasn't actually completed until more than 100 years later, in 1881. There are five gates in the main arena from which the matadors arrive and leave in addition to other functions.

Why is this bullring different than others? As the geometrically keen may notice, Sevilla's bullring is not in fact shaped like a circle. Instead, it takes the shape of an oval. Additionally, there is one prized gate in which the matador may exit, but only if he has gained the three "trophies" of his bullfight—two ears and the tail of the bull that he fights. Only when the matador completes this task does he have permission to exit through the ring's most important gate, which in Sevilla is called Puerta del Principe (Prince's Gate). The Sevillan Salida a Hombros occurs in the gate directly under the balcony where the royal family is intended to sit—hence the gate's name. (Does the royal family ever travel south of Madrid to watch a bullfight at Sevilla? Good question. Not really. Apparently, Juan Carlos liked to bring his daughter to the fights, but no precedent has yet been set by his son, Felipe, new king of Spain as of June 2014.)

In addition to the bullring, visitors can view a museum showcasing the bullring's history, including some of its celebrity bullfighters like Juan Belmonte, Joselito El Gallo, and their very spectacular costumes (silver, gold, silk). Entrance to both the museum and the bullring is by guided tour (you cannot guide yourself), which is offered in both English and Spanish (simultaneously). The tour takes about 40 minutes, but it is quite informative, and frankly, better than you would do on your own. The tours run roughly every 20 minutes, though times do vary. Additionally, should you desire to see a live bullfight, Sevilla's season runs from Easter Sunday to October 12 and includes around 20-25 fights in total. Prices for the fights vary, with the most expensive tickets costing upwards of €100. These seats will be right at the front, out of the sun, near all the action. Substantially cheaper tickets can be bought for seats across the stadiu.

i Tapas €3-8.75. Fish €12. Rice €10. Dessert €6. ☒ Open daily Apr-Oct 9:30am-9pm, Nov-Mar 9:30am-7pm.

CATHEDRAL
Av de la Constitución   CATHEDRAL
☎902 09 96 92 www.facebook.com/maravilaibiza

What's so special about Sevilla's Cathedral? A few things. First, it's the third-largest church in the world and the largest Gothic cathedral in the world. Second, its interior has the largest nave of any other Cathedral in Spain (42 meters high). And third, it's the burial site of our favorite explorer Christopher Columbus.

Sevilla's mammoth cathedral, located in the heart of the city center (actually, it may very well be the heart of the city, since everything seems to revolve around it), was constructed starting in 1402 and finished in a timely 104 years, during 1506. The locals who decided to build this new cathedral are reported to have said during the time "Let us build a church so beautiful and so grand that those who see it finished will think we are mad."

Maybe they were a bit mad after all. The cathedral has four facades, 15 doors, 80 chapels, 11,520 square meters in total floor space, and the world's largest altarpiece. Like many Catholic cathedrals of the time, the cathedral was built on the site of a 12th-century Moorish structure, the Almohad Mosque. The cathedral was intended to display Sevilla's newfound wealth and power after the period of Reconquista. Although the cathedral is built in the gothic style, it still retains a few traces of Moorish influence from the mosque, like the court in which visitors enter (the Patio de los Naranjos) and the then-minaret now-bell tower Giralda.

Alright, alright, cool history, big church we get it. But where are Columbus's remains? We know that's all you care about. His tomb is located just off the entrance to the cathedral. on the south side at the Puerta de San Cristóbal. No, this isn't where he was originally buried, which was in Valladolid, Spain, where

get a room!

Find more recommendations over at **www.letsgo.com**.

THE SEVILLA INN INN $$

C. Angeles, 11 ☎954 21 95 41 http://sevillabackpackers.es

The Sevilla Inn also has a prime location, just steps away from the Cathedral, the Alcázar of Sevilla, and the center of the city. Tucked away in the corner of Calle Ángeles, the hostel may not look like much from the outside, but once you step through its glass doors and up the stairs to its first floor and set of rooms, you'll realize you're inside what the owner calls a "typical" Sevillian household, complete with windy staircases, mosaic tiles, and plenty of windows. The kitchen is bright and accommodating, while the rooms are large with extremely comfortable bunk beds and storage lockers. On the first floor, the Inn offers a common room with a television, board games, couches, and outlets, as well as two bathrooms with showers (which surprisingly don't get too crowded). Walk up the stairs through the kitchen and you'll find yourself on the next floor. Keep going up, and you have a remarkable terrace, where the hostel offers paella making classes and drinking nights (€1 sangria!).

You're in for a relaxing and comfortable stay when you book at this backpacker's hostel. However, given the demand (especially during the summer time), you may be placed in a room (usually a single) in another building near the one that houses Sevilla Inn's reception. Wi-Fi in these buildings is quite spotty, so feel free to visit the main building for less spotty (though still not the best) Wi-Fi. Storage locks are available for purchase, and unlike many hostels. the reception may not provide you a map of the city right off the bat. Ask for one when you arrive; you'll be needing it.

i Mixed dorms €17-18. Privates €24-29. ☼ Reception 24hr. Check out by 11am.

sevilla

he died. His remains were shortly thereafter transferred to Sevilla, and then jumped around a bit (if you can say that about remains). In 1795, they ended up at the Havana Cathedral in Cuba, which Columbus had first encountered in his voyage of 1492. Upheaval from the 1902 Cuban revolution led Spain to transfer his remains to Sevilla, their resting place today. Visit for the history, the architecture, or Columbus. You're bound to learn a thing or two.

i €8, students under 25 €4. ⏰ Open M 11am-3:30pm, Tu-Sa 11am-5pm, Su 2:30-6pm.

FOOD

BAR ZURBARÁN
Pl. de Zurbaran

TAPAS $

☎954 22 96 34

Visit Bar Zurbarán for a taste of authentic Spain—warning, not for the faint of heart. This little nook, near Sevilla's famous "mushroom" structures, yet still hidden from the city's main touristy avenues, serves up platters of southern Spain's most famous dishes. Not sure what caracoles are? How about cola de toro? Huevas planchas? Better buy a Spanish dictionary or keep up with Google translate before heading to Zurbarán. (For the uninformed, those menu items are, respectively: snails, oxtail, and grilled frog eggs.) No, the waiters don't speak very good English, and menus are offered only in Spanish, but that's a good sign, right? You'll be hard-pressed to hear anything other than Spanish in this restaurant, in addition to the little plaza it occupies. Plus, tapas prices from €1 just go to show that this place is far from a tourist trap.

Despite the slightly frightening menu items listed, you'll still be able to find something for your non-adventurous palette. Try some classic croquettas (croquettes, small breadcrumbed dumpling-like tapas, only fried and stuffed with mashed potatoes or cream and Iberian ham), Jamon Iberico, and delicious tomato and olive oil paste with baguettes or other breads. Your satisfaction at this restaurant honestly depends on whether or not you have a dictionary in hand.

i Tapas €1-2. Raciones €4-8. ⏰ Open daily 8am-midnight.

LOS COLONIALES
Pl. Cristo De Burgos, 19

RESTAURANT $$

☎954 50 11 37 www.tabernacoloniales.es

Located in a city that's full of expensive tourist traps and a central plaza known for these traps, Los Coloniales provides its guests with authentic food and great service, all for a cheap cost. The restaurant has a dimly lit, intimate feel about it, with beautiful mosaic tiling and pots and pans hung up on the walls, just like your mom's kitchen. Eat inside, at the bar, or at a table (near to which hang large, chunky legs of Iberian ham) and enjoy a fair amount of people watching while savoring large portions of quail egg and chorizo, cheese fritters, or tenderloin with port sauce.

The staff is friendly and well versed in English (it is located in a touristy area, after all), and often the place can get so packed near dinnertime (anywhere from 8pm-10:30pm) that reservations may be necessary for those hoping to beat the crowds. Sip on some delicious white or red wine while watching a fútbol game with some energized fans. If you're looking for a spot to try some tapas, this is it. Additionally, Los Coloniales is popular among both locals and tourists, so while you'll have the typical German, British, American crowd, you may also strike up a conversation with a true, born and bred Sevillian (we challenge you to find these in the city center. They'll be of great use to you later).

i €2-15. ⏰ Open daily 12:30pm-12:15am.

NIGHTLIFE

The city is great for nightlife, but where do you go? Check out Calle Alemeda, near the center of the city, or Los Remedios. Also, during the summer, most locals head to the river or to nearby terraces, so walk in that direction and you're sure to find something for you.

BABILONIA

CLUB

Av. García Morato

Part indoor-part outdoor, perfect for the summer months. The club Babilonia, one of the hottest in Sevilla, has a beautiful ambiance to it. There are flickering candles that glow in the darkness, tropical palms (fake or real, we don't actually know) and thick curtains decorating the club, twinkling lights dangling from the trees, and well-dressed patrons. Like its name may suggest, Babilonia feels like a desert oasis (especially given the scorching midsummer Sevillan temperatures). The club has four different bars with plenty of drinks to go around, in addition to a number of plush seating arrangements for even the most relaxed of partygoers. There is a VIP section, coat check, and concierge service for those who desire it.

People say it feels modern, chic, and chill—when you want it to be. But if you're looking for a "relaxing" night of drinking and bar hopping, you're better off doing just that—bar hopping. Babilonia is a full-fledged club, opening at 11pm and closing only when the sun rises at 7am. Still, if you get tired after dancing the night away, you do have plenty of seats on which to rest—but only for a minute! Plenty of hookah to go around as well.

How much does it cost? That depends. Do you look nice enough? Do the bouncers like you? Work on those two things, and we'll get back to you. But seriously, you may find yourself charged anywhere from €10-30 depending on the night, if you are female, or if you're dressed well enough to suit the posh, Moroccan style of the discoteca. Drinks can also be a little pricy as well, which isn't too surprising. Better botellón before visiting the club, or else be prepared to break your bank for a night.

i Mixed drinks €6-10. Cover varies. 🕑 Open Th-Sa 11pm-7am in summer.

ESSENTIALS

Practicalities

- **TOURIST OFFICES:** The city's main tourist office is located at la plaza del Triunfo, near the Cathedral and the Alcázar. Visit for a map, directions, restaurant recommendations, etc. Its staff speaks a number of languages, including English and French.

Emergency

- **EMERGENCY NUMBERS:** ☎112. **Ambulance:** ☎061.

- **POLICE:** Patio de Banderas: ☎954 28 95 64.

- **PHARMACIES:** Most pharmacies follow the typical siesta schedule, opening at regular business hours, taking a break mid afternoon, and reopening until close. If you need to visit one from 2-5pm or after about 8-8:30pm, know that each neighborhood has a rotating system of Farmacia de Guardias. Each pharmacy location at one point or another in each neighborhood of the city takes on the responsibility of being the all-night or all-day pharmacy. Check out the dates and times of these openings on the window of every pharmacy or in a local newspaper.

- **MEDICAL SERVICES: Hospital Universitario Virgen del Rocío:** Manuel Siurot ☎955 01 20 00. **Hospital Universitario Virgen Macarena:** 34 Dr. Fedriani ☎955 00 80 00.

sevilla

Getting There

Sevilla is the capital of Andalucia, which means it's a very well connected city, both within and without. You can get to Sevilla from most parts of Spain by bus, train, or plane, and from Portugal by bus.

By Plane

The San Pablo airport is the region's main airport and connects with airports throughout Spain and Europe. It's located six miles outside of the main city, so you'll need to take a bus or taxi into Sevilla. The airport is relatively small (it only has one terminal) and serves low-cost carriers like Vueling and Ryanair. Taxis outside of the main terminal can take you to the city center for €15-22, and the trip lasts around 15 minutes. Alternatively, the airport offers a busline, Especial Aeropuerto, that runs to and from the airport, stopping at the two bus stations and the train station along the way.

By Train

Sevilla has one train station, Sevilla San Justa, which has AVE long distance and short distance trains to cities like Granada, Malaga, Cordoba, and Madrid. The train station is located on Avenida de Kansas City, and from here travelers can take buses that connect with the city center and the city's two bus stations. The ticket office is open daily from 8am-10pm and can be reached at ☎954 53 76 26. Coffee shops and restaurants are also located throughout the station in case you get hungry.

By Bus

Sevilla has two bus stations, la Estación del autobuses Plaza de Armas and the station at Prado de San Sebastián, the latter of which is about a 15-minute walk from the bus station. San Sebastián primarily serves the Andalucia region, like Ronda, Tarifa, Granada, and Cordoba. (☎954 41 71 11) Plaza de Armas primarily serves cities outside of the Andalucia region and Portugal. (☎954 90 80 40 or 954 90 77 37) Sevilla buses to and from the city center also connect with these stations. Check www.andalucia.com for more information.

Getting Around

Sevilla is a fairly well connected city that has a taxi, bus, and metro system, in addition to a tram that runs through the city center. Currently, its metro has one line with 22 stops, and runs 11 miles through the city and its metropolitan area. It starts at Ciudad Expo and ends at Olivar Quinto. Alternatively, you can use its city tram (tranvia, Metro Centro), which runs through different spots at the city center. The tram leaves from Plaza Nueva, and follows Avenida de la Constitucion past the Cathedral, stopping at the Archivo de Indias and then at San Fernando (Puerta Jerez), and terminates at the Prado de San Sebastian. It also runs in the opposite direction. Fares cost €1.20.

By Bus

Sevilla's buses are the heart and soul of its metro system. The buses cover all neighborhoods in the city and run from around 6am to 11:30pm, with night buses leaving from Prado de San Sebastian from 12am-2am. The city has "circular" buses (C3 and C4) that circle around the city center, while C5 follows a smaller route inside the center. Fares are €1.20. Visit www.tussam.es (in Spanish) for more information.

For travelers who are staying a day, one option for a potentially cheaper fare is one-day card (€4.50) for unlimited travel. Also consider a three-day card (€8.50). If you're staying for even longer, consider getting a Tarjeta Mulltiviaje, a card for which you pay a refundable €1.50 deposit. You then can pay €5 for 10 journeys without transfer (using more than one line), or €7 for 10 journeys with transfer. You can recharge at kiosks or estancos (tobacco sellers).

ibiza

You've read about it. You've seen it in the Wanted's music video for "Glad you Came." You can only dream about the party capital of the world, Ibiza, but somehow you're here and somehow you need to figure it all out, fast—before your money's gone and your massive hangover's a little too massive for comfort.

In order to fully experience Ibiza Town, the island's biggest nightlife hub, you'll need to bake in the sun all day, party on a few booze cruises, and, at 3am, hit the clubs just as everything's getting exciting. Expect little sleep and lots of debauchery (you don't know what goes on in the place until you've actually arrived). Look out for free entrance passes on the beach (since a €60 entrance fee will do a little more than break your bank) and bustling bars perfect for a pregame.

But Ibiza Town isn't just party central. During the daytime, when you're not lounging on one of the city's many crystalline beaches, check out the city center, where amidst a labyrinth of narrow, cobbled roads and beautiful white and blue cottages you'll find a Renaissance-era castle, cathedral, and some incredible ocean views.

It's a city with many faces but one thing's assured: you're in for a good time.

SIGHTS

CASTLE OF IBIZA
CASTLE
www.ibiza-spotlight.com

It's safe to say that when most young people visit Ibiza, touring castles isn't the first thing on their mind. But if you aren't too hung over from partying or sunburned from hours spent lying on the beach, hiking up to the city's historic center is well worth your time. Located in Eivissa, this ancient, fortified city within a city retains traces of Muslim civilization, though the building standing today hails from the 16th century. A gaunt cathedral designed in Gothic style occupies the highest point of Dalt Via. Construction for Ibiza's cathedral began in the 13th century, and rumor has it that it was built over a mosque. Today, it maintains a trapezoidal bell tower and a polygonal apse with five chapels. Although it's precariously perched on a steep hill above the Mediterranean Sea, the cathedral isn't going anywhere any time soon. It's brusque and concrete, strengthened by large buttresses.

Close to the cathedral are a number of museums, including the Puget museum, which is located in a palace that belonged to the noble Palou de Comasema family and dates back to the 15th century. Also make sure to stop by the Archaeological Museum of Ibiza and Formentera, whose collection includes various odds and ends, like coins, from the Prehistoric age all the way to the Islamic medieval times.

Perhaps the best thing about the "castle" of Dalt Via is the views that it offers. Walk along the fortified walls of this old city and gaze out into the turquoise Mediterranean—a view you're likely not to forget any time soon, no matter how much partying you've done on the island. You can see almost everything from the port to Bossa Beach. The sunbathers. The booze cruises. If you keep wrapping around the castle, you'll also happen upon some cannons (models, of course) that were used to defend the city against invasion.

FOOD

If you're coming to Ibiza to party all night long, your wallet—and your stomach—will be feeling pretty empty. Food in the city can be expensive, especially the closer you get to the water, but don't let that keep you from eating! (Because trust us, in order to survive financially on the island, people sometimes forgo eating for clubbing.)

BIORGANIC

ORGANIC $

Av. Espana, 11   ☎971 39 36 21   www.biorganicibiza.com

If you're looking for cheap, quick, and healthy good eats for picnics on the beach, try Biorganic, a small cornerstone on Avanida Espana, Eivissa's main road. With all the great perks of a farmer's market, like local produce and lots of carrots, and prices that won't break your bank, this store is the perfect place to load up for a few days. You can cook yourself a meal with garbanzo beans (€2.67) or egg noodles (€2.99) or buy a premade meal like paella (€4.89). Food here is guaranteed to be fresh, bright, and delicious. Fresh fruit and vegetables—finally, you've found some! No scurvy for you in Ibiza—produce is stored in wooden crates near the front of the market, while dried goods like organic chips and beans are stored near the back. Mineral water (a must have) is also available cheap; as are juices, yogurts, and other cool summertime treats.

Biorganic also has a smoothie bar near the front of its store, just after the check out line. Mix and match your favorite fruits and vegetables for a refreshing drink that will fuel you for another day on the beach and under the sun. The store is located in the heart of Ibiza Town, just a quick walk from the beach, and as its name entails, you're guaranteed fresh produce whenever you want it (as

get a room!

Find more recommendations over at **www.letsgo.com**.

HOSTEL GIRAMUNDO

HOSTEL $$

Carrer de Ramon Muntaner, 55   ☎971 30 76 40   www.hostalgiramundoibiza.com

Cheap is a word rarely used in Ibiza. So as far as cheap accommodations go—forget it. You might as well try hiding out in Pacha's bathrooms for the night.

Kidding, of course. But if you're hoping to save a buck or two, you're best off staying at Hostal Giramundo, an open air, party crazy, young adult (not "youth") hostel located steps away from the beach (which one?). While the hostel doesn't offer too many social activities and events like some in other cities (but let's be honest, located in this city, pub crawls are not necessary), Giramundo does offer its guests an awesome desayuno of cafe con leche, zumo de naranja (orange juice), and a delicious croissant. But it's not just about the food—the hostel has a full bar, its own restaurant downstairs (which, as you'll find, will be significantly cheaper than anything else along the beach), outdoor patios, and a third-floor terrace great for pre-gaming for the island's famous clubs.

Its staff is very knowledgeable about Ibiza Town and can give you advice about how to get into the clubs for a discounted price (walking along the beach midday isn't a bad idea). The building is colorful, fun, and inviting—but with an open and bright layout come a few drawbacks. Naturally, the place is pretty sandy (it is steps away from the beach, after all). Wi-Fi, though free and available in the common rooms, is spotty at best. Sometimes, it will take an hour to connect to the Internet, if not more. Prepare yourself. Additionally, there is only one shower on each floor. Decision time. Forgo showering for a few days and instead bathe in the ridiculously salty Mediterranean, or battle it out among fellow hostellers. Win-win?

i *Mixed and female-only rooms €22-33. Privates € 44-55. ⏰ Reception 24hr. Check out by 11am.*

long as you visit between the hours of 9am-10pm). Gluten free food is offered as well!

i €1-10 for anything you could possibly desire. ☼ Open daily 9am-10pm.

CAN FLOW
TAPAS $$

Carrer des Passadis, 8   ☎653 77 24 44 www.biorganicibiza.com

Are you one of those people who likes eating cute bites of fancy-looking food? And you want to be vegan/gluten free/raw/whatever other weird diet you can think of? Ibiza Town has just the place for you! Can Flow (why the name, we don't know) has healthy, green tapas-sized meals for anyone and everyone, meat-eaters and plant-eaters alike. With bite-sized food comes bite-sized prices too—especially for Ibiza. Prices for meals range from €6-25. Try salmon tartar, veggie burgers, chicken burgers (anything burgers, really), and lots of fish. The plates themselves are so artistically done you may be afraid to eat. But then eat, because the food is fresh, filling, and of course, delicious.

Can Flow's food is organic and self-described "ecological" too, so your body will thank you after all that... partying during the night. And to add to the great food, you'll get a casual, laid back atmosphere too. Almost like you're eating your mom's best cuisine, all dolled up on a shining white platter, except in Ibiza, where you'll probably do things at which your mom would cringe. A lot.

i Tapas €6. Racions €8-15. ☼ Open daily 11am-1:30am.

MAR A VILA
TAPAS $$

Av. Ignasi Wallis, 16   ☎971 31 47 78 www.facebook.com/maravilaibiza

Ah, tapas. The only type of food you can afford in Ibiza Town. Kidding (but are we?). If you're going to do tapas, might as well do them right. Head over to Mar a Vila, a chic and beautifully decorated restaurant located in the heart of the city's center. Get your fill of five-star bites, like calamari, anchovy toast, mussels, and even chocolate. Tapas are modern, creative, and come in surprising combinations—peppers stuffed with goat cheese? Pickled mussels? The restaurant's name does have "mar" in it, after all. They're bound to have pretty darn good seafood.

For an inexpensive price, you and your friends can dine at the bar, at a table, or in the secret garden-esque, beautiful courtyard, which is decorated white and modestly with hanging plants and simple chairs and tables. It's refreshing to eat in a budget restaurant that tries hard not to look the best, but actually serve the best food to its guests. Food here is prepared and served artistically—plates are definitely worth a few Instagram posts. We only wish we could sneak back into the kitchen to watch the chefs work their magic.

Since you'll probably only chow down on a few plates of tapas, you may have room for some dessert. If not, make room. Lick your fingers after sampling some rich chocolate truffles, strawberry ice cream, or red wine compote. In fact, come back another time—just for dessert. Your taste buds will forever thank you.

i Tapas €3-8.75. Fish €12. Rice €10. Dessert €6. ☼ Open M-F 8:30am-midnight, Sa 11am-4:30pm and 7pm-midnight.

NIGHTLIFE

AMNESIA
CLUB

Ctra. Ibiza a San Antonio, Km 5   ☎971 19 80 41 www.amnesia.es

It's tough to recommend just one club in Ibiza when the entire island is basically known for one thing and one thing only: partying. But one club everyone seems to rave about is Amnesia (warning: not actually located in Ibiza Town! Sorry folks, it's over in San Antonio instead). Known for its local, Spanish vibe and crazy ice cannon machine (more on that later), this place is worth remembering. Or not. You know you're in for a good time when you visit a club called Amnesia.

ibiza

It's one of Ibiza's originals, founded in the 1970s, and most the famous, though perhaps overshadowed in recent pop culture by other giants like Privilege or Pacha. (Though it HAS won a number of "Best Global Club" awards in recent history.) The club was originally founded to accommodate hippies who wanted to "expand their minds" in the mysterious, bohemian island of Ibiza. Nowadays an eclectic mix of people visit the club, but that wanderlust, free-for-all ambience remains. Although the club is no longer open air (sad, we know), it still has two major rooms—a main dance floor and a terrace, the latter of which is only covered by a glass ceiling that you probably won't even notice at all when partying hard (you may notice it if you're still standing at daybreak, since sunlight floods the place). The club, currently run by Cream, invites a great mix of DJs to man the club—house music, techno, trance. Like all clubs on the island, Amnesia is "good" on certain day(s)—those days being Sundays and Mondays. Mondays are Cocoon nights (Sven Väth's big party) and can cost from €40-55. Amnesia is also known for hosting its famous foam party nights on Sundays (hygienic… we think not). Non-Monday/Sunday nights at the club are relatively inexpensive (for Ibiza!), costing around €25-40 depending on the profile of the DJ.

A night at Amnesia is one you'll never forget! Well…

i €25-40, €40-55 on M and Su. ☒ Generally open midnight-6am.

ESSENTIALS

Getting There

Ibiza is an island. That means no cars, trains, or buses will ever be able to reach Ibiza (unless man makes some sort of underwater bus, but that'll probably take a while). You have three options: airplane, ferry, swim. Let's just count that last one out. Major Spanish airports have direct flights to Ibiza, from cities like Madrid, Barcelona, Valencia, and Sevilla. Vueling, Ryanair, and Iberia are going to be your best bets for airlines. Round-trip prices (unless you're planning on staying there a while) can range—a lot. Ryanair will always be the cheapest (€90 round trip), but the cost can get as expensive as €400. Ryanair veterans know, cheap comes at a price. Not your greatest airline (first come first serve seating), but once you get to Ibiza you'll be thanking yourself for saving on plane tickets early on. Flights from Valencia, the closest airport, last around 45min.

Getting Around

Welcome to the land of horrible buses. Well, they're fine; really, they just don't run that often or late. Line 10 runs from the airport into Ibiza Town, and back. Other lines cross the island. Check http://ibizabus.com/ibiza/lineas for a comprehensive list of bus schedules and stop locations. The island itself is pretty small, but not small enough to cross by foot in a timely manner (believe us, we've tried). Check out the taxi service as well at www.turismoibiza.com/taxi. Rates start at €3.25 and cost anywhere from €0.98-1.65 per km.

santiago de compostela

Santiago de Compostela is the lively and multicultural capital of Galicia. For Christians, it is famous for being the burial grounds of St. James, one of the 12 apostles of Christ. It is the end destination for many travelers walking the Camino de Santiago (Way of St. James) pilgrimage. Many travel through Great Britain, France, and ultimately Spain to arrive in Santiago, receive their certificates of completion of the pilgrimage, visit the Cathedral of Santiago de Compostela and attend the pilgrims mass.

The mass, held weekly on Fridays, serves to celebrate the completion of the journey and honor the spiritual walk that many have completed. Due to the significance of the Camino in Santiago, the town has great respect for the pilgrims, who hail from all around the world. They bring great tourism to the city, whose stone streets and structures are both an idyllic resting place and lively finish line. The town has one of the most beautiful cathedrals in Spain, gorgeous open parks and museums, exciting streets and bars in the evening, and open arms toward all travelers.

SIGHTS

SANTO DOMINGO DE BONAVAL PARK

PARK

Santo Domingo de Bonaval Park is a mid-sized park in Santiago de Compostela located behind the Museum of Galician People, and is one of the top 10 attractions in Santiago de Compostela. However, while it is a nice park, there are much nicer parks in the area, specifically one along Ave de Xoan Carlos I, which is between the USC campus and the city. Regardless, if you're at the Museum of Galician People, the Santo Domingo de Bonaval Park is worth going to.

The park has many different terraces. On the bottom, closest to the street, you'll find pretty flowers, large trees with people's clothes hanging on them to naturally dry, and a stone fountain. As you ascend the park, there are more stone structures (with little to see or do with them) and a large field surrounded by flowers that makes for a good picnic location in the shade. As you continue to rise, you'll see another field with a path going through it, and a stone wall that separates a second field that overlooks the city. All of these fields are lush, shady, and good places for picnics or a good vantage point. Connected to the second field is is a very pretty multi-colored structure with a tall, lone tree in the middle that encloses another large, open field..

i Free. ☒ Open in summer daily 8am-11pm, in winter daily 9am-8pm.

BOTAFUMEIRO

RELIGIOUS CEREMONY

Praza do Obradoiro   ☎981 56 93 27 www.catedraldesantiago.es

Botafumeiro refers to a religious ceremony held during the pilgrim's mass in the cathedral of Santiago de Compostela. Literally, the Botafumeiro means "smoke expeller" in Galician. Its famous thurible where incense is burned during mass, weighing over 50 kilos, is 1.6 meters in height. Typically, the Botafumeiro is on exhibition in the cathedral, but during special religious holidays such as Christmas, St. James Day, Three King's Day, and Easter, it is used for ceremonial purposes.

The Botafumeiro is taken off display and filled with charcoal and incense. It is then tied elaborately to a rope, and then suspended from the middle of the ceiling of the cathedral by a pulley. It is initially pushed, and then eight tiraboleiros pull the ropes and cause it to swing high over the crowds from one side of the cathedral to another. It swings fast and dispenses thick clouds of incense and reaches over 20 meters in height.

It's expensive for the ceremony to take place, so it is only done once a week to honor the pilgrims, plus special circumstances like the aforementioned holidays. However, if a group is unable to attend the ceremony on one of those days, they can contact the pilgrim center and have a ceremony arranged for a price of €300. It's one of the greatest attractions in Santiago, and it's worth attending even if you are not religious. Make sure to come early and get seats on the side, instead of facing the altarpiece.

i Free. ☒ Occurs F at 7:30pm, but arrive an hour early.

santiago de compostela

MUSEO DE POBO GALEGO (MUSEUM OF GALICIAN PEOPLE)

MUSEUM

Hotel Bonaval, Rúa de Bonaval ☎981 58 36 20 www.museodopobo.es

El Museo do Pobo Galego, or the Museum of Galician People, is about five minutes northeast from the center of Santiago de Compostela and matches the city's enormous stone fashion. Upon entering and passing the ticket counter, you will walk through a beautiful lush courtyard in the middle of the entire building. As you continue into the museum, there is series of three grand stone staircases that spiral up towards the different museum exhibitions.

The museum is incredibly large, is well lit with nice wooden floors, and has tons to see. There are several rooms featuring just art, including local paintings, photography from Steffan and Mikael Mörling, religious portraits, portraits of commoners, landscape paintings, a ceramics section, and painted china. There are also lots of cultural exhibitions, including a church recreation, historical shoes and clothing collection, massive boat replicas, a musical instruments archive, bedroom and kitchen displays, and a series of miniature houses from over the centuries. Additionally, there are historic craftsmanship stations, including a loom, cobbling station, horseback riding mantles, and two separate sections for stone smithing and carpentry.

The museum is free to enter on Sundays, but none of the information is available in different languages (just Galician dialect). Once you're finished, you can grab a meal from one of the restaurants nearby or take a stroll through the park connected in the back of the museum..

i General admission €3. ☼ Open Tu-Sa 10:30am-2pm and 4pm-7:30pm, Su and holidays 11am-2pm.

FOOD

ENTRE PEDRAS

CAFE $

Rua Hospitalino 18 ☎981564097 www.facebook.com/entre.pedras.veg/info

Entre Pedras is a local vegan cafe located north of the cathedral. The restaurant is very quirky, and on the walls there are paintings of animals eating dinner and playing cards, handmade art hanging from the ceiling, and framed water-color pictures (mostly of nature) lining the building. Basically, it's a hipster's paradise. They've got Christmas lights up year round, and speakers that play a mix of indie, Spanish music and jazz. It's relatively small, could fit about 50 patrons, and has one narrow bar extending through the middle of it.

The menu is incredibly cheap and even more brief. The first page is drinks, including different types of coffees, juices, and infusions. All of the options are natural, and they're all less than about €2.50. The second and final page are the meal options, which are also limited. The food includes veggie or tofu burgers, tostas, bocatas, and patacas bravas con aioli. All of these options are under €4. The food portions are large for the price you pay, and very savory. Moreover, the bar has local wines, beers, and any cocktails you desire.

Entre Pedras is cheap and delicious—'nough said. The restaurant is open for dinner, so make sure to swing by (even if just for a juice), especially if you're staying at one of the many nearby hostels.

i €5 or less. ☼ Open daily 7:30pm-2:30am.

CAFE CASINO

CAFE $

Rúa do Vilar, 35 ☎981 57 75 03 www.cafecasino.es

Café Casino is located on Rua do Vilar, a popular tourist street in front of the cathedral. The restaurant has a limited outdoor seating, but the inside is spacious and decorated in a classic, regal fashion. There are elaborate light fixtures hanging from the high, crown-molded ceilings, as well as ornate wooden wall panels that have framed watercolor pictures hanging from them, all of which

For more recommendations, visit **www.letsgo.com.**

🏨 CASA FELISA
Porta da Pena, 5

HOSTEL $$

☎981 58 26 02 www.casafelisa.es

Casa Felisa is located northwest of the city center and cathedral on a street packed with restaurants and hostels. The hostel is well favored by the internet travel community, as well as the hostel's garden restaurant downstairs, which has received exceptional reviews and serves a delectable grilled octopus (pulpo a la plancha). Unless you have a swipe card you'll have to enter the hostel through the restaurant and be checked in at the indoor bar seating. The hostel operators have a friendly and old golden retriever whom you might run into, and the lobby is clean and has free maps of the town that feature recommended attractions.

Casa Felisa has three floors, with shared bathrooms on each level for the hostel guests. The rooms vary by size, and some have several beds whereas the large privates typically just have one large bed. In the rooms there are desks, a closet space for towels and extra bed sheets, a safe to keep some belongings, and some of the rooms have a window that opens out to the street. Rooms that are situated against the street are obviously louder than rooms that face away from it because the hostel's walls are relatively thin. So much for sleep! Lol jk—if you are a very light sleeper, then this may be a problem, but otherwise the sound is not too bad since the streets clear out pretty soon in the evening.

The bathrooms are cleaned daily and have a towel basket, sink, toilet, and large shower. The facilities are, for the most part, clean, but you may find some cobwebs hanging in the corner of the ceiling above the shower. However, the service staff are very friendly and would assist you with any concerns about cleanliness. Nobody's trying to get sued here. The hostel has free Wi-Fi, but you need to request the password in order to receive it, and sometimes you may face limited connectivity issues.

i Privates €25. Doubles €45. ☒ Reception 24hr.

are for sale. There's a combination of wooden seats and cushioned armchairs against the wall. Further back, towards the bar and pastry section of the cafe, are high top glass tables with leather chairs. The restaurant is huge, and could hold over 100 people easily. In the center of the dining room is a grand piano. You'll find a projector screen on the back wall and elegant mirrors along the side walls, above the wooden panels.

Café Casino has very extensive drink options, including coffees, infusions, chocolate drinks, and a large variety of alcoholic beverages. They serve breakfast, lunch, and dinner, and, in addition to classic options like eggs and bacon and hamburgers, they serve local delicacies such as octopus, and traditional Spanish appetizers and salads. Finally, they also serve great gelato at the front entrance.

While the restaurant is a bit pricier than other options around, the ambience, service, and food quality more than justify the price. It's a great, all-purpose restaurant for whatever time of the day you visit. The only downside is that there is no free public Wi-Fi.

i Appetizers €6. Meals €10. ☒ Open daily 9am-1am.

santiago de compostela

O PARIS
CAFE $

Rúa dos Bautizados, 11 ☎981 57 18 64 https://es-es.facebook.com/oparisdc

O Paris is a French cafe and a local favorite. It's located just outside of Toural Square, towards the park and University of Santiago de Compostela (USC) campus. They generally attract a younger crowd, and have an extensive menu and large bar. The restaurant has a few outdoor tables on a patio under protection from the rain. They're bar has plenty of seating, with four tables along the wall, a few in the open space in the middle of the restaurant, and extra seating in the back for those who wish to get larger meals from the menu instead of just tapas and drinks.

O Paris serves a combination of French, Spanish, and American food. They have delicious hamburgers of many different varieties, salads, tostas, fish options, bar food such as chicken fingers, and a menu del dia, which includes a starter, entree, bread, drink, and dessert for only €12. The restaurant has modern decorations, and the kitchen has open windows that you can see into from next to the bar. The bathrooms are clean, and they've got free Wi-Fi if you ask one of the waiters or bartenders for a password. If you're looking for a solid brunch, light dinner, or quick drink, O Paris certainly hits the spot.

i Appetizers €4. Entrees €10. ☼ Open M-F 10am-1am, Sa 10am-2:30am.

NIGHTLIFE

BAR ALBAROQUE
BAR

Pl. Cervantes

Bar Albaroque is located in Plaza Cervantes directly across from Cervantes, the vinoteca. They're a small place that functions as a cafe during the day, bar in the early evening, and dance club at night. Inside, they have a small seating area around a long bar that curves around to the back of the room. At the end of the bar is access to another room, which has tables for meals and another television for watching sports. The main room is simply decorated in wooden sports bar fashion. There's a large television that is across from the bar, and close to the entrance is the kitchen, which has a few tables in front of it.

In the evenings, the bar staff clear out all of the tables and chairs and turn the area into a dance floor. By midnight, mostly everything is cleared out but there usually is no crowd yet, aside from the people who were there for meals and have chosen to stay into the evening. The party usually gets started around 1am. Typically, the crowd tends to be a younger demographic and the bar attracts many students from the local university.

i Drinks €2-5. ☼ Open M-Sa midnight-2am.

HAWAII'S EDER
BAR

Rúa do Vilar, 47 ☎981 556 452

Hawaii's Eder is a sports bar in the heart of Santiago, next to Praza de Praterias. It's decorated with Hawaiian everything. Surfboards on the walls next to framed pictures of the beach, wooden tables with Palm tree paintings in them, lights with tribal waves across them, a giant shark hanging over the entrance next to the bar, statues of Hawaiian women in bathing suits with leis around their neck, and a giant mural of a volcano in between the two flat screen televisions. When you enter, there's a very large bar with smaller TVs overhead, and in the back of the restaurant are the tables with menus next to the napkins. The menus are in a variety of different languages, and they serve typical bar food, appetizers, ice cream, and drinks for all under €8. The place is filled with tourists and pilgrims during sporting events, but unless it's a major match then the bar isn't too densely populated.

It's the perfect place to grab a beer and watch a match before heading out to a club or bar hopping for the evening. The service is exceptionally friendly, but can be slow if the bar is very populated. Hawaii's Eder has free Wi-Fi. You know the drill, all you have to do is ask a waiter for the password. Finally, when you order a beer, you'll be given complementary chips and olives on the side.

i Appetizers €4. Entrees €8. Beer €2. ☼ Open M-Sa midnight-2am.

ESSENTIALS

Practicalities

- **TOURIST OFFICE: Oficina Municipal de Turismo** has maps and thorough information on accommodations as well as a 24hr. interactive information screen outside. (R. Vilar, 63 ☎98 155 51 29 www.santiagoturismo.com *i* On R. Vilar 1 block toward Cathedral from Pr. Toural. *i* English, French, German, Portuguese, Italian, Galician, and other languages spoken. ☼ Open daily 9am-9pm.) **Oficina de Turismo de Galicia** has information on the rest of Galicia, and on festivals. (R. Vilar, 30 ☎98 158 40 81 www.turgalicia.es *i* On R. Vilar between Pr. Toural and Cathedral, on opposite side of street from Municipal Tourism Office but closer to Cathedral. ☼ Open M-F 10am-8pm, Sa 11am-2pm and 5-7pm, Su 11am-2pm.) **Oficina del Xacobeo,** in the same building, provides information on the Camino de Santiago. (R. Vilar, 30 ☎98 158 40 81 ☼ Open M-F 10am-8pm.)

- **CURRENCY EXCHANGE:** Banco Santander has **Western Union** services and a 24hr. **ATM** outside, and cashes American Express Travelers Cheques commission-free. (Pl. Galicia, 1 ☎98 158 61 11 *i* On right side of Pl. Galicia with your back to the old town. ☼ Open Apr-Sept M-F 8:30am-2pm; Oct-Mar Sa 8:30am-1pm.)

- **INTERNET ACCESS: Ciber Nova 50** has fast computers and pay phones. (R. Nova, 50 ☎98 156 41 33 *i* On R. Nova 1 block toward the Cathedral from Pr. Toural. €0.45 for 12min., €2 per hr. ☼ Open M-F 9am-midnight, Sa-Su 10am-11pm.)

- **ENGLISH-LANGUAGE BOOKS: Libraria Couceiro** has several shelves of books in English. (Pr. Cervantes, 6 ☎98 156 58 12 *i* From Pl. Galicia, take R. Orfas into old city; it becomes R. Caldeirería, then R. Preguntoiro, and the bookstore is immediately to the left on Pr. Cervantes. ☼ Open M-F 10am-noon and 4-9pm, Sa 10am-noon and 5-9pm.)

- **POST OFFICE: Correos** has a Lista de Correos and fax. (R. Orfas ☎98 158 12 52 www.correos.es *i* Take Cantón do Toural from Pr. Toural 2 blocks to R. Orfas. ☼ Open M-F 8:30am-8:30pm, Sa 9am-2pm.)

Emergency

- **POLICE: Policía Local.** (Pr. Obradoiro, 1 ☎98 154 23 23 *i* On Pr. Obradoiro across from Cathedral.)

- **MEDICAL SERVICES: Hospital Clínico Universitario** has a public clinic across from the emergency room. (Tr. Choupana ☎98 195 00 00 *i* Take bus #1 from R. Senra toward Hospital Clínico. ☼ Clinic open M-Sa 3-8pm, Su 8am-8pm.)

- **PHARMACY: Farmacia R. Bescansa** has been around since 1843—stop in to gawk at the classic 19th-century decor, even if you don't need anything. (Pl. Toural, 11 ☎98 158 59 40.)

Getting There

By Bus

ALSA (☎91 327 05 40 www.alsa.es) runs buses from: Astorga (€21-25 ☼ 5hr., 4 per day 4:15am-7:30pm); Barcelona (€72-86 ☼ 17hr., 3 per day 10am-10:50pm); Bilbao (€49 ☼ 9-11hr., 4 per day 10:30am-1:45am); Burgos (€40 ☼ 8½hr., daily at 1:15pm); León (€28 ☼ 6hr., daily at 4:45pm); Madrid (€44-54 ☼ 8-9hr.; M-Th 5 per day 7:30am-12:30am,

F-Sa 4 per day 7:30am-12:30am); Salamanca (€26-31 ☼ 6-7hr.; M-F 3pm and 1:10am, Sa 5pm and 1:10am, Su 3pm and 1:10am).

RENFE (www.renfe.es) trains arrive from: A Coruña (€7-15 ☼ 40min.; M-F 20 per day 5:35am-10:15pm, Sa 18 per day 6:55am-9:55pm, Su 17 per day 6:55am-9:55pm); Bilbao (€48 ☼ 11hr., daily at 9:15am); Burgos (€42 ☼ 8hr., 2 per day at 12:12 and 3:25pm.); Madrid (€47-53 ☼ 7-9hr. 3 per day 3-10:30pm).

Ryanair (www.ryanair.com) has flights to Santiago's **Lavacolla Airport** (SCQ; ☼ 30min. bus from bus station or city center) from: Alicante, Barcelona (El Prat), Madrid, Málaga, Reus, Frankfurt (Hahn), London (Stansted), and Rome. **Iberia** (www.iberia. es) flies to Santiago from Bilbao, Sevilla, and Valencia.

Getting Around

Most of the old city is closed off to all but foot traffic, so the easiest way to get around is to walk. For those venturing farther afield, **buses** (€1, with *bono* €0.55) are a good way to get around, though not particularly frequent on weekends. Bus #2 and 5 go to the bus station; bus #6 goes to the train station. **Freire** (☎98 158 81 11) runs buses (€3 ☼ 30min.) from R. Doutor Teixeiro and the bus station to the airport. There are **taxi** stands at the bus and train stations and at Pl. Galicia and Pr. Roxa. Otherwise, call **Radio Taxi** (☎98 156 92 92) or **Eurotaxi** (☎67 053 51 54).

spain essentials

MONEY

Tipping and Bargaining

Native Spaniards rarely tip more than their spare change, even at expensive restaurants. If you make it clear that you're a tourist—especially an American—they might expect you to tip more. Don't feel like you have to tip, as the servers' pay is almost never based on tips.

Bargaining is common and necessary in open-air and street markets. If you are buying a number of things, like produce,you can probably get a better deal if you haggle. Do not barter in malls or established shops.

Taxes

Spain has a 10% value added tax (IVA) on all means and accommodations. The prices listed in Let's Go include IVA unless otherwise mentioned. Retail goods bear a much higher 21% IVA, although the listed prices generally include this tax. Non-EU citizens who have stayed in the EU fewer than 180 days can claim back the tax paid on purchases at the airport. Ask the shop where you have made the purchase to supply you with a tax return form, but stores will only provide them for purchases of around €50-100. Due to the economic crises sweeping Europe, don't be surprised if Spain increases its VAT even more.

SAFETY AND HEALTH

Local Laws and Police

Travelers are not likely to break major laws unintentionally while visiting Spain. You can contact your embassy if arrested, although they often cannot do much to assist you beyond finding legal counsel. You should feel comfortable approaching the police, although few officers speak English. There are several types of police in Spain. The policía nacional wear blue or black uniforms and white shirts; they guard government buildings, protect dignitaries, and deal with criminal investigations (including theft). The policía local wear blue uniforms, deal more with local issues, and report to the mayor or town hall in each municipality. The guardia civil wear olive-green uniforms and are responsible for issues more relevant to travelers: customs, crowd control, and national security. Catalonia also has its own police force, the Mossos d'Esquadra. Officers generally wear blue and occasionally sport berets or other interesting headgear. This police force is often used for crowd control and deals with riots.

Drugs and Alcohol

Recreational drugs are illegal in Spain, and police take these laws seriously. The legal drinking age is 16 in Asturias and 18 elsewhere. In Asturias, however, it is still illegal for stores to sell alcohol to those under age 18. Spain has the highest road mortality rates in Europe, and one of the highest rates of drunk driving deaths in Europe. Recently, Spanish officials have started setting up checkpoints on roads to test drivers' blood alcohol levels. Do not drive while intoxicated and be cautious on the road.

Terrorism

Until very recently, Basque terrorism was a serious concern for all travelers in Spain. A militant wing of Basque separatists called the Euskadi Ta Askatasuna (ETA; Basque Homeland and Freedom) continued to have an active presence well into the 2000s, but has recently taken a more dormant stance. Historically, ETA's attacks have been politically targeted and were not considered random terrorist attacks that endanger regular civilians. In January 2011, ETA declared a "permanent and general cease-fire," and at this point, many of ETA's leaders have been arrested. The group has also announced a "definitive cessation of its armed activity."

LANGUAGE

There are four main languages spoken in Spain, along with a slew of less widely spoken ones. Here are the ones you're likely to come across.

Spanish/Castellano

Castilian or Spanish is the official language of Spain. Spain's Spanish is distinct from its Western Hemisphere counterparts in its hallmark lisp of the z and soft c and its use of the vosotros form (second-person plural).

Catalan/Valenciancatalà/Valencià

Along the Mediterranean coast from Alicante up to the French border, the main language spoken is Catalan, along with its close relative Valencian. Throughout the regions of Catalonia, Valencia and the Balearic Islands, as well as parts of Aragon, this Romance language sounds to most ears like a combination of Spanish, Italian, and French. It's also the official language of the small principality of Andorra. Never imply that Catalan is a dialect of Spanish—this is untrue and will turn the entire nation of Andorra against you.

Basque/Euskara

Basque looks extraterrestrial—full of z's, x's, and k's—but the Basques don't care how pretty their language looks; they just care about preserving it. After decades of concerted efforts by Franco to wipe euskara out, it is still the official language of about 600,000 people, though you won't need to know a word of it to get by in País Vasco's main cities.

Galician/Galego

Somewhere between Spanish and Portuguese falls Galician, spoken in Galicia, in the northwest corner of the peninsula. As with Basque, you won't need your Spanish-Galician dictionary to get by, though it'll probably help with most menus.

Other Languages

In the British territory of Gibraltar, English is spoken, of course, though the locals also speak a creole known as Llanito. Languages you're less likely to come across in your travels include Asturian, spoken along parts of the northern coast; Leonese, in the area around Astorga; Extremaduran, in Extremadura; Aranese, in the valley around Vielha; Aragonese, in the mountains of Aragon north of Huesca; and Caló, spoken by the Romanior gypsy community across Spain.

spain

SWEDEN

With the design world cooing over bright, blocky Swedish furniture and college students donning designs from H&M, Scandinavia's largest nation has earned a reputation abroad for its chic style. At home, Sweden's struggle to balance a market economy with its generous social welfare system stems from it belief that all citizens should have access to education and healthcare. This neutral nation's zest for spending money on butter instead of guns has also shored up a strong sense of national unity, from reindeer herders in the Lappland forests to bankers in bustling Stockholm.

greatest hits

- **POSEIDON, LOOK AT ME NOW:** Take a cruise along the archipelago in Stockholm (p. 904) for a breathtaking tour through nature. Maybe you'll spot some Wildlings along the way.

- **A CHANCE OF MEATBALLS:** Hungry in Stockholm? Head to **Husmans Deli** (p. 908) for a huge portion of the classic dish: Swedish meatballs.

- **BE A SQUARE:** From afternoon coffee chats to protests, **Lilla Torg** (p. 916) is the perfect people-watching square in little Malmö.

stockholm

To put it simply, Stockholm is the real deal: a veritable Mordor-Death Star combo of everything that is young, hip, and Anglophone. You'll find artisanal hot dog stands next to Gatsby-themed speakeasies next to garlic bars and kebab-Vietnamese fusion. It's like Narnia in modern form, and you'll absolutely love it.

Stockholm is probably the best place for backpackers in Scandinavia (if not Europe). The sheer size and vibrancy of the city means that you have every kind of accommodation at your disposal from nature cabins to Betty-Boop themed free-pasta compounds. There is something for even the pickiest travellers here. The nightlife, like in any big city, is diverse and affordable, while the food never disappoints: whether it's noodles or meatballs, burgers or buffets, Stockholm does it and it does it well.

Like the other Nordic countries, the standard of living is high here, and that means that prices are a bit above what you're used to. If you want to eat out twice a day, go to bars and museums, and stay at a nice hostel, it may be hard to spend less than 80 USD a day. Nonetheless, it always feels like money well spent here: whether you take quiet stroll in a park, visit a Viking exhibit, or grab beers on a boat heading around the archipelago, you will be amazed at how fun and diverse an experience in Stockholm can be.

ACCOMMODATIONS

CITY HOSTEL
HOSTEL $$

Fleminggatan 19   ☎8 410 03 830 www.cityhostel.se

In Hollywood, hostels are often portrayed as the travelling equivalent of Animal House: the drinking is non-stop, the baby-making is on point, and some guy named Hans is playing the guitar. On your travels, though, you might have found most hostels to be full of more snoring men than hedonistic youth—until City Hostel. This place feels vibrant, fun and new. The rooms are spacious and come with their own lockers, while the community kitchen and bathrooms are both spotless and quite large. The hostel offers little treats like laundry service and their own guidebook to Stockholm (though you already have us!)—but most importantly, the clientele is almost entirely college students. With shared rooms at around 250 SEK a night, it's an excellent deal.

i Singles 450 SEK. Doubles 600 SEK. Dorms 220-250 SEK. ☒ Reception 9am-6pm.

CITY BACKPACKERS' HOSTEL
HOSTEL $

Upplandsgatan 2a   ☎8 20 69 20 www.citybackpackers.org

The place looks like it was designed by Andy Warhol on a mescaline trip, and we mean that in the best way possible: an average walk down the hallway takes you past vintage skateboards, 50's TV sets, and posters featuring North Korea's national ski team. It's the kind of place that's youthful and artistic without being cheesy, and its young clientele and cleverly-designed social spaces might make it the best hostelling experience you'll have in Sweden. Though the basic price of a room is the same as in other places around Stockholm, we recommend you shell out extra here for the breakfast: they have a full-time chef who serves a six-part meal with everything from sandwiches and yogurt to juice and fruit plates.

i Singles 600 SEK. Doubles 890 SEK. Dorm 190-280 SEK. ☒ Reception 8am-midnight.

SKANSTULLS
HOSTEL $$

Ringvägen 135   ☎8 643 02 04 www.skanstulls.se

Skanstulls is the same price as other Stockholm hostels but with much nicer amenities. Book collection? You got it. Free pasta? Done. Actual wooden bunk-beds that don't feel like prison cots? Check, check, check. Its location in Södermalm means you are 10 minutes away from some of Europe's best-rated nightlife and restaurants, and the mass of people in the kitchen at dinnertime makes it incredibly easy to make friends.

i *Singles 500 SEK. Doubles 600 SEK. Dorms 220-250 SEK. ☾ Reception 9am-8pm.*

2KRONOR
HOSTEL $

Surbrunnsgatan 44 ☎8 22 92 30 www.2kronor.se

2kronor is a nice place to stay for the price and location. The rooms are spacious and the kitchen and common room are well-equipped. One slight frustration here is that reception closes at 11am and does not reopen until 3pm, so you can't check-in early and you need to get special codes to enter the building. On a plus side though, they sell metro tickets, breakfast vouchers, and selfie sticks. Just ask at reception.

i *Singles 495 SEK. Doubles 590 SEK. Dorms 195 SEK. ☾ Reception M-F 7:30am-11am and 3pm-6pm, Sa-Su 8am-3pm.*

HOTEL MICRO
HOTEL $$

Tegnérlunden 8 ☎8 545 45 569 www.hotelmicro.se

Somehow the Japanese idea of sleeping in pods has become attractive across the globe in recent years, and now you, too, can sleep in an artsy, glorified closet! Hotel Micro is located right off of Stockholm's main walkway, Drottninggatan, and is directly in front of peaceful Tegnér Park. The facilities are certainly nicer than you'll find in most hostels. Each room (even the singles) comes with a desk, mirror, and bunk beds, so it's a (relatively) inexpensive alternative if you're looking for somewhere to decompress for a day or two. However, all of the bathrooms and showers are communal, though the lobby bar and 24-hour service make up for this small inconvenience.

i *Singles 495 SEK. Doubles 1090 SEK. 15% discount often available if booked directly on web-site. ☾ Reception 24hr.*

RED BOAT MÄLAREN
HOSTEL $$

Södermälarstrand Kajplats 10 ☎8 644 43 85 www.theredboat.com

Have you heard "I'm On A Boat" too many times and want to know what all the hype is about? Now, for around 350 SEK a night, you can find out! The Red Boat Mälaren is anchored off of Stockholm's Södermalm neighborhood and has an interior best described as "Pirates of the Caribbean." There's a great selection of Swedish beers and snacks on board, and if you shell out extra for the breakfast, you can get a tasty filling of meats, cheeses, and fruit all washed down with Muesli and yogurt. The Wi-Fi only works in the social spaces and the rooms are a bit cramped and poorly-ventilated, but the bathrooms are surprisingly clean and the selfie opportunities are endless. Note that the boat is stationary, but may rock back and forth during heavy winds; we'd advise anyone only to stay a night or two, but that advice goes especially for those with motion sickness.

i *It's the boat in the harbor in Södermalm. Singles 590 SEK. Doubles 750 SEK. 4-bed dorms 350 SEK. ☾ Reception 24hr.*

SIGHTS

VASA MUSEUM (VASAMUSEET)
MUSEUM

Universitetsgata 13 ☎8 519 54 800 www.vasamuseet.se

A wooden monument to King Gustav Adolf's small penis, the Vasa ship was commissioned in 1626 and was supposed to be the largest seagoing vessel of its day. Unfortunately, the guy whose job it was to say "Wait! You can't put 64 cannons on a boat like that. It'll sink!" was sick the day the Vasa took off, so in 1628, the entire Swedish government watched as their life savings sank beneath the waves of Stockholm's harbor. Thankfully, the ship has been dredged up from

top 5 apps to use in stockholm

1. SWEDISH BY NEMO: As Nelson Mandela said, "When you speak to a man in his mother tongue, you are speaking to his heart." We almost feel guilty writing that because we know you'll only use this app to get laid, but at least you'll be snatching hearts in a foreign language!

2. FOOD LOVERS STOCKHOLM: Crowd-sourced, impartial reviews of restaurants and wine bars throughout Stockholm. Can't shine a candle to StreetKak (below) but we suppose it has its plebian charm.

3. MUSEUMS IN STOCKHOLM: Easy and simple—an offline guide to Stockholm's most popular museums. Includes times, short descriptions, and a map

4.TRANSIT MAP STOCKHOLM: Though the train system here is nothing like New York's, it can still be tricky to navigate. With this offline map, you can search where the stations are and which trains service them. Easy, simple, super practical.

5. STREETKAK: Do you ever find a food cart that you simply can't find again? You no longer have to hit Craigslist's Missed Connections because now there's an app for that! With StreetKak, you can watch Stockholm's food carts move in real time and see what they're serving. If you're broke and looking for cheap eats, this may just be the best option next to selling plasma.

the seafloor and is on full display at the museum today. For just 100 SEK, you can relive all the hubris and ambition of 17th century Sweden while avoiding the scurvy and drowning that followed it.

i *130 SEK, students 100 SEK, free for under 18.* ☒ *Open daily 8:30am-6pm.*

NORDISKA MUSEUM (NORDISKA MUSEET)
MUSEUM
Djurgårdsvägen 6-16   ☎8 519 54 600 www.nordiskamuseet.se

This museum covers all aspects of life in Sweden from holiday practices, to clothing, to the indigenous Sami minority and seeks to impress upon visitors the diversity of Nordic tradition. While some displays may be a tad excessive on the details (trust us, you don't need to know all seven kinds of biscuits Swedes ate in the 19th century) it's nonetheless one of the coolest museums you'll find in Stockholm.

i *100 SEK, free for under 18. Free Sept-May on Wednesdays 5pm-8pm.* ☒ *Open M-Tu 10am-5pm, W 10am-8pm, Th-Su 10am-5pm.*

ARMY MUSEUM
MUSEUM
Riddargatan 13   ☎21 98 20 00 www.armemuseum.se

Guns! Tanks! Bombs! If any of these words gives you a brain-boner, the Army Museum should be your #1 stop in Stockholm. It traces the history of the Swedish military from the past to the present—covering everything from the 30 Years War to the Napoleonic Wars to World War II—and even has machine guns and uniforms you can play with. The exhibits are incredible and make this a perfect place for anyone with an interest in military history. Or Sweden. Or vaguely attractive mannequins in revealing poses.

i *80 SEK, students 50 SEK, free for under 19.* ☒ *Open June-Aug daily 10am-5pm; Sept-May Tu 11am-10pm, W-Su 11am-5pm.*

SPIRITS MUSEUM
MUSEUM
Djurgårdsvägen 38   ☎8 121 31 310 www.spritmuseum.se

At the Spirits Museum, you can learn everything you never knew about Swedes' love-hate relationship with alcohol: how it brings together families, how it tears

sweden

apart relationships, how it smells great when you mix in a lil' cinnamon or cardamom and oh my god this smelling room is getting me high on spice. The art exhibit at the entrance walks you through the last 30 years of advertising from Absolut Vodka, and we have to say that these posters are just as cool as anything you'll see in art museums. After that, you can walk through exhibits on the history of beer, fumble your way through a hangover simulation, and lie down in a movie theater that tries to immerse you in one man's boozy night out. It's the kind of place we'd refer to unironically as "meta," and (because we know this is the only thing you're wondering) you can book tastings if you call in advance.

i *100 SEK, students 90 SEK. ⚅ Open M 10am-6pm, Tu 10am-8pm, W-Su 10am-6pm.*

FOTOGRAFISKA
MUSEUM
Stadsgårdshamnen 22 ☎8 509 00 500 www.fotografiska.eu

Like most modern art museums, this place seems bizarre to the uninitiated: the opening exhibit features a lot of boob and sideboob, but we're not sure what the deeper meaning is. Nonetheless, the photographs on display here are some of the most interesting you'll find in Europe, with exhibits from the world's leading nature photographers, fashion designers, and artists making a constant rotation in the galleries. For art-fars and confused tourists alike, it's an incredible place to spend the day—even if you're only pretending to understand that photo of a headless horse.

i *120 SEK, students 90 SEK. ⚅ Open daily 9am-11pm.*

SWEDISH HISTORY MUSEUM
MUSEUM
Narvavägen 13-17 ☎8 519 55 600 www.historiska.se

This museum's main attraction is its Viking collection and damn is it impressive: rings, swords, graves, ever runestones are all on display. If that weren't enough, you can participate in activities like mock archeology digs, archery practice, and sailing on a replica Viking boat because we are all Vikings on the inside. Additionally, there's an interactive exhibit on the prehistory of Sweden that walks you through the entire country's history up until today. This museum feels like it was built for adults with the attention span of a carrot and the wondrous curiosity of a child, and we love it!

i *100 SEK, students 80 SEK, free for under 18. ⚅ Open June-Aug daily 10am-6pm, Sept-May Tu 11am-5pm, W 11am-8pm, Th-Su 11am-5pm, closed Mondays.*

IKEA
SHOPPING
Kungens kurva ☎77 570 05 00

Is IKEA "the" place to hang out in Stockholm? Probably not, unless you're a. over 80 or b. seriously convinced that Yin-Yang Tables are going to turn your life around. Nonetheless, a trip to Sweden without IKEA would be more sacrilegious than not eating a single baguette in France, so head over to this wonder emporium when you have the chance. Unfortunately, it's about 20min. outside of Stockholm by bus, but IKEA's free shuttle leaves from outside the central train station every hour. Once there, you'll be struck by how Ikéaic (?) everything is: the sofas are plush, the meatballs are succulent, and the shoppers are a healthy mix of tourists, Swedes and more tourists. Even if you're not looking to buy something, it's surprisingly fun to simply visit this altar of consumption and see what all the hubbub is about.

i *Free shuttle buses leave every hour starting at 10am from Vasagatan 10 to Kungens kurva, ride takes about 20-30min. ⚅ Open daily 10am-7pm.*

GRÖNA LUND AMUSEMENT PARK
AMUSEMENT PARK
Lilla Allmänna Gänd 9 ☎8 587 50 100 www.gronalund.com

Do you need the threat of serious bodily harm to make you feel alive? Instead of joining a fight club, why not just come down to Gröna Lund and push the limits of what human beings define as fun? Whether it's The Eclipse (a giant

stockholm

43mph "wave swinger" that only requires you be 4 feet tall) or the Fritt Fall Tilt (which drops you from a dizzying 250 feet in the sky), there's something for everyone here. Thankfully the park also has accommodations for the less crazy of us, like bumper cars and a "haunted house" (though we can only imagine shareholders screaming "pussy!" every time a customer gets on the carousel). NOTE: if you want an authentically terrifying experience, put on the Lord of the Rings soundtrack as you make your way through the orc-hordes of six year olds running around the park grounds.

i *110 SEK.* ☉ *Hours vary, usually open 11am-10pm during the summer, but check calendar online for the most up-to-date opening and closing times.*

ARCHIPELAGO
CRUISE
Strandvägen berth no 15 and 16 ☎8 519 54 800
www.stromma.se/en/stockholm/excursions/day-trips/archipelago-tour-with-guide
The archipelago is a breathtaking tour through nature. Over the course of three hours, you sit back and cruise through Game of Thrones-style scenery: dramatic inlets, lakes, forested islands—hell, we may have even seen a piece of the Wall and some Wildlings along the way. Some of the most interesting spots are Tegelön Island and the little rock outcroppings that shoot out of the sea before you reach Tynningö. Our recommendation: try and book a boat that goes to Vaxholm Island; the port and nature there feel more Nordic than Odin shopping at Ikea.

i *260 SEK.* ☉ *Tours leave M-F at 10:30am, noon, 1:30pm, and 3pm; Sa-Su at noon. Trip takes 2.5-3 hrs.*

FOOD

HUSMANS DELI
DELI $
inside Östermalms Saluhall at Östermalmstorg ☎8 553 40 480 www.husmansdeli.se
Sweden without meatballs is like middle school without awkward outfits and photos: it might exist, but our sources tell us your experience is woefully inauthentic if you miss it. When it comes to these tiny bundles of animal flesh, we haven't yet found a place that tastes as good as Husman's Deli. For 95 SEK, you get a huge portion of meatballs, mashed potatoes, and juniper berry jam, all floating in enough succulent gravy to drown any sorrow. For the price and portions, this place is a must-go; even better, it's located in a complex with a dozen other shops selling fruit, cheese, and meatballs of their own.

i *Entrees 80-120 SEK.* ☉ *Open M-Th 9:30am-6pm, F 9:30am-7pm, Sat 9:30am-4pm; closed Sundays.*

CHUTNEY
INDIAN $
Katarina Bangata 19 ☎8 640 30 10 www.chutney.se/om-chutney
Located in Stockholm's trendy Södermalm neighborhood, this place has all the charm of a hippie Indian restaurant. For 98 SEK, you order from a preset menu that includes dishes with rice, stewed vegetables, and several kinds of chutney. That's good enough, but the real reason to go here is the portions: you can get seconds (even thirds) for free, and there are enormous plates of carrots, salad, breads, and sauces that you can use to spice up or enhance your dish. It's an excellent choice for the budget traveller.

i *Entrees 98 SEK.* ☉ *Open M-F 11am-10pm, Sa noon-10pm, Su noon-9pm.*

PONG THAI BUFFET
THAI $$
Drottninggatan 71 C ☎8 20 45 63 pongasian.se/pong-buffe
Swedes are huge on Thai food, so if you're sick of meatballs and kebab, you can find Pad Thai on practically every corner here. At Pong Thai Buffét, you can scarf down as much food as you can take for only 168 SEK. That may sound like a lot, but remember that it's all-you-can-eat in one of world's most expensive

stockholm

cities, and the selection is huge: spring rolls, noodles, satay, orange chicken, chicken fingers, coconut beef, stir fry, lychees, mandarins, cream pudding... we're practically singing "My Favorite Things" as we write out the list.

i *All-you-can-eat buffet 168 SEK.* 🍴 *Lunch buffet open M-F 10:30am-2pm. Dinner open M-Th 5pm-10pm, F 5pm-11pm, Sa noon-11pm, Su noon-10pm.*

FRICK & HAGBERG AB
BURGERS $

Food truck, address varies ☎70 355 92 81 www.frickochhagberg.se

This food truck changes locations every day, but trust us: it's worth the trek. These burgers would even have Gollum purring "my precious." They're 100% organic and absolutely delicious; our order, the Original, came with gruyère cheese, onion, pickles, mayo, and meat that was flavorful and enlightening. With an average price of about 80 SEK, these burgers are both filling and affordable. And they even have veggie options! To find them, follow their FB page for weekly updates on locations.

i *Burgers 75-90 SEK. Double patties, add on 45 SEK.* 🍴 *Open daily 11am-1pm and 5-7pm.*

KOH PHANGAN
THAI $$

Skånegatan 57 ☎8 642 50 40 www.kohphangan.se/sodermalm

In wintertime—when Swedes spend months on end fighting darkness and snow—we imagine this place is a cheery reminder of what non-Stalingrad weather looks like. In summer, though, tourists might find the tiki-torches, strobe lights, and beach-bar more like the venue for a tacky Sweet 16 than a genuine foodie destination. To its credit, though, Koh Phangan serves a mean Mai Tai and decent rosés (around 70 SEK a glass), while the chicken pad thai and complimentary fish sauce salad are also quite tasty. This place is a hit with locals and could be a genuinely fun place to start out the night—just be prepared to spend in the 200 SEK range if you want to feel full and satisfied.

i *Entrees 150 SEK.* 🍴 *Open M-F 4pm-1am, Sa-Su noon-1am. Kitchen closes at midnight; bar open until closing.*

URBAN DELI
SWEDISH $$

Nytorget 4 ☎8 599 09 180

Urban Deli is part upscale grocery store, part restaurant-bar, and the food tastes like what Zeus would eat after a particularly long-night of nectar and nymph-boning. The Iberian ham plate (145 SEK) and Fiskgoyta (mussel/salmon fish pot; 205 SEK) are definitely recommended, while the chocolate almond pudding is likely the closest mankind will ever get to orgasm in culinary form. The drink menu is about twice as good as the food listing, and most beers go for around 80 SEK. It's certainly on the pricier end of things, but if you're going to treat yourself on a night out this is the place to do it.

i *Entrees 150 SEK.* 🍴 *Open daily 8am-10pm.*

HURRY CURRY
INDIAN $

Slöjdgatan 11 ☎8 23 30 80 www.hurrycurry.se

This Indian restaurant doesn't engage in the huge portions (or vegan tomfoolery) of Södermalm's Chutney, but the food is equally good. While the menu is admittedly limited, the butter chicken is a bargain at 90 SEK, and the vegetarian options (our personal favorite: vego vindaloo) are also pretty tasty. Like a onenight-stand, though, it's best to dip in and out rather than linger too long here; the place can get crowded and is much more suited to a quick meal than a drawn-out dinner.

i *Entrees 100 SEK.* 🍴 *Open M-Sa 11am-9pm, Su noon-5pm.*

RAMEN KIMAMA
JAPANESE $

Birger Jarlsgatan 93 ☎8 15 55 39 www.kimamma.se/ramen

Some of best ramen in Stockholm and possibly Scandinavia. This place has all the classics—shoyu, shio, miso—each sprinkled with garlic, boiled egg, bamboo shoots, pork, and, of course, noodles. The broth is perfect, and the food itself had an incredible aroma. We went for the shoyu ramen with an Asahi beer and were not disappointed in the least. For those with less soupy inclinations, they also have standard fare like gyoza, yaki soba, kimchi, and more. The drinks are reasonably priced (50 SEK for beers, 90 SEK for wines) and most main dishes are around 115 SEK or more.

i Ramen 115 SEK. Alcoholic drinks 50-90 SEK. ☑ Open M-F 11:30am-2:30pm and 5pm-9:30pm; Sa 5pm-9:30pm, Su 5pm-9pm.

VIGARDA
BURGERS $

Norrlandsgatan 13   ☎8 505 24 466 www.vigarda.se/mood

An excellent place for a quick, cheap burger in Stockholm's Östermalm neighborhood. Though it's a more upscale joint, the prices aren't bad by Stockholm standards: the bacon cheeseburger goes for 75 SEK, while the burger of the month (when we visited, 'Thai spice" with coriander and chili) is 95 SEK (fries and salad included). In a true act of gluttony, our researcher threw in an extra 50 SEK to make his cheeseburger a double and did not regret it. Perhaps not as good a burger as Frick & Hagberg, but certainly worth a quick visit.

i Burgers 75-100 SEK. ☑ Open M-Tu 11am-9pm, W-Sa 11am-11pm, Su 11am-7pm.

JOHAN & NYSTRÖM COFFEE CONCEPT STORE
CAFE $

Swedenborgsgatan 7   ☎8 702 20 40 johanochnystrom.se

You'll see an Espresso House or Wayne's Coffee on every block in this city, but Johan & Nyström beats them all with its engaging staff, cheap pastries, and décor of a mini Scandinavian Williamsburg. The staff here told us it was the best coffee shop in Stockholm, and their cappuccinos and cardamom buns positively convinced us of that. This place is an absolute must-go coffee lovers, whether you're stepping in for a quick macchiato or preparing for a forlorn, day-long affair with your computer and a sandwich.

i Coffee 30-60 SEK. Pastries 30 SEK. ☑ Open M-F 7:30am-6pm, Sa 10am-4pm, Su 11am-4pm.

MUGGEN
CAFE $

Götgatan 24   ☎8 642 50 40 www.muggen.se

Do you want scones best described as "bitchin'"? Paninis and salads that won't break the bank, and coffee that's fresher than a new pair of Jordans? At Muggen, you can get all these and more in the heart of Södermalm, Stockholm's coolest neighborhood. Our personal rec: go for the House croque. With gouda, oregano and juicy ham, it's a delectably sinful sandwich that goes great with the cappuccinos and ironic neckbeards you'll see everywhere here.

i Coffee 30 SEK. Pastries 30 SEK. Sandwiches 115 SEK. ☑ Open M-F 8am-11pm, Sa-Su 8am-10pm.

NIGHTLIFE

GARLIC AND SHOTS
BAR

Folkungagatan 8   ☎8 640 84 46 www.garlicandshots.co

As you may have guessed, Swedes really don't beat around the bush when it comes to names: this place is indeed a garlic-themed restaurant and bar. Though you may choke through nausea and bad breath as you make your way down the menu, the prices here are unbeatable: each of their 101 shots—with flavors such as garlic and bourbon, tequila and chili, and vodka and licorice—costs 50 SEK. For biohazard reasons, you may want to bring a pack of breath mints or at least a 48-hour abstinence pledge if you end up going, but the location in the hip Södermalm neighborhood makes this one of Let's Go's favorite bars in Stockholm.

i Shots 50 SEK. ☑ Open M-F 5pm-11pm, Sa-Su 5pm-11:30pm.

AIFUR
BAR

Västerlånggatan 68b   ☎8 20 10 55 www.aifur.se

Let's say your life flashes before your eyes. You've definitely had some accomplishments: that Little League game you won, that trip to London you took, that "girlfriend" you had in 6th grade. But all of those mean nothing if you haven't tried mead. Part honey, part wine, all deliciousness, it's an ancient beverage with more flavors than Paris Hilton has STDs. At Aifur, a Viking-themed cellar in Stockholm's Gamla Stan neighborhood, you can sample this holy nectar while surrounded by waiters dressed in medieval garb. The outfits and prices may make it seem like a bit of a tourist trap, but it's the kind of tourist trap Let's Go 100% embraces.

i Mead 80 SEK. ☼ Open M-Th 5pm-11pm, F-Sa 5pm-1am, closed Sundays.

CARMEN
BAR

Tjärhovsgatan 14   ☎8 641 24 12

One native informant cheerily referred to Carmen's clientele as "a melting pot," explaining: "you've got students and musicians, winos and drunks, grandparents and tattoo artists...basically everyone besides Batman!" And while the place is certainly no Bruce Wayne in hiding (it's a simple dive bar—what you see is what you get), the prices are great by Swedish standards. Beers (including imports like Brooklyn IPA) are in the 50-65 SEK, while mixed drinks clock in at around 100 SEK or more. It's a cheap spot to get your buzz on, though the size of the crowd and the 1am closing time mean that it's best to come here earlier in the night before moving on to bigger and better things.

i Beers 50-65 SEK. Mixed drinks 100 SEK. ☼ Open daily 4pm-1am.

EXIT BAR & LOUNGE
BAR

Götgatan 53   ☎8 644 77 77 www.exitloungebar.se

Though this bar's name is about as inspired as "Bathroom on the Left," we still like the place. The atmosphere here is quiet and subdued, with a slightly older clientele who look like extras from a James Bond film (or, given the number of requests for Old Fashioneds, perhaps Mad Men). It's much better for cocktails than beers, so be sure you order correctly: we highly recommend the Dark and Stormy and Lynchburg Lemonade. Exit is great for a quiet drink before moving on to rowdier locales; seeing as you're across the street from Södermalm's Medborgarplatsen station and surrounded by other cool bars and restaurants, the world is your oyster.

i Drinks 100 SEK. ☼ Open M-F 3pm-1am, Sa-Su 2pm-1am.

TIKI ROOM
BAR

Birkagatan 10   ☎8 33 15 55 www.mellowbar.com

Do you want to drink alcohol out of a carved Polynesian chest with 3 foot-long straws? Who are we kidding—you'd have to be the ultimate bougie bitch to think that wasn't cool. With the Tiki torches, calypso music, and a drink called "Missionary's Downfall," what more could you want from a kitschy bar? This place is pretty average price-wise (cocktails are in the 160 SEK), but the atmosphere can't be beat.

i Drinks 150 SEK. ☼ Open M-Th 4pm-midnight, F-Sa 4pm-1am, closed Sundays.

BERNS
CLUB

Skånegatan 57   ☎8 642 50 40 www.berns.se

Every city has its massive, multi-story nightclub that you "have" to go to: New York has Studio 54, Prague has Karlovy Lázně, and Stockholm has Berns. It looks like a massive, repurposed royal ballroom, and we've been told Edith Piaf used to sing here; if that's the case, though, she probably did not write La Vie en Rose about this place. To start off, the cover charge is a bit high—200 SEK after 10pm— and the bouncers, in true Stockholm style, can be very dismissive and intimidating to non-locals. With its minimum age of 23, Berns is also clearly shooting for an older crowd, but still expect a 30+ minute wait if you're getting there late at night. If you really hate nightlife, our best recommendation is to come here early in the evening for a cocktail: you're paying mostly for the scenery anyway, so why not enjoy your G&T without a sweaty Swede getting his pheromones on you at 1 in the morning?

i *Cover 200 SEK after 10pm on weekends. Mixed drinks 100 SEK.* ☑ *Hours in different clubs/floors vary, usually open 11pm-3am.*

TWEED   BAR

Lilla Nygatan 5   ☎8 506 40 082 www.tweedbar.se

If Casablanca is your favorite film, rest assured that you'll always have Tweed. It's the kind of place where you sit back in a Chesterfield armchair and talk about beating the Gerries; a 40's-style lounge that transports you back to the classiest days of the empire over bourbons and a cuban cigar. If that weren't enough, they cook up some mean burgers to temper your boozy nostalgia, though in the 195-220 SEK range, it may be best to come here for after-dinner shenanigans. Tweed's main room is unfortunately closed for much of the summer but its rooftop bar, The Sanchez, remains open.

i *Drinks 120 SEK.* ☑ *Open M-Th 5pm-midnight, F-Sa 5pm-1am, closed Sundays.*

ESSENTIALS
Practicalities

- **TOURIST OFFICES:** Stockholm Visitor Center (Kulturhuset, Sergels Torg 5 ☎8 508 28 508. ☑ Open May-Sept M-F 9am-7 pm, Sa 9am-4pm and 6pm July-Aug, Su 10am-4pm.)

- **CURRENCY EXCHANGE:** Possible at Arlanda Airport and stores such as 24Money and Forex (the latter of which probably has the most competitive rates). The best bet may be simply to withdraw cash from an ATM, though: the exchange rates are not much different than what you'll get in stores.

- **ATMS:** You can pay for almost everything in Sweden with debit or credit cards, but the Central Train Station and most chain stores like 7-11 will have an ATM (Bankomat in Swedish). ATMs and currency exchange are also available at Stockholm Airport and are easy to locate along major pedestrian streets such as Drottninggatan and the T-Centralen metro stop.

- **LUGGAGE STORAGE:** You can hire lockers in public areas such as Cityterminalen, the bus station directly connected to Stockholm Central Station. Average costs are about 70 SEK for 24hrs in a medium-sized box, 90 SEK for a large box, and 120 SEK for an extra large box

- **LAUNDROMATS:** Most hostels offer laundry services either for free or at a low cost (City Backpackers: machines are free, soap is 50 SEK; City Hostel 30 SEK). Independent laundromats include Tvättomaten i Stockholm (Västmannagatan 61B ☎8 34 64 80. ☑ Open M-F 8:30am-6:30pm, Sa 9:30am-1pm, closed on Sundays.) This laundromat is often better for dry-cleaning needs—if you're just washing a sack of dirty clothing, it will cost at least 100 SEK.

- **INTERNET:** Wi-Fi is available widely throughout Stockholm, with hotspots in the Stockholm Visitor Center, Arlanda Airport, Central Station, and most hostels and hostels. Additionally, certain chain stores you'll see on every corner—such as Espresso House and Wayne's Coffee—also offer free connectivity. There's also an app called the Free Wi-Fi Map, which helps you identify places near to you and provides any necessary login information

- **POST OFFICE:** Centralposthuset (Vasagatan 28-34) in the center of Stockholm is a massive, century-old building designed by the Swedish architect Ferdinand Boberg.

Emergency

- **EMERGENCY NUMBER:** ☎112

- **POISON CONTROL:** ☎8 33 12 31, open 8am-5pm
- **24-HOUR EMERGENCY MEDICAL ADVICE:** ☎1177
- **SUICIDE HOTLINE:** ☎20 22 00 60, nationellahjalplinjen.se, open M-Th 5am-10pm.
- **RFSL STOCKHOLM (FOR COUNSELING ON LGBTQ-RELATED ISSUES):** ☎8 501 62 970, www.rfsl.se
- **LATE-NIGHT PHARMACIES:** 24-Hour Apoteket Pharmacy (CW Scheele, Klarabergsgatan 64, near T-Centralen ☎8 45 481 30.)
- **HOSPITALS:** Non-Swedish citizens need identification, insurance papers, and a photocopy of their passport when visiting a public hospital. As always, call the emergency services at 112 if you need an ambulance or other kinds of medical help. Generally, in-patient care is free but you (or your insurer) have to pay the costs of outpatient care. Stockholm South (Sjukhusbacken 10 ☎8 616 10 00. 24hr emergency room.)

Getting There

By Plane

Arlanda is Stockholm's main airport, located about 23 miles away from the city's center. It is the largest airport in Sweden and services the majority of domestic and international flights coming into Stockholm (though a smaller number of aircraft also land at Bromma Airport, to the northwest of the city).The easiest and quickest way to get from the airport to the heart of Stockholm is to take the Arlanda Express, a train running every 15min. between the airport and Central Station. For people under 25, the price of a one-way ticket is 150 SEK, while adults over the age of 25 must pay 280 SEK. The main advantage of taking the Express is that the trip takes only around 20 min. Tickets can be booked online (www.arlandaexpress.com) or at kiosks in the airport/train station. The earliest airport express train from the city center leaves at 4:35am.

By Bus

The Flygbussarna buses leave every 15min. from both Arlanda and City Terminalen (connected to Central Station) on a trip that takes roughly 35-40min. Tickets can be booked online (www.flygbussarna.se) and cost 99 SEK for adults and 89 SEK for students.

By Taxi

Taxis are much more expensive than buses and trains and, with wait times, will probably make your trip to the airport/city center longer than it needs to be. Nonetheless, you can book companies like Taxi Stockholm to pick you up for a fixed price: 520 SEK to the airport and 620 SEK from the airport.

Getting Around

Public Transportation

Stockholm does not do transportation on the honor system; you must swipe your card to access all trams, subways, and buses. Cards can be purchased at the stations and most major bus stops; note that you must pay an initial fee of 20 SEK to get the card itself, but then can fill it up indefinitely. Single-use ticket 36 SEK (students 20 SEK); 24-hour ticket 70 SEK; 7-day 300 SEK (students 180 SEK).

Stockholm Card: This card gives you free access to public transportation and discounts at a number of museums, restaurants, and parking spaces. The full list of attractions and prices are available on the official Stockholm tourist website (www.visitstockholm.com/en/Stockholmcard/), but sample prices are: 1 adult for 2 days 765 SEK; 1 adult for 3 days 895 SEK.

By Train

Stockholm Central Station (Centralplan 15, Main Hall open daily 5am-12:15am; rail lines open M-F 5am-1:15am, Sa-Su 5am-2:15am) is the main hub for local, national, and international trains coming into the city. Long distance buses such as Swebus also drop off here.

By Taxi

Taxi Stockholm (☎8 15 00 00, www.taxistockholm.se). Prices vary depending on the number of passengers, the time of day, and the length of the trip, but for a sample ride: a taxi ride on weekend nights with two people booked in advance starts at 45 SEK, goes up 9.5 SEK a minute in addition to 13.6 SEK per kilometer. Be wary of black taxis—individuals with a car offering to drive you places for cash. You'll often see them outside of crowded clubs and bars in Södermalm. They're illegal, unlicensed, and potentially dangerous. Uber is widely available in Stockholm, though their prices don't differ dramatically from standard cabs (especially during surge pricing).

malmö

Malmö straddles a number of identities. It's a medieval town with plenty of old architecture to show for it, but it also boasts stunning skyscrapers, beautiful parks, and a huge immigrant population that makes it one of Sweden's most diverse cities. It's a foodie's paradise, with many of its younger, vibrant neighborhoods offering everything from organic Middle Eastern to Mexican-Turkish fusion, and on the nightlife front you'll find your fair share of German beer houses and music clubs.

The cash-strapped traveller will be happy to know that Malmö is much cheaper than Stockholm. The city itself is a 30-minute train ride from Copenhagen and only 15 minutes from the Swedish town of Lund, so you're ideally placed to explore new shores. Just avoid plundering them when you land.

ACCOMMODATIONS

MERCURE HOTEL   HOTEL $$

Stadiongatan 21   ☎40 672 85 70 www.mercure-hotel-malmo.com

Have you heard that Malmö is the Vegas of Sweden? No? Maybe because we just made that up. But if you theoretically wanted a luxurious bachelor party, a room here would be the place to do it. For the low price of just 550 SEK, you can book a sizable wood-paneled double with TV, Wi-Fi, and a King-Solomon-style breakfast buffet. Though this place is essentially a 4-star hotel going for 2-star prices, that trade-off comes at a cost: the hotel is located in a removed part of town whose nearest attractions are a shopping mall and apartment blocks. Thankfully, you're only 10 minutes away from downtown by public transport, so the revelry can continue into the city.

i Singles 500 SEK. 🕐 Reception 24hr.

STF VANDRARHEM   HOSTEL $

Rönngatan 1   ☎40 611 62 20 www.hihostels.com/hostels/malmo-city

Malmö does not have much of a hostelling culture, so this place is one of your only choices if you're looking to economize. The hostel has all the amenities a backpacker needs (kitchens, clean bathrooms, a central location, and helpful staff) and the prices are pretty standard for Scandinavia. It's not a party hostel nor a particularly exciting place to stay, but if you need a good, cheap bed to come home to at night, this hostel is a great choice.

i Doubles 850 SEK. Dorms 330 SEK. Hostelling International members get 50 SEK discount. 🕐 Reception open Tu-Sa 8am-8pm, Su-M 8am-4pm.

SIGHTS

SLOTTSPARKEN AND MALMÖ CASTLE

Fågelbacken

PARK
☎20 34 45 00

Yes, it's called "Slottsparken." Haha. Grow up. Unfortunately, this place does not offer the liberal sexual dalliances that its name implies to English-speakers, but it's still a gorgeous place for a walk. The small lakes and reservoirs along the paths give this park a serene feel, and the giant boathouses and nearby Torso skyscraper give the impression that its planners watched Woody Allen's Manhattan and felt inspired. Head to the northern part of the park and you'll approach its giant slott (stop giggling, it means 'castle'. Ok, we giggle too). You're going to see your fair share of castles in Scandinavia, but Malmö Castle is particularly impressive: it was built in the 15th century and served as one of the strongholds of Denmark. Like any good adolescent, this castle went through a lot of identities from coin-minting, to party-holding, to prison. The castle today stands as a museum, or technically museums, including the City Museum, where you can learn about the culture and history of Malmö; the Technology and Maritime Museum, where you can walk onto a submarine; and the Malmö Art Museum, which boasts a large collection of Swedish art and furniture.

i Park free. Castle 40 SEK. ☼ Park open 24hrs. Castle open daily 10am-5pm.

LILLA TORG

intersection of Larochegatan and Hjulhamnsgatan

SQUARE

If you've got a degree in people-watching, Lilla Torg is an excellent spot for you. Meaning "little square" in Swedish, it's where you'll find the native Malmö-ites eating, shopping, and drinking coffee every afternoon. Everything from casual afternoon chats to protests to counter-protests happen here. In a city that can sometimes feel small, sterilized, and underwhelming, Lilla Torg is a welcome dose of excitement and youth culture.

i Free. ☼ Open 24hrs.

RIBERSBORGS OPEN-AIR BATHHOUSE

Limhamnsvägen, Brygga 1

SAUNA
☎46 26 03 66 www.ribersborgskallbadhus.se

The Ribersborgs Kallbadhus is the epitome of the sauna experience: whether you want to steam up, jump in the Baltic, or kick back with an espresso or two, this place is a definite must-go in Malmö. There are three bathhouses—one male, one female, one mixed—and we must say there's something oddly liberating about sizing up everybody's junk in a room full of naked strangers (be sure to man-spread because that is how you establish dominance.) Bring your own lock and towel (you're not allowed to wear clothes inside) and enjoy your day of detoxing before the inevitable retoxing.

i Sauna 55 SEK. ☼ Open May-Aug M-Tu 9am-8pm, W 9am-9pm, Th-F 9am-8pm; Sa-Su 9am-6pm; Sept-Apr M-Tu 10am-7pm, W 10am-8pm, Th-F 10am-7pm, Sa-Su 9am-4pm.

FOOD

BAR BURRITO

Fersensväg 14

MEXICAN $
☎40 615 32 78 www.barburrito.se

Bar Burrito was easily Let's Go's best food experience in Malmö—this place makes its own dough and throws a big middle finger to the establishment by putting garlic sauce in the burritos (note to Chipotle: you're slacking). The food is fresh and affordable: a burrito with guac will put you back 69 SEK and the home-made lemonade is only 15 SEK. Eating here is as satisfying as watching Gandhi punch Hitler in the face—and we mean that in the best possible way.

i Burrito or burrito bowl 69 SEK. Frozen yogurt 20-30 SEK. Lemonade 15 SEK. ☼ Open M-Th 11am-8pm, F 11am-9pm, Sa noon-9pm, Su noon-7pm.

sweden

NORDIC STREETFOOD

Food truck, address varies

SWEDISH $$

☎706 20 20 94 facebook.com/nordicstreetfood

The food truck phenomenon has hit Sweden faster than reality hit Eddie Murphy's career after Pluto Nash, and Nordic Streetfood is a perfect example of that. For the last two years, the humble van has been serving up delicious, locally-sourced food with an interesting Swedish touch. Our recommendation: the pulled pork burger. With beets. And coleslaw. Or the chanterelle (mushroom) wrap. Everything here, as Shakespeare would say, is "on fleek."

i *Sandwiches and burgers 100 SEK.* ⓩ *Check on their FB page (facebook.com/nordicstreetfood) for weekly schedules and locations.*

DONER KEBAB

Sankt Johannesgatan 1E

TURKISH $

☎40 30 09 11

Do you want hunks of garlic beef wrapped in the oily goodness of a pancake-sized wrap? Basically, this is your place if you're in search of tasty, spiced meats. It's as healthy as bathing in gasoline, but no one goes to a Turkish fast food joint if they're trying to slim down. Our recommendation is to go for the durum doner (easily one of the tastiest we had in Malmö) though the shawarma is equally good.

i *Wraps 69 SEK.* ⓩ *Open M-F 11am-8pm, Sa-Su 11am-7pm.*

SALTIMPORTEN CANTEEN

Grimsbygatan 24

SWEDISH $

☎70 651 84 26

This restaurant is like a cat. It refuses to work for your attention and only gives you the time of day when it feels like it…by which we mean this place is only open for two hours a day. And closed on weekends—it's like they're daring you to try and get in. If you do manage to make it between noon and 2pm though, you'll be blown away. The menu changes every day and only has a few items, but the food is always cooked to perfection: whether pork chops, prime rib, or chili with thyme and cauliflower, it's fresh, delicious, and at 85 SEK, it's pretty cheap. Though the riverside warehouse the restaurant is housed in looks a little sketch, don't shy away. We can't recommend this place enough!

i *Entreés 85-100 SEK.* ⓩ *Open M-F noon-2pm.*

NIGHTLIFE

BIERHAUS

Drottninggatan 36

BAR

☎40 23 60 01 www.bierhaus.se

Located right off of Malmö's main pedestrian street, this beer house feels ridiculously authentic. They've got every kind of beer imaginable at knockout prices: though we're partial to the Berliner Kindl and Warsteiner Pilsner, practically everything here is tasty and Teutonic. Whatever you order, we highly recommend shelling out money for the currywurst—part sausage, part curry ketchup, it's the ultimate drunk food to set your night in the right direction.

i *Beers 100 SEK.* ⓩ *Open Tu-Th 4pm-1am.*

BIERHAUS MALMÖ

Norra Parkgatan 2

CLUB

☎40 23 60 01 www.bierhaus.se

This is one of Malmö's biggest and best clubs. Even though our Scandinavia researcher would prefer getting cholera to going clubbing, even he had to admit this place was fun. The clientele is usually a mix of young professionals and a college-age crowd, and the space is big enough (between the patio, lounge room, bar, and music stage) to find your own groove. Start off at the bar to try one of the 20 beers on tap here. Then get ready to dance the night away. The music can range from house to hip hop to 80s rock. If all the music and bumping is getting you claustrophobic, step outside. You're in the heart of Malmö's

malmö

coolest pub neighborhood, so you're sure to find something here that won't kill your vibe.

i Cover varies depending on performers. Beers 150 SEK. ☿ Open Tu-Sa 4pm-1am.

MALMÖ BRYGGHUS

BAR

Bergsgatan 33 ☎40 20 96 85

If your average beer intake include Keystone and Miller Lite, congrats on being a patriot. But we encourage you expand your horizons a bit by visiting the Brygghus, Malmö's only microbrewery. Though the giant metal vats give off a Breaking Bad vibe, the beer here is so high quality, it's clear they pour all of their time into making it. You can't go wrong with the tap selection—Pilsner, lagers and a few IPA's—but for the more adventurous, their monthly selection is where it's at. Even better, they offer tasting tours (at roughly 250 SEK) and a full food menu to battle the beer hangover you might have the next morning.

i Beer 30-150 SEK. Tasting tour 250 SEK. Bar snacks 100 SEK. ☿ Open M-Tu 5pm-11pm, W-Th 4pm-1am, F-Sa 4pm-3am, closed Sundays.

ESSENTIALS
Practicalities

- **TOURIST OFFICES:** Malmö Turistbyrå (Börshuset, Skeppsbron. ☎40 34 12 00. www.malmotown.com. ☿ Open M-F 9am-5pm, Sa-Su 10am-2pm.)

- **CURRENCY EXCHANGE:** Possible at Malmö Airport and stores such as Forex (which has three locations in Malmö, including in Central Station).

- **ATMS:** Swedbank and Nordea ATMs are located throughout Malmö (especially along crowded pedestrian streets such as Scheelevägen and the area directly adjacent to Slottsparken) and many give you an option of withdrawing in Swedish Kronor, Danish Kronor, or Euros.

- **LUGGAGE STORAGE:** If you're not storing your luggage at a hostel or hotel, you can rent out a small, medium or large lockers at Malmö Central Station (available for periods of 12 and 24 hours or longer; can use coins or card).

- **GLBT SERVICES:** Next to Stockholm, Malmö may be the most gay-friendly city in Sweden—you'll find plenty of gay bars in the area around Folkets Park (for a full list of clubs, bars and restaurants, consult the Malmö city website www.malmotown.com/en/article/gay-friendly-places/).

- **INTERNET:** Almost all cafes have free Wi-Fi (you'll find plenty of Swedish national chains, such as Espresso House, alongside independent coffee shops). You'll also get connectivity at the City Library (Kung Oscars väg 11) and major train stations such as Central Station and Triangeln.

- **POST OFFICE:** Posten Företagscenter (Krossverksgatan 7 ☎40 15 58 92. ☿ Open M-F 8am-6pm.)

Emergency

- **EMERGENCY NUMBER:** ☎112

- **LOCAL POLICE:** ☎77 114 14 00

- **POISON CONTROL:** ☎20 22 00 06

- **SWEDISH NATIONAL SUICIDE HOTLINE:** ☎31 711 24 00

- **RFSL MALMÖ:** ☎40 10 33 21, for questions related to the organization and LGBTQ-related issues. ☿ Phone available Tuesdays and Thursdays from 12pm to 4pm.

- **24 HOUR MEDICAL ADVICE:** ☎1177

- **LATE-NIGHT PHARMACIES:** Apoteket Gripen (Bergsgatan 48 ☎77 145 04 50. ☿ Open daily 8am-10pm.)

- **HOSPITALS:** For emergencies, always call ☎112 for an ambulance or ☎1177 for medical advice. If you are not a Swedish citizen, make sure to bring your passport and insurance information if you go to the doctor. Vårdcentralen Granen (Grangatan 11 ☎40 623 42 00. ☼ Best time for drop-ins is weekdays 10am-12pm and 1-3pm, but primary care and phone lines are open 8am-5pm on weekdays.)

Getting There

Malmö Airport (known previously as Sturup) is 17 miles away from the city center and services both Malmö and Lund. There are several daily flights between here and Stockholm, as well as other Scandinavian and continental European cities. The cheapest and quickest way to get from the airport to the city center is to take the shuttle bus, Flygbussarna, directly from the departures terminal. Tickets can be purchased online (www.flygbussarna.se/en/malmo) or at the airport at a price of 105 SEK for adults and 95 SEK for children. The bus takes 30-40 minutes to arrive at Malmö Central Station.

As elsewhere in Sweden, cabs to and from the airport are more expensive than public transportation. Cheaper rides from companies such as Taxi 23 (☎40 23 23 23) go for a flat rate of 359 SEK. Always confirm the fare with the driver before getting in the car.

Getting Around

Public Transportation

Jojo: To use public transportation, you must first purchase a Jojo card. The card costs 20 SEK (available at Malmö Central Station) and you can then add as many fares as you want onto it. Each ride costs 22 SEK, but you get a 20% discount (ie price of 17 SEK per ride) if you upload more than 200 SEK onto the card.

Malmö City Card: This card gives discounts at around 600 separate places, whether that be 50% off at public museums, 10% off taxi rides, or free dessert at restaurants. The card also provides 24 hours of free parking and can be purchased via an app or in person at the Tourist Information office. Full price offerings are available online, but the 1 day for 1 adult and 2 kids is 170 SEK, while 2 days is 200 SEK.

By Taxi

Taxis are not as expensive here as they are in Stockholm, though prices change depending on time of day and number of passengers. The following are prices for an average 10 km/15-minute trip (though there's an extra tax if you're traveling after 9 o'clock on weekends). RD Taxi (☎20 30 03 00): 241 SEK. Taxi Kurir (☎40 700 00): 245-261 SEK. Taxi Skåne (☎40 33 03 30): 263 SEK.

lund

College students make up about half of Lund's population. That young population means that there are cheap eats galore—everything from vegetarian and sushi to kebab and dumplings—and a very active nightlife. As it's such a small place, there isn't much of a backpacker's scene; in fact, Lund only has one hostel, though there are reasonably priced hotels and B&Bs as well.

That might seem a bit limiting for the young traveller, but you'll probably stay here only day or two in the first place; the town is roughly the size of a medium pizza, and you can see all the main sights in a single day. Nevertheless, Lund has plenty of hidden charm: whether its touring the Tolkien-esque cottages or finding bargains at the student thrift shops, there are plenty of ways to fall in love with this town. Do note, though, that while the medieval cathedral and botanical park are certainly

lund

beautiful places to walk through, in summer, the whole town tends to be as dead as Al Gore's presidential hopes. So if you're looking for wild college parties, try to come while school is still in session.

ACCOMMODATIONS

WINSTRUP HOSTEL
HOSTEL $

Winstrupsgatan 3 ☎723 290 800 www.winstruphostel.se

You'd think that being the only hostel in town would make these guys drunk on power; that they, like some budget-travel version of Monsanto, would jack up prices and give substandard service because it's a monopoly. However, the accommodations here actually went above and beyond: all of the beds in the shared rooms have lamps, power outlets, and curtains that effectively turn them into mini-cubbies. You can actually stay here without ever interacting with the other people in your room, and the introvert in us loves that! Moreover, the place comes equipped with a full kitchen and offers 25% discounts at a cafe around the corner. It's comfortable and affordable and, along with love, that's all you need.

i Dorms 275 SEK. Linens 65 SEK. Laundry 50 SEK. Breakfast 69 SEK. ☑ Reception open 7am-11am and 3pm and 8pm.

CHECKINN B&B
B&B $$

Hantverksgatan 6 ☎723 290 800 www.checkinn.se

CheckInn is run by the same people who own Winstrup, and clearly they're doing something right: the place is cute and cheap while still maintaining a hotel-level quality of service. The cheaper rooms go for around 600 SEK a night, but each usually has a bathroom, TV, air conditioner, and wooden floors (because only peasants decorate with shag carpet). It's a short walk away from the train station and might be the comfiest accommodation you'll find while here—if you're only staying a night or two, we highly recommend this place!

i Studio apartment 600-900 SEK. Doubles 800-1000 SEK. Breakfast included. ☑ Reception open 7am-11am and 3pm and 8pm.

SIGHTS

LUND CATHEDRAL
CHURCH

Kyrkogatan 6 www.lundsdomkyrka.se

Every city has something to be proud of. Lund is no different with its massive medieval cathedral that is absolutely beautiful to look at. It has been here for close to 1000 years, and whatever botox the building uses is clearly working: the stonework is immaculate, the arches are perfectly preserved, and the pews inside have got more wood than most mornings. The cathedral is an imposing landmark, and, better yet, is five minutes away from all the parks, museums and restaurants you'll want to visit while on a trip to Lund. If you're lucky, you may even come during one of the free tours of the cathedral, which are offered daily during the summer.

i Free. ☑ Open M-F 8am-6pm, Sa 9:30am-5pm, Su 9:30am-6pm.

BOTANICAL GARDEN
GARDEN

Östra Vallgatan 20 ☎46 222 73 20 www.botaniskatradgarden.se

This garden, managed by Lund University, boasts over 7000 species of plants and some beautifully curated walking paths. The place is swarming with flowers, trees, blackbirds (who, like Poe's Raven, quoth "uh uh, nevermore!" when you try to pet them), and a number of greenhouses and tranquil ponds. Spend an afternoon walking through this historic garden—it has been around since the 1600s—and learning about our world's greener friends.

i Free. ☑ Open daily May-Sept 6am-9:30pm; Oct-Apr 6am-8pm.

sweden

LUND UNIVERSITY

UNIVERSITY

University kids make up about half of the population in this town of 80,000, so it only makes sense you should drop by their alma mater. The campus covers a significant portion of Lund proper and includes everything from medieval towers to French-style style gardens and palatial ivy-lined libraries. The campus also hosts the Historiska Museum, the second-largest museum, in Sweden, as well as a number of beautiful tree-lined gardens. Look smart and see what your college years could've looked like without Netflix.

i Free.

RUNESTONE MOUND

MONUMENT

on Lund University's campus, off Paradisgatan

These runes are a stone's throw away from Lund University's main buildings and are arranged in a curious pattern on a raised mound. We've heard tell that coming here at midnight and whispering "bloody murder" three times will summon the ghost of Ivar the Boneless, but thankfully that's not too much cause for concern. Probably a good guy to grab a beer with. The stones themselves are incredibly old and fascinating to look at. Most of them are eulogies to fallen warriors, with inscriptions like "here lies Björn, a fighter of wide renown," but others are much longer and more artistically written out. Though our Old Norse skills leave a lot to be desired, it's entirely possible the bigger inscriptions say something like "End of the World Sale: all axes half off at Leif's Wonder Emporium, December 31st, 999 A.D." (Note: this is actually not possible.)

FOOD

HUMMUS BAR

MIDDLE EASTERN $

Bangatan 8 ☎12 63 00

The entrance to this place has an illustrated guide on how to eat hummus with pita, but thankfully informs its customers that they won't judge if you use a fork. Thanks, Hummus Bar. You the real MVP. And we say that not only for your tolerance of our primitive ways, but also because of the wallet-friendly Middle Eastern goodness of all your dishes. Our recommendation: the falafel (65 SEK) comes wrapped in a blanket of tahini and hummus and also includes two small side salads.

i Wraps 65-85 SEK. ☒ Open M-F 11am-7pm, Sa noon-7pm; closed Sundays.

WOKERIAN

ASIAN $

Knut Den Stores Torg 2 ☎12 23 23

This popular student haunt fries up tasty dumplings and serves them fast. The restaurant is directly in sight of the train station and not far from the university, and with most dishes in the 70-90 SEK range, it's filling and affordable. They cook up a full menu of Chinese and Japanese dishes, so this is an ideal spot if you're looking to spoon noodles, kung pao chicken, or maki rolls into your eager mouth.

i Entrees 70-100 SEK. ☒ Open M-Sa 11am-9pm, Su noon-8pm.

LUND SALUHALLEN

FOOD COURT $$

Mårtenstorget 1

You'll find plenty of saluhallen throughout Scandinavia, and Lund's is pretty typical: there are about 15 restaurants, a couple delis, and, for those of you looking to spend half your paycheck on a shot of vodka, a Systembolaget liquor store. We're huge fans of Persian food and highly recommend Shiraz Restaurant (the chicken kebab, at 85 SEK, gave us a whole new perspective on life), though other spots like Thai Way and Wasabi Sushi are also tasty. Our best advice: get lost in here and let the food choose you.

i Prices vary. The delis are a bit more upscale, though both the Thai and Persian places are in the 85SEK range. ☒ Open M-W 10am-6pm, Th-F 10am-7pm, Sa 9:30am-3pm; closed Sundays.

CAFÉ & CREPERIE OSKAR

Klostergatan 14C

CAFE $

☎72 329 08 00

Café Oskar is truly an excellent spot for breakfast and snacks. Whether you're looking to nibble on a crêpe or plow through a week's worth of sandwiches and coffee, the prices are affordable and the food is delectable. If you're a guest at Winstrup, CheckInn, or Hotel Oskar, you get a 25% discount here, and the breakfast buffet—with all the classic Scandinavian trappings like eggs, cured meats and marmalade—is excellent for both light eaters and food juggernauts.

i *Coffee 25 SEK. Pastries 70 SEK.* ☼ *Open M-F 7am-5pm, Sa-Su 8am-5pm.*

NIGHTLIFE

CAFÉ ARIMAN

Kungsgatan 2

BAR, CLUB

☎46 13 12 63 www.ariman.se

This place seems to be Lund's loud, leftwing answer to Starbucks. By day it's a cafe filled wall to wall with neckbeards and berets, but at night it becomes a club and bar that's a major hit with students. Unfortunately, the DJs take off during the summer, but it's still a good place for quick beers or a cocktail as you debate Liechtenstein's critique of the Hamburger Palpability Theorem or whatever intellectual people talk about.

i *No cover. Drinks 70 SEK.* ☼ *Open M-Sa 11am-late (usually 3am on weekends), Su 3pm-11pm.*

ESSENTIALS

Practicalities

- **TOURIST OFFICE:** Lunds Turistbyrå (Botulfsgatan 1A ☎46 35 50 40. www.visitlund.se. ☼ Open M-F 10m-6pm, Sa 10am-3pm, Su 11am-3pm.)

- **CURRENCY EXCHANGE:** There are two Forex locations in Lund: Bankgatan 8 and at Botulfsgatan 2.

- **ATMS:** There are a number of ATMs in the shopping area adjacent to Central Station. It's the first place you will see when you arrive at the train station

- **LUGGAGE STORAGE:** Lockers are available at Lund Central Station (payable by credit card or coins). Medium sized luggage costs 50 SEK per day. Larger lockers are available for 60 SEK a day.

- **INTERNET:** Wi-Fi is available at the central station, tourist center, public library (Lund Stadsbibliotek—Sankt Petri Kyrkogatan 6), and most cafes.

- **POST OFFICE:** Posten Företagscenter Lund City (Gasverksgatan 3A ☎10 436 10 35. ☼ Open M-F 8am-6pm.)

Emergency

- **EMERGENCY NUMBER:** ☎112

- **LOCAL POLICE:** ☎77 114 14 00

- **MEDICAL ADVICE:** ☎1177

- **SWEDISH NATIONAL SUICIDE HOTLINE:** ☎31 71 124 00

- **PHARMACIES:** Apotek Hjärtat (Mårtenstorget 12 ☎40 54 05 223 51. ☼ Open M-F 9am-8pm, Sa 9am-7pm, Su 10am-7pm.)

- **HOSPITALS:** For emergencies, always call ☎112 for an ambulance or ☎1177 for medical advice. If you are not a Swedish citizen, make sure to bring your passport and insurance information if you go to the doctor. Skane University Hospital in Lund (Getingevägen 4 ☎17 10 00.)

Getting There

Lund is serviced by Malmö Airport. The cheapest and quickest way to get from the airport to the city center is to take the shuttle bus, Flygbussarna directly from the departures terminal. Tickets can be purchased online (www.flygbussarna.se/en/malmo) or at the airport for 105 SEK. The airport flat rate for a cab from Taxi Skåne is 445 SEK, and other companies have similar prices

Getting Around

Public Transportation

Lund is tiny and there's little need to use public transportation here, but the town does have an extensive bus network which uses the Jojo card. The card costs 20 SEK and you then upload as many fares as you want onto it. Each ride costs 22 SEK, but you get a 20% discount (17 SEK per ride) if you upload more than 200 SEK onto the card.

Malmö City Card: This card gives discounts at around 600 separate places, whether that be 50% off at public museums, 10% off taxi rides, or free dessert and extra burgers at restaurants. The card also provides 24 hours of free parking and can be purchased via an app or in person at the Tourist Information office. Full price offerings are available online, but the 1 day for 1 adult and 2 kids is 170 SEK while 2 days is 200 SEK.

By Taxi

Taxi Lund 121212 (☎046 12 12 12.) Generally, weekend prices are 35 SEK as a base, 11.50 SEK per km and 5 SEK per minute, though the exact rates change depending on time of day and number of people.

sweden essentials

VISAS

Sweden is a member of the EU, and also a member of the Schengen area. Citizens of Australia, Canada, New Zealand, the US, and many other non-EU countries do not need a visa for stays of up to 90 days. However, if you plan to spend time in other Schengen countries, note that the 90-day period of time you are allowed to visit without a visa applies cumulatively to all Schengen countries.

MONEY

Despite being a member of the EU, Sweden is not in the Eurozone and uses the Swedish krona (SEK or kr.) as its currency.

In restaurants, a gratuity or service charge is often included, in which case you don't have to tip. If no gratuity is added, tip your server 5-10%, or to round up the bill to the nearest 10. To tip a taxi driver, also just round up the bill.

ATMs in Sweden are common and convenient. They are often located in airports, train stations and major pedestrian areas. The two major international money networks are MasterCard/Maestro/Cirrus and Visa/PLUS. To find out what out-of-network or international fees you may be subject to by using ATMs, call your bank.

ALCOHOL

There is no minimum age in Sweden to purchase alcohol under 2.25% ABV in supermarkets. The minimum age to purchase alcohol in restaurants and bars, or alcohol above 2.25% in supermarkets is 18. To purchase alcohol from a Systembolaget, you must be 20. Bars, clubs, and discos often have age restrictions higher than 18, and are usually either 20 or 23. Remember to drink responsibly and to never drink and drive. The legal blood alcohol content (BAC) for driving in Sweden is under 0.02%, significantly lower than the US limit of 0.08%.

ESSENTIALS

You don't have to be a rocket scientist to plan a good trip. (It might help, but it's not required.) You do, however, need to be well prepared, and that's what we can do for you. Essentials is the chapter that gives you all the nitty-gritty you need to know for your trip: the hard information gleaned from 56 years of collective wisdom and several months of furious fact-checking. Planning your trip? Check. Where to find Wi-Fi? Check. The dirt on public transportation? Check. We've also thrown in communications info, safety tips, and a phrasebook, just for good measure. Plus, for overall trip-planning advice from what to pack (money and as little underwear as possible) to how to take a good passport photo (it's physically impossible; consider airbrushing), you can also check out the Essentials section of www.letsgo.com.

greatest hits

- **WE ARE ONE.** Poli Sci majors may think of the EU as a bureaucratic nightmare, but it's awesome for you—the Schengen Agreement allows you to move between most European countries without going through customs. (p. 927)

- **WE ARE ONE, PART TWO.** We have mixed feelings about the euro. On one hand, it's awfully convenient to have one currency for most of Europe. On the other hand, the exchange rate is awful. (p. 928)

- **ONE-EURO FLIGHTS.** Yes, it's true—budget airlines are a wonderful thing. We've compiled the continent's cheapest and most convenient. (p. 929)

- **WE AREN'T REALLY ONE.** As integrated as Europe becomes, they'll always speak some wildly different languages. Enter our handy dandy phrasebook. Can you say "Traveling is awesome"? Can you say it in Czech? (p. 934)

planning your trip

DOCUMENTS AND FORMALITIES

We're going to fill you in on visas and work permits, but don't forget the most important one of all: your passport. **Remember to bring your passport!**

Visas

Those lucky enough to be EU citizens do not need a visa to globetrot throughout the
continent. You citizens of Australia, Canada, New Zealand, the US, and most other
non-EU countries do not need a visa for stays of up to 90 days, but this three-month
period begins upon entry into any of the countries that belong to the EU's **freedom of
movement** zone. Those staying longer than 90 days may apply for a longer-term visa;
consult an embassy or consulate for more information.

Double-check entrance requirements at the nearest embassy or consulate for up-
to-date information. US citizens can also consult http://travel.state.gov. Admittance
to a country as a traveler does not include the right to work, which is authorized only
by a **work permit.** You should check online for the process of obtaining a work permit
in the country you are planning to work in.

---

entrance requirements

- **PASSPORT:** Required for citizens of Australia, Canada, New Zealand, and the US.

- **VISA:** For most EU countries, required for citizens of Australia, Canada, New Zealand,
  and the US only for stays longer than 90 days.

- **WORK PERMIT:** Required for all foreigners planning to work in the EU.

TIME DIFFERENCES

Most of Europe is on Central European Time, which is 1hr. ahead of Greenwich Mean
Time (GMT) and observes Daylight Saving Time during the summer. This means that
it is 6hr. ahead of New York City, 9hr. ahead of Los Angeles, 1hr. ahead of the British
Isles, 8hr. behind Sydney, and 10hr. behind New Zealand. However, the UK, Ireland,
and Portugal are on Western European Time (subtract 1hr. from Central European
Time)—a.k.a. Greenwich Mean Time. In addition, Greece and some parts of Eastern
Europe are on Eastern European Time (add 1hr. to Central European Time).

money

GETTING MONEY FROM HOME

Stuff happens. When stuff happens, you might need some money. When you need
some money, the easiest and cheapest solution is to have someone back home make
a deposit to your bank account. Otherwise, consider one of the following options.

Wiring Money

Arranging a **bank money transfer** means asking a bank back home to wire money to a
bank wherever you are. This is the cheapest way to transfer cash, but it's also the
slowest and most agonizing, usually taking several days or more. Note that some

banks may only release your funds in local currency, potentially sticking you with a poor exchange rate; inquire about this in advance.

Money transfer services like **Western Union** are faster and more convenient than bank transfers—but also much pricier. Western Union has many locations worldwide. To find one, visit www.westernunion.com or call the appropriate number: in Australia ☎1800 173 833, in Canada 800-235-0000, in the UK 0808 234 9168, in the US 800-325-6000, or in France 08 00 90 04 07. Money transfer services are also available to **American Express** cardholders and at selected **Thomas Cook** offices.

US State Department (US Citizens Only)

In serious emergencies only, the US State Department will help your family or friends forward money within hours to the nearest consular office, which will then disburse it according to instructions for a US$30 fee. If you wish to use this service, you must contact the Overseas Citizens Services division of the US State Department. (☎+1 202-501-4444, from US 888-407-4747)

WITHDRAWING MONEY

ATMs are readily available in most major European destinations. To use a debit or credit card to withdraw money from a cash machine (ATM) in Europe, you must have a four-digit Personal Identification Number (PIN). If your PIN is longer than four digits, ask your bank whether you can just use the first four or whether you'll need a new one. Credit cards don't usually come with PINs, so if you intend to hit up ATMs in Europe with a credit card to get cash advances, call your credit card company before leaving to request one.

money

TIPPING

Europe is nowhere near homogenous when it comes to common tipping practices, but suffice it to say that no one tips quite as much as Americans. We sometimes include tipping customs in the **Essentials** section of each chapter. When in doubt, check the bill to make sure tip isn't included, and then see what those around you do. Then hope that those around you aren't overly generous or horribly stingy.

TAXES

Members of the EU have value added tax (VAT) of varying percentages. Non-European Economic Community visitors who are taking goods home may be refunded this tax for certain purchases. To claim a refund, fill out the form you are given at the shop and present it with the goods and receipts at customs upon departure.

the euro

Despite what many dollar-possessing Americans might want to hear, the official currency of 16 members of the European Union—Austria, Belgium, Cyprus, Estonia, Finland, France, Germany, Greece, Ireland, Italy, Luxembourg, Malta, the Netherlands, Portugal, Slovakia, Slovenia, and Spain—is the euro.

Still, the currency has some important—and positive—consequences for travelers hitting more than one eurozone country. For one thing, money-changers across the eurozone are obliged to exchange money at the official, fixed rate and at no commission (though they may still charge a small service fee). Second, euro-denominated traveler's checks allow you to pay for goods and services across the eurozone, again at the official rate and commission-free. For more info, check a currency converter (such as www.xe.com) or www.europa.eu.int.

getting around

BY PLANE

Commercial Airlines

For small-scale travel on the continent, *Let's Go* suggests **budget airlines** (below) for budget travelers, but more traditional carriers have made efforts to keep up with the revolution. The **Star Alliance Europe Airpass** offers low economy-class fares for travel within Europe to 220 destinations in 45 countries. The pass is available to non-European passengers on Star Alliance (www.staralliance.com) carriers. **EuropebyAir's** snazzy FlightPass also allows you to hop between hundreds of cities in Europe and North Africa. (☎+1 888-321-4737 www.europebyair.com Most flights US$99.)

In addition, a number of European airlines offer discount coupon packets. Most are only available as tack-ons for transatlantic passengers, but some are standalone offers. Most must be purchased before departure, so research in advance. For example, **oneworld** (www.oneworld.com), a coalition of 10 major international airlines, offers deals and cheap connections all over the world, including within Europe.

The recent emergence of no-frills airlines has made hopscotching around Europe by air increasingly affordable. The following resources will be useful not only for crisscrossing countries but also for those ever-popular weekend trips to nearby international destinations.

- **BMIBABY:** To and from most major European cities, and a few less major ones. (www.bmibaby.com)

- **EASYJET:** Who knew London had so many airports? EasyJet did. (www.easyjet.com)

- **RYANAIR:** A budget traveler's dream, Ryanair goes most everywhere, especially in France and Italy. (www.ryanair.com)

- **PEGASUS:** For your inner Bellerophon. (www.flypgs.com)

- **TRANSAVIA:** What every Northern European dreams of: cheap flights to the Mediterranean. (www.transavia.com)

- **WIZZ AIR:** Short hops from Krakow to Paris. (www.wizzair.com)

BY TRAIN

Trains in Europe are generally comfortable, convenient, and reasonably swift. Second-class compartments are great places to meet fellow travelers. Make sure you are on the correct car, as trains sometimes split at crossroads. Towns listed in parentheses on European train schedules require a train switch at the town listed immediately before the parentheses.

You can either buy a **railpass,** which allows you unlimited travel within a particular region for a given period of time, or rely on buying individual **point-to-point** tickets as you go. Almost all countries give students or youths (under 26, usually) direct discounts on regular domestic rail tickets, and many also sell a student or youth card that provides 20-50% off all fares for up to a year.

BY BUS

Though European trains and railpasses are extremely popular, in some cases buses prove a better option. Often cheaper than railpasses, **international bus passes** allow unlimited travel on a hop-on, hop-off basis between major European cities. **Busabout,** for instance, offers three interconnecting bus circuits covering 29 of Europe's best bus hubs. (☎+44 845 026 7514 www.busabout.com. 1 circuit in high season starts at US$729, students US$705.) **Eurolines,** meanwhile, is the largest operator of Europe-wide coach services. We get misty-eyed just thinking about their unlimited 15- and 30-day passes to 41 major European cities. (www.eurolines.com)

- **WWW.RAILEUROPE.COM:** Info on rail travel and railpasses.

- **POINT-TO-POINT FARES AND SCHEDULES:** www.raileurope.com/us/rail/fares_schedules/index.htm allows you to calculate whether buying a railpass would save you money.

- **WWW.RAILSAVER.COM:** Uses your itinerary to calculate the best railpass for your trip.

- **WWW.ROME2RIO.COM:** Plan routes between destinations by rail, bus, ferry, and more.

getting around

safety and health

In any type of crisis, the most important thing to do is **stay calm.** Your country's embassy abroad is usually your best resource in an emergency; registering with that embassy upon arrival in the country is a good idea. The government offices listed in the **Travel Advisories** feature at the end of this section can provide information on the services they offer their citizens in case of emergencies abroad.

Whenever necessary, *Let's Go* lists specific concerns and local laws in the **Essentials** section of the relevant chapter. Basically, if you want to read about prostitution in Amsterdam, just flip back.

travel advisories

The following government offices provide travel information and advisories:

- **AUSTRALIA: Department of Foreign Affairs and Trade.** (☎+61 2 6261 1111 www.smartraveller.gov.au)

- **CANADA: Department of Foreign Affairs and International Trade.** Call or visit the website for the free booklet *Bon Voyage, But...* (☎+1-800-267-6788 www.international.gc.ca)

- **NEW ZEALAND: Ministry of Foreign Affairs and Trade.** (☎+64 4 439 8000 www.safetravel.govt.nz)

- **UK: Foreign and Commonwealth Office.** (☎+44 845 850 2829 www.fco.gov.uk)

- **US: Department of State.** (☎888-407-4747 from the US, +1-202-501-4444 elsewhere http://travel.state.gov)

PRE-DEPARTURE HEALTH

Matching a prescription to a foreign equivalent is not always easy, safe, or possible, so if you take **prescription drugs,** carry up-to-date prescriptions or a statement from your doctor stating the medications' trade names, manufacturers, chemical names, and dosages. Be sure to keep all medication with you in your carry-on luggage.

Immunizations and Precautions

Travelers over two years old should make sure that the following vaccines are up to date: MMR (for measles, mumps, and rubella); DTaP or Td (for diphtheria, tetanus, and pertussis); IPV (for polio); Hib (for *Haemophilus influenzae* B); and HepB (for Hepatitis B). For recommendations on immunizations and prophylaxis, check with a doctor and consult the **Centers for Disease Control and Prevention (CDC)** in the US (☎+1 800-232-4636 www.cdc.gov/travel) or the equivalent in your home country.

keeping in touch

BY EMAIL AND INTERNET

Hello and welcome to the 21st century, where you're rarely more than a 5min. walk from the nearest Wi-Fi hot spot, even if sometimes you'll have to pay a few bucks or buy a drink for the privilege of using it. **Internet cafes** and the occasional free internet terminal at a public library or university are listed in the **Practicalities** sections of cities that we cover.

Wireless hot spots make internet access possible in public and remote places. Unfortunately, they also pose security risks. Hot spots are public, open networks that use unencrypted, unsecured connections. They are susceptible to hacks and "packet sniffing"—the theft of passwords and other private information. To prevent problems, disable "ad hoc" mode, turn off file sharing and network discovery, encrypt your email, turn on your firewall, beware of phony networks, and watch for over-the-shoulder creeps.

BY TELEPHONE

If you have internet access, your best—i.e., cheapest, most convenient, and most tech-savvy—means of calling home is probably our good friend **Skype** (www.skype.com). You can even videochat if you have one of those new-fangled webcams. Calls to other Skype users are free; calls to landlines and mobiles worldwide start at US$0.023 per minute, depending on where you're calling.

For those still stuck in the 20th century, **prepaid phone cards** are a common and relatively inexpensive means of calling abroad. Each one comes with a Personal Identification Number (PIN) and a toll-free access number. You call the access number and then follow the directions for dialing your PIN. To purchase prepaid phone cards, check online for the best rates; www.callingcards.com is a good place to start. Online providers generally send your access number and PIN via email, with no actual "card" involved. You can also call home with prepaid phone cards purchased abroad.

Another option is a **calling card,** linked to a major national telecommunications service in your home country. Calls are billed collect or to your account. Cards generally come with instructions for dialing both domestically and internationally. Placing a collect call through an international operator can be expensive but may be necessary in case of an emergency. You can frequently call collect without even possessing a company's calling card just by calling its access number and following the instructions.

international calls

To call Europe from home or to call home from Europe, dial:

1. THE INTERNATIONAL DIALING PREFIX. To call from Australia, dial ☎0011; Canada or the US, ☎011; Ireland New Zealand, the UK, and most of Europe, ☎00.

2. THE COUNTRY CODE OF THE COUNTRY YOU WANT TO CALL. To call Australia, dial ☎61; Austria, ☎43; Belgium, ☎32; Canada, ☎1; Croatia, ☎385; Czech Republic, ☎420; Denmark, ☎45; France, ☎33; Germany, ☎49; Greece, ☎30; Hungary, ☎36; Ireland, ☎353; Italy, ☎39; the Netherlands, ☎31; Norway ☎47; New Zealand, ☎64; Poland ☎48; Portugal, ☎351; Slovenia ☎386; Spain, ☎34; Sweden ☎46; the UK, ☎44; the US, ☎1.

3. THE CITY/AREA CODE. Let's Go lists the city/area codes for cities and towns in Europe opposite the city or town name, next to a ☎, as well as in every phone number. If the first digit is a zero (e.g., ☎020 for Amsterdam), omit the zero when calling from abroad (e.g., dial ☎20 from Canada to reach Amsterdam).

4. THE LOCAL NUMBER.

keeping in touch

Cellular Phones

The international standard for cell phones is **Global System for Mobile Communication (GSM)**. To make and receive calls in Europe, you will need a GSM-compatible phone and a **SIM (Subscriber Identity Module) card,** a country-specific, thumbnail-size chip that gives you a local phone number and plugs you into the local network. Many SIM cards are prepaid, and incoming calls are frequently free. You can buy additional cards or vouchers (usually available at convenience stores) to "top up" your phone. For more information on GSM phones, check out www.telestial.com. Companies like **Cellular Abroad** (www.cellularabroad.com) and **OneSimCard** (www.onesimcard.com) rent cell phones and SIM cards that work in a variety of destinations around the world.

BY SNAIL MAIL
Sending Mail Home from Europe
Airmail is the best way to send mail home from Europe. Write "airmail," *"par avion,"* or the equivalent in the local language on the front. For simple letters or postcards, airmail tends to be surprisingly cheap, but the price will go up sharply for weighty packages. Surface mail is by far the cheapest, slowest, and most antiquated way to send mail. It takes one to two months to cross the Atlantic and one to three to cross the Pacific—good for heavy items you won't need for a while, like souvenirs that you've acquired along the way.

Receiving Mail in Europe
There are several ways to arrange pickup of letters sent to you while you are abroad, even if you do not have an address of your own. Mail can be sent via **Poste Restante** (General Delivery). Address Poste Restante letters like so:

Napoleon BONAPARTE
Poste Restante
City, Country

The mail will go to a special desk in the city's central post office, unless you specify a local post office by street address or postal code. It's best to use the largest post office, since mail may be sent there regardless. Bring your passport (or other photo ID) for pickup; there may be a small fee. If the clerks insist that there is nothing for you, ask them to check under your first name as well. *Let's Go* lists post offices in the **Practicalities** section for each city we cover. It is usually safer and quicker, though more expensive, to send mail express or registered. If you don't want to deal with Poste Restante, consider asking your hostel or accommodation if you can have things mailed to you there. Of course, if you have your own mailing address or a reliable friend to receive mail for you, that will be the easiest solution.

climate

Europe is for lovers, historians, architects, beach bums, and…weather nerds? In fact, the smallest continent has quite the diverse climate. Southern Europe is known for the warm weather surrounding the Mediterranean Sea. This area has warm, wet winters and hot, dry summers. Northern Europe is marked by temperate forests, where cold arctic air in winter contrasts with hot summers. In between sits the exception: the mile-high Alps, where things are generally colder and wetter.

AVG. TEMP. (LOW/HIGH), PRECIP.	JANUARY			APRIL			JULY			OCTOBER		
	°C	°F	mm	°C	°F	mm	°C	°F	mm	°C	°F	mm
Amsterdam	-1/4	30/39	68	4/13	39/55	49	13/22	55/72	77	7/14	45/57	72
Athens	6/13	43/55	62	11/20	52/68	23	23/33	73/91	6	15/24	59/75	51
Barcelona	6/13	43/55	31	11/18	52/64	43	21/28	70/82	27	15/21	59/70	86
Berlin	-3/2	27/36	46	4/13	39/55	42	14/24	57/75	73	6/13	43/55	49
Brussels	-1/4	30/39	66	5/14	41/57	60	12/23	54/73	95	7/15	45/59	83
Budapest	-4/1	25/34	37	7/17	45/63	45	16/28	61/82	56	7/16	45/61	5
Dublin	1/8	34/46	67	4/13	39/55	45	11/20	52/68	70	6/14	43/57	70
Istanbul	3/8	37/46	109	7/16	45/61	46	18/28	64/82	34	13/20	55/68	81
Lisbon	8/14	46/57	111	12/20	54/68	54	17/27	63/81	3	14/22	57/72	62
London	2/6	36/43	54	6/13	43/55	37	14/22	57/72	57	8/14	46/57	57
Madrid	2/9	36/48	39	7/18	45/64	48	17/31	63/88	11	10/19	50/66	53
Marseille	2/10	36/50	43	8/18	46/64	42	17/29	63/84	11	10/20	50/68	76
Paris	1/6	34/43	56	6/16	43/61	42	15/25	59/77	59	8/16	46/61	50
Prague	-5/0	23/32	18	3/12	37/54	27	13/23	55/73	68	5/12	41/54	33
Rome	5/11	41/52	71	10/19	50/66	51	20/30	68/86	15	13/22	55/72	99
Venice	1/6	34/43	37	10/17	50/63	78	19/27	66/81	52	11/19	52/66	77
Vienna	-4/1	25/34	39	6/15	43/59	45	15/25	59/77	84	7/14	45/57	56

To convert from degrees Fahrenheit to degrees Celsius, subtract 32 and multiply by 5/9. To convert from Celsius to Fahrenheit, multiply by 9/5 and add 32. The mathematically challenged may use this handy chart:

°CELSIUS	-5	0	5	10	15	20	25	30	35	40
°FAHRENHEIT	23	32	41	50	59	68	77	86	95	104

measurements

Like the rest of the rational world, Europe uses the metric system. The basic unit of length is the meter (m), which is divided into 100 centimeters (cm) or 1000 millimeters (mm). One thousand meters make up one kilometer (km). Fluids are measured in liters (L), each divided into 1000 milliliters (mL). A liter of pure water weighs one kilogram (kg), the unit of mass that is divided into 1000 grams (g). One metric ton is 1000kg. Gallons in the US and those in Britain are not identical: one US gallon equals 0.83 Imperial gallons. Pub aficionados will note that an Imperial pint (20 oz.) is larger than its US counterpart (16 oz.).

MEASUREMENT CONVERSIONS	
1 inch (in.) = 25.4mm	1 millimeter (mm) = 0.039 in.
1 foot (ft.) = 0.305m	1 meter (m) = 3.28 ft.
1 yard (yd.) = 0.914m	1 meter (m) = 1.094 yd.
1 mile (mi.) = 1.609km	1 kilometer (km) = 0.621 mi.
1 ounce (oz.) = 28.35g	1 gram (g) = 0.035 oz.
1 pound (lb.) = 0.454kg	1 kilogram (kg) = 2.205 lb.
1 fluid ounce (fl. oz.) = 29.57mL	1 milliliter (mL) = 0.034 fl. oz.
1 gallon (gal.) = 3.785	1 liter (L) = 0.264 gal.

measurements

phrasebook

ENGLISH	ITALIAN	FRENCH	SPANISH	PORTU-GUESE	DANISH	TURKISH
Hello	Buongiorno	Bonjour	Hola	Olá	Hej	Merhaba
Goodbye	Arrivederci	Au revoir	Adiós	Até logo	Farvel	İyi günler/İyi akşamlar
Yes	Sì	Oui	Si	Sim	Ja	Evet
No	No	Non	No	Não	Nej	Hayır
Please	Per favore	S'il vous plaît	Por favor	Por favor	Må jeg bede	Lütfen
Thank you	Grazie	Merci	Gracias	Obrigado/a	Tak	Teşekkur ederim
You're welcome	Prego	De rien	De nada	De nada	Selv tak	Bir şey değil
Sorry!	Mi scusi!	Désolé!	¡Perdón!	Desculpe!	Undskyld	Pardon!
My name is...	Mi chiamo...	Je m'appelle...	Me llamo...	O meu nome é...	Jeg hedder...	Ismim...
How are you?	Come sta?	Comment êtes-vous?	¿Cómo estás?	Como você está?	Hvordan har De det?	Sen nasılsın?
I don't know.	Non lo so.	Je ne sais pas.	No sé.	Eu não sei.	Jeg kender ikke	Bilmiyorum.
I don't understand.	Non capisco.	Je ne comprends pas.	No entiendo.	Não entendo.	Jeg forstår jeg ikke	Anlamadım.
Could you repeat that?	Potrebbe ripetere?	Répétez, s'il vous plaît?	¿Puede repetirlo?	Você pode repetir?	En gang til?	Lütfen o tekrarla?
Do you speak English?	Parla inglese?	Parlez-vous anglais?	¿Hablas español?	Fala inglês?	Taler du engelsk?	İngilizce biliyor musun?
I don't speak ___.	Non parlo italiano.	Je ne parle pas français.	No hablo castellano.	Eu não falo português.	Jeg kan ikke tale dansk	Türkçe okuyorum.
Why?	Perché?	Pourquoi?	¿Por qué?	Porque?	Hvorfor	Neden?
Where is...?	Dov'è...?	Où est?	¿Dónde está...?	Onde é...?	Hvor er...?	...nerede?
What time is it?	Che ore sono?	Quelle heure est-il?	¿Qué hora es?	Que horas são?	Hvad er klokken?	Saat kaç?
How much does this cost?	Quanto costa?	Combien ça coûte?	¿Cuánto cuesta esto?	Quanto custa?	Hvad koster det?	Ne kadar bu bedeli do?
I am from the US.	Sono degli Stati Uniti.	Je suis des Etats-Unis.	Soy de los Estados Unidos.	Eu sou de os Estados Unidos.	Jeg er fra de USA.	Ben ABD geliyorum.
I have a visa/ID.	Ho un visto/carta d'identità.	J'ai un visa/identification.	Tengo una visa/identificación.	Eu tenho um visto/identificação.	Jeg har et visum/identifikation.	Benim bir vizem/ID var.
I have nothing to declare.	Non ho nulla da dichiarare.	Je n'ai rien à déclarer.	No tengo nada para declarar.	Não tenho nada a declarar.	Jeg har intet at erklære.	Duyurmak için benim hiçbirşeyim yok.
I will be here for less than three months.	Sarò qui per meno di tré mesi.	Je serai ici pour moins de trois mois.	Estaré aquí por menos de tres meses.	Eu estarei aqui há menos de três meses.	Jeg vil være her i mindre end tre måneder.	Ben üçten az ay için burada olacağım.
One-way	Solo andata	Aller simple	Ida	Ida	En vej	Tek yön
Round-trip	Andata e ritorno	Aller-retour	Ida y vuelta	Ida e volta	Rundtur	Gidiş dönüş
Hotel/hostel	Albergo/ostello	Hôtel/auberge	Hotel/hostel	Hotel/albergue	Hotel/vandrerhjem	Otel/pansiyon
I have a reservation.	Ho una prenotazione.	J'ai une réservation.	Tengo una reserva.	Tenho uma reserva.	Jeg har en reservation.	Benim bir koşulum var.
Single/double room	Camera singola/doppia	Chambre pour un/deux	Habitación simple/doble	Quarto individual/duplo	Enkelt-værelse	Tek/çift kişilik

ENGLISH	ITALIAN	FRENCH	SPANISH	PORTU-GUESE	DANISH	TURKISH
I'd like...	Vorrei...	Je voudrais...	Me gustaría...	Gostaria...	Jeg vil gerne...	Ben bir ... seveceğim.
Check, please!	Il conto, per favore!	L'addition, s'il vous plaît!	¡La cuenta, por favor!	A conta, por favor!	Må jeg bede om regningen!	Hesap, lütfen!
I feel sick.	Mi sento male.	Je me sens malade.	Me siento mal.	Eu me sinto doente.	Jeg føler mig syg.	Ben hastayım.
Get a doctor!	Telefoni un dottore!	Va chercher un médecin!	¡Llama un médico!	Chamar um doutor!	Ringe til en læge!	Doktor ihtiyacim!
Hospital	Ospedale	Hôptal	Hospital	Hospital	Hospital	Hastane
I lost my passport/luggage.	Ho perso il mio passaporto/i miei bagagli.	J'ai perdu mon passeport/bagage.	He perdido mi pasaporte/equipaje.	Eu perdi o meu passaporte/a minha bagagem.	Jeg har mistet mit pas/min bagage.	Ben benim pasaportumu/bagajimi kaybettim.
Help!	Aiuto!	Au secours!	¡Socorro!	Socorro!	Hjælpe!	Imdat!
Leave me alone!	Lasciami stare!/Mollami!	Laissez-moi tranquille!	¡Déjame en paz!	Deixe-me em paz!	Lad mig være i fred!	Beni yalnız bırak!
Go away!	Vattene!	Allez-vous en!	¡Vete!	Vá embora!	Gå!	Git başımdan!
Call the police!	Telefoni alla polizia!	Appelez les flics!	¡Llama la policia!	Chamar a polícia!	Ringede til politiet.	Polis çağırın!

ENGLISH	GERMAN	DUTCH	CZECH	HUNGARIAN	GREEK PRONUNCIATION
Hello	Hallo/Tag	Dag/Hallo	Dobrý den	Szervusz	yah sahs
Goodbye	Auf Wiedersehen/Tschüss	Tot ziens	Nashledanou	Viszontlátásra	yah sahs
Yes	Ja	Ja	Ano	Igen	neh
No	Nein	Nee	Ne	Nem	oh-hee
Please	Bitte	Alstublieft	Prosím	Kérem	pah-rah-kah-LO
Thank you	Danke	Dank u wel	Děkuji	Köszönöm	Ef-hah-ree-STO
You're welcome	Bitte	Alstublieft	Prosím	Kérem	pah-rah-kah-LO
Sorry!	Es tut mir leid!	Sorry!	Promiňte!	Elnézést!	sig-NO-mee
My name is...	Ich bin...	Mijn naam is...	Mé jméno je...	A nevem...	meh LEH-neh
How are you?	Wie geht's (geht es Ihnen)?	Hoe gaat het?	Jak se máš?	Hogy vagy?	tee KAH-neh-teh
I don't know.	Ich weisse nicht/Keine Ahnung.	Ik weet het niet/Geen idee.	Nevím.	Nem tudom.	dthen KSER-o
I don't understand.	Ich verstehe nicht.	Ik begrijp het niet.	Nerozumím.	Nem értem.	dthen kah-tah-lah-VEH-no
Could you repeat that?	Können Sie wiederholen?	Kunt u dat herhalen?	Můžete opakovat, že?	Meg tudnád ismételni ezt?	bor-EE-teh na ep-an-a-LAH-vet-eh ahv-TO
Do you speak English?	Sprechen Sie Englisch?	Spreekt u Engels?	Mluví anglicky?	Beszél angolul?	mee-LAH-teh sng-lee-KAH
I don't speak ____.	Ich kann kein Deutsch.	Ik spreek geen Nederlands.	Nemluvím Česky.	Nem tudok (jól) magyarul.	dthen meel-AOH eh-lee-nee-KAH
Why?	Warum?	Waarom?	Proč?	Miért?	gee-ah-TEY
Where is...?	Wo ist...?	Waar is...?	Kde je...?	Hol van...?	poo EE-ne
What time is it?	Wie spät ist es?	Hoe laat is het?	Kolik je hodin?	Hány óra van?	tee O-rah EE-neh
How much does this cost?	Wie viel (kostet das)?	Wat kost het?	Kolik to stojí?	Menny be kerül?	PO-so kos-TI-dzeh ahv-TO
I am from the US.	Ich bin von Amerika.	Ik ben uit de VS.	Já jsem ze Spojených států.	Én vagyok az Egyesült Államok.	EE-meh ap-OH tiss een-o-MEN-ess pol-ee-TEE-ess
I have a visa/ID.	Ich habe ein Visum/eine ID.	Ik heb een visum/ID.	Mám víza/ID.	Van egy vízumot.	EH-oh mia theh-OH/ray-sey/tahf-TOH-tay-ta
I have nothing to declare.	Ich habe nichts zu verzollen.	Ik heb niets aan te geven.	Nemám nic k procelní.	Nekem van egy azor osřója.	Dthen EH-oh TEE-poh-teh na day-LO-so

phrasebook

ENGLISH	GERMAN	DUTCH	CZECH	HUNGARIAN	GREEK PRO-NUNCIATION
I will be here for less than three months.	Ich reste hier für weniger als drei Monate.	Ik blijf hier minder dan drie maanden.	I tady bude za méně než tři měsíce.	Én itt leszek kevesebb, mint három hónap.	Tha EE-meh eth-OH gee-ah lig-OH-teh-ro ap-OH treess MAY-ness
One-way	Einfache	Enkele reis	Jedním směrem	Csak oda	mon-OH-drom-OSS
Round-trip	Hin und zurück	Rondreis	Zpáteční	Oda-vissza	met ep-eess-tro-FACE
Hotel/hostel	Hotel/Herberge	Hotel/hostel	Hotel/ubytovna	Hotel/szálló	kse-no-dtho-HEE-o/ksen-OH-na
I have a reservation.	Ich habe eine Reservierung.	Ik heb een reservering.	Mám rezervaci.	Foglaltam asztalt.	EH-oh CAHN-ee KRA-tay-say
Single/double room	Einzelzimmer/Doppelzimmer	Eenpersoonskamer / Tweepersoonskamer	Jednolůžkový/dvoulůžkový pokoj	Egyágyas / kétágyas szoba	mo-NO-klin-oh/DIE-klin-oh
I'd like...	Ich möchte...	Ik wil graag...	Prosím...	kérek...	THAH EE-the-lah
Check, please!	Die Rechnung, bitte!	Mag ik de rekening!	Paragon, prosím!	A számlát, kérem!	oh lo-ghah-ree-yah-SMOS, pah-rah-kah-LO
I feel sick.	Ich bin krank.	Ik ben ziek.	Je mi špatně.	Rosszul érzem magam.	EE-meh AH-rose-tose
Get a doctor!	Hol einen Arzt!	Haal een dokter!	Najít lékaře!	Orvost!	PAH-re-te HEN-ah yiah-TROH
Hospital	Krankenhaus	Ziekenhuis	Nemocnice	Orvos	no-so-ko-MEE-o
I lost my passport/luggage.	Ich habe mein Reisepass/Gepäck verloren.	Ik heb mijn paspoort/bagage verloren.	Ztratil jsem pas/ zavazadla.	Elveszítettem az útlevelemet/ Elfelejtettem a poggyász.	EH-ah-sa toh dthaya-vah-tee-ri-o/vah-LEE-tsah moo
Help!	Hilfe!	Help!	Pomoc!	Segíts nekem!	vo-EE-thee-ah
Leave me alone!	Verloren gehen!	Laat me met rust!	Nech mě být!	Hagyj békén!	a-FIS-te me EE-si-kho (m.)/ EE-si-khee (f.)
Go away!	Geh weg!	Ga weg!	Prosím odejděte!	Távozzék!	FOO-geh
Call the police!	Ruf die Polizei!	Bel de politie!	Zavolejte policii!	Hívja a rendőrséget!	kah-LESS-ee teen ah-stih-noh-MIH-ah

let's go online

Plan your next trip on our spiffy website, **www.letsgo.com.** It features full book content, the latest travel info on your favorite destinations, and tons of interactive features: read blogs from our trusty Researcher-Writers, browse our photo library, watch exclusive videos, check out our newsletter, find travel deals, follow us on Facebook, and buy new guides. Plus, if this Essentials wasn't enough for you, we've got even more online. We're always updating and adding new features, so check back often!

essentials

INDEX

index

d

index

index

n

index

index

W

Y

Z

ACKNOWLEDGMENTS

WILL THANKS: Priyanka, for learning to not be scared when I get out of my chair quickly; Emma, for the same thing and also for the banana chips and protecting the M&Ms from #jeweltheives; Jim, Patrick, and Bryant, for the guidance and support; Rakesh Khurana, for almost paying for our lunch at Spice that one time; Travis Morrison and Kelly Clarkson; Tim, for teaching me more than I needed to know about the Oslo Tinder scene and for teaching Norwegian high schoolers how to write good; Claire, for the snaps à la Melancholia; Shaun, for keeping true to the straight and narrow path, such as your grandfather wanted; Western Union, for the ease of your international transfers; Zeb; Zeb's dad; William Caxton; Ryan, for the bushwhacker intel; Petey, for everything; Ana, for encountering the Kafkaesque. To Miles: The fall (bababadalgharaghtakamminarronnkonnbronntor nerronntuonnthunntrovarrhounawnskawn- toohoohoordenenthur — nuk!) of a once wallstrait oldparr is retaled early in bed and later on life down through all christian minstrelsy (Blog Post 28). Adam: thanks!

PRIYANKA THANKS: Will and Emma, for being the best co-workers and Pokemon masters I could ever ask for. Thank you for probably a little too much fun in the office, for gluten-free food outings, and for an unforgettable summer. Chesters_Treasure for being the official Let's Go Neopet that we always forgot about. Thanks to my nine kickass RWs: Adam for chasing waterfalls and always making me worry. Ana for marginalia that would make cry laughing and for warning me to not give blowjobs and get into knife fights. Claire for completing your Let's Go experience and letting me vicariously return to Rome through your pictures and stories. Miles for your writing style and for being our only RW to end up in a prison (renovated into a hostel, of course). Petey for Snapchats, for Froggyland, and for bringing Let's Go back to Croatia. Ryan for your beard, your calming voice which makes Will fangirl, and for drinking all the beer. Shaun for being the golden child of our RWs this year and for petting a kangaroo. Tim (aka Baby Doll) for all your snark that was at times unpublishable and for sharing your Tinder stories with us. And of course, Zeb for being a trooper in Cuba, being one of our bravest RWs, and for taking Let's Go to the final frontier. Thank you all for being amazing. I am so glad I got to know each and every one of you.

DIRECTOR OF PUBLISHING Will Holub-Moorman
EDITORIAL DIRECTOR Priyanka Sen

PRESIDENT, HARVARD STUDENT AGENCIES Patrick Scott
GENERAL MANAGER, HARVARD STUDENT AGENCIES Jim McKellar

ABOUT LET'S GO

THE STUDENT TRAVEL GUIDE

Let's Go publishes the world's favorite student travel guides, written entirely by Harvard students. Armed with pens, notebooks, and a few changes of underwear stuffed into their backpacks, our student researchers go across continents, through time zones, and above expectations to seek out invaluable travel experiences for our readers. Because we are a completely student-run company, we have a unique perspective on how students travel, where they want to go, and what they're looking to do when they get there. If your dream is to grab a machete and forge through the jungles of Costa Rica, we can take you there. If you'd rather bask in the Riviera sun at a beachside cafe, we'll set you a table. In short, we write for readers who know that there's more to travel than tour buses. To keep up, visit our website, www.letsgo.com, where you can sign up to blog, post photos from your trips, and connect with the Let's Go community.

TRAVELING BEYOND TOURISM

We're on a mission to provide our readers with sharp, fresh coverage packed with socially responsible opportunities to go beyond tourism. Each guide's Beyond Tourism sections share ideas about responsible travel, study abroad, and how to give back to the places you visit while on the road. To help you gain a deeper connection with the places you travel, our fearless researchers scour the globe to give you the heads-up on both world-renowned and off-the-beaten-track opportunities. We've also opened our pages to respected writers and scholars to hear their takes on the countries and regions we cover, and asked travelers who have worked, studied, or volunteered abroad to contribute first-person accounts of their experiences.

FIFTY-SIX YEARS OF WISDOM

Let's Go has been on the road for 56 years and counting. We've grown a lot since publishing our first 20-page pamphlet to Europe in 1960, but over five decades and 75 titles later, our witty, candid guides are still researched and written entirely by students on shoestring budgets who know that train strikes, stolen luggage, food poisoning, and marriage proposals are all part of a day's work. Meanwhile, we're still bringing readers fresh new features, such as a student-life section with advice on how and where to meet students from around the world; a revamped, user-friendly layout for our listings; and greater emphasis on the experiences that make travel abroad a rite of passage for readers of all ages. And, of course, *Europe 2016* is still brimming with editorial honesty, a commitment to students, and our irreverent style.

THE LET'S GO COMMUNITY

More than just a travel guide company, Let's Go is a community that reaches from our headquarters in Cambridge, MA, all across the globe. Our small staff of dedicated student editors, writers, and tech nerds comes together because of our shared passion for travel and our desire to help other travelers get the most out of their experience. We love it when our readers become part of the Let's Go community as well—when you travel, drop us a postcard (67 Mt. Auburn St., Cambridge, MA 02138, USA), send us an email (feedback@letsgo.com), or sign up on our website (www.letsgo.com) to tell us about your adventures and discoveries.

For more information, updated travel coverage, and news from our researcher team, visit us online at www.letsgo.com.

HELPING LET'S GO. If you want to share your discoveries, suggestions, or corrections, please drop us a line. We appreciate every piece of correspondence, whether a postcard, a 10-page email, or a coconut. Visit Let's Go at **www.letsgo.com** or send an email to:

feedback@letsgo.com, subject: "Let's Go Europe"

Address mail to:

Let's Go Europe, 67 Mount Auburn St., Cambridge, MA 02138, USA

In addition to the invaluable travel advice our readers share with us, many are kind enough to offer their services as researchers or editors. Unfortunately, our charter enables us to employ only currently enrolled Harvard students.

Maps © Let's Go and Avalon Travel

Distributed by Publishers Group West.
Printed in Canada by Friesens Corp.

ISBN-13: 978-1-61237-049-1
Fifty-sixth edition
10 9 8 7 6 5 4 3 2 1

Let's Go Europe is written by Let's Go Publications, 67 Mt. Auburn St., Cambridge, MA 02138, USA.

QUICK REFERENCE

YOUR GUIDE TO LET'S GO ICONS

📚	*Let's Go* recommends	☎	Phone numbers
i	Other hard info	🕰	Hours

EMERGENCY PHONE NUMBERS (POLICE)

Austria	☎133	Ireland	☎999
Belgium	☎101	Italy	☎113
Croatia	☎192	The Netherlands	☎911
Czech Republic	☎158	Norway	☎112
Denmark	☎114	Poland	☎997
France	☎17	Portugal	☎112
Germany	☎110	Slovenia	☎133
Great Britain	☎999	Spain	☎092
Greece	☎100	Sweden	☎112
Hungary	☎107	General Emergency (Europe)	☎112

USEFUL PHRASES

ENGLISH	FRENCH	GERMAN	ITALIAN	SPANISH
Hello/Hi	Bonjour/Salut	Hallo/Tag	Ciao	Hola
Goodbye/Bye	Au revoir	Auf Wiedersehen/ Tschüss	Arrivederci/Ciao	Adiós/Chau
Yes	Oui	Ja	Sì	Sí
No	Non	Nein	No	No
Excuse me!	Pardon!	Entschuldigen Sie!	Scusa!	¡Perdón!
Thank you	Merci	Danke	Grazie	Gracias
Go away!	Va t'en!	Geh weg!	Vattene via!	¡Vete!
Help!	Au secours!	Hilfe!	Aiuto!	¡Ayuda!
Call the police!	Appelez la police!	Ruf die Polizei!	Chiamare la polizia!	¡Llame a la policía!
Get a doctor!	Cherchez un médecin!	Hol einen Arzt!	Chiamare un medico!	¡Llame a un médico!
I don't understand	Je ne comprends pas	Ich verstehe nicht	Non capisco	No comprendo
Do you speak English?	Parlez-vous anglais?	Sprechen Sie Englisch?	Lei parla inglese?	¿Habla inglés?
Where is...?	Où est...?	Wo ist...?	Dov' è...?	¿Dónde está...?

TEMPERATURE CONVERSIONS

°CELSIUS	-5	0	5	10	15	20	25	30	35	40
°FAHRENHEIT	23	32	41	50	59	68	77	86	95	104

MEASUREMENT CONVERSIONS

1 inch (in.) = 25.4mm	1 millimeter (mm) = 0.039 in.
1 foot (ft.) = 0.305m	1 meter (m) = 3.28 ft.
1 mile (mi.) = 1.609km	1 kilometer (km) = 0.621 mi.
1 pound (lb.) = 0.454kg	1 kilogram (kg) = 2.205 lb.
1 gallon (gal.) = 3.785L	1 liter (L) = 0.264 gal.